32387

DATE			

ENCYCLOPEDIA

OF

AMERICAN SHIPWRECKS

BRUCE D. BERMAN

Published by The Mariners Press Incorporated
Boston, Massachusetts
Third Printing - 1973

Copyright © 1972 by The Mariners Press Incorporated

Library of Congress Catalog Card Number 71-181861

ISBN: 0-913352-01-2

Printed in the United States of America

Soft cover edition - ISBN: 0-913352-00-4

INTRODUCTION

In presenting this *Encyclopedia of American Shipwrecks* to the public, I feel a certain satisfaction and a certain humility. The satisfaction comes from knowing that this book sets a new standard for published compendia of shipwrecks. The humility comes from realizing the magnitude of the task, and knowing that it is not yet finished.

What I have done is to collect the pertinent data on every shipwreck of whose occurrence in American waters I could find hard evidence. After eight years of hard work, I have files of more than 50,000 documented shipwrecks in American territorial waters. From these files I have selected over 13,000 by excluding from the list all vessels of less than 50 gross tons. What is left is over ten times larger than any other published directory.

The shipwrecks documented here extend from the pre-Revolutionary era to a few months ago. They lie from 10 to 700 feet deep, in both the coastal and inland waterways of the United States. They were barks, barges, tankers, and floating palaces, and everything in between. They flew the flags of many nations. They foundered, burned, capsized, exploded, collided, or were scuttled by hostile action in time of war.

I have done my best to include every kind of shipwreck (subject only to the tonnage restriction) that might attract the interest of my fellow mariners, whether the interest focusses on fishing or treasure hunting or salvaging or just visiting and taking pictures.

My own interest is two-man submarines, designing and building them, although when I began I was strictly a diver, in New England and the Great Lakes. I began this compilation for my own use, but I was goaded on by dissatisfaction with the shipwreck information that was in print. Too much of it is superficial, embedded in adventure stories to make it "interesting," and scanty on the precise details of how-when-where. In the course of my work, wrecks never before listed have turned up in obvious sources that a serious author could not have ignored. Therefore, I grew steadily more aware that I was making the first attempt at a precise and complete collection.

Two things have decided me on publication at this time. One is the conviction that it would be a shame to withhold this collection any longer. The other is that the nearer the list gets to completion, the greater is the effort of finding each addition. In offering this work to the public, I hope I am enlisting some friendly collaboration in extending this collection as far as possible.

I invite all interested readers to write me at The Mariners Press, 755 Boylston Street, Boston, Massachusetts, 02116, with their findings and inquiries.

I wish to acknowledge here my gratitude for the help of my family and friends, without whose encouraging aid none of my work would have been possible.

Boston, Mass.   Bruce D. Berman
December, 1971

How to Use This Book

The shipwrecks are listed alphabetically by name of vessel within six separate sections, each devoted to a geographical region, with unidentified wrecks listed in a seventh section.

Section One
Maine
New Hampshire
Massachusetts
Rhode Island
Connecticut
New York
Pennsylvania
New Jersey
Delaware
Maryland
District of Columbia
plus Nova Scotia

Section Two
Virginia
North Carolina
South Carolina
Georgia
Florida

Section Three
Alabama
Mississippi
Louisiana
Texas

Section Four
California
Oregon
Washington
Alaska
plus Baja California, Mexico
and British Columbia (parts)

Section Five
Minnesota
Wisconsin
Illinois
Indiana
Michigan
Ohio
Pennsylvania
New York
including all Great Lake Ports

Section Six
Iowa
West Virginia
Indiana
Kentucky
Tennessee
Arkansas
Missouri
Oklahoma
Kansas
Nebraska
South Dakota
North Dakota
Montana
including all vessels shipwrecked on such rivers as: Arkansas, Brazos, Cumberland, Mississippi, Missouri, Ohio, Red, Tennessee, Yellowstone

Section Seven
Unidentified Shipwrecks

v

The list is in tabular form, consisting of columns for displaying the salient features of each wreck opposite the name of the vessel. The name entered for the ship is the name given at the time of its registry. Its name may have changed subsequently - if so, the fact is duly noted in the furthest column under "Place and Comment." There also the location of the event is given, in precise bearings where possible, or the current location of the wreck. The complete order of the columnar material is:

Name of Vessel- As indicated, name at registry, plus the flag under which the vessel is sailing (if other than American).

Rig- The kind of vessel, designated according to its function or how it is propelled.

Tons- The number of tons, gross tonnage being meant, except where the figure is followed by an asterisk (*), in which case it is net tons.

Built- The year the vessel was commissioned.

Date- Month-day-year of the shipwreck, unless otherwise clearly specified.

Cause- Cause of the ship's sinking or being wrecked.

Place and Comment- As indicated above, location, aliases or re-commissioned names of the vessel, and any comment that adds credibility to the event here recorded.

Key to Abbreviations

Name of Vessel - Flag

Aus.	Australian
Bel.	Belgium
Braz.	Brazilian
Br.	British
Can.	Canadian
Dan.	Denmark
Fin.	Finland
Fr.	French
Ger.	German
Grk.	Greek
Hon.	Honduran
It.	Italian
Nor.	Norwegian
Rus.	Russian
Sp.	Spanish
Sw.	Swedish
Ven.	Venezualean
Y.S.	Yugo-Slav

Rig

Brg.	Barge
Clipper	Clipper
Cnl.bt.	Canalboat
Ct.	Catamaran
Drg.	Dredge
El.b.	Electric Battery
El.c.	Electric Cable
El.o.	Electric screw, oil
El.s.	Electric screw, steam
El.w.o.	Electric stern wheel, oil
Frgt.	Freighter
Ga.ct.	Gas catamaran
Ga.h.	Gas hydrofoil
Ga.o.s.	Gas-oil screw
Ga.s.	Gas Screw
Ga.w.	Gas stern wheel
H.bt.	Houseboat
Jt.g.	Gas water jet
Jt.o.	Oil water jet
Ol.ct.	Oil catamaran
Ol.h.	Oil screw hydrofoil
Ol.p.	Oil side wheel
Ol.s.	Oil screw
Ol.w.	Oil stern wheel
Sail	Sail
Sch.	Schooner
Sch.b.	Schooner-barge
Scow	Scow
Sloop	Sloop
St.p.	Steam side wheel
St.s.	Steam screw
St.w.	Steam stern wheel
Sub.	Submarine
Tk.	Tanker
Tug	Towing
Ycht.	Yacht
Ywl.	Yawl

NO.	NAME OF VESSEL	RIG	TONS	BUILT	DATE		CAUSE	PLACE AND COMMENT
1	A One	-	391	1941		1961	Unknown	100 yds. 135° from Raritan Bay Channel Lighted Buoy 35. Depth 24'.
2	ABL 151	Brg.	391	1941	Apr 20	1954	Foundered	In Turning Basin No.1, Calumet River, Del. Steel vessel.
3	A.B. Spelman	C.bt.	103	1902	Aug 23	1923	Foundered	St. Charles River, Canada.
4	A. Barcud	Sch.	-	-		1888	Unknown	New Harbour, Nova Scotia.
5	A.C. Dodge	Brg.	-	-		1952	Unknown	1200 yds. 59° True from Ready Island, Delaware River.
6	A.C. Dodge	Ol.s.	1,147	1942	May 25	1952	Collided	With tanker MICHAEL. Off Reedy Island, Del. Steel vessel.
7	A.C. Nickerson	St.s.	64	1864	Mar 25	1894	Lost	New York, N.Y.
8	A.E. Sterns	Sch.	-	-	Oct 10	1876	Unknown	Kent Swamp, Block Island, R.I.
9	A.F. Kindberg	Sch.	226	1865	Nov 29	1919	Stranded	Cape Porpoise, Me.
10	A.G. Blair	Sch.	-	-	Sep 17	1887	Unknown	Mount Desert, Me.
11	A.G. Heisler (Br.)	Sch.	-	-	Jun 10	1897	Unknown	Cahoons Hollow, Mass.
12	A.G. & P. Co. No. 13	Brg.	124	1931	Feb 14	1941	Foundered	31-31 N. 70-42 W.
13	A.G. & P. Co. No. 43	Scow	138	1941	Oct 14	1957	Foundered	About 3 miles E of Falkner's Island, S of Madison, Conn. Steel vessel.
14	A.G. Pease	Sch.	74	1854	Jul 10	1920	Foundered	Sailed from Narragansett Bay, R.I. and has not since reported.
15	A.G. Ropes	Sch.	2,438	1884	Dec 26	1913	Foundered	Forked River, N.J. All 5 lives lost.
16	A.H. Bowman	Sch.	-	-		1885	Unknown	Point Judith, R.I.
17	A.H. Glover	Steamer	-	-	Lost 1800's		Unknown	Off Race Point, Mass.
18	A.H. Hurlburt	Sch.	301	1917	Dec 26	1890	Unknown	2-3/4 miles S of Narragansett L.S. Station, R.I. 41-23-12 N. 71-27-50 W.
19	A.H. Olwine	Brg.	1,077	1917	Aug 18	1944	Stranded	Newport, R.I. Length 204'.
20	A. Heaton	Sch.	166	1851	Jan 24	1907	Stranded	Outer Brewster Island, Boston, Mass.
21	A.J. Broadman	Sch.	-	-	Jul 18	1891	Unknown	North of Block Island, R.I.
22	A.J. McIntosh	Ga.s.	78	1912	Oct 2	1914	Burned	At dock, Severn side, near Annapolis, Md.
23	A.J. Miller	Sch.	110	1878	Nov 9	1913	Foundered	Long Island Sound, N.Y.
24	A.J. Ruddy	Brg.	523	1929	Apr 23	1945	Collided	North Brothers Island, N.Y.
25	A.L. Page	St.s.	94	1909	Dec 11	1926	Burned	Berkeley, Pa.
26	A.M. Andrews	Brg.	247	1919	Apr 28	1933	Foundered	Brooklyn, N.Y.
27	A.M. Burham	Sch.	-	-	May 19	1895	Unknown	Handkerchief Shoals, Mass.
28	A.P. Emerson	Sch.	243	1873	Dec 3	1906	Foundered	Off Cape Sable, Newfoundland.
29	A. Piatt Andrew	Sch.	141	1912	Aug 20	1918	War Loss	55 miles S of Canso, Nova Scotia. Sunk by German raider TRIUMPH.
30	A.R. Co. 7	Brg.	251	1912	Jun 2	1952	Foundered	3 miles west-half-south of Hens & Chicken Lightship, Mass. Steel vessel.
31	A.R. Co. 8	Brg.	316	1915	Nov 16	1950	Foundered	Off Finn's Ledge, Boston, Mass. Steel vessel.
32	A. Roger Hickey	Ol.s.	52	1925	Feb 2	1927	Stranded	Wellfleet, Mass.
33	A.S. & R. Hammond	Sch.	-	-	Jun 29	1890	Unknown	Whaleman Shoal, Mass.
34	A.T. Gifford	Ga.s.	86	1883	Jun 9	1913	Foundered	Sailed from New Bedford, Mass. & has not since reported. On whaling voyage.
35	A.W. Embrey	Brg.	338	1895	Oct 5	1917	Stranded	Wolf Trap Bar, Chesapeake Bay.
36	A.W. Thompson	Sch.	-	-	Mar 19	1887	Collided	Willett Point, Long Island, N.Y.
37	A. Woodall	Ga.s.	92	1903	Dec 8	1924	Burned	Turkey Point Light, Chesapeake Bay. All 7 lives lost.
38	Abacena	Ga.y.	92	1912	Sep 30	1929	Burned	City Island, N.Y.
39	Abbie and Eva Hooper	Sch.	321	1874	Nov 18	1911	Stranded	Vineyard Sound, Mass.
40	Abbie G. Cole	Sch.	273	1891	Dec 15	1910	Stranded	Vineyard Haven Shoals, Mass.
41	Abbie H. Hodgman	Sch.	-	-	Nov	1891	Unknown	Shovelful Shoal, Mass.
42	Abbie P. Crammer	Sch.	305	-	Sep 26	1888	Unknown	42-39-30 N. 70-42-28 W. 1-3/4 miles WSW of Davis Neck L.S. Station, Mass.
43	Abbie S	Sch.	53	1882	Jun 4	1915	Stranded	Kitts-Hammack Beach, Del.
44	Abbie S. Walker	Sch.	-	-	Apr 10	1894	Unknown	Provincetown, Mass.
45	Abbott W. Lewis	Sch.	-	-	Mar 6	1890	Unknown	Milk Island Bar, Mass.
46	Abby Thaxter	Sch.	-	-	Sep 17	1889	Unknown	Whitehead, Me.
47	Abby Wasson	Sch.	-	-	Dec 11	1887	Unknown	Pollock Rip, Mass.
48	Abby Weld	Sch.	-	-	Apr 18	1888	Foundered	Baker's Island, Mass.

NO.	NAME OF VESSEL	RIG	TONS	BUILT	DATE	CAUSE	PLACE AND COMMENT
49	Abden Keene	Sch.	-	-	Lost 1800's	Unknown	Peaked Hill, Mass.
50	Abdon Keene	Sch.	53	1860	Sep 9 1913	Stranded	Mescongus, Me.
51	Abel E. Babcock	Sch.	812	-	Nov 27 1898	Unknown	42-18-45 N. 70-54-32 W. 3/4 mile NW of Point Allerton L.S. station, Mass.
52	Abel W. Parker	Sch.	-	-	Lost 1800's	Unknown	Orleans, Mass.
53	Abenaki	Sch.	176	1894	Oct 1 1917	Foundered	15 miles SW of Seguin Island, Me.
54	Abertina (Br.)	Bark	-	-	Apr 29 1903	Unknown	Off Muskeget Shoal, Martha's Vineyard, Mass.
55	Abogado	Ol.s.	73	1926	Nov 25 1964	Burned	At Tebbston on the Magothy, Anne Arundel County, Md.
56	Abram Collerd	Brg.	217	1869	Sep 11 1905	Collided	With steamer MAINE. New York, N.Y.
57	Absecon	Brg.	914	1918	May 9 1944	Collided	With st.s. STERLINGTON & st.s. EMPIRE CURZON. In New York Harbor, N.Y.
58	Acadia	Ga.s.	56	1925	1959	Foundered	Off City Island, N.Y.
59	Achilles	St.s.	764	-	Jun 6 1887	Unknown	41-10 N. 71-37 W. 2 miles S of Block Island L.S. Station, R.I. Coal cargo.
60	Acorn	Sch.	400	-	Summer 1891	Unknown	Beaver Tail, R.I.
61	Acorn	Sloop	-	-	Apr 14 1828	Unknown	Lost on Halifax Station, Nova Scotia. 18 gun armament. 115 lives lost.
62	Active	St.s.	60	1892	Jul 12 1933	Burned	Hog Island, Pa.
63	Active	Sch.	-	-	Oct 25 1895	Unknown	Old Beach, Block Island, R.I.
64	Active	Sloop	-	-	Oct 18 1899	Unknown	Wood End, Mass.
65	Acushia	Ol.s.	135	1917	Jun 20 1929	Burned	Halifax, Nova Scotia.
66	Acushnet	Ol.s.	63	1929	Jul 10 1947	Collided	With ol.s. RAINBOW. Approx. 125 miles E of Pollock Rip, Mass.
67	Acusionet	Steamer	-	-	Aug 10 1870	Unknown	West of Point Judith, R.I.
68	Ada A. Kennedy	Sch.	633	-	Oct 11 1893	Unknown	Sow & Pigs Reef, Cuttyhunk Island, Mass. Coal cargo.
69	Ada Ames	Sch.	199	1860	Aug 29 1910	Stranded	Nantucket Shoals, Mass.
70	Ada Barker	Sch.	-	-	Jan 13 1891	Unknown	Near Portland, Me.
71	Ada H. Penere	Sch.	-	-	Lost 1800's	Unknown	Chatham, Mass.
72	Ada Herbert	Sch.	-	-	Apr 22 1884	Unknown	East of Block Island, R.I.
73	Ada J. Campbell	Sch.	-	-	Nov 12 1899	Unknown	Wood End, Mass.
74	Ada K. Damon	Sch.	94	1875	Dec 26 1909	Stranded	Ipswich, Mass.
75	Ada L. Harris	Sch.	-	-	Nov 1872	Unknown	Nantucket Shoals, Mass.
76	Adalaide	Sch.	-	-	Unknown	Unknown	Point Judith, R.I.
77	Addie	Sch.	-	-	Jun 1803	Unknown	West part of Hyannis Harbor, Mass.
78	Addie	Sch.	80	1867	Jan 24 1907	Stranded	Turtle Island Ledge, Me.
79	Addie B. Bacon	Sch.	-	-	Sep 10 1889	Stranded	Delaware Breakwater.
80	Addie B. Bacon	Brg.	422	1874	Feb 10 1908	Stranded	Flynns Knoll, New York Bay, N.Y.
81	Addie Fuller	Sch.	217	1867	Aug 19 1912	Stranded	Cutler Head, Me.
82	Addie G. Begans	Sch.	-	-	Jul 26 1895	Stranded	Pollock Rip, Mass.
83	Addie Jordan	Brg.	376	1873	Dec 15 1907	Stranded	Manasquan, N.J.
84	Addie M. Bird	Sch.	-	-	Aug 9 1887	Unknown	Campo Bello, New Brunswick.
85	Addie M. Story	Sch.	61	1867	Oct 4 1912	Stranded	Rocky Harbor, Newfoundland.
86	Addie P. Avery	Sch.	332	-	Jan 3 1878	Unknown	42-03-18 N. 70-04-42 W. 1/2 mile N of Highland L.S. Station, Truro.
87	Addison Center	Sch.	-	-	Nov 9 1900	Storm	Off Race Point, Mass.
88	Adelaide	St.p.	734	1853	Jun 19 1880	Collided	With GRAND REPUBLIC. Sank immediately. New York, N.Y.
89	Adele Trudell	Sch.	-	-	Nov 24 1891	Unknown	Romer Shoal, New York Harbor, N.Y.
90	Adeline Townsend	Sch.	231	1854	Jan 12 1909	Collided	With st.s. MOHICAN. Cape Henlopen, Del. All 6 lives lost.
91	Admiral	Bark	-	-	Apr 1 1891	Unknown	North Beach, Md.
92	Admiral Dewy	Brg.	303	1898	Jan 24 1918	Burned	Newark, N.J.
93	Admiral Dupont	St.p.	750	1847	Jun 8 1865	Collided	With STADACONA. Off Cape May, N.J. Formerly British "Anglia".
94	Adolph Obrig	Bark	1,448	1881	Apr 10 1907	Foundered	Sailed from New York, N.Y. & has not since been reported. All 18 lives lost.
95	Adonis (Dutch)	Bark	-	-	Mar 3 1859	Foundered	200 yds. offshore from San Alfonso Retreat, Takanassee, N.J. Depth 25'.
96	Adrea	Brg.	372	1905	May 8 1913	Foundered	Off Rocky Point, Conn.

NO.	NAME OF VESSEL	RIG	TONS	BUILT	DATE		CAUSE	PLACE AND COMMENT
97	Adriana	Ol.y.	56	1927	Sep 20	1932	Burned	Montauk Point, Long Island, N.Y. 1 life lost (11).
98	Adrianna	Sch.	-	-	Jan 3	1884	Unknown	West of Block Island, R.I.
99	Advance	St.s.	2,458	1883	Jul 2	1923	Stranded	Off Shut In Island, Halifax, Nova Scotia. Iron vessel.
100	Adventure	Sail	-	-		1699	Unknown	Near Montauk Point, N.Y. 41-05 N. 71-51 W. Valued at $2 million.
101	Adventure	Yacht	-	-	Sep 25	1801	Unknown	Wood End, Mass.
102	Adventure II	Ol.s.	119	1911	Mar 20	1943	Burned	Grave Light, Mass.
103	Adventurer	Ol.s.	-	-	Dec 17	1969	Foundered	About 15 miles, 112° from Nantucket Shoals Lightship. 40-25.1 N. 69-10-00 W.
104	Adverse	Ol.s.	55	1934	Aug 7	1937	Burned	14 miles SE of Pollock Rip Lightship, Mass.
105	Aebna	Sch.	-	-	Aug 31	1894	Foundered	Handkerchief Shoals, Mass.
106	Aeneas	-	-	-	Oct 23	1805	Unknown	At night off coast of Newfoundland. 340 lives lost.
107	Aeolus	Ol.s.	-	-	Jun 3	1942	Unknown	42-05 N. 66-50 W. Trawler.
108	Aeroc	Brg.	350	1891	Jan 19	1966	Unknown	Maffitt Ledge, Boston Harbor, Mass. 42-21-30 N. 70-53-42 W. Depth 36'.
109	AEtna	Sch.	-	-	Sep 30	1913	Stranded	Petit Manan Light, Nova Scotia.
110	Afton	Sch.	87	1853	Jan 15	1887	Unknown	Cranberry Island Bar, Me.
111	Agawam	St-p.	-	-	Jul 28	1854	Burned	East Haddam, Conn.
112	Agnes	Sch.	-	-	Apr	1889	Unknown	Fisherman Island, Me.
113	Agnes	Sch.	-	-	Nov 27	1898	Unknown	Point Judith, R.I.
114	Agnes	Sch.	-	-	Nov 27	1898	Unknown	Provincetown, Mass.
115	Agnes E. Manson	Sch.	852	-	May 6	1903	Unknown	Rose & Crown Shoal, entrance to Nantucket Sound, Mass. 174' length.
116	Agnes Howard	Brg.	582	1914	Dec 4	1940	Stranded	Green Hills, Long Island, N.Y. All life (1) lost.
117	Agnes Manning	Sch.	-	-	Nov 26	1889	Collided	Fenwick Island, Md.
118	Agnes Manning	Sch.	-	-	Dec 2	1891	Unknown	Pasque Island, Mass.
119	Agnes R. Bacon	Sch.	396	-	Feb 11	1888	Unknown	Brant Rock, Mass. 42-05-36 N. 70-38-15 W. Coal cargo.
120	Agnes R. Murray	Brg.	233	1922	Nov 24	1940	Foundered	Lock No. 10, Cranesville, N.Y.
121	Agnes S. Quillin	Sch.	197	1891	Nov 16	1938	Stranded	Smith Point, Potomac River, Md.
122	Agnes V. Gleason	Sch.	70	1899	Dec 30	1907	Stranded	Boothbay, Me.
123	Aimejean	Ol.y.	165	1926	Jun 22	1932	Burned	Squantum, Mass.
124	Ajax	St.p.	332	1848	Oct	1853	Foundered	Cape Cod, Mass. 6 lives lost.
125	Ajax	St.s.	356	1919	Oct 6	1934	Burned	Tenants Harbor, Me.
126	Alabama	Sch.	-	-	Jul 4	1891	Unknown	Gun Rock Point, Me.
127	Alanson A. Summer	Brg.	249	1869	Dec 14	1907	Stranded	Watch Hill, R.I.
128	Alanson S. Page	St.s.	144	1856		1866	Burned	Philadelphia, Pa.
129	Alaric	Brg.	-	-	Aug 2	1887	Unknown	Seal Island, Nova Scotia.
130	Alaska	Sch.	-	-	Oct 16	1800	Unknown	Nauset Bar, Mass.
131	Alaska	Sch.	855	1894	Feb 18	1907	Stranded	Peaked Hill Bars, Mass. All 4 lives lost.
132	Albany	Sch.	650	1889	Nov 16	1922	Stranded	Man-O-War Rock, New York Harbor, N.Y.
133	Albatross	Ol.s.	83	1918	Mar 24	1932	Foundered	Boston Light Ship, Mass.
134	Albemarle	St-p.	80	1818	May 1	1825	Burned	Philadelphia, Pa. Used as ferryboat.
135	Albert	Ol.s.	-	-	Oct 10	1942	Unknown	41-05 N. 70-30 W. Fisherman.
136	Albert J. Stone	St.s.	306	1913	Aug 4	1916	Stranded	Warren Point, Buzzards Bay, Mass. Steel vessel.
137	Albert Jameson	Sch.	-	-	Nov 29	1891	Unknown	Monhegan Island, Me.
138	Albert L. Butler	Sch.	-	-	Nov 27	1898	Unknown	Peaked Hill, Mass.
139	Albert M.	Brg.	375	-	Jan 26	1895	Foundered	Off Point Judith, R.I. 1-1/4 miles SSE of Monomoy Pt. L.S. Station.
140	Albert T. Stearns	Sch.	508	-	Apr 27	1903	Unknown	41-31-02 N. 70-00-09 W.
141	Albert W. Black	Ga.s.	54	1892	Aug 14	1931	Collided	With st.s. GRIPSHOLM. Georges Banks, Newfoundland.
142	Albert W. Tinible	Sch.	-	-	Lost 1800's		Unknown	Off Orleans, Mass.
143	Albert Woodbury	Sch.	-	-	Lost 1800's		Unknown	Monomoy, Cape Cod, Mass.
144	Alberta	Ol.s.	-	-		1950	Unknown	Provincetown Harbor, Mass. 42-02.7 N. 70-11-00 W. Depth 12'.

NO.	NAME OF VESSEL	RIG	TONS	BUILT	DATE	CAUSE	PLACE AND COMMENT
145	Albertina	St.p.	558	1882	May 9 1932	Burned	152nd Street and East River, N.Y.
146	Albertina	Bark	701	-	Jul 1 1904	Unknown	41-39-52 N. 69-55-42 W. 2 miles S of Old Harbor L.S. Station.
147	Alcaea	Bark	403	1883	Dec 16 1907	Foundered	Sailed from Philadelphia, Pa. & has not since reported. All 7 lives lost.
148	Alcona	St.s.	1,191	1878	Nov 6 1913	Burned	Bay of Isles, Nova Scotia.
149	Alden	Ol.s.	79	1917	Feb 22 1957	Burned	About 8 miles off Thatcher's Buoy, Rockport, Mass. 42-41-30 N. 70-19-24 W.
150	Alder Point	-	-	-	Sep 18 1937	Unknown	46-45 N. 56-27 W.
151	Alena Covert	Sch.	-	-	Sep 11 1889	Unknown	Delaware Breakwater.
152	Alert	St.s.	170	1874	Dec 16 1905	Collided	With car float, Hell Gate, N.Y.
153	Alert	Ga.s.	145	1906	Dec 4 1906	Stranded	Port au Port, Newfoundland. 1 life lost.
154	Alert	St.s.	126	1862	Mar 9 1921	Foundered	Bridgeport, Conn.
155	Alert	Ol.s.	78	1917	Apr 25 1929	Foundered	Highland Light, N.J.
156	Alert	Ol.s.	-	-	Oct 10 1942	Foundered	South of Martha's Vineyard, Mass. 41-05 N. 70-30 W.
157	Alex Anderson	Sch.	738	1892	Oct 2 1916	Foundered	Off Massachusetts coast.
158	Alex Gibson	Brg.	-	-	Unknown	Unknown	Cape May Inlet, N.J. 10.1 miles, 087° from the north jetty light. Depth 28'.
159	Alex Gibson	Sch.	2,154	1877	Nov 28 1915	Stranded	Off McCreigh Shoal, N.J.
160	Alexander	Sch.	-	-	May 12 1879	Unknown	West of Block Island, R.I.
161	Alexander Campbell	Sch.	-	-	Nov 27 1888	Unknown	Block Island, R.I.
162	Alexander Macomb	Frgt.	9,172	-	Jul 3 1942	War Loss	41-40 N. 66-52 W. or 41-39 N. 66-32 W. German Submarine.
163	Alexandria	Sch.	-	-	May 27 1887	Unknown	Shovelful Shoal, Mass.
164	Alexina	Sch.	-	-	Oct 11 1890	Collided	Grosse Island, St. Lawrence River.
165	Alfred and Edwin	Ol.s.	109	1872	Dec 19 1926	Foundered	Brooklyn, N.Y. Iron vessel.
166	Alfred Keen	Sch.	-	-	Lost 1800's	Unknown	Off Race Point, Mass.
167	Alfred W. Fiske	Sch.	395	-	Oct 19 1801	Unknown	Monomoy, Mass. 41-30-00 N. 69-55-55 W. Length 136'.
168	Algiers	St.s.	2,294	1876	Nov 1 1925	Abandoned	37-35-00 N. 69-23-00 W. Iron vessel.
169	Alhambra	St.s.	764	1865	May 2 1875	Stranded	Cape Sable, Nova Scotia.
170	Alianza (Can.)	Sch.	359	1897	Feb 9 1896	Unknown	42-43-36 N. 70-46-30 W. 3/4 mile S of Plum Is. L.S. Station. Coal cargo.
171	Alice	St.p.	326	1845	Jul 22 1852	Burned	Bridgeport, Conn.
172	Alice	Brg.	-	-	Nov 25 1888	Unknown	Cohasset, Mass.
173	Alice	Brg.	-	-	Dec 7 1890	Abandoned	Off Lunenburg, Nova Scotia.
174	Alice	St.p.	99	1892	Aug 30 1913	Exploded	At Corapolis, Pa. 8 lives lost.
175	Alice	Brg.	250	1904	Jun 15 1925	Stranded	Sanquist Head, Mass.
176	Alice	St.s.	154	1897	Jan 28 1935	Foundered	Erie Basin, Brooklyn, N.Y.
177	Alice B. Phillips	Sch.	-	-	Mar 29 1890	Collided	Absecon, N.J.
178	Alice C. Jordan	Sch.	-	-	May 3 1899	Unknown	Race Point, Mass.
179	Alice E. Clark	Sch.	1,621	1898	Sep 16 1898	Run down	In Vineyard Sound, Mass.
180	Alice I. McCrowdis	Sch.	-	-	Jul 1 1909	Stranded	Long Island Ledge, Penobscot Bay, Me.
181	Alice J. Crabtree	Sch.	-	-	Jul 6 1887	Unknown	Liscombe, Nova Scotia.
182	Alice J. Crabtree	Sch.	-	-	Sep 12 1891	Unknown	Handkerchief Shoals, Mass.
183	Alice J. Crabtree	Sch.	378	1891	Aug 7 1914	Stranded	Port Joli Head, Nova Scotia.
184	Alice J. Hathaway	Ol.s.	89	1916	Dec 6 1950	Burned	Approx. 74 miles ESE of Nantucket Lightship, Mass.
185	Alice M. Colburn	Sch.	1,603	1896	Jan 3 1923	Stranded	Egg Rock, Manchester, Mass. 42-33-48 N. 70-44-17 W. Length 225'.
186	Alice M. Doughty II	Ol.s.	50	1930	Jan 24 1967	Collided	With tanker EMERILLO. About 10 miles from Portland Lightship, Me.
187	Alice M. Lawrence	Sch.	3,132	1906	Dec 5 1914	Stranded	Tuckumuck Shoal, Vineyard Sound, Mass. 41-24-13 N. 70-13-00 W.
188	Alice M. Ridgeway	Sch.	-	-	Dec 11 1891	Foundered	East of Watch Hill Light, R.I. Total loss. Salt cargo.
189	Alice Oakes	Sch.	-	-	Apr 30 1885	Unknown	North side of Nantucket Island, Mass.
190	Alice Oakes	Sch.	-	-	Aug 17 1891	Unknown	Hyannis, Mass.
191	Alice Raymond	Sch.	-	-	Lost 1800's	Unknown	Race Point, Mass.
192	Alice Roy	Bark	-	-	Aug 1887	Abandoned	Off New York.

NO.	NAME OF VESSEL	RIG	TONS	BUILT	DATE	CAUSE	PLACE AND COMMENT
193	Alice S. Hawkes	Sch.	63	1877	Sep 1 1905	Burned	Plymouth, Mass.
194	Alice Sheridan	Brg.	373	1919	Oct 1 1945	Collided	With Royal Netherlands vessel. Off St. George, Staten Island, N.Y.
195	Alice T. Boardman	Sch.	-	-	Feb 1 1802	Unknown	Hardings Beach, Mass.
196	Alice T. Boardman	Sch.	123	1873	Jan 4 1907	Stranded	Handkerchief Shoal, Mass. 1 life lost.
197	Alice T. Clark	C.bt.	116	1891	Jun 25 1922	Burned	State Dock, Verona Beach, N.Y.
198	Alida	Sch.	-	-	1885	Unknown	5 miles west of Point Judith, R.I.
199	Alida B	C.bt.	118	1899	Jun 7 1911	Foundered	Off Captain Island, Long Island Sound, N.Y.
200	Aline	Ol.s.	75	1905	Jun 1957	Lost	In Gowanus Canal, off the 9th Street Bridge, Brooklyn, N.Y.
201	Allegheny	Brg.	914	1917	Mar 31 1942	War Loss	1 mile south of Paramour Bay, Md. Sunk by enemy action.
202	Allen	Sch.	-	-	Oct 22 1894	Unknown	Fishers Island, N.Y.
203	Allen Goren	Sch.	-	-	Jan 9 1886	Unknown	West of Point Judith, R.I.
204	Allen Greene	Sch.	442	1874	Mar 17 1911	Stranded	Long Island, Bay of Fundy, Nova Scotia. 1 life lost.
205	Allen H. Jones	Sch.	-	-	Nov 27 1898	Unknown	Provincetown, Mass.
206	Allentown	Sch.	-	-	1888	Unknown	Cohasset, Mass.
207	Allentown	Sch.	842	1908	Mar 31 1917	Collided	With st.s. COAMO. Off Highlands, N.J.
208	Allie H. Belden	Sch.	-	-	Mar 12 1888	Unknown	Delaware Bay.
209	Allison	Sloop	-	-	Aug 8 1802	Unknown	Watch Hill, R.I.
210	Allison White	Brg.	269	1880	Oct 24 1917	Foundered	Off Jamestown, R.I.
211	Alma	Sch.	-	-	Sep 25 1888	Unknown	Vineyard Haven, Mass.
212	Alma	Sch.	134	1882	Jun 10 1907	Abandoned	St. John, New Brunswick.
213	Alma E.A. Holmes	Sch.	1,208	1896	Oct 10 1914	Collided	With SS BELFAST. Near Bakers Island, Marblehead, Mass. 42-28-06 N. 70-44-54 W.
214	Almeda Willey	Sch.	547	1874	Jul 28 1911	Abandoned	Swans Island, Me.
215	Almeida	Sch.	-	-	Apr 12 1896	Unknown	Race Point, Mass.
216	Almirante	St.s.	5,010	1909	Sep 6 1918	Collided	With USS HISKO. 39-21-12 N. 74-12-48 W. Also known as "Flour Wreck".
217	Almon Bacon	Sch.	-	-	Nov 5 1885	Unknown	East by South of Point Judith, R.I.
218	Aloha	Sch.	138	1901	Jun 4 1915	Burned	25 miles S of Ellis Bay, Anticosti, Nova Scotia.
219	Aloma	Ol.s.	60	1924	Feb 7 1931	Foundered	Nantucket Lightship, Mass.
220	Alsenborn	Steamer	-	-	Jan 11 1891	Unknown	Delaware Bay.
221	Altamaha	Bark	343	-	Mar 19 1893	Unknown	41-37-00 N. 69-57-24 W. 2-1/4 miles S of Chatham L.S. Station. Lumber cargo.
222	Altana M. Jagger	Sch.	132	1890	Jul 8 1932	Stranded	Watch Hill, R.I.
223	Altona (Br.)	Bark	530	-	Jan 11 1906	Unknown	41-31-48 N. 70-02-24 W. 2 miles SW of Monomoy L.S. Station, Mass.
224	Alum Chive (Br.)	-	-	-	Mar 7 1913	Exploded	Baltimore, Md. 40 lives lost.
225	Alva	-	-	-	Feb 14 1885	Unknown	Tuckernuck Flats, Nantucket, Mass.
226	Alva	St.s.	1,151	-	Jul 24 1892	Unknown	41-32-43 N. 69-53-52 W. Pollock Rip, Mass. Wood vessel of 256' length.
227	Alva L. McCrowdis	Sch.	-	-	Nov 1 1887	Unknown	Fishman's Harbor, Nova Scotia.
228	Amanda E.	Sch.	-	-	Nov 16 1801	Unknown	Chatham Roads, Mass.
229	Amanda E.	Sch.	-	-	Mar 5 1802	Unknown	Point Judith, R.I.
230	Amazon	Brg.	-	-	Lost 1800's	Unknown	Race Point, Mass.
231	Amazon	-	-	-	Jan 24 1890	Unknown	Race Rock, N.Y.
232	Azores	-	-	-	Pre-WWII	Unknown	42-10 N. 66-20 W.
233	Azua	Sch.	114*	1918	May 14 1930	Collided	With st.s. CITY OF ATLANTA. 74-10 N. 39-00 W. 3 lives lost (7).
234	Ambrose Channel Relief Lightship	St.s.	664	-	1960	Unknown	8.5 miles, 094° from Sandy Hook Light. 40-27-12 N. 73-49-06 W. Depth 100'. Lies east to west.
235	Amelia	Sch.	-	-	Apr 30 1864	Unknown	Near Point Judith, R.I.
236	Amelia G. Joeland	Sch.	-	-	Dec 13 1890	Unknown	Chatham, Mass.
237	Amelia M. Percira	Ol.s.	106	1928	May 16 1932	Burned	Cornfield Lightship, Conn.
238	Amelia M. Pereira	Ol.s.	100	-	Pre-WWII	Unknown	41-16-30 N. 71-40-00 W. 4-3/4 miles, 119° True from Sandy Pt. Light, R.I.
239	Amelia M. Price	Sch.	58	1869	Dec 19 1905	Collided	With st.p. BALTIMORE. Point No Point, Md. 1 life lost.

NO.	NAME OF VESSEL	RIG	TONS	BUILT	DATE	CAUSE	PLACE AND COMMENT
240	America	St.s.	107	1875	Jun 6 1930	Burned	Sandy Point, Md.
241	America	St.s.	297	1908	Jul 29 1932	Burned	Dark Island Shoal, St. Lawrence River. Steel vessel. 7 lives lost (15).
242	America	St.p.	689	1895	Feb 15 1937	Burned	Dyckman Street & Hudson River, N.Y. Iron vessel.
243	America	Brg.	242	1925	May 17 1942	Stranded	North of George Washington Bridge, North River, N.Y.
244	America	Ol.s.	64	1930	Mar 14 1949	Foundered	3-1/2 miles ENE of Thatcher's Buoy, Gloucester, Mass.
245	American	Brg.	836	1898	Oct 14 1925	Foundered	Absecon Light, N.J. Steel vessel.
246	American Boy	Ga.y.	79	1917	Apr 16 1936	Burned	Two Tree Shoals, near New London, Conn.
247	American Chief	Sch.	-	-	Lost 1800's	Unknown	Between Orleans and Nauset, Mass.
248	American Eagle	Sch.	-	-	Jun 21 1870	Unknown	South of Point Judith, R.I.
249	American Eagle	Brg.	311	-	Jan 26 1895	Foundered	Off Point Judith, R.I. Coal cargo.
250	American Lloyds	Brg.	460	-	Nov 18 1888	Unknown	42-02-48 N. 70-03-42 W. 1/2 mile ESE of Highland L.S. Station, Mass.
251	American Soldier	Brg.	422	1918	May 1 1941	Collided	With POUGHKEEPSIE SOQONY. In vicinity of New London, in New York State Barge Canal.
252	American Team	Sch.	376	1876	Mar 30 1918	Foundered	Off Winter Quarter Light, Md.
253	Americus	Scow	170	1898	Apr 18 1925	Collided	With st.s. BRONX. Brooklyn, N.Y.
254	Amos Briggs	Sch.	93	1868	Apr 14 1921	Stranded	Off Sandy Hook, N.J.
255	Anadir	Sch.	73	1867	1900	Foundered	Off Port Jefferson, N.Y.
256	Anahuac	St.s.	863	1920	Apr 15 1923	Stranded	Fortunes Rock, near Biddeford, Me. Steel vessel.
257	Anastasia	Brg.	1,313	1919	Feb 15 1933	Foundered	Off Barnegat Light, N.J. 39-57 N. 73-53 W. All (4) lives lost.
258	Andover	Ga.s.	113	1930	Dec 10 1938	Foundered	Between Orleans & Old Harbor L.S. Stations, Cape Cod, Mass.
259	Andrea G.	Ol.s.	107	1928	May 21 1964	Burned	About 50 miles ESE off Shelburne, Nova Scotia.
260	Andrew Axton	St.p.	99	1903	Jan 18 1906	Burned	Duquesne, Pa.
261	Andrew E. Hathaway	Ol.s.	51	1923	Aug 10 1929	Burned	Round Shoals Buoy, Mass.
262	Andrew Fletcher	St.p.	160	1865	Dec 20 1872	Burned	Staten Island, N.Y.
263	Andrew H. Edwards	Sch.	-	-	Jun 26 1888	Unknown	Island Beach, N.J.
264	Andrew J. Snyder	Brg.	292	1902	Sep 7 1918	Foundered	Arlington, N.Y.
265	Andrew J. York	Sch.	-	-	Sep 6 1891	Unknown	7-1/4 miles NW by 1/4N from Nantucket Light, Mass.
266	Andria Doria (It.)	Ol.s.	29,100	-	Jul 26 1956	Collided	With Swedish STOCKHOLM. 40-29-30 N. 69-50-36 W. Depth 225'.
267	Angela	Sch.	-	-	May 20 1858	Unknown	1-1/4 miles WNW of Cross Rip, Mass.
268	Angelia B. Nickerson	Steamer	-	-	Lost 1800's	Unknown	Provincetown, Mass.
269	Angeline Corning	St.s.	98	1852	Nov 21 1872	Burned	Guttenburg, N.J.
270	Anglo-Saxon	-	-	-	Apr 27 1863	Wrecked	Cape Race, Newfoundland. 237 lives lost.
271	Angie B. Watson	Ga.s.	65	1902	Oct 11 1896	Foundered	Block Island, R.I.
272	Angie L. Marshall	Ol.s.	109	1917	Aug 16 1930	Stranded	Bakers Island, Mass.
273	Angler	Sch.	93	1852	Mar 25 1931	Stranded	Burges, Newfoundland.
274	Anglo-Saxon	-	-	-	May 26 1911	Stranded	Duck Island, Long Island Sound.
275	Anita	Sch.	-	-	May 2 1888	Unknown	Point Judith, R.I.
276	Anita Owen	Brig	-	-	Dec 1 1885	Unknown	Nantasket Beach, Mass.
277	Ann	Sch.	-	-	Aug 6 1896	Unknown	Orleans, Mass.
278	Ann Hooper	Brg.	1,900	1915	Feb 7 1942	Foundered	4 miles E by N of Brigantine Shoals, N.J.
279	Ann Louisa Lockwood	Sch.	338	1869	May 23 1914	Stranded	Wallon River, Nova Scotia.
280	Ann Marie Tracy	St.s.	150	1899	Oct 2 1948	Collided	With st.s. ELIZA JANE NICHOLSON. Off pier 64, North River, N.Y.
281	Ann Thomson	Brg.	252	1891	Aug 10 1906	Foundered	Point Lookout, Md.
282	Anna	Bark	-	1874	Nov 25 1891	Unknown	Anticosti Island, Gulf of St. Lawrence.
283	Anna	Sch.	488	-	Apr 29 1907	Stranded	Campbello Island, New Brunswick.
284	Anna A. Holton	Sch.	-	-	Oct 16 1889	Unknown	Provincetown, Mass.
285	Anna B. Jacobs	Sch.	-	-	Mar 20 1885	Unknown	East of Block Island, R.I.
286	Anna Camp	Sch.	83	1883	Dec 24 1921	Foundered	Chesapeake Bay.
287	Anna Camp	Sch.	83	1883	Nov 19 1926	Burned	Chesapeake Bay, Md.

NO.	NAME OF VESSEL	RIG	TONS	BUILT	DATE	CAUSE	PLACE AND COMMENT
288	Anna D. Price	Sch.	-	-	Lost 1800's	Unknown	Off Peaked Hill, Mass.
289	Anna E. Ketchum	Sch.	-	-	Jul 9 1888	Unknown	Peaked Hill, Mass.
290	Anna E. Young	St.s.	66	1872	May 21 1932	Burned	Kearny, N.J.
291	Anna Elizabeth	Sch.	-	-	Nov 9 1890	Unknown	Chatham, Mass.
292	Anna & Ella Benton	Sch.	-	-	Sep 10 1889	Unknown	North Beach, Md.
293	Anna Kenny	C.bt.	103	1890	Jun 21 1912	Foundered	4 miles south of Poughkeepsie, N.Y.
294	Anna L. Sanboon	Sch.	-	-	Aug 5 1897	Unknown	Monomoy Point, Mass.
295	Anna M.	Sloop	-	-	Nov 10 1897	Unknown	Block Island, R.I.
296	Anna M. Dalton	C.bt.	106	1912	Oct 26 1930	Collided	With unknown vessel. Champlain, Quebec.
297	Anna R.	Brg.	405	1905	Feb 5 1913	Foundered	Bartlett Reef, Long Island, N.Y. All lives (2) lost.
298	Anna R. Eaton	Sch.	-	-	Jun 23 1875	Unknown	Kent Swamp, Block Island, R.I.
299	Annapolis	St.p.	485	1892	Oct 29 1935	Burned	Baltimore, Md.
300	Annapolis	Brg.	1,371	1918	Feb 17 1945	Collided	With submarine. In Block Island Sound, N.Y. 41-17 N. 71-38 W. Length 228'.
301	Annie	Smack	-	-	Aug 18 1899	Unknown	Quonochontaug, R.I.
302	Annie Bliss	Sch.	334	1871	Aug 11 1909	Abandoned	110 miles SW of Briar Island, Nova Scotia.
303	Annie Bulger	Brg.	233	1906	Feb 26 1918	Foundered	New York Harbor, N.Y.
304	Annie Conant	Lighter	-	-	Apr 1 1936	Unknown	42-21-45 N. 70-39-05 W.
305	Annie E. Lane	Sch.	-	-	Sep 18 1801	Unknown	Nantucket Shoal, Mass.
306	Annie E. Moore	Sch.	-	-	Aug 27 1890	Unknown	Handkerchief Shoal, Mass.
307	Annie E. Randolph	Sch.	-	-	May 9 1897	Unknown	Orleans, Mass.
308	Annie G.	Sch.	-	-	May 19 1888	Unknown	East of Block Island, R.I.
309	Annie Godfrey	Sch.	-	-	Jan 9 1884	Unknown	East of Block Island, R.I.
310	Annie H. Smith	Sch.	1,487	1876	May 6 1917	Foundered	Off Fire Island, N.Y.
311	Annie J. Russell	Sch.	-	-	Jun 25 1890	Unknown	Peaks Island, Me.
312	Annie L. Henderson	Sch.	428	1880	Sep 1 1906	Burned	Bangor, Me.
313	Annie L. McKeen	Sch.	-	-	Oct 28 1891	Unknown	Downing Cove, Nova Scotia.
314	Annie L. Wilcox	Ol.s.	158	1878	Jul 26 1934	Stranded	Shagwong Reef in Long Island Sound, N.Y.
315	Annie Laura (Br.)	Sch.	-	-	Jun 8 1802	Unknown	Shovelful, Mass.
316	Annie M. Ash	Sch.	1,258	1888	Jan 20 1907	Foundered	Off Fire Island, N.Y.
317	Annie Pendleton	-	-	-	1961	Unknown	580 yds. 353° from Noank Light, Fishers Island Sound, Conn. 41-19.0 N. 71-59.3 W.
318	Annie Perry	Sch.	116	1903	Aug 3 1918	Torpedoed	35 miles west of Seal Island, Nova Scotia.
319	Annie R. Lewis	Sch.	216	1873	Jun 6 1914	Foundered	Off Brazil Rock, Nova Scotia.
320	Annie and Reuben	Sch.	128	1891	Mar 22 1943	Foundered	Off Seaside Park, N.J.
321	Annie Sargent	Sch.	-	-	May 10 1890	Unknown	Westport, Me.
322	Annie Sargent	Sch.	66	1861	Oct 16 1907	Stranded	Bayville Creek, Long Island, N.Y.
323	Annie Steel	Sch.	-	-	Jan 9 1884	Unknown	East of Block Island, R.I.
324	Annie Steel	Sch.	-	-	Sep 6 1886	Unknown	Southwest of Block Island, R.I.
325	Annie Whiting	Sch.	-	-	Jun 28 1883	Unknown	Southwest of Block Island, R.I.
326	Annis	Sch.	-	-	Nov 16 1883	Unknown	Nauset, Mass.
327	Anthony Benton	Sch.	-	-	Oct 15 1885	Unknown	East of Watch Hill Point, R.I.
328	Anthony McCue	Brg.	485	1914	Nov 8 1925	Foundered	Dunkirk, N.Y.
329	Antietam	Ol.s.	63	1890	Oct 18 1928	Stranded	Gay Head, Mass.
330	Antioch	Bkn.	986	1876	Mar 27 1913	Stranded	Oquan Beach, N.J.
331	Antoinette	St.p.	1,118	-	Jan 28 1889	Foundered	41-17-45 N. 70-16-36 W. 3 miles SSE of Muskeget L.S. Station. Depth 50'.
332	Antoinette	St.s.	221	1888	Oct 14 1921	Stranded	Ruffle Bar, Jamaica Bay, N.Y.
333	Anton Von Driel (Bel.)	-	-	-	Dec 29 1919	Sank	Newfoundland. 26 lives lost.
334	Aquatic	Brig	361	-	Feb 24 1893	Unknown	Sow & Pigs Reef, Cuttyhunk Island, Mass. Sugar cargo.
335	Aquebogue	C.bt.	138	1906	Dec 5 1922	Foundered	Lake Oneida, N.Y.

NO.	NAME OF VESSEL	RIG	TONS	BUILT	DATE		CAUSE	PLACE AND COMMENT
336	Aquehonga	St.p.	290	1912	Nov 18	1935	Foundered	Piermont, N.J.
337	Ara	Ol.y.	314	1922	Jul 20	1927	Stranded	Southwest Harbor, Me. Steel vessel.
338	Arab	-	-	-	Apr	1871	Unknown	Exact location not known. See C.G.S. Chart 1208.
339	Arandau	Frgt.	1,334	-	Jan 23	1900	Unknown	41-26-30 N. 70-48-00 W. Steel vessel.
340	Aransas	Sc.b.	1,312	1919	Jan 29	1928	Foundered	Barnegat Light, N.J. All lives (4) lost.
341	Arbic	Sch.	-	-	Jun 23	1879	Unknown	Stephens Cove, Block Island, R.I.
342	Arbittrator	Sch.	106	1897	Dec 13	1916	Foundered	Sailed from New York, N.Y. & has not since reported. All lives (6) lost.
343	Arbutus	Sch.	120	1893	Jul 25	1913	Stranded	Shipigan, New Brunswick.
344	Arcadia	Sch.	127	1901	May 30	1913	Stranded	Wolf Cove, Nova Scotia.
345	Arcaisa	Sch.	-	-	Aug 11	1893	Unknown	Chatham, Mass.
346	Archer & Reeves	Sch.	-	-	Jul 28	1891	Unknown	Brandywine Shoal, Delaware Bay.
347	Arco No.7	Brg.	251	-	Jun 5	1952	Unknown	41-25-30 N. 71-07-23 W. Steel vessel. Fuel cargo. Length 120'.
348	Arco No.8	Brg.	316	-	Nov	1950	Unknown	42-23-24 N. 70-55-10 W. Steel vessel. Fish oil cargo. Length 130'.
349	Arctic	St.s.	-	-	Sep 27	1854	Collided	Cape Race, Newfoundland. Owned by Collins Line. 350 lives lost.
350	Arctic	St.p.	350	1852	Jul 15	1858	Burned	Pittsburgh, Pa.
351	Arcturus	Sch.	-	-	May	1866	Unknown	41-30-40 N. 70-35-30 W. Depth 56'.
352	Ardandher	Steamer	-	-	Apr 23	1800	Unknown	Robinsons Hole, Vineyard Sound, Mass.
353	Ardmore	Sch.	821	1895	Apr 16	1913	Foundered	Barnegat, N.J.
354	Argo	Sch.	-	-	Oct 16	1885	Unknown	Fishers Island, N.Y.
355	Arianna Bateman	Sch.	63	1871	Oct 20	1933	Collided	With unknown vessel. Maryland Point, Md.
356	Ariel	Sloop	54	1857	Sep 21	1908	Burned	New York, N.Y.
357	Ariel	Ga.s.	81	1930	Sep 21	1939	Foundered	Off Nantucket Island, Mass.
358	Arion	Ga.y.	66	1906	Nov 3	1912	Burned	Manchester, Mass.
359	Ariosa	St.s.	140	1885	Jan 4	1906	Stranded	Romer Shoal, N.Y.
360	Arizona	St.s.	765	1868	Dec 1	1922	Burned	Cape Vincent, N.Y.
361	Arkona	Sch.	133	1901	Dec 15	1918	Stranded	Forteau Bay, Labrador.
362	Arlington	Sch.	592	1883	Aug 17	1909	Stranded	Long Beach, N.Y.
363	Arlyn	Frgt.	3,304	-	Aug 28	1942	War Loss	Off Newfoundland. 51-55 N. 55-50 W.
364	Armitage Brearly	St.s.	160	1863	Dec 5	1918	Stranded	Stone Harbor, N.J.
365	Armitage Brearly	St.s.	237	1863	Dec 5	1918	Stranded	Stone Harbor, N.J. See No. 364.
366	Arona (Br.)	Sch.	-	1837	Mar 13	1898	Unknown	Handkerchief Shoals, Mass.
367	Arrow	St.p.	290	1837	Aug 6	1865	Exploded	Haverstraw, N.Y. 5 lives lost.
368	Arrow	St.y.	82	1901	Jan 2	1925	Foundered	Baltimore, Md.
369	Arrow	Ga.y.	55	1917	Sep 21	1938	Foundered	Bristol, R.I.
370	Artenius Tiwell	Sch.	-	-	Sep 23	1889	Unknown	Shovelful Shoals, Mass.
371	Arthur	Sch.	-	-	Jan 3	1887	Unknown	Margaret Harbor, Cape Brenton, Nova Scotia.
372	Arthur Clifford	Sch.	84	1865	May 24	1908	Collided	With st.s. GOVERNOR DINGLEY. Thatchers Island, Mass.
373	Arthur D. Bissell	St.s.	137	1881	Nov 8	1910	Burned	Little Fairy, N.J.
374	Arthur M. Gibson (Br.)	Sch.	-	-	May 21	1896	Unknown	Handkerchief Shoals, Mass. Depth 47'.
375	Arthur Sewall	Ship	3,209	1899	Apr 3	1907	Foundered	Sailed from Philadelphia, Pa. & has not since reported. All 28 lives lost.
376	Artic	-	2,856	-	Sep 27	1854	Collided	With French St.s. VESTA. 60 miles SE of Cape Cod, Mass.
377	Artist	Sch.	-	-	Apr 6	1888	Unknown	Napatree Point, R.I.
378	Arundel	Brg.	418	1902	Apr 9	1916	Foundered	Barnegat, N.J.
379	Arundo (Dutch)	St.s.	5,163	-	Apr 28	1942	War Loss	40-11-04 N. 73-41-12 W. or 40-10-25 N. 73-40-57 W. Belmar, N.J. Depth 60'.
380	Arvesta	Sch.	505	-	Mar 2	1893	Unknown	41-27-12 N. 71-25-33 W. 2 miles NE of Narragansett L.S. Station. Coal cargo.
381	Asa H. Perrere	Sch.	-	-	Oct 17	1890	Unknown	Chatham, Mass.
382	Asa Wilgus	St.s.	412	1857	Sep 3	1860	Snagged	Weston, Md.
383	Ashford	St.s.	132	1883	Nov	1919	Foundered	Near Schenectady, N.Y.

NO.	NAME OF VESSEL	RIG	TONS	BUILT	DATE	CAUSE	PLACE AND COMMENT
384	Ashland	St.s.	762	-	May 17 1879	Unknown	41-21-50 N. 71-29-48 W. 1/2 mile W of Point Judith L.S. Station, R.I.
385	Ashland	Sch.	901	1898	Mar 3 1916	Stranded	Off Minots Ledge Light, Mass. 194' length.
386	Asia	Ship	1,500	-	Feb 20 1898	Wrecked	Great Round Shoal, Mass. Hemp cargo.
387	Astra (Dan.)	Frgt.	2,705	-	Mar 30 1951	Collided	10.5 miles 97-1/2° True from Atlantic City Light, N.J. REMOVED.
388	Atalanta	Brg.	370	1881	Jan 17 1906	Stranded	Seal Island, Penobscot Bay, Me.
389	Atlantic	St.p.	1,112	1846	Nov 27 1846	Stranded	Fishers Island, N.Y. 42 lives lost. Wrecked.
390	Atlantic (Br.)	St.s.	-	-	Apr 1 1873	Wrecked	Off Nova Scotia. Owned by White Star Line. 547 lives lost.
391	Atlantic	St.p.	653	1857	Mar 31 1876	Unknown	Chesapeake Bay. Ferryboat.
392	Atlantic	Brg.	399	1899	Nov 28 1921	Stranded	Seabright, N.J.
393	Atlantic Beach	Drg.	178	1908	Oct 10 1934	Burned	Pelham Bay, N.Y.
394	Atlantic States	Tanker	8,537	-	Apr 5 1945	Unknown	42-07 N. 70-00 W. SALVAGED.
395	Atlantic Sun	Ol.s.	11,355	1941	Nov 22 1943	War Loss	Enroute from Reykjavik, Iceland to New York. Steel vessel. Sunk by enemy action.
396	Atlantis	Bark	-	-	Jun 30 1888	Unknown	St. Barbe, Newfoundland.
397	Atlas	Brg.	423	1880	Feb 4 1905	Collided	With steamer KATAHDIN, Long Island, N.Y.
398	Atrato (Br.)	Sch.	-	-	Nov 9 1801	Unknown	Handkerchief Shoals, Mass.
399	Aug. Demarest	C.bt.	122	1888	Dec 13 1917	Stranded	Duck Island, Conn.
400	Augusta (Br.)	Frigate	-	-	1777	Unknown	In Delaware Channel, off New Jersey. Reported to have carried treasure.
401	Augusta	St.p.	218	1838	Sep 1863	Stranded	Hell Gate, N.Y.
402	Augusta	Brig	355	-	Mar 24 1884	Unknown	41-12-00 N. 71-35-24 W. 1/8 mile NNW of Block Is. L.S. Station. General cargo.
403	Augustus J. Fabens	Sch.	-	-	Mar 15 1891	Unknown	Boothbay Harbor, Me.
404	Augustus W. Yates	Sch.	-	-	Lost 1800's	Unknown	Provincetown, Mass.
405	Austin Locke	Sch.	-	-	Dec 10 1885	Unknown	South side of Nantucket Island, Mass. Salt cargo.
406	Avabelle	Sch.	-	-	Nov 10 1897	Unknown	Block Island, R.I.
407	Avalon	Sch.	-	-	Jun 9 1800	Unknown	Nauset, Mass.
408	Avalon	Ga.s.	124	1903	Oct 29 1927	Collided	With st.s. PRESIDENT WILSON, Cape Cod, Mass. 11 lives lost (14).
409	Ave Maria	Ga.s.	57	1926	Jul 18 1928	Collided	With ol.s. MERRIMAC. Watch Hill, R.I.
410	Avenger	Sch.	-	-	Aug 24 1890	Unknown	Watch Hill Reef, R.I.
411	Aviator	Ga.s.	264	1918	Nov 6 1924	Stranded	Sandy Point, Newfoundland.
412	Aviator	Ga.s.	264	1918	Feb 24 1919	Stranded	St. Lawrence Harbor, Newfoundland.
413	Aviel	Sloop	-	-	Aug 8 1802	Unknown	Quonochontaug, R.I.
414	Avon	Ship	1,573	1884	Apr 5 1918	Foundered	Sailed from New York, N.Y. & has not since reported. All lives (17) lost.
415	Ayr	Sch.	-	-	Oct 14 1890	Ashore	On rocks at Napatree Point, R.I.
416	Ayricola	Sch.	-	-	Oct 21 1894	Unknown	Napatree Point, R.I.
417	Azalea City	Frgt.	5,588	-	Feb 16 1942	War Loss	Off east coast of United States.
418	Azores	Ol.s.	114	1911	Jun 1 1932	Burned	Lower East Pubnico, Nova Scotia.
419	B 101	Brg.	801	1933	Feb 10 1955	Foundered	Off coast of Rhode Island. Steel vessel.
420	B. & B. No.8	C.bt.	235	1924	Oct 22 1943	Collided	Sank in center of Hudson River, off 74th Street, N.Y.
421	B. & B. No.10	C.bt.	235	1926	Oct 22 1943	Collided	Sank in center of Hudson River, off 74th Street, N.Y.
422	B. & B. No.13	C.bt.	235	1927	Jan 31 1937	Foundered	In barge canal at Brewerton, N.Y.
423	BC-2596	Scow	195	1943	Nov 13 1957	Foundered	About 5 miles W by S of Burnt Island Whistler, 1 mile SSE of Mosher's Ledge, Me.
424	BC-2890	Scow	195	1944	Aug 31 1954	Foundered	In harbor at Seaport, Me. Wood vessel.
425	B.C. Smith	Sch.	-	-	Mar 9 1891	Unknown	Near Lunenburg, Nova Scotia.
426	B and E	Ol.s.	-	-	1957	Unknown	41-16.8 N. 69-00.8 W. Fisherman. length 64'.
427	B.F. Macomber	Ol.s.	257	1913	Jul 20 1946	Foundered	1.1 nautical miles, 100° True N from Harbor Refuge Lt., Cape Henlopen, Del.
428	B.O. Haskins	Sch.	-	-	May 31 1895	Unknown	Off Nauset, Mass.
429	B.P. Fout	Brg.	125	1905	Dec 21 1917	Unknown	Thompson's Point, N.J.
430	BS No.1	Brg.	195	1944	Oct 1964	Foundered	In Seekonk River, off East Providence, R.I.
431	BS No.94	Brg.	417	1943	Jan 17 1951	Foundered	41-28-00 N. 70-57-20 W. 1 mile S1/2E from Green Buoy #3, Buzzards Bay, Mass.

NO.	NAME OF VESSEL	RIG	TONS	BUILT	DATE		CAUSE	PLACE AND COMMENT
432	B.S. Ford	Brg.	278	1877	Oct 23	1960	Foundered	About 500 yds. off entrance to Honga River, Md. Iron vessel.
433	B.W. O'Hara	Brg.	227	1903	May 11	1914	Foundered	New York Harbor, N.Y.
434	B.Y. 11	Brg.	157	-	Jan 15	1926	Foundered	New York, N.Y.
435	Baby Blue	Brg.	463	1907	Apr 6	1918	Collided	With unknown barge. New York, N.Y.
436	Baden	Brg.	1,128	1892	Dec 31	1905	Stranded	41-29-00 N. 70-57-30 W. Buzzards Bay, Mass. Steel Vessel. All lives (6) lost.
437	Bailey	Brg.	349	1896	Nov 21	1923	Stranded	Chesapeake Canal.
438	Baker	Brg.	996	1876	Dec 21	1905	Burned	Off Atlantic City, N.J.
439	Baker Brothers	Sch.	100	1881	Sep 30	1909	Foundered	23rd. Street and North River, New York, N.Y.
440	Baker Palmer	Sch.	2,792	1901	Dec 11	1915	Foundered	34-21 N. 64-47 W.
441	Baja	Sch.	678	1895	Feb 5	1907	Foundered	Off Atlantic City, N.J. All lives (3) lost.
442	Balloon	St.p.	204	1839	Oct 29	1872	Burned	Philadelphia, Pa.
443	Balsa	Sch.	557	1919	Apr 23	1925	Stranded	Romer Shoal, Sandy Hook, N.Y.
444	Baltic	St.p.	372	1848	Jul 21	1876	Burned	Albany, N.Y.
445	Baltimore	St.p.	850	1888	Jan 6	1926	Burned	Rock Hall, Md. Iron vessel.
446	Baltimore	Brg.	1,307	1916	Dec 31	1952	Collided	With tug ELLEN M. BOUCHARD. In Arthur Kill of Kreicherville, Staten Island, N.Y.
447	Bannent	-	-	-	Oct 24	1897	Unknown	Narragansett Pier, R.I.
448	Banshee	Sloop	57	1880	Oct 1	1924	Stranded	Henderson Harbor, N.Y.
449	Baravia	Ga.y.	1,227	1891	Jan 23	1914	Foundered	Off Montauk Point, Long Island, N.Y.
450	Barbadoes	Brg.	93	1911	Oct 24	1930	Foundered	Atlantic City, N.J. 8 lives lost (11).
451	Barbara G.	St.s.	-	-		1957	Unknown	41-11-51 N. 71-22-06 W. About 8.75 miles, 72° from Block Is. Southeast Light, R.I.
452	Barbara and Gail	Ol.s.	76	1929	Dec 18	1961	Foundered	41-20 N. 69-45 W. On Rose & Crown Shoal, Mass. Depth 18'.
453	Barcelona	Steamer	-	-	Sep 15	1890	Unknown	Red Island, St. Lawrence River.
454	Barge #20	Brg.	-	-		1959	Unknown	39-53-32 N. 75-08-21 W. Buoyed.
455	Baroness	Brg.	1,295	1890	Nov 10	1910	Foundered	15 miles SW of Fire Island Light, N.Y. Steel vessel.
456	Bartie Pierce	Scow	201	1913	Jan 24	1889	Unknown	Canso, Nova Scotia.
457	Baspaco	Sch.	101	1874	Oct 29	1921	Burned	Port Reading, N.J.
458	Bat	St.s.	1,399	1891	Aug 20	1906	Stranded	Grand Manan, New Brunswick.
459	Bay Port	Steamer	-	-	Dec 14	1916	Stranded	Cape Cod Canal, Mass.
460	Bay Ridge	Steamer	-	-	Aug 11	1888	Unknown	Long Island Sound.
461	Bay State (Br.)	Ga.s.	156	1913	Oct	1899	Wrecked	Off coast of Massachusetts.
462	Bay State	St.s.	2,262	1895	Dec 2	1927	Stranded	Liverpool Harbor, Nova Scotia.
463	Baylies Wood	Sch.	-	-	Sep 23	1916	Stranded	Cape Elizabeth, Me.
464	Bayonne	Brg.	97	-	Apr 3	1887	Unknown	Cape Henlopen, Del.
465	Bayudrici	Frgt.	2,908	-	Sep 13	1961	Hurricane	Off Rossnille, N.Y.
466	Beacon	Sch.	341	1886	Jul 20	1877	Unknown	South of Block Island, R.I.
467	Bear Ridge	Brg.	-	Unknown	Apr 7	1909	Foundered	Watch Hill, R.I.
468	Beatrice	Sch.	-	-	Aug 6	1890	Wrecked	38-55-30 N. 74-45-28 W. Cape May Inlet, N.J. Depth 47'.
469	Beatrice	Tanker	-	-	Apr 27	1935	Unknown	Black River, Nova Scotia.
470	Beatrice & Rose	Ol.s.	80	1918	Nov 2	1949	Stranded	42-21-25 N. 70-42-15 W.
471	Beaufort	Brg.	944	1914	Nov 20	1945	Stranded	3/4 mile off Good Harbor Beach, Gloucester, Mass.
472	Beaver	Brg.	342	-	Nov 27	1898	Stranded	Race Rock Lighthouse, N.Y.
473	Beaver Tail	St.p.	284	1896	Sep 21	1938	Unknown	Vineyard Haven Harbor, Mass.
474	Bedevind (Nor.)	Frgt.	2,908	-	Apr 30	1942	War Loss	41-34-35 N. 71-22-42 W. 1-1/4 miles N of Conanicut Island. Length 110'.
475	Belle	Sch.	-	-	Mar 5	1872	Stranded	39-48-30 N. 72-49-00 W. Wreck on side. Depth 192'.
476	Belle A. Nause	Sch.	-	May 20	1890	Unknown	Peaked Hill, Mass.
477	Belle F. Mesick	Brg.	350	1904	Feb 26	1918	Foundered	Cahoon Hollow, Mass.
478	Belle Halladay	Sch.	355	1869	Dec 13	1910	Collided	With sch. GEN'L. E.S. GREELEY. 1 mile W of Pollock Rip Shoal Lt., Mass.

NO.	NAME OF VESSEL	RIG	TONS	BUILT	DATE	CAUSE	PLACE AND COMMENT
480	Belle Higgins	Sch.	-	-	Feb 26 1890	Collided	Shinnecock, Long Island, N.Y.
481	Belle Hindy	Sch.	-	-	Mar 30 1896	Unknown	Long Shoal, Nantucket, Mass.
482	Belle O'Neil	Sch.	-	-	Dec 29 1883	Unknown	Beaver Tail, R.I.
483	Belle R. Hull	Sch.	-	-	Feb 11 1896	Unknown	Watch Hill, R.I. Total loss.
484	Belle Wooster	Sch.	479	1878	Dec 11 1902	Foundered	60 miles east of Cape Ann, Mass. Length 129'.
485	Belleville (Nor.)	Frgt.	-	-	Dec 1957	Unknown	41-26-42 N. 71-21-00 W. or 41-26-38 N. 71-20-51 W. Steel vessel. Rubber cargo.
486	Belmont	Bark	533	-	Apr 9 1894	Unknown	Peaked Hill Bars, Provincetown, Mass. Sugar cargo.
487	Belmont	St.w.	198	1856	May 7 1859	Burned	Pittsburgh, Pa.
488	Belvidere	Sch.	-	-	Dec 21 1891	Unknown	Spencer Island, Nova Scotia.
489	Ben Franklin	Sloop	316	1872	Nov 9 1909	Stranded	Sandwich, Mass.
490	Ben and Joseph	Ol.s.	-	-	Jun 3 1942	Unknown	42-05 N. 66-50 W. Fisherman.
491	Ben Venue	Steamer	-	-	Nov 10 1891	Unknown	Sandgate, Nova Scotia.
492	Benjamin A. Smith	Ga.s.	146	1908	Aug 3 1923	Stranded	Flat Island, Nova Scotia.
493	Benjamin B. Odell	St.s.	2,011	1911	Feb 22 1937	Burned	Marlboro, Newport, R.I. Steel vessel. Length 263'.
494	Benjamin Cole	Sch.	-	-	Lost 1800's	Unknown	Mussle Bar, near Watch Hill, R.I.
495	Benjamin D. Prince	Sch.	-	-	Aug 4 1899	Unknown	Beaver Tail, R.I.
496	Benj. E. Weeks	Sch.	77	1867	Nov 1 1920	Stranded	New York, N.Y.
497	Benjamin Gartside	Sch.	-	-	Oct 5 1889	Collided	2-1/2 miles NW of Handkerchief Shoals, Mass.
498	Benjamin Rush	St.p.	142	1847	Jun 2 1848	Burned	Pittsburgh, Pa.
499	Benjamin M. Wallace	Ga.s.	77	1905	Jul 14 1929	Burned	Thatchers Island, Mass.
500	Benjamin O. Colonna	Ol.s.	145	1903	Oct 26 1948	Collided	With tanker TULLAHOMA. Near Hooper's Island, Md.
501	Benmore	Bark	1,478	1870	Jul 10 1924	Foundered	New York, N.Y. Iron vessel.
502	Berkley	Sch.	650	1904	Feb 26 1918	Stranded	Off Block Island, R.I. Wood vessel. Length 180'.
503	Berkley	Brg.	223	1869	Oct 10 1905	Foundered	New Haven, Conn.
504	Berkshire	St.p.	649	1864	Jun 8 1864	Burned	Poughkeepsie, N.Y. 35 lives lost.
505	Berkshire	Brg.	1,192	1889	May 23 1909	Foundered	Off Sandy Hook, N.J. Steel vessel.
506	Bernard F. Guinan	Brg.	322	1903	Feb 18 1920	Ice	Yonkers, N.Y.
507	Berrien	Ol.s.	132	1906	Jan 11 1935	Burned	Newark, N.J.
508	Bert	Brg.	314	1919	Apr 22 1948	Burned	Cilco Terminal Co. wharf, Bridgeport Harbor, Conn.
509	Bertha F. Walker	Sch.	676	1879	Nov 12 1911	Stranded	41-27-00 N. 70-48-20 W. Robinsons Hole, Naushon Island, Mass.
510	Bertha J. Fellows	Sch.	-	-	1885	Unknown	Monomoy, Mass.
511	Bertha L. Barker	Sch.	85	1895	Apr 7 1916	Foundered	New York, N.Y. All lives lost (13).
512	Bertha Miner	C.bt.	105	1908	Apr 11 1924	Foundered	South Amboy, N.J.
513	Bertie Baxter	Sch.	55	1884	Mar 10 1918	Foundered	Egg Island, N.J.
514	Bertie B. Smith	Sch.	-	-	Jul 6 1886	Unknown	Southwest of Block Island, R.I.
515	Bess	Sloop	-	-	Oct 2 1897	Unknown	Point Judith, R.I.
516	Bessie	Sch.	-	-	Jul 23 1889	Unknown	Catch Harbor, Nova Scotia.
517	Bessie	St.s.	185	1881	Sep 4 1908	Burned	Verplank, N.Y.
518	Bessie C. Beach	Sch.	341	1880	Dec 6 1912	Stranded	Nepeague Beach, Long Island, N.Y.
519	Bessie J.	Brg.	800	1907	Oct 8 1907	Unknown	Narragansett Bay, R.I. Coal cargo.
520	Bessie M. Divine	Sch.	-	-	Sep 20 1896	Unknown	Block Island, R.I.
521	Bethayres	Sc.b.	955	1902	Oct 26 1926	Foundered	Shinnecock Light, N.Y.
522	Bettina	Ol.s.	121	1901	Apr 7 1928	Collided	With USCG Patrol Boat CAHOONE. 40-06 N. 77-44 W.
523	Betty Alden	St.p.	775	1908	Nov 28 1929	Burned	Boston, Mass.
524	Bill R. Hill	Sch.	-	-	Feb 11 1896	Wrecked	On east beach at Watch Hill, R.I. Coal cargo.
525	Bill Stowe	Sch.	460	-	Dec 3 1887	Unknown	Narragansett Pier Beach, R.I. 41-26-12 N. 71-26-30 W. Stone cargo.
526	Bird	St.p.	50	1850	Dec 1 1855	Collided	With PALMETTO. Red Bank, N.J.
527	Bit Bob	Ga.y.	51	1905	Feb 23 1920	Burned	New York, N.Y.

NO.	NAME OF VESSEL	RIG	TONS	BUILT	DATE		CAUSE	PLACE AND COMMENT
528	Black Hawk	-	-	-		1965	Unknown	Woods Hole, Vineyard Sound, Mass. 41-30-44 N. 70-40-05 W.
529	Black Point	St.s.	5,353	1918	May 5	1945	War Loss	41-18-55 N. 71-25-33 W. 3-3/4 miles SE of Pt. Judith Lighthouse. 12 lives lost.
530	Black Warrior	St.p.	1,556	1852	Feb 20	1858	Stranded	Rockaway, N.Y.
531	Blanche	Sch.	109	1899	Jan 3	1918	Burned	Portland Head, Newfoundland.
532	Blanche Ring	Ol.s.	68	1921	Dec 19	1929	Burned	Boston, Mass.
533	Blizzard	Sch.	-	-	Nov 3	1890	Unknown	Lunenburg, Nova Scotia.
534	Blue Book	Brg.	368	1885	Nov 23	1916	Foundered	Off Penfield Reef, Conn.
535	Blue Haven	Brg.	417	1909	Oct 25	1925	Stranded	Long Beach, N.Y.
536	Blue Hummer	Brg.	304	1911	Feb 20	1934	Foundered	Stamford, Conn.
537	Blue Jay	Sch.	-	-	Jul 30	1896	Unknown	Point Judith, R.I.
538	Blue Point	Brg.	300	1900	Jan 18	1918	Foundered	Whitestone, Long Island, N.Y.
539	Blue Ribbon	Brg.	432	1910	Sep 21	1938	Foundered	New London, Conn.
540	Bluebird	Sch.	1,618	1918	Mar 6	1932	Foundered	Perth Amboy, N.J.
541	Bob Connell	St.w.	78	1864	Jun 29	1901	Stranded	Pittsburgh, Pa.
542	Bobb	Sch.	-	-	Jan 10	1883	Unknown	Block Island, R.I.
543	Bohemian	St.s.	72	1906	Jun 13	1935	Collided	With barge GREAT LAKE DREDGE NO.52. New York Harbor, N.Y.
544	Bonanza	Brg.	-	-	Aug 31	1886	Unknown	Watch Hill, R.I.
545	Bone Wreck	-	-	-		1903	Unknown	Opposite Lookout Tower at Island Beach Park, 1-1/2 miles N of Barnegat Inlet, N.J.
546	Bonita	Ol.s.	79	1918	Apr 18	1926	Foundered	Barnegat, N.J.
547	Bonnie Bill	Ol.s.	50	1952	Mar 30	1962	Stranded	On Gay Head, Martha's Vineyard, Mass.
548	Bonnie Breeze	Ol.s.	167	1930	Jan 5	1957	Foundered	42-06 N. 67-42 W. On Georges Bank, Mass. Steel vessel.
549	Bonnie Doon	Sch.	570	1876	Sep 18	1891	Unknown	Canso, Nova Scotia.
550	Boston	Bkn.	570	1876	Dec 6	1906	Stranded	Stone Horse Shoal, Mass.
551	Boston	St.s.	259	1847	Jul 28	1854	Collided	With bark PLYMOUTH. Oak Orchard, N.Y.
552	Boston	Sch.	-	-	Jul 15	1890	Unknown	Mill Creek, Penobscot River, Me.
553	Boston Floating Lifeboat Station	Ol.s.	-	-		1950	Unknown	42-20-32 N. 71-01-28 W. 1,300 yds. 287° True from monument, Castle Hill, Boston Harbor, Mass.
554	Bouquet	Brg.	306	1881	Apr 15	1906	Foundered	Off Quonochontaug, R.I.
555	Bourne	Brg.	1,626	1921	Mar 13	1934	Foundered	Portland, Me.
556	Boyd & Leeds	Sch.	-	-	Aug 5	1897	Unknown	Race Point, Mass.
557	Braddock	Sch.	678	1895	Apr 28	1923	Foundered	Off Point Judith, R.I. 1 life lost. Length 176'.
558	Bradford C. French	Sch.	-	-	May 6	1894	Unknown	Dickens Point, Block Island, R.I.
559	Bragauza	Sch.	-	-	Feb 4	1802	Unknown	Race Point, Mass.
560	Bragauza	Sloop	-	-	Oct 26	1899	Unknown	Wood End, Mass.
561	Brazoria	St.s.	423	1883	Aug 26	1910	Stranded	Absecon Bar, N.J. Iron vessel.
562	Bridgeport	C.bt.	125	1880	Sep 28	1905	Collided	With st.s. NEW YORK. Off Yonkers, N.Y.
563	Bridgeport	-	-	-	Nov	1913	Unknown	St. Lawrence River. 26 lives lost.
564	Brig Carrick	Brig	-	-	May 19	1847	Foundered	St. Lawrence River. 170 lives lost.
565	Brig Florence	Brig	-	-	Aug	1840	Foundered	Newfoundland. 60 lives lost.
566	Brigadier	Ol.s.	92	1929	Oct 17	1960	Collided	With ol.s. BETHCOASTER. At Schaefers Dock, Chesapeake & Delaware Canal, Md.
567	Bright	Brg.	2,176	1918	Sep 17	1940	Stranded	Sharp's Island, Chesapeake Bay, Md.
568	Brilliant	Brg.	319	1881	Jul 23	1911	Foundered	Off Fort Adams, Newport, R.I.
569	Brilliant	Tanker	9,131	-	Jan 25	1943	War Loss	46-13 N. 58-38 W. Off Halifax, Nova Scotia. 12 lives lost (55).
570	Brinda P. Pendleton	Sc.b.	1,522	1918	Apr 16	1946	Burned	42-19-52 N. 71-00-05 W. 1,560 yds. 288° True from Spectacle Is. Rear Range Light, Mass. Length 220'. Depth 34'.
571	Bristol	St.p.	2,962	1867	Mar 18	1889	Burned	Newport, R.I. 77 lives lost.
572	Bristol	-	-	-	Nov 21	1836	Wrecked	Far Rockaway, N.Y. 77 lives lost.
573	Bristol	Sch.	653	1904	Sep 4	1910	Collided	With Italian st.s. DINNAMARE. Barnegat, N.J.

NO.	NAME OF VESSEL	RIG	TONS	BUILT	DATE	CAUSE	PLACE AND COMMENT
574	Bristol	St.p.	226	1905	1932	Foundered	Stamford, Conn. Steel vessel.
575	Britannia	St.s.	66	1883	Oct 1 1921	Stolen	Jersey City, N.J. Vessel stolen from pier and has not been located.
576	British Freedom (Br.)	Tanker	6,995	-	Jan 14 1945	War Loss	44-27-30 N. 63-27-30 W.
577	British Prudence (Br.)	Tanker	-	-	Mar 23 1942	War Loss	45-28 N. 56-13 W.
578	Brittania	Brg.	1,169	1869	May 16 1909	Unknown	41-11-18 N. 71-36-15 W. 3/4 mile SW of Block Island L.S. Station, R.I.
579	Broadway	St.p.	755	1869	Sep 19 1917	Burned	New York, N.Y.
580	Bronx No.4	St.s.	100	1893	Sep 29 1943	Foundered	Pier 5, Staten Island, N.Y.
581	Brookline	Ol.s.	196	1931	Apr 29 1954	Foundered	About 160 miles SE by 1/2 mile E of Canso, Nova Scotia.
582	Brooklyn	Sch.	70	1869	Mar 26 1920	Stranded	St. Marys River, Md.
583	Brooklyn	Brg.	1,880	1883	Mar 29 1936	Foundered	Kill Van Kull, West New Brighton, Staten Island, N.Y. Iron vessel.
584	Brownstone	Brg.	176	1869	Feb 15 1943	Foundered	At Black Walnut Bar, Great Choptank River, Md.
585	Brumfield	Sch.	-	-	Sep 1 1895	Unknown	Sugar Reef, Watch Hill, R.I.
586	Brunette	St.s.	274	1867	Feb 1 1870	Collided	With SANTIAGO DE CUBA. Squan, N.J. Steel vessel. 2 lives lost.
587	Brunette	Sch.	-	-	Sep 19 1889	Unknown	Searsport Harbor, Me.
588	Brunswick	Brg.	680	1912	May 11 1966	Foundered	In Chesapeake Bay, Md. 38-32 N. 76-25 W.
589	Buaco	Sch.	-	-	Jul 1 1889	Unknown	Beaver Tail, R.I.
590	Bucephelus	Sch.	-	-	Feb 1 1882	Unknown	Nantasket Beach, Mass.
591	Budget	Brg.	363	1871	Nov 27 1898	Unknown	Vineyard Haven Harbor, Mass. Coal cargo.
592	Buena Ventura	Sch.	1,660	1871	Dec 7 1906	Foundered	Off Montauk Point, N.Y.
593	Buffalo	St.p.	429	1854	Jun 29 1854	Foundered	New York, N.Y.
594	Buffalo	Sloop	482	1882	Jul 18 1908	Foundered	Fishers Island Sound, N.Y.
595	Buffalo	St.s.	131	1885	Nov 21 1913	Burned	Staten Island, N.Y.
596	Bunker Hill	St.p.	310	1835	Oct 30 1841	Stranded	Saybrook, Conn.
597	Bunker Hill	St.p.	457	1837	Sep 2 1851	Burned	Tonawanda, N.Y.
598	Burns Bros. No.82	Brg.	227	1894	May 19 1950	Foundered	At coal piers, South Amboy, N.J.
599	Burnside	Sch.	855	-	Apr 20 1913	Foundered	12 miles south of Fire Island Lightship, N.Y.
600	Bushrod W. Hill	Sch.	-	-	Jul 14 1889	Collided	Cape Cod, Mass.
601	Bushwick	Brg.	269	1927	Oct 2 1948	Collided	With st.s. ELIZA JANE NICHOLSON. In North River, New York City, N.Y.
602	Byrnes Sisters	C.bt.	128	1893	Aug 1 1924	Foundered	Waterford, N.Y.
603	C1	Brg.	518	1906	Aug 31 1928	Foundered	New York, N.Y.
604	C.B. Clark	Sch.	194	1866	Sep 30 1916	Stranded	Long Island City, N.Y.
605	C.B. Hamilton	Bark	-	-	Dec 28 1866	Unknown	Near Point Judith Light, R.I.
606	C.B. Hazeltine	Sch.	-	-	Mar 12 1888	Unknown	Delaware Bay.
607	C.B. Payne	Sch.	-	-	Jun 6 1883	Unknown	Northwest of Block Island, R.I.
608	C.B. Rossell	Brg.	178	1880	Aug 24 1906	Foundered	Off Poplar Island, Md.
609	C.B. Wood	Sch.	236	1867	Jul 12 1909	Stranded	Patridge Island, St. John, New Brunswick.
610	C.C. Lane	Sch.	321	1873	Mar 19 1906	Stranded	42-19-38 N. 70-53-25 W. Boston Lighthouse, Mass. Length 130'.
611	C.E. Schmidt	Sch.	-	-	Lost 1800's	Unknown	Off Chatham, Mass.
612	C.E. Trumbell	Sloop	-	-	Lost 1800's	Unknown	Off Peaked Hill Bars, Mass.
613	C.G. Donehue	C.bt.	107	1882	Sep 30 1909	Foundered	32nd. Street, South Brooklyn, N.Y.
614	C. Graham	Sch.	-	-	Jan 24 1887	Unknown	Near Halifax, Nova Scotia.
615	C.H. Frances	Ol.s.	73	1895	Oct 24 1931	Stranded	Long Island Sound, N.Y.
616	C.H. Sprague	Tanker	-	-	Oct 5 1931	Unknown	42-20-24 N. 70-40-47 W.
617	C.H. Tucker	C.bt.	227	1890	Feb 5 1909	Collided	With unknown dredge. Hell Gate, N.Y.
618	C.J. Kerry	Brg.	-	-	1961	Unknown	Lower Hudson River, N.Y. 2,245 yds. 013° from Lower Hudson River Light #23. 41-21-1 N. 73-57.8 W. Depth 74'. Lies in northerly direction. Oil cargo.
619	C.L. Haines	St.s.	125	1890	Dec 17 1920	Stranded	East India Rocks, Conn.
620	C.L. & T. Co. No.268	Scow	134	1905	Sep 27 1930	Foundered	Love Point Lighthouse, Chesapeake Bay, Md.

NO.	NAME OF VESSEL	RIG	TONS	BUILT	DATE	CAUSE	PLACE AND COMMENT
621	C.T. No.5	Brg.	177	1891	Nov 13 1904	Foundered	Long Island Sound.
622	CRR No. 10	Brg.	-	-	Dec 24 1900	Unknown	Monomoy, Cape Cod, Mass.
623	C.W. Dexter	Sch.	91	1858	May 12 1915	Foundered	4 miles E of Little River, Me.
624	C.W. Loche	Sch.	-	-	Jul 1888	Collided	Portsmouth, N.H.
625	C.W. Lock	Sch.	-	-	Apr 15 1886	Unknown	Napatree Point, R.I.
626	C.W. Morse	Steamer	-	-	Aug 1 1897	Unknown	Race Point, Mass.
627	C.W. Morse	St.s.	509	1889	Jul 17 1916	Foundered	New York, N.Y. Sailed and never reported. All lives (25) lost.
628	C. Vanderbuilt	Steamer	-	-	Jan 4 1859	Unknown	Fishers Island, Conn.
629	C.Y. Davenport	St.s.	52	1863	Apr 10 1872	Exploded	Jersey City, N.J. 6 lives lost.
630	Cachalot	St.y.	174	1901	Jun 21 1925	Burned	Southport, Conn.
631	Caddo	Brg.	432	1910	Aug 26 1921	Foundered	7 miles, 169° from Barnegat Inlet, N.J. Depth 64'. Steel vessel.
632	Caddo	St.s.	10,172	1942	Nov 23 1942	War Loss	38-21-00 N. 55-43-00 W. Sunk by enemy action. Steel vessel.
633	Cadet	Sch.	-	-	Unknown	Unknown	South of Manasquan Inlet, 3 miles offshore, Point Pleasant, N.J. Depth 73'.
634	Calabria	Brg.	-	-	Sep 24 1899	Unknown	Monomoy Point, Cape Cod, Mass.
635	Calatco No.2	Ol.s.	101	1918	Nov 13 1946	Burned	Oswego Harbor, N.Y.
636	California	Ol.s.	82	1917	Sep 15 1955	Foundered	In Ipswich Bay, off Rockport, Mass.
637	California	Ol.s.	-	-			42-40-25 N. 70-34-19 W. Ex-sub chaser converted to fisherman. See No.636.
638	Calvin	Brg.	415	1908	Jan 29 1930	Foundered	Patuxent River, Md.
639	Calvin B. Orcutt	Sch.	950	-	Dec 23 1896	Unknown	41-41-42 N. 69-54-48 W. 1/2 mile offshore, opposite Old Harbor L.S. Station.
640	Calvin F. Baker	Sch.	567	-	Nov 27 1898	Unknown	42-19-47 N. 70-52-55 W. Shag Rocks, Broad Sound, Boston, Mass. Length 144'.
641	Calvin P. Harris	Sch.	-	-	Lost 1800's	Unknown	Off Race Point L.S. Station, Cape Cod, Mass.
642	Calvin Tomkins	St.s.	187	1888	Dec 14 1920	Foundered	Near Bridgeport, Conn. 2 lives lost (13).
643	Cambria	St.s.	85	1871	Feb 4 1920	Burned	Jersey City, N.J.
644	Cambridge	St.p.	1,337	1867	Feb 10 1886	Stranded	Old Man Ledge, Me.
645	Camellia	Bark	-	-	Sep 9 1891	Unknown	Scatarie, Cape Breton, Nova Scotia.
646	Cameo	Sch.	243	1878	Apr 2 1933	Foundered	Bucksport, Me.
647	Camilla May Page	Sch.	688	1905	Nov 18 1928	Stranded	Portsmouth, N.H.
648	Canary	Sch.	-	-	Dec 21 1899	Unknown	Muskeget, Mass.
649	Canisteo	Sc.b.	671	1891	Nov 17 1924	Foundered	Monhegan, Me.
650	Cannonbury (Br.)	St.s.	1,676	-	Mar 28 1888	Unknown	Old Man Shoal, Nantucket Island, Mass. Iron vessel. Sugar cargo.
651	Can't Help It	Sch.	-	-	Apr 1891	Collided	Off Halifax, Nova Scotia.
652	Canton	Sch.	531	1899	Apr 28 1923	Foundered	Off Point Judith, R.I. Length 167'.
653	Cape Ann	Ol.s.	79	1929	Mar 6 1948	Stranded	On Nauset Beach, Cape Cod, Mass., near Nauset Lighthouse.
654	Cape Cod	Sch.	-	-	Jul 19 1802	Unknown	Provincetown, Mass.
655	Cape Cod	St.s.	557	1900	Feb 5 1927	Collided	With st.s. MICHAEL TRACY. Astoria Ferry, N.Y. 1 life lost (25).
656	Cape Fear	St.s.	2,795	1919	Oct 29 1920	Collided	With st.s. CITY OF ATLANTA. 41-28-30 N. 71-21-00 W. Concrete vessel. 19 lives lost (44).
657	Capital City	Brg.	440	1875	Feb 23 1917	Foundered	Block Island Sound, R.I. 1 life lost.
658	Capt. Mathiasen	St.s.	117	1899	Apr 20 1928	Burned	Gravesend Bay, N.Y.
659	Capt. Matt	Ol.s.	57	1922	Mar 18 1937	Foundered	Near Eatona Neck, N.Y.
660	Car of Commerce	St.p.	127	1836	Apr 5 1838	Foundered	Philadelphia, Pa.
661	Carara	Bark	-	-	Jun 28 1888	Unknown	Squam Beach, N.J.
662	Carch	Sch.	-	-	Dec 19 1890	Unknown	Camp Island, Me.
663	Carl D. Lothrop	Sch.	-	-	Lost 1800's	Unknown	Off Race Point, Mass.
664	Carlos French	Brg.	433	1899	Dec 20 1914	Foundered	Off Bartletts Reef, Long Island Sound.
665	Carlotta	Sch.	-	-	Dec 31 1895	Unknown	Tuckernuck Shoal, Mass.
666	Carmac	Ol.s.	224	1929	Sep 18 1953	Stranded	On Watch Hill Reef, R.I. Steel vessel.
667	Carmania	St.p.	321	1896	Mar 12 1924	Foundered	Fall River, Mass. Steel vessel.

NO.	NAME OF VESSEL	RIG	TONS	BUILT	DATE	CAUSE	PLACE AND COMMENT
668	Carniola	Bark	-	1944	Oct 2 1891	Unknown	Bryon Island, Gulf of St. Lawrence.
669	Carol and Estelle	Ol.s.	63	1944	Nov 18 1960	Burned	Approx. 30 miles SSE of Round Shoals Buoy, Mass.
670	Carolina	Brg.	334	1897	Feb 22 1912	Collided	With barge ELLEN S. JENNINGS. Poplar Island, Chesapeake Bay, Md.
671	Carolina	St.s.	5,093	1896	Jun 2 1918	Torpedoed	38-57 N. 73-06 W. 13 lives lost. German Submarine Activities 1st World War.
672	Carolina	C.bt.	100	1912	Nov 24 1931	Collided	With ferry FORT LEE. Hudson River, N.Y.
673	Caroline	Sch.	-	-	Apr 8 1889	Unknown	Cove Point Bar, Md.
674	Caroline	St.s.	63	1875	Aug 6 1922	Burned	Brooklyn, N.Y.
675	Caroline Ann Cornelier	Sch.	200	-	Spring 1876	Unknown	Short Beaver Tail, R.I.
676	Caroline Kunesle	Sch.	-	-	Jun 10 1877	Unknown	South of Block Island, R.I.
677	Carolyn	St.s.	2,241	1889	Jan 10 1912	Stranded	Metinic Island, Me. Steel vessel.
678	Carpender	Sc.b.	1,566	1906	Dec 12 1933	Foundered	Ocean City, Md.
679	Carrie A. Lane	Sch.	-	-	Dec 27 1890	Unknown	Napatree Point, R.I.
680	Carrie C.	Sch.	-	-	Aug 21 1899	Unknown	Wood End, Cape Cod, Mass.
681	Carrie C. Miles	Sch.	106	1871	Oct 15 1907	Stranded	Dry Romer Shoal, N.Y.
682	Carrie Clark	Sch.	1,298	1874	Nov 28 1921	Foundered	Northwest of Highland Light, N.J. All lives (3) lost.
683	Carrie E. Look	Sch.	530	1890	Dec 8 1916	Foundered	Perth Amboy, N.J.
684	Carrie E. Philips	Sch.	-	-	Aug 13 1897	Unknown	Wood End, Mass.
685	Carrie E. Sayward	Sch.	-	-	Nov 27 1898	Storm	Provincetown, Mass.
686	Carrie E. Wright	Sch.	58	1868	Mar 3 1916	Stranded	Cedar Point, Chesapeake Bay.
687	Carrie L. Paysire	Sch.	-	-	Nov 26 1898	Unknown	Chatham, Mass.
688	Carrie Lida	Sloop	-	-	Nov 27 1898	Storm	Provincetown, Mass.
689	Carrie M. Richardson	Sch.	-	-	Jan 12 1887	Unknown	Off Race Point L.S. Station, Mass.
690	Carrie S. Roderick	Ol.s.	73	1927	Dec 16 1932	Foundered	Off Highland Light, Mass.
691	Carrie W.	Sch.	-	-	Jan 11 1887	Unknown	Highland Light, Mass.
692	Carroll	Sc.b.	1,281	1920	Feb 16 1930	Foundered	Cape May, N.J. All lives (4) lost.
693	Cartagena	St.s.	1,532	1901	Jul 1 1907	Stranded	Cape Negro, Nova Scotia.
694	Casco Bay	Ol.s.	93	1928	Jun 25 1964	Foundered	About 5 miles northwest of Cashes Buoy, Gulf of Maine.
695	Caspian	Ol.s.	94	1936	Mar 16 1953	Foundered	About 48 miles SSE of Five Fathom Lightship and 48 miles due E of Assateague Island, Md.
696	Cassandra	St.s.	1,284	1864	Feb 5 1867	Stranded	Brigantine Shoals, N.J.
697	Cassie	Brg.	948	1890	Oct 24 1917	Stranded	Sandy Hook, N.J. Steel vessel.
698	Castagna (It.)	Bark	843	-	Feb 17 1914	Unknown	41-53-40 N. 69-57-18 W. 3-1/2 miles S of Cahoons Hollow L.S. Station.
699	Castalia	St.s.	3,599	1890	Jan 11 1919	Foundered	Off Sable Island, Nova Scotia. 4 lives lost.
700	Castillian	Sch.	-	-	Aug 30 1890	Unknown	Bald Porcupine Island, Me.
701	Castine	St.s.	69	1889	Jun 8 1935	Stranded	Bay Leges, Vinalhaven, Me. 3 lives lost (68).
702	Castleton	Brg.	412	1899	Oct 1 1907	Collided	With st.p. ROCHESTER. New York, N.Y.
703	Castor	St.s.	73	1891	Mar 7 1923	Foundered	New York, N.Y.
704	Catalina	Sch.	57	1857	Jul 18 1905	Stranded	Rockland, Me.
705	Catawamteak	Sch.	148	1864	Apr 29 1922	Foundered	43-27-53 N. 69-18-59 W.
706	Catherine	Ol.s.	159	1915	Dec 31 1933	Stranded	Canso Harbor, Nova Scotia.
707	Catherine C	Ol.s.	75	1937	Sep 12 1964	Burned	Approx. 10 miles east of Burin, Newfoundland.
708	Catherine Connolly	C.bt.	106	1912	Nov 23 1922	Unknown	Sylvan Beach, Oneida Lake, N.Y.
709	Catherine and Ellen	Sch.	145	1902	Jun 29 1911	Collided	With st.s. NACOOCHEE. Cape Cod, Mass.
710	Catherine G. Howard	Sch.	122	1905	Apr 21 1907	Stranded	Off Seguin, Me.
711	Catherine Horan	Brg.	481	1916	Oct 23 1917	Stranded	Green Hill, R.I.
712	Catherine Nichols	Sch.	-	-	Dec 15 1839	Foundered	Nahant Rocks, Mass.
713	Cathie C. Berry	Sch.	-	-	Jan 29 1899	Unknown	Peaked Hill Bars, Mass.
714	Catonsville	Sc.b.	1,281	1919	Jan 29 1928	Foundered	Barnegat Light, N.J. All lives (4) lost.

NO.	NAME OF VESSEL	RIG	TONS	BUILT	DATE	CAUSE	PLACE AND COMMENT
715	Catonsville	Brg.	2,236	1919	Feb 6 1937	Foundered	17-1/2 miles east by north, 3/4 mile north from Chesapeake Light Vessel.
716	Cavaire	Sch.	-	-	Jan 12 1802	Unknown	Wood End, Mass.
717	Caviare	Sch.	-	-	Dec 16 1896	Unknown	Provincetown, Mass.
718	Cayru (Braz.)	Frgt.	5,152	-	Mar 8 1942	War Loss	39-05 N. 73-47 W.
719	Cecelia M. Dunlap	Brg.	835	1876	Sep 12 1931	Foundered	Scotland Lightship, N.Y. Iron vessel. 40-25-52 N. 73-55-09 W. Depth 60'.
720	Cecelia McIlvaine	Brg.	489	1901	Jul 13 1921	Stranded	Scarborough Beach, R.I.
721	Cecil P. Stewart	Brg.	1,216	1919	Feb 17 1927	Stranded	Harvey Cedars, N.J.
722	Celena Delorme	C.bt.	99	1900	May 19 1923	Stranded	Point-a-Citrouille, St. Lawrence River.
723	Centennial	Sch.	-	-	Aug 5 1896	Unknown	Peaked Hill, Mass.
724	Centennial	Sch.	115	1876	Mar 7 1923	Stranded	Bliss Island, New Brunswick.
725	Central States	St.s.	63	1872	Nov 17 1933	Foundered	Clyde, N.Y.
726	Chaika	Ol.y.	81	1917	Oct 19 1931	Foundered	Chesapeake Bay, Md.
727	Chalmet	Sch.	-	-	Oct 27 1893	Unknown	Pollock Rip, Mass.
728	Champion	St.p.	1,419	1859	Nov 8 1879	Collided	With British bark LADY OCTAVIA. Cape Henlopen, Del. Steel vessel. 31 lives lost.
729	Champion	Sch.	-	-	Nov 27 1898	Unknown	Provincetown, Mass.
730	Chancellor	St.s.	383	1910	Jul 31 1928	Burned	Rosebank, Staten Island, N.Y. 3 lives lost (12).
731	Charger	Sch.	-	-	Jan 1887	Unknown	Ipswich, Mass.
732	Charlemagne Tower, Jr.	St.s.	1,825	1886	Mar 26 1914	Foundered	Off Barnegat, N.J.
733	Charles A. Gilberg	Brg.	234	1896	Aug 1 1913	Foundered	Off Norwalk, Conn.
734	Charles A. Ropes	Sch.	485	1890	Nov 28 1911	Abandoned	75 miles SE of Cape Henlopen, Del.
735	Charles A. Smith	Ol.s.	54	1903	Jul 30 1950	Foundered	Tuckernuck Flats, Nantucket, Mass. Coal cargo.
736	Charles Atkinson	Sch.	68	1862	Oct 13 1913	Foundered	Near Charity Ledge, off Baileys Island, Me.
737	Charles B. Sanford	St.s.	151	1871	Jun 9 1917	Stranded	At Mattinicock Point, Long Island.
738	Charles C. McIlvaine	Brg.	522	1912	Sep 6 1923	Burned	Nantasket, Mass.
739	Charles Dennis	Brg.	-	-	May 1 1890	Unknown	South Amboy, N.J. Steel vessel.
740	Charles E. Dunlap	Sch.	1,609	1904	Jul 22 1919	Stranded	Whales Back, Kennebec River, Me.
741	Charles E. Raymond	Sch.	500	-	Winter 1868	Unknown	Far Rockaway Beach, N.Y.
742	Charles E. Sears	Sch.	169	1874	Nov 27 1905	Stranded	Long Gully, 1/4 mile north of Beaver Tail, R.I.
743	Charles E. Wyman	Sch.	234	1882	May 30 1919	Foundered	Chatham, Mass.
744	Charles F. Prichard	Brg.	861	1904	Oct 23 1937	Foundered	Off Sable Island, Nova Scotia.
745	Charles F. Sampson	Sch.	745	-	Feb 18 1891	Unknown	11-1/2 miles SE from water tower off Atlantic City, N.J.
746	Charles G. Hill	Brg.	192	1864	Dec 1 1906	Foundered	41-27-38 N. 71-02-03 W. Near Hen & Chickens Lightship. Coal Cargo.
747	Charles H. Baxter	Brg.	523	1930	May 19 1950	Burned	Off Marlborough, N.Y.
748	Chas. H. Burton	Sch.	514	1873	Oct 11 1905	Stranded	Due to an explosion at South Amboy, N.J.
749	Charles H. Sprague	Sch.	318	1882	Jul 13 1913	Foundered	Westfield, N.Y.
750							Monhegan Island, Me.
751	Charles H. Trickey	Sch.	281	1879	Jan 1 1920	Stranded	Cape Porpoise, Me.
752	Charles H. Wolston	Sch.	350	1883	Nov 17 1911	Stranded	41-25-25 N. 70-02-15 W. Coal cargo. Length 133'.
753	Charles J. Willard	Sch.	253	1874	Sep 18 1909	Collided	With wreck. Vineyard Sound, Mass.
754	Charles K. Buckley	Sch.	507	1890	Apr 15 1914	Stranded	Off Long Branch, N.J. 8 lives lost.
755	Charles Kennedy, Jr.	St.s.	135	1902	1944	Foundered	Sank at Pig Iron dock, Elizabethport, N.J.
756	Charles L. Mitchell	Sch.	-	-	Feb 11 1883	Unknown	Fishers Island, N.Y.
757	Charles Lawrence	Sch.	436	1874	Nov 9 1914	Foundered	Point Judith, Long Island Sound.
758	Charles Loring	Bark	552	1878	Feb 2 1907	Collided	With st.s. SENECA. Off Sandy Hook, N.J.
759	Charles Luling	Sch.	195	1873	Dec 13 1913	Stranded	East end of Middle Ground, Vineyard Haven, Mass.
760	Charles McAllister	St.s.	195	1878	Apr 21 1924	Foundered	Foot of 29th Street, Brooklyn, N.Y. Iron vessel.
761	Charles McWilliams	St.s.	83	1862	Mar 9 1922	Foundered	Bridgeport Harbor, Conn.
762	Charles R. Stone	St.s.	55	1873	Nov 7 1924	Burned	Bayonne, N.J.

NO.	NAME OF VESSEL	RIG	TONS	BUILT	DATE	CAUSE	PLACE AND COMMENT
763	Charles S. Ashley	Ol.s.	74	1927	Mar 3 1936	Collided	With ol.s. THE FRIARS. Georges Bay, Mass.
764	Charles S. Griffin	C.bt.	96	1883	Oct 1 1909	Foundered	Morris Canal Basin, New York, N.Y.
765	Charles S. Haight	St.s.	7,198	1944	Apr 2 1946	Foundered	Off Rockport, Mass. 42-40-38 N. 70-35-03 W. Steel Vessel.
766	Charles S. Rogers	Sch.	-	1864	May 31 1879	Collided	Off Cape Cod, Mass.
767	Charles Thomas	St.s.	1,155	1864	Nov 7 1868	Collided	With GENERAL MEADE. Sandy Hook, N.J.
768	Charles W. Church	Sch.	844	1894	Oct 31 1914	Foundered	38-18-00 N. 70-58-00 W.
769	Charles W. Morse	Sch.	-	-	May 1888	Unknown	Southern part of Newport Harbor, R.I.
770	Charles W. Parker	Sch.	57	1883	Apr 23 1907	Stranded	Absecon Inlet, N.J.
771	Charleston	St.p.	94	1887	Feb 10 1906	Stranded	Wolf Island Shute, Me.
772	Charley Woolsey	Sch.	207	1865	Jul 25 1908	Collided	With st.s. MAINE. Cornfield Light, Conn.
773	Charlie and Willie	Sch.	123	1849	Oct 30 1923	Burned	New York, N.Y.
774	Charlott Fish	Sch.	-	-	Dec 1892	Unknown	Monomoy, Mass.
775	Charlotte	Sch.	-	-	Dec 22 1839	Unknown	Nantasket Beach, Mass.
776	Charlotte	Ga.s.	77	1917	Dec 9 1931	Stranded	Sea Girt Light, N.J.
777	Charlotte	Brg.	431	1905	Jan 8 1942	Stranded	Southwest Point Lookout, Md.
778	Charlotte A. Maxwell	Sch.	688	1917	Mar 27 1923	Stranded	Off False Hook Shoal, Sandy Hook, N.J.
779	Charlotte L. Morgan	Sch.	70	1854	Apr 16 1905	Stranded	Southern Island, Me.
780	Charlotte M.	Ol.s.	119	1945	Feb 26 1962	Burned	About 2.1 miles ENE of Minot's Light, Cohasset, Mass.
781	Charnley	St.s.	83	1882	Jul 15 1922	Burned	Port Jefferson Harbor, New York, N.Y.
782	Charter Oak	St.p.	439	1838	Mar 4 1850	Burned	New York, N.Y.
783	Chatham	St.s.	5,649	-	Aug 27 1942	War Loss	Off Newfoundland. 51-52-00 N. 55-30-00 W.
784	Chattanooga	Bark	527	-	Jun 25 1888	Unknown	Fourth Cliff, Mass. 42-06-18 N. 70-38-54 W. Salt cargo.
785	Chattanooga	Sch.	-	-	Dec 12 1890	Unknown	Orleans, Mass.
786	Chehegan	Sch.	-	-	Feb 11 1897	Unknown	East of Block Island, R.I.
787	Chelsea	Ol.s.	556	1919	Feb 10 1957	Stranded	North of Thatchers Island, Rockport, Mass. 42-38-53 N. 70-34-10 W. Length 170'.
788	Chemung	Sch.	671	1891	Dec 3 1921	Foundered	Off Dumplings Bell Buoy, Newport, R.I. Length 158'.
789	Cherokee	Tug	-	-	Feb 26 1918	Storm	Delaware Capes. Operated by U.S. Navy. 23 lives lost.
790	Cherokee	St.s.	267	1892	Nov 8 1936	Foundered	At dock, foot of East 7th Street, New York, N.Y. Steel vessel. All lives (1) lost.
791	Cherokee	St.s.	5,896	1925	Jun 15 1942	War Loss	42-11 N. 69-25 W. Off Massachusetts coast. Sunk by enemy action.
792	Cherubim	Sch.	98	1873	Apr 9 1918	Foundered	Off Wolf Trap, Chesapeake Bay.
793	Cheslyme	St.p.	50	1914	Nov 9 1938	Foundered	Mouth of Oyster River, Saybrook, Conn.
794	Chester R. Lawrence	Sch.	123	1874	Oct 24 1913	Stranded	Fishermans Island, near Boothbay Harbor, Me.
795	Chicopee	St.s.	172	1851	Jul 28 1869	Burned	Maurice River, N.J.
796	Chief Powhatan	Ol.w.	93	1927	Jun 19 1957	Foundered	At Mile No.4, Allegheny River, Pa. Steel vessel.
797	Chillion	Sch.	-	-	Apr 4 1891	Collided	Thatchers Island, Mass.
798	China Arrow	St.s.	8,403	1920	Feb 5 1942	War Loss	37-44-00 N. 73-18-00 W. Steel vessel. Sunk by enemy action.
799	Chippewa	Brg.	421	1917	Dec 8 1917	Foundered	Off Point Judith, R.I. All lives (3) lost.
800	Choapa (Chil.)	Frgt.	1,700	-	Sep 21 1944	Collided	With British tanker VOCO. 40-13-00 N. 73-44-52 W. Depth 150'.
801	Chris Olsen	St.s.	54	1907	Apr 19 1948	Burned	At Mariners Harbor, Staten Island, N.Y.
802	Chrystenah	St.p.	571	1866	Nov 16 1920	Stranded	New Rochelle, N.Y.
803	Cienfuegos	Sch.	1,915	1902	May 27 1922	Foundered	Southwest of Barnegat Buoy, N.J.
804	Cigar Joe	Ol.s.	78	1944	Dec 30 1963	Collided	With unknown object. About 25 miles SE of Gloucester, Mass.
805	Cinderella	Sch.	57	1836	Nov 12 1898	Stranded	Fire Island Inlet, N.Y.
806	Circassian	Brig	-	-	1896	Unknown	Off Chatham, Mass.
807	Cities Service No.4	Brg.	810	1929	Jan 24 1936	Foundered	4 miles E of Cornfield Lightship, Conn. Steel vessel.
808	City of Albany	St.p.	458	1863	Oct 6 1894	Burned	New York, N.Y.
809	City of Annapolis	St.s.	1,923	1913	Feb 24 1927	Collided	With st.s. CITY OF RICHMOND. Smiths Point, Chesapeake Bay. Steel vessel.
810	City of Athens	St.s.	3,648	1911	May 1 1918	Collided	With French cruiser LA GLORIE. Off Atlantic City, N.J. 66 lives lost.

NO.	NAME OF VESSEL	RIG	TONS	BUILT	DATE	CAUSE	PLACE AND COMMENT
811	City of Augusta	Sch.	-	-	Lost 1800's	Unknown	Off Peaked Hill, Mass.
812	City of Baltimore	St.s.	2,379	1911	Jul 29 1937	Burned	Seven Foot Knoll, Chesapeake Bay, Md. Steel vessel.
813	City of Birmingham	St.s.	3,066	1888	Nov 4 1907	Foundered	Castle Island, Boston Bay, Mass. Iron vessel.
814	City of Brunswick	St.s.	5,850	1921	Aug 26 1921	Stranded	Sisters Rocks, southwest of Halifax, Nova Scotia. Steel vessel.
815	City of Columbus	St.s.	2,200	1884	Jan 18 1884	Unknown	41-21-36 N. 70-50-55 W. Devils Bridge Reef, Gay Head, Mass. Iron vessel. Length 275'. 99 lives lost. Used as passenger vessel.
816	City of Detroit	C.bt.	118	1875	Apr 18 1906	Burned	St. George, N.Y.
817	City of Ellsworth	Sch.	-	-	Nov 27 1889	Unknown	Boon Island, Me.
818	City of Georgetown	Sch.	599	1902	Feb 2 1913	Collided	With German st.s. PRINZ OSKAR. Delaware Capes.
819	City of Gloucester	Sch.	-	-	Jun 1 1879	Storm	On Whalemans Shoal, Chatham, Mass.
820	City of Hartford	St.p.	814	1852	1886	Stranded	Parson's Point, Rye Beach, N.Y. Renamed "Capitol City" in 1883.
821	City of Hudson	St.p.	444	1863	Jan 8 1890	Burned	Albany, N.Y.
822	City of Lawrence	St.p.	1,678	1867	Jul 2 1907	Stranded	Eastern Point, New London, Conn. Iron vessel.
823	City of Montreal	Sch.	1,130	1861	Nov 27 1909	Stranded	Plymouth Bay, Mass.
824	City of New London	St.p.	696	1863	Nov 27 1871	Burned	Norwich, Conn. 17 lives lost.
825	City of Orleans	Sch.	2,347	1919	Nov 13 1923	Foundered	Off Fenwick Island Lightship, Del.
826	City of Philadelphia	-	-	-	Sep 9 1854	Wrecked	Cape Race, Newfoundland.
827	City of Rockland	St.p.	1,696	-	Sep 2 1923	Unknown	42-32-44 N. 70-48-08 W. Between Misery Island and Little Misery Island, Beverly, Mass. Wood vessel. Length 274'. General cargo. Wreck demolished.
828	City of Rome	St.s.	1,908	1881	May 7 1914	Burned	Off Ripley, about 30 miles west of Dunkirk, N.Y.
829	City of Salisbury	Frgt.	-	-	Apr 22 1938	Unknown	42-22-26 N. 70-51-35 W. Near Northeast Graves, Broad Sound, Mass. Length 419'.
830	City of Stamford	St.s.	427	1907	Oct 27 1931	Collided	With barge MARLBORO NO.5. East River, New York, N.Y.
831	City of Toledo	St.p.	796	1891	Sep 30 1932	Burned	Tonawanda, N.Y. Steel vessel.
832	City of Troy	St.p.	1,527	1876	Apr 5 1907	Burned	Bobbs Ferry, N.Y.
833	City of Utica	Steamer	-	-	Dec 16 1890	Unknown	Long Island Sound, N.Y.
834	City of Yonkers	St.s.	170	1884	Jul 24 1940	Foundered	At pier 32, North River, New York City, N.Y.
835	Civita Carrara (It.)	-	-	-	Jun 29 1888	Unknown	Manasquan Inlet, N.J. Marble cargo.
836	Clara	Sch.	828	1896	Jan 12 1922	Foundered	Off Sea Girt, N.J.
837	Clara	St.s.	75	1877	Jan 16 1947	Foundered	Foot of Oak Street, Greenpoint, Brooklyn, N.Y.
838	Clara A. Donnell	Sch.	1,177	1889	Jul 7 1922	Stranded	Off Nantucket Shoals, Davis Bank, Mass.
839	Clara Bell	-	-	-	Mar 1872	Unknown	Off Highland Light, Mass. Total loss. One survivor.
840	Clara E. Comee	Sch.	138	1888	Jul 21 1912	Foundered	Providence River, R.I.
841	Clara E. Rogers	Sch.	144	1872	Jun 2 1906	Collided	With st.p. vessel. Off Vineyard Haven Lightship, Mass.
842	Clara Goodwin	Brig	407	-	May 3 1803	Unknown	Monomoy Point, Mass.
843	Clara J. Adams	Sch.	-	-	Sep 19 1881	Unknown	East end of Peaked Hill Bars, Mass. Cargo of ice.
844	Clara Jane	Sch.	-	-	Feb 20 1801	Unknown	Orleans, Mass.
845	Clara Jane	Sch.	124	1864	Jan 10 1913	Stranded	Eastern Point, Gloucester, Mass.
846	Clara Leavitt	Sch.	456	-	Nov 27 1898	Unknown	41-21-10 N. 70-47-30 W. 1-1/2'miles E of Gay Head L.S. Station, Marthas Vineyard, Mass. Length 127'. Clay cargo.
847	Clara Louise	Ol.s.	103	1928	Dec 3 1953	Burned	7 miles south by west of Boone Island, Me.
848	Clara M. Leonard	Sch.	56	1875	Dec 17 1921	Stranded	Off Point Lookout, Md.
849	Clara McWilliams	St.s.	50	1874	May 8 1937	Burned	At city dock, Malden, N.Y.
850	Clara Egan	Brg.	240	1918	May 30 1945	Foundered	Oneida Lake, N.Y.
851	Clarella II	Ol.y.	60	1929	Sep 4 1930	Burned	Cape May, N.J.
852	Clarence Blakeslee	St.s.	87	1898	Jan 6 1918	Foundered	Off Block Island, R.I.
853	Clarence H. Venner	Sch.	-	-	Aug 14 1899	Unknown	Shovelful Shoals, Mass.
854	Clarence H. Venner	Sch.	934	1890	Jul 19 1914	Stranded	Cape Sable, Nova Scotia.
855	Clarissa Allen	Sch.	-	-	Mar 15 1896	Unknown	Point Judith, R.I.

NO.	NAME OF VESSEL	RIG	TONS	BUILT	DATE	CAUSE	PLACE AND COMMENT
856	Clasco	Ga.s.	68	1908	Aug 9 1933	Burned	Rockaway Beach, Long Island, N.Y.
857	Cleary Bros. No.56	Brg.	367	1926	May 20 1935	Burned	Rikers Island, East River, N.Y.
858	Cleary Bros. No.58	Brg.	367	1927	May 20 1935	Burned	Rikers Island, East River, N.Y.
859	Cleary Bros. No.59	Brg.	429	1918	Feb 26 1945	Foundered	East breakwater, Bridgeport Harbor, Conn.
860	Cleary Bros. No.60	Brg.	367	1927	May 20 1935	Burned	Rikers Island, East River, N.Y.
861	Cleary Bros. No.66	Brg.	366	1927	May 20 1935	Burned	Rikers Island, East River, N.Y.
862	Cleary Bros. No.80	Brg.	366	1930	May 20 1935	Burned	Rikers Island, East River, N.Y.
863	Clement	Brig	-	-	Lost 1800's	Storm	On Whale Rock, Chatham, Mass.
864	Cleo Chileot	Sch.	-	-	Jan 9 1886	Unknown	East of Watch Hill, R.I.
865	Cleopatra	St.s.	1,045	1865	1890	Collided	With CRYSTAL WAVE. At sea, off Delaware Capes.
866	Cleopatra	St.s.	415	1919	Jul 12 1933	Burned	Thames River, Conn.
867	Cleveland	St.p.	579	1837	1854	Burned	Tonawanda, N.Y.
868	Clifford	Sch.	-	-	Jun 15 1887	Unknown	South Gull Rocks, Nova Scotia.
869	Clifford (Br.)	Sch.	-	-	Apr 28 1897	Unknown	Wood End, Mass.
870	Clifford I. White	Sch.	305	1889	Aug 13 1916	Stranded	Spectacle Island, Nova Scotia.
871	Clifton	St.p.	175	1837	Dec 1860	Burned	Kinderhook, N.Y.
872	Clifton	Sch.	-	-	Dec 31 1888	Unknown	West of Point Judith, R.I.
873	Clifton (Br.)	Sch.	-	-	Jan 6 1896	Unknown	Shoveful Shoals, Mass.
874	Clifton	St.p.	280	1883	Jun 8 1909	Burned	Pittsburgh, Pa.
875	Climax	St.s.	119	1872	Aug 19 1934	Burned	Jersey City, N.J.
876	Clina	Sch.	-	-	Dec 23 1887	Unknown	Off Orleans, Mass.
877	Clinton D. Harryman	Brg.	721	1910	Oct 22 1925	Foundered	Bartlett Reef Light, Conn. Steel vessel.
878	Clover	Brg.	-	-	Oct 17 1890	Unknown	Off Point Judith, R.I.
879	Clytie	Sch.	-	-	Sep 30 1891	Unknown	Matinicu, Me.
880	Coal King	Sch.	1,417	1878	Sep 3 1907	Foundered	Montauk Point, Long Island, N.Y.
881	Coal Port	Brg.	529	1907	Oct 20 1913	Foundered	Off Point Judith, R.I.
882	Coal Valley	St.w.	226	1864	Dec 19 1891	Burned	Pittsburgh, Pa.
883	Coast Transit Co. No.2	Brg.	263	1907	Jan 6 1935	Foundered	Astoria, Long Island, N.Y.
884	Coasting Schooner	Sch.	-	-	Dec 8 1786	Unknown	Lovells Island, Boston Harbor, Mass.
885	Coastwise	St.s.	268	1900	Jul 10 1920	Foundered	Near Fire Island, N.Y.
886	Codorus	St.s.	2,165	1892	Dec 10 1917	Stranded	Chatham, New Brunswick. Steel vessel.
887	Cohasset	Sch.	965	1903	Jan 22 1907	Burned	Canton, Md.
888	Cohasset	Brg.	2,577	1893	Nov 17 1948	Collided	With tug TERN. In Chesapeake Bay, vicinity of Whartons Point. Steel vessel. 40-22-00 N. 72-20-00 W.
889	Coimbra (Br.)	Tanker	3,976*	-	Jan 15 1942	War Loss	With s.s. PRESIDENT WILSON. 33-51-00 N. 75-45-00 W. Steel vessel.
890	Coldwater	St.s.	5,110	1920	Sep 1 1933	Collided	1 mile north of Highland Light, Mass.
891	Coleraine	Sch.	954	1899	Apr 4 1915	Stranded	Off Maine coast. 44-19-00 N. 63-09-00 W. Steel vessel. Sunk by enemy action.
892	Collamer	St.s.	5,112	1920	Mar 5 1942	War Loss	Nantucket Sound, Mass.
893	Colleen	Ol.s.	78	1925	Dec 2 1932	Burned	Castle Hill, R.I.
894	Colmar	Brg.	244	1897	Oct 7 1927	Foundered	Kettle Cove, Manchester, Mass.
895	Colombo	Ol.s.	97	1940	Nov 29 1945	Foundered	Wood End, Mass.
896	Colonial (Br.)	Sch.	-	-	Oct 14 1801	Unknown	Saybrook, Conn.
897	Colonial	St.p.	54	1905	Jun 11 1911	Burned	Rondeau, Canada.
898	Colonial	St.s.	1,713	1882	Nov 13 1914	Stranded	Barcelona, N.Y. Iron vessel. 3 lives lost (31).
899	Colonial	St.p.	538	1885	Sep 1 1925	Burned	Stamford, Conn.
900	Col. L.F. Peck	C.bt.	166	1887	Apr 26 1907	Foundered	Off Barnstable, Mass.
901	Columbia	-	-	-	1851	Unknown	Sailed from New York, N.Y. & has not since reported. All lives (11) lost.
902	Columbia	St.s.	174	1890	Dec 24 1909	Foundered	Off Barnstable, Mass.
903	Columbia	St.p.	332	1902	Feb 17 1910	Burned	Moss Side Landing, Pa.

NO.	NAME OF VESSEL	RIG	TONS	BUILT	DATE		CAUSE	PLACE AND COMMENT
904	Columbia	Sch.	152	1923	Aug 24	1927	Foundered	Sable Island, Nova Scotia. All lives (23) lost.
905	Columbia	Ol.s.	60	1915	Jun 10	1946	Foundered	65 miles east of Nantucket Light, Mass.
906	Columbia	Brg.	359	1911	Dec 16	1942	Collided	With ol.s. LILLIAN ANNE. Sank off Drum Point Light, Patuxent River, Md.
907	Columbia	Ol.s.	85	1896	Oct 19	1948	Collided	With st.s. BOWGRAN. In the cut off channel off North Point, Md. Steel vessel.
908	Columbian	Brg.	356	1864	Sep 4	1913	Foundered	Dunkirk, N.Y.
909	Columbus	St.p.	416	1829	Nov 27	1850	Burned	Point Lookout, Md. 9 lives lost.
910	Comet	St.s.	97	1904	Jun 17	1925	Burned	Brooklyn, N.Y.
911	Comet	St.s.	77	1901	May 26	1939	Foundered	At pier, Arlington, Staten Island, N.Y.
912	Commack	C.bt.	128	1893	Oct 22	1918	Collided	With unknown vessel. Pendleton, N.Y.
913	Commack	Sch.	1,446	1918	Jan 20	1925	Stranded	Sandy Hook, N.J.
914	Commander	Sch.	-	Lost 1800's			Unknown	Off Race Point L.S. Station, Mass.
915	Commander	St.s.	74	1872	Mar 16	1929	Burned	North River, N.Y.
916	Commerce	St.w.	198	1856	May 7	1859	Burned	Pittsburgh, Pa.
917	Commerce	Brg.	517	1919	Sep 26	1939	Foundered	41-24-10 N. 71-11-15 W. 3 miles south of Sakonnet Point, R.I. Length 114'.
918	Commodore	Steamer	-	-	Aug 9	1863	Unknown	South of Point Judith, R.I.
919	Commodore	St.p.	984	1848	Dec 27	1866	Stranded	Hortons Point, N.Y.
920	Commonwealth	St.p.	1,732	1855	Dec 29	1865	Burned	Groton, Conn. 1 life lost.
921	Commonwealth	Ga.s.	141	1913	Apr 8	1927	Burned	Shelburne, Nova Scotia. 12 lives lost (20).
922	Concordia	St.s.	1,681	1862	May 1	1872	Stranded	Cape Brenton Island, Nova Scotia. Steel vessel.
923	Confidence	Brg.	163	1901	Jan 26	1919	Burned	Newark, N.J.
924	Confidence	Tanker	-	-	Nov 5	1940	Unknown	42-24-30 N. 70-39-05 W.
925	Connaught	-	-	-	Oct 7	1860	Burned	Off Massachusetts coast.
926	Connecticut	Sch.	-	-	Sep 25	1883	Unknown	East of Block Island, R.I.
927	Connecticut	Sch.	-	-	Apr 15	1891	Unknown	Newcastle, N.H.
928	Connecticut	Sch.	99	1847	Nov 7	1903	Foundered	41-38-12 N. 69-54-46 W. Southeast of Chatham Light, Mass. Length 80'.
929	Connecticut	Ol.s.	57	1946	Sep 29	1948	Foundered	West 1/4 north, 3-3/4 miles from Gay Head Lighthouse, Mass. Length 60'.
930	Constellation	Ol.s.	137	1902	May 10	1931	Stranded	Gay Head, Mass.
931	Convenient	Sch.	-	-	Jan 10	1883	Unknown	Block Island, R.I.
932	Convoy	Brg.	332	1914	Oct 21	1953	Burned	At Amasses Landing, New Gretna, N.J.
933	Copy	Sch.	86	1854	Oct 15	1912	Stranded	Eatons Neck, Long Island, N.Y.
934	Coquette	St.p.	221	1867	Mar 24	1868	Stranded	Long Beach, N.J.
935	Cora	Brg.	389	1901	Oct 12	1916	Foundered	Point Judith, R.I. 1 life lost.
936	Cora C. Meadow	Sch.	-	-	Dec 14	1896	Unknown	Bearses Shoal, R.I.
937	Cora Green	Sch.	247	1875	Jun 2	1915	Collided	With sch. JAMES YOUNG. Seguin Island, Me.
938	Corbin	Sch.	954	1899	Jan 10	1911	Stranded	42-05-09 N. 70-10-24 W. 1/2 mile NW of Peaked Hill L.S. Station, Mass. Coal cargo. Length 180'. All lives (5) lost.
939	Coree E. Smith	Sch.	95	1899	Jul 12	1897	Unknown	Shoveful Shoals, Mass.
940	Corinna	St.s.	58	1899	Sep 12	1915	Burned	Brooksville, Me.
941	Corinne	St.s.	54	1864	Feb 28	1877	Snagged	Cape May, N.J.
942	Corinthian	St.y.	161	1903	Oct 24	1925	Burned	Salem, N.J.
943	Corinthian	Ol.s.	177	1917	Sep 19	1949	Collided	With st.s. MOMACFIR. 37 miles south, 1/2 mile east of Halifax Lightship, N.S.
944	Corn Planter	St.w.	50	1851	Feb 12	1857	Ice	West Monterey, Pa.
945	Cornelius H. Delamater	Sch.	-	1870	Jan 3	1915	Stranded	Off Clinton, N.Y.
946	Cornelius Hargraves	Sch.	79	1874	Oct 30	1890	Unknown	Barnegat, N.J.
947	Cornell	Ol.s.	68	1893	Nov 4	1955	Foundered	In Hudson River, off Tarrytown Lights, in area of Tarrytown, N.Y.
948	Cornell No.20	Ol.s.	-	-	Jan 31	1953	Foundered	Off coast of New Jersey & sank about 40-25 N. 73-55 W.
949	Cornelia	Tanker	-	-	Jul 8	1933	Unknown	42-23-05 N. 70-45-05 W.
950	Cornfield Lightship	-	-	-		1927	Unknown	Saybrook, Conn.

NO.	NAME OF VESSEL	RIG	TONS	BUILT	DATE		CAUSE	PLACE AND COMMENT
951	Cornish	St.s.	1,827	1923	Jun 4	1943	War Loss	North Atlantic Ocean. Steel vessel. Sunk by enemy action.
952	Cornwallis	-	5,458	-	Dec 3	1944	Unknown	44-01-00 N. 68-20-00 W.
953	Corona	Ga.s.	120	1901	Feb 26	1916	Stranded	Green Island, Nova Scotia.
954	Corrotoman	Brg.	334	1890	Sep 17	1924	Foundered	Brown's Shoals, Delaware Bay.
955	Corvalis	St.s.	2,922	1919	Jun 16	1925	Burned	Sandy Hook, N.J.
956	Corvallis	Frgt.	2,922*	-	Pre-WWII		Unknown	39-39-00 N. 73-13-00 W. See No. 955.
957	Corvin	Frgt.	-	-	Pre-WWII		Stranded	41-28-00 N. 70-57-20 W. Struck Sow & Pigs Reef and drifted. Steel vessel.
958	Cory	Brg.	339	-	Oct 12	1916	Foundered	Off Point Judith, R.I.
959	Cottage City	Steamer	-	-	Feb 4	1893	Unknown	Chatham Bar, Mass.
960	Council Bluffs	St.w.	203	1857	May 7	1859	Burned	Pittsburgh, Pa.
961	Courageous	Ol.s.	77	1926	Sep 27	1953	Foundered	About 9-1/2 miles off Ocean City Inlet, N.J.
962	Cova	Sloop	-	-	Sep 1	1895	Unknown	Brentons Point, R.I.
963	Cox & Green	Sch.	-	-	Nov 26	1888	Unknown	Toddy Rocks, Nantasket Beach, Hull, Mass.
964	Coyote	Frgt.	-	-	Jan 11	1932	Unknown	42-22-06 N. 70-43-06 W.
965	Cremona	St.w.	178	1856	May 7	1859	Burned	Pittsburgh, Pa.
966	Creole	St.w.	1,056	1862	Mar 17	1868	Burned	Squan, N.J.
967	Crescent	St.s.	68	1872	Jan 13	1929	Stranded	Brooklyn, N.Y.
968	Crew Levick No.5	Brg.	513	1920	Apr 11	1923	Foundered	Off Fenwick Shoal Lightship, Del.
969	Crew Levick No.9	Brg.	209	1921	Feb 21	1925	Foundered	Philadelphia, Pa. Iron vessel. All lives (2) lost.
970	Cricket	Brg.	-	-	Sep 28	1890	Unknown	Five Fathom Bank, Del.
971	Croatan	Brg.	416	1901	Oct 3	1940	Foundered	Off Coast Guard Station, Shipbottom, N.J.
972	Crocodile	Sloop	-	-	Oct 8	1898	Unknown	Quanochoutaug, N.J.
973	Cuckoo	Sch.	-	-	Oct 12	1882	Unknown	Point Judith, R.I.
974	Culdirri	Bkn.	-	-	Mar 23	1898	Unknown	South side of Nantucket Island, Mass. Lumber cargo.
975	Cullen No.18	Sc.b.	923	1900	May 28	1938	Burned	480 yds. off Penobscot Coal Co. dock, Searsport, Me.
976	Cullen No.180	Brg.	424	1915	Apr 17	1918	Collided	With barge LIBERTY. East River, N.Y.
977	Cumberland	Sch.	413	1874	Sep 24	1907	Foundered	Wolf Point, New Brunswick.
978	Cumberland	St.s.	50	1868	Mar 17	1917	Stranded	Green Island, Vinalhaven, Me.
979	Curlew	St.s.	343	1856	Nov 5	1863	Collided	With LOUISIANA. Point Lookout, Md.
980	Cutchogue	C.bt.	137	1906	Dec 2	1921	Collided	With lock wall. Barge Canal Lock No.13, near Fonda, N.Y.
981	Cyclone	Drg.	84	1939	May 10	1940	Burned	At Timber Creek, N.J.
982	Cynthia (Br.)	-	-	-	May 22	1889	Collided	St. Lawrence River. 8 lives lost.
983	Cyrus Chamberlain	Sch.	-	-	Lost 1800's		Unknown	Peaked Hill Bars, Mass.
984	D 18	Brg.	581	1903	Nov 5	1961	Foundered	Off Newport, R.I. 41-35-00 N. 71-16-45 W.
985	D 36	Scow	607	1903	Nov 11	1913	Stranded	Ranes Head, Boston Harbor, Mass.
986	D.B. Haskins	Sch.	-	-	Jun 1	1885	Unknown	Nauset, Mass.
987	D.E.	Scow	201	1917	Dec 28	1938	Stranded	Tonawanda, N.Y.
988	D.E. Vanwickle	Brg.	373	1898	Jan 8	1911	Foundered	Off Cornfield Reef, Conn.
989	D. Gifford	Sch.	253	1862	Apr 10	1906	Stranded	Field Rocks, Mass.
990	D.S. Stetson	St.s.	52	1857	Oct 3	1893	Burned	Georgetown, District of Columbia.
991	D. Sawyer	-	-	-	Jan 11	1890	Unknown	Seal Island, Nova Scotia.
992	D.T. Helm	St.s.	64	1893	Jul 14	1929	Burned	Martinsville, N.Y.
993	D.T. Sheridan	Ol.s.	267	1939	Nov 5	1948	Foundered	At Lobster Point, Mohegan Island, Me. Steel vessel.
994	Decian (Br.)	-	-	-	Apr 7	1872	Wrecked	Halifax, Nova Scotia.
995	Dalas Hill	Sch.	-	-	Nov 28	1888	Unknown	Tenants Harbor, Me.
996	Dalzellido	St.s.	103	1918	Jun 19	1946	Burned	Pier 24, Brooklyn, N.Y.
997	Damietta & Joanna	Sch.	-	-	Apr 16	1801	Unknown	Shovelful Shoals, Mass.
998	Damon	Sch.	-	-	Nov 20	1890	Unknown	Chatham, Mass.

NO.	NAME OF VESSEL	RIG	TONS	BUILT	DATE	CAUSE	PLACE AND COMMENT
999	Dandy	St.s.	115	1888	Oct 12 1929	Burned	Worton Point, Chesapeake Bay, Md.
1000	Daniel B. Fearing	Sch.	1,240	-	May 6 1896	Unknown	42-01-00 N. 70-01-30 W. 1 mile N of Pamet River L.S. Station. Length 216'.
1001	Daniel D. Perry	Scow	289	1908	Aug 24 1916	Foundered	Strawberry Island, Niagara River.
1002	Daniel G. O'Day	C.bt.	138	1909	May 18 1929	Stranded	Rotterdam, N.Y.
1003	Daniel I. Tenney	Sc.b.	1,701	-	Nov 07 1898	Unknown	Off Sandy Neck, Barnstable, Mass. Length 212'.
1004	Daniel M. French	Sch.	-	1867	Dec 11 1889	Wrecked	Mussel Bar, Napatree Point, west of Watch Hill Light, R.I. Lumber cargo.
1005	Daniel McLoud	Sch.	295	1867	Dec 25 1916	Stranded	Nantucket, Mass.
1006	Daniel S. Miller	St.s.	605	1862	Jun 24 1910	Burned	Highland, N.Y. Renamed "Poughkeepsie" in 1900.
1007	Daniel Webster	Sch.	-	-	Oct 22 1890	Unknown	Cornfield Point, Conn.
1008	Darby	Sch.	1,513	1899	Feb 5 1907	Foundered	Off Atlantic City, N.J.
1009	Darien	Brg.	944	1914	May 2 1948	Foundered	Off Atlantic City, N.J.
1010	Dart	Sch.	-	-	Mar 16 1890	Unknown	Chesapeake Bay.
1011	Dauntless	St.p.	301	1876	Oct 13 1922	Burned	Gloucester, N.J.
1012	Dauntless No.2	St.s.	87	1889	Apr 17 1938	Unknown	Foot of 18th Street, Brooklyn, N.Y.
1013	David	Sch.	-	-	Lost 1800's	Unknown	Off Pamet River L.S. Station, Mass.
1014	David A. Barry	Sch.	300	1832	Summer 1875	Unknown	1 mile north of Beaver Tail (west side), R.I.
1015	David Brown	St.p.	190	1832	Nov 10 1836	Foundered	Havana-New York.
1016	David Currie	Sch.	151	1866	Dec 20 1907	Foundered	Duck Island, Conn.
1017	David D.	Sch.	-	-	Sep 29 1891	Unknown	Sheep Harbor, Nova Scotia.
1018	David E. Baxter	Brg.	173	1889	May 8 1908	Foundered	St. George, Staten Island, N.Y.
1019	David F. Lowe	Sch.	-	-	Jun 20 1891	Unknown	Broad Cove, Nova Scotia.
1020	David Faust	Sch.	216	1854	Sep 3 1911	Stranded	Port Clyde, Me.
1021	David Foss	Sch.	-	-	Nov 29 1888	Unknown	Great Point, Nantucket, Mass.
1022	David Goddard	C.bt.	110	1881	Oct 30 1917	Foundered	Rouses Point, N.Y.
1023	David H. Atwater	St.s.	2,438	1919	Apr 2 1942	War Loss	37-37-00 N. 75-10-00 W. Steel vessel. Sunk by enemy action.
1024	David J. Lee	Sch.	-	-	Mar 23 1886	Unknown	Nauset Beach, Mass.
1025	David K. Akin	Ga.s.	50	1882	Apr 26 1938	Foundered	2 miles west of Pollock Rip Lightship, Mass.
1026	David S. Siner	Sch.	-	-	Nov 3 1889	Unknown	Off Newport, R.I.
1027	David Taylor	Bark	-	-	May 21 1890	Unknown	Lockport, Nova Scotia.
1028	David Wallace	Sch.	1,103	1884	Aug 7 1915	Foundered	Off Matinieus, Me.
1029	Davis Palmer	Sch.	2,965	1905	Dec 26 1909	Foundered	About 1 mile outside entrance to channel, Broad Sound, Boston, Mass. Length 305'. Coal cargo. All lives (14) lost.
1030	Dawn	St.s.	399	1857	Dec 27 1869	Stranded	Pecks Beach, N.J.
1031	Dawson City	Sch.	-	-	Oct 24 1803	Foundered	Peaked Hill Bars, Mass.
1032	Dayton	Brg.	252	1930	Jan 8 1960	Foundered	At Mariners Harbor, Staten Island, N.Y.
1033	Daytona	Sc.b.	1,313	1919	Oct 10 1925	Foundered	Five Fathom Bank Light, N.J.
1034	De Brook (Br.)	Frigate	-	-	1798	Unknown	Off Lewes, Del. Valued at $500,000. Reported located.
1035	Decator Oakes	Sch.	-	-	Sep 18 1889	Unknown	Whitehead, Me.
1036	Decorra	Sch.	181	1866	Sep 6 1907	Abandoned	Nash Island, Me.
1037	Deepwater	Brg.	3,376	1904	Mar 6 1932	Foundered	Panamour Bank Buoy, Md. Steel vessel. All lives (5) lost.
1038	Deer Lodge	St.s.	6,187	1919	Feb 18 1943	War Loss	Off Fire Island, N.Y. Steel vessel. Sunk by enemy action.
1039	Defense	Sch.	-	-	Mar 10 1779	War Loss	Off Bartletts Reef, Waterford, Conn. Connecticut privateer. Estimated to be valued at over $200,000. Length 98'. Depth ranges from 6' to 35'.
1040	Delawanna	Sch.	698	1905	Nov 30 1905	Foundered	Off Minots Ledge Lighthouse, North Scituate, Mass. Iron vessel. Length 318'. See No.1041.
1041	Delaware	Sch.	-	-	Oct 5 1899	Unknown	Shovelful Shoals, Mass.
1042	Delaware	Sc.b.	2,461	-	Nov 27 1898	Foundered	Near Collamore Ledge, North Scituate, Mass. Steel vessel. Coal cargo. 4 lives lost.
1043	Delaware	Steamer	1,646	-	Jul 9 1898	Burned	1.7 miles off beach at Bay Head & 2.6 miles, 155° from Manasquan Inlet, Point Pleasant, N.J. Owned by Clyde Lines. Wood vessel. Length 251'. Depth 68'. $250,000.

NO.	NAME OF VESSEL	RIG	TONS	BUILT	DATE		CAUSE	PLACE AND COMMENT
1044	Delaware	St.s.	166	1858	Jul 28	1909	Collided	With wharf, Philadelphia, Pa.
1045	Delaware	Brg.	294	1874	Jan 10	1907	Stranded	Fishers Island, N.Y.
1046	Delaware	St.s.	50	1891	Apr 23	1925	Burned	Poughkeepsie, N.Y.
1047	Delia	Sch.	775	-	Mar 8	1937	Unknown	46-38-00 N. 53-15-00 W.
1048	Delia C. Smith	Ol.s.	59	1926	Aug 22	1931	Foundered	Georges Bay, Mass.
1049	Delia Hinds	Sch.	-	-	Oct 9	1889	Unknown	Mount Desert, Me.
1050	Del-Mar-Va	Ol.s.	106	1926	Mar 2	1951	Collided	With ol.s. HERBERT R. O'CONOR. About 2 miles east of Sandy Point Ferry Terminal.
1051	Delta	Sch.	-	-	May 23	1887	Unknown	Near St. Johns, Newfoundland.
1052	De Mory Gray	Sch.	401	1874	Nov 8	1912	Stranded	Northport Bay, Long Island, N.Y.
1053	Diadem	Sch.	-	-	Mar 2	1888	Foundered	Off Thatcher's Island, Mass.
1054	Diadem	Sch.	67	1855	Jul 25	1906	Stranded	Ash Island, Penobscot Bay, Me.
1055	Diana	Sch.	123	1903	Nov 12	1913	Stranded	Shag Harbor, Nova Scotia.
1056	Dick L	Brg.	324	1926	Sep 19	1928	Stranded	Port Jefferson, N.Y.
1057	Diggs	Frgt.	1,041	-	Pre-WWII		Unknown	38-54-54 N. 74-23-00 W.
1058	Dighton	Sloop	282	1896	Nov 6	1919	Foundered	Off Faulkners Island, Conn.
1059	Dire	Sloop	-	-	Jun 25	1803	Unknown	Block Island, R.I.
1060	Dispatch	St.s.	52	1872	Feb 23	1925	Stranded	Harlem River, N.Y.
1061	Ditto	Sloop	-	-	Sep 7	1899	Unknown	Watch Hill, R.I.
1062	Diver	Sloop	141	1886	Oct 13	1927	Foundered	North Rye Beach, N.Y. 2 lives lost (3).
1063	Dixie	Ol.y.	73	1908	Aug 17	1939	Foundered	5 miles SE of Ocean City, N.J. Steel vessel.
1064	Dixie Sword	St.s.	3,283	1919	Feb 13	1942	Foundered	41-32-58 N. 69-58-50 W. 1/4 mile northeast of Stone Horse Buoy, Bearses Shoal, Nantucket Sound, Mass. Steel vessel. Length 324'. Copper cargo.
1065	Dixon Chemicals	Brg.	1,054	1959	Nov 26	1961	Foundered	41-02-30 N. 71-29-45 W. South of Block Island, R.I. Steel vessel. Sulfuric acid.
1066	Dolly Vasden	Sch.	-	-	Feb 14	1885	Unknown	Tuckernuck Flats, Nantucket, Mass. Coal cargo.
1067	Dolphin	Sch.	-	-	Dec 15	1891	Unknown	Bond Island, Me. (Boon Island).
1068	Dolphin	St.w.	121	1860	Apr 11	1867	Burned	Pittsburgh, Pa.
1069	Dolphin	Ga.s.	-	-		1960	Unknown	830 yds., 192° from Coney Island Light, N.Y. Speedboat. Depth 27'.
1070	Dom Pedro	Brg.	193	1876	Feb 21	1906	Collided	With dock. New York, N.Y.
1071	Dominion Halsyd (Can.)	-	227	-	Oct 24	1942	Unknown	43-07-05 N. 70-17-45 W. 8 miles E by S1/2S magnetic from Boon Island. Depth 330'.
1072	Donna T. Briggs	Sch.	204	1891	Sep 5	1916	Foundered	Casco Bay, between Portland Lightship and Portland Head, Me.
1073	Dora	Sch.	825	1896	Oct 1	1915	Foundered	Fenwick Island, Md.
1074	Dora A. Lawson	Sch.	125	1889	Dec 29	1909	Stranded	Canso, Nova Scotia.
1075	Dora Mathews	Sch.	392	-	Sep 18	1902	Unknown	41-35-53 N. 69-58-12 W. 3/4 mile NE1/4E of Monomoy L.S. Station. Length 136'.
1076	Dora M. French	Sch.	-	-	Oct 1	1893	Unknown	Shovelful Shoal, Mass.
1077	Doreen Lee	Ol.s.	75	1928	May 18	1960	Foundered	40-51-00 N. 70-48-00 W. Fisherman. Length 85'. Depth 174'.
1078	Doris F. Amero	Ol.s.	60	1936	Jan 14	1955	Lost	About 94 miles SE by 1/2S of Gloucester, Mass.
1079	Doris Gertrude	St.s.	96	1879	Aug 11	1922	Burned	About 145 miles ESE of Pollock Rip Lightship, about 130 miles E of New York, N.Y.
1080	Dorothea	Brg.	393	1905	Nov 14	1919	Stranded	Montauk, Long Island, N.Y.
1081	Dorothy	St.s.	2,873	1918	Sep 1	1929	Collided	With st.s. EURANA. Smiths Point, Md. 2 lives lost (32).
1082	Dorothy	Sch.	2,088	1904	Aug 14	1918	Torpedoed	Off Anglesea, N.J.
1083	Dorothy B. Barrett	Sch.	488	1943	Nov 8	1914	Foundered	Sailed from Philadelphia, Pa., and has not since reported. All lives (8) lost.
1084	Dorothy Belle	Ol.s.	59	1943	Nov 8	1947	Foundered	Yarmouth Sound, Yarmouth, Nova Scotia.
1085	Dorothy & Ethel III	Ol.s.	60	1930	Nov 12	1961	Burned	About 40 miles SE of Nantucket Island, Mass.
1086	Dorothy and Mary	Sch.	2,872	1903	Mar 25	1923	Stranded	Stone Horse Shoal, off Monomoy Point, Mass. Length 295' Coal cargo.
1087	Dorothy Palmer	Sch.	1,024	-	Feb 20	1893	Unknown	41-24-38 N. 70-55-58 W. 1-1/8 mile WSW of Cuttyhunk L.S. Station, Mass.
1088	Douglas Dearborn	Sch.	-	-	Nov 11	1901	Unknown	Little Round Shoal, Mass.
1089	Douglas Haynes	Sch.	-	-	Oct 13	1890	Unknown	Brentons Reef, R.I.
1090	Douglas Staynes							

NO.	NAME OF VESSEL	RIG	TONS	BUILT	DATE		CAUSE	PLACE AND COMMENT
1091	Dove	Sch.	–	–	Apr 29	1887	Unknown	Bordens Reef, Newport, R.I.
1092	Dredge No.6 (Blue Jay)	Drg.	–	–	Oct 10	1931	Unknown	42-20-56 N. 70-41-05 W. Blue Jay lost while towing dredge.
1093	Dredge No.12	Brg.	330	–	Jan 19	1939	Burned	Off Bayonne, N.J.
1094	Duchess	St.s.	400	1860	Sep 12	1902	Burned	Albany, N.Y.
1095	Dudley Farlin	Sch.	–	–	Dec 28	1891	Unknown	Off Maine coast.
1096	Dudley Pray	St.s.	215	1890	Feb 13	1908	Stranded	Rockport, Mass.
1097	Dunlo	Sch.	840	1898	Sep 12	1914	Foundered	Harbor of Refuge, Del.
1098	Dunmore	Sch.	581	1905	Dec 30	1921	Foundered	Off Minots Ledge, Mass. All lives (2) lost.
1099	Dunmurry	Steamer	–	–	Aug 29	1891	Unknown	Off Halifax, Nova Scotia.
1100	Dunozella	Sch.	–	–	Feb 16	1899	Unknown	Eel Point, Nantucket, Mass.
1101	Duroc	Sch.	–	–	May 10	1890	Unknown	Roaring Bull Ledge, Me.
1102	Dynafuel	Ol.s.	3,100	1946	Nov 15	1963	Collided	With Norwegian FERNVIEW. 41-33-34 N. 70-51-39 W. Buzzards Bay, Mass. REMOVED.
1103	E.A. Hooper	Sch.	–	–	Jan 3	1879	Unknown	West of Block Island, R.I.
1104	E.A. Williams	Sch.	–	–	Sep 8	1891	Unknown	Monomoy Beach, Mass.
1105	E. Arcularius	Sch.	99	1851	Nov 15	1909	Stranded	Vineyard Sound, Mass.
1106	E.B. Potter	C.bt.	81	1909	Nov 15	1936	Foundered	Lake Champlain, Burlington, Vermont.
1107	E.C. Hay	Sch.	63	1873	Jun 28	1906	Collided	With Danish st.s. C.F. TIETGEN. Off Desbrosses Street, New York, N.Y.
1108	E.C. Knight	Steamer	–	–	Oct 15	1887	Collided	Little Egg Harbor, N.J.
1109	E. Chambers	Sch.	–	–		1888	Unknown	Off Dibby Strait, Nova Scotia.
1110	E. Madison Hall	Ol.s.	212	1878	Mar 31	1942	Foundered	Turkey Point, Chesapeake Bay.
1111	E.G. Irwin	Sch.	188	1865	Dec 12	1907	Collided	With tug DAUNTLESS. Point No Point, Md.
1112	E. and G.W. Hinds	Sch.	115	1874	May	1906	Stranded	Plympton, Nova Scotia.
1113	E.H. Taylor	Sch.	63	1898	Apr 1	1924	Stranded	Three Sisters, Chesapeake Bay.
1114	E.I. DuPont	St.p.	103	1845	Jun 14	1856	Stranded	Jamaica, N.Y.
1115	E.K. Davison	St.w.	98	1901	Nov 2	1926	Foundered	West Tarentum, Pa. 2 lives lost (8).
1116	E.L. Dow	Sch.	401	–	Feb 12	1899	Unknown	41-20-46 N. 70-00-08 W. 1-1/2 miles SE of Coskata L.S. Station, Mass.
1117	E.L. Higgins	Sch.	–	–	Nov 15	1888	Unknown	Near Boston, Mass.
1118	E. & L. Marts	Sch.	317	–	Mar 17	1876	Unknown	42-03-20 N. 70-14-40 W. 1/4 mile S of Race Point Light, Mass. Coal cargo.
1119	E.M. Ashley	C.bt.	134	1895	Aug 24	1922	Foundered	East River, N.Y.
1120	E.M. Card	St.s.	204	1920	Apr 3	1945	Burned	Red Hook Flats, Brooklyn, N.Y. Steel vessel.
1121	E.M. Clark	St.s.	9,647	1921	Mar 18	1942	War Loss	North Atlantic. Sunk by enemy action.
1122	E.M. Duffield	Sch.	92	1851	Jan 1	1908	Foundered	Bridgeport, Conn.
1123	E.R. Cashin	Scow	307	1918	Oct 8	1934	Stranded	Off Faulkners Island, Conn.
1124	E.R. Haggett	Brg.	696	1910	Oct 5	1927	Foundered	Brigatine Gas Buoy, N.Y.
1125	E.S. Johnson	Sch.	90	1882	Jun 9	1928	Foundered	Rock Point, Md.
1126	E.T. Williams	St.s.	97	1898	Oct 5	1921	Burned	Drum Point, Patuxent River, Md.
1127	E.W. Merchant	Sch.	–	–	Jul 9	18	Unknown	Shovelful Shoals, Mass.
1128	EX-PC 469	Ol.s.	–	–		1961	Unknown	Swinburne Island vicinity, New York Harbor. 40-34.5 N. 74-03.4 W. U.S. Navy vessel.
1129	Eagle	St.s.	392	1853	Dec 1	1866	Stranded	Cape Sable, Nova Scotia.
1130	Eagle	Sloop	–	–	Oct 15	1902	Capsized	Off Gay Head, Mass.
1131	Eagle	St.s.	65	1887	Jul 11	1927	Foundered	Gurnet, N.H.
1132	Eagle	Ol.s.	159	1943	Jan 15	1967	Burned	About 75 miles east of Cape Cod, Mass.
1133	Eagle Boat No.42	Ol.s.	–	–	Jun 15	1931	Unknown	42-22-26 N. 70-43-23 W.
1134	Eagle Boat	Ol.s.	430	–	Pre-WWII		Unknown	41-24-18 N. 70-57-54 W. Sow & Pigs Reef, Cuttyhunk, Mass. Navy Patrol Craft.
1135	Eagle's Wing	St.p.	409	1854	Jul 24	1861	Burned	Pawtucket, R.I.
1136	Eaglet	Sch.	130	1882	Jul 10	1906	Collided	With French cruiser JURIEN DE LA GRAVIERE. North River, N.Y.
1137	Earl & Nettie	Sch.	–	–	Apr 11	1894	Unknown	Block Island, R.I.
1138	Earl P. Mason	Sch.	–	–	Aug 22	1888	Unknown	Point Judith, R.I.

NO.	NAME OF VESSEL	RIG	TONS	BUILT	DATE	CAUSE	PLACE AND COMMENT
1139	Earthquake	Scow	384	1904	Oct 15 1918	Foundered	Dunkirk, N.Y. Steel vessel.
1140	East Boston	St.p.	164	1834	Mar 4 1857	Burned	Boston, Mass. Ferryboat.
1141	East Wind	Sch.	-	-	Feb 10 1892	Unknown	Point Judith, R.I.
1142	Eastern Light	Sch.	85	1847	Nov 9 1911	Stranded	Pumpkin Rock, Boothbay Harbor, Me.
1143	Eastern Shore	St.p.	831	1885	Jan 4 1928	Burned	Bay Shore, Md. Iron vessel.
1144	Eastern Star	Sch.	-	-	Lost 1800's	Unknown	Point Judith, R.I.
1145	Easton	Sc.b.	531	1899	May 5 1929	Foundered	Block Island, R.I.
1146	Ebb	Ol.s.	259	1929	Jul 28 1942	War Loss	43-18 N. 63-50 W. Steel vessel. Sunk by enemy action.
1147	Eben Dole	Sch.	-	-	Oct 22 1890	Unknown	Freshwater Cove, Mass.
1148	Eben Fisher	Sch.	300	-	Sep 12 1892	Unknown	41-26-00 N. 70-24-06 W. Marthas Vineyard Island, Mass. Stone cargo.
1149	Eckie	Brg.	309	1920	Mar 11 1952	Foundered	In Chesapeake Bay, about 15 miles S of Annapolis, Md. Steel vessel.
1150	Eclipse	St.s.	106	1859	Nov 27 1869	Stranded	Jersey City, N.J.
1151	Eclipse	St.p.	99	1905	Dec 8 1917	Burned	Coraopolis, Pa.
1152	Economy	St.p.	239	1853	Jun 30 1854	Burned	New York, N.Y.
1153	Eddie B. Blount	Ol.s.	62	1889	Aug 31 1954	Hurricane	At Popasquash Point, Bristol, R.I.
1154	Eddie H. Weeks	Sch.	-	-	Dec 4 1891	Unknown	Block Island, R.I.
1155	Eddie Pierce	Sch.	-	-	Sep 26 1888	Abandoned	Highland Light, Mass.
1156	Edgar Baxter	St.s.	60	1869	Nov 7 1924	Burned	Tremley Point, N.J. 6 lives lost (7).
1157	Edgar G. Barratt	C.bt.	104	1908	Mar 4 1924	Foundered	Pellecare Islands, Lake Champlain.
1158	Edgar Randall	Sch.	-	-	Dec 4 1896	Unknown	Race Point, Mass.
1159	Edgar W. Murdock	Sch.	1,451	1902	Jun 18 1917	Stranded	Grand Manan, New Brunswick.
1160	Edgemere	Brg.	261	-	Mar 27 1946	Collided	With CAPE HOPE. 40th and East River, New York, N.Y.
1161	Edith	Brg.	-	-	May 8 1891	Collided	Chesapeake Bay.
1162	Edith	St.s.	50	1880	Oct 4 1909	Burned	Gibsons Island, Magothy River, Md.
1163	Edith	Brg.	516	1899	Jun 19 1942	Burned	Frankfort, Me.
1164	Edith C. Rose	Ol.s.	146	1920	May 11 1939	Collided	With ol.s. ISABELLE PARKER. About 115 miles east by south of Boston Light, Mass.
1165	Edith and Elinor	Ol.s.	134	1929	Nov 25 1931	Collided	With st.s. GYPSUM PRINCE. Baccaro, Nova Scotia. 6 lives lost (12).
1166	Edith L. Boudreau	Ol.s.	93	1930	Oct 5 1967	Stranded	Between Nantucket and Marthas Vineyard, Mass.
1167	Edith L. Conley	Sch.	-	-	Sep 20 1896	Unknown	Handkerchief Shoals, Mass.
1168	Edith L. Gandy	Sch.	-	-	Oct 22 1891	Unknown	Shovelful Shoals, Mass.
1169	Edith Nute	Ga.s.	985	1917	Mar 27 1922	Stranded	41-39-53 N. 69-57-14 W. 1/2 mile N of Chatham L.S. Station, Mass.
1170	Edith T. Gandy	Sch.	-	-	Oct 23 1891	Unknown	Monomoy Beach, Mass.
1171	Edmund	Sch.	-	-	Lost 1800's	Unknown	Off Chatham, Mass.
1172	Edmund F. Black	Ga.s.	66	1909	Jul 6 1919	Collided	With st.s. MAGUNKOOK. Georges Bank, 1 life lost.
1173	Edmund Phinney	Bark	751	1873	Dec 14 1907	Stranded	Sandy Hook, N.J.
1174	Edna	St.s.	53	1882	Jun 14 1927	Burned	Hackensack, N.J.
1175	Edna A. Pogue	Sch.	162	1883	Mar 5 1911	Collided	With Norwegian st.s. FORTUNA. Cedar Point, Md.
1176	Edna Harwood	Ga.s.	-	-	Lost 1800's	Unknown	Northeast of Nauset, Mass.
1177	Edna Wallace Hopper	Ga.s.	136	1901	Sep 19 1906	Stranded	Port au Port Bay, Newfoundland.
1178	Eduardo	Steamer	-	-	Jul 20 1889	Unknown	Cutler Harbor, Me.
1179	Edward A. Ryan	Brg.	236	1917	Sep 25 1928	Stranded	Federal Lock, Troy, N.Y.
1180	Edward B. Winslow	Sch.	2,046	1918	Dec 12 1928	Stranded	40-27 N. 71-50 W.
1181	Edward E. Briry	Sch.	1,613	1896	Dec 14 1917	Stranded	Little Round Shoal, Nantucket Sound, Mass. Coal cargo.
1182	Edward Easton	Brg.	344	-	Oct 3 1900	Unknown	42-40-15 N. 70-34-00 W. South end of Dry Salvages, Rockport, Mass.
1183	Edward F. Cullen	Brg.	292	1901	Feb 15 1908	Stranded	New Haven, Conn.
1184	Edward H. Cole	Sch.	1,789	1904	May 31 1918	Torpedoed	39-10-18 N. 73-20-30 W. Off Barnegat, N.J.
1185	Edward H. Nortan	Sch.	-	-	Feb 12 1887	Unknown	Narragansett Pier Beach, R.I.
1186	Edward H. Smead	Sch.	-	-	Nov 27 1898	Unknown	Block Island, R.I.

NO.	NAME OF VESSEL	RIG	TONS	BUILT	DATE	CAUSE	PLACE AND COMMENT
1187	Edward J. Lawrence	Sch.	3,350	1908	Dec 27 1925	Burned	Portland, Me.
1188	Edward M. Laughlin	Sch.	-	-	Nov 4 1897	Unknown	Point Judith, R.I.
1189	Edward Monk	C.bt.	99	1900	Apr 21 1917	Stranded	Quebec, Canada.
1190	Edward N. Wigton	St.s.	81	1875	Oct 21 1926	Burned	Brighton, N.Y.
1191	Edward Oliney, Jr.	Brg.	337	1904	Nov 25 1916	Foundered	Long Island Sound, N.Y.
1192	Edward S. Eveleth	Sch.	88	1883	Sep 20 1922	Stranded	Mouth of Essex River, Mass.
1193	Edward Smith	Sch.	440	1896	Sep 23 1925	Stranded	Richibucto, New Brunswick.
1194	Edward Stewart	Sch.	398	1883	Mar 7 1916	Stranded	Cranberry Isles, Me.
1195	Edward T. Buchanan	St.s.	106	1919	Aug 1955	Burned	At 152nd Street and Harlem River, New York, N.Y.
1196	Edward T. Dalzell	St.s.	96	1900	Oct 26 1926	Collided	With st.s. WALTER JENNINGS. Brooklyn, N.Y.
1197	Edwin Booth	C.bt.	102	1893	Nov 10 1920	Foundered	Rouses Point, N.Y.
1198	Edwin L. Pilsbury	St.s.	83	1906	Jan. 10 1948	Burned	Cunningham Flats, Boston, Mass.
1199	Effie M. Lewis	Ol.s.	104	1928	Nov 22 1941	Foundered	Delaware Bay.
1200	Effort	Sch.	-	-	Lost 1800's	Unknown	Chatham, Mass.
1201	Egan Sisters	Brg.	280	1924	Oct 25 1937	Stranded	Frenchman's Island, Lake Oneida, N.Y.
1202	Eglantine	Ga.s.	99	1902	Jan 24 1913	Stranded	Taylors Head Isle, Nova Scotia.
1203	El Dorado	St.s.	3,531	1884	Jan 1 1913	Foundered	Sailed from Baltimore, Md. & has not since reported. Iron vessel. 39 lives lost.
1204	El Sol	St.s.	6,008	1910	Mar 11 1927	Collided	With unknown vessel. New York, N.Y. Steel vessel. 1 life lost (47).
1205	Eldora	Sch.	-	-	Aug 30 1891	Unknown	Brown Island, Me.
1206	Eldora	Sch.	52	1881	Nov 5 1906	Foundered	52 miles NNW, Cultivator Shoals, Me.
1207	Eldorado	St.s.	96	1893	Dec 16 1908	Burned	Phippsburg, Me.
1208	Eleanor	Ga.s.	53	1897	Jan 14 1935	Foundered	Chester River, Chester, Pa.
1209	Eleanor Nickerson	Ol.s.	143	1927	Feb 5 1932	Collided	With Belgian st.s. JEAN JABOT. 43-05 N. 63-45 W. 21 lives lost (27).
1210	Eleazer Boynton	Sch.	88	1883	Aug 9 1911	Collided	With st.s. CAMDEN. Rockland Harbor, Me.
1211	Electa Bailey	Sch.	344	-	Jan 21 1901	Unknown	41-39-30 N. 69-59-55 W. Chatham, Mass. Length 118'.
1212	Elgin	Sloop	-	-	Nov 2 1894	Unknown	Monomoy Beach, Mass.
1213	Elgrudor	St.y.	103	1903	Dec 5 1925	Burned	Pelham Bay, N.Y. Steel vessel.
1214	Elihio Thompson	St.slp.	896	-	Aug 18 1897	Unknown	Pollock Rip, Mass. Iron vessel. Length 198'.
1215	Elisa C.	Brg.	542	1923	Jan 30 1940	Foundered	Southeast of Blackstone Island, Md.
1216	Eliza J. Pendleton	Sch.	751	1891	Feb 22 1905	Abandoned	At sea, off Fire Island, N.Y.
1217	Eliza Jane	Sch.	-	-	Oct 18 1890	Unknown	Shelbourne, Nova Scotia.
1218	Eliza Levensaler	Sch.	159	1882	Oct 21 1916	Stranded	Monhegan Island, Me.
1219	Elizabeth	Sloop	-	-	Lost 1800's	Unknown	2-1/2 miles north of Point Judith, R.I.
1220	Elizabeth	Sch.	-	-	Dec 23 1890	Unknown	Digby Gut, Nova Scotia.
1221	Elizabeth	St.p.	1,079	1867	Oct 22 1901	Burned	New York, N.Y. Ferryboat.
1222	Elizabeth	Brg.	354	1904	Feb 14 1914	Foundered	Off Bartlett's Reef, Long Island Sound.
1223	Elizabeth Ann	Sch.	-	-	Nov 6 1891	Unknown	Seal Ledges, Nova Scotia.
1224	Elizabeth Ann	Ol.s.	77	1917	Apr 1 1951	Burned	At New London, Conn.
1225	Elizabeth de Hart	Sch.	-	-	Jul 4 1888	Unknown	Cape Henlopen, Del.
1226	Elizabeth E. Vane	Brg.	405	1905	Oct 19 1911	Collided	With st.s. COLUMBIA. Baltimore Harbor, Md.
1227	Elizabeth Freeman	Sch.	1,665	1920	Oct 22 1927	Burned	St. Johns, Mass.
1228	Elizabeth Howard	Sch.	142	1916	Nov 7 1923	Stranded	Porter's Island, Halifax, Nova Scotia.
1229	Elizabeth Jane	Sch.	-	-	May 1887	Unknown	Cape Anguille, Newfoundland.
1230	Elizabeth Levansaler	Sch.	-	-	Oct 18 1895	Unknown	Race Point, Mass.
1231	Elizabeth M. Cook	Sch.	-	-	Apr 19 1892	Unknown	Monomoy, Mass.
1232	Elizabeth Palmer	Sch.	3,065	1903	Jan 26 1915	Collided	With SS WASHINGTON. Off Fenwick Island Lightship, Del.
1233	Elizabeth Scott Moore	Sch.	798	1917	Sep 4 1955	Foundered	Off Glen Cove Yacht Club, Glen Cove, N.Y.
1234	Elizabeth Silsbee	Ga.s.	153	1905	Jan 24 1909	Stranded	Blanche Point, Nova Scotia.

NO.	NAME OF VESSEL	RIG	TONS	BUILT	DATE	CAUSE	PLACE AND COMMENT
1235	Elk	Brg.	299	1901	Dec 14 1907	Stranded	Off Watch Hill, R.I.
1236	Elk	Sch.	139	1848	Aug 23 1918	Foundered	Off Monhegan Island, Me.
1237	Elk	Ol.s.	123	1910	Sep 11 1944	Stranded	Seal Island, Nova Scotia.
1238	Ella	Sch.	-	-	Lost 1800's	Unknown	Point Judith, R.I.
1239	Ella	Sch.	-	-	Mar 23 1888	Unknown	Chatham, Mass. (Bar).
1240	Ella	Sch.	-	-	Nov 27 1888	Unknown	Rehoboth, Del.
1241	Ella A. Call	Sch.	59	1893	Sep 24 1917	Foundered	Off Reedy Island, Del.
1242	Ella Francis	Sloop	-	-	Nov 27 1898	Unknown	Provincetown, Mass.
1243	Ella G. Eells	Sch.	256	1891	Jul 4 1906	Stranded	Libby Island, Me. 4 lives lost.
1244	Ella M. Goodwin	Sch.	121	-	Jan 21 1911	Foundered	Sailed from Newfoundland for Gloucester, Mass. Lost in Gulf of Maine.
1245	Ella M. Storer	Sch.	449	1873	Dec 12 1914	Stranded	42-34-57 N. 70-40-24 W. Entrance to Gloucester Harbor, Mass. Length 135'.
1246	Ella May	Sch.	96	1864	Dec 11 1911	Stranded	York, Me. 1 life lost.
1247	Ella Powell	Sch.	140	1872	Oct 11 1906	Foundered	Off New London, Conn. 1 life lost.
1248	Ella Rose	Sch.	59	1857	Nov 16 1907	Stranded	Sheep Island Ledge, near Vinal Haven, Me.
1249	Ellen	St.s.	54	1917	May 6 1923	Burned	On Raritan River, between Perth Amboy & New Brunswick, N.J.
1250	Ellen A. Swift	Sch.	131	1882	Jan 15 1919	Foundered	Sailed from New Bedford, Mass. & has not since reported. All lives (14) lost.
1251	Ellen B.	Sloop	-	-	Oct 24 1888	Unknown	Block Island, R.I.
1252	Ellen F. Gleason	Sch.	72	1898	Feb 5 1907	Collided	With British st.s. WINIFREDIAN. 300 miles NE of Boston, Mass.
1253	Ellen Lincoln	Sch.	-	-	Dec 31 1895	Unknown	Nauset Beach, Mass.
1254	Ellen M. Feeley	Brg.	265	1920	Nov 30 1936	Foundered	In New York State Barge Canal, Cleveland, N.Y.
1255	Ellen M. Mitchell	Sch.	379	1875	May 16 1907	Stranded	Stanley Ledge, west of Great Wass Island, Me.
1256	Ellen Morrison	Sch.	-	-	Oct 16 1894	Unknown	Shovelful Shoals, Mass.
1257	Ellen S. Jennings	Brg.	330	1890	Feb 22 1912	Collided	With barge CAROLINA (also sank). Poplar Island, Chesapeake Bay, Md.
1258	Ellen T. Marshall	Ol.s.	124	1919	Dec 15 1933	Burned	Cape Sable, Nova Scotia. 3 lives lost (27)
1259	Ellery Wright	Ol.s.	151	1929	Feb 19 1966	Burned	In New York Harbor, about 300' off Liberty Island, N.Y.
1260	Ellie F. Long	Sch.	-	-	Apr 15 1891	Unknown	Frier Island, Nova Scotia.
1261	Ellie L. Smith	Sch.	331	1878	Dec 18 1876	Unknown	Nauset Beach, Mass.
1262	Ellis P. Rogers	Brg.	68	1878	Dec 23 1907	Collided	With st.s. MAURETANIA. New York, N.Y.
1263	Elmar	Ga.s.	51	1925	Nov 25 1950	Lost	At pier, City Island, N.Y.
1264	Elmir Roberts	Ga.s.	784	1918	Aug 22 1919	Burned	41-05 N. 62-18 W.
1265	Elsie G. Silva	Ol.s.	106	1915	Feb 14 1927	Stranded	Cape Cod, Mass.
1266	Elsie M. Smith	Sch.	-	-	Mar 5 1891	Unknown	Cape Cod, Mass.
1267	Elsie M. Smith	Ga.s.	-	-	Feb 14 1902	Unknown	Chatham Bar, Cape Cod, Mass.
1268	Elva L. Spurling	Ga.s.	74	1904	Aug 1 1922	Collided	With st.s. LAKE FLOURNEY. Southeast of Nauset Light, Mass.
1269	Elwood Burton	Sch.	-	-	Mar 19 1902	Unknown	Handkerchief Shoals, Mass.
1270	Elwood Burton	Sch.	394	-	Oct 14 1904	Unknown	42-05-09 N. 70-11-30 W. 1-1/4 miles WNW of Peaked Hill L.S. Station, Mass.
1271	Emerald	Ga.s.	124	1924	Mar 26 1925	Stranded	Georges Bank.
1272	Emily	Sch.	-	-	Jan 20 1899	Unknown	Watch Hill, R.I.
1273	Emily A. Foote	Ol.s.	113	1875	Aug 23 1930	Foundered	Harbor of Refuge, Breakwater, Del.
1274	Emily A. Staples	Sch.	86	1872	Oct 30 1911	Stranded	Port Clyde, Me.
1275	Emily Baxter	Sch.	53	1873	Nov 26 1910	Stranded	Fire Island Inlet, N.Y.
1276	Emily E. Burton	Sch.	88	1871	Nov 20 1925	Foundered	James Point, Md.
1277	Emily F. Northam	Sch.	332	1883	Nov 27 1926	Stranded	Cranberry Island, Me.
1278	Emily & Jennie	Sch.	-	-	Apr 8 1888	Unknown	Harvey Cedar, N.J.
1279	Emily Mansfield	Ol.s.	54	1883	Nov 1 1957	Burned	At Darien, Conn.
1280	Emily T. Sheldon	Brig	425	-	Mar 22 1886	Unknown	East end of Peaked Hill Bars, Mass. Ice cargo.
1281	Emma	Sch.	-	-	Lost 1800's	Unknown	Nauset Beach, Mass.
1282	Emma	Sch.	-	-	Nov 26 1888	Unknown	Rehoboth, Del.

NO.	NAME OF VESSEL	RIG	TONS	BUILT	DATE	CAUSE	PLACE AND COMMENT
1283	Emma	Sch.	354	-	Nov 27 1898	Foundered	Off Sandy Neck, Barnstable, Mass. Length 127'. Coal cargo.
1284	Emma	Sch.	64	1864	Nov 4 1914	Foundered	Oyster Bay, N.Y.
1285	Emma	Sch.	54	1871	Jan 24 1940	Stranded	On inner bay ledges of Penobscot Bay, Me.
1286	Emma Bacon	Sch.	-	-	Lost 1800's	Unknown	Point Judith, R.I.
1287	Emma D. Endicott	Sch.	-	-	Jan 1 1902	Unknown	Chatham, Mass.
1288	Emma G. Edwards	Sch.	-	-	Apr 1 1879	Unknown	2 miles northeast of Tuckernuck, Mass.
1289	Emma J. Chesbro	Sch.	86	1869	Jun 11 1914	Storm	Connecticut River, Conn.
1290	Emma K. Small	Sch.	-	-	Jun 5 1883	Foundered	North of Block Island, R.I.
1291	Emma K. Smalley	Sch.	-	-	Dec 9 1891	Unknown	Chatham Bar, Cape Cod, Mass.
1292	Emma M. Dyer	Sch.	-	-	Nov 27 1899	Unknown	Off Cape Cod, Mass.
1293	Emma R.	Brg.	251	1903	Sep 8 1906	Foundered	New York, N.Y.
1294	Emma R. Harvey	Sch.	286	1872	Dec 4 1906	Stranded	Digby Gut, Nova Scotia. 2 lives lost.
1295	Emmett McLoughlin, Jr.	Brg.	331	1924	Sep 21 1938	Stranded	Gravesend, N.Y.
1296	Empire Knight (Br.)	Frgt.	7,244	-	Feb 11 1944	Unknown	43-07-00 N. 70-25-39 W. Depth over 200'.
1297	Empire Ocean (Br.)	Frgt.	6,755	-	Aug 4 1942	Unknown	46-37-00 N. 53-05-00 W. Depth 120'.
1298	Empire State	Drg.	-	-	Oct 6 1899	Unknown	Cahoons Hollow, Mass.
1299	Empire Story (Br.)	Frgt.	10,000	-	May 4 1942	Unknown	44-18-00 N. 66-24-00 W. Bay of Fundy.
1300	Empire Sun	Frgt.	6,952	-	Feb 7 1942	Unknown	43-55-00 N. 64-22-00 W.
1301	Empress	Sch.	-	-	Oct 29 1891	Unknown	Kennebunk River, Me.
1302	Empress	Sch.	-	-	Oct 9 1897	Unknown	Monomoy Point, Mass.
1303	Empress	Sch.	120	1856	Jan 8 1912	Stranded	Cape Elizabeth, Me.
1304	Empress Bay	El.s.	531	1929	Jun 25 1958	Collided	In the East River, foot of Manhattan Bridge, New York, N.Y.
1305	Empress of Ireland		-	-	May 29 1914	Collided	St. Lawrence River. Canadian vessel. 1,024 lives lost.
1306	Endeavor	St.w.	200	1854	Jun 14 1859	Burned	Pittsburgh, Pa.
1307	Enos B. Phillips	Sch.	409	-	Feb 19 1893	Unknown	42-17-10 N. 70-51-50 W. 2 miles ESE of Point Allerton L.S. Station, Mass.
1308	Enos Soule	Sch.	1,386	1869	May 12 1914	Stranded	On Brigantine Shoals, N.J.
1309	Enterprise	St.p.	75	1857	Jan 22 1867	Exploded	New York, N.Y.
1310	Enterprise	St.s.	204	1866	May 26 1874	Stranded	Fishers Island, N.Y.
1311	Ephrata	Sch.	954	1899	Apr 29 1923	Stranded	Near Shag Rock, Long Island, N.Y.
1312	Erie	St.p.	497	1837	Aug 9 1841	Burned	Off Silver Creek, N.Y. 242 lives lost.
1313	Erie	Sch.	-	-	Nov 14 1890	Unknown	Near Damriscotta, Me.
1314	Erna	Bark	-	-	Sep 13 1889	Abandoned	Barnegat Shoals, Nova Scotia.
1315	Ernst T. Lee	Sch.	-	-	Apr 14 1890	Unknown	Dochet Island, Me.
1316	Ervin J. Luce	Sch.	127	1892	Nov 8 1931	Foundered	Race Point, Cape Cod, Mass. 1 life lost (4).
1317	Escort	Ol.s.	-	-	Feb 6 1889	Unknown	Buzzards Bay, Mass. 5.25 miles, 110° True from Dumpling Rock Lighthouse.
1318	Esme	Steamer	-	-	Feb 6 1889	Unknown	Near Barrington, Nova Scotia.
1319	Esperanto	Sch.	140	1906	May 30 1921	Foundered	Off Sable Island, Nova Scotia.
1320	Essex (Br.)	Frigate	-	-	Mar 12 1741	Unknown	In channel, off east side of Deadman's Island, Magalena, Nova Scotia. Depth 80'.
1321	Essex	St.s.	389	1885	Jun 5 1923	Foundered	Beach Haven, N.J.
1322	Essex	Ol.s.	92	1916	Dec 8 1939	Foundered	Easterly end of Long Island Sound, N.Y.
1323	Essex	St.s.	3,018	1890	Sep 26 1941	Foundered	Off southeast coast of Block Island, R.I. Steel vessel. 41-08-38 N. 71-33-00 W.
1324	Essie M.L.	Sch.	-	-	Nov 4 1889	Unknown	45-19 N. 60-35 W.
1325	Esso Manhattan	Tanker	10,172	-	Mar 29 1943	War Loss	25 miles off Ambrose Lightship, N.Y. SALVAGED.
1326	Estelle	Brg.	182	1884	May 8 1912	Collided	With British st.s. ANTAEUS. Newcastle, Del.
1327	Estelle McGeeney	Brg.	307	1918	Jul 8 1948	Foundered	In North River, N.Y.
1328	Estelle Phinney	Sch.	922	1891	Dec 27 1907	Collided	With sch. ELIZABETH PALMER. Barnegat, N.J. 1 life lost.
1329	Ester Ward	Sch.	-	-	Dec 28 1892	Unknown	Chatham, Mass.
1330	Esther Ann	Sch.	753	1909	Oct 9 1920	Collided	With st.s. DUQUESNE. 38-21-00 N. 74-40-00 W.

NO.	NAME OF VESSEL	RIG	TONS	BUILT	DATE	CAUSE	PLACE AND COMMENT
1331	Ethel	Bark	-	-	May 7 1801	Unknown	Monomoy Beach, Mass.
1332	Ethel Marion	O1.s.	70	1927	Mar 18 1930	Foundered	Nantucket, Mass.
1333	Ethel Maud	Sch.	-	-	May 2 1897	Unknown	Race Point, Cape Cod, Mass.
1334	Ethel N.	Sch.	-	-	Dec 31 1930	Unknown	42-22-45 N. 70-39-30 W.
1335	Ethel Swift	Sch.	-	-	Lost 1800's	Unknown	Peaked Hill Bars, Mass.
1336	Ethel Ward	Sch.	-	-	Dec 28 1898	Unknown	Off Cape Cod, Mass.
1337	Etna	Sch.	-	-	Oct 7 1891	Unknown	Sandy Hook, N.J.
1338	Etta A. Stimpson	Sch.	314	-	Dec 9 1902	Unknown	42-02-10 N. 70-36-30 W. High Pine Ledge, Duxbury Beach, Mass. Length 125'.
1339	Etta M. Story	Sch.	55	1860	Apr 30 1911	Stranded	Block Island, R.I. 9 lives lost.
1340	Eugene F. Moran	St.s.	176	1906	Dec 8 1917	Foundered	Off Absecon, N.J. 1.2 miles, 104° from bell buoy at Absecon Inlet, N.J.
1341	Eugene F. Moran	Tug			1918	Unknown	39-20-50 N. 74-21-03 W. 1.2 miles, 104° from bell buoy at Absecon Inlet, N.J. Depth 30'. Lies on hard sand bar. Wreck demolished.
1342	Eugenia	Brg.	-	-	Oct 28 1890	Unknown	Jones Inlet, Long Island, N.Y.
1343	Eugenia	O1.s.	100	1908	Jul 1 1928	Stranded	Beaver Tail Point, R.I.
1344	Eugenie	Sch.	95	1883	Oct 14 1923	Stranded	Bald Head, Cape Small Point, Me.
1345	Eunice - Lilian	O1.s.	72	1936	Jun 12 1958	Collided	With CLIPPER. About 135 miles ESE of Pollock Rip, Mass.
1346	Eureka	Sch.	-	-	Oct 23 1891	Unknown	Middleton, Nova Scotia.
1347	Eureka	St.s.	223	1892	Nov 11 1914	Stranded	Wilsons Point, Conn.
1348	Eureka	Ga.s.	84	1919	May 18 1928	Burned	Indian Island, North River, N.Y.
1349	Eureka No.80	Brg.	393	1914	Jun 4 1941	Foundered	Bridgeport Harbor, Conn.
1350	Eva C. Yates	Sch.	-	-	Sep 27 1887	Unknown	Fire Island Bar, N.Y.
1351	Eva Divesty	Sch.	-	-	Oct 12 1889	Unknown	Eaton's Neck, Long Island, N.Y.
1352	Eva Lendel	Sch.	-	-	Aug 24 1898	Unknown	Chatham, Mass.
1353	Eva Leonard	Sch.	-	-	Jan 13 1895	Unknown	Ragged Point, Newport, R.I.
1354	Eva May	Sch.	-	-	Oct 21 1892	Unknown	Handkerchief Shoal, Mass.
1355	Evangeline	St.s.	314	1889	Jul 10 1930	Burned	Rockaway, Long Island, N.Y.
1356	Evans	Lighter	-	-	Jun 28 1935	Unknown	42-21-00 N. 70-42-50 W.
1357	Evelyn	Sch.	-	-	Oct 5 1895	Unknown	Block Island, R.I.
1358	Evelyn	St.s.	57	1884	Oct 25 1930	Burned	Brooklyn, N.Y.
1359	Evelyn	Ga.s.	69	1913	Apr 12 1917	Burned	Bay Shore, N.Y.
1360	Evelyn M. Thompson	Ga.s.	97	1908	Jul 12 1918	Stranded	Siaconset, Mass.
1361	Evelyn W. Hinkly	Sch.	698	1905	Oct 1 1917	Foundered	New London, Conn.
1362	Evening Star	Tanker	-	-	Unknown	Unknown	38-51-33 N. 74-37-05 W. Cape May Inlet, N.J. Demolished. Depth 40'.
1363	Evening Star	Brg.	250	1900	Apr 12 1914	Foundered	Off Hell Gate, N.Y.
1364	Evolution	Sch.	202	1889	Apr 3 1921	Foundered	Nantucket Shoals, Mass.
1365	Evzone	O1.s.	93	1944	Dec 16 1952	Foundered	23 miles SSE of Matinicus Rock Light, Me.
1366	Ewan Crerar	Brig	-	-	Mar 9 1860	Unknown	Near Boston Light, Mass.
1367	Excelsior	Sc.b.	855	-	Feb 16 1898	Unknown	Handkerchief Shoals, Mass. Length 192'.
1368	Excelsior	Brg.	518	1901	Sep 6 1907	Stranded	Off Watch Hill, R.I.
1369	Exeter	O1.s.	114	1930	Apr 16 1938	Burned	70 miles S by E of Sable Island, Nova Scotia.
1370	Exminster	St.s.	4,986	-	Apr 19 1942	Unknown	41-47-07 N. 70-29-05 W. Freighter. Partially removed by blasting. Depth 31'.
1371	Expedite	Sch.	-	-	1891	Unknown	Sand Point, Long Island, N.Y.
1372	Experimenter	O1.y.	129	1939	Dec 31 1939	Foundered	In Hudson River, off Ossining, N.Y.
1373	Express	St.p.	275	1841	Oct 22 1878	Foundered	Point No Point, Md.
1374	Express	Sch.	-	-	Nov 6 1889	Abandoned	Cape Cod, Mass.
1375	Express	St.p.	1,023	1864	May 11 1933	Foundered	Brooklyn, N.Y. Iron vessel.
1376	F.A. Allen	Sch.	535	1872	Nov 11 1915	Stranded	Reedy Island, Delaware Bay.
1377	F.A. Willey	Bkn.	-	-	Lost 1800's	Unknown	Off Cahoons Hollow, Mass.

NO.	NAME OF VESSEL	RIG	TONS	BUILT	DATE	CAUSE	PLACE AND COMMENT
1378	F.B. Scarborough	Ol.s.	75	1911	Aug 13 1940	Collided	With ol.s. POCAHONTAS. 5 miles above Coles Point, Chesapeake Bay.
1379	F.C. Pendleton	Sch.	408	1882	About 1925	Foundered	In Seal Harbor, Me.
1380	F.F. Clain	Brg.	1,327	1919	Mar 24 1958	Foundered	In the Delaware River, about 1,000 feet off Thompson's Point, N.J.
1381	F.F. Clain	Brg.	963	1913	Feb 17 1942	Foundered	Off Barnegat, N.J.
1382	F.H. Beckwith	St.s.	196	1904	Sep 22 1937	Foundered	Off Cape May Inlet, N.J.
1383	F.H. Odiorne	Sch.	323	-	Jul 12 1888	Unknown	41-33-12 N. 70-02-16 W. 4 miles southwest of Monomoy L.S. Station, Mass.
1384	F.H. Smith	Sch.	-	-	Nov 27 1898	Unknown	Provincetown, Mass.
1385	F.L. Hayes	-	-	-	1952	Unknown	Chesapeake and Delaware Canal. Vessel may have been removed.
1386	F.M. Allen	Sch.	-	-	Nov 20 1895	Unknown	Napatree Point, R.I.
1387	F.M. Lamb	C.bt.	88	1891	Apr 13 1913	Foundered	St. Lawrence River.
1388	F.W. Fredson	Sch.	-	-	May 4 1890	Unknown	Old Schooner Point, Block Island, R.I.
1389	F.Y. Robertson	St.s.	65	1888	Nov 24 1939	Burned	State Barge Canal, near St. Johnsville, N.Y.
1390	Faerder	Bark	-	-	Jul 14 1889	Unknown	Sable Island, Nova Scotia.
1391	Fair Star	Ol.s.	63	1951	Dec 5 1961	Foundered	In the Absecon Inlet, off Atlantic City, N.J.
1392	Fairfax	St.s.	2,551	-	Nov 27 1898	Unknown	Sow & Pigs Reef, Cuttyhunk Island, Mass. Length 270'.
1393	Fairfield	Sch.	-	-	Jan 24 1890	Unknown	Small Point, Me.
1394	Fairfield	St.s.	2,551	1919	Jun 9 1921	Stranded	Governors Island, Boston, Mass.
1395	Fairport	Brg.	212	1909	Jan 16 1929	Stranded	Little Hell Gate, N.Y.
1396	Fairport	Frgt.	6,168	-	Jul 16 1942	War Loss	North Atlantic. 27-00-00 N. 64-25-00 W. Convoy #AS-4.
1397	Faith	St.s.	94	1918	Jan 8 1927	Foundered	Green Ledge Light, N.Y. Steel vessel.
1398	Falcon	St.s.	176	1879	Aug 22 1912	Collided	With st.s. AMAGANSETT, Handkerchief Shoal, Mass.
1399	Falcon	Ol.s.	54	1929	Aug 31 1967	Foundered	41-38-00 N. 69-56-00 W.
1400	Fall River	Sch.	850	1898	Jan 25 1908	Foundered	40 miles southwest of Block Island, R.I.
1401	Fall River	Brg.	1,759	1911	Nov 1 1932	Foundered	Brigantine Buoy, N.J. 39-19-36 N. 74-13-12 W. or 39-19-36 N. 74-12-54 W. Also reported as freighter. Depth 70'. Readings show 7' rise in 74' of water.
1402	Falmouth	Ol.s.	124	1924	Jun 23 1926	Burned	Sable Island, Nova Scotia.
1403	Fame	Sch.	130	1905	May 28 1908	Collided	With British st.s. BOSTON. 70 miles off Maine coast. 18 lives lost.
1404	Fannie	Brg.	948	1890	Jan 8 1908	Foundered	Barnegat, N.J. Steel vessel.
1405	Fannie H. Stewart	Sch.	351	1882	May 8 1915	Foundered	Near McCories Shoal, off Cape May, N.J.
1406	Fanny B. Tucker	Brg.	-	-	Jun 24 1889	Collided	Gulf of Maine.
1407	Fantee	Bark	652	-	Sep 19 1896	Unknown	41-25-08 N. 70-53-29 W. 1 mile E by S of Cuttyhunk L.S. Station, Mass.
1408	Farmer R. Walker	Sch.	-	-	Nov 27 1899	Storm	Off Race Point, Cape Cod, Mass.
1409	Farmount	Bark	-	-	Feb 13 1888	Unknown	Bayhead L.S. Station, N.J.
1410	Fashion	Sloop	-	-	Oct 2 1892	Unknown	Southwest of Fort Adams, R.I.
1411	Favorite	Sch.	-	-	1839	Storm	Gloucester Harbor, Gloucester, Mass. Off historical value.
1412	Favorite	Sch.	-	-	Oct 16 1884	Unknown	East of Block Island, R.I.
1413	Fawn	Sch.	-	-	Lost 1800's	Unknown	Off Orleans, Mass.
1414	Fawn	Brg.	-	-	1950	Unknown	Hudson River, N.Y. 750 yds., 305.5° True from spire, Poughkeepsie, N.Y. Depth 60'.
1415	Fear Not	Sch.	-	-	Oct 12 1890	Unknown	Jeddore, Nova Scotia.
1416	Fearless	Sch.	-	-	Dec 4 1890	Unknown	Gaspe, Quebec, Canada.
1417	Felicia and Grace	Ol.s.	195	1945	Mar 23 1963	Burned	About 60 miles west of Chatham, Mass.
1418	Felix	Sch.	1,174	1891	Mar 1 1914	Foundered	Off Fire Island, N.Y. Steel vessel.
1419	Feniam Ram, Jr.	Sub	-	-	1883	Foundered	While under tow. In Long Island Sound, off New Haven, Conn. Minature submarine. Steel vessel. Built by John P. Holland. Off Historical value.
1420	Ferdinand Bol	Frgt.	3,704	-	Jul 29 1942	War Loss	45-21-00 N. 59-29-00 W.
1421	Ferland	Sch.	-	-	Jul 6 1891	Unknown	Spectacle Island, Nova Scotia.
1422	Fidilia	Brg.	-	-	Sep 26 1894	Unknown	Pollock Rip, Mass.
1423	Fiherman	Sch.	174	1889	Jan 22 1907	Foundered	Off Cape Elizabeth, Me.

NO.	NAME OF VESSEL	RIG	TONS	BUILT	DATE	CAUSE	PLACE AND COMMENT
1424	Fillet	St.s.	537	1899	Oct 3 1928	Foundered	Montauk Point, N.Y.
1425	Fillmore	Sch.	50	1849	Mar 6 1907	Stranded	Boston Harbor, Boston, Mass.
1426	Finance	Sch.	-	1888	Jan 27 1888	Unknown	Shilburne, Nova Scotia.
1427	Finance	St.s.	2,603	1882	Nov 26 1908	Collided	With British st.s. GEORGIC. Sandy Hook, N.J. Iron vessel.
1428	Financier	St.w.	309	1864	Apr 12 1866	Burned	Economy, Pa. 10 lives lost.
1429	Finback	Ga.s.	159	1916	Aug 23 1919	Stranded	5 miles south of Cape Fullerton, Hudson Bay.
1430	Flannery Boys	St.s.	77	1883	Sep 7 1928	Burned	North River, N.Y.
1431	Fleetwing	Sch.	-	-	Mar 2 1891	Unknown	Near Biddeford Pool, Me.
1432	Flit	Ga.y.	50	1903	Dec 21 1922	Stranded	Marthas Vineyard, Mass.
1433	Flora A. Newcomb	Sch.	-	-	Mar 12 1888	Unknown	Lewes, Del.
1434	Flora and Agnes	Sch.	71	1880	Sep 29 1923	Foundered	Chesapeake Bay. All lives (3) lost.
1435	Flora B	Steamer	-	-	Mar 28 1887	Unknown	Port George, Nova Scotia.
1436	Flora Dell	Sch.	-	-	Jun 28 1889	Unknown	Western Block Island, Nova Scotia.
1437	Flora L. Oliver	Ga.s.	116	1912	Jun 17 1930	Burned	South Highland Light, Mass. 40-20-00 N. 67-49-00 W.
1438	Florence	Sch.	75	1871	Jun 25 1917	Foundered	Off Eatons Neck, Long Island Sound, N.Y.
1439	Florence	Ol.s.	102	1882	Jun 22 1947	Foundered	In the Race, east of Fisher's Island, N.Y.
1440	Florence E. McNaughton	Brg.	357	1896	Jun 7 1923	Foundered	Elk River, Md.
1441	Florence Elliott	Sc.b.	455	1917	Nov 16 1924	Foundered	New Haven, Conn.
1442	Florence K	Ol.s.	79	1917	Oct 16 1935	Foundered	3 miles off Cape Cod Canal, Mass.
1443	Florence Leland	Sch.	343	1882	Oct 16 1910	Abandoned	40-38-00 N. 64-00-00 W.
1444	Florence Marie	Brg.	233	1903	Jun 4 1914	Foundered	Penfield Light, Conn.
1445	Florence Nowell	Sch.	-	-	Oct 24 1891	Collided	Pollock Rip, Mass.
1446	Florence O'Brien	Brg.	345	1905	Feb 4 1917	Foundered	Betterton, Md.
1447	Florence Pearl	Sch.	-	-	May 25 1899	Unknown	Shovelful Shoals, Mass.
1448	Florence Russell	Sch.	60	1890	Oct 30 1913	Foundered	Off Shippan Point, Conn.
1449	Florence Thurlow	Sch.	1,042	1906	May 12 1920	Collided	With st.s. LARAMIE. Southeast Sea Girt, N.J.
1450	Florida	Sch.	-	-	Nov 10 1801	Unknown	Cahoons Hollow, Mass.
1451	Florida	Sch.	-	-	Feb 16 1891	Unknown	Handkerchief Shoal, Mass.
1452	Florizel	-	-	-	Feb 24 1918	Wrecked	Cape Race, Newfoundland. Red Cross vessel. 92 lives lost.
1453	Flushing	St.p.	107	1830	Dec 17 1856	Burned	Machias, Me.
1454	Flushing	Ol.s.	129	1957	Sep 7 1963	Foundered	In Hell Gate Channel, N.Y.
1455	Fly Away	Sch.	159	1854	Jun 1 1911	Stranded	Spruce Island, New Brunswick.
1456	Flyer	St.y.	50	1903	Jul 13 1919	Burned	Sag Harbor, N.Y. 3 lives lost.
1457	Flying Dart	Sch.	-	-	Jan 6 1887	Abandoned	Handkerchief Shoal Light, Mass.
1458	Flying Dutchman	Sail	-	-	May 5 1896	Unknown	Cahoons Hollow, Mass.
1459	Foam	St.s.	324	1919	May 17 1942	War Loss	Vineyard Sound, Mass. 41-29-30 N. 70-37-30 W. Depth 56'.
1460	Force	Sloop	53	1867	Sep 1 1915	Foundered	43-21-00 N. 63-10-00 W. Steel vessel. Sunk by enemy action.
1461	Ford City	St.p.	93	1889	Mar 28 1915	Burned	Lynbrook, Long Island, N.Y.
1462	Fordham	St.p.	728	1887	Apr 7 1913	Burned	Allegheny River, Pittsburgh, Pa.
1463	Forest City	Sch.	-	1903	Oct 13 1889	Abandoned	Shooter Island, N.Y. Iron vessel.
1464	Forest Holm (Br.)	Steamer	-	-	May 5 1896	Unknown	Handkerchief Shoal Light, Mass.
1465	Forest Prince	Bark	350	-	Dec 24 1852	Unknown	41-15-48 N. 70-11-52 W. Opposite Long Pond, Nantucket Island, Mass.
1466	Fort Mercer	Tanker	10,266	-	Feb 17 1952	Unknown	41-37-57 N. 69-46-00 W. Northeast of Pollock Rip Lightship. Length 504'.
1467	Fortuna	Sch.	-	-	Jan 13 1896	Run Down	Off Highland Light, Mass.
1468	Fortuna	Brg.	612	1883	May 9 1915	Foundered	Off Mount Desert Island, Me.
1469	Foster	Sch.	841	1898	Sep 8 1917	Foundered	Off New Jersey coast.
1470	Four Brothers	Sch.	-	-	Nov 24 1896	Unknown	Common Point Cove, Block Island, R.I.
1471	Four Sisters	Sch.	-	-	May 4 1888	Unknown	Prince Edward Island, Canada.

NO.	NAME OF VESSEL	RIG	TONS	BUILT	DATE	CAUSE	PLACE AND COMMENT
1472	Fram	Brg.	220	1890	Mar 18 1917	Foundered	Philadelphia, Pa.
1473	Frances	Ol.s.	64	1943	Jun 21 1947	Foundered	15 miles southwest of Hen and Chickens Lightship, R.I.
1474	Frances L. Taussig	Sch.	1,080	1918	Apr 5 1929	Collided	With st.s. SANDWICH. Vineyard Haven, Mass.
1475	Frances S. Grueby	Ga.s.	140	1912	Sep 22 1923	Collided	With ga.s. COMMONWEALTH. Boston Harbor, Boston, Mass.
1476	Frances Salman	St.s.	2,609	1919	Jan 17 1942	War Loss	Disappeared between St. Johns and Corner Brook, Newfoundland.
1477	Francis B. Thurber	C.bt.	131	1880	Nov 20 1906	Collided	With submerged wreck. Cornfield Lightship, Long Island Sound.
1478	Francis E. Powell	St.s.	7,096	1922	Jan 27 1942	War Loss	North Atlantic. Steel vessel. Sunk by enemy action.
1479	Francis Goodnow	Sch.	350	1890	Apr 29 1923	Stranded	At McKenney Point, Cape Elizabeth, Me.
1480	Francis Hatch	Sch.	-	-	Lost 1800's	Unknown	Off Chatham, Mass.
1481	Francis J. O'Hara, Jr.	Ga.s.	117	1904	Aug 20 1918	War Loss	55 miles south of Canso, Nova Scotia. Sunk by German raider TRIUMPH.
1482	Francis J. Reichert	St.s.	72	1872	Mar 17 1923	Collided	With Norwegian st.s. ALMERA. East of Greenville Channel Buoy, New York Harbor.
1483	Francis Mulqueen	Brg.	415	1913	Dec 11 1916	Foundered	Off Brenton Reef Lightship, Long Island Sound.
1484	Francis Perkins	Sch.	-	-	1887	Unknown	Tom's River, N.J.
1485	Francis S. Hampshire	Sch.	1,055	1881	Dec 9 1913	Foundered	Off Block Island, R.I.
1486	Francis S. Orne	Sch.	-	-	Jun 15 1891	Unknown	Shovelful Shoals, Mass.
1487	Francis Skiddy	St.p.	1,183	1851	Nov 5 1864	Stranded	Staatsberg, N.Y.
1488	Francis Whalen	Sch.	-	-	May 17 1801	Unknown	Handkerchief Shoal, Mass.
1489	Frank	Brg.	330	1928	May 23 1939	Stranded	Off Hewletts Point, Long Island, N.Y.
1490	Frank A. Lowery	C.bt.	226	1916	Nov 23 1922	Foundered	Near Sylvan Beach, Lake Oneida, N.Y.
1491	Frank Foster	Sch.	-	-	Nov 23 1898	Unknown	Provincetown, Mass.
1492	Frank Fowler	St.w.	67	1901	Mar 17 1937	Burned	Pittsburgh, Pa.
1493	Frank G. Rich	Sch.	105	1883	Jul 2 1905	Stranded	Liscomb, Nova Scotia.
1494	Frank Herbert	Sch.	-	-	Dec 18 1889	Unknown	Narragansett Pier, R.I.
1495	Frank Jenkins	Brg.	375	1904	May 28 1923	Stranded	Hell Gate, N.Y.
1496	Frank Leaming	Sch.	257	1873	Nov 11 1915	Foundered	Off Stanford, Conn.
1497	Frank Miller	Brg.	274	1887	Dec 14 1910	Foundered	Hell Gate, N.Y.
1498	Frank P. Scully	Brg.	363	1888	Dec 6 1916	Foundered	Near Faulkners Island, Long Island Sound.
1499	Frank Pendleton	Sch.	1,393	1874	Mar 8 1917	Foundered	Ambrose Channel, N.Y.
1500	Frank R. Diggs	Brg.	480	1913	Jan 1 1946	Foundered	Rogue's Harbor, below Chesapeake and Delaware Canal, Del.
1501	Frank Ryan	C.bt.	106	1906	Jul 4 1929	Burned	Mechanicsville, N.Y.
1502	Frankie J. Smith	C.bt.	99	1884	Apr 1 1912	Ice	Whitehall, N.Y. Crushed by ice.
1503	Franklin	St.p.	2,183	1850	Jul 17 1854	Stranded	Moriches, N.Y.
1504	Franklin	Sch.	-	-	Nov 25 1888	Unknown	Provincetown, Mass.
1505	Franklin	Sch.	-	-	May 1 1891	Unknown	Near Merigomish, Nova Scotia.
1506	Franklin	Brg.	338	1901	Sep 27 1928	Collided	With st.s. JOHN M. WORTH, Clason Point, N.Y.
1507	Franklin	St.p.	663	1876	Oct 28 1932	Burned	Philadelphia, Pa. Iron vessel.
1508	Franklin Pierce	Sch.	-	-	Apr 4 1883	Unknown	Block Island, R.I.
1509	Fransisco	Bark	-	-	Lost 1800's	Unknown	Off Chatham, Mass.
1510	Fred A. Carl	Sch.	-	-	Dec 7 1825	Unknown	Watch Hill Beach, R.I.
1511	Fred A. Emerson	Sch.	122	1890	Aug 5 1914	Foundered	Nantucket Shoals, Mass.
1512	Fred A. Small	Sch.	619	1886	Mar 12 1909	Stranded	41-29-27 N. 69-57-10 W. Little Round Shoal, Mass. Length 142'.
1513	Fred B. Balano	Sch.	263	1890	Dec 30 1918	Stranded	Great Wass Island, Me.
1514	Fred C. Holden	Sch.	137	1872	May 30 1913	Foundered	Damariscotta Island, Me.
1515	Fred & Elmer	Sch.	-	-	Jan 30 1874	Unknown	Provincetown, Mass.
1516	Fred and Jessie	C.bt.	116	1890	Jun 28 1922	Foundered	Albany, N.Y.
1517	Fred Munster	Brg.	523	1929	May 19 1950	Burned	At South Amboy, N.J.
1518	Fred Smith	Sch.	-	-	Aug 27 1890	Unknown	Mosquito Island, Me.
1519	Fred Snow	Sch.	106	1855	Feb 27 1915	Foundered	Off Conanicut Island, R.I. All lives (5) lost.

NO.	NAME OF VESSEL	RIG	TONS	BUILT	DATE	CAUSE	PLACE AND COMMENT
1520	Fred T. Kellers	Brg.	194	1897	Mar 1 1914	Foundered	Off Stratford, Conn.
1521	Fred Tyler	Sch.	114	1848	Oct 27 1920	Foundered	Biddeford Pool, Me.
1522	Fred W. Thurlow	Sch.	1,191	1901	Apr 9 1927	Foundered	Highland Light, N.J.
1523	Fred Walton	Sch.	-	-	Sep 22 1890	Unknown	Pollock Rip, Mass.
1524	Frederica	Sch.	56	1889	Sep 15 1908	Foundered	Delaware Bay.
1525	Frederick	Bark	-	-	Jan 10 1883	Unknown	Off Pleasant Bay, Chatham, Mass.
1526	Fred'k Lenning	St.s.	75	1883	Nov 20 1928	Burned	Coxsackie, N.Y.
1527	Frederick Roessner	Sch.	406	1890	Jan 16 1915	Foundered	38-40-00 N. 72-14-00 W.
1528	Frederick Willenbrock	Brg.	395	1907	Feb 14 1914	Foundered	Off Bartlett's Reef, Long Island Sound.
1529	Freehold	St.s.	220	1903	May 7 1941	Foundered	Off Buoy No.6, Lisbon Range, Delaware Bay, N.J.
1530	Friedricke	Bark	434	-	Jan 10 1883	Unknown	41-46-12 N. 69-55-42 W. Opposite Orleans L.S. Station. See No.1525.
1531	Friendship II	Ol.s.	67	1913	Aug 31 1954	Foundered	6 miles SE of No Mans Land, off Massachusetts coast.
1532	Frisco	Frgt.	2,699	-	Jan 12 1942	Unknown	44-50-00 N. 60-20-00 W.
1533	Fuller Palmer	Sch.	3,060	1908	Jan 12 1914	Foundered	Off Highland Light, Mass. Coal cargo.
1534	G.A. Hayden	Sch.	107	1857	Apr 15 1909	Stranded	Point Judith, R.I.
1535	G.F. Brady	St.s.	238	1897	Oct 25 1926	Foundered	Irvington, N.Y. Steel vessel. 2 lives lost (10).
1536	G.F. McCaffrey	Brg.	505	1918	May 19 1950	Burned	At South Amboy, N.J.
1537	G.G. Bennett	Brg.	479	1919	Feb 28 1936	Foundered	2-1/2 miles NNE of Smith Point Light, Potomac River entrance, Chesapeake Bay, Md.
1538	G.L. 142	Brg.	564	1955	Dec 18 1963	Foundered	Off Rockland, Me. Steel vessel.
1539	G.M. Porter	Sch.	143	1871	Jan 12 1914	Stranded	Nantucket Sound, Mass.
1540	G.N. Soffron	Ol.s.	88	1943	Nov 30 1949	Stranded	Off Blanche Point, Nova Scotia.
1541	G. Stanley	Sch.	-	-	Dec 29 1890	Unknown	Quoddy Head, Me.
1542	G.T. Forbush	Ol.s.	125	1951	Mar 27 1954	Burned	At Fox's Island on Maryland-Virginia line.
1543	G.W. Patterson	Brg.	1,047	1919	Nov 10 1934	Collided	With SS GEZINA. Near Vineyard Haven, Marthas Vineyard, Mass.
1544	G.W. Rawley	Sch.	-	-	Nov 25 1888	Unknown	Edgartown, Mass.
1545	Galatea	Sch.	65	1905	Jul 14 1914	Stranded	Off Cape Cod, Mass.
1546	Gale	Ol.s.	-	-	Apr 27 1937	Unknown	42-26-04 N. 70-37-33 W. Fisherman.
1547	Galway Castle (Br.)	-	-	-	Sep 12 1918	Torpedoed	Atlantic coast. 189 lives lost.
1548	Game Cock	Sch.	59	1851	Apr 9 1906	Stranded	Stonington, Me.
1549	Garda	Bark	-	-	Jul 29 1890	Unknown	Sable Island, Nova Scotia.
1550	Gardiner Colby	Sch.	-	-	May 8 1887	Unknown	South of Block Island, R.I.
1551	Gardiner G. Deering	Sch.	-	-	Feb 18 1891	Unknown	Sow and Pigs Ledge, Mass.
1552	Gardiner G. Deering	Sch.	1,982	1903	Jul 4 1930	Burned	Brookville, Me.
1553	Gardner Pattison	Brg.	408	1926	Nov 25 1950	Foundered	Off Bedloes Island, N.Y.
1554	Garnet	Sch.	-	-	Nov 24 1890	Unknown	Willingate, Nova Scotia.
1555	Garret	Brg.	2,301	1921	Sep 7 1944	Stranded	Under Triborough Bridge, N.Y.
1556	Gaspee	St.s.	113	1893	Sep 21 1938	Stranded	India Point Railroad Bridge, Providence, R.I.
1557	Gazelle	St.w.	204	1854	Jun 14 1859	Burned	Pittsburgh, Pa.
1558	Geestemunde	Steamer	-	-	Sep 12 1889	Unknown	Absecon Beach, N.J.
1559	Gem	Slaver	-	-	1850	Unknown	West side of Brenton Cove, Newport, R.I., Fort Adams.
1560	General	Drg.	792	1926	Oct 16 1955	Foundered	In Housatonic River near Stratford, Conn. Steel vessel.
1561	General A.E. Burnside	St.s.	72	1862	Sep 18 1895	Burned	New York, N.Y.
1562	General Adelbert Ames	Sch.	476	1881	Jan 21 1914	Stranded	41-32-30 N. 69-59-35 W. 1 mile SE of Monomoy Pt. L.S. Station. Lumber cargo.
1563	General Gordon	Sch.	-	-	Dec 2 1887	Unknown	Whitehead Harbor, Nova Scotia.
1564	General Hall	Sch.	-	-	Apr 4 1891	Collided	Nauset Light, Mass.
1565	General Howard	Sch.	-	-	Sep 19 1887	Unknown	Faulkner's Island, Long Island Sound, N.Y.
1566	Gen'l J.A. Dumont	St.p.	309	1862	Dec 22 1914	Burned	Seven Side, Md.
1567	General Meigs	St.s.	267	1892	Oct 27 1926	Foundered	New York, N.Y. Steel vessel.

NO.	NAME OF VESSEL	RIG	TONS	BUILT	DATE		CAUSE	PLACE AND COMMENT
1568	General Palmer	Sch.	-	-		1888	Unknown	Cold Spring Inlet, N.J.
1569	General Scott	Sch.	-	-	Lost	1800's	Unknown	Off Highland Light, Mass.
1570	General Scott	Sch.	83	1848	Mar 26	1913	Stranded	Quoddy Bay, Me.
1571	General Sheridan	Sch.	-	-	Oct 16	1800	Unknown	Highland Light, Mass.
1572	General Slocum	-	-	-	Jun 15	1904	Burned	Hell Gate, East River, N.Y. 1,021 lives lost.
1573	Genesta	Ga.s.	90	1904	Jul 28	1921	Collided	With schooner MARY G. DUFF. Browns Bank, Fishery Grounds, Mass.
1574	Geneva	C.bt.	114	1897	Nov 12	1925	Stranded	Sylvan Beach Light, Conn.
1575	Geneva Mertis	Ol.s.	50	1876	Oct 15	1919	Collided	With unknown vessel. Rockaway Inlet, N.Y.
1576	Genzam	Ga.s.	148	1931	Jan 14	1949	Burned	At Henry B. Nevin's Shipyard, City Island, N.Y.
1577	George A. Tuck	Sch.	-	-	Nov 9	1889	Unknown	New London, Conn.
1578	George A. Upton	Sch.	-	-	Aug 8	1896	Unknown	Newport, R.I.
1579	George & Albert	Sch.	-	-	Nov 17	1887	Unknown	Wood Island, Me.
1580	George Albree	St.w.	181	1854	Sep 9	1865	Burned	Pittsburgh, Pa.
1581	George Appold	St.s.	1,370	1865	Jan 9	1889	Stranded	Montauk Point, N.Y.
1582	George B. Marble	Sch.	-	-	Sep 5	1892	Unknown	Chatham Roads, Mass.
1583	George Campbell	Sch.	111	1893	Jan 26	1914	Stranded	Woods Island, Newfoundland.
1584	George Cromwell	St.p.	802	1862	Jan 5	1877	Stranded	Off Cape St. Mary, Newfoundland. 30 lives lost.
1585	George D. Edmunds	Sch.	541	1904	Aug 16	1919	Burned	300 miles SE of Nantucket, Mass.
1586	George E. Bently	Sch.	-	-	Apr 27	1895	Unknown	North of Block Island, R.I.
1587	George E. Walcott	Sch.	1,553	1890	Jul 30	1916	Burned	Black Tom, N.J.
1588	George Edwin	Sch.	99	1871	Jul 4	1906	Foundered	Off Grand Manan, New Brunswick.
1589	Geo. F. Bass	C.bt.	125	1910	Nov 7	1922	Collided	With Standard Oil barge. West of Rochester, N.Y.
1590	George F. Brown	Sch.	-	-	Dec 1	1889	Unknown	Long Beach, Conn.
1591	George F. Edmands	Sch.	-	-	May 14	1890	Unknown	Handkerchief Shoals, Mass.
1592	George F. Keen	Sch.	70	1864	Dec 25	1910	Burned	Marblehead, Mass.
1593	George F. Morse	St.s.	153	1878	Aug 28	1917	Burned	Barren Island, N.Y.
1594	George Gress	Sch.	67	1885	Sep 20	1940	Stranded	Birch Point, Bar Harbor, Me.
1595	George H. Bent	Sch.	-	-		1888	Sunk	Delaware Breakwater, Del.
1596	George H. Lubee	Ga.s.	73	1902	May 24	1913	Stranded	Penobscot Bay, Me.
1597	George H. Meckins	Sch.	80	1872	Jan 4	1929	Stranded	Point Lookout, Md.
1598	George H. Squires	Sch.	-	-	Lost	1800's	Unknown	Off Nauset, Mass.
1599	George Henry	Sch.	-	-	Jun 18	1891	Unknown	Delaware Bay.
1600	George Hudson	St.s.	149	1880	Aug 24	1918	Stranded	Watch Hill, R.I.
1601	Geo. K. Kirkham	St.s.	95	1900	Jun 24	1935	Burned	Hudson River, N.Y.
1602	George Killam	Sch.	-	-	Jul 1	1889	Collided	West Quoddy Head, Me.
1603	George Law	St.p.	240	1852	Aug 27	1894	Burned	Bridgeton, N.J.
1604	George Law	St.p.	480	1856	Aug 27	1901	Burned	Camden, N.J. Ferryboat.
1605	George M. Adams	Sch.	-	-	Lost	1800's	Unknown	Nauset, Mass.
1606	George May	Brg.	300	1891	Nov 14	1921	Foundered	Delaware River, near Philadelphia, Pa.
1607	George McCaffrey	C.bt.	172	1887	Apr 4	1908	Foundered	Penfield Reef, Long Island Sound, N.Y.
1608	George N. Orr	St.s.	2,872	1896	Dec 7	1917	Stranded	Savage Harbor, Prince Edward Island, Canada.
1609	George P. Davenport	Sch.	1,461	-	Jan 19	1901	Unknown	41-25-24 N. 70-51-30 W. 2-1/4 miles E by S of Cuttyhunk L.S. Station.
1610	George P. Halleck	Sch.	-	-	Oct 28	1889	Unknown	Tom's River, N.J.
1611	George P. Hudson	Sch.	2,258	1900	Jul 11	1914	Collided	With SS MIDDLESEX. Great Round Shoal, Mass. Length 266'. 3 lives lost.
1612	George R. Skolfield	Sch.	1,728	1885	Feb 5	1920	Stranded	Sea Isle, N.J.
1613	George R. Smith	Sch.	-	-	Nov 24	1802	Unknown	Monomoy Point, Cape Cod, Mass.
1614	George R. Smith	Sch.	128	1867	Jul 3	1922	Burned	Duxbury, Mass.
1615	George S. Repplier	Brg.	395	1913	Dec 5	1942	Foundered	Off West Breakwater, New Haven Harbor, Conn.

NO.	NAME OF VESSEL	RIG	TONS	BUILT	DATE		CAUSE	PLACE AND COMMENT
1616	George S. Tarbell	Sch.	-	-	Aug 19	1888	Unknown	Pollock Rip, Mass.
1617	George S. Tarbell	Sch.	525	-	Nov	1892	Unknown	41-19-20 N. 71-05-15 W. 1/2 mile SE of Browns Ledge, Rhode Island Sound.
1618	George Savage	Sch.	-	-	Jul 28	1889	Unknown	Jamaica Island, N.H.
1619	George T. Oliphant	St.P.	122	1863	Jan 14	1880	Collided	With WARREN. New York, N.Y.
1620	George V. Jordan	Sch.	615	1874	Aug 6	1906	Stranded	41-31-32 N. 69-55-00 W. 4-1/2 miles ESE of Monomoy Pt. L.S. Station, Mass.
1621	Geo. W. Anderson	Sch.	-	-	Mar 12	1888	Unknown	Lewes, Del.
1622	George W. Anderson	Sch.	224	1873	Jan 26	1914	Foundered	Off Thatchers Island, Mass.
1623	Geo. W. Cushing	Sch.	-	-	Dec 27	1888	Unknown	Richmonds Island, Me.
1624	Geo. W. Danielson	Steamer	-	-	Jan 10	1883	Unknown	Block Island, R.I.
1625	George W. Elzey, Jr.	Sch.	696	1903	Feb 27	1932	Collided	With USCG Cutter ACUSHNET. Near Cross Rip Lightship, Nantucket Sound, Mass.
1626	George W. Krebs	Sch.	62	1852	Nov 29	1909	Stranded	St. Jeromes Creek, Md.
1627	George Walker (Br.)	Ship	-	-	Lost 1800's		Unknown	Point Judith, R.I.
1628	George Washington	St.P.	804	1862	Jan 20	1877	Stranded	French Mistaken Point, Newfoundland. 25 lives lost.
1629	George Weems	St.P.	447	1858	Jun 10	1871	Burned	Baltimore, Md.
1630	George Willard	Sch.	-	-	Oct 20	1890	Unknown	Lockport, Nova Scotia.
1631	Georgette	Brg.	-	-	Jun 22	1887	Unknown	West of Block Island, R.I.
1632	Georgia (Br.)	-	-	-	Aug 4	1863	Wrecked	Sable Island, Nova Scotia.
1633	Georgia	Sch.	350	1873	Feb 10	1909	Stranded	Munroe Island, Me.
1634	Georgia	Ga.s.	105	1909	Jul 10	1918	Collided	With st.s. BRISTOL. 6 miles north of Great Round Shoal, Mass.
1635	Georgia D. Jenkins	Sch.	471	1903	Nov 4	1927	Foundered	Fox Island Thoroughfare, Me.
1636	Georgiana	-	-	-	May 1	1891	Unknown	Gabarus, Nova Scotia.
1637	Georgiana	Sch.	122	1905	Dec 6	1929	Stranded	Cape St. George, Newfoundland.
1638	Georgiana Fe	-	-	-	Dec 20	1924	Unknown	42-04-24 N. 70-19-50 W.
1639	Georgie D. Loud	Sch.	175	1872	Sep 15	1904	Abandoned	50 miles NE of Cape Cod, Mass.
1640	Georgietta	Bark	459	-	Jun 22	1887	Unknown	41-12-42 N. 71-35-06 W. 1 mile north of Block Island L.S. Station, R.I.
1641	Georgina M.	Sch.	-	-	Dec 20	1924	Unknown	42-04-24 N. 70-19-50 W. 3-1/2 miles WSW of Race Point, Mass.
1642	Georgina M	Ol.s.	103	1928	Dec 19	1928	Collided	With schooner COPPERFIELD. Boston, Mass.
1643	Gerald A. Kelleher	Brg.	256	1929	Nov	1959	Lost	At owners terminal, Weehawken, N.J.
1644	Gerald J. Killian	Brg.	269	1925	Feb 1	1943	Stranded	In North River, vicinity of Hoboken, N.J., ferries.
1645	Germania	Bark	-	-	Nov 26	1889	Unknown	Long Branh, N.J.
1646	Gertie S. Winsor	Sch.	-	-	Feb 17	1896	Unknown	Race Point, Cape Cod, Mass.
1647	Gertrude	Sch.	-	-	May 9	1890	Collided	Hog Island Roads, Portland, Me.
1648	Gertrude	Brg.	115	1894	Apr 30	1908	Abandoned	Patapsco River, Md.
1649	Gertrude Abbott	Sch.	-	-	Nov 25	1888	Unknown	Toddy Rocks, Nantasket Beach, Hull, Mass.
1650	Gertrude L. Trundy	Sch.	485	1883	Sep 4	1905	Abandoned	Off Thatchers Island, Mass.
1651	Gertrude M. Fauci	Ol.s.	126	1930	Feb 5	1936	Foundered	62-13-00 N. 43-45-00 W.
1652	Gertrude Maria (Dan.)	Sch.	-	-	Feb 12	1793	Unknown	Between Lovell's Island, Boston Harbor and Brush Island. Cohasset, Mass.
1653	Gertrude Parker	Ol.s.	115	1929	Jun 5	1946	Collided	With ol.s. SKILLIGOLEE. 40 miles SSE of Thatchers Light, Mass.
1654	Giberton	Sch.	841	1890	Sep 16	1903	Foundered	Brown Shoal, Del.
1655	Giovanni	Bark	-	-	Feb 18	1907	Wrecked	Between Highland and High Head L.S. Station, Cape Cod, Mass. Total loss.
1656	Girard	Sch.	841	1890	Feb 18	1907	Stranded	Highland Light, Truro, Mass. Length 186'. Coal cargo. 2 lives lost.
1657	Gladstone	Sch.	-	-	Oct 2	1801	Unknown	Wood End, Mass.
1658	Gladstone	Sch.	102	1886	Jan 25	1914	Stranded	Francois Harbor, Newfoundland.
1659	Gladys	Sch.	-	-	Jan 21	1887	Stranded	Cheboxgue Point, Nova Scotia.
1660	Gladys II	Ol.s.	51	1922	Apr 10	1948	Foundered	Foot of 27th Street, Brooklyn, Mass.
1661	Gladys M. Taylor	Sch.	967	1918	Aug 9	1928	Stranded	Penobscot Bay, Me.
1662	Glasgow (Br.)	-	-	-	Jul 31	1865	Burned	Nantucket Island, Mass.
1663	Gleaner	Sch.	-	-	Jan 16	1890	Unknown	Murder Island, Nova Scotia.

NO.	NAME OF VESSEL	RIG	TONS	BUILT	DATE	CAUSE	PLACE AND COMMENT
1664	Gleason	Ycht.	-	-	Jun 7 1888	Unknown	Chesapeake Bay.
1665	Glen	Sch.	-	-	Feb 13 1890	Unknown	Little Duck Island, Me.
1666	Glen Rock	Brg.	308	1921	Oct 7 1957	Foundered	Off the J.P. Duffy Co. dock at 25-50 Borden Ave., Long Island City, N.Y.
1667	Glendale	Brg.	-	-	1956	Unknown	41-47-22 N. 70-30-58 W. Cape Cod Bay, Sagamore Beach, Mass. Depth 7'.
1668	Glendower	Sc.b.	855	1894	Jan 3 1930	Collided	With st.s. CITY OF ELWOOD. Brooklyn, N.Y.
1669	Glenmore	Brg.	265	-	May 19 1950	Burned	South Amboy Coal Docks, South Amboy, N.J.
1670	Glenside	Brg.	974	1917	Nov 21 1944	Stranded	Sandwich, Mass.
1671	Glenullen	Sch.	73	1883	Oct 25 1906	Stranded	Machias Bay, Me.
1672	Glenwood	Sch.	1,600	-	Feb 22 1893	Unknown	42-18-19 N. 70-50-57 W. Hardings Ledge, Hull, Mass. Coal cargo.
1673	Gloria	Steamer	-	-	Unknown	Unknown	12.2 miles, 066° from the Absecon Inlet Bell Buoy, Little Egg Inlet, N.J.
1674	Gloucester	Ol.s.	167	1930	Feb 15 1960	Stranded	On Sandwich Point, off Halifax, Nova Scotia. Steel vessel.
1675	Go. Bodwell	St.s.	170	1892	Mar 23 1931	Burned	Swans Island, Me.
1676	Golden Ball	Sch.	291	1890	Jan 28 1909	Stranded	Jonesport, Me.
1677	Golden Belt	Sch.	-	-	Oct 7 1891	Unknown	Tusket, Nova Scotia.
1678	Golden Ray	Sch.	58	1869	Nov 24 1905	Foundered	Plum Gut, N.Y.
1679	Golden Rod	Sch.	132	1899	Mar 12 1906	Stranded	Burger, Newfoundland.
1680	Golden Sheaf	Bkn.	-	-	May 24 1896	Unknown	Pollock Rip, Mass.
1681	Goldsboro	St.s.	681	1882	Feb 27 1912	Stranded	Brandywine Shoals, Delaware Bay.
1682	Goldsmith Maid	Sch.	-	-	Nov 5 1888	Unknown	Boston, Mass.
1683	Gordon C. Baird	Brg.	240	1922	Oct 7 1942	Collided	With st.s. M. & J. TRACY. While moored at foot of 139th Street & East River, N.Y.
1684	Gordon C. Cooke	Brg.	2,023	1918	Apr 12 1947	Foundered	Between Fenwick Island & Winterquarter Shoal, off coast of Delaware. Steel.
1685	Governor Al Smith	Ol.s.	92	1928	Sep 3 1949	Collided	With Norwegian SS JAN. Approx. 25 miles SE of Liverpool Buoy, Nova Scotia.
1686	Governor Andrew	St.p.	495	1874	Jun 18 1911	Burned	East Boston, Mass. 2 lives lost.
1687	Gov. Bodwell	St.s.	140	1892	Jan 26 1924	Foundered	Swans Island, Me.
1688	Gov. Foss	Ol.s.	130	1911	Apr 2 1929	Stranded	Cape May Harbor, N.J.
1689	Governor Fuller	Ol.s.	85	1927	Aug 14 1930	Burned	Great Round Shoal, Mass.
1690	Gov. J.G. Smith	Sch.	-	-	Lost 1800's	Unknown	Race Point, Mass.
1691	Governor Marshall	Ol.s.	131	1921	Nov 28 1927	Stranded	Shelburne Harbor, Nova Scotia.
1692	Governor Powers	Sch.	1,962	1905	Sep 11 1918	Collided	With st.s. SAN JOSE. Nantucket Sound, Mass. Length 237'.
1693	Governor Prence	Ol.s.	83	1917	Oct 24 1929	Burned	Cape Cod Canal, Mass.
1694	Governor Robie	Sch.	1,712	1883	Nov 28 1921	Foundered	Northwest of Hogland Light, N.J. All lives (3) lost.
1695	Grace	Sch.	877	1900	Jan 12 1922	Foundered	Off Sea Girt, N.J.
1696	Grace A. Martin	Sch.	3,129	1904	Jan 4 1914	Foundered	30 miles south of Matincus Island, Me.
1697	Grace C. Hadley	Sch.	-	-	May 25 1895	Unknown	Shovelful Shoals, Mass.
1698	Grace Davis	Sch.	401	1873	Oct 4 1916	Foundered	Off Louisburg, Nova Scotia.
1699	Grace and Evelyn	Ol.s.	81	1927	Jan 25 1932	Burned	Off Highland Light, Mass.
1700	Grace G. Bennett	Sch.	210	1893	1956	Foundered	In Chester River, Crumpton, Md.
1701	Grace P. Willard	Sch.	107	1891	May 17 1919	Collided	With rock drill. East River, N.Y.
1702	Grace and Rosalie	Ol.s.	50	1925	Sep 14 1945	Stranded	Off Big Cranberry Island, Me.
1703	Grace Van Dusen	Sch.	303	1874	Apr 12 1922	Stranded	Alongside Red Buoy, near Lubec, Me.
1704	Gracie	Sloop	-	-	Nov 27 1898	Unknown	Provincetown, Mass.
1705	Grafton	Sch.	531	1899	Jan 24 1908	Foundered	40 miles southwest of Block Island, R.I. All lives (3) lost.
1706	Gramercy	Ol.s.	64	1926	Feb 1966	Lost	In Newton Creek, Long Island City, N.Y.
1707	Grampus	Sch.	-	-	Sep 24 1890	Unknown	Shovelful Shoals, Mass.
1708	Grand Republic	St.p.	1,760	1878	Apr 26 1924	Burned	Foot of West 155th Street, N.Y.
1709	Granite State	St.p.	887	1853	Jun 1883	Burned	Old Saybrook, Conn. 3 lives lost.
1710	Granite State	Sch.	-	-	Lost 1800's	Unknown	Off Pleasant Bay, Chatham, Mass.
1711	Granville R. Bacon	Sch.	385	1911	Dec 20 1933	Stranded	Weekapang Point, R.I. Length 133'.

NO.	NAME OF VESSEL	RIG	TONS	BUILT	DATE	CAUSE	PLACE AND COMMENT
1712	Gray Eagle	Sch.	-	-	Oct 17 1890	Unknown	Wellfleet, Cape Cod, Mass.
1713	Great Isaac	Ol.s.	1,117	1944	Apr 16 1947	Collided	With Norwegian MV BANDEIRANTE. 39-39-30 N. 73-56-36 W. Steel vessel.
1714	Great West	St.w.	230	1855	Jul 15 1858	Burned	Pittsburgh, Pa.
1715	Grecian	Sch.	-	-	Lost 1800's	Unknown	Off Pleasant Bay, Chatham, Mass.
1716	Grecian	St.s.	2,827	1900	May 27 1932	Collided	With st.s. CITY OF CHATTANOOGA. 41-06-18 N. 71-33-06 W. 2-3/4 miles south of Block Island Southeast Light, R.I. Steel vessel. Length 263'. 4 lives lost (36).
1717	Greenwich	St.s.	70	1906	Nov 19 1948	Burned	In Johnsons Creek, Bridgeport, Conn.
1718	Grey Eagle	Sch.	-	-	Oct 17 1890	Unknown	Wellfleet, Mass. See No.1712.
1719	Greyhound	Ga.y.	103	1910	Oct 2 1929	Burned	Lloyds Harbor, N.Y.
1720	Griswold	St.s.	133	1899	Aug 17 1921	Foundered	New Haven, Conn.
1721	Grouse	Ol.s.	-	-	Sep 21 1963	Unknown	42-40-24 N. 70-34-29 W. West side of Little Dry Salvages, Rockport, Mass. U.S. Navy mine sweeper. Length 136'. Wood vessel.
1722	Guard	Brig	797	-	Oct 18 1884	Unknown	Watch Hill Race, R.I. Coal cargo.
1723	Guinn	Sloop	-	-	Aug 13 1888	Unknown	Napatree Point, R.I.
1724	Gulftrade	St.s.	7,776	1920	Mar 10 1942	War Loss	39-50-56 N. 73-49-30 W. or 39-43-42 N. 74-01-21 3.6 miles, 120° from Barnegat Inlet, N.J. Southerly Wreck Lighted Gong Buoy, 9,000 yds. 116° True from Abandoned Lighthouse, Barnegat, N.J. Tanker. Sunk by enemy action. Depth 75'.
1725	Gurnet	Sch.	-	-	Dec 17 1888	Abandoned	Off Lynn, Mass.
1726	Gwendoline Steers	Ol.s.	149	1888	Dec 20 1962	Foundered	In Huntington Bay, Long Island Sound, between Lloyd's Neck & Eaton's Neck, N.Y. Ocean going tug. Iron vessel.
1727	Gwennie	Sch.	1,087	1902	Jan 24 1908	Foundered	25 miles NE of Barnegat, N.J. All lives (5) lost.
1728	Gypsum	St.s.	141	1889	Jan 2 1919	Burned	Northport, N.Y.
1729	Gypsum King	St.s.	562	1899	Jan 22 1906	Stranded	St. Marys Reef, off Grand Manan, New Brunswick.
1730	Gypsum Prince (Br.)	St.s.	1,970*	-	May 3 1942	War Loss	1.2 miles, 117° from light on south end of rock breakwater, 1.1 miles off tip of Cape Henlopen, Del. 38-48-00 N. 75-04-00 W. Demolished & cleared to 50' depth.
1731	H.A. Dening	Sch.	133	1887	Nov 6 1894	Unknown	Watch Hill, R.I.
1732	H. and A. Morse	St.s.	95	1885	May 14 1905	Burned	Crossman Dock, Raritan River, N.J.
1733	H.B. Bates	C.bt.	-	-	Feb 15 1912	Ice	Whitehall, N.Y.
1734	H.B. Hussey	Brg.	545	-	Aug 31 1887	Unknown	Handkerchief Shoals, Mass. Coal cargo.
1735	H.B. Sichel	Sl.b.	963	1912	Jul 9 1951	Burned	At Port Reading, N.J.
1736	H.C. French	C.bt.	142	1888	Mar 19 1906	Stranded	New Haven, Conn.
1737	H.C. Higginson	Sch.	-	-	Nov 25 1888	Unknown	Nantasket Beach, Hull, Mass.
1738	H.C. Libby	Brg.	-	-	Jul 20 1897	Unknown	Nantucket Shoal, Mass.
1739	H.C. Rowe & Co.	St.s.	500	1886	Oct 31 1922	Burned	Shelter Island Sound, off Sag Harbor, Long Island, N.Y.
1740	H. Eldridge	Sch.	-	-	Jul 20 1889	Unknown	Tusket Island, Nova Scotia.
1741	H.F. Hallett	Brg.	350	1889	Oct 22 1907	Foundered	Faulkners Island, Conn.
1742	H.J. Wheeler	St.s.	421	1919	Aug 30 1949	Burned	At Hoboken, N.J.
1743	H.L. Parnell	Brg.	413	1912	May 31 1941	Burned	Jersey City, N.J.
1744	H.M. Rowley	Sch.	-	-	Jun 30 1897	Unknown	Block Island, R.I.
1745	H.M.S. Hussar (Br.)	Frigate	-	-	Sep 13 1780	Collided	Off Pot Rock, Hell Gate, New York Harbor, N.Y. 28 gun armament. Reported to have carried $500,000 to $5 million in gold & silver. No detailed explanation made mention of treasure during court martial of Captain Charles M. Pole.
1746	H.M.S. Faithful Steward (Br.)	Frigate	-	-	1785	Wrecked	Off Rehoboth Beach, Del. Reported to have carried $500,000 in gold.
1747	H.M.S. Tilbury (Br.)	Frigate	-	-	1757	Lost	Cape Breton, off Louisbourg, Nova Scotia. Reported to have carried $500,000.
1748	H. & N.Y.T. Co. No.32	Brg.	551	1913	Feb 20 1934	Foundered	Stamford, Conn.
1749	H.P. Dilworth	St.p.	123	1900	Jan 19 1910	Burned	Rices Landing, Pa.
1750	H. Prescott	Sch.	-	-	Nov 13 1891	Collided	Near Boston, Mass.

NO.	NAME OF VESSEL	RIG	TONS	BUILT	DATE		CAUSE	PLACE AND COMMENT
1751	H.S. Inc. No.11	Brg.	258	-	May 18	1948	Collided	With SS GYPSUM PRINCE. Off pier 6, Staten Island, N.Y.
1752	H.S. Inc. No.73	Brg.	314	-	Nov 6	1948	Stranded	On reef at Execution Lighthouse in Long Island Sound, 1 mile from New Rochelle. N.Y.
1753	H.S. Inc No.86	Brg.	366	1911	Mar 18	1959	Foundered	In East River at south side of Green Street Pier, Brooklyn, N.Y. Steel vessel.
1754	H.S. Lanfair	Sch.	402	1884	May 1	1917	Stranded	St. Johns Island, Me.
1755	H.T. Hedges	Sch.	239	1868	May 22	1908	Foundered	Whitestone, N.Y.
1756	H.T. Townsend	Sch.	-	-	Feb 14	1885	Unknown	Tuckernuck Flats, Nantucket, Mass. Mahogony cargo.
1757	H.W. Godfrey	Sch.	-	-	Oct 7	1890	Unknown	Hereford Bar, N.J.
1758	Hail Columbia	St.w.	116	1848	Apr 19	1852	Collided	Beaver, Pa.
1759	Haleyon	St.s.	89	1875	Oct 18	1923	Foundered	Coney Island, N.Y. 2 lives lost (19).
1760	Halsey	St.s.	7,088	1920	May 5	1942	War Loss	North Atlantic. Sunk by enemy action.
1761	Hamilton Fish	Sch.	1,616	1856	Mar 6	1906	Foundered	Off Barnegat, N.J.
1762	Hammond	Sch.	693	1895	Apr 12	1918	Stranded	Holly Beach, N.J.
1763	Hampshire	Sch.	830	1900	Mar 10	1918	Foundered	Off Five Fathom Bank Lightship, N.J. All lives (4) lost.
1764	Hampton	Sch.	-	-	Dec 10	1888	Unknown	George's Island, Me.
1765	Hannah	Bark	-	-	Nov 25	1888	Unknown	Lewes, Del.
1766	Hannah A. Lennen	St.s.	136	1901	Jun 16	1944	Collided	With tanker BEUNA VISTA. Harbor end of channel, entrance to Delaware Bay.
1767	Hannah E. Shubert	Sch.	398	-	Mar 9	1886	Unknown	Peaked Hill Bars, Provincetown, Mass.
1768	Hannah F. Carleton	Sch.	225	1884	Nov 24	1911	Foundered	Handkerchief Shoal, Mass.
1769	Hanover No.1	Sc.b.	915	1898	Sep 28	1935	Foundered	51 miles south of Fenwick Island Whistling Buoy, Md.
1770	Harbor	St.s.	50	1891	Aug 30	1912	Burned	Maurice River, N.J.
1771	Harby	Brg.	162	1919	Jul 5	1940	Foundered	Newton Creek, Brooklyn, N.Y.
1772	Harding Highway	St.p.	652	1884	Feb 14	1926	Foundered	Christiana River, Del. Iron vessel. All lives (18) lost.
1773	Harford	Brg.	2,240	1921	Jan 14	1948	Foundered	Off Sandy Hook Light, N.J.
1774	Harmona	Sch.	-	-	Oct 21	1892	Unknown	Handkerchief Shoals, Mass.
1775	Harmony	Ga.s.	119	1904	May 1	1924	Stranded	Rockaway Beach, N.Y.
1776	Harold	Scow	-	-	Sep 27	1903	Unknown	Staten Sound, off Sewaren, N.J. Cargo of silver ingots. Eighty per cent of the 7,678 ingots were recovered off and/or on Story's Flat.
1777	Harold B. Cousens	Sch.	379	1882	Nov 29	1918	Stranded	East Gloucester, Mass. Length 139'.
1778	Harold C. Beacher	Sch.	363	1883	Jul 18	1914	Stranded	Scattaric Island, Nova Scotia.
1779	Haroldine	Sch.	-	-	Nov 8	1895	Unknown	Nauset Light, Mass.
1780	Harrie M. Young	Sch.	-	-	Nov 27	1898	Unknown	Provincetown, Mass.
1781	Harriet B.	Sch.	447	1920	Mar 27	1925	Stranded	Campobello, New Brunswick.
1782	Harriet C. Kerlin	Sch.	-	-	Aug 10	1895	Unknown	Pollock Rip, Mass.
1783	Harriet E. Ford	Sch.	50	1870	Jul 8	1911	Stranded	Love Point Light, Chesapeake Bay, Md. 2 lives lost.
1784	Harriet E. Winne	Brg.	386	1864	Nov 14	1907	Stranded	Plumb Island, N.Y.
1785	Harriet S. Jackson	Bark	497	-	Sep 20	1898	Unknown	41-35-14 N. 69-58-41 W. 3/8 mile ESE of Monomoy L.S. Station, Mass.
1786	Harrison	Brg.	312	1893	Jul 10	1909	Burned	Providence, R.I.
1787	Harrison	St.s.	217	1907	Jun 13	1950	Burned	Ben Davis Shoal, Del.
1788	Harry	Steamer	-	-	Sep 28	1895	Unknown	Eastsoutheast of Brentons Lightship, R.I.
1789	Harry A. Barry	Sch.	-	-	Feb 20	1887	Unknown	South of Point Judith, R.I. 41-21-46 N. 71-28-48 W.
1790	Harry A. Keeler	Brg.	345	1903	Jan 25	1928	Foundered	Newport, R.I.
1791	Harry A. Wheeler	Brg.	253	1891	Oct 24	1914	Stranded	Off Bridgeport, Conn.
1792	Harry Bumm	St.s.	51	1864	May 27	1872	Exploded	New York, N.Y. 3 lives lost.
1793	Harry C. Sheppard	Sch.	213	1870	Jul 30	1911	Abandoned	South of Boston Light, Mass.
1794	Harry E.	Steamer	-	-		1895	Unknown	On Brenton Reef, R.I.
1795	Harry Friend	Sch.	-	-	Oct 21	1893	Unknown	On Shoveful Shoal, Mass.
1796	Harry Howard	Brg.	538	1922	Oct 17	1930	Stranded	Newport, R.I.
1797	Harry K. Fooks	Ol.s.	184	1921	Sep 10	1941	Collided	With st.s. E.J. CODD. 1,000 yds. from Hens & Chickens Whistling Buoy, Del.

NO.	NAME OF VESSEL	RIG	TONS	BUILT	DATE	CAUSE	PLACE AND COMMENT
1798	Harry Knowlton	Sch.	317	1890	Feb 11 1907	Collided	With st.p. LARCHMONT. 41-15-45 N. 71-49-30 W. About 3 miles SE of Watch Hill Light, R.I. Length 130'. Coal cargo.
1799	Harry Messer	Sch.	627	1880	Dec 24 1908	Stranded	Northeast part of Handkerchief Shoal, off Monomoy Point, Mass. Coal cargo.
1800	Harry R. Conners	Brg.	230	1903	May 25 1916	Stranded	Harlem River, N.Y.
1801	Harry Rush	Brg.	956	1908	Feb 17 1942	Foundered	Barnegat, N.J.
1802	Harry Stewart	Sch.	-	-	Apr 26 1892	Unknown	Shovelful Shoal, Mass.
1803	Harry W. Haynes	Sch.	295	1890	Mar 17 1917	Stranded	Cashier's Ledge, Me. All lives (4) lost.
1804	Harsimus	St.s.	112	1882	Jan 25 1927	Burned	Port Richmond, N.Y.
1805	Hartwelson	St.s.	3,078	1902	May 5 1943	Foundered	On Bantam Rock, Sheepscot Bar, Me. 43-27-00 N. 70-00-00 W. Freighter.
1806	Harvest	St.s.	345	1864	Apr 2 1869	Burned	Point Judith, R.I.
1807	Harvest Home	Sch.	78	1870	1906	Collided	With British vessel. Off Cape Cod, Mass.
1808	Harvester	Sch.	106	1892	Oct 19 1912	Stranded	Car Rock, Yarmouth, Nova Scotia.
1809	Harvester	Brg.	558	1910	May 31 1933	Stranded	Van Wies Point, Hudson River, N.Y.
1810	Hastings	St.s.	165	1885	Oct 24 1906	Burned	Off Shippan Point, Conn.
1811	Hastings	Sch.	84	1871	Sep 15 1911	Unknown	Rockport Harbor, Me.
1812	Hattie Burcham	Ol.s.	-	-	1960	Unknown	Old Bare Shoal, Delaware Bay. West of shoal about 6,190 yds. 88° 15' from tower.
1813	Hattie G. Dixon	Bkn.	528	1876	May 13 1906	Stranded	Chappaquiddick Island, Mass.
1814	Hattie H. Barbour	Sch.	301	1883	Apr 10 1917	Foundered	Off Cape Cod, Mass.
1815	Hattie J. Philips	Sch.	-	-	Nov 30 1880	Unknown	Handkerchief Shoal, Mass.
1816	Hattie M. Crowell	Sch.	-	-	Oct 22 1891	Abandoned	Off Long Cove, Me.
1817	Hattie Thomas	St.s.	56	1890	Jan 29 1928	Foundered	Elm Park, Staten Island, N.Y.
1818	Hauppauge	Sch.	1,446	1918	May 25 1918	Torpedoed	38 miles off Blackfish Bank, Md.
1819	Havana	Sch.	1,617	1900	Jan 11 1922	Foundered	Mantoloking, N.J. 2 lives lost.
1820	Hazard	Sloop	-	-	Nov 12 1714	Unknown	Cohasset, Mass.
1821	Hazel Mitchell	Brg.	377	1907	Apr 16 1929	Stranded	St. George, N.Y.
1822	Hazel R. Knight	Brg.	236	1919	Nov 17 1927	Collided	With st.p. F.W. SARGENT, Buffalo, N.Y.
1823	Hecla	Ol.s.	53	1923	Feb 15 1961	Foundered	In the Delaware River off New Castle, Del.
1824	Hector	Sch.	-	-	Nov 27 1898	Unknown	Vineyard Haven, Mass.
1825	Helen	Sch.	-	-	Jan 27 1800	Unknown	Orleans, Cape Cod, Mass.
1826	Helen	Sch.	-	-	Mar 4 1891	Unknown	Cape Elizabeth, Me.
1827	Helen	Brg.	388	1901	Jan 7 1908	Stranded	Fishers Island, N.Y.
1828	Helen	Sch.	149	1864	May 6 1917	Foundered	Bay of Fundy, Nova Scotia.
1829	Helen	Sch.	1,285	1911	Jan 12 1922	Foundered	Off Sea Girt, N.J.
1830	Helen	St.s.	73	1880	Jul 20 1931	Foundered	Long Island Sound, N.Y.
1831	Helen A. Wyman	Sch.	1,717	1881	Nov 19 1911	Foundered	Montauk Point, N.Y.
1832	Helen Augusta	Sch.	-	-	Dec 27 1887	Collided	Off Faulkners Island, N.Y.
1833	Helen B. Crosby	Sch.	1,776	1906	Oct 11 1906	Stranded	Inner Bay Ledge, Penobscot Bay, Me.
1834	Helen E. Cunningham	Brg.	269	1924	Sep 28 1942	Stranded	Yonkers, N.Y.
1835	Helen F. Smith	Brg.	457	1920	Dec 1 1941	Stranded	South of Troy, N.Y.
1836	Helen F. Whitten	Sch.	-	-	Sep 9 1896	Unknown	Newport, R.I.
1837	Helen F. Whittin	Sch.	134	1890	Aug 6 1907	Foundered	Blanc Sablong, Newfoundland.
1838	Helen G. King	Sch.	147	1867	Feb 27 1916	Stranded	Cape Cod Canal, Mass.
1839	Helen G. Moseley	Sch.	566	1898	Jun 4 1898	Unknown	Bearses Shoal, Mass. Length 146'.
1840	Helen J. Seitz	Sch.	2,547	1905	Feb 9 1907	Stranded	Beach Haven, N.J.
1841	Helen L. Smith	Sch.	-	-	Lost 1800's	Unknown	Point Judith, R.I.
1842	Helen M.	Ol.s.	77	1926	Feb 1 1957	Foundered	About 22 miles east by south from Thatcher's Buoy, off Rockport, Mass.
1843	Helen M. Fairlamb	Sch.	74	1903	Apr 15 1922	Foundered	Nantuxent Point, Delaware Bay.
1844	Helen M. Mathiasen	St.s.	137	1891	Jun 22 1935	Burned	Pier 21, Brooklyn, N.Y.

NO.	NAME OF VESSEL	RIG	TONS	BUILT	DATE	CAUSE	PLACE AND COMMENT
1845	Helen Mar	Sch.	-	-	Nov 11 1887	Unknown	Handkerchief Shoal, Mass.
1846	Helen Maud (Br.)	Sch.	-	-	May 29 1803	Unknown	Shovelful Shoal, Mass.
1847	Helen R	Brg.	284	1904	Oct 5 1909	Stranded	Flushing, N.Y.
1848	Helen R. Cullen	Brg.	295	1901	Feb 15 1908	Stranded	New Haven, Conn.
1849	Helen R. Low	Sch.	-	-	Mar 1 1892	Unknown	Provincetown, Mass.
1850	Helen Thompson	Sch.	-	-	Apr 22 1891	Unknown	Horse Shoe Shoal, Mass.
1851	Helena	Sch.	-	-	Jan 1 1887	Unknown	North Beach, Md.
1852	Helena	Sch.	-	-	May 3 1899	Unknown	Peaked Hill, Mass.
1853	Helena	Sch.	619	1893	Jan 30 1909	Unknown	42-10-00 N. 70-42-12 W. Entrance to New Inlet, Fourth Cliff L.S. Station, Mass.
1854	Helena	Sch.	184		Apr 21 1913	Stranded	Near Port Clyde, Me.
1855	Helene	Sch.	-	-	Mar 1873	Unknown	Point Allerton, Mass.
1856	Helja Silva	Ol.s.	140	1918	Nov 9 1926	Stranded	Shelburne Light, Nova Scotia.
1857	Henlopen	Brg.	765	1917	Aug 29 1936	Foundered	9.2 miles, bearing 125° from south standpipe at Margate City, N.J.
1858	Henrietta A. Whitney	Sch.	217	1896	Aug 6 1924	Burned	Eastport, Me.
1859	Henrietta Collyer	Sch.	58	1880	Oct 10 1925	Stranded	Port Jefferson, N.Y.
1860	Henry	Sch.	-	-	Feb 11 1802	Unknown	Peaked Hill, Mass.
1861	Henry A. Burnham	Bark	-	-	Sep 15 1890	Unknown	Seal Island, Nova Scotia.
1862	Henry A. Paul	Sch.	-	-	Lost 1800's	Unknown	Race Point, Mass.
1863	Henry B. Fiske	Sch.	-	-	Sep 7 1803	Unknown	Monomoy Point, Mass.
1864	Henry B. Fiske	Sch.	847	1901	Jan 23 1910	Stranded	Nantucket Island, Mass. Length 182'. All lives (8) lost.
1865	Henry C. Cadmus	Brg.	611	1905	Apr 14 1911	Foundered	Beavertail Lighthouse, R.I. 1 life lost.
1866	Henry C. Rowe	St.s.	220	1883	Nov 17 1923	Collided	With st.s. ST. LOUIS. North River, N.Y. 1 life lost (7).
1867	Henry Clay	Sch.	841	1890	Apr 6 1917	Foundered	Off Montauk Point, N.Y.
1868	Henry Clay	St.p.	386	1851	Jul 28 1852	Burned	Hudson River, Yonkers, N.Y. 70 lives lost.
1869	Henry D. May	Sch.	278	1871	Feb 25 1913	Foundered	Off Long Island Sound, N.Y.
1870	Henry D. McCord	St.s.	69	1872	Apr 18 1926	Burned	Brooklyn, N.Y.
1871	Henry E. Eckford	St.p.	153	1824	Apr 27 1841	Exploded	New York, N.Y. Used as coal barge.
1872	Henry Endicott	Brg.	866	1908	Sep 18 1939	Foundered	41-55-00 N. 70-29-00 W. 2-1/4 miles ESE of Manomet Point, Plymouth, Mass. Wood vessel. Length 200'. Carrying locomotive. Moderate currents in area.
1873	Henry F. Kreger	Sch.	1,250	1903	Oct 26 1921	Stranded	Little Round Shoal, Mass. Length 203'. Plaster cargo.
1874	Henry Failing	Sch.	1,976	1883	Feb 26 1918	Foundered	Off Block Island, R.I.
1875	Henry Ford	Ga.s.	155	1922	Jun 16 1928	Stranded	Bonne Bay, Newfoundland.
1876	Henry Graff	St.w.	250	1855	May 7 1859	Burned	Pittsburgh, Pa.
1877	Henry H. Seavy	Sch.	-	-	Jan 25 1875	Unknown	South of Point Judith, R.I.
1878	Henry J. Jordan	Brg.	380	1908	Dec 11 1951	Burned	While moored at Dolan's Bulkhead in Greenwich, Staten Island, N.Y.
1879	Henry J. May	Sch.	866	1891	May 27 1876	Unknown	Southwest Point, Block Island, R.I.
1880	Henry L. Pechham	St.s.	54	1862	Jun 29 1910	Burned	Isleboro, Me.
1881	Henry L. Wait	St.s.	76	1902	Nov 3 1908	Burned	College Point, N.Y.
1882	Henry Lange	Sch.	-	-	Jun 5 1929	Burned	Elm Park, N.Y.
1883	Henry Lippet	Sch.	-	-	Lost 1800's	Unknown	Off Pamet River, Cape Cod, Mass.
1884	Henry M. Clark	Sch.	-	-	Aug 25 1891	Unknown	Atlantic City, N.J.
1885	Henry M. Stanley	Sch.	118	1890	Dec 1 1909	Stranded	Bay of Islands, Newfoundland.
1886	Henry Morrison	St.p.	146	1854	Apr 6 1898	Burned	Winthrop, Mass.
1887	Henry Nowell	Bkn.	-	-	Lost 1800's	Unknown	Pollock Rip, Mass.
1888	Henry R. Tilton	Sch.	-	-	Nov 26 1898	Unknown	Stoney Beach, Mass.
1889	Henry S. Little	Sch.	-	-	Lost 1800's	Unknown	Pollock Rip, Mass.
1890	Henry S. Wyman	Sch.	-	-	Jun 13 1896	Unknown	East of Block Island, R.I.
1891	Henry Steers	Brg.	368	1911	Jan 26 1918	Burned	Port Newark, N.J.

NO.	NAME OF VESSEL	RIG	TONS	BUILT	DATE		CAUSE	PLACE AND COMMENT
1892	Henry Sutton	Sch.	602	1879	Oct 18	1906	Foundered	Sailed from Cheverie, Nova Scotia & has since not reported. All lives (7) lost.
1893	Henry W.	Sch.	-	-	Jan 25	1875	Unknown	South of Point Judith, R.I.
1894	Henry Wardell	Sch.	69	1862	Dec 26	1909	Foundered	Perth Amboy, N.J. All lives (1) lost.
1895	Henry Warner	Bark	-	-	Jul 26	1891	Unknown	Centerville, Nova Scotia.
1896	Henry Washington	Sch.	-	-	Apr 30	1895	Unknown	Pollock Rip, Mass.
1897	Henry Whitney	Sch.	146	1869	Jan 26	1905	Stranded	Newport, R.I.
1898	Henry Willis	Sch.	80	1884	Nov 18	1911	Foundered	Menunketesuck Point, Conn. 2 lives lost.
1899	Henry Withington	Sch.	527	1874	Mar 5	1917	Stranded	Scituate, Mass.
1900	Herald	Sch.	499	1883	Apr 4	1915	Foundered	100 miles west of Sea Island, New Brunswick.
1901	Herbert	St.s.	349	1910	Aug 6	1924	Collided	Nahant, Mass. 42-25-05 N. 70-51-25 W. 2 miles east of East Point.
1902	Herbert	Brg.	735	1918	Sep 30	1944	Foundered	Off Barnegat, N.J.
1903	Herbert D. Maxwell	Sch.	772	1905	May 16	1910	Collided	With st.s. GLOUCESTER. Off Annapolis, Md. 4 lives lost.
1904	Herbert Parker	Ol.s.	137	1919	May 16	1932	Burned	Off Ambrose Channel Lightship, N.Y.
1905	Hercules	St.s.	155	1880	Dec 14	1907	Collided	With obstruction. 41-18-50 N. 71-47-00 W. 3-1/2 miles ENE of Watch Hill L.S. Station, R.I. Tug. Iron vessel.
1906	Hercules	Sch.	755	1870	Aug 12	1916	Foundered	Off Yarmouth, Fairway Buoy, Nova Scotia. Iron vessel.
1907	Hercules	St.s.	233	1906	Apr 21	1917	Collided	With st.s. ATLANTA. Boston Harbor, Mass.
1908	Herman F. Kimball	Sch.	125	1888	Sep 5	1918	Stranded	Trundys Reef, Me.
1909	Herman Frasch	St.s.	3,803	1910	Oct 5	1918	Collided	With st.s. GEORGE G. HENRY. Off Cape Sable, Nova Scotia. Steel vessel.
1910	Herman Winter	St.s.	2,638	1887	Mar 7	1944	Stranded	41-20-57 N. 70-50-30 W. Devils Bidge Reef, Gay Head, Marthas Vineyard, Mass. Iron vessel. Length 271'. Tanker (also reported as freighter).
1911	Hermione	Sloop	-	-	Nov 1	1782	Aground	Sank east of New London Harbor entrance, Conn. Connecticut privateer. Depth 30'. Reported to have carried $100,000 in gold specie.
1912	Hermit	Sch.	70	1893	Dec 15	1906	Collided	With st.s. MONTEREY. Off Sandy Hook, N.J.
1913	Hero	Brg.	180	1891	Oct 20	1913	Foundered	At Brandywine Lighthouse, Del.
1914	Hero	Ol.s.	159	1945	Feb 19	1961	Collided	With ledge. About 1 mile east of Hen & Chicken Light Buoy, Mass. Steel vessel.
1915	Heroine	St.s.	296	1899	Jun 19	1920	Foundered	41-18-18 N. 71-33-42 W. 5 miles southwest of Point Judith, R.I. Steel vessel.
1916	Hesper	Ga.s.	98	1884	Apr 30	1919	Stranded	Delaware Capes.
1917	Hesperus	Sch.	135	1917	Oct 7	1935	Foundered	Boston Harbor, Mass. Historical value.
1918	Hesperus	Ol.s.	-	-	Feb 13	1893	Stranded	Off Cape Cod, Mass.
1919	Highlander	Brig	-	-	Apr 26	1924	Storm	Ashore on Fishers Island, N.Y. Lumber cargo.
1920	Highlander	St.p.	1,310	1902	Feb 20	1961	Burned	Foot of West 155th Street, N.Y. Steel vessel.
1921	Hilda Garston	Ol.s.	150	1945			Unknown	41-26-54 N. 71-02-06 W. 1 mile south of Old Cook Rock, Hen & Chickens Reef, Mass. Fisherman. Length 90'. Steel vessel. Depth 50'. Intact. Salvage attempted.
1922	Hilda Marie	Ol.s.	78	1917	Aug 23	1932	Burned	Five Fathom Bank Lightship, N.J.
1923	Hillsborough	St.s.	328	1916	May	1952	Foundered	At Hudson Heights, N.J.
1924	Hillville	Brg.	-	-	Unknown		Unknown	South of Manasquan Inlet, 3 miles offshore, Point Pleasant, N.J. Depth 76'.
1925	Hinckley	St.s.	232	1901	Aug 3	1929	Stranded	Stony Point, N.Y.
1926	Hippodrome	St.s.	315	1862	Nov 17	1886	Stranded	Cape May, N.J. Used as coal barge.
1927	HMCS Saint Clair	-	1,060	-	Jul 13	1945	Unknown	41-27-42 N. 71-06-20 W. Destroyer. Steel vessel. Length 314'. 4,600 yds., 216° True from Two Mile Rock, Westport.
1928	Hobomok	St.s.	119	1864	Aug 25	1866	Burned	Thomas Point, Md.
1929	Hockomock	Ga.s.	50	1904	Aug 28	1917	Stranded	Off Isaac Harbor, Nova Scotia.
1930	Holbrook	St.s.	79	1864	May 23	1929	Stranded	Waterford, N.Y. 1 life lost (9).
1931	Holliswood	St.s.	75	1879	Oct 10	1925	Stranded	Bergen Point Light, N.J.
1932	Holly	Brg.	219	1892	Dec 19	1919	Foundered	Chester, Pa.
1933	Holy Name	Ol.s.	52	1893	May 21	1960	Foundered	Off Rockport, Mass., east by north from Thatcher's Buoy.
1934	Homer K. Martin	C.bt.	96	1891	Apr 25	1913	Foundered	Whitehall, N.Y.

NO.	NAME OF VESSEL	RIG	TONS	BUILT	DATE	CAUSE	PLACE AND COMMENT
1935	Honesdale	Brg.	277	1874	Jan 10 1907	Stranded	Fishers Island, N.Y.
1936	Hoop-La	Ol.s.	80	1917	Jan 10 1940	Foundered	15 miles east of Gurnet Point Light, Plymouth, Mass.
1937	Hopatcong	St.p.	854	1885	Aug 7 1905	Burned	Hoboken, N.J.
1938	Hopatcong	Brg.	563	1885	Dec 6 1910	Foundered	New York Bay, N.Y. Iron vessel.
1939	Horace A. Allyn	Sch.	859	1904	Aug 12 1928	Foundered	Absecon Light, N.J.
1940	Horace G. Morse	Sch.	437	1890	Jan 19 1907	Stranded	Bliss Island, New Brunswick. 2 lives lost.
1941	Horace W. Macomber	Sch.	-	-	Feb 7 1802	Unknown	Nauset, Mass.
1942	Horatio Babson	Sch.	-	-	Mar 19 1876	Unknown	Peaked Hill, Mass.
1943	Horatio Hall	St.s.	3,167	1898	Mar 10 1909	Collided	With st.s. H.F. DIMOCK. 41-32-20 N. 69-54-08 W. 1 mile south by east of bell buoy, Pollock Rip Slue, Mass. Steel vessel. Length 300'. Freighter.
1944	Hornet	St.s.	93	1849	May 9 1860	Burned	Peekskill, N.Y.
1945	Hornet	Slp.b.	578	1883	Dec 18 1925	Collided	With slp.b. VIRGINIA PALMER. Bath Beach, N.Y.
1946	Howard	St.s.	179	1882	Mar 6 1911	Stranded	Jones Beach, Long Island, N.Y.
1947	Howard	Brg.	2,219	1921	Mar 21 1942	Stranded	North River, N.Y. Also reported lost in September.
1948	Howard B. Peck	Sch.	472	1890	Feb 15 1908	Stranded	Fire Island, N.Y.
1949	Howard Dail	Sch.	77	1872	Feb 17 1915	Burned	Madison, Md.
1950	Howard E.	Sc.b.	436	1918	Feb 15 1939	Foundered	1 mile south of Stratford Point Lighthouse, near Bridgeport, Conn.
1951	Howard L. Neff	Brg.	353	1897	Jan 25 1922	Foundered	Patapsco River, Md.
1952	Howard Russell	Sch.	63	1881	Dec 15 1921	Foundered	Mackerel Cove, Swans Island, Me.
1953	Howard Sisters	Brg.	488	1918	Oct 17 1930	Stranded	Newport, R.I.
1954	Howard Williams	Sch.	-	-	Jan 30 1891	Unknown	Absecon, N.J.
1955	Howard Wood	Brg.	561	1918	Oct 10 1925	Foundered	Hog Island, Pa. All lives (3) lost.
1956	Howard Wood	Brg.	760	1917	Apr 28 1928	Foundered	Absecon Light, N.J.
1957	Howard Wood	Brg.	598	1889	Dec 22 1944	Foundered	Worten's Point, 24 miles south of Chesapeake City, Md.
1958	Hudson	Sch.	-	-	Jul 6 1887	Unknown	Green Island, Me.
1959	Hugh Blair	C.bt.	106	1881	Nov 1908	Foundered	Port Liberty, N.Y.
1960	Humbolds	Sch.	-	-	Oct 12 1899	Unknown	Monomoy Point, Mass.
1961	Humboldt	St.p.	2,181	1851	Dec 6 1853	Stranded	Near Halifax, Nova Scotia. 1 life lost.
1962	Hume	Sch.	84	1843	Mar 21 1916	Stranded	Off Portsmouth, N.H.
1963	Hungaria	Steamer	-	-	Feb 19 1860	Wrecked	Cape Sable, Nova Scotia. 205 lives lost.
1964	Hunter No.2	St.w.	69	1863	Mar 7 1910	Burned	Pittsburgh, Pa. See No.1964.
1965	Hunter No.2	St.p.	91	1863	Mar 10 1910	Burned	McKeesport, Pa.
1966	Huntress	Sch.	-	-	Dec 28 1891	Unknown	Browney Island, Me.
1967	Huntsville	St.s.	817	1858	Dec 19 1877	Burned	Off Little Egg Harbor Light, N.J.
1968	Hustler	St.s.	192	1891	Sep 6 1931	Burned	Shadyside, N.J.
1969	Hustler	Ol.s.	93	1923	Dec 9 1965	Collided	With British ALAUNIA. Off pier 18, Hudson River, New York, N.Y.
1970	Hutchinson	Brg.	1,034	1923	Jul 9 1951	Burned	Reading Terminal, Port Reading, N.J.
1971	Hyena	Sch.	-	-	Aug 28 1890	Unknown	Wood End, Cape Cod, Mass.
1972	Hygrade No.2	Brg.	503	1929	Jun 13 1931	Burned	Sewaren, N.J.
1973	Hygrade No.6	Brg.	706	1928	Sep 5 1937	Stranded	Arlington, N.J. Steel vessel.
1974	Hyperton	Brg.	-	-	Oct 20 1888	Collided	Off Absecon, N.J.
1975	I.E. Brown	Ol.s.	80	1906	Nov 30 1962	Foundered	Off Staples Coal Wharf, Warren, R.I.
1976	Iberia	Sc.b.	1,208	1919	Oct 10 1925	Foundered	Five Fathom Bank Light, N.J.
1977	Ice King	St.s.	138	1877	Dec 28 1913	Stranded	Off Sandy Hook, N.J.
1978	Ida	Brg.	385	1902	Dec 30 1907	Foundered	41-20-00 N. 71-29-06 W. 2 miles south of Point Judith L.S. Station, R.I.
1979	Ida	Sch.	72	1877	Oct 1 1914	Stranded	Sow and Pigs Ledge, Vineyard Sound, Mass.
1980	Ida E. Latham	-	-	-	Mar 12 1888	Unknown	Long Island Sound, N.Y.
1981	Ida and Joseph II	Ol.s.	50	1943	Nov 3 1944	Foundered	Off Thatchers Island, Mass.

NO.	NAME OF VESSEL	RIG	TONS	BUILT	DATE	CAUSE	PLACE AND COMMENT
1982	Ida May	Sch.	–	–	Apr 13 1889	Unknown	Handkerchief Shoal, Mass.
1983	Idaho	St.s.	522	1864	Dec 23 1865	Stranded	Barnegat, N.J.
1984	Idaho	Sch.	81	1860	Oct 1 1897	Stranded	Great Gull Isle, Me.
1985	Ideal	St.s.	149	1906	Jan 1 1945	Stranded	Staten Island, N.Y.
1986	Idelia A. Moore	Sch.	55	1870	Apr 11 1918	Foundered	Herring Bay, Md. All lives (3) lost.
1987	Idler	St.s.	57	1886	Jul 24 1912	Collided	With st.s. OLD COLONY, New York, N.Y.
1988	Idlewild	Sch.	–	–	Jun 6 1884	Unknown	Sand Hill Cove, Point Judith, R.I.
1989	Ilion	Brg.	143	1890	Dec 14 1917	Stranded	Coney Island, N.Y.
1990	Illinois	Frgt.	5,447	–	Jun 2 1942	War Loss	North Atlantic. 24-00 N. 60-00 W. Sunk by enemy action.
1991	Illinoise	Sch.	–	–	Jun 12 1880	Unknown	West of Point Judith, R.I.
1992	Ime	–	–	–	Dec 30 1917	Collided	With MONT BLANC, Halifax, Nova Scotia. 1,158 lives lost.
1993	Imperator	St.s.	93	1886	Sep 9 1912	Collided	With st.s. RIVERSIDE. Philadelphia, Pa.
1994	Inca	St.s.	90	1898	Jul 13 1918	Stranded	No Mans Land, Mass. 42-02-50 N. 70-20-48 W. Fisherman.
1995	Independence	Sch.	–	–	Jun 20 1862	Unknown	North of Point Judith, R.I.
1996	Independence	St.p.	361	1828	Sep 28 1836	Stranded	Bangor, Me.
1997	Independence Hall	St.s.	5,050	–	Mar 8 1942	War Loss	43-55-00 N. 59-55-00 W. Off Halifax, Nova Scotia. Freighter.
1998	India Arrow	St.s.	8,327	1921	Feb 4 1942	War Loss	38-33-30 N. 73-50-06 W. 15 miles east of Five Fathom Bank, Atlantic City, N.J.
1999	Indian (Br.)	–	–	–	Nov 21 1859	Wrecked	Nova Scotia. 27 lives lost.
2000	Indian	Ga.s.	92	1913	Jun 20 1956	Foundered	At Fielder's Atlantic Boat Yard, Rockaway, N.Y.
2001	Ingomar	Ol.s.	143	1904	Feb 17 1936	Stranded	Plum Island, 2 miles north of Knobbs Beach Coast Guard Station, Mass.
2002	Innis	St.s.	112	1863	Jun 15 1905	Burned	Bartletts Point, N.Y.
2003	Interboro	St.s.	122	1882	Dec 22 1911	Burned	Mount St. Vincent, N.Y.
2004	Interstate	Brg.	502	1916	Nov 30 1916	Foundered	Off Cove Point Light, Chesapeake Bay.
2005	Invader	Sloop	–	–	1960	Unknown	Lower Hudson River, N.Y. Off Day Line Pier at West Point, N.Y.
2006	Ioannis P. Goulandris	Frgt.	3,750	–	Dec 1 1942	War Loss	Western edge of the "Mud Hole", Long Branch, N.J. 40-15-54 N. 73-47-38 W.
2007	Iowa	Sch.	1,606	1900	Feb 5 1917	Foundered	Off Sandy Hook, N.J. All lives (5) lost.
2008	Ira A. Allen	Brg.	199	–	Nov 12 1905	Collided	With steamer POWHATAN. Off Pomham Light, R.I.
2009	Ira and Abby	Sch.	–	–	Nov 27 1898	Unknown	Point Judith, R.I.
2010	Ira D. Sturgis	Sch.	235	1873	Feb 15 1906	Stranded	Near Indian River, Del.
2011	Ira Laffrimier	Sch.	–	–	Jul 14 1897	Unknown	Nauset, Mass.
2012	Ireland	Bark	–	–	Sep 27 1887	Unknown	Bryer Island, Nova Scotia.
2013	Irene	Sch.	–	–	Sep 21 1898	Unknown	Mussel Bar, Watch Hill, R.I.
2014	Irene	Brg.	246	1881	Jun 26 1918	Foundered	7 miles northeast of Baltimore, Md. All lives (2) lost.
2015	Irene	Sc.b.	1,208	1913	May 26 1934	Foundered	Off Barnegat Light, N.J.
2016	Irene and Helen	Ol.s.	88	1927	May 30 1932	Burned	Nantucket Lightship, Mass.
2017	Irma A	Ol.s.	80	1917	Apr 15 1930	Burned	Nantucket, Mass.
2018	Irma-Pauline	Ol.s.	58	1943	Mar 6 1951	Stranded	625 yds., 142° True from Cape May East Jetty Light, N.J. Fisherman. Depth 34'.
2019	Iron Queen	Sc.b.	1,348	1887	Jul 16 1926	Foundered	Cudlam Beach Light, N.J.
2020	Iroquois	St.s.	80	1883	Jul 16 1930	Foundered	Cayuga, N.Y.
2021	Irvington	St.s.	398	1907	Oct 29 1914	Foundered	Off Pond Island, Me. Steel vessel.
2022	Irwin	Sc.b.	1,304	1913	Aug 12 1928	Foundered	Atlantic City, N.J.
2023	Isaac Burpee	Sch.	–	–	Jan 25 1891	Unknown	Digby Gut, Nova Scotia.
2024	Isaac Carlton	Sch.	455	–	Jan 9 1886	Unknown	42-08-16 N. 70-41-00 W. 1-1/2 miles south of Fourth Cliff L.S. Station, Mass.
2025	Isaac Collins	Sch.	–	–	Nov 7 1898	Unknown	Provincetown, Mass.
2026	Isaac H. Borden	Sch.	–	–	Sep 9 1888	Unknown	Point Judith, R.I.
2027	Isaac H. Tillyer	Sch.	598	–	Jun 22 1900	Unknown	41-25-12 N. 70-54-38 W. 1/6 mile SSE of Cuttyhunk L.S. Station, Mass.
2028	Isaac Jackson	Bark	641	–	Jan 22 1897	Unknown	Pasque Island, Vineyard Sound, Mass. Salt cargo.
2029	Isaac Newton	St.p.	1,332	1846	Feb 5 1863	Exploded	Fort Washington, N.Y. 9 lives lost.

NO.	NAME OF VESSEL	RIG	TONS	BUILT	DATE	CAUSE	PLACE AND COMMENT
2030	Isaac P. Smith	St.p.	286	1851	Oct 25 1873	Burned	West Haven, Conn.
2031	Isabel	St.p.	421	1894	Sep 28 1915	Stranded	Shippan Point, Conn.
2032	Isabella Gill	Sch.	585	1891	Aug 17 1906	Foundered	Sailed from New York, N.Y. & has not since reported. All lives (8) lost.
2033	Isabella H	St.s.	248	1915	Sep 28 1925	Foundered	Oswego Harbor, N.Y.
2034	Isabelle Parker	Ol.s.	110	1925	May 10 1939	Collided	With ol.s. EDITH C. ROSE. About 150 miles east by south of Boston Light, Mass.
2035	Isaiah K. Stetson	Sch.	313	1882	Mar 14 1920	Foundered	Off Nantucket, Mass. 4 lives lost.
2036	Isiah Hart	Sch.	-	-	Aug 16 1897	Unknown	Pollock Rip, Mass.
2037	Isiah K. Stetson	Sch.	-	-	May 31 1898	Unknown	Shovelful Shoal, Mass.
2038	Island Belle	Sch.	-	-	Jan 9 1884	Unknown	East of Block Island, R.I.
2039	Island City	Sch.	423	1871	Aug 15 1906	Stranded	Shediac, New Brunswick.
2040	Island Queen	St.p.	1,213	1925	Sep 7 1947	Burned	Monongahela River, Pittsburgh, Pa. Steel vessel.
2041	Islander	St.p.	118	1871	Sep 16 1909	Burned	Alexandria Bay, N.Y.
2042	Italy	Scow	339	1914	Apr 19 1920	Burned	Brooklyn, N.Y.
2043	Itasca	Sch.	75	1879	Aug 20 1920	Collided	With U.S. Submarine No.8. Off Brenton Reef, R.I.
2044	Ithaca	St.s.	105	1891	Aug 6 1922	Foundered	Off Atlantic City, N.J.
2045	Ithaca	St.s.	1,462	1906	Aug 11 1946	Burned	Brighton Marine Repair Yard, West New Brighton, New York, N.Y. Steel vessel.
2046	Iva & Abbey	Sch.	-	-	Nov 27 1898	Unknown	Point Judith, R.I.
2047	Ivanhoe	Sch.	-	-	Lost 1800's	Unknown	Monomoy Beach, Mass.
2048	Ivanhoe	St.s.	119	1900	Feb 17 1924	Collided	With st.s. GERRY. Kill von Kull, New York Harbor, N.Y. 1 life lost (7).
2049	Ivanhoe	Ol.s.	52	1931	Oct 4 1967	Burned	20 miles southeast of Block Island, R.I.
2050	Izetta	Sch.	199	1865	May 11 1916	Stranded	Waketown, New Brunswick.
2051	J.A. Croswell	Sch.	56	1908	Oct 26 1936	Foundered	Northeast of Poplar Island, Eastern Bay, Md.
2052	J.A. Hatfield	Sch.	-	-	Lost 1800's	Unknown	Off Peaked Hill, Mass.
2053	J.A. Hill	Brg.	229	1903	Oct 26 1925	Foundered	Monomoy Beach, Mass.
2054	J.A. Holmes	Sch.	167	1867	Sep 8 1917	Foundered	Perth Amboy, N.J.
2055	J. Arthur Lord	Sch.	212	1881	Dec 27 1916	Stranded	Off Barnegat, N.J.
2056	J.B. King Co. No.17	Sloop	357	-	Oct 19 1903	Unknown	Bay of Fundy, Canada.
2057	J.B. Woodbury	Sch.	-	-	1878	Unknown	42-18-19 N. 70-50-57 W. Hardings Ledge, Mass.
2058	J.C. Austin	St.s.	143	1886	Dec 5 1921	Foundered	Monomoy Point, Mass.
2059	J.C. McClain	Ga.w.	57	1924	May 31 1955	Burned	Southeast of Greensledge Lighthouse, N.Y.
2060	J.D. Ingraham	Sch.	-	-	Nov 27 1898	Unknown	At Point Marion, Pa. 600 yds. below mouth of Chest River on right bank of Monongahela River.
2061	J.D. Scott	St.p.	87	1876	Nov 22 1906	Stranded	Vineyard Haven, Mass.
2062	J.D. Secor	St.p.	101	1854	Dec 7 1866	Burned	Off Pultneyville, N.Y.
2063	J. Dallas Marvil	Sch.	160	1889	Jun 15 1910	Collided	Blackwell Island, N.Y.
2064	J.E. Leonard	St.p.	83	1903	Jun 23 1905	Burned	With st.s. EVERETT. Sandy Point, Md.
2065	J.G. Babcock	Sch.	-	-	Lost 1800's	Unknown	Redstone Creek, Pa.
2066	J.G. Fell	Sch.	-	-	Jan 19 1899	Unknown	Off Orleans, Mass.
2067	J.H. Carey	Brg.	360	1911	Nov 26 1890	Unknown	Mussel Bar, Watch Hill, R.I.
2068	J.H. Cooper	Brg.	360	1911	Nov 12 1941	Collided	Shovelful Shoal, Mass.
2069	J.H. Eels	Sch.	-	-	Mar 16 1887	Unknown	With st.s. LUS POZOS. Pier 73, North River, New York, N.Y.
2070	J.H.G. Perkins	Sch.	59	1867	Oct 3 1908	Stranded	Nauset, Mass.
2071	J.H. Rutter	Sch.	1,224	1873	Oct 23 1918	Collided	Goat Island, Cape Porpoise, Me.
2072	J. Henry Edmunds	Sch.	284	1889	Feb 1 1910	Collided	With st.s. TEXAN. Off pier 20, North River, New York, N.Y.
2073	J. Henry Edmonds	Ga.s.	72	1893	Mar 13 1928	Stranded	With st.s. WILLIAM H. TAYLOR. Sandy Hook, N.J.
2074	J. Howell	Sch.	-	-	Dec 1 1883	Unknown	Cape Henlopen, Del.
2075	J. Howell Leeds	Sch.	414	1881	Dec 1 1918	Stranded	Southwest of Block Island, R.I.
2076	J.I. Worthington	Sch.	-	-	Nov 6 1888	Unknown	Lockport, Nova Scotia.
							Near Mount Desert, Me.

NO.	NAME OF VESSEL	RIG	TONS	BUILT	DATE		CAUSE	PLACE AND COMMENT
2077	J.J. Hagerty	St.s.	53	1882	Dec 6	1928	Collided	With st.s. THOMAS TRACEY. Hunts Point Light, N.Y.
2078	J. Kennedy	Sch.	-	-	Oct 16	1883	Unknown	Sugar Reef, R.I.
2079	J.M. Harlow	Sch.	232	1874	Sep 20	1912	Stranded	St. Martins, New Brunswick.
2080	J.M. Movalves	Sch.	-	-	Lost 1800's		Unknown	Chatham, Mass.
2081	J.N. Harris	St.s.	207	1854	Aug 15	1857	Collided	With METROPOLIS. Falkland Island, Conn. 13 lives lost.
2082	J. Nickerson	Sch.	179	1879	May 13	1905	Stranded	Johns Island Ledge, Me.
2083	J. Norman Riley	Ol.s.	406	1928	Aug 3	1931	Burned	Sewaren, N.J.
2084	J.O. Webster	Sch.	431	1919	May 13	1931	Stranded	Norwalk, Conn. (Island).
2085	J.P. McAllister	St.s.	133	1909	May 18	1934	Burned	Brooklyn, N.Y.
2086	J.P. Wyman	Sch.	-	-	Lost 1800's		Unknown	Peaked Hill, Mass.
2087	J. Palmer	Brig	300	-	Fall	1838	Unknown	Short Beaver Tail, R.I.
2088	J.R. Baldwin	Brg.	267	1864	Jan 21	1933	Foundered	Milton, N.Y.
2089	J.R. Bodwell	Sch.	224	1874	Oct 16	1916	Foundered	Sandy Hook, N.J.
2090	J.S. Cosgrove	St.w.	58	1858	Mar 28	1868	Collided	With bridge. Pittsburgh, Pa.
2091	J.S. Glover	Sch.	56	1868	Oct 15	1907	Foundered	Marsh Harbor, Me.
2092	J.S. Lamprey	Sch.	306	1877	May 17	1913	Foundered	Off Mispich Cape, St. Johns, New Brunswick.
2093	J.V. Davenport	Ol.s.	56	1929	Feb 6	1939	Stranded	Terrapin Sand Point, Tangier Sound, Md.
2094	J.W. Campbell	Sch.	-	-	Jan 16	1885	Unknown	South of Nauset, Mass.
2095	J.W. Durant	Sch.	-	-	Dec 1	1890	Unknown	Shulee, Nova Scotia.
2096	J.W. Knight	Sch.	-	-	Jun 25	1889	Unknown	Chesapeake Bay.
2097	J.W. Roberts	Sch.	-	-	Jun 28	1890	Unknown	Cape St. John, Newfoundland.
2098	J.W. Tillett No.26	Brg.	491	1920	Dec 30	1947	Collided	With barge MAINE. In Delaware River near Penns Grove.
2099	J.W. Wendt	Ship	-	-	Mar 21	1889	Unknown	Island Beach, N.J.
2100	Jacintha	Ol.s.	110	1937	May 30	1959	Collided	With trawler SWALOW. About 160 miles southeast by east of Boston, Mass.
2101	Jack Heffern	Brg.	287	1928	Nov 11	1942	Foundered	At Baldwinsville, near Syracuse, N.Y.
2102	Jackie B.	Ol.s.	63	1929	Apr 6	1963	Burned	6 miles off Thatcher's Buoy, Rockport, Mass.
2103	Jackson	Brg.	438	1918	Feb 6	1946	Stranded	Broke loose from pier at 34th Street & East River and stranded at Welfare Is.N.Y.
2104	Jacob A. Stamler	Ship	1,198	1856	Feb 17	1916	Burned	New York, N.Y.
2105	Jacob M. Haskell	Sch.	1,778	1901	May 31	1918	Torpedoed	Off Barnegat, N.J. 39-36-00 N. 73-01-30 W.
2106	Jacob S. Winslow	Sch.	910	1889	Mar 1	1914	Stranded	On southern shore, Block Island, R.I. Lumber cargo. Length 181'.
2107	Jake	Ol.s.	56	1915	Aug 25	1959	Foundered	43-44-18 N. 69-41-32 W. Off coast of Maine, about 3 miles SE of Seguin Light. Tug. Depth 190'.
2108	James	Sch.	-	-	Oct 7	1889	Sunk	Stonington, Conn.
2109	James A. Brown	Sch.	198	1859	Nov 5	1908	Foundered	60 miles southwest of Cape Elizabeth, Me.
2110	James A. Cox	St.s.	61	1874	Apr 30	1928	Foundered	Rockaway Beach, N.Y. 1 life lost (7).
2111	James A. Garfield	Sch.	73	1881	Aug 1	1916	Stranded	Gulf of St. Lawrence.
2112	James A. Garfield	Sch.	61	1881	Aug 7	1917	Collided	With st.s. VENATOR. Cove Point, Chesapeake Bay.
2113	James A. Parsons	Sch.	-	-	Nov 23	1897	Unknown	Orleans, Mass.
2114	James A. Parsons	Sch.	219	1860	Jun 20	1918	Stranded	St. Jeromes, Md.
2115	James A. Stetson	Sch.	65	1868	May 29	1906	Stranded	Amherst, Magdalen Islands, New Brunswick.
2116	James B. Anderson	Sch.	163	1871	Aug 10	1919	Foundered	Potomac River.
2117	James B. Deperty	Sch.	-	-	Oct 27	1894	Unknown	Handkerchief Shoals, Mass.
2118	James B. Johnson	Sch.	-	-	Jan 25	1890	Unknown	Forke River, N.J.
2119	James Boyce	Sch.	453	1877	Oct 10	1909	Stranded	Mussel Ridge Channel, Pleasant Island, Me.
2120	James Bradley	St.s.	51	1864	Aug 6	1914	Burned	Cow Bay, N.Y.
2121	James Cavanaugh	Brg.	246	1918	Sep 10	1941	Foundered	Onandaga Lake, N.Y.
2122	James D. Leary	St.s.	76	1886	Oct 25	1905	Burned	Newark Bay, N.J.
2123	James Driman	Sch.	-	-	Lost 1800's		Unknown	Race Point, Cape Cod, Mass.

NO.	NAME OF VESSEL	RIG	TONS	BUILT	DATE		CAUSE	PLACE AND COMMENT
2124	James Duffield	Sch.	187	1889	Apr 30	1912	Stranded	Cape Henlopen, Del.
2125	James E. English	Brg.	285	1873	Dec 14	1907	Stranded	41-19-00 N. 71-47-48 W. 3 miles ENE of Watch Hill L.S. Station, R.I.
2126	James E. Longstreet	Frgt.	7,176	1907		1944	Unknown	41-49-45 N. 70-02-54 W. Length 422'. Used as target ship by US Navy. See No.2139.
2127	James E. O'Day	C.bt.	140	1907	Nov 8	1930	Foundered	Sylvan Beach, N.Y.
2128	James E. Stansbury	Sch.	51	1871	Jan 8	1906	Stranded	Cedar Point, Md.
2129	James E. Trott	Sch.	59	1870		1928	Foundered	Jacks Bay, Calvert County, Md.
2130	James F. Murphy	Tug	-	-		1961	Unknown	780 yds. 332-1/2° from dome, Sailors Snug Harbor, New York Harbor. Depth 27'.
2131	James G. Blaine	Sch.	555	1867	Jul 8	1908	Stranded	Oswego, N.Y.
2132	James H. Robinson	C.bt.	97	1881	May 26	1909	Foundered	Brooklyn, N.Y.
2133	James H. Tripp	Sch.	-	-	Oct 23	1891	Unknown	Provincetown, Mass.
2134	James Horan	Brg.	549	1918	Sep 14	1929	Burned	Wainers, N.J.
2135	James J. Duffy	Brg.	379	1904	Jul 16	1917	Collided	With St.y. UNITED STATES. Off Shady Side, N.J.
2136	James L. Malay	Sch.	174	1864	Jul 30	1930	Foundered	42-30-00 N. 70-42-00 W. Off Marblehead, Mass.
2137	James Logan	St.s.	201	1914	Nov 17	1917	Collided	With st.s. LEXINGTON. New York, N.Y.
2138	James Longstreet	Frgt.	7,176	-	Oct 26	1943	War Loss	Off New Jersey coast. 40-27-00 N. 74-00-00 W.
2139	James Longstreet		-	-		1950	Unknown	Cape Cod Bay, Mass. Approx. 6,710 yds. 0° 30' True from spire, East Brewster, Ma.
2140	James M. Flanagan	Sch.	-	-	Apr 29	1893	Unknown	Chatham, Mass.
2141	James M. Hall	Sch.	87	1879	Nov 15	1906	Stranded	Long Branch, N.J.
2142	James M. Hudson	Sc.b.	1,011	1917	Mar 7	1925	Foundered	Boston Light, Mass. All lives (4) lost.
2143	James M. Tucker	C.bt.	118	1897	Apr 20	1918	Foundered	Port Reading, N.J.
2144	James Moriarty	Brg.	314	1904	Nov 29	1936	Stranded	1,000 feet west of Barge Canal Terminal, Little Falls, N.Y.
2145	Jas. Nichols	Sch.	-	-	Jul 5	1891	Unknown	Schooner Ledge, Cuttyhunk, Mass.
2146	James O'Donnell	Brg.	502	1920	May 19	1950	Burned	At South Amboy Coal docks, South Amboy, N.J.
2147	James P. Ward	C.bt.	103	1903	Jul 5	1930	Stranded	Edgewater, N.J.
2148	James Parker, Sr.	Sch.	116	1856	Dec 14	1907	Stranded	Callenders Point, Conn.
2149	James Rothwell	Sch.	498	1884	Oct 11	1917	Stranded	St. Mary's Bay, Newfoundland.
2150	James Rouke	Sch.	-	-	Feb 12	1891	Unknown	North Haven, Me.
2151	James Rumsey	St.p.	341	1845	Nov 4	1853	Burned	New York, N.Y. Used as ferryboat.
2152	James Rumsey	St.p.	671	1867	Feb 20	1891	Sunk	New York, N.Y. Used as ferryboat.
2153	Jas. S.T. Stranahan	St.s.	127	1883	May 23	1910	Burned	Clason Point, N.Y.
2154	James S. Steele	Sch.	78	1892	Sep 2	1907	Stranded	Vineyard Sound, Mass.
2155	James Sheridan	Brg.	934	1908	Jan 26	1946	Foundered	Off Rhode Island coast. Steel vessel.
2156	James Sheridan	Brg.	1,991	1918	Jan 20	1960	Foundered	About 1/2 mile SE of Buoy 8B, Long Island Sound, near Saybrook, Conn. Steel vessel.
2157	James Watson	Sch.	-	-	Mar 12	1887	Unknown	Outside Great Point, Nantucket, Mass. Lime and lumber cargo.
2158	James Wood	St.w.	328	1856	May 7	1859	Burned	Sugar Creek, Pittsburgh, Pa.
2159	James Young	Sch.	261	1866	Jun 7	1918	Foundered	Off Portland Lightship, Me.
2160	Jan Melchers	Bark	-	-	May 2	1888	Foundered	Fenwick Island Shoal, Del. Floated off and believed sunk near by.
2161	Jane	Ga.y.	69	1908	Apr 13	1932	Burned	Baltimore, Md.
2162	Jane Arden	Ol.w.	54	1930	Dec 26	1955	Burned	At mile 8.0 on Monongahela River, Pa.
2163	Jane Ingram	Sch.	-	-	Jan	1890	Unknown	Prospect Harbor, Me.
2164	Jane L. Newton	Sch.	-	-	Oct 18	1890	Unknown	Off Chatham, Mass.
2165	Jane Walton	Tug	-	-		1966	Foundered	Northwest of Maffitt Ledge, off Green Island, Boston Harbor, Mass. Depth 28'.
2166	Jason (Br.)	Ship	1,512	-	Dec 5	1893	Foundered	42-00-30 N. 70-01-06 W. NNW of Pamet River, Truro, Mass. Iron vessel. Jute cargo.
2167	Jean	Sch.	971	1917	Jan 21	1928	Collided	With st.s. CITY OF GLASGOW. Gas Buoy, N.J.
2168	Jean and Patricia	Ol.s.	65	1906	Nov 16	1953	Burned	13 miles south 1/2 east, off Gloucester Harbor, Gloucester, Mass.
2169	Jeanne	Brg.	316	1930	Nov 15	1953	Foundered	At College Point, N.Y.
2170	Jed F. Duren	Sch.	-	-	May 25	1889	Unknown	Near Boston, Mass.
2171	Jennie	Sloop	-	-	May 5	1894	Unknown	Point Judith, R.I.

NO.	NAME OF VESSEL	RIG	TONS	BUILT	DATE	CAUSE	PLACE AND COMMENT
2172	Jennie	Sch.	-	-	Jun 2 1895	Unknown	Quonochontang, R.I.
2173	Jennie	Brg.	382	1901	Dec 30 1907	Stranded	41-21-50 N. 71-28-43 W. 150 yds. southeast of Point Judith L.S. Station, R.I.
2174	Jennie A. Cheney	Sch.	301	-	Aug 6 1887	Unknown	East Spindle Reef, Watch Hill, R.I. Also reported as "Cheney".
2175	Jennie B. Hodgdon	Sch.	118	1891	Jul 22 1914	Stranded	Caraquet, New Brunswick.
2176	Jennie C. May	Sch.	882	-	Feb 2 1902	Unknown	42-04-38 N. 70-07-24 W. 1-3/4 miles E of Peaked Hill L.S. Station, Mass.
2177	Jennie E. Meseng	Sch.	-	-	Aug 16 1802	Unknown	Monomoy, Mass.
2178	Jennie and Florence Cahill	Brg.	168	1889	Mar 22 1906	Foundered	Oyster Bay, N.Y.
2179	Jennie French Potter	Sch.	1,993	1899	May 18 1909	Stranded	Half Moon Shoal, Nantucket Sound, Mass. Coal cargo.
2180	Jennie G. Pillsbury	Sch.	154	1882	Nov 27 1906	Stranded	Two-Blush Reef, Penobscot Bay, Me.
2181	Jennie Gray	St.w.	161	1857	May 7 1859	Burned	Pittsburgh, Pa.
2182	Jennie Green Bank	Sch.	-	-	Oct 23 1899	Unknown	Monomoy Point, Mass.
2183	Jennie and Julia	Ol.s.	64	1931	Sep 6 1953	Stranded	Off Dolliver's Neck, Gloucester Harbor, Mass.
2184	Jennie Phinny	Sch.	-	-	Jul 28 1890	Unknown	Pollock Rip, Mass.
2185	Jersey Belle	Steamer	-	-	Lost 1920's	Unknown	38-58-06 N. 74-47-09 W. About 2 miles off beach at Montgomery Ave., Wildwood, N.J.
2186	Jess B. Shaw	Brg.	739	1910	Sep 21 1938	Foundered	Fall River, Mass.
2187	Jesse Barlow	Sch.	276	1889	Dec 17 1907	Collided	With st.s. LEHIGH. Pollock Rip, Mass.
2188	Jesse Hart, 2d	Sch.	225	1866	Apr 30 1919	Foundered	Apple River, Nova Scotia.
2189	Jesse L. Leach	Sch.	247	1863	Dec 2 1922	Foundered	South of Thatchers Island, Mass.
2190	Jesse W. Starr	Sch.	-	-	Jun 15 1891	Unknown	Shoveful Shoal, Mass.
2191	Jesse W. Starr	Sch.	307	1874	Feb 27 1906	Abandoned	37-33 N. 74-36 W. 6 lives lost.
2192	Jessie L. Boyce	Sch.	196	1861	Jan 10 1907	Stranded	Stimpsons Island, Me.
2193	Jessie Lena	Sch.	347	1883	Mar 13 1912	Stranded	Timber Island, Me.
2194	Jeuil	-	475	-	May 20 1943	Unknown	Sound Beach, Long Island, N.Y. Depth 67'.
2195	Jewess	St.p.	352	1839	Nov 11 1854	Stranded	Barnegat, N.J.
2196	Joanna	Ol.s.	149	1881	May 22 1930	Burned	Sewaren, N.J.
2197	Job H. Jackson, Jr.	Sch.	1,159	1889	Jan 5 1895	Unknown	42-05-06 N. 70-08-18 W. 1 mile east of Peaked Hill L.S. Station, Mass.
2198	Joe	Sch.	119	-	Aug 9 1886	Stranded	Bunkers Ledge, Me.
2199	Joel Cook	Sch.	390	-	Jan 9 1886	Unknown	42-11-12 N. 70-42-30 W. 1-3/4 miles N of Fourth Cliff L.S. Station, Mass.
2200	Joel Cook	Lighter	-	-	Aug 18 1938	Unknown	42-21-45 N. 70-40-25 W.
2201	Joffre	Ol.s.	140	1918	Aug 9 1947	Burned	10 miles SE by E of Eastern Point, Gloucester, Mass.
2202	John	-	-	-	Nov 3 1703	Unknown	Georges Island, Mass.
2203	John A. Bridges	Sch.	2,086	1878	Dec 26 1909	Foundered	Off Barnegat, N.J. All lives (6) lost.
2204	John A. Matterson	Sch.	-	-	May 25 1885	Unknown	Sandy Point, Block Island, R.I.
2205	John B. Carrington	Sch.	388	1874	Apr 23 1914	Stranded	At Bull Dog Beach, Campbello, New Brunswick.
2206	John Beattie	Sch.	-	-	Aug 16 1887	Unknown	Plum Island, N.Y.
2207	John Bossert	Sch.	601	1904	Feb 15 1916	Burned	Seabright, N.J. 1 life lost.
2208	John Bunyan	Brg.	-	-	Jan 21 1889	Unknown	Boston Harbor, Mass.
2209	John C. Baxter	Brg.	145	-	Aug 23 1935	Burned	Off Stoops Point, near Fairlee Creek, eastside Chesapeake Bay, Md. Explosion.
2210	John C. Fitzpatrick	Sch.	-	-	Mar 11 1802	Unknown	Shoveful Shoals, Mass.
2211	John C. Gregory	Sch.	379	1884	May 4 1905	Collided	With st.s. ONTARIO. Off Gay Head, Marthas Vineyard, Mass.
2212	John C. Meyer	Bkn.	932	1902	Nov 28 1925	Stranded	Machias Bay, Me.
2213	John C. Smith	Sch.	451	1904	Oct 5 1904	Unknown	41-32-30 N. 70-00-12 W. Shovelful Shoal, Monomoy Point, Mass. Lumber cargo.
2214	John C. Wyman	Brg.	268	1873	Dec 14 1907	Stranded	Watch Hill, R.I.
2215	John Cadwallader	Sch.	137	1853	Nov 18 1910	Stranded	Cape Elizabeth, Me.
2216	John Crookford	Sch.	-	-	Aug 9 1885	Unknown	Mussel Bar, R.I.
2217	John Douglass	Sch.	189	1873	Oct 13 1909	Stranded	Mussel Ridge Channel, White Head Island, Me.
2218	John Dwight	St.s.	153	1896	Apr 6 1923	Foundered	Off Cuttyhunk Light, Vineyard Sound, Mass. All lives (8) lost.

NO.	NAME OF VESSEL	RIG	TONS	BUILT	DATE	CAUSE	PLACE AND COMMENT
2219	John E. Berwind	St.s.	75	1888	Feb 16 1931	Foundered	Stapleton, Staten Island, N.Y.
2220	John E. Enright	Brg.	278	1921	Jun 30 1929	Foundered	Rotterdam Junction, N.Y.
2221	John E. Sanford	Sch.	-	-	Nov 3 1887	Unknown	Newburyport Bar, Mass.
2222	John Endicott	St.s.	483	-	Sep 9 1900	Unknown	Off Hardings Ledge, Hull, Mass. Wood vessel. Length 168'.
2223	John F. Kennedy	Ol.s.	-	-	1969	Burned	42-03.5 N. 69-53.8 W. Off Massachusetts coast. Depth 262'. Fisherman.
2224	John F. McIlvaine	Brg.	414	1903	May 10 1923	Stranded	On Egg Harbor Bar, N.J.
2225	John Fuller	St.s.	93	1864	May 23 1929	Stranded	Waterford, N.Y.
2226	John G. Olsen	St.s.	134	1900	Aug 4 1935	Burned	Pier 31, Brooklyn, N.Y.
2227	John Garrett	St.s.	108	1880	Jun 13 1928	Burned	Port Morris, N.Y.
2228	John Griffith	St.p.	56	1845	Jul 1867	Burned	Philadelphia, Pa.
2229	John H. Forshew	Brg.	369	1941	May 5 1964	Foundered	In East River, New York, N.Y.
2230	John H. May	Sch.	363	1883	Dec 24 1912	Stranded	Sandy Hook, N.J.
2231	John H. McMames	Sch.	-	-	Lost 1800's	Unknown	Between Cahoons Hollow and Nauset, Mass.
2232	John H. McManus	Sch.	-	-	Mar 5 1889	Unknown	Cape Cod, Mass.
2233	John H. Perry	Sch.	-	-	Oct 4 1888	Unknown	Sow and Pigs Reef, Mass.
2234	John H. Winstead	Sch.	841	1912	Sep 14 1920	Foundered	Montauk Point Light, Long Island, N.Y.
2235	John H. Winstead	Sc.b.	1,160	1922	Dec 5 1927	Foundered	Sea Girt Lighthouse, N.J.
2236	John Harvey	Brig	-	-	Nov 27 1898	Unknown	Point Judith, R.I.
2237	John Howard	Brg.	490	1917	Dec 3 1919	Stranded	Plymouth, Mass.
2238	John J. Burdee	Brig	-	-	Jan 19 1804	Unknown	Watch Hill Point, R.I.
2239	John J. Fallon	Ol.s.	125	1908	Oct 29 1930	Stranded	Plum Island, Mass.
2240	John J. Ward	Sch.	295	1865	Mar 6 1907	Stranded	Lewes, Del.
2241	John Jay	St.p.	214	1850	Jul 29 1856	Burned	Caldwell, N.Y. 6 lives lost.
2242	John K. Hammitt	St.s.	61	1863	Dec 1 1890	Burned	Albany, N.Y.
2243	John L. Merrill	Sch.	-	-	Lost 1800's	Unknown	Off Peaked Hill, Mass.
2244	John Lane	C.bt.	105	1904	Aug 29 1923	Foundered	North River, N.Y.
2245	John Linsey	Sch.	-	-	Nov 11 1887	Unknown	Bearse's Shoal, Mass.
2246	John M. Ball	Sch.	-	-	Aug 19 1890	Unknown	Wood End, Cape Cod, Mass.
2247	John M. Hathaway	Ol.s.	52	1925	Sep 6 1959	Foundered	At Centerboard Yacht Club, Front Street, South Portland, Me.
2248	John Mago	Sch.	-	-	Oct 16 1879	Unknown	Watch Hill Reef, R.I.
2249	John Mann	Sch.	-	-	Jul 16 1886	Unknown	West of Block Island, R.I.
2250	John Mantia	Ol.s.	84	1928	Jun 16 1932	Foundered	Off Highland Light, Mass.
2251	John Mettler	Bark	-	-	Nov 25 1888	Unknown	Cape Ann, Mass. 28 lives lost.
2252	John Minturn	Sch.	-	-	Feb 15 1846	Grounded	Squam Beach, N.J.
2253	John Morris	Sch.	-	-	Jun 1 1874	Unknown	Dickens Reef, Narragansett Pier, R.I.
2254	John McMakin	St.w.	158	1853	Aug 1860	Burned	Lewes, Del.
2255	John N. Sherwood	Sch.	-	-	Jun 5 1889	Ashore	At Watch Hill, R.I.
2256	John N. Winstead	Brg.	-	-	Unknown	Unknown	South of Manasquan Inlet, 3 miles offshore, Point Pleasant, N.J. Depth 75'.
2257	John Neilson	Brg.	344	1849	Aug 19 1905	Stranded	New York, N.Y.
2258	John P. Kelsey	Sch.	-	-	Dec 7 1891	Unknown	Handkerchief Shoals, Mass.
2259	John R. Ericsson	Ol.s.	78	1921	Sep 30 1930	Burned	Highland Light, Mass.
2260	John R. Manta	Sch.	147	1904	Nov 9 1934	Foundered	Sailed from Providence, R.I. & has not since reported. All lives (31) lost.
2261	John Paul	Sch.	1,509	-	Feb 10 1893	Unknown	41-21-25 N. 71-35-50 W. Green Hill Point, R.I. Coal cargo.
2262	John Paul	Sch.	410	1891	Jul 12 1914	Foundered	41-27-00 N. 70-23-20 W. 4-1/2 miles west of Cross Rip Lightship, Nantucket Sound, Mass. Length 137'. 1 life lost.
2263	John Proctor	Sch.	498	1873	Sep 13 1909	Stranded	Cape Henlopen, Del.
2264	John R. Parsons	Brg.	204	1891	Nov 29 1913	Foundered	In Lake Ontario, near Oswego, N.Y.
2265	John R. Williams	St.s.	396	1913	Jun 24 1942	War Loss	38-45-00 N. 74-55-00 W. Steel vessel. Sunk by enemy action.

NO.	NAME OF VESSEL	RIG	TONS	BUILT	DATE	CAUSE	PLACE AND COMMENT
2266	John Rommie, Jr.	Sch.	-	1874	Lost 1800's	Unknown	Race Point, Cape Cod, Mass.
2267	John S. Beacham	Sch.	234	1874	Apr 3 1917	Foundered	Cape Sable, Nova Scotia.
2268	John S. Bennett (Br.)	Bark	301	-	Nov 8 1909	Unknown	41-15-50 N. 71-33-05 W. 5-1/2 miles SW 1/2 S of Point Judith Whistle Buoy, R.I.
2269	John S. Parker (Br.)	Sch.	-	1891	Nov 7 1801	Unknown	Orleans, Mass.
2270	John S. Parsons	Brg.	203	1891	Dec 8 1910	Stranded	Rock Shoal, St. Lawrence River, N.Y.
2271	John S. Presson	Sch.	92	1874	May 8 1910	Stranded	Burnt Island, Port Clyde, Conn.
2272	John S. Thompson	Brg.	239	1895	Nov 23 1916	Foundered	Long Island Sound, N.Y.
2273	John Schmults	Sch.	59	1884	Feb 26 1925	Foundered	Brooklyn, N.Y.
2274	John Simmons	Sch.	-	-	Nov 13 1890	Unknown	Plum Island, Mass.
2275	John Stockham	Sch.	-	-	Dec 19 1890	Unknown	Near Faulkners Island, Long Island, N.Y.
2276	John T. Gulliman (Br.)	Sch.	-	-	Aug 17 1801	Unknown	Shovelful Shoal, Mass.
2277	John T. Hughes	Brg.	490	1917	Aug 8 1922	Collided	With dredge. Hell Gate, N.Y.
2278	John T. Manson	Sch.	387	-	Aug 5 1881	Unknown	41-08-39 N. 71-35-40 W. Black Rock, Block Island, R.I. Coal cargo.
2279	John T. Pratt	St.s.	60	1882	Mar 25 1910	Burned	Glen Cove, N.Y.
2280	John T. Williams	Sch.	-	-	Sep 23 1803	Unknown	Orleans, Mass.
2281	John Taylor	St.s.	643	1863	Jun 18 1876	Burned	Hudson, N.Y.
2282	John Tracy	St.s.	2,469	1919	Jan 8 1927	Foundered	Off Highland Light, Truro, Mass. Steel vessel. Length 253'. All lives (26) lost.
2283	John V. Craven	St.s.	183	1891	Dec 29 1920	Collided	With Dutch st.s. NIEUW AMSTERDAM. New York, N.Y. 2 lives lost (7).
2284	John W. Brown	Ol.s.	52	1891	Jun 23 1961	Unknown	At Howells Point, Md.
2285	John W. Clark	C.bt.	99	1890	Apr 15 1908	Foundered	South Boston, Mass.
2286	John W. Hall	Sch.	346	1890	Mar 12 1912	Stranded	Ocean City, Md.
2287	John W. Richmond	St.p.	487	1838	Sep 3 1843	Burned	Hallowell, Me.
2288	John Welsh	Brg.	-	-	1888	Unknown	Point Judith, R.I.
2289	John Welch, Jr.	Brig	316	-	Mar 3 1888	Unknown	Point Judith, R.I. 41-22-18 N. 71-32-54 W. Coal cargo.
2290	John Wethered	Sch.	69	1867	Aug 18 1915	Foundered	Chesapeake Bay, Md.
2291	Johnathan Cone	Sch.	-	-	Dec 19 1898	Unknown	Mussel Bar, Watch Hill, R.I.
2292	Jonathan Cone	Sch.	122	1855	Jun 6 1923	Foundered	Off Sakonnet Point, R.I.
2293	Johnson No.17	Brg.	134	1906	Jul 10 1916	Burned	Black Tom Island, New York Harbor, N.Y. Due to explosion. 1 life lost.
2294	Jonas H. French	St.s.	195	1899	Sep 28 1914	Foundered	Off Minots Light, Mass.
2295	Jonathan Bourne	Sch.	708	-	Mar 4 1896	Unknown	Pollock Rip, Mass.
2296	Jonathan May	Sch.	326	-	Mar 17 1877	Unknown	41-41-42 N. 69-55-18 W. Opposite Old Harbor L.S. Station, Mass.
2297	Jonathan Sawyer	Sch.	399	1886	Nov 6 1907	Stranded	Cape Porpoise, Me.
2298	Jonesport	Brg.	1,322	1919	Feb 18 1937	Foundered	38-17-33 N. 75-00-00 W.
2299	Jordan L. Mott	Sch.	138	1874	Nov 27 1898	Unknown	Provincetown, Mass.
2300	Jordan L. Mott	Sch.	1,938	1881	Nov 14 1911	Stranded	Mouth of Georges River, Me.
2301	Joseph B. Thomas	Sch.	438	1919	Oct 15 1913	Foundered	3 miles southwest of Cape Cod, Mass.
2302	Joseph Bannigan	Brg.	438	1919	Mar 24 1891	Unknown	Long Branch, N.J.
2303	Joseph Cleary	Brg.	438	1919	Jun 4 1941	Foundered	Bridgeport Harbor, Conn.
2304	Joseph E. Hooper	Sc.b.	2,233	1921	Nov 15 1945	Foundered	1-1/2 miles south by east of Fenwicks Island, Md., off Atlantic coast.
2305	Joseph Fitch	Sch.	-	-	Oct 29 1880	Unknown	Sugar Reef, R.I.
2306	Joseph G. Ray	Sch.	1,253	1901	Nov 24 1911	Stranded	Tail of Horseshoe, Va., Chesapeake Bay.
2307	Joseph G. Stover	Sch.	-	-	Sep 27 1887	Unknown	Pleasant Bay, Chatham, Mass.
2308	Joseph H. Conn	St.w.	264	1856	May 7 1869	Burned	Pittsburgh, Pa.
2309	Joseph Hall	Sch.	-	-	Dec 7 1888	Collided	Off Cape Cod, Mass.
2310	Joseph Hammond	Sch.	74	1836	Aug 17 1909	Stranded	Plum Island, N.Y.
2311	Joseph Hay	Sch.	188	1864	Feb 11 1906	Stranded	Sow & Pigs Islands, Mass.
2312	Joseph J. Flannery	St.s.	107	1881	Jan 25 1927	Burned	Port Richmond, N.Y.
2313	Joseph P. Mesquita	Sch.	122	1916	Dec 9 1917	Stranded	White Head, Nova Scotia.

NO.	NAME OF VESSEL	RIG	TONS	BUILT	DATE	CAUSE	PLACE AND COMMENT
2314	Joseph S. Furlong	St.s.	64	1904	Aug 30 1928	Burned	Lock 7, State Barge Canal, N.Y.
2315	Joseph S. Zeman	Sch.	1,956	1919	Feb 3 1922	Stranded	Matinia Ledge, Penobscot Bay, Me.
2316	Joseph V. Connolly	St.s.	7,176	1945	Jan 29 1948	Lost	40-48-00 N. 52-48-00 W. Steel vessel.
2317	Joseph W. Drayton	Brg.	437	1907	Feb 15 1908	Stranded	New Haven, Conn.
2318	Joseph W. Fish	Sch.	-	-	Jun 2 1891	Unknown	Near Burnt Island, Me.
2319	Joseph Warren	Ol.s.	-	-	Jan 25 1899	Unknown	Wood End, Cape Cod, Mass.
2320	Josephine	Ol.s.	84	1922	Oct 6 1958	Collided	With st.s. INVINCIBLE. At mouth of Newton Creek, in East River, N.Y.
2321	Josephine B. Knowles	Sch.	-	-	Aug 17 1886	Unknown	Napatree Point, R.I.
2322	Josephine De Costa	Ol.s.	114	1910	Sep 15 1929	Stranded	Blonde Rock, Nova Scotia.
2323	Josephine Elliot	Sch.	391	1890	Jan 9 1908	Foundered	Sailed from New York, N.Y. & has not since reported. All lives (7) lost.
2324	Josephine G. Colyer	Sch.	-	-	Jul 20 1885	Unknown	North of Block Island, R.I.
2325	Josephus (Br.)	Ship	-	-	1849	Unknown	1 mile north of Highland Light, Cape Cod, Mass.
2326	Josiah R. Smith	Sch.	-	-	Aug 7 1895	Unknown	3-3/4 miles southeast of Cuttyhunk L.S. Station, Mass.
2327	Josiah Whitehouse	Sch.	-	-	Oct 12 1890	Unknown	3-3/4 miles north by west 1/2 west of Gay Head, Marthas Vineyard, Mass.
2328	Josie	Sch.	83	1870	Jun 9 1915	Collided	With British schooner VIRGINIA. Newport, R.I.
2329	Josie F.	Sch.	-	-	Sep 29 1895	Unknown	Napatree Point, R.I.
2330	Josie R. Burt	Sch.	760	1882	Aug 30 1911	Foundered	Barnegat, N.J.
2331	Joyce Card	St.s.	123	1892	Mar 7 1931	Burned	Brooklyn, N.Y. 5 lives lost (8).
2332	Julia	Sch.	57	1878	Sep 13 1907	Collided	With st.s. ISLANDER. Coney Island, N.Y.
2333	Julia	Ol.s.	52	1925	Dec 10 1929	Burned	Cape Ann, Mass.
2334	Julia A. Berkele	Sch.	168	1866	Jul 29 1917	Foundered	Tarpaulin Cove, Mass.
2335	Julia A. Tate	Sch.	-	-	May 10 1884	Unknown	Point Judith, R.I.
2336	Julia A. Trubee	Sch.	412	1880	Mar 7 1914	Unknown	38-00-00 N. 66-00-00 W.
2337	Julia Baker	Sch.	108	1860	Feb 1 1908	Stranded	Milbridge, Me.
2338	Julia Costa	Sch.	107	1888	Jul 5 1908	Collided	With schooner MIRANDA. Highland Light, Mass.
2339	Julia Davis	Sch.	58	1907	Jan 2 1908	Collided	With unknown barge. Fishers Island, N.Y.
2340	Julia E. Pratt	Sch.	-	-	1884	Unknown	Great Point Rip, Mass.
2341	Julia E. Whalen	Sch.	-	-	Lost 1800's	Unknown	Race Point, Cape Cod, Mass.
2342	Julia Elizabeth	Sch.	-	-	Mar 30 1881	Unknown	Catumet Reef, Watch Hill, R.I.
2343	Julia Luckenbach	St.s.	3,100	1882	Jan 3 1913	Collided	With British st.s. INDRAKULA. Chesapeake Bay. Steel vessel. 16 lives lost.
2344	Julia and Martha	Sch.	117	1833	Jul 4 1911	Stranded	Cuttyhunk Island, Mass.
2345	Julia R. Dempsey	Sch.	833	1904	Aug 29 1913	Foundered	Winter Quarter Lightship, N.J.
2346	Julia S. Bailey	Sch.	322	-	Lost 1800's	Unknown	Off Race Point, Cape Cod, Mass. Length 124'.
2347	Julie-Ann	Ol.s.	159	1946	Mar 18 1953	Burned	50 miles from Shelburne, Nova Scotia, light.
2348	Juliet	Sch.	-	-	Jan 9 1889	Unknown	Cape Ann, Mass.
2349	June Bright	Sch.	-	-	Feb 4 1891	Unknown	Brandywine Shoal, Delaware Bay.
2350	June K.	Ol.s.	50	-	Jul 31 1959	Unknown	42-00-39 N. 70-32-03 W. 3 miles east of Gurnet Light, Plymouth, Mass. Tug.
2351	Juneal	Ol.s.	84	1928	Aug 19 1935	Burned	25 miles east of Nantucket Lightship, Mass. 4 lives lost (8). Explosion.
2352	Juniper	Brg.	473	1914	Feb 10 1925	Collided	With st.s. CITY OF ATLANTA. Chesapeake Bay.
2353	Juno (Span.)	Frigate	-	-	Oct 27 1802	Foundered	20 miles east of Cape May, N.J.; Delaware Bay. 34-gun armament. All lives (425) lost. Depth 180'. Cargo valued at $300,000.
2354	Juno	Sch.	119	1905	Feb 1880	Storm	Provincetown, Mass.
2355	Juno	Sch.	-	-	Mar 14 1916	Stranded	Lockeport, Nova Scotia.
2356	Junojaes	Ol.s.	57	1946	Mar 6 1954	Foundered	65 miles SW of No Mans Land Island, Mass.
2357	Juvigny	St.s.	2,309	1920	Jan 31 1927	Collided	With British st.s. VALEMORE. Delaware River, Pa. Steel vessel.
2358	Kadosh	Bark	-	1872	Dec 26 1872	Unknown	Point Allerton, Hull, Mass.
2359	Kanawha	St.y.	128	1896	Nov 28 1907	Burned	Gurnet Bay, Brunswick, Me.
2360	Kanised	Ga.y.	61	1909	Mar 30 1922	Burned	Morris Heights, N.J.

NO.	NAME OF VESSEL	RIG	TONS	BUILT	DATE		CAUSE	PLACE AND COMMENT
2361	Karlanna	St.s.	178	1906	Jan 19	1920	Stranded	Cold Springs, N.J.
2362	Kars (Br.)	St.s.	5,420	-	Feb 23	1942	War Loss	44-15-00 N. 63-09-00 W. Tanker. Depth 240'.
2363	Kaskaskia	St.s.	2,934	1918	Jan 31	1920	Burned	New York, N.Y.
2364	Katahdin	Brg.	-	-	Sep 23	1898	Unknown	Monomoy Point, Cape Cod, Mass.
2365	Katahdin	St.s.	1,380	1895	Oct 23	1917	Collided	With Japanese st.s. TOKUYAMA MARU. Off Chester, Pa. 1 life lost.
2366	Kate B. Ogden	Sch.	625	1883	Sep 29	1914	Foundered	41-30-00 N. 63-30-00 W.
2367	Kate E. Morse	Sch.	-	-	Sep 11	1889	Unknown	Delaware Bay.
2368	Kate G. Robinson	Sch.	-	-	Oct 6	1800	Unknown	Peaked Hill, Mass.
2369	Kate Harding (Br.)	Bark	-	-	Nov 30	1892	Unknown	Off Highland Light, Mass.
2370	Kate Jones	Tug	-	-	Jun 4	1891	Collided	Chesapeake Bay.
2371	Kate M. Hilton	Sch.	-	-	Lost 1800's		Unknown	Off Nauset, Mass.
2372	Kate & Mary	Sch.	-	-	Oct 15	1802	Unknown	Quonochontaug, R.I.
2373	Kate McNamara	Sch.	65	1873	Feb 11	1908	Burned	Tilghmans Island Wharf, Choptank River, Md.
2374	Katherine Howard	Brg.	583	1913	Dec 4	1940	Stranded	Green Hills, R.I. Length 120'.
2375	Katherine & Mary	Ol.s.	75	1917	May 28	1955	Foundered	About 35 miles off coast of New Jersey. 38-33-00 N. 74-06-00 W.
2376	Katherine Nichols	Sch.	-	-	Dec 15	1839	Unknown	Nahant, Mass.
2377	Katherine W	St.s.	59	1895	Feb 1	1911	Exploded	Jersey City, N.J. All lives (6) lost.
2378	Kathleen Ann	St.s.	133	1914	Nov 8	1944	Burned	Waterford, N.Y.
2379	Kathleen Sheridan	Brg.	2,336	1919	Jun 26	1964	Foundered	In Arthur Kill, off Pralls Island, New York Harbor, N.Y.
2380	Kathryn	St.p.	67	1890	Dec 8	1907	Burned	Pittsburgh, Pa.
2381	Katie D. Seavey	Sch.	66	1902	Jan 15	1946	Foundered	Cuttyhunk Island, Mass.
2382	Katie Feeney	Brg.	480	1941	May 28	1941	Burned	1-1/2 miles west of Sylvan Beach, Lake Oneida, N.Y.
2383	Katie J. Barrett	Sch.	-	-	Feb 16	1890	Unknown	Nauset, Mass.
2384	Katie McGovern	C.bt.	174	1888	Jan 10	1910	Foundered	Shippan Point, Conn.
2385	Katie Ranger	Sch.	-	-	Dec 18	1887	Foundered	Off Absecon, N.J.
2386	Katie Woods	Brg.	359	1903	Feb 14	1914	Foundered	Off Bartlett's Reef, Long Island Sound.
2387	Keansburg	St.p.	498	1878	Apr 16	1928	Burned	Newburgh, N.Y.
2388	Keelnorth	Brg.	462	1918	Feb 21	1936	Stranded	Off Mount Vernon, N.Y.
2389	Kelsey	Brg.	203	-	Nov 28	1904	Foundered	New York, N.Y.
2390	Kennebec	Sch.	187	1886	Apr 25	1923	Stranded	Perry, Me.
2391	Kennebec	St.s.	2,183	1901	Jun 18	1921	Foundered	Near Barnegat Light, N.J. Steel vessel.
2392	Kennebec	Sch.	2,048	1883	Feb 5	1917	Foundered	Off Sandy Hook, N.J.
2393	Kenneth E. Healing	Ol.s.	180	1927	May 19	1950	Burned	At South Amboy, N.J.
2394	Kenneth Lang	C.bt.	120	1914	Nov 13	1925	Stranded	Sylvan Beach, N.Y.
2395	Kenneth W. McNeil	Brg.	261	1903	May 2	1907	Foundered	New York, N.Y.
2396	Kenny Girls	Brg.	388	1903	May 31	1941	Burned	Jersey City, N.J.
2397	Kenny and Jenny	Ol.s.	-	-	Apr 2	1969	Unknown	Cape Cod Bay, Cape Cod Canal Approach, Mass. 41-28-50 N. 70-31-55 W. 1-3/4 miles, 69° True from East Chop Lighthouse, Marthas Vineyard, Mass. Steel vessel. Length 282'. 7 lives lost (36). Freighter.
2398	Kenosha	St.s.	1,697	1894	Jul 24	1909	Foundered	Fire Island, N.Y. 42-19-47 N. 70-52-55 W. Shag Rocks, Broad Sound, Boston Harbor, Mass. Coal cargo.
2399	Kent	St.p.	142	1839	Nov 25	1857	Burned	Gloucester Point, N.J. Renamed "Oscar Thompson" Aug. 12, 1856.
2400	Kent	Brg.	365	1900	Sep 14	1944	Foundered	37-52-00 N. 76-10-00 W.
2401	Kenwood	Sch.	929	1901	Feb 4	1926	Foundered	Scituate, Mass.
2402	Kershaw	St.s.	2,741	1899	May 31	1927	Collided	With st.s. PRESIDENT GARFIELD. 41-28-50 N. 70-31-55 W.
2403	Keystone	Sc.b.	841	-	Feb 25	1900	Unknown	Jersey City, N.J.
2404	Kill von Kull	St.p.	1,191	1858	Oct 16	1889	Burned	New York, New York. Used as ferryboat.
2405	Killarney	Ol.s.	157	1917	Jul 25	1957	Burned	41-47-36 N. 67-57-48 W. While under tow. Fisherman.
2406	King Philip	St.p.	169	1832	Nov 16	1867	Burned	Jersey City, N.J.

NO.	NAME OF VESSEL	RIG	TONS	BUILT	DATE	CAUSE	PLACE AND COMMENT
2407	King Philip	-	-	-	Apr 7 1935	Unknown	42-22-03 N. 70-37-11 W. Small wreck. Depth 210'.
2408	Kingdon	Brg.	421	1908	Dec 16 1917	Foundered	South Norwalk, Conn.
2409	Kingfisher	St.s.	301	1902	Jun 20 1926	Burned	Gull Island Light, Mass. Steel vessel.
2410	Kingfisher	St.s.	353	1918	Sep 20 1918	Torpedoed	43-31-00 N. 61-53-00 W.
2411	Kings County	St.p.	467	1861	Nov 2 1868	Burned	Hunter's Point, N.Y. Used as ferryboat.
2412	Kingston	Sch.	1,070	1875	Jul 4 1906	Foundered	Off Shinnecock, N.Y. 1 life lost.
2413	Kingsway	Sch.	1,272	1918	Jan 22 1929	Burned	Broad Cove, Eastport, Me.
2414	Kit Carson	Sch.	211	1877	Apr 12 1915	Stranded	Narragansett Bay, R.I.
2415	Klondyke	Brg.	1,563	1921	Feb 3 1942	Stranded	Junction of Elk and Susquehanna Rivers, Turkey Point, Md. Steel vessel. 26 lives lost (38).
2416	Klotowah	St.y.	88	1902	May 12 1916	Burned	St. Lawrence River. Steel vessel.
2417	Knickerbocker	St.p.	858	1843	Jan 4 1865	Stranded	Smith's Point, Md.
2418	Knickerbocker	Sch.	954	1899	Nov 4 1915	Foundered	Off Montauk Point, N.Y. 3 lives lost.
2419	Knickerbocker	Sch.	2,381	1893	Oct 19 1915	Foundered	North of Barnegat Inlet, N.J. 3 lives lost.
2420	Knoxville	St.p.	1,240	1854	Dec 22 1856	Burned	New York, N.Y.
2421	Kohinoor	Sch.	841	1890	Mar 3 1916	Stranded	Off Minot's Ledge Lighthouse, Mass. 4 lives lost. Length 186'.
2422	Kolon	Sch.	150	1866	Jun 5 1914	Foundered	Halifax, Nova Scotia.
2423	L.A. Buzby	C.bt.	117	1892	Jan 31 1919	Collided	With st.s. McALLISTER. New York, N.Y.
2424	L.B. Curtis	Brg.	177	1880	Jul 8 1908	Burned	Boston Harbor, Boston, Mass.
2425	L.B. Hatch	Sch.	-	-	Oct 25 1891	Wrecked	Off Seal Island, Nova Scotia.
2426	L.B. Shaw	Brg.	1,251	1918	Jul 2 1935	Burned	West end entrance to Cape Cod Canal, Buzzards Bay, Mass.
2427	L.B. Shaw	Brg.	967	1908	Jul 1 1939	Foundered	Off coast of Wildwood, N.J. 38-54-54 N. 74-23-00 W. Depth 126'.
2428	L.B. Snow	Sch.	-	-	Lost 1800's	Burned	Off Highland Light, Mass.
2429	L. Boyer	St.s.	197	1888	Sep 23 1914	Burned	Jamaica Bay, N.Y.
2430	L.C. Foster	Sch.	-	-	Oct 10 1894	Unknown	Block Island, R.I.
2431	L.E. Muller	Brg.	229	1892	Mar 9 1919	Foundered	Port Reading, N.Y.
2432	L.E. Williams	Sch.	100	1875	Oct 5 1930	Foundered	Travers Point, Md.
2433	L.F. Gould	Sch.	-	-	Lost 1800's	Unknown	Pleasant Bay, Chatham, Mass.
2434	L. Herbert Taft	Sch.	1,492	1901	Dec 19 1912	Stranded	Romer Shoals, New York Bay, N.Y.
2435	L.J. Witmove	Sch.	-	-	Oct 21 1897	Unknown	Shovelful Shoal, Mass.
2436	L. & L. 100	Brg.	341	1917	Aug 2 1938	Foundered	State Barge Canal, near Canajoharie, N.Y.
2437	L.L. Hamlin	Sch.	147	1871	Jun 5 1921	Stranded	South Bristol, Me.
2438	L.M. Lamond	Sch.	-	-	Jun 14 1877	Unknown	South of Block Island, R.I.
2439	L.P.	Sch.	-	-	May 20 1892	Unknown	Nauset, Mass.
2440	L.Q.C. Wishart	Sch.	238	1867	Dec 5 1910	Stranded	Brigantine Shoals, N.J.
2441	L.S. Liviring	Sch.	-	-	Aug 28 1886	Unknown	West of Block Island, R.I.
2442	L.T. Whitmore	Sch.	296	1874	May 31 1916	Burned	Spencer Island, Nova Scotia.
2443	L. & W.B.C. Co. No.1	Brg.	852	1892	Aug 9 1942	Collided	With st.s. EUREKA. 42-28-45 N. 70-45-12 W. 2 miles SW by S of Newcomb Ledge Buoy, Marblehead, Mass. Length 192'. Coal cargo.
2444	L. & W.B.C. Co. No.1	Brg.	862	-	Jan 11 1945	Foundered	Boston Harbor, Mass. Length 195'. Coal cargo.
2445	L. & W.B.C. Co. No.3	Brg.	1,117	1904	Mar 1 1943	Foundered	Hortons Point, Long Island, N.Y.
2446	L. & W.B.C. Co. No.3	Sch.	852	1892	Nov 11 1919	Collided	With st.s. CAMDEN. Boston, Mass.
2447	L. & W.B.C. Co. No.5	Sc.b.	953	-	Nov 11 1942	Unknown	41-12-20 N. 71-31-30 W. 2-1/2 miles NE from Old Harbor, Block Island, R.I. Length 194'. Coal cargo.
2448	L. & W.B.C. Co. No.6	Brg.	685	1892	Feb 28 1943	Foundered	Hortons Point, Long Island, N.Y.
2449	L. & W.B.C. Co. No.7	Brg.	685	1892	Jan 25 1945	Foundered	Off Montauk Point, N.Y.
2450	L. & W.B.C. Co. No.7	Brg.	685	1892	Dec 27 1933	Stranded	Nantucket Island, Mass. Coal cargo.
2451	L. & W.B.C. Co. No.9	Sc.b.	678	1895	Jun 5 1937	Collided	1 mile east of Race Rock Lighthouse, Warwick, R.I.

NO.	NAME OF VESSEL	RIG	TONS	BUILT	DATE	CAUSE	PLACE AND COMMENT
2452	L. & W.B.C. Co. No.10	Brg.	862	1893	Aug 15 1946	Burned	Fall River, Mass.
2453	L. & W.B.C. Co. No.11	Brg.	862	1893	Jan 11 1945	Foundered	Off Boston Light, Boston, Mass.
2454	L. & W.B.C. Co. No.12	Brg.	911	1898	Jul 15 1943	Foundered	Off Brenton Reef Lightship, Newport, R.I.
2455	L. & W.B.C. Co. No.12	Sch.	862	1893	May 15 1919	Foundered	Race Point, Cape Cod, Mass.
2456	L. & W.B.C. Co. No.15	Brg.	953	1900	Nov 11 1942	Foundered	Block Island, R.I.
2457	La Chameau (Fr.)	Frigate	-	-	Aug 25 1725	Foundered	Off rocks between Portenove Island & Louisburg, Nova Scotia. Depth 72'. Valued at $500,000 in gold. This vessel has been located and is being worked.
2458	La Libertie (Fr.)	Frigate	-	-	Dec 11 1719	Unknown	2 miles off St. Esprit, Nova Scotia. Depth 72'. Valued at over $500,000.
2459	La Rosa	Ol.s.	-	-	1952	Unknown	1,900 yds., 302° True from Deer Island Lighthouse, Boston Harbor, Mass. F/V.
2460	Lackawanna	St.s.	340	1900	Aug 15 1915	Collided	With barge NANTICOKE. Off Handkerchief Shoal Lightship, Mass. Steel vessel.
2461	Lackawanna	Brg.	277	1873	Jul 1 1918	Burned	Mystic River, Conn.
2462	Lady Antrim	Brg.	87	1857	Mar 19 1906	Foundered	Off Marblehead, Mass. 3 lives lost.
2463	Lady Franklin	Sch.	-	-	May 1 1891	Unknown	Merigomish, Nova Scotia.
2464	Lady of the Lake	Bark	-	-	May 6 1890	Unknown	Block Island, R.I., 1/2 mile north of Life Saving Station.
2465	Lady of the Lake	Bark	552	-	May 15 1890	Unknown	Governor Point, Block Island, R.I.
2466	Lady Leavitt	Sch.	-	-	Apr 21 1893	Unknown	Provincetown, Mass.
2467	Lady of the Ocean	Sch.	-	-	Aug 14 1889	Unknown	Watch Hill, R.I., on rocks at Napatree Point. Lime cargo. Total loss.
2468	Laela Bell	Sch.	-	-	Jun 20 1884	Unknown	North of Block Island, R.I.
2469	Laforrest L. Simmons	Ol.s.	154	1909	Aug 12 1955	Collided	With CONNIE. About 1 mile north of Sharp's Island, Md.
2470	Laine Cobb	Sch.	-	-	Lost 1800's	Unknown	Chatham, Mass.
2471	Lake Allen	-	2,015	-	Dec 3 1942	War Loss	Off Nova Scotia. 45-32-00 N. 60-35-00 W.
2472	Lake Calvenia	St.s.	2,364	1919	1921	Collided	With st.s. H.H. ROGERS. Chesapeake Bay. Steel vessel. 1 life lost (29).
2473	Lake Crystal	Brg.	2,015	1918	Feb 14 1946	Foundered	Off Watch Hill, R.I. Steel vessel. Length 254'.
2474	Lake Frampton	St.s.	2,622	1918	Jul 12 1920	Collided	Atlantic City, N.J. Steel vessel. 2 lives lost (32).
2475	Lake Hemlock	Brg.	2,015	1918	Dec 13 1957	Foundered	In Long Island Sound, about 2 miles N of 28 Foot Lump, 25 miles W of New London, Conn. Steel vessel.
2476	Lake Houghton	St.s.	2,038	1918	Jun 11 1918	Stranded	Cranberry Isle, Nova Scotia. Steel vessel.
2477	Lake Oswego	Frgt.	2,398	-	Feb 17 1942	War Loss	43-14-00 N. 64-45-00 W. Off Maine coast.
2478	Lakeview (Can.)	Bark	726	-	Apr 14 1909	Unknown	Nomansland Island, Mass. Salt cargo.
2479	Lammont Dupont	Frgt.	5,102	-	Apr 23 1942	War Loss	27-10-00 N. 57-10-00 W. North Atlantic. Sunk by enemy action.
2480	Lana V. Rose	Sch.	-	-	Oct 10 1894	Unknown	Handkerchief Shoal, Mass.
2481	Landseer	Sch.	1,372	1874	Mar 13 1907	Foundered	Off Absecon, N.J.
2482	Lanie Cobb	Sch.	243	1874	Sep 17 1915	Stranded	West Quoddy Head, Me.
2483	Lansford	Sch.	830	1908	Jul 21 1918	Shell Fire	41-42-30 N. 69-51-08 W. 3-1/2 miles E of Old Harbor L.S. Station, Mass. Sunk by enemy action. Coal cargo.
2484	Lantana	Brg.	-	-	Jan 1 1891	Unknown	St. Mary Bay, Nova Scotia.
2485	Larchmont	St.p.	1,605	1885	Feb 11 1907	Collided	With schooner HARRY KNOWLTON. 41-16-00 N. 71-49-18 W. About 3 miles SE of Watch Hill Light, R.I. Length 250'. 123 lives lost.
2486	Larnie B. Shaw	Ga.s.	79	1899	Feb 5 1932	Foundered	Off Cape May Jetty, N.J. Iron vessel. All lives (7) lost.
2487	Laura Belle	Sch.	-	-	May 5 1887	Foundered	Point Michaux, Nova Scotia. Struck iceberg.
2488	Laura Brown	Sch.	-	-	Lost 1800's	Unknown	Off Highland, Mass.
2489	Laura E. Gammage	Sch.	426	-	Feb 20 1884	Unknown	East of Block Island, R.I.
2490	Laura E. Messer	Sch.	-	-	Jan 12 1894	Unknown	Pollock Rip, Mass. Coal cargo.
2491	Laura L. Sprague	Sch.	-	-	Dec 22 1894	Unknown	Handkerchief Shoal, Mass.
2492	Laura Loon	Sch.	-	-	Feb 6 1886	Unknown	East of Block Island, R.I.
2493	Laura Messer	Sch.	-	-	Jan 12 1875	Unknown	Sandy Point, Block Island, R.I.
2494	Laura Robinson	Sch.	-	-	Apr 7 1800	Unknown	Pollock Rip, Mass.
2495	Laurissa	Sch.	-	-	Jan 24 1890	Unknown	Near Machias, Me.

NO.	NAME OF VESSEL	RIG	TONS	BUILT	DATE		CAUSE	PLACE AND COMMENT
2496	Lavinia Campbell	Sch.	-	-	Oct 14	1883	Unknown	Southwest of Block Island, R.I.
2497	Lawrence	Drg.	202	1925	Jan 1	1942	Burned	Hartford, Conn.
2498	Lawrence Haines	Sch.	256	1883	Oct 2	1905	Collided	With st.p. NANTASKET. College Point, R.I.
2499	Lawrence Murdock	Sch.	67	1882	Apr 22	1924	Foundered	Buzzards Bay, Mass.
2500	Lawrence N. McKenzie	Sch.	-	-	Mar 21	1890	Unknown	Cedar Creek, N.J.
2501	Leah F.	Ol.s.	179	1942	Jun 4	1949	Foundered	20 miles SE of Gloucester, Mass.
2502	Leander A. Knowles	Sch.	464	-	Feb 13	1880	Unknown	Handkerchief Shoal, Mass. Ice cargo.
2503	Leander V. Beebe	Sch.	749	-	Nov 27	1898	Stranded	42-16-17 N. 70-49-25 W. Black Rock, North Cohasset, Mass. Coal cargo.
2504	Lehman Blew	Sch.	-	-	Nov 18	1890	Unknown	Pope Island, Del.
2505	Leigh No.3	Brg.	-	-	Nov 11	1919	Unknown	42-24-02 N. 70-50-00 W. About 1-1/2 miles east of wreck "Romance", Broad Sound.
2506	Lemuel Burrows	St.s.	7,610	1917	Mar 14	1942	War Loss	39-18-12 N. 74-15-54 W. 5 miles off Atlantic City, N.J. Steel vessel.
2507	Lenape	St.s.	5,179	1912	Nov 18	1925	Burned	Delaware Breakwater, Del. Steel vessel. 1 life lost (104).
2508	Lennie	Sch.	-	-	Dec 27	1889	Unknown	Sandy Cove, Nova Scotia.
2509	Leomontin	Brig	200	-	Lost 1853-4		Unknown	Short Beaver Tail, R.I.
2510	Leon Walter	Ol.s.	75	1953	Mar 23	1964	Collided	With HESS BUNKER. 6 miles southeast of Manasquan Inlet, N.J.
2511	Leona	Sloop	-	-	Apr 20	1802	Unknown	Quonachontang, R.I.
2512	Leonard J. Busby	St.s.	126	1894	Jan 13	1935	Foundered	Hudson, N.Y.
2513	Leonna	Sch.	-	-	Apr 16	1801	Unknown	Nantucket Shoals, Mass.
2514	"L'Essui"	Brig	61	1873	Apr 5	1850	Unknown	Nantasket Beach, Hull, Mass.
2515	Lester A. Forsyth	St.s.	61	1873	Dec 28	1924	Burned	Coxsackie, N.Y.
2516	Lester A. Forsyth	St.s.	-	-	Jan 30	1915	Foundered	Fort Montgomery, N.Y.
2517	Lester A. Lewis	Sch.	-	-	Nov 27	1898	Unknown	Wood End, Cape Cod, Mass.
2518	Lester A. Lewis	Sch.	-	-	Mar 30	1889	Unknown	Long Branch, N.J.
2519	Letha May	Sch.	-	-	Nov 27	1898	Unknown	Provincetown, Mass.
2520	Letharna	Steamer	-	-	Aug 22	1890	Unknown	Soldiers Ledge, Nova Scotia.
2521	Lethe Linwood	Sch.	-	-	Jun 5	1885	Unknown	East of Block Island, R.I.
2522	Letgo	Ga.y.	51	1915	Aug 11	1941	Stranded	Foot of Rushmore Ave., Mamaroneck, N.Y.
2523	Lettie G. Howard	Sch.	-	-	Nov 24	1894	Unknown	Highland Light, Mass.
2524	Lettie Wells	Sch.	-	-	Jan 24	1887	Unknown	Mosquito Island, Me.
2525	Levanter	Sch.	-	-	Lost 1800's		Unknown	Off Peaked Hill Bars, Mass.
2526	Leviathan	St.s.	537	1853	Mar 20	1856	Burned	Sandy Hook, N.J.
2527	Leviathian	St.s.	109	1899	Jan 12	1927	Collided	With car float. East River, N.Y.
2528	Levin J. Marvel	Sch.	183	1891	Aug 12	1955	Foundered	At North Beach, Chesapeake Bay, Md.
2529	Lewis Clark	Steamer	-	-	Sep 5	1888	Unknown	Cape Henlopen, Del.
2530	Lewis H. Giles	Sch.	-	-	Oct 12	1802	Unknown	Wood End, Mass.
2531	Lewis H. Giles	Sch.	135	1893	Oct 24	1906	Stranded	Wood Island, Newfoundland.
2532	Lewis H. St. John	Sch.	1,741	1885	Apr 24	1924	Stranded	Lubec Bay, Me.
2533	Lewis Jane	Sch.	-	-	May 21	1896	Unknown	Chatham, Mass.
2534	Lewis K. Cottingham	Sch.	524	1883	Jan 18	1916	Stranded	Seal Island, Nova Scotia. All lives (8) lost.
2535	Lewiston	Steamer	900	1856	Sep 6	1898	Stranded	Point Judith, R.I. Removed a week later.
2536	Lexington (Br.)	Frigate	-	-	Sep 21	1780	Unknown	East River, near Hell Gate, N.Y. Estimated value $1 million (not proved).
2537	Lexington	Sch.	-	-	Lost 1800's		Unknown	Off Chatham, Mass.
2538	Lexington	St.p.	488	1835	Jan 13	1840	Burned	Eaton's Neck, N.Y. 156 lives lost (160). Valued at $75,000. Reported located. Nothing to date recovered or mention of actual location.
2539	Liassa	Sch.	-	-	Sep 3	1801	Unknown	Monomoy, Mass.
2540	Liberty	St.p.	150	1864	Jan 4	1866	Burned	Cedar Point, Md.
2541	Liberty	Sch.	856	1896	May 10	1918	Foundered	41-24-36 N. 71-00-24 W. 1-1/2 miles NE of Buzzards Bay Tower, Mass.
2542	Liberty	Brg.	247	1918	Nov 8	1935	Foundered	Struck guard gate in canal at Little Falls, N.Y.

NO.	NAME OF VESSEL	RIG	TONS	BUILT	DATE	CAUSE	PLACE AND COMMENT
2543	Lexington	St.s.	1,248	1891	Jan 2 1935	Collided	With SS JANE CHRISTENSON. East River, N.Y. Iron vessel. 7 lives lost (59).
2544	Libtery	St.s.	171	1891	Feb 25 1942	Stranded	Off pier 88, North River, New York, N.Y.
2545	Liby (Br.)	Sch.	-	-	Jan 3 1801	Unknown	Nauset, Mass.
2546	Liet. Sam Mengel	Brg.	907	1918	Oct 16 1935	Foundered	4 miles east by south of Boston Lightship, Mass.
2547	Lightburn(e)	St.s.	6,429	1919	Feb 10 1939	Stranded	41-08-58 N. 71-32-54 W. 1/4 mile south of Block Island Southeast Light, R.I. Steel vessel. Length 416'. Tanker. Fuel cargo. Depth 25'.
2548	Lightning	Sch.	-	-	Sep 20 1887	Unknown	Scituate, Mass.
2549	Lila	Sloop	-	-	Nov 27 1898	Unknown	Provincetown, Mass.
2550	Lilian	Sch.	99	1873	Apr 1 1926	Stranded	Long Island, Me.
2551	Lillian	St.s.	3,482	1920	Feb 6 1939	Collided	With German SS WIEGAND. 13 miles E of Barnegat Lightship, N.J. 40-01-30 N. 73-31-40 W. Steel vessel.
2552	Lillian B. Jones	Sch.	-	-	Jan 6 1889	Unknown	Petit Menan, Me.
2553	Lillian E. Kerr	Ol.s.	-	-	Nov 13 1942	Unknown	42-38-00 N. 68-35-00 W. Trawler.
2554	Lillie A. Wilson	Sch.	56	1873	May 23 1911	Foundered	Vineyard Sound, Mass.
2555	Lilly (Can.)	Sch.	380	-	Jan 3 1901	Unknown	41-48-36 N. 69-55-50 W. 2-1/4 miles S of Nauset L.S. Station, Mass. Coal cargo.
2556	Lily	St.s.	99	1889	Jul 31 1924	Foundered	Wilson, N.Y.
2557	Lina	Sch.	-	-	Oct 24 1890	Unknown	Parrsboro, Nova Scotia.
2558	Linah C. Kaminski	Sch.	443	1882	Dec 4 1915	Collided	With Spanish st.s. CONDE WILFREDO. 36-02-00 N. 78-22-00 W.
2559	Lincoln	Ol.s.	79	1917	Nov 22 1931	Burned	Liverpool, Nova Scotia.
2560	Linden	Sch.	-	-	Feb 14 1885	Unknown	Tuckernuck Flats, Nantucket, Mass. Cargo of logwood.
2561	Linseed	-	-	-	Dec 20 1926	Foundered	Hudson River, N.Y. 45 lives lost.
2562	Linta	Ol.s.	73	1905	Mar 26 1948	Capsized	32 miles east of Thatcher's Buoy, off Gloucester, Mass.
2563	Lion	St.w.	209	1863	Jan 13 1877	Ice	Pittsburgh, Pa.
2564	Lionessa	Sch.	-	-	Lost 1800's	Unknown	Peaked Hill, Mass.
2565	Liria	Ga.y.	60	1921	Aug 26 1938	Foundered	Off Scituate, Mass.
2566	Little Jennie	Sch.	-	-	Sep 27 1892	Unknown	Race Point, Cape Cod, Mass.
2567	Little Nancy	Ol.s.	71	1944	Oct 4 1953	Foundered	11 miles NE by E of Island Light, off Cape Cod, Mass.
2568	Little Star	Ol.s.	85	1927	Sep 18 1955	Stranded	Off Block Island, near coast of Connecticut.
2569	Lively	Sch.	-	-	Jul 8 1781	Unknown	Off Montauk Point, Long Island, N.Y. Connecticut privateer. 14-gun vessel. Reported to have carried undisclosed amount of gold. Depth 36'.
2570	Lizzie B. Barker	Sch.	-	-	Jun 5 1885	Unknown	East of Block Island, R.I.
2571	Lizzie Cochran	Sch.	-	-	Sep 21 1882	Unknown	Point Judith, R.I.
2572	Lizzie Cochran	Sch.	188	1870	May 27 1908	Foundered	Vineyard Haven, Mass. All lives (5) lost.
2573	Lizzie D	St.s.	122	1907	Oct 19 1922	Foundered	Sailed from Brooklyn, N.Y. & has since not reported. All lives (8) lost.
2574	Lizzie D. Small	Sch.	190	1866	Nov 28 1922	Stranded	On Horse Neck Beach, Westport, Mass.
2575	Lizzie Evans	C.bt.	117	1880	Jul 2 1907	Foundered	Race Point, Cape Cod, Mass.
2576	Lizzie Gorffin	Sch.	-	-	Nov 1 1801	Unknown	Race Point, Cape Cod, Mass.
2577	Lizzie Lane	Sch.	231	1874	Jun 3 1921	Burned	West Dublin Bay, Nova Scotia.
2578	Lizzie M. Center	Sch.	-	-	Jun 28 1901	Unknown	In Muskeget Channel, Mass.
2579	Lizzie M. Parsons	Sch.	655	1902	Feb 15 1925	Stranded	Atlantic City, N.J.
2580	Lizzie Major	Sch.	-	-	Jan 25 1887	Unknown	Nashawena, Mass.
2581	Lizzie Smith	Sch.	-	-	Sep 3 1800	Unknown	Monomoy, Mass.
2582	Lizzie V. Hall	Sch.	196	1878	Apr 5 1922	Stranded	Port Reading, N.J.
2583	Lizzie W. Hannum	Sch.	-	-	Apr 10 1895	Unknown	On Great Ledge, Buzzards Bay, Mass.
2584	Lizzie Wilson	Sch.	-	-	Aug 18 1887	Collided	South of Barnegat, N.J.
2585	Lizzie Young	Sch.	-	-	Nov 16 1890	Unknown	Handkerchief Shoal, Mass.
2586	Llewellyn Howland	St.s.	2,748	1888	Apr 21 1924	Foundered	41-26-12 N. 71-20-50 W. 1 mile SSE of Brenton Point, on Seal Ledge, R.I. Steel.
2587	Lloyd	Bark	-	-	Dec 23 1839	Unknown	Nantasket Beach, Hull, Mass.

NO.	NAME OF VESSEL	RIG	TONS	BUILT	DATE	CAUSE	PLACE AND COMMENT
2588	Lloyd H. Dalzell	St.s.	202	1927	Apr 19 1954	Burned	At Commercial Wharf, foot of Atlantic Basin, Brooklyn, N.Y.
2589	Lochinvar	Ga.s.	57	1907	Oct 15 1932	Stranded	Portland Head Light, Me.
2590	Locust	Drg.	250	-	Apr 27 1940	Burned	Thames River, Conn.
2591	Locust Point	St.s.	462	1853	Jul 3 1864	Collided	With MATANZAS. Off Absecon, N.J. 17 lives lost.
2592	Loderick Bill	Sch.	-	-	Oct 18 1897	Unknown	Peaked Hill, Mass.
2593	Logan	Sch.	955	1901	Sep 18 1917	Stranded	Off Cape Cod, Mass.
2594	Lois A. Conrad	Sch.	-	-	Oct 18 1936	Unknown	46-22-00 N. 60-10-00 W.
2595	Lois V. Chaples	Sch.	230	1875	Nov 2 1911	Foundered	Nantucket Sound, Mass.
2596	Loma Doone	Sch.	-	-	May 24 1898	Unknown	Chatham, Mass.
2597	Lone Star	Brg.	436	1922	Aug 3 1940	Foundered	Federal dock, Troy, N.Y.
2598	Long Island	St.s.	163	1885	Nov 19 1924	Burned	North Bergen, N.J.
2599	Long Island	St.s.	300	1912	Sep 18 1936	Foundered	1 mile southwest of Red Nine No.6, inside Overfall, Delaware Bay. 7 lives lost.
2600	Longfellow	St.s.	414	-	Sep 9 1904	Unknown	41-56-36 N. 69-58-30 W. Opposite Cahoons Hollow L.S. Station, Mass. Length 146'. Cargo of explosives.
2601	Look Out	Sch.	-	-	Lost 1800's	Unknown	Off Pamet River, Cape Cod, Mass.
2602	Lorana	Brig	-	-	Mar 2 1857	Unknown	Nantasket Beach, Hull, Mass.
2603	Lord Mayo	Sch.	-	-	Oct 13 1890	Unknown	Clark's Head, Nova Scotia.
2604	Lorraine	Ol.s.	98	1885	Apr 9 1950	Foundered	Off Windmill Point, Chesapeake Bay.
2605	Lottie	Brg.	657	1907	Sep 19 1928	Foundered	Lewes, Del.
2606	Lottie B. (Br.)	Sch.	-	-	May 10 1893	Unknown	Nauset Beach, Mass.
2607	Lottie Beard	Sch.	303	1866	Oct 16 1913	Abandoned	39-50-00 N. 69-48-00 W.
2608	Lottie Bell	Sch.	-	-	Nov 18 1891	Unknown	Mud Island, Nova Scotia.
2609	Lottie Byrnes	Sch.	97	1876	Oct 21 1912	Stranded	Newfoundland.
2610	Lottie G. Merchant	Ga.s.	117	1901	Sep 13 1918	Collided	With schooner MARY F. BARRETT. 18 miles SE of Monhegan Island, Me. 1 life lost.
2611	Lottie S. Haskins	Sch.	-	-	Sep 3 1886	Unknown	Race Point, Cape Cod, Mass.
2612	Lottie S. Haskins	Sch.	-	-	Nov 16 1895	Unknown	Race Point, Cape Cod, Mass.
2613	Lotus	Bark	-	-	Jan 4 1887	Unknown	Long Beach, Long Island, N.Y.
2614	Lotus	Brg.	148	1881	Oct 8 1906	Foundered	Off Cohansey Point, N.J.
2615	Louis	St.s.	89	1863	Oct 16 1876	Stranded	Coney Island, N.Y.
2616	Louis O'Donnell	Sch.	81	1910	Aug 7 1933	Burned	Lyons, N.Y.
2617	Louisa Robinson	Sch.	-	-	Nov 22 1890	Unknown	Great Egg Harbor, N.J.
2618	Louisa Smith	Sch.	-	-	Oct 17 1890	Unknown	In Broad Sound, Boston Harbor, Boston, Mass.
2619	Louise	St.p.	1,351	1864	May 11 1933	Foundered	Brooklyn, N.Y. Steel vessel.
2620	Louise	Ga.s.	66	1883	Jul 3 1937	Stranded	Napatree Point, R.I.
2621	Louise B. Marshall	Ol.s.	120	1918	May 4 1932	Burned	Off Cape Sable Island, Nova Scotia.
2622	Louise C. Cabral	Sch.	96	1904	Feb 13 1910	Burned	Provincetown, Mass.
2623	Louise D. Rathbun	Sch.	302	-	Jan 31 1882	Unknown	42-08-48 N. 70-41-24 W. 1 mile south of Fourth Cliff L.S. Station, Mass.
2624	Louisiana	St.p.	1,126	1854	Dec 14 1874	Collided	With FALCON. Chesapeake Bay. Machinery salvaged for "Carolina" (1877).
2625	Love Point	St.p.	618	1884	Mar 11 1909	Burned	Love Point, Md.
2626	Lucerne	Ga.y.	99	1920	Aug 4 1937	Burned	1/4 mile east of Sag Harbor, N.Y.
2627	Lucia	St.s.	6,744	1912	Oct 17 1918	Torpedoed	38-05-00 N. 50-50-00 W. Steel vessel. 4 lives lost.
2628	Lucia Porter	Sch.	-	-	Aug 1 1898	Unknown	Peaked Hill Bars, Mass.
2629	Lucie Wheatley	Sch.	189	1875	Jan 1 1928	Collided	With st.s. ANNE ARUNDEL. Baltimore, Md.
2630	Lucinda Nickerson	Sch.	-	-	Sep 27 1876	Unknown	Peaked Hill, Mass.
2631	Lucy A. Nichols	Bark	1,395	1882	Nov 27 1898	Unknown	42-16-17 N. 70-49-25 W. Black Rock, North Cohasset, Mass. Coal cargo.
2632	Lucy E. Friend	Sch.	470	1882	Nov 14 1910	Foundered	Fenwick Island, Md.
2633	Lucy Hughes	Brg.	535	1919	Jun 10 1926	Foundered	Off Gloucester, Mass.
2634	Lucy Jones	Sch.	-	-	Dec 27 1887	Unknown	Great Point, Nantucket, Mass. Coal cargo.

NO.	NAME OF VESSEL	RIG	TONS	BUILT	DATE		CAUSE	PLACE AND COMMENT
2635	Lucy M. Collins	Sch.	-	-	Aug 20	1891	Unknown	Ipswich, Mass.
2636	Lucy & Mary	Ol.s.	64	1929	Jun 26	1967	Foundered	Approx. 65 miles southeast of Cape Cod, Mass.
2637	Lucy Neff	St.s.	946	1893	Dec 15	1915	Foundered	Off Fenwick Island, Md.
2638	Lucy S. Blossom	Sch.	-	-	Feb 15	1886	Unknown	Southeast of Watch Hill Point, R.I.
2639	Ludlow	St.w.	76	1847	Oct 10	1849	Collided	With ALLEGHENY CLIPPER. Pittsburgh, Pa.
2640	Ludlow	Brg.	413	1899	Nov 3	1914	Burned	Pier 22, Brooklyn, N.Y.
2641	Ludlow	Brg.	219	1904	Jan 5	1915	Stranded	Hell Gate, N.Y.
2642	Lugano	Sch.	174	1867	Nov 15	1906	Stranded	Point Judith, R.I. 3 lives lost.
2643	Lunet	Sch.	-	-	Gale	1898	Foundered	192° magnetic from Tarpaulin Cove Lighthouse, Naushon Island, Me. Coal cargo.
2644	Luther E. Hooper	Sc.b.	2,190	1920	Feb 26	1927	Foundered	41-19-45 N. 71-25-53 W. 3 miles southeast of Point Judith, R.I. Coal cargo.
2645	Luvina	Ga.s.	51	1911	Aug 10	1926	Burned	Nyack, N.Y.
2646	Lyala Skolfield	Ship	-	-	Apr 19	1891	Unknown	Bateman Beach, R.I. Also reported as "Lydia" Skolfield.
2647	Lydia B. Cowperthwaite	Brg.	271	1856	May 29	1907	Foundered	Long Island Sound, N.Y.
2648	Lyman M. Law	Sch.	1,300	-	Feb 1	1803	Unknown	Pamet River, Cape Cod, Mass.
2649	Lyonnais	-	-	-	Nov 2	1856	Collided	Nantucket Island, Mass. 260 lives lost.
2650	M-35	Scow	-	-		1961	Unknown	In area N of Matinicock Point Shoal Lighted Bell Buoy #21. About 1-1/2 miles north of Matinicock Point, Long Island Sound, N.Y. Sand cargo. Depth 55'.
2651	M.C. Haskell	Sch.	351	1866	Aug 20	1905	Stranded	41-34-08 N. 69-54-33 W. 4-1/2 miles W by S of Monomoy Point L.S. Station, Mass. Length 115'. Coal cargo. 1 life lost.
2652	M. Coulbourn	Sch.	63	1871	Mar 4	1909	Stranded	Nanticoke, Md.
2653	M.E. Dooks	Sch.	-	-	Jul 16	1890	Unknown	Jeddore, Nova Scotia.
2654	M.H. Fuller	Brg.	433	1889	Feb 9	1913	Foundered	6 miles west of Cornfield Lightship, Long Island Sound.
2655	M.H. Perkins	Sch.	76	1876	Aug 27	1906	Stranded	Rockport, Mass.
2656	M.H. Read	Sch.	160	1854	Oct 10	1911	Stranded	Boston Harbor, Mass.
2657	M.J. Laughton	Sch.	-	-	Dec 2	1887	Unknown	Musquah New Brunswick.
2658	M.J. Woods	Brg.	457	1931	Jan 30	1948	Foundered	In New Haven Harbor, New Haven, Conn. While under tow of tug SKIPPER.
2659	M.K. Rawley	Sch.	302	1874	Nov 15	1914	Stranded	1 mile NE of Spruce Island, New Brunswick.
2660	M.K. Wilson	St.s.	76	1851	Aug 3	1854	Burned	Saybrook, Conn.
2661	M.L. St. Pierre	Sch.	-	-	Dec 20	1889	Unknown	Whitehead, Me.
2662	M.L. Wetherell	Sch.	69	1865	Jan 10	1910	Stranded	Ipswich, Mass.
2663	M.M. Merriman	Sch.	-	-	Oct 7	1891	Unknown	Shoveiful Shoal, Mass.
2664	M. Massey	St.s.	105	1862	Nov 9	1883	Burned	Chester, Pa.
2665	M.P. Grace	Sch.	1,934	1875	Nov 13	1906	Stranded	Shinnecock, N.Y.
2666	M.P. Howlett	St.s.	53	1868	Nov 28	1912	Burned	Cramer Hill, N.J.
2667	M.P. Warmuth	Brg.	89	1918	May 20	1924	Stranded	Grassy Sound, N.J.
2668	M.V.B. Chase	Sch.	457	1882	Aug 4	1915	Foundered	Sandy Hook, N.J. 2 lives lost.
2669	Mabel	Sch.	-	-	Oct 24	1890	Unknown	Isle a Haute, Me.
2670	Mabel E. Goss	Sch.	95	1890	May 10	1921	Stranded	Sullivan Falls, Me.
2671	Mabel G	St.s.	69	1893	Mar 24	1922	Burned	Schuylkill River, Philadelphia, Pa. Iron vessel.
2672	Mabel I. Meyers	Bkn.	750	1891	Jul 30	1915	Collided	With USS NEBRASKA. Off Cape Cod, Mass.
2673	Mabel L. Barton	St.s.	204	1905	Jul 25	1924	Foundered	Providence, R.I.
2674	Mabel McGreeney	Brg.	315	-	Feb 25	1938	Stranded	East River, New York, N.Y.
2675	Mabel Purdy	Sch.	-	-	Dec 18	1891	Unknown	Machiasport, Me.
2676	Mackinac	-	-	-	Aug 18	1925	Exploded	Narragansett Bay, R.I. 47 lives lost.
2677	Madagascar	Sch.	112	1845	Dec 5	1911	Stranded	Off Plymouth, Mass.
2678	Madelyne J. Meseck	St.s.	89	1929	Oct 22	1955	Foundered	In Caven Point Channel, New York Harbor, N.Y.
2679	Madison	Brg.	441	1917	Dec 8	1917	Foundered	Off Point Judith, R.I. All life (1) lost.
2680	Madison	Sch.	229	1873	Sep 12	1920	Foundered	Patapsco River, Md.

NO.	NAME OF VESSEL	RIG	TONS	BUILT	DATE	CAUSE	PLACE AND COMMENT
2681	Mae	Ol.s.	69	1928	May 5 1929	Burned	Bridgeport, Conn.
2682	Magellan	Ol.s.	90	1930	Oct 15 1965	Burned	41-13-00 N. 68-47-00 W.
2683	Maggie A. Fisk	Sch.	418	1893	Feb 7 1880	Unknown	42-05-09 N. 70-11-00 W. 1 mile west of Peaked Hill L.S. Station, Mass.
2684	Maggie A. Phillips	Sch.	95	-	May 31 1906	Foundered	Sailed from Baltimore, Md. & has not since reported. All lives (6) lost.
2685	Maggie Abbot	Sch.	-	-	Oct 23 1898	Unknown	Watch Hill, R.I. Total loss.
2686	Maggie C. Accles	C.bt.	110	1905	Apr 10 1923	Stranded	Cohoes, N.Y.
2687	Maggie Cummings	Sch.	-	-	Dec 26 1891	Unknown	Ashore on Napatree Point, R.I.
2688	Maggie J. Chadwick	Sch.	-	-	Jul 10 1892	Unknown	Handkerchief Shoal, Mass.
2689	Maggie J. Smith	Sch.	701	-	Nov 10 1887	Unknown	41-26-18 N. 71-26-25 W. North end of Little Neck, Bass Rocks, Narragansett, R.I.
2690	Maggie & Lilly	Sch.	-	-	Lost 1800's	Unknown	Off Race Point, Cape Cod, Mass.
2691	Maggie M.	Bark	-	-	Nov 13 1888	Unknown	Cape Negro Island, Nova Scotia.
2692	Maggie M. Keogh	Sch.	-	-	Sep 18 1897	Unknown	Wood End, Cape Cod, Mass.
2693	Maggie and May	Sch.	122	1891	Aug 8 1908	Collided	With German st.s. FREGA. La Have, Nova Scotia. 9 lives lost.
2694	Maggie Mitchell	Sch.	-	-	Sep 4 1873	Unknown	Pleasant Bay, Chatham, Mass.
2695	Maggie Sullivan	Sch.	-	-	May 9 1894	Unknown	Handkerchief Shoal, Mass.
2696	Magic Safety	Ol.s.	71	1901	Aug 3 1887	Burned	Kingston, N.Y.
2697	Maglona	Sch.	-	-	Sep 3 1887	Unknown	French Mistaken Point, Newfoundland.
2698	Magnet	Sch.	-	-	Aug 2 1889	Unknown	Nash Island, Me.
2699	Magnolia	Ol.s.	167	1930	Dec 16 1961	Foundered	Off Georges Banks, about 120 miles SE of Boston Light, Mass. Steel vessel.
2700	Maguire	Ol.s.	66	1915	Apr 11 1944	Burned	Warton Point, Md.
2701	Maid of the Mist	Ga.s.	72	1866	Sep 24 1920	Foundered	Off Cape Henlopen, Del.
2702	Maiden Creek	St.s.	5,031	1919	Dec 31 1942	Foundered	70 miles off Block Island, R.I. 40-10-00 N. 72-02-00 W. Steel vessel. Freighter. Position as reported is doubtful.
2703	Main, Bremen, Saale	-	-	-	Jun 30 1900	Burned	Hoboken, N.J. German vessel. 145 lives lost.
2704	Maine	St.s.	2,395	1891	Feb 4 1920	Stranded	Execution Rocks, N.Y. Steel vessel.
2705	Maine	Brg.	1,110	1912	Jan 2 1951	Foundered	In Chesapeake and Delaware Canal, Md.
2706	"Maine" of Bath	-	-	-	Oct 1 1841	Unknown	Scituate, Mass.
2707	"Maine" of Dennis	-	-	-	Dec 30 1842	Unknown	Cohasset, Mass.
2708	Mainsett	Sch.	-	-	Jan 25 1900	Storm	Watch Hill, R.I.
2709	Majestic	Sch.	1,108	1891	Jun 10 1910	Foundered	Off Cape Cod, Mass. 1 life lost.
2710	Major	St.s.	1,864	1889	Nov 13 1913	Foundered	30 miles NW of White Fish Point, Lake Ontario, Niagara Falls, N.Y.
2711	Major	St.s.	60	1904	Aug 25 1926	Foundered	Philadelphia Point, Pa.
2712	Major Wheeler	Frgt.	3,431	-	Feb 28 1942	War Loss	Off east coast of United States.
2713	Malcolm	Brg.	449	1909	Sep 21 1938	Foundered	New London, Conn.
2714	Malden	St.s.	5,054	1907	Sep 17 1921	Collided	With st.s. JONANEY. 41-01-00 N. 71-53-00 W. Between Shinnecook and Montauk Lights, N.Y. Steel vessel.
2715	Malicor	St.s.	268	1886	Aug 19 1934	Burned	Jersey City, N.J.
2716	Maloha	Ga.s.	67	1928	Nov 20 1945	Stranded	Off Asbury Park, N.J.
2717	Malta	Steamer	-	-	Unknown	Unknown	100 yds. offshore at 9th Avenue, Belmar, N.J. Depth 20'.
2718	Malvern	Sch.	844	1899	Mar 26 1922	Foundered	Off Fort Wadsworth, N.Y.
2719	Malvern	Sc.b.	844	1899	Sep 7 1925	Foundered	Montauk Point, N.Y.
2720	Manchester	St.p.	293	1852	Jul 1 1853	Burned	Pittsburgh, Pa.
2721	Mandalay	St.s.	1,120	1889	May 28 1939	Collided	With SS ACADIA. New York Harbor, N.Y. Iron vessel.
2722	Manhassett	Ga.s.	112	1902	Mar 25 1915	Stranded	East end of Long Island, N.Y.
2723	Manhattan	Brg.	879	-	Oct 15 1882	Unknown	41-18-42 N. 71-50-12 W. 1 mile east of Watch Hill L.S. Station, R.I.
2724	Manhattan	Steamer	-	-	Nov 26 1889	Collided	Fenwick Island, Md.
2725	Manhattan	St.s.	1,892	1891	Mar 1 1910	Burned	Portland, Me. 1 life lost.
2726	Manhattan	St.p.	1,197	1902	Mar 12 1939	Burned	Tottenville, N.Y. Iron vessel.

NO.	NAME OF VESSEL	RIG	TONS	BUILT	DATE	CAUSE	PLACE AND COMMENT
2727	Manie Saunders	Sch.	279	1883	Aug 24 1917	Collided	With st.s. PORTUGUESE PRINCE. Off Chatham, Mass. 4 lives lost.
2728	Manokin	Brg.	1,289	1919	Aug 23 1944	Collided	With st.s. WALTER D. NOYES. 41-40-52 N. 70-41-12 W. 1-1/4 miles west of Wings Neck Lighthouse, Cape Cod Canal, Mass. Coal cargo. REMOVED.
2729	Manomet	Sch.	-	1901	Jan 29 1802	Unknown	Wood End, Cape Cod, Mass.
2730	Manomet	Ga.s.	73	1901	Dec 17 1915	Burned	Thatchers Island, Mass.
2731	Manuel P. Domingos	Ol.s.	123	1946	May 8 1949	Foundered	58 miles S by E of Halifax, Nova Scotia.
2732	Manxman (Br.)	-	-	-	Dec 18 1919	Lost	Nova Scotia. 40 lives lost.
2733	Mao III	Ol.s.	80	1918	Feb 9 1928	Stranded	Provincetown, Mass.
2734	Mao IV	Ol.s.	83	1917	Jun 9 1941	Foundered	148 miles east, 1/2 mile south from Pollock Rip, Mass., 40 miles from #3 Buoy.
2735	Maple Hill	Sc.b.	911	1897	Dec 10 1926	Collided	With barge in tow of st.s. WM.G. HOWARD. Sand's Point, N.Y.
2736	Marcena Johnson	St.s.	50	1864	Mar 28 1866	Burned	Holbrook Island, Me.
2737	Marcena Mumford, Jr.	Sch.	-	-	Aug 2 1884	Unknown	Beaver Tail, R.I.
2738	Marcus Edwards	Sch.	-	-	May 3 1891	Unknown	Squam River, Mass.
2739	Marcus Edwards	Sch.	227	1875	Dec 15 1910	Foundered	Cape Cod, Mass. All lives (5) lost.
2740	Marechal Foch	Ga.s.	134	1919	Oct 11 1922	Stranded	Sable Island, Nova Scotia.
2741	Margaret	Sch.	117	1869	Nov 24 1918	Stranded	Point Wolf, Nova Scotia.
2742	Margaret	St.s.	203	1904	Dec 30 1912	Collided	With submerged wreck. Near Avalon, N.J. 1 life lost.
2743	Margaret A. Amelia	Sch.	-	-	Mar 14 1887	Unknown	Sandy Hook, N.J.
2744	Margaret B	Ol.s.	-	-	1951	Unknown	4,700 yds., 330° True from Harbor of Refuge North End Light, Delaware Bay, Del. Fisherman. Depth 67'.
2745	Margaret F. Biglow	C.bt.	104	1891	Sep 21 1913	Foundered	St. Lawrence River.
2746	Margaret Julia Howard	Brg.	502	1918	Nov 27 1920	Collided	With British st.s. CLIFFTOWER, New York, N.Y.
2747	Margaret M. Feeley	C.bt.	108	1913	Nov 9 1932	Stranded	Captain's Island, N.Y.
2748	Margaret Olsen	St.s.	78	1890	May 4 1929	Collided	With tug JOSEPH A. GINDER. Brooklyn, N.Y.
2749	Margee and Pat	Ol.s.	52	1908	Nov 12 1947	Foundered	Off George's Bank, Mass.
2750	Margie Smith	Sch.	61	1875	Oct 17 1912	Stranded	Newfoundland.
2751	Margurerite	Sch.	108	1883	Sep 9 1916	Foundered	Boston Harbor, Boston, Mass.
2752	Maria	Bark	-	-	Jul 18 1888	Unknown	Bird Rocks, Gulf of St. Lawrence.
2753	Maria Adelaide	Sch.	-	-	Sep 18 1890	Unknown	Cuttyhunk Island, Mass.
2754	Maria Dagwell	C.bt.	110	1890	Jul 19 1919	Collided	With st.s. TOWNSMAN. New York, N.Y.
2755	Maria Norwood	Brg.	-	-	May 13 1890	Unknown	Rose & Crown Shoal, Mass.
2756	Maria O. Tell	Sch.	-	-	Sep 24 1890	Unknown	Pollock Rip, Mass.
2757	Mariam Howlett	Ga.s.	69	1877	Sep 17 1910	Burned	Cramer Hill, N.J.
2758	Mariana	Frgt.	3,110		Mar 6 1942	War Loss	North Atlantic. 27-45-00 N. 67-00-00 W.
2759	Marie C. Beazley	Sch.	2,414	1918	Feb 5 1920	Burned	Fenwick Island Light, Md.
2760	Marie De Ronde	Brg.	2,376	1918	Dec 19 1935	Burned	14 miles from Fire Island Lightship, N.J.
2761	Marie F. Cummins	Sch.	548	1884	Nov 14 1908	Stranded	12 miles south of Delaware Breakwater, Del.
2762	Marie Hooper	Brg.	2,190	1920	Dec 28 1944	Foundered	5-3/4 miles west by south, half south of Hen & Chickens Lightship, Mass.
2763	Marie Thomas	St.s.	188	1906	Dec 3 1910	Burned	Milton, Del.
2764	Marieanne Buchanan	Ol.s.	108	1888	Jan 6 1951	Burned	1/2 mile east of Hart's Island, N.Y.
2765	Marietta & Mary	St.s.	58	1930	May 18 1953	Foundered	30 miles east of Highland Light (now Cape Cod Light), Mass.
2766	Marigold	St.s.	115	1863	Nov 30 1875	Burned	New York, N.Y.
2767	Marilda	Ga.y.	58	1914	Jul 11 1931	Burned	Manhasset, Long Island, N.Y.
2768	Marine Merchant	St.s.	6,639	1944	Apr 14 1961	Foundered	42-49-00 N. 69-46-00 W. Platts Bank, Mass. Steel vessel. Broke up.
2769	Mariner	St.p.	147	1862	Mar 13 1879	Stranded	Baltimore, Md. Used as ferryboat.
2770	Mariner	Ga.s.	57	1920	Aug 1955	Foundered	At Quincy Shipbuilding and Yacht Repair Co., Quincy, Mass.
2771	Mariner	Yacht	-	-	1956	Burned	41-35-57 N. 70-48-24 W. 1 mile east of West Island, Fairhaven, Mass.
2772	Marion	Brg.	951	1899	Oct 28 1938	Foundered	40-07-15 N. 73-57-15 W. 4 miles SE, 1/2 mile S of Asbury Park, N.J. Depth 55'.

NO.	NAME OF VESSEL	RIG	TONS	BUILT	DATE	CAUSE	PLACE AND COMMENT
2773	Marion B	Brg.	510	1915	Dec 8 1917	Foundered	Off Beavertail Lighthouse, Conanicut Island, R.I. All lives (2) lost.
2774	Marion Chappell	Sc.b.	1,595	1899	Oct 10 1924	Foundered	Fenwick Island Light, Md.
2775	Marion Draper	Sch.	-	-	Lost 1800's	Unknown	Pleasant Bay, Chatham, Mass.
2776	Marion E. Rockhill	Sch.	284	1867	Aug 22 1905	Stranded	Amagansett Bay, N.Y.
2777	Marion E. Turner	Ga.s.	84	1902	May 24 1914	Stranded	Off Shellbourne, Nova Scotia.
2778	Marion O'Boyle	Brg.	2,200	1918	Nov 12 1923	Foundered	Off Fenwick Island Shoal, Del. 3 lives lost (5).
2779	Marion Olsen	St.s.	87	1881	Aug 22 1931	Burned	Brooklyn, N.Y.
2780	Mariposa (Br.)	-	-	-	Oct 1895	Stranded	St. Lawrence River.
2781	Maritana (Br.)	Ship	991	-	Nov 3 1861	Unknown	42-19-47 N. 70-52-54 W. Shag Rocks, Broad Sound, Boston, Mass.
2782	Marjorie Parker	Ol.s.	51	1925	Jul 15 1929	Foundered	Cape Cod, Mass.
2783	Marjorie Parker	Ol.s.	76	1923	Aug 31 1954	Foundered	At Fairhaven, Mass.
2784	Marjorie Parker	Ol.s.	76	1923	Jul 28 1941	Stranded	White Point Beach, Nova Scotia.
2785	Marjory Brown	Sch.	-	-	Oct 5 1802	Unknown	Wood End, Cape Cod, Mass.
2786	Marjory Brown	Sch.	1,210	1889	Oct 20 1913	Foundered	Off Long Island coast, N.Y.
2787	Mark Pendleton	Sch.	-	-	Nov 12 1801	Unknown	Pollock Rip, Mass.
2788	Mars	St.s.	278	1890	Sep 13 1942	Foundered	41-56-16 N. 70-29-33 W. 2-1/4 miles east of Manomet Point, Plymouth, Mass. Tug. Iron vessel. Length 117'. Possible collision with tanker BIDWELL.
2789	Marsala	Sch.	80	1882	Dec 5 1916	Stranded	Magdalen Island, Gulf of St. Lawrence.
2790	Marsala	Ol.s.	54	1910	Sep 1 1953	Burned	14 miles SE of Chatham Buoy, Chatham, Mass.
2791	Marshall Perrin	Sch.	-	-	Lost 1800's	Unknown	Off Pleasant Bay, Chatham, Mass.
2792	Marshall Perrin	Sch.	149	1859	Nov 16 1907	Stranded	Wood Island, Me. 2 lives lost.
2793	Martha	St.p.	447	1852	Oct 4 1904	Unknown	Billingsport, N.J. Renamed "West Side" on Jan. 24 1884.
2794	Martha A. Berry	Brig	335	-	Jun 28 1883	Unknown	41-38-00 N. 70-02-24 W. 3-1/2 miles NW of Monomoy L.S. Station, Monomoy Island.
2795	Martha E. McCabe	Sch.	345	1888	Mar 20 1906	Foundered	Barnegat, N.J.
2796	Martha Stevens	St.s.	283	1862	Jul 20 1909	Collided	With st.s. CONFIDENCE. New York Harbor, N.Y. Iron vessel. 1 life lost.
2797	Martin	Ol.s.	141	1918	1934	Burned	Mispillion River at Delaware Bay.
2798	Martin Kehoe	St.s.	111	1885	Aug 4 1926	Foundered	Rockaway Inlet, N.Y.
2799	Martin Van Buren	Bkn.	7,176	1943	Feb 14 1945	War Loss	44-28-00 N. 63-28-00 W. Steel vessel. Sunk by enemy action.
2800	Mary	St.s.	58	1859	Jan 31 1802	Unknown	Marblehead, Mass.
2801	Mary	Sch.	-	-	Mar 15 1875	Collided	With SHADY SIDE. New York Harbor, N.Y.
2802	Mary	Sch.	174	1893	Nov 1 1888	Collided	Near Boston, Mass.
2803	Mary	St.s.	360	1882	Jun 3 1906	Burned	Waddington, N.Y.
2804	Mary	St.s.	138	1912	Apr 12 1908	Burned	Boston, Mass.
2805	Mary	Ol.s.	54	1919	May 30 1928	Burned	Gloucester, Mass.
2806	Mary A	Ol.s.	56	1925	Apr 12 1933	Foundered	Off Georges Bank, Nova Scotia. All lives (8) lost.
2807	Mary A	Ol.s.	-	-	Jun 3 1950	Stranded	On rocks off Criehaven, Ragged Island, Me.
2808	Mary A. Boardman	St.s.	483	1862	Jan 8 1866	Stranded	Romar Shoals, N.Y.
2809	Mary A. Drury	Sch.	477	-	Dec 31 1887	Unknown	41-22-10 N. 71-28-48 W. 1/4 mile north of Point Judith L.S. Station, R.I.
2810	Mary A. Fee	C.bt.	127	1912	Nov 23 1922	Foundered	Sylvan Beach, Lake Oneida, N.Y.
2811	Mary A. Fisher	Sch.	-	-	Oct 11 1882	Unknown	East of Watch Hill, R.I.
2812	Mary A. Hall	Sch.	381	1882	May 29 1919	Burned	New York Harbor, N.Y.
2813	Mary A. Hood	Sch.	380	-	Apr 8 1894	Unknown	Nantasket Beach, Hull, Mass.
2814	Mary A. Killen	Sch.	435	-	Feb 3 1886	Unknown	42-10-00 N. 70-42-12 W. Entrance to New Inlet, Fourth Cliff L.S. Sta., Scituate, Mass. Cargo of sugar.
2815	Mary A. White	Brg.	90	1883	Jun 30 1940	Burned	Boston Harbor, Boston, Mass.
2816	Mary A. White	Sloop	-	-	Jul 1 1940	Unknown	42-23-30 N. 70-40-25 W.
2817	Mary Adelaide Randall	Sch.	-	-	Apr 19 1894	Unknown	Handkerchief Shoals, Mass.
2818	Mary Adelaide Randall	Sch.	1,116	1891	Dec 28 1911	Stranded	Block Island, R.I.

NO.	NAME OF VESSEL	RIG	TONS	BUILT	DATE	PLACE AND COMMENT
2819	Mary Agusta	Sch.	198	1867	Jul 2 1914	Walkers Point, Kennebunk, Me.
2820	Mary Ann McCann	Sch.	178	1869	Jul 9 1916	Seaconnet River, R.I.
2821	Mary Anna	Ol.s.	75	1905	Nov 12 1931	Carteret, N.J.
2822	Mary Arnold	St.s.	73	1905	Nov 24 1940	In Block Island Sound.
2823	Mary B. Howard	Brg.	642	1914	Jul 6 1942	Hen & Chickens Lightship, Mass.
2824	Mary B. Mitchell	Sch.	1,229	1888	Dec 26 1915	Off Auburn Lightship, N.Y. 1 life lost.
2825	Mary Bradford Peirce	Sch.	1,133	1919	Jul 17 1931	Cape Brenton, Nova Scotia.
2826	Mary C. Hartz	Steamer	-	-	Aug 4 1801	Race Point, Mass.
2827	Mary Cabral	Sch.	-	-	Nov 27 1898	Provincetown, Mass.
2828	Mary Canas	Ol.s.	51	1944	Aug 2 1954	145 miles ESE of Pollock Rip Lightship, Mass.
2829	Mary Chilton	St.p.	922	1916	Nov 28 1929	Nantasket Pier, Hull, Mass.
2830	Mary Cobb	Sch.	334	-	Oct 24 1875	Chatham, Mass.
2831	Mary Costello	C.bt.	227	1916	Nov 24 1940	Lock 10, New York State Barge Canal, Cranesville, N.Y.
2832	Mary Curtis	Sch.	435	1874	Oct 15 1915	Nantucket Bar, Nantucket Island, Mass. All lives (7) lost.
2833	Mary Doane	Sch.	4	-	Apr 4 1885	Off Highland Light, Mass.
2834	Mary E. Harty	Ga.s.	122	1901	Aug 9 1921	Seal Island, Nova Scotia.
2835	Mary E. Joyce	Brg.	261	1924	Jun 13 1928	With st.s. COHOES. Yonkers, N.Y.
2836	Mary E. Link	Sch.	-	-	Jul 9 1893	Monomoy Beach, Mass.
2837	Mary E. Lynch	Sch.	185	1890	Dec 5 1919	With st.s. PHOENIX. North River, N.Y. 4 lives lost (5).
2838	Mary E. McHale	Sch.	-	-	Lost 1800's	Quonochontaug, R.I.
2839	Mary E. Morris	Sch.	-	-	Jan 5 1889	Barnegat, N.J.
2840	Mary E. O'Hara	Ol.s.	108	1922	Jan 21 1941	1/2 mile east of Finns Ledge Buoy, entrance to Boston Harbor, Mass. Collision with barge WINIFRED SHERIDAN. 18 lives lost (23).
2841	Mary E. Plys	Sch.	224	1891	Jan 1 1920	Cape Porpoise, Me.
2842	Mary E. Sheridan	Brg.	447	1917	Jun 12 1931	Clyde, N.Y.
2843	Mary and Elizabeth	Ol.s.	64	1926	Aug 18 1932	Kent Island, Md.
2844	Mary Ella	Ol.s.	86	1925	Mar 14 1939	1 mile off Poplar Island Gas Buoy, Chesapeake Bay, Md.
2845	Mary Ellen	Sch.	-	-	Dec 27 1890	Chesapeake Bay.
2846	Mary Ellen	Sch.	-	-	Apr 4 1898	Off Point Judith, R.I.
2847	Mary Evans	Bark	-	-	Lost 1800's	Off Highland L.S. Station, Mass.
2848	Mary F. Curtis	Ol.s.	135	1903	Feb 17 1952	Off Shelburne Light, Shelburne, Nova Scotia.
2849	Mary F. Cushman	Sch.	86	1872	Jul 5 1918	Nantucket Sound, Mass.
2850	Mary F. Pennell	Sch.	251	1868	Jul 6 1915	Off Wells Beach, Me. All lives (5) lost.
2851	Mary F. Oike	Sch.	125	1872	Apr 23 1906	East Point, Prince Edwards Island, Canada.
2852	Mary F. Sears	Ga.s.	113	1912	Jun 13 1918	Thatcher's Island, Mass.
2853	Mary Farrow	Sch.	-	-	Nov 30 1802	Monomoy Point, Mass.
2854	Mary Farrow	Sch.	99	1845	Dec 31 1911	Nantucket Sound, Mass.
2855	Mary G. Maynard	Sch.	735	1920	Jul 14 1930	38-40-00 N. 60-06-00 W.
2856	Mary Grace	Ol.s.	69	1936	Sep 22 1946	With ol.s. WHALER. 10 miles ESE of Pollock Rip Lightship, Mass.
2857	Mary H. Keeler	Sc.b.	1,587	1903	Jan 19 1929	Absecon Lighthouse, N.J.
2858	Mary H. Stockhom	Sch.	-	-	Nov 10 1881	Watch Hill Reef, R.I.
2859	Mary Isabel	Sch.	65	1866	Nov 24 1907	Reed Creek Point, Long Island, N.Y.
2860	Mary J. Castner	Sch.	433	-	Sep 5 1894	41-37-20 N. 69-55-00 W. 3 miles SSE of Chatham L.S. Station, Mass. Iron ore cargo.
2861	Mary J. Elliot	Sch.	53	1849	Nov 10 1910	Machiasport, Me.
2862	Mary J. Oliver	C.bt.	101	1904	Dec 14 1928	Pier 53, North River, N.Y.
2863	Mary J. Walker	St.s.	61	1891	Mar 10 1932	Christiana River, Del.
2864	Mary Jane	Sch.	-	-	Oct 6 1890	Near Cape Tormentine, Nova Scotia.

NO.	NAME OF VESSEL	RIG	TONS	BUILT	DATE		CAUSE	PLACE AND COMMENT
2865	Mary Jane	Sch.	–	–	Oct 6	1890	Unknown	Joarmain Island, Nova Scotia.
2866	Mary and Joseph	Ol.s.	–	–	Sep 1	1966	Unknown	41-18-37 N. 70-06-02 W. 1,250 yds., 279° from Nantucket East Breakwater Light, Mass. Fisherman. Depth 20'. Visible.
2867	Mary and Joseph	Ol.s.	72	1932	May 20	1948	Lost	About 20 miles northeast of Thatcher's Island, Mass.
2868	Mary and Julia	Ol.s.	98	1930	Aug 28	1956	Collided	With CAP'N BILL. About 120 miles east half north of Pollock Rip Light, 3 miles west of Pollock Rip Channel, Mass.
2869	Mary L. Cushing	Ship	–	–	Apr 30	1887	Unknown	West of Block Island, R.I.
2870	Mary Lee Newton	Sch.	112	1868	Nov 15	1906	Stranded	Boston Harbor, Boston, Mass.
2871	Mary M.	Ol.s.	120	1910	Nov 27	1951	Unknown	41-24-34 N. 70-57-41 W. West side of Sow & Pigs Reef, Cuttyhunk Island, Mass.
2872	Mary Malia	C.bt.	120	1910	Nov 23	1922	Foundered	Sylvan Beach, Oneida Lake, N.Y.
2873	Mary Monk	Brg.	322	1900	Dec 20	1922	Stranded	Off Sunken Meadows, N.Y.
2874	Mary Natt	Sch.	–	–	Dec 1	1886	Unknown	Point Judith, R.I.
2875	Mary P. Mosquita	Ol.s.	84	1901	Nov 26	1936	Stranded	2-1/2 miles east of Dutch Plains Coast Guard Station, Montauk, Long Island, N.Y.
2876	Mary S. Ewing	Sch.	59	1878	Apr 3	1915	Foundered	Point Lookout, Chesapeake Bay. All lives (3) lost.
2877	Mary Sears	Ol.s.	143	1926	Jun 25	1929	Burned	Sable Island, Nova Scotia.
2878	Mary Steele	Sch.	69	1866	Jun 5	1907	Foundered	Eastern Point, Mass.
2879	Mary T. Morrissey	Brg.	197	1914	Mar 31	1933	Foundered	Oneida Lake, N.Y.
2880	Mary Theresa	Sch.	–	–	Dec 5	1891	Unknown	Tangiers Island, Nova Scotia.
2881	Mary V. Duncan	Sch.	56	1870	Feb 25	1906	Collided	With schooner WILLIAN AND JAMES. Chesapeake Bay.
2882	Mary W.	Ol.s.	80	1917	Nov 21	1953	Burned	72 miles east by south, about 13 miles off Phipanney's Bank, Gloucester, Mass.
2883	Mary Weaver	Sch.	222	1866	Oct	1918	Stranded	Sheepscott River, Me.
2884	Maryland	Brg.	625	1891	Dec 4	1912	Foundered	Ludlam Beach, N.J.
2885	Maryland	St.p.	871	1902	Jan 22	1915	Burned	Magothy River, Md. Steel vessel.
2886	Maryland	St.s.	2,419	1890	Dec 26	1916	Foundered	39-00-00 N. 67-00-00 W. Steel vessel. All lives (34) lost.
2887	Mascotta	Bark	–	–	Feb 18	1891	Collided	New York Harbor, N.Y.
2888	Mascotte	Bark	–	–	Feb 12	1888	Unknown	Rehoboth Beach, Del.
2889	Massachusetts	Brg.	270	1873	Jan 21	1913	Foundered	Near New London, Conn.
2890	Massachusetts	Sch.	141	1901	Mar 28	1913	Stranded	Miquelon Island, Nova Scotia.
2891	Massacoit	Frgt.	–	–	Jan 22	1931	Unknown	42-24-26 N. 70-39-00 W.
2892	Massasoit	Ship	–	–	Dec 11	1844	Unknown	Point Allerton, Hull, Mass.
2893	Matanzas	Sch.	1,579	1901	Jan 27	1908	Stranded	Montauk, Long Island, N.Y.
2894	Matchless	St.s.	163	1912	Jul 20	1914	Burned	Arthur Kills, N.Y.
2895	Mathew S. Greer	Sch.	112	1910	Jan 7	1929	Stranded	Buzzards Bay, Mass.
2896	Mathiasen Line	St.s.	58	1892	Apr 14	1933	Stranded	Bogota, N.J.
2897	Mathiasen Line	St.s.	95	1887	Aug 15	1947	Collided	Off end of pier 33, with Philippine vessel NUNSUCO. East River, N.Y.
2898	Mathiasen Sisters	St.s.	167	1882	Jun 15	1929	Stranded	Jones Inlet, Long Island, N.Y.
2899	Matiana	Sch.	88	1908	Dec 18	1910	Stranded	Rockland Bay, Me.
2900	Matilda	Brig	–	–	Jul 18	1876	Unknown	South of Point Judith, R.I. Cargo valued at $200,000.
2901	Mattakeesett	Sch.	77	1898	Mar 5	1911	Stranded	Peaked Hill Bar, Cape Cod, Mass.
2902	Mattie D. Brundage	Sch.	71	1895	Sep 21	1910	Stranded	Round Island, Beaver Harbor, Nova Scotia.
2903	Mattie E. Atwood	Sch.	–	–	Dec 18	1887	Abandoned	38-20-00 N. 74-20-00 W.
2904	Mattie E. Eaton	Sch.	–	–	Nov 25	1888	Unknown	Nantasket Beach, Hull, Mass.
2905	Mauch Chunk	Brg.	529	1908	Apr 24	1926	Unknown	Narragansett, R.I.
2906	Maud	Sch.	–	–	Jul 15	1890	Collided	Nauset, Mass.
2907	Maud Briggs	Sch.	–	–	Dec 28	1801	Unknown	Nauset, Mass.
2908	Maud H. Dudley	Sch.	–	–	Nov 11	1897	Unknown	On Wickapeset, near Watch Hill, R.I.
2909	Maud M. Story	Sch.	75	1882	Nov 20	1905	Stranded	Sambro, Nova Scotia.
2910	Maud Maloch	Sch.	116	1868	Jan 19	1907	Stranded	Otter Point, Me.

NO.	NAME OF VESSEL	RIG	TONS	BUILT	DATE	CAUSE	PLACE AND COMMENT
2911	Maud S	Sch.	79	1883	Nov 21 1921	Stranded	Haskells Ledge, Stonington, Me.
2912	Maud Seward	Sch.	143	1875	Jan 1 1910	Stranded	Marthas Vineyard, Mass.
2913	Maude L. Foster	Brg.	423	1918	Oct 27 1934	Collided	With unknown vessel. Hudson River, N.Y.
2914	Maude Sherwood	Sch.	638	1883	Jul 5 1907	Collided	With sch. BAKER PALMER. Race Point, Cape Cod, Mass.
2915	Maurice Tracy	St.s.	2,468	1916	Jun 17 1944	Collided	With st.s. JESSE BILLINGSLEY. 39-53-10 N. 73-58-45 W. Steel vessel. Freighter. Demolished. Depth 65'.
2916	Max C.	Sch.	-	-	Aug 29 1939	Unknown	47-01-00 N. 60-18-00 W.
2917	May	Steamer	-	-	Lost 1800's	Unknown	Off Race Point, Cape Cod, Mass.
2918	May	C.bt.	169	1887	May 11 1907	Stranded	Wards Island, N.Y.
2919	May Archer	St.s.	125	1906	May 20 1934	Stranded	Quincy, Mass.
2920	May Brown	Sch.	59	1882	Dec 13 1909	Burned	Pea Patch Island, Delaware River.
2921	May Flower	St.p.	1,354	1849	Dec 16 1851	Stranded	Girard, Pa.
2922	May Queen	St.p.	349	1852	Aug 16 1854	Burned	Cedar Grove, N.J.
2923	May Riley	Sch.	-	-	Lost 1800's	Unknown	Off Peaked Hill, Mass.
2924	Maywood	Sch.	925	1890	Dec 16 1910	Foundered	Off Cape Cod, Mass.
2925	Mazeppa	Bark	-	-	Jul 4 1888	Unknown	Seal Island, Nova Scotia.
2926	Meddo No.1	Scow	218	1902	Sep 12 1931	Burned	Bucksport, Me.
2927	Meddo No.2	Scow	206	1903	Sep 12 1931	Burned	Bucksport, Me.
2928	Medford	Ol.s.	243	1928	Oct 21 1945	Collided	With USAT THOMAS H. BARRY. 122 miles NE of Nantucket, Mass.
2929	Melinda Reilly	C.bt.	104	1914	Nov 14 1925	Stranded	Sylvan Beach, N.Y.
2930	Melissa Trask	Sch.	236	1880	Sep 22 1922	Stranded	Millers Island, Medomac River, Me.
2931	Melmerby	Bark	-	-	Oct 12 1890	Unknown	Roys Island, Nova Scotia.
2932	Melrose	Sch.	-	-	Oct 30 1802	Unknown	Monomoy Point, Mass.
2933	Memento	Sch.	-	-	Nov 18 1879	Unknown	Watch Hill Reef, R.I.
2934	Menawa	Sch.	211	1864	Jul 12 1908	Collided	With USS MAYFLOWER. Long Island Sound, N.Y.
2935	Menumetrick	Sch.	-	-	Feb 27 1893	Burned	Ashore on Watch Hill Point, R.I. Cargo of vitriol.
2936	Meritz	-	-	-	Jul 2 1930	Unknown	42-30-15 N. 70-39-20 W.
2937	Merlin (Br.)	Frigate	-	-	1777	Unknown	In Delaware Channel between Hog Island and New Jersey coast. Depth 30'. Reported to have carried treasure.
2938	Meropi	-	2,650	-	Feb 2 1942	Unknown	44-14-00 N. 62-41-00 W.
2939	Merril C. Hart	Sch.	191	1866	Nov 7 1909	Collided	With British bark JOHN S. BENNET. Off Block Island, R.I. All lives (5) lost.
2940	Merrimac	St.s.	1,991	1862	Jul 10 1887	Stranded	Near Little Hope Island, Nova Scotia. Iron and wood vessel.
2941	Merrimac	Sch.	640	1906	Apr 10 1918	Stranded	Rehoboth, Del.
2942	Merryconeag	St.s.	165	1888	Nov 29 1918	Burned	Orrs Island, Me.
2943	Mertle B. Crowley	Sch.	2,824	1907	Jan 23 1910	Stranded	Wasque Shoal, Nantucket Sound, Mass.
2944	Messenger	St.w.	1855	1855	Dec 7 1861	Stranded	Rochester, Pa.
2945	Messenger	Brg.	410	1908	Oct 11 1931	Burned	Edgewater, N.J.
2946	Meteor	Brig	-	-	Dec 21 1869	Unknown	West of Point Judith, R.I.
2947	Meteor	Sch.	-	-	Dec 19 1890	Unknown	Louisburg, Cape Breton, Nova Scotia.
2948	Meteor	St.s.	2,324	1901	Jul 10 1926	Stranded	Off Block Island, R.I. Steel vessel.
2949	Metinic	Sch.	261	1901	Feb 26 1916	Foundered	Sailed from New York, N.Y. & has not since reported. All lives (6) lost.
2950	Metis	St.s.	1,359	1865	Aug 30 1872	Collided	Long Island Sound. 30 lives lost. Off Watch Hill, R.I. With sch. NETTIE CUSHING.
2951	Metropolitan	St.s.	71	1892	Nov 19 1935	Stranded	In barge canal near Gasport, N.Y.
2952	Metropolitan No.1	-	-	-			South of Bedioes Island, New York Harbor, N.Y. Depth 24'.
2953	Mexico	-	-	-	Jan 2 1837	Wrecked	Hempstead Beach, N.Y. 62 lives lost.
2954	Michael David	Tug	-	-			44-07-36 N. 68-52-56 W. Penobscot Bay, Me. Length 65'. Depth 45'.
2955	Michael Dempsey	Brg.	522	1907	Dec 8 1917	Foundered	Off Beachhaven, N.J. All lives (3) lost.
2956	Michael F. Densmore	Ol.s.	99	1929	Aug 24 1957	Foundered	At Georges Bank, off Provincetown, Mass.

NO.	NAME OF VESSEL	RIG	TONS	BUILT	DATE		CAUSE	PLACE AND COMMENT
2957	Michael Howard	Brg.	502	1918	Mar 18	1942	Foundered	New York Harbor, N.Y.
2958	Michael L.	Brg.	271	1933	Nov 24	1943	Stranded	Lock No.13, New York State Barge Canal, N.Y.
2959	Midland	St.s.	1,535	1895	Jan 26	1924	Burned	Washington, D.C. Steel vessel.
2960	Mildred A. Pope	Sch.	90	1890	Jun 29	1907	Collided	With st.p. PURITAN. Off Falkners Island, Conn.
2961	Mildred McNally	Brg.	494	1910	Jul 14	1931	Foundered	Chesapeake and Delaware Canal, Del.
2962	Mildred Robinson	Ga.s.	121	1903	Jun 16	1931	Stranded	Magdalen Islands, Prince Edward Island, Canada.
2963	Mildred V. Nunan	Sch.	79	1903	Feb 26	1912	Stranded	Cape Porpoise, Me.
2964	Miles M. Merry	Sch.	1,589	1901	Feb 17	1909	Stranded	Moriches, N.Y.
2965	Miles Standish	Sch.	-	-	Lost 1800's		Unknown	Highland Light, Mass.
2966	Miles Standish	Tug	-	-		1960	Unknown	About 150 ft. south of 9th Street Bridge over Gowanus Canal (west side), New York Harbor, N.Y. Visible.
2967	Miller	Sch.	-	-	Oct 4	1841	Unknown	Nantasket Beach, Hull, Mass.
2968	Millville	Sc.b.	1,213	1919	Dec 2	1927	Foundered	Sea Girt, N.J.
2969	Milton	Ol.s.	115	1925	Jun 2	1935	Burned	13 miles, 114° from Nauset Beach Light, Mass.
2970	Mima A. Reed	Sch.	-	-	Sep 11	1889	Unknown	Delaware Breakwater.
2971	Mimmie F. Paine	Sch.	-	-	Nov 25	1888	Unknown	Provincetown, Mass.
2972	Mimmie Kinnie	Sch.	-	-	Sep 4	1875	Unknown	West of Point Judith, R.I.
2973	Mineola	St.s.	367	-	Unknown		Unknown	Off Newport, R.I.
2974	Minerva	Sch.	56	1896	Feb 11	1910	Stranded	Cape Ann, Mass.
2975	Mingue	Sch.	-	-	Nov 27	1898	Unknown	Off Provincetown, Mass.
2976	Minnie	Sch.	-	-	Jan 13	1874	Unknown	Short Beach, Winthrop, Mass.
2977	Minnie C. Murray	C.bt.	117	1909	Nov 10	1924	Burned	Wilbur Basin, N.Y.
2978	Minnie D. Kennelly	Brg.	371	1904	Feb 4	1916	Foundered	Long Island Sound.
2979	Minnie & Gussie	Sch.	-	-	Jan 30	1891	Unknown	Cape Henlopen, Del.
2980	Minnie & Irwin	Steamer	-	-	Aug 29	1893	Unknown	Off Provincetown, Mass.
2981	Minnie Rowan	Sch.	678	1867	Feb 13	1894	Unknown	Near Collamore Ledge, North Scituate, Mass. Coal cargo.
2982	Minnie Slauson	Sch.	317	-	Sep 24	1915	Foundered	Hyannis Harbor, Mass.
2983	Miranda	Steamer	-	-	Jun 20	1886	Unknown	Point Judith, R.I.
2984	Miranda	Sch.	108	1893	Dec 20	1912	Stranded	Bonne Bay, Newfoundland.
2985	Miss Atlantic City	Brg.	118	1929	Sep 12	1945	Burned	Anglesa Harbor, N.J.
2986	Miss Point Judith	Ol.s.	67	1959	Jun 23	1961	Collided	With ol.s. M/S MONTEVIDEO. At entrance to Buzzards Bay, Mass.
2987	Mist	Ol.s.	-	-	Apr 8	1936	Unknown	42-23-36 N. 70-39-18 W. Trawler.
2988	Misletoe	St.p.	362	1872	Oct 5	1924	Burned	Sandy Hook, N.J.
2989	Mockingbird	Ol.s.	112	1936	Apr 27	1967	Foundered	Approx. 75 miles east of Cape May, N.J.
2990	Modens	Sch.	-	-	Jun	1878	Foundered	Off Cape Cod, Mass. During storm.
2991	Mohawk	Ship	-	-	Dec 17	1841	Unknown	Point Allerton, Hull, Mass.
2992	Mohawk	St.s.	194	1843	Oct 9	1854	Stranded	Saybrook, Conn.
2993	Mohawk	Sch.	913	1882		1918	Foundered	Sailed from New York, N.Y. & has not since reported. All lives (10) lost.
2994	Mohawk	St.s.	535	1890	Aug 9	1922	Stranded	Castle Hook, N.J.
2995	Mohawk	St.s.	4,623	1908	Jan 1	1925	Burned	Fourteen Bank Light, Delaware Bay. Steel vessel.
2996	Mohawk	St.s.	5,896	1926	Jan 25	1935	Collided	With Norwegian S.S. TALISMAN. 40-01-24 N. 73-54-19 W. 6.7 miles off beach, Mantoloking, N.J. Steel vessel. 45 lives lost (164). Depth 76'. Ward Line.
2997	Moldavia (Br.)	St.s.	154	1898	May 23	1918	Torpedoed	Off Atlantic coast. Troop carrier. 53 lives lost.
2998	Mollie Barton	C.bt.	238	1885	Jul 12	1906	Collided	With French warship. North River, New York, N.Y.
2999	Mollie Rhodes	Sch.	-	-	Dec 15	1910	Foundered	Little Round Shoal, Nantucket, Mass. All lives (5) lost.
3000	Mollie Trim	Sch.	-	-	Jan 9	1886	Unknown	Off Calf Island, Boston Harbor, Mass.
3001	Moluncus	Brig	-	-		1885	Unknown	Off Block Island, R.I.
3002	Mondego	Sch.	-	-	May 1	1900	Foundered	Off Nauset Beach, Mass. Lost in fog.

NO.	NAME OF VESSEL	RIG	TONS	BUILT	DATE	CAUSE	PLACE AND COMMENT
3003	Monitor	St.s.	146	1862	Feb 27 1887	Stranded	Tolchester, Md.
3004	Monitor	Sch.	110	1886	Nov 28 1914	Stranded	Codroy Island, Newfoundland.
3005	Monitor	St.w.	221	1901	Feb 16 1925	Collided	With st.s. LA BELLE. Old Lock Three, Monongahela River, Pa. 1 life lost (9).
3006	Monmouth	St.p.	184	1836	Oct 14 1856	Collided	With brig WOODWARD. Baltimore-New York.
3007	Monmouth	Sch.	-	-	Jan 4 1882	Unknown	Watch Hill Reef, R.I.
3008	Monmouth	Sch.	-	-	Jul 30 1887	Collided	Off Cape Cod, Mass.
3009	Monohansett	St.p.	465	1862	Aug 3 1904	Stranded	Salem, Mass.
3010	Mont Blanc	-	-	-	Dec 30 1917	Collided	With IMO. Halifax, Nova Scotia. 1,158 lives lost.
3011	Monte Tabor (It.)	Bark	567	-	Sep 14 1896	Unknown	42-05-30 N. 70-10-24 W. 1 mile NNW of Peaked Hill L.S. Station, Mass.
3012	Montague	St.p.	410	1853	Dec 8 1853	Burned	New York, N.Y. Used as ferryboat.
3013	Montana	Sch.	852	1870	Jan 21 1907	Foundered	Off Block Island, R.I. Lumber cargo.
3014	Montara	St.s.	2,562	1881	Aug 13 1920	Stranded	Louisburg, Nova Scotia.
3015	Montcalm	-	9,784	-	Jan 24 1942	Unknown	44-17-00 N. 62-42-00 W.
3016	Montezuma	Sch.	-	-	Dec 23 1888	Unknown	Brier Island, Nova Scotia.
3017	Montgomery	St.s.	787	1858	Jan 7 1877	Collided	With SEMINOLE. 38 miles SW of Cape May, N.J. 17 lives lost.
3018	Monticello	Sch.	-	-	Jul 1 1902	Unknown	On Schooner Reef, Cuttyhunk, Mass.
3019	Moonbeam	Sch.	-	-	Oct 27 1893	Unknown	Pollock Rip, Mass.
3020	Moonbeam	Sch.	-	-	May 3 1905	Unknown	Off Point Judith, R.I.
3021	Moonlight	Sch.	198	1855	Dec 19 1933	Burned	Off Jonesport, Me.
3022	Moonstone	Yacht	-	-	Oct 15 1943	Unknown	23.7 miles offshore, Indian River Inlet, Del. 38-29-00 N. 74-33-18 W. Depth 124'.
3023	Moosic	Brg.	274	1874	May 3 1909	Stranded	Falkner Island, Conn.
3024	Mooween	Sch.	122	1904	Dec 12 1911	Stranded	Great Island, Lunenburg, Nova Scotia.
3025	Mopang	Sch.	77	1884	Nov 7 1906	Stranded	Gayhead, Mass.
3026	Morancy	Sch.	198	1868	Feb 27 1907	Foundered	70 miles south of Monhegan Island, Me.
3027	Moravia (Ger.)	-	-	-	Feb 12 1899	Wrecked	Sable Island, Nova Scotia.
3028	Moritz	St.s.	-	-	Jul 2 1930	Unknown	42-30-15 N. 70-39-20 W.
3029	Morjan	Ga.y.	84	1906	Oct 11 1927	Burned	Bear Creek, Md.
3030	Morning Star	Sch.	-	-	Aug 27 1895	Unknown	Shovelful Shoal, Mass.
3031	Morning Star	St.p.	277	1893	Aug 28 1913	Burned	Monongahela City, Pa.
3032	Moro Castle	Bark	-	-	Nov 25 1888	Unknown	Delaware Breakwater.
3033	Moro Castle	Brg.	-	-	Jul 16 1890	Unknown	Absecon, N.J.
3034	Morris E. Wilson	Sch.	-	-	Sep 20 1891	Unknown	Guyon Island, Nova Scotia.
3035	Morro Castle	El.s.	11,520	1930	Sep 8 1934	Burned	Sea Girt, N.J. Steel vessel. Owned by Ward Lines. 126 lives lost (549).
3036	Mortimer R. Swan	Brg.	103	1894	Nov 12 1910	Foundered	Jersey City, N.J.
3037	Moses B. Bramhall	Sch.	-	-	Oct 21 1891	Unknown	Entrance to New York Harbor, N.Y.
3038	Moses Webster	Sch.	488	-	Nov 28 1885	Unknown	41-32-30 N. 70-00-14 W. Shovelful Shoal, Mass. Sugar cargo.
3039	Mott Haven	Sch.	-	-	Dec 25 1885	Unknown	Southeast of Point Judith, R.I.
3040	Mount Hope	Sch.	-	-	Dec 23 1800	Unknown	Pollock Rip, Mass.
3041	Mount Pleasant	St.p.	177	1835	Dec 10 1844	Foundered	New York-Philadelphia. 12 lives lost.
3042	Mountaineer	St.p.	513	1846	Jun 26 1850	Stranded	Cape Henlopen, Del.
3043	Mower	Sch.	-	-	Jul 4 1888	Unknown	Near Matinicus Island, Me.
3044	Multnomah	Sch.	124	1889	Jun 16 1910	Stranded	Off Cape Ann, Mass.
3045	Muridita	Sch.	-	-	Jul 10 1899	Unknown	Pollock Rip, Mass.
3046	Muriel	Sch.	120	1904	Aug 3 1918	Torpedoed	45 miles west of Seal Island, Nova Scotia.
3047	Mutual	St.s.	84	1890	Jan 3 1930	Collided	With ferry W.R. Hearst. Erie Basin, Brooklyn, N.Y.
3048	Myndert Starin	Brg.	203	-	Mar 3 1906	Foundered	Weehawken, N.J.
3049	Myra B. Weaver	Sch.	525	-	Nov 9 1800	Unknown	Handkerchief Shoal, Mass.
3050	Myra W. Spear	Sch.	156	1888	Dec 28 1908	Foundered	20 miles west of Highland Light, Mass. 3 lives lost.

NO.	NAME OF VESSEL	RIG	TONS	BUILT	DATE		CAUSE	PLACE AND COMMENT
3051	Myron L. Hyman	Ol.s.	377	1907	Oct 2	1962	Foundered	At Long Island Sound, Port Jefferson Dumping Ground, N.Y. Steel vessel.
3052	Myronus	Sch.	283	1865	Aug 12	1907	Collided	With st.s. TENNESSEE. 5 miles NE of Eaton's Neck, Long Island, N.Y. 4 lives lost.
3053	Myrtle F.	Slp.ycht	-	-	Sep 3	1890	Unknown	Pollock Rip, Mass.
3054	Mystery	-	-	-	Jul 10	1887	Capsized	Jamaica Bay, Long Island, N.Y. 25 lives lost.
3055	Mystery	Sch.	-	-	Nov 10	1887	Unknown	Jerry's Point, N.H.
3056	Mystery	Bark	-	-	Feb 3	1888	Unknown	Near Lockport, Nova Scotia.
3057	Mystery	Ga.y.	137	1905	Feb 23	1920	Burned	New York, N.Y. Steel vessel.
3058	Mystic	Sch.	259	1908	Nov 8	1916	Foundered	Sailed from Perth Amboy, N.J. & has not since reported. All lives (7) lost.
3059	Mystic	Ol.s.	90	1925	Jun 12	1931	Stranded	Sankaty Head, Mass.
3060	McAllister Bros. No.34	Brg.	187	1883	Apr 23	1919	Collided	With st.s. TRANSFER NO.16. Greenville, N.J.
3061	McCarren Boys	St.s.	75	1886	Apr 15	1931	Burned	Turkey Point, N.Y.
3062	McCormick	Sloop	68	1904	Nov 19	1921	Burned	Phippsburg, Me.
3063	McDonough	St.p.	272	1826	May 8	1839	Burned	Little Egg Harbor, N.J. Also registered as "Macdonough".
3064	McGowen	Lighter	-	-	Aug 8	1930	Unknown	42-21-10 N. 70-43-00 W.
3065	McKie No.12	Brg.	206	1944	Sep 5	1953	Stranded	At entrance to harbor, Gloucester, Mass.
3066	N.B. Starbuck	St.s.	101	1863	Oct 17	1928	Burned	New York, N.Y.
3067	N.B. Starbuck	St.s.	72	1865	Oct 17	1928	Burned	New York, N.Y. See No.3066.
3068	N.E. Ayer	Sch.	249	1865	Apr 6	1917	Abandoned	40-22-00 N. 71-37-00 W.
3069	N.E.T. Co. No.10	Scow	197	1881	Mar 19	1906	Foundered	Off New Haven Breakwater, Conn.
3070	N.E.T. Co. No.61	Scow	197	1882	Jan 1	1906	Foundered	Off Duck Island, Conn.
3071	N.E. Turner	Ga.s.	724	1917	May 31	1919	Abandoned	39-00-00 N. 59-30-00 W.
3072	Nahant	Brg.	1,289	1919	Jan 21	1947	Collided	With Nowegian tanker. Off Finns Point Range in Delaware River.
3073	Nahant	Brg.	196	-	Mar 26	1952	Burned	Cape Cod Cannal, Buzzards Bay, Mass.
3074	Nancy	Sch.	86	1868	Apr	1907	Stranded	Port Kent, N.Y.
3075	Nancy Jane	Ol.w.	60	1942	Oct 8	1953	Burned	Landing at Jordan, Pa., mile 117, Monongahela River.
3076	Nanna Scully	Brg.	474	1917	Mar 21	1943	Foundered	Bridgeport, Conn.
3077	Nantasket	St.p.	739	1902	Nov 28	1929	Burned	Nantasket Pier, Mass.
3078	Nantasket	Sch.	655	1882	Dec 25	1909	Stranded	North of entrance to Scituate Harbor, Mass. Lumber cargo.
3079	Nanticoke	Sch.	730	1900	May 15	1919	Foundered	Off Isle of Shoals, N.H. All lives (7) lost.
3080	Nantucket	Ol.s.	71	1923	Jan 23	1954	Foundered	35-00 N. 75-00 W.
3081	Narragansett	-	-	-	Jun 11	1880	Collided	Long Island Sound. 27 lives lost.
3082	Narragansett	Sloop	54	1883	Sep 7	1910	Stranded	Nayatt Point, R.I.
3083	Narragansett	St.s.	125	1873	Aug 13	1938	Burned	Pier 32, Brooklyn, N.Y.
3084	Nassau	St.s.	400	1898	Apr 26	1924	Burned	Foot of West 155th Street, N.Y.
3085	Nat Ayer	Sch.	148	1865	Oct 21	1910	Stranded	Deer Island, Boston Harbor, Boston, Mass.
3086	Nat Sutton	St.s.	66	1887	May 27	1946	Burned	At Canal Terminal, foot of Columbia Street, Brooklyn, N.Y.
3087	Natalie B. Nickerson	Na.s.	128	1901	Jul 12	1907	Collided	With British st.s. ROMANIC. Nantucket, Mass. 3 lives lost.
3088	Natalie Hammond	Ol.s.	110	1913	Jul 29	1937	Foundered	18 miles E 1/2 S Eastern Point, Gloucester, Mass. 42-33 N. 70-15 W.
3089	Nathan Clifford	Sch.	-	-	Aug 15	1887	Unknown	Boothbay, Me.
3090	Nathaniel Cogswell	Bark	-	-	Nov 3	1861	Unknown	Off Scituate, Mass.
3091	Natrona	Brg.	423	1905	Mar 29	1920	Collided	With st.s. COWBOY. Philadelphia, Pa.
3092	Nautilus	St.s.	128	1853	Jan 27	1872	Burned	Off Cape Cod, Mass.
3093	Navessink	-	-	-	May 7	1928	Foundered	New York Harbor, N.Y. 18 lives lost.
3094	Nay Aug	Sc.b.	843	1890	Dec 20	1932	Collided	Off Cape May, N.J.
3095	Nearchus	Brg.	1,271	1873	Feb 23	1912	Burned	Off Point Judith, R.I.
3096	Neches	St.s.	2,609	1919	Aug 27	1930	Collided	With scow MULLIGAN NO.3. Fort Wadsworth, N.Y. Steel vessel. 1 life lost (24).
3097	Nellie	Brig	-	-	Dec 1	1880	Unknown	Fishers Island, N.Y.
3098	Nellie	Brg.	206	1905	Oct 21	1932	Burned	Off Gibson Island, Md.

NO.	NAME OF VESSEL	RIG	TONS	BUILT	DATE		CAUSE	PLACE AND COMMENT
3099	Nellie A. Walker	Sch.	-	-	Apr 2	1891	Foundered	Boon Island, Me.
3100	Nellie B	Sch.	-	-	Dec 27	1891	Unknown	Rable Ledges, Nova Scotia.
3101	Nellie Bowers	Sch.	-	-	Feb 25	1888	Unknown	Richmond Island, Me.
3102	Nellie C. Raine	Sch.	-	-	Mar 16	1890	Unknown	Delaware Bay.
3103	Nellie D. Vaughn	Sch.	-	-	Jul 12	1888	Unknown	Watch Hill Point, R.I.
3104	Nellie Eaton	Sch.	118	1874	Apr 3	1924	Stranded	Chance Harbor, New Brunswick. All lives (3) lost.
3105	Nellie F. Sawyer	Sch.	284	1873	Sep 24	1913	Foundered	Pollock Rip Shoals, Mass.
3106	Nellie J. Day	Sch.	-	-	Apr 9	1891	Unknown	Boon Island, Me.
3107	Nellie Lamper	Sch.	327	-	Oct 21	1897	Unknown	41-50-30 N. 69-56-21 W. 1/2 mile SSE of Nauset L.S. Station, Mass.
3108	Nellie M. Nixon	Sch.	-	-	Apr 20	1891	Unknown	Man-of-War Rock, Nova Scotia.
3109	Nellie R	Brg.	297	1920		1940	Foundered	1/2 mile east of Fire Island Lighthouse, N.Y.
3110	Nellie S. Jarrell	Sch.	-	-		1887	Collided	Near Barnegat, N.J.
3111	Nellie T	Brg.	255	1904	Nov 14	1919	Collided	With unknown vessel. Brooklyn, N.Y.
3112	Nelly Bly	Sch.	57	1890	Nov	1917	Foundered	Black Walnut Cove, Md.
3113	Nelson Harvey	Sch.	-	-	May 14	1889	Unknown	Narragansett Bay, R.I.
3114	Neosho	Sch.	1,857	1888	Aug 18	1919	Foundered	Off Fenwick Light Vessel, Del.
3115	Neptune	St.s.	1,244	1863	Dec 5	1865	Stranded	Long Island, N.Y.
3116	Neptune	St.s.	166	1864	Jan 3	1866	Exploded	Sandy Hook, N.J. 1 life lost.
3117	Neptune	Ol.s.	53	1943	Oct 16	1945	Foundered	75 miles off Boston Lightship, Mass.
3118	Neptune	Brg.	54	1939	Feb 22	1957	Foundered	At Point Morris, East River, New York, N.Y. Steel vessel.
3119	Nettie B. Dobbin	Sch.	97	1875	Apr 28	1910	Abandoned	Off Nantucket Island, Mass.
3120	Nettie Champion	Sch.	445	1881	Dec 27	1909	Abandoned	38-00-00 N. 70-00-00 W.
3121	Nettie Cushing	Sch.	117	1867	Apr 13	1906	Stranded	Cornfield Sand Shoal, Conn.
3122	Nettie Walker	Sch.	-	-	Feb 1	1882	Unknown	Toddy Rocks, Mass.
3123	New Berne	Ol.s.	194	1903	Sep 20	1933	Burned	Chesapeake Bay. Iron vessel. 1 life lost (8).
3124	New Boxer	Sch.	60	1845	Jan 5	1912	Stranded	Isle au Haut, Me.
3125	New Castanet	St.s.	52	1898	May 11	1924	Foundered	Albany, N.Y.
3126	New Empire	Brig	-	-	Jan 19	1857	Unknown	Cohasset, Mass.
3127	New England	St.p.	852	1862	May 8	1884	Stranded	Grindstone Ledge, Me. Renamed City of Portland on July 9, 1873.
3128	New England	-	-	-	Oct 27	1833	Exploded	Connecticut River. 20 lives lost.
3129	New England	St.p.	261	1833	May 31	1838	Collided	With sch. CURLEW. Boon Island, Me. 1 life lost.
3130	New Era	-	-	-	Nov 13	1854	Wrecked	Off New Jersey coast. 300 lives lost.
3131	New Hampshire	Sch.	1,055	-	Dec 9	1913	Foundered	Block Island Sound, R.I.
3132	New Hampshire	Ship	2,600	-	Jul 26	1922	Foundered	42-34-16 N. 70-44-45 W. Off Graves Island, Manchester, Mass. Length 196'. Depth 30'. Has historical value. Popular dive area.
3133	New Jersey	St.p.	85	1836	Mar 15	1856	Burned	Philadelphia, Pa. 51 lives lost. Used as ferryboat.
3134	New Jersey	St.s.	324	1862	Feb 26	1870	Burned	Sharps Island, Chesapeake Bay, Md.
3135	New Jersey	St.s.	478	1902	Jul 10	1914	Collided	With Norwegian SS NANCHIONIEL. Off Sandy Hook, N.J.
3136	New Orleans	St.p.	1,564	1872	Oct 11	1917	Foundered	38-41-00 N. 74-51-00 W. 1 life lost.
3137	New York	St.p.	155	1824	Aug 22	1826	Burned	Petit Manan, Me.
3138	New York	St.p.	994	1852	May 21	1894	Burned	Camden, N.J.
3139	New York	Sch.	1,688	1899	Oct 23	1907	Foundered	15 miles SW of Montauk Point, Long Island, N.Y.
3140	New York	St.p.	1,974	1887	Oct 20	1908	Burned	Newburgh, N.Y. Steel vessel. 4 lives lost.
3141	New York	St.s.	770	1889	Jul 18	1932	Burned	Fresh Kills Creek, Staten Island, N.Y. Iron vessel.
3142	New York	Brg.	523	1923	Jan	1964	Foundered	At foot of Columbia Street, Brooklyn, N.Y.
3143	New York Marine Co. #6	St.s.	179	1904	Feb 17	1926	Foundered	Brooklyn, N.Y.
3144	New Yorker	St.p.	2,571	1909	Mar 1	1940	Burned	Marlboro, N.Y. Steel vessel.
3145	Newark	St.w.	71	1845	Apr 16	1847	Exploded	Pittsburgh, Pa.

NO.	NAME OF VESSEL	RIG	TONS	BUILT	DATE	CAUSE	PLACE AND COMMENT
3146	Newark	St.s.	59	1883	Dec 15 1906	Burned	Camden, N.J.
3147	Newbay	Ol.s.	178	1928	Jul 7 1950	Foundered	Off Canso Banks, Nova Scotia. 60-35-00 N. 45-17-00 W.
3148	Newfoundland	Ol.s.	93	1930	Jan 26 1961	Burned	At 25 miles due east of Texas Tower 32, off coast of Long Island, N.Y.
3149	Newhall	Ol.s.	167	1927	Nov 2 1959	Burned	At Black Tom Basin, Jersey City, N.J.
3150	Newport	Brg.	1,321	1919	Aug 18 1946	Foundered	Between Asbury Park and Long Branch, N.J., 14 miles offshore.
3151	Newton	Ship	699	-	Dec 25 1865	Unknown	Nantucket Island, Mass. Iron vessel.
3152	Niagara	St.p.	411	1849	Jan 26 1868	Burned	Jersey City, N.J. Used as ferryboat.
3153	Niagara	Sch.	112	1899	May 4 1910	Stranded	Cranberry Island, Nova Scotia.
3154	Nil Desperandum	Sch.	79	1861	1908	Stranded	Penobscot Bay, Me.
3155	Nile	Sch.	87	1856	Dec 7 1914	Stranded	Ash Point, Me.
3156	Nimrod	Scow	99	-	Sep 1905	Stranded	Derby, Conn.
3157	Nina	Ol.s.	48	1933	Apr 21 1952	Burned	8 miles north by east of Salvages Buoy, off Gloucester, Mass.
3158	Nirvana	Ga.s.	81	1893	Oct 12 1925	Collided	With st.s. ABSECON. Nauset Buoy, Mass.
3159	Nodoc	Sch.	189	1882	Dec 29 1908	Abandoned	Cape Ann, Mass.
3160	Nomad	Ga.y.	78	1918	Nov 16 1924	Foundered	Old Field Point, Long Island Sound, N.Y.
3161	No-Name	Scow	-	-	Oct 4 1963	Unknown	41-30-10 N. 70-50-54 W. 5 miles S of Sconticut Neck, Fairhaven, Mass. Rock cargo.
3162	Nora	Brg.	761	1904	Sep 15 1903	Unknown	41-11-06 N. 71-36-24 W. 1 mile S of Block Island L.S. Station, R.I. Coal cargo.
3163	Norfolk	Sch.	589	1894	Feb 11 1918	Foundered	Off Block Island, R.I.
3164	Norma	Ga.s.	111	1907	Apr 28 1920	Stranded	Near Point Lookout, N.Y.
3165	Norman	Brg.	372	1867	Jan 31 1924	Collided	With st.s. EL ESTERO. Off Governors Island, N.Y.
3166	Normandic	Ol.s.	79	-	Jan 9 1954	Burned	At Deal Island, Md., upper thoroughfare, near breakwater.
3167	Norness (Pan.)	Ol.s.	6,007	1884	Jan 14 1942	Unknown	40-26-00 N. 70-50-00 W.
3168	Norombega	Sch.	310		Jun 16 1910	Collided	With st.s. MILLS. Off Fire Island, N.Y.
3169	Norscott	Tanker	-		1961	Unknown	1,375 yds., 192° from Ship John Shoal Light, Delaware Bay Main Channel, N.J. and Del. Sunken "skin" of tanker. Buoyed.
3170	Norseman	-	-		Mar 20 1899	Wrecked	Off Marblehead, Mass.
3171	North American	St.s.	2,317	1913	Sep 13 1967	Foundered	About 29 miles off Nantucket Light. 40-46-00 N. 68-53-00 W.
3172	North America	St.p.	430	1827	Jan 26 1839	Ice	Albany, N.Y.
3173	North Carolina	St.s.	618	1861	Jan 30 1903	Stranded	Hartford Inlet, N.J. Steel vessel.
3174	North Gaspe (USAT)	-	-	-	Pre-WWII	Unknown	46-33-00 N. 53-04-00 W.
3175	North Star	Ol.s.	79	1919	Mar 28 1951	Burned	13 miles east by south 1/2 south from Mt. Desert Rock, Me.
3176	North Star	St.s.	3,159	1901	Aug 8 1919	Stranded	Green Island, Nova Scotia. Steel vessel.
3177	Northern Light	St.p.	241	1847	Jan 18 1849	Burned	Pittsburgh, Pa.
3178	Northern Light	Sch.	139	1865	Nov 13 1925	Stranded	Rockland, Me.
3179	Northern No.8	Brg.	673	1916	Jan 16 1924	Stranded	Off Long Branch, N.J.
3180	Northern No.17	Sc.b.	961	1918	Mar 10 1928	Stranded	Absecon Light, N.J.
3181	Northern No.19	Brg.	739	1918	May 23 1927	Collided	With submerged object. Romer Shoals, N.Y.
3182	Northern No.30	Sc.b.	1,264	1918	Mar 10 1928	Foundered	Absecon Light, N.J.
3183	Northern No.34	Sch.	1,946	1919	Feb 4 1924	Stranded	Off False Hook, N.J.
3184	Northern No.35	Sc.b.	3,051	1920	Feb 14 1927	Foundered	Five Fathom Bank Lightship, N.J.
3185	Northumberland	Ol.s.	169	1897	Oct 24 1955	Foundered	40-22-00 N. 73-31-00 W.
3186	Northwind	Sch.	-	-	1960	Unknown	500 yds., 079° from Cupola City, City Island Harbor, L.I.S., N.Y. Depth 16'.
3187	Norumbega	St.s.	304	1902	May 1934	Burned	Quincy, Mass.
3188	Norumbega	Sch.	126	1890	Apr 23 1906	Collided	With sch. EDITH L. ALLEN. Fenwick Island, Md.
3189	Norvana	Frgt.	2,677	-	Jan 18 1942	War Loss	Off east coast of United States.
3190	Norwalk	St.s.	110	1908	Sep 24 1932	Burned	College Point, N.Y.
3191	Notter	St.s.	130	1885	Aug 15 1909	Foundered	Cornfield Point, Conn.
3192	Nova Julia	Ol.s.	67	1930	Mar 23 1934	Stranded	Currituck Beach Lighthouse, Mass.

NO.	NAME OF VESSEL	RIG	TONS	BUILT	DATE	CAUSE	PLACE AND COMMENT
3193	Novadoc (Can.)	Frgt.	2,250	-	Mar 1 1947	Foundered	22 miles east of Portland, Me. Entire crew (24) lost.
3194	Number 1	Brg.	877	-	Nov 27 1898	Unknown	42-18-45 N. 70-54-32 W. Toddy Rocks, off Point Allerton, Hull, Mass.
3195	Number 4	Brg.	920	-	Nov 27 1898	Unknown	See No. 3194 for location.
3196	Number Six	Sch.	910	1898	Apr 3 1915	Stranded	On Hen and Chicken Shoal, Cape Henlopen, Del. All lives (5) lost.
3197	No.7	Sch.	957	1907	Oct 6 1918	Collided	With USS MONITOR. New York, N.Y.
3198	Number Seven	Sch.	898	1898	Mar 14 1920	Foundered	Block Island Sound, R.I. All lives (6) lost.
3199	No.7	Drg.	246	-			At Horn Pier of the N.Y., N.H. & Hartford Railroad, on Northern Ave., Boston.
3200	Number Eight	Sch.	924	1899	Jul 20 1916	Collided	With st.s. COMUS. Off Seagirt, N.J.
3201	Number Nine	Sch.	909	1899	Apr 3 1915	Stranded	On Hen and Chicken Shoal, Cape Henlopen, Del. All lives (5) lost.
3202	No.9	Drg.	-	-	Oct 20 1931	Unknown	42-21-45 N. 70-41-20 W.
3203	No.9	Ol.s.	299	1920	Dec 21 1951	Foundered	In slip at 53rd Street, Brooklyn, N.Y. Steel vessel.
3204	Number Ten	Sch.	897	1898	Mar 14 1920	Foundered	Off Montauk Point, Long Island, N.Y. 1 life lost.
3205	Number Eleven	Sch.	953	1899	Feb 28 1906	Foundered	10 miles ESE of Fenwick Island Lightship, Md. 5 lives lost.
3206	Number Twelve	Sch.	930	1899	Feb 4 1916	Collided	With st.s. HOWARD, off Point Judith, R.I. 3 lives lost.
3207	Number Fifteen	Sc.b.	912	1899	Feb 24 1927	Foundered	Off Graves Island, Mass. 42-22-00 N. 70-52-05 W.
3208	Number Sixteen	Sch.	929	1899	Feb 12 1912	Stranded	Great Point, Nantucket Sound, Mass.
3209	Number Seventeen	Sch.	935	1899	Nov 16 1922	Stranded	Man-O-War Rock, New York, N.Y.
3210	Number Eighteen	Brg.	936	1899	Apr 22 1933	Collided	With dredge CREST. East River, N.Y.
3211	No.19	Scow	281	1920	Mar 3 1938	Stranded	In Scituate Harbor, Mass.
3212	No.78	Scow	681	1914	Sep 11 1937	Foundered	1 mile SE of Scotland Lightship, N.J.
3213	No. 201	St.s.	197	1919	Sep 20 1933	Stranded	North Arlington, N.J.
3214	Number Twenty	Sc.b.	940	1899	Feb 4 1926	Foundered	Barnegat, N.J. All lives (3) lost.
3215	Number Twenty-one	Sc.b.	905	1901	Feb 4 1926	Foundered	Barnegat, N.J. 1 life lost (3).
3216	Number Twenty-two	Sch.	936	1898	Jan 17 1909	Foundered	Barnegat, N.J. All lives (5) lost.
3217	Number Twenty-six	Sch.	1,566	1906	Nov 25 1907	Foundered	Barnegat, N.J. Steel vessel.
3218	Number Twenty-eight	Sc.b.	1,035	1899	Feb 4 1926	Foundered	Barnegat, N.J. All lives (3) lost.
3219	Nyoda	Ol.s.	52	1918	Jun 11 1954	Collided	With FLYING CLOUD. Sank 27 miles SSE of Eastern Point Light, Gloucester, Mass.
3220	O.B. Jennings	St.s.	10,289	1917	Aug 4 1918	Torpedoed	74-00-00 N. 36-40-00 W. Steel vessel. 1 life lost.
3221	O.D. Witherell	Sch.	631	1874	Apr 21 1911	Stranded	Fenwick Island Light, Del.
3222	OMCC No.4	Brg.	1,048	1920	Jan 13 1959	Foundered	About 400 yds. west of St. George Delaware Bridge in Chesapeake and Delaware Canal, Del. Steel vessel.
3223	Oak Point	Brg.	356	1926	Jan 8 1956	Stranded	On Romer Shoal, off Coney Island, N.Y.
3224	Oakey L. Alexander	St.s.	5,284	1919	Mar 3 1947	Stranded	At Cape Elizabeth, Me. Steel vessel.
3225	Oakland	Sch.	926	1890	Oct 16 1913	Foundered	42-01-54 N. 70-02-18 W. 2 miles N of Pamet River L.S. Station, Mass.
3226	Oakwoods	Sch.	137	1880	Nov 24 1919	Collided	With American submarine R-3. Off Cape Cod Canal, Mass.
3227	O'Brien	St.s.	59	1899	Mar 25 1924	Collided	With st.s. DIAMOND S. North River, N.Y.
3228	Observation	St.p.	122	1888	Sep 7 1932	Burned	East River, N.Y. 72 lives lost (127). Fire due to explosion.
3229	Ocean	St.s.	658	1849	Nov 24 1854	Collided	With British ship CANADA. Boston, Mass. 5 lives lost.
3230	Ocean	Ol.s.	-	-	Apr 26 1938	Unknown	42-23-19 N. 70-35-33 W. Trawler.
3231	Ocean Belle	Sch.	-	-	Nov 28 1889	Unknown	Thumb Cape, Nova Scotia.
3232	Ocean Nymph	-	-	-	May 1853	Unknown	Off Massachusetts coast.
3233	Ocean View	Ol.s.	108	1884	Sep 21 1938	Foundered	Long Island Sound, N.Y. 6 lives lost (23).
3234	Ocean Wave	Ol.s.	79	1943	Mar 13 1964	Burned	About 65 miles S of Montauk Point, N.Y.
3235	Oceana	Sch.	-	1887	Apr 2 1887	Unknown	Off Duxbury Beach, Plymouth, Mass.
3236	Oceanica	St.s.	1,490	1881	Jul 2 1919	Burned	Montreal, Canada.
3237	Oceanus	St.s.	1,996	1865	May 24 1868	Burned	New York, N.Y.
3238	Oceanus	Sch.	-	-	Sep 28 1890	Unknown	Off Delaware Capes.
3239	Octoraro	Brg.	807	1919	Jan 25 1935	Foundered	Delaware Bay, Del.

NO.	NAME OF VESSEL	RIG	TONS	BUILT	DATE		CAUSE	PLACE AND COMMENT
3240	Odell	Sch.	141	1873	Jul 9	1921	Stranded	Portland Harbor, Me.
3241	Odessa	Brig	-	-	Mar 2	1857	Unknown	Stoney Beach, Mass.
3242	Ohio	St.p.	412	1829	Jul 6	1832	Exploded	New York, N.Y.
3243	Ohio	Ol.s.	159	1944	Apr 7	1964	Foundered	At Eastern Point, Gloucester, Mass. Steel vessel.
3244	Oil Transfer No.17	Brg.	706	1928	Dec 4	1930	Burned	Troy, N.Y. Steel vessel.
3245	Oil Valley	St.w.	209	1865	Apr 4	1870	Collided	With bridge. Emlenton, Pa.
3246	O'Keefe V	Ol.s.	51	1953	Jul 1	1966	Burned	At 3-1/2 miles NE of Buzzards Bay Light Tower, Buzzards Bay, Mass.
3247	Oklahoma	St.s.	5,853	1908	Jan 4	1914	Foundered	58 miles south of Sandy Hook, N.J. Steel vessel. 26 lives lost.
3248	Old Colony	St.p.	741	1904	Nov 28	1929	Burned	Boston, Mass.
3249	Old Glory	Ol.s.	75	1929	Apr 8	1947	Foundered	South-southeast, 55 miles from Shelburne, Nova Scotia.
3250	Old Point Comfort	St.p.	643	1886	Aug 22	1920	Burned	Baltimore, Md. Iron vessel.
3251	Olga	St.s.	2,496	1919	Mar 12	1942	War Loss	North Atlantic. Steel vessel. Sunk by enemy action.
3252	Olive Etta	Scow	51	1917	Sep 15	1928	Foundered	Boothbay, Me.
3253	Olive M. Williams	Ol.s.	50	1928	Sep 1	1954	Storm	At Fairhaven, Mass. 41-54.8 N. 68-01.9 W. Fisherman.
3254	Oliver A. Arnold	St.s.	50	1863	Feb 14	1894	Burned	New York, N.Y.
3255	Oliver Ames	Sch.	456	1866	Oct 20	1913	Stranded	Indian Island, New Brunswick.
3256	Oliver Chase	Sch.	-	-	May 24	1893	Unknown	Off Point Judith, R.I.
3257	Oliver Dyer	Sch.	-	-	Nov 25	1888	Unknown	Jerry's Point, N.H.
3258	Oliver Mitchell	Sch.	320	1864	Sep 26	1911	Collided	Plum Island, Long Island Sound, N.Y. With st.s. MILLINOCKET.
3259	Olivia A. McMullen	Sch.	-	-	Mar 30	1889	Unknown	Jeddore, Nova Scotia.
3260	Olivia Brown	Ol.s.	82	1927	Jul 4	1953	Foundered	35 miles southeast from Seal Island, Gloucester, Mass.
3261	Olson	Ol.s.	56	1947	Apr 17	1961	Foundered	Off Manasquan, N.J.
3262	Olympia	Sch.	77	1899	Jun 17	1913	Collided	With British st.s. SAGAMORE. 40 miles south of Sable Island, Nova Scotia.
3263	Olympia	Ol.s.	73	1900	Oct 25	1964	Collided	With unknown object. About 13 miles SE of Gloucester, Mass.
3264	Olympic	St.s.	59	1896	Oct 17	1916	Foundered	Wood End Light, Cape Cod, Mass. 1 life lost.
3265	One-Oh-One	Brg.	801	-	Feb 10	1955	Foundered	41-18-00 N. 71-38-30 W. 3-1/2 miles S of Charleston Inlet, R.I. Steel vessel.
3266	Onglo	Brig	-	-	Dec 12	1887	Unknown	Great Point, Nantucket, Mass. Sugar cargo.
3267	Onondaga	St.s.	2,696	1905	Jun 28	1918	Stranded	41-17-40 N. 71-53-00 W. 1/10 mile west of Sugar Reef, Watch Hill, R.I. Steel vessel. Length 275'. Freighter. Depth 50'. General cargo.
3268	Onteora	St.p.	1,213	1908	Sep 21	1936	Burned	Bear Mountain on Hudson River, N.Y. Steel vessel.
3269	Oregon	St.p.	1,004	1845	Oct 22	1863	Collided	With CITY OF BOSTON. New York, N.Y.
3270	Oregon (Br.)	St.s.	7,375	-	Mar 14	1886	Collided	15 miles out to sea from Fire Island Inlet, on south shore of Long Island, N.Y. Length 501'. Beam 54'. Depth 130'.
3271	Oregon	Ol.s.	6,754	1941	Dec 10	1941	Foundered	20 miles south of Nantucket Shoals, Mass. 41-20-00 N. 70-02-00 W. Steel vessel. Cargo of African wool.
3272	Orlando V. Wootten	Sch.	677	1901	Apr 8	1922	Stranded	Off Barnegat, N.J.
3273	Orinoco	Sch.	120	1902	Aug 18	1909	Foundered	Sambro, Nova Scotia. 11 lives lost.
3274	Orio VI	Ga.s.	79	1917	Aug 16	1926	Collided	With st.s. BARWICK. Brooklyn, N.Y.
3275	Oriole	St.p.	75	1900	Mar 28	1915	Burned	Allegheny River, Pittsburgh, Pa.
3276	Oriole	Sch.	145	1908	Aug 12	1916	Collided	With Norwegian st.s. BORGHILD. 40 miles SW of Seal Island, Nova Scotia.
3277	Orissa	-	-	-		1857	Unknown	Off Nauset Beach, Mass.
3278	Orleans	Brg.	1,602	1916	Aug 18	1946	Foundered	Off New Jersey coast. 40-18-54 N. 73-53-27 W. Depth 68'.
3279	Ormond	Sc.b.	1,313	1919	Jan 3	1926	Foundered	Highlands, N.J. All lives (4) lost.
3280	Orteantan	St.s.	2,293	1880	Nov 9	1915	Foundered	Sailed from New York, N.Y. & has not since reported. All 36 lives lost.
3281	Osana	Ga.y.	81	1919	Jul 9	1932	Burned	Off Squantum, Mass.
3282	Osceola	Brg.	1,621	-	Apr 2	1942	Unknown	42-00-00 N. 77-00-00 W. Off Massachusetts coast.
3283	Osprey	Ol.s.	64	1943	Jul 31	1952	Burned	Approx. 3 miles east of Asbury Park, N.J.
3284	Ostrea	Ga.s.	68	1887	Jan 1	1929	Burned	Bridgeport, Conn.

NO.	NAME OF VESSEL	RIG	TONS	BUILT	DATE	CAUSE	PLACE AND COMMENT
3285	Ottawa	St.s.	94	1884	Dec 14 1910	Burned	Cape Vincent, N.Y.
3286	Otter	Sch.	-	-	Jan 13 1891	Unknown	Bellport, Long Island, N.Y.
3287	Ousatonic	St.p.	81	1825	Sep 27 1833	Burned	Leonardtown, Md.
3288	Overseas	St.s.	75	1903	Jun 9 1925	Burned	Federalsburg, Md.
3289	Owego	St.s.	483	1853	Nov 29 1867	Stranded	Van Buren, N.Y. 5 lives lost.
3290	Oxford	Sch.	836	1899	Jan 31 1921	Stranded	Sandwich, Mass.
3291	Ozelia	Sch.	-	-	May 11 1887	Unknown	Whale's Back Ledge, Me.
3292	PC 1203	Ol.s.	-	-	Jul 18 1963	Unknown	41-30-55 N. 70-22-20 W. Center of Horseshoe Shoal, Nantucket Sound, Mass. U.S. Navy Patrol Craft. Steel vessel. Length 173'.
3293	P.E. Wharton	Sch.	76	1896	Jan 28 1909	Stranded	North Beach, Md.
3294	P.S. Lindsey	Sch.	-	-	Apr 11 1888	Unknown	Rockaway, Long Island, N.Y.
3295	P.R.R. 701	Brg.	310	1907	Sep 4 1907	Foundered	Off Watch Hill, R.I.
3296	P.R.R. No.100	Brg.	306	1923	Jul 28 1941	Foundered	At pier 14, South Wharves, Philadelphia, Pa.
3297	P.R.R. 704	Brg.	196	-	Dec 19 1905	Collided	With pier, Elizabethport, N.J.
3298	Paladium	Sch.	-	-	Apr 30 1881	Unknown	Southwest of Point Judith, R.I.
3299	Pallas	Sch.	-	-	Dec 3 1882	Unknown	Off Nauset Beach, Mass.
3300	Palma (Br.)	-	-	-	Dec 30 1881	Wrecked	Off Nova Scotia.
3301	Palmella	St.s.	595	1867	Jun 30 1870	Lost	New York, N.Y.
3302	Palmer	Brg.	-	-	Unknown	Unknown	Atlantic City, N.J. 39-21-19 N. 74-11-31 W. Depth 58'.
3303	Palmetto	St.s.	705	1851	Mar 21 1858	Stranded	Off Block Island, R.I.
3304	Palmetto	Ol.s.	174	1916	Mar 5 1968	Foundered	36-28-00 N. 73-35-05 W. 140 miles offshore.
3305	Pan-Massachusetts	St.s.	11,015	1943	Jun 6 1953	Collided	With st.s. PHOENIX. In Delaware River. Steel vessel.
3306	Pan Pennsylvania	St.s.	11,017	1943	Apr 16 1944	War Loss	40-23-20 N. 69-36-30 W. Off New Jersey coast. Tanker. 15 lives lost (81).
3307	Pan Royal	St.s.	5,627	1918	Aug 27 1943	Collided	With st.s. GEORGE DAVIS. While in convoy 100 miles off New York, N.Y. 36-40-00 N. 67-20-00 W. Steel vessel. Freighter. Convoy number UGS-5.
3308	Panola	St.w.	199	1858	May 7 1859	Burned	Pittsburgh, Pa.
3309	Panther	Sch.	-	-	Apr 21 1893	Unknown	Provincetown, Mass.
3310	Panuco	St.s.	192	1882	Jun 2 1926	Foundered	Brooklyn, N.Y.
3311	Panuco	St.s.	3,570	1917	Aug 18 1941	Burned	Pier 27, Brooklyn, N.Y. Steel vessel. 5 lives lost (35).
3312	Paolina	Ol.s.	60	1926	Feb 14 1952	Unknown	Off Nantucket Lightship, Mass.
3313	Paragon	St.s.	142	1898	May 21 1930	Collided	With st.s. SOCONY 9. Kill Von Kull, N.Y.
3314	Pardon G. Thomson	Sch.	171	1884	Jul 26 1907	Stranded	Grand Manan Island, New Brunswick.
3315	Park City	St.s.	391	1898	Aug 8 1951	Foundered	40-04-00 N. 73-59-00 W.
3316	Parker M. Whitmore	Ship	474	-	Aug 23 1890	Unknown	Louis Head, Nova Scotia.
3317	Parks	Sloop	190	-	May 7 1915	Burned	Eaton's Neck, Long Island, N.Y.
3318	Parthenia	St.s.	552	1856	Aug 7 1870	Burned	Falkner Island, Conn.
3319	Passaic	Brg.	88	1913	May 8 1930	Burned	Bayonne, N.J.
3320	Passyunk	St.s.	-	1922	May 5 1957	Burned	On New Jersey bank of Delaware River, 1/4 mile south of Bridgeport, N.J.
3321	Patapsco	Brg.	325	1915	Nov 16 1926	Stranded	St. Marys River, Md.
3322	Paterson	St.p.	1,057	1886	Dec 29 1906	Collided	With sch. FLORA. North River, N.Y. Iron vessel. 1 life lost.
3323	Patricia	Tug	-	-	1966	Unknown	Off the northwest end of Great Brewster Island, Boston Harbor, Boston, Mass.
3324	Patrician	Sch.	125	1905	Mar 15 1912	Stranded	Delaware Breakwater.
3325	Patriot	Bark	-	-	May 23 1889	Unknown	Jordan Bay, Nova Scotia. 10 lives lost.
3326	Pattie Morrisette	Brg.	516	1902	Jul 14 1931	Foundered	Chesapeake and Delaware Canal, Del.
3327	Pattie Morrisette	Brg.	971	1917	Jan 24 1935	Foundered	Off Five Fathoms Bank, N.J. All lives (3) lost.
3328	Patty Sue	Ol.s.	-	-	Oct 1 1969	Unknown	41-16.3 N. 70-20.3 W. Fisherman. Length 51'. Depth 61'.
3329	Paul & Essie	Sch.	-	-	Sep 7 1891	Unknown	Black Point, Nova Scotia.
3330	Paul Jones	St.p.	157	1837	Jun 3 1845	Exploded	Baltimore, Md. 4 lives lost.

NO.	NAME OF VESSEL	RIG	TONS	BUILT	DATE	CAUSE	PLACE AND COMMENT
3331	Paul La Point	Brg.	360	1923	Aug 1 1966	Foundered	At Powell & Minnock Brick Works dock, Hudson River, Coeymans, N.Y.
3332	Paul Palmer	Sch.	2,193	1902	Jun 15 1913	Burned	42-04-48 N. 70-08-00 W. 5 miles east of Race Point Light, Mass.
3333	Paul & Thomas	Sch.	-	-	Nov 20 1880	Unknown	Fishers Island, N.Y.
3334	Paul & Thompson	Sch.	-	-	Mar 12 1888	Collided	Lewes, Del.
3335	Pauline M. Boland	Ol.s.	59	1925	Sep 29 1930	Burned	Highland Light, Mass.
3336	Paulmino	Ol.s.	57	1943	Apr 3 1959	Stranded	Off Nauset Beach, Cape Cod, Mass.
3337	Paurechita	Sch.	-	-	Nov 3 1889	Unknown	Peaked Hill, Mass.
3338	Pavilion	Sch.	-	-	Jul 6 1891	Unknown	West Quoddy, Me.
3339	Pawtuckaway	Sch.	-	-	Sep 9 1896	Unknown	Off Point Judith, R.I.
3340	Paxinos	Sch.	-	-	Apr 11 1802	Unknown	Pollock Rip, Mass.
3341	Paxinox	Sch.	-	-	Mar 14 1802	Unknown	Off Wood End, Cape Cod, Mass.
3342	Paxtang	Sch.	954	-	Sep 5 1900	Unknown	42-44-39 N. 70-46-54 W. 1/2 mile NE of Plum Island L.S. Station, Mass.
3343	Pearce	Brg.	944	1913	Sep 30 1944	Foundered	Off Barnegat, N.J.
3344	Pearl	Sch.	76	1858	Oct 5 1905	Collided	With unknown vessel. Chesapeake Bay.
3345	Pearl Nelson	Sch.	123	1881	Aug 30 1914	Stranded	Isle of Shoals, N.H. 2 lives lost.
3346	Pedro Varela	Sch.	89	1853	Jul 1 1918	Foundered	Sailed from New Bedford, Mass. & has not since reported. Whaler.
3347	Peekskill	St.s.	190	1889	Dec 12 1910	Burned	Verplanck Point, N.Y.
3348	Pell S.C. Vought	Sch.	77	1862	Apr 27 1913	Stranded	Little Gull Island, Long Island Sound.
3349	Pemberton	Sch.	839	1899	Feb 13 1907	Burned	41-31-14 N. 70-37-38 W. 1-1/2 miles east by north of Nobska Lighthouse, Woods Hole, Mass.
3350	Pendleton	El.s.	10,448	1944	Feb 18 1952	Foundered	41-35-10 N. 69-57-45 W. Off Monomoy Island, Mass. Tanker. Steel vessel. About 980 yds.; 83.5° True from southeast stack, New Bedford, Mass.
3351	Penn	Brg.	476	1905	Oct 7 1911	Foundered	Race Rock Light, Long Island Sound, N.Y.
3352	Penn	Sch.	1,849	1913	Jan 8 1923	Stranded	Southwest end of Block Island, R.I.
3353	Pennington	Brg.	967	1917	Jan 11 1947	Burned	Off coast of New Jersey.
3354	Pennsylvania	St.s.	76	1894	Feb 5 1935	Stranded	Coopers Creek, Camden, N.J.
3355	Pennsylvania	Ol.w.	94	1931	Jan 15 1940	Burned	At Shippingport, Pa.
3356	Penobscot	Sch.	358	1882	May 11 1908	Stranded	Two Bush Island, Me.
3357	Penobscot	St.s.	223	1901	Feb 12 1931	Burned	Guntove Ledge, Me.
3358	Pentagoet	-	333	-	Nov 27 1898	Foundered	Off Highland Light, Mass.
3359	Pentland Firth (Br.)	Ol.s.	500	-	Sep 22 1942	Unknown	40-25-19 N. 73-52-05 W. Patrol craft. Depth 50'.
3360	Percy	Sch.	-	-	Nov 15 1897	Unknown	Off Block Island, R.I.
3361	Percy	Sch.	-	-	Jan 19 1901	Storm	Off Block Island, R.I.
3362	Peregrine II	Ol.s.	109	1926	May 27 1956	Burned	At Delaware Bay Shipbuilding Co. wharf, Leesburg, N.J.
3363	Perevian	Ship	-	-	Dec 26 1877	Unknown	Off Peaked Hill, Mass.
3364	Perit	Sch.	590	-	Jan 17 1877	Unknown	41-47-00 N. 69-55-42 W. 3/4 mile north of Orleans L.S. Station, Mass.
3365	Perkasie	Sch.	956	1908	Jul 8 1909	Foundered	Off Barnegat, N.J.
3366	Perry	St.p.	255	1846	May 21 1896	Burned	Wilmington, Del. Renamed "Delaware" in 1841.
3367	Persephone (Pan.)	Ol.s.	5,055	-	May 25 1942	War Loss	39-46-28 N. 74-02-00 W. 2.8 miles, 075° from the north jetty at Barnegat Inlet, N.J. Tanker. Steel vessel. Depth 50'.
3368	Perserverance	Sch.	-	-	Lost 1800's	Unknown	Off Race Point, Mass.
3369	Perseverance	Brg.	673	1885	Dec 12 1885	Unknown	42-05-20 N. 70-12-09 W. 1 mile NE by E of Race Point L.S. Station, Mass.
3370	Persis Hinckley	Brig	-	-	Lost 1800's	Unknown	Off Highland Light, Mass.
3371	Peruvian	Ship	-	-	Dec 26 1873	Wrecked	Off Peaked Hill Bar, Cape Cod, Mass.
3372	Peter C. Schultz	Sch.	437	1874	Oct 11 1916	Foundered	Georges Bank, Atlantic Ocean.
3373	Peter Howard	Brg.	490	1918	Oct 30 1922	Stranded	Scusset Breakwater, Sandwich, Mass.
3374	Petrel	St.y.	110	1898	Jun 7 1921	Burned	Newburgh, N.Y.

NO.	NAME OF VESSEL	RIG	TONS	BUILT	DATE		CAUSE	PLACE AND COMMENT
3376	Phantom	Sch.	-	-	Nov 27	1899	Storm	Off Plymouth, Mass.
3377	Phantom II	Ga.s.	58	1946	Jul 12	1951	Burned	At City Island Yacht Basin, New York, N.Y.
3378	Phelena Miner	C.bt.	104	1888	May 23	1914	Collided	With unknown dredge. Elizabethport, N.J.
3379	Phil Mar	Ol.s.	68	1943	Jul 17	1966	Foundered	15 miles, 060° True, from Chesapeake Light Station.
3380	Phil Sheridan	Sch.	-	-	Feb 27	1887	Abandoned	Boston, Mass.
3381	Philip & Grace	Ol.s.	101	1942	Apr 17	1968	Burned	90 miles ESE of Provincetown, Mass.
3382	Philip J. Kenny	St.s.	142	1884	Jan 19	1923	Burned	Off Ambrose Channel, N.Y.
3383	Phillip R.	Brg.	305	1913	Nov 15	1954	Foundered	At foot of Hillman Street, New Bedford, Mass.
3384	Philomena Manta	Sch.	-	-	Nov 27	1888	Unknown	Provincetown, Mass.
3385	Phinias W. Sprague	Sch.	-	-	Lost 1800's		Unknown	Off Chatham, Mass.
3386	Phincas W. Sprague	Sch.	789	-	Sep 14	1889	Unknown	Chatham Bar, Mass. See No.3385.
3387	Phipeas H. Gay	Sch.	109	1888	Sep 3	1907	Foundered	Boston Harbor, Boston, Mass.
3388	Phoenix	St.s.	98	1850	Mar 25	1866	Foundered	Cape May, N.J.
3389	Phoenix (Br.)	Sch.	-	-	May 16	1896	Unknown	Orleans, Mass.
3390	Phoenix (Can.)	Sch.	406	1898	Nov 29	1902	Unknown	3-1/2 miles south by east of Monomoy L.S. Station, Mass.
3391	Phoenix	Sch.	901	1898	Feb 3	1926	Stranded	New York, N.Y. All lives (3) lost.
3392	Phoenix	St.s.	14,179	1944	Jun 6	1953	Collided	With PAN-MASSACHUSETTS. In Delaware River. Steel vessel. Exploded, burned & sank. 2,900 yds. 95° True from Baker Range Rear Light. Depth 44'. Lies SE to NW.
3393	Piedmont	St.s.	448	1853	Jun 6	1865	Burned	Cape Elizabeth, Me. Renamed "Potomac" in 1858.
3394	Pierre Dionne	C.bt.	103	1889	Oct 26	1912	Foundered	Louise Basin, Quebec, Canada.
3395	Pilgrim	Sch.	1,215	1897	May 10	1918	Foundered	Buzzards Bay, Vineyard Sound, Mass.
3396	Pilgrim	St.s.	261	1891	Mar 27	1937	Burned	Bayonne, N.J.
3397	Pilot	St.p.	163	1854	Feb	1857	Stranded	Sandy Hook, N.J.
3398	Pilot Boat	-	361	-	Apr 27	1939	Collided	With OSLOFJORD. 40-27-45 N. 73-49-30 W. Off Sandy Hook, N.J. Depth 80'.
3399	Pine Forest	Sch.	910	1897	Jan 10	1911	Stranded	Peaked Hill Bar, Cape Cod, Mass. All lives (5) lost.
3400	Pinta (Dutch)	Frgt.	500	-	May 8	1963	Collided	With CITY OF PERTH. 40-12-30 N. 73-50-24 W. 7.4 miles off Asbury Park, N.J.
3401	Pinthis	Ol.s.	1,111	1919	Jun 10	1930	Collided	With st.s. FAIRFAX. Tanker. 42-09-18 N. 70-33-48 W. Off Scituate, Mass. All lives (19) lost. Depth 84'. Length 206'. Fuel cargo.
3402	Pinzi	Sch.	-	-	Lost 1800's		Unknown	Harbor Neck Point, Block Island, R.I.
3403	Pioneer	Steamer	-	-	Jul 21	1890	Unknown	St. Lawrence River.
3404	Pioneer	Sch.	-	-	Nov 5	1890	Unknown	Arisaig, Nova Scotia.
3405	Pioneer	Brg.	376	1872	Nov 24	1912	Stranded	3/4 mile WNW of Point Judith L.S. Station, R.I.
3406	Pioneer	St.s.	64	1864	Nov 23	1915	Foundered	Off Barnstable Light, Cape Cod Bay, Mass.
3407	Pioneer	Ol.s.	233	1918	Oct 15	1926	Burned	Peaked Hill Light, Mass.
3408	Pioneer	Ol.s.	83	1892	Oct 2	1938	Foundered	About 200 miles east of Nantucket Light, Mass.
3409	Pipestone County	St.s.	5,102	1919	Apr 21	1942	War Loss	37-43-00 N. 66-16-00 W. Steel vessel. Sunk by enemy action.
3410	Pittsburgh	St.p.	68	1831	Jan 25	1832	Ice	Pittsburgh, Pa.
3411	Pittsburgh	St.p.	148	1891	Nov 30	1910	Burned	Ambridge, Pa.
3412	Pittsburgh	Ol.w.	71	1930	Mar 6	1964	Foundered	Near 6th Street and River Avenue, Pittsburgh, Pa.
3413	Placidia	Ga.s.	52	1897	Sep 21	1938	Foundered	Off Newport, R.I.
3414	Pliney (Br.)	Steamer	1,671	-	May 13	1882	Foundered	Deal Beach, N.J. Grounded during storm. Depth 26'.
3415	Plow City	St.s.	3,282	1920	May 9	1942	War Loss	39-08-00 N. 69-57-00 W. Steel vessel. Freighter. Sunk by enemy action.
3416	Plum Point	Brg.	330	1928	Sep 9	1952	Stranded	In Long Island Sound, off Sands Point Light, N.Y.
3417	Plymouth	Brg.	474	1916	Mar 31	1924	Foundered	Long Branch, N.J.
3418	Plymouth	St.s.	373	1892	Jan 27	1938	Foundered	At Cape Cod Canal, Cape Cod, Mass. Iron vessel. 1 life lost (17).
3419	Plymouth Rock	Sch.	-	-	Apr 11	1888	Unknown	Provincetown, Mass.
3420	Plimouth Rock	Sch.	-	-	Dec 11	1890	Unknown	Near Barrington, Nova Scotia.
3421	Pocahontas	-	-	-	Dec 23	1839	Unknown	Plum Island, Boston Harbor, Mass.

NO.	NAME OF VESSEL	RIG	TONS	BUILT	DATE		CAUSE	PLACE AND COMMENT
3422	Pocahontas	Sch.	1,382	-	Jan 12	1890	Unknown	Off Black Rock, Block Island, R.I.
3423	Pochasset	Sch.	-	-	Jul 15	1897	Unknown	Off Orleans, Cape Cod, Mass.
3424	Pochasset	Sch.	254	1874	Nov 21	1920	Stranded	Off Cape Elizabeth, Me.
3425	Pocono	Sc.b.	698	1905	Sep 5	1930	Foundered	Atlantic Highlands, N.J. Steel vessel.
3426	Pocopson	Brg.	721	1906	Oct 17	1936	Foundered	1-1/2 miles northeast of Shark River L.S. Station, N.J. 40-12-04 N. 73-59-14 W.
3427	Pohatcong	Sc.b.	843	1890	Nov 17	1924	Foundered	Monhegan, Me. All lives (3) lost.
3428	Point Comfort	St.p.	629	1886	Sep 17	1919	Stranded	Esopus Island, N.Y.
3429	Pointer	Slp.ycht.	-	-	Feb 3	1899	Unknown	Off Race Point, Cape Cod, Mass.
3430	Polar Land	-	4,130	-	Nov 9	1919	Vanished	Off Nova Scotia. All lives (51) lost.
3431	Polar Wave	Sch.	-	-	May 22	1901	Unknown	Off Block Island, R.I.
3432	Polias	St.s.	2,564	1919	Feb 6	1920	Stranded	Penobscot Bay, Me. Concrete vessel. 11 lives lost.
3433	Poling Bros. No.2	Ol.s.	159	1863	Mar 12	1940	Foundered	Off Captain Island, Long Island, N.Y. Iron vessel.
3434	Poling Bros. No.18	Ol.s.	248	1926	Jul 19	1952	Burned	In East River, off 60th Street, New York, N.Y.
3435	Pollux	-	-	-		1943	Unknown	46-45-00 N. 55-29-00 W.
3436	Pollyanna	Ol.s.	123	1915	Aug 5	1951	Foundered	Off Cape Brenton, Nova Scotia.
3437	Pontiac	Ga.s.	116	1906	Oct 7	1916	Stranded	Handkerchief Shoal, Mass.
3438	Pontin 227	Brg.	234	1916	Jun 8	1966	Burned	At Port Richmond, N.Y.
3439	Ponyer Overtier	Steamer	-	-	Sep 15	1899	Unknown	Off Orleans, Mass.
3440	Porter F. Roberts	Sch.	-	-	Aug 6	1890	Unknown	Sherbrooke, Nova Scotia.
3441	Port Hunter (Br.)	St.s.	-	-	Nov 2	1918	Unknown	On south side of Hedge Fence Shoal, Nantucket Sound, Mass. 41-29-42 N. 70-33-07 W.
3442	Port Nicholson (Br.)	Frgt.	5,338	-	Jun 16	1942	Unknown	Steel vessel. General cargo. Dive during slack water. 42-09-00 N. 69-22-30 W. Depth 106 fathoms.
3443	Port Royal	Brg.	298	1895	Dec 14	1910	Stranded	Hell Gate, N.Y.
3444	Portland	St.s.	2,284	-	Nov 26	1898	Foundered	Off Peaked Hill Bars, Provincetown, Mass. Passenger vessel. Wood vessel. 157 lives lost. General cargo. Length 280'. No reports of recovery of the reported cargo of gold and tin valued at from $150,000.
3445	Portland Packet	Sch.	91	1885	Jul 16	1916	Foundered	Sailed from New York, N.Y. & has not since reported. All lives (3) lost.
3446	Potomac	St.w.	169	1857	May 7	1859	Snagged	Pittsburgh, Pa.
3447	Potomac	Brg.	763	-	Nov 9	1909	Unknown	200 yds. south of Cape Cod Canal, Cape Cod Bay, Mass. Stone cargo.
3448	Pottstown	Brg.	974	1917	Nov 17	1944	Foundered	Northeast of Cape Cod Canal Breakwater, Mass. Demolished.
3449	Pottsville	St.s.	72	1864	Nov 17	1911	Burned	Wilson Point, Conn.
3450	Poudent (Br.)	Sch.	-	-	Feb 10	1895	Unknown	Handkerchief Shoal, Mass.
3451	Poughkeepsie	St.s.	810	1862	Jun 26	1910	Burned	Highland, N.Y.
3452	Pow Wow	Sch.	-	-	Lost 1800's		Unknown.	Between Cahoons Hollow and Pamet River, Cape Cod, Mass.
3453	Powhatan	-	-	-	Apr 16	1854	Grounded	Long Beach, N.Y. 311 lives lost.
3454	Powhatan	St.s.	2,898	1894	Nov 25	1916	Burned	Off Block Island, R.I.
3455	Powhatan	Ol.s.	61	1931	Apr 10	1961	Collided	With st.s. SOUTH AFRICAN PIONEER. About 34 miles SE of Cape May, N.J.
3456	Precurser	St.s.	57	1885	Jun 14	1912	Burned	Port Jefferson, N.Y.
3457	Premier	Sch.	138	1910	Nov 29	1916	Stranded	Canso, Nova Scotia.
3458	Preston H. Burr	Brg.	320	1928	Dec 4	1940	Stranded	On Gilgo Beach, Long Island, N.Y.
3459	Prima Dinna	Brg.	210	1873	Oct 22	1907	Foundered	Faulkners Island, Conn.
3460	Princess Anne	St.s.	3,629	1897	Feb 6	1920	Stranded	Rockaway Shoals, N.Y. Steel vessel.
3461	Princess Augusta (Br.)	Frigate	-	-	Dec 27	1738	Unknown	On Hummock, north tip of Sandy Point, Block Island, R.I. Valued at $100,000.
3462	Princess Beatrice	Steamer	-	-	Sep 16	1890	Unknown	New Harbor, Nova Scotia.
3463	Princeton	St.s.	435	1845	Apr 20	1854	Ice	Barcelona, N.Y.
3465	Princeton	St.s.	458	1901	Oct 24	1923	Burned	Camden, N.J. Steel vessel.
3466	Principessa Margharta di Piemonte	Bark	-	-	Mar 12	1891	Unknown	Hen and Chicken Shoal, Del.

NO.	NAME OF VESSEL	RIG	TONS	BUILT	DATE	CAUSE	PLACE AND COMMENT
3467	Priscilla	Sch.	-	-	Aug 23 1893	Unknown	Napatree Point, R.I.
3468	Priscilla Smith	Sch.	120	1900	Feb 1 1915	Stranded	Shelburn, Nova Scotia.
3469	Professor Morse	Steamer	-	-	Apr 23 1883	Unknown	North of Block Island, R.I.
3470	Progress	Brg.	262	1896	May 1 1917	Foundered	Off Ship John Light, Delaware River.
3471	Progress	Ol.s.	117	1913	May 31 1930	Burned	Highland Light, Mass. 41-13-00 N. 69-37-00 W.
3472	Promised Safety	Sch.	-	-	Nov 20 1895	Unknown	Off Brenton Point, R.I.
3473	Property	Ol.w.	114	1932	Dec 19 1962	Burned	At Lamples Landing, a point 16 miles above Pittsburgh, Pa., Monongahel River.
3474	Prospect	Sch.	-	-	Mar 11 1840	Unknown	Ipswich Bay, Mass.
3475	Prospect	Sch.	-	-	Mar 15 1887	Abandoned	Off Chatham, Mass.
3476	Providence	Ship	-	-	Sep 28 1697	Unknown	Off Harding's Ledge, Mass.
3477	Providence	Sch.	-	-	Feb 28 1883	Unknown	Off Chatham, Cape Cod, Mass.
3478	Pure Oil Co. No.5	Ol.s.	223	1910	Mar 7 1930	Burned	Kearny, N.J. 3 lives lost (7).
3479	Puritan	Sch.	664	-	Dec 16 1896	Unknown	1 mile north of Fourth Cliff L.S. Station, Mass.
3480	Puritan	Sch.	80	1887	Sep 18 1905	Stranded	Canso, Nova Scotia.
3481	Puritan	Sch.	116	1886	Aug 17 1920	Foundered	Bridgewater, Nova Scotia. 1 life lost.
3482	Puritan	Sch.	149	1922	Jun 23 1922	Stranded	Sable Island, Nova Scotia. 1 life lost.
3483	Putski (Swedish)	Frgt.	-	-	Late 1940's	Unknown	41-13-08 N. 71-33-25 W. 500 yds. southwest of Old Briton Rock, R.I. Steel vessel.
3484	Python	Sch.	-	-	Sep 9 1891	Collided	Pollock Rip Shoal, Mass.
3485	Quattro	Bark	-	-	Feb 17 1887	Unknown	Ocean City, Md.
3486	Queen	St.p.	196	1855	Jul 21 1872	Burned	Eastport, Me.
3487	Queen	Sch.	160	1906	Mar 24 1920	Burned	City Island, N.Y. Steel vessel.
3488	Queen City	St.s.	115	1881	Mar 14 1907	Burned	Sakonnet Point, R.I.
3489	Queens	St.p.	802	1877	Nov 9 1918	Burned	New York, N.Y.
3490	Queensboro	St.p.	254	1893	Feb 15 1920	Foundered	Off Clason Point Road, N.Y.
3491	Quilp	Sch.	-	-	Lost 1800's	Unknown	Entrance to Cuttyhunk Pond, Mass. (May have been lost Oct. 14, 1889).
3492	Quoddy	Sch.	-	-	Aug 4 1888	Unknown	Handkerchief Shoal, Mass.
3493	Quonnapowitt	Ga.s.	117	1903	Oct 8 1913	Stranded	Off Highland Light, Mass.
3494	R.A. Allen	Bark	576	-	Jul 3 1887	Unknown	Handkerchief Shoal, Mass.
3495	R.A. Allen	Bark	-	-	Dec 1892	Unknown	Handkerchief Shoal, Mass.
3496	R.B. Spedden	Sch.	84	1874	Jun 29 1929	Stranded	Ragged Point, Md.
3497	R.B. White	Sch.	481	1912	Sep 7 1916	Foundered	Sailed from Philadelphia, Pa. & has not since reported. All lives (8) lost.
3498	R. Bowers	Sch.	435	1879	Jul 25 1916	Foundered	Off Canadian coast.
3499	R.C. Reynolds	St.p.	469	1896	Apr 28 1926	Burned	Newburgh, N.Y.
3500	R.C. & T. Co. No.386	Scow	158	1920	Jun 24 1924	Foundered	Curtis Bay, Md.
3501	R.F. Hart	Sch.	-	-	Lost 1800's	Unknown	Off Race Point, Cape Cod, Mass.
3502	R.G. Moran	Sch.	-	-	May 25 1887	Unknown	Mount Desert, Me.
3503	R.H. Daley	Scow	-	-	Feb 8 1887	Ice	Long Island Sound.
3504	R.J. Wilson	Scow	272	-	Nov 1 1905	Foundered	Off Bridgeport, Conn.
3505	R.L. Tay	Sch.	151	1857	Sep 9 1914	Collided	With SS STANDISH. Off Deer Island, Boston Harbor, Boston, Mass.
3506	R.L. Tay	Sch.	-	-	May 14 1890	Unknown	Off Chatham, Mass.
3507	R.P. Chase	Sch.	102	1857	Oct 9 1907	Stranded	Outer Black Rocks, Me.
3508	R.P. Resor	St.s.	7,451	1935	Feb 26 1942	War Loss	39-47-45 N. 73-25-50 W. Off Atlantic coast, 18 miles east of LaBallette, Barnegat, N.J. Tanker. Steel vessel. Sunk by enemy action. 45 lives lost. Cleared to 50' depth.
3509	R.R. Thomas	Sch.	1,393	1876	Jan 7 1915	Foundered	Off Shinnecock Light, Long Island, N.Y.
3510	R.T. Rundlett	Sch.	271	1892	Jun 29 1916	Foundered	New York, N.Y. All lives (7) lost.
3511	R.W. Genn	Sch.	-	-	Dec 23 1870	Unknown	Nantasket Beach, Hull, Mass.
3512	R.W. Griffin, Jr.	Ol.s.	81	1945	Jul 11 1958	Collided	With British CITY OF KARACHI. 40-10-00 N. 70-38-00 W.

NO.	NAME OF VESSEL	RIG	TONS	BUILT	DATE	CAUSE	PLACE AND COMMENT
3513	Race Horse	Sch.	-	-	Dec 30 1890	Unknown	Pollock Rip, Mass.
3514	Race Horse	Sch.	105	1865	Sep 27 1908	Stranded	Casco Bay, Me.
3515	Racer	Sch.	68	1868	Oct 27 1907	Foundered	Bridgeport, Conn.
3516	Rachel Vaneman	Sch.	-	-	Jan 4 1878	Unknown	Narragansett Pier Beach, R.I.
3517	Radio 1	Sch.	-	-	Nov 22 1935	Unknown	44-41-00 N. 62-21-00 W.
3518	Radnor	Sch.	678	1895	Jan 31 1921	Stranded	Entrance to Cape Cod Canal, Cape Cod Bay, Sandwich, Mass.
3519	Rainbow	Ol.s.	92	1929	Nov 10 1947	Foundered	Entrance to Yarmouth Harbor, Nova Scotia.
3520	Raleigh	St.s.	339	1872	Mar 9 1927	Foundered	Newark, N.J.
3521	Ralph Brown	Ol.s.	119	1914	Feb 10 1926	Stranded	Off Gloucester, Mass. 3 lives lost (21).
3522	Ralph F. Hodgdon	Sch.	90	1884	Dec 29 1906	Burned	Off Race Point, Cape Cod, Mass.
3523	Ralph M. Eaton	Sch.	-	-	Lost 1800's	Unknown	Bay of Islands, Newfoundland.
3524	Rambler	C.bt.	107	1900	Sep 25 1922	Foundered	St. Lawrence River, above Quebec, Canada.
3525	Ramos	Brg.	1,208	1919	Jun 30 1933	Foundered	Scotland Lightship, N.J. 40-25-27 N. 73-54-06 W. Depth 75'.
3526	Ranger	Sch.	-	-	Nov 12 1897	Unknown	Off Chatham, Mass.
3527	Raphael Semmes	Frgt.	6,027	-	Jun 28 1942	War Loss	North Atlantic. 29-30-00 N. 64-30-00 W.
3528	Rapidan	Sch.	-	-	Aug 24 1893	Unknown	Narragansett Pier, R.I.
3529	Rattler	Sch.	82	1859	Jun 25 1905	Stranded	Todd Head, Nova Scotia.
3530	Raymond T. Maull	Sch.	-	-	Lost 1800's	Unknown	Off Race Point, Mass.
3531	Raymond T. McNally	Brg.	457	1906	Apr 10 1929	Foundered	Off Highlands, N.J.
3532	Raymonde	Ol.s.	87	1929	Jan 26 1966	Stranded	2 miles south of Race Point, off Provincetown, Mass.
3533	Reardon Bros.	Brg.	236	1917	May 19 1935	Burned	Hudson River, N.Y.
3534	Rebecca A. Toulane	Sch.	-	-	Apr 11 1894	Unknown	Bearses Shoal, R.I.
3535	Rebecca Bartlett	Sch.	-	-	May 20 1889	Unknown	Shovelful Shoal, Mass.
3536	Rebecca J. Moulton	Sch.	-	-	Feb 16 1890	Unknown	Pollock Rip, Mass.
3537	Rebecca R. Douglas	Sch.	360	-	Sep 17 1926	Collided	Pollock Rip Slue, Mass. Coal cargo.
3538	Rebecca R. Douglas	Sch.	475	1894	Apr 28 1943	Foundered	North Atlantic.
3539	Rebecca Shepherd	Sch.	411	1873	Dec 4 1907	Stranded	Pollock Rip Shoal, Mass.
3540	Rebecca W. Hudell	Sch.	-	-	Sep 1 1878	Unknown	West of Block Island, R.I.
3541	Rebecca W. Huddell	Sch.	256	1869	Apr 22 1909	Stranded	East Libbey Island, Me.
3542	Red Ash	St.s.	117	1888	Jul 7 1927	Burned	Staten Island, N.Y.
3543	Red Feather	Brg.	471	1917	Oct 19 1922	Collided	With st.s. CAPE COD. New London, Conn.
3544	Red Jacket	St.p.	424	1848	Apr 24 1868	Burned	Elizabethport, N.J.
3545	Red Jacket	Sch.	116	1860	Jan 6 1911	Stranded	Thumb Cap Island, Me.
3546	Red Lion	Brg.	455	1916	Aug 15 1919	Stranded	Man-O-War Rock, East River, N.Y.
3547	Red Rover	Sloop	-	-	Feb 20 1893	Unknown	North of Block Island, R.I.
3548	Red Rover	Sch.	-	-	May 16 1898	Unknown	Peaked Hill, Mass.
3549	Red-Skin	Ol.s.	104	1940	May 3 1949	Stranded	1 mile NW of Matinicus Island, off Rockland, Me.
3550	Red Star Coal Barge 38	Brg.	-	-	1952	Unknown	445 yds., 303° True from Stamford Harbor Front Range Light #1, Stamford Harbor, West Channel, Conn. Depth 15'. Lies N and S direction.
3551	Red Star Barge No.52	Brg.	-	-	1961	Unknown	1,525 yds., 049° from Old Field Point Light, L.I.S., Conn.
3552	Red Star Barge No.57	Brg.	637	1952	Jun 25 1966	Storm	Approx. 1,350 yds. from East Breakwater Lake, near harbor entrance, Bridgeport, Conn.
3553	Red Star T. & T. Co.28	Brg.	282	1908	Oct 25 1925	Stranded	High Hill Beach, N.Y.
3554	Red Wing	St.s.	98	1889	Dec 27 1926	Burned	Hays, Pa.
3555	Redstart	Ol.s.	99	1936	Aug 31 1954	Hurricane	30 miles SE of Nantucket Lightship, New Bedford, Mass.
3556	Redwood (Br.)	Brig	-	-	Lost 1800's	Unknown	North of Point Judith, R.I.
3557	Refuge	Ga.y.	53	1928	May 8 1933	Burned	Ellsworth, Me.
3558	Regina	Sch.	-	-	May 8 1898	Unknown	Off Block Island, R.I.

NO.	NAME OF VESSEL	RIG	TONS	BUILT	DATE			CAUSE	PLACE AND COMMENT
3559	Reichert Brothers	St.s.	85	1873	Sep	3	1930	Burned	New York, N.Y.
3560	Reigh Count	Frgt.	6,734	-	Jun	5	1942	War Loss	44-08-00 N. 63-16-00 W.
3561	Reindeer	St.p.	790	1850	Sep	3	1852	Exploded	Bristol Landing, Saugerties, Hudson River, N.Y. 37 lives lost.
3562	Reliable	Ol.s.	79	1917	Jul	5	1948	Burned	About 8 miles from Barnegat Lightship, N.J.
3563	Reliance	Bark	841	-	Feb	20	1893	Unknown	Southwest of Block Island, R.I.
3564	Reliance	Lighter	-	-	Aug	3	1933	Unknown	42-21-25 N. 70-42-00 W.
3565	Relief	St.s.	79	1873	Mar	21	1939	Burned	Kearny, N.J.
3566	Relief Lightship WAL	-	-	-			1961	Unknown	In vicinity of Ambrose Channel Lightship Station, off New York & New Jersey.
3567	Republic	Ga.s.	99	1915	Feb	15	1925	Collided	With unknown vessel. Cape Sable, Nova Scotia. 2 lives lost (19).
3568	Republic (Br.)	St.s.	15,379	1900	Jan	23	1909	Collided	With FLORIDA. 40-28-40 N. 69-38-40 W. 20 miles southwest of Nantucket South Shoals Lightship. Passenger vessel. Steel vessel. Length 570'. Beam 68'. 6 lives lost (1600). First use of "wireless" for summoning aid. The Republic was outbound for Naples. Vessel operated by White Star Lines. Vessel foundered while under tow of U.S. Coast Guard, making for shallow waters. Depth 185' to 225' and located north of wreck "Andria Doria". Reported to have carried over $2 million in gold, but this remains to be proved.
3569	Rescue	Ga.s.	60	1854	Oct	28	1919	Stranded	Diamond Point, Johnsons Bay, Lubec, Me.
3570	Resolute	St.w.	59	1914	Oct	20	1927	Foundered	Monongahela River, Pa.
3571	Restless	St.w.	475	1904	Mar	12	1939	Burned	Tottenville, Staten Island, N.Y.
3572	Restless	Ol.s.	-	-	Oct	4	1942	Unknown	42-30-00 N. 70-25-00 W. Fisherman.
3573	Rex	Brg.	519	1895	May	3	1911	Foundered	7 miles west of Point Judith, R.I.
3574	Rhode Island	Sch.	-	-	Dec	27	1800	Unknown	Off Brenton Reef, R.I.
3575	Riberia	Bark	-	-	Dec	2	1887	Unknown	East Sandwich, Mass.
3576	Ricameron	Sch.	1,072	1890	Mar	28	1922	Foundered	Middle Rip, South Shoals, Mass.
3577	Richard	Sloop	183	1893	Sep	20	1923	Burned	Merrymeeting Bay, Me.
3578	Richard	St.w.	247	1908	Dec	10	1940	Burned	Charleroi, Pa. Steel vessel.
3579	Richard Card	St.s.	182	1904	Oct	1	1944	Foundered	North side of pier, foot of 31st Street, Brooklyn, N.Y.
3580	Richard J. Nunan	Ol.s.	92	1904	Feb	5	1953	Stranded	43-09-00 N. 70-08-00 W.
3581	Richard Jackson	Brg.	230	1880	Mar	6	1913	Foundered	New York, N.Y.
3582	Richard K. Fox	Sch.	-	-	Dec	30	1886	Storm	Off West Chatham, Mass.
3583	Richard Law	Sch.	-	-	Jun	9	1891	Unknown	Monomoy Point, Mass.
3584	Richard Law	Sch.	-	-	Jul	14	1896	Unknown	Off Nauset Beach, Mass.
3585	Richard M. Johnson	Sch.	-	-	Jan	26	1887	Unknown	Plum Island, N.Y.
3586	Richard Morrell	Sch.	-	-	Oct	12	1888	Unknown	Coney Island, N.Y.
3587	Richard S. Leaming	Sch.	-	-	Feb	9	1899	Unknown	Orleans, Mass.
3588	Richard S. Leaming	Sch.	487	1918	Dec	18	1904	Unknown	Long Shoal, Nantucket, Mass.
3589	Richard T. Green	Sch.	1,467	1900	Jan	10	1917	Burned	Morgan, N.J.
3590	Richard Wainwright	Sch.	133	1900	Oct	10	1907	Stranded	Bay of St. George, Newfoundland. 1 life lost.
3591	Richardson	Sc.b.	694	1895	Oct	10	1925	Burned	Rockland, Me.
3592	Richmond	Ga.s.	107	1891	Aug	17	1932	Collided	With Norwegian st.s. GISLA. Delaware River. Steel vessel. 3 lives lost (7).
3593	Right Arm	St.s.	238	1891	Apr	22	1923	Stranded	Absecon Inlet, N.J.
3594	Ring Dove	Sch.	-	-	Nov	6	1890	Unknown	Off Chatham, Mass.
3595	Ringleader	Sch.	-	-	Dec		1801	Unknown	Hyannis Harbor Flats, Mass.
3596	Ringleader	St.s.	121	1889	Dec	21	1917	Burned	Alexandria Bay, N.Y.
3597	Rio Tercero (Argen.)	Frgt.	4,866	-	Jun	22	1942	War Loss	39-15-00 N. 72-30-00 W.
3598	Rio Tinto	Brg.	419	1911	Aug	9	1920	Foundered	South of Camden, N.J. Steel vessel. 1 life lost.
3599	Rising Star	Sch.	-	-	Feb	10	1888	Unknown	Rye Beach, N.H.
3600	Rising Sun	Sch.	80	1852	Apr	10	1906	Stranded	Drakes Island, Me.

NO.	NAME OF VESSEL	RIG	TONS	BUILT	DATE	CAUSE	PLACE AND COMMENT
3601	Rita Howard	Brg.	616	1914	Nov 3 1931	Stranded	Watch Hill, R.I.
3602	Rival	Sch.	-	-	Lost 1800's	Unknown	Off Race Point, Cape Cod, Mass.
3603	River Queen	St.p.	578	1864	Jul 8 1911	Burned	Washington, D.C.
3604	Riverside	Sch.	-	-	Jan 1888	Unknown	McGlathery Island, Me.
3605	Rob Hadfeld	C.bt.	103	1883	Aug 10 1911	Foundered	Mechanicsville, N.Y.
3606	Rob Roy	Ga.s.	111	1900	Aug 3 1918	Torpedoed	35 miles west of Seal Island, Nova Scotia.
3607	Rob Roy	Brg.	466	1907	Oct 5 1933	Foundered	Barnegat, N.J.
3608	Robejan	Ga.s.	61	1928	Jul 1966	Burned	Between White Rocks and the Maryland Yacht Club, Md.
3609	Robert	Brg.	396	1883	Jun 30 1914	Stranded	Faulkners Island, Conn.
3610	Robert B. Smith	Sch.	-	-	Lost 1800's	Unknown	Off Peaked Hill, Mass.
3611	Robert Byron	Sch.	-	-	May 3 1899	Unknown	Off Race Point, Cape Cod, Mass.
3612	Robert C. Bonham	Ol.s.	113	1925	May 31 1941	Burned	Foot of 6th Street, Jersey City, N.J.
3613	Robert C. McQuillen	Sch.	464	1891	Dec 19 1909	Foundered	Mystic, Conn. All lives (7) lost.
3614	Robert Egan	Brg.	233	1923	May 30 1945	Foundered	Oneida Lake, N.Y.
3615	Robert Fulton	St.p.	368	1835	Oct 23 1844	Foundered	Sturgeon Point, N.Y. 3 lives lost.
3616	Robert H. Colley	Tanker	11,651	-	Oct 4 1942	War Loss	North Atlantic. 59-06-00 N. 26-18-00 W. 26 lives lost (61). Convoy #HX-209.
3617	Robert Hedger	Brg.	523	1928	May 19 1950	Exploded	At South Amboy, N.J.
3618	Robert Jenkins	St.w.	95	1893	Nov 1 1924	Burned	Grays Landing, Monongahela River, Pa.
3619	Robert Lockhart	Tug	-	-	Jan 21 1890	Unknown	Napatree Point, R.I.
3620	Robert and Mary	C.bt.	105	1887	1919	Foundered	Rouses Point, N.Y.
3621	Robert Mowe	Sch.	-	-	Jun 24 1895	Unknown	Hyannis Harbor, Cape Cod, Mass.
3622	Robert and Richard	Sch.	140	1915	Jul 22 1918	Torpedoed	25 miles southeast of Cape Porpoise, Me.
3623	Robert Rodgers	St.s.	142	1881	Oct 11 1913	Burned	New York, N.Y.
3624	Robert T. Graham	Sch.	70	1835	Oct 14 1911	Exploded	Fire Island, N.Y.
3625	Robert W	Sch.	93	1847	Jan 12 1923	Stranded	York Beach, Me.
3626	Roberta Dee	Ol.s.	64	1941	Sep 26 1956	Stranded	Off Point Judith and Block Island, R.I.
3627	Robin Hood	St.s.	6,887	1919	Apr 15 1942	War Loss	North Atlantic. Steel vessel. Sunk by enemy action.
3628	Rochester	St.s.	6,836	1920	Jan 30 1942	War Loss	37-10-00 N. 73-58-00 W. Steel vessel. Sunk by enemy action.
3629	Rockville	Brg.	943	1922	Dec 27 1952	Stranded	Struck concrete pier while under tow in East River, in vicinity of 45th St., N.Y.
3630	Rocky Glen	Sch.	-	-	Jun 6 1895	Unknown	Shovelful Shoal, Mass.
3631	Roderick C. McNeil	Brg.	215	1903	Nov 19 1914	Foundered	Off Penfield Reef, Long Island, N.Y.
3632	Rodney Parker	Sch.	440	1874	Nov 7 1914	Stranded	Cranberry Islands, Me.
3633	Roger Bruny	Sch.	-	-	Nov 25 1802	Unknown	Monomoy Point, Mass.
3634	Roger C. Sullivan	St.s.	179	1918	Mar 5 1931	Stranded	Old Cock Ledge, Long Island, N.Y.
3635	Roger Drury	Sch.	360	1872	Jan 12 1918	Foundered	Biddeford Pool, Me.
3636	Rogers	Sch.	-	-	Apr 6 1893	Unknown	Handkerchief Shoal, Mass.
3637	Rolla	-	-	-	Dec 1820	Unknown	Off Eastham, Mass.
3638	Romance	St.s.	1,240	1898	Sep 9 1936	Stranded	42-23-43 N. 70-51-46 W. Steel vessel. Passenger vessel. Length 245'. 2-1/2 miles southeast of East Point, Nahant, Mass.
3639	Romo	Bark	-	-	Jul 28 1887	Unknown	On Nantucket South Shoal, Mass.
3640	Ronald & Dorothy	Ol.s.	-	-	Jan 18 1943	Unknown	41-31-05 N. 75-50-35 W. 350 yds., 302° True from Negro Lighted Bell Buoy #5.
3641	Ronald and Mary Jane	Ol.s.	141	1941	May 20 1953	Burned	20 miles off coast of Shelbourne, Nova Scotia.
3642	Roosevelt	St.s.	126	1906	Oct 7 1938	Burned	Edgewood Park, Alexandria Bay, N.Y.
3643	Rosa Mueller	Sch.	282	1882	Jul 29 1909	Burned	Brewer, Me.
3644	Rosalie	St.s.	299	1903	1921	Foundered	Hudson River, N.Y.
3645	Rose	Brg.	262	1892	Nov 1 1916	Foundered	Maurice River, N.J.
3646	Rose	Sc.b.	443	1917	Nov 11 1933	Foundered	Ludlam Beach Gas Buoy, N.J. 1 life lost (3).
3647	Rose	Brg.	467	1929	Nov 24 1958	Foundered	In the Hudson River at Coxsackie, N.Y.

NO.	NAME OF VESSEL	RIG	TONS	BUILT	DATE	CAUSE	PLACE AND COMMENT
3648	Rose Cabral	Sch.	-	-	Jan 25 1801	Unknown	Wood End, Cape Cod, Mass.
3649	Rose & Lucy	Ol.s.	70	1930	Jan 4 1964	Collided	With ol.s. ST. ANNA MARIA. About 18 miles northeast of Rockport, Mass.
3650	Rose Marie Feeney	Brg.	461	1905	Feb 14 1914	Foundered	Off Bartlett's Reef, Long Island Sound, N.Y.
3651	Rose Mary Mello	Ol.s.	56	1926	Aug 31 1954	Hurricane	In New Bedford Harbor, Fairhaven, Mass.
3652	Rose Standish	St.p.	309	1863	Jun 8 1900	Burned	Calais, Me.
3653	Rose Standish	St.p.	993	1912	Nov 28 1929	Burned	Boston, Mass.
3654	Rosetta McLoughlin	Brg.	199	1912	Sep 21 1938	Stranded	Gravesend Bay, N.Y.
3655	Roseway	Sch.	291	1907	Sep 11 1926	Stranded	Wolfville, Nova Scotia.
3656	Rover	Sch.	-	-	Oct 23 1889	Unknown	Chesapeake Bay.
3657	Rover	Sch.	-	-	Apr 21 1893	Unknown	Off Provincetown, Mass.
3658	Roxana	Yacht	-	-	Sep 10 1935	Unknown	42-20-39 N. 70-40-43 W.
3659	Royal Arcanum	Sch.	-	-	Jan 25 1888	Unknown	St. Croix Bay, Nova Scotia.
3660	Royal Arch	Sch.	422	-	Nov 29 1894	Unknown	41-34-52 N. 69-55-15 W. Monomoy, Cape Cod, Mass.
3661	Rudolph	St.s.	200	1898	Sep 25 1918	Collided	With USS ST. LOUIS. New York, N.Y.
3662	Ruggles	St.s.	104	1859	Jul 23 1901	Burned	Nyack, N.Y.
3663	Rush	Ga.s.	145	1918	Aug 26 1918	Torpedoed	44-30-00 N. 58-03-00 W.
3664	Rusland (Bel.)	-	-	-	Mar 17 1877	Collided	With remains of wreck. 200 yds. offshore from San Alfonso Retreat, Takanassee, N.J. Depth 28'.
3665	Russell 2	St.s.	77	1916	Oct 14 1949	Foundered	At Eaton's Neck, N.Y.
3666	Russell 10	St.s.	55	1903	Jun 21 1939	Foundered	Hell Gate, off East 90th Street, New York, N.Y.
3667	Russell 29	Brg.	721	1938	Nov 25 1956	Burned	Linden, N.J. Steel vessel.
3668	Ruth	Sch.	89	1881	Jan 13 1913	Stranded	New London Light, Conn.
3669	Ruth	Brg.	224	1916	Mar 21 1942	Stranded	Brooklyn, N.Y.
3670	Ruth Conway	Ol.s.	113	1909	Oct 30 1946	Collided	With tugs HUSTLER and 110. 1 mile east of railroad bridge, in Chesapeake & Delaware Causeway.
3671	Ruth Conway	Ol.s.	113	1909	Oct 7 1965	Foundered	About 1 mile west of Thimble Shoal Light in Chesapeake Bay.
3672	Ruth Darling	Sch.	-	-	Mar 27 1889	Collided	Five Fathom Bank, N.J.
3673	Ruth E. Merrill	Sch.	3,003	1904	Jan 12 1924	Foundered	Vineyard Sound, Mass.
3674	Ruth E. Pember	Ga.s.	94	1901	Dec 15 1917	Collided	With unknown vessel. Off Scotland Light, N.Y.
3675	Ruth and Margaret	Ol.s.	121	1915	Aug 15 1948	Foundered	In Middle Ground, Buzzards Bay, Mass.
3676	Ruth Mildred	Ol.s.	70	1922	Mar 16 1932	Burned	Off Chesapeake Lightship, Md.
3677	Ruth Robinson	Sch.	496	1874	Oct 1 1916	Stranded	West Cape, Prince Edward Island, Canada.
3678	Ruth Shaw	Brg.	485	1916	Nov 11 1939	Foundered	2 miles SE of Jones Inlet Buoy, Long Island, N.Y. 40-29-00 N. 73-45-00 W.
3679	Rutherford	Sch.	955	1901	Feb 20 1921	Stranded	Off Cape Cod, Mass.
3680	Ryan	St.s.	126	1890	Mar 14 1917	Foundered	Perth Amboy, N.J.
3681	Rye	Brg.	392	1907	Aug 31 1911	Foundered	Off Point Judith, R.I.
3682	Rye Cliff	St.p.	427	1898	Sep 28 1918	Burned	Sea Cliff, N.Y.
3683	S-21	Ol.s.	-	-	Unknown	"Sunk"	43-36-53 N. 69-59-24 W. Submarine. Sunk for experimental purposes. Depth 25 fathoms.
3684	S.A. Rudolph	Sch.	-	-	Sep 10 1889	Unknown	Delaware Breakwater.
3685	S.B. Franklin	Sch.	-	-	Oct 23 1891	Unknown	Gurnet Point, Plymouth, Mass.
3686	S.C. Noyes	Sch.	-	-	Feb 2 1884	Unknown	East of Block Island, R.I.
3687	S.E. Davis	Sch.	79	1867	Mar 16 1906	Stranded	Clark Island, Me.
3688	S.E. Graham	Ol.s.	1,591	1943	Aug 7 1958	Burned	In East Narragansett Bay, between Jamestown and Newport, R.I. Steel vessel.
3689	S.E. Vincent	Brg.	290	1902	Jan 2 1918	Foundered	Off Throggs Point, N.Y.
3690	S.F. Maker	Sch.	-	-	Nov 6 1803	Unknown	Ting Shoal, Nantucket, Mass.
3691	S.G. Wilbur	-	604*	Pre-WWII	Unknown	Unknown	38-14-18 N. 74-44-42 W. 18 miles offshore, Ocean City, Md. Depth 97'.
3692	S.H. Bassett	Brg.	205	1912	Mar 31 1933	Foundered	Lake Oneida, N.Y.
3693	S. Hale	Sch.	125	1864	Feb 11 1907	Foundered	Off Stratford, Conn.

NO.	NAME OF VESSEL	RIG	TONS	BUILT	DATE	CAUSE	PLACE AND COMMENT
3694	S. Hammond	Sch.	-	-	Oct 1 1889	Unknown	Near Portland, Me.
3695	S.J. Dailey, Jr.	C.bt.	154	1914	May 5 1935	Collided	With tug DEWEY. Off pier 6, East River, N.Y.
3696	S.K.F. James	Sch.	-	-	Mar 18 1890	Unknown	Farrel Island, Me.
3697	S.L. Clark	St.s.	125	1893	Jun 16 1928	Foundered	Mindenville, N.Y.
3698	S.M. Bird	Sch.	517	1874	Jan 10 1910	Stranded	Pollock Rip Slue, Mass.
3699	S.N. Hayens	Sch.	-	-	Aug 30 1887	Collided	New York Bay.
3700	S.P. Willard	Sch.	127	1892	Dec 28 1912	Stranded	Guyon Island, Nova Scotia.
3701	S.R. Lane	Sch.	72	1873	Apr 5 1907	Foundered	Mile End, Boston, Mass.
3702	S.S. Bicmove	Sch.	-	-	Oct 20 1890	Unknown	Off Hyannis, Mass.
3703	SS Chaparro	-	1,505	-	Oct 27 1918	War Loss	39-40-48 N. 73-55-00 W. 120°, 10 miles from Barnegat, N.J.
3704	S.S. Hudson	Sch.	429	1869	Aug 29 1907	Burned	SE of Little Hope, Nova Scotia.
3705	S.S. Seranbon	Sch.	-	-	Oct 5 1894	Unknown	1 mile southwest of Mishaum Point, entrance to Buzzards Bay, Mass.
3706	S.S. Silvia	Sch.	-	-	Jun 5 1887	Unknown	East of Block Island, R.I.
3707	S.S. Winneconne	-	1,869	-	Jun 2 1918	War Loss	39-26-00 N. 72-50-00 W. German Submarine Activities 1st World War.
3708	S.S. Wyckoff	St.s.	267	1864	Mar 13 1913	Collided	With st.s. HEROINE. New York Harbor, N.Y. 2 lives lost.
3709	S.T. Co. No.5	Brg.	95	1902	Nov 23 1924	Foundered	Off Belfast, Me.
3710	S. Thomas Browne	Tug	-	-	Jul 24 1892	Unknown	Off Watch Hill, R.I.
3711	S.W. Pring	Brg.	350	1889	Feb 15 1908	Foundered	Cornfield Point, Conn.
3712	Sabao	Sch.	-	-	Oct 13 1889	Unknown	Jones Inlet, Long Island, N.Y.
3713	Sabastiana C.	Ol.s.	-	-	Apr 20 1966	Unknown	42-36-45 N. 70-39-26 W. Fisherman.
3714	Sadie Scism	C.bt.	116	1901	Jun 5 1925	Foundered	Hudson River, N.Y.
3715	Sadie Willcut	Sch.	365	1874	Apr 30 1911	Collided	With sch. GEORGE D. EDMANDS. Off Cape Cod, Mass.
3716	Saetia	St.s.	2,873	1918	Nov 9 1918	Collided	With mine. 10 miles southeast of Fenwick Island, Md.
3717	Sagamore	Sch.	1,415	1891	May 12 1907	Collided	With Norwegian st.s. EDLA. Off West Chop Lighthouse, Marthas Vineyard, Mass.
3718	Sagamore	St.s.	130	1909	Jan 7 1919	Burned	Northport, N.Y.
3719	Sagamore	St.s.	2,592	1920	Jan 14 1934	Stranded	Prouts Neck, Me. Steel vessel.
3720	Sagamore	Ol.s.	87	1898	Jan 15 1937	Foundered	3 miles east of Brigantine Shoals, N.J.
3721	Sagua	Sch.	1,585	1901	Mar 1 1914	Foundered	20 miles SW of Montauk Point, Long Island, N.Y.
3722	Sagunta (Span.)	Frigate	-	-	1813	Unknown	Isles of Shoals, N.H. Reported to be carrying $2 million in gold.
3723	Sailor	Brg.	611	1905	Apr 14 1911	Foundered	Beavertail Light, R.I.
3724	Saint Ann	Ol.s.	58	1939	Jul 21 1959	Foundered	About 135 miles east and 1/2 mile south of Round Shoal Buoy, Nantucket Sound.
3725	St. Anthony	Ol.s.	115	1946	Jan 4 1958	Foundered	About 110 miles off Eastern Point Light, Gloucester, Mass.
3726	St. Anthony	Ol.s.	90	1945	Jan 12 1963	Burned	In Cape Cod Bay, Mass.
3727	St. Augustine (USS)	Ol.s.	147	1941	Unknown	War Loss	38-04-00 N. 74-06-00 W. Attacked by USS SOLAR.
3728	St. Bernadette	St.s.	-	-	May 8 1953	Foundered	About 8 miles southwest of Mt. Desert, Me.
3729	St. Bernard (Br.)	Sch.	-	-	Jul 8 1802	Unknown	Wood End, Cape Cod, Mass.
3730	St. Christopher	Ol.s.	139	1944	May 15 1946	Foundered	58 miles east by south from Eastern Point Light, Gloucester, Mass.
3731	St. Christopher	Ol.s.	146	1942	Aug 5 1949	Burned	30 miles SE of Monhegan Island, Me.
3732	St. Clair (Can.)	Ol.s.	-	-	Unknown	Unknown	Inner Mayo Ledge, Westport, Mass. Bearing 4,600 yds., 216° True from Two Mile Rock Spindle. Destroyer. Depth 65'.
3733	St. Croix	Sch.	234	1866	Aug 31 1920	Stranded	Vineyard Sound, Mass.
3734	St. Daniel	Brg.	467	1914	Dec 11 1916	Foundered	Off Brenton Reef Lightship, Long Island Sound, R.I.
3735	St. Elmo	Sch.	-	-	Mar 31 1898	Unknown	Rose and Crown, Nantucket, Mass.
3736	St. John	Brig	-	-	Oct 7 1849	Unknown	Minot's Ledge, Boston, Mass.
3737	St. Leon	Sch.	83	1871	Mar 15 1912	Stranded	Pigeon Hill Bay, Me.
3738	St. Louis	Brg.	599	1864	Feb 18 1914	Stranded	Cape Vincent, N.Y.
3739	St. Louis	St.s.	10,230	1895	Jan 8 1920	Burned	Hoboken, N.J. Steel vessel.
3740	St. Marys	St.p.	688	1872	Dec 5 1907	Burned	Benedict, Md. 1 life lost.

NO.	NAME OF VESSEL	RIG	TONS	BUILT	DATE		CAUSE	PLACE AND COMMENT
3741	St. Nicholas	Sch.	-	-	Feb 16	1898	Unknown	Monomoy Point, Mass.
3742	St. Nicholas	Ol.s.	165	1947	Aug 23	1963	Burned	About 80 miles SE of Georges Basin, Cape Cod, Mass.
3743	St. Paul	Ol.s.	71	1945	Nov 29	1945	Stranded	Dolivers Point, Gloucester, Mass.
3744	St. Rita	Ol.s.	52	1926	Jan 15	1955	Foundered	39-10-00 N. 72-06-00 W. 120 miles southeast of Ambrose Lightship.
3745	St. Rosalie	Ol.s.	56	1926	Aug 17	1943	Foundered	Monhegan Island, Me.
3746	St. Therese	Ol.s.	71	1944	Jul 1	1961	Collided	With log. Off Cape Porpoise, Me.
3747	St. Thomas	Sch.	742	-	Sep 13	1801	Unknown	Muskeget Shoal, Nantucket Sound, Mass.
3748	St. Victoria	Ol.s.	98	1945	Dec 9	1963	Burned	42-00-00 N. 67-55-00 W.
3749	Saitia	-	-	-	Pre-WWII		Unknown	38-14-18 N. 74-44-54 W. Depth 84'.
3750	Salem	Brg.	2,873	1900	Apr 3	1932	Foundered	Brigantine Gas Buoy, N.J. All lives (3) lost. 39-06-48 N. 74-32-54 W.
3751	Salisbury	Frgt.	703	-	Pre-WWII		Unknown	42-22-26 N. 70-51-35 W. Depth 130'.
3752	Sallie	Brg.	379	1905	Dec 16	1917	Foundered	South Norwalk, Conn.
3753	Sallie Ann	Sch.	58	1866	Nov 15	1909	Foundered	Black Hall Point, Conn.
3754	Sallie B.	Sch.	-	-	Oct 20	1895	Unknown	Off Monomoy Beach, Mass.
3755	Sallie B	Sch.	286	1861	Apr 10	1906	Foundered	Casco Bay, Me. 4 lives lost.
3756	Sallie C. Norton	Sch.	-	-	Oct 21	1888	Unknown	Off Cape May, N.J.
3757	Sallie E. Ludlam	Sch.	-	-	Mar 18	1802	Unknown	Handkerchief Shoal, Mass.
3758	Sallie E. Ludlam	Sch.	237	1873	Jun 17	1917	Collided	With s.s. COROZAL. New York Harbor, N.Y.
3759	Sallie I'on	Sch.	550	1884	Jun 30	1912	Burned	Portland, Me.
3760	Sallie T. Charter	Sch.	125	1892	Sep 29	1891	Collided	Faulkner Island, Long Island Sound.
3761	Sally Purnell Beswick	Sch.	107	1855	Jun 28	1919	Foundered	Sandypoint Light, Md.
3762	Sally W. Ponder	Sch.	70	1930	Oct 9	1916	Foundered	New Bedford, Mass.
3763	Salvatore	Ol.s.	71	1947	Apr 1	1949	Burned	65 miles SE by S of Cape May, N.J.
3764	Salvatore and Grace	Sch.	915	1917	Jul 24	1966	Foundered	About 5 miles SSE of Eastern Point Buoy, Gloucester, Mass.
3765	Sam C. Mengel	Brg.	594	1924	Jun 2	1918	Torpedoed	38-07-00 N. 73-46-00 W.
3766	Sam Demarest	Brg.	-	-	Jan 25	1959	Foundered	At New York Central Loading Dock at 63rd St. & Hudson River, N.Y.
3767	Sam Mengel	Ol.s.	99	1915	Oct 16	1935	Unknown	42-20-16 N. 70-41-00 W.
3768	Sam Weller	Sch.	1,082	1875	Dec 17	1954	Burned	At Arundel Yard, Fairfield, Md.
3769	Samar	Sch.	-	-	Mar 25	1909	Foundered	Highlands, N.J.
3770	Same H. Walker	Sch.	-	-	Dec 30	1884	Unknown	Off Chatham, Mass.
3771	Sammy Ford	Sch.	79	1880	Feb 14	1885	Unknown	Tuckernuck Flats, Nantucket, Mass. Coal cargo.
3772	Samuel C. Holmes	Sch.	-	-	Nov 15	1906	Stranded	Off Long Branch, N.J.
3773	Samuel C. Throp	Sch.	-	-	Jan 6	1890	Unknown	Southeast of Block Island, R.I.
3774	Samuel Casbner	Sch.	-	1857			Wrecked	On beach 1 mile north of Narragansett Pier, R.I. Coal cargo.
3775	Samuel Colpel	Brg.	-	-	Jan 25	1888	Unknown	Mud Island, Nova Scotia.
3776	Samuel H. Hartman	St.s.	245	1891	Jul 25	1923	Foundered	Delaware Bay.
3778	Samuel H. Sharp	Sch.	236	1862	Jan 25	1907	Stranded	Cape May, N.J.
3779	Samuel Hart	Sch.	210	1871	Nov 9	1922	Foundered	Casco Bay, Me.
3780	Samuel J. Goucher	Sch.	2,547	1904	Nov 12	1911	Stranded	Isle of Shoals, N.H.
3781	Samuel M. Denny	Ol.s.	122	1921	Nov 8	1938	Foundered	Near Old James Island, Pa.
3782	Samuel Marquand, Jr.	C.bt.	101	1882	May 17	1918	Foundered	Erie Basin, N.Y.
3783	Samuel W. Tilton	Sch.	937	-	Nov 27	1898	Unknown	Hull Beach, Nantasket, Mass.
3784	San Diego	Cruiser	-	-	Jul	1918	Collided	With mine. Fire Island, N.Y. 50 lives lost.
3785	San Francisco	St.p.	2,272	1853	Dec 24	1853	Foundered	At sea. 39-00-00 N. 59-00-00 W. 164 lives lost.
3786	San Francisco	Steamer	-	-	Jun 13	1898	Unknown	Peaked Hill Bar, Mass.
3787	San Gil (Pan.)	Frgt.	1,957*	-	Feb 4	1942	War Loss	38-06-06 N. 74-37-00 W. 26.5 miles offshore, Winter Quarter Beach, Md. Stands 25' high in 117' of water.
3788	San Jose (Span.)	Frigate	-	-		1752	Unknown	New London, Conn. Estimated value to be $250,000.

NO.	NAME OF VESSEL	RIG	TONS	BUILT	DATE		CAUSE	PLACE AND COMMENT
3789	San Jose	St.s.	3,358	1904	Jan 17	1942	Collided	With st.s. SANTA ELISA. 39-15-00 N. 74-04-00 W. Steel vessel. Depth 105'.
3790	San Joseph (Span.)	-	-	-	Nov 24	1752	Unknown	New London, Conn. See No.3788.
3791	San Saba	St.s.	2,458	1879	Oct 4	1918	Collided	With mine. 15 miles SE of Barnegat, N.J. Iron vessel. 30 lives lost (37).
3792	Sandalphin	Sch.	-	-	Jun 7	1881	Unknown	39-43-48 N. 73-56-39 W. Depth 80'. Cleared and demolished. Sugar Reef, R.I.
3793	Sandcraft	St.s.	2,054	1918	Jul 2	1950	Collided	With st.s. MELROSE. In narrows of New York Harbor, N.Y. Steel vessel. 1,325 yds., 268° True from spire, Visitation Convent. Depth 47'.
3794	Sandmate	Drg.	-	-		1951	Unknown	630 yds., 195° True from Newark Bay Light #9, Newark Bay, N.J. Depth 35'.
3795	Sandy Hook	St.s.	1,559	1880	Oct 28	1931	Burned	Jersey City, N.J. Iron vessel.
3796	Sandy Hook	St.s.	361	1902	Apr 27	1939	Collided	With st.s. OSLDJORD. 40-27-45 N. 73-49-30 W. 1/2 mile outside Ambrose Lightship. Steel vessel. Pilot boat.
3797	Sankaty	Ol.s.	-	-	Unknown		Unknown	49-55-18 N. 70-26-48 W. Fisherman. 2 miles E of Manomet Gong Buoy. Depth 118'.
3798	Sankaty	St.s.	677	1911	Jun 30	1924	Burned	New Bedford, Mass.
3799	Sansego	Ol.s.	133	1944	Feb 12	1964	Foundered	Off Southampton, N.Y.
3800	Santa Maria	Ol.s.	79	1931	Apr 18	1964	Burned	About 35 miles east of Chatham, Mass.
3801	Santa Rita	St.s.	-	-	Jul 9	1942	War Loss	North Atlantic. 26-11-00 N. 55-40-00 W. Sunk by enemy action.
3802	Santa Rosa	Sch.	695	1918	May 7	1928	Collided	With submerged derelict. 40-32-00 N. 64-10-00 W.
3803	Santiago	Sch.	1,917	1902	Dec 1	1904	Collided	With steamer PHILADELPHIA. Off Delaware Breakwater, Del.
3804	Santino	Sch.	2,491	1917	Feb 18	1923	Foundered	East of Nantucket Lightship, Mass.
3805	Santo Antonio	Ol.s.	79	1918	Sep 10	1955	Foundered	In Ipswich Bay, off Braces Cove, about 7 miles out of Gloucester, Mass.
3806	Sara A. Johnson	Brg.	412	1908	Apr 5	1923	Collided	With British st.s. SOUTHWAY. Near Statue of Liberty, New York Harbor.
3807	Sara Fort	-	-	-	Apr	1879	Wrecked	Off Peaked Hill Bar, Cape Cod, Mass.
3808	Sarah	Brg.	296	1889	Oct 12	1929	Collided	With GEORGE W. LOFT. Bay Ridge, N.Y.
3809	Sarah Ann Carpenter	Ol.s.	65	1883	Sep 23	1938	Foundered	Stonington Harbor, Conn.
3810	Sarah Babcock	Sch.	-	-	Apr 21	1883	Unknown	Fishers Island, N.Y.
3811	Sarah C. Smith	Sch.	-	-	Apr 7	1801	Unknown	Off Race Point, Cape Cod, Mass.
3812	Sarah C. Smith	Sch.	297	1868	Jul 8	1905	Collided	With steamer GOV. DINGLEY. Portland Head, Me.
3813	Sarah C. Wharf	Sch.	51	1871	Aug 11	1910	Stranded	Cape Cando, Nova Scotia.
3814	Sarah C. Whorf	Sch.	-	-	Lost 1800's		Unknown	Off Race Point, Cape Cod, Mass.
3815	Sarah Doe	Bark	-	-	Jan 17	1888	Unknown	Fisher's Island, N.Y.
3816	Sarah E. Lee	Sch.	-	-	Feb 7	1891	Unknown	Near Shelbourne, Nova Scotia.
3817	Sarah E. Thatcher	C.bt.	102	1902	Apr 15	1923	Foundered	North River, N.Y.
3818	Sarah Godfrey	Sch.	-	-	Lost 1800's		Unknown	Off Cahoons Hollow, Mass.
3819	Sarah Graham	Sch.	-	-	Apr	1870	Unknown	North of Beaver Tail, R.I.
3820	Sarah L.	Sch.	-	-	Jun 8	1868	Unknown	Near Point Judith Light, R.I.
3821	Sarah L. Davis	Sch.	180	1871	Mar 23	1918	Stranded	Rockport, Mass.
3822	Sarah L. Simmons	Sch.	252	1874	Sep 11	1889	Unknown	Pollock Rip, Mass.
3823	Sarah O. Fell	Sch.	-	-	Aug 3	1918	Stranded	Nantucket Island, Mass.
3824	Sarah Potter	Sch.	-	-	Aug 28	1894	Unknown	Pollock Rip, Mass.
3825	Sarah Potter	Sch.	359	-	Mar 19	1803	Unknown	Handkerchief Shoal, Mass.
3826	Sarah Quinn	Sch.	-	-	Oct 3	1889	Collided	Hart's Island, N.Y.
3827	Sarah Quinn	Sch.	-	-	Jan 1	1885	Unknown	Fishers Island, N.Y.
3828	Sarah W. Blake	Sch.	-	-	Jan 1	1882	Collided	West of Point Judith, R.I.
3829	Sarah W. Lawrence	Sch.	1,369	1886	Feb 14	1909	Stranded	Cape Henlopen, Del.
3830	Saratoga	Brg.	292	1920	Nov 14	1935	Foundered	3 miles below Bowers, Del. Steel vessel.
3831	Sardinian	Sch.	124	1859	Apr 18	1907	Stranded	Metinic Island, Me.
3832	Sasanoa	Sch.	-	-		1888	Unknown	Near Hull, Mass.
3833	Satellite	St.s.	381	1894	Nov 20	1915	Burned	New York Harbor, N.Y.

NO.	NAME OF VESSEL	RIG	TONS	BUILT	DATE		CAUSE	PLACE AND COMMENT
3834	Satellite	St.s.	381	1894	Jul 22	1924	Foundered	Percy Beach Light, Catskill, N.Y.
3835	Savannah	Brg.	944	1914	Feb 18	1948	Foundered	Off Mannasquan, N.J.
3836	Saxon	Ol.s.	78	1885	May 7	1928	Foundered	Nantucket, Mass.
3837	Say When	St.y.	87	1888	Dec 21	1917	Burned	Alexandria Bay, N.Y.
3838	Sceptre	Sch.	125	1901	Oct 21	1907	Stranded	Scatary Island, Nova Scotia.
3839	Schoodic	Ol.s.	84	1907	Feb 22	1947	Burned	Drum Point, Patuxent River, Md.
3840	School Girl	Sch.	-	-	Nov 27	1898	Unknown	Off Provincetown, Mass.
3841	Scott Brothers	Brg.	140	1888	Sep 11	1911	Foundered	Bridgeport, Conn.
3842	Scranton	Brg.	588	1889	Dec 16	1910	Foundered	Off Chatham, Mass.
3843	Scully	Sch.	1,542	1878	Mar 30	1919	Foundered	Entrance to Inner Harbor, Delaware Breakwater.
3844	Sea Bird	St.p.	489	1866	May 9	1932	Burned	152nd Street and East River, N.Y.
3845	Sea Bird	Sch.	-	-	Jul 30	1898	Unknown	Nauset Beach, Mass.
3846	Sea Gannet	St.y.	124	1904	Aug 3	1910	Burned	Tuckers Light, N.J.
3847	Sea Hag	Ol.s.	81	1918	Jul 29	1949	Foundered	39-47-05 N. 73-50-05 W. 4 miles off Barnegat Lightship, N.J.
3848	Sea King	Ol.s.	64	1926	Mar 1	1956	Foundered	About 115 miles south of Montauk Point Light, Long Island, N.Y.
3849	Sea King	Ol.s.	78	1917	Aug	1959	Foundered	In the Shrewsbury River off Highlands, N.J. Depth 14'.
3850	Sea King	Ol.s.			Mar	1963	Wrecked	100 yds. south of the south jetty at Barnegat Inlet, N.J. Fisherman. Length 110'. Salvage has failed.
3851	Sea Lion	Sch.	-	-	Lost 1800's		Unknown	North of Orleans, Mass.
3852	Sea Port	Brg.	523	-	Nov 14	1957	Lost	In vicinity of Sandy Hook, N.J.
3853	Sea Prince	Brg.	564	-	Mar 31	1958	Collided	With MARGARET McALLISTER. About 3-1/2 miles SE of Scotland Lightship, entrance to New York, N.Y. harbor.
3854	Sea Queen	Ol.s.	76	1947	Feb 8	1966	Burned	At pier 73, East River, New York, N.Y.
3855	Sea Saw IV	Ol.s.	63	1963	May 12	1964	Burned	About 5 miles north of Shark Island Light in Chesapeake Bay.
3856	Sea Serpent	Sloop	-	-	Dec 16	1896	Unknown	Block Island, R.I.
3857	Seabird	Sch.	-	-	Jun 4	1891	Unknown	Off Libbey Island, Me.
3858	Seaboard	Tug	-	-	Oct 28	1965	Unknown	41-22-17 N. 70-09-14 W. About 9,800 yds., 253° from Nantucket Light. Length 58'.
3859	Seaconnet	St.s.	188	1880	May 29	1905	Stranded	Shinnecock Beach, N.Y.
3860	Seaconnet	St.s.	3,372	1918	Apr 29	1923	Foundered	41-22-10 N. 70-59-00 W. South of Vineyard Sound Light, Mass. Freighter. Length 318'. Steel vessel. 7 lives lost.
3861	Seagull	Sch.	-	-	Feb 16	1891	Collided	Grassy Bay, N.J.
3862	Seahorse	Ga.y.	69	1921	Sep 27	1929	Burned	Sag Harbor, N.Y.
3863	Seaquester	Ol.s.	63	1950	Jun	1966	Unknown	On Lake Champlain, Vermont.
3864	Searsport	Brg.	1,159	-	Nov 12	1911	Foundered	1 mile south of Fire Island, N.Y. Steel vessel. All lives (5) lost.
3865	Searsport	Sc.b.	1,321	1919	Feb 4	1926	Foundered	Barnegat Gas Buoy, N.J. 1 life lost (4).
3866	Searsville	Sch.	-	-	Oct 17	1871	Unknown	Pollock Rip, Mass.
3867	Sebago	Sch.	307	1883	Mar 17	1906	Stranded	Beaver Harbor, New Brunswick.
3868	Secausus	St.s.	919	1873	Nov 3	1935	Burned	In ferry slip, foot of Bay Ridge Ave., Brooklyn, N.Y.
3869	Security	Brg.	402	1904	Dec 16	1919	Foundered	Chesapeake Bay.
3870	Sedona	Sch.	-	-	Mar 31	1888	Unknown	Libbey Island, Me.
3871	Seer	Ol.s.	60	1938	Oct 24	1946	Stranded	Cape May, N.J.
3872	Seiner	St.s.	346	1922	Jan 13	1929	Foundered	41-05-00 N. 67-10-00 W. All lives (21) lost.
3873	Seminole	Ol.s.	278	1897	Apr 12	1947	Collided	With ELISHA LEE. 1-1/4 miles NE of Thimble Shoal Light, Chesapeake Bay.
3874	Senator	Sch.	110	1893	Jan 31	1922	Foundered	Off Dipper Harbor, New Brunswick.
3875	Senator Gardner	Sch.	129	1900	Jun 6	1915	Exploded	180 miles NW of St. Pierre, Newfoundland.
3876	Senator Penrose	St.s.	63	1875	Dec 21	1926	Collided	With unknown barge. Governors Island, N.Y. Iron vessel.
3877	Seneca	St.p.	313	1849	Jun 30	1872	Burned	New York, N.Y. Used as ferryboat.
3878	Seneca	St.s.	2,963	1894	Jan 9	1928	Burned	New York, N.Y.

NO.	NAME OF VESSEL	RIG	TONS	BUILT	DATE	CAUSE	PLACE AND COMMENT
3879	Seneca	Sc.b.	2,208	1884	Feb 18 1928	Collided	With st.s. SIBONEY. Sandy Hook, N.J. Iron vessel.
3880	Senora	Sch.	54	1865	Sep 5 1924	Foundered	Choptank River, Md.
3881	Sereena	Ga.y.	51	1912	Aug 30 1936	Burned	Fresh Kills, Staten Island, N.Y.
3882	Serena S. Kendall	Sch.	136	1876	Oct 1 1912	Foundered	Off Cape Cod, Mass. All lives (4) lost.
3883	Service	St.s.	406	1870	Mar 25 1924	Burned	Northport, N.Y.
3884	Seth H. Linthicum	Brg.	1,026	1921	Jun 19 1935	Stranded	4 miles SE of Barnegat Light, N.J.
3885	Seth M. Todd	Sch.	-	-	Mar 26 1803	Unknown	Monomoy Point, Mass.
3886	Seth M. Todd	Sch.	194	1875	Sep 14 1920	Stranded	Parrsboro River, Nova Scotia.
3887	Seven-Eight-Nine	Brg.	541	-	Dec 11 1915	Collided	Off Sakonnet, R.I.
3888	Seven-Eight-Six	Sch.	500	-	Mar 14 1926	Foundered	Off Plymouth, Mass.
3889	Seven-Oh-Two	Sch.	934	-	Jul 2 1932	Unknown	41-46-48 N. 70-29-30 W. Scusset Breakwater, Cape Cod Canal, Mass.
3890	Shadow	Sch.	-	-	Mar 12 1891	Unknown	Orleans, Mass.
3891	Shamokin	Brg.	-	-	Jun 26 1894	Unknown	Pollock Rip, Mass.
3892	Shamokin	Sc.b.	829	1904	May 11 1925	Foundered	Scotland Lightship, N.Y.
3893	Shamrock	Sch.	-	-	Aug 23 1800	Unknown	Off Block Island, R.I.
3894	Shamrock	-	-	-	Jul 9 1842	Exploded	St. Lawrence River. 68 lives lost.
3895	Shannon	Ol.s.	95	1930	Dec 15 1954	Foundered	45 miles ESE of Cape May, N.J.
3896	Shanunga	Ship	546	-	Feb 12 1852	Unknown	Tom Nevers Head, Nantucket Island, Mass.
3897	Sharpshooter	Ga.s.	57	1867	May 7 1928	Collided	With st.s. LACKAWANNA. Vineyard Sound, Mass.
3898	Sharpshooter	Brg.	525	1917	May 19 1950	Burned	At South Amboy, N.J.
3899	Shawmont	Sch.	954	1900	Aug 17 1909	Foundered	Off Shinnecock, N.Y. All lives (5) lost.
3900	Shawmut	Bkn.	468	1866	Dec 1 1908	Stranded	Yellowhead Island, Machias Bay, Me.
3901	Shawmut	Brg.	250	1889	Nov 1 1909	Collided	With st.s. AMERICA. Buffalo Harbor, N.Y.
3902	Sheila	Ol.y.	161	1930	Aug 24 1932	Burned	Squantum, Mass.
3903	Shenandoah	Sch.	841	1890	Oct 29 1909	Collided	With st.s. POWHATAN. 41-31-45 N. 69-57-38 W. Nantucket Sound, Mass. 1 life lost.
3904	Shenandoah	Ga.s.	110	1890	Aug 27 1912	Collided	With sch. ADDIE M. LAWRENCE. Near Nantucket Island, Mass.
3905	Shenandoah	Sch.	3,406	1890	Oct 20 1915	Foundered	Off Fire Island, N.Y.
3906	Shepherd King	Sch.	121	1905	Jul 12 1907	Collided	With Russian st.s. SARATOV. Nantucket Island, Mass.
3907	Shepherd Knapp	St.p.	186	1845	1856	Burned	New York, N.Y.
3908	Sherry and Scott	Ol.s.	68	1954	Apr 26 1955	Stranded	About 2 miles SE of Sable River, Nova Scotia.
3909	Sherwood	Brg.	1,281	1919	Jan 21 1947	Stranded	Wilkes Ledge, Buzzards Bay, Mass.
3910	Shetucket	St.s.	183	1844	May 7 1870	Stranded	Cape May, N.J.
3911	Shippan	St.p.	553	1866	May 7 1870	Burned	Stamford, Conn.
3912	Shrub	-	-	1912	Aug 6 1931	Unknown	On Bridges Reef, York Harbor, Me. Total loss. Lighthouse tender. Length 100'.
3913	Siesta	Ol.s.	132	1919	Unknown	Unknown	Off Long Beach, N.Y.
3914	Silas Might	Sch.	-	-	Lost 1800's	Unknown	Narragansett Pier, R.I.
3915	Silas T. Webster	Ga.s.	63	1925	May 14 1949	Foundered	1/2 mile SE of Eastpoint Light, 500 to 800 yards off Thompsons Beach, N.J.
3916	Silex	St.s.	143	1892	Dec 13 1918	Ice	1-1/2 miles north of Essex, Conn.
3917	Silvanus	St.s.	2,202	1919	Nov 28 1921	Foundered	Shrewsbury Rock Gas Buoy, N.J.
3918	Silver Dart	Sch.	-	-	Sep 13 1896	Unknown	Off Highland Light, Mass.
3919	Silver Heels	Sch.	134	1872	Jan 5 1911	Stranded	Shovelful Shoals, Cape Cod, Mass.
3920	Silver Ray	Tanker	2,626*	-	Feb 2 1942	War Loss	43-54-00 N. 64-16-00 W.
3921	Silver Spray	Sch.	-	-	Jan 21 1801	Unknown	Monomoy Beach, Mass.
3922	Silver Spray	Sch.	-	-	Apr 3 1899	Unknown	Monomoy Point, Mass.
3923	Silver Spray	Sch.	124	1872	Sep 1 1912	Stranded	Monomoy, Mass.
3924	Silver Spray	Sch.	194	1873	Apr 13 1916	Foundered	20 miles south of Portland, Me.
3925	Silvia Slide	Sch.	-	-	May 24 1882	Unknown	Off Point Judith, R.I.
3926	Simon Flake	Sch.	-	-	Oct 17 1800	Unknown	Monomoy Point, Mass.

NO.	NAME OF VESSEL	RIG	TONS	BUILT	DATE		CAUSE	PLACE AND COMMENT
3927	Sinbad	Sch.	-	-	Dec 5	1888	Unknown	Muscle Ridge Channel, Me.
3928	Sinbad V	Ga.y.	50	1915	May 22	1928	Burned	Little Sheepscot River, Me.
3929	Singleton Palmer	Sch.	2,859	1904	Nov 6	1921	Collided	With st.s. APACHE. Off Delaware coast. 1 life lost.
3930	Sinker	Bark	-	-	Nov 21	1890	Unknown	Mizzen Bank, Nova Scotia.
3931	Sintram	Sch.	2,259	1920	Nov 19	1921	Collided	With st.s. DAVID McKELVY. North of Highland Light, Truro, Mass.
3932	Sir Sidney Smith	-	-	-	Dec 21	1812	Unknown	On Bass Rip, off Siaconset, Nantucket Island, Mass. No survivors. Depth 48'.
3933	Skippack	Sch.	739	1913	May 3	1924	Collided	With st.s. J.E. O'NEIL. Delaware Bay.
3934	Smith	Sch.	200	-	Summer	1892	Unknown	Beaver Tail, R.I.
3935	Smuggler	Sch.	-	-	Dec 30	1895	Storm	Off Cahoons Hollow, Mass.
3936	Snipe	St.s.	411	1919	Jun 21	1923	Stranded	Seal Island, Nova Scotia. Steel vessel.
3937	Snow Maiden	Sch.	-	-	Jan 24	1956	Unknown	41-59-00 N. 70-37-12 W. Brown's Bank, Plymouth, Mass.
3938	Snow Daisy	Sch.	-	-	Jan 10	1883	Unknown	Off Block Island, R.I.
3939	Snug Harbor	St.s.	2,388	1917	Aug 15	1920	Collided	With sch. POTTSVILLE. Point Light Buoy, Long Island, N.Y. Steel vessel.
3940	Sobbay	Sch.	-	-	Dec 6	1709	Unknown	Near Boston Neck, Mass.
3941	Sodonia Curley	Sch.	79	1892	Aug 27	1919	Foundered	Wolf Trap, Chesapeake Bay.
3942	Sol	Ol.s.	77	1925	Jul 24	1951	Foundered	20 miles S of Cashe's Banks Buoy, off Maine coast.
3943	Solus	Sch.	839	1899	Jun 20	1915	Collided	With st.p. CITY OF TAUNTON. Off Brenton Reef Lightship, R.I.
3944	Solverg J.	Ol.s.	-	-	May 7	1969	Unknown	41-30-45 N. 68-11-12 W. Cultivator Shoals, Mass. Fisherman. Depth 148'.
3945	Somerset (Br.)	Frigate	-	-	Nov	1778	Unknown	Near Highland Light, close to Dead Man's Hollow, Mass.
3946	Somerset	Sch.	629	1905	Feb 10	1918	Foundered	Off Ambrose Light, N.Y.
3947	Sonja Maersk	Frgt.	1,909	-	Jun 5	1942	War Loss	44-29-00 N. 63-32-00 W.
3948	Soo City	St.s.	670	1888	Dec 2	1908	Foundered	Gulf of St. Lawrence. All lives (19) lost.
3949	Soolo	Sch.	963	-	Nov 16	1892	Unknown	3,500 yds. northeast of Pollock Rip Slue Lightship, Mass.
3950	Sophie Kranz	Sch.	622	-	Jan 31	1886	Unknown	West end of Peaked Hill Bars, Provincetown, Mass.
3951	South Sea	Ol.s.	75	1917	Jun 30	1959	Stranded	On sand bar off Tuckernuck Island, Mass. 41-17-00 N. 70-15-30 W.
3952	South Shore	St.p.	874	1906	Oct 31	1926	Foundered	Port Newark, N.J. Steel vessel.
3953	Southern Sword	Brg.	2,180	1918	Mar 18	1946	Foundered	Fenwick's Island, Md. Steel vessel.
3954	Southland	Ga.s.	72	1907	May 18	1922	Burned	Verplanks, N.Y.
3955	Southland	Frgt.	-	-	Dec 2	1930	Unknown	42-16-35 N. 70-36-26 W. Depth 148'.
3956	Southland	St.s.	1,521	1917	May 25	1933	Burned	Massachusetts Bay, Mass. See No.3955.
3957	Sparkling Wave	Sch.	-	1879	May 15	1879	Storm	Shovelful Shoal, Mass.
3958	Spartan	St.s.	1,596	1883	Mar 19	1905	Stranded	Block Island, R.I. Iron vessel.
3959	Spartel	Sch.	132	1868	Jan 23	1919	Foundered	Sailed from Kittery, Me. & has not since reported. All lives (5) lost.
3960	Spentonbush No.1	Ol.s.	87	1903	Jun 13	1931	Burned	Carteret, N.J.
3961	Spitfire	St.p.	221	1846	Oct 12	1849	Burned	New York, N.Y.
3962	Splendid	St.p.	209	1832	Apr 11	1855	Stranded	Cold Spring, N.Y.
3963	Spring	Sc.b.	1,780	1904	Mar 6	1932	Foundered	Cape May, N.J. All lives (4) lost.
3964	Squanto	Ol.s.	133	1901	Nov 30	1931	Stranded	Sandy Point, St. George, Nova Scotia.
3965	Squantum	St.s.	248	1888	Jan 16	1924	Foundered	Brooklyn, N.Y. Steel vessel.
3966	Stamford	St.p.	284	1863	Sep 16	1900	Stranded	Cohasset Rocks, Mass. Renamed "John Endicott" on July 14, 1900.
3967	Standard Oil Co. #58	Sch.	-	-	Feb 22	1899	Unknown	Off Race Point, Cape Cod, Mass.
3968	Star	Brg.	89	-	Sep 12	1905	Foundered	New York, N.Y.
3969	Star of the Sea	Ol.s.	63	1946	Aug 14	1958	Burned	Off Cape Cod, Mass. 42-02-00 N. 69-04-00 W.
3970	Star of the Sea	Ol.s.	85	1943	Feb 3	1960	Burned	About 22 miles southwest of Block Island, R.I.
3971	Starble	Sloop	-	-	Mar 10	1804	Unknown	Wood End, Cape Cod, Mass.
3972	Starlight	St.s.	437	1864	Oct 5	1866	Stranded	Barnegat, N.J.
3973	Starlight	St.s.	335	1890	Nov 23	1914	Burned	Rock Creek, Md.
3974	Starr King	Bark	367	-	Nov 12	1875	Unknown	White Horse Rock, Manomet, Plymouth, Mass. 41-56-12 N. 70-33-24 W.

NO.	NAME OF VESSEL	RIG	TONS	BUILT	DATE	CAUSE	PLACE AND COMMENT
3975	Starry Flag	Sch.	-	-	Lost 1800's	Unknown	Off Peaked Hill, Mass.
3976	State of Virginia (Br)	-	-	-	Jul 15 1879	Stranded	Sable Island, Nova Scotia. 9 lives lost.
3977	Staten Island	St.s.	-	-	Jul 30 1871	Exploded	New York, N.Y. Ferryboat. 100 lives lost.
3978	Steel City	St.w.	297	1926	Jun 5 1941	Foundered	Monongahela River, at Penn. Railroad Panhandle Bridge, Pittsburgh, Pa. Steel.
3979	Steel Queen	St.w.	177	1901	Oct 16 1926	Burned	Pittsburgh, Pa.
3980	Stella Lee	Sch.	-	-	Jun 25 1890	Collided	Thatchers Island, Mass.
3981	Stella M. Kenyon	Sch.	-	-	Dec 12 1890	Unknown	Jamaica Bay, Long Island, N.Y.
3982	Stella Moren	St.p.	215	1890	Mar 7 1908	Stranded	Lock No.2, Pa. 3 lives lost.
3983	Stephen G. Hart	Bkn.	605	1879	Jan 28 1911	Stranded	Sow & Pigs Reef, Cuttyhunk Island, Vineyard Sound, Mass.
3984	Stephen R. Jones	St.s.	4,387	1915	Jun 28 1921	Stranded	Cape Cod Canal, Mass. 41-62-00 N. 70-33-00 W. Steel vessel.
3985	Stephen Raymond	Sch.	-	-	Nov 1893	Unknown	Hyannis Harbor, Cape Cod, Mass.
3986	Sterling	Sch.	2,364	1884	Jan 9 1912	Foundered	Off Block Island, R.I.
3987	Stetson and Ellison	Sch.	56	1872	1906	Foundered	Delaware Bay.
3988	Stiletto	Ol.s.	136	1910	Apr 3 1930	Stranded	Forth River, N.J.
3989	Stolt Dagali (Nor.)	Tanker	19,150	-	Nov 22 1964	Collided	22 miles to sea from Manasquan Inlet, N.J. Depth 150'. 13 lives lost.
3990	Stonington	Sch.	1,072	1866	Mar 24 1911	Foundered	Pollock Rip, Cape Cod, Mass. 2 lives lost.
3991	Storm King	Sch.	-	-	May 9 1800	Unknown	Off Block Island, R.I.
3992	Storm King	Sc.b.	1,262	1870	Nov 16 1892	Unknown	41-34-40 N. 69-55-30 W. 5,000 yards north of Pollock Rip Lightship, Mass.
3993	Storm Petrel	Sch.	174	1870	Dec 6 1930	Foundered	Off Watch Hill, R.I. All lives (6) lost.
3994	Stormy Weather	Ol.s.	58	1925	Jan 18 1950	Foundered	East Beach, Quonochontaug, R.I.
3995	Strafford	Sc.b.	678	1895	Nov 17 1924	Foundered	Monhegan, Me.
3996	Stray	Sch.	-	-	Sep 8 1869	Unknown	Narragansett Pier, R.I.
3997	Strickland	Sch.	50	-	Spring 1873	Unknown	Brentons Reef, R.I.
3998	Stroudsburg	Sch.	693	1896	Apr 14 1923	Foundered	Northeast of Browns Shoal, Del. 4 lives lost.
3999	Stuartline	St.s.	78	1879	Mar 22 1932	Burned	Arthur Kills, Staten Island, N.Y.
4000	Sturdy	Ga.y.	52	1905	Aug 4 1915	Stranded	Off Fort McHenry, Md.
4001	Sub Chaser #60	-	-	-	1918	Unknown	40-25-40 N. 73-51-09 W. 2 miles north of Shewsbury Rocks, N.J. 1.4 miles offshore.
4002	Sudi Junior	Yacht	-	-	Oct 1 1959	Unknown	125 yds., 180° from Cape May East Jetty Light #22, Cape May Harbor, N.J. Depth 22'. Lies E to W.
4003	Suffolk	Sc.b.	855	1894	Jan 4 1926	Stranded	Montauk Whistling Buoy, N.Y.
4004	Suffolk	St.s.	4,607	1911	Dec 11 1943	Foundered	40-43-00 N. 71-58-00 W. or 40-52-48 N. 71-13-12 W. Steel vessel. Freighter.
4005	Sultan	Sch.	-	-	Dec 11 1890	Unknown	Whitehead, Nova Scotia.
4006	Sumner R. Mead	Sloop	1,035	1873	Oct 13 1913	Stranded	300 yards north of Cahoons Hollow L.S. Station, Wellfleet, Mass.
4007	Sun	St.p.	278	1825	Sep 1 1928	Burned	Sandy Hook, N.J.
4008	Sunbeam	Sch.	-	-	Nov 26 1888	Unknown	Quoddy Head, Mass.
4009	Sunbeam	Sch.	-	-	Dec 1 1890	Unknown	Whitehead, Nova Scotia.
4010	Sunbury	Sch.	1,544	1899	Aug 17 1910	Foundered	Fenwick Island Light, Del.
4011	Sunny & Joy	Ol.s.	-	-	Unknown	Foundered	East of Indian Hill, Plymouth, Mass. Fisherman.
4012	Sunny Side	St.p.	742	1866	Dec 1 1875	Ice	West Park, N.Y. 11 lives lost.
4013	Sunrise	Ship	-	-	Apr 6 1889	Unknown	Delaware Breakwater.
4014	Sunshine	Sch.	-	-	Aug 9 1891	Unknown	Off Watch Hill Point, R.I.
4015	Superior	Ol.s.	107	1932	Nov 10 1953	Foundered	Off Dwyer's Ledge, Gloucester, Mass.
4016	Supply 3	Ol.s.	66	1921	Jan 30 1920	Foundered	Brooklyn, N.Y. All lives (3) lost.
4017	Surge	St.s.	302	1916	Jun 23 1927	Collided	With st.s. OZARK. Peaked Hill Bar, Mass. Steel vessel. 3 lives lost (22).
4018	Susan	Sch.	-	-	Mar 6 1890	Unknown	Field Point, Long Island, N.Y.
4019	Susan and Mary	Sch.	124	1905	Nov 1 1911	Stranded	Point Allerton, Mass. 42-18-55 N. 70-51-36 W. Fisherman.
4020	Susan R. Stone	Sch.	-	-	May 5 1890	Unknown	Off Race Point, Cape Cod, Mass.
4021	Susan Snow	Ol.s.	53	1949	Mar 26 1966	Foundered	3 miles SSE of Manasquan Inlet, N.J.

NO.	NAME OF VESSEL	RIG	TONS	BUILT	DATE	CAUSE	PLACE AND COMMENT
4022	Susan Stetson	Sch.	140	1867	Nov 5 1907	Foundered	50 miles SE of Biddeford Pool, Me.
4023	Susan Stone	Sch.	-	-	Lost 1800's	Unknown	Orleans, Mass.
4024	Susie E.	Sch.	-	-	Aug 1 1890	Unknown	Seal Ledge, Nova Scotia.
4025	Susquehanna	St.p.	-	1826	May 9 1826	Exploded	Nescopeck, Pa. 3 lives lost.
4026	Susquehanna	Brg.	314	1850	Apr 22 1907	Foundered	Off Cornfield Point, Conn. All lives(1) lost.
4027	Susquehanna	Brg.	290	1874	Jul 4 1918	Burned	Mystic River, Conn.
4028	Swallow	Sch.	-	-	Oct 17 1800	Unknown	Off Point Judith, R.I.
4029	Swallow	St.p.	426	1837	Apr 7 1845	Stranded	Athens, N.Y. 15 lives lost.
4030	Swan	St.p.	306	1862	Mar 10 1869	Collided	With FANITA. Above Salem, N.J.
4031	Swawa	Sloop	-	-	Lost 1800's	Unknown	Napatree Point, R.I.
4032	Sweepstakes	Sch.	-	-	Mar 11 1802	Unknown	Shovelful Shoal, Mass.
4033	Swiftscout	St.s.	8,300	1921	Apr 18 1945	War Loss	37-30-00 N. 72-45-00 W. Sunk by enemy action.
4034	Swordfish	Brig	-	-	Dec 1864	Unknown	Toddy Rocks, Mass.
4035	Sylvan Dell	St.p.	440	1872	Jul 16 1919	Burned	Salem Creek, Salem, N.J.
4036	Sylvania	Sch.	136	1910	Aug 21 1918	War Loss	90 miles SE of Canso, Nova Scotia. Sunk by German Raider TRIUMPH.
4037	Sylvester Mahan	C.bt.	110	1880	Aug 15 1909	Foundered	Jones Inlet, N.J.
4038	Sylvia (Br.)	St.s.	1,708	-	Mar 14 1908	Unknown	41-23-58 N. 70-57-55 W. East side of Sow & Pigs Reef, Cuttyhunk Island, Mass. Steel vessel. Passenger carrier.
4039	Sylvia M. Nunan	Sch.	56	1893	Feb 27 1911	Collided	With sch. GRAYLING. Thatcher's Island, Mass.
4040	Sylvister Whealen	Sch.	-	-	Nov 22 1898	Unknown	Off Race Point, Cape Cod, Mass.
4041	T.B. Garland	Sch.	-	-	Aug 20 1893	Unknown	Bearses Shoal, Mass.
4042	T.B. Harris	Sch.	-	-	Oct 7 1890	Abandoned	Near Portland, Me.
4043	T.B. Witherspoon	Sch.	364	-	Jan 13 1886	Unknown	South side of Nantucket Island, Mass. Cocoa cargo.
4044	T. Charlton Henry	Sch.	2,421	1902	Jun 23 1907	Collided	With British st.s. CHELSTON. Fire Island, N.Y.
4045	T.J. Hooper	Sc.b.	722	1908	Jan 9 1926	Foundered	Highlands, N.J. All lives (3) lost.
4046	T.J. Hooper	Sc.b.	2,197	1918	Jan 23 1935	Foundered	38-26-06 N. 74-23-42 W. 31 miles offshore, near Fenwick Island Shoal, Del. Stands 38' high in 135' of water.
4047	T.M. Nicholson	Sch.	128	1904	Jan 1 1924	Foundered	Bay of Islands, Gulf of St. Lawrence. all lives (8) lost.
4048	T. Morris Perot	Sch.	308	1875	Sep 28 1913	Foundered	After collision with st.s. SHAWMUT. Off Fenwick Island, Md.
4049	T. Remick	Brig	367	-	Mar 5 1889	Unknown	300 yards north of North Scituate L.S. Station, Mass.
4050	T.W. Allan	Sch.	113	1870	Nov 19 1919	Foundered	Sailed from New Bedford, Mass. & has not since reported. All lives (26) lost.
4051	T.W. Cooper	Sch.	158	1889	Jul 17 1914	Stranded	Off Point Judith, R.I.
4052	T.W.O. Co. No.28	Brg.	312	1917	Mar 1 1930	Burned	Staten Island, N.Y.
4053	T.W. Spencer	Sch.	71	1874	Jan 15 1920	Stranded	Off South Norwalk, Conn.
4054	Tabor	Sch.	963	1912	Feb 27 1920	Collided	With st.s. DOVER. 1 mile east of Tarpaulin Cove Lighthouse, Naushon Island, Vineyard Sound, Mass.
4055	Taborfjell (Nor.)	Frght.	1,339*	-	Apr 30 1942	Unknown	42-20-00 N. 69-10-00 W. Depth over 600'.
4056	Talbot	Brg.	2,229	1921	Oct 28 1938	Burned	Delaware Breakwater.
4057	Talisman	Ol.s.	74	1917	1965	Foundered	At 1-1/2 miles SSW of Gooseberry Island, Mass.
4058	Tamaulipas	St.s.	6,943	1919	Apr 9 1942	War Loss	North Atlantic. Steel vessel.
4059	Tarantula	Ga.y.	159	1913	Oct 24 1918	Collided	With Dutch st.s. FRISIA. Between New York and Halifax, Nova Scotia. Steel vessel.
4060	Tariff	Brig	-	-	Mar 26 1840	Unknown	Cohasset Rocks, Cohasset, Mass.
4061	Taro	St.y.	87	1890	Sep 20 1922	Foundered	Off Noyes Beach, R.I.
4062	Tartar	Ga.s.	126	1904	Aug 1 1915	Stranded	Barnegat, N.J.
4063	Taunton	Sch.	318	1893	Apr 28 1923	Foundered	Off Point Judith, R.I.
4064	Taylor	Brg.	525	1920	Aug 12 1941	Foundered	1/2 mile SW by W from Brenton Reef Lightship, R.I. 41-25 N. 71-23 W.
4065	Teaser	St.s.	216	1899	May 29 1914	Foundered	Off Atlantic City, N.J.
4066	Teazer	Ol.s.	97	1905	Mar 25 1948	Foundered	In Cabot Straight, 14 miles NW of St. Pauls Island, Gulf of St. Lawrence.

NO.	NAME OF VESSEL	RIG	TONS	BUILT	DATE		CAUSE	PLACE AND COMMENT
4067	Tedesco	Bark	-	-	Jan 19	1857	Unknown	Swampscott, Mass.
4068	Teka	Brg.	389	1917	Jan 13	1942	Collided	With ol.s. CALATCO NO.2. New York, N.Y.
4069	Telegraph	St.p.	127	1847	Jun 28	1870	Collided	With DANIEL DREW. Rhinebeck, N.Y.
4070	Telumah	Sch.	230	1866	Sep 30	1922	Stranded	St. John, New Brunswick.
4071	Tempest	St.p.	80	1849	Oct 1	1866	Burned	New York, N.Y.
4072	Temple	Sc.b.	963	1912	Feb 4	1947	Collided	With st.s. WAGON BOX. At Red Hook Flats, N.Y.
4073	Tena A. Cotton	Sch.	377	1883	Feb 4	1907	Stranded	Ocean City, Md.
4074	Tennessee	Brg.	-	-		1950	Wrecked	41-23-48 N. 71-00-42 W. Vineyard Sound, Mass. Demolished.
4075	Teresa D. Baker	Sch.	87	1867	May 2	1911	Foundered	Granite Point, Mass.
4076	Terranova	Sch.	138	1906	Mar 16	1914	Stranded	Pamet River, Cape Cod, Mass.
4077	Teutonic	Scow	253	1892	Oct 8	1907	Foundered	Greenwich, Conn. 1 life lost.
4078	Texas	Sch.	1,627	-	Apr 6	1905	Unknown	41-06-45 N. 71-35-40 W. 4 miles SSW of New Shoreham L.S. Station, R.I.
4079	Texel	Frgt.	3,210	-	Jun 2	1918	War Loss	38-58-00 N. 73-13-00 W. German Submarine Activities 1st World War.
4080	Thames	St.s.	560	1883	Apr 24	1930	Burned	Captains Island, Conn. 16 lives lost (26).
4081	Thaxter	Sch.	843	1899	Mar 15	1912	Foundered	12 miles SE of Shinnecock, N.Y. All lives (4) lost.
4082	The Bang	Ga.s.	79	1917	Jan 26	1924	Burned	Clason Point, East River, N.Y.
4083	The Boston Floating Hospital	St.s.	672	1906	Jun 1	1927	Burned	Boston, Mass. Steel vessel.
4084	The Bruce	Ship	-	1891	Feb 11	1891	Unknown	Bayonne, N.J.
4085	The Leader	St.p.	131	1913	Sep 27	1910	Burned	Economy, Pa.
4086	The Ima	Ol.s.	52	1938	Apr 10	1936	Foundered	25 miles off New York Lightship, N.Y.
4087	Thelma Ann	Ol.s.	70	1938	Unknown		Lost	Above Lock 8, at mile 91 in the Monongahela River, off Point Marion, Pa.
4088	Theodora Palmer	Sc.b.	1,042	1900	Dec 9	1927	Foundered	Brigatine Gas Buoy, N.J.
4089	Theodore	Brg.	126	1882	Jul 30	1916	Burned	Jersey City, N.J.
4090	Theodore Birely	Steamer	-	-	Jan 18	1887	Unknown	Taunton, Mass.
4091	Theodore Roosevelt	Sch.	125	1901	Oct 31	1913	Stranded	Centerville, Nova Scotia.
4092	Theresa A.	Ol.s.	138	1944	Sep 12	1950	Foundered	About 100 miles east by north of Nantucket Lightship.
4093	Theresa and Dan	Ol.s.	60	1931	Dec 11	1942	Stranded	Highland Light Station, Mass.
4094	Theresa Wolf	Sch.	307	1874	Oct 16	1909	Foundered	15 miles SW of Seguin, Me.
4095	Theresa Wolf	Sch.	307	1874	Aug 11	1911	Stranded	41-40-18 N. 69-55-30 W. 1-1/2 miles south of Old Harbor L.S. Station, Mass.
4096	Theta (Br.)	Sch.	-	-	Jun 15	1801	Unknown	Peaked Hill, Mass.
4097	Thetis	St.y.	118	1901	Jul 10	1925	Burned	Mattapoisett, Mass.
4098	Thetis	St.s.	79	1920	Nov 11	1924	Stranded	New Rochelle, N.Y.
4099	Thirley (Br.)	St.s.	4,888	-	Jan 23	1942	War Loss	43-19-00 N. 66-20-00 W.
4100	Thistle	Sch.	-	-	Oct 20	1890	Unknown	Canso, Nova Scotia.
4101	Thomas B. Reed	Sloop	-	-	Nov 27	1898	Unknown	Off Provincetown, Mass.
4102	Thomas B. Wattson	St.s.	134	1868	Feb 2	1928	Foundered	Greenville, N.J.
4103	Thomas Bonndage	Sch.	-	-	May 8	1899	Unknown	Shovelful Shoal, Mass.
4104	Thomas Borden	Sch.	-	-	Apr 10	1802	Burned	In Hyannis Harbor, Cape Cod, Mass.
4105	Thomas Brumidge	Sch.	-	-	Apr 5	1898	Unknown	Off Race Point, Mass.
4106	Thomas Brundage	Sch.	72	1895	Nov 12	1915	Stranded	Monomoy Point Light, Mass.
4107	Thomas Bulger	Brg.	265	1900	Feb 11	1925	Collided	With B. & O. Railroad bridge. Bayonne, N.J.
4108	Thomas E. Hulse	St.p.	314	1851	Mar 30	1875	Ice	New York, N.Y.
4109	Thomas Edison Mulqueen	Brg.	432	1914	Jan 3	1917	Foundered	Off Point Judith, R.I.
4110	Thomas H. O'Leary	Brig	940	1910	Dec 4	1940	Stranded	1 mile east of Green Hills, R.I.
4111	Thomas Hale	Brg.	207	1896	Feb 5	1917	Foundered	Brooklyn, N.Y.
4112	Thomas Hix	Sch.	99	1847	Apr 7	1913	Stranded	Southwest Harbor, Me.
4113	Thomas Holden (Br.)	Sch.	-	-	Oct 19	1899	Unknown	Cahoons Hollow, Mass.

NO.	NAME OF VESSEL	RIG	TONS	BUILT	DATE		CAUSE	PLACE AND COMMENT
4114	Thomas J. Cunningham	Brg.	279	1927	Jun 18	1945	Collided	With o.l.s. GLORIA O. Near Schenectady, N.Y.
4115	Thomas J. Horan	Brg.	306	1909	Jul 25	1916	Foundered	Off Plum Island, N.Y.
4116	Thomas J. Lanigan	Brg.	333	1926	Jan 1	1963	Foundered	In Hudson River, off Hoboken, N.J.
4117	Thomas J. Owen	Sch.	68	1863	Feb 8	1906	Burned	Sayreville, N.J.
4118	Thomas J. Yorke	Steamer	-	-	Jan 27	1887	Unknown	Delaware River.
4119	Thomas R. Phillsbury	Sch.	-	-	Jan 13	1883	Unknown	Off Point Judith, R.I.
4120	Thomas R. Woolley	Sch.	104	1872	Nov 28	1921	Stranded	Montauk Point, Long Island, N.Y.
4121	Thomas Sheridan, Jr.	Brg.	343	1919	Apr 22	1948	Burned	At Cilco Terminal Co. wharf, Bridgeport Harbor, Conn.
4122	Thomas Tomlinson	Brg.	422	1918	Aug 3	1942	Foundered	Execution Rocks Light Station, Long Island Sound, N.Y. Depth 87'.
4123	Thomas Tracy	St.s.	2,443	1916	Sep 14	1944	Stranded	Rehoboth Beach, Del. Reported also as 7,143 Gross Tons.
4124	Thomas Tracy	St.s.	176	1919	Nov 16	1926	Foundered	Atlantic City, N.J.
4125	Thomas W.H. White	Sch.	213	1867	Dec 20	1919	Foundered	Sailed from Vineyard Haven, Mass. & has not since reported. All lives (5) lost.
4126	Thomas W. Hyde	Sch.	-	-	Jul 15	1893	Unknown	Shovelful Shoal, Mass.
4127	Thomaston	Sc.b.	693	1895	Apr 25	1925	Collided	With st.s. LONDON EXCHANGE. Delaware River. 1 life lost (4).
4128	Thor	Bark	-	-	Jul 29	1888	Unknown	Musquidobout River, Nova Scotia.
4129	Thrasher	Sch.	-	-	Lost 1800's		Unknown	Handkerchief Shoal, Mass.
4130	Three Rivers	St.s.	1,110	1910	Jul 4	1924	Burned	Cove Point, Md. Steel vessel. 10 lives lost (134).
4131	Three Sisters	Sch.	302	1872	Aug 7	1908	Stranded	Bakers Island, Me.
4132	Three Sisters	Brg.	535	1920	Dec 1	1924	Foundered	College Point, N.Y.
4133	Thunderbolt	St.p.	244	1851	Mar 26	1855	Burned	Chester, Pa.
4134	Thurmond	St.s.	1,252	1890	Dec 26	1909	Stranded	Seaside Park, N.J.
4135	Ticeline	St.s.	99	1896	Nov 22	1920	Collided	With st.s. CORRECTION. New York, N.Y.
4136	Ticker	Sch.	-	-	Apr	1873	Unknown	Short Beaver Tail, R.I.
4137	Ticonderoga	-	-	-	Sep 30	1918	Torpedoed	Off Atlantic coast. 213 lives lost.
4138	Ticonic	St.p.	99	1832	Oct	1836	Stranded	Hallowell, Me.
4139	Tide	St.w.	79	1900	Nov 1	1924	Burned	Grays Landing, Monongahela River, Pa.
4140	Tilbury (Br.)	Frigate	-	-	Jun 11	1757	Unknown	4 miles off Cape Brenton, Nova Scotia. Depth 68'. Reported to be valued at over $500,000.
4141	Tillie	Brg.	202	1880	Sep 22	1917	Foundered	Off Wolfe Trap Light, Chesapeake Bay.
4142	Tillie E.	Sch.	-	-	Aug 6	1881	Unknown	Off Point Judith, R.I.
4143	Timrod	Yacht	-	-	Jul 18	1958	Unknown	42-19-45 N. 70-00-11 W. About 1,450 yds., 13° from stack on Thompson Island, Boston Harbor, Mass. Depth 23'.
4144	Tip Top	Brg.	410	1906	Oct 11	1931	Foundered	Edgewater, N.J.
4145	Tipperary	Scow	305	1918	Oct 28	1934	Stranded	Off Faulkners Island, Conn.
4146	Titania	St.s.	73	1875	Aug 11	1908	Collided	With British st.s. KINGSTON. Charlotte, N.Y. Iron vessel.
4147	Tivoli	St.p.	704	1894	Nov 26	1915	Burned	Off Kent Island, Md. Steel vessel. 5 lives lost.
4148	Tivoli	Brg.	-	-	Nov 2	1895	Unknown	Pollock Rip, Mass.
4149	Tohickon	Sc.b.	739	1913	Dec 12	1932	Stranded	Buzzards Bay, Mass.
4150	Tolchester	St.p.	1,098	1878	May 15	1941	Burned	At pier 16, Light Street, Baltimore, Md. Iron vessel.
4151	Tolten (Chil.)	St.s.	1,014*	1886	Mar 14	1942	Unknown	39-54-12 N. 73-48-18 W. 12.6 miles off beach. Freighter. Depth 90'.
4152	Tom Beattie	Sch.	140	1886	Nov 16	1925	Stranded	Dipper Harbor, New Brunswick.
4153	Tonkawe II	Ga.y.	68	1928	Aug 8	1932	Burned	Hampton Bays, Long Island, N.Y.
4154	Top Sergeant	St.s.	155	1892	Feb 3	1946	Foundered	East River, off East 85th Street, N.Y. Steel vessel.
4155	Topa Topa	St.s.	5,356	1920	Aug 28	1942	War Loss	North Atlantic. Steel vessel. Sunk by enemy action.
4156	Toronto	Brig	433	1903	Nov 25	1886	Unknown	200 yards NE of Watch Hill L.S. Station, R.I.
4157	Trader	Scow	291	1903	Jul 8	1908	Foundered	Strawberry Island, Niagara River, N.Y.
4158	Traffic	St.s.	203	1892	Apr 30	1925	Burned	City Island, N.Y.
4159	Transco No.4	Ga.s.	53	1923	Aug 24	1928	Burned	Rexford, N.Y.

NO.	NAME OF VESSEL	RIG	TONS	BUILT	DATE	CAUSE	PLACE AND COMMENT
4160	Transmarine No.113	Brg.	197	1921	Jun 9 1937	Foundered	In State Canal, near Athens Light, N.Y. Steel vessel.
4161	Transmarine No.115	Brg.	197	1921	Nov 29 1935	Foundered	Collided with B. & A. Bridge, Albany, N.Y. Steel vessel.
4162	Transmarine No.126	Brg.	218	1922	Dec 27 1932	Foundered	Off Tarrytown Light, N.Y. Steel vessel.
4163	Transport	St.s.	162	1900	Mar 22 1933	Foundered	Brooklyn, N.Y.
4164	Traveler	Sch.	172	1869	Aug 12 1907	Stranded	East Reef, Long Island Sound.
4165	Tremont	Brig	-	-	Oct 7 1844	Unknown	Off Point Allerton, Hull, Mass.
4166	Trenton	Sch.	-	-	Dec 3 1890	Unknown	Woods Hole, Mass.
4167	Trenton	St.p.	688	1902	Jan 30 1926	Foundered	Trenton, N.J.
4168	Trevorton	Sch.	1,763	1901	Jan 10 1911	Stranded	Peaked Hill Bar, Cape Cod, Mass. 42-05-06 N. 70-10-00 W. All lives (7) lost.
4169	Trimount	Ol.s.	124	1908	May 7 1931	Collided	With st.s. NEW YORK, Long Island Sound, N.Y. 3 lives lost (7).
4170	Triton	Sloop	-	-	Jul 8 1802	Unknown	Nauset Beach, Mass.
4171	Trojan	St.p.	280	1842	Aug 9 1851	Burned	New York, N.Y. 4 lives lost.
4172	Trojan	Sch.	-	-	Dec 5 1891	Unknown	Near Cranberry Isles, Me.
4173	Trojan	St.s.	2,632	1888	Jan 21 1906	Collided	With st.s. NACOOCHEE. 41-22-33 N. 71-00-24 W. Vineyard Haven, Mass. Iron vessel. Length 260'. Passenger carrier.
4174	Truro	Brg.	1,631	1917	May 26 1934	Foundered	North Barnegat Lightship, N.J. 2 lives lost (5).
4175	Truxton	-	-	-	1943	Unknown	46-45-00 N. 55-29-00 W. US Navy vessel.
4176	Tryall	Sch.	-	-	Lost 1800's	Unknown	Off Point Judith, R.I.
4177	Tuckahoe	Brg.	466	1913	Apr 1949	Foundered	In Chesapeake Bay, Md., near Smith's Point.
4178	Tuna Lady	Ol.s.	52	1927	Nov 14 1956	Burned	Bridgers Boast Basin, Sandspoint Harbor, Waretown, N.J.
4179	Tunkhannock	Sch.	843	1891	Oct 18 1914	Foundered	Off Barnegat, N.J.
4180	Tunnel Ridge	Sch.	911	1898	Apr 3 1915	Stranded	1 mile north of Highland Light, Cape Cod, Mass.
4181	Tuscarora	St.s.	2,386	1890	Dec 6 1917	Foundered	Sailed from Montreal, Canada and has not since reported. All lives (30) lost.
4182	Twilight	Sch.	-	-	Aug 31 1890	Unknown	Advocate Harbor, Nova Scotia.
4183	Twilight	Sch.	59	1858	Oct 12 1907	Foundered	Sailed from West Side, New Brunswick & has not since reported. All (4) lives lost.
4184	Twilight	St.p.	466	1868	Oct 24 1923	Burned	Camden, N.J. Iron vessel.
4185	Two Brothers	Sch.	-	-	Mar 3 1891	Unknown	Yarmouth, Nova Scotia.
4186	Two Brothers	Sch.	-	-	Apr 20 1897	Unknown	Nantucket Bar, Mass.
4187	Two Brothers	St.p.	71	1884	Jan 12 1908	Foundered	Lock No.4, Ohio River, Pa.
4188	Two Brothers	St.s.	139	1881	Apr 20 1928	Burned	Rockaway Point, Long Island, N.Y.
4189	Two Forty	Sch.	-	-	May 10 1801	Unknown	Off Race Point, Mass.
4190	Tyr (Nor.)	St.s.	4,625	-	Mar 9 1942	War Loss	43-40-00 N. 71-10-00 W.
4191	U-853 (Ger.)	Ol.s.	-	-	May 5 1945	"Sunk"	Submarine - Steel vessel. Double hull construction. Length 231'. Depth 125'. 7 miles east of Sand Point, Block Island, R.I. Attempted salvage in 1967. Submarine contains an estimated $500,000 quantity of mercury.
4192	U.S. 103	Brg.	306	1919	Nov 25 1923	Foundered	Troy, N.Y. Concrete vessel.
4193	U.S. 110	Brg.	294	1919	Mar 7 1924	Foundered	Brooklyn, N.Y. Concrete vessel.
4194	U.S. 117	Brg.	303	1919	Aug 14 1922	Foundered	Troy, N.Y. Concrete vessel.
4195	U.S. 244	Brg.	294	1919	Aug 17 1929	Stranded	Erie Canal, N.Y.
4196	U.S.L. No.1	Brg.	302	-	Mar 30 1931	Burned	Kingston, N.Y.
4197	U.S.L. No.2	Brg.	301	-	Mar 30 1931	Burned	Kingston, N.Y.
4198	U.S. Navy Patrol	Ol.s.	280	-	1950	Burned	41-28-13.5 N. 71-01-41.5 W. On Hen & Chickens Reef, Mass. Steel vessel. Used as bombing target. Bow section salvaged. Remains demolished.
4199	U.S. Navy Torpedo Retriever Boat	Ol.s.	-	-	1957	Unknown	41-07 N. 71-41 W. Southwest Ledge, R.I. Length 63'.
4200	U.S.S. Bass	Ol.s.	2,506	-	Jul 24 1945	Unknown	41-01-09 N. 71-32-50 W. Steel vessel. Length 341'. Depth 120'. 7-1/2 miles south of Block Island Southeast Light, R.I.

NO.	NAME OF VESSEL	RIG	TONS	BUILT	DATE	CAUSE	PLACE AND COMMENT
4201	U.S.S. Jacob Jones	-	-	-	Feb 28 1942	Unknown	Bow section: 38-39-12 N. 74-28-42 W. 10' high in 102'. Stern section: 38-37-00 N. 74-23-12 W. 28' high in 117' of water. 28 miles offshore from Indian River Inlet, Del.
4202	U.S.S. St. Augustine	-	-	-	Unknown	Exploded	38-04-00 N. 74-06-00 W. Attacked by S.S.S. SOLAR.
4203	U.S.S. San Diego	-	13,680	-	Jul 19 1918	War Loss	Off Long Island Sound. Battle cruiser. Length 503'. Beam 69'. Depth 120'.
4204	U.S.S. Triana	St.s.	306	-	Mar 15 1891	Unknown	41-25-11 N. 70-55-02 W. 1/4 mile WSW of Cuttyhunk Island, Mass. Iron vessel.
4205	U.S.S. YMS 14	Ol.s.	207	-	Jan 11 1945	Unknown	42-22-06 N. 70-54-53 W. 4,040 yds., 275.5° True from Graves Light, Broad Sound, Boston, Mass. Mine Sweeper. Steel vessel. Length 136'.
4206	U.S.S. YSD	Derrick	-	-	Dec 1957	Unknown	41-16-24 N. 70-49-08 W. U.S. Navy vessel. Steel vessel. Length 132'. Between Old Man Rock and No Mans Land Island, Mass.
4207	U.S.S. Yankee	Cruiser	6,225	-	Sep 23 1908	Unknown	41-32-30 N. 70-52-40 W. 3/4 mile south by east 3/4 east of Phinney Rock, Buzzards Bay, Mass. Iron vessel. Length 391'.
4208	Ulrica	Sch.	-	-	Dec 16 1896	Unknown	Off Nantasket Beach, Hull, Mass.
4209	Ulysses	-	-	-	1802	Unknown	Off Provincetown, Mass.
4210	Ulysses	St.p.	239	1864	Jan 10 1878	Stranded	Rockland, Me.
4211	Umberto Primo	Bark	-	-	Mar 13 1891	Unknown	Romer Shoal, N.Y.
4212	Umpire	Sch.	-	-	Jun 4 1890	Unknown	Bunker Island, Nova Scotia.
4213	Uncle Abe	St.s.	94	1864	Nov 12 1911	Burned	Wilson Point, Conn.
4214	Uncle John	Ol.s.	76	1918	Nov 12 1947	Foundered	1 to 2 miles east-southeast of No.7 Buoy, entrance to New Bedford, Mass.
4215	Uncle Paul	Brg.	67	1900	Sep 5 1908	Foundered	41-31-50 N. 70-51-45 W. Fisherman.
4216	Uncle Sam	St.s.	57	1862	May 22 1866	Stranded	Fox Island, N.Y.
4217	Uncle Sam	Ol.s.	81	1917	Jul 24 1938	Stranded	Old Man Ledge, Me.
4218	Undaunted	Sch.	1,768	-	Dec 26 1913	Foundered	Brace's Cove, Eastern Point, Gloucester, Mass.
4219	Undercliff	Ga.s.	50	1948	1943	Foundered	Off Forked River, N.J.
4220	Union	-	-	-	Feb 20 1810	Unknown	In Curtiss Bay, at Smith's Boat Yard, Baltimore, Md.
4221	Union	St.p.	296	1844	Dec 15 1878	Burned	Off Baker's Island, Mass. Cargo of metal.
4222	Union	St.p.	546	1862	Jul 17 1929	Burned	New York, N.Y.
4223	Union	Brg.	495	1862	Nov 30 1927	Foundered	Port Richmond, N.Y. Used as ferryboat.
4224	Union Star	St.p.	163	1861	Oct 16 1862	Burned	Chesapeake and Delaware Canal, Md.
4225	Unique	Sch.	-	-	Jul 9 1890	Unknown	New York, N.Y. Was originally schooner and converted to steam in 1862.
4226	Unique (Can.)	Sch.	-	-	Jul 10 1917	Collided	Bald Tusket, Nova Scotia.
4227	United States	Brg.	426	1916	May 7 1937	Foundered	With submerged wreck. 41-24-13 N. 70-13-00. On east end of Tuckernuck Shoal, Nantucket Sound, Mass. Coal cargo.
4228	United Workman	C.bt.	101	1891	Nov 14 1912	Burned	In Kill Von Kull, near Bayonne, N.J.
4229	Universe	Brg.	420	1915	Apr 2 1926	Foundered	Near Rochester, N.Y.
4230	Uranus	Steamer	-	-	May 10 1887	Unknown	New York, N.Y.
4231	Valchem	El.s.	10,416	1942	Mar 26 1959	Collided	Off Rehoboth, Del.
4232	Vale Riyal	Brg.	944	1914	Aug 24 1942	Stranded	With SANTA ROSA. 20 miles east of Atlantic City, N.J. Steel vessel.
4233	Valiant	Ol.s.	93	1963	Jun 6 1967	Collided	At Cape Cod Canal, Sandwich, Mass. 41-46-48 N. 70-29-30 W.
4234	Valkyore	Sloop	-	-	Nov 10 1897	Unknown	With unknown object. 80 miles east of Nantucket Island, Mass.
4235	Valkyrie	Yach	-	-	1950	Unknown	Off Block Island, R.I.
4236	Valparaiso	Brg.	-	-	Unknown	Unknown	Located 3/4 mile from the end of breakwater, 100 feet to starboard of east side of channel inbound, Gloucester Harbor, Gloucester, Mass.
4237	Valvoline No.6	Brg.	160	-	Jul 7 1942	Stranded	South of Manaquan Inlet, 3 miles offshore, Point Pleasant, N.J. Depth 65'.
4238	Vamoose	Sch.	-	-	Dec 5 1898	Unknown	Off Barren Island, Brooklyn, N.Y.
4239	Van	Frgt.	-	-	May 16 1935	Unknown	Northeast of Block Island, R.I. 41-12-44 N. 71-33-00 W. 42-26-24 N. 70-40-16 W. Demolished.
4240	Van Gilder (Fr.)	Sch.	251	-	Mar 29 1885	Unknown	41-24-13 N. 70-13-00 W. Stone cargo.

NO.	NAME OF VESSEL	RIG	TONS	BUILT	DATE	CAUSE	PLACE AND COMMENT
4241	Vandalia	Sch.	-	-	Nov 20 1892	Unknown	Off Watch Hill, R.I.
4242	Varanger (Nor.)	Tanker	5,505	-	Jan 25 1942	War Loss	39-00-30 N. 74-05-00 W. Wildwood, N.J. Steel vessel, 39 feet high in 126' of water. Also spelled "Varranger" and listed as 9,305 Gross Tons.
4243	Varuna	Sch.	52	1929	Jun 21 1930	Collided	With ol.y. SHADOW K. Rye Beach, N.Y.
4244	Vasco Da Gama	Ol.s.	88	1928	Aug 6 1931	Burned	Brown's Bank, Mass.
4245	Vega	Ol.s.	84	1946	Jan 11 1961	Foundered	About 3 miles, 009° off the Shark River Breakwater, N.J. Steel vessel.
4246	Ventura	Sch.	118	1930	May 28 1888	Unknown	Near Calais, Me.
4247	Venture II	Ol.s.	118	1930	Oct 1 1949	Foundered	8 miles due east of Highland Light, off Massachusetts coast.
4248	Venus	Sch.	-	-	Aug 1877	Unknown	West of Point Judith, R.I.
4249	Venus	Sch.	-	-	Nov 27 1899	Storm	At Plymouth, Mass.
4250	Veritas	Sch.	-	-	Dec 2 1891	Unknown	Yankee Jack Shoal, Nova Scotia.
4251	Vermilion	Sch.	1,208	1919	Sep 14 1920	Collided	With unknown obstruction. Near Montauk Point Light, N.Y.
4252	Vermillion	Brg.	1,208	-	1923	Unknown	8 miles west by south of Dickens Point, Block Island, R.I.
4253	Vermont	Brg.	270	1873	Nov 18 1911	Foundered	Plum Island, N.Y. 2 lives lost.
4254	Verona	St.s.	149	1902	Nov 27 1907	Burned	Highland Falls, N.Y.
4255	Vesta	Sch.	-	-	Oct 29 1883	Unknown	Louis Point, Block Island, R.I.
4256	Vesta	Sch.	119	1866	Jul 21 1916	Abandoned	5 miles east of Seal Island, Nova Scotia.
4257	Vesta	Tanker	-	-	Apr 26 1938	Unknown	42-21-50 N. 70-39-48 W.
4258	Vesta R. Gates	Sch.	-	-	Mar 1884	Unknown	Nantucket Island, Mass. Coal cargo.
4259	Vicksburg	Sch.	-	-	Jun 20 1890	Unknown	Off Chatham, Mass.
4260	Victor	Sch.	-	-	Nov 22 1889	Unknown	Gut of Cannipsett, Mass.
4261	Victor & Ethan	Ga.s.	94	1908	Oct 13 1916	Collided	With st.s. HARRY LUCKENBACH. Off No Mans Land, Mass.
4262	Victor Lynn	Ga.s.	94	1905	Mar 10 1924	Burned	White Haven, Md.
4263	Victoria	Sch.	-	-	Jun 12 1875	Unknown	Marsh Cove, Point Judith, R.I.
4264	Victorious	Brg.	447	1916	Apr 26 1931	Stranded	Fishers Island, N.Y.
4265	Victory	Ol.s.	54	1945	Jul 24 1953	Burned	75 miles SW of Atlantic City, N.J.
4266	Vigilant	Steamer	-	-	Nov 27 1898	Unknown	Off Provincetown, Mass.
4267	Vigilant	St.s.	98	1902	Aug 19 1934	Burned	Jersey City, N.J.
4268	Viking	Sch.	-	-	Sep 15 1802	Unknown	Off Monmoy Beach, Mass.
4269	Viking	Ol.s.	77	1917	Aug 15 1948	Collided	With ol.s. BONNIE, 41-43-00 N. 66-29-00 W.
4270	Viking	Ol.s.	67	1931	Oct 20 1966	Foundered	Approx. 11-1/2 miles southeast of NoMansLand, Mass.
4271	Villanova	Ol.s.	86	1942	Feb 22 1964	Collided	About 25 miles SE of Gloucester, Mass.
4272	Vinalhaven	St.s.	186	1892	Nov 10 1938	Foundered	Rockland, Me.
4273	Vineland	St.s.	148	1863	Sep 18 1888	Lost	Baltimore, Md.
4274	Vineyard	Sch.	215	1874	Oct 10 1919	Foundered	Hantsport, Nova Scotia.
4275	Vineyard Sound Lightship	-	538	-	Sep 14 1944	Foundered	41-23-48 N. 71-00-58 W. 6,600 yds., 251° True from Cuttyhunk Light, Mass. Steel vessel. Length 112'. All lives (12) lost.
4276	Vinita	St.y.	-	-	Jun 10 1888	Unknown	Off Point Judith, R.I.
4277	Vinland	Sch.	965	1896	Jul 4 1906	Burned	Off Rikers Island, N.Y.
4278	Viola (Br.)	Sch.	-	-	Oct 22 1892	Unknown	Handkerchief Shoal, Mass.
4279	Viola	Bkn.	193	1910	Sep 5 1917	Foundered	Sailed from New Bedford, Mass., and has not since reported. All lives (19) lost.
4280	Violet Blossom	Brg.	374	1907	Feb 20 1913	Collided	With st.s. McALLISTER BROS. New York, N.Y.
4281	Virginia	Brg.	1,500	-	Nov 27 1898	Unknown	Near Black Rock, North Cohasset, Mass. Coal cargo.
4282	Virginia	C.bt.	142	1911	Dec 13 1917	Foundered	Off Kelsey Point, Conn.
4283	Virginia	Ga.y.	91	1918	Nov 27 1922	Stranded	Off Port Jefferson, N.Y.
4284	Virginia	Ol.s.	76	1926	Nov 9 1928	Stranded	Cahoon's Hollow, Cape Cod, Mass.
4285	Virginia	Ol.s.	53	1937	Sep 6 1967	Burned	At Nelson Point, Mattawoman Creek, Charles County, Md.

NO.	NAME OF VESSEL	RIG	TONS	BUILT	DATE		CAUSE	PLACE AND COMMENT
4286	Virginia Dare	Sch.	1,569	1919	Jan 17	1930	Stranded	New London, Conn.
4287	Virginia H. Hudson	Sch.	579	1871	Sep 15	1906	Foundered	Hereford, N.J.
4288	Virginia R.	Ol.s.	51	1927	Jul 23	1933	Collided	With ol.s. NEWTON. 43-05-00 N. 67-00-00 W.
4289	Virginian (Br.)	-	-	-	Mar	1895	Stranded	Near Boston, Mass.
4290	Virginian	Brg.	309	1902	Dec 2	1906	Stranded	Branford, Conn.
4291	Viscava	-	-	-	Oct 29	1890	Collided	Barnegat, N.J. 70 lives lost.
4292	Visitor	St.s.	70	1892	Jan 2	1920	Burned	Sewaren, N.J. Steel vessel.
4293	Visitor	St.s.	70	1892	Apr 26	1925	Burned	Flushing, Long Island, N.Y.
4294	Vizcaya	Steamer	-	-	Oct 30	1890	Collided	Off Barnegat, N.J.
4295	Volunteer	St.s.	136	1887	Mar 10	1922	Foundered	Off Bridgeport, Conn.
4296	Volunteer	St.s.	92	1888	Dec 12	1928	Collided	With st.s. CHESTER W. CHAPIN. East River, N.Y. 1 life lost (10).
4297	Vulcan	St.ycht.	-	-	Aug 3	1802	Unknown	Quonochontaug, R.I.
4298	Vulcan	Sch.	-	-	Oct 23	1891	Unknown	Nantucket Island, Mass.
4299	Vulcan	Sch.	-	-	Dec	1893	Unknown	Costaka Beach, Nantucket Island, Mass. Lime cargo.
4300	W.A. Crocker	Sch.	-	-	Apr 27	1888	Unknown	Long Cove Harbor, Me.
4301	W.A. Dubosque	Sch.	-	-	Jul 22	1888	Unknown	Stradsmouth Island, Mass.
4302	W.A. Marshall	Brg.	506	1903	Jan 7	1922	Foundered	Near Boston Lightship, Mass. 42-22-00 N. 70-44-00 W.
4303	W.B. Daisby	Sch.	-	-	Lost 1800's		Unknown	Off Chatham, Mass.
4304	W.C. Richardson	St.s.	3,818	1902	Dec 8	1909	Foundered	Buffalo, N.Y. Steel vessel. 5 lives lost.
4305	W.D. Brinnier	Brg.	334	1910	Aug 31	1911	Foundered	Narragansett Bay, R.I.
4306	W.E. Barker	Brg.	264	1894	Sep 26	1909	Foundered	Sharps Island, Me.
4307	W.E. and W.L. Tuck	Sch.	416	1883	Apr 9	1916	Stranded	Suttons Island, Me.
4308	W.H. Fredson	Sch.	654	-	May 4	1890	Foundered	41-11-27 N. 71-36-00 W. 1/2 mile south of Block Island L.S. Station, R.I.
4309	W.H. Oler	Sch.	693	-	Mar 11	1901	Unknown	High Head Life Saving Station, Truro, Cape Cod, Mass.
4310	W.J. Townsend	Ol.s.	133	1876	Jan 16	1944	Foundered	Bayonne, N.J. Concrete vessel.
4311	W. Jaffrey	Frgt.	5,663	1918	Feb 8	1942	War Loss	43-36-00 N. 60-30-00 W.
4312	W.L. Steed	St.s.	6,182	1918	Feb 2	1942	War Loss	North Atlantic. Steel vessel. Sunk by enemy action. 2.6 miles offshore, Fenwick Island, Md. Depth 50'. 34 lives lost (38).
4313	W.L. Webster	St.s.	73	1882	Jun 3	1919	Collided	With unknown obstruction. Brooklyn, N.Y.
4314	W.M. Goodspeed	Ga.s.	95	1908	Jun 2	1919	Collided	With st.s. SWELL. 41-40-00 N. 68-25-00 W.
4315	W.O. Nettleton	Sch.	-	-	May 20	1898	Foundered	2-1/2 miles southwest by south of Coskata L.S. Station, Mass.
4316	W.O. Nettleton	Sch.	55	1859	Nov	1917	Stranded	Seaconnet River, R.I.
4317	W.P. O'Hara	Sch.	-	-	Jul 31	1892	Unknown	Off Peaked Hill, Mass.
4318	W.S. & A.L. Rogers	C.bt.	106	1889	Dec	1916	Foundered	New York, N.Y.
4319	W.T. Bell	Sch.	234	1887	Feb 22	1927	Stranded	Bayville, N.Y. Iron vessel.
4320	W.W. Stewart	Sch.	294	1866	Oct 12	1909	Burned	Buffalo, N.Y.
4321	Wabash	St.s.	1,186	1856	Mar 13	1920	Foundered	Off Richmond Island, Me.
4322	Wade Hampton	St.s.	123	1877	Nov 16	1923	Foundered	Delaware Bay.
4323	Wadena	Sch.	1,076	-	Mar 11	1802	Foundered	Monomoy Beach, Cape Cod, Mass.
4324	Wake	Sch.	-	-		1891	Unknown	Near Brenton Reef Lightship, R.I.
4325	Wakefield	Brg.	287	1885	May 27	1930	Foundered	Horseshoe, Delaware River.
4326	Waldron Holmes	Sch.	59	1851	Feb 1	1908	Stranded	Point Francis, Me.
4327	Walpole	St.p.	145	1854	Apr 7	1863	Stranded	Minots Ledge, Mass. 2 lives lost.
4328	Walter F. Parker	Sch.	-	-	Sep 3	1889	Collided	Delaware Bay.
4329	Walter Irving	Sch.	-	-	Jan 2	1878	Unknown	Peaked Hill, Mass.
4330	Walter J. Schloefer	C.bt.	138	1887	Mar 19	1906	Stranded	New Haven, Conn.
4331	Walter Miller (Br.)	Sch.	-	-	Jun 10	1897	Unknown	Off Nauset Beach, Mass.
4332	Walter P. Goulart	Sch.	84	1904	May 12	1912	Stranded	Shelburne, Nova Scotia.

NO.	NAME OF VESSEL	RIG	TONS	BUILT	DATE		CAUSE	PLACE AND COMMENT
4333	Waltham	Sch.	523	1889	Oct 27	1925	Stranded	Shearbrook, Nova Scotia.
4334	Waltham	Ol.s.	82	1904	Jul 9	1932	Stranded	Off Block Island, R.I.
4335	Waltham II	Ol.s.	80	1918	Jan 8	1935	Stranded	No Mans Land, Mass.
4336	Walton	Brg.	523	1896	Aug 12	1928	Foundered	Sandy Point, Md. All lives (2) lost.
4337	Wamsetta	Ol.s.	76	-	-	-	Unknown	41-18-00 N. 70-52-00 W. Vineyard Sound approach, Gay Head, Mass. Fisherman.
4338	Wamsutta	Ol.s.	76	-	Mar 19	1964	Unknown	41-19-06 N. 70-51-37 W. 2-1/2 miles SSW of Gay Head Light, Mass. See No.4337.
4339	Wanda	Slp.ycht.	-	-	Aug 30	1800	Unknown	Off Highland, Mass.
4340	Wanderer	Bark	303	1878	Aug 26	1924	Stranded	41-25-18 N. 70-56-36 W. West end of Cuttyhunk Island, Mass.
4341	Warn Boys, Jr.	C.bt.	140	-	Jun 24	1934	Foundered	Shadyside, N.J.
4342	Warren	St.s.	821	1875	Sep 8	1907	Stranded	Fall River, Mass.
4343	Warren Brown	C.bt.	106	1882	Jul	1909	Foundered	Newburgh, N.Y.
4344	Warren Gates	Sch.	-	-	Mar 25	1883	Unknown	Off Point Judith, R.I.
4345	Warren Gates	Sch.	73	1870	Sep 21	1907	Stranded	Southold, N.Y.
4346	Warren Sawyer	Sch.	380	-	Dec 22	1884	Unknown	South side of Nantucket Island, Mass. Cotton cargo.
4347	Warrior	Sch.	-	-	Lost 1800's		Unknown	Sand Point, R.I.
4348	Warsaw	Sloop	-	-	Apr 30	1841	Unknown	Off Cohasset, Mass.
4349	Warsteed	Sch.	-	-	May 28	1896	Unknown	Quonochontaug, R.I.
4350	Washington	St.p.	339	1825	May 14	1831	Collided	With CHANCELLOR LIVINGSTON. Long Island Sound. 2 lives lost.
4351	Washington Irving	St.p.	3,104	1913	Jun 1	1926	Collided	With barge in tow by st.s. THOMAS E. MORAN. New York, N.Y. Steel vessel. 3 lives lost (310).
4352	Washingtonian	St.s.	6,648	1914	Jan 26	1915	Collided	With sch. ELIZABETH PALMER. Off Fenwick L.S. Station, Del. 1 life lost.
4353	Wasp	Brg.	2,140	-	Jun 12	1903	Storm	Off Clarks Point, Mass.
4354	Waterton	Frgt.	343	-	Jan 23	1942	Unknown	47-07-00 N. 59-34-00 W.
4355	Wathen	Ol.s.	343	-	Nov 16	1944	Unknown	41-46-15 N. 70-28-50 W. Sandwich Town Beach, Mass. Tug. Steel vessel.
4356	Wau-Kon	St.s.	61	1883	May 17	1919	Burned	Tonawanda, N.Y.
4357	Wave	Sch.	-	-	Aug 19	1884	Unknown	Off Watch Hill Point, R.I.
4358	Wave	Ol.s.	-	-	Sep 21	1936	Unknown	42-22-45 N. 70-39-25 W. Trawler.
4359	Wave Crest	Sch.	-	-	Sep 8	1881	Unknown	Black Rock, Block Island, R.I.
4360	Wave Crest	Sch.	-	-	Mar 31	1888	Unknown	Hereford Inlet, N.J.
4361	Wave Marker III	Ol.s.	78	1929	Oct 18	1967	Foundered	At 6 miles off Holdgate, N.J.
4362	Wawaset	St.p.	258	1863	Aug 8	1873	Burned	Chatterton's Ledge, Potomac River. 13 lives lost.
4363	Wawenock	Sch.	325	1907	Jan 14	1929	Stranded	McGlatherys Island, Me.
4364	Wayne	Sch.	820	1895	Apr 16	1913	Foundered	22 miles NE of Barnegat, N.J.
4365	Wayne	Sc.b.	436	1918	Aug 17	1932	Foundered	Off Sea Isle City, N.J.
4366	Wayne	Brg.	-	-		1932	Unknown	39-05-00 N. 74-37-30 W. 4.7 miles, 119° from the Townsend Inlet Bridge, N.J. Stands 12' high in 46' of water.
4367	Waywood (Br.)	Brig	-	-	Lost 1800's		Unknown	West of Point Judith, R.I.
4368	Weehawken	Sch.	448	1896	Nov 9	1915	Foundered	Off Minots Ledge Lighthouse, Mass. 3 lives lost.
4369	Welcome	Sch.	-	-	Lost 1800's		Unknown	Off Race Point, Cape Cod, Mass.
4367	Welcome R. Beebe	Sch.	400	-	Aug 5	1896	Unknown	41-58-48 N. 69-59-54 W. 2 miles north-half-west of Cahoons Hollow L.S. Station, Mass. Ice cargo.
4368	Wellesley	Sch.	1,306	1919	Apr 16	1923	Foundered	Southwest of Northeast End Lightship, N.J.
4369	Wellington	St.s.	334	1905	Feb 5	1926	Collided	With st.s. ARDMORE. Brigantine Shoals, N.J. Steel vessel.
4370	Wellington	-	334	-		1940	Unknown	Little Egg Inlet, N.J. 39-26-48 N. 74-12-48 W. 9.4 miles from Bell Buoy at Absecon Inlet, bearing 054°. Depth 57'. See No.4369.
4371	Wenonah II	Ga.y.	143	1920	Jul 16	1929	Burned	Hempstead, N.Y. 1 life lost (9).
4372	Wentworth	Sch.	350	-	Oct 13	1904	Unknown	41-41-20 N. 69-55-12 W. Off Chatham, Mass.
4373	Wesgleland	Steamer	-	-	Lost 1800's		Unknown	Off Nauset, Mass. Also reported as "Wergleland".

NO.	NAME OF VESSEL	RIG	TONS	BUILT	DATE		CAUSE	PLACE AND COMMENT
4374	Wesley Abbott	Sch.	-	-	Jul 30	1898	Unknown	Off Chatham, Mass.
4375	Wesley Bellis	Brg.	320	1927	Mar 7	1944	Collided	With US Naval vessel No.292. While moored at 30th Street & East River, N.Y.
4376	West Imboden	Frgt.	5,751	-	Apr 21	1942	War Loss	41-14-00 N. 65-55-00 W.
4377	West Jaffrey	St.s.	5,663	1919	Feb 8	1942	Foundered	43-36-00 N. 66-30-00 W. Steel vessel. Freighter.
4378	West Point	St.p.	409	1860	Aug 13	1862	Collided	With GEORGE PEABODY. Ragged Point, Ptomac River. 76 lives lost.
4379	West Port	Sch.	-	-	Oct 23	1800	Unknown	Brentons Point, R.I.
4380	West River	St.s.	261	1907	Apr 19	1931	Burned	Wilmington, Del.
4381	West Shore	St.s.	196	1882	Sep 15	1912	Stranded	Chesapeake Bay.
4382	West Virginia	Sch.	1,564	1898	Sep 29	1909	Foundered	1-1/2 miles southeast of Pollock Rip Shoals Lightship, Mass.
4383	West Wind	Sch.	-	-	May 8	1895	Unknown	Spouting Pock Point, Newport, R.I.
4384	Westchester	St.s.	312	1853	Jul 21	1866	Collided	With sch. PECONIC. Absecon, N.J.
4385	Western	St.s.	415	1908	Nov 22	1926	Stranded	Shelburne, Nova Scotia. Steel vessel.
4386	Western Belle	Sch.	1,097	1876	Dec 23	1917	Foundered	Fenwick Island, Del. All lives (4) lost.
4387	Western Port	St.s.	453	1853	Jan 26	1866	Stranded	Off Cape Cod, Mass.
4388	Wethea	Ga.s.	63	1912	Sep 12	1945	Burned	Off Corsons Inlet, N.J.
4389	Weybosset	Sch.	-	-	Aug 13	1890	Burned	Pollock Rip Shoal, Mass.
4390	Wheeler & Howes	Brg.	256	1887	Oct 14	1917	Stranded	East Haven, Conn.
4391	Whidah	-	-	-	Apr	1717	Foundered	Off Wellfleet, Cape Cod, Mass. Valued at $250,000 in gold & silver.
4392	Whip	Ga.s.	64	1882	Jun 25	1914	Burned	At Salem, Mass.
4393	Whistler	Sch.	-	-	Apr 21	1893	Unknown	Provincetown, Mass.
4394	Whitaker	Sch.	-	-	Dec 4	1853	Unknown	Near Wellfleet, Cape Cod, Mass.
4395	White Band	Sch.	1,816	1879	Jan 24	1908	Foundered	Cape Henlopen, Del. All lives (6) lost.
4396	White Band	Brg.	366	1881	Dec 6	1916	Foundered	Near Faulkners Island, Long Island Sound.
4397	White Band	Brg.	490	1918	May 15	1919	Foundered	High Pine Ledge, Mass. All lives (2) lost.
4398	White Marsh	Brg.	433	1908	May 31	1933	Stranded	Off Plymouth, Mass.
4399	White Rock	Sch.	-	-	Jul 25	1890	Unknown	New York Bay.
4400	White Squall	-	-	-		1868	Unknown	On outer bars northeast of Cahoons Hollow L.S. Station, Cape Cod, Mass.
4401	White Wing	Sch.	-	-	Sep 20	1887	Unknown	Fourth Cliff, Scituate, Mass.
4402	Whiteport	Brg.	423	1923	Oct 29	1955	Foundered	3 miles below Bay Bridge on SW side of Vern River, Md.
4403	Whitehead	St.s.	136	1861	Sep 1	1872	Burned	New London, Conn.
4404	Whitman	Sch.	477	1901	Mar 6	1913	Stranded	42-21-28 N. 70-54-00 W. 3 miles north of Point Allerton L.S. Station, Hull, Mass. Phosphate cargo.
4405	Wiconisco	Sc.b.	956	1907	Oct 12	1927	Foundered	Sakonnet Light, R.I.
4406	Wild Cat	Ga.s.	84	1917	Nov 14	1935	Foundered	Ackroys Point, Piscataqua River, N.H.
4407	Wild Flower	Sch.	55	1872	Apr 16	1919	Foundered	Tilghmans Island, Md.
4408	Wild Pigeon	Sch.	-	1886	Oct 10	1886	Unknown	East of Block Island, R.I.
4409	Willeimsplein	Frgt.	5,489	-	Oct 5	1942	Unknown	46-40-00 N. 53-38-00 W.
4410	Willet	St.s.	74	1892	Nov 29	1935	Burned	Troy, N.Y.
4411	Wm. A. Carroll	St.s.	74	1906	Mar 17	1948	Foundered	Foot of Baltis Street, Brooklyn, N.Y.
4412	Wm. A. Grozier	Sch.	116	1865	Jul 1	1913	Foundered	Off New Bedford, Mass.
4413	William A. Jamison	St.s.	229	1910	Mar 17	1919	Collided	With st.s. LEXINGTON. Near pier 15, East River, New York, N.Y.
4414	William A. Maillies	Sch.	-	-		Lost 1800's	Unknown	Off Race Point, Cape Cod, Mass.
4415	William A. Morse	Sch.	-	-	Nov 27	1898	Unknown	Provincetown, Mass.
4416	William A. Street	C.bt.	123	1880	May 7	1907	Stranded	Fort Ann Creek, N.Y.
4417	Wm. B. Diggs	Brg.	475	1913	Mar 7	1929	Foundered	Shrewsbury, N.J.
4418	Wm. B. Diggs	Brg.	1,041	1918	Sep 3	1934	Foundered	Off Hereford Lighthouse Breakwater, Del. 38-56-29 N. 74-41-56 W. Depth 42'.
4419	William B. Orr	Sch.	-	-	Apr 28	1891	Unknown	Delaware Bay.
4420	William B. Palmer	Sch.	1,805	1896	Sep 29	1910	Stranded	Davis Shoals, Nantucket Island, Mass.

NO.	NAME OF VESSEL	RIG	TONS	BUILT	DATE		CAUSE	PLACE AND COMMENT
4421	William B. Rambo	Sch.	99	1894	Dec 26	1909	Stranded	Broadkiln Creek, Del.
4422	William Boardman	Sch.	-	-	Jul 5	1891	Unknown	Off Chatham, Mass.
4423	William Booth	Sch.	545	1903	May 7	1928	Collided	With sch. HELEN BARNET GRING. Chatham, Cape Cod, Mass.
4424	Wm. Boyce Thompson	St.s.	7,061	1921	Nov 17	1924	Burned	Trembly Point, N.J. Steel vessel.
4425	William C. Carnegie	Sch.	2,663	1900	May 1	1909	Stranded	Moriches, N.Y.
4426	Wm. C. Redfield	St.s.	370	1865	Jun 20	1910	Burned	Athens, N.Y.
4427	William Chisholm	St.s.	1,581	1884	Jul 16	1916	Burned	Cape Cod, Canal, Mass. Iron vessel.
4428	William D. Becker	Sch.	1,046	1892	Apr 7	1907	Stranded	Off Barnegat, N.J.
4429	Wm. D. Hilton	Sch.	324	1871	May 23	1919	Foundered	Rockland, Me.
4430	William Duren	Sch.	101	1867	Jun 11	1907	Stranded	Western Duck Rock, Monhegan, Me.
4431	William E. Barnes	Sch.	-	-	Nov 2	1887	Unknown	Off Nauset Light, Mass.
4432	William E. Lee	Sch.	-	-	Jul 25	1883	Unknown	Southwest of Block Island, R.I.
4433	William E. McDonald	Sch.	-	-	Jul 31	1897	Unknown	Great Point, Mass.
4434	William Emerson	Sch.	-	-	Lost 1800's		Unknown	Peaked Hill, Mass.
4435	William F. Campbell	Sch.	211	1893	Apr 28	1906	Foundered	Off Owlshead, Me.
4436	Wm. F. Havemeyer	St.s.	110	1875	Jul 28	1907	Burned	New York, N.Y.
4437	William F. McCormack	Brg.	476	1920	May 19	1950	Burned	At South Amboy Coal dock, South Amboy, N.J.
4438	William G. Bartlett	Sch.	-	-	Mar 12	1888	Unknown	Cape Henlopen, Del.
4439	William G.R. Mowry	Sch.	-	-	Dec 5	1893	Unknown	Northeast of Block Island, R.I.
4440	William Gillum	Sch.	-	-	Aug 4	1890	Unknown	Shovelful Shoal, Mass.
4441	William Guindon	C.bt.	103	1888	Jun	1915	Foundered	South Brooklyn, N.Y.
4442	William H. Brinsfield	Sch.	-	-	Apr 19	1890	Unknown	Chesapeake Bay.
4443	Wm. H. Coates	St.s.	195	1900	Jul 19	1924	Stranded	Green Island, Troy, N.Y.
4444	Wm. H. Conner	Sch.	1,514	1877	Apr 22	1909	Collided	With sch. HUGH KELLY. Sandy Hook, N.J.
4445	William H. Dicks	Sch.	-	-	Aug 29	1939	Unknown	46-54-00 N. 56-48-00 W.
4446	William H. Fredson	Sch.	-	-	May 4	1890	Unknown	Block Island, R.I.
4447	William H. Higgins	Sch.	593	-	Mar 31	1898	Unknown	42-05-00 N. 70-10-00 W. 1/4 mile NNW of Peaked Hill L.S. Station, Mass.
4448	William H. Jordan	Sch.	498	-	Jan 2	1888	Unknown	41-11-06 N. 71-36-24 W. 1 mile south of Block Island L.S. Station, R.I. Also reported as "William H. Jourdan" Coal cargo.
4449	William H. Killigrew	Ol.s.	74	1928	Mar 20	1956	Foundered	About 40 miles east of Nantucket Lightship, Mass.
4450	William H. Machen	St.s.	3,922	1916	Jul 7	1943	Foundered	42-57-00 N. 70-30-00 W. Off New Hampshire coast. Steel vessel.
4451	William H. Mitchell	Sch.	-	-	Aug 24	1888	Unknown	Apple River, Nova Scotia.
4452	William H. McCleve	Brg.	238	1868	Jul 28	1910	Foundered	Off Watch Hill, R.I.
4453	William H. Oaks	Sch.	-	-	Jun 5	1885	Foundered	East of Block Island, R.I.
4454	William H. Rowe	Sch.	53	1886	Jul 12	1888	Foundered	Nauset Beach, Mass.
4455	William H. Starbuck	Ga.s.	226	1903	Aug 10	1918	Torpedoed	41-45-00 N. 67-10-00 W.
4456	William H. Taylor	St.s.	241	1871	Sep 21	1924	Burned	Jersey City, N.J.
4457	William H. Treice	Sch.	277	1907	Lost 1800's		Unknown	Point Judith, R.I.
4458	William H. Vanderbilt	Brg.	241	1871	Aug 19	1905	Stranded	New York, N.Y. All lives (2) lost.
4459	William H. Wessels	Brg.	277	1907	Apr 28	1908	Collided	With st.s. ISLANDER. Sands Point, Long Island, N.Y.
4460	William H. Yerkes	Tanker	320	1927	Apr 16	1938	Unknown	42-21-50 N. 70-39-48 W.
4461	William J. Mahoney	Brg.	-	-	Mar 23	1964	Foundered	Off the boardwalk, Coney Island, N.Y.
4462	William L. Bunoughs	Sch.	241	1873	Jan 19	1889	Unknown	Handkerchief Shoal, Mass.
4463	William L. Elkins	Sch.	445	1908	Dec 6	1915	Stranded	Cape Elizabeth, Me.
4464	William L. Hooper	Brg.	107	1927	Feb	1942	Foundered	Lewes, Del. Steel vessel.
4465	William L. Putnam	Ol.s.	167	1870	Mar 15	1942	Collided	With st.s. ROANER. 15 miles SE of Seal Island, Me.
4466	William M. Bird	Sch.	-	-	May 23	1893	Unknown	Handkerchief Shoal, Mass.
4467	Wm. M. Everett	Sch.	167	1870	Nov 18	1898	Foundered	Shelter Island, N.Y.

NO.	NAME OF VESSEL	RIG	TONS	BUILT	DATE		CAUSE	PLACE AND COMMENT
4468	Wm. M. Gaffney	Sch.	74	1877	Jun 24	1913	Stranded	Maitland, Nova Scotia.
4469	William Maloney	St.s.	165	1891	Nov 15	1924	Foundered	Newport, R.I. All lives (12) lost.
4470	William Marshall	Sch.	-	-	Feb 14	1899	Foundered	3 miles WSW of Coskata L.S. Station, Mass. Lost during gale.
4471	William Marshall	Sch.	305	1874	Dec 11	1906	Unknown	42-03-18 N. 70-04-42 W. 1/2 mile north of Highland L.S. Station, Truro, Mass.
4472	William Mason	Sch.	-	-	Jun	1891	Unknown	Machias Bay, Me.
4473	William Mason	Sch.	465	1872	Dec 18	1916	Foundered	St. Marys Bay, Nova Scotia. All lives (6) lost.
4474	William Matheson	Sch.	111	1875	May 28	1915	Stranded	Magdalen Islands, Gulf of St. Lawrence.
4475	Wm. Montgomery	St.s.	101	1889	Dec 1	1912	Foundered	Lake Champlain, N.Y.
4476	William Morgan	Sch.	86	1861	Jan 4	1875	Foundered	Sandy Hook, N.J.
4478	William McGee	Sch.	85	1865	May 15	1908	Foundered	Sea Isle City, N.J.
4479	William O'Brien	St.s.	5,211	1915	Apr 18	1920	Foundered	Sailed from New York, N.Y. & has not since reported. All lives (40) lost.
4480	William P. Donnelly	St.s.	54	1903	Jun 25	1922	Burned	Verona Beach, Oneida Lake, N.Y. 1 life lost.
4481	William P. Hood	Sch.	665	-	Mar 11	1900	Unknown	Orleans, Mass.
4482	William Penn	St.p.	141	1819	Mar 4	1834	Burned	Philadelphia, Pa.
4483	William R. Huston	Sch.	548	1874	Apr 20	1915	Foundered	42-34-00 N. 57-40-00 W. Off St. John, New Brunswick.
4484	William Rice	Sch.	133	1869	Nov 7	1912	Stranded	Boothbay, Me.
4485	William Riley	Sch.	-	-	Aug 21	1889	Collided	Off Sandy Hook, N.J.
4486	William S. Bartlett	Sch.	-	-	Mar 12	1888	Unknown	Off Cape Henlopen, Del.
4487	William S. Keeler	Brg.	476	1908	Jul 10	1934	Collided	With tanker TYDOL. Between Execution and Gangway Rocks, Long Island, N.Y.
4488	Wm. S. Ronan	C.bt.	105	1894	Nov 15	1921	Foundered	Shady Side Basin, N.J.
4489	William S. Scull	Sch.	409	-	Jul 16	1877	Unknown	South of Block Island, R.I. 41-08-39 N. 71-35-40 W. Phosphate cargo.
4490	William Slater	Sch.	-	-	Dec 5	1888	Unknown	Off Chatham, Mass.
4491	William Smith	Sch.	-	-	Lost	1800's	Unknown	Nauset, Mass.
4492	William T. Donnell	Sch.	538	1883	Jan 4	1913	Stranded	Maces Bay, New Brunswick.
4493	William Thomas	Sch.	106	1849	Nov 4	1925	Stranded	Annisquam Bar, Mass.
4494	William V.O. Driscoll	Brg.	335	1928	Oct 14	1965	Collided	With el.s. HOUSTON. On the Hudson River near Poughkeepsie, N.Y.
4495	William V.R. Smith	St.s.	207	1905	Mar 11	1920	Stranded	New York, N.Y.
4496	William W. Curtin	Brg.	398	1898	Mar 7	1920	Foundered	Off Kent Island, Md.
4497	William Voorhis	Sch.	89	1866	Nov 2	1907	Unknown	With dock, New York, N.Y.
4498	William Wilson	Sch.	-	-	Jan 16	1896	Unknown	Monomoy Point, Mass.
4499	William Wray	St.p.	70	1838		1857	Stranded	Camden, N.J.
4500	Williamsport	Steamer	1,283	-	May 12	1902	Stranded	Pollock Rip, Mass. Iron vessel.
4501	Williamsburg	Sch.	319	1899	Nov 6	1917	Foundered	Cornfield Light, Conn.
4502	Willie DeWolf	Sch.	-	-	Dec 25	1885	Unknown	East of Block Island, R.I.
4503	Willie H. Higgins	Sch.	-	-	Mar 31	1898	Unknown	Peaked Hill, Mass.
4504	Willie and Ida	Steamer	-	-	Nov 21	1889	Unknown	Cuttyhunk Island, Mass.
4505	Willie Sheridan	C.bt.	132	1908	Feb 9	1925	Stranded	North Brothers Island, N.Y.
4506	Willis G. Fisher	C.bt.	100	1888	May 12	1918	Collided	With lighthouse. North Pulpit Point, Lake Champlain.
4507	Willis & Guy	Sch.	199	1873	Aug 9	1917	Stranded	Pamaquid Point, Me.
4508	Wilmington	Drg.	80	1927	Jun 29	1945	Foundered	Cedar Point, Chesapeake Bay, in vicinity of Patuxent River, Md.
4509	Wilmington	Brg.	1,371	1915	Jan 1	1945	Foundered	Off Block Island Sound, R.I.
4510	Wilmington	Brg.	766	1917	Dec 14	1954	Collided	3,700 yds., 224° True from Chester Range Front Light, Delaware River. Length 110'. Depth 6'.
4511	Wilson Small	St.p.	258	1851	Aug 9	1867	Collided	With MARY AUGUSTA. Poplar Island, Md. 3 lives lost.
4512	Wilson and Willard	Sch.	52	1884	Aug 15	1909	Stranded	Kittery, Me.
4513	Winceco	St.s.	188	1905	Feb 21	1929	Foundered	Cornfield Light, Conn.
4514	Winchester	Sch.	303	1882	Oct 15	1918	Foundered	Off Cape Cod, Mass.
4515	Wind	Ol.s.	115	1906	Oct 12	1953	Burned	44-25-00 N. 66-35-00 W. About 20 miles SSE of Cross Island.

NO.	NAME OF VESSEL	RIG	TONS	BUILT	DATE	CAUSE	PLACE AND COMMENT
4516	Winifred Sheridan	Brg.	934	1907	Pre-WWII	Unknown	42-23-00 N. 70-53-40 W. Steel vessel. 2 miles NE of Deer Island, Boston, Mass.
4517	Winneconne	St.s.	1,869	1907	Jun 18 1918	Torpedoed	39-26-00 N. 72-05-00 W.
4518	Winnegance	Sch.	-	-	Feb 18 1899	Unknown	Muskeget, Mass.
4519	Winnegance	Sch.	1,327	-	Oct 14 1943	Unknown	42-02-32 N. 70-16-00 W. West of Race Point, Mass.
4520	Winnie Lang	Sch.	-	-	Dec 3 1890	Unknown	Napatree Point, R.I.
4521	Winnie Lawry	Sch.	-	-	Oct 1 1899	Unknown	Off Chatham, Mass.
4522	Winnie Lawry	Sch.	246	1874	Apr 28 1912	Stranded	Rockport, Mass.
4523	Winona	Brg.	53	1909	Feb 25 1920	Burned	Alexandria Bay, N.Y.
4524	Winsor	Sch.	1,034	-	Dec 2 1946	Unknown	42-09-00 N. 70-34-00 W. Off Marshfield, Mass. Coal cargo.
4525	Witch Hazel	Sch.	251	1872	Nov 12 1911	Stranded	New Haven, Conn. 3 lives lost.
4526	Wonder	Sch.	-	-	Mar 18 1891	Unknown	Fox Point, Nova Scotia.
4527	Woodbury	Sch.	735	1899	Feb 5 1907	Stranded	Highland Light, Cape Cod, Mass.
4528	Woodbury M. Snow	Sch.	107	1883	May 31 1916	Burned	Rockport, Me.
4529	Woodmencey	St.s.	82	1901	Jul 9 1932	Burned	Harlem River, New York, N.Y.
4530	Worcester	Sch.	625	1904	Nov 27 1921	Stranded	Woodbury, N.J.
4531	Wreath	Sch.	-	-	Jul 11 1888	Unknown	Bass Harbor, Me.
4532	Wreath	Bark	-	-	Apr 1 1889	Unknown	Near Prospect Harbor, Me.
4533	Wright	St.s.	96	1893	Jan 2 1927	Stranded	Long Beach, N.Y.
4534	Wyoming	Brg.	-	-	Dec 14 1890	Unknown	Saybrook, Conn.
4535	Wyoming	Brg.	277	1874	Jul 4 1918	Burned	Mystic River, Conn.
4536	Wyoming	Sch.	3,730	1909	Mar 12 1924	Foundered	Off Chatham, Mass. All lives (14) lost.
4537	Ximena	Sch.	-	-	Jan 25 1890	Unknown	Near Machias, Me.
4538	YMS 14 (USS)	-	-	-	Jan 11 1945	Unknown	42-22-06 N. 70-54-53 W. Depth 33'.
4539	YP 387 (USS)	-	-	-	May 20 1942	Unknown	39-01-15 N. 74-39-18 W. Depth 25'. May have been removed.
4540	Yale	St.s.	312	1907	Sep 25 1930	Foundered	42-12-00 N. 69-07-00 W.
4541	Yankee	Frgt.	-	-	Pre-WWII	Unknown	41-12-00 N. 68-59-00 W.
4542	Yankee	Frgt.	-	-	Pre-WWII	Unknown	40-20-00 N. 73-16-30 W. Depth 98'.
4543	Yankee	St.s.	2,418	1890	Jun 11 1918	Collided	With Italian SS ARGENTINA. Off Fire Island, N.Y. Steel vessel. See No.4542.
4544	Yankee	Brg.	531	1902	Feb 4 1920	Stranded	Brooklyn, N.Y.
4545	Yankee	Ol.s.	141	1921	Jun 9 1940	Burned	70 miles SE of Highland Light, Mass.
4546	Yankee Doodle	Sch.	-	-	Sep 13 1891	Unknown	Penfield Reef, Long Island Sound.
4547	Yankee Maid	Sch.	58	1858	Feb 2 1906	Stranded	Seal Island, Me.
4548	Yawl Princess	-	-	-	Oct 14 1967	Unknown	42-17-18 N. 71-00-12 W.
4549	Yeada	Yacht	-	-	May 25 1890	Unknown	New York Bay.
4550	Yemassee	Sch.	1,257	1879	Dec 29 1916	Foundered	15 miles SE of Boston Lightship, Mass.
4551	Yolanda	Ga.y.	108	1919	Jun 17 1934	Burned	Rocky Point, N.J.
4552	Young America	St.s.	359	1853	Sep 2 1874	Stranded	Oak Orchard, N.Y.
4553	Young Brothers	Sch.	897	1890	Jun 29 1910	Burned	Richmond, Me.
4554	ZPG-3 (U.S. Navy)	Blimp	-	-	Jul 6 1960	Unknown	39-41-00 N. 73-48-00 W. Depth 60'. Partially salvaged.
4555	Zeller No.18	Ol.s.	370	1927	Aug 18 1961	Burned	At West New York, N.J.
4556	Zenobia	Sch.	-	-	Jul 24 1898	Unknown	Orleans Beach, Mass.
4557	Zephy	Sch.	-	-	Oct 28 1901	Unknown	Wood End, Cape Cod, Mass.
4558	Zephy	Sch.	-	-	Oct 17 1896	Unknown	North of Block Island, R.I.
4559	Zero	Brg.	331	1926	Sep 21 1938	Foundered	Gravesend Bay, N.Y.
4560	Zulma	Bark	-	-	Jan 6 1887	Unknown	Off Nauset, Mass.
4561	44	Brg.	230	-	Nov 17 1924	Burned	Tremley Point, N.J.
4562	65-H	Brg.	216	1908	Jan 22 1939	Stranded	Lawrence Point, off Astoria, N.Y.
4563	506	Brg.	-	-	1961	Unknown	3,600 yds., 147.5° from Fort Delaware Light, Main Channel, Delaware River.

NO.	NAME OF VESSEL	RIG	TONS	BUILT	DATE	CAUSE	PLACE AND COMMENT
4563	506	Sc.b.	934	1908	Jul 7 1932	Stranded	39-33-57 N. 75-32-37 W. Length 195'. Beam 35'. Depth 30'.
4564	702	Sch.	934	1908	Jul 21 1918	Shell Fire	Cape Cod, Mass.
4565	703	Sch.	680	1912	Jul 21 1918	Shell Fire	4 miles off Cape Cod, Mass.
4566	740	Brg.	527	1912	Jul 21 1918	Shell Fire	4 miles off Cape Cod, Mass.
4567	766	Sch.	924	1900	Aug 10 1917	Foundered	Cape Cod, Mass.
4568	782	Sc.b.	495	1899	Mar 14 1926	Foundered	12.5 miles southwest of Shinnicock Light, Long Island, N.Y.
4569	786	Sloop	541	1880	Dec 11 1915	Collided	Plymouth, Mass.
4570	789	Sch.	532	1880	Nov 24 1916	Foundered	With unknown schooner. Seaconnet, R.I. All lives (3) lost.
4571	792	Brg.	368	1888	Nov 12 1927	Foundered	Long Island Sound, N.Y.
4572	801	Brg.	363	1888	Nov 12 1927	Foundered	Off Watch Hill, R.I.
4573	806						Off East Watch Hill, R.I.

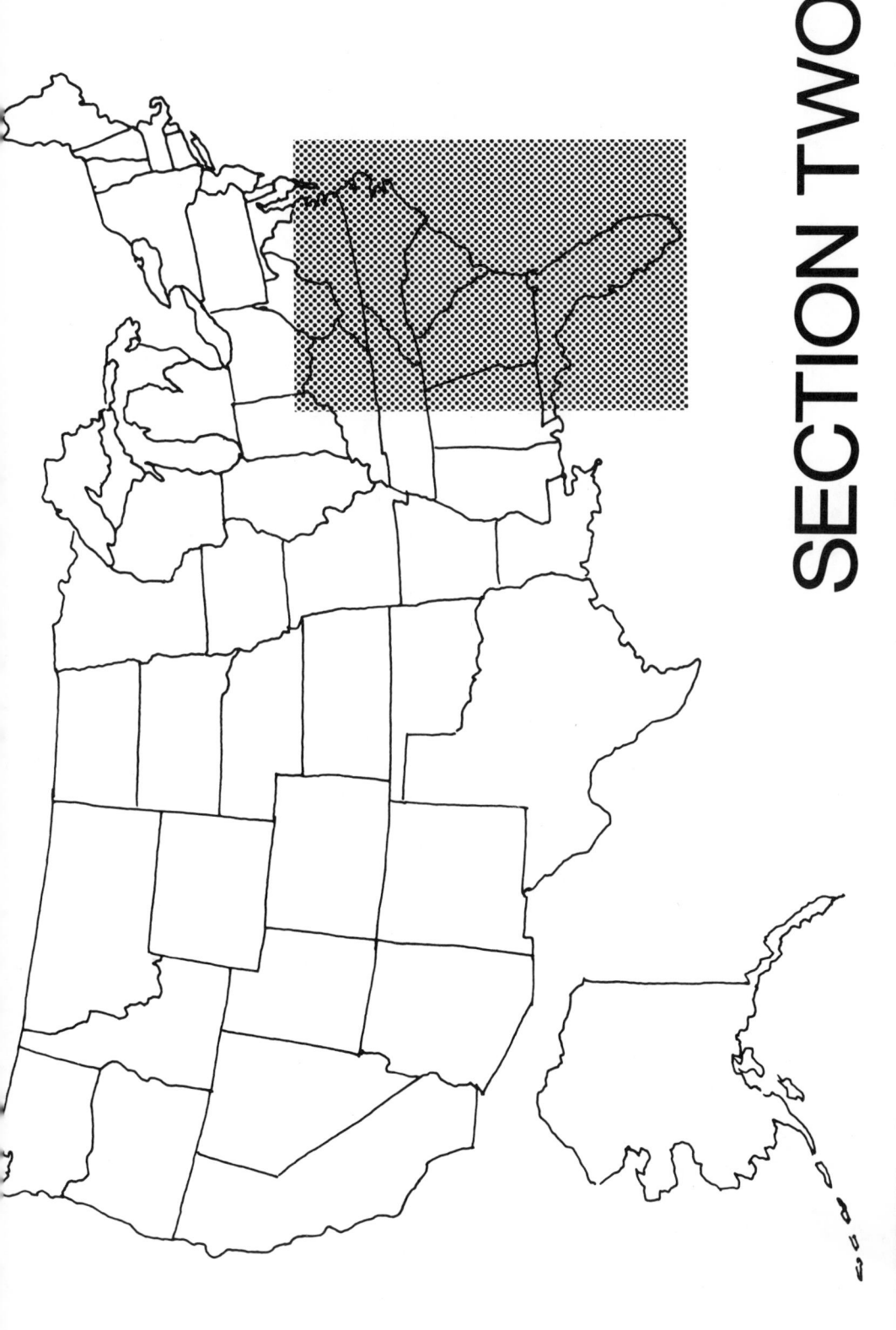

NO.	NAME OF VESSEL	RIG	TONS	BUILT	DATE		CAUSE	PLACE AND COMMENT
1	A.B. Goodman	Sch.	-	-	Apr 4	1881	Unknown	Near Creed Hill Life Saving Station, Diamond Shoals, N.C. 1 life lost.
2	A. Ernest Mills	Sch.	918	1919	May 3	1929	Stranded	North of Currituck Beach Light, Currituck Beach, N.C. 3 lives lost (9).
3	A.F. Crockett	Sch.	-	-	Feb 7	1885	Unknown	Ocracoke, N.C.
4	A.G.T. No.34	Brg.	265	1937	Nov 22	1946	Foundered	Pensacola Bay, Fla. Steel vessel.
5	A.H. Schultz	St-p.	164	1849	Feb 17	1865	Exploded	Cox Ferry, James River, Va. 4 lives lost. Also known as "CSS SCHULTZ".
6	A.L. & M. Townsend	Sch.	-	-	Jul 7	1891	Unknown	Off Cape Lookout, N.C.
7	A.M. Hathaway	St.s.	217	1873	Sep 2	1914	Stranded	Dibidue Island, Georgetown, S.C.
8	A.P. Hurt	St-p.	96	1915	Mar 6	1923	Foundered	Wilmington, N.C. Steel vessel.
9	A.P. Richardson	Sch.	-	-	Sep 26	1894	Unknown	Ocracoke, N.C.
10	A.S. Davis	Clipper	1,400	1875	Oct 22	1878	Unknown	Wrecked approaching Hampton Roads, Va. 1 survivor.
11	A.S. Willers	Sch.	-	-	Sep	1857	Unknown	Off Cape Hatteras, N.C.
12	A.W. Thompson	Brg.	2,279	1901	Nov 6	1928	Foundered	60 miles south of Brunswick, Ga. 2 lives lost (6).
13	Aaron Reppard	Sch.	459	-	Aug 16	1899	Unknown	13 miles north from Big Kinnakeet L.S. Station, off Gull Shoal, N.C. 3-masted vessel.- Coal cargo. 5 lives lost.
14	Abbie H. Gheen	Sch.	266	1880	Feb 13	1916	Stranded	Metomkin Isle, Va.
15	Aberlady Bay	Steamer	-	-	May 10	1889	Unknown	Off Lookout Shoals, N.C.
16	Accoma	St.s.	2,551	1918	Feb 11	1919	Foundered	26-08-00 N. 62-34-00 W.
17	Accomac	Brg.	440	1928	Jan 20	1937	Stranded	On Windmill Point Bar, Va.
18	Acme	Tanker	6,878	-	Mar 17	1942	Unknown	12 miles, 148° from Cape Hatteras Light, N.C. 35-06-00 N. 75-23-00 W. SALVAGED.
19	Ada F. Whitney	Sch.	-	-	Sep 22	1885	Unknown	Poyners Hill, N.C.
20	Ada Gray	Sch.	-	-		1888	Unknown	Little Island, Va.
21	Ada P. Gould	Bark	-	-		1891	Abandoned	Near Cape Charles Lightship, Va.
22	Adam W. Spies	Sch.	1,222	1884	Dec 1	1906	Stranded	40 miles west of Stirrup Key, Fla.
23	Adamantine	Sch.	-	-	Nov	1867	Unknown	Bodie Inlet, N.C.
24	Addie	Sch.	55	1885	Mar 2	1903	Stranded	Bull Island, S.C.
25	Addie F. Cole	Sch.	76	1867	Apr 15	1908	Foundered	North Anclote Channel, Fla.
26	Addie Henry	Sch.	-	-	Apr 14	1895	Unknown	Ocracoke, N.C.
27	Addie Morrill	Bkn.	654	1882	Oct 3	1907	Foundered	Cape Hatteras, N.C.
28	Adelaide Baker	Bark	-	-	Jan 30	1889	Unknown	Coffin Patches, Fla.
29	Adelaide Day	St.s.	686	1917	Nov 8	1927	Stranded	Off Cape Hatteras, N.C.
30	Adeline	St.s.	70	1903	May 12	1924	Burned	Fort Pierce, Fla.
31	Admiral	St.s.	68	1903	May 1	1920	Foundered	Off Frying Pan Lightship, N.C.
32	Adonis	Bark	-	-	Feb 23	1887	Unknown	Tybee Island, Ga.
33	Adventure	Ol-y.	57	1926	Jan 19	1941	Foundered	20 to 30 miles southwest of Winterquarter Lightship, Va.
34	Afoundria	Frgt.	5,010	-	May 5	1942	Unknown	20-00-00 N. 73-30-00 W. North of Cuba.
35	Agamemnon	Ship	-	-	Mar 25	1859	Unknown	Currituck Beach, N.C.
36	Agawam	Ga.y.	50	1905	Mar 16	1922	Foundered	Northeast of Diamond Shoal Lightship, off Cape Hatteras, N.C.
37	Agnes Boston	Brg.	-	-	Mar 14	1889	Unknown	Dam Neck Mills, Va.
38	Agra	-	-	-	Apr 20	1942	Unknown	Off Cape Hatteras, N.C.
39	Aid Harrington	-	-	-	May 23	1851	Unknown	Caffeys Inlet, N.C.
40	Alabama	Sch.	881	1911	Jan 9	1912	Foundered	50 miles southwest of Cape Hatteras, N.C. 4 lives lost.
41	Albany	St-p.	168	1846	Oct 9	1852	Stranded	Apalachicola, Fla.
42	Albatross	Ol.s.	372	1918	Feb 2	1940	Stranded	Off Ocracoke Island, N.C. 35-03-00 N. 75-55-00 W. Trawler. Depth 28'.
43	Albemarle	Brig	-	-	Sep 7	1853	Unknown	Off Hatteras, N.C.
44	Albemarle	Steamer	-	-	Oct 27	1864	Unknown	Plymouth, N.C. Confederate ram.
45	Albert Meyer	Sch.	459	1896	Dec 31	1927	Stranded	Florida Keys, Fla.
46	Alberta	Sch.	77	1882	Jul 1	1925	Stranded	Toms Cove, Va.
47	Alcoa Guide	Frgt.	4,834	-	Apr 16	1942	War Loss	35-34-00 N. 70-08-00 W. Off North Carolina coast.

NO.	NAME OF VESSEL	RIG	TONS	BUILT	DATE		CAUSE	PLACE AND COMMENT
48	Alcoa Shipper	Frgt.	5,491	-	Apr 30	1942	War Loss	37-49-00 N. 65-15-00 W. Off Virginia coast.
49	Alela	Ga.y.	70	1913	May 20	1923	Burned	Beaufort, N.C.
50	Alert	Ga.s.	99	1888	Nov 24	1914	Stranded	Nassau Bar, Fla.
51	Alex J. Gibson	Brg.	431	1901	Dec 19	1927	Foundered	Chesapeake Bay, Va.
52	Alexander Cooper	Steamer	-	-	Aug 22	1863	Burned	Near Cape Fear, N.C. Confederate blockade-runner.
53	Alexander Jones	St.s.	134	1877	Oct 14	1910	Stranded	Favey Rock, Fla. Iron vessel.
54	Alexis L. DuPont	Ol.s.	150	1919	Jan 26	1928	Foundered	Cape Lookout, N.C.
55	Alfred Brabrook	Sch.	563	-	Mar 7	1899	Wrecked	2 miles north of Gull Island L.S. Station, north of Cape Hatteras, N.C.
56	Alfred Thomas	Sch.	-	-	Mar 10	1867	Unknown	New Inlet, N.C.
57	Alhambra	Sch.	-	-	Aug 26	1837	Unknown	Off Bodie Island, N.C.
58	Alice	Sch.	61	1882	May 7	1906	Stranded	Chincoteague Cove, Va.
59	Alice	Brg.	260	1882	Apr 23	1919	Burned	Portsmouth, Va.
60	Alice Ann	Ol.s.	79	1918	Mar 14	1950	Foundered	In vicinity of False Cape, Va.
61	Alice C. Price	St.p.	283	1853	Jun 16	1864	Torpedoed	St. John's River, Fla.
62	Alice Holbrook	Sch.	722	1890	Apr 16	1913	Stranded	Hillsboro Inlet, Fla.
63	Alice Lord	Sch.	373	1902	Jan 13	1915	Foundered	37-16-00 N. 71-06-00 W. 1 life lost.
64	Alice M. Guthrie	Ga.s.	89	1901	Jun 2	1918	Collided	With st.s. ANSON M. BANGS. 3 miles east of Cape Henry, Va.
65	Alice Murphy	Sch.	425	1874	Apr 3	1915	Foundered	Off Cape Hatteras, Fla.
66	Alice Tebb	St.s.	2,426	1920	Sep 28	1940	Foundered	At sea, about 160 miles north of Jacksonville, Fla.
67	Allan Jackson	Tanker	6,635	-	Jan 19	1942	War Loss	35-00-00 N. 74-22-00 W. 60 miles off Cape Hatteras, N.C. Length 453'.
68	Allegheney	Brg.	-	-	Mar 31	1942	Unknown	37-33-30 N. 75-24-15 W. Depth 74'. Also known as "Alleghany".
69	Alliance	Steamer	-	-	Mar 4	1869	Unknown	Off Hatteras Inlet, N.C.
70	Allie R. Chester	Sch.	-	-	Jan 20	1889	Unknown	Outer edge of Diamond Shoals, Cape Hatteras, N.C. Phosphate cargo. 5 lives lost.
71	Alligator	St.p.	69	1888	Nov 5	1909	Burned	Cross Cut Lake, Fla.
72	Alma	St.s.	165	1901	Sep 12	1920	Burned	Mattamuskeet Lake, N.C.
73	Alonzo	Sch.	-	-	Aug 24	1841	Unknown	Currituck Beach, N.C.
74	Alpena	Sch.	970	1901	Dec 4	1924	Foundered	St. Andrews Bay, Fla.
75	Alpha	St.s.	107	1857	Oct 7	1865	Exploded	Albemarle Sound, N.C.
76	Alpha	Ga.y.	79	1917	Feb 7	1922	Foundered	31-32-00 N. 78-52-00 W.
77	Alphild	Bark	-	-	Feb 27	1893	Unknown	Off Cape Fear, N.C.
78	Altamaha	St.s.	2,667	1908	Jun 26	1923	Stranded	Pensacola, Fla. Steel vessel.
79	Amaganset	St.s.	145	1879	Jul 13	1922	Stranded	Off Cobbs Island, Va.
80	Amagansett	Ol.s.	226	1954	Nov 20	1964	Foundered	Off the Cove Banks between Drum Inlet & Cape Lookout Lighthouse, N.C.
81	Amanda	Sch.	-	-	Jul 26	1887	Unknown	Pensacola, Fla.
82	Amanda Coons	Brig	-	-	Nov 11	1858	Unknown	Currituck Beach, N.C.
83	Amanda Winants	St.p.	257	1864	Sep 28	1874	Foundered	Georgetown, S.C. 16 lives lost.
84	Amazon	Bark	318	-	Dec 21	1861	"Sunk"	4 miles SSE off Fort Sumter and 3 miles ESE of the light on Morris Island, Charleston Harbor, S.C. Stone cargo. Part of "Stone Fleet" to block harbor by Union forces during Civil War.
85	Amazon	St.p.	372	1856	Feb	1866	Snagged	Savannah River, Ga. Steel vessel.
86	Amazone	Bkn.	1,167	1902	Jul 4	1925	Burned	27-25-00 N. 79-30-00 W.
87	Amazone (Dutch)	Frgt.	677*	-	May 7	1942	Unknown	27-23-39 N. 80-03-08 W. Depth 42'. Wreck demolished.
88	Amelia M. Price	Sch.	58	1869	Dec 19	1905	Collided	With st.p. BALTIMORE. Point No Point, Md. 1 life lost.
89	Amelia Zeman	Sch.	738	1920	Feb 10	1920	Foundered	Sailed from Norfolk, Va. & has not since reported. All lives (9) lost.
90	America	St.p.	460	1849	Jan 29	1851	Foundered	Off Cape Hatteras, N.C.
91	America	Ship	418	-	Jan 20	1862	"Sunk"	On south edge of Rattlesnake Shoal, Maffitt's Channel, Charleston, S.C. 2nd "Stone Fleet" used to block harbor by Union forces during Civil War.
92	America	Bark	-	-	Dec 24	1876	Unknown	Chicamacomico, N.C.

NO.	NAME OF VESSEL	RIG	TONS	BUILT	DATE	CAUSE	PLACE AND COMMENT
93	American	Bark	329	-	Dec 21 1861	"Sunk"	4 miles SSE off Fort Sumter and 3 miles ESE of the light on Morris Island, Charleston Harbor, S.C. Stone cargo. Used by Union forces to block harbor.
94	American Trader	Sch.	-	-	Aug 24 1841	Unknown	Currituck Beach, N.C.
95	Amicus	Bark	-	-	Apr 2 1891	Unknown	Near Apalachicola, Fla.
96	Amy Dora	St.s.	-	-	Oct 7 1889	Unknown	Watchapregue Inlet, Va.
97	Andrew Hicks	Bark	303	1867	Dec 8 1917	Foundered	Off Cape Henry, Va.
98	Andrew Jackson	St.p.	139	1829	Dec 4 1830	Exploded	Savannah, Ga. 2 lives lost.
99	Andrew Jackson	Frgt.	5,990	-	Jul 12 1942	War Loss	23-32-00 N. 81-02-00 W. Southeast of Key West, Fla.
100	Andrew Johnson	Steamer	-	-	Oct 5 1866	Unknown	2 miles north of Chaffey's Inlet Coast Guard Station, Currituck Inlet, N.C.
101	Andrew McDonald	Sc.b.	2,218	1919	Feb 20 1937	Foundered	About 11 miles north of Paramour Gas Buoy, Va.
102	Angela (It.)	Bark	-	-	Mar 4 1883	Unknown	1/4 mile east of northern end of Kitty Hawk Beach, N.C. Iron cargo. Depth 20'.
103	Angelo	St.p.	122	1893	Sep 27 1906	Stranded	Pensacola Bay, Fla.
104	Anna M. Record	Sch.	1,259	1906	Jan 26 1924	Foundered	Off Cape Lookout, N.C.
105	Anna May	Ol.s.	-	-	Dec 9 1931	Unknown	Off Diamond Shoals, N.C. Trawler.
106	Anna R. Bishop	Sch.	448	1880	Dec 25 1909	Foundered	Sailed from Jacksonville, Fla. & has not since reported. All lives (7) lost.
107	Anna R. Heidritter	Sch.	-	-	Mar 1 1942	Unknown	Ocracoke Inlet, N.C.
108	Annawan	St.p.	163	1855	Jun 28 1856	Burned	Wheeling, Va.
109	Annchen	Brg.	-	-	Jul 18 1888	Unknown	Off Cape Hatteras, N.C.
110	Anne Comber	Sch.	-	-	Jan 17 1908	Unknown	Pamlico Sound, N.C.
111	Annie	St.s.	72	1899	Apr 5 1918	Exploded	Elizabeth City, N.C. 4 lives lost.
112	Annie E. Blackman	Sch.	-	-	Oct 25 1889	Unknown	2.5 miles off New Inlet, N.C. Coal cargo. 6 lives lost.
113	Annie E. Pierce	Sch.	-	-	Feb 22 1892	Unknown	Little Kinnakeet, N.C. 1 life lost.
114	Annie F. Kimball	Sch.	401	1895	Jan 8 1912	Foundered	Cape Hatteras, N.C. 7 lives lost.
115	Annie McFarland	Brig	-	-	Jan 30 1873	Unknown	Currituck Beach, N.C.
116	Antelope	St.p.	181	1849	Feb 20 1850	Stranded	Hog Island, Va.
117	Anthony D. Nicholas	Sch.	680	1904	Feb 28 1928	Burned	Monte Del Canejo Light, Fla.
118	Anthony R	Brg.	348	1924	Sep 1960	Foundered	At Atlantic Creosoting Co. dock, Portsmouth, Va.
119	Antilla	Sch.	-	-	Nov 6 1846	Unknown	Nags Head, N.C.
120	Antonia	Ol.s.	68	1932	Jun 4 1961	Burned	About 13 miles off coast of Palm Beach, Fla.
121	Antonica	St.w.	563	-	Dec 19 1863	Wrecked	3 miles south of the southern tip of Smith's Island, on west side of Frying Pan Shoals, N.C. Blockade runner.
122	Aphrodite	St.s.	1,098	1864	Oct 15 1864	Stranded	Core Sound, N.C.
123	Arabian	Ol.s.	109	1905	Sep 15 1863	Wrecked	Near Cape Fear, N.C. Blockade runner.
124	Arago	Brg.	240	1869	Oct 3 1928	Stranded	Eastern Sambo Key, Fla.
125	Arasapha	St.sch.	201	-	Jan 30 1915	Stranded	Old Point, Va. Iron vessel.
126	Arawak (Br.)	Frgt.	322	-	Sep 23 1941	Unknown	29-36-00 N. 80-54-00 W. Hull completely burned. Depth 60'.
127	Archer	Ship	-	-	Dec 21 1861	"Sunk"	4 miles SSE off Fort Sumter and 3 miles ESE of the light on Morris Island, Charleston, S.C. Part of "Stone Fleet" used by Union forces to block harbor.
128	Argon	Sch.	923	-	Dec 1844	Unknown	Off Cape Lookout, N.C.
129	Ariadne	St.s.	-	1864	Feb 7 1873	Stranded	Oregon Inlet, N.C.
130	Ario	Tanker	6,952	-	Mar 15 1942	Torpedoed	34-20-00 N. 75-29-00 W. Off North Carolina. 8 lives lost (34). Depth 89'.
131	Ario Pardee	Sch.	198	-	Dec 29 1884	Unknown	Wash Woods, N.C.
132	Ariosto	St.sch.	2,265	-	Dec 24 1899	Unknown	3 miles south of Hatteras Inlet, N.C.
133	Arizona Sword	Brg.	3,161	1946	Jan 13 1961	Foundered	About 10 miles east of West Palm Beach, Fla. Steel vessel.
134	Arleville H. Peary	Sch.	311	1874	Oct 31 1908	Stranded	False Cape, Va.
135	Armenia	St.p.	398	1848	Jan 5 1886	Burned	Alexandria, Va.
136	Arroyo	Steamer	-	-	Feb 20 1910	Unknown	Portsmouth, Va.
137	Arthur	Brg.	-	-	Jul 26 1887	Abandoned	Near Tortugas, Fla.

NO.	NAME OF VESSEL	RIG	TONS	BUILT	DATE		CAUSE	PLACE AND COMMENT
138	Arthur C. Wade	Sch.	699	1884	Mar 26	1907	Stranded	St. Helena Shoals, Savannah River, S.C.
139	Asa T. Stowell	Sch.	419	1891	Sep 22	1906	Foundered	Gulf of Mexico. Sailed from Pensacola, Fla. All lives (7) lost.
140	Asher Ayers	St.p.	188	1865	Jan 9	1866	Burned	Darien, Ga. 6 lives lost.
141	Ashkabad (Rus.)	Frgt.	3,164	-	Apr 29	1942	War Loss	34-22-41 N. 76-21-41 W. 16.9 miles, 153° from Cape Lookout Light, N.C. Wreck demolished. Depth 60'.
142	Ashley	Brig	-	-	Jun 2	1842	Unknown	Off Cape Fear, N.C.
143	Astoria	Bark	-	-	Jan 29	1842	Unknown	Hatteras Inlet, N.C.
144	Atlanta	St.p.	158	1854	Mar 1	1858	Stranded	Body Island, N.C.
145	Atlanta	St.s.	1,054	1864	Oct 15	1865	Foundered	36-03-00 N. 72-30-00 W. 48 lives lost.
146	Atlantic	St.s.	221	1902	Sep 21	1906	Collided	With st.s. NAVAHOE. Cape Fear River, N.C.
147	Atlantic	St.s.	188	1894	Sep 10	1925	Foundered	Cooper River, S.C.
148	Atlantic	St.s.	95	1897	Sep 10	1925	Burned	Satilla River, Ga.
149	Atlantic Sun	Tanker	11,355	-	Mar 21	1942	Unknown	Beaufort Sea Buoy. SALVAGED.
150	Atlas	Tanker	7,137	-	Apr 9	1942	War Loss	34-27-00 N. 76-16-00 W. 15.6 miles from lighthouse, Cape Lookout, N.C. Depth 115'. 2 lives lost (34).
151	Atosaras	Ga.y.	162	1911	Dec 13	1921	Burned	Long Shoal River, N.C.
152	Auburn	Sch.	633	1906	Dec 23	1909	Foundered	Sailed from Jacksonville, Fla. and has not since reported. All lives (9) lost.
153	Augusta	St.p.	157	1833	Apr 1	1835	Burned	Augusta, Ga. 4 lives lost.
154	Augusta	St.p.	132	1840	Jan 15	1847	Collided	With EUFALA. Apalachicola, Fla.
155	Augusta	St.p.	1,310	1853	Dec 31	1877	Lost	Savannah, Ga. Redocumented "Magnolia" in 1868.
156	Augusta	St.w.	512	1905	Jun 28	1931	Stranded	Altamah River, Ga. Steel vessel.
157	Augusta Dinsmore	St.s.	850	1863	Jan 11	1869	Stranded	Cape Lookout, N.C. 23 lives lost.
158	Augusta G. Hilton	Sch.	1,562	1918	Aug 18	1933	Foundered	37-29-00 N. 40-50-00 W.
159	Augustus Moore	Sch.	-	-	Apr 15	1853	Unknown	Kitty Hawk, N.C.
160	Aurora	Sch.	-	-	Jun	1837	Unknown	Ocracoke Bar, N.C.
161	Aurora	Bark	-	-	Dec 30	1888	Unknown	Warsaw Sound, Ga.
162	Aurora	St.s.	98	1894	Jan 21	1923	Burned	Near Buzzard Island Point, Appomattox River, Va.
163	Australia	Tanker	11,728	-	Mar 16	1942	War Loss	35-07-18 N. 75-22-03 W. Off North Carolina coast. 4 lives lost (40). Wreck demolished. Depth 42'.
164	Avio	Sch.	473	1890	Jul 6	1924	Burned	Port St. Joe, Fla.
165	Axtell J. Byles	Tanker	8,955	-	Apr 18	1942	War Loss	4 miles off Whimble Shoals Buoy. SALVAGED.
166	B. C. Phillips	St.p.	86	1909	Jan 20	1922	Foundered	Near Coffeys Bluff, Ga.
167	B.T. Martin	Brig	-	-	Jul 24	1861	Unknown	Chicamacomico, N.C.
168	Badger	Steamer	-	-	Sep 10	1864	Wrecked	Cape Fear Bar, N.C. Confederate blockade runner.
169	Bagdad	Sch.	790	1918	Oct 27	1921	Foundered	Sailed from Key West, Fla. and has not since reported. All lives (8) lost.
170	Bainbridge	Sch.	566	1900	Feb 4	1929	Stranded	Nags Head, N.C.
171	Baja California	-	811*	-	Jul 18	1942	Unknown	25-29-00 N. 82-27-00 W.
172	Balila	Ol.s.	79	1916	Jan 17	1947	Burned	35 miles east of Cape Henry, Va.
173	Balsa	Sch.	557	1919	Mar 7	1922	Stranded	Smiths Island, Va.
174	Baltic	Sch.	-	-	Nov	1857	Unknown	Currituck Beach, N.C.
175	Baltimore	Bark	692	1888	Jan 22	1908	Foundered	Sailed from Hampton Roads, Va. and has not since reported. All lives (9) lost.
176	Bangor	Brg.	1,158	1893	Dec 7	1912	Stranded	Hampton Roads, Va. Steel vessel.
177	Barbara Ann Macphie	Brg.	266	1904	Jun 12	1952	Burned	In Bulls Bay Creek, N.C.
178	Barnegat	Brg.	-	-	Mar 31	1942	Unknown	37-33-30 N. 75-24-15 W. Depth 75'.
179	Barnett	St.w.	311	1865	Dec 1	1871	Collided	With survey schooner. Apalachicola, Fla.
180	Barnstable	St.s.	1,210	1887	Sep 13	1919	Foundered	Off Tybee Light, Ga. 4 lives lost.
181	Barnstable	Brg.	1,626	1921	Apr 11	1934	Stranded	Winter Quarter Buoy, Va.
182	Basil Lamar	St.p.	236	1833	Jun 18	1834	Burned	Savannah, Ga.

NO.	NAME OF VESSEL	RIG	TONS	BUILT	DATE		CAUSE	PLACE AND COMMENT
183	Bath	Brg.	1,192	1889	Dec 15	1905	Foundered	Cape Charles, Va. Steel vessel. All lives (6) lost.
184	Bay Queen	St.p.	298	1892	Jul 21	1921	Burned	Hillsboro River, Tampa, Fla.
185	Bayard Hopkins	Sch.	269	1895	Jan 10	1919	Foundered	Sailed from Norfolk, Va. and has not been reported. All lives (6) lost.
186	Bazely	Tug	-	-	Dec 10	1864	Wrecked	Off Jamesville Bluff, Roanoke River, N.C. Confederate vessel. Depth 18'.
187	Beachwood	Sch.	841	1890	May 27	1922	Foundered	Southwest of Fenwick Lightship.
188	Bear Ridge	Sc.b.	910	1898	Sep 29	1927	Collided	With submerged derelict. Hereford Inlet Light, Fla.
189	Beatrice	Ga.y.	79	1917	Jan 27	1927	Collided	With st.s. LAGO. Cape Hatteras, N.C.
190	Beauregard	Steamer	-	-	Dec 11	1863	Wrecked	Carolina Beach, N.C. Confederate blockade runner.
191	Beauty St. Joseph	Ol.s.	92	1928	May 8	1933	Burned	Off Cape Henry, Va.
192	Bedfordshire	Ol.s.	-	-	May	1942	Unknown	Cape Lookout, N.C. Trawler.
193	Belfast	Sc.b.	944	1913	Jan 8	1929	Stranded	Southport, N.C.
194	Belgian Airman (Bel.)	Frgt.	6,959	-	Apr 14	1945	Unknown	80 miles east of Nags Head, N.C. 1 life lost.
195	Bella	St.s.	1,281	1906	Jun 18	1922	Foundered	25-37-00 N. 74-40-00 W. Steel vessel.
196	Belle	Packet	340	1833	Aug 15	1836	Wrecked	On Bodie Island, N.C.
197	Belle	Brig	-	-	Jul	1850	Unknown	Diamond Shoals, N.C.
198	Belle	St.p.	74	1903	Apr 26	1911	Burned	Choctawhatchie Bay, Fla. 4 lives lost.
199	Belle Isle	Ol.s.	75	1917	Feb 18	1952	Foundered	On beach near Cape Henry Lighthouse, Va.
200	Belle O'Neill	Sch.	467	1881	Feb 4	1909	Foundered	Lookout Shoals, N.C.
201	Bellingham	St.s.	5,345	1920	Sep 22	1942	War Loss	70-00-00 N. 10-30-00 W. Steel vessel.
202	Belmont	Sc.b.	1,491	1891	Jan 25	1940	Foundered	Entrance to Tampa Bay, Fla. Steel vessel. All lives (4) lost.
203	Ben	Brg.	369	1903	Dec 18	1921	Foundered	29-51-00 N. 84-05-00 W.
204	Bendigo	Steamer	-	-	Jan 4	1864	Wrecked	Lockwoods Folly Inlet, N.C. Confederate blockade runner.
205	Benjamin A. Van Brunt	Sch.	1,191	1891	Sep 20	1925	Collided	With USS MILWAUKEE. 36-56-00 N. 74-46-00 W.
206	Benj. C. Firth	Sch.	888	1890	Jun 28	1909	Foundered	Martins Industry Shoal, S.C.
207	Benjamin Dickerman	Bark	-	-	Oct 18	1880	Unknown	Off Cape Hatteras, N.C. 1 life lost.
208	Benjamin F. Poole	Sch.	1,555	1886	Jan 29	1914	Foundered	Sailed from Wilmington, N.C. and has not since reported. All lives (8) lost.
209	Benjamin M. Wallace	Sch.	-	-	Mar 26	1904	Unknown	Chicamacomico, N.C.
210	Benjamin W. Robinson	Sch.	-	-	Apr 10	1877	Unknown	Chicamacomico, N.C.
211	Benson H. Riggin	Ol.s.	111	1942	Dec 3	1953	Foundered	In Ocracoke Inlet, N.C.
212	Benwood (Nor.)	Frgt.	2,388*	-	Apr 9	1942	Unknown	25-03-30 N. 80-19-30 W.
213	Berks	Brg.	379	1899	Sep 3	1913	Stranded	Gull Rock, Pamlico Sound, N.C. 2 lives lost.
214	Bertha	Sch.	-	-	May 21	1887	Unknown	Morris Island, S.C.
215	Bertha	Brg.	310	1898	Dec 6	1918	Foundered	2 miles below Hog Shoal Gas Buoy.
216	Bertie	Brg.	756	1947	Mar 17	1956	Foundered	About 5 miles south of Wolf Trap-light in Chesapeake Bay, Va. Steel vessel.
217	Bessie Brown	Sch.	260	1884	May 5	1915	Stranded	Off Cobb Isle Life Saving Station, Va.
218	Bessie Morris	Sch.	-	-	Nov 17	1887	Unknown	False Cape, Va.
219	Bessie Whiting	Sch.	559	1882	Jan 11	1918	Stranded	Perico Island, Fla.
220	Beverly	Brg.	308	1882	Nov 15	1948	Burned	At City Point Oil Terminal, Inc., dock, Hopewell, Va. Steel vessel.
221	Bill Nye	Sch.y.	80	1893	Aug 7	1933	Stranded	Fernandina, Fla.
222	Billy Bowlegs	Sch.	-	-		1840	Unknown	At entrance to Apalachicola Bay, Fla. Vessel belonged to privateer. Valued at over $4 million.
223	Birch Lake	Brg.	-	-	Apr 7	1943	Unknown	8 miles out from Sand Shoal Inlet, Wreck Island, Va. 37-15-00 N. 75-37-24 W.
224	Biscayne	St.p.	276	1888	Apr 12	1913	Stranded	Pine Island, North River, Fla.
225	Black Squall	Brig	-	-	Apr 8	1861	Unknown	Ocracoke, N.C.
226	Black Warrior	Sch.	-	-	Feb 10	1862	Burned	Off Fort Cobb at Cobb's Point, N.C. Confederate vessel.
227	Bladen	St.p.	63	1853	Jun	1853	Unknown	Norfolk, Va.
228	Bladen McLaughlin	Steamer	-	-	May 6	1853	Unknown	Kitty Hawk, N.C.
229	Blaisdell	Sch.	-	-	May	1875	Unknown	Off Cape Hatteras, N.C.

NO.	NAME OF VESSEL	RIG	TONS	BUILT	DATE		CAUSE	PLACE AND COMMENT
230	Blanche	St.s.	94	1878	Nov 5	1947	Foundered	Cape Fear River Channel, N.C., below entrance to Maritime Basin. Steel vessel.
231	Blanche	Sch.	-	-	Dec 18	1890	Unknown	Ocracoke Inlet, N.C.
232	Blanche C. Pendleton	Sch.	880	1920	Jan 21	1922	Collided	With st.s. I.C. WHITE. Off Bodies Island, N.C.
233	Blanche Hopkins	Sch.	-	-	Apr 11	1905	Unknown	Gull Shoal, N.C.
234	Blink (Nor.)	-	-	-	Feb 11	1942	Unknown	Off Cape Hatteras, N.C. 17 lives lost.
235	Bloody Marsh	Tanker	10,195	1943	Jul 2	1943	War Loss	31-25-00 N. 78-45-00 W. Steel vessel. 3 lives lost (78).
236	Bluefields	Sch.	281	1904	Oct 17	1923	Stranded	Perdido Bay, Fla. 4 lives lost (9).
237	Bluefields	St.s.	736	1866	Jan 4	1908	Foundered	Cape Hatteras, N.C. All lives (18) lost. Iron vessel.
238	Boatwright	St.p.	184	1835	Apr 23	1838	Stranded	Indian River, Fla.
239	Bonnets of Blue	St.p.	71	1833	Jul 1	1833	Foundered	Savannah to Mobile.
240	Boringer	St.s.	-	-	Apr 6	1891	Unknown	Ocracoke Inlet, N.C.
241	Bosiljka (Y.S.)	Frgt.	1,810*	-	Jun 19	1942	Unknown	24-58-03 N. 81-52-15 W. Wreck demolished. Depth 27'.
242	Boyd C. Taylor	St.w.	242	1891	Feb	1909	Foundered	Wheeling, W.Va.
243	Braganza	Sch.	95	1892	Oct 11	1903	Unknown	Key West, Fla.
244	Brainbridge	Brig	-	-	Aug 21	1863	Unknown	Off Cape Hatteras, N.C. Federal vessel used during Civil War.
245	Brainbridge	Sch.	-	-	Feb 5	1929	Unknown	Nags Head, N.C.
246	Brazos	Sch.	226	1902	Nov 3	1917	Stranded	Tortugas, Fla.
247	Brazos	Frgt.	4,497	-	Jan 13	1942	War Loss	34-30-00 N. 75-30-00 W. Off North Carolina coast.
248	Brewster	Steamer	-	-	Nov 29	1909	Unknown	Middle of Diamond Shoals, Cape Hatteras, N.C.
249	Brewster	Ga.s.	516	1878	Apr 21	1922	Collided	With st.s. LAKE STERLING. James River, Va. 1 life lost.
250	Bride of Lorne	-	-	-	Apr 1	1887	Unknown	Pensacola, Fla.
251	Bris	-	-	-	Apr 21	1942	Unknown	34-27-00 N. 75-19-00 W. Also reported lost August 8, 1942.
252	British Splendour [Br.]	Tanker	4,172*	-	Apr 6	1942	War Loss	35-09-36 N. 75-18-24 W. Off Diamond Shoals, N.C. Depth 46'. 12 lives lost.
253	Bronx	Sloop	-	-	Jun 21	1892	Unknown	Beaufort Harbor, N.C.
254	Bronx	St.s.	57	1882	Oct 7	1923	Foundered	Off Pensacola Bar, Fla.
255	Bronx Barge Corp. No.1	Brg.	308	1898	Jan 28	1926	Foundered	Frying Pan Shoals, N.C.
256	Brooklyn	Brg.	154	1887	May 10	1926	Stranded	Lake Worth Inlet, Fla.
257	Broward	Drg.	165	1923	Apr 11	1924	Burned	Hollywood Lake, Fla.
258	Brown Bros.	Bark	870	1875	Nov 13	1916	Foundered	Sailed from Savannah, Ga., and has not since reported. All lives (12) lost.
259	Brown Dick	St.w.	56	1855	Nov 23	1862	Burned	Wheeling, Va.
260	Bruce	St.s.	84	1922	Sep 8	1925	Burned	White City, Fla.
261	Brunswick	St.s.	89	1896	Oct 19	1926	Burned	Awendaw River, S.C.
262	Brunswick	Brg.	473	1914	Jul 1	1933	Foundered	Winter Quarter Lightship, Va.
263	Buarque (Braz.)	St.s.	-	-	Feb 15	1942	Unknown	Kill Devil Hills, N.C. 35-56-00 N. 75-32-00 W.
264	Buckeye	St.p.	74	1896	Jul 27	1921	Burned	Point Pleasant, W.Va.
265	Buddy Lynn	Ol.s.	64	1958	Feb 11	1961	Foundered	About 15 miles south of Rebecca Shoal Light, 45 miles west of Key West, Fla.
266	Busiris	Sch.	250	-	Oct 23	1889	Unknown	Off Poyners Hill L.S. Station, N.C.
267	Buttonwood	St.s.	2,848	1919	Jan 31	1923	Burned	Lynhaven Roads, near Cape Henry, Va.
268	Buxton	St.s.	161	1863	Apr 20	1922	Burned	Berkley, Va. Iron vessel.
269	Byam	Sch.	58	1896	Jan 20	1928	Foundered	Chesapeake Bay, Va.
270	Byron D. Benson	Tanker	7,053	-	Apr 3	1942	Unknown	36-10-00 N. 75-13-00 W. Off North Carolina coast. Depth 80'. 9 lives lost (37).
271	C.C. Overton	Brig	-	-	Feb 1	1878	Unknown	Ocracoke Inlet, N.C.
272	C.C. Thorn	Sch.	-	-	Jun 2	1846	Unknown	Off New Inlet, N.C.
273	C.D. Fry	St.w.	332	1865	Oct 26	1871	Snagged	32 miles below Columbus, Ga.
274	C.H. Evans	St.s.	57	1890	Dec 4	1907	Burned	Bull Head Bluff, Ga.
275	C.S. Glidden	Sch.	-	-	Mar 17	1903	Unknown	Off Cape Lookout, N.C.
276	C.S. Pearcy	St.p.	148	1910	Sep 13	1917	Burned	Little Kanawha River, W.Va.
277	C.W. Lyon	St.p.	98	1905	Nov 14	1911	Foundered	Cape Fear River, N.C. Steel vessel. 1 life lost.

NO.	NAME OF VESSEL	RIG	TONS	BUILT	DATE	CAUSE	PLACE AND COMMENT
278	C.W. Mills	Sch.	371	1904	May 1 1921	Burned	South of Tortugas, Fla.
279	Caldwell	St.w.	51	1859	Mar 14 1865	Burned	Fayetteville, N.C.
280	Caldwell H. Colt	Sch.	64	1887	Feb 16 1922	Stranded	Tortugas, Fla. 7 lives lost.
281	Caledonia	St.s.	459	1853	Feb 28 1869	Stranded	Cape Hatteras Inlet, N.C.
282	Cambridge	St.p.	462	1846	Sep 16 1853	Burned	Reppahannock River, Va.
283	Camden	Ol.s.	58	1891	Dec 8 1953	Foundered	200 yards south of Black Can Buoy #87, off Windmill Point, Va., on the James R.
284	Campello	St.s.	2,469	1919	Apr 13 1922	Burned	Claremont, Va.
285	Cando	St.p.	74	1899	Jun 10 1907	Foundered	Huntington, W.Va.
286	Cape Fear	Steamer	-	-	Jan 1865	Wrecked	Cape Fear River, N.C. Confederate blockade runner.
287	Cape Hatteras Lightship	-	320	-	Aug 1827	Unknown	Aground on Whalebone Inlet, opposite Ocracoke Island, N.C. 2 lives lost.
288	Captain Bartlett	Drg.	320	-	Aug 1827	Unknown	Aground on Whalebone Inlet, opposite Ocracoke Island, N.C. 2 lives lost.
289	Capt. Charlie Lewis	Ol.s.	194	1925	Jan 21 1930	Burned	Miami, Fla.
290	Capt. Fritz	St.w.	149	1951	Dec 29 1961	Stranded	About 3-3/4 miles, 192° from Cape Lookout, N.C. Steel vessel.
291	Capt. John A. Nelson	Ga.y.	57	1892	Sep 19 1930	Burned	Cedar Tree Landing, Fla. 1 life lost (8).
292	Caribsea	St.s.	2,609	1919	Mar 11 1942	War Loss	Morehead City Shipyard, N.C. 10 miles east of Cape Lookout Lighthouse, N.C. 34-35-43 N. 76-18-02 W. Steel vessel. Wreck demolished. Depth 100'.
293	Carisco	St.s.	927	1912	Jan 21 1925	Foundered	James River, Va. Steel vessel.
294	Carl D. Lothrop	Sch.	-	-	Oct 21 1889	Unknown	Cape St. George, Fla.
295	Carl Gerhard (Swed.)	Steamer	1,504	-	Sep 23 1929	Unknown	1 mile north of Kill Devil Hills Coast Guard Station, N.C. Length 265'.
296	Carolina	Brg.	334	1897	Feb 22 1912	Collided	Cargo of plaster rock. Depth 24'. With barge ELLEN S. JENNINGS. Poplar Island, Chesapeake Bay, Md.
297	Carolina King	Ol.s.	82	1928	Nov 4 1962	Burned	At Little River, S.C.
298	Caroline	Ol.s.	109	1918	Aug 11 1939	Foundered	Cumberland Sound, Fla.
299	Carolyn	St.s.	3,209	1912	Apr 7 1943	War Loss	34-52-00 N. 69-58-00 W. Steel vessel. Freighter. Sunk by enemy action.
300	Carrie A. Norton	Sch.	559	1882	Feb 6 1910	Stranded	False Cape, Va.
301	Carrie & Hattie	Sloop	-	-	Mar 25 1887	Unknown	Charleston, S.C.
302	Carrie Holmes	Sch.	-	-	Oct 31 1887	Unknown	Cape Henry, Va.
303	Carrie Strong	Sch.	473	1882	Jul 1916	Foundered	26-12-00 N. 88-35-00 W. All lives (7) lost.
304	Carroll	Brig	-	-	Feb 8 1837	Foundered	1 mile south of Cape Lookout Light, N.C.
305	Carroll	Brg.	300	1895	Jan 26 1926	Foundered	Cape Romain Light, N.C. All lives (11) lost.
306	Carroll A. Deering	Sch.	2,114	1919	Jan 31 1921	Stranded	Off Cape Hatteras, N.C. All lives (11) lost.
307	Casket	Bark	107	1856	Sep 13 1892	Unknown	Off Frying Pan Shoals, N.C.
308	Casper Heft	Sch.	107	1856	Dec 24 1906	Stranded	Smiths Point, Va.
309	Cassie F. Bronson	Sch.	1,124	1886	Sep 17 1906	Stranded	Near Cape Fear, N.C.
310	Cassimir	St.s.	5,030	1920	Feb 26 1942	Collided	With st.s. LARA. Halfway between Cape Fear and Cape Lookout, N.C. 33-54-06 N. 77-48-57 W. Steel vessel. Tanker. Also reported as "Cassimer".
311	Cassius	Sch.	-	1888	Feb 12 1854	Unknown	Off Cape Hatteras, N.C.
312	Castleton	St.p.	1,587	1888	Mar 2 1918	Burned	Norfolk, Va.
313	Catahoula	St.s.	5,030	1920	Apr 5 1942	War Loss	19-16-00 N. 68-42-00 W. Steel vessel. Sunk by enemy action.
314	Catherine G. Scott	Sch.	739	1918	Oct 14 1930	Foundered	Cape Hatteras, N.C. 3 lives lost (7).
315	Catherine L. Brown	Ol.s.	129	1919	Feb 27 1947	Foundered	Southeast half south from Chesapeake Lightship, about 50 miles off Portsmouth, Virginia.
316	Catherine M. Monahan	Sch.	896	1905	Aug 24 1910	Abandoned	14 miles south of Cape Hatteras, N.C.
317	Catherine W. May	Sch.	-	-	Dec 19 1887	Unknown	Cape Henry, Va.
318	Cecilia Cohen	Sch.	1,102	1920	Aug 7 1921	Foundered	Off Cape Henry, Va.
319	Ceiba	-	-	-	Mar 15 1942	Unknown	Off Nags Head, N.C.
320	Central America	Steamer	2,141	1852	Sep 12 1857	Foundered	95 miles east of Cape Romain, S.C., and 127 miles south, 1/2 west of Cape Fear.

NO.	NAME OF VESSEL	RIG	TONS	BUILT	DATE		CAUSE	PLACE AND COMMENT
	Central America							Length 272'. Originally named "George Law". 423 lives lost. The cargo was insured for over $1.25 million. Reported to have carried over $1.5 million in gold. Rescue ship gave the following location: 31-25 N. 77-10 W.
321	Chamois	St.p.	125	1836	Oct 31	1842	Exploded	River Junction, Fla.
322	Chansfield	Sch.	-	-	Feb	1860	Unknown	Albemarle Sound, N.C.
323	Charles	Sch.	-	-	Nov	1859	Unknown	Off Nags Head, N.C.
324	Charles A. Dean	Sch.	1,143	1919	Dec 14	1926	Stranded	Frying Pan Shoals, N.C.
325	Charles A. Witler	Sch.	219	1904	Aug 26	1905	Collided	With sch. JOHN BOSSERT. Diamond Shoals, N.C.
326	Charles Benton	St.s.	202	1863	Jan 15	1866	Foundered	At sea. 35-49-00 N. 78-25-00 W.
327	Charles C. Dame	Sch.	598	-	Oct 14	1893	Unknown	8 miles offshore on Frying Pan Shoals, in line with the Cape Fear L.S. Station, North Carolina. 3 masted vessel.
328	Charles C. Lister, Jr.	Sch.	-	-	Jan 26	1891	Unknown	Cape Hatteras, N.C.
329	Charles D. Stanford	Sch.	714	1918	Mar 10	1932	Foundered	Cape Hatteras, N.C. All lives (8) lost.
330	Charles Downing	St.p.	112	1842	Jun 22	1855	Burned	Wilmington, N.C. Renamed "Calhoun" in 1849.
331	Charles F. Tuttle	Sch.	776	1886	Sep 17	1906	Abandoned	Charleston, S.C.
332	Chas. G. Joyce	Sch.	122	1882	May 13	1944	Foundered	McArthur Causeway Docks, Miami, Fla.
333	Charles H. Valentine	Sch.	639	1884	Aug 29	1911	Stranded	Cape Fear, N.C.
334	Charles Hartridge	St.p.	201	1851	Feb 4	1856	Burned	Westlake, Ga.
335	Charles J. Dumas	Sch.	697	1904	Dec 26	1911	Stranded	Pea Island, near Nags Head, N.C.
336	Charles L. Mitchell	Sch.	597	1881	Dec 8	1906	Abandoned	Off Cape Henry, Va.
337	Charles Morand	St.s.	-	-	Jul 26	1890	Unknown	39-42-00 N. 73-23-00 W.
338	Charles S. Hirsch	Sch.	620	1901	Oct 29	1908	Stranded	Paul Gamiels Hill, N.C. 2 lives lost.
339	Charles W. Alcott	Sch.	296	1873	Jun 24	1918	Foundered	50 miles southeast of Hog Island, Va.
340	Charles W. Parker, Jr.	St.s.	277	1909	Mar 26	1910	Foundered	Sailed from Norfolk, Va., and has not since reported. All lives (17) lost. Last report sighted vessel 18 miles off Atlantic City, N.J.
341	Charleston II	Packet	492	1839	Sep 21	1849	Burned	At sea. Off Cape Lookout, N.C. Length 128'.
342	Charleston	St.p.	112	1821	Oct 28	1835	Foundered	Charleston, S.C.
343	Charlotte	Ga.s.	53	1920	Jan	1946	Foundered	James River, at City Point, Hopewell, Va.
344	Charmer	Sch.	-	-	Mar 4	1899	Unknown	Portsmouth, N.C.
345	Charmer	Sch.	1,885	1881	Dec 3	1912	Stranded	Middle Grounds, Chesapeake Bay, Va.
346	Chatham	St.p.	57	1850	Mar 14	1865	Burned	Fayetteville, N.C. Confederate vessel destroyed by Union forces.
347	Chatham	St.s.	2,728	1885	Jan 14	1910	Stranded	North jetty, St. Johns River, Fla. Iron vessel.
348	Chatham	El.o.	228	1944	Oct 14	1968	Burned	At Savannah, Ga.
349	Chelsea	Ol.s.	197	1905	Feb 1	1938	Burned	Cape Fear River, N.C.
350	Chenango	Steamer	-	-	Apr 20	1942	Unknown	Kill Devil Hills, N.C.
351	Chester Sun	Tanker	-	-	Mar 10	1942	Unknown	Big Kinnakeet, N.C.
352	Chetolah	St.y.	91	1891	May 19	1911	Burned	James River, Va.
353	Chevalier	St.p.	67	1901	May 22	1907	Burned	Huntington, W.Va. (Ohio River).
354	Chilore	St.s.	8,310	1922	Jul 15	1942	War Loss	34-39-00 N. 75-34-00 W. Freighter. Steel vessel. Sunk by enemy action.
355	Chimo	St.s.	2,525	1918	Sep 7	1920	Burned	Seven Mile Reach, Va.
356	China Arrow	Tanker	8,403	-	Feb 5	1942	War Loss	37-59-30 N. 75-11-30 W. 1 mile WNW of Buoy #5, Winter Quarter Shoals, Va.
357	Choptank	Brg.	376	1897	Sep 27	1929	Burned	Bayport, Va.
358	Cibao (Nor.)	Steamer	-	-	Dec 4	1927	Unknown	At mouth of Hatteras Inlet, N.C.
359	Ciltvaira	Tanker	-	-	Jan 20	1942	Unknown	Gull Shoal, N.C.
360	Cities Service Denver	St.s.	9,316	1921	Mar 24	1941	Burned	130 miles east of Charleston, S.C. Steel vessel. 20 lives lost (40).
361	Cities Service Empire	St.s.	8,103	1918	Mar 3	1942	War Loss	25 miles north of Bethel Shoals Gas Buoy, Fla. Steel vessel. Tanker. Also reported lost February 22, 1942. Sunk by enemy action. 12 lives lost (50).
362	Cities Service Petrol	St.s.	9,343	1920	Jul 14	1933	Burned	34-00 N. 75-22 W. Steel vessel. 2 lives lost (38).

NO.	NAME OF VESSEL	RIG	TONS	BUILT	DATE		CAUSE	PLACE AND COMMENT
363	City of Alma	St.s.	5,446	1920	Jun 2	1943	War Loss	82-30-00 N. 23-00-00 W. Steel vessel. Sunk by enemy action.
364	City of Atlanta	St.s.	5,269	1904	Jan 19	1942	War Loss	12 miles south of Wimble Shoals Buoy, N.C. Steel vessel. Sunk by enemy action.
365	City of Bath	St.p.	496	1862	Feb 10	1867	Burned	35-23-48 N. 75-15-42 W. Freighter. Depth 41'. 75% loss of life.
366	City of Birmingham	St.s.	5,861	1923	Jun 6	1942	War Loss	Cape Hatteras, N.C. 22 lives lost.
367	City of Dublin	St.p.	147	1897	Sep	1905	Stranded	35-04-00 N. 70-46-00 W. Steel vessel. Sunk by enemy action.
368	City of Eufaula	St.p.	216	1912	Feb 11	1921	Burned	Dublin, Ga.
369	City of Everglades	Ga.s.	93	1921	May 17	1928	Burned	Near Neals Landing, Fla.
370	City of Fayetteville	St.s.	149	1902	Sep 30	1913	Foundered	Collier City, Fla.
371	City of Fayetteville	Brg.	540	1939	Dec 10	1960	Burned	Fayetteville, N.C. Steel vessel.
372	City of New York	St.s.	574	1852	Jan 13	1862	Stranded	In the Cape Fear River, N.C. Steel vessel.
373	City of New York	Ol.s.	8,272	1930	Mar 29	1942	War Loss	Cape Hatteras, N.C.
374	City of Philadelphia	St.s.	542	1896	Oct 14	1919	Burned	Off North Carolina coast. 35-12 N. 74-40 W. Steel vessel. 33 lives lost.
375	City of Port Huron	Ol.s.	62	1946	Feb 7	1966	Foundered	Punta Rassa, Fla.
376	City of Richmond	Brg.	2,013	1913	Oct 5	1964	Foundered	Approximately 22 miles ESE of Port Everglades Sea Buoy, Fla.
377	City of St. Helens	Ga.s.	2,135	1917	Mar 23	1920	Burned	Off Charleston, S.C.
378	City of Sarasota	St.s.	125	1911	Nov 5	1919	Foundered	32-20-00 N. 77-40-00 W.
379	City of Tampa	St.s.	88	1887	Jun 29	1921	Burned	Tampa, Fla.
380	City of Vera Cruz	-	-	1877	Aug 29	1880	Foundered	Near Bay Point Light, Fla.
381	City of Washington	Sch.	2,410	1877	Jul 10	1917	Stranded	Off Florida coast. 68 lives lost.
382	Clara Davidson	Sch.	-	-	Feb 7	1876	Unknown	Elbow Reef, Florida Straits, Fla.
383	Clara E. Bergen	Sch.	-	-	Jun 26	1905	Unknown	Off Hatteras Inlet, N.C.
384	Clare	Ga.y.	65	1923	Jun 23	1925	Burned	Durants, N.C.
385	Clarence H.	Sch.	-	-	Dec 9	1903	Unknown	Point Comfort, Va. 5 lives lost.
386	Clarendon	St.p.	140	1833	Jan 11	1839	Burned	Oak Island, N.C. 5 lives lost.
387	Clarendon	St.s.	143	1860	Mar 14	1865	Burned	St. Catherines Island, Ga.
388	Clarion	St.p.	217	1842	May 1	1845	Burned	Fayetteville, N.C. Confederate vessel destroyed by Union forces.
389	Clemmie Travers	Sch.	85	1885	Sep 18	1936	Stranded	Guyandotte, Va.
390	Clifford N. Carver	Sch.	1,101	1900	Apr 2	1913	Stranded	Against stone breaker at Norfolk, Va.
391	Clifton	St.p.	256	1864	May 18	1909	Stranded	Tennessee Reef, Fla.
392	Clintonia	Sch.	1,876	1881	Apr 4	1915	Foundered	Beaufort, N.C.
393	Clyde	St.s.	96	1862	Oct 14	1897	Burned	50 miles southeast of Diamond Shoals Lightship, N.C. Iron vessel.
394	Clythia (Nor.)	Bark	-	-	Jan 22	1894	Unknown	Key West, Fla. Steel vessel.
395	Codorus	Bark	-	-	Aug 4	1886	Unknown	0.8 miles north of the Virginia-North Carolina boundary and south of False Cape, Va. 150 yards offshore. Marble cargo.
396	Col. Thomas F. Austin	Ga.s.	83	1902	Feb 24	1916	Stranded	Off Diamond Shoals, N.C.
397	Colthraps	St.s.	5,134	1920	Sep 5	1922	Burned	Off Cape Fear Lighthouse, N.C.
398	Columbia	St.p.	121	1819	Nov 14	1824	Stranded	Pensacola, Fla. 1 life lost.
399	Columbia	St.p.	149	1900	Mar 13	1911	Burned	Sullivan Island, S.C.
400	Columbia	Ga.s.	58	1891	Nov 1	1925	Stranded	Milton, Fla.
401	Comanche	St.s.	3,856	1895	Oct 17	1925	Burned	Charleston, S.C.
402	Comanche	Ol.s.	63	1952	Jan 6	1963	Burned	Jacksonville, Fla. Steel vessel. 1 life lost.
403	Comet	Sch.	-	-	Jan 7	1846	Unknown	25-02-00 N. 82-62-00 W.
404	Comet	St.p.	496	1865	Nov	1865	Snagged	Ocracoke Inlet, N.C.
405	Comet	St.p.	181	1857	Dec 2	1865	Stranded	Hawkinsville, Ga.
406	Comet	Ga.y.	65	1906	Aug 9	1935	Burned	Hawkinsville, Ga.
407	Commerce	St.p.	124	1836	1839		Exploded	Foot of 24th Avenue, Miami, Fla.
408	Commodore	St.s.	940	1863	Mar 3	1867	Burned	Apalachicola River, Fla. 5 lives lost. / Off Cape Hatteras, N.C.

NO.	NAME OF VESSEL	RIG	TONS	BUILT	DATE	CAUSE	PLACE AND COMMENT
409	Commodore Bartlett	St.s.	58	1901	Jun 10 1928	Burned	Elizabeth City, N.C.
410	Comol Rico	St.s.	5,034	1919	Apr 4 1942	War Loss	20-46-00 N. 66-46-00 W. Steel vessel. Sunk by enemy action.
411	Concord	St.s.	155	1853	Feb 20 1886	Burned	Washington, N.C.
412	Condor (Br.)	Steamer	-	-	Oct 1 1864	Wrecked	On north reef near Swash Channel Bar, off Fort Fisher, N.C. Blockade runner.
413	Coniscliffe	Ship	-	-	Aug 24 1842	Unknown	Outer Diamond Shoal, east of Cape Hatteras, N.C. 7 lives lost. Salt cargo.
414	Coniscliffe	Sch.	441	1891	Apr 7 1921	Burned	27-21-00 N. 79-31-00 W.
415	Connecticut	Brg.	473	1915	Jun 10 1931	Burned	New Bern, N.C.
416	Conserva	St.s.	-	-	Mar 23 1889	Unknown	Winter Quarter Shoal, Va.
417	Constitution	St.s.	944	1863	Dec 26 1865	Stranded	Cape Lookout, N.C. 40 lives lost.
418	Cora A	Sch.	370	1889	Mar 6 1916	Foundered	36-42-00 N. 57-18-00 W.
419	Coral Isle	Ol.s.	69	1950	Jan 18 1968	Collided	With submerged object. Northeast of Toggerhead Light, Tortugas, off Key West, Fla.
420	Corapeake	Sch.	234	1894	Jun 15 1936	Burned	North River Bar, N.C.
421	Cordelia E. Hays	Sch.	-	-	Jan 15 1905	Unknown	Off Cape Hatteras, N.C.
422	Corea	Ship	356	-	Dec 21 1861	"Sunk"	4 miles SSE off Fort Sumter and 3 miles ESE of the light on Morris Island, Charleston, S.C. Stone cargo. Used by Union forces to block harbor entrance.
423	Cornelia	Sch.	60	1866	Aug 10 1905	Foundered	Back Creek, Va.
424	Cornelius H. Callaghan	Sch.	1,341	1916	Jan 10 1924	Stranded	St. Andrews Bar, Fla.
425	Corydon	St.s.	2,351	1918	Sep 9 1919	Foundered	Off Florida coast. Steel vessel. 27 lives lost (36).
426	Cossack	Bark	254	-	Dec 21 1861	"Sunk"	4 miles SSE off Fort Sumter and 3 miles ESE of the light on Morris Island, Charleston, S.C. Stone cargo. Used by Union forces to block harbor entrance.
427	Courier	Ship	381	-	Dec 21 1861	"Sunk"	Part of "Stone Fleet". See No. 426 for location.
428	Courier	Ol.s.	138	1941	Jan 15 1965	Burned	Approximately 80 miles off Cape Henry, Va.
429	Cragsill	St.s.	80	1917	Feb 27 1891	Unknown	Cape Hatteras, N.C.
430	Crane	St.s.	591	1881	Jul 31 1929	Burned	Bennetts Creek, N.C.
431	Crescent	Sch.	465	1883	Feb 27 1916	Foundered	Off Cape Hatteras, N.C.
432	Crescent	Clipper	942	1854	Jan 26 1920	Foundered	150 miles southeast of Pensacola, Fla.
433	Crest of the Wave	Sch.	-	-	Apr 1870	Wrecked	On Wreck Island, 15 miles north of Cape Charles, Va. All lives lost.
434	Crissie Wright	St.p.	396	1840	Jan 11 1886	Unknown	Lookout Shoals, N.C. 6 lives lost.
435	Croton	Ol.s.	57	1898	May 10 1867	Collided	With sch. TWO MARYA. Cape Henry, Va. 6 lives lost.
436	Crystal Wave	Sch.	-	-	Sep 17 1931	Burned	Hilton Head Island, S.C.
437	Cumberland	Steamer	-	-	Oct 8 1837	Unknown	Core Bank, N.C.
438	Curlew	St.p.	201	1851	Feb 7 1862	Unknown	Near Fort Forrest, Manns Harbor, N.C. Confederate gun-boat. Iron hull.
439	Cusseta	Sch.	113	1871	Feb 5 1856	Collided	With UNION. Apalachicola River, Fla.
440	Custus W. Wright	St.p.	141	1829	Jan 24 1908	Foundered	Newport News, Va. All lives (4) lost.
441	Cygnet	Sch.	317	1881	Oct 7 1834	Burned	Alexandria, Va.
442	D.D. Haskell	St.s.	321	1863	May 9 1905	Stranded	Near Ocracoke Inlet, N.C. (Core Bank, N.C.)
443	D.H. Mount	Sch.	547	1891	Oct 23 1865	Foundered	Cape Hatteras, N.C. - Jacksonville, Fla. 24 lives lost.
444	D. Howard Spear	Brig	-	-	Mar 9 1911	Foundered	33-00-00 N. 76-55-00 W.
445	D.W. Hall	Drg.	242	1925	Jun 14 1842	Unknown	Hatteras Inlet, N.C.
446	Dania	Sch.	-	-	Feb 15 1958	Foundered	About 1500 feet to the eastward of Cut "F" Channel, in Tampa Bay, Fla.
447	Daniel Chase	St.p.	119	1853	Nov 1867	Unknown	Ocracoke Inlet, N.C.
448	Daniel P. Shenfelder	Brg.	1,035	1851	Mar 1859	Burned	Charles City, Va.
449	Daniel Webster	Brg.	1,018	1903	Oct 3 1866	Foundered	180 miles off Tybee Island, Ga.
450	Dansonia	Sch.	-	-	Oct 1925	Foundered	Berkley, Va.
451	Danube	Sch.	178	1887	May 14 1844	Unknown	Bodie Island, N.C.
452	Dare	Sch.	50	1887	Jan 7 1864	Burned	North of North Inlet, N.C. Confederate blockade runner.
453	Dauntless	Brg.	267	1878	Sep 18 1907	Collided	With barge ARTHUR. Pinners Point, Va.
454	David				Jun 7 1931	Burned	Norfolk Harbor, Va. Iron vessel.

NO.	NAME OF VESSEL	RIG	TONS	BUILT	DATE	CAUSE	PLACE AND COMMENT
455	David B	Ol.s.	57	1949	May 6 1963	Foundered	About 35 miles northwest of Tampa Seabuoy, Tampa, Fla.
456	David H. Atwater	Frgt.	2,438	-	Apr 2 1942	War Loss	37-37-00 N. 75-10-00 W. Winter Quater Shoals, Va. Steel vessel. Depth 67'.
457	David W. Hunt	-	-	-	Nov 26 1888	Abandoned	34-30-00 N. 72-30-00 W.
458	Davy Crockett	Sch.	85	1876	Jul 8 1909	Stranded	South Pass, Tampa Bay, Fla.
459	Debby D.	Ol.s.	64	1954	Oct 10 1966	Foundered	Near Key West, Fla.
460	Dee	-	-	-	Feb 6 1864	War Loss	Off New Inlet, Cape Fear, N.C. Confederate blockade runner lost during action with USS COLUMBIA.
461	Deer	St.p.	130	1852	Feb 26 1879	Burned	Newbern, N.C.
462	Defender	St.p.	514	1881	Jan 3 1905	Exploded	Huntington, W.Va. 9 lives lost.
463	Delisle	St.s.	3,478	1919	May 4 1942	War Loss	Off Florida coast. Steel vessel. Sunk by enemy action.
464	Delta	Sch.	317	1892	Sep 30 1926	Stranded	Delray, Fla. 1 life lost (6).
465	Delvalle	St.s.	5,032	1919	Apr 12 1942	War Loss	16-51-00 N. 72-25-00 W. Steel vessel. Sunk by enemy action.
466	Dendron	Sch.	592	1904	Feb 7 1918	Foundered	13 miles northwest of Hog Island Light, Va.
467	Desert Light	-	-	-	Apr 16 1942	Unknown	Oregon Inlet, N.C.
468	Desire	Ol.s.	82	1913	Mar 9 1951	Burned	6 miles off coast of Venice, Fla.
469	Dessoug	Sch.	1,382	1864	Oct 21 1908	Foundered	17 miles northeast of Winter Quarter Shoal, Va. Iron vessel.
470	Dexter	Sch.	51	1871	Jun 25 1919	Collided	With st.s. LIZZIE COLBURN. Norfolk, Va.
471	Diamond Shoals Light-ship	Steamer	-	-	Aug 6 1918	Unknown	Off Cape Hatteras, N.C. Length 124'.
472	Diamond State	Brg.	380	1898	Jun 10 1931	Burned	New Bern, N.C.
473	Diamonfield	Sch.	374	1903	Sep 1917	Foundered	Off Tillman, Fla. All lives (7) lost.
474	Diane	St.s.	118	1905	Aug 14 1948	Burned	Colonna's Shipyard, Elizabeth River, Norfolk, Va.
475	Dictator	Bark	-	-	Mar 27 1891	Unknown	Near Cape Henry, Va.
476	Dixie Arrow	St.s.	8,046	1921	Mar 26 1942	War Loss	25 miles south by west of Cape Hatteras Lighthouse, N.C. 34-53-30 N. 75-44-42 W. Steel vessel. Tanker. 11 lives lost (33). Sunk by enemy action. Demolished.
477	Dixie Crystal	Ol.s.	123	1895	Sep 21 1945	Stranded	Nun Buoy 152, opposite Vilano Beach, St. Augustine, Fla.
478	Dr. W.J. Newbill	St.s.	94	1906	Nov 10 1907	Burned	Carters Creek, Va.
479	Dolphin	St.p.	133	1835	Dec 19 1836	Exploded	St. Johns Bar, Fla.
480	Dom Pedro II	Sch.	489	1878	Feb 14 1914	Stranded	Horseshoe Shoal, Chesapeake Bay, Va.
481	Donna Christina	Sch.	174	1899	Apr 9 1915	Foundered	60 miles southeast of Cape San Blas, Fla. Capsized in storm. All lives (7) lost.
482	Dorado	Brg.	842	1963	Aug 18 1967	Foundered	18-17-00 N. 64-57-00 W.
483	Dorchester	Brg.	358	1898	Apr 1 1918	Foundered	Off Smith Point, Va.
484	Doris Kellogg	St.s.	5,030	1920	Dec 29 1932	Burned	32-41-00 N. 77-30-00 W. Steel vessel.
485	Dorothea L. Brinkman	Sch.	698	1919	Mar 22 1924	Stranded	Oregon Inlet, N.C.
486	Dorothy	St.s.	74	1891	Dec 15 1919	Foundered	Brunswick, Ga.
487	Dorothy T.	St.w.	131	1923	Apr 16 1934	Foundered	Bells Ferry, Ga.
488	Dos Hermanos	Steamer	-	-	Sep 13 1884	Unknown	Off Frying Pan Shoals, N.C. 2 lives lost.
489	Doswell S. Edwards	Ol.s.	93	1926	Dec 8 1952	Foundered	At Beaufort Inlet, Beaufort, N.C.
490	Douglas Hall	St.p.	122	1900	Sep 12 1914	Burned	Leon, W.Va.
491	Douglas Hevey	Sch.	-	-	Apr 4 1888	Unknown	Frying Pan Shoals, N.C.
492	Douro	St.s.	180	-	Oct 11 1863	Wrecked	On beach above Fort Fisher, N.C. Iron vessel. Confederate blockade runner. Depth 23'. No salvage reported after destruction of vessel.
493	Dove	Bark	151	-	Jan 20 1862	"Sunk"	On south edge of Rattlesnake Shoal, Maffitt's Channel, Charleston, S.C. Stone cargo. Used by Union forces to block harbor. Second "Stone Fleet".
494	Dovrefjeld	Sch.	1,858	1882	Feb 28 1919	Foundered	32 miles east of Cape Hatteras, N.C.
495	Dragoon	Ga.s.	70	1926	Mar 7 1957	Collided	With floating object. Off Port Everglades, Fla.
496	Dredge Hester	St.p.	206	1889	Jul 23 1911	Burned	Clearwater, Fla.
497	Druid Hill	Brg.	1,281	1919	Sep 21 1942	Foundered	Near No.7 Buoy, Thimble Shoals Channel, opposite Little Creek, Va.

NO.	NAME OF VESSEL	RIG	TONS	BUILT	DATE	CAUSE	PLACE AND COMMENT
498	Dudley Farlin	Sch.	-	-	Dec 26 1890	Unknown	Bodie Island, N.C.
499	Dulcimer (Br.)	Bark	290	-	Feb 2 1883	Unknown	East of Hatteras Inlet, N.C.
500	Duncan McRae	St.p.	215	1835	Jun 8 1841	Exploded	Johnson Landing, Ga. 3 lives lost. Also documented as "Duncan".
501	Dunham Wheeler	Sch.	1,926	1917	Nov 15 1930	Foundered	28-11-10 N. 80-19-40 W. Depth 72'.
502	E.B. Wharton	Sch.	-	-	Jan 31 1878	Unknown	Off Ocracoke, N.C.
503	E.C. Mowett	Bark	1,123	1868	Mar 5 1914	Abandoned	26-44-00 N. 74-11-00 W. Iron vessel.
504	E.E. Simpson	St.s.	109	1877	Oct 28 1929	Stranded	Saint Andrews Bay, Fla.
505	E.H. Blum	Tanker	11,615	-	Feb 16 1942	War Loss	36-57-00 N. 75-52-00 W. SALVAGED.
506	E.H. Clark	Tanker	9,647	-	Mar 18 1942	War Loss	34-49-30 N. 75-33-00 W. 1 life lost (48).
507	E.J. Bullock	St.s.	6,630	1920	Dec 2 1938	Foundered	Off S.W. Dry Tortugas, Fla. Steel vessel. 3 lives lost (36).
508	E.M. Skinner	Sch.	76	1883	May 20 1921	Stranded	Off Cape Romain, S.C.
509	E.M. Willis II	Ga.s.	67	1917	Jan 3 1929	Burned	Ocracoke Inlet, N.C.
510	E.S. Newman	Sch.	393	-	Oct 11 1896	Unknown	2 miles south of Pea Island L.S. Station, Pea Island, N.C.
511	Ea	Steamer	2,632	-	Mar 15 1902	Unknown	Outer tip of Lookout Shoals, 12 miles from Cape Lookout Lighthouse, N.C.
512	Eagle	St.p.	200	1852	Jan 29 1854	Burned	Below Columbus, Ga. 4 lives lost.
513	Eagle	St.p.	1,532	1862	Mar 4 1870	Stranded	Bodie Island, N.C.
514	Eagle	Sloop	-	1900	Mar 29 1905	Foundered	Near Sarasota, Fla.
515	Early Bird	Sch.	58	1880	Mar 7 1929	Stranded	Ship Shoals, Assateague, Va.
516	East Coast	Ol.s.	275	1892	May 27 1944	Foundered	20-05-00 N. 72-14-00 W.
517	Eastern Shore	Ol.s.	426	1883	Apr 26 1949	Burned	At Goodwin Inland Boat Industry dock, Great Bridge, Va. Iron vessel.
518	Eastern Sword	-	3,785	-	May 4 1942	Unknown	25-17-00 N. 83-57-00 W.
519	Eclipse	St.p.	98	1865	Dec 28 1866	Exploded	Perrysburg, Ga. 4 lives lost.
520	Eclipse	Ga.s.	66	1906	Dec 3 1919	Burned	1 mile below Fort Jackson, Ga.
521	Edda	Bark	-	-	May 10 1891	Unknown	In the Straits of Florida, Fla.
522	Edenton	St.s.	265	1871	May 31 1930	Burned	Mount Gould, N.C.
523	Edith	St.s.	3,382	1915	Jun 6 1942	War Loss	14-33-00 N. 74-35-00 W. Steel vessel. Sunk by enemy action.
524	Edith B. Everman	Sch.	-	-	Oct 31 1887	Unknown	Cape Henry, Va.
525	Edith L. Allen	Sch.	969	1890	Jun 17 1906	Foundered	At sea. 26-10-00 N. 79-38-00 W.
526	Edith and May	Sch.	128	1891	Mar 22 1906	Stranded	Berry Island, Bahamas.
527	Edna Harwood	Sch.	-	1918	Nov 31 1882	Unknown	Off Cape Hatteras, N.C. 1 life lost.
528	Edna M. McKnight	Sch.	1,326	1918	Dec 7 1926	Foundered	Cape Henry, Va.
529	Edna M. Smith	Bark	816	1903	Apr 3 1915	Foundered	70 miles east of Cape Hatteras, N.C. 5 lives lost.
530	Edward	Bark	274	-	Jan 20 1862	"Sunk"	On south edge of Rattlesnake Shoal, Maffitt's Channel, Charleston, S.C. Sunk by Union forces to block harbor entrance. Second "Stone Fleet".
531	Edward	Brg.	319	-	Oct 15 1905	Burned	Wolf Trap Light, Va.
532	Edward D. McNair	St.p.	71	1836	Sep 29 1841	Stranded	Newbern, N.C.
533	Edward F. Clark	Sch.	601	1910	Feb 7 1917	Foundered	14 miles off Norfolk, Va.
534	Edward G. Taublane	Sch.	-	-	Feb 7 1888	Unknown	35-18-00 N. 73-10-00 W.
535	Edward J. Berwind	C.bt.	278	1881	Apr 23 1919	Burned	Portsmouth, Va.
536	Edward J. Berwind	Sch.	1,141	1894	Jan 30 1908	Abandoned	35-25-00 N. 71-58-00 W.
537	Edward Luckenbach	St.s.	401	1899	Apr 3 1915	Foundered	False Capes, Va. Steel vessel. 15 lives lost.
538	Edward Luckenbach	St.s.	7,934	1916	Jul 1 1942	War Loss	North of Key West, Fla. 24-57-03 N. 81-54-00 W. Steel vessel. Freighter. Depth 67'. Wreck demolished.
539	Edward R. Baird, Jr.	Sch.	279	1903	Sep 14 1956	Foundered	In Tangier Sound, Va.
540	Edward R. Smith	Sch.	565	1911	Jan 24 1943	Stranded	Off Virginia coast.
541	Edward S. Stearns	Sch.	-	-	Mar 4 1895	Unknown	Durants, N.C.
542	Edward Smith	Sch.	-	-	Oct 23 1890	Unknown	Doboy Bank, Ga.
543	Edward T. Stotesbury	Sch.	1,446	1900	Oct 17 1910	Stranded	Knights Key, Fla. 1 life lost.

NO.	NAME OF VESSEL	RIG	TONS	BUILT	DATE		CAUSE	PLACE AND COMMENT
544	Edward Wood	Sch.	-	-	Nov 23	1850	Unknown	Currituck Inlet, N.C.
545	Edwin Shaw	St.w.	266	1924	Jan 10	1932	Burned	Savannah, Ga.
546	Edwina	Sch.	459	1879	Aug 26	1911	Stranded	Charleston, S.C.
547	Edwina H. Redmond	Sch.	56	1887	Jun 3	1915	Foundered	Southeast of Cape Henry, Va.
548	Effingham	St.s.	6,421	1919	Mar 30	1942	War Loss	70-28-00 N. 35-44-00 W. Steel vessel. Sunk by enemy action.
549	El Captain (Span.)	Galleon	-	-		1717	Unknown	Northwest end of New Providence Island. Valued at $200,000.
550	Elba	Sch.	-	-	Dec 3	1864	Wrecked	Cape Fear, N.C. Confederate blockade runner.
551	Eleanor T.	Sch.	-	-	Feb 4	1870	Unknown	Carolina Beach, N.C. 5 lives lost.
552	Eleazer W. Clark	Sch.	934	1891	Nov 16	1909	Stranded	Frying Pan Shoals, N.C.
553	Electric	Sch.	-	-	Aug 21	1876	Unknown	Off Cape Fear, N.C.
554	Eliza	Bark	-	-	Nov 28	1853	Unknown	Wash Woods, N.C. 1 life lost.
555	Elizabeth	Steamer	-	-	Sep 24	1863	Burned	Lockwoods Folly, N.C. Confederate blockade runner.
556	Elizabeth	St.p.	-	-	Jan 8	1887	Unknown	Cape Henry. Va.
557	Elizabeth	Ga.s.	58	1913	Jul 22	1934	Burned	Maw Point, N.C.
558	Elizabeth	St.s.	3,482	1919	Nov 4	1935	Stranded	2-1/2 miles north of Miami Sea Buoy, Miami, Fla. Steel vessel.
559	Elizabeth A. Baizley	Sch.	-	-	Sep 28	1894	Unknown	Cape Fear, N.C. Also reported lost on October 18, 1894.
560	Elizabeth E. Vane	Brg.	405	1905	Oct 19	1911	Collided	With st.s. COLUMBIA. Baltimore Harbor, Md.
561	Elizabeth Massey [Br.]	Frgt.	2,598*	-	Feb 19	1942	Unknown	28-09-10 N. 80-00-40 W. Depth 240'. Length 240'.
562	Elizabeth T. Doyle	Sch.	781	1903	Jul 30	1918	Foundered	3 miles southwest of Diamond Shoals, N.C.
563	Elk Garden	Sch.	847	1900	May 28	1922	Foundered	North of Hog Island, Va.
564	Ella	St.p.	-	-	Dec 3	1864	Burned	South end of Marshall Shoal, Smith's Island, N.C. Iron vessel. Confederate blockade runner. Has been located by modern diver.
565	Ella A. Dempsey	Brg.	388	1875	Aug 13	1919	Foundered	Off Wachapreague, Va. Iron vessel.
566	Ella L. Davenport	Sch.	543	1891	Mar 1	1916	Abandoned	31-39-00 N. 62-36-00 W.
567	Ella May	St.p.	147	1863	Jul 3	1872	Burned	Pensacola, Fla.
568	Ella Pierce Thurlow	Sc.b.	1,509	1918	Mar 23	1932	Foundered	Off Frying Pan Lightship, S.C. 33-54-00 N. 77-05-30 W. Length 180'. Depth 75'.
569	Ellen M. Adams	Sch.	90	1876	Dec 20	1909	Foundered	North Anclote Channel, Fla.
570	Ellen S. Jennings	Brg.	330	1890	Feb 22	1912	Collided	With barge CAROLINA (also sank). Poplar Island, Chesapeake Bay, Md.
571	Ellis	Steamer	-	-	Feb 9	1862	Unknown	Off Fort Cobb, on Cobb's Point on the Pasquotank River, N.C. Lost in Civil War.
572	Elm City	Sch.	672	1880	Mar 24	1912	Foundered	Cape Hatteras, N.C. 2 lives lost.
573	Eloisa	St.p.	154	1834	Dec 31	1834	Burned	Columbus, Ga.
574	Elsie A. Bayles	Sch.	296	1883	Apr 5	1916	Stranded	New Inlet, N.C. 2 lives lost.
575	Elvira Ball	Sch.	869	1907	Feb 8	1909	Abandoned	130 miles east of Cape Charles, Va.
576	Emelle E. Birdsall	Sch.	491	1874	Feb 4	1908	Collided	With st.s. JEFFERSON. Winter Quarter Shoal, Va. 3 lives lost.
577	Emerald	Ship	518	-	Jan 20	1862	"Sunk"	On south edge of Rattlesnake Shoal, Maffitt's Channel, Charleston, S.C. Second "Stone Fleet" used by Union forces to block harbor entrance.
578	Emerett	Sch.	659	1919	Mar 4	1931	Foundered	31-43-00 N. 73-20-00 W. All lives (7) lost.
579	Emilee (Emilie)	Bark	-	-	Jan 5	1845	Unknown	36-45-00 N. 75-40-00 W.
580	Emilia Gloria	Sch.	59	1903	Apr 7	1918	Foundered	Pensacola Bay, Fla.
581	Emily	St.p.	144	1845	May 27	1849	Exploded	Apalachicola, Fla. 7 lives lost.
582	Emily B. Sonder	-	-	-	Dec 10	1878	"Sank"	Off Cape Hatteras, N.C. 38 lives lost.
583	Emily I. White	Sch.	352	1901	Feb 11	1916	Stranded	Off Bull Island, S.C.
584	Emily of London	Steamer	-	-	Feb 10	1864	Burned	Above Masonboro Inlet, N.C. Confederate blockade runner.
585	Emma C. Cotton	Sch.	-	-	Dec 27	1895	Unknown	Pea Island, N.C.
586	Emma C. Middleton	Sch.	-	-	Jan 4	1905	Unknown	Off Cape Fear, N.C.
587	Emma C. Rommell	Sch.	-	-	Jan 8	1884	Unknown	Gull Shoal, N.C.
588	Emma F. Angell	Sch.	862	1883	Apr 7	1916	Collided	With British st.s. CHEPSTON CASTLE. Off Virginia coast.
589	Emma J. Warrington	Sch.	-	-	Oct 4	1893	Unknown	Off Paul Gamiels Hill L.S. Station, opposite Duck, N.C.

NO.	NAME OF VESSEL	RIG	TONS	BUILT	DATE	CAUSE	PLACE AND COMMENT
590	Emma K. Reed	Ol.s.	94	1904	May 3 1934	Collided	With unknown vessel. Hampton Roads, Va.
591	Emma L. Cottingham	Sch.	522	1875	Jun 1 1906	Foundered	At sea. 26-58-00 N. 85-10-00 W. 5 lives lost.
592	Emma M. Robinson	Sch.	63	1881	May 16 1920	Stranded	Jensen, Fla.
593	Emma S	Sch.	50	1885	Oct 1906	Foundered	Off Charleston, S.C. All lives (4) lost.
594	Empecinadp	Sch.	-	-	1815	Unknown	Off Amalia Island, Fla. Armament of 6 guns.
595	Empire Dryden	St.s.	-	-	Apr 19 1942	Unknown	Off Oregon Inlet, N.C. Freighter.
596	Empire Gem (Br.)	Tanker	10,600	-	Jan 23 1942	Unknown	35-01-24 N. 75-29-44 W. Broken in two. Depth 137'.
597	Empire Mica	-	4,676	-	Jun 29 1942	Unknown	29-18-50 N. 85-21-00 W. Depth 58'.
598	Empire Steel (Br.)	-	-	-	Mar 24 1942	Unknown	Off Wash Woods, N.C.
599	Empire Thrush (Br.)	Frgt.	3,836*	-	Apr 14 1942	War Loss	35-11-48 N. 75-15-19 W. 13 miles, 108° from Cape Hatteras Light, N.C. Depth 48'. Wreck demolished.
600	Emulous	Sch.	-	-	Jan 22 1825	Unknown	Off Kitty Hawk, N.C.
601	Enchantress	Sch.	371	-	Aug 31 1893	Wrecked	Lockwoods Folly, N.C. Cargo of lumber.
602	Endeavor	St.s.	315	1896	Apr 15 1925	Burned	Weems, Va. Steel vessel.
603	Energy	Brg.	-	-	Oct 14 1891	Collided	Off Capes of Virginia, Va.
604	Ensis	-	-	-	Apr 4 1942	Unknown	Off Cape Hatteras, N.C.
605	Enterprise	Steamer	-	-	Dec 27 1882	Unknown	Off Mauls Point, N.C. 3 lives lost.
606	Enterprise	Sch.	-	-	Oct 27 1918	Unknown	Chicamacomico Banks.
607	Enterprise	Sch.	-	-	Oct 27 1822	Unknown	New Inlet, N.C.
608	Enterprize	Brig	-	-	Oct 9 1837	Unknown	Bodie Island, N.C. 1 life lost.
609	Ephram Williams	Brg.	491	-	Dec 22 1884	Unknown	North of Diamond Shoals, N.C.
610	Equipoise (Pan.)	Frgt.	3,872*	-	Mar 27 1942	War Loss	Caffeys Inlet, N.C. 36-15-30 N. 74-51-06 W. 38 lives lost.
611	Erl King	St.s.	-	-	Dec 16 1891	Unknown	Long Reef, Fla.
612	Escambia	Brig	-	-	Mar 25 1840	Unknown	Frying Pan Shoals, N.C.
613	Esk	Sch.	-	-	Sep 8 1888	Unknown	Watchapreague, Va.
614	Esmeralda	St.s.	219	1897	Sep 18 1926	Foundered	Miami, Fla. Steel vessel. 1 life lost (6).
615	Esparta	St.s.	3,365	1904	Apr 9 1942	War Loss	17 miles, 120° True from St. John's L.V., Jacksonville, Fla. Steel vessel. Sunk by enemy action. Depth 36'. 30-50-45 N. 81-09-58 W.
616	Esperanza	Ga.s.	677	1917	Feb 13 1923	Stranded	19-05-00 N. 69-05-00 W.
617	Esso Aruba	Tanker	8,773	-	Aug 28 1942	War Loss	17-55-00 N. 74-50-00 W. SALVAGED.
618	Esso Augusta	Tanker	11,237	-	Jun 15 1942	War Loss	36-52-00 N. 75-51-00 W. SALVAGED.
619	Esso Baton Rouge	Tanker	7,989	-	Apr 8 1942	War Loss	31-13-00 N. 80-05-00 W. 3 lives lost (39). SALVAGED.
620	Esso Boston	St.s.	7,698	1938	Apr 12 1942	War Loss	Approximately 21-45-00 N. 60-00-00 W. Steel vessel. Sunk by enemy action.
621	Esso Gettysburg	Ol.s.	10,172	1942	Jun 10 1943	War Loss	31-00-00 N. 79-15-00 W. Sunk by enemy action. 55 lives lost (70). Tanker.
622	Esso Nashville	Tanker	7,943	-	Mar 21 1942	War Loss	North of Frying Pan Shoals, N.C. Stern section salvaged. Depth of bow is 55'.
623	Estelle	Ol.s.	164	1880	Mar 15 1927	Foundered	Thimble Light, Va.
624	Estelle Randall	St.s.	211	1898	Jan 17 1910	Burned	Columbia, N.C. 1 life lost.
625	Ethan Allen	St.p.	513	1859	Sep 22 1901	Stranded	Off Jacksonville, Fla. Used as ferryboat.
626	Ethel	Sch.	-	-	Apr 5 1890	Foundered	Off Cape Canaveral, Fla.
627	Ethel	Bark	734	1881	Sep 17 1906	Stranded	Singleton Swash, S.C. 2 lives lost.
628	Ethel	Ga.s.	718	1918	Oct 23 1918	Foundered	St. Augustine, Fla.
629	Ethel A. Merritt	Sch.	-	-	Apr 7 1890	Collided	Off Cape Hatteras, N.C.
630	Ethel De Mary	St.s.	58	1934	Feb 4 1935	Stranded	Alligator River, N.C. All lives (2) lost.
631	Ethel V. Boynton	Bkn.	739	1890	Jun 2 1915	Stranded	30-15-00 N. 74-30-00 W.
632	Etta M. Barter	Sch.	-	-	Feb 27 1895	Unknown	Portsmouth, N.C.
633	Eugene	Sch.	-	-	Jan 22 1883	Unknown	Ocracoke, N.C.
634	Eulalia	St.p.	231	1896	Apr 25 1910	Burned	Beresford, Fla.
635	Eureka	St.s.	-	-	May 6 1888	Collided	36-45-00 N. 74-52-00 W.

NO.	NAME OF VESSEL	RIG	TONS	BUILT	DATE	CAUSE	PLACE AND COMMENT
636	Eureka II	Ga.s.	81	1921	Dec 14 1930	Burned	Cape Florida, Fla. 3 lives lost (133).
637	Eva B. Douglas	Sch.	1,093	1886	Mar 7 1920	Abandoned	37-52-00 N. 71-23-00 W.
638	Evelyn	Ol.s.	60	1892	Oct 30 1926	Burned	Wilmington, N.C. Steel vessel.
639	Evening Star	St.p.	2,014	1863	Oct 3 1866	Foundered	About 100 miles off Tybee Island, Ga. 247 lives lost.
640	Evening Star	Ol.s.	74	1947	Jan 31 1958	Burned	In Gulf of Mexico, 20 miles west of Key West, Fla.
641	Evergreen	Sch.	-	-	Jan 1849	Unknown	Currituck Beach, N.C.
642	Everett Webster	Sch.	476	1883	Apr 12 1907	Abandoned	Off Cape Hatteras, N.C. 41-41-00 N. 57-10-00 W.
643	Explorer	Tug	-	-	Dec 12 1919	Unknown	Off Nags Head, N.C.
644	Ezra	Bark	-	-	Sep 1869	Unknown	Bodie Island, N.C.
645	F.A. Kilburn	St.s.	997	1904	Jun 14 1918	Burned	American Shoals Light, Fla.
646	F.A. Tupper	Sch.	-	-	Mar 1 1876	Unknown	South of Chicamacomico Beach, N.C.
647	F.H. Odiorne	Sch.	323	1871	May 9 1919	Foundered	Off Chincoteague, Va.
648	F.L. Carney	Bark	-	-	Jan 22 1882	Unknown	Off Hatteras Inlet, N.C. 10 lives lost.
649	F.W. Abrams	St.s.	9,310	1920	Jun 11 1942	War Loss	34-59-30 N. 75-48-30 W. Off North Carolina coast. Steel vessel. Tanker. Wreck has been demolished.
650	Fair Dealer	Sch.	-	-	Oct 9 1887	Unknown	Folly Island, S.C.
651	Fair Haven	St.s.	474	1863	Apr 9 1864	Stranded	Cape Henry, Va.
652	Fairbanks	Steamer	-	-	Dec 9 1870	Unknown	Off Hatteras Inlet, N.C.
653	Fairlee	Drg.	503	1908	Aug 31 1955	Foundered	About 16-59-00 N. 73-40-00 W. Steel vessel.
654	Fairport	St.s.	6,165	1942	Jul 16 1942	War Loss	27-00-00 N. 64-25-00 W. Steel vessel. Sunk by enemy action.
655	Fairy Queen	St.w.	169	1854	Oct 21 1860	Stranded	Buffington Island, Parkersburg, Va.
656	Falcon	St.p.	185	1850	Aug 23 1851	Stranded	Apalachicola, Fla.
657	Fannie and Fay	Sch.	233	1885	Jun 29 1925	Foundered	Dry Tortugas, Fla.
658	Fannie Insley	Sch.	59	1883	Aug 20 1940	Foundered	Off Windmill Point, Va.
659	Fannie Mae	St.s.	99	1901	Nov 5 1935	Foundered	1 mile ESE of Windmill Point Light, Va.
660	Fannie Reiche	Sch.	463	1892	Dec 23 1905	Collided	With sch. MARTHA E. WALLACE. Off Winter Quarter Light, Va.
661	Fanny	St.p.	-	-	Feb 10 1862	Burned	On Pasquotank River, above Fort Cobb, N.C. Converted to Confederate gunboat.
662	Fanny and Jenny	St.p.	-	-	Feb 10 1864	Burned	Near the channel at Masonboro Inlet, N.C. Confederate blockade runner.
663	Fanny Sprague	St.s.	89	1872	Apr 30 1917	Stranded	Fort George Inlet, Fla.
664	Fayetteville	St.p.	264	1852	May 18 1853	Exploded	Smithville, N.C.
665	Fearless	St.s.	128	1864	Nov 15 1866	Stranded	Beaufort, N.C.
666	Fenimore	St.p.	1,634	1892	Jun 22 1918	Burned	Norfolk, Va. 2 lives lost.
667	Fides B. Scott	Ga.s.	61	1921	Mar 21 1924	Burned	Jupiter, Fla.
668	Fire Island	Ol.s.	138	1912	Apr 15 1947	Collided	At City Yacht Basin, Miami, Fla.
669	Fitz J. Babson	Sch.	69	1871	Feb 27 1914	Foundered	Sailed from Jacksonville, Fla., and has not since reported. All lives (7) lost.
670	Flambeau	St.s.	766	1861	Mar 1 1867	Foundered	Off Fort Fisher, N.C. Also reported as being 850 Gross Tons.
671	Flamingo	Ga.y.	84	1913	Jun 24 1935	Burned	Pilkingtons Yacht Basin, Fort Lauderdale, Fla.
672	Fleetwood III	Ga.y.	55	1922	Sep 18 1926	Stranded	Miami, Fla.
673	Flirt	St.s.	1,365	1917	Jan 30 1919	Burned	26-30-00 N. 68-54-00 W.
674	Float No.1	Brg.	592	1885	Mar 1 1912	Foundered	Mobjack Bay, Va.
675	Flora	Ship	-	-	Mar 28 1840	Unknown	Off Frying Pan Shoals, N.C.
676	Flora	Brg.	180	1887	1924	Collided	With unknown vessel. Cape Fear River, N.C.
677	Flora Rogers	Sch.	376	1879	Oct 23 1908	Stranded	Bodys Island, N.C.
678	Florence	St.p.	158	1841	Dec 17 1845	Snagged	Albany, Ga.
679	Florence C. Magee	Sch.	1,081	-	Feb 26 1894	Unknown	About 1 mile from Bodie Island Lighthouse, Bodie Island, N.C. 4-masted vessel.
680	Florence Howard	Sch.	863	1909	Nov 14 1922	Foundered	Sailed from Georgetown, S.C., and has not since reported. All lives (8) lost.
681	Florence I. Lockwood	Sch.	299	1867	Dec 6 1906	Stranded	Chincoteague Inlet, Va.
682	Florence and Lillian	Sch.	252	1874	Sep 19 1921	Foundered	Southwest of Chincoteague Lighthouse, Va.

NO.	NAME OF VESSEL	RIG	TONS	BUILT	DATE		CAUSE	PLACE AND COMMENT
683	Florence Luckenbach	St.s.	5,049	1910	Jan 29	1942	War Loss	12-55-00 N. 80-33-00 W. Steel vessel. Sunk by enemy action.
684	Florence O'Brien	Brg.	345	1905	Apr 12	1918	Foundered	2 miles off Stingray Point Light, Va. All life (1) lost.
685	Florence Randall	Sch.	741	-	Aug 16	1899	Unknown	2 miles north of Gull Island Light, N.C.
686	Florence Shay	Sch.	405	1867	Nov 12	1908	Stranded	Virginia Beach, Va. 2 lives lost.
687	Florence Witherbee	St.s.	84	1873	Feb 14	1907	Collided	With st.s. ACCOMAC. Pensacola, Fla.
688	Florida	St.p.	144	1834	May 17	1842	Stranded	North Edisto, S.C.
689	Florida	St.slp.	-	-	Nov 28	1864	Collided	Above Newport News, Va. Length 191'. Beam 27'. Confederate vessel. Depth 45'.
690	Florida	Sch.	1,071	1871	Aug 29	1912	Collided	With British steamer KERNWOOD. In Hampton Roads, Va. Iron vessel.
691	Florida	Drg.	582	1910	Aug 29	1961	Burned	At Escort and Submarine piers, Norfolk, Va.
692	Florie	Steamer	-	-	Sep 10	1864	Burned	Cape Fear Bar, N.C. Confederate blockade runner.
693	Foam	Sch.	64	1863	Oct 30	1907	Foundered	100 miles east of Cape Henry, Va.
694	Formosa	Bark	-	-	Feb 20	1893	Unknown	Off Diamond Shoals, N.C.
695	Fort Pierce	Sch.	2,196	1919	Oct 24	1923	Foundered	Off Assiteague Light, Va.
696	Fortuna	Ga.s.	105	1920	Sep 29	1949	Burned	At Bull River, in St. Helena Sound, Beaufort, S.C.
697	Fortune	Bark	292	-	Dec 21	1861	"Sunk"	4 miles SSE off Fort Sumter and 3 miles ESE of the light on Morris Island, Charleston Harbor, S.C. Used by Union forces to block harbor. "Stone Fleet".
698	Fortune	St.s.	142	1875	Feb 1	1920	Foundered	Off Jekyl Island, Ga. All lives (13) lost.
699	Frances	St.s.	352	1864	Dec 31	1867	Stranded	Above New Inlet, N.C.
700	Frances	Sch.	677	1887	Feb 1	1910	Stranded	Off Cape Hatteras, N.C. All lives (8) lost.
701	Frances Courtney	Ga.s.	56	1912	Mar 28	1914	Exploded	Monday Point, Va.
702	Frances Henrietta	Bark	407	-	Dec 21	1861	"Sunk"	4 miles SSE off Fort Sumter and 3 miles ESE of the light on Morris Island, Charleston, S.C. Used by Union forces to block harbor entrance. "Stone Fleet".
703	Francis E. Powell	Tanker	7,096	-	Jan 27	1942	War Loss	37-27-48 N. 75-16-42 W. 17 miles off Parramore Island, Va. 4 lives lost (32).
704	Francis E. Waters	Sch.	147	-	Oct 24	1889	Unknown	Nags Head, N.C. 6 lives lost.
705	Francis O'Boyle	Brg.	2,200	1919	Jan 16	1924	Foundered	Off Cape Henry Light, Va.
706	Francis V. Sylvia	Ga.s.	93	1904	Nov 16	1943	Foundered	25 miles south of Miami, Fla.
707	Franconia	St.s.	-	-	Jul 29	1890	Unknown	Fernandina, Fla.
708	Frank B. Witherbee	Sch.	504	1908	Oct 3	1913	Collided	With st.s. CITY OF ATLANTA. Off Diamond Shoal Lightship, Va.
709	Frank Butler	Sch.	74	1869	Oct 23	1906	Stranded	Windmill Point, Chesapeake Bay, Va.
710	Frank E. Swain	Sch.	433	1909	Jan 9	1915	Foundered	75 miles southeast of Cape Henry, Va. All lives (7) lost.
711	Frank Harrington	Sch.	-	-	Jan 28	1890	Stranded	Tybee Beach, Ga.
712	Frank M. Deering	Sch.	1,891	1916	Feb 6	1923	Stranded	Near Cobbs Island, Va.
713	Frank M. Low	Sch.	542	1909	Feb 4	1912	Burned	Cape Romain, S.C.
714	Frank M. McGear	Sch.	-	-	Oct 26	1889	Unknown	Whale's Head Light, N.C.
715	Frank W. Cummiskey, Jr.	Brg.	351	1896	Apr 9	1907	Foundered	Off Newport, Va. All lives (2) lost.
716	Franklin	St.p.	193	1819	Sep 14	1850	Stranded	Currituck, N.C.
717	Franklin	St.w.	181	1851	Jan	1854	Burned	Apalachicola River, Fla. 1 life lost.
718	Franklin Baker 2d	Ga.s.	93	1925	Nov 15	1943	Stranded	Off Fort Lauderdale, Fla.
719	Franklin Woodruff	Sch.	-	-	Feb 23	1889	Unknown	South Edisto, S.C.
720	Fred R.	Brg.	307	1920	Sep	1960	Foundered	At Atlantic Creosoting Co., Inc. dock, Portsmouth, Va.
721	Fred W. Chase	Sch.	-	-	Feb 3	1887	Unknown	Folly Island, S.C.
722	Fred Walton	-	441	-	Aug 17	1899	Wrecked	On Hog Shoal, Portsmouth, N.C.
723	Freddie Hencken	Sch.	500	1892	Sep 12	1912	Stranded	San Blas Shoals, near Apalachicola, Fla.
724	Freddie L. Porter	Sch.	-	-	Jan 21	1887	Abandoned	Tortugas, Fla.
725	Freddie W. Alton	Sch.	86	1867	Oct 11	1909	Collided	With dock. Key West, Fla.
726	Frederick W. Day	Sch.	613	1901	Sep 17	1914	Foundered	7 miles off Charleston Lighthouse, S.C.
727	Fredericksburg	St.p.	199	1827	Dec 29	1845	Foundered	Fredericksburg, Va.
728	Freeman Rawdon	St.p.	493	1850	Oct 16	1856	Foundered	Cape Hatteras, N.C. Renamed "City of Savannah" in 1856.

NO.	NAME OF VESSEL	RIG	TONS	BUILT	DATE	CAUSE	PLACE AND COMMENT
729	Frying Pan Shoals Lightship	–	–	–	–	–	–
730	Fulton City	St.w.	199	1857	Dec 31 1862	Burned	Above Fort Caswell, Cape Fear River, N.C.
731	Future	Sch.	613	1900	Nov 11 1858	Snagged	Buffington Island, Parkersburg, Va. 5 lives lost.
732	G.A. Kohler	Sch.	1,462	1919	Jan 3 1913	Foundered	34-08-00 N. 75-10-00 W. 3 lives lost.
733	G.J. Cherry	Sch.	533	1909	Aug 22 1933	Stranded	Cape Hatteras, N.C.
734	G.T. Melton	St.p.	347	1899	Mar 1 1927	Foundered	Cape Hatteras, N.C.
735	G.W. Carpenter	Sch.	–	–	Jan 31 1907	Stranded	Lumber City, Ga.
736	Gamaliel	Bark	–	–	Apr 1867	Unknown	Creeds Hill, N.C.
737	Garland	Bark	243	–	Jan 27 1888	Abandoned	29-04-00 N. 75-27-00 W.
738.-	Gasparilla	–	–	–	Dec 21 1861	"Sunk"	4 miles SSE off Fort Sumter and 3 miles ESE of the light on Morris Island, Charleston, S.C. Used by Union forces to block harbor. Known as "Stone Fleet".
					1821	Unknown	On Bell Bar, at mouth of Boca Grande Pass, Fla. Pirate vessel. Reported to have carried $10 million in gold bullion.
739	Gaston	Sch.	1,442	1865	Mar 25 1912	Stranded	Cobb Island, Va.
740	Gatherer	Sch.	1,469	1874	Nov 29 1909	Foundered	Off Virginia coast. Square-rigged sailing vessel converted to barge. Located in area of Assateague, Va. Coal cargo.
741	Gelmer	Drg.	–	–	Pre-WWII	Unknown	29-19-00 N. 84-55-00 W. Depth 88'.
742	General Berry	St.p.	144	1863	Jun 19 1869	Foundered	Savannah, Ga.
743	General Hooker	St.p.	266	1864	Mar 26 1866	Burned	Charleston, S.C. 8 lives lost.
744	General J.B. Carr	St.s.	157	1892	Oct 29 1923	Burned	Fairfield Canal, Fla.
745	General Lyon	St.s.	1,076	1864	Mar 25 1865	Burned	Off Cape Hatteras, N.C. 400 lives lost.
746	General Mathews	St.s.	469	1901	Mar 22 1930	Burned	Norfolk, Va.
747	General S.E. Merwin	Sch.	–	–	Mar 4 1901	Unknown	Gull Shoal, N.C.
748	General Shepley	St.p.	134	1864	Jan 27 1867	Burned	Ossabaw Island, Ga.
749	General U.S. Grant	St.s.	58	1863	Aug 2 1869	Burned	Jacksonville, Fla.
750	Genessee	St.y.	212	1900	Oct 1925	Stranded	Zero, Fla. Steel vessel.
751	Geo. A. Lawry	Sch.	108	1886	Dec 17 1913	Foundered	Sailed from Jacksonville, Fla., and has not since reported. All lives (6) lost.
752	George A. McFadden	Sch.	1,070	1888	Jan 27 1910	Stranded	Diamond Shoals, N.C.
753	George C. Bell	Ol.s.	88	1929	Jan 1 1948	Collided	With USS YP-629. At the eastern end of main channel in Miami Harbor, Fla.
754	George C. Collins	St.s.	234	1862	Mar 27 1865	Stranded	St. John's River, Fla.
755	George D. Bolster	Ga.s.	72	1908	Dec 5 1929	Stranded	Lookout Shoals, N.C.
756	George E. Klinck	Sch.	569	1904	Mar 8 1941	Foundered	70 miles south by east of Diamond Shoal Lightship, N.C.
757	George E. Maltby	Brig	–	–	Jan 7 1867	Unknown	Off Cape Hatteras, N.C.
758	George F. Phillips	Sch.	270	1901	Feb 5 1910	Abandoned	33-25-00 N. 73-40-00 W.
759	George Farwell	St.s.	977	1895	Oct 6 1906	Stranded	Cape Henry, Va.
760	George H. Bradley	St.s.	99	1871	Sep 7 1929	Burned	Ocran, Va.
761	George L. Fessenden	Sch.	394	–	Apr 27 1898	Wrecked	1 mile north of Chicamacomico L.S. Station, off New Inlet, N.C. Stone cargo. 3-masted vessel. 4 lives lost.
762	George M. Adams	Sch.	–	–	May 1 1897	Unknown	Nags Head, N.C.
763	George MacDonald	St.s.	10,164	1943	Jun 29 1960	Foundered	32-25-00 N. 78-05-00 W. Steel vessel.
764	George N. Reed	Sch.	493	1911	Jun 20 1915	Stranded	10 miles south of Bodie Island, N.C.
765	George Page	St.p.	410	1853	Mar 10 1862	Burned	Quantico, Va.
766	George R. Congdon	Sch.	–	–	Jan 31 1901	Unknown	Off Cape Hatteras, N.C.
767	George R. Vreeland	Sch.	423	1873	Jan 21 1908	Foundered	Sailed from Hampton Roads, Va., and has not since reported. All lives (7) lost.
768	George S. Marts	Sch.	–	–	Apr 16 1887	Unknown	Cape Hatteras, N.C. 2 lives lost.
769	George Taulane, Jr.	Sch.	465	1882	Sep 18 1909	Foundered	Sailed from Belfast, Ga., and has not since reported. All lives (7) lost.
770	George W. Truitt, Jr.	Sch.	779	1904	Feb 20 1928	Stranded	Ocracoke Inlet, N.C.
771	George W. Wells	Sch.	2,970	1900	Sep 3 1913	Stranded	Ocracoke Island, N.C.

NO.	NAME OF VESSEL	RIG	TONS	BUILT	DATE	CAUSE	PLACE AND COMMENT
772	George Washington	St.p.	243	1851	Apr 1863	Burned	Port Royal, S.C.
773	George Weems	St.s.	416	1874	May 20 1908	Burned	Frying Pan Shoals, N.C.
774	Georgena	Ga.y.	64	1912	Jan 16 1913	Burned	Savannah River, Ga.
775	Georges Creek	St.s.	448	1853	Aug 22 1863	Foundered	Cape Hatteras, N.C.
776	Georgia	Sch.	1,318	1915	Dec 9 1917	Foundered	Chincoteague, Va.
777	Georgian	St.p	120	1830	Dec 26 1833	Snagged	Roanoke, Ga.
778	Georgiana C. McCaw	St.p.	700	-	Jun 2 1864	Burned	Off the western bar, 1/4 mile west of Fort Caswell and Bay Light Batteries, N.C. Confederate blockade runner.
779	Georgie L. Drake	Sch.	465	1883	Dec 31 1909	Abandoned	35-05-00 N. 71-47-00 W.
780	Glad Tidings	Sch.	654	1883	Oct 16 1907	Stranded	Nassau Bar, Ga.
781	Glenrath	Steamer	-	-	Oct 1 1890	Unknown	Off Cape Lookout, N.C.
782	Glory	Steamer	-	-	Aug 26 1933	Unknown	Off Nags Head, N.C.
783	Glyndon	St.s.	2,220	1919	Mar 22 1924	Foundered	34-30-00 N. 74-00-00 W. Steel vessel. 3 lives lost (25).
784	Golden Liner	Steamer	-	-	Apr 27 1863	Wrecked	Cape Fear River, N.C. Confederate blockade runner.
785	Good News	Bkn.	712	1889	Jun 3 1910	Abandoned	29-42-00 N. 74-26-00 W.
786	Governor	St.p.	644	1846	Nov 20 1861	Foundered	Charleston, S.C. 7 lives lost.
787	Gov. Ames	Sch.	1,778	1888	Dec 13 1909	Stranded	Wimble Shoals, N.C. 11 lives lost.
788	Governor Jackson	Sch.	-	-	Aug 22 1888	Unknown	Winter Quarter Shoal, Va.
789	Governor Safford	St.p.	307	1884	Jul 24 1908	Foundered	Bogue Inlet, N.C.
790	Governor Troup	St.p.	154	1859	May 29 1865	Burned	Below Augusta, Ga. 40 lives lost.
791	Grace Deering	Brg.	627	1877	Nov 1 1906	Foundered	Off Miami, Fla.
792	Gracie D. Buchanan	Sch.	1,140	1888	Feb 10 1910	Stranded	Nassau Inlet, Fla.
793	Gracie D. Chambers	Sch.	379	1875	Feb 13 1919	Foundered	Currituck Beach, N.C.
794	Gradco Pioneer	Ol.s.	70	1944	Jun 20 1965	Burned	About 1 mile north of the sea buoy off Miami Beach, Fla.
795	Green Seas	Ol.s.	65	1942	Apr 16 1952	Foundered	In Gulf of Mexico, 70 miles southwest of Tampa, Fla.
796	Greenwood	St.w.	47	1848	Aug 21 1850	Exploded	Kanawha, Va. 2 lives lost.
797	Grey Eagle	St.p.	51	1850	May 1 1857	Burned	Wheeling, Va.
798	Grey Eagle	Bark	-	-	Feb 12 1888	Unknown	Little Island Beach, Va.
799	Grey Hound	St.p.	380	1863	Nov 27 1864	Burned	Hog Island, James River, Va.
800	Gulf of America	St.s.	4,805*	1942	Apr 11 1942	War Loss	30-16-37 N. 81-13-43 W. Tanker. Depth 60'. Steel vessel. Sunk by enemy action.
801	Gulf City	Steamer	-	-	Jun 11 1869	Unknown	Off Lookout Shoals, N.C. 22 lives lost.
802	Gulf King	Ol.s.	66	1954	May 22 1961	Burned	At St. Augustine, Fla., about 1/4 mile from the mouth of the San Sebastian River, on the east bank.
803	Gulfbelle	St.s.	7,104	1936	Oct 20 1943	Collided	With st.s. GULFLAND. Off Palm Beach, Fla. Steel vessel.
804	Gulfland	St.s.	5,276	1918	Oct 20 1943	Collided	With st.s. GULFBELLE. At Palm Beach, Fla. 26-56-00 N. 80-01-00 W. Steel vessel.
805	Gulfport	Drg.	682	1930	Feb 14 1943	Foundered	18 miles off Clearwater, Fla. Steel vessel.
806	Gulfstate	St.s.	6,882	1920	Apr 3 1943	War Loss	24-22-00 N. 80-18-00 W. Steel vessel. Tanker. Sunk by enemy action. 31 lives lost.
807	Gunbor (Nor.)	Frgt.	1,121*	-	Jun 14 1942	Unknown	24-56-55 N. 81-46-33 W. Wreck demolished.
808	Gwalia	St.s.	415	1907	Dec 4 1925	Foundered	Egmont Key, Fla. Steel vessel.
809	Gypsum Empress	Sch.	779	1893	May 17 1917	Foundered	34-40-00 N. 47-00-00 W. 4 lives lost.
810	Gypsum Prince (Br.)	Frgt.	1,970*	-	Mar 3 1942	War Loss	38-48-00 N. 75-04-00 W. Wreck demolished. Depth 50'.
811	Gypsy Girl	Ol.s.	52	1945	Jul 17 1950	Burned	2-1/3 miles north of North Jetty Range Line, harbor entrance, Fernandina, Fla.
812	H.A. Dewitt	Sch.	-	-	Jun 16 1891	Abandoned	Off Egmont Key, Fla.
813	H.C. Drewer	Ol.s.	54	1926	Jan 28 1953	Foundered	Off Cape Lookout Shoals, northeast of Diamond Shoals Lightship, N.C.
814	H.G. Johnson	Bark	1,082	1877	Apr 14 1908	Stranded	Cumberland Bar, Ga.
815	H.L. Cook	St.p.	123	1842	Mar 1855	Foundered	Darien, Ga.
816	H.M.S. Winchester[Br.]	-	-	-	Sep 1695	Foundered	Off Key Largo, Fla. Warship. 60-gun vessel. All 400 lives lost. Located in 1940.

NO.	NAME OF VESSEL	RIG	TONS	BUILT	DATE		CAUSE	PLACE AND COMMENT
817	H. & S. No.11	Scow	284	1913	Feb 8	1918	Stranded	Denmans Island, Gulf of Georgia.
818	H.S. Smith	St.p.	230	1848	Mar 24	1850	Burned	30 miles below Columbus, Ga. 4 lives lost.
819	H.W. McColly	Sch.	-	1881	Oct 5	1881	Unknown	Gull Shoal, N.C.
820	Hackensack	St.s.	113	1863	Oct 13	1870	Burned	Portsmouth, Va.
821	Hagan	St.s.	6,401	1919	Aug 12	1942	War Loss	32-00-00 N. 77-30-00 W. Steel vessel. Sunk by enemy action.
822	Haleakala	St.s.	5,587	1919	Sep 8	1926	Foundered	25-00-00 N. 66-00-00 W. Steel vessel. All lives (35) lost.
823	Half Moon	Ol.s.	63	1944	Mar 1	1952	Foundered	5 miles off Hatteras Inlet, N.C.
824	Halsey	Tanker	7,088	-	May 6	1942	War Loss	27-14-00 N. 80-03-00 W. Steel vessel. Depth 58'.
825	Hamburg	St.p.	216	1838	Oct 24	1846	Burned	Savannah, Ga.
826	Hamilton	St.s.	341	1884	Feb 27	1917	Foundered	Roanoke River, N.C. 1 life lost.
827	Hampton	Steamer	-	-	Apr 3	1865	Burned	Near Fort Darling, James River, Va. Confederate vessel.
828	Hampton	Ol.s.	52	1897	Jun 20	1928	Burned	Hampton Roads, Va.
829	Hanging Rock	St.w.	98	1859	Nov 14	1861	Stranded	Cannelton, Va.
830	Harkaway	Bark	-	-	Nov 30	1885	Unknown	Caffeys Inlet, N.C.
831	Harold J. McCarthy	Sch.	312	1893	Mar 25	1911	Stranded	Lake Worth, Fla. 1 life lost.
832	Harpagon (Br.)	Frgt.	2,600	-	Apr 19	1942	Unknown	2 miles east of Cape Hatteras Light, N.C.
833	Harpathian (Br.)	Steamer	4,588	-	Jun 5	1918	War Loss	60 miles off coast of Currituck, N.C. Sunk by German Submarine Activities 1st World War. Also reported as "Harpatheon".
834	Harriet C. Kerlin	Sch.	517	1884	Feb 6	1911	Stranded	Hatteras Shoals, N.C.
835	Harriet Deford	St.s.	149	1864	Apr 7	1865	Burned	Indian River, Fla.
836	Harriet N. Rogers	Sch.	-	-	Jan 15	1873	Unknown	Bodie Island, N.C.
837	Harriet Thomas	Sch.	-	-	Nov 1	1877	Unknown	Virginia Beach, Va.
838	Harry F. Hooper	Sch.	726	1912	Feb 15	1916	Abandoned	Off Cape Hatteras, N.C.
839	Harry F. Sinclair	Tanker	6,151	-	Apr 11	1942	War Loss	34-10-00 N. 76-35-00 W. Steel vessel. 10 lives lost (36). SALVAGED.
840	Harry P. Simmons	Sch.	-	-	Oct 23	1889	Unknown	Cape Henry, Va.
841	Harry Prescott	Sch.	433	1882	Jan 18	1912	Foundered	Cape Hatteras, N.C. 3 lives lost.
842	Harry T. Hayward	Sch.	1,203	1902	Oct 16	1910	Stranded	Hillsboro Light, Fla. 3 lives lost.
843	Harvest	Bark	314	-	Dec 21	1861	"Sunk"	4 miles SSE off Fort Sumter and 3 miles ESE of the light on Morris Island, Charleston, S.C. Used by Union forces to block harbor. Part of "Stone Fleet".
844	Harvest	Sch.	-	-	Nov 17	1875	Unknown	Off Nags Head, N.C.
845	Harvester	Bark	-	-	Nov 2	1887	Unknown	Near Cape Henry, Va.
846	Hattie Gage	St.s.	184	1889	Jun 29	1918	Stranded	Oregon Inlet, N.C. 1 life lost.
847	Hattie L. Fuller	Sch.	-	-	Apr 13	1877	Unknown	Oregon Inlet, N.C.
848	Hattie Lollies	Sch.	-	-	Apr 7	1889	Unknown	Nags Head, N.C.
849	Hattie N. Gove	Sch.	-	-		1888	Unknown	Off Port Royal Bar, S.C.
850	Hattie P. Simpson	Sch.	1,296	1891	Mar 21	1914	Foundered	Off Cape Lookout, N.C. 6 lives lost.
851	Hattie Perry	Sch.	-	-	Sep 29	1890	Unknown	Cape Henry, Va.
852	Hattie S. Clark	Sch.	-	-	May 15	1890	Unknown	Frying Pan Shoals, N.C.
853	Havana	-	-	-	Jan 6	1934	Collided	With reef off coast of Florida. Operated by Ward Lines. 1 life lost.
854	Heather IV	Ol.s.	178	1966	Nov 12	1966	Burned	At Broward Marine, Inc., Fort Lauderdale, Fla.
855	Hebe	St.w.	-	-	Aug 23	1863	Burned	Between Fort Fisher and Masonboro Inlet, N.C. Confederate blockade runner. Iron vessel.
856	Hebe (Dutch)	Frgt.	1,140*	-	Apr 11	1942	Unknown	33-08-40 N. 78-15-00 W. Depth 95'.
857	Hector	-	-	-	Pre-WWII		Unknown	33-00-00 N. 79-05-00 W. Depth 50'.
858	Hedo	Ol.s.	58	1938	Aug 2	1967	Burned	At York River Yacht Haven, Gloucester Point, Va.
859	Helen E. Taft	Sch.	1,197	1904	Jan 29	1908	Collided	With Swedish st.s. UPPLAND. Cape Lookout, N.C.
860	Helen G. Moseley	Sch.	566	1883	Jan 26	1908	Abandoned	20 miles east of Cape Henry, Va.
861	Helen H. Benedict	Sch.	770	1881	Feb 6	1914	Stranded	6-1/2 miles north of Bodie Island Light, N.C.

NO.	NAME OF VESSEL	RIG	TONS	BUILT	DATE	CAUSE	PLACE AND COMMENT
862	Helen Lee	Ol.s.	64	1954	Feb 29 1964	Foundered	Off Key West, Fla. 24-11-00 N. 84-18-00 W.
863	Helen T	Brg.	436	1916	Dec 27 1917	Stranded	Off Jupiter Light, Fla.
864	Helen Thomas	Sch.	1,470	1903	Mar 5 1912	Stranded	Cape Charles Shoals, Va.
865	Helma	Ga.s.	172	1925	Sep 10 1960	Hurricane	at 148 N.W. North River Drive, Miami River, Miami, Fla.
866	Henrietta	Sch.	950	-	Oct 25 1873	Unknown	Off Frying Pan Shoals, N.C.
867	Henrietta Hill	Sch.	-	-	Aug 24 1899	Unknown	Portsmouth, N.C.
868	Henrietta Pierce	Sch.	-	-	Jan 16 1853	Unknown	Kitty Hawk, N.C.
869	Henry	Sloop	-	-	Jun 1813	Unknown	Ocracoke Inlet, N.C.
870	Henry A. Litchfield	Sch.	593	1867	Aug 12 1907	Burned	Cape Henry, Va.
871	Henry G. Fay	Sch.	-	-	Apr 1 1876	Unknown	Caffeys Inlet, N.C.
872	Henry Norwell	Bkn.	-	-	Jul 7 1896	Unknown	Gull Shoals, N.C.
873	Henry P. Simmons	Sch.	650	-	Oct 23 1889	Unknown	At Pebble Shoals, Wash Woods, N.C. 7 lives lost.
874	Henry Shultz	St.p.	208	1824	Apr 22 1825	Burned	Augusta, Ga.
875	Henry W. Cramp	Sch.	1,629	1896	Nov 15 1914	Stranded	Off Cape Lookout, N.C. 33-50-00 N. 75-35-00 W.
876	Henry Weiler	Sch.	400	1900	Oct 5 1912	Abandoned	4 miles SSE off Fort Sumter and 3 miles ESE of the light on Morris Island,
877	Herald	Ship	274	-	Dec 21 1861	"Sunk"	Charleston, S.C. Used by Union forces to block harbor. Part of "Stone Fleet".
878	Herbert May	Sch.	384	1906	Feb 7 1922	Stranded	On Marguesas Reef, Fla.
879	Hercules	St.s.	163	1905	Jun 9 1923	Foundered	30-43-00 N. 79-35-00 W.
880	Hercules	St.p.	800	1892	Aug 22 1933	Burned	Stone Point, Va.
881	Hereward	Sch.	90	1874	Dec 9 1917	Foundered	Stump Pass, Fla.
882	Herman Oelrichs	Sch.	76	1894	Dec 22 1910	Stranded	Cape San Blas Shoals, Fla.
883	Hermitage	Sc.b.	2,111	1919	Nov 22 1924	Foundered	30-16-00 N. 79-43-00 W. Steel vessel.
884	Heroine	Sch.	-	-	Oct 1841	Unknown	Whales Head, N.C.
885	Hesperides	Steamer	-	-	Oct 9 1897	Unknown	Off Cape Hatteras, N.C.
886	Hess Mariner	El.s.	10,564	1945	Oct 6 1961	Lost	31-10-00 N. 79-09-00 W. Steel vessel. Exploded and broke into two pieces.
887	Hester A. Seward	Sch.	124	-	Jan 6 1895	Unknown	Ocracoke Inlet, N.C.
888	Hettie J. Dorman	Sch.	88	-	May 5 1900	Unknown	Off Cape Hatteras, N.C.
889	Hiawatha	Ol.s.	647	1926	Sep 30 1931	Burned	Eastport, Fla.
890	Hilda	Sch.	149	1877	Feb 6 1907	Stranded	Diamond Shoals, N.C. All lives (7) lost.
891	Hildegarde	St.s.	53	1898	May 29 1928	Stranded	Fenwick Island, S.C.
892	Hilton	Ga.s.	57	1925	Dec 18 1937	Stranded	1 mile southwest of Cartsfort Light, Fla.
893	Hjalmar	Sch.	1,141	1891	Dec 18 1910	Foundered	Carrabelle, Fla.
894	Holliswood	Brg.	537	1893	Jun 30 1920	Foundered	110 miles southeast of Cape San Blas, Fla.
895	Home	St.p.	376	1837	Oct 9 1837	Foundered	Off Cape Hatteras (Ocracoke), N.C. 96 lives lost. Length 220'. Beam 22'.
896	Honduras	St.p.	-	1861	1870	Stranded	Key West, Fla.
897	Hope	Bark	-	-	Sep 15 1887	Abandoned	30-42-00 N. 79-30-00 W.
898	Horatio	Ship	-	-	Apr 2 1820	Unknown	Off Diamond Shoals, N.C. 8 lives lost.
899	Horatio L. Baker	Sch.	829	1888	Mar 1 1915	Foundered	26-02-00 N. 78-00-00 W.
900	Horse	Sch.	-	-	Jan 31 1838	Unknown	Currituck Beach, N.C.
901	Howard Smith	Sch.	-	-	Oct 23 1891	Unknown	Doboy Bank, Ga.
902	Hudson	Ol.s.	124	1893	Dec 19 1946	Foundered	On jetties at entrances to St. John River, Fla.
903	Hugh Kelly	Sch.	792	1892	Apr 2 1915	Foundered	60 miles east of Cape Hatteras, N.C.
904	Hunley (David)	Sub.	-	-	Feb 17 1864	"Sunk"	5-1/2 miles ENE from Fort Sumter, Charleston, S.C. Confederate vessel. All lives (7) lost. In successfully sinking USS HOUSATONIC, the submarine was lost. First time in naval history that submarine was used in sinking vessel.
905	Hunter	Sch.	-	-	Aug 19 1837	Unknown	Kitty Hawk, N.C. 2 lives lost.
906	Huntress	Ga.y.	76	1906	Jan 6 1913	Burned	Cape Kennedy, Fla. 3 lives lost.

NO.	NAME OF VESSEL	RIG	TONS	BUILT	DATE		CAUSE	PLACE AND COMMENT
907	Huron	St.s.	541	-	Nov 24	1877	Wrecked	Short distance offshore from Nags Head, N.C. 100 lives lost. Depth 26'.
908	Hurryup II	Ga.s.	51	1922	Mar 15	1945	Foundered	Bellhaven, N.C.
909	Ida	Sloop	-	-	Mar 18	1890	Unknown	Cape Charles, Va.
910	Ida B. Silsbee	Sch.	-	-	Aug 18	1879	Unknown	Off Cape Hatteras, N.C.
911	Ida C. Schoolcraft	Sch.	-	-	Jul 1	1902	Unknown	Core Bank, N.C.
912	Ida Lawrence	Sch.	-	-	Dec 4	1902	Unknown	Ocracoke, N.C.
913	Ida M. Silva	Sch.	55	1903	May 24	1922	Foundered	Off Pensacola, Fla.
914	Idabelle	Ga.s.	113	1923	May 17	1930	Burned	Back River, Ga.
915	Idler	Ga.y.	122	1901	Jan 25	1915	Stranded	Diamond Shoals, Cape Hatteras, N.C. All lives (12) lost.
916	Illinois	St.s.	5,447	1920	Jun 2	1942	War Loss	24-00-00 N. 60-00-00 W. Steel vessel. Sunk by enemy action.
917	Imogene	Ga.s.	59	1903	Nov 22	1940	Burned	At May River, Bluffton, S.C.
918	Independent	Sch.	2,253	1889	Nov 14	1908	Foundered	Hog Island, Va. All lives (5) lost.
919	Independence	Ol.s.	65	-	Dec 10	1964	Burned	About 17 miles west of Tarpon Springs, Fla.
920	India	Ship	366	1953	Jan 20	1862	"Sunk"	On south edge of Rattlesnake Shoal, Maffitts Channel, Charleston, S.C. Used by Union forces to block harbor. Part of 2nd "Stone Fleet".
921	Indus	Brig	-	-	Dec 18	1837	Unknown	Off Cape Hatteras Inlet, N.C.
922	Ingomar	Ol.y.	143	1903	Feb 21	1931	Stranded	Cape Fear Light, N.C. Steel vessel.
923	Iola	St.s.	72	1908	Jul 6	1912	Burned	Tampa Bay, Fla.
924	Ira	Sch.	75	1908	Oct 24	1909	Foundered	Cedar Keys, Fla.
925	Ira	St.s.	60	1891	Apr	1924	Foundered	Altamaha River, Ga.
926	Irene	Brg.	491	1876	Jan 28	1906	Abandoned	At sea. 25 miles southeast of Cape Lookout, N.C.
927	Irene Thayer	Sch.	-	-	Nov 19	1892	Unknown	Oregon Inlet, N.C.
928	Irma	Sch.	614	1917	Apr 29	1925	Stranded	Bodie Island, N.C.
929	Iron Age	Steamer	-	-	Jan 11	1864	Burned	Lockwoods Folly Inlet, N.C. Federal (Union) gunboat.
930	Isaac Collins	Sch.	98	1889	Nov 21	1911	Stranded	Biscayne Bay, Fla.
931	Isaac L. Clark	Sch.	-	-	Dec 17	1884	Unknown	Off Diamond Shoals, N.C.
932	Isabella Parmenter	Sch.	979	1920	Oct 21	1925	Foundered	Cape Henry, Va. 36-53-00 N. 74-45-00 W.
933	Isis	St.p.	130	1837	Jan 5	1842	Burned	Tampa, Fla.
934	Island Belle	St.s.	132	1892	Mar 25	1926	Stranded	Key West, Fla.
935	Islander	St.s.	119	1883	Jun 2	1926	Burned	Southport, N.C.
936	Isle of Iona	Steamer	-	-	Dec 13	1914	Unknown	Ocracoke, N.C.
937	Islington	Ship	-	-	Mar 16	1820	Unknown	Off Cape Hatteras, N.C.
938	Israel W. Durham	Brg.	329	1872	May 27	1907	Stranded	Bird Shoal, N.C. Iron vessel.
939	Istria	Bark	-	-	Jun	1868	Unknown	Diamond Shoals, N.C. 23 lives lost.
940	Ivie	Brg.	1,227	1891	May 10	1916	Collided	With st.s. BERKSHIRE. Hampton Roads, Va. Steel vessel.
941	J.A. Moffett, Jr.	Ol.s.	9,788	1921	Jul 8	1942	War Loss	24-45-00 N. 80-42-00 W. Tanker. Steel vessel. 1 life lost (43). SALVAGED.
942	J.B. Holden	Sch.	-	-	Oct 11	1903	Unknown	Paul Gamiels Hill, N.C.
943	J.B. Walker	Sch.	2,136	1879	Apr 4	1924	Burned	Scotland, Va.
944	J.C. McNaughton	Sch.	-	-	Apr 8	1899	Unknown	Durants, N.C.
945	J. Carlton Hudson	Sch.	880	1904	Feb 19	1916	Foundered	Off Hog Island, Va. All lives (4) lost.
946	J.D. Swain	St.p.	228	1859		1869	Stranded	Escambia River, Fla.
947	J.F. Becker	Sch.	167	1904	Apr 26	1903	Unknown	Oregon Inlet, N.C.
948	J.F. Whitcomb	Sch.	412	- -	Mar 24	1907	Stranded	Assateague Beach, Va.
949	J. Frank Seavey	Sch.	412	1888	Mar 3	1920	Foundered	Florida Straits.
950	J.G. Carver	St.w.	197	1902	Feb 15	1948	Foundered	On the Altamaha River, near Doctortown, Ga.
951	J.H. Lockwood	Sch.	-	1870	Nov 20	1876	Unknown	Chicamacomico, N.C.
952	J.J. Stewart	Sch.	51		Dec 11	1906	Foundered	James River, Va.
953	J.L.M. Curry	St.s.	7,176	1942	Mar 8	1943	Foundered	66-53-00 N. 14-17-00 W. Steel vessel.

NO.	NAME OF VESSEL	RIG	TONS	BUILT	DATE		CAUSE	PLACE AND COMMENT
954	J. Manchester Haynes	Sch.	795	1885	Feb 26	1919	Abandoned	35-33-00 N. 70-49-00 W.
955	J. Means	Sch.	-	-	Oct 12	1874	Unknown	Bodie Island, N.C.
956	J.P. Bickley	Sch.	-	-	Mar	1849	Unknown	Off Cape Hatteras, N.C.
957	J.P. Huppman	Brg.	436	1903	Apr 1	1947	Collided	With unknown vessel. At Sewells Point, Hampton Roads, Va.
958	J.R. Teel	Sch.	870	1889	Nov 9	1913	Stranded	Bogue Isle, N.C. 1 life lost.
959	J.S. Underhill	St.s.	123	1853	Dec 24	1878	Burned	Wilmington, N.C.
960	J.W. Dresser	Bkn.	602	-	Jul 22	1895	Wrecked	Outer Diamond Shoals, Cape Hatteras, N.C.
961	J.W. Everman	Brg.	-	-	Apr 10	1887	Unknown	Cape Charles, Va.
962	J.W. Gaskill	Sch.	-	-	Feb 16	1891	Unknown	Pea Island, N.C.
963	Jackson	St.s.	454	1853	Sep 12	1868	Burned	Cape Lookout, N.C. Renamed "Patapsco" in 1858.
964	Jacob Jones	-	-	-	Feb 28	1942	Unknown	38-39-12 N. 74-28-42 W. 10' high in 102' of water. U.S. Navy vessel.
965	Jacob W. Hook	Sch.	677	1918	Nov 11	1928	Foundered	Cape Hatteras, N.C. 3 lives lost (7).
966	James A. Lweis	Ol.s.	190	1905	May 4	1936	Burned	Off Wind Mill Point, Va. Steel vessel.
967	James B. Anderson	Sch.	-	-	Jan 21	1889	Unknown	Durants, N.C.
968	James C. Clifford	Sch.	377	1886	Apr 14	1909	Abandoned	60 miles southeast of Pensacola, Fla.
969	James Chrisropher	St.p.	243	1853	Jan 13	1866	Burned	Savannah River, Ga.
970	James D. Dewell	Sch.	603	1882	Sep 17	1906	Foundered	Off Charleston, S.C. All lives (7) lost.
971	James Davidson	Sch.	451	1891	Aug 26	1911	Foundered	Off Charleston, S.C.
972	James Gibbon	St.p.	116	1830	Aug 28	1840	Exploded	Richmond, Va. 3 lives lost.
973	James H. Neff	Sch.	-	-	Dec 17	1890	Unknown	2-1/2 miles south of Oak Island L.S. Station, Cape Fear, N.C.
974	James M. Hamlen	Bark	-	-	Aug 28	1903	Unknown	Off Cape Lookout, N.C.
975	James Rudd	Sch.	-	-	Mar 22	1890	Unknown	Lookout Shoals, N.C. Also reported as "Joseph Rudd".
976	James Sprunt	St.s.	7,177	1943	Mar 10	1943	War Loss	19-49-00 N. 74-38-00 W. Steel vessel. Sunk by enemy action.
977	James T. Hatfield	Sch.	-	-	Jan 18	1846	Unknown	Wash Woods, N.C.
978	James W. Brooks	Sch.	-	-	Jan 17	1904	Unknown	South side of Lookout Shoals, N.C.
979	James W. Haig	Sch.	-	-	Sep 26	1882	Unknown	Durants, N.C.
980	James W. Howard	Sch.	1,655	1920	Dec 14	1925	Collided	With Italian st.s. LIVENZA. Cape Lookout, N.C.
981	James Woodall	Steamer	-	-	Jan 12	1896	Unknown	New Inlet, N.C.
982	Jamie Carlton	Sch.	-	-	Jun 7	1890	Unknown	Off Cape Charles, Va.
983	Jane	Sch.	-	-	Jun	1851	Unknown	Cape Hatteras, N.C.
984	Jane C. Harris	Sch.	-	-	Feb 25	1900	Unknown	Oregon Inlet, N.C.
985	Jane Henderson	Ship	-	-	Jun 21	1860	Unknown	Wash Woods, N.C.
986	Jane Nichols	St.p.	68	1851	Apr 24	1859	Exploded	Wheeling, Va. Used as ferryboat.
987	Jane Palmer	Sch.	3,138	1904	Dec 18	1920	Abandoned	36-06-00 N. 65-31-00 W.
988	Java Arrow	St.s.	8,327	1921	May 5	1942	War Loss	27-30-00 N. 80-08-00 W. Steel vessel. Sunk by enemy action. SALVAGED.
989	Javelin	Ga.y.	57	1907	Sep 8	1927	Burned	Dunedin, Fla.
990	Jaxshipco No.4	Brg.	75	1920	Apr 1	1920	Foundered	Miami, Fla.
991	Jay	Sloop	-	-	Feb 20	1825	Wrecked	Off Smith Island, Va.
992	Jeanie Lippitt	Sch.	742	1880	Dec 22	1908	Stranded	Winter Quarter Shoal, Va. 7 lives lost.
993	Jeff	Ol.s.	137	1888	Oct 15	1954	Foundered	About 30 miles due east of Miami, Fla.
994	Jemina F. III	Ga.y.	149	1908	Sep 18	1926	Foundered	Biscayne Bay, Fla. Steel vessel.
995	Jennie Beasley	Sch.	-	-	Jan 26	1886	Unknown	Currituck Inlet, N.C.
996	Jennie Lockwood	Sch.	433	1882	Feb 13	1906	Stranded	Pea Island, N.C.
997	Jennie N. Huddell	Sch.	279	1870	Feb 4	1910	Stranded	Carters Shoal, Chincoteague, Va.
998	Jennie Sweeney	Sch.	643	1875	Jun 14	1906	Foundered	Cape Fear Bar, N.C.
999	Jenny Lind	St.p.	246	1847	Sep 6	1854	Stranded	Savannah, Ga.
1000	Jermiah Smith	Sch.	409	1888	Mar 14	1920	Foundered	200 miles east of Hampton Roads, Va.
1001	Jerome	Sch.	53	1881	Apr 9	1907	Stranded	Mobjack Bay, Va.

NO.	NAME OF VESSEL	RIG	TONS	BUILT	DATE	CAUSE	PLACE AND COMMENT
1002	Jesse W. Starr	Sch.	307	1874	Feb 27 1906	Abandoned	37-33-00 N. 74-36-00 W. 6 lives lost.
1003	Jessie	-	-	-	1875	Unknown	Off Brazos, Fla. Valued at $100,000.
1004	Jessie A. Bishop	Sch.	754	1908	Jan 1 1912	Stranded	Nassau Inlet, Fla.
1005	Jessie G. Noyes	Sch.	1,376	1917	Mar 3 1927	Foundered	37-31-00 N. 69-00-00 W. 3 lives lost (11).
1006	Jewell	St.w.	75	1918	Feb 1926	Foundered	Oconec River, Ga.
1007	Joel F. Sheppard	Sch.	567	1889	Nov 20 1911	Burned	Harborton, Va.
1008	John A. Buttrick	Sch.	-	-	Mar 30 1903	Unknown	Cape Fear, N.C. 1 life lost.
1009	John B. Manning	Sch.	1,190	1889	Apr 5 1915	Foundered	20 miles north of Cape Hatteras, N.C. Vessel was found in "bottom-up" position.
1010	John Boushell	Sch.	-	-	Jan 28 1851	Unknown	Albemarle Sound, N.C. 4 lives lost.
1011	John C. Calhoun	St.p.	165	1859	Apr 28 1860	Exploded	Brainbridge, Ga. 8 lives lost.
1012	John D. Gill	El.s.	11,641	1942	Mar 12 1942	War Loss	33-50-30 N. 77-30-30 W. Steel vessel. Tanker. Sunk by enemy action. Demolished. Depth 44'. Partially visible. 23 lives lost (49).
1013	John E. Devlin	Sch.	1,107	1900	Jan 10 1908	Stranded	Metomkin, Va.
1014	John E. Wales	Ol.s.	88	1918	Apr 18 1930	Stranded	Neuse River, N.C.
1015	John Ena	Ship	2,842	1892	Feb 19 1926	Foundered	35-25-00 N. 70-45-00 W. Steel vessel.
1016	John Floyd	Sch.	-	-	Dec 14 1882	Unknown	Diamond Shoals, N.C.
1017	John Francis	Sch.	322	1897	May 29 1919	Stranded	Egmont Key, Fla.
1018	John G. Whildin	Sch.	51	1839	Sep 5 1915	Foundered	Near Cape San Blas, Fla. All lives (9) lost.
1019	John H. McNally	Brg.	381	1902	Jan 11 1910	Collided	With st.s. MARYLAND. Bush Bluff Lightship, Va.
1020	John Hancock	St.s.	7,176	1942	Aug 18 1942	War Loss	19-41-00 N. 76-50-00 W. Steel vessel. Sunk by enemy action.
1021	John Henry Sherman	Ga.s.	77	1924	Sep 17 1928	Stranded	Garden Key, Dry Tortugas, Fla.
1022	John I. Clark	St.s.	50	1907	Mar 16 1944	Foundered	Norfolk, Va.
1023	John I. Snow	Sch.	196	1888	Jan 14 1907	Stranded	Portsmouth, N.C. (Beach).
1024	John J. Hanson	Sch.	628	1885	Feb 15 1914	Abandoned	36-20-00 N. 72-30-00 W.
1025	John J. Shay	St.s.	-	-	Aug 24 1887	Unknown	Coosa River, Ga.
1026	John M. Keen	Sloop	64	1894	Jul 5 1916	Stranded	Pensacola, Fla.
1027	John M. Morehead	Ol.s.	72	1924	Oct 15 1954	Lost	Off Southport, N.C.
1028	John Maxwell	Sch.	532	1899	Nov 1 1912	Stranded	New Inlet, N.C. 6 lives lost.
1029	John Morgan	St.s.	7,176	1943	Jun 1 1943	Collided	With st.s. MONTANA. Cape Henry, Va. 36-53-00 N. 76-00-00 W. Steel vessel.
1030	John McLean	St.p.	133	1837	Nov 15 1838	Stranded	New Smyrna, Fla.
1031	John N. Parker	Sch.	-	-	Jan 8 1884	Unknown	Hatteras Inlet, N.C.
1032	John R.P. Moore	Sch.	99	1877	Oct 31 1939	Foundered	Norfolk, Va.
1033	John R. Rees	Sch.	81	1872	Oct 10 1906	Foundered	Off Dymers Wharves, Va.
1034	John R. Zimmerman	Brg.	336	1893	Nov 29 1906	Stranded	Mouth of Elizabeth River, Va.
1035	John Rice	St.s.	782	1863	Oct 14 1889	Stranded	Ocracoke, N.C.
1036	John Rose	Sch.	626	1883	Aug 29 1911	Abandoned	33-12-00 N. 77-00-00 W.
1037	John S. Deering	Sch.	478	1801	Mar 5 1906	Stranded	37-05-00 N. 71-50-00 W.
1038	John S. Emery	Bkn.	919	1890	Oct 3 1923	Foundered	30-32-00 N. 66-38-00 W.
1039	John S. Wood	Sch.	-	-	Apr 7 1889	Unknown	Wash Woods, N.C.
1040	John Sevier	St.s.	7,176	1942	Apr 6 1943	War Loss	20-17-00 N. 73-52-00 W. North of Cuba. Freighter. Steel vessel. Sunk by enemy action. Convoy #GUAM-83.
1041	John Shay	Sch.	111	1835	Apr 17 1889	Unknown	Cape Hatteras, N.C. 6 lives lost.
1042	John T. Lamar	St.p.	-	-	Dec 8 1835	Snagged	Relee, Ga.
1043	John Twohy	Sch.	1,019	1891	Oct 9 1913	Stranded	On Cape Fear, N.C.
1044	John W. Callahan	St.p.	202	1907	Mar 25 1923	Stranded	White River, Fla.
1045	John W. Fredericks Jr.	St.s.	214	1914	Jan 1919	Foundered	Sampit River, S.C.
1046	John W. Hall	Sch.	346	1890	Mar 12 1912	Stranded	Ocean City, Md.
1047	John Young	Sch.	-	-	Sep 30 1890	Unknown	Colts Island, Va.

NO.	NAME OF VESSEL	RIG	TONS	BUILT	DATE	CAUSE	PLACE AND COMMENT
1048	Jonas Sparks	Sch.	-	-	Apr 14 1867	Unknown	Beaufort Bar, N.C.
1049	Jose Olaverri	Sch.	661	1885	Jul 23 1908	Stranded	Bull Island, S.C.
1050	Joseph A. O'Brien	Brg.	218	1874	Jul 11 1912	Burned	Albermarle Sound, N.C.
1051	Joseph B. Thomas	Sch.	1,564	1900	Mar 21 1909	Stranded	Fowey Rocks, Fla.
1052	Joseph Baker	Bark	-	-	Jan 31 1891	Unknown	Near Fort Jefferson, Fla.
1053	Joseph E. Coffee	St.p.	207	1846		Stranded	Hatteras Inlet, N.C. Also known as "CSS Winslow" and CSS Warren Winslow". 38-28-00 N. 74-58-42 W.
1054	Joseph E. Hooper	Brg.	-	-			Off Hog Island, Va.
1055	Joseph F. Clinton	Sch.	553	1904	May 8 1917	Foundered	Off coast of South Carolina. 29 lives lost.
1056	Joseph F. Luckenbach		-	-	May 15 1914	Wrecked	Tail of Horseshoe, Chesapeake Bay, Va.
1057	Joseph G. Ray	Sch.	1,253	1901	Nov 24 1911	Stranded	Oak Island Light, N.C.
1058	Joseph H. Neff	Sch.	-	-	Dec 17 1890	Unknown	25-57-00 N. 83-57-00 W. Steel vessel. Tanker. Sunk by enemy action.
1059	Joseph M. Cudahy	St.s.	6,949	1921	May 4 1942	War Loss	36-21-00 N. 71-41-00 W.
1060	Joseph P. Cooper	Sch.	315	1905	Nov 29 1918	Foundered	Outer point of Lookout Shoals, Cape Lookout, N.C.
1061	Joseph W. Brooks	Sch.	728	-	Jan 17 1904	Unknown	22-23-00 N. 97-03-00 W.
1062	Joseph W. Hawthorn	Sch.	585	1891	Jan 14 1914	Foundered	Chesapeake Bay.
1063	Joseph Wilde	Sch.	-	-	Aug 26 1889	Collided	3/4 mile south of Kill Devil Hills L.S. Station, N.C. 3 lives lost.
1064	Josephine	Sch.	-	-	Apr 3 1915	Wrecked	Scotland, Va.
1065	Josephus	Sch.	1,646	1876	Apr 4 1924	Burned	Tortugas Reef, Fla.
1066	Joshua H. Marvell	Sch.	-	-	Jul 25 1887	Unknown	Chicamicomico, N.C. 11 lives lost.
1067	Josie Troop	Bark	-	-	Feb 23 1889	Unknown	On south edge of Rattlesnake Shoal, Maffitt's Channel, Charleston, S.C.
1068	Jubilee	Bark	233	-	Jan 20 1862	"Sunk"	Used by Union forces to block harbor. Part of 2nd "Stone Fleet".
1069	Judge Pennewill	Sch.	439	1906	Jun 9 1912	Foundered	Charleston, S.C.
1070	Judy	Ga.s.	68	1943	Nov 29 1963	Foundered	100 miles east of Savannah, Ga.
1071	Julia	Ga.s.	91	1882	Jan 13 1916	Stranded	Little River, S.C.
1072	Julia Moffett	St.w.	56	1860	Aug 1 1861	Burned	Tyler, Va.
1073	Julia P. Cole	Sch.	495	1904	Jan 21 1910	Foundered	Off Cape Hatteras, N.C.
1074	Julian J. Fleetwood	St.s.	52	1896	Mar 20 1923	Foundered	Mouth of North River, N.C. 4 lives lost.
1075	Juliet L. Hopkins	Sch.	78	1884	Apr 6 1920	Foundered	Off Old Plantation Creek, Va.
1076	June	Sloop	-	-	Aug 11 1899	Unknown	Oregon Inlet, N.C.
1077	Juno	St.s.	62	1876	Jul 22 1923	Foundered	Beaufort, N.C. Iron vessel. 1 life lost (9).
1078	Juno	Ga.y.	68	1929	Apr 28 1938	Foundered	10 miles south of St. Georges Light, St. Andreas, Fla.
1079	Kaimoku	St.s.	6,367	1919	Aug 8 1942	War Loss	56-32-00 N. 32-15-00 W. Steel vessel. Sunk by enemy action.
1080	Kallskeg		-	-	Apr 7 1942	Unknown	35-12-00 N. 75-13-00 W.
1081	Kanawha	St.s.	2,182	1902	Mar 16 1916	Foundered	33-08-00 N. 73-42-00 W. Steel vessel. 7 lives lost.
1082	Kanawha Valley	St.w.	126	1857	Aug 1 1861	Burned	Cannelton, Va.
1083	Karina T.	Ol.s.	81	1954	Mar 7 1962	Storm	At Chincoteague, Va.
1084	Kassandra Louloudis	Frgt.	3,184*	-	Mar 19 1944	Unknown	35-10-30 N. 75-22-45 W. or 35-10-18 N. 75-21-18 W. About 9.5 miles, 121° from tower at Cape Hatteras, N.C. Steel vessel. Wreck demolished. Greek registry.
1085	Kate		-	-	Jul 12 1863	Wrecked	Smith's Island, N.C. Confederate blockade runner.
1086	Kate Cannon	St.s.	50	1887	Aug 2 1920	Collided	With st.s. LAKE ELLENORAH. Charleston, S.C. 1 life lost (6).
1087	Kate E. Gifford	Sch.	149	-	Aug 29 1893	Unknown	Off Oak Island L.S. Station, Oak Island, N.C.
1088	Kate McLarin	St.p.	54	1859	May 29 1860	Exploded	Elizabethtown, N.C. 3 lives lost.
1089	Kate Spencer	Sch.	-	-	Oct 7 1904	Unknown	Cape Lookout, N.C.
1090	Kate Wentworth	Sch.	-	-	Nov 18 1886	Unknown	Bogue Banks, N.C. 1 life lost.
1091	Katherine	Brg.	94	1901	Apr 24 1908	Foundered	20 miles west of Ship Shoal, Va.
1092	Katherine	St.p	89	1909	Jun 27 1917	Foundered	Savannah River, Ga.
1093	Katherine D. Perry	Sch.	1,125	1891	Dec 17 1911	Stranded	Off Fisherman's Island, Cape Charles, Va. 37-02-20 N. 75-56-12 W.

NO.	NAME OF VESSEL	RIG	TONS	BUILT	DATE	CAUSE	PLACE AND COMMENT
1094	Katie	St.p.	190	1867	1881	Lost	Savannah, Ga.
1095	Katie Brady	Brg.	-	-	Sep 1 1890	Unknown	Hampton Roads, Va.
1096	Kemah	Ga.y.	58	1907	Sep 18 1926	Foundered	Miami, Fla.
1097	Kennebec	St.p.	480	1845	Apr 9 1870	Burned	Gloucester Point, Va.
1098	Kennedy	St.p.	140	1901	Feb 24 1914	Burned	St. Johns River, Fla.
1099	Kensington	Ship	357	-	Dec 21 1861	"Sunk"	4 miles SSE off Fort Sumter and 3 miles ESE of the light on Morris Island, Charleston, S.C. Used by Union forces to block harbor. Part of "Stone Fleet".
1100	Kensington	-	-	-	Jan 27 1871	Collided	Cape Hatteras, N.C. 150 lives lost.
1101	Kentucky	St.s.	996	1897	Feb 4 1910	Foundered	200 miles south of Cape Hatteras, N.C.
1102	Keshena	St.s.	427	1919	Jul 19 1942	War Loss	Off Hatteras Inlet, N.C. Steel vessel. Sunk by enemy action. Tug. Demolished. 34-59-30 N. 74-45-48 W.
1103	Key West	St.s.	713	1862	Oct 12 1870	Stranded	Cape Hatteras, N.C.
1104	Key West	Ol.s.	347	1928	Jan 10 1942	Burned	Cocoa, Fla.
1105	Kilgore	Brig	-	-	Aug 24 1842	Wrecked	On Currituck Beach, N.C.
1106	Kimtoo	Ol.s.	63	1953	Jan 18 1955	Stranded	1 mile northwest of Anna Maria, Fla.
1107	King Fish	Ol.s.	117	1955	Jan 11 1958	Burned	At Goose Creek, near Hobucken, N.C.
1108	Kingfisher	St.s.	441	1863	Nov 13 1866	Foundered	Cape Hatteras, N.C. 4 lives lost.
1109	Kingston Ceylonite	-	500	-	Jun 17 1942	War Loss	36-49-39 N. 75-52-09 W. British. Trawler. Depth 40'. Demolished.
1110	Kit	Ol.s.	88	1924	Aug 26 1964	Hurricane	At Neptune Marina, Miami Beach, Miami, Fla.
1111	Kitty Woodall	Ol.s.	103	1905	Oct 12 1934	Collided	With M/V B.S. FORD, Alligator River and Pungo River Canal, N.C.
1112	Knoxville City	St.s.	5,686	1921	Jun 1 1942	War Loss	21-10-00 N. 83-47-00 W. North of Cuba. Steel vessel. Freighter. Sunk by enemy action. 25% of lives lost.
1113	Kochalene	St.p.	127	1903	1922	Foundered	Alabama River, Ga.
1114	Kon-Tiki	Ol.s.	58	1953	Dec 9 1954	Burned	At West Pass, Fla.
1115	Korsholm (Swed.)	-	1,418*	-	Apr 13 1942	Unknown	28-12-10 N. 80-29-16 W. Freighter. Wreck demolished. Depth 50'.
1116	Kyma	Ol.s.	98	1928	Dec 7 1958	Foundered	About 147 miles ENE of Norfolk, Va.
1117	Kyzikes (Gr.)	-	2,627	-	Dec 4 1927	Unknown	1.5 miles north of Kill Devil Hills Coast Guard Station, N.C. Length 226'. Depth 36'. 4 lives lost.
1118	L.B. Shaw	-	967	-	Pre-WWII		38-54-54 N. 74-23-00 W.
1119	L.C. Ballard	Sch.	-	-	Apr 13 1915	Unknown	1/2 mile south of Gull Island Light, N.C.
1120	L.C. Richmond	Ship	340	-	Dec 21 1861	"Sunk"	4 miles SSE off Fort Sumter and 3 miles ESE of light on Morris Island, Charleston, S.C. Used by Union forces during Civil War to block harbor.
1121	L & D Fisk	Sch.	-	-	Nov 23 1880	Unknown	Diamond Shoals, N.C. 6 lives lost.
1122	L. McNeill	St.p.	145	1899	Jun 8 1916	Stranded	Mosquito Inlet, Fla.
1123	La Republic	Steamer	-	-	Feb 1871	Unknown	Off Cape Lookout, N.C. Also known as "La Republique".
1124	Lady Drake	-	-	-	May 5 1942	Unknown	Oregon Inlet, N.C. 35-45-00 N. 75-24-00 W.
1125	Lady Fish	Ol.s.	115	1916	May 9 1940	Burned	Isle of Hope, Ga.
1126	Lady of the Lake	Sch.	-	-	Jul 14 1888	Unknown	Dawson Shoals, Va.
1127	Lady Whidbee	Sch.	-	-	Jan 17 1860	Unknown	New Inlet, N.C.
1128	Laertes (Dutch)	Frgt.	3,629*	-	May 3 1942	Unknown	28-28-48 N. 80-22-00 W. Freighter. Wreck demolished. Depth 38'. Also reported as "Laertis".
1129	Lake City	St.s.	2,485	1917	Oct 5 1918	Collided	With st.s. JAMES McGEE. Off Key West, Fla. Steel vessel. 30 lives lost. Also reported as being "torpedoed".
1130	Lakewood	Sch.	586	1900	Apr 29 1907	Collided	With Norwegian st.s. LIVINGSTONE. Off Cape Hatteras, N.C.
1131	Lambert Tree	Sch.	-	-	Feb 17 1841	Unknown	Off Ocracoke, N.C.
1132	Lamplighter	St.p.	186	1835	Feb 15 1841	Foundered	East Pass, Fla. 19 lives lost.
1133	Lancaster	Sch.	1,284	1874	Dec 9 1917	Foundered	Chincoteague, Va. All lives (5) lost.
1134	Lancaster Olympice	Tanker	5,335	-	Jan 31 1942	War Loss	36-01-00 N. 75-30-00 W. Off North Carolina coast.

NO.	NAME OF VESSEL	RIG	TONS	BUILT	DATE	CAUSE	PLACE AND COMMENT
1135	Lancing	-	-	1916	Apr 7 1942	Unknown	Off Cape Hatteras, N.C.
1136	Larimer	Sch.	1,584	-	May 28 1922	Foundered	North of Hog Island, Va. 1 life lost.
1137	Laura	St.p.	61	1862	Oct 4 1866	Snagged	Augusta, Ga.
1138	Laura A. Barnes	Sch.	629	1918	Jun 1 1921	Stranded	Bodie Island, N.C.
1139	Laura M. Lunt	Sch.	567	1867	Mar 4 1914	Abandoned	Off coast of North Carolina.
1140	Lavinia M. Snow	Sch.	354	1893	Mar 7 1930	Foundered	Cape Hatteras, N.C.
1141	Laura Nelson	Sch.	-	-	Mar 30 1895	Unknown	Bodie Island, N.C.
1142	Laurie V. Grove	Brg.	324	1891	Nov 28 1915	Burned	Mattapony River, Va.
1143	Le Roy	St.p.	83	1836	Oct 28 1840	Exploded	Iola, Fla. 6 lives lost.
1144	Leading Breeze	Sch.	-	-	Nov 23 1901	Unknown	Portsmouth, N.C.
1145	Lehigh	Drg.	414	-	Feb 24 1942	Stranded	2-1/2 miles NNW of Coast Guard Station, Ocracoke Island, N.C.
1146	Leibre	Tanker	7,075	-	Apr 2 1942	War Loss	34-17-00 N. 76-12-00 W. 9 lives lost (34). SALVAGED.
1147	Lejok	Sch.	371	1901	Mar 4 1920	Foundered	29-12-00 N. 79-10-00 W.
1148	Lena Breed	Sch.	-	-	Dec 4 1888	Unknown	Diamond Shoals, N.C.
1149	Leonidas	Bark	231	-	Dec 21 1861	"Sunk"	4 miles SSE off Fort Sumter and 3 miles ESE of light on Morris Island, Charleston, S.C. Used by Union forces to block harbor. Part of "Stone Fleet".
1150	Leonidas	Ga.s.	920	1918	Aug 11 1918	Burned	35-57-00 N. 65-59-00 W.
1151	Leonie	Ga.s.	164	1917	Sep 1 1961	Burned	At Miami, Fla.
1152	Leonora	Sch.	458	1874	Jan 8 1908	Stranded	Diamond Shoals, Cape Hatteras, N.C. 5 lives lost.
1153	Leroy	Sch.	-	-	Oct 5 1842	Unknown	Big Kinnakeet, N.C.
1154	Leroy	St.s.	209	1874	Nov 16 1926	Foundered	St. Andrews Bar, Fla.
1155	Leslie	St.s.	2,609	1919	Apr 4 1942	War Loss	28-35-00 N. 80-19-00 W. 3 miles southeast of Hetzel Shoals Gas Buoy, Fla. Steel vessel. Freighter. Sunk by enemy action.
1156	Leverine	Brg.	180	1907	Jun 18 1920	Stranded	Off Cape Fear Bar, N.C.
1157	Levi Davis	Tug	669	1881	Nov 29 1896	Unknown	Oak Island, N.C.
1158	Levi S. Andrews	Sch.	308	-	Mar 1 1914	Foundered	Norfolk, Va. All lives (7) lost.
1159	Lewis	Ship	-	-	Dec 21 1861	"Sunk"	4 miles SSE off Fort Sumter and 3 miles ESE of light on Morris Island, Charleston, S.C. Used by Union forces during Civil War to block harbor.
1160	Lewis H. Goward	Sch.	1,191	1895	Apr 1 1921	Burned	Near Key West, Fla.
1161	Libbie	Ga.s.	66	1908	Apr 26 1932	Burned	Kings Ferry, Fla.
1162	Liberator	St.s.	7,720	1918	Mar 19 1942	War Loss	Off Diamond Shoals Buoy, off Cape Hatteras, N.C. 35-14-00 N. 75-33-00 W. Steel vessel. Freighter. Sunk by enemy action.
1163	Liberty	St.w.	261	1857	Dec 27 1862	Snagged	Twelve Pole Creek, Va.
1164	Liberty	-	-	-	Mar 17 1915	Unknown	Off Cape Lookout, N.C.
1165	Liberty	Ol.s.	125	1896	Jan 3 1943	Stranded	71-53-00 N. 21-59-00 W.
1166	Liberty	Ol.s.	63	1953	Mar 3 1960	Foundered	About 200 miles southwest of Fort Myers, Fla.
1167	Ligero	Brig	-	-	Mar 27 1820	Unknown	Off east Florida in the New Bahamas Canal. 18-gun armament.
1168	Lillian Luckenbach	St.s.	6,369	1919	Mar 27 1943	Collided	With st.s. CAPE HENLOPEN. 35-58-00 N. 75-25-00 W. Steel vessel. Freighter. Wreck demolished. Convoy #ON-48.
1169	Lillie	St.s.	53	1883	Jun 8 1906	Burned	Southport, N.C.
1170	Lillie Ernestine	Sch.	68	1872	Mar 15 1922	Stranded	Wachapreague Beach, Va.
1171	Lillie F. Schmidt	Sch.	-	-	Mar 9 1893	Unknown	Ocracoke, N.C.
1172	Lily White	Sch.	55	1883	Dec 23 1910	Burned	Tampa, Fla. 3 lives lost.
1173	Lincoln	Sc.b.	855	1894	Apr 21 1925	Foundered	Chincoteague, Va.
1174	Little David	Ol.s.	58	1944	Feb 1 1960	Foundered	While enroute from Fort Myers, Fla., to Port Sutton, Fla. Steel vessel.
1175	Little Rock	St.p.	156	1837	Apr 3 1840	Stranded	Boeuf River, Fla.
1176	Lizzie B. Willey	Sch.	573	1881	Apr 10 1915	Foundered	31-35-00 N. 38-56-00 W. Off Cape Lookout, N.C.
1177	Lizzie Chadwick	Sch.	472	1883	Mar 3 1906	Abandoned	Off Cape Hatteras, N.C.

NO.	NAME OF VESSEL	RIG	TONS	BUILT	DATE	CAUSE	PLACE AND COMMENT
1178	Lizzie E. Dennison	Sch.	528	1890	Mar 10 1918	Stranded	Hetzel Shoal, Fla.
1179	Lizzie Godfrey	Sch.	77	1890	Jul 12 1914	Stranded	Chincoteague Inlet, Va.
1180	Lizzie H. Partrick	Sch.	471	1883	Nov 27 1911	Stranded	Cape Lookout Shoals, N.C.
1181	Lizzie S. Haynes	Sch.	436	-	Oct 24 1889	Unknown	Bodie Island, N.C. 5 lives lost.
1182	Lizzie S. James	Sch.	-	-	Mar 12 1900	Unknown	Ocracoke, N.C.
1183	Ljubica Matkovic	-	-	-	Jun 24 1942	Unknown	Core Bank, N.C. Possibly small freighter.
1184	Lone Star No.1	Brg.	775	1929	Apr 27 1932	Stranded	Chesapeake Bay, Va.
1185	Lorena	St.p.	287	1895	Feb 3 1916	Burned	Point Pleasant, W.Va.
1186	Loring C. Ballard	Sch.	660	1884	Apr 3 1915	Stranded	Gull Shoal, N.C.
1187	Lotta Lee	Sch.	-	-	Mar 1876	Unknown	Hatteras Inlet, N.C.
1188	Lottero Bertollo	Bark	-	-	Sep 28 1891	Unknown	St. Catherine Sound, Ga.
1189	Lottie	Brg.	425	1909	Dec 9 1917	Foundered	Off Black Fish Bank, Va.
1190	Louanna	Ol.s.	74	1953	Dec 10 1959	Foundered	In the Tampa, Fla., area. 27-55-00 N. 82-28-00 W.
1191	Louisa M	Sch.	412	1918	Dec 8 1920	Foundered	Off Currituck Light, N.C.
1192	Louisa Matilda	Packet	313	1820	Aug 24 1827	Wrecked	On Bodie Island, N.C. Length 97'.
1193	Louisburg	St.p.	894	1863	Apr 24 1870	Burned	Cedar Keys, Fla.
1194	Louis H	Brg.	323	1884	May 2 1919	Burned	Sombrero Key Light, Fla.
1195	Louise G	Ga.y.	82	1918	Mar 2 1921	Burned	25-00-00 N. 77-00-00 W.
1196	Louise Greer	St.s.	108	1890	Jan 10 1927	Collided	With st.s. HOWARD. Craney Island Light, Va. 2 lives lost (7).
1197	Louise Howard	Sch.	173	1917	Apr 14 1921	Stranded	On bar entrance to Beaufort Harbor, S.C.
1198	Low Tide	Ol.s.	63	1952	Oct 10 1953	Foundered	At Arcas Keys, Fla.
1199	Lowell	St.w.	124	1849	Mar 24 1851	Collided	With S.F. VINTON. Captina Island, Wheeling, Va. 15 lives lost.
1200	Lubrafol (Pan.)	Tanker	4,588*	-	May 9 1942	Unknown	29-14-00 N. 80-10-00 W.
1201	Lucie Marmet	St.p.	185	1903	Oct 5 1914	Burned	Charleston, W.Va.
1202	Lucile Ross	Ol.s.	61	1893	Apr 4 1950	Burned	In the Roanoke River, off the pier at Jamesville, N.C.
1203	Lucretia	Brg.	285	1903	Dec 12 1922	Foundered	On Portsmouth Flats, Elizabeth River, Va.
1204	Lucretia	Brg.	285	1903	Dec 22 1926	Foundered	Georgetown, S.C.
1205	Lucretia	Brg.	285	1903	Jul 28 1935	Stranded	Point of shoal in Shallotte River, N.C.
1206	Lucy Russell	Sch.	-	-	Jun 21 1903	Unknown	Gull Shoal, N.C.
1207	Luella A. Snow	Sch.	-	-	Sep 13 1891	Abandoned	Cape Lookout, N.C.
1208	Luis G. Rabel	Sch.	582	1883	Nov 18 1906	Stranded	Bulls Island, S.C.
1209	Lula M. Quillin	Sch.	129	1863	Dec 9 1917	Stranded	Pamlico Sound, N.C.
1210	Luna	Sch.	297	1899	Jul 29 1918	Stranded	Portsmouth Island, N.C.
1211	Lunaria	Ga.y.	64	1911	Dec 28 1913	Stranded	Jeltic, Georgetown, S.C.
1212	Luola Murchison	Sch.	-	-	Oct 3 1883	Unknown	Kitty Hawk, N.C.
1213	Luther C. Ward	St.s.	106	1882	Nov 7 1914	Foundered	Off Scotland Light, N.C.
1214	Luther T. Garretson	Sch.	572	1884	Dec 26 1915	Foundered	Charleston, S.C.
1215	Lycoming	Brg.	389	1901	Jan 28 1942	Foundered	Near Thimble Shoal Light, Chesapeake Bay, Va.
1216	Lydia A. Willis	Sch.	-	-	Aug 18 1899	Wrecked	Off Ocracoke Inlet, N.C. 2 lives lost.
1217	Lynn	Brg.	441	1914	Feb 16 1926	Stranded	Lake Worth Inlet, Fla.
1218	Lynnhaven	Ol.s.	65	1917		Burned	In Fernandina Beach Harbor, Fla.
1219	Lynx	St.p.	-	-	Sep 25 1864	Burned	Near Half Moon Battery, about 5 miles above Fort Fisher, N.C. Confederate blockade runner.
1220	M.A. Forbes	Bark	-	-	May 1870	Unknown	Currituck Beach, N.C.
1221	M.B. Davis	Sch.	-	-	Dec 8 1917	Unknown	Bogue Inlet, N.C.
1222	M. and E. Henderson	Sch.	387	-	Nov 30 1879	Unknown	Near north bank of New Inlet, N.C. Cargo of phosphate rock. 4 lives lost.
1223	M.J. Haynie	-	-	-	May 24 1911	Unknown	35-04-00 N. 75-50-00 W.
1224	M.W. Chapin	St.s.	217	1856	Mar 22 1868	Burned	City Point, Va.

NO.	NAME OF VESSEL	RIG	TONS	BUILT	DATE		CAUSE	PLACE AND COMMENT
1225	Mabel	Sch.	1,336	1901	Oct 13	1923	Foundered	26-26-00 N. 75-30-00 W.
1226	Mabel L. Phillips	Sch.	-	-	Oct	1889	Abandoned	Cape Hatteras, N.C.
1227	Mabel Rose	Sch.	-	-	Oct 11	1903	Unknown	Wash Woods, N.C.
1228	Machodoc	Brg.	367	1899	May 25	1931	Foundered	Mosquito Point, Va.
1229	Macon	St.p.	152	1826	Feb 5	1835	Exploded	Charleston, S.C. 4 lives lost.
1230	Madalene Cooney	Sch.	790	1892	Dec 28	1911	Collided	With st.s. WARRINGTON. 12 miles north of Cape Hatteras, N.C. All lives (9) lost.
1231	Madam Queen II	Ol.s.	67	1961	Dec 17	1961	Burned	Off Ft. Meyers Beach, Fla.
1232	Madeleine	St.s.	74	1893	Jun 10	1912	Abandoned	12 miles southeast of Cape Lookout Lightship, N.C.
1233	Madrugada	Ga.s.	1,613	1917	Aug 15	1918	Shell Fire	37-50-00 N. 74-55-00 W.
1234	Maetopolis	-	-	-	Jan 31	1878	Wrecked	Off North Carolina coast. 100 lives lost.
1235	Maggie J. Lawrence	Sch.	-	-	Feb 10	1896	Unknown	Pea Island, N.C.
1236	Maggie S. Hart	Sch.	679	-	Dec 18	1909	Foundered	Sailed from Jacksonville, Fla., and has not since reported. All lives (8) lost.
1237	Maggie Todd	Sch.	136	1873	Aug 22	1918	Foundered	100 miles northwest of Egmont Keys, Fla.
1238	Magic City	St.s.	315	1876	Feb 16	1910	Collided	With st.s. PARTHIAN. Mayport, Fla.
1239	Magnet	St.w.	98	1846	Dec 14	1852	Exploded	Grand View Island, Va. 10 lives lost.
1240	Magnolia	St.p.	260	1851	Jan 12	1852	Exploded	St. Simon Sound, Ga. 13 lives lost.
1241	Magnolia	Sch.	-	-	Dec 3	1852	Unknown	Chicamacomico, N.C. 1 life lost.
1242	Magnolia	St.p.	66	1855	Feb 19	1858	Exploded	Cape Fear River, N.C. 11 lives lost.
1243	Majestic	Bark	297	-	Jan 20	1862	"Sunk"	On south edge of Rattlesnake Shoal, Maffitt's Channel, Charleston Harbor, S.C. Used by Union forces to block harbor during Civil War. 2nd "Stone Fleet".
1244	Malay	Tanker	8,206	-	Jan 19	1942	War Loss	35-25-00 N. 75-23-00 W. Steel vessel. 3 lives lost (43). SALVAGED.
1245	Malchase	St.s.	3,515	1920	Apr 9	1942	War Loss	34-38-00 N. 75-56-00 W. Steel vessel. Sunk by enemy action.
1246	Malcolm B. Seavey	Sch.	1,247	1901	Aug 28	1911	Foundered	Cape Romain, S.C. 1 life lost.
1247	Maltran	St.s.	3,513	1920	Jul 5	1943	War Loss	18-11-00 N. 74-57-00 W. Steel vessel. Sunk by enemy action.
1248	Mamie T.	Sch.	63	1867	Nov 9	1919	Unknown	36-18-00 N. 75-43-00 W.
1249	Manaway	Steamer	-	-	Sep 3	1918	Collided	With st.s. G.S. ALLYN. Windmill Point, Va.
1250	Manhassett	St.s.	4,772	1934	Mar 28	1887	Unknown	Norfolk, Va.
1251	Manuela	St.s.	4,772	1934	Jun 24	1942	War Loss	34-30-00 N. 75-40-00 W. Steel vessel. Freighter. Sunk by enemy action.
1252	Manzanillo (Cuban)	Frgt.	1,025	-	Aug 12	1942	War Loss	24-20-00 N. 81-50-00 W. Depth "deep".
1253	Marana	Ol.s.	93	1922	Dec 28	1965	Foundered	Approximately 18 miles off the coast of Miami, Fla.
1254	Marcia	Bark	356	-	Jan 20	1862	"Sunk"	On south edge of Rattlesnake Shoal, Maffitt's Channel, Charleston Harbor, S.C. Used by Union forces during Civil War to block harbor. 2nd "Stone Fleet".
1255	Margaret	Brig	-	-	Jul 24	1850	Unknown	Off Diamond Shoal, N.C.
1256	Margaret A. May	Sch.	536	1884	Aug 26	1911	Foundered	Kiawah Island, S.C. All lives (10) lost.
1257	Margaret H. Vane	Sch.	246	1901	Aug 24	1908	Stranded	Cobbs Island, Va.
1258	Margaret Haskell	Sch.	2,114	1904	Feb 27	1916	Foundered	29-50-00 N. 75-45-00 W.
1259	Margaret Scott	Bark	330	-	Jan 20	1862	"Sunk"	On south edge of Rattlesnake Shoal, Maffitt's Channel, Charleston Harbor, S.C. Used by Union forces during Civil War to block harbor. 2nd "Stone Fleet".
1260	Margaret Thomas	Sch.	1,427	1904	Feb 29	1924	Stranded	Off Mosquito Lagoon, Fla.
1261	Margarette Tunnell	Sch.	-	-	Feb 13	1906	Unknown	Cape Fear, N.C.
1262	Marguedora	Ga.y.	58	1902	Aug 23	1905	Burned	Carrabelle River, Fla.
1263	Marguerite	Ol.s.	86	1903	Apr 5	1933	Burned	Spruells Bridge, N.C.
1264	Marguerite Egan	C.bt.	124	1909	Jun 30	1933	Burned	Berkeley, N.C.
1265	Marguerite M. Wemyss	Sch.	582	1919	Nov 22	1924	Collided	With st.s. CITY OF MONTGOMERY. Cape Lookout Light, N.C.
1266	Maria Fernanda	Ol.s.	50	-	Apr 14	1968	Foundered	Approximately 15 miles east of Port Royal Sea Buoy, off coast of South Carolina.
1267	Maria O. Teal	Sch.	1,125	1890	Jan 14	1915	Foundered	23-00-00 N. 64-00-00 W.
1268	Maria Theresa	Ship	330	-	Dec 21	1861	"Sunk"	4 miles SSE off Fort Sumter and 3 miles ESE of light on Morris Island, Charleston, S.C. Used by Union forces during Civil War to block harbor. "Stone Fleet".

NO.	NAME OF VESSEL	RIG	TONS	BUILT	DATE	CAUSE	PLACE AND COMMENT
1269	Marie Gilbert	Ga.s.	586	1906	Apr 20 1907	Stranded	Masson Bar, near Mayport, Fla.
1270	Marie Palmer	Sch.	1,904	1900	Dec 17 1909	Stranded	Frying Pan Shoals, N.C.
1271	Marion	Brig	-	-	Nov 4 1842	Unknown	Bodie Island, N.C.
1272	Marion	St.s.	206	1905	Feb 22 1907	Burned	Wadmalaw Sound, S.C. 24 lives lost.
1273	Marion Grimes	Sch.	72	1868	Sep 25 1906	Stranded	Assateague Beach, Va.
1274	Mariposa	St.s.	1,089	1864	Oct 9 1870	Foundered	Off Florida coast. 36 lives lost.
1275	Mark E. Singleton	Ol.s.	99	1965	Aug 1 1967	Burned	Off Egmont Key, Tampa Bay, Fla. 27-36-00 N. 82-45-00 W.
1276	Mark Pendleton	Sch.	534	1890	Jun 26 1918	Stranded	Cobb Island, Va.
1277	Marlboro	St.p.	272	1851	Dec 22 1853	Exploded	Charleston, S.C. 14 lives lost.
1278	Marlyn	Ol.s.	83	1926	Jan 1947	Foundered	Off coast of Norfolk, Va.
1279	Marore	St.s.	8,215	1922	Feb 26 1942	War Loss	35-42-38 N. 75-16-42 W. 3-1/2 miles off Whimble Shoals, N.C. Freighter. Steel vessel. Sunk by enemy action. Depth 90'.
1280	Marshall Nye	St.s.	204	1854	Jan 17 1862	Stranded	Hatteras Inlet, N.C.
1281	Martha	Sch.	-	-	Jan 10 1867	Unknown	Currituck Beach, N.C.
1282	Martha	Sch.	-	-	Mar 4 1893	Unknown	Off Cape Hatteras, N.C.
1283	Martha E. Wallace	Sch.	1,108	1902	Dec 21 1910	Stranded	Cape Lookout Shoals, N.C.
1284	Martha Helen	St.s.	75	1878	Feb 6 1910	Burned	Jacksonville, Fla. 1 life lost.
1285	Martha S. Bement	Sch.	479	1881	Dec 16 1909	Foundered	Sailed from Jacksonville, Fla., and has not since reported. All lives (7) lost.
1286	Martha Stevens	St.s.	247	1862	Apr 13 1922	Burned	Berkley, Va. Steel vessel. Also reported as iron vessel.
1287	Martin S. Ebel	Sch.	-	-	Nov 5 1895	Unknown	Big Kinnakeet, N.C.
1288	Mary	Sch.	-	-	Dec 22 1839	Unknown	Ocracoke, N.C.
1289	Mary	St.w.	143	1849	Feb 14 1852	Burned	Below Fort Gaines, Ga.
1290	Mary A. Trainor	Sch.	-	-	Jan 27 1890	Unknown	Off Cape Hatteras, N.C.
1291	Mary Anna	Sch.	-	-	Sep 8 1846	Unknown	Off Cape Hatteras, N.C.
1292	Mary B. Baird	Sch.	908	1890	Jun 27 1912	Foundered	33-15-00 N. 74-24-00 W.
1293	Mary Barry	Bkn.	608	1882	Mar 17 1913	Foundered	33-28-00 N. 75-30-00 W.
1294	Mary Bear	Sch.	-	-	Sep 9 1881	Foundered	New Topsail Inlet, N.C.
1295	Mary C. Carroll	Sch.	-	-	Mar 15 1891	Unknown	Watchapreague, Va.
1296	Mary C. Hughes	Brg.	500	1917	Dec 14 1921	Foundered	Cape Hatteras, N.C.
1297	Mary C. Ward	Sch.	-	-	Jan 26 1900	Unknown	Pamlico Sound, N.C. 5 lives lost.
1298	Mary D. Cranmer	Sch.	-	-	Oct 31 1887	Unknown	Dam Neck Mills, Va.
1299	Mary De Costa	Ol.s.	147	1909	Dec 22 1945	Foundered	Lucretia Light, 10 miles east of Miami, Fla.
1300	Mary E. Eskridge	Sch.	378	1911	Dec 31 1911	Stranded	Big Kinnakeet, N.C.
1301	Mary Ellen	Brig	-	-	Jul 1850	Unknown	Off Diamond Shoals, N.C.
1302	Mary J. Fisher	Sch.	-	-	Aug 24 1881	Unknown	Off Lockwoods Folly, N.C.
1303	Mary J. Haynie	Sch.	-	-	May 24 1911	Unknown	Ocracoke, N.C.
1304	Mary J. Russell	Sch.	372	1893	Jan 31 1910	Collided	With Cuban st.s. OLINDA. 29-50-00 N. 73-30-00 W.
1305	Mary L. Crosby	Sch.	487	1889	Jun 2 1915	Foundered	Off Cape Hatteras, N.C.
1306	Mary L. Vankirk	Sch.	-	-	Feb 5 1882	Unknown	Off New Inlet, N.C.
1307	Mary Manson Gruener	Sch.	715	1908	Oct 1 1923	Foundered	28-09-00 N. 71-00-00 W.
1308	Mary S. Eskridge	Sch.	-	-	Dec 31 1911	Unknown	Big Kinnakeet, N.C.
1309	Mary Sanford	St.s.	757	1863	Nov 13 1871	Stranded	Cape Hatteras, N.C.
1310	Mary Turcan	Brig	-	-	Unknown	Unknown	Off Currituck, N.C.
1311	Mary Varney	Bark	-	-	Apr 5 1856	Unknown	Off Cape Hatteras, N.C.
1312	Mary W. Morris	Sch.	-	-	Oct 27 1893	Unknown	Oak Island, N.C.
1313	Mascot	Brg.	348	1889	Jan 26 1908	Foundered	Thimble Shoal, Va.
1314	Maside	Steamer	-	-	Dec 14 1920	Unknown	Fort Macon, N.C.
1315	Massachusetts	St.p.	97	1817	Mar 25 1818	Stranded	Off Cape Hatteras, N.C.

NO.	NAME OF VESSEL	RIG	TONS	BUILT	DATE		CAUSE	PLACE AND COMMENT
1316	Massachusetts	Drg.	472	1914	Apr 10	1928	Foundered	Fowey Rock Light, Fla.
1317	Massasoit	Sch.	1,377	1889	Nov 15	1914	Stranded	Off Smiths Island, Va.
1318	Matagorda	Brg.	1,312	1919	Jul 3	1933	Foundered	Winter Quarter Lightship, Va.
1319	Matanzas	St.s.	862	1860	Nov 15	1868	Burned	Cape Hatteras, N.C. Steel vessel.
1320	Mathilda	Ship	-	-	Oct 27	1897	Unknown	Bodie Island, N.C.
1321	Matilda	Ga.s.	69	1927	Dec 7	1949	Foundered	3 miles east of Smith Point Lighthouse, Chesapeake Bay, Va.
1322	Matilda D. Borda	Sch.	827	1891	Aug 21	1917	Foundered	Off Gull Shoals, N.C.
1323	Mattie E. Hiles	Sch.	-	-	Oct 30	1892	Unknown	Currituck Inlet, N.C.
1324	Maud Spurling	Sch.	53	1895	Apr 26	1908	Stranded	Pensacola Bar, Fla.
1325	Maude B. Krum	Sch.	687	1883	Apr 20	1915	Foundered	Sailed from St. Andrews, Fla., and has not since reported. All lives (7) lost.
1326	Mauna Loa	Sch.	-	-	Jan 26	1877	Unknown	25-40-00 N. 74-20-00 W.
1327	Maurice R. Shaw	Sch.	803	1912	Feb 15	1916	Foundered	Whimble Shoal, N.C. All lives (4) lost.
1328	Maurice R. Shaw, Jr.	Brg.	632	1917	Feb 16	1933	Foundered	Winter Quarter Shoal, Va.
1329	Maurice R. Shaw, Jr.	Brg.	598	1917	Nov 4	1942	Foundered	4 miles from Point Jupiter Light, Fla.
1330	Maurice R. Thurlow	Sch.	1,270	1920	Oct 14	1927	Stranded	Diamond Shoal, Fla.
1331	May Garner	St.s.	101	1893	Jul 10	1921	Burned	Brunswick, Ga.
1332	Mayflower	St.s.	93	1894	Mar 26	1920	Burned	Plymouth, N.C.
1333	Mayport	St.s.	2,551	1919	Jan 27	1920	Stranded	Roncador Reef, Fla.
1334	Mechanic	Ship	335	-	Jan 20	1862	"Sunk"	On south edge of Rattlesnake Shoal, Maffit's Channel, Charleston, S.C. Used by Union forces to block harbor during Civil War. Part of second "Stone Fleet".
1335	Mechanic	St.p.	215	1856	Aug 15	1891	Stranded	Jacksonville, Fla.
1336	Medford	Sch.	1,351	1900	Oct 11	1909	Stranded	Key West, Fla. 1 life lost.
1337	Meitowax	El.o.	199	1927	Oct 19	1963	Lost	About 40 miles from Norfolk, Va. Steel vessel.
1338	Melbourn P. Smith	Sch.	650	1909	Sep 23	1923	Foundered	31-50-00 N. 71-58-00 W.
1339	Melrose	Sch.	693	1880	Feb 15	1908	Stranded	Cape Hatteras, N.C.
1340	Menemon Sanford	St.p.	904	1854	Dec 9	1862	Burned	Carysfort Reef, Fla.
1341	Menominee	St.s.	441	1919	Mar 31	1942	War Loss	Near Paramour Buoy, off Virginia coast. Steel vessel. Tug. 37-32-00 N. 75-26-00 W.
1342	Merak	Steamer	3,024	-	Aug 6	1918	War Loss	Diamond Shoals, off Little Kinnakeet, N.C. Sunk by enemy action.
1343	Mercy T. Trundy	Sch.	-	-	Apr 24	1882	Unknown	Cape Fear, N.C.
1344	Messenger	Bark	216	-	Jan 20	1862	"Sunk"	On south edge of Rattlesnake Shoal, Maffit's Channel, Charleston Harbor, S.C. Used by Union forces to block harbor during Civil War. Part of 2nd "Stone Fleet".
1345	Messenger	Ga.s.	77	1918	Oct 14	1940	Stranded	1 mile south of Jupiter Light, Fla.
1346	Meta & Margaret	Ol.s.	50	1936	Mar 6	1962	Storm	Below Kill Devil Coast Guard Station at Kitty Hawk, N.C.
1347	Meteor	Ship	324	-	Dec 21	1861	"Sunk"	4 miles SSE off Fort Sumter and 3 miles ESE of light on Morris Island, Charleston, S.C. Used by Union forces to block harbor. Part of "Stone Fleet".
1348	Metropolis	St.s.	879	-	Jan 31	1878	Foundered	4-1/2 miles north of Life Station #4 and 3 miles south of Currituck Light, N.C. Length 198'. 85 lives lost. Cargo of general stores.
1349	Miantonomi	St.p.	245	1850	Jun 16	1867	Stranded	St. Johns Bar, Fla. Renamed "Taminend" in 1853.
1350	Michael	Ol.s.	88	1954	Sep 11	1964	Foundered	In Atlantic Ocean off coast of Georgia.
1351	Mielero	St.s.	5,596	1917	Jan 26	1920	Foundered	31-45-00 N. 78-40-00 W. Steel vessel. 22 lives lost (40).
1352	Mignon	St.y.	-	-	Sep 9	1890	Unknown	Off Cape Fear, N.C.
1353	Mikawe	Ol.s.	61	1916	Sep	1944	Burned	In LaFayette River, near Norfolk Country Club, Va.
1354	Mildred	St.s.	343	1902	Nov	1914	Collided	With sch. BRAZOS. 7 miles south of Egmont Bar, Fla.
1355	Mildred Silva	Ol.s.	87	1928	Jan 31	1945	Burned	25 miles eastnortheast of Cape Henry, Va.
1356	Milledgeville	Packet	399	1835	Oct 23	1839	Wrecked	20 miles north of Cape Hatteras, N.C.
1357	Miller Brothers	Ol.s.	63	1952	Nov 2	1963	Foundered	About 2 miles south of Turtle Mound, 7 miles south of New Smyrna Beach, Fla.
1358	Millie	Brg.	153	1889	Sep 18	1926	Foundered	Miami, Fla.
1359	Millie R. Bohannan	Sch.	686	1891	Feb 17	1919	Foundered	28-35-00 N. 83-40-00 W.

NO.	NAME OF VESSEL	RIG	TONS	BUILT	DATE		CAUSE	PLACE AND COMMENT
1360	Millinocket	Frgt.	3,274	-	Jun 17	1942	War Loss	23-12-00 N. 79-58-00 W. North of Cuba.
1361	Milton	Sch.	-	-	Apr 27	1898	Unknown	Off Bodie Island, N.C.
1362	Mindora	St.s.	161	1884	Jan 22	1915	Stranded	Frying Pan Shoals, N.C.
1363	Minerva	Sch.	64	1891	Sep 27	1906	Foundered	Pensacola Bay, Fla.
1364	Minerva	Sch.	222	1863	Jun 25	1920	Stranded	Anastasia Island, Fla.
1365	Minnie	Sch.	-	-	Apr 12	1882	Unknown	Cape Fear, N.C.
1366	Minnie Bergen	Sch.	387	-	Aug 17	1899	Unknown	1-1/2 miles northeast of Chicamacomico L.S. Station, N.C.
1367	Minnominee	Tanker	-	-	Mar 31	1942	War Loss	Off Parramore Banks, Wachapreague, Va. 37-32-00 N. 75-26-00 W.
1368	Minquass	St.p.	160	1864	Apr 7	1865	Burned	Neuse River, N.C.
1369	Miramar	Ga.y.	96	1912	Sep 3	1941	Foundered	McKay's River, St. Simons Island, Brunswick, Ga.
1370	Mirlo (Br.)	Tanker	6,679	-	Aug 16	1918	Collided	With mine. Opposite Whimble Shoals Light Buoy. 35-36-00 N. 75-20-00 W. 10 lives lost. Gasolene cargo.
1371	Mispillion	Ol.s.	143	1942	Jul 14	1965	Burned	On North River Thorofare Marsh, Beaufort, N.C.
1372	Miss Campeche	Ol.s.	56	1951	Jan 8	1958	Foundered	In Gulf of Mexico, about 60 miles northwest of Dry Tortugas, Fla.
1373	Miss Carolina	Ol.s.	63	1927		1965	Foundered	In the Cape Fear River, N.C.
1374	Miss Constance	Ol.s.	63	1928		1965	Foundered	At Hopewell, Va.
1375	Miss Pamlico	Ol.s.	70	1954	Jan 20	1960	Stranded	On Oregon Inlet, N.C.
1376	Miss Powerama	Ol.s.	64	1955	Jan 31	1962	Stranded	Off Passage Key, Tampa Bay, Fla.
1377	Miss Sarah	Ol.s.	64	1954	Dec 1	1962	Burned	At East Key, about 50 miles southwest of Key West, Fla.
1378	Mississippi	St.p.	2,008	1862	May 12	1869	Stranded	Hillsboro Inlet, Fla.
1379	Modern Greece	St.s.	1,000	-	Jun 27	1862	Wrecked	Near New Inlet, 1/2 mile north of Federal Point, N.C. Schooner rigged. Confederate blockade runner. Depth 40'. 200 yards offshore.
1380	Mohican	St.s.	2,255	1904	May 10	1925	Burned	Cape Canaveral Light, Fla. Steel vessel.
1381	Mollie J. Saunders	Sch.	-	-	Dec 11	1890	Unknown	Off Bodie Island, N.C.
1382	Mollie S. Look	Sch.	572	1904	Feb 13	1908	Stranded	Hillsboro Inlet, N.C.
1383	Momie T	Sch.	590	1904	Jan 27	1920	Stranded	Currituck Inlet, N.C.
1384	Monitor	Steamer	-	-	Dec 30	1862	Foundered	2 miles north of Outer Diamond Shoal, N.C. Steel top deck. Hull of wood construction. Federal gun-boat. Lost while under tow of RHODE ISLAND.
1385	Monocacy	Brg.	466	1913	Feb	1956	Burned	On Pasquotank River, Elizabeth City, N.C.
1386	Monroe	St.s.	4,704	1903	Jan 30	1913	Collided	With st.s. NANTUCKET. Off Hog Island, Va. Steel vessel. 41 lives lost.
1387	Monroe	Drg.	338	1924	Jan 7	1953	Burned	At St. Lucie Yard, near Stuart, Fla.
1388	Monroe County	Ol.s.	129	1927	Sep 15	1928	Burned	Key West, Fla.
1389	Montana	Sch.	-	-	Dec 11	1904	Unknown	Pea Island, N.C. 1 life lost.
1390	Monterey	Sch.	-	-	Mar 7	1851	Unknown	Cape Lookout, N.C.
1391	Montezuma	Ship	424	-	Jan 20	1862	"Sunk"	On south edge of Rattlesnake Shoal, Maffitt's Channel, Charleston Harbor, S.C. Used by Union forces during Civil War to block harbor. Part of 2nd "Stone Fleet".
1392	Montrose W. Houck	Sch.	1,104	1911	Feb 18	1913	Stranded	Currituck Beach, N.C.
1393	Moon	Brig	-	-	May 8	1845	Unknown	Off Nags Head, N.C.
1394	Moore No.3	Brg.	215	1914	Apr 14	1927	Foundered	Great Isaac Light, Fla.
1395	Mormackite	St.s.	6,195	1945	Oct 7	1954	Lost	Sank off Cape Hatteras, N.C. Steel vessel.
1396	Morris and Cliff	Sch.	132	1890	Jan 15	1926	Stranded	Bogue Inlet, N.C.
1397	Mount Dirfys (Gr.)	St.s.	-	-	Dec 29	1936	Unknown	33-36-40 N. 77-51-30 W. 15 miles, 161° from Cape Fear Lighthouse, N.C.
1398	Mountaineer	Steamer	-	-	Dec 25	1852	Unknown	Kitty Hawk, N.C.
1399	Munger T. Ball	Tanker	5,104	-	May 4	1942	War Loss	24-57-00 N. 84-00-00 W.
1400	Munnatawket	Ol.s.	204	1890	Aug 6	1935	Burned	East River, Va.
1401	Muscogee	St.p.	117	1837	May 23	1838	Foundered	Cape Florida, Fla. 3 lives lost.
1402	Mutual Safety	St.p.	420	1842	Oct 11	1846	Stranded	St. Johns River, Fla.
1403	Myrna Loy	Ol.s.	69	1945	Dec 7	1951	Burned	30 to 35 miles southeast of Winter Quarter Lightship, about 54 miles from Virginia

NO.	NAME OF VESSEL	RIG	TONS	BUILT	DATE	CAUSE	PLACE AND COMMENT
1404	Myrtle Tunnell	Sch.	-	-	Mar 9 1906	Unknown	Off Cape Fear, N.C.
1405	McDonough	Sch.	-	-	Jun 13 1844	Unknown	Kitty Hawk, N.C.
1406	N.A.D. Co. No.5	Brg.	254	1912	May 28 1912	Foundered	25-56-00 N. 96-25-00 W.
1407	N.A.D. Co. No.6	Brg.	254	1912	May 28 1912	Foundered	25-56-00 N. 96-25-00 W.
1408	N. Boynton	Brg.	-	-	Apr 17 1889	Unknown	Poyner Hill, N.C.
1409	N.H. Burrow	Sch.	252	1874	Feb 13 1916	Stranded	Hog Island, Va.
1410	Naeco	St.s.	5,372	1918	Mar 23 1942	War Loss	34-02-54 N. 76-34-24 W. Steel vessel. Tanker. Kerosene cargo. 24 lives lost (38).
1411	Nahmeoka	Ga.y.	101	1921	May 22 1922	Stranded	Sunk by enemy action. Sand bar in Moores Inlet, N.C.
1412	Nancy Hanks	Sch.	1,162	1917	Jan 10 1926	Stranded	Florida Reef, Fla.
1413	Nancy Jane	Ol.s.	63	1954	Jan 30 1968	Foundered	Off Chincoteague, Va.
1414	Nancy Moran	Ol.s.	212	1941	Dec 26 1941	Collided	With SS PC 451. About 18 miles east of Port Everglades, Fla. Steel vessel. 26-02-00 N. 79-56-00 W.
1415	Nandoma	Ga.s.	51	1910	Feb 29 1948	Burned	At Ancelote Anchorage, Fla.
1416	Nannie B	St.s.	85	1887	Mar 26 1906	Stranded	Bennetts Point, S.C.
1417	Nannie C. Bohlin	Sch.	130	1890	Oct 18 1909	Stranded	Garden Key, Tortugas, Fla.
1418	Nansemond	Steamer	-	-	Apr 3 1865	Burned	Near Fort Darling, James River. Wood vessel. Confederate vessel.
1419	Narragansett	St.p.	576	1836	Oct 28 1847	Stranded	Mosquito Inlet, Fla.
1420	Nashville	St.p.	1,220	1854	Feb 28 1863	Burned	Ogeechee River, Ga.
1421	Nassauvian	Ol.s.	547	1919	Apr 27 1930	Burned	Jacksonville, Fla.
1422	Nat Meader	Sch.	278	1885	Jun 26 1918	Foundered	Off Cape Hatteras, N.C.
1423	Nathan Esterbrook, Jr.	Sch.	713	-	Feb 20 1893	Wrecked	2-1/2 miles north of Little Kinnakeet, N.C. 1 life lost.
1424	Nathaniel Lank	Sch.	-	-	Jan 22 1891	Unknown	New Inlet, N.C.
1425	Nautilus	St.p.	898	1854	Aug 10 1856	Stranded	Last Island, Ga. 20 lives lost.
1426	Nautilus	Ol.s.	65	1930	Dec 28 1946	Foundered	At Cape Hatteras, near Avon, N.C.
1427	Ned P. Walker	Sch.	98	1881	Aug 23 1913	Stranded	80 miles east of Pensacola, Fla.
1428	Nellie Floyd	Sch.	457	1879	Sep 18 1906	Foundered	18 miles southwest of Frying Pan Shoal Light, N.C. 1 life lost.
1429	Nellie Potter	Sch.	61	-	Apr 8 1889	Unknown	Ocracoke Life Saving Station, N.C.
1430	Nellie Wadsworth	Sch.	-	-	Dec 5 1885	Unknown	North side of Hatteras Inlet, N.C. 1 life lost.
1431	Nelson E. Newbury	Sch.	658	1882	Sep 17 1906	Foundered	Off Charleston, S.C. 6 lives lost.
1432	Nepenthe	Ga.y.	84	1917	Sep 18 1926	Foundered	Miami, Fla.
1433	Nepenthe	Ga.s.	84	1917	Jan 24 1932	Burned	Travernier Key, Fla.
1434	Nettie Shipman	Sch.	338	1884	Feb 12 1919	Abandoned	26-16-00 N. 73-34-00 W.
1435	Neuse	Brg.	464	1909	Dec 26 1939	Foundered	2 miles southeast of North River, Albemarle Sound, N.C.
1436	Neva Nag	Sch.	-	-	Oct 15 1888	Abandoned	Off Cape Henry, Va.
1437	Nevada	St.s.	914	1864	Jun 5 1868	Stranded	Cape Hatteras, N.C. 1 life lost.
1438	New England	Ship	369	-	Jan 20 1862	"Sunk"	On south shoal of Rattlesnake Shoal, Maffitt's Channel, Charleston Harbor, S.C. Used by Union forces to block harbor. Part of 2nd "Stone Fleet".
1439	New Jersey	St.s.	14,949	-	Sep 5 1923	Unknown	1 mile east of Diamond Shoal Lightship, N.C. Depth 435'. U.S. Battleship.
1440	New Moon	Ol.s.	64	1954	Oct 7 1957	Collided	With ALCOA PARTNER. 100 miles northwest of Dry Tortugas, Fla.
1441	New Munnerlyn	St.w.	193	1867	May 1 1867	Lost	Apalachicola, Fla.
1442	New York	St.p.	281	1822	Oct 4 1823	Stranded	Cape Hatteras, N.C.
1443	New York	Brg.	584	1892	Feb 13 1962	Foundered	In the South River, about 1 mile north of the South River Post Office, and 1/2 mile from the Neuse River, N.C. Iron vessel.
1444	Newburyport	Ship	341	-	Jan 20 1862	"Sunk"	On south edge of Rattlesnake Shoal, Maffitt's Channel, Charleston Harbor, S.C. Used by Union forces to block harbor. Part of 2nd "Stone Fleet".
1445	Newport News	St.p.	1,064	1883	Dec 29 1924	Foundered	Pearl Beach, Va. Iron vessel.
1446	Ney	Sch.	-	-	Apr 8 1889	Unknown	Windmill Point, Va.

NO.	NAME OF VESSEL	RIG	TONS	BUILT	DATE		CAUSE	PLACE AND COMMENT
1447	Nicarao	Frgt.	1,445	-	May 15	1942	War Loss	25-20-00 N. 74-19-00 W. Off Florida Keys.
1448	Nickeliner	Ol.s.	2,249	1938	May 13	1943	War Loss	21-25-00 N. 76-40-00 W. Also reported as 21-31-00 N. 76-48-00 W. Steel vessel. Sunk by enemy action. Convoy #NC-18.
1449	Night Hawk	St.p.	300	1864	Sep 29	1864	Burned	On Federal Shoals, off New Inlet, N.C. Confederate blockade runner.
1450	Nineveh	Bark	-	-	Jan 24	1903	Unknown	Off Cape Fear, N.C.
1451	Noble	Bark	274	-	Jan 20	1862	"Sunk"	On south edge of Rattlesnake Shoal, Maffitt's Channel, Charleston Harbor, S.C. Part of second "Stone Fleet".
1452	Nomis	Sch.	460	1919	Aug 16	1935	Stranded	6 miles south of Coast Guard Station, Hatteras Inlet, N.C.
1453	Nordal (Pan.)	Frgt.	3,848	-	Jun 24	1942	Unknown	34-41-30 N. 75-35-06 W.
1454	Nordhav (Nor.)	Bark	2,846	-	Aug 17	1918	Unknown	Off Bodie Island, N.C. Linseed oil cargo.
1455	Norfolk	St.s.	1,012	1900	Sep 30	1945	Burned	At Claremont, Va. Steel vessel.
1456	Norlandia	St.s.	2,689	1919	Jul 4	1942	War Loss	19-39-00 N. 69-10-00 W. Steel vessel. Sunk by enemy action.
1457	Norlavore	St.s.	2,713	1919	Feb 24	1942	War Loss	28-00 N. 80-00-00 W. Off Florida east coast. Also reported as being lost off Diamond Shoals, N.C. Steel vessel. Freighter. Sunk by enemy action.
1458	Norman H. Davis	Drg.	664	1911		1942	Burned	At Key West, Fla. Steel vessel.
1459	North America	St.s.	1,651	1864	Dec 22	1864	Foundered	At sea. 31-10-00 N. 78-40-00 W. 197 lives lost.
1460	North Carolina	St.p.	370	1838	Jul 26	1840	Collided	With GOVERNOR DUDLEY. On route between Wilmington and Charleston, S.C.
1461	North Carolina	St.p.	861	1852	Jan 29	1859	Burned	Smith Point, Va. 1 life lost.
1462	North Carolina	Steamer	-	-	Sep	1864	Unknown	Off Cape Fear River, N.C. Confederate gun-boat.
1463	North Heath	-	-	-	Jan	1865	Unknown	Cape Fear River, N.C. Blockade runner.
1464	North State	Ga.s.	75	1918	Nov 28	1936	Foundered	West Cape Point Shoals, N.C.
1465	North West	Sch.	616	1884	Jul 13	1916	Foundered	Off Cape Romain, S.C.
1466	Northeastern	Steamer	-	-	Dec 27	1904	Unknown	Cape Hatteras, N.C.
1467	Northern Light	Brg.	2,351	1888	Nov 8	1930	Foundered	25-03-00 N. 80-13-00 W. Steel vessel. 5 lives lost (6).
1468	Northern No.29	Brg.	1,267	1918	Dec 10	1933	Foundered	Beach Haven, Va.
1469	Northern Sword	St.s.	2,948	1918	Feb 8	1943	Collided	With unknown vessel. 10-28-00 N. 79-32-00 W. Steel vessel.
1470	Northwestern	St.s.	1,645	1881	Mar 22	1920	Stranded	Matanzas Inlet, Fla. 1 life lost.
1471	Northwind	Ol.s.	112	1944	Feb 27	1954	Foundered	1/2 mile north of Gun Cay Light, off Florida coast.
1472	Norvana	St.s.	2,677	1920	Jan 18	1942	War Loss	Probable loss off Cape Hatteras, N.C. Steel vessel. Sunk by enemy action.
1473	Norwalk	Frgt.	2,157	-	Jan 10	1943	Unknown	28-18-00 N. 80-00-00 W. North of Cuba.
1474	Nor'wester	Clipper	1,267	1854	Feb	1872	Burned	At Key West, Fla.
1475	Number Five	Sch.	1,120	1900	Dec 9	1917	Foundered	37-50-00 N. 65-52-00 W. Steel vessel.
1476	No.300	Brg.	438	1926		1943	Wrecked	Point Pleasant, W.Va. Steel vessel. Destroyed by flood.
1477	No. B-29	Brg.	344	1939	Sep 18	1955	Foundered	In Tampa Bay, Tampa, Fla. Steel vessel.
1478	Nuova Ottavia	-	-	-	Mar 1	1876	Wrecked	Off Currituck Beach, N.C.
1479	Nutfield	-	-	-	Feb 4	1864	Wrecked	Off New River Inlet, N.C. Blockade runner.
1480	O.B. Jennings	Tanker	10,000	-	Aug 4	1918	War Loss	60 miles southeast of Cape Henry, Va. 1 life lost. German Submarine Activities.
1481	O.G. Scott	Sch.	98	-	Oct 14	1930	Unknown	35-13-00 N. 75-22-00 W.
1482	O.H. Vessels	Ol.s.	98	1908	Jul 7	1933	Burned	Pungo River, N.C.
1483	O.M. Clark	St.s.	872	1913	Oct 27	1918	Burned	Lamberts Point, Va.
1484	Oak	St.p.	151	1856	May 28	1866	Burned	Savannah, Ga. 9 lives lost.
1485	Oak	Brg.	302	-	Mar 19	1906	Stranded	Thimble Shoal, Chesapeake Bay.
1486	Oakmar	St.s.	5,766	1920	Mar 20	1942	War Loss	36-41-00 N. 68-50-00 W. Off Virginia coast. Tanker. Steel vessel. Sunk by German submarine activities.
1487	Ocean	Brig	-	-	Jul	1850	Unknown	Off Diamond Shoals, N.C.
1488	Ocean Breeze	Ol.s.	65	1942	Mar 6	1948	Burned	East by north at Whimble Shoals Buoy, about 90 miles south of Cape Henry, Va.
1489	Ocean Queen	Ol.s.	96	1942	Nov 16	1966	Collided	With German M/V LUTJENBURG. Near sea buoy about 10 miles off Sulivan Island, S.C.
1490	Ocean Venture (Br.)	Frgt.	4,278*	-	Feb 8	1942	Unknown	37-03-35 N. 74-55-20 W.

NO.	NAME OF VESSEL	RIG	TONS	BUILT	DATE		CAUSE	PLACE AND COMMENT
1491	Ocean Venus (Br.)	Frgt.	4,272*	-	May 3	1942	Unknown	28-23-28 N. 80-17-43 W. Wreck demolished. Depth 40'.
1492	Ocmulgee	St.p.	57	1902	Aug 13	1905	Foundered	Durhams Bluff, Ga.
1493	Ogir (Nor.)	Bark	547	-	Oct 10	1894	Wrecked	On Cape Fear Bar, Oak Island, N.C.
1494	Ohio	St.p.	361	1898	Feb 9	1916	Burned	Parkersburg, W.Va.
1495	Ohioan	St.p.	104	1833	Apr 23	1836	Burned	Ocheesee, Fla. 1 life lost.
1496	Ohioan	St.s.	6,078	1920	May 8	1942	War Loss	26-31-00 N. 79-59-00 W. 4 miles off Boyington Inlet, Fla. Freighter. Steel vessel. Sunk by enemy action.
1497	Okeechobee	Drg.	116	1925	Sep 23	1947	Foundered	2 miles east of Gadsden Point in Tampa Bay, Fla.
1498	Okesa	St.s.	2,551	1918	Aug 23	1920	Burned	Claremont, Va.
1499	Oklahoma	Tanker	9,264	-	Apr 8	1942	War Loss	31-13-00 N. 80-05-00 W. 19 lives lost (38). SALVAGED.
1500	Old River	Ol.s.	299	1928	Nov 28	1947	Burned	Lower Matacumbe Key, Fla.
1501	Olean	Tanker	9,119	-	Mar 15	1942	War Loss	34-21-00 N. 76-29-00 W. 6 lives lost (42). SALVAGED.
1502	Olga	Sch.	308	1881	Apr 26	1911	Abandoned	53 miles south of Egmont Key, Fla.
1503	Olga	Frgt.	2,496	-	Mar 11	1942	War Loss	21-15-00 N. 76-35-00 W. North of Cuba.
1504	Olinda (Braz.)	Frgt.	2,521	-	Feb 18	1942	Unknown	37-55-00 N. 74-00-00 W. Depth 100 fathoms.
1505	Olive Thurlow	Bkn.	660	-	Dec 5	1902	Unknown	Off Lookout Bight, N.C. Lumber cargo. 1 life lost.
1506	Olympic		-	-	Feb 23	1942	Unknown	Kill Devil Hills, N.C.
1507	Onondaga	Frgt.	1,440*	-	Jul 24	1942	War Loss	24-40-00 N. 78-44-00 W. North of Cuba.
1508	Onawa	Ga.s.	71	1925	May 23	1965	Foundered	Approximately 100 miles off Fort Myers, Fla.
1509	Oneida	St.s.	2,309	1920	Jul 13	1942	War Loss	20-17-00 N. 74-06-00 W. Steel vessel. Sunk by enemy action.
1510	Oneida	St.s.	2,664	1919	May 4	1943	War Loss	31-24-00 N. 72-20-00 W. Steel vessel. Sunk by enemy action.
1511	Oniota	St.p.	411	1849	Nov 12	1867	Foundered	Cape Fear, N.C. Used as ferryboat.
1512	Ontario	Bark	-	-	Winter	1845	Unknown	Off Diamond Shoals, N.C.
1513	Ontelaunce	Brg.	738	1913	Dec 4	1941	Foundered	10 miles south of Cape Lookout, N.C.
1514	Oran Sherwood	Sch.	-	-	Oct 29	1837	Unknown	Currituck Beach, N.C.
1515	Oregon	St.p.	68	1846	Sep 6	1854	Stranded	Savannah, Ga.
1516	Orient	Sch.	93	1875	Apr 18	1908	Stranded	Cape Lookout, N.C.
1517	Oriental	St.s.	1,202	1861	May 14	1862	Stranded	Bodie Island, N.C. Steel vessel.
1518	Orline St. John	Bark	250	-	Feb 21	1854	Unknown	Off Diamond Shoals, Cape Hatteras, N.C.
1519	Orono	St.p.	97	1900	Mar 5	1911	Burned	Apalachicola, Fla.
1520	Orrie V. Drisco	Sch.	-	-	Dec 22	1891	Unknown	Cape Canaveral, Fla.
1521	Orville Horwitz	Sch.	-	-	Mar 11	1887	Unknown	Winter Quarter Shoal, Va.
1522	Oscar E. Edwards	Sch.	86	1922	Jan 18	1924	Burned	Little Bay, Norfolk, Va.
1523	Osceola	St.p.	144	1837	Nov 25	1846	Exploded	Cheraw, S.C.
1524	Osceola	St.s.	117	1848	Nov 2	1861	Stranded	Savannah, Ga.
1525	Osceola	St.p.	52	1907	May 10	1911	Stranded	Altamaha River, Ga.
1526	Osiris	Ga.y.	137	1911	Feb 12	1921	Burned	Miami, Fla.
1527	Otherne G. Scott	Sch.	-	-	Oct 14	1930	Unknown	35-13-00 N. 75-22-00 W.
1528	Otho	St.s.	4,839	1920	Apr 3	1942	War Loss	34-38-00 N. 69-38-00 W. Also reported as 36-38-00 N. 69-38-00 W. Steel vessel. Sunk by enemy action.
1529	Outbound	Ol.s.	136	1917	Jun 25	1944	Foundered	Riding Rock, Bahamas Banks, off Florida coast.
1530	Outing	Sloop	-	-	Jan 18	1887	Unknown	Gilbert's Bar, Fla.
1531	Oyster Bay	St.s.	84	1864	May 24	1876	Burned	Jacksonville, Fla. Also reported as "Oyster Boy".
1532	P.B. Savery	Sch.	-	-	Aug 11	1851	Unknown	Chicamacomico, N.C.
1533	P.T. Barnum	Sch.	667	1890	Dec 19	1906	Abandoned	30 miles east of Bodie Island, N.C.
1534	Pacific	Brg.	399	1901	Nov 20	1938	Stranded	Parrimare Buoy, Va.
1535	Pactolus	Sch.	1,199	1865	Jun 2	1907	Foundered	Off Hog Island, Va.
1536	Pajaro (Span.)	Galleon	-	-		1820	Unknown	Off east Florida in the New Bahama Canal.

NO.	NAME OF VESSEL	RIG	TONS	BUILT	DATE	CAUSE	PLACE AND COMMENT
1537	Palatka	Sch.	-	-	Apr 10 1889	Abandoned	Cape Hatteras, N.C.
1538	Palatka	St.s.	73	1923	Dec 3 1926	Foundered	Mandarin Point, Fla. 4 lives lost (5).
1539	Palestro	Steamer	-	-	Aug 9 1900	Unknown	Off Cape Hatteras, N.C.
1540	Palmetto	St.p.	136	1848	Oct 9 1852	Stranded	Apalachicola, Fla.
1541	Pamela Ann	Ol.s.	55	1950	Mar 23 1959	Burned	About 10 miles, 190° from black can buoy, Fort Myers Beach, Fla.
1542	Pampero	St.p.	379	1850	Dec 4 1866	Foundered	Cape Romano, Fla.
1543	Pan-Massachusetts	St.s.	8,201	1918	Feb 19 1942	War Loss	28-27-00 N. 80-08-00 W. Off Florida coast. Tanker. Steel vessel. Sunk by enemy action. 20 lives lost (38).
1544	Papa Jon	Ol.s.	74	1952	Nov 18 1965	Burned	2 miles south of Sarasota Bridge, Sarasota, Fla.
1545	Papoose	St.s.	5,939	1921	Mar 18 1942	War Loss	34-09-06 N. 76-40-30 W. 15 miles southwest of Cape Lookout, N.C. Tanker. Steel vessel. 2 lives lost (34). Sunk by enemy action.
1546	Pardee	Sch.	-	-	Dec 24 1884	Unknown	Off Nags Head, N.C.
1547	Parkins	Ol.s.	133	1923	Dec 21 1942	Foundered	Beaufort, N.C. Fisherman. 34-41-09 N. 76-43-18 W.
1548	Parrot	Sch.	-	-	Apr 7 1889	Unknown	Albemarle Sound, N.C.
1549	Pasadena	Sch.	596	1880	Nov 21 1905	Stranded	Fernandina, Fla.
1550	Passaic	Sch.	875	1896	May 27 1922	Foundered	Southwest of Fenwick Island Lightship.
1551	Patadeline	Ol.s.	51	1943	May 21 1956	Burned	At Bahia Mar Yacht Basin, Fort Lauderdale, Fla.
1552	Patapsco	Steamer	-	-	Sep 12 1868	Unknown	Off Cape Lookout, N.C.
1553	Pathfinder (Br.)	Sch.	-	-	Nov 2 1862	Burned	2 miles west of Little River Inlet, N.C. Blockade runner.
1554	Pathfinder	St.s.	74	1917	Jul 3 1925	Burned	East River, Va.
1555	Patricia	Ol.y.	60	1922	Aug 18 1926	Foundered	Fort Lauderdale, Fla.
1556	Patriot	Sch.	-	-	Jan 1813	Stranded	Off Nags Head, N.C.
1557	Pauline	Bark	-	-	Jul 7 1890	Unknown	Southport, N.C.
1558	Pauline M. Boland	Ol.s.	62	1925	Mar 15 1964	Foundered	About 42 miles southeast of Assateague Island, Va.
1559	Peconic	St.s.	1,855	1881	Aug 28 1905	Foundered	Off Fernandina, Fla. Iron vessel. 20 lives lost.
1560	Peconic	Ol.s.	186	1879	Jun 27 1950	Foundered	Off starboard edge of Cape Charles Channel, Cape Charles, Va.
1561	Pee Dee	St.p.	138	1845	Jan 27 1858	Stranded	St. Augustine, Fla.
1562	Peerless	Steamer	-	-	Oct 31 1861	Unknown	Off Cape Hatteras, N.C.
1563	Peerless	St.p.	50	1903	Oct 11 1909	Foundered	Boot Key, Fla.
1564	Peggy H	Ol.s.	77	1917	Jun 20 1926	Burned	Hampton, Va.
1565	Peggy Sue	Ol.s.	69	1959	Dec 12 1964	Foundered	Approximately at 24-19-00 N. 82-56-00 W.
1566	Pendleton	St.p.	250	1824	May 8 1832	Burned	Savannah, Ga.
1567	Pendleton Brothers	Sch.	970	1903	Mar 17 1913	Stranded	Torugas Reefs, Fla.
1568	Pendleton Sisters	Sch.	798	1900	Dec 15 1905	Stranded	Chincoteague, Va.
1569	Pendulum	St.p.	215	1851	Mar 8 1862	Foundered	Hampton Roads, Va.
1570	Penmar	St.s.	5,868	1920	Sep 23 1942	War Loss	58-12-00 N. 34-35-00 W. Steel vessel. Sunk by enemy action.
1571	Pennsylvania	Brig	-	-	Sep 24 1847	Unknown	Off Diamond Shoals, N.C.
1572	Pennsylvania Sun	Frgt.	11,373	-	Jul 15 1942	War Loss	24-12-00 N. 82-35-00 W. Sunk by enemy action. 2 lives lost (59). SALVAGED.
1573	Penobscot	St.p.	494	1843	Sep 12 1857	Foundered	Hog Island, Va. Renamed "Norfolk" in 1857.
1574	Pensacola	Brg.	466	1914	Mar 1956	Burned	In Pasquotank River, N.C.
1575	Peri	Bark	261	-	Jan 20 1862	"Sunk"	On south edge of Rattlesnake Shoal, Maffitt's Channel, Charleston Harbor, S.C. Used by Union forces to block harbor. Part of second "Stone Fleet".
1576	Perserverance	Ol.s.	85	1918	1943	Foundered	Mouth of Lynnhaven River, Va.
1577	Peru	St.w.	128	1848	Feb 3 1852	Ice	Below Wheeling, Va.
1578	Peter	Brg.	453	1902	May 8 1935	Burned	Pensacola Bay, Fla.
1579	Peter Demill	Bark	340	-	Dec 21 1861	"Sunk"	4 miles SSE off Fort Sumter and 3 miles ESE of the light on Morris Island, Charleston, S.C. Used by Union forces to block harbor. Part of "Stone Fleet".
1580	Pevensey	-	-	-	Jun 9 1864	Wrecked	Bogue Inlet, N.C. Confederate blockade runner.

NO.	NAME OF VESSEL	RIG	TONS	BUILT	DATE	CAUSE	PLACE AND COMMENT
1581	Phantom	St.s.	500	-	Sep 23 1863	Burned	Near Rich Inlet, S.C. Iron vessel. Confederate blockade runner. Depth 35'.
1582	Philadelphia	St.p.	504	1859	Apr 4 1874	Stranded	Hog Island, Va.
1583	Phoebe Crosby	Sch.	1,048	1921	Oct 10 1921	Stranded	Southeast jetty at Georgetown, S.C.
1584	Phoenix	Ship	404	-	Dec 21 1861	"Sunk"	4 miles SSE off Fort Sumter and 3 miles ESE of light on Morris Island, Charleston Harbor, S.C. Used by Union forces to block harbor. Part of "Stone Fleet".
1585	Pickett	Steamer	-	-	Sep 6 1862	Unknown	Washington, N.C. Federal (Union) gun-boat.
1586	Piedmont	St.s.	90	1892	Jan 5 1919	Foundered	Off Cape Henry, Va. 3 lives lost.
1587	Pilgrim	Bark	1,629	1893	Dec 13 1914	Foundered	36-40-00 N. 68-24-00 W. 1 life lost.
1588	Pilot	St.s.	217	1849	Feb 8 1852	Stranded	Charleston, S.C.
1589	Pilot	St.s.	193	1880	Dec 16 1917	Collided	With st.s. BERKSHIRE. Hampton Roads, Va.
1590	Pilot No.2	St.w.	93	1847	Aug 22 1852	Snagged	Wheeling, Va.
1591	Pinar del Rio	St.s.	2,504	1895	Jun 8 1918	Torpedoed	36-15-00 N. 73-55-00 W. Sunk by German submarine during 1st World War.
1592	Pine Grove	Brg.	256	1892	Sep 9 1929	Burned	Norfolk, Va.
1593	Pine Ridge	El.s.	10,417	1943	Jan 16 1961	Broke-up	About 95 miles east of Cape Hatteras, N.C. Steel vessel. Vessel broke in two, bow section, including bridge, lost in heavy weather.
1594	Pioneer	Brig	-	-	Aug 24 1842	Stranded	On northeast end of Ocracoke Island, N.C. 1 life lost. Salt cargo.
1595	Pioneer	Steamer	-	-	1889	Unknown	Ocracoke, N.C.
1596	Pipestone County	Frgt.	5,102	1925	Apr 21 1942	War Loss	37-43-00 N. 66-16-00 W. Off Virginia coast. 25% of lives lost.
1597	Piute	Ol.s.	79		Jan 27 1927	Stranded	Mosquito Inlet, Fla.
1598	Planter	St.p.	116	1832	Mar 20 1836	Collided	With REINDEER. Fort Gaines, Ga.
1599	Planter	St.s.	499	1876	Jun 17 1914	Burned	Fort Myers, Fla.
1600	Planter	Sch.	530	1886	Aug 15 1921	Foundered	24-18-00 N. 81-08-00 W.
1601	Play House	Brg.	436	1914	Nov 14 1941	Unknown	In harbor, Savannah River, Ga.
1602	Pleasantville	-	-	-	Jun 8 1942	Unknown	Off Cape Hatteras, N.C. Presumed to be freighter lost during war.
1603	Pocahontas	St.p.	428	1829	Jan 18 1862	Stranded	Cape Hatteras, N.C.
1604	Pocomoke	Sch.	827	-	Jan 9 1912	Foundered	50 miles southwest of Cape Hatteras, N.C.
1605	Poling Bros. No.3	Ol.s.	157	1910	Nov 5 1943	Burned	Southwest of New Point Light, Va.
1606	Pontiac	Ship	-	-	Feb 1871	Burned	Off Cape Lookout, N.C.
1607	Pope Catlin	St.s.	118	1853	Aug 28 1899	Burned	Brunswick, Ga.
1608	Portland	Frgt.	2,648	-	Feb 11 1943	Unknown	34-29-39 N. 76-25-39 W. 9.1 miles, 150° from light at Cape Lookout, N.C. Steel vessel. Depth 48'.
1609	Potomac	Ship	356	-	Dec 21 1861	"Sunk"	4 miles off Fort Sumter and 3 miles ESE of light on Morris Island, Charleston Harbor, S.C. Used by Union forces to block harbor. "Stone Fleet".
1610	Potosi	Sch.	-	-	Mar 17 1891	Unknown	Charleston, S.C.
1611	Powell	St.s.	1,218	1900	Apr 6 1920	Foundered	30 miles southwest of Diamond Shoal Lightship, N.C. Steel vessel.
1612	Powhatan	St.p.	181	1817	Sep 20 1823	Exploded	Norfolk, Va.
1613	Premium	Sch.	-	-	Jan 8 1837	Unknown	Mouth of Ocracoke Inlet, N.C.
1614	Prescott Palmer	Sch.	2,811	1902	Jan 20 1914	Foundered	34-08-00 N. 66-46-00 W. 1 life lost.
1615	Prince Umberto	Bark	-	-	Oct 31 1888	Unknown	Duck Key, Fla.
1616	Prins Mauritz (Dutch)	Steamer	1,328	-	Apr 3 1915	Lost	Off Cape Hatteras, N.C. Length 285'. 59 lives lost.
1617	Prins Valdemar	Bkn.	1,338	1892	Jan 10 1926	Foundered	Miami, Fla. Steel vessel.
1618	Priscilla	Bkn.	364	-	Aug 18 1899	Foundered	5 miles south of Gull Shoal Life Saving Station, N.C. 4 lives lost.
1619	Priscilla L. Ray	Sch.	712	1891	Feb 16 1920	Stranded	Northwest Passage, Key West, Fla.
1620	Proteus	St.s.	4,836	1900	Aug 19 1918	Collided	With st.s. CUSHING. 31 miles south of Diamond Shoals, N.C. Steel vessel. 1 life lost. 34-48-54 N. 75-54-30 W.
1621	Puerto Rican	St.s.	6,076	1919	Mar 9 1943	War Loss	66-44-00 N. 10-41-00 W. Steel vessel. Sunk by enemy action.
1622	Pulaski	St.p.	687	1837	Jun 14 1838	Exploded	New River Inlet, N.C. 141 lives lost.
1623	Quick	Brig	-	-	Mar 1867	Unknown	Oregon Inlet, N.C.

NO.	NAME OF VESSEL	RIG	TONS	BUILT	DATE	CAUSE	PLACE AND COMMENT
1624	Quincy	St.s.	396	1857	Dec 20 1863	Foundered	Cape Hatteras, N.C. 16 lives lost.
1625	Quinebaug	St.s.	186	1844	Jul 20 1865	Stranded	Morehead City, N.C.
1626	Quoque	St.s.	2,540	1918	Jan 12 1920	Stranded	6 miles off Carysfort Light, Fla.
1627	R. B. Forbes	Steamer	329	-	Feb 25 1862	Unknown	Currituck Beach, N.C. Federal (Union) gun-boat.
1628	R. B. Thompson	Sch.	-	-	Jul 3 1873	Unknown	Off Cape Hatteras, N.C. 9 lives lost.
1629	R. B. Trueman	Ga.s.	78	1918	Jun 18 1924	Burned	Jacksonville, Fla.
1630	R. D. Bibber	Sch.	769	1884	Sep 17 1906	Stranded	Frying Pan Shoals, N.C.
1631	R. E. Bell	St.p.	87	1865	Jul 6 1867	Foundered	Waccamaw River, S.C. 7 lives lost.
1632	R. K. Mabey	St.p.	137	1854	Feb 5 1897	Burned	Brunswick, Ga. Also reported as "R.L. Mabey".
1633	R. W. Brown	Sch.	-	-	Dec 11 1848	Unknown	Off New Inlet, N.C. 3 lives lost.
1634	Racer	Sch.	-	-	Jul 1850	Unknown	Diamond Shoals, N.C. 3 lives lost.
1635	Rachel A. Collins	Sch.	-	-	Mar 12 1888	Unknown	Cape Hatteras, N.C.
1636	Rachel W. Stevens	Sch.	1,211	1898	Dec 2 1924	Foundered	Cape Hatteras, N.C.
1637	Raleigh	Steamer	-	-	May 7 1864	Unknown	Cape Fear River, N.C. Confederate gun-boat.
1638	Raleigh	St.p.	868	1865	Dec 24 1867	Burned	Off Charleston, S.C. 24 lives lost.
1639	Ralph	Brig	-	-	Dec 22 1837	Unknown	Wash Woods, N.C.
1640	Ramos	St.s.	843	1885	Jul 11 1916	Foundered	Off North Carolina coast. Steel vessel. 11 lives lost.
1641	Ranger	Steamer	-	-	Jan 11 1864	Burned	1 mile west of Lockwood's Folly Inlet, N.C. Blockade runner. Depth 20'.
1642	Raphael Semmes	St.s.	6,027	1920	Jun 28 1942	War Loss	29-30-00 N. 64-30-00 W. Steel vessel. Sunk by enemy action.
1643	Raritan	St.s.	2,649	1919	Feb 28 1942	Stranded	Seward Edge, Frying Pan Shoals, N.C. Steel vessel. Freighter.
1644	Rattler	Clipper	538	1852	Dec 8 1853	Unknown	Near Norfolk, Va.
1645	Ravenswood	Bkn.	-	-	Oct 13 1893	Unknown	Chicamacomico, N.C.
1646	Ravenswood	St.p.	430	1867	Mar 31 1895	Lost	Jacksonville, Fla.
1647	Raymond H	St.p.	55	1905	Oct 2 1907	Burned	Newton, Ga. 2 lives lost.
1648	Raymond T. Maull	Sch.	538	1881	Mar 21 1906	Stranded	Gull Shoal, N.C.
1649	Rebecca Barton	St.s.	353	1864	Mar 17 1866	Foundered	Off Key West, Fla.
1650	Rebecca C. Scott	Sch.	813	1919	Oct 27 1930	Collided	With st.s. ATLAS. 36-39-00 N. 74-00-00 W.
1651	Rebecca Clyde	St.s.	446	1863	Sep 17 1876	Stranded	Portsmouth, N.C. 13 lives lost.
1652	Rebecca Sims	Ship	400	-	Dec 21 1861	"Sunk"	4 miles SSE off Fort Sumter and 3 miles ESE of the light on Morris Island, Charleston Harbor, S.C. Used by Union forces to block harbor. "Stone Fleet".
1653	Red Wing	Sch.	-	-	Oct 22 1891	Unknown	Indian River Inlet, Fla.
1654	Regulus	Sch.	-	-	Jan 5 1846	Unknown	On Hatteras Shoal, N.C.
1655	Relief	Ga.s.	74	1917	Oct 9 1923	Burned	Tybee Island, Ga.
1656	Relief No.5	Brg.	87	-	Sep 18 1926	Foundered	Miami, Fla.
1657	Republic	St.s.	5,287	1920	Feb 21 1942	War Loss	27-00-38 N. 80-02-37 W. Off Jupiter Light, Fla. Tanker. Steel vessel. Sunk by enemy action. 5 lives lost (34). Wreck demolished. Depth 40'.
1658	Resource	Sch.	-	-	Mar 15 1942	Unknown	Off Kill Devils Hill, N.C. Presumed freighter.
1659	Revenue	Sloop	-	-	Dec 1818	Unknown	Currituck Inlet, N.C.
1660	Rhea	Ol.s.	63	1953	Jan 3 1966	Foundered	At False Cape, 5 miles offshore and about 3 miles north of Cape Canaveral, Fla.
1661	Richard F.C. Hartley	Sch.	469	1888	Sep 2 1913	Stranded	Off Bodie Island, N.C. 2 lives lost.
1662	Richard H. Wyatt	Sch.	-	-	Jan 31 1851	Unknown	Off Cape Hatteras, N.C.
1663	Richard S. Spofford	Sch.	488	1894	Dec 25 1894	Unknown	Entrance to Ocracoke Inlet, N.C. 1 life lost.
1664	Richland	St.p.	160	1842	Jan 14 1849	Exploded	Brittons Ferry, S.C. 15 lives lost.
1665	Richmond	Steamer	-	-	Apr 5 1865	Burned	Drewy's Bluff, James River, Va. Confederate flagship. Ironclad vessel.
1666	Richmond	Sch.	1,719	1919	Jan 5 1920	Stranded	Jacksonville, Fla.
1667	Richmond	Sch.	288	1909	Sep 18 1926	Stranded	Fort Lauderdale, Fla.
1668	Richmond	St.s.	893	1902	Sep 30 1945	Burned	Claremont Wharf, James River, Va. Steel vessel.
1669	Richmond Cedar Works 1	Brg.	223	1896	Jun 29 1933	Burned	James River, Va.

NO.	NAME OF VESSEL	RIG	TONS	BUILT	DATE		CAUSE	PLACE AND COMMENT
1670	Richmond Cedar Works 1	Brg.	381	1894		1955	Hurricane	At Western Fork, Bell's Mill Landing, Wlizabeth River, near Gilberton, Va.
1671	Richmond Cedar Works 2	Brg.	394	1903	Dec 22	1953	Foundered	In Fatty Creek, mouth of Pasquotank River, N.C. Steel vessel.
1672	Richmond Cedar Works 3	Brg.	283	1888		1955	Hurricane	At Western Fork, Bell's Mill Landing, Elizabeth River, near Gilberton, Va.
1673	Richmond Cedar Works 7	Brg.	291	1898		1955	Hurricane	At Western Fork, Bell's Mill Landing, Elizabeth River, near Gilberton, Va.
1674	Rigulas	Sch.	-	-	Jan 5	1846	Unknown	Off Cape Hatteras Shoal, N.C.
1675	Rio	Sch.	-	-	Dec	1853	Unknown	Bodie Island, N.C.
1676	Rio Blanco		-	-	Apr 1	1942	Unknown	East of Cape Hatteras, N.C. Presumed freighter.
1677	Ripogenus	St.s.	2,369	1919	Nov 8	1932	Collided	With st.s. EVANSVILLE. Off Cape Henry, Va.
1678	Roanoke	Steamer	-	-	Apr 3	1865	Burned	Near Fort Darling, James River, Va. Confederate vessel.
1679	Robert	Brg.	278	1917	Oct 9	1918	Foundered	Key West, Fla.
1680	Robert A. Snyder	Sch.	375	1891	Sep 14	1917	Stranded	St. Andrews Bar, Fla.
1681	Robert F. Brattan	Sch.	53	1881	Feb 29	1916	Stranded	Rappahannock River, Va.
1682	Robert Fulton	St.p.	187	1839	Jul 9	1843	Snagged	Iola, Fla.
1683	Robert Graham Dun	Sch.	595	1881	Apr 6	1915	Foundered	36-04-00 N. 73-32-00 W. 1 life lost.
1684	Robert Grier	Brg.	403	1905	Oct	1921	Burned	Great Bridge, Va.
1685	Robt. H. Lockwood	St.s.	112	1883	Jul 1	1956	Foundered	At Charleston, S.C. Iron vessel.
1686	Robert H. McCurdy	Sch.	735	1903	Dec 19	1920	Foundered	35-30-00 N. 73-15-00 W.
1687	Robert H. Stevenson	Sch.	1,290	1902	Jan 13	1906	Stranded	Diamond Shoals, N.C. 12 lives lost.
1688	Robert L. Bean	Sch.	1,335	1920	Feb 17	1926	Stranded	San Rosa Island, Fla.
1689	Robert Martin	St.p.	247	1849	Nov 21	1853	Exploded	Cheraw, S.C. 6 lives lost.
1690	Robert McCarrell	Sch.	-	-	Feb 26	1891	Unknown	Savannah River, Ga.
1691	Robert P. Doherty	Ol.s.	65	1943	Nov 17	1965	Foundered	At South Shores Light, off the coast of St. Marks, Fla.
1692	Robert W. Dasey	Sch.	-	-	Aug 17	1899	Unknown	3/4 mile from Little Kinnakeet L.S. Station, Little Kinnakeet, N.C.
1693	Robert Walsh	Sch.	-	-	Mar 8	1854	Unknown	Off Cape Hatteras, N.C. 10 lives lost.
1694	Robin Hood	Ship	395	-	Dec 21	1861	"Sunk"	4 miles SSE off Fort Sumter and 3 miles ESE of the light on Morris Island, Charleston Harbor, S.C. Used by Union forces to block harbor. "Stone Fleet".
1695	Robin Hood	Frgt.	6,887	-	Apr 15	1942	War Loss	37-10-00 N. 73-58-00 W. Off Virginia coast.
1696	Rochester	Tanker	6,836	-	Jan 30	1942	War Loss	37-10-00 N. 73-58-00 W. Off Virginia coast. 3 lives lost (35).
1697	Rodney	Brig	-	-	Jun 20	1848	Unknown	Off Cape Fear, N.C.
1698	Rodney Phillips MacPhie, Jr.	Brg.	392	1916	Jul	1959	Foundered	Near Plymouth, N.C.
1699	Roger Moore	Sch.	-	-	Oct 30	1899	Unknown	Big Kinnakeet, N.C.
1700	Rogist	Ol.s.	146	1929	Nov 12	1942	Collided	With U.S. Naval Patrol Craft SC 330. 7 miles southeast of Cape Charles Light-house, Va.
1701	Rosalie	Ol.s.	130	1942	Jan 25	1964	Burned	Off Plantation Key, Fla.
1702	Rose Innes	Bkn.	835	1881	Oct 30	1907	Stranded	St. Simons Island, Ga.
1703	Rose Murphy	St.s.	1,991	1918	Jan 25	1927	Foundered	Sand Key Light, Fla. Steel vessel.
1704	Rose McDavitt	Sch.	59	1924	Mar 18	1891	Unknown	Smith Point, Va.
1705	Rosecliff 2nd	Ga.y.	938	1877	Jun 24	1935	Burned	Fort Lauderdale, Fla.
1706	Rosedale	St.p.	901	1917	Apr 13	1922	Burned	Berkley, Va.
1707	Rosemary	Sch.	54	1943	Nov 7	1930	Burned	Key West, Fla.
1708	Rosie II	Ol.s.	127	1859	Apr 1	1954	Foundered	About 90 miles due north of Dry Tortugas Island, off Florida coast.
1709	Rotary	St.s.	126	1883	Dec 31	1882	Burned	Edenton, N.C.
1710	Rover	Sch.	247	1911	Jul 19	1916	Foundered	Off Cape Hatteras, N.C.
1711	Rowland H. Wilcox	Ol.s.	2,551	1918	Sep 30	1943	Foundered	94 miles east of Nags Head, N.C.
1712	Roy H. Beattie	St.s.	79	1924	Apr 18	1919	Burned	29-50-00 N. 66-30-00 W. 2 lives lost.
1713	Ruby Lee II	Ga.s.	131	1903	Jul 4	1941	Stranded	Mouth of St. John's River, near Jacksonville, Fla.
1714	Rubylee	Ga.y.			Apr 30	1930	Foundered	Olympia, Fla.

NO.	NAME OF VESSEL	RIG	TONS	BUILT	DATE	CAUSE	PLACE AND COMMENT
1715	Rufus King	St.s.	7,176	1942	Jul 7 1942	Stranded	Between Cape Lookout and Morton Island, N.C. Steel vessel.
1716	Rugged	Ga.s.	52	1905	Jul 15 1943	Burned	50 miles southeast of Miami, Fla.
1717	Ruhama Shaw	Brg.	473	1915	Dec 8 1917	Foundered	Off Black Fish Bank, Va.
1718	Rusius	Sch.	-	-	Oct 23 1889	Unknown	Currituck Lighthouse, N.C.
1719	Ruth	Brg.	435	1908	Dec 9 1917	Foundered	Off Black Fish Bank, Va.
1720	Ruth	St.p.	173	1910	Jan 31 1918	Ice	McMechen, W.Va.
1721	Ruth	Frgt.	4,833	-	Jun 29 1942	War Loss	21-44-00 N. 74-05-00 W. Southeast of Cuba.
1722	Ruxton No.2	Ol.s.	97	1934	Dec 28 1960	Foundered	About 6 miles due east of Port Everglades, Fla.
1723	S-16 (USS)	Ol.s.	-	-	Mar 2 1945	"Sunk"	24-25-13 N. 82-02-24 W. Submarine sunk for experimental purposes.
1724	S.D. Carleton	Sch.	1,874	1890	Mar 25 1912	Stranded	Cobbs Island, Va.
1725	S.G. Hart	Sch.	-	-	Aug 10 1898	Unknown	Off Little Kinnakeet, N.C.
1726	S.G. Haskell	Sch.	681	1891	Feb 27 1914	Foundered	32-01-00 N. 74-00-00 W.
1727	S.G. Wilder	Sc.b.	604	1887	Jul 3 1933	Foundered	Fenwick Island. 38-14-18 N. 74-44-42 W. 3 lives lost (5).
1728	S.M. Manning	St.p.	202	1858	Mar 12 1860	Exploded	Hawkinsville, Ga. 3 lives lost.
1729	S.O. Co.No.90	Sch.	2,019	1900	Sep 26 1906	Foundered	Off Tortugas, Fla. All lives (9) lost.
1730	S.P. Blackburn	Sch.	1,756	1896	Jan 26 1913	Foundered	34-40-00 N. 70-35-00 W.
1731	S.S. Lewis	Sch.	-	-	Sep 1876	Unknown	Off Cape Hatteras, N.C.
1732	S.S. Merida	St.s.	6,207	1906	May 12 1911	Collided	With st.s. ADMIRAL FARRAGUT. Steel vessel. Passenger carrier. Much has been written about this vessel and to provide best information, it will be listed here. The following locations have been given: 55 miles east of Cape Charles, Va.; Mouth of Chesapeake Bay.; 168 miles north of Diamond Shoals, 55 miles east of Cape Charles, Va.; 37-02-00 N. 74-47-00 N. 74-39-00 W.; 37-17-00 N. 74-39-00 W.; 37-23-30 N. 74-42-00 W. This vessel obviously carried a certain amount of monies and/or gold. How much has not really been ascertained. The following reports have been made: $500,000 in silver; $500,000 in copper; $5 million in gold. It is of this author's opinion that more research is necessary and that a moderate amount of money may be recovered, but to cover the expenses in finding and salvaging will not be a likely possiblity.
1733	S. Warren Hall	Sch.	-	-	Apr 5 1898	Unknown	Portsmouth, N.C.
1734	Sa-La	Ol.s.	55	1947	Jun 4 1952	Burned	Between New Ground and Rebecca Light, Fla.
1735	St. Augustine	Sub.	-	-	Unknown	"Sunk"	38-04-00 N. 74-06-00 W. Attacked by USS SOLAR.
1736	St. Cathan (Br.)	Ol.s.	210	-	Apr 11 1942	Unknown	33-09-00 N. 78-16-26 W. Depth 95'.
1737	St. Catharis	Sch.	-	-	Apr 16 1891	Wrecked	South of Chicamacomico Beach, N.C.
1738	St. Johns	Sch.	-	-	Mar 17 1890	Unknown	Hatteras Inlet, N.C.
1739	St. Lucie	St.p.	165	1888	Oct 18 1906	Foundered	Elliotts Key, Fla. Steel vessel. 21 lives lost.
1740	Saint Matthew	St.p.	174	1836	Dec 6 1851	Stranded	Darien, Ga.
1741	St. Nicholas	Sch.	841	1890	Feb 7 1916	Foundered	Frying Pan Shoals, N.C.
1742	St. Paul	Bkn.	471	1890	Nov 7 1916	Foundered	5 miles north of St. Lucie Inlet, Fla.
1743	St. Rita	Ol.s.	80	1918	Jan 13 1932	Stranded	Kitty Hawk, N.C. Fisherman.
1744	Saitia	-	2,873	-	Unknown	Unknown	18 miles offshore, Ocean City, Md. 38-14-18 N. 74-44-54 W. Depth 84'.
1745	Sallie Bissell	Sch.	-	-	Mar 4 1895	Unknown	Portsmouth, N.C.
1746	Salvor II	Scow	53	1920	Sep 27 1931	Foundered	26° N., 26 miles off Florida coast.
1747	Sam Beery	St.p.	185	1853	Jan 12 1856	Stranded	Masonboro Inlet, N.C. 1 life lost.
1748	Sam Brown	St.p.	491	1903	Feb 2 1916	Burned	Huntington, W.Va. 11 lives lost.
1749	Sam Eddy	Sch.	-	-	Feb 1869	Unknown	Frying Pan Shoals, N.C.
1750	Sam Houston	St.s.	7,176	1942	Mar 31 1943	War Loss	15-00-00 N. 63-20-00 W. Steel vessel. Sunk by enemy action.
1751	Sam Jones	St.p.	154	1839	Sep 6 1854	Stranded	Savannah, Ga.
1752	Samay	Ga.s.	56	1926	Oct 21 1961	Burned	At Miami Beach, Fla.

NO.	NAME OF VESSEL	RIG	TONS	BUILT	DATE	CAUSE	PLACE AND COMMENT
1753	Samuel C. Loveland, Jr.	Brg.	1,288	1911	Nov 17 1948	Foundered	At sea. About 120 miles northwest of Egmont Key, Tampa Bay, Fla. Steel vessel.
1754	Samuel Dillaway	Sch.	739	1886	Jan 4 1916	Stranded	St. Helena Bar, S.C.
1755	Samuel Eddy	Sch.	-	-	Feb 1869	Unknown	Frying Pan Shoals, N.C.
1756	Samuel Faunce	St.s.	87	1912	Jan 29 1920	Foundered	Sailed from Wilmington, N.C. for Key West, Fla., and has not since reported.
1757	Samuel L. Russell	Sch.	179	1869	Jan 8 1906	Foundered	Iron vessel. All lives (13) lost.
1758	Samuel MacManemy	Sch.	-	-	Mar 10 1887	Unknown	Chesapeake Bay. All lives (5) lost.
1759	Sam'l T. Beacham	Sch.	185	1898	Mar 30 1913	Collided	Apalachicola, Fla.
1760	Samuel W. Hall	Sch.	-	-	Dec 24 1897	Unknown	With British st.s. TEODORO de LARRINAGA. Florida Straits, Fla.
1761	Samuel W. Hathaway	Sch.	1,038	1902	Aug 26 1924	Foundered	Chicamacomico, N.C.
1762	Samuel W. Tilton	Sch.	-	-	Feb 17 1898	Unknown	Cape Hatteras, N.C.
1763	Samuel Welsh	Bkn.	-	-	Feb 25 1888	Unknown	Chicamacomico, N.C.
1764	Samuel Wood	Sch.	51	1867	Jan 20 1917	Burned	Whales Head, N.C.
1765	San Antonio	Bark	-	-	Jan 21 1890	Unknown	Rappahannock River, Va.
1766	San Delfino (Br.)	Tanker	4,800*	-	Apr 9 1942	War Loss	35-37-48 N. 74-56-36 W. 28 lives lost. Depth 188'.
1767	San Domingo	Sch.	-	-	Nov 27 1888	Abandoned	34-16-00 N. 73-00-00 W.
1768	San Gil (Pan.)	Frgt.	1,957*	-	Feb 2 1942	War Loss	38-06-06 N. 74-37-00 W. Stands 25' high in 117' of water.
1769	San Jacinto	St.s.	6,069	1903	Apr 22 1942	War Loss	31-11-00 N. 70-45-00 W. Off Georgia coast. Freighter. Steel vessel. Sunk by enemy action. 25% of lives lost.
1770	San Jocinto	El.s.	11,257	1945	Mar 25 1964	Burned	In Atlantic Ocean, off Norfolk, Va. Steel vessel.
1771	San Marcos	-	-	-	Unknown	Unknown	Off southwestern tip of Tangier Island, Chesapeake Bay, Va. Demolished.
1772	San Pedro	-	-	-	1717	Unknown	West of Gorda Key, Bahamas. Valued at over $500,000.
1773	San Snipe	Ga.s.	69	1882	1950	Foundered	At Norfolk, Va.
1774	Sand Dollar	Ol.s.	52	1956	Nov 9 1964	Stranded	Approximately 15 miles south of Ponce De Leon Inlet, Fla.
1775	Sanders	St.s.	74	1903	Apr 18 1907	Unknown	Little River Bar, N.C.
1776	Sandusky	Ship	-	-	Aug 28 1881	Unknown	Off Cape Hatteras, N.C.
1777	Sangamon	St.p.	108	1832	Mar 1 1835	Stranded	Kent River, Fla.
1778	Santa Catalina	St.s.	6,507	1943	Apr 24 1943	War Loss	30-59-00 N. 76-07-00 W. Off Georgia coast. Freighter. Steel vessel.
1779	Santa Claus	Ga.s.	78	1922	Mar 30 1927	Burned	St. Augustine, Fla.
1780	Santa Cristina	Ga.s.	2,119	1917	Jul 8 1919	Burned	25 miles off Key West, Fla.
1781	Santa Margharita (Span)	Galleon	-	-	1595	Unknown	Lost off Biscayne, Fla. Also reported off Merritt Island, Fla. Value $7 million.
1782	Santa Rita	St.s.	8,379	1941	Jul 9 1942	War Loss	26-11-00 N. 55-40-00 W. Steel vessel. Sunk by enemy action.
1783	Santa Rosa (Span.)	Galleon	-	-	Unknown	Unknown	Due south of Key West, Fla. Unlikely this vessel exists or contains the amount of wealth claimed at $30 million.
1784	Santiago	St.s.	3,325	1906	Mar 11 1924	Foundered	Off Cape Hatteras, N.C. Steel vessel. 25 lives lost (35).
1785	Santiago De Cuba	Frgt.	989*	-	Aug 12 1942	War Loss	24-20-00 N. 81-50-00 W. Depth over 600'. Cuban registry.
1786	Santore	St.s.	7,117	1918	Jun 17 1942	War Loss	1-1/4 miles northeast of No.2 CB Gas Buoy off Virginia coast. 36-54 N. 75-46 W. Steel vessel. Freighter. Convoy #KS-511. Sunk by enemy action.
1787	Sarah A. McNally	Sch.	-	-	Mar 15 1891	Unknown	Lambert Point, Va.
1788	Sarah D. Fell	Sch.	578	1882	Aug 10 1911	Abandoned	Near Cape Lookout, N.C.
1789	Sarah D.J. Rawson	Sch.	292	-	Feb 9 1905	Wrecked	Off Cape Lookout Shoals, N.C.
1790	Sarah J	Ol.s.	99	1946	Jan 14 1961	Foundered	At Oregon Inlet, N.C.
1791	Sarah Quinn	Sch.	113	1868	May 13 1930	Stranded	Cobbs Island, Va.
1792	Saturn	Brg.	328	1896	Mar 2 1914	Foundered	Bluff Head, Pamlico Sound, N.C.
1793	Savannah	St.p.	305	1838	Nov 28 1841	Foundered	Cape Hatteras, N.C. 8 lives lost.
1794	Savannah	Sch.	584	1901	Dec 27 1912	Stranded	Frying Pan Shoals, N.C.
1795	Savannah	Brg.	466	1912	Dec 18 1946	Foundered	Inland Waterway at Lockwood Folly, N.C.
1796	Saxon	Brg.	555	1862	Oct 12 1907	Stranded	Gull Island, N.C. 3 lives lost.

NO.	NAME OF VESSEL	RIG	TONS	BUILT	DATE		CAUSE	PLACE AND COMMENT
1797	Schuylkill	Sch.	841	1890	Oct 5	1915	Foundered	Chincoteague Shoals, Va.
1798	Scotia	Sch.	406	1883	Dec 30	1911	Foundered	Marsh Island, S.C.
1799	Scotia	Sch.	406	1883	Apr 20	1918	Foundered	Off Bogue Inlet, N.C.
1800	Scurry	Ga.y.	55	1914	Feb 20	1941	Burned	Coot Bay, Fla.
1801	Sea Bird	St.p.	-	-	Feb 10	1862	War Loss	Off Fort Cobb, on Cobb's Point, Pasquotank River, N.C. Confederate flagship. Wood vessel. Rammed by USS Commodore Perry.
1802	Sea Bird	Ga.y.	81	1918	May 22	1927	Foundered	28-24-00 N. 80-35-00 W.
1803	Sea King	Sch.	1,491	1877	Apr 4	1924	Burned	Scotland, Va.
1804	Sea Thrush	St.s.	5,447	1920	Jun 28	1942	War Loss	22-38-00 N. 60-59-00 W. Steel vessel. Sunk by enemy action.
1805	Seabright	Steamer	-	-	Sep 18	1901	Unknown	Oak Island, N.C.
1806	Seafarer	Ol.s.	63	1952	Oct 1	1952	Foundered	28-36-00 N. 80-35-00 W.
1807	Seagull	Ol.s.	69	1905	Feb 14	1937	Foundered	Linen Island, Va.
1808	Seaman	Sch.	-	-	Mar 5	1837	Unknown	New River Inlet, N.C.
1809	Secretary Marcy	St.s.	153	1847	Mar 7	1851	Stranded	Cape Lookout, N.C.
1810	Sedgwick	Sch.	605	1890	Feb 11	1922	Foundered	Sailed from Charleston, S.C., and has not since reported. All lives (6) lost.
1811	Seminole	St.p.	319	1854	Dec 20	1855	Burned	Jacksonville, Fla.
1812	Seminole	Ga.y.	174	1904	Jun 24	1935	Burned	Fort Lauderdale, Fla. Steel vessel. 1 life lost (5).
1813	Seminole	Brg.	173	1911	Oct 4	1942	Foundered	25-52-00 N. 79-20-00 W. Steel vessel.
1814	Senateur Duhamel (Br.)	Ol.s.	739	-	May 6	1942	Unknown	34-33-00 N. 76-36-18 W. 5.6 miles, 222° from Cape Lookout Light, N.C. Fisherman.
1815	Seth Low	St.s.	236	1861	Nov 2	1881	Burned	Jacksonville, Fla.
1816	Severn	St.s.	113	1891	Nov 16	1925	Burned	Elizabeth River, Va.
1817	Severn	Brg.	339	1897	Jan 28	1926	Foundered	Frying Pan Shoals, N.C. All lives (2) lost.
1818	Shamokin	Sch.	900	1904	Feb 21	1916	Foundered	Cape Henry, Va.
1819	Sherman	St.s.	619	1861	Jan 10	1874	Foundered	Off Cape Fear Light, N.C. Steel vessel.
1820	Shiawassee III	Ol.s.	142	1926	Feb 15	1947	Burned	65 miles off Florida coast.
1821	Shiloh	Sch.	-	-	Mar 17	1876	Unknown	Durants, N.C.
1822	Shiloh	Ga.s.	75	1895	Sep 22	1929	Burned	Tolls Point, Va.
1823	Shrimp Queen	Ol.s.	79	1953	Apr 15	1956	Foundered	In Yucatan Channel, 250 miles southwest of Egmont Key, Fla. Steel vessel.
1824	Simmons	Sch.	62	1890	Jan 29	1926	Foundered	Hollywood, Fla.
1825	Slobodna	Steamer	-	-	Mar 17	1887	Unknown	Molasses Reef, Fla.
1826	Soli Deo Gloria	Bark	-	-	Oct 19	1891	Unknown	Nassau Inlet, Fla.
1827	Sophia (Br.)	Bark	-	-	Nov 4	1862	Burned	3-1/2 miles west of Masonboro Inlet, N.C. Blockade runner.
1828	Sophia	St.s.	286	1855		1866	Foundered	Apalachicola, Fla. Steel vessel.
1829	South America	Packet	605	1832	Dec 21	1861	"Sunk"	4 miles SSE off Fort Sumter and 3 miles ESE of the light on Morris Island, Charleston Harbor, S.C. Used by Union forces to block harbor. "Stone Fleet".
1830	South Carolina	St.p.	173	1853	Jan 12	1860	Burned	Apalachicola, Fla.
1831	South West	Sch.	569	1904	Jul 13	1916	Foundered	Off Charleston, S.C. All lives (5) lost.
1832	Southern Districts	Ol.s.	3,337	1944	Dec 6	1954	Foundered	South of Cape Hatteras, N.C. Presumed lost in bad weather. Steel vessel.
1833	Southern Isles	Ol.s.	3,325	1943	Oct 5	1951	Foundered	Approximately 190 miles southeast of Cape Hatteras, N.C. Steel vessel.
1834	Southland	St.p.	261	1903	Nov	1911	Stranded	Dublin, Ga.
1835	Spellbourne	Sch.	-	-	Oct	1873	Unknown	Off Cape Hatteras, N.C.
1836	Spero	Bark	-	-	Dec 24	1910	Unknown	Hatteras Inlet, N.C.
1837	Spring Chicken	Ol.s.	103	1915	Apr 5	1944	Foundered	35 miles east of Cape Henry, Va.
1838	Spunkie	Steamer	-	-	Feb 9	1864	Unknown	West of Fort Caswell, near Cape Fear, N.C. Blockade runner.
1839	Staffa	Steamer	2,146	-	Jan 16	1897	Unknown	1/2 mile south of boundary line of Virginia and North Carolina.
1840	Stampede	Sch.	-	-	Feb 4	1882	Unknown	Off Cape Fear, N.C.
1841	Standard	Drg.	175	1926	Mar 14	1944	Burned	Arlington, Fla.
1842	Standish	St.s.	109	1862	May 24	1866	Burned	Savannah River, Ga.

NO.	NAME OF VESSEL	RIG	TONS	BUILT	DATE	CAUSE	PLACE AND COMMENT
1843	Stanley H. Minor	Sch.	696	1902	Mar 8 1907	Stranded	Frying Pan Shoals, N.C.
1844	Stanley M. Seaman	Sch.	1,060	1908	Aug 5 1918	Torpedoed	34-59-00 N. 73-18-00 W.
1845	Star of the Sea	Sch.	967	1887	Oct 26 1911	Stranded	Florida Reefs, Fla.
1846	State of Georgia	St.p.	1,204	1852	Oct 5 1866	Stranded	Currituck, N.C. Redocumented "Andrew Johnson" in 1866.
1847	Steel Barge No.2	Brg.	2,217	1889	Jan 23 1935	Foundered	Off Black Fish Bank Buoy, Va. Steel vessel. All lives (6) lost.
1848	Steelmaker	St.s.	6,176	1920	Apr 19 1942	War Loss	Off Charleston, S.C. Freighter. Steel vessel. Sunk by enemy action.
1849	Stella B. Kaplan	Sch.	1,078	1891	Sep 18 1911	Stranded	Chesapeake Bay, Va.
1850	Stephen Young	Brig	200	–	Jan 20 1862	"Sunk"	On south edge of Rattlesnake Shoal, Maffitt's Channel, Charleston, S.C. Used by Union forces to block harbor. Part of second "Stone Fleet".
1851	Stillman F. Kelley	Sch.	685	1905	Sep 14 1909	Stranded	Salt Key Bank, Fla.
1852	Stone 6	Ol.s.	71	1890	May 1959	Foundered	In Cape Fear River, Eagle Island, Wilmington, N.C.
1853	Stormy Petrel	Steamer	–	–	Dec 15 1864	Burned	New Inlet, Cape Fear River, N.C. Blockade runner.
1854	Stranger	Sch.	595	1918	Sep 15 1927	Burned	Tampa, Fla.
1855	Strathairly (Br.)	St.s.	1,236	–	Mar 24 1891	Unknown	Chicamicomico, N.C. Iron ore cargo. 19 lives lost.
1856	Submarine L-24 (Br.)	Ol.s.	–	–	Jan 10 1924	"Sunk"	Off Cape Hatteras, N.C. 48 lives lost.
1857	Success	Bark	–	–	Jan 15 1879	Unknown	Bodie Island, N.C.
1858	Sue Williams	Sch.	–	–	Mar 24 1890	Unknown	Chicamicomico, N.C.
1859	Suloide	Frgt.	1,879	–	Mar 26 1943	Unknown	34-32-48 N. 76-53-42 W. 8.4 miles off Bogue Banks, Cape Lookout, N.C. Demolished. Depth 59'.
1861	Summit	St.s.	70	1872	Mar 19 1924	Foundered	James River, Va.
1861	Sun	Sch.	84	–	Jan 13 1854	Unknown	Beaufort Inlet, N.C.
1862	Sun	St.p.	255	1898	Feb 2 1909	Stranded	Apalachicola, Fla.
1863	Sunbeam	Bark	255	1856	Oct 30 1911	Stranded	Sapelo Island, Ga.
1864	Sunbeam	Sch.	–	–	Dec 17 1919	Unknown	Off Currituck, N.C. 18 lives lost.
1865	Sunshine	Ga.s.	64	1917	Dec 25 1949	Burned	At Cross Key, 50 miles south of Miami, Fla.
1866	Superior	St.p.	617	1862	Apr 20 1911	Burned	Norfolk, Va.
1868	Superior	St.p.	570	1862	Apr 20 1911	Burned	Norfolk, Va.
1868	Supertest	Ol.s.	51	1942	Apr 2 1958	Stranded	On St. George Island, Fla.
1869	Susan B	Sch.	455	1919	Nov 17 1924	Foundered	Winter Quarter Light, Va.
1870	Susan Preston MacPhie	Brg.	272	1908	Jul 1959	Foundered	Near Plymouth, N.C.
1871	Svanen	Bark	–	–	Mar 23 1890	Unknown	Fernandina Bar, Fla.
1872	Swan	Ol.s.	50	1908	Apr 27 1927	Burned	Milton, Fla.
1873	Sweet Pea	Ol.s.	77	1942	Nov 12 1959	Burned	In the Neuse River, off Cypress Point, N.C.
1874	Swiftscout	St.s.	8,300	–	Apr 18 1945	Unknown	37-30-00 N. 72-45-00 W. Off Virginia coast. 1 life lost (47).
1875	Swordfish	Ga.y.	151	1901	Apr 29 1921	Burned	Near Amelia, Fla.
1876	Sylph	St.p.	290	1844	Mar 31 1868	Burned	Jacksonville, Fla.
1877	Sylvan Grove	St.p.	283	1858	Jan 9 1891	Burned	Wilmington, N.C.
1878	Sylvia C. Hall	Sch.	384	1891	Mar 18 1915	Stranded	Lookout Shoals, N.C. Lumber cargo.
1879	T.H. Anderson	Ol.s.	62	1942	Oct 15 1949	Collided	With wreck of San Marcos, in Tangier Sound, Va.
1880	T.J. Hooper	–	2,197	Pre-WWII		Unknown	38-26-06 N. 74-23-42 W. 38' high in 135' of water.
1881	T.J. Hooper	St.s.	456	1921	Mar 18 1941	Stranded	Off Assateague, Va.
1882	Tallac	St.s.	1,380	1895	Feb 24 1920	Stranded	18 miles south of Cape Henry, Va.
1883	Tallahassee	Steamer	–	–	Jan 15 1865	Wrecked	Near Cape Fear, N.C. Confederate gun-boat.
1884	Talofa	Ol.s.	83	1910	Oct 24 1940	Burned	Near Moore's Beach, N.C.
1885	Tamarack	Ga.y.	157	1913	Dec 4 1921	Burned	Pamlico Sound, N.C. Steel vessel.
1886	Tamarco	Sch.	686	1903	Sep 24 1932	Foundered	Flagler Beach, Fla. 1 life lost (7).
1887	Tamaulipas	Tanker	6,943	–	Apr 9 1942	War Loss	34-31-30 N. 76-01-48 W.25 miles, 113° from Cape Lookout Light, N.C. Steel vessel. Sunk by enemy action, 2 lives lost (37).

NO.	NAME OF VESSEL	RIG	TONS	BUILT	DATE		CAUSE	PLACE AND COMMENT
1888	Tangier	Brg.	433	1909	Sep 19	1916	Foundered	Off York River, Va.
1889	Taxan	Frgt.	7,005	-	Mar 11	1942	War Loss	21-34-00 N. 76-28-00 W. North of Cuba. Steel vessel.
1890	Telegraph	Clipper	1,069	1851	Jan 26	1857	Burned	At Savannah, Ga.
1891	Tempest	St.p.	105	1835	Nov 26	1838	Snagged	Ocheesee, Fla.
1892	Tenas	Brg.	2,212	1919	Mar 16	1942	Foundered	35-15-00 N. 75-30-00 W. Off Diamond Shoals, N.C.
1893	Tenedos	Bark	245	-	Dec 21	1861	"Sunk"	4 miles SSE off Fort Sumter and 3 miles ESE of the light on Morris Island, Charleston Harbor, S.C. Used by Union forces to block harbor. "Stone Fleet".
1894	Tennessee	St.p.	1,148	1854	Oct 25	1865	Foundered	At sea, off Savannah, Ga. All lives (34) lost. Captured as Confederate steamer and documented "Republic" on May 12, 1865.
1895	Tennessee	-	-	-	Apr 11	1942	Unknown	Cape Lookout, N.C.
1896	Texan	Frgt.	4,427*	-	Mar 11	1942	War Loss	22-05-00 N. 77-36-30 W. See No.1889.
1897	Thames	St.s.	644	1862	Apr 6	1869	Burned	West side of Diamond Shoals, Cape Hatteras, N.C.
1898	Thames	St.s.	447	1889	Oct 22	1921	Foundered	North of Jupiter Lighthouse, Fla.
1899	The Everlasting	Ol.s.	70	1963	Nov 24	1967	Burned	In the Intercoastal Waterway, North Miami, Fla.
1900	The Josephine	Sch.	638	1890	Apr 3	1915	Stranded	Kill Devil Hill, N.C. 3 lives lost.
1901	The Sea Gypsy	Ol.s.	63	1953	Dec 9	1957	Foundered	About 300 miles west of Key West, Fla.
1902	Thendara	St.y.	58	1886	Oct 20	1926	Foundered	Key West, Fla.
1903	Theodore D. Wagner	St.p.	604	1866	Oct 20	1866	Burned	At sea. 31-00-00 N. 74-00-00 W.
1904	Theodore Weems	St.s.	926	1884	Mar 27	1915	Collided	With SS HEREDIA. Tampa Bay, Fla.
1905	Thistleroy	Steamer	-	-	Dec 28	1911	Unknown	4 miles, 183° from Cape Lookout Light and 1-1/2 miles from Cape Point, N.C.
1906	Thomas A. Goddard	Sch.	643	1874	Dec 2	1905	Stranded	Nags Head, N.C.
1907	Thomas A. Scott	St.s.	1,052	1863	Mar 23	1887	Foundered	200 miles off Cape Canaveral, Fla.
1908	Thomas B. Garland	Sch.	348	1881	Oct 27	1921	Stranded	Tampa, Fla.
1909	Thomas C. Eaton	Sch.	77	1882	Dec 14	1919	Stranded	Smith Point, Va.
1910	Thomas Clooney	Brg.	574	1906	Feb 15	1927	Foundered	Baypoint, Fla.
1911	Thomas Collyer	St.p.	189	1850	Sep 11	1897	Burned	Off coast of Florida. Renamed "City of Brunswick" in 1886.
1912	Thomas F. Pollard	Sch.	707	1890	Oct 1	1920	Foundered	Off Cape Henry, Va.
1913	Thomas Foulks	St.s.	104	1861	Jan 14	1866	Burned	Claremont, Va.
1914	Thomas G. Smith	Sch.	513	1883	Apr 10	1910	Stranded	Core Bank, N.C.
1915	Thomas J. Lancaster	Sch.	-	-	Oct 5	1881	Unknown	New Inlet, N.C. 7 lives lost.
1916	Thomas J. Martin	Sch.	-	-	Jan 9	1883	Unknown	Caffeys Inlet, N.C.
1917	Thomas Morgan	St.s.	52	1873	Aug 27	1911	Foundered	Charleston, S.C.
1918	Thomas S. Dennison	Sch.	1,491	1900	Jan 3	1913	Foundered	100 miles south of Pascagoula, Fla.
1919	Thomas Sinnickson	Sch.	-	-	Oct 12	1885	Unknown	Off Cape Hatteras Inlet, N.C.
1920	Thomas Swan	St.s.	462	1853	Jan 16	1864	Stranded	Cape Henry, Va.
1921	Thomas W. Haven	Sch.	435	1891	Oct 3	1891	Abandoned	Off Charleston, S.C.
1922	Thomas Winsmore	Sch.	403	1891	Dec 22	1915	Foundered	29-20-00 N. 73-08-00 W.
1923	Thorn	St.s.	594	1862	Mar 4	1865	Torpedoed	Cape Fear River, N.C.
1924	Three Friends	Sch.	-	1905	Feb 9	1900	Unknown	Portsmouth, N.C.
1925	Tifton	Sch.	-	-	Jan 29	1926	Foundered	Hillsboro Light, Fla. 2 lives lost (8).
1926	Tiger	-	-	-	Jun	1585	Unknown	Ocracoke Inlet, N.C. Flagship of Sir Richard Greenville.
1927	Tiger	St.s.	5,992	1917	Mar 31	1942	War Loss	2 miles true from Buoy No.2 CB, off Chesapeake Bay entrance. Steel vessel. Tanker. 36-46-06 N. 75-46-06 W. Sunk by enemy action. 1 life lost (42).
1928	Timandra	Ship	1,579	1885	Mar 6	1917	Foundered	Sailed from Norfolk, Va., and has not since been reported. All lives (19) lost.
1929	Timor	Ship	289	-	Dec 21	1861	"Sunk"	4 miles SSE off Fort Sumter and 3 miles ESE of the light on Morris Island, Charleston, S.C. Used by Union forces to block harbor. "Stone Fleet".
1930	Tinqua	Clipper	668	1852	Jan 12	1855	Unknown	Off Cape Hatteras, N.C.
1931	Tobyhanna	Sch.	836	1891	Feb 6	1917	Stranded	Off Winter Quarter Lightship, Va.

NO.	NAME OF VESSEL	RIG	TONS	BUILT	DATE	CAUSE	PLACE AND COMMENT
1932	Tonawanda	St.s.	752	1863	Mar 28 1866	Stranded	Grecian Shoals, Fla.
1933	Tondelavo	Ga.s.	55	1946	Nov 17 1946	Foundered	Off Georgia coast.
1934	Tornado	Ol.s.	56	1947	May 18 1962	Foundered	In Pensacola Bay, off Florida coast.
1935	Torpedo	St.s.	-	1894	Apr 3 1865	Burned	Near Fort Darling, James River, Va. Tug. Wood vessel.
1936	Tourist	St.s.	284	1831	Jun 4 1907	Burned	Albemarle Sound, N.C.
1937	Trader	St.p.	76	1831	Jan 25 1832	Ice	Parkersburg, Va.
1938	Transfer No.8	St.s.	131	1891	Dec 15 1950	Foundered	In St. Johns River, Jacksonville, Fla. Iron vessel.
1939	Trident	Sch.	-	-	Jun 14 1842	Unknown	Off Bodie Island, N.C.
1940	Trillora II	Ga.s.	64	1917	Jun 25 1946	Burned	At Bucksport, S.C.
1941	Triumph	St.s.	52	1863	Sep 8 1870	Burned	James River, Va.
1942	Tropic	Ga.y.	126	1925	Jun 24 1935	Burned	Fort Lauderdale, Fla.
1943	True Briton	Ship	-	-	Feb 1 1889	Unknown	Rebecca Shoals, Fla.
1944	Tuckahoe	St.p.	80	1836	Jun 13 1841	Burned	Guyandotte, Va.
1945	Tuscaloosa City	St.s.	5,686	1920	May 4 1942	War Loss	18025-00 N. 81-31-00 W. Steel vessel. Sunk by enemy action.
1946	Twilight	St.s.	644	1865	Nov 14 1865	Stranded	Cape Fear River, N.C.
1947	Twilight	Sch.	376	1874	Sep 16 1906	Capsized	50 miles off Charleston, S.C. 6 lives lost.
1948	Twilight	Ga.y.	65	1915	Apr 28 1926	Burned	West Palm Beach, Fla.
1949	Two Boys	St.p.	102	1865	Feb 8 1870	Exploded	Sapelo Sound, Ga. Steel vessel.
1950	Two Brothers	Ol.s.	67	1916	Mar 4 1967	Foundered	At Key West, Fla.
1951	Two Sisters	Sloop	-	-	Mar 12 1888	Unknown	Hampton Roads, Va.
1952	Tzenny Chandris (Ger.)	Steamer	9,010	-	Nov 13 1937	Unknown	40 miles northeast of Diamond Shoals Lightship, N.C. 7 lives lost.
1953	U-85 (Ger.)	Sub	-	-	Apr 14 1942	War Loss	South of Whimble Shoals, near Nags Head, N.C. Steel vessel.
1954	U-352 (Ger.)	Sub	500	-	May 9 1942	War Loss	23-1/2 miles, 187° from Cape Lookout Light, N.C. Depth 109'.
1955	U-701 (Ger.)	Sub	-	-	Jul 7 1942	War Loss	Off Cape Hatteras, N.C. Steel vessel.
1956	USS Columbia	St.p.	542	1865	Feb 6 1864	"Shelled"	Mouth of Masonboro Inlet, N.C. Lost during Civil War.
1957	USS Commodore Jones	St.w.	542	1916	May 6 1864	Collided	With torpedo. In James River off Jones' Point, Va. Length 154'. Lost during Civil War.
1958	USS Cumberland	Sloop	1,726	-	Mar 8 1862	Rammed	Entrance to James River, Va. Ironclad vessel. Armament of 24 guns. Was sunk by CSS Virginia. 121 lives lost.
1959	USS Congress	Steamer	1,869	-	Mar 8 1862	Burned	Near Newport News, above Signal Point, Va. Length 180'.
1960	USS Despatch	-	-	-	Oct 10 1891	Burned	Assateague, Va.
1961	USS Housatonic	St.slp.	1,240	-	Feb 17 1864	"Sunk"	Off Charleston, S.C. 5-1/2 miles east-north-east from Fort Sumter. Length 208'. Sunk by CSS Hunley (David) which was first successful use of submarine in battle. Both vessels were lost and would be of valuable interest historically.
1962	USS Monitor	Steamer	776	-	Dec 29 1862	Foundered	While under tow by USS Rhode Island. Approximately 1/2 mile off Cape Hatteras Lighthouse, N.C. Length 172'. Beam 41.5'. Hull was of wood construction. Armored with 8" wrought-iron plate. Would be of great value historically.
1963	USS New Jersey	St.w.	14,949	-	Sep 5 1923	Unknown	1 mile off the Diamond Shoals Light Vessel, N.C. Length 435'.
1964	USS Otsego	St.w.	974	-	Dec 9 1864	Burned	Off Jamesville Bluff, Roanoke River, N.C. Destroyed by "torpedo".
1965	USS Peterhoff	St.s.	1,200	-	Mar 6 1864	"Rammed"	South of New Inlet and about 1 mile offshore and south of Sheep Head Rock. Length 210'. Rammed by USS Monticello. Located in 1963.
1966	USS Shawsheen	St.w.	180	-	May 7 1864	Burned	In James River (off Pickett's farm), Va. Tug. Length 118'.
1967	USS Southfield	St.w.	750	-	Apr 19 1864	"Rammed"	Off Plymouth, N.C. in the Roanoke River. Length 200'. Sunk by CSS Albemarle.
1968	USS Underwriter	St.p.	341	-	Feb 2 1864	Burned	Neuse River, off New Bern, N.C. Off Foster's Wharf. Length 170'.
1969	USS Weehawken	Steamer	844	1862	Dec 6 1863	Unknown	East of beacon off Morris Island, S.C. Iron monitor type vessel.
1970	Union	St.p.	141	1831	Jan 25 1832	Burned	Parkersburg, Va.
1971	Union	St.p.	209	1852	Feb 5 1856	Collided	With CUSSETA. Apalachicola River, Fla.
1972	Urbano	Bark	-	-	Jan 17 1889	Unknown	Pensacola, Fla.

NO.	NAME OF VESSEL	RIG	TONS	BUILT	DATE		CAUSE	PLACE AND COMMENT
1973	Utility	St.s.	77	1899	Feb 21	1932	Burned	St. Johns River, Fla.
1974	Vahadah	Ga.s.	54	1921		1948	Foundered	At Palm Beach, Fla.
1975	Valkyrie	Ga.s.	58	1915	Nov 3	1947	Stranded	Medecis Creek, 10 miles north of St. Augustine, Fla.
1976	Valley City	St.s.	318	1859	Jan 30	1882	Foundered	Cape San Blas, Fla.
1977	Valley Gem	St.p.	156	1897	Feb	1919	Foundered	Morgantown, W.Va.
1978	Valparaiso	Ship	400	-	Jan 20	1862	"Sunk"	On south edge of Rattlesnake Shoal, Maffitt's Channel, Charleston Harbor, S.C. Used by Union forces to block harbor. Part of second "Stone Fleet".
1979	Van Buren	St.p.	94	1833	Dec 5	1834	Burned	Columbus, Ga.
1980	Vandalia	Ga.s.	141	1898	Jan 27	1913	Burned	St. Petersburg, Fla. 1 life lost.
1981	Vandore	Frgt.	8,016	-	Jan 23	1942	Unknown	35-00-00 N. 75-25-00 W.
1982	Vapor	Sch.	-	-	Nov 5	1885	Unknown	Cape Fear Bar, N.C.
1983	Varuna	-	-	-	Oct 20	1870	"Sank"	Off Florida coast. 72 lives lost.
1984	Venetia	Ga.y.	81	1920	Feb 24	1939	Burned	Fort Myers, Fla.
1985	Venmore	St.s.	8,016	1921	Jan 23	1942	War Loss	5 to 15 miles southeast of Diamond Shoals, N.C. Steel vessel. Sunk by enemy action. See No. 1981. Also reported as "Venore". 21 lives lost.
1986	Venus (Br.)	Steamer	1,100	-	Oct 21	1863	Burned	North of New Inlet, about 2 miles north of Gatlin's Battery, between Flag Pond Hill and Dick's Bay, N.C. Wood vessel with iron plating. Length 265'.
1987	Venus	Ol.s.	100	1966	Nov 18	1966	Burned	At Broward Marine, Inc., Fort Lauderdale, Fla.
1988	Vera Cruz	St.s.	1,340	1864	Apr 12	1866	Stranded	Bodie Island, N.C.
1989	Vera Cruz	Brig	500	-	May 8	1903	Foundered	Off Dry Shoal Point, Portsmouth, N.C. 1 life lost.
1990	Verona	Ol.s.	60	1933	Jul 14	1965	Burned	At foot of Front Street, Beaufort, N.C.
1991	Versailles	St.p.	83	1831	Jan 10	1835	Snagged	Apalachicola, Fla.
1992	Vesta	St.s.	500	-	Jan 11	1864	Burned	4 miles below and to the west of Tubb's Inlet, N.C. Iron vessel. Blockade runner.
1993	Vester	Ol.s.	134	1876	Feb 16	1939	Burned	2-1/2 miles west of Minnesot Beach, N.C.
1994	Vestris (Br.)	-	-	-	Nov 12	1928	"Sank"	Off Virginia Capes. 110 lives lost.
1995	Vililla	Brig	-	-	May 25	1891	Unknown	Currituck Beach, N.C.
1996	Victor	St.s.	1,339	1864	Oct 20	1872	Foundered	Jupiter Light, Fla.
1997	Victor C. Records	Sch.	293	1902	Feb 16	1920	Foundered	35 miles southwest of Lookout Lightship, N.C.
1998	Victoria S	Sch.	754	1918	Aug 23	1925	Foundered	Ocracoke Beach, N.C.
1999	Victory	Sch.	-	-	Feb 6	1837	Unknown	Off Bodie Island, N.C.
2000	Victory	Clipper	670	1851	Feb 9	1861	Wrecked	Near Cape Henry, Va.
2001	Victory	St.s.	337	1918	May 11	1921	Burned	Off Matanzas Inlet, Fla. 29-27-14 N. 80-52-50 W. Depth 81'.
2002	Viking	Ol.s.	52	1926	Dec 23	1943	Burned	7 miles east of Gratton Beach, Fla.
2003	Vindeggen (Nor.)	St.s.	3,179	1926	Jun 8	1918	Torpedoed	Off Currituck, N.C. Cargo of copper, wool and hides.
2004	Vineyard	Brig	-	-		1830	Unknown	Off Long Key, Fla.
2005	Viola W. Burton	Sch.	-	-	May 27	1889	Unknown	Big Kinnakeet Life Saving Station, N.C.
2006	Viola W. Tunis	Brg.	264	1865	May 6	1912	Foundered	25 miles southwest by west of the Cape Hatteras Lightship, N.C.
2007	Virginia	St.p.	548	1853		1862	Burned	Fredericksburg, Va.
2008	Virginia	Sch.	704	1877	Aug 30	1906	Foundered	Cape Fear, N.C.
2009	Virginia	St.p.	79	1905	Oct 17	1910	Foundered	Boca Chica, Fla.
2010	Virginia	St.s.	220	1904	Aug 24	1912	Burned	Elizabeth City, N.C.
2011	Virginia	St.s.	2,027	1905	May 24	1919	Burned	Smiths Point, Va. Steel vessel. 8 lives lost (207).
2012	Virginia Dare	Ol.s.	220	1888	Jan 31	1935	Stranded	Currituck Sound, N.C. Iron vessel.
2013	Virginia Lee Hickman	Sch.	-	-	Jan 26	1888	Unknown	St. Augustine Bar, Fla.
2014	Virginia May	Ol.s.	53	1951	Oct 1	1951	Foundered	175 miles west of Port Myers, Fla.
2015	Virginia Pendleton	Sch.	1,547	1919	Nov 1	1927	Foundered	28-45-00 N. 76-30-00 W. 3 lives lost (10).
2016	Virginia Rulon	Sch.	280	1874	Jul 18	1916	Foundered	Off Cape Hatteras, N.C.
2017	Virginia Sinclair	St.s.	6,151	1930	Mar 7	1943	War Loss	20-11-00 N. 74-04-00 W. Steel vessel. Freighter. Sunk by enemy action.

NO.	NAME OF VESSEL	RIG	TONS	BUILT	DATE	CAUSE	PLACE AND COMMENT
2018	Volador II (Span.)	Sch.	-	-	May 25 1815	Foundered	Off Pensacola, Fla. Armament 10 guns. 2 lives lost.
2019	Volant	Brig	-	-	Sep 1862	Unknown	New Inlet, N.C.
2020	Volunteer	St.p.	-	-	Feb 23 1873	Foundered	Nags Head, N.C.
2021	Voucher	Ship	-	-	Nov 19 1817	Foundered	Off Chicamacomico, N.C.
2022	W.D. Anderson	St.s.	10,227	1921	Feb 22 1942	War Loss	About 14 miles east of Stewart, Fla. 25-41-00 N. 80-00-00 W. Tanker. Steel vessel. 1 life lost (36). Sunk by enemy.
2023	W.E. Hutton	St.s.	7,076	1920	Mar 18 1942	War Loss	34-30-06 N. 76-54-18 W. 11 miles off Bogue Banks at Salterpath, bearing 248°, 20-1/2 miles from Cape Lookout Light, N.C. Tanker. Steel vessel. 13 lives (36) lost. Sunk by enemy action. Depth 41'. Wreck demolished.
2024	W.H. Hoodless	Ol.s.	112	1907	Jan 17 1929	Stranded	Smith Jetty, Georgetown, S.C.
2025	W.H. Van Name	Sch.	97	1872	Mar 31 1906	Collided	With submerged barge ARK. Hampton Beach, Va.
2026	W.J. Colle	Sch.	450	1922	Dec 21 1930	Foundered	Key West, Fla.
2027	W.J. Townsend	Ol.s.	289	1944	Dec 15 1962	Stranded	At Oregon Inlet, N.C. Went aground on reef.
2028	W.L. Steed	Tanker	3,798*	-	Feb 2 1942	War Loss	38-25-00 N. 75-00-00 W. Depth 45'.
2029	W. Osborne Holland	Ol.s.	115	1935	Jul 20 1955	Burned	Near Young's Island, S.C.
2030	W.P. Anderson	Ol.s.	82	1923	Oct 15 1954	Lost	Off Southport, N.C.
2031	W.T. Gibbons	St.s.	-	-	Sep 9 1856	Foundered	Off Nags Head, N.C. Rigged with sail.
2032	Wabash	St.p.	131	1841	Dec 12 1842	Stranded	Fort Gaines, Ga.
2033	Walling III	Ol.s.	66	1953	Oct 15 1958	Foundered	About 70 miles SSW of Saibel Light, Fla. 25-37-00 N. 83-43-00 W.
2034	Walter	Sch.	100	1875	Oct 21 1932	Collided	With st.s. ELEANOR BOLING. Off Fort Pierce, Fla.
2035	Walter J. Doyle	Sch.	-	-	Mar 1852	Unknown	Off Beaufort Bar, N.C.
2036	Walter Raleigh	St.p.	-	-	Aug 5 1845	Burned	Georgetown, S.C.
2037	Walter S. Massey	Bark	157	1832	Jan 18 1889	Foundered	Off Hatteras Shoals, N.C.
2038	Waltham	Sch.	-	-	May 4 1874	Unknown	Bodie Island, N.C.
2039	Wanderer	St.p.	84	1897	Mar 24 1909	Foundered	Money Key, Florida Bay, Fla.
2040	Warner Moore	Sch.	443	1883	Jun 3 1914	Stranded	Cobb Island, Va. 3 lives lost.
2041	Warren B. Potter	Sch.	368	1879	Sep 3 1918	Stranded	Cape Charles, Va.
2042	Washington	St.s.	472	1865	Oct 14 1870	Burned	Cape Fear River, N.C.
2043	Washington	Ol.s.	127	1923	Jan 20 1928	Burned	Norfolk, Va.
2044	Washington	Brg.	346	1897	Jun 29 1933	Burned	Fork Swam, James River, Va.
2045	Washington	Brg.	143	-	Jan 29 1939	Burned	Shipyard River, S.C.
2046	Wasp	St.s.	53	1859	Jun 1 1870	Burned	James River, Va.
2047	Wasp	St.s.	641	1905	Jun 19 1919	Burned	Pensacola Bay, Fla.
2048	Water Nymph	St.p.	130	1833	Jan 26 1834	Burned	Milligan Island, Ga. 2 lives lost.
2049	Wateree	St.p.	160	1843	Dec 6 1850	Stranded	Pee Dee River, S.C.
2050	Wave	Steamer	-	-	Mar 5 1885	Unknown	Cape Fear River, N.C. 3 lives lost.
2051	Wave	Sch.	67	1884	Nov 3 1908	Burned	Tampa, Fla.
2052	Wave	Sch.	-	-	Dec 9 1937	Unknown	Currituck Beach, N.C.
2053	Welaka	St.p.	256	1851	Dec 2 1857	Stranded	St. John's River, Fla.
2054	Wellfleet	Sch.	600	1900	Mar 6 1911	Stranded	Diamond Shoals, N.C.
2055	Wellfleet	St.s.	430	1921	Mar 2 1943	Collided	With st.s. EDW. L. DOHENY. 33-02-00 N. 74-49-00 W. Steel vessel.
2056	Wellington	Sch.	970	1918	Sep 10 1928	Foundered	Cape Hatteras, N.C.
2057	Wesley M. Oler	Sch.	-	-	Dec 5 1902	Foundered	34-10-00 N. Hatteras Inlet, N.C. 10 lives lost.
2058	West Notus	St.s.	5,492	1920	Jun 1 1942	War Loss	34-10-00 N. 68-20-00 W. Off North Carolina coast. Freighter. Steel vessel.
2059	Western Star	Sch.	-	-	Sep 11 1877	Unknown	Bodie Island, N.C.
2060	Western Virginia	St.p.	82	1829	Jan 25 1832	Wrecked	Parkersburg, Va.
2061	Westland	Brg.	989	1918	Dec 5 1941	Foundered	7 miles south of Cape Lookout Sea Buoy, N.C.
2062	Westmoreland	Ol.s.	114	1921	Oct 10 1926	Burned	McGuires Wharf, Va.

NO.	NAME OF VESSEL	RIG	TONS	BUILT	DATE	CAUSE	PLACE AND COMMENT
2063	Westmoreland	Brg.	1,593	1916	Oct 3 1939	Foundered	Off Cape Henry, Va. 36-56-45 N. 75-57-30 W. Demolished. Depth 50'.
2064	Wetherby	St.p	-	-	Dec 2 1893	Unknown	Off Diamond Shoals, N.C.
2065	Whereaway	Ga.s.	70	1918	Dec 5 1962	Foundered	At Colyer Island, off Lake Park, Fla.
2066	White Haven	Brg.	1,293	1919	Jul 4 1933	Foundered	Winter Quarter Lightship, Va.
2067	Widgeon	St.s.	56	1864	Apr 8 1867	Burned	Jacksonville, Fla.
2068	Wilbert S. Bartlett	Sch.	741	1918	Dec 19 1925	Stranded	Off Jupiter, Fla.
2069	Wild Dayrell	St.p	440	-	Feb 3 1864	Burned	Near New Topsail Inlet, N.C. Blockade runner.
2070	Willena	Ga.p	50	1907	Jan 28 1910	Stranded	St. Andrews Bar, Fla.
2071	William	Sch.	-	-	Aug 29 1837	Unknown	Off Cape Lookout, N.C.
2072	William A. Morse	Ga.s.	77	1896	Feb 6 1937	Stranded	Off Charleston, S.C. 31-17-00 N. 79-04-00 W.
2073	William A. Rockefeller	St.s.	14,054	1921	Jun 28 1942	War Loss	35-11-00 N. 75-07-00 W. Off North Carolina coast. Tanker. Steel vessel. Sunk by enemy action.
2074	William B. Blades, Jr.	St.s.	62	1902	Dec 20 1921	Burned	Norfolk, Va.
2075	Wm. B. Diggs	-	1,041*	1874	Pre-WWII	Unknown	38-56-35 N. 74-41-54 W.
2076	William B. Herrick	Sch.	499	1874	Mar 6 1916	Foundered	26-59-00 N. 73-03-00 W.
2077	William C. May	Sch.	710	1912	Jun 21 1920	Foundered	37-24-00 N. 71-30-00 W.
2078	William Carlton	Ship	-	1874	May 15 1818	Unknown	Kill Devil Hills, N.C.
2079	William Cobb	Sch.	424	1874	Nov 6 1918	Abandoned	37-40-00 N. 62-40-00 W.
2080	Wm. D. Sanner	Ol.s.	260	1903	Dec 1 1938	Collided	With SS LEVENBAND. 2 miles northwest of Cape Henry Light, Va. Steel vessel.
2081	Wm. Donnelly	Sch.	98	1860	Dec 4 1914	Stranded	Off Virginia coast. 2 lives lost.
2082	William Drayton	Packet	370	-	Feb 24 1833	Wrecked	At New Inlet, near Currituck, N.C.
2083	William F. Dunn	Sch.	70	1924	Feb 12 1932	Foundered	Tangier Island, Va.
2084	William Fisher	St.s.	63	1862	Feb 24 1889	Burned	Alexandria, Va.
2085	William G. Gibbons	St.p.	174	1865	Apr 27 1866	Burned	Hershman Lake, Ga.
2086	William Gibbons	St.p.	294	1834	Oct 12 1836	Stranded	Bodie Island, N.C.
2087	William H. Allison	Sch.	-	-	Feb 3 1896	Unknown	Cape Fear, N.C.
2088	William H. Bailey	Sch.	480	1878	Mar 8 1907	Abandoned	Off Cape Hatteras, N.C.
2089	Wm. H. Davidson	Sch.	-	-	Dec 12 1910	Unknown	Paul Gamiels Hill, N.C.
2090	Wm. H. Hopkins	Sch.	-	-	Jun 21 1891	Unknown	Off Big Kinnakeet, N.C.
2091	Wm. H. Keeney	Sch.	-	-	Mar 27 1890	Unknown	Little Kinnakeet, N.C.
2092	William H. Kenzal	Sch.	-	-	Apr 5 1900	Stranded	Cape Hatteras, N.C.
2093	William H. Macy	Sch.	2,163	1883	Apr 5 1915	Stranded	Near Wash Woods Life Saving Station, Va.
2094	Wm. H. Meekins	Sch.	79	1874	Dec 22 1918	Stranded	Chincoteague Inlet, Va.
2095	Wm. H. Shubert	Sch.	-	-	Feb 16 1903	Foundered	Bodie Island, N.C.
2096	Wm. H. Skinner	Sch.	262	1893	Feb 15 1908	Abandoned	45 miles ENE of Frying Pan Shoals, N.C.
2097	William H. Sumner	Sch.	572	1891	Sep 8 1919	Stranded	Top Sail Inlet, N.C.
2098	William H. Yerkes	Sch.	1,498	1901	Feb 7 1915	Stranded	Frying Pan Shoals, N.C.
2099	Wm. Henry	Sch.	52	1870	Nov 24 1904	Stranded	Old Point, Va.
2100	William Hooper	St.s.	7,177	1942	Jul 4 1942	War Loss	75-55-00 N. 27-14-00 W. Steel vessel. Sunk by enemy action.
2101	Wm. J. Lermond	Sc.b.	887	1885	Oct 5 1923	Foundered	Lynn Haven, Va.
2102	Wm. J. Lermond	Sch.	887	1885	Dec 22 1908	Foundered	Currituck Beach, N.C.
2103	William J. Quillen	Sch.	695	1904	Mar 13 1915	Collided	With Norwegian S.S. LALY. Off Cape Hatteras, N.C.
2104	William Watson	Sch.	-	-	Nov 15 1840	Foundered	Bodie Island, N.C.
2105	William Jenkins	St.p.	1,011	1855	Jan 19 1861	Burned	Savannah, Ga.
2106	William L. Walker	Sch.	592	1882	Oct 29 1907	Foundered	40 miles south of Cape Lookout, N.C.
2107	Wm. Lee	Ship	311	-	Jan 20 1862	"Sunk"	On south edge of Rattlesnake Shoal, Maffitt's Channel, Charleston Harbor, S.C. Sunk by Union forces to block harbor. Part of second "Stone Fleet".
2108	William Lowndes	St.p.	220	1823	Dec 28 1823	Burned	Flowery Gap, S.C.

NO.	NAME OF VESSEL	RIG	TONS	BUILT	DATE		CAUSE	PLACE AND COMMENT
2109	William Muir	Brig	-	-	Apr 1	1871	Unknown	Currituck Beach, N.C.
2110	William R.	Ol.s.	57	1951	Dec 8	1962	Collided	With trawler MISS JEANNETTE. 25-00 N. 83-00 W. In area of Dry Tortugas, Fla.
2111	William R. Wilson	Sch.	1,385	1908	Jan 13	1912	Stranded	Pickles Reef, Fla.
2112	William Russell	Sch.	63	1907	Nov 29	1925	Foundered	Olympia, Fla.
2113	William Selden	St.p.	378	1851	May 10	1862	Burned	Norfolk, Va.
2114	William W. Converse	Sch.	745	1886	Oct 18	1910	Stranded	Halifax River Beach, Fla. 3 lives lost.
2115	Willie H. Child	Sch.	626	1888	Aug 17	1911	Stranded	Beach Gull Shoal, N.C.
2116	Wilmington	St.p.	229	1829	Dec 10	1838	Stranded	Biscayne Bay, Fla.
2117	Winifred A. Foran	Sch.	858	1881	Feb 13	1906	Abandoned	Off Cape Hatteras, N.C.
2118	Winifred S. Shuster	Sch.	1,481	1904	Oct 27	1911	Stranded	Isaac Shoal, Fla.
2119	Winthrop	Sch.	841	1898	May 27	1915	Foundered	15 miles from Assateague Light, Va.
2120	Winthrop	St.s.	189	1920	Jul 15	1920	Foundered	Cape Henry, Va. Steel vessel. 2 lives lost (18).
2121	Witchcraft	Clipper	1,130	1850	Apr 8	1861	Foundered	Cape Hatteras, N.C.
2122	Withlacoochee No.9	Brg.	119	1901	Jun 12	1906	Foundered	Port Inglis, Fla.
2123	Wolseley	Bark	-	-	Apr 11	1889	Unknown	Big Kinnakeet Life Saving Station, N.C.
2124	Wonderland	Brg.	259	1906	Jul 8	1917	Foundered	Belleville, W.Va.
2125	Wood	-	-	-	Jun 3	1942	Unknown	28 miles, 188° from Cape Lookout Lighthouse, N.C.
2126	Wustrow (Ger.)	Brig	-	-	Aug 29	1893	Wrecked	West of Oak Island Life Saving Station, N.C.
2127	Y.P. 389	Ol.s.	86	1819	Jun 19	1942	Unknown	Cape Hatteras, N.C. Anti-submarine chaser.
2128	Yankee	St.p.	86	1819	Mar 7	1822	Snagged	Alexandria, Va.
2129	Yenrut	St.s.	541	1891	Oct 20	1918	Foundered	25-00-00 N. 72-15-00 W. Steel vessel. 5 lives lost.
2130	York	-	-	-	Aug 9	1861	Unknown	Off Cape Hatteras, N.C. Reported as Confederate privateer vessel.
2131	York	Frgt.	1,660*	-	Unknown		Unknown	22 miles offshore from the Wright Brothers Monument, Kill Devil Hills, N.C. 36-03-30 N. 75-12-36 W. Depth 100'.
2132	Yorkmar	St.s.	5,612	1919	Oct 9	1943	War Loss	56-35-00 N. 19-24-00 W. Steel vessel. Sunk by enemy action.
2133	Zaccheus Sherman	Sch.	767	1880	Feb 28	1913	Stranded	Gull Shoal, N.C.
2134	Zalophus	Ga.y.	300	1922	Feb 4	1932	Stranded	Sarasota, Fla.
2135	Zenith	Ga.s.	58	1914	Oct 16	1949	Burned	At junction of Satilla River and St. Andrews Sound, near Brunswick, Ga.
2136	65	Brg.	221	1910	May 12	1932	Foundered	Phillip Inlet, Fla.
2137	66	Brg.	221	1910	May 12	1932	Foundered	Phillip Inlet, Fla.
2138	604 Steel	Brg.	1,257	1906	Apr 14	1927	Foundered	Cape Charles, Va. Steel vessel.

SECTION THREE

NO.	NAME OF VESSEL	RIG	TONS	BUILT	DATE		CAUSE	PLACE AND COMMENT
1	A.B. Chambers	St.p.	410	1854	Sep 24	1860	Snagged	Mouth of Missouri River.
2	A.B.L. 61	Brg.	292	1923	May 23	1942	Foundered	At Tarpley Lower Light, Mile 461.7, near Greenville, Miss. Steel vessel.
3	A.B.L. 92	Brg.	486	1939	Aug 1	1943	Foundered	Near Galveston, Texas. Steel vessel.
4	A.B.L. 106	Brg.	486	1927	Jul 22	1946	Lost	Whiteman's Fleet, above Gretna, La., west bank of Mississippi River. Steel vessel.
5	A.B.L. 140	Brg.	486	1936	May 29	1946	Foundered	Off Ashbrook Light, Lower Mississippi River. Steel vessel.
6	A.B.L. 145	Brg.	486	1936	Feb 10	1943	Foundered	14 miles below Lake Providence, La. Steel vessel.
7	A.B.L. 968	Brg.	620	1951	Mar 30	1955	Foundered	In Mississippi River, about Mile 437.1, 5-1/2 miles above Vicksburg, Miss. Steel vessel.
8	ACBL	Brg.	1,054	1958	Sep 9	1965	Foundered	Approximately Mile 90, in Lower Mississippi River.
9	A.C.H.	Brg.	258	1890	Mar 8	1914	Stranded	Old River, Texas.
10	ACO 22	Brg.	623	1954	Apr 12	1961	Collided	With st.s. BRAGE. At New Orleans, La. Steel vessel.
11	A.G. Brown	St.p.	150	1857	Dec 30	1868	Collided	With German TEUTONIC. 45 miles below New Orleans, La.
12	A.G.T. No.34	Brg.	265	1937	Feb 1	1959	Collided	With Dolphin Island Bridge, Ala. Steel vessel.
13	A.J.L.	Ol.s.	64	1954	Jul 1	1960	Stranded	Off coast of Mexico, about 40 miles south of Brazos Santiago Pass, Texas.
14	A.L. Bisso	St.s.	434	1899	Sep 19	1947	Foundered	In Mississippi River, foot of Walnut Street, New Orleans, La. Steel vessel.
15	Aaron	St.p.	261	1848	Oct 8	1849	Burned	New Orleans, La.
16	Aberdeen	St.p.	209	1848	Dec 21	1851	Snagged	Devil Shoals, Ala.
17	Acadia	St.p.	343	1859	Jul 17	1863	Burned	Yalobusha River, Miss.
18	Active	St.w.	105	1867	Jan 29	1877	Lost	Brashear, La.
19	Addie F. Cole	Sch.	76	1867	Apr 15	1908	Foundered	North Anclote Channel, Fla.
20	Adriatic	Ol.s.	120	1953	Feb 25	1960	Foundered	22-20-00 N. 109-10-00 W.
21	Advance	St.w.	166	1853	Nov 14	1859	Snagged	Peavey Ledge, Ala.
22	Adventurer	Ol.s.	201	1928	Nov 22	1932	Burned	San Lazarus Cape, Mexico.
23	Afton	St.p.	287	1851	Apr 13	1855	Burned	Yazoo River, Miss.
24	Afton, Jr.	St.p.	155	1856	Dec 8	1858	Snagged	19 miles above Baton Rouge, La.
25	Ahwaneda	Ga.s.	71	1912	May 28	1917	Stranded	Boco de Carrizal, Mexico.
26	Aimee	Ol.y.	101	1924	Feb 12	1932	Burned	Puerto Escondido, Mexico.
27	Ajax	St.p.	120	1836	Mar 3	1841	Snagged	Jeanerette, La.
28	Ajax	Drg.	136	1910	Mar 6	1947	Foundered	Lake Ponchartrain, about 6 miles south by east of Tchefunta River Lighthouse, La.
29	Ala	Ol.s.	59	1952	Jul 16	1963	Stranded	About 7 miles northeast of Green's Bayou, Texas.
30	Alabama	St.p.	218	1817		1824	Collided	With NATCHEZ. New Orleans, La.
31	Alabama	St.p.	194	1826	May 8	1826	Burned	Vernon, Ala.
32	Alabama	St.p.	162	1841	Feb 12	1847	Snagged	Covington, La.
33	Alabama	St.p.	213	1852	Mar 15	1856	Exploded	Minden, La. 9 lives lost.
34	Alabama	Ol.w.	162	-	Sep 24	1925	Burned	Claiborne's, Ala.
35	Alamo	St.p.	66	1849	Jun 1	1856	Lost	At 19 Mile Post, west of Harvey Locks, Intracoastal Canal, La.
36	Alatok	Ol.s.	70	1942	Sep 23	1965	Burned	Between the mouths of the San Benard and Colorado Rivers, Texas.
37	Albatross	Ol.s.	50	1944	Mar 29	1955	Burned	Atchafalaya Bay, La.
38	Albert	Brg.	140	1906	Aug 25	1911	Foundered	Trinity Bay, Texas. 4 lives lost.
39	Albert Gallatin	St.p.	94	1839	Dec 21	1841	Exploded	Alacrane Reef, Mexico. 1 life lost.
40	Albert	Sch.	56	1893	Aug 16	1916	Foundered	Lake Providence, La.
41	Albert Pearce	St.p.	401	1863	May 19	1867	Burned	28-40-00 N. 88-22-00 W. Steel vessel. Freighter. Gulf of Mexico.
42	Alcoa Puritan	St.s.	6,759	-	May 6	1942	War Loss	Bayou Plaquemine, La.
43	Alexander Porter	St.p.	156	1839	Mar 9	1841	Snagged	Prudhomme Landing, La.
44	Alexander Speer	St.w.	171	1864	Nov 12	1866	Snagged	Bonnet Carre, La.
45	Alexandria	St.p.	95	1820	Feb 1	1823	Stranded	New Orleans, La.
46	Alexandria	Ga.s.	85	1906	Feb 5	1931	Burned	Chandeleur Island, La.
47	Alfhild	Bark	-	-	Oct 1	1891	Unknown	

NO.	NAME OF VESSEL	RIG	TONS	BUILT	DATE		CAUSE	PLACE AND COMMENT
48	Alfred	Ol.s.	68	1918	Nov 26	1942	Stranded	At Tamaulipas, Mexico.
49	Alfred G. Rose	St.w.	126	1857	Sep 27	1860	Snagged	Demopolis, Ala.
50	Alice	St.p.	149	1900	Sep 29	1915	Stranded	New Orleans, La.
51	Alice	Ol.s.	52	1912	Oct 31	1945	Burned	3 miles east of Vermilion Locks, La.
52	Alice	Ol.s.	97	1961	Dec 3	1962	Foundered	In Gulf of Mexico, approximately 20 miles NNE of Progreso Yucatan, Mexico.
53	Alice B. Miller	St.p.	90	1904	Mar 26	1915	Burned	Vicksburg, Miss.
54	Alice M	St.p.	185	1865	Oct 3	1867	Stranded	Galveston, Texas.
55	Alice W. Glaze	St.w.	161	1853	Mar	1857	Burned	Bayou Sara, La.
56	Allegheny	Sch.	396	1904	May 20	1921	Foundered	26-42-00 N. 86-48-00 W. Steel vessel.
57	Allen Glover	St.p.	241	1847	Apr 20	1854	Collided	With P. DALMAU. Alexandria, La.
58	Aloe	St.p.	242	1867	Jan 26	1869	Snagged	Battleground, La.
59	Alone	St.w.	80	1864	Jul 5	1868	Snagged	Bayou Lafourche, La.
60	Altair	Ol.s.	84	1946	Jun 3	1961	Foundered	22-35-00 N. 86-30-00 W. Steel vessel.
61	Alton	St.p.	344	1847	May 7	1855	Burned	Yazoo River, Miss.
62	Amatlan (Mex.)	Frgt.	-	-	Sep 4	1942	Unknown	22-48-00 N. 97-20-00 W.
63	Amazon	St.p.	296	1827	Nov 21	1831	Snagged	Palmyra Island, Miss.
64	Amazone	St.s.	677	-	May 7	1942	Unknown	27-23-39 N. 80-03-00 W. Steel vessel. Depth 42'.
65	Ambassador	St.p.	324	1851	Feb 25	1854	Burned	Mobile, Ala.
66	America	St.w.	427	1898	Aug 13	1926	Foundered	New Orleans, La.
67	American	St.p.	190	1902	Apr 4	1915	Burned	Mobile, Ala.
68	American Belle	Ol.s.	199	1940	Feb 2	1950	Burned	35 miles north of Cedros Island, Mexico.
69	American Clipper	Ol.s.	225	1928	Jan 16	1955	Stranded	About 3 miles west of Manzanillo Point, Mexico.
70	Amiga Mia	Ol.s.	63	1936	Nov 18	1954	Burned	At entrance to Brazos Santiago Pass, Texas. 26-04-00 N. 97-07-45 W.
71	Amor Da Patria	Ol.s.	68	1926	Dec 27	1952	Foundered	In bay at Cape San Lucas, Mexico.
72	Anaconda	Brg.	2,217	1921	Feb 7	1946	Foundered	28-28-00 N. 86-17-00 W.
73	Anastasia	Ol.s.	61	1952	Feb 8	1959	Stranded	In Gulf of Mexico, about 2 miles northwest of Lobos Island.
74	Ancient Mariner	Ol.s.	54	1960	Jul 17	1967	Burned	Southeast of Cameron, La. 20-40-00 N. 93-05-00 W.
75	Andes	St.w.	197	1910	Jul 1	1931	Foundered	Plaquemine, La.
76	Andrew Jackson	St.p.	98	1833	May 16	1838	Snagged	Mobile, Ala.
77	Andrew Jackson	Frgt.	5,999	-	Jul 12	1942	Unknown	23-32-00 N. 81-02-00 W.
78	Angelos	Ol.s.	132	1944	Jun 8	1956	Burned	In Gulf of Mexico, about 60 miles south by east of Point Au Fer Light, off Louisiana coast. 28-27-05 N. 91-34-00 W.
79	Angie	Ol.s.	52	1957	Sep 20	1967	Storm	At Brownsville, Texas.
80	Anglo-Celt	St.p.	367	1853	May 21	1855	Collided	With LOUISIANA. New Orleans, La. 1 life lost.
81	Anglo-Norman	-	-	-	Dec 14	1850	Exploded	New Orleans, La. 100 lives lost.
82	Anglo-Norman	St.p.	558	1849	Apr 7	1862	Burned	New Orleans, La.
83	Ankla	Sch.	285	1915	Oct 12	1920	Stranded	24-02-00 N. 97-46-00 W.
84	Anna	St.p.	156	1849	Sep 3	1852	Snagged	Atchafalays Bayou, La.
85	Anna E	St.p.	86	1864	Nov 15	1871	Snagged	Bayou Teche, La.
86	Anna Laura McKenney	Sch.	1,021	1917	Mar 3	1921	Stranded	Off Puerto, Mexico.
87	Anna M.	Ol.s.	259	1941	Jun 16	1954	Burned	18 miles southwest of San Martin Island, Mexico.
88	Anna M.	Sch.	100	1954	Feb 15	1963	Burned	About 55 miles south-southeast of Aransas Pass, Texas.
89	Anna Tardy	St.p.	71	1900	Nov 15	1905	Snagged	Miggs Ferry, Red River, La.
90	Anne Hardy	Ol.s.	56	1946	Nov 15	1951	Foundered	About 25-10-00 N. 83-20-00 W.
91	Annie	St.p.	200	1863		1889	Burned	Point Clear, Ala.
92	Annie Murphy	Sch.	589	1905	May 2	1923	Stranded	South of Chandeleur Light, Gulf of Mexico.
93	Antelope	St.p.	587	1853	Sep 27	1864	Snagged	New Orleans, La.
94	Antionette	Sch.	299	1907	Nov 15	1916	Stranded	90 miles east of Progresso, Mexico.

NO.	NAME OF VESSEL	RIG	TONS	BUILT	DATE		CAUSE	PLACE AND COMMENT
95	Antoinette Douglas	St.p.	242	1849	Nov 25	1850	Exploded	Alabama River. 9 lives lost.
96	Anton Wilbert	St.p.	52	1900	Jan 22	1909	Burned	Franklin, La.
97	Anton Wilbert	St.p.	185	1920	Sep 3	1923	Burned	Bayou Plaquemine, La.
98	Apalachicola	St.p.	148	1843	May	1848	Burned	Kings Rocks, Ala.
99	Apalachicola	Ol.s.	59	1958	Oct 15	1961	Burned	About 50 miles northwest of Campeche, Mexico.
100	Arawak	-	201	-	Sep 23	1941	Unknown	29-36-00 N. 80-54-00 W.
101	Ardilla (Span.)	Bkn.	-	-		1808	Foundered	Gulf of Mexico. 18-gun vessel. All lives lost.
102	Argo	St.p.	99	1856	May 25	1863	Burned	Sunflower River, Miss.
103	Arkadia	St.s.	2,206	-	Oct 11	1910	Foundered	Sailed from New Orleans, La., and has not since reported. All lives (37) lost.
104	Arkansas	St.w.	246	1852	Jan 26	1856	Snagged	Mobile River, Ala.
105	Arkansas	St.w.	154	1856	Feb 19	1859	Snagged	Bayou Sara, La.
106	Arkansas No.4	St.p.	281	1844	Jun 21	1849	Collided	With GENERAL HAMER. Rigolets, La.
107	Arkansas No.5	St.p.	162	1845	Jun 5	1856	Snagged	Mobile, Ala.
108	Arkansaw	St.p.	51	1820		1827	Snagged	Mobile, Ala.
109	Arkla	St.w.	68	1904	Jun 16	1934	Burned	Patterson, La.
110	Arrow	Ol.s.	152	1943	Nov 11	1955	Burned	About 50 miles northeast of Aransas Pass, Texas.
111	Athenian	St.p.	110	1838	Jul 15	1841	Burned	Grand Prairie, La.
112	Atlanta	St.p.	330	1865	Jan 12	1877	Snagged	Tomigbee River, Ala.
113	Atlanta	Ol.s.	55	1951	Dec 18	1957	Foundered	Vicinity of Mustang Island, Corpus Christi, Texas. 27-47-00 N. 97-07-00 W.
114	Atlantic No.2	St.w.	53	1863	Oct 9	1865	Snagged	Demopolis, Ala.
115	Attakapas	St.p.	123	1827	Sep 29	1831	Burned	Algiers, La.
116	Augusta	St.p.	290	1834	Jun 4	1846	Stranded	Brazos River, Texas. 8 lives lost.
117	Augustus B. Harris	Ol.s.	75	1942	Jan 25	1951	Burned	Near Mile Post 13, west of Harvey, La., on Gulf Intracoastal Canal.
118	Aurora	Tanker	7,050	-	May 10	1942	War Loss	28-35-00 N. 90-00-00 W. 1 life lost (45). SALVAGED.
119	Austin	St.p.	603	1860		1876	Unknown	Mississippi River. Steel vessel. Captured as Confederate steamer "Donegal" and redocumented on Nov. 11, 1865.
120	Autocrat	St.p.	846	1847	Feb 10	1851	Collided	With MAGNOLIA. Bayou Goula, La. 10 lives lost.
121	Autocrat	St.p.	662	1860	Apr 10	1868	Burned	Algiers, La.
122	Aztec	Ol.s.	67	1926	Dec 6	1952	Foundered	7 miles off Rosarita Beach, Mexico.
123	BB 5	Brg.	964	1932	Dec 17	1963	Foundered	At Mile 24.9 (Ahp) and Cable Crossing, in Mississippi River at Buras, La.
124	B.C. Levi	St.w.	110	1862	Mar 9	1869	Snagged	Shreveport, La.
125	B.E. Clark	St.p.	199	1853	May 30	1860	Burned	New Orleans, La.
126	B and J	Ol.s.	53	1949	May 16	1963	Foundered	About 25 miles south of Port Isabel, Texas.
127	B.J. Adams	St.p.	497	1860	Aug 9	1866	Burned	New Orleans, La.
128	BL 203	Brg.	612	1949	Nov 26	1958	Foundered	At Mile 885, Lower Mississippi River. Steel vessel.
129	B.M. Runyan	St.p.	443	1857	Jul 21	1864	Snagged	Gaines Landing, Miss. 100 lives lost.
130	B.P. Cheney	St.p.	247	1859	Jul 14	1863	Burned	Yazoo River, Miss.
131	Baddacock	St.s.	426	1920	Nov 25	1920	Stranded	Near Port Aransas, Texas. Steel vessel.
132	Badger State	St.w.	127	1852	Dec 14	1862	Stranded	Chain of Rocks, Mississippi River.
133	Badger State	Ol.s.	1,538	1912	Jan 14	1946	Foundered	Mouth of Grijalva River, Gulf of Mexico. Steel vessel.
134	Bags	Ol.s.	50	1952	Mar 22	1967	Burned	24-24-00 N. 82-25-00 W.
135	Baja California (Hon.)	Frgt.	811*	-	Jul 18	1942	War Loss	25-29-00 N. 82-27-00 W.
136	Baltic	St.p.	407	1832	Apr 1	1842	Collided	With MAID OF KENTUCKY. Fort Adams, Miss.
137	Baltic	St.p.	399	1856	Nov 3	1860	Exploded	Mobile, Ala. 20 lives lost.
138	Baltic	St.p.	604	1860	May 6	1861	Burned	Algiers, La.
139	Baltimore	St.p.	637	1853	Dec 13	1859	Snagged	Chain of Rocks, Mississippi River.
140	Bar Pilot	Ol.s.	57	1964	Oct 16	1965	Foundered	Approximately 2 miles southwest of Pass A Loutre Whistle Buoy, off coast of Louisiana, Gulf of Mexico.

NO.	NAME OF VESSEL	RIG	TONS	BUILT	DATE	CAUSE	PLACE AND COMMENT
141	Barbara Jean	Ol.s.	57	1947	May 21 1964	Burned	29-15-00 N. 89-51-00 W.
142	Baroid Express	Ol.s.	97	1959	Dec 27 1965	Foundered	28-38-00 N. 90-15-00 W.
143	Barugo	Sch.	2,497	1918	Oct 9 1920	Stranded	North of Tampico, Mexico.
144	Bay Queen	St.p.	471	1896	Mar 27 1929	Burned	Mobile, Ala.
145	Bay Ridge	Brg.	79	1867	Nov 2 1917	Foundered	Progreso, Mexico.
146	Bayard (Nor.)	Frgt.	2,160	-	Jul 6 1942	Unknown	29-19-00 N. 88-50-00 W.
147	Bayou Belle	St.w.	168	1855	Oct 1860	Snagged	Cahaba River, Ala.
148	Bayou City	St.p.	271	1859	Sep 27 1860	Exploded	Trinity Bay, Texas. 7 lives lost.
149	Bayou Sara	St.p.	244	1833	Apr 2 1840	Burned	Algiers, La.
150	Beacon	St.p.	175	1848	1852	Snagged	Lake Pontchartrain, La.
151	Beaver	St.w.	51	1837	Feb 7 1842	Burned	Shreveport, La.
152	Beaver	St.p.	70	1884	Jul 5 1916	Foundered	Mobile River, Ala.
153	Becky Sue	Ol.s.	63	1952	Dec 14 1958	Stranded	On Boca Chica Beach, Texas, 100 feet south of the south jetties of Brazos Santiago Pass.
154	Bect No.2	Ol.s.	97	1966	Sep 5 1967	Burned	In Block 175, Eugene Island area, off coast of Louisiana, Gulf of Mexico.
155	Bees Wing	St.p.	133	1844	Mar 17 1845	Burned	Port Hudson, La. 1 life lost.
156	Belfast	St.p.	780	1854	Nov 19 1860	Stranded	Lake Providence, La.
157	Belfast	St.w.	156	1857	Mar 7 1868	Burned	Tombigbee River, Ala.
158	Bella Donna	St.p.	152	1864	Aug 12 1865	Snagged	50 miles below Alexandria, La.
159	Bellatrix	Ol.s.	63	1952	Jan 16 1964	Foundered	In Gulf of Mexico. 26-15-00 N. 82-08-00 W.
160	Belle of Arkansas	St.p.	224	1842	Aug 6 1850	Lost	New Orleans, La.
161	Belle Claire	Brg.	793	1956	Jan 12 1960	Burned	In the Deer Island Field, about 18 miles southwest of Morgan City, La. Steel.
162	Belle Creole	St.p.	120	1822	Mar 13 1829	Snagged	Natchitoches, La.
163	Belle of Jefferson	St.p.	69	1889	Jun 30 1907	Foundered	New Orleans, La.
164	Belle Poule	St.p.	157	1841	Jul 2 1849	Snagged	Mobile, Ala.
165	Belle Prince	St.p.	68	1879	Jun 26 1907	Foundered	Natchez, Miss.
166	Belle Zane	-	-	-	Jan 8 1845	"Sank"	Mississippi River. 75 lives lost.
167	Belmont	-	1,521*	-	Pre-WWII	Unknown	27-37-00 N. 82-52-00 W.
168	Belvidere	St.p.	808	1851	Oct 5 1868	Stranded	Indianila, Texas. Redocumented "Texas" on Dec. 2, 1865.
169	Ben	Brg.	2,200	1919	Sep 2 1941	Foundered	Gulf of Mexico.
170	Ben Franklin	-	-	1856	Mar 13 1836	Exploded	Mobile, Ala. 20 lives lost.
171	Ben Franklin	St.p.	732	1856	Oct 21 1858	Burned	Ashton, Miss.
172	Ben Hur	St.p.	284	1887	Mar 20 1916	Foundered	Duckport, La. 1 life lost.
173	Ben Lee	St.w.	122	1852	Dec 13 1856	Snagged	Mobile, Ala.
174	Ben McCulloch	St.w.	80	1860	May 26 1868	Burned	Monroe, La. 3 lives lost. Was used as Confederate steamer during Civil War.
175	Ben Sherrod	St.p.	393	1836	May 8 1837	Burned	Black Hawk, La. 72 lives lost.
176	Benefit	St.p.	213	1863	Apr 6 1867	Burned	Starke Landing, Ala.
177	Benjamin Brewster	Tanker	5,950	-	Jul 9 1942	War Loss	29-03-00 N. 90-09-00 W. Steel vessel. Demolished. Depth 15'. 26 lives lost (42).
178	Bentwood	-	2,389	-	Apr 9 1942	Unknown	24-03-30 N. 80-19-30 W. Probably coastal trader lost during war. Also known as "Benwood".
179	Bernadette	Ol.s.	63	1951	Nov 5 1959	Foundered	At Arcas Key, near Campeche, Mexico.
180	Bertha	St.s.	56	1906	Mar 16 1917	Foundered	Off Port Aransas, Texas. All lives (9) lost.
181	Bertha H	Ol.s.	52	1955	Nov 17 1957	Stranded	On Washington Beach, Mexico.
182	Bertha V	Ol.s.	88	1954	Jul 23 1964	Burned	At Freeport, Texas.
183	Bertrand	St.p.	145	1844	Jan 11 1850	Snagged	Bayou Sorrel, La.
184	Bessie H. Dantzler	St.s.	108	1901	Mar 6 1926	Burned	Lake Pontchartrain, La.
185	Betty Ann	Ol.s.	70	1938	May 24 1954	Burned	In Lake Ponchartrain, near Gulfport, Miss.
186	Betty Powell	St.p.	166	1854	May 17 1859	Burned	Galveston, Texas.

NO.	NAME OF VESSEL	RIG	TONS	BUILT	DATE	CAUSE	PLACE AND COMMENT
187	Betty Sca	Ol.s.	72	1953	Mar 21 1966	Stranded	On beach, about 12 miles south of Aransas Pass, Texas.
188	Beverly Jean	Ol.s.	64	1954	Sep 20 1967	Storm	At Brownsville, Texas.
189	Big Horn	St.w.	312	1865	Apr 10 1873	Foundered	Bayou Bartholomew, La.
190	Big Louie	Ol.s.	53	1956	Apr 26 1958	Foundered	In Mississippi River, about 100 feet off left bank near Audubon Park, La., at mile point 6.
191	Big Mama	Ol.s.	73	1954	Jan 10 1962	Stranded	On Boca Chica Beach, Texas, about 1/4 mile south of the South Brazos Santiago jetty.
192	Bill Henderson	St.w.	104	1864	Feb 18 1876	Stranded	New Orleans, La.
193	Bill Holmes	Ol.s.	65	1953	Sep 10 1961	Storm	Freeport, Texas.
194	Billy (Bowlegs) Rogers	-	-	-	1840	Unknown	At west Pass, entrance to Apalachicola Bay, Fla. Pirate of Gulf area. Reported to have lost up to as much as $4 million in treasure.
195	Billy Boy	Ol.s.	50	1943	Aug 14 1957	Burned	In Mississippi River at 12 mile point on east bank, foot of Ravan Street, Harahan, La.
196	Bio Bio	St.p.	822	1859	Mar 22 1863	Burned	New Orleans, La.
197	Black Diamond	Brg.	121	1875	Oct 11 1906	Collided	With st.s. JOSEPHINE, Mobile, Ala.
198	Black Gold	Ol.s.	103	1927	Dec 16 1955	Foundered	Gulf of Mexico, 29-05-00 N. 95-32-00 W.
199	Black Hawk	St.p.	137	1833	Apr 3 1838	Foundered	Red River, La. 5 lives lost.
200	Blanche	St.p.	84	1906	Dec 21 1919	Foundered	Warrior River, Ala.
201	Blonde Rebel	Ol.s.	63	1943	Aug 10 1961	Stranded	Off Mexican coast, about 18 miles south of Port Isabel, Texas.
202	Blue Chip	Ol.s.	70	1943	Jan 2 1958	Foundered	In entrance to San Pedro River, Frontera Tobasco, Mexico.
203	Blue Fin	Ol.s.	79	1954	May 21 1957	Foundered	10 miles south of Port Aransas jetties, Port Aransas, Texas.
204	Blue Ridge	Ga.y.	72	1917	Nov 12 1921	Foundered	New Orleans, La. Missing from port.
205	Blue Stack No.79	Brg.	669	1951	Mar 1 1954	Stranded	13 miles west of Edgmont Key, 27-35-00 N. 83-06-00 W. Steel vessel.
206	Blue Star	Ol.s.	281	1943	Jun 10 1956	Stranded	At East Triangulas Island, Gulf of Mexico, near Campeche, Mexico.
207	Blue Water I	Brg.	641	1957	Oct 6 1964	Storm	In Gulf of Mexico, in Block 104, West Delta, off coast of Louisiana.
208	Bluff City	St.p.	252	1854	Oct 20 1859	Stranded	Sayder Landing, Yazoo River, Miss.
209	Bob	Brg.	589	1916	Dec 8 1916	Foundered	Gulf of Mexico. All lives (40) lost.
210	Bob Blanks	St.p.	265	1903	Mar 2 1912	Burned	Raccouri Landing, La.
211	Bob Francis	Ol.s.	51	1941	Sep 4 1950	Burned	In Gulf Intracoastal Waterway at mile 116, west of Harvey Lock, La.
212	Boca Chica	Ol.s.	65	1957	Jan 22 1968	Foundered	About 50 miles south of Port Isabel, Texas, in Gulf of Mexico.
213	Bogue Homer	St.p.	105	1836	1837	Snagged	Mobile, Ala.
214	Bogue Houma	St.p.	114	1839	Apr 14 1843	Snagged	Bayou de Glaize, La.
215	Bois d'Arc	St.p.	182	1843	Dec 8 1847	Snagged	Bayou Plaquemine, La.
216	Bolikow	Brg.	2,551	1918	Dec 23 1920	Burned	Galveston, Texas. 4 lives lost (15).
217	Bonita	St.p.	211	1857	May 7 1860	Burned	Bayou Sara, La.
218	Bonne Fortune	Ol.s.	98	1937	Oct 4 1964	Hurricane	Vicinity of Buoy #5, Lower Mobile Bay, Ala.
219	Boreta	St.s.	3,349	1918	Jul 14 1920	Burned	Near Tampico, Mexico.
220	Bosiljka (Yugo-Slav.)	Frgt.	1,810*	-	Jun 19 1942	Unknown	24-58-00 N. 82-00-00 W.
221	Bounty	Ol.s.	52	1944	Nov 15 1953	Burned	On beach at Padre Island, 40 miles north of Port Isabel, Texas.
222	Bradford C. French	Sch.	968	1884	Jul 15 1916	Foundered	60 miles east of South Pass, Miss.
223	Brazos	Ol.s.	74	1951	May 20 1959	Burned	While moored at docks of the Tidewater Seafood Co., Freeport, Texas.
224	Breakwater	St.s.	1,065	1880	Oct 4 1918	Stranded	Point Zapotitlan, Mexico. Iron vessel. 1 life lost.
225	Bridgewater	St.p.	160	1837	Dec 1 1859	Snagged	Vicksburg-New Orleans.
226	Brilliant	-	-	-	Sep 29 1851	Exploded	Mississippi River. 100 lives lost.
227	British Pride	Ol.s.		1951	Oct 15 1952	Foundered	23-50-00 N. 86-30-00 W.
228	Brownsville	St.p.	99	1845	Jun 11 1849	Snagged	Brownsville, Texas.
229	Bruce	Brg.	358	1904	Feb 15 1908	Stranded	Galveston, Texas.
230	Brunette	St.p.	207	1842	Jan 28 1847	Snagged	Millikins Bend, La.

NO.	NAME OF VESSEL	RIG	TONS	BUILT	DATE	CAUSE	PLACE AND COMMENT
231	Buccaneer	Ol.s.	64	1954	Nov 8 1965	Foundered	About 20 miles west of Southwest Pass, off coast of Louisiana.
232	Buck Elk	St.p.	58	1900	Sep 21 1909	Foundered	Vicksburg, Miss.
233	Buckeye	St.p.	170	1837	Mar 1 1844	Collided	With DeSOTO, Atchafalaya, La. 80 lives lost. Also reported as occurring on Feb. 28, 1844.
234	Buckpasser	Ol.s.	51	1945	Apr 4 1968	Burned	In the Atchafalaya River, approximately 1/2 mile north of Eugene Island Light, La.
235	Bull	Ol.s.	59	1956	Apr 17 1965	Foundered	At 2 miles SSW of West Cameron Jetties, La.
236	Butchie Boy	Ol.s.	60	1958	Mar 14 1967	Collided	With submerged object. About 150 miles south of Brownsville, Texas.
237	CB 220	Brg.	639	1951	Jun 2 1958	Foundered	In Mississippi River at New Orleans, La., off Congress Street Wharf. Steel.
238	CB 1417	Brg.	780	1952	Sep 9 1965	Hurricane	At New Orleans, La.
239	C.C. Wehrum	Sch.	395	1887	Jan 6 1924	Stranded	El Cuyo, Mexico.
240	C.J. Reynolds	St.p.	71	1901	Aug 3 1915	Burned	Baton Rouge, La.
241	CL 602	Brg.	885	1964	Apr 21 1965	Foundered	In Mississippi River at Vicksburg, Miss.
242	C.M. Boggs	Ol.s.	86	1943	Jul 19 1959	Collided	With submerged object. About 4 miles off Southwest Pass of the Mississippi River.
243	C.M. Depew	St.s.	176	1901	Sep 11 1961	Foundered	In the San Jacinto River, Houston, Texas. Steel vessel.
244	C.M. Pate	St.p.	82	1904	Aug 14 1912	Burned	Gramercy, La. 2 lives lost.
245	CNC 64	Brg.	952	1964	Sep 10 1965	Foundered	In Mississippi River in vicinity of Westwego & Destrehan, La.
246	C.P. Baker	Brg.	3,891	1945	Jun 30 1964	Foundered	28-25-00 N. 91-34-00 W.
247	C.T. 408	Brg.	406	1935	Mar 23 1952	Foundered	Mile 177.3, Upper Mississippi River. Steel vessel.
248	C.T. 500	Brg.	401	1937	Jul 2 1955	Foundered	Near foot of Walnut Street, New Orleans, La. Steel vessel.
249	CU 708	Brg.	633	1941	Jul 30 1969	Foundered	At West Delta Blocl 136, 30 miles south of Grand Terre Island, La.
250	C.W. Dorrance	St.p.	340	1857	Jan 15 1870	Snagged	Alabama River.
251	C. Connor	St.p.	144	1845	Jan 3 1848	Snagged	Bayou Catalpa, La.
252	C. Woodhouse		–	–	1877	Unknown	Off Brazos, Texas.
253	Caddo	St.p.	188	1848	Feb 15 1852	Foundered	New Orleans, La.
254	Caicos Trader	Ol.s.	142	1944	Mar 20 1949	Foundered	About 60 miles off coast of Yucatan, Mexico.
255	California	St.p.	269	1850	Apr 4 1853	Snagged	16 miles below Greenville, Miss.
256	Camarones	Ol.s.	137	1944	Jan 22 1953	Foundered	17-45-00 N. 88-00-00 W.
257	Campeche Gal	Ol.s.	64	1957	Jul 21 1959	Burned	At Campeche Banks, off Mexico.
258	Canebrake	St.p.	162	1840	Jan 1 1845	Stranded	Warsaw, Ala.
259	Cannon Ball	Ol.s.	56	1951	Dec 2 1953	Foundered	In Gulf of Mexico, at the seaward end of the north jetties, at Santiago Brazos Pass.
260	Canonchet	St.p.	147	1851	Oct 16 1857	Burned	Mobile, Ala.
261	Cape Horn	Sch.	77	1903	Sep 18 1919	Foundered	Off Point Isabel Light, Texas.
262	Capitol	St.p.	448	1855	Jun 28 1862	Burned	Liverpool, Miss.
263	Capitola	St.p.	137	1860	Nov 15 1865	Snagged	Shreveport, La.
264	Captain Bud	St.s.	203	1898	Jul 16 1937	Burned	Vicksburg, Miss. Steel vessel.
265	Captain Eddie	Drg.	333	1944	Nov 9 1957	Burned	At Jahncke Shipyard, Madisonville, La.
266	Captain Gene	Ol.s.	65	1945	Jun 23 1957	Burned	In Gulf of Mexico, about 25 miles northeast of Port Isabel, Texas.
267	Captain George	St.w.	134	1907	Jul 7 1930	Foundered	Monola Landing, La. 2 lives lost (19).
268	Captain Irish	Ol.s.	63	1953	Dec 17 1959	Burned	In Gulf of Mexico, about 185 miles southeast of Port Isabel, Texas.
269	Captain Irish	Ol.s.	74	1963	Feb 25 1965	Stranded	On Arcas Reef, off coast of Mexico, Gulf of Mexico.
270	Capt. Jimmie	Ol.s.	74	1950	Jan 17 1962	Burned	In Gulf of Mexico, 12 miles south of Joseph Harbor and about 35 miles east of Cameron, La.
271	Captain Joe	Ol.s.	74	1957	Feb 13 1968	Collided	With submerged object. 20 miles SSE of Horn Island Sea Buoy, Gulf of Mexico.
272	Captain Pete	Ol.s.	69	1953	Jun 22 1966	Collided	With west jetty. At Freeport, Texas.
273	Captain Robert	Ol.s.	66	1946	Feb 28 1962	Stranded	On Mexican coast, about 30 miles south of Vera Cruz, Mexico.
274	Captain Sam	St.s.	92	1873	Jan 28 1920	Collided	With barge GEN'L PETTIBONE. 5 miles off Beaumont, Texas.
275	Captain Steve	Ol.s.	71	1958	Aug 18 1968	Stranded	On sand bar, approximately 3 miles north of Port Mansfield, Texas.

NO.	NAME OF VESSEL	RIG	TONS	BUILT	DATE	CAUSE	PLACE AND COMMENT
276	Captain Walling	Ol.s.	59	1952	May 16 1959	Stranded	About 3 miles south of Bryant Beach, Texas.
277	Capt. Wes Robinson	Ol.s.	81	1941	Sep 1946	Burned	Pascagoula River, Pascagoula, Miss.
278	Captiva II	Ga.y.	279	1915	Apr 6 1942	Burned	Corpus Christi, Texas.
279	Carabesset	St.p.	202	1863	May 1 1870	Snagged	Labadieville, La.
280	Carl Tide	Ol.s.	185	1957	Dec 18 1965	Foundered	In Gulf of Mexico. 28-54-00 N. 90-40-00 W.
281	Carma	Ol.y.	149	1913	Feb 1 1934	Foundered	Mazatlan, Mexico.
282	Carol Faye	Ol.s.	111	1953	Nov 27 1959	Burned	Off the Louisiana coast, near Tiger Shoals.
283	Carolina Explorer	Ol.s.	50	1954	Dec 20 1963	Foundered	Off Bayou La Betre, Ala.
284	Caroline	St.p.	78	1828	Mar 12 1834	Burned	Plaquemine, La.
285	Caroline	-	-	-	Mar 5 1854	Snagged	Mississippi River. 50 lives lost.
286	Caroline	St.w.	198	1863	May 15 1870	Snagged	Red River, La.
287	Carolyn	St.w.	72	1922	Nov 25 1934	Burned	Glandale, Miss.
288	Carrabulle	St.s.	5,030	1920	May 26 1942	War Loss	26-18-00 N. 89-28-00 W. Tanker. Steel vessel. 22 lives lost. Sunk by enemy action.
289	Carrie B. Schwing	St.p.	98	1904	Feb 28 1912	Burned	Bayou Natchez, La.
290	Carrie B. Schwing	St.w.	63	1912	Jan 17 1946	Foundered	Standard Oil dock, Baton Rouge, La.
291	Carrie Poole	St.w.	154	1865	Jul 27 1870	Burned	Algiers, La.
292	Carrie Thomas	-	-	-	1880	Unknown	Off Padre Island, Texas.
293	Carrollton	St.p.	185	1831	Oct 11 1836	Exploded	Baton Rouge, La. 15 lives lost.
294	Caspian	St.p.	199	1832	May 6 1840	Burned	Mobile, Ala.
295	Caspian	St.p.	248	1851	Mar 3 1854	Snagged	Red River, La.
296	Castine	St.s.	836	1893	Dec 11 1924	Foundered	South West Pass, La. Steel vessel.
297	Catania	St.s.	3,347	1881	Jan 7 1920	Stranded	South Pass, Mississippi River, La. Iron vessel.
298	Catherine	St.s.	55	1897	Jan 21 1928	Burned	Slidell, La.
299	Catherine J	Ol.s.	54	1953	Apr 19 1957	Foundered	In Mississippi River, near Poverty Point, La. Steel vessel.
300	Cathy and Barney	Ol.s.	54	1945	Sep 19 1963	Burned	About 30 miles south of East Cote Blanche Bay, La.
301	Cauto	St.s.	3,570	1916	Nov 28 1937	Stranded	Off western breakwater at Puerto Mexico, Mexico. Steel vessel.
302	Cavalier	Ol.s.	57	1951	Nov 26 1965	Collided	With north jetty. At entrance to Port Isabel Harbor, Port Isabel, Texas.
303	Caviare	Sch.	62	1891	Jul 7 1916	Foundered	Alacrane Reef, Mexico.
304	Celeste Joan	Ol.s.	57	1951	Jan 29 1966	Stranded	About 1000 yards west of Fort Jefferson, Dry Tortugas, Gulf of Mexico.
305	Celestino Arias	Ol.s.	63	1952	Sep 26 1955	Foundered	300 miles northeast of Palmas Point, Mexico.
306	Cephas Starret	Sch.	-	-	Mar 29 1888	Unknown	Galveston Island, Texas.
307	Ceres	St.p.	217	1853	Oct 9 1862	Exploded	St. Joseph Island, La. 12 lives lost.
308	Chalmette	Ol.s.	108	1915	Nov 25 1957	Foundered	In Mississippi River, Algiers, La. Steel vessel.
309	Champion	St.p.	148	1843	Apr 7 1849	Exploded	New Orleans, La. 3 lives lost.
310	Champion No.5	St.p.	184	1863	Apr 26 1864	Burned	Red River, La.
311	Chancellor	St.p.	440	1833	Apr 30 1841	Burned	Oyster Bayou, La. 6 lives lost.
312	Charles Belcher	St.p.	823	1852	Feb 4 1854	Burned	New Orleans, La. 2 lives lost.
313	Charles Braley	Ga.s.	3,253	1917	Jul 25 1922	Burned	Off Tampico, Mexico. Steel vessel.
314	Charles K. Schull	Sch.	884	1889	Feb 4 1917	Foundered	Gulf of Mexico.
315	Charles L. Bass	St.p.	103	1836	Nov 22 1842	Snagged	Mobile, Ala.
316	Charles May	St.p.	94	1913	Oct 18 1916	Foundered	Mobile River, Ala.
317	Chas. Schreiner	Ol.s.	68	1952	Oct 3 1967	Foundered	Off Matagorda, Texas.
318	Charleston	St.p.	84	1835	Mar 17 1842	Snagged	Natchez, Miss.
319	Charleston	St.p.	133	1843	May 1848	Snagged	Gibsons Reach, Ala.
320	Charlie Mason	Ol.s.	180	1937	Jun 9 1956	Burned	About 2-1/2 miles off Cameron, La., in Gulf of Mexico.
321	Charm	St.p.	223	1860	Jul 1863	Burned	Big Black River, Miss.
322	Charmer	St.p.	667	1859	Feb 10 1861	Burned	Lauderdale, La. 5 lives lost.

NO.	NAME OF VESSEL	RIG	TONS	BUILT	DATE		CAUSE	PLACE AND COMMENT
323	Cherokee	St.p.	74	1827	Dec 17	1827	Burned	Red River, La.
324	Cherokee	Ol.s.	194	1943	Jun 29	1953	Collided	With tug SWANEE. In Mississippi Sound, 2 miles southeast of Rigolets Bridge, near New Orleans, La.
325	Cherokee	Ol.s.	75	1954	Dec 20	1959	Burned	About 65 miles south of Freeport, Texas.
326	Chicopee	Sch.	55	1909	Sep 29	1915	Foundered	Gulf of Mexico. All lives (9) lost.
327	Chief	St.s.	230	1893	Nov 9	1936	Burned	Atreco dock, in Naches River, Texas. 4 lives lost (11).
328	Chieftain	St.p.	322	1840		1844	Snagged	Choctaw Bend, Mississippi River.
329	Chillicothe	St.p.	253	1837		1838	Snagged	Mississippi River.
330	Chingarora	St.p.	367	1850	Aug 15	1851	Burned	Lake Pontchartrain, La.
331	Chippewa	St.p.	150	1832	Mar 25	1841	Snagged	Mobile, Ala.
332	Choctaw	St.p.	107	1833	Aug 5	1836	Snagged	St. James, La.
333	Choctaw	St.p.	136	1831	Feb 5	1842	Snagged	Mobile, Ala.
334	Choctaw	St.p.	99	1899	Dec 21	1916	Burned	Palo Alta Ledge, Mississippi River.
335	Choctaw	St.s.	96	1884	Mar 18	1922	Burned	Melrose Landing, Miss.
336	Chuckadee II	Ol.s.	72	1943	Oct 18	1963	Collided	With south jetty. Near No.1 Buoy, in Aransas Pass, Texas.
337	Cincinnati	St.p.	276	1851	May 23	1853	Stranded	Brazos, Texas.
338	Cinderella	St.p.	125	1837	Mar 28	1841	Snagged	Bayou Plaquemine, La.
339	Cities Service Empire	Tanker	8,103	-	Feb 22	1942	Unknown	28-00-00 N. 80-22-00 W.
340	Cities Service Toledo	St.s.	8,192	1918	Jun 12	1942	War Loss	29-02-00 N. 92-50-00 W. Tanker. Steel vessel. 15 lives lost (45). Sunk by enemy action. Demolished.
341	City Belle	St.p.	153	1855	May 5	1864	"Gunfire"	Alexandria, La.
342	City Belle	St.p.	215	1854	May 5	1864	Burned	Eggbend, La.
343	City of Cairo	St.p.	894	1864	Sep 1	1873	Burned	New Orleans, La.
344	City of Greenwood	St.p.	97	1899	Nov 16	1906	Snagged	Torras, Red River, La.
345	City of Houston	Ga.s.	1,519	1917	Aug 6	1917	Burned	Orange, Texas.
346	City of Madison	St.p.	419	1860	Sep	1863	Exploded	Vicksburg, Miss. 156 lives lost. Cargo of ammunition.
347	City of Mobile	St.p.	209	1898	Jul 5	1916	Foundered	Mobile River, Ala.
348	City of San Diego	Ol.s.	306	1931	Jan 18	1953	Burned	33 miles south of Coronado Islands, Mexico.
349	City of Shreveport	St.p.	176	1908	Oct 14	1919	Burned	Near Monroe, La.
350	City of Waco	-	-	-	Nov 8	1875	Burned	Galveston, Texas. 53 lives lost.
351	Clara Barrett	Brg.	587	1926	Mar 21	1957	Collided	With bridge pier. At Greenville, Miss. Steel vessel.
352	Clara Marie	Ol.s.	73	1945	Aug 24	1957	Foundered	About 5 miles northwest of San Hipolite Point, Mexico.
353	Clara Woodhouse	-	-	-		1877	Unknown	Off Brazos, Texas.
354	Clarabell	St.p.	200	1860	Jul 24	1864	Burned	Caroline Landing, Miss.
355	Clare	St.s.	3,372	1915	May 20	1942	War Loss	21-33-00 N. 84-39-00 W. Freighter. Steel vessel. Sunk by enemy action.
356	Clare Ann K	Ol.s.	61	1947	Oct 22	1966	Storm	About 30 miles ESE of mouth of Cameron, La., jetties.
357	Claribel	Ol.s.	63	1891	Oct 10	1947	Burned	On the Intracoastal Canal, 2-1/2 miles west of Freeport, Texas.
358	Clarke Oil Tank No.1	Brg.	304	1901	Dec 23	1911	Stranded	Sabine Pass, Texas.
359	Clarke Oil Tank No.2	Brg.	382	1901	Dec 15	1911	Foundered	Sabine Pass, Texas.
360	Clarke Oil Tank No.3	Brg.	518	1902	Mar 28	1907	Foundered	Galveston Harbor, Texas.
361	Clarksville	St.p.	307	1839	Jun 30	1841	Snagged	Red River Cutoff, La. 2 lives lost.
362	Clemence S	Ol.s.	61	1947	Feb 17	1955	Foundered	60 miles south of Port Isabel, Texas. Steel vessel.
363	Cleona	St.p.	185	1850	Sep 20	1854	Burned	Alexandria, La.
364	Cleona	St.w.	125	1864	Oct 3	1870	Foundered	Liberty, Texas.
365	Cleopatra	St.p.	151	1852	Dec 6	1852	Burned	Below Catahoula, La. 3 lives lost.
366	Climax	St.p.	58	1893	Jul 28	1907	Stranded	Carters Point, Miss.
367	Climax	St.w.	56	1910	Jul 24	1924	Foundered	New Orleans, La. 5 lives lost (12).
368	Clinton	St.p.	267	1844	Mar 21	1847	Burned	Bonnet Carre, La. 6 lives lost.

NO.	NAME OF VESSEL	RIG	TONS	BUILT	DATE		CAUSE	PLACE AND COMMENT
369	Clinton Hayes	Ol.s.	64	1959	Nov 27	1965	Burned	Approximately 3 miles west of Campeche Harbor, Campeche, Mexico.
370	Clipper	St.p.	242	1865	Oct 5	1865	Burned	70 miles above Mobile, Ala. 8 lives lost.
371	Coastal 2	Brg.	547	1940	Feb 9	1952	Burned	At Warrior Asphalt Corp. dock, Holt, Ala. Steel vessel.
372	Col. Bowie	St.s.	1,363	1917	Apr 11	1921	Foundered	22-34-00 N. 97-37-00 W. 7 lives lost (22).
373	Colonel Edwards	St.p.	216	1856	Dec 12	1857	Burned	Below Shreveport, La. 9 lives lost.
374	Colonel Fremont	St.w.	74	1850	Oct 24	1854	Snagged	Tombigbee River, Ala.
375	Colonel Harney	St.p.	132	1844	Oct 12	1846	Stranded	Brazos, Texas. 15 lives lost.
376	Colonel Moore	Brg.	647	1916	Apr 20	1927	Foundered	Pass Cavalo, Texas.
377	Colonel Rufus Ingalls	St.s.	65	1862	Jun 15	1897	Foundered	Velasco, Texas.
378	Colonel Yell	St.p.	233	1847	Jul 13	1847	Stranded	Aransas Pass, Texas.
379	Colorado	St.p.	97	1850	Mar 1	1853	Stranded	Below La Grange, Texas.
380	Columbia	St.p.	222	1825	Dec 21	1827	Burned	Fort St. John, La.
381	Columbia	St.p.	131	1826	Oct 11	1833	Snagged	St. Rose, La.
382	Columbia	St.p.	140	1835	Nov 17	1838	Stranded	New Orleans, La.
383	Columbia	St.p.	92	1894	Aug 9	1908	Burned	New Orleans, La.
384	Columbia	St.p.	138	1903	Feb 27	1910	Stranded	Grand Levee, La. 1 life lost.
385	Columbia	-	-	-		1931	Unknown	Off Point Tasco, Mexico. Valued at $500,000.
386	Columbia	Ol.s.	153	1944	Dec 3	1961	Foundered	About 110 miles west of Acapulco, Mexico.
387	Columbus	Ol.s.	213	1930	Dec 25	1953	Burned	In Manzanillo Bay, Mexico.
388	Combat	Ol.s.	142	1942	Jan 3	1958	Burned	In Gulf of Mexico, about 45 miles south of Tuxpam, Mexico.
389	Comet	St.p.	154	1819		1823	Snagged	New Orleans, La.
390	Comet	Ol.s.	115	1935	Feb 21	1961	Burned	In vicinity of Mazatlan, Mexico.
391	Como	St.p.	367	1866	Apr 28	1867	Burned	Trinity River, Texas. 1 life lost.
392	Compadre	Ol.s.	85	1929	Jul 20	1953	Burned	On Mississippi River, about halfway between the head of the Pass and the mouth of the Pass.
393	Concordia	-	-	-	Sep 16	1848	Exploded	Plaquemine, La. 28 lives lost.
394	Conqueror	St.p.	398	1847	May 16	1861	Burned	New Orleans, La.
395	Conquest	St.p.	209	1899	Sep 20	1909	Foundered	New Orleans, La.
396	Constante (Span.)	-	-	-		1727	Foundered	Gulf of Mexico. 60-gun warship. Reported to be carrying treasure of silver valued at $5 million. Also known as "San Antonio".
397	Constitution	St.p.	262	1830	Jan 12	1838	Stranded	Matagorda, Texas.
398	Convoy	St.p.	749	1846	Mar 8	1849	Burned	Natchez, Miss. 2 lives lost.
399	Coosa Belle	St.w.	229	1855	Apr 24	1860	Snagged	Bridgeport, Ala.
400	Coquette	St.w.	238	1859	Mar 20	1867	Snagged	Selma, Ala.
401	Coquette	Sch.	-	-	Feb 28	1891	Unknown	Near Galveston, Texas.
402	Cora Anderson	St.p.	658	1856	Jan 18	1861	Snagged	Lake Providence, La.
403	Coral Sands	Ol.s.	63	1953	Oct 21	1955	Stranded	Near Aransas Pass, Texas.
404	Coral Sands	Ol.s.	52	1955	Dec 7	1957	Foundered	In Gulf of Campeche, Mexico.
405	Cordelia Ann	St.w.	82	1862		1868	Snagged	Red River, La.
406	Corinne	St.p.	183	1844	Feb 28	1851	Exploded	McDonoughville, La. 15 lives lost.
407	Corinne Dean	Ol.s.	91	1932	Dec 15	1935	Burned	Sabine River, Texas. Steel vessel.
408	Corinthian	St.s.	398	1863	Dec 23	1871	Foundered	Gulf of Mexico. 1 life lost.
409	Cornelia	St.p.	647	1865	Nov 16	1870	Burned	Algiers, La.
410	Corozal	St.p.	283	1883	Jan 18	1912	Burned	New Orleans, La.
411	Correo	St.w.	89	1847	May 20	1856	Snagged	Mobile, Ala.
412	Corsair	St.s.	95	1884	Sep 29	1915	Foundered	New Orleans, La. Iron vessel. 4 lives lost.
413	Cotton Plant	St.p.	72	1821	May 7	1828	Snagged	Whites Landing, Ala.
414	Cotton Plant	St.p.	260	1831	Dec 4	1832	Burned	New Orleans, La.

NO.	NAME OF VESSEL	RIG	TONS	BUILT	DATE	CAUSE	PLACE AND COMMENT
415	Cotton Plant	St.p.	59	1859	Jul 23 1863	Foundered	Vicksburg, Miss.
416	Cougar	Ol.s.	57	1951	Feb 16 1959	Foundered	In Gulf of Mexico, about 65 miles southeast of Tampico, Mexico.
417	Courage	Ol.s.	68	1943	Dec 15 1953	Stranded	150 miles south of Port Isabel, Texas, in Gulf of Mexico, 1/2 mile off Mexican coast.
418	Courier	St.p.	140	1846	Mar 9 1849	Snagged	Davant, La.
419	Creole	St.p.	192	1839	Feb 22 1841	Burned	Torras, La. 34 lives lost.
420	Creole	St.p.	122	1847	Dec 27 1850	Burned	New Orleans, La.
421	Crescent	St.p.	115	1841	Feb 18 1842	Snagged	Tchula, La.
422	Crescent	St.p.	547	1850	Feb 4 1854	Burned	New Orleans, La.
423	Crescent	St.p.	678	1863	Dec 11 1868	Burned	New Orleans, La. Steel vessel.
424	Crescent City	St.p.	257	1841	Feb 1 1843	Snagged	Peach Tree, Ala.
425	Crescent City	St.s.	146	1887	Apr 15 1924	Burned	Bayou Sara, Ala.
426	Crisp Wilkinson	Ol.s.	64	1953	Jan 1957	Foundered	In Campeche Bay, Gulf of Mexico.
427	Cuba	St.p.	285	1850	Apr 20 1856	Snagged	Davis Ledge, 89 miles above Mobile, Ala. 7 lives lost.
428	Cuba	St.p.	562	1837	Jun 12 1859	Foundered	Galveston, Texas.
429	Cuba	St.w.	168	1864	Nov 11 1867	Exploded	Alexandria, La. 7 lives lost.
430	D.A. McGee	Ol.s.	104	1944	Jul 28 1959	Burned	About 5 miles east of Lake Calcasieu Locks, La.
431	D-B	Ol.s.	57	1948	Feb 6 1955	Burned	About 10 miles SSE of Galveston, Texas.
432	D.B. 301	Brg.	341	1929	Feb 14 1950	Foundered	In Mississippi River, off Bohemia Point, La. Steel vessel.
433	D.B. 364	Brg.	321	1935	May 7 1954	Stranded	In Mobile Bay, Ala., at entrance to Gulf Intracoastal Waterway. Steel vessel.
434	D.B. 1107	Brg.	396	1931	Sep 8 1945	Foundered	Mississippi River, opposite Algiers, La. Steel vessel.
435	D.B. 1110	Brg.	431	1931	Sep 19 1947	Foundered	Freeport Sulphur Co. loading dock, Port Sulphur, La. Steel vessel.
436	D.B. Moseby	St.p.	164	1849	Oct 19 1854	Burned	St. Patrick, La. 1 life lost.
437	D.H. Blunk	St.s.	98	1863	Nov 19 1865	Snagged	Brown's Landing, La.
438	D.L.V.	Ol.s.	52	1945	Jan 25 1964	Stranded	About 70 miles south of Brownsville, Texas.
439	D.N. Co. No.103	Brg.	342	1912	Aug 9 1927	Foundered	Punta Arena, Mexico.
440	D.W. McLean	-	-	-	Nov 9 1891	Unknown	Off Chiltepec, Mexico.
441	Daiho II	Ol.s.	81	1924	Jun 11 1961	Foundered	Approximately 23-03-00 N. 111-30-00 W. In Mexican waters.
442	Daisy Farlin	Sch.	466	1891	Nov 18 1919	Foundered	31-00-00 N. 80-10-00 W.
443	Dalmacia	Ol.s.	73	1923	Oct 15 1959	Foundered	In Mississippi River, east of Freemason Island, La.
444	Daniel Boone	St.p.	169	1844	Sep 10 1853	Collided	With SOUTHERN BELLE. College Point, La.
445	Daniel Boone	St.p.	381	1854	Dec 13 1859	Snagged	Above Vicksburg, Miss.
446	Daniel O'Connell	St.p.	193	1833	Mar 11 1838	Snagged	Princeton, Miss.
447	Daniel Pratt	St.p.	293	1847	Oct 26 1854	Exploded	Mobile, Ala. 3 lives lost.
448	Daniel Webster	St.p.	345	1835	May 6 1850	Snagged	New Orleans, La.
449	Danny	Ol.s.	80	1949	May 10 1963	Foundered	East-northeast of Port Isabel, Texas. Steel vessel.
450	Daryl Wayne	Ol.s.	64	1954	Apr 1965	Foundered	In Gulf of Campeche, off coast of Mexico.
451	Dave W.	Ol.s.	64	1953	Apr 6 1966	Collided	With M/V MISS PHYLLIS. 35 miles northwest of Campeche, Mexico.
452	David McKelvy	St.s.	6,820	1921	May 13 1942	War Loss	28-55-10 N. 90-35-00 W. Tanker. Steel vessel. 17 lives lost (42). Sunk by enemy action. Cleared to acceptable depth.
453	David White	St.p.	636	1853	Feb 17 1867	Exploded	Columbia, Miss. 35 lives lost.
454	Dayton	St.p.	90	1835	Sep 12 1845	Exploded	Aransas Pass, Texas. 10 lives lost.
455	Dean E. Brown	Sch.	719	1907	Sep 17 1917	Foundered	Mobile, Ala. All lives (9) lost.
456	Decatur	St.p.	113	1825	1828	Snagged	Fort St. John, La.
457	De De	St.w.	80	1856	Mar 27 1858	Snagged	Black Bayou, La.
458	Delaware Sun	Sch.	3,708	1903	Dec 18 1917	Collided	With jetty. Entrance to Sabine River, Texas. Steel vessel.
459	Delisle	St.s.	3,478	1919	Nov 24 1943	War Loss	47-19-00 N. 52-27-00 W. Steel vessel. Sunk by enemy action.
460	Del Norte	St.w.	115	1846	1849	Snagged	Rio Grande, Texas.

NO.	NAME OF VESSEL	RIG	TONS	BUILT	DATE		CAUSE	PLACE AND COMMENT
461	Dell-D	Ol.s.	59	1952	Jul	1960	Stranded	In channel, off coast of Freeport, Texas.
462	Delta	St.p.	396	1849	May 10	1858	Burned	Algiers, La.
463	Denebola	Ol.s.	83	1944	Mar 20	1959	Burned	About 25 miles east of Port Aransas, Texas.
464	Dereld	Ol.s.	59	1945	Dec 16	1954	Burned	2 miles northeast of Tortugas Light, in Gulf of Mexico.
465	Desco	Ol.s.	63	1953	May 28	1966	Unknown	At 127° from Aransas Jetties, Aransas Pass, Texas.
466	De Soto	St.p.	104	-	Dec 9	1865	Exploded	Pascagoula, Miss. 11 lives lost. Used as ferryboat.
467	De Soto	-	-	-	Feb 28	1844	Collided	With BUCKEYE, Mississippi River. 80 lives lost.
468	DeSoto	St.p.	390	1860	Apr 1	1867	Burned	Grand View, La.
469	DeSoto	St.p.	1,600	1859	Dec 31	1870	Burned	Below New Orleans, La.
470	Despatch	St.p.	105	1835	Dec 30	1842	Stranded	Mobile, Ala.
471	Detroit	Sch.	1,166	1893	Apr 27	1919	Collided	With st.s. AUGUSTA. South Pass, Mississippi River. Steel vessel.
472	Dew Drop	St.p.	184	1858	May 25	1863	Burned	Quiver River, Miss.
473	Dewey	Ol.s.	144	1941	Aug 16	1956	Burned	5 miles west of Calcasieu Bar and 3/4 mile offshore Holly Beach, La.
474	Dial	St.s.	98	1891	Sep 27	1907	Foundered	New Orleans, La. 1 life lost.
475	Diana	St.p.	296	1845	Jan 23	1850	Collided	With OHIO. Pilot Station, New Orleans, La.
476	Diana	St.p.	239	1858	Apr 12	1863	Burned	Bayou Teche, La.
477	Diane	Ol.y.	61	1912	Aug 5	1932	Foundered	Off San Lucas Bay, Mexico.
478	Dick Fulton No.2	St.w.	98	1860	Feb 2	1866	Exploded	New Orleans, La. 4 lives lost.
479	Die Vernon	St.p.	578	1859	Feb 10	1867	Snagged	Australia, Miss.
480	Dixie	St.p.	106	1860	Oct 20	1860	Snagged	Campti, La.
481	Dixie Dandy	Ol.s.	63	1947	Dec 31	1957	Foundered	About 12 miles from Port Aransas, Texas, on Padre Island.
482	Doctor Franklin	St.p.	280	1843	Mar 8	1846	Burned	New Orleans, La.
483	Doctor Walling	Ol.s.	59	1952	Feb 3	1960	Stranded	On Padre Island, Texas, about 15 miles north of Port Mansfield Pass.
484	Doctor Watson	St.p.	141	1844	Oct 26	1846	Foundered	New Orleans, La.
485	Dollie Webb	St.w.	139	1859	May 5	1861	Burned	Algiers, La.
486	Dolphin	Ol.s.	57	1962	Jan 3	1967	Stranded	About 70 miles south of Brownsville, Texas, on the coast of Mexico.
487	Domenico	Bark	-	-	Jun	1890	Unknown	Chandeleur Island, La.
488	Doncelyn	Ol.s.	66	1952	Jan 8	1966	Collided	With unknown object. About 28-40-00 N. 91-50-00 W. Steel vessel.
489	Donna Jean	Ol.s.	52	1954	Jul 28	1966	Burned	At Trinity Shoal, Texas.
490	Donna K	Ol.s.	88	1954	Jan 20	1961	Collided	With trawler. About 26-00-00 N. 86-00-00 W.
491	Dora Allison	Sch.	339	1884	Aug 17	1915	Stranded	Galveston, Texas.
492	Doris	Sch.	382	1903	Aug 15	1915	Foundered	Gulf of Mexico. All lives (7) lost.
493	Dorothy	Sch.	70	1904	Jul 6	1916	Foundered	Off Petit Bois Island, Mobile, Ala. 7 lives lost.
494	Dorothy Gloria	Ol.s.	52	1950	Jul	1967	Collided	With submerged object. 2 miles southeast of South Pass Lighted Whistle Buoy, in the Gulf of Mexico.
495	Dorothy Lee	Ol.s.	102	1941	Nov 11	1953	Foundered	Off Hipolito Point, Mexico.
496	Double Dipper	Ol.s.	55	1958	Apr 13	1962	Storm	About 50 miles east of Tampico, Mexico.
497	Doubloon	St.p.	293	1859	Jun 24	1867	Burned	New Orleans, La.
498	Dove	St.p.	176	1856		1866	Snagged	Pearl River, Miss.
499	Dover	St.p.	172	1833	Apr 1	1840	Snagged	Mobile, Ala.
500	Dover	St.s.	617	1873	Oct 2	1912	Stranded	St. Johns River, La. Iron vessel.
501	Drag O Net	Ol.s.	65	1953	Mar 17	1965	Foundered	About 19-50-00 N. 92-10-00 W.
502	Dredge	-	-	-	Mar 26	1936	Unknown	26-20-50 N. 82-07-00 W. Used for pipe line installment.
503	Dredge Hester	St.p.	205	1889	Jul 23	1911	Burned	Clearwater, Fla.
504	Driftwood	Ol.s.	73	1953	Jan 21	1959	Foundered	Northeast of Progreso, Mexico.
505	Drue Ann	Ol.s.	61	1957	Oct 13	1963	Stranded	At the entrance to ship channel, Port Isabel, Texas.
506	Dubuque	-	-	-	Aug 15	1837	Collasped	Mississippi River. 27 lives lost.
507	Duke W. Goodman	St.w.	196	1858	Nov	1865	Burned	Rainwater, Ala.

NO.	NAME OF VESSEL	RIG	TONS	DATE			BUILT	CAUSE	PLACE AND COMMENT
508	Duncan F. Kenner	St.p.	493	May 20	1860		1859	Burned	New Orleans, La.
509	Dunham Wheeler	Sch.	1,926	Pre-WWII			-	Unknown	28-11-10 N. 80-19-40 W. Depth 80'.
510	Dwight	Ol.s.	64	Jan 16	1962		1954	Stranded	On a reef in Gulf of Mexico, about 10 miles northeast of Vera Cruz, Mexico.
511	Dwight	Ol.s.	74	Oct 22	1966		1955	Foundered	About Mile 61.8 Ahp, Mississippi River, La.
512	E.A. Ogden	St.p.	249	Apr 1	1850		1847	Snagged	Brazos River, Texas.
513	E.D. King	St.p.	108		1850		1848	Stranded	Mobile, Ala.
514	E.E. Simpson	Tanker	-	Pre-WWII			-	Wrecked	30-03-12 N. 85-37-16 W. Wreck was located in 1936 and was partially visible.
515	ELB 110	Brg.	799	Sep	1965		1965	Hurricane	At New Orleans, La.
516	E.V. Toomer	Ol.s.	81	Nov 26	1958		1933	Collided	With submerged rock. At Arcas Key, Campeche, Mexico.
517	Eagle		-	Pre-WWII			-	Snagged	25-52-00 N. 82-20-00 W.
518	Eagle	St.p.	188	Nov 26	1825		1818	Snagged	New Orleans, La.
519	Eagle	St.p.	118	Oct 15	1846		1843	Burned	Mobile, Ala.
520	Eagle	St.p.	162	Apr 25	1909		1880	Foundered	Point Celeste, La. 8 lives lost.
521	East Point	Ol.s.	185	Apr 12	1968		1941	Burned	In Lake Borgne, about Mile 40 outside Intracoastal Canal, Miss.
522	Eastern Sword	Frgt.	61	May 4	1942		-	Unknown	25-17-00 N. 83-57-00 W.
523	Ebba	Ship	3,785	Feb 15	1889		-	Unknown	Chandeleur Island, La.
524	Echo	St.p.	-	Jan 28	1842		1836	Snagged	Natchitoches, La.
525	Echo	St.s.	158	Apr 8	1949		1883	Collided	With Ol.s. H.C. WHITEMAN. At Gretna, La. Iron vessel.
526	Eclipse	St.p.	136	Aug 20	1826		1823	Snagged	Black Hawk, La.
527	Eclipse	St.p.	168	Feb 21	1860		1852	Foundered	New Orleans, La.
528	Eddie	St.w.	1,117	Jan 30	1869		1864	Snagged	Bogue Phalia, La.
529	Edgar F. Coney	St.s.	50	Jan 28	1930		1904	Foundered	29-22-00 N. 93-00-00 W. All lives (14) lost.
530	Edgar F. Conway		153	Pre-WWII			158	Unknown	29-32-00 N. 93-00-00 W.
531	Edgar F. Luckenbach	St.s.	158	Aug 12	1939		1916	Collided	With dock. Bienville Street dock, New Orleans, La. Steel vessel.
532	Edgar Randall	Sch.	6,013	Dec 14	1906		1894	Collided	With Dutch st.s. DELTA. Off Mobile, Ala.
533	Editor	St.p.	62	May 6	1861		1851	Burned	Algiers, La.
534	Edna	St.p.	246	Jun 4	1847		1842	Exploded	Columbia, La. 20 lives lost.
535	Edward Bates		183	Aug 9	1848		-	Exploded	Mississippi River. 53 lives lost.
536	Edward E. Barrett	Sch.	-	Jul 5	1916		1883	Stranded	On Ship Island, Miss.
537	Edward F. Dix	St.p.	69	Jun 15	1865		1864	Snagged	Alexandria, La.
538	Edward F. Williams	Sch.	296	Dec 3	1913		1863	Stranded	Entrance to Galveston Harbor, Texas.
539	Ed. Howard	St.p.	52	Jun 28	1862		1852	Burned	Liverpool, Miss. Burned as Confederate steamer "General Polk".
540	Edward J. Gay	St.p.	390	Jul 17	1863		1859	Burned	Yalobusha River, Miss.
541	Edward Luckenbach	St.s.	823	Jul 2	1942		-	War Loss	24-56-00 N. 81-53-00 W.
542	Edwin	Brg.	5,041	Feb 1	1914		1906	Burned	Buffalo Bayou, Texas.
543	Edwin E. Crozat	Ol.s.	262	Nov 12	1946		1902	Burned	Bayou Bienvenue, New Orleans, La.
544	Effort	St.p.	108	Sep 3	1838		1836	Snagged	Franklin, La.
545	El Capitan (Span.)	Galleon	80		1717		-	Unknown	Northwest end of New Providence Island, Fla. Treasure ship valued at $1/2 million.
546	El Capitan II	Ol.s.	-	Jun 11	1927		1925	Burned	Natchez, Miss.
547	El Gallo	Sch.	118	Oct 10	1917		1917	Stranded	Tampico, Mexico.
548	El Maria	Ol.s.	630	Dec 13	1963		1952	Foundered	About 50 miles southwest of Tuxpan Reef, Gulf of Mexico.
549	El Mozo	St.s.	63	Jul 21	1913		1890	Burned	New Orleans, La.
550	El Vivo	St.s.	103	Apr 24	1945		1902	Foundered	At 9 Mile Point, opposite Westwego, La. Steel vessel.
551	Electra	Ol.s.	199	Jan 22	1955		1943	Burned	About 8 miles east of Aransas Pass, Texas.
552	Elginshire	St.s.	77	Apr 20	1890		-	Unknown	Anagada de Afuera Reef, Mexico.
553	Elite	St.w.	-	Mar 5	1852		1849	Foundered	Smithfield, Texas.
554	Eliza Battle	St.p.	79	Mar 1	1858		1852	Burned	Kemps Ledge, Tombigbee River, Ala. 29 lives lost.
555	Elizabeth	St.p.	315	May 30	1827		1819	Burned	Mobile, Ala.

NO.	NAME OF VESSEL	RIG	TONS	BUILT	DATE	CAUSE	PLACE AND COMMENT
556	Elizabeth	St.w.	53	1839	Apr 3 1845	Exploded	Mississippi River. Renamed "Kittanning" in 1842.
557	Elizabeth	St.s.	4,727	1918	May 20 1942	War Loss	21-41-00 N. 84-54-00 W. Steel vessel. Sunk by enemy action.
558	Elizabeth Massey	Frgt.	2,598*	-	Feb 19 1942	War Loss	28-09-10 N. 80-00-40 W.
559	Elizabeth O	St.p.	71	1919	Jan 11 1921	Foundered	Tombigbee River, Ala.
560	Elizabeth O	St.w.	71	1919	Jun 7 1930	Burned	Mobile, Ala.
561	Ella Andrews	St.s.	64	1879	Jan 7 1926	Foundered	Thomas Point, Baton Rouge, La. Iron vessel. 1 life lost (8).
562	Ella C. Andrews	Ol.s.	59	1878	Apr 18 1933	Stranded	Dog Keys Pass, Miss.
563	Ella Hughes	St.w.	212	1867	Mar 17 1880	"Sunk"	Near New Orleans, La.
564	Ellen C. Burke	Sch.	92	1902	Oct 13 1927	Stranded	Gulf of Mexico.
565	Elma F.	Ol.s.	50	1892	Feb 1946	Foundered	Mississippi River, New Orleans, La.
566	Elmer E. Randall	Sch.	56	1893	Sep 26 1906	Foundered	75 miles off Mobile, Ala.
567	Elnora	St.w.	332	1865	Feb 24 1868	Stranded	Robson, La.
568	Elsie U	Ol.s.	99	1943	Nov 8 1968	Foundered	About 20 miles south of Brownsville, Texas in Mexican waters.
569	Emblem	St.p.	120	1836	Apr 18 1839	Foundered	Mobile, Ala. 5 lives lost.
570	Emerald	St.p.	123	1836	1837	Snagged	Mississippi River.
571	Emerald	St.p.	419	1859	Jan 5 1868	Snagged	Cat Island, Penton, Miss. 3 lives lost.
572	Emily Cooney	Sch.	73	1902	Aug 16 1916	Foundered	Alacrane Reef, Mexico. 1 life lost.
573	Emily P. Wright	Sch.	97	1884	Aug 23 1914	Stranded	Madre Island, off Mexican coast.
574	Emma	St.w.	189	1859	Jun 20 1865	Snagged	Shreveport, La.
575	Emma	Ol.s.	72	1950	Jul 15 1952	Burned	In Gulf of Mexico, 14 miles north of Chiltepec Lighthouse. 18-55 N. 94-25 W.
576	Emma Betts	St.w.	79	1858	May 25 1863	Burned	Quiver River, Miss.
577	Emma Boyd	St.w.	172	1863	Aug 26 1864	Snagged	Selma, Miss.
578	Emma L. Cottingham	Sch.	522	1875	Jun 10 1906	Foundered	26-58-00 N. 85-10-00 W. 5 lives lost.
579	Emma Watts	St.w.	111	1852	Sep 22 1858	Snagged	Mobile, Ala.
580	Emperor	St.p.	396	1848	Jul 1 1856	Stranded	Mobile, Ala.
581	Empire Mica (Br.)	Tanker	4,676*	-	Jun 29 1942	War Loss	29-18-51 N. 85-21-05 W. Steel vessel. Depth 50'.
582	Empire Parish	St.p.	279	1859	May 28 1864	Burned	New Orleans, La.
583	Empress	St.p.	304	1850	Jun 29 1858	Burned	Algiers, La.
584	Eneanore	-	-	-	Jun 5 1916	Capsized	Mississippi River. 30 lives lost.
585	Enterprise	St.p.	106	1844	Aug 21 1846	Exploded	Reynosa, Mexico. 5 lives lost.
586	Enterprise	St.p.	70	1856	Sep 22 1858	Snagged	Mobile, Ala.
587	Envoy	St.p.	113	1848	Oct 17 1850	Burned	Matagorda Bay, Texas.
588	Esmeraldas	Ol.s.	125	1943	May 19 1955	Stranded	At northeast point, Brenton Island, La.
589	Esperanza	St.s.	4,764	1901	Nov 24 1924	Stranded	Tampico, Mexico. Steel vessel. 1 life lost (48).
590	Esso Barge No.202	Brg.	664	1916	Jun 18 1945	Collided	With SS WILLIAM CROMPTON. At mile 196.5, Mississippi River, near White Castle, La. Steel vessel.
591	Ethel Walling	Ol.s.	66	1953	Jul 9 1961	Foundered	In Gulf of Mexico, 36 hours off Arcas Light, running 326° for Aransas Pass, Texas.
592	Etta B	Ga.s.	90	1895	Jan 25 1923	Stranded	Todos Santos Islands, Mexico.
593	Eugene	St.s.	70	1889	Jul 30 1914	Burned	Houston, Texas.
594	Eureka	St.p.	110	1845	Nov 6 1847	Snagged	McNeil Bar, Ala.
595	Eureka	St.w.	112	1847	Nov 20 1851	Collided	With CORINNE. Tombigbee River, Ala.
596	Euterpe	St.s.	823	1864	Jan 10 1870	Burned	Galveston, Texas.
597	Eva	Sch.	277	1880	Apr 20 1910	Stranded	Alta Bar, Mexico.
598	Eva	Ga.y.	62	1924	Sep 7 1943	Burned	New Orleans, La.
599	Eva Rose	Ol.s.	63	1946	Jan 21 1957	Collided	With submerged object, Gulf of Mexico, 24 miles north of Aransas Pass, Texas.
600	Evelyn Jewell	Ol.s.	69	1943	Nov 26 1952	Foundered	About 60 miles south of Aransas, Texas, 15 miles offshore in Gulf of Mexico.
601	Exit	St.p.	158	1847	Oct 28 1850	Snagged	Campti, La.
602	Exmoor	St.s.	4,986	1919	Jun 18 1942	War Loss	19-53-00 N. 86-30-00 W. Steel vessel. Sunk by enemy action.

NO.	NAME OF VESSEL	RIG	TONS	BUILT	DATE	CAUSE	PLACE AND COMMENT
603	Explorer	Ol.s.	61	1947	May 20 1951	Lost	In Gulf of Mexico, 70 miles south of Santiago Brazos Light, Mexico.
604	Explorer	Ol.s.	691	1944	Aug 24 1956	Capsized	About: 14-58-00 N. 94-00-00 W.
605	Express Mail	St.p.	244	1841	Apr 27 1846	Snagged	Campti, La.
606	Express No.2	St.p.	59	1837	Jul 25 1840	Exploded	Blakely, Ala. 6 lives lost.
607	F. 12	Brg.	519	1916	Nov 15 1918	Burned	Galveston, Texas. All life (1) lost.
608	F.A. Goebel	St.p.	61	1886	Aug 23 1907	Foundered	Monroe, La.
609	F.B. Williams	St.p.	86	1893	Jan 13 1912	Burned	Belle River, Bayou Teche, La.
610	F.M. Owens	St.p.	129	1910	Sep 29 1915	Foundered	New Orleans, La. 1 life lost.
611	F.M. Streck	St.p.	198	1844	Oct 6 1859	Snagged	Mobile, Ala.
612	Fair Moon	Ol.s.	64	1954	Sep 20 1958	Foundered	Near mouth of St. Bernard River, 5 miles south of the Brazos River, Texas.
613	Fairfield	St.w.	157	1854	Oct 13 1858	Snagged	Alabama River.
614	Fairhope	St.s.	93	1901	Nov 21 1905	Burned	Fairhope, Ala.
615	Fairhope	St.s.	114	1899	Jan 22 1918	Foundered	28-55-00 N. 89-04-00 W. 2 lives lost.
616	Falcon	St.p.	295	1849	Oct 8 1849	Burned	New Orleans, La.
617	Falcon	St.p.	177	1852	Apr 24 1855	Burned	Algiers, La.
618	Falls City	St.w.	183	1855	Apr 19 1864	Foundered	Loggy Bayou, La.
619	Fanny	St.p.	195	1864	Jun 9 1871	Foundered	Galveston, Texas. 32 lives lost.
620	Farmer	St.p.	158	1849	Mar 23 1853	Exploded	Baton Rouge, La. 43 lives lost.
621	Fashion	St.p.	1,194	1865	Dec 27 1866	Burned	75 yards south of South Pier on Mustang Island, Texas.
622	40 Fathom No.12	Ol.s.	50	1945	Dec 10 1955	Stranded	Gulf of Mexico, bearing 192° True, 28 miles from Au Fer Reef Lighthouse. Steel.
623	Fearless	Ol.s.	73	1953	Mar 8 1961	Foundered	Yalobusha River, Miss.
624	Ferd Kennett	St.p.	591	1861	Jul 17 1863	Burned	About 5.5 miles south-southwest of Freeport Buoy, Freeport, Texas.
625	Ferninand Magellan	Ol.s.	54	1951	Oct 31 1959	Foundered	Gulf of Mexico. 4 lives lost (5).
626	Fidget	Ga.y.	50	1886	Oct 7 1923	Foundered	Gulf of Mexico, about 60 miles northeast of Port Isabel, Texas.
627	Flagship	Ol.s.	63	1944	Dec 20 1954	Stranded	About 1 mile south of Caminatta Pass Bridge, Grand Isle, La.
628	Flamingo	Ol.s.	105	1946	Mar 29 1957	Burned	Mobile, Ala.
629	Flirt	St.w.	198	1859	Jul 18 1867	Collided	With TIMOUR. Tunica, Miss.
630	Flora	St.p.	112	1848	Jan 1852	Exploded	Locopolis, Miss.
631	Flora Temple	St.p.	180	1858	Jul 24 1863	Foundered	Off Campeche, Mexico.
632	Florence Friede	Ol.s.	76	1953	Nov 22 1964	Stranded	Fort Morgan, Ala.
633	Florence Harvey	Sch.	340	1918	Jan 3 1922	Snagged	Warrenton, Miss.
634	Florence Miller No.3	St.w.	236	1864	Mar 3 1869	Burned	Padre Island, Texas.
635	Florette	Ga.s.	54	1900	Dec 2 1938	Burned	Cahawba, Ala. 1 life lost.
636	Florida	St.p.	247	1827	Apr 4 1828	Foundered	Approximately 12 miles north of Port O'Connor, Texas.
637	Flossie R. Shaw	Ol.s.	63	1952	Oct 12 1967	Stranded	Cat Island, Miss.
638	Fluorine	Bark	386	1881	Sep 27 1906	Foundered	Gulf of Mexico.
639	Flyton	Brg.	553	1902	Nov 17 1906	Snagged	Tombigbee River, Ala.
640	Forest Monarch	St.p.	212	1848	Apr 14 1855	Stranded	Bayou Sara, La.
641	Fort Adams	St.p.	137	1825	Dec 9 1836	Stranded	San Jose del Cabo, Mexico.
642	Fort Bragg	St.s.	705	1910	Nov 5 1915	Snagged	Alexandria, La.
643	Fort Gibson	St.p.	96	1842	Nov 18 1842	War Loss	27-35-00 N. 83-11-00 W. Steel vessel. Sunk by enemy action.
644	Fort Lee	El.s.	10,198	1943	Nov 2 1944	Wrecked	Off Yucatan, Mexico.
645	Forth	Steamer	-	-	1849	Burned	Frailes Bay, Mexico.
646	Fortuna	Ga.s.	50	1920	May 30 1926	Stranded	Campeche River, Mexico.
647	Fortuna	Sch.	85	1883	Feb 23 1928	Stranded	Beached on shores in Gulf of Mexico about 30 miles south from piers on the Gulf side of Padre Island, Texas. 27-10-00 N. 97-20-00 W.
648	Four Kids	Ol.s.	101	1944	Dec 2 1953	Snagged	Mobile, Ala.
649	Fox	St.p.	91	1834	Aug 6 1840		

NO.	NAME OF VESSEL	RIG	TONS	BUILT	DATE		CAUSE	PLACE AND COMMENT
650	Fox	St.w.	74	1855	Mar 28	1861	Gunfire	Above raft, Red River, La.
651	Fox	Ol.s.	58	1878	Feb 13	1956	Foundered	In Atchafalaya River, Morgan City, La.
652	Frances	Ol.s.	178	1947	Apr 23	1958	Foundered	Gulf of Mexico, 3 miles SSW of Grand Isle, La. Steel vessel.
653	Frances Troop	St.p.	-	-	Aug 14	1890	Unknown	Salinas Cruz, Mexico.
654	Frank L. Baske	Ol.s.	243	1930	Oct 4	1965	Foundered	In Mississippi River at approximately 103 Mile Ahp, La.
655	Frank R. Hill	St.p.	109	1905	Dec 24	1907	Foundered	New Orleans, La.
656	Franklin No.2	-	-	-	Aug 22	1852	Collapsed	Mississippi River. 32 lives lost.
657	Franklin Pierce	St.p.	348	1853	Apr 18	1855	Burned	Yazoo River, Miss. Renamed "Texan" in 1855.
658	Fred P. Litchfield	Sch.	1,045	1876	Sep 26	1906	Foundered	Gulf of Mexico. 26-00-00 N. 87-50-00 W.
659	Fred W. Ayer	Sch.	387	1903	Sep 22	1920	Stranded	Ship Island, Miss.
660	Freestone	St.w.	150	1858	Sep 27	1865	Snagged	Yazoo City, Miss.
661	Fridleif	Bark	-	-	Jan	1889	Unknown	Vera Cruz, Mexico.
662	Friend	Ol.s.	74	1958	Jul 5	1960	Collided	With ol.s. MASTER ALLEN. In Gulf of Campeche. 18-44-00 N. 92-54-00 W.
663	Frontier	St.p.	109	1843	Jun 19	1846	Stranded	Port Isabel, Texas.
664	Fulton	St.p.	114	1846	Mar 15	1849	Snagged	Shreveport, La.
665	G.A. Bayard	St.p.	140	1836	Dec 26	1836	Collided	With DANIEL O'CONNELL. Coles Point, Mississippi River.
666	G.C.T. Co. No.9	Brg.	210	1912	Jan 18	1922	Foundered	24-07-00 N. 95-33-00 W.
667	G.C.T. Co. No.16	Brg.	197	1912	Feb 21	1912	Foundered	Gulf of Mexico.
668	G.R. Co. 4	Brg.	117	1937	Jul 19	1957	Foundered	In Mississippi River, Buras, La. Steel vessel.
669	GWG 201	Brg.	1,254	1955	Sep 10	1964	Collided	With lead barge. In the Fay Blackman Tow, at Mile 404.6, Lower Mississippi River.
670	G.W. Robertson	St.p.	204	1910	Jun 25	1916	Burned	Greenville, Miss.
671	Gail-D	Ol.s.	77	1953	Feb 13	1960	Foundered	In Gulf of Mexico, about 270 miles southeast of Port Isabel, Texas.
672	Gainesville	St.p.	221	1839	Mar 31	1843	Collided	Mobile, Ala.
673	Galveston	St.p.	545	1845	Nov 25	1851	Stranded	Ship Island, Miss.
674	Galveston	St.p.	945	1857	Apr 2	1862	Burned	New Orleans, La.
675	Gamma	St.p.	89	1903	Sep 26	1906	Foundered	Mobile, Ala.
676	Ganges	St.p.	155	1836	May 17	1841	Burned	Vicksburg, Miss.
677	Gasparilla	Flagship				1821	Unknown	At the mouth of Charlotte River, Fla. or at Belle Bar, at mouth of Boca Grande Pass, Fla. Reported to be worth some $10 million. Pirate vessel.
678	Gayle	Ol.s.	171	1941	Jan 6	1958	Foundered	In Gulf of Mexico, off Louisiana coast. 21-15-00 N. 91-30-00 W.
679	Gazelle	St.p.	82	1844	May	1847	Foundered	Reynosa, Mexico.
680	Gelmer	Drg.	-	-	Pre-WWII		Unknown	29-19-00 N. 84-55-00 W. About 18 miles southeast of Cape St. George. Depth 78'.
681	Gem	St.p.	97	1898	Feb 10	1914	Burned	Mississippi River, Hahnville, La. 6 lives lost.
682	General Bradley	Ol.s.	78	1947	Jul	1960	Storm	Off Coatzacoalcos, Mexico. Steel vessel.
683	General Brown	St.p.	224	1825	Feb 24	1830	Burned	Mobile, Ala.
684	Gen. Brown	-	-	-	Nov 25	1838	Exploded	Mississippi River. 60 lives lost.
685	General Bryan	St.p.	72	1839	Feb 16	1842	Snagged	Sabine River, Texas.
686	Gen. Clark	Ol.s.	54	1948	Jul 19	1961	Burned	About 50 miles southwest of Freeport, Texas.
687	Gen. Collier	-	-	-	May 6	1839	Exploded	New Orleans, La. 26 lives lost.
688	General Crowder	St.w.	252	1895	Feb 7	1927	Burned	Slidell, La.
689	General Herran	St.p.	65	1849	Jan 9	1850	Capsized	New Orleans, La.
690	General Lee	St.s.	199	1895	Dec 13	1910	Foundered	Fairhope, Ala.
691	General Patton	Ol.s.	83	1947	Jan 2	1955	Foundered	In Gulf of Mexico, about 100 miles SE of Port Isabel, Texas. Steel vessel.
692	General Pike	St.p.	308	1843	Apr 18	1849	Burned	Point Coupee, La. 1 life lost.
693	General Pike	St.p.	248	1856	May 6	1861	Burned	Algiers, La.
694	General Quitman	St.p.	615	1859	Oct 21	1868	Snagged	Angola, La.
695	General Ransom	St.w.	115	1865	Apr 10	1868	Burned	Algiers, La.
696	Genevieve H	Ol.s.	63	1927	Feb 3	1955	Foundered	10 miles south of Turtle Bay, Mexico.

NO.	NAME OF VESSEL	RIG	TONS	BUILT	DATE	CAUSE	PLACE AND COMMENT
697	George C. Greer	St.s.	426	1919	1942	Unknown	In Gulf of Mexico.
698	George Calvert	St.s.	7,191	1942	May 20 1942	War Loss	Gulf of Mexico. 22-55-00 N. 84-26-00 W. Steel vessel. Freighter. Sunk by enemy action.
699	George Collier	St.p.	402	1835	1839	Foundered	Mississippi River. 26 lives lost.
700	George K.	Ol.s.	61	1893	Oct 23 1947	Foundered	In Mississippi River, on left descending bank, at Mile 460.9 Ahp, La. Steel.
701	George Moulton	Sch.	-	-	Dec 10 1891	Unknown	Vera Cruz, Mexico.
702	George Washington	St.p.	355	1825	1831	Burned	New Orleans, La.
703	George Washington	St.p.	309	1836	Apr 21 1842	Burned	New Orleans, La.
704	George Washington	St.p.	303	1845	Jan 14 1852	Exploded	Grand Gulf, Miss. 17 lives lost.
705	Geo. Wolfe	-	-	-	Aug 23 1873	"Blown up"	Mississippi River. 30 lives lost.
706	Georgia	St.p.	135	1837	Mar 29 1842	Burned	Lafayette, La.
707	Georgia	St.p.	326	1851	Jan 28 1854	Exploded	Lake Pontchartrain, La. Between 25 and 60 lives lost.
708	Georgian	Ol.s.	52	1954	Jan 19 1961	Foundered	In vicinity of Cayo Arcas, off coast of Campeche, Mexico.
709	Germania	Bark	-	-	Dec 12 1887	Unknown	Porto Macao, Mexico.
710	Geronimo	Ol.s.	85	1953	Jun 1 1959	Burned	About 45 miles northeast of Palamas Point, Mexico.
711	Gertrude	St.p.	70	1864	Sep 21 1864	Foundered	College Point, La. 6 lives lost.
712	Gertrude A. Somerville	Sch.	556	1917	Oct 24 1921	Foundered	Gulf of Mexico. All lives (7) lost.
713	Gertrude Summers	Sch.	64	1871	Jun 8 1912	Foundered	Gulf of Mexico.
714	Gimick	Ol.s.	108	1943	Feb 23 1951	Stranded	25 miles north of Padre Island Coast Guard Station, Texas.
715	Gipsy	St.p.	298	1848	Dec 7 1854	Burned	Torras, La. 5 lives lost.
716	Gladiator	St.p.	99	1834	Jan 18 1838	Snagged	Liverpool, Miss.
717	Gladiator	St.s.	146	1863	Feb 10 1900	Burned	Gretna, La.
718	Glen-Rae	Ol.s.	67	1950	Sep 1 1959	Stranded	On beach about 20 miles north of Aransas Pass, Texas.
719	Glide	St.w.	232	1863	Jan 13 1869	Exploded	New Orleans, La.
720	Glide No.3	St.w.	225	1864	Nov 15 1865	Snagged	Shreveport, La.
721	Globe	St.p.	481	1842	Jun 17 1851	Stranded	Brazos, Texas.
722	Gloria	Ol.s.	63	1952	Mar 8 1960	Burned	At Campeche, Mexico.
723	Gloria Colita	Sch.	202	1939	Sep 26 1941	Stranded	9 miles northeast of Freeport, Texas. 29-02 N. 95-10 W. Also known as "Gloria Coleta".
724	Gold Shield	St.w.	550	1890	Apr 29 1939	Foundered	At Todd Johnson Dry Dock, New Orleans, La. Steel vessel.
725	Golden City	St.p.	3,373	1863	Feb 22 1870	Stranded	Cape San Lazaro, Mexico.
726	Golden Duchess	Ol.s.	63	1952	May 3 1960	Stranded	Near Obero, Mexico.
727	Golden State	Sch.	1,094	1901	Feb 17 1922	Burned	29-29-00 N. 85-50-00 W.
728	Golden West	Ol.s.	63	1953	Dec 30 1961	Burned	About 40 miles south of Freeport, Texas.
729	Gossamer	St.w.	114	1865	Sep 22 1869	Foundered	Campti, La.
730	Governor Morton	St.p.	150	1865	Feb 7 1868	Stranded	Grand Isle, La.
731	Governor Morton	St.s.	50	1863	Feb 15 1868	Burned	Grand Isle, La.
732	Governor Morton	Clipper	1,430	1851	Jul 1 1877	Burned	At mouth of Mississippi River. Length 196'. Cotton cargo.
733	Governor Pease	St.p.	240	1857	Feb 26 1858	Burned	Trinity River, Texas.
734	Governor Yell	St.p.	104	1841	Oct 12 1843	Lost	New Orleans, La.
735	Grace Devers	St.w.	116	1920	May 24 1931	Foundered	Salina Point, La.
736	Grace & George	Ol.s.	239	1941	Jul 9 1954	Burned	In the Calcasieu River at the wharf of John Santos Carinhas, Cameron, La.
737	Grampus	St.p.	297	1827	May 13 1840	Exploded	Mouth of Mississippi River. 2 lives lost.
738	Grand	St.p.	124	1905	May 17 1921	Burned	Bayou Teche, La.
739	Grand Duke	St.p.	508	1859	Sep 25 1863	Burned	Shreveport, La.
740	Grand Turk	Sch.	540	1916	Nov 15 1924	Stranded	San Fernando, Mexico.
741	Grapeshot	St.p.	179	1855	May 8 1858	Burned	Galveston Bay, Texas.
742	Grecian	St.p.	156	1824	May 24 1826	Burned	New Orleans, La.

NO.	NAME OF VESSEL	RIG	TONS	BUILT	DATE	CAUSE	PLACE AND COMMENT
743	Green's Pride	Ol.s.	54	1959	Sep 9 1961	Stranded	On Mexican coast, about 70 miles south of Port Isabel, Texas.
744	Grenville Power Unit	Brg.	85	1950	Sep 10 1965	Hurricane	In Mississippi River between the Huey P. Long Bridge and West Kenner, La.
745	Grenada	St-p.	217	1851	May 6 1861	Burned	Algiers, La.
746	Grey Eagle	St.p.	177	1847	Jan 18 1850	Snagged	Grand River, La.
747	Greyhound	Ol.s.	165	1928	Aug 9 1929	Stranded	San Hipolits, Mexico.
748	Griffin	Sch.	367	1893	Apr 21 1920	Stranded	Petit Bois Island, Miss.
749	Guide	Sch.	144	1887	Dec 17 1909	Stranded	Geronimo Island, Mexico.
750	Gulf America	Tanker	4,805*	-	Apr 11 1942	War Loss	30-16-37 N. 81-13-43 W. Steel vessel. Depth 62'.
751	Gulf Prince	Tanker	6,560	-	May 13 1942	War Loss	28-32-00 N. 91-00-00 W. Gulf of Mexico. SALVAGED.
752	Gulf Stream	Ol.s.	74	1948	Feb 12 1960	Stranded	On western end of Timbalier Island, La.
753	Gulf Trader	Ol.s.	62	1957	Jan 15 1959	Stranded	On Mexican coast, 130 miles south of Port Isabel, Texas.
754	Gulf Trader	Ol.s.	63	1952	Nov 23 1960	Foundered	In Gulf of Mexico, about 2.5 miles south of Port Isabel, Texas.
755	Gulfland	Tanker	5,272	-	Oct 21 1943	War Loss	26-56-00 N. 80-01-00 W. Steel vessel. Also reported as being sunk on Jan. 31, 1943.
756	Gulfoil	St.s.	5,188	1912	May 16 1942	War Loss	28-08-00 N. 89-46-00 W. Steel vessel. 21 lives lost (40). Sunk by enemy action.
757	Gulfpenn	St.s.	8,862	1921	Mar 13 1942	War Loss	28-29-00 N. 89-17-00 W. Tanker. Steel vessel. 13 lives lost (38). Sunk by enemy action.
758	Gulfstag	El.s.	12,775	1944	Oct 24 1966	Burned	In Gulf of Mexico. Steel vessel.
759	Gulfstate	Tanker	7,612	-	Apr 3 1943	War Loss	24-22-00 N. 80-18-00 W.
760	Gunbor	Frgt.	1,121	-	Jun 14 1942	Unknown	25-00-00 N. 81-45-00 W.
761	Gussie	St.p.	998	1872	Sep 27 1906	Stranded	Dauphin Island, Ala. Iron vessel.
762	Guyton No.1	Brg.	235	1908	Dec 11 1916	Foundered	Port Aransas, Texas.
763	Guyton No.3	Brg.	54	1912	Jan 25 1918	Stranded	North of Jurez Point, Mexico.
764	Guyton No.9	Brg.	288	1916	Jul 22 1918	Foundered	23-58-00 N. 81-02-00 W.
765	Guyton No.10	Brg.	149	1909	Jan 3 1911	Foundered	Gulf of Mexico.
766	Guyton No.10	Brg.	88	1917	Jan 16 1918	Foundered	Gulf of Mexico.
767	Gypsy Girl	Ol.s.	63	1947	Jul 23 1954	Foundered	About 20 miles offshore, about 40 miles SE of Port Aransas Jetties, Texas.
768	H.A. Harvey, Jr.	St.p.	59	1892	Oct 30 1908	Burned	Mount Pleasant, La. Steel vessel.
769	H.C. Whiteman	Ol.s.	177	1892	Feb 4 1963	Collided	With WASHINGTON CARRIER, Mississippi River, about 600 feet off the Southern Pacific Wharf, Algiers, La.
770	H.D. Mears	St.w.	338	1860	Jul 25 1863	Burned	Sunflower River, Miss.
771	H. Kinney	St.p.	130	1844	May 28 1848	Exploded	Wilkins Landing, Ala. 7 lives lost.
772	H.M. Carter	St.p.	97	1901	Nov 21 1908	Burned	Palo Alto, La. 11 lives lost.
773	H.M. Wright	St.p.	366	1852	Mar 1 1857	Snagged	Haileys Cutoff, La.
774	H.R.W. Hill	St.p.	602	1852	Oct 31 1860	Exploded	Baton Rouge, La. 39 lives lost.
775	H.T. De Bardeleben	St.s.	426	1920	Apr 14 1934	Foundered	South Pass, La. Steel vessel.
776	Haavund	Bark	-	-	Feb 28 1889	Unknown	Chandeleur Island, La.
777	Halo	St.s.	6,986	1920	May 20 1942	War Loss	21 miles off Southwest Pass, La. 28-42-00 N. 90-08-00 W. Tanker. Steel vessel. 39 lives lost (42). Sunk by enemy action.
778	Halsey	-	4,339	-	May 6 1942	Unknown	27-23-00 N. 80-08-00 W. Freighter. Steel vessel. Depth 50'.
779	Hamlet (Nor.)	St.s.	3,994*	-	May 27 1942	War Loss	28-32-00 N. 91-30-00 W. Tanker. Steel vessel.
780	Hampton Roads	St.s.	2,689	-	Jun 1 1942	War Loss	23-00-00 N. 85-42-00 W. Freighter. Steel vessel. Sunk by enemy action.
781	Hardwood	St.w.	177	1914	Sep 15 1931	Stranded	Jonesville, La.
782	Harkaway	St.p.	288	1843	Jan 1 1849	Stranded	Donaldsonville, La.
783	Harold Kaffie	Ol.s.	57	1950	Jan 30 1957	Foundered	About 38 miles south of Brazos Santiago Pass, Texas.
784	Harp	St.p.	132	1837	Jun 27 1838	Snagged	Frog Bayou, La.
785	Harry K. Fooks	Sch.	276	1902	Oct 19 1910	Foundered	Gulf of Mexico. 5 lives lost.

NO.	NAME OF VESSEL	RIG	TONS	BUILT	DATE		CAUSE	PLACE AND COMMENT
786	Harry Luckenbach	St.s.	6,366	1919	Mar 16	1943	War Loss	50-38-00 N. 34-46-00 W. Steel vessel. Sunk by enemy action.
787	Harry Morse	Sch.	1,365	1871	Jul 5	1916	Collided	With sch. EMMA LORD. Mobile Bay, Ala. All lives (8) lost.
788	Harry of the West	Clipper	1,050	1855	Nov	1865	Burned	Near mouth of Mississippi River.
789	Hartford City	St.p.	150	1856	Jul 24	1863	Burned	Tallahatchie River, Miss.
790	Harvester	St.p.	530	1896	Sep 30	1909	Foundered	Donaldsonville, La. 1 life lost.
791	Hastings	St.w.	191	1857	Apr 23	1864	Snagged	Alexandria, La.
792	Hattie	Brg.	84	1882		1898	Stranded	Sabine Pass Lighthouse, Texas.
793	Haydee	St.p.	144	1847	Jun 14	1851	Snagged	Ouachita River, La.
794	Hazel Dell	St.w.	169	1857	Jan 5	1866	Snagged	Demopolis, Ala. 4 lives lost.
795	Heedless	Ol.s.	53	1945	Jan 29	1962	Foundered	Gulf of Mexico. 28-30-00 N. 88-50-00 W. Steel vessel.
796	Helen	St.p.	169	1843	Aug 8	1846	Snagged	Sartartia, Miss.
797	Helen	St.p.	292	1850	May 12	1855	Burned	Mobile, Ala.
798	Helen Burke	St.w.	365	1908	Sep 5	1932	Foundered	Mobile River, Ala.
799	Helen Lane	St.p.	143	1915	Jun 30	1919	Foundered	Berwick, La.
800	Helen McGregor	St.p.	341	1825	Dec 23	1832	Collided	With HERALD. Mobile, Ala.
801	Helen S.	Ol.s.	105	1957	Nov 27	1965	Stranded	At Petit Pois Island, Ala.
802	Helen Story	Sch.	58	1893	Feb 1	1913	Stranded	Matagorda Peninsula, Texas.
803	Heloise	St.w.	109	1922	Jun 1	1948	Burned	At River View docks, Tuscaloosa, Ala.
804	Hempstead	St.p.	75	1844	Jul 21	1848	Snagged	New Orleans, La.
805	Henderson	St.p.	123	1818	Apr 27	1825	Collided	With BALIZE, Claiborne, Ala.
806	Henrietta	Sch.	-	-	Apr 7	1888	Unknown	Aransas Pass, Texas.
807	Henrietta	St.p.	62	1893	Jun 30	1906	Burned	Bayou Felix, La.
808	Henrietta J. Powell	Sch.	316	1883	Oct 26	1914	Burned	En route from Pascagoula, Miss., to Cuba.
809	Henry Ames	St.p.	777	1864	Aug	1874	Snagged	Waterproof, La. 2 lives lost.
810	Henry A. Homeyer	St.p.	222	1863	Jan 12	1868	Burned	Trenton, La.
811	Henry Clay	St.p.	190	1819	Dec 7	1826	Snagged	Sisemores Landing, Ala.
812	Henry Clay	St.p.	257	1857	Apr 22	1863	Burned	Vicksburg, Miss.
813	Henry Howell	St.w.	144	1857	Jan 20	1860	Burned	Blanton Landing, Red River, La.
814	Henry Thane	St.w.	148	1923	Dec 17	1927	Foundered	Rosedale, Miss.
815	Henry von Phul	St.p.	709	1860	Nov 13	1866	Burned	Burnside, La. 6 lives lost.
816	Herald	St.p.	133	1825	Dec 23	1832	Collided	With HELEN McGREGOR. Mobile, Ala.
817	Hercules	St.w.	165	1826	Dec 26	1828	Collided	With brig EMERY. Montgomery, La.
818	Hercules	St.p.	161	1839	Jan 3	1842	Burned	Tuscahoma, Ala.
819	Hercules	Drg.	1,140	1917	Mar 9	1932	Burned	Filter, Miss.
820	Heredia	St.s.	4,740	1908	May 19	1942	War Loss	Gulf of Mexico. 28-30-25 N. 90-59-30 W. Freighter. Steel vessel. Sunk by enemy action. 25 to 75 per cent of lives lost.
821	Heroine	St.w.	94	1851	Mar 13	1855	Exploded	Blakeley Ledge, Ala. 3 lives lost.
822	Heron	Ol.s.	50	1903	Dec 11	1949	Foundered	24-00 N. 85-00 W.
823	Hettie	St.p.	119	1898	Oct 13	1920	Collided	With st.s. HULVER. New Orleans, La.
824	Hewitt	St.s.	5,398	1914	Jan 20	1921	Foundered	Sailed from Sabine, Texas, for Boston, Mass., and has not since reported. Steel vessel. All lives (42) lost.
825	Hico	Ol.s.	144	1943	Feb 17	1957	Storm	Gulf of Mexico, 35 miles east of Cameron, La. 29-40-00 N. 92-50-00 W.
826	High Flyer	St.s.	6,124	1944	Apr 17	1947	Exploded	In Texas City, Texas. Steel vessel. Destroyed.
827	High Tide	Ol.s.	64	1954	Apr 25	1961	Burned	Gulf of Mexico, about 6 miles southwest of Obregon, Mexico.
828	Highlander	St.p.	87	1829	Apr 3	1834	Foundered	Burlington, Miss.
829	Hill Billy	Ol.s.	67	1964	Jul 4	1968	Burned	Offshore from Carmen, Campeche, Mexico.
830	Hinds	St.p.	130	1836	May 7	1840	Foundered	Natchez, Miss. 51 lives lost. Also reported that 400 lives were lost.
831	Hoo Hoo	St.p.	82	1894	Oct 8	1906	Burned	Vermillion Bay, La.

NO.	NAME OF VESSEL	RIG	TONS	BUILT	DATE	CAUSE	PLACE AND COMMENT
832	Hope	St.p.	75	1821	1825	Snagged	Bayou Sara, La.
833	Hope	St.w.	193	1855	May 25 1863	Burned	Ft. Pemberton, Yazoo River, Miss.
834	Hope	St.p.	218	1859	Nov 29 1867	Snagged	Yazoo River, Miss.
835	Hopper	Brg.	280	1901	Mar 13 1913	Burned	Galveston, Texas.
836	Horace M. Bickford	Sch.	503	1907	Nov 21 1925	Foundered	25-15-00 N. 86-21-00 W.
837	Houma	St.w.	105	1906	Sep 20 1926	Burned	Harvey, La.
838	Houston	Drg.	690	1912	Jan 21 1932	Burned	New Orleans, La.
839	Houtex	Ol.s.	92	1918	Feb 3 1937	Burned	In Intracoastal Waterway near Barataria, La.
840	Howard L. Brookshire	Ol.s.	63	1958	Jan 8 1962	Storm	About 60 miles south of Brownsville, Texas.
841	Huasteca Grande	St.s.	735	1908	Apr 25 1920	Stranded	Panuco River, Mexico. Steel vessel.
842	Huckster	Ol.s.	56	1945	Jan 5 1954	Foundered	45 miles south of the mouth of the Rio Grande River, in Gulf of Mexico, 1 mile off Mexican coast.
843	Hugoma	St.s.	2,182	1901	Feb 20 1907	Collided	With French cruiser KIEBER. New Orleans, La.
844	Hulda Bee	Ol.s.	62	1946	Aug 4 1964	Burned	At the north slip of Port Isabel Ship Basin, Port Isabel, Texas.
845	Humble	Brg.	299	1907	Jun 26 1911	Burned	Port Arthur, Texas. 1 life lost.
846	Hunter	St.p.	103	1831	Sep 15 1835	Exploded	Calvert, Ala. 3 lives lost. Renamed "DON JUAN" on Nov. 14, 1833.
847	Hunter	St.p.	149	1832	Apr 4 1836	Burned	Tombigbee River, Ala.
848	Hunter	St.w.	53	1910	Mar 3 1933	Burned	Vicksburg, Miss.
849	Huntress	St.w.	138	1862	Dec 30 1865	Stranded	Alexandria, La.
850	Huntress	Ol.s.	78	1917	Feb 28 1933	Burned	Ensenada, Mexico.
851	Huron	St.p.	183	1829	Sep 20 1833	Snagged	Rodney, Miss.
852	Huron	St.w.	168	1851	Feb 23 1855	Snagged	Atchafalaya River, La.
853	Husky III	Ol.s.	95	1939	Aug 26 1944	Burned	353 miles above mouth of Mississippi River.
854	Ida	St.p.	77	1860	Apr 13 1865	Torpedoed	Blakeley River, Ala.
855	Ida Lewis	–	–	–	1875	Unknown	Off Brazos, Texas.
856	Ida May	St.w.	220	1858	Dec 28 1865	Snagged	100 miles below Shreveport, La.
857	Ida Rees	St.w.	221	1863	Feb 28 1873	Snagged	Sabine River, Texas.
858	Ida Rees No.2	St.w.	284	1865	Jun 20 1871	Foundered	Mississippi River.
859	Ida S. Brooks	Sch.	72	1901	Oct 18 1922	Stranded	Isla de las Mujeres, Yucatan, Mexico.
860	Idaho	St.p.	62	1863	Nov 26 1867	Exploded	New Orleans, La. 2 lives lost.
861	Idaho	St.w.	153	1863	Jan 10 1869	Snagged	Columbia, La.
862	Idaho	Ol.s.	50	1944	Nov 3 1963	Burned	In Berwick Bay, near Berwick, La.
863	Ideal	St.s.	147	1924	Nov 26 1952	Foundered	At Algiers Iron Works Shipyard, Algiers, La.
864	Ilda	Ol.s.	52	1945	Oct 8 1949	Stranded	About 30 miles south of Port Isabel Jetties, Port Isabel, Texas.
865	Illinois	St.p.	579	1847	Aug 29 1849	Burned	New Orleans, La.
866	Illinois	Brg.	67	1925	Aug 20 1942	Foundered	Mattagorda Bay, Texas.
867	Imogen	St.p.	51	1903	Jun 17 1909	Foundered	Yazoo City, Miss.
868	Imperial	St.p.	494	1894	Mar 26 1912	Burned	New Orleans, La.
869	Independence	St.p.	1,376	1851	Feb 16 1852	Stranded	Matagorda Bay, Texas. 6 lives lost.
870	Independence	St.p.	613	1851	Apr 27 1853	Stranded	Margarita Island, Mexico.
871	Independent	St.s.	164	1901	Dec 9 1927	Foundered	New Orleans, La. Steel vessel. 2 lives lost.
872	Indiana	St.w.	134	1923	Feb 24 1937	Burned	Natchez, Miss.
873	Indianola	St.w.	146	1859	Aug 10 1863	Snagged	20 miles below Warrenton, Miss.
874	Ingomar	St.w.	110	1858	Feb 7 1867	Snagged	Plaquemine, La.
875	Intrepid	Ol.s.	95	1917	Apr 12 1929	Burned	San Jose del Cabo, Mexico.
876	Invader	Ol.s.	254	1929	Mar 2 1961	Stranded	Near Roca Partida, Mexico. 19-00-00 N. 112-07-00 W.
877	Invincible	St.p.	210	1836	Jan 1844	Snagged	English Turn, La.
878	Ione	Ol.s.	108	1944	1951	Burned	In Bayou Sauvage, New Orleans, La.

NO.	NAME OF VESSEL	RIG	TONS	BUILT	DATE	CAUSE	PLACE AND COMMENT
879	Iowa	St.p.	143	1843	Jan 17 1837	Burned	Fairfield, Ala.
880	Irene	St.p.	76	1844	Apr 1 1850	Lost	Mobile, Ala.
881	Irene	St.w.	211	1864	Nov 10 1868	Snagged	20 miles below Shreveport, La.
882	Iron City	St.w.	190	1864	Feb 23 1868	Snagged	Below Alexandria, La.
883	Isaac Collins	Sch.	98	1889	Nov 21 1911	Stranded	Biscayne Bay, Fla.
884	Isaac T. Campbell	Sch.	586	1879	Aug 27 1909	Foundered	450 miles off Louisiana coast. 2 lives lost.
885	Island Trader	Ol.s.	89	1917	Aug 22 1944	Stranded	Chinchorro Reef, Mexico.
886	Islander	Ol.s.	63	1953	Nov 9 1961	Collided	With US Coast Guard Cutter GENTIAN. 28-43-05 N. 95-06-05 W.
887	Isora	St.p.	124	1842	Apr 30 1842	Snagged	Craig Ferry, Ala.
888	Istrouma	St.p.	253	1896	Sep 29 1915	Foundered	Baton Rouge, La.
889	Ivanhoe	St.p.	197	1834	Aug 6 1840	Snagged	Mobile, Ala.
890	J.A. Bisso	Ol.s.	224	1906	Nov 7 1957	Foundered	28-46-00 N. 90-41-30 W. Enroute from Sabine, Texas to New Orleans, La. Steel.
891	J.A. Cotton	St.p.	549	1861	Jan 11 1863	Burned	Bayou Teche, La. Burned as Confederate vessel.
892	J.A. Hatry	Sch.	-	-	Nov 28 1890	Unknown	Coatzacoalcos, Mexico.
893	J.A. Moffitt, Jr.	St.s.	9,788	-	Jun 8 1942	War Loss	24-45-00 N. 80-42-00 W. Tanker. Steel vessel.
894	J.B. Chauvin	St.p.	112	1916	Nov 8 1916	Burned	Teche River, La.
895	J.B. Lewis	St.w.	162	1900	Aug 25 1926	Foundered	New Orleans, La.
896	J.B. Rabel	Bkn.	450	1882	Dec 7 1915	Stranded	Petit Bois Island, Miss.
897	JC 1700	Brg.	799	1964	Sep 9 1965	Storm	In harbor of New Orleans, La.
898	J.C. Atlee	St.p.	87	1886	Sep 15 1918	Burned	Jonesville, La.
899	J.C. Burdett	St.p.	85	1893	Sep 29 1915	Foundered	New Orleans, La.
900	J.C. Werner, Jr.	St.w.	95	1918	Feb 7 1934	Foundered	Melville, La.
901	J.D. Hinde	St.s.	111	1863	Nov 1 1869	Snagged	Trinity River, Texas.
902	J.E. Trudeau	St.p.	242	1889	Feb 29 1912	Burned	Belle River, La. 10 lives lost.
903	J.F. Pargoud	St.p.	522	1860	Jul 14 1863	Burned	Yazoo City, Miss.
904	J.G. Blackford	St.w.	248	1864	Jan 13 1871	Burned	Wetumpka, Ala.
905	J.J. McCarthy	Ol.s.	139	1891	May 9 1951	Foundered	In Mississippi River, Texas. Iron vessel.
906	J.J. Warren	St.p.	132	1858	Jan 29 1859	Snagged	Sabine River, Texas.
907	J.L. McLean	St.p.	271	1849	Mar 4 1854	Snagged	Grenada, Miss.
908	J.M. Jones	St.w.	134	1911	Mar 17 1929	Burned	Coles Creek, La.
909	J.M. Jones	St.w.	134	1911	Mar 14 1931	Burned	Fitler's Landing, Miss.
910	J.O. Ellison	St.s.	555	1909	Jun 15 1914	Foundered	Gulf of Mexico.
911	J.S.	St.p.	292	1901	Jun 25 1910	Burned	Bad Axe Island, Mississippi River. 2 lives lost.
912	J.S. Chenoweth	St.p.	309	1851	Sep 17 1855	Foundered	Algiers, La.
913	J.W. Clise	Sch.	845	1904	Aug 5 1940	Foundered	26-50-00 N. 88-10-00 W.
914	J.W. Somerville	Sch.	547	1919	Oct 24 1921	Foundered	Gulf of Mexico. All lives (8) lost.
915	Jack Pharr	Ol.s.	62	1944	Sep 3 1963	Foundered	In Gulf of Mexico, about 80 miles south of Freeport, Texas.
916	Jackie Ann	Ol.s.	56	1947	Feb 25 1956	Collided	With JAY MAMA. In Gulf of Mexico, about 13 miles NNE of Tuxpam, Mexico.
917	Jackson	St.w.	84	1860	Apr 2 1862	Burned	New Orleans, La.
918	Jacob Luckenbach	St.s.	6,570	1910	May 8 1927	Stranded	10-07-00 N. 85-49-00 W. Steel vessel.
919	Jas. A. Carney	St.p.	199	1894	Jul 5 1916	Foundered	Mobile River, Ala.
920	Jas. B. Cobb	Ol.s.	76	1905	Mar 10 1964	Foundered	In Snow's Creek, on the Black Warrior-Tombigbee Rivers, about Mile 399.4, north of Mobile, Ala. Steel vessel.
921	James Clooney	Ol.s.	51	1943	Mar 6 1955	Foundered	On Broussards Beach, 5.5 miles east of Cameron, La., 1/2 mile offshore.
922	Jas. T. Staples	St.s.	365	1908	Jan 9 1913	Exploded	Tombigbee River, Ala. 16 lives lost.
923	James Trabue	St.p.	300	1854	Feb 16 1855	Snagged	Campti, La.
924	Jan R	Ol.s.	73	1953	Sep 11 1961	Hurricane	At dock, Port Lavaca, Texas.
925	Jan T	Ol.s.	67	1962	Apr 19 1968	Stranded	On Alacran Reef, Gulf of Mexico.

NO.	NAME OF VESSEL	RIG	TONS	BUILT	DATE	CAUSE	PLACE AND COMMENT
926	Jane Smith	Ol.s.	216	1948	May 19 1950	Stranded	At Melville, La., after collision with bridge. Steel vessel.
927	Janis Walker	Ol.s.	184	1953	May 6 1961	Burned	About 2-3/4 miles west of Block 131, Vermillion Parish, off Louisiana coast.
928	Japonica	Ol.s.	66	1906	Sep 6 1941	Burned	Near Rockport, Texas.
929	Java Arrow	St.s.	8,328	-	May 5 1942	War Loss	27-30-00 N. 80-08-00 W.
930	Jayhawk	Ol.s.	94	1939	Jan 1 1946	Foundered	Mile 335, Mississippi River. Steel vessel.
931	Jeff Davis	St.p.	107	1847	Oct 10 1850	Snagged	Sartaria, Miss.
932	Jefferson	St.w.	74	1851	Feb 26 1852	Snagged	Campti, La.
933	Jefferson	St.s.	99	1896	Sep 29 1915	Foundered	New Orleans, La. Iron vessel.
934	Jennie Hubbs	St.w.	220	1863	Dec 27 1868	Foundered	Natchez, Miss.
935	Jennie Louise	St.p.	77	1890	Oct 29 1913	Burned	At Berwick, La.
936	Jennie S. Hall	Sch.	450	1881	Aug 14 1916	Foundered	Gulfport, Miss. All lives (7) lost.
937	Jesse C. Barbour	Sch.	1,908	1919	Jun 3 1922	Burned	St. Joseph Island, Texas.
938	Jessie	-		-	1875	Unknown	Off Brazos, Texas. Said to be worth $100,000.
939	Jessie	St.w.	187	1866	Jul 3 1875	Unknown	New Orleans, La. Used as ferryboat.
940	Jessie A. Bishop	Sch.	754	1908	Jan 1 1912	Stranded	Nassau Inlet, Fla.
941	Jewess	St.p.	150	1839	Oct 28 1841	Snagged	Canton, Ala.
942	Jewess	St.p.	206	1862	Dec 28 1868	Snagged	Mobile, Ala.
943	Jim Gilmer	St.p.	115	1846	Mar 13 1851	Snagged	Soda Lake, La. 2 lives lost.
944	Jim Turner	St.p.	212	1853	Apr 27 1853	Snagged	Rowland, La.
945	Jimmie Boy	Ol.s.	94	1945	Jan 8 1950	Foundered	10 miles south of Roca Partida, Revilla Gigido Islands, Mexico. Steel vessel.
946	Jimmy & Renie	Ol.s.	61	1953	Mar 26 1959	Burned	Off Arcas Keys, Fla.
947	Joan of Arc	Ol.s.	56	1951	Dec 25 1959	Stranded	Off Grande Isle, La.
948	Joe B. Chaffe	St.w.	55	1906	Sep 8 1934	Foundered	Westwego, La.
949	Joe Davis	St.p.	218	1842	Dec 10 1843	Snagged	Plaquemine, La.
950	Joe Ed	Ol.s.	54	1945	Aug 8 1954	Burned	6 miles upstream from mouth of the San Bernard River, Texas. Steel vessel.
951	Joe-Gal	Ol.s.	74	1954	Feb 5 1955	Burned	In Campeche Bay, Mexico.
952	Joe L. Hill	Ol.s.	79	1875	Jul 7 1965	Foundered	In Mississippi River, at 9 Mile Point, La.
953	Joe M.	Ol.s.	67	1948	Mar 9 1960	Foundered	At San Luis Pass, Texas.
954	Joetta	St.p.	50	1949	Feb 2 1950	Foundered	Between Freeport and Matagorda Bay, Texas.
955	John A. Patten	St.p.	229	1906	Nov 4 1910	Burned	Bridgeport, Ala.
956	John A. Wood	St.w.	687	1870	Dec 8 1925	Burned	Baton Rouge, La.
957	John C. Fremont	St.w.	315	1854	May 1863	Collided	With MODERATOR. Grand Gulf, Miss. Renamed "Horizon" on March 1, 1863.
958	John Duncan	St.p.	265	1839	Dec 30 1844	Snagged	Tuscaloosa, Ala.
959	John E. Coon	Ol.s.	112	1955	Mar 29 1962	Foundered	At Mile 227 AHP, Mississippi River, Baton Rouge, La. Steel vessel.
960	John F.	Ol.s.	56	1909	Jul 18 1966	Foundered	At dock on Brays Bayou, Houston, Texas.
961	John Francis	Sch.	322	1897	Oct 17 1922	Stranded	Cozumel Island, Yucatan, Mexico.
962	John G. North	Brg.	336	1881	May 14 1919	Burned	Cabo San Lucas Bay, Mexico.
963	John I. Brady	St.s.	118	1891	Jun 26 1911	Burned	Port Arthur, Texas. Iron vessel.
964	John L. Avery	St.p.	323	1853	Mar 9 1854	Snagged	Fort Adams, Miss. 40 lives lost. Also reported lost at New Orleans, La.
965	John Linton	St.p.	307	1836	Apr 19 1845	Snagged	New Orleans, La.
966	John M. Emery	St.s.	1,560	1919	Jan 13 1920	Foundered	Off Brazos River Bar, Galveston, Texas.
967	John & Mary	Ol.s.	63	1952	Jul 25 1958	Burned	About 15 miles southeast of Freeport Bar, Texas.
968	John Peirce	Sch.	405	1888	Dec 26 1920	Foundered	23-02-00 N. 86-20-00 W.
969	John Raine	St.p.	541	1858	Jan 17 1867	Burned	Greenville, Miss. 59 lives lost.
970	John Ray	St.w.	86	1859	Aug 5 1860	Snagged	Pine Prairie, La.
971	John Sealy	St.s.	113	1910	Nov 21 1919	Collided	With st.s. PAULSBORO. Sabine Pass, Texas. 1 life lost.
972	John Swasey	St.p.	274	1851	Feb 16 1853	Burned	New Orleans, La. 3 lives lost.
973	John W. Dana	Sch.	556	1900	Dec 7 1915	Stranded	Chandeleur Islands, La.

NO.	NAME OF VESSEL	RIG	TONS	BUILT	DATE		CAUSE	PLACE AND COMMENT
974	John Walsh	St.p.	809	1858	May 22	1863	Burned	Fort Pemberton, Miss.
975	John Warner	St.p.	391	1856	May 15	1864	Burned	Red River, La.
976	Jordan Bros.	Ol.s.	84	1953	Apr 16	1960	Foundered	About 65 miles NNW of Arcas Island, Mexico.
978	Joseph Anthony	Ol.s.	58	1949	Feb 9	1955	Foundered	About 20 miles SSE of Port Aransas Bar, Gulf of Mexico.
979	Joseph Bisso	St.s.	110	1903	Sep 29	1915	Foundered	New Orleans, La.
980	Joseph Bisso	St.w.	169	1916	Jul 13	1946	Burned	Louisiana Ave. and Mississippi River, New Orleans, La. Steel vessel.
981	Jos. Favre-Baldwin	St.s.	50	1902	Sep 27	1906	Burned	Fairport, Miss.
982	Joseph H. Davis	Ol.s.	135	1876	Mar 2	1959	Burned	28-39-00 N. 90-54-00 W.
983	Joseph Holden	St.w.	222	1856	Apr 7	1859	Snagged	Twelve Mile Bayou, La.
984	Joseph M. Cudahy	St.s.	6,949	-	May 5	1942	War Loss	24-57-00 N. 84-10-00 W. Tanker. Off Florida (west coast). Depth 300'.
985	Joseph Pierce	St.p.	533	1864	Jul 31	1865	Exploded	Palmyra Landing, Miss. 12 lives lost.
986	Josephine	St.s.	254	1860	Jun	1879	Burned	Rigolets, La.
987	Josephine	Sch.			Oct 18	1887	Unknown	Matagorda Peninsula, Texas.
988	Josephine	St.s.	774	1886	Sep 27	1906	Collided	With barge BLACK DIAMOND. Mobile, Ala.
989	Josephine Savage	St.p.	465	1857	Jan 8	1859	Burned	Tunica Island, Natchez, Miss.
990	Judge Porter	St.p.	203	1859	Mar 13	1860	Burned	Lake Pontchartrain, La. 7 lives lost.
991	Judy Lane	Ol.s.	83	1955	Dec 16	1963	Foundered	About 3 miles east of Santana, Mexico.
992	Jujubee	Ol.s.	59	1958	Nov 30	1959	Burned	About 4 miles south of Colorado River, Matagorda Bay, Texas.
993	Julie	Ol.s.	64	1957	Feb 10	1968	Collided	With submerged object. 80 miles southeast of Galveston Sea Buoy, Galveston, Texas.
994	Julie Ann	Brg.	3,118	1957	Mar 13	1968	Collided	At Block 276, Eugene Island, La. 28-26-00 N. 91-27-00 W.
995	Juniata	St.p.	110	1832	Oct 11	1842	Snagged	Mobile, Ala.
996	Justice	St.p.	117	1864	Jun 9	1870	Foundered	Liberty, Texas to Galveston, Texas.
997	K - D	Ol.s.	57	1948	Apr 25	1949	Burned	Off coast of Brownsville, Texas.
998	Kankakee	St.s.	84	1865	Jun 11	1871	Foundered	New Orleans, La. 1 life lost.
999	Kansas	St.p.	111	1836	Nov 4	1841	Exploded	Claiborne, Ala.
1000	Karen Bradley	Ol.s.	85	1953	Nov 9	1953	Foundered	On reef at Arcas Island, Bay of Campeche, Mexico.
1001	Kate Adams	-	-	-	Dec 24	1888	Burned	Mississippi River. 23 lives lost.
1002	Kate Dale	St.p.	428	1856	May 25	1865	Burned	Mobile, Ala.
1003	Kate Feore	Sch.	383	1902	Sep 20	1909	Foundered	Gulf of Mexico. 2 lives lost.
1004	Kathy D	Ol.s.	73	1951	Dec 29	1960	Foundered	Gulf of Mexico, about 35 miles northeast of Port Isabel, Texas. Steel vessel.
1005	Katy Sue	Ol.s.	63	1953	Feb 5	1966	Collided	With submerged object. Eastsoutheast of Pass Cavallo Light. 28-02 N. 95-45 W.
1006	Kellogg	St.p.	1,178	1898	Mar 21	1928	Foundered	New Orleans, La. Steel vessel.
1007	Kelly K.	Ol.s.	52	1957	Nov 4	1961	Foundered	On Port Mansfield jetty, Port Mansfield, Texas.
1008	Kermac XVI	Ol.s.	68	1943	Aug 2	1955	Foundered	Gulf of Mexico. 29-15-00 N. 89-55-00 W.
1009	Keturah	Ol.s.	77	1925	Jun 20	1957	Hurricane	About 11 miles off Galveston Bar, Texas.
1010	Key Largo	Ol.s.	59	1958	Jun 24	1965	Foundered	At Sargent Beach, Texas.
1011	Kiva	Ga.s.	69	1917	Oct 1	1939	Burned	Gulf of Mexico, off entrance to Southwest Pass, Mississippi River.
1012	Knoxville	-	-	-	Dec 17	1850	Exploded	New Orleans, La. 19 lives lost.
1013	Knoxville	St.p.	349	1848	Jul 3	1855	Burned	New Orleans, La. 4 lives lost.
1014	Kokomo	Ol.s.	141	1944	Aug 18	1964	Burned	Southeast of Freeport, Texas.
1015	Korsholm	-	-	-	Apr 13	1942	Unknown	28-12-10 N. 80-29-15 W. Presumed freighter lost during war. Depth 60'.
1016	L.E. Patton	St.w.	94	1894	Aug 26	1926	Foundered	Convent, La. Steel vessel. All lives (9) lost.
1017	L.H. Marrero	St.s.	163	1905	Jan 22	1946	Burned	Off Louisiana Ave., in Mississippi River, New Orleans, La. Steel vessel.
1018	L.P. Featherstone	Brg.	838	1908	Aug 15	1915	Stranded	Galveston, Texas.
1019	L.T.C. No.16	Brg.	283	1932	May 10	1948	Collided	With barge L.T.C. No.15. Approximately 1 mile upstream from Huey Long Bridge, near New Orleans, La.
1020	L. Dillard	St.w.	56	1865	Jan 31	1867	Snagged	Soda Lake, La.
1021	La Crosse	St.w.	186	1856	Apr 12	1864	Burned	Eggbend, La.

NO.	NAME OF VESSEL	RIG	TONS	BUILT	DATE		CAUSE	PLACE AND COMMENT
1022	La Fourche	St.p.	398	1888	Sep 20	1907	Burned	Twelve Mile Point, La.
1023	Lacon	St.p.	118	1845	Mar	1846	Snagged	Yazoo River, Miss.
1024	Lady Franklin	St.w.	207	1860	Jan 31	1867	Burned	Algiers, La.
1025	Lady Grace	St.p.	144	1881	Sep 27	1906	Stranded	Mobile, Ala.
1026	Lady Jane	Ol.s.	50	1945	Apr 5	1952	Burned	About 4 miles northeast of anchor basin in the Brownsville Ship Channel, Texas.
1027	Lady Lynn	Ol.s.	65	1953	Apr 4	1960	Collided	With Liberian freighter DORIEFS. 24-04-00 N. 86-29-00 W.
1028	Lady Mae	Ol.s.	50	1946	Jul 13	1951	Stranded	About 15 miles north of Coast Guard Station, on Padre Island, Texas.
1029	Lady Washington	St.p.	96	1832	Jan 9	1836	Snagged	Natchez, Miss.
1030	Laetres	St.s.	3,629	-	May 3	1942	War Loss	28-28-48 N. 80-23-00 W. Depth 50'.
1031	Lama	St.p.	68	1844	May 29	1847	Exploded	Camargo, Mexico.
1032	Laura L. Sprague	Sch.	594	1890	Mar 18	1913	Stranded	Mobile Bar, Mobile, Ala.
1033	Laurel	Sch.	-	-	Dec 31	1888	Unknown	Matagorda Island, Texas.
1034	Lawrence	St.s.	259	1895	Aug 16	1915	Foundered	Harrisburg, Texas.
1035	Lea	-	-	-		1880	Unknown	Matamoras, Mexico. Said to be valued at $100,000.
1036	Leah Ann	Ol.s.	79	1956	Jun 8	1967	Burned	About 3.5 miles south of Houma, La., the Houma Navigation Canal.
1037	Lebanon	St.w.	225	1855	May 27	1864	Burned	Greenville, Miss.
1038	Lecompte	St.p.	238	1855	Mar 27	1861	Burned	Mobile, Ala.
1039	Lecompte	St.p.	250	1856	Apr 16	1861	Snagged	Campti, La.
1040	Leeville	Ol.s.	59	1954	Jul 31	1961	Burned	Gulf of Mexico, about 7 miles south of Belle Pass, La.
1041	Lelia No.7	St.w.	134	1851	May 4	1853	Burned	Algiers, La.
1042	Leo Huff	Ol.s.	157	1941	Dec 5	1947	Burned	29-35-00 N. 93-14-00 W.
1043	Leona	St.p.	232	1856	Dec 16	1859	Snagged	Coushatta, La.
1044	Leopard	St.p.	73	1822	Aug 5	1825	Snagged	Point Chicot, La.
1045	Leora M. Thurlow	Sch.	213	1891	Apr 21	1920	Stranded	Chincorro Reef, Yucatan, Mexico.
1046	Leslie	-	2,609	-	Apr 12	1942	Unknown	28-35-00 N. 80-19-00 W. Probable freighter lost during war.
1047	Lewis Brothers (Br.)	Sch.	-	-	Pre-WWII		Unknown	30-09-30 N. 88-29-15 W. Depth 45'.
1048	Lewis Cass	St.s.	7,176	1943	Jan 25	1943	Stranded	2 miles southwest of Northern Point, Guadalupe Island, Mexico. Steel vessel.
1049	Lexington	St.p.	230	1836		1842	Snagged	Napoleon, La.
1050	Liah Tuna	St.p.	646	1853	Feb 4	1854	Burned	New Orleans, La.
1051	Libbie Shearn	Sch.	58	1900	Nov 2	1911	Stranded	Aransas Pass, Texas.
1052	Lt. W. Robinson III	Ol.s.	57	1945	May 31	1948	Burned	Off coast, Freeport, Texas.
1053	Lightwood	St.w.	133	1884	Nov 27	1925	Burned	Rosedale, Miss.
1054	L'il Texan	Ol.s.	51	1958	Feb 8	1960	Burned	About 65 miles SSE of Eugene Island Light, off Louisiana coast.
1055	Lillian B	Ga.s.	58	1905	Jul 6	1916	Foundered	Tampico, Mexico.
1056	Lillie	St.p.	580	1893	Sep 3	1906	Foundered	Trinity, La.
1057	Lilly	St.w.	190	1865	Jan 10	1868	Snagged	Tuscaloosa, Ala.
1058	Lindbar	Ol.s.	85	1925	Aug 4	1958	Burned	At Lower Mississippi, at Mile 381. Steel vessel.
1059	Linde No.5	Drg.	231	1909	Jul 16	1936	Burned	8 miles from Port Bolivar, Texas.
1060	Lion	St.p.	160	1843	Oct 5	1846	Burned	Mobile, Ala.
1061	Lioness	St.p.	160	1832	May 19	1833	Exploded	Montgomery, Ala. 15 lives lost.
1062	Lisboa	Ol.s.	64	1926	Apr 14	1931	Burned	Magdallen, Mexico.
1063	Little Cracker	Ol.s.	56	1949	Dec 10	1966	Burned	In Atchafalya Bayou, 1 mile west of Berwick, La.
1064	Little Lorraine	Ol.s.	66	1953	Feb 5	1955	Stranded	About 2 miles east of Chiltepec, Mexico.
1065	Little Mitch	Ol.s.	76	1953	Feb 1	1960	Burned	Approximately 40 miles southeast of Port Aransas, Texas.
1066	Little Pardner	Ol.s.	64	1957	Feb 15	1960	Foundered	In Gulf of Mexico, vicinity of Frontera, Mexico.
1067	Little Red	Ol.s.	82	1930	Oct 23	1966	Foundered	On Main Pass, near Block 46, in Mississippi River, La.
1068	Little Rufus	St.p.	278	1903	Jan 14	1914	Burned	Near Natches, Miss.
1069	Live Oak	St.p.	64	1845	Jun 4	1846	Snagged	New Orleans, La.

NO.	NAME OF VESSEL	RIG	TONS	BUILT	DATE	CAUSE	PLACE AND COMMENT
1070	Lizzie A. Williams	Sch.	188	1892	Jul 13 1917	Collided	With unknown tanker. Gulf of Mexico.
1071	Lizzie Lake	St.w.	53	1855	Dec 7 1859	Snagged	Guadalupe River, Texas.
1072	Lizzie Lee	St.p.	101	1856	Jan 15 1857	Snagged	Twelve Mile Bayou, La.
1073	Lizzie Prien	Sch.	95	1884	Oct 3 1913	Stranded	Near Mulege, Mexico.
1074	Lochinvar	Ol.s.	96	1928	Jun 12 1966	Burned	In Black Levee Canal at Empire, La.
1075	Lockport	St.p.	54	1908	Jul 19 1920	Foundered	Gretna, La.
1076	Lodi	St.p.	91	1843	Dec 27 1845	Snagged	Grand River, La.
1077	Logan	St.p.	70	1834	Jul 23 1836	Collided	With CASPIAN. Alexandria, La.
1078	Loless Maurine	Ol.s.	65	1960	Feb 7 1967	Foundered	About 50 miles south of Tampico, Mexico. 21-35-00 N. 97-20-00 W.
1079	Lone Star	St.w.	121	1859	Mar 1 1860	Snagged	Trinity River, Texas.
1080	Lone Star	Ol.s.	164	1943	Jul 13 1951	Burned	In Galveston Bay, 2,600 feet southwest of black can buoy No.45, Texas.
1081	Longhorn	Ol.s.	67	1950	Mar 16 1960	Burned	About 25 miles SSE of Beacon Eugene Lykes, Morgan City, La.
1082	Lonnie Dale	Ol.s.	76	1953	Jan 20 1955	Foundered	23-00-00 N. 85-50-00 W.
1083	Lotawanna	St.w.	479	1867	Jun 30 1874	Lost	New Orleans, La.
1084	Lottie Carson	Ga.s.	284	1881	Sep 19 1941	Collided	With Mexican CAMPECHE. At Mazatlan, Mexico.
1085	Lotus	St.w.	153	1856	Aug 20 1858	Snagged	Montgomery, La.
1086	Loufayterry	Ol.s.	56	1954	Nov 17 1955	Foundered	On Wine Island, La.
1087	Louisa	St.p.	393	1851	Mar 2 1855	Snagged	Harrisonburg, La.
1088	Louisa No.2	St.w.	57	1856	May 1859	Snagged	Bayou Bartholomew, La.
1089	Louise	St.s.	126	1887	Oct 18 1905	Stranded	Near Pointe a la Hache, La.
1090	Louise R.	Ol.s.	57	1951	Jan 15 1961	Stranded	About 30 miles north of Tuxpan, Mexico. 21-05-00 N. 97-01-00 W.
1091	Louise Ray	Ol.s.	52	1927	Nov 4 1937	Stranded	Anacapa Island, Mexico.
1092	Louisiana	-	-	-	Aug 1841	Exploded	Mississippi River. 20 lives lost.
1093	Louisiana	St.p.	376	1848	Nov 15 1849	Exploded	New Orleans, La. 86 lives lost. See No. 1092.
1094	Louisiana	St.s.	1,056	1850	May 31 1857	Burned	Galveston, Texas. 55 lives lost.
1095	Louisiana	St.s.	2,674	1919	Oct 28 1926	Collided	With st.s. MADISON. South Pass, La. Steel vessel. 1 life lost (29).
1096	Louisiana Belle	St.w.	89	1859	Jun 1 1862	Burned	Red River, La.
1097	Lua	Ol.s.	60	1952	Jan 23 1963	Foundered	About 2 miles northeast of Brazos Santiago jetties, off coast of Port Isabel, Texas.
1098	Lubrofol	St.s.	4,588	-	May 9 1942	War Loss	29-14-00 N. 80-10-00 W.
1099	Luchador	Ol.s.	67	1954	Nov 6 1968	Foundered	About 45 miles west of Campeche, Mexico.
1100	Lucile	Ol.s.	63	1952	Oct 15 1959	Stranded	On Lobos Island, in Gulf of Mexico.
1101	Lucky Star	Ol.s.	66	1947	Dec 3 1956	Foundered	In Gulf of Mexico, about 70 miles south of Port Isabel, Texas.
1102	Lucy Walker	St.p.	182	1843	Oct 25 1844	Exploded	New Orleans, La. 18 lives lost.
1103	Luda	St.p.	244	1841	Jan 8 1846	Collided	Plaquemine, La.
1104	Luda	St.w.	93	1851	Feb 20 1855	Snagged	Red River, La.
1105	Ludlow	Sch.	762	1900	May 27 1925	Burned	Gulfport, Miss.
1106	Luna	St.p.	321	1846	May 17 1850	Collided	With DUCHESS. Donaldsonville, La. 5 lives lost.
1107	Luzerne	St.p.	179	1852	Jan 28 1864	Lost	Crawford Ledge, Mississippi River.
1108	Lyco T	Ol.s.	64	1956	Mar 11 1964	Stranded	About 200 yards north of the north jetty, Port Isabel, Texas.
1109	Lyco XX	Ol.s.	64	1957	Jun 24 1968	Burned	About 8 miles south of Galveston, Texas.
1110	Lydia	Bark	-	-	Nov 1887	Unknown	Campeche, Mexico.
1111	Lydia H. Roper	Sch.	321	1875	Mar 16 1925	Foundered	Pilot Town, Miss.
1112	Lydia M. Deering	Sch.	1,224	1889	Aug 16 1915	Foundered	25-39-00 N. 92-46-00 W. 3 lives lost.
1113	Lysistrata	Ol.y.	64	1937	Dec 1 1938	Burned	Mobile, Ala.
1114	M-65	Brg.	898	1958	Mar 31 1961	Foundered	In Mississippi River, near Baton Rouge, La. Steel vessel.
1115	M.A. Bowlin	Ol.s.	61	1943	Oct 18 1965	Burned	In Lake Constance, 10 miles southwest of Pecan Island, La.
1116	MBL	Brg.	770	1954	Sep 10 1965	Hurricane	Near Baton Rouge, La.

NO.	NAME OF VESSEL	RIG	TONS	BUILT	DATE	CAUSE	PLACE AND COMMENT
1117	M. Carney	St.p.	75	1913	Jul 7 1916	Collided	With dam lock #12. Warrior River, La.
1118	M.G.O. Co., No.11	Brg.	326	1914	Jul 13 1915	Burned	Panuco River, Mexico.
1119	M.P. Co. No.7	Sch.	2,130	1919	Oct 7 1921	Burned	East of Tampico, Mexico. 2 lives lost.
1120	MTC 602	Brg.	262	1955	Sep 10 1965	Hurricane	In Mississippi River, near Baton Rouge, La.
1121	MV 656	Brg.	911	1956	Sep 23 1960	Collided	With st.s. TRIMBLE'S FORD. Mile 170 Ahp, lower Mississippi River, near Burnside, La. Steel vessel.
1122	Madeleine	Sch.	463	1902	Dec 21 1914	Stranded	Chandeleir Island, Gulf of Mexico.
1123	Madison	St.p.	322	1835	Jan 21 1838	Snagged	Way, Miss.
1124	Madison	St.p.	399	1853	Aug 6 1866	Burned	Gretna, La.
1125	Maertis	-		Unknown		Unknown	28-28-48 N. 80-22-00 W.
1126	Magenta	St.p.	782	1861	Jul 14 1863	Burned	Above Yazoo City, Miss.
1127	Magnolia	St.p.	596	1845	Jul 8 1855	Burned	Baton Rouge, La. 8 lives lost.
1128	Magnolia	St.p.	160	1850	Jun 12 1856	Stranded	Vicksburg, Miss. 3 lives lost.
1129	Magnolia	St.p.	824	1859	Jul 14 1863	Burned	Above Yazoo City, Miss.
1130	Magnolia	St.p.	72	1907	Mar 6 1921	Burned	Allemands, La.
1131	Magnolia Banner	St.p.	151	1855	Jul 3 1855	Burned	Baton Rouge, La. 8 lives lost.
1132	Magyar	St.p.	135	1849	Jan 4 1854	Exploded	35 miles east of Galveston, Texas.
1133	Maid of Arkansas	St.p.	213	1840	Nov 3 1842	Burned	Carrollton, La.
1134	Majestic	St.w.	201	1864	Oct 22 1865	Burned	Pointe Coupee, La.
1135	Major A. Harris	St.p.	102	1852	Feb 6 1857	Exploded	Galveston, Texas. 1 life lost.
1136	Major Aubry	St.p.	79	1853	Nov 1858	Snagged	Berwick, La.
1137	Major Gen. Henry Gibbins	St.s.	5,766	-	Jun 23 1942	War Loss	24-35-00 N. 87-45-00 W. Steel vessel. Sunk by enemy action.
1138	Malcolm B. Toomer	Ol.s.	78	1954	Nov 11 1966	Foundered	Southwest of South West Pass, off Mississippi River.
1139	Mamie Higgins	St.s.	77	1879	Apr 28 1925	Burned	Houston Ship Channel, Texas.
1140	Mammoth Cave	St.p.	96	1849	May 3 1852	Collided	With GRENADA. Little Sunflower River, Miss.
1141	Mandan	St.p.	127	1819	Nov 20 1824	Stranded	Vicksburg, Miss.
1142	Manharton (Br.)	St.s.		-	Pre-WWII	Unknown	30-12-26 N. 88-20-04 W. Freighter.
1143	Marengo	St.p.	326	1844	Aug 24 1848	Collided	With HARRY HILL. Clarksville, Miss. 3 lives lost.
1144	Margaret	Ol.s.	158	1908	Sep 9 1965	Hurricane	In Mississippi River, 1000 feet upriver from Louisiana Ave. Wharf, New Orleans.
1145	Margaret M.	Ol.s.	143	1944	May 23 1957	Foundered	About 12 miles from the Aransas South Jetty Light, Texas, in Gulf of Mexico, on a course of 125°. Steel vessel.
1146	Margate	Brg.	199	1926	Dec 28 1943	Burned	Galveston, Texas.
1147	Marguedora	Ga.y.	58	1902	Aug 23 1905	Burned	Carrabelle River, Fla.
1148	Maria	St.p.	692	1844	Nov 21 1846	Collided	With SULTAN. Natchez, Miss. 30 lives lost.
1149	Maria Burt	St.p.	319	1846	Jun 25 1851	Foundered	Galveston, Texas.
1150	Maria Denning	St.p.	691	1856	May 11 1866	Burned	Algiers, La.
1151	Maria Hein	St.p.	310	1864	Feb 27 1866	Burned	Red River, La.
1152	Marian	Sch.	258	1889	May 17 1907	Stranded	Tupilco, Mexico.
1153	Marian	Ol.s.	65	1953	May 6 1968	Collided	With submerged object. Westnorthwest of Campeche, Mexico.
1154	Marie	Ol.s.	76	1952	Jan 5 1960	Foundered	In Gulf of Mexico, about 30 miles south of Port Isabel, Texas. Steel vessel.
1155	Marie Theresa	-		-		Unknown	Off Padre Island, Texas. Also known as "Marie Therese".
1156	Marilyn Rose	Ol.s.	199	1950	Aug 7 1955	Stranded	On Asuncion Island, Mexico.
1157	Marine Transit Company Barge No.12	Brg.	395	1941	Jan 26 1950	Foundered	In Mississippi River, at Vicksburg Highway and Railway Bridge, Vicksburg, Miss.
1158	Marine Transit Company Barge No.14	Brg.	761	1944	Nov 17 1966	Foundered	In Mississippi River, off Burnside, La.
1159	Mariner	St.p.	98	1836	Mar 10 1841	Snagged	Pecan Point, La.

NO.	NAME OF VESSEL	RIG	TONS	BUILT	DATE	CAUSE	PLACE AND COMMENT
1160	Marion	St.p.	139	1835	Dec 9 1835	Collided	New Orleans, La.
1161	Marion	St.w.	133	1854	Jan 7 1859	Snagged	Soda Lake, La.
1162	Marion N. Cobb	Sch.	459	1902	Nov 28 1925	Foundered	28-50-00 N. 87-30-00 W.
1163	Mark R. Cheek	St.p.	122	1860	Mar 31 1865	Burned	Ouachita City, La. Used as ferryboat.
1164	Markatana	H.bt.	262	1904	Dec 31 1942	Burned	Black Bayou, La.
1165	Marmora	St.p.	261	1836	Dec 23 1837	Burned	Red River, La.
1166	Marmora	St.w.	177	1857	Feb 15 1867	Burned	Lake Providence, La.
1167	Marowijne	-	-	-	Aug 13 1915	Lost	Gulf of Mexico. 87 lives lost.
1168	Marquette	St.p.	126	1842	Jul 1 1845	Exploded	New Orleans, La. 13 lives lost. Also reported as "Marquitte".
1169	Mars	St.p.	61	1820	Dec 6 1822	Stranded	Cantrell Church, La.
1170	Marshal Ney	St.p.	486	1847	Oct 8 1849	Burned	New Orleans, La.
1171	Martha	Sch.	91	1897	May 17 1917	Stranded	14 miles south of Rio Grande, Texas.
1172	Martha H. Hennan	St.p.	77	1904	Jul 5 1916	Foundered	Mobile River, Ala.
1173	Marvin D.	Ol.s.	55	1936	Jul 27 1940	Burned	29 miles west of Harvey, La.
1174	Mary	St.w.	202	1866	Nov 6 1868	Snagged	Black Warrior River, Ala.
1175	Mary	St.p.	198	1899	Sep 27 1906	Foundered	Mobile, Ala.
1176	Mary A. Bell	St.w.	80	1918	Dec 24 1929	Foundered	Clayton, La.
1177	Mary Ann	Ol.s.	109	1947	Aug 20 1952	Foundered	45 miles south-southwest from Geronimo Island, Mexico.
1178	Mary B	St.p.	84	1903	Mar 31 1906	Collided	With log. Belle Point, La.
1179	Mary Clifton	St.p.	207	1849	Feb 26 1855	Snagged	Tait Shoals, Ala.
1180	Mary Crane	St.w.	111	1862	Jan 8 1863	Burned	Lake Cormorant, Miss.
1181	Mary E. Forsythe	St.p.	621	1862	Jun 4 1873	Stranded	Chandeleur Island, Miss.
1182	Mary E. Silveria	Sch.	93	1904	Aug 16 1915	Foundered	Gulf of Mexico. All lives (9) lost.
1183	Mary Ellen	Sch.	-	-	May 3 1890	Unknown	Gulf of Mexico.
1184	Mary Express	St.p.	54	1836	1840	Burned	Mobile, Ala.
1185	Mary G. Dantzler	Sch.	490	1915	Jul 5 1916	Foundered	Off Ship Island, Miss. All lives (8) lost.
1186	Mary Hill	St.p.	234	1858	Nov 22 1865	Snagged	Trinity River, Texas.
1187	Mary Lou	Ol.w.	91	1932	Feb 21 1933	Burned	Bayou Plaquemine, La.
1188	Mary McDonald	St.p.	563	1866	Jun 12 1873	Burned	Gillman Landing, Mississippi River.
1189	Mary Shaw	St.s.	74	1862	Nov 3 1900	Snagged	Mobile, Ala.
1190	Marylee	Ol.s.	64	1954	Oct 31 1962	Foundered	In the Yucatan Channel. About 24-00 N. 85-00 W.
1191	Masco II	Ol.s.	260	1925	Mar 19 1959	Burned	In the Mermentau River, about 8 miles upstream from the Lake Arthur, La., bridge. Steel vessel.
1192	Massachusetts	-	-	-	1921	Unknown	30-17-48 N. 87-18-42 W. Visible.
1193	Mathilda Jane	St.p.	87	1845	Mar 1849	Snagged	New Orleans, La. Used as ferryboat.
1194	Mattie	St.w.	149	1863	May 14 1867	Snagged	Bayou Bartholomew, La.
1195	Maude Palmer	Sch.	1,745	1900	Aug 26 1915	Foundered	Gulf of Mexico. All lives (11) lost.
1196	Maverick	Brg.	2,955	1964	Sep 9 1965	Hurricane	In the Mississippi River Delta.
1197	May A. Bruner	St.w.	172	1865	Feb 3 1866	Burned	Mouth of Red River, La.
1198	May Fisher	St.p.	52	1875	Oct 17 1905	Foundered	Baton Rouge, La.
1199	May Flower	St.p.	262	1845	Oct 1872	Burned	Mobile, Ala. Redocumented "Ella May".
1200	Mediator	St.p.	421	1852	Jan 4 1856	Burned	St. Joseph, La.
1201	Medora	St.p.	210	1835	Nov 22 1842	Snagged	McGrews, Ala.
1202	Melodeon	St.p.	244	1849	Dec 14 1850	Collided	With GEORGE W. KENDALL. Plaquemine, La. 3 lives lost.
1203	Memphis	St.p.	462	1843	Nov 3 1847	Snagged	Profit Island, La.
1204	Merchant	St.p.	64	1840	Oct 3 1842	Stranded	West Temalier, La. 8 lives lost.
1205	Merchant	St.p.	305	1835	Oct 4 1842	Stranded	West Temalier, La. 8 lives lost.
1205	Mercury	Brg.	1,949	1945	Nov 1 1966	Foundered	About 25 miles south-southwest of Tampico, Mexico.

NO.	NAME OF VESSEL	RIG	TONS	BUILT	DATE		CAUSE	PLACE AND COMMENT
1206	Meriwether	Ga.s.	147	1917	Jul 8	1921	Burned	Lake Pontchartrain, La.
1207	Messenger	St.p.	389	1852	Aug 30	1859	Burned	Bayou Sara, La.
1208	Meteor	St.p.	162	1847	Oct 2	1850	Burned	Long View, La. 3 lives lost.
1209	Meteor	St.p.	542	1851	Apr 29	1852	Snagged	Matagorda, Texas.
1210	Meteor	St.p.	220	1863	Jul 27	1886	Burned	New Orleans, La.
1211	Mexico	St.p.	120	1859	Mar 18	1865	Burned	Point Isabel, Texas.
1212	Miami	-	-	-	Jan 30	1866	Exploded	Mississippi River. 150 lives lost.
1213	Mike Jr.	Ol.s.	64	1953	Nov 15	1965	Foundered	About 200 miles due south of New Orleans, La.
1214	Mildred Runyon	St.p.	54	1904	Oct 22	1918	Collided	With obstruction. Near McDowell, Ala.
1215	Millville	Sch.	365	1887	Jan 7	1913	Stranded	Near Fort Morgan, Ala.
1216	Mingo	Sch.	397	1904	Mar 19	1920	Collided	With unknown steamer. Southwest Pass, Miss. Steel vessel. 2 lives lost.
1217	Minimax Elevator	Ol.s.	72	1964	Mar 15	1966	Foundered	In Gulf of Mexico, South Pelto Area, Block 20, La.
1218	Minnehaha	St.p.	531	1857	May 15	1865	Burned	New Orleans, La.
1219	Minnehaha	St.p.	351	1864	May 15	1865	Burned	New Orleans, La.
1220	Minnesotta	St.w.	142	1857	May	1863	Burned	Greenville, Miss.
1221	Minnie	Sch.	-	-	Aug 19	1888	Unknown	Ship Shoal, La.
1222	Minnie	St.p.	63	1898	Apr 1	1907	Foundered	Morgan City, La.
1223	Minnie and Clara	Ol.s.	61	1943	Feb 22	1954	Foundered	About 155 miles south of Brazos Santiago Pass, Gulf of Mexico, about 15 miles from Mexican coast.
1224	Mira A. Pratt	Sch.	-	-	Jan 16	1888	Unknown	Tompico, Mexico.
1225	Miss Auburn	Ol.s.	58	1951	Nov 12	1954	Foundered	On Arcus Reef, 70 miles NNW of Campeche, Mexico.
1226	Miss Barbara Ann	Ol.s.	63	1953	Aug 12	1959	Collided	With ol.s. BELVEDERE. About 40 miles east-southeast of Freeport, Texas.
1227	Miss Betty	Ol.s.	124	1954	Nov 16	1961	Burned	In Intracoastal Canal, about 6 miles west of La Rose, La.
1228	Miss California	Ol.s.	155	1838	Jun 23	1941	Foundered	6 miles northwest of Cedros Island, Mexico.
1229	Miss Carmen Louise	Ol.s.	66	1954	Jan 1	1958	Burned	Gulf of Mexico, about 30 miles south of Alvarado, Mexico.
1230	Miss Carrie	Ol.s.	64	1957	Sep 9	1961	Hurricane	About 10 miles south of Port Isabel, Texas, on Mexican coast.
1231	Miss Catherine	Ol.s.	62	1947	Jan 31	1960	Burned	About 10 miles southwest of Sabine, Texas.
1232	Miss Connie	Ol.s.	64	1956	Dec 1	1967	Stranded	On beach, 1 mile north of Brown Cedar Cut, on Texas coast.
1233	Miss Ellen	Ol.s.	59	1950	Jun 9	1965	Collided	With unlighted platform. Gulf of Mexico, Block 87, Ship Shoal area.
1234	Miss Emmy	Ol.s.	64	1956	Jun 30	1957	Foundered	On Alacran Reef, Gulf of Mexico.
1235	Miss Eva	Ol.s.	59	1958	Jan 10	1962	Storm	About 60 miles south of Brownsville, Texas.
1236	Miss Gina	Ol.s.	57	1950	Dec 20	1960	Collided	With ol.s. MISS LIBERTY. Gulf of Mexico, about 45 miles northeast of Port Isabel, Texas.
1237	Miss Hartley	Ol.s.	65	1953	Jul 28	1956	Foundered	In Campeche Bay, Mexico.
1238	Miss Hayes	Ol.s.	64	1958	Nov 4	1967	Stranded	On Matagorda Peninsula, approximately 70 miles northeast of Corpus Christi, Texas.
1239	Miss Liberty	Ol.s.	75	1953	Feb 25	1965	Foundered	About 1 mile offshore, southeast of Raccoon Point, La.
1240	Miss Lillie	Ol.s.	64	1949	Feb 11	1962	Collided	With unknown object, North of Lobos Island, off coast of Mexico.
1241	Miss Lisa	Ol.s.	50	1963	Jan 24	1964	Stranded	On Arcas Reef, off Mexican coast. Steel vessel.
1242	Miss Mildred	Ol.s.	64	1959	Nov 9	1960	Stranded	At entrance to port at Galveston, Texas.
1243	Miss Patricia	Ol.s.	59	1957	Dec 9	1964	Collided	With tow of barges. In Block 86, Vermilion Bay, La.
1244	Miss Trade Winds	Ol.s.	83	1953	Jan 9	1956	Burned	About 100 miles south of Brownsville, Texas, in Gulf of Mexico.
1245	Miss Wanda Dene	Ol.s.	64	1953	Sep 7	1958	Collided	With submerged object. 200 miles southeast of Brownsville, Texas.
1246	Missouri Belle	St.p.	165	1834	Oct 24	1834	Collided	With BOONS LICK. Kenner, La. 15 lives lost.
1247	Mr. Arjo	Ol.s.	64	1958	Jun 26	1965	Collided	With submerged object. About 40 miles south-southwest of Port Aransas, Texas.
1248	Mr. Bill	Ol.s.	132	1954	Jun 4	1959	Collided	With British CLEVELAND. 5 miles southeast of Belle, Pass, La. Steel vessel.
1249	Mittie Stephens	St.p.	224	1863	Feb 11	1869	Burned	Caddo Lake, La. Many lives lost.
1250	Mobile	St.p.	194	1831	Mar 3	1831	Burned	Claiborne, Ala.
1251	Mobile	St.p.	230	1836	Oct 6	1837	Stranded	Lake Pontchartrain, La.

NO.	NAME OF VESSEL	RIG	TONS	BUILT	DATE	CAUSE	PLACE AND COMMENT
1252	Mobile	St.p.	282	1860	May 20 1863	Burned	Yazoo City, Miss.
1253	Mohican	St.p.	371	1830	Feb 19 1842	Exploded	New Orleans, La. 12 lives lost. Also reported lost Feb. 2, 1842.
1254	Mohican	St.p.	398	1848	Feb 4 1854	Burned	New Orleans, La.
1255	Mohican	St.s.	2,255	-	Pre-WWII	Unknown	28-23-54 N. 80-32-12 W. Depth 32'.
1256	Moira (Nor.)	St.s.	744	-	Jun 17 1942	War Loss	25-35-00 N. 96-20-00 W. Steel vessel. Reported as tanker. More likely freighter.
1257	Mollie McPike	St.w.	303	1864	Nov 8 1871	Stranded	Turner's Ledge, Mississippi River.
1258	Mona Lisa	Ol.s.	311	1951	May 30 1953	Burned	12-50-00 N. 91-05-00 W.
1259	Monarch	Ol.s.	131	1941	Feb 6 1962	Foundered	About 3/4 mile north of Clipperton Island, Mexico.
1260	Monmouth	St.p.	135	1836	Oct 30 1837	Collided	With ship TREMONT. Profit Island, Mississippi River. 300 lives lost.
1261	Monongahela Belle	St.w.	74	1854	Mar 8 1859	Burned	Austin, Miss.
1262	Monroe	St.p.	128	1845	Nov 1847	Stranded	Rio Grande, Texas.
1263	Monroe	St.p.	183	1848	Mar 20 1854	Capsized	Above Natchez, Miss. 30 lives lost.
1264	Monroe	St.p.	299	1896	Sep 29 1915	Collided	With st.s. CLARA. New Orleans, La.
1265	Monsson	St.p.	267	1863	Dec 26 1868	Snagged	Red River, La.
1266	Montana	St.p.	1,003	1865	Dec 14 1876	Burned	Guaymas, Mexico.
1267	Montgomery	St.p.	407	1843	Nov 7 1851	Burned	New Carthage, Miss. 2 lives lost.
1268	Montgomery	St.p.	314	1854	Feb 20 1858	Burned	Algiers, La.
1269	Montgomery	Brg.	294	1920	Jan 27 1943	Foundered	25-27-00 N. 80-45-00 W. Steel vessel.
1270	Monticello	St.p.	94	1829	Mar 29 1833	Snagged	Bayou Plaquemine, La.
1271	Morgan	Ol.s.	94	1918	Mar 21 1931	Foundered	Cape San Lazaro, Mexico.
1272	Morning Star	Ol.s.	121	1940	Mar 30 1952	Foundered	3 miles northeast of Ceralbo Island, Mexico.
1273	Morning Star II	-	-	-	1863	Burned	Off Texas coast. Vessel sunk and burned by Confederates.
1274	Moro	St.p.	132	1858	Feb 26 1861	Stranded	Spanish Bluffs, La.
1275	Motive	St.w.	67	1845	Jun 26 1850	Snagged	Mobile, Ala.
1276	Motto	St.p.	82	1836	Nov 24 1838	Exploded	Sabine, Texas. 5 lives lost.
1277	Mount Vernon	St.p.	148	1820	Dec 10 1831	Stranded	Pascagoula, Miss.
1278	Mountain Girl	St.s.	-	-	May 21 1890	Unknown	Gulf of Mexico.
1279	Munger T. Ball	St.s.	5,104	1920	May 4 1942	War Loss	25-17-00 N. 83-57-00 W. Also given as 25-17-00 N. 83-17-00 W. Tanker. Steel vessel. 33 lives lost (37). Sunk by enemy action.
1280	Munisla	St.s.	1,697	1916	Sep 9 1919	Foundered	Sailed from Mobile, Ala., for Cuba, and has not since reported. Steel vessel. All lives (28) lost.
1281	Muscle No.2	St.p.	168	1846	Sep 13 1849	Snagged	Yazoo River, Miss.
1282	Muskingum	St.p.	127	1822	Mar 19 1829	Snagged	Natchitoches, La.
1283	Mustang	St.p.	67	1849	Jan 1852	Burned	Alexandria, La.
1284	Mustang	St.p.	172	1860	Jun 24 1869	Stranded	Trinity River, Texas.
1285	Mustang	Ol.s.	57	1951	Jan 10 1962	Foundered	In Gulf of Mexico, about 10 miles south of Port Isabel, Texas.
1286	Mutiny	Ol.s.	52	1944	Mar 10 1956	Burned	14 miles north of Port Isabel, Texas.
1287	Mystic	St.s.	75	1953	Jun 19 1956	Foundered	Off Vera Cruz, Mexico. 19-35-00 N. 94-45-00 W.
1288	MacGregor	-	-	-	Dec 30 1888	Unknown	Off coast of Yucatan, Mexico.
1289	N.A.D. Co. No.9	Brg.	325	1912	Feb 8 1914	Burned	Fronteria, Mexico.
1290	N.A.D. Co. No.10	Brg.	366	1912	Feb 8 1914	Burned	Fronteria, Mexico.
1291	NBC 387	Brg.	430	1937	May 19 1965	Burned	At Breaux Oil Co. dock, on Bayou Lafourche in Lockport, La.
1292	N.H. Breaux	St.w.	131	1925	Feb 28 1944	Burned	Bayou Lafourche, Lockport, La.
1293	Nan M. Dantzler	Sch.	224	1882	Nov 8 1906	Abandoned	Off Coatzacoalcos, Mexico. 1 life lost.
1294	Nancy F.	Ol.s.	63	1952	Jul 7 1959	Burned	Off the coast of Texas, 60 miles south of Sabine Light.
1295	Naniope	St.p.	114	1850	Sep 15 1852	Snagged	Atchafalaya Bayou, La.
1296	Napoleon	St.p.	315	1818	May 17 1822	Snagged	Grand Gulf, Miss.
1297	Nardy Boy	Ol.s.	63	1953	Jul 14 1958	Foundered	Near jetties at Freeport, Texas.

NO.	NAME OF VESSEL	RIG	TONS	BUILT	DATE		CAUSE	PLACE AND COMMENT
1298	Nashville	St.p.	194	1822	Feb 22	1826	Snagged	St. James, La.
1299	Natchez	St.p.	206	1823	Sep 4	1835	Burned	New Orleans, La.
1300	Natchez	St.p.	698	1853	Feb 4	1854	Burned	New Orleans, La. 3 lives lost.
1301	Natchez	St.p.	714	1855	Apr 4	1863	Burned	Castleman, Miss.
1302	Natchez	St.p.	800	1860	Apr	1863	Burned	Burtonia, Miss.
1303	Natchez	St.p.	388	1849	Mar 10	1866	Foundered	Mobile Bay, Ala.
1304	Naughty Girl	Ol.s.	74	1954	Nov	1967	Burned	Off Port Mansfield Pass, Port Mansfield, Texas.
1305	Naumkeag	St.w.	326	1863	Jan 19	1867	Burned	Erie, Ala. 3 lives lost.
1306	Navarre	Ol.s.	65	1953	Feb 10	1955	Burned	118 miles northeast by north of Point Palmas, Mexico.
1307	Navigator	St.p.	69	1834		1838	Snagged	Mississippi River.
1308	Navigator	St.w.	243	1862	Feb 6	1867	Snagged	Loggy Bayou, La.
1309	Nelfred	Ga.s.	56	1897	Jun 13	1944	Foundered	75 miles north of Tampico, Mexico.
1310	Nellie Brown	St.s.	56	1878	Jul 22	1921	Foundered	Gretna, La. Iron vessel.
1311	Nelly Rose	Ol.s.	52	1954	Sep 24	1965	Foundered	In Gulf of Mexico, about 20 miles southeast of Grand Isle, La.
1312	Nemo	Ol.s.	123	1926	Sep 17	1958	Stranded	Off Rio Soto La Marina, Mexico, about 150 miles south of Port Isabel, Texas.
1313	Neponset	Ol.s.	95	1906	Aug 2	1929	Foundered	Acapulco, Mexico.
1314	Neptune	St.p.	133	1833	Feb 10	1842	Burned	Mobile, Ala.
1315	Neptune No.2	St.p.	257	1859	May 13	1859	Burned	Harrisburg, Texas.
1316	Neskleetia	Ol.s.	96	1891	Nov 21	1933	Foundered	South Alijos Rocks, Mexico.
1317	Nettie Franklin	Sch.	102	1901	Aug 18	1915	Foundered	Galveston, Texas. 2 lives lost.
1318	New Brunswick	St.p.	178	1832	Oct 28	1833	Burned	Vicksburg, Miss.
1319	New Falls City	St.p.	880	1858		1864	Burned	80 miles below Shreveport, La.
1320	New Haven	St.p.	92	1882	Jan 9	1910	Foundered	Demopolis, Ala.
1321	New Jersey	St.s.	6,414	1921	May 28	1942	War Loss	18-32-00 N. 82-28-00 W. Steel vessel. Sunk by enemy action.
1322	New Orleans	St.p.	371	1811	Jul 14	1814	Snagged	Baton Rouge, La.
1323	New Orleans	St.p.	324	1815	Dec 1	1818	Snagged	New Orleans, La.
1324	New Orleans	St.w.	146	1857	Jun 26	1864	Lost	Liverpool, Miss. Lost as Confederate vessel "CSS W.H. IVY".
1325	New Orleans	St.p.	913	1880	Jul 20	1928	Burned	Slidell, La.
1326	New York	St.p.	365	1837	Sep 5	1846	Foundered	Galveston, Texas to New Orleans, La. 17 lives lost.
1327	New York	St.w.	199	1862	Mar 21	1870	Burned	New Orleans, La.
1328	Newark	Ga.s.	162	1887	Sep 29	1920	Stranded	San Carlos Point, Mexico.
1329	Niagara	St.p.	121	1829	Mar 21	1834	Snagged	Opelousas, La.
1330	Niagara	St.p.	125	1836	Dec 17	1841	Collided	Montgomery, Ala.
1331	Nicholas Biddle	St.p.	139	1836	Jul 15	1837	Snagged	Lake Providence, La. 10 lives lost.
1332	Nick C	Ol.s.	72	1930	Aug 2	1940	Stranded	15 miles inside Point Eufenio, Mexico.
1333	Nick Hill	St.w.	97	1851	May 12	1853	Stranded	Trinity River, Texas.
1334	Nightingale	St.s.	815	1864	Jan 29	1868	Stranded	Vera Cruz, Mexico. 7 lives lost.
1335	Nile	St.p.	149	1859	Nov 5	1859	Burned	Benton, Ala.
1336	Nimrod	St.p.	210	1844	Aug 6	1850	Lost	New Orleans, La.
1337	Nina Simms	St.p.	327	1860	Jun 17	1869	Snagged	60 miles below Bayou Sara, La.
1338	Nokomis	Sch.	295	1897	Dec 25	1905	Foundered	28-00-00 N. 88-00-00 W.
1339	Nola	Ga.s.	595	1919	Nov 9	1922	Burned	Southwest of Southwest Pass, Gulf of Mexico. Steel vessel.
1340	Nola 2	Brg.	1,847	1945	Oct 17	1959	Stranded	Gulf of Campeche, about 42 miles south of Coatzacoalcos, Mexico. Steel vessel.
1341	Nola Gladys	Ol.s.	67	1950	Apr 25	1964	Burned	Gulf of Mexico, about 40 miles north of Vera Cruz, Mexico.
1342	Nolan R.	Ol.s.	69	1945	Jun 20	1965	Collided	With unknown vessel. Approximately 40 miles southwest of Freeport, Texas.
1343	Nominee	St.p.	213	1848	Oct 11	1854	Snagged	Mississippi River at "Britts Ledge".
1344	Norfolk	St.p.	219	1838	Jul 2	1849	Snagged	Mobile, Ala.
1345	Norlindo	St.s.	2,686	1920	Mar 4	1942	War Loss	24-57-00 N. 84-00-00 W. Freighter. Steel vessel. Sunk by enemy action.

NO.	NAME OF VESSEL	RIG	TONS	BUILT	DATE		CAUSE	PLACE AND COMMENT
1346	Norma	St.p.	188	1839	Jun 1	1846	Snagged	Mobile Bay, Ala.
1347	Norma	St.p.	378	1852	Feb 11	1855	Snagged	President Island, Princeton, Miss.
1348	Norman	Brg.	853	1862	Aug 4	1917	Foundered	2.5 miles southwest of Orleans Bay, New Orleans, La.
1349	Norman	-	-	-	May 8	1925	Capsized	Mississippi River. 22 lives lost.
1350	North Alabama	St.p.	341	1832	Oct 30	1842	Stranded	Natchez, Miss.
1351	North America	St.p.	1,440	1851	Feb 27	1852	Stranded	30 miles from Acapulco, Mexico.
1352	North Bend	St.p.	120	1841	Oct 9	1846	Stranded	Perthshire, Miss. 16 lives lost.
1353	North Star	St.p.	157	1837	Feb 25	1842	Exploded	Tuscaloosa, Ala. 16 lives lost.
1354	North Star	St.p.	82	1857	Mar 11	1858	Foundered	Grand Gulf, Miss.
1355	North Star	Ol.s.	188	1942	May 12	1952	Stranded	Off Todos Santos Island, near Ensenada, Mexico.
1356	Northern Light	Ol.s.	169	1937	Jun 27	1955	Burned	5 miles southwest of Descanso Point, Mexico.
1357	Northwestern	St.s.	2,207	1901	Feb 10	1920	Burned	Port Neches, Texas. Steel vessel. 1 life lost.
1358	Norwalk	-	2,157	-	Jan 10	1943	Unknown	28-18-00 N. 80-00-00 W. Presumed freighter lost during war.
1359	Nueces	Ol.s.	83	1927	Mar 8	1956	Foundered	Mobile Bay, Ala.
1360	Nuevo Currutaco	Brg.	-	-	Sep 19	1889	Unknown	Gulf of Mexico.
1361	No. 573	Ol.s.	170	1943	Sep	1958	Foundered	In slip owned by Freeport Sulphur Co., at Bay Ste. Elaine, Terrebonne Parish, La. Steel vessel.
1362	Oaxaca (Mex.)	St.s.	4,351	-	Jul 26	1942	War Loss	28-23-00 N. 96-11-00 W. Steel vessel.
1363	Ocean Venus	St.s.	4,272	-	May 3	1942	War Loss	28-23-28 N. 80-17-43 W. Freighter. Steel vessel.
1364	Ocean Wave	St.p.	272	1854	Aug 20	1871	Exploded	Point Clear, Ala. 75 lives lost.
1365	Octararo	St.p.	110	1841	Feb 21	1843	Snagged	Bayou Plaquemine, La.
1366	Odd Fellow	St.p.	97	1845	Dec 20	1848	Stranded	Diamond Island, La.
1367	Oella	St.p.	77	1848	Dec 22	1850	Snagged	Red Church, Lower Mississippi River.
1368	Offshore	Ol.s.	68	1956	Dec 14	1963	Foundered	In Block 107, West Cameron, La.
1369	Ogontz	St.s.	5,037	1919	May 19	1942	War Loss	23-30-00 N. 86-37-00 W. Steel vessel. Sunk by enemy action.
1370	Ohio	St.w.	179	1924	Mar 27	1931	Foundered	Natchez, Miss.
1371	Ohioan	St.s.	6,078	-	May 8	1942	War Loss	26-31-00 N. 79-59-00 W. Steel vessel. Freighter.
1372	Old Glory	Ol.s.	58	1941	Nov 24	1946	Foundered	8 miles WSW of San Martin Island, Mexico.
1373	Old Hickory	Brg.	887	1920	Dec 27	1940	Foundered	New Orleans Harbor, Mississippi River. Steel vessel.
1374	Olive	St.p.	115	1847	Sep 2	1848	Exploded	Chehaw, Ala. 1 life lost.
1375	Olive	Sch.	172	1891	Sep 27	1906	Foundered	Mobile River, Ala.
1376	Olive Branch	St.p.	697	1863	Jul 12	1871	Foundered	Liberty Island, Mississippi River.
1377	Olympia	Ol.s.	117	1927	Apr 7	1950	Foundered	At Santa Margarita Islands, Mexico.
1378	Olympic	St.s.	770	1901	Oct 24	1917	Foundered	85 miles off Puerto Mexico, Mexico.
1379	Onandaga	St.w.	1,440	-	Jul 24	1912	Unknown	24-40-00 N. 75-44-00 W.
1380	Onward	St.p.	241	1864	Nov 17	1867	Burned	Bells Ledge, Alabama River, Ala. 11 lives lost.
1381	Opelousas	St.p.	100	1852	Nov 12	1857	Collided	With GALVESTON. Galveston, Texas. 18 lives lost.
1382	Opelousas	St.p.	944	1857	Nov 15	1857	Collided	With GALVESTON. Berwick Bay, La. 18 lives lost. See No.1381.
1383	Ophelia	Ol.s.	113	1832		1838	Snagged	Tuscaloosa, Ala.
1384	Orange	Ol.s.	130	1903	Jan 30	1960	Burned	In the Intracoastal Canal at Mile 57, east in Mississippi Sound. Steel vessel.
1385	Oregon	-	-	-	Mar 1	1851	Exploded	Mississippi River. 60 lives lost.
1386	Orion	St.s.	127	1906	Mar 1	1945	Collided	With SS MORTON PRINCE. 27-48-36 N. 97-22-48 W.
1387	Orizaba	St.p.	595	1858	Jun 15	1865	Stranded	Liberty, Texas. Formerly C.S.S. Orizaba. (Confederate vessel).
1388	Orline St. John	St.p.	349	1847	Mar 4	1850	Burned	Bridgeport, Ala. 41 lives lost. Reported lost Mar 2, 1850 with 100 lives lost.
1389	Oronoko	-	367	1837	Apr 21	1838	Exploded	Mississippi River. 100 lives lost.
1390	Oronoko	St.p.	149	1842	Oct 6	1842	Burned	New Orleans, La.
1391	Osage	St.p.	149	1820	Feb 24	1824	Snagged	Coffeeville, Ala.
1392	Osage	St.p.	129	1841	Mar 22	1844	Burned	Donaldsonville, La.

NO.	NAME OF VESSEL	RIG	TONS	BUILT	DATE	CAUSE	PLACE AND COMMENT
1393	Osceola	St.p.	125	1849	Dec 8 1859	Snagged	Mobile, Ala.
1394	Osceola	Ol.s.	64	1955	Mar 8 1964	Stranded	About 60 miles west-northwest of Campeche, Mexico.
1395	Otis	Sch.	292	1898	Sep 21 1917	Foundered	Pascagoula, Miss. All lives (7) lost.
1396	Otto	St.p.	163	1832	Jan 6 1836	Collided	Lake Pontchartrain, La.
1397	Ouachita	St.w.	91	1908	Sep 12 1924	Burned	Wilton, La.
1398	PDC 1	Brg.	800	1956	Aug 16 1966	Collided	With unknown object. Commercial Barge dock, Mobile River, Ala.
1399	P. Miller	St.p.	153	1838	Mar 28 1842	Snagged	Red River, La.
1400	P.N. Ellis	Ol.s.	52	1918	Apr 23 1953	Foundered	3 miles below Morgan City, La., in the Atchafalaya River. Steel vessel.
1401	Paladin	Ol.s.	75	1928	Jul 20 1951	Burned	About 1 mile south of intersection St. Johns River and Intercoastal Waterway. 30-21-00 N. 81-26-00 W.
1402	Palatine	Ol.s.	63	1906	Apr 21 1927	Burned	Mobile, Ala.
1403	Palmetto	St.p.	533	1846	Jan 9 1851	Stranded	Matagorda Bay, Texas.
1404	Palomino	Ol.s.	60	1958	Dec 28 1966	Burned	Gulf of Mexico, 35 miles north of Coatzacoalcos, Mexico.
1405	Pamela M.	Ol.s.	85	1962	Nov 5 1965	Foundered	In South Pass area, East Bay, Block 37, off Louisiana.
1406	Pan American - 20	Ol.s.	79	1942	May 5 1963	Foundered	Gulf of Mexico, off Louisiana coast, about 30 miles south-southwest of Eugene Island Light.
1407	Pan Massachusetts	St.s.	8,201	-	Feb 19 1942	War Loss	28-27-00 N. 80-08-00 W. Tanker. Steel vessel.
1408	Panola	St.p.	136	1839	Jun 28 1842	Snagged	Bayou Pigeon, La.
1409	Panola	St.p.	89	1863	Oct 3 1865	Snagged	Grand Bayou, La.
1410	Panther	St.w.	137	1910	Feb 1 1928	Burned	Yazoo River, Miss.
1411	Panther	Ol.s.	57	1951	Feb 13 1960	Stranded	On the beach, 18 miles north of Obregon, Mexico.
1412	Papa Delta	Ol.s.	60	1947	Jul 21 1959	Foundered	In Gulf of Mexico, about 40 miles southeast of Port Isabel, Texas. Steel vessel.
1413	Paragon	Ol.s.	79	1953	Nov 30 1957	Foundered	Gulf of Campeche, 60 miles northeast of Coatzacoalcos, Mexico. Steel vessel.
1414	Pasadena	Sch.	596	1880	Nov 1905	Stranded	Fernandina, Fla.
1415	Pathfinder	St.p.	137	1841	Feb 8 1845	Burned	Rodney, Miss. 7 lives lost.
1416	Patricia II	Ol.s.	65	1926	Feb 9 1966	Foundered	Approximately 70 miles northeast of Cotay, Mexico.
1417	Patrick Henry	St.p.	161	1840	Feb 18 1850	Foundered	Algiers, La.
1418	Patton	Brg.	98	1910	Nov 30 1917	Foundered	29-04-00 N. 94-57-00 W.
1419	Paul	Ga.s.	91	1910	Jan 27 1912	Collided	With British st.s. HEREDIA. Poverty Point, Mississippi River, La.
1420	Paul Clifford	St.p.	99	1831	Oct 23 1833	Collided	With MISSOURIAN. Tunica, Miss.
1421	Paul Harwood	St.s.	6,610	-	Jul 7 1942	War Loss	28-26-00 N. 88-38-00 W. Steel vessel. Tanker. SALVAGED.
1422	Paul Jones	St.p.	353	1855	Jul 1863	Burned	Big Black River, Miss.
1423	Pearl	St.p.	184	1851	Jan 1 1854	Collided	With NATCHEZ, Bayou Sara, La. 7 lives lost.
1424	Peconic	St.s.	1,855	1881	Aug 28 1905	Foundered	Off Fernandina, Fla. Iron vessel. 20 lives lost.
1425	Peerless	St.p.	349	1858	May 27 1860	Burned	New Orleans, La.
1426	Pegasus	Ol.s.	50	1929	Jun 12 1948	Burned	Whiskey Bay, La., 16 miles out of Terrebonne Parish.
1427	Pelican	St.p.	260	1847	Aug 23 1856	Burned	Biloxi, Miss.
1428	Pelican	St.p.	362	1856	Feb 24 1858	Burned	Francis, Miss.
1429	Pelican	St.s.	58	1904	Jan 18 1938	Foundered	New Orleans, La.
1430	Pelican	Drg.	181	1936	Jul 6 1952	Burned	In the channel of the Tchefuncta River, opposite Jahncke's Shipyard, New Orleans.
1431	Pelican Driller	Ol.s.	89	1954	Aug 9 1957	Foundered	In Gulf of Mexico, about 18 miles south of Belle Pass, La. Steel vessel.
1432	Penelope	St.p.	121	1842	Oct 15 1846	Burned	Mobile, Ala.
1433	Pennsylvania	-	-	-	Jun 13 1858	Exploded	Mississippi River. 160 lives lost.
1434	Penny B.	Ol.s.	67	1951	Jan 19 1966	Foundered	At Shell Island Pass, La.
1435	Peoria City	St.p.	459	1864	Feb 21 1869	Snagged	Coles Creek, Miss.
1436	Percy Swain	St.p.	135	1910	Jul 23 1922	Foundered	Rifle Point, La.
1437	Perserverance	St.p.	827	1852	Oct 3 1856	Burned	Powder House, Texas.
1438	Persian	-	-	-	Nov 1840	Exploded	Mississippi River. 24 lives lost.

NO.	NAME OF VESSEL	RIG	TONS	BUILT	DATE	CAUSE	PLACE AND COMMENT
1439	Peruvian	St.p.	226	1831	Jun 7 1833	Exploded	Natchez, Miss., 50 lives lost.
1440	Peter Tellen	St.p.	738	1854	Dec 22 1858	Stranded	Greenville, Miss.
1441	Peters Lee	St.p.	463	1899	Aug 8 1913	Foundered	Lake Providence, La., 1 life lost.
1442	Petro Pete	Ol.s.	57	1957	Nov 15 1962	Foundered	About 20 miles offshore, Grand Isle, La. Steel vessel.
1443	Petrolia No.2	St.w.	91	1864	Jan 14 1871	Snagged	Black River, La.
1444	Peytona	St.p.	685	1859	Jul 14 1863	Burned	Sataria, Miss.
1445	Philadelphia	St.p.	179	1862	Mar 1 1868	Stranded	Aransas Pass, Texas. Redocumented as screw steamer, June 22, 1865.
1446	Philomene	Ol.s.	63	1952	May 14 1959	Collided	With barge in tow by ol.s. LISA R. Gulf of Mexico, 100 miles southwest of New Orleans, La.
1447	Phoenix	St.p.	205	1829	Jul 16 1832	Burned	Albemarle, La.
1448	Phoenix Shaw	Ol.s.	64	1954	Jan 19 1966	Collided	With submerged object. 12 miles south of Freeport, Texas jetties.
1449	Phyllis	Ga.s.	67	1944	Apr 26 1953	Burned	Off Port Isabel, Texas.
1450	Phyllis Jean	Ol.s.	53	1949	Sep 20 1961	Foundered	In Gulf of Mexico, about 70 miles south of Port Isabel, Texas.
1451	Pilot	St.p.	128	1836	May 18 1839	Snagged	Tuscaloosa, Ala.
1452	Pilot Boy	St.s.	233	1905	Aug 18 1916	Foundered	10 miles off Port Aransas, Texas. 6 lives lost.
1453	Pine Hill	St.w.	73	1864	Jun 1865	Snagged	Tucker's Bar, Red River, La.
1454	Piney Woods	St.p.	79	1844	Oct 6 1848	Burned	Springfield, Miss. 15 lives lost.
1455	Pink Gold	Ol.s.	53	1950	Sep 1 1955	Burned	About 120 miles southwest of Campeche, Mexico.
1456	Pioneer	St.w.	50	1866	Sep 14 1870	Foundered	Trenton, La.
1457	Pioneer	St.s.	63	1867	1872	Burned	New Orleans, La.
1458	Pioneer	Ga.s.	277	1914	Nov 29 1915	Burned	Port O'Conner, Texas. Steel vessel.
1459	Piota	St.p.	293	1858	Jun 4 1859	Burned	Carrollton, La. 2 lives lost.
1460	Pittsburgh	St.p.	132	1823	May 14 1828	Snagged	Prairie Bluff, Ala.
1461	Pittsburgh	St.p.	144	1836	Jan 14 1838	Snagged	Baton Rouge, La.
1462	Planet	St.p.	604	1856	Feb 1 1864	Stranded	College Point, La.
1463	Planter	St.p.	119	1843	Aug 20 1845	Snagged	Alexandria, La.
1464	Planter	St.p.	182	1852	Dec 30 1857	Snagged	Fort Adams, Miss.
1465	Pleasure Bay	St.p.	378	1890	Jun 4 1922	Burned	Madisonville, La.
1466	Plough Boy	St.p.	81	1834	1837	Exploded	Mississippi River. 3 lives lost.
1467	Plough Boy	St.p.	142	1834	Jan 14 1839	Snagged	Mobile, Ala.
1468	Pocahontas	Ol.s.	50	1945	Aug 16 1960	Collided	With ol.s. LADY MEL. In Gulf of Mexico, about 25 miles ESE of Port Isabel, Texas.
1469	Point Comfort	Ol.s.	207	1885	Jan 9 1963	Collided	With Navy tanker MAUMEE. At the Texico Oil Co. dock, Houston Ship Channel, Galena Park, Texas. Iron vessel.
1470	Point Loma	Ol.s.	148	1928	Jul 8 1932	Stranded	Off Point San Roque, Mexico.
1471	Poland	St.w.	161	1857	Jan 2 1865	Collided	With IDAHO. Yazoo River, Miss. 12 lives lost.
1472	Polaris	Ol.s.	65	1946	Dec 1954	Burned	29-14-00 N. 91-54-00 W.
1473	Ponce De Leon	Ol.s.	58	1948	Sep 16 1956	Stranded	On Mexican coast, about 150 miles south of Brazos Santiago Pass, Texas.
1474	Port Allen	St.w.	88	1888	Jun 19 1937	Foundered	Baton Rouge, La.
1475	Portsmouth	Brg.	1,159	1903	Oct 4 1927	Foundered	Freeport, Texas. Steel vessel.
1476	Post Boy	St.p.	140	1836	Mar 28 1842	Snagged	Enlish Turn, La.
1477	Post Boy	St.p.	259	1825	Mar 31 1842	Snagged	New Orleans, La.
1478	Post Boy	St.p.	157	1851	Jan 10 1858	Exploded	New Orleans, La. 3 lives lost.
1479	Potomac	St.p.	198	1844	Jul 1 1846	Stranded	Galveston, Texas.
1480	Potomska	St.s.	287	1854	Jul 15 1866	Stranded	Saluda, Texas.
1481	Potosi	St.p.	121	1834	1836	Snagged	Mississippi River.
1482	Premier III	Ol.s.	64	1954	Jun 27 1965	Foundered	Off coast of Catoche, Mexico. 23-00 N. 87-00 W.
1483	Prince Lucien	Ship	-	-	Aug 7 1889	Unknown	Chandeleur Island, La.
1484	Prince of Wales	St.p.	572	1860	Jul 14 1863	Burned	Yazoo City, Miss.

NO.	NAME OF VESSEL	RIG	TONS	BUILT	DATE		CAUSE	PLACE AND COMMENT
1485	Princess	St.p.	687	1852	Oct 6	1854	Burned	Fort Adams, Miss. 2 lives lost.
1486	Princess	St.p.	715	1855	Feb 28	1859	Exploded	Baton Rouge, La. 70 lives lost.
1487	Princess Julanne	Ol.s.	53	1951	Jul 24	1959	Foundered	Near South Jetty, Freeport, Texas.
1488	Princeton	St.p.	251	1847	Jan 5	1851	Collided	With ALAMO, Ouachita River, La. 1 life lost.
1489	Privateer	St.p.	146	1833	Nov 27	1837	Snagged	Natchitoches, La.
1490	Progress	Ol.s.	64	1945	Nov 12	1954	Foundered	On Mexican coast of the Gulf of Mexico, about 80 miles south of Brownsville, Texas.
1491	Progress	Ol.s.	65	1953	Nov 6	1967	Foundered	Off New Orleans, La. 27-45-00 N. 28-45-00 W.
1492	Protector	St.p.	156	1834	Apr 7	1834	Burned	Claiborne, Ala.
1493	Protector	Ol.s.	116	1882	Jun 6	1954	Foundered	10 miles southeast of Galveston, Texas. Iron vessel.
1494	Pure Lubell	Brg.	1,296	1891	Mar 23	1932	Burned	New Orleans, La. Steel vessel. 1 life lost (7).
1495	Putnam	St.p.	109	1845	Feb 13	1848	Stranded	Little Tombigbee, Ala.
1496	Pyramus	Brg.	2,384	1919	Feb 15	1921	Foundered	North of Tampico, Mexico.
1497	Quarter Boat 357	Brg.	104	1934	Dec 15	1947	Foundered	In Pass Aux Herons Channel, La.
1498	Quee Queg	Ol.s.	144	1943	Dec 19	1952	Foundered	19-35-00 N 87-10-00 W. About 14 miles off coast of Mexico.
1499	Queen	Ol.s.	55	1929	Sep 6	1947	Foundered	10 miles south of Todos Santos Ilas, near Ensenada, Mexico.
1500	Queen Anne II	Ol.s.	64	1955	Nov 8	1956	Stranded	On Alacran Reef, Yucatan Peninsula, Mexico.
1501	Queen City	St.p.	318	1843	May 24	1846	Exploded	Natchez, Miss. 12 lives lost.
1502	Queen Conch	Ol.s.	50	1945	Nov 21	1957	Burned	At Campeche Banks, Mexico.
1503	Queenie B	Ol.s.	75	1954	Feb 21	1962	Foundered	In Gulf of Mexico, about 20 miles south of Port Isabel, Texas.
1504	Quintana	Sch.	-		Oct 7	1887	Unknown	Pelican Island Shoals, Texas.
1505	Quo Vadis	Ol.s.	73	1952	Apr 20	1962	Stranded	On beach in Mexico, about 70 miles south of Rio Grande River.
1506	RBL 627	Brg.	627	1962	Sep 9	1965	Hurricane	At New Orleans, La., Point Landing Fleet, 108 Mile, Mississippi River.
1507	R.B. Taney	St.p.	301	1857	Oct 27	1865	Stranded	Mobile, Ala.
1508	R.C. Oglesby	St.p.	115	1849	Feb 1	1851	Snagged	Lake Bistineau, La.
1509	R.E. Hill	St.w.	103	1863	Aug 26	1865	Snagged	Greenwood, Miss. 1 life lost.
1510	R.F. Sass	St.w.	238	1855	May 9	1860	Snagged	Glover, Miss. 17 lives lost.
1511	RGT 5708	Brg.	724	1957	Oct 4	1964	Hurricane	At Jefferson Parish, La.
1512	RGT 5831	Brg.	662	1958	Oct 4	1964	Hurricane	At Jefferson Parish, La.
1513	R.J. Lackland	St.p.	710	1857	May 22	1863	Burned	Below Port Pemberton, Miss.
1514	R.K. Dunkerson	St.w.	115	1863	Mar 22	1866	Snagged	Shreveport, La.
1515	R.M. Parker	St.s.	6,779	-	Aug 13	1942	War Loss	28-47-00 N. 90-45-00 W. Tanker. Steel vessel. Also known as "R.M. Parker, Jr.".
1516	RO 5	Brg.	1,166	1959	Apr	1960	Foundered	Gulf of Mexico, off coast of New Orleans, La. Steel vessel.
1517	R.W. Adams	St.p.	399	1857	Dec 15	1858	Stranded	Alexandria, La.
1518	R.W. Gallagher	St.s.	7,989	1938	Jul 11	1942	War Loss	28-32-00 N. 90-59-00 W. Tanker. Steel vessel. 8 lives lost (52). Sunk by enemy action.
1519	R.W. Powell	St.p.	349	1855	Aug 20	1861	Snagged	Plaquemine, La.
1520	Rachel	Sch.	528	1919	Jun 29	1933	Stranded	Fort Morgan, La.
1521	Rachel Emery	Bkn.	673	1883	May 19	1911	Collided	With Italian st.s. DELPHINE. 80 miles south of New Orleans, La.
1522	Rachel Miller	St.w.	212	1863	May 9	1867	Stranded	Decatur, Ala.
1523	Rambler	St.p.	93	1847	Oct 3	1848	Foundered	Black River, La.
1524	Rambler	St.s.	288	1899	Nov 13	1921	Foundered	Northeast of Arcas Key, Yucatan, Mexico.
1525	Randolph	St.p.	549	1833	Mar 2	1841	Snagged	Carrollton, La. 1 life lost. Renamed "John Randolph" on Jan. 2, 1837.
1526	Rangely	Ol.s.	197	1942	May 27	1957	Foundered	28-49-30 N. 91-42-15 W. Steel vessel.
1527	Ranger	St.w.	86	1856	Feb 15	1859	Burned	Carthage, Miss.
1528	Rapide	St.p.	188	1819	Jan 21	1823	Burned	New Orleans, La.
1529	Ravenswood	St.p.	177	1852	Jul 16	1859	Burned	Waggaman, La. 1 life lost.
1530	Rawleigh Warner	St.s.	3,663	1912	Jun 22	1942	War Loss	28-57-00 N. 89-13-00 W. or 28-53-00 N. 89-13-00 W. Tanker. Steel vessel. All lives (33) lost. Sunk by enemy action.

NO.	NAME OF VESSEL	RIG	TONS	BUILT	DATE		CAUSE	PLACE AND COMMENT
1531	Raymond	Brg.	326	1904	Nov 7	1916	Foundered	Galveston Island, Texas.
1532	Red River	St.p.	97	1899	Feb 17	1907	Foundered	Alexandria, La.
1533	Red Rover	St.p.	435	1828		1836	Collided	With MAGNET, Red River, La.
1534	Reina Del Mar	Ol.s.	914	1942	Feb 17	1949	Burned	Offshore at San Martin Island, Mexico.
1535	Reindeer	St.p.	104	1834	Jan 5	1837	Burned	Point Pleasant, La.
1536	Reindeer	St.p.	177	1845	Nov 10	1845	Snagged	Angola, Miss.
1537	Reliable	Ol.s.	70	1954	May 5	1967	Burned	In Gulf of Campeche, Mexico, 120° northwest.
1538	Reliance	Ga.s.	70	1905	Sep 27	1923	Burned	Phoenix, La. 6 lives lost (16).
1539	Reliance	Ol.s.	50	1927	Oct 22	1958	Burned	About 4 miles east of Belle River Landing and 15 miles north of Morgan City, La.
1540	Republic	St.p.	699	1855	Jul	1863	Burned	Yazoo City, Miss.
1541	Republic	St.s.	5,287	-	Mar 21	1942	War Loss	27-00-38 N. 80-02-37 W. Tanker. Steel vessel. Depth 34'.
1542	Rescue	St.p.	207	1859	Dec	1860	Snagged	Tompkins Bluff, Ala. 3 lives lost.
1543	Reserve	St.p.	115	1837	May 14	1842	Stranded	Tompkins Bluff, Ala.
1544	Resolute	Ol.s.	63	1952	Sep 4	1958	Foundered	On South Jetties, Galveston, Texas.
1545	Restless	St.s.	133	1918		1924	Foundered	Tampico, Mexico.
1546	Return	St.p.	125	1832	Oct 5	1834	Snagged	Princeton, Miss.
1547	Reub White	St.p.	110	1856	Feb 3	1861	Stranded	Harvey Canal, La.
1548	Richmond	St.w.	359	1866	Dec 2	1869	Snagged	Below Shreveport, La.
1549	Ridgley	St.p.	97	1847	Jun 28	1849	Burned	Recourse Cutoff, La.
1550	Rifleman	St.p.	230	1819	Nov 19	1824	Burned	Cahawba, Ala.
1551	Rip Tide	Ol.s.	148	1955	Feb 3	1960	Foundered	In Gulf of Mexico, vicinity of Eugene Island. Steel vessel.
1552	Roanoke	St.p.	262	1836	Jan 23	1842	Stranded	Woods Bluff, Ala. 1 life lost.
1553	Roanoke	Ol.s.	139	1943	Jul 23	1952	Foundered	In Gulf of Mexico, about 24 miles east of Aransas Pass, Texas.
1554	Robert Campbell, Jr.	St.p.	421	1860	Sep 28	1863	Burned	Millikins Bend, La.
1555	Robert E. Lee	St.s.	5,184	1924	Jul 30	1942	War Loss	28-37-00 N. 88-20-00 W. Passenger vessel. Steel vessel. Escourted. Sunk by enemy action. 25% of lives lost.
1556	Robert Emmet	St.p.	147	1846	May 26	1847	Snagged	Mobile, Ala.
1557	Robert Rhea	St.w.	182	1908	Jul 25	1931	Burned	Mobile, Ala.
1558	Robert Waterman	St.p.	199	1857	Nov 5	1859	Stranded	Bayou Lafourche, La. Steel vessel.
1559	Roberta	St.p.	94	1903	Dec 31	1905	Foundered	Grand Ecrore, La. 2 lives lost.
1560	Rob Roy	St.p.	236	1823	Mar 7	1837	Burned	New Orleans, La.
1561	Rob Roy	St.p.	110	1845	May 9	1846	Burned	New Orleans, La.
1562	Robin Hood	Sch.	1,983	1918	Jun 25	1924	Burned	24-00-00 N. 82-48-00 W.
1563	Rockaway No.2	St.p.	324	1850	Apr 29	1854	Burned	Bayou Sara, La.
1564	Rodolph	St.p.	150	1836	Jan 14	1849	Snagged	New Orleans, La.
1565	Rosa	St.p.	265	1851	Jun 9	1856	Snagged	Lake End, La.
1566	Rose Croix	Ol.s.	67	1954	Oct 2	1961	Stranded	At Pass Cavallo, Texas.
1567	Rose Ella	Ol.s.	62	1944	Feb 15	1951	Foundered	In Gulf of Mexico, about 140 miles southeast of jetty, Port Isabel, Texas.
1568	Rose Franks	St.w.	240	1866	Mar 18	1871	Burned	15 miles up Red River, La.
1569	Rose Wallace Bradley	Ol.s.	65	1953	Jan 15	1957	Foundered	20-00-00 N. 92-00-00 W. Northeast of Cayos Arcos.
1570	Rover	Ga.w.	50	1925	Aug	1949	Foundered	In Red River, near mouth of the Black River, New Orleans, La. Steel vessel.
1571	Rowena	St.p.	225	1842	Mar 20	1844	Burned	Mobile, Ala.
1572	Rowena Burgman	Ol.s.	60	1943	Dec 29	1960	Burned	In Gulf of Mexico, about 8 miles ENE of Aransas Pass, Texas.
1573	Roxy	Ol.s.	130	1942	Apr 17	1952	Stranded	On the north jetties at Santiargo Brazos Pass, at Port Isabel, Texas.
1574	Ruby	St.p.	98	1843	Mar 9	1845	Collided	With RED ROVER, Fort Stoddart, Ala. 2 lives lost.
1575	Rufus Putnam	St.p.	68	1822	Dec 28	1825	Snagged	Point Chicot, La.
1576	Ruma	Ol.s.	54	1947	Jan 28	1949	Burned	About 5 miles west of Camanaba Pass, west of Grand Isle, off coast of Louisiana.
1577	Rush Krodel	St.w.	194	1924	Dec 9	1938	Burned	Natchez, Miss.

NO.	NAME OF VESSEL	RIG	TONS	BUILT	DATE	CAUSE	PLACE AND COMMENT
1578	Ruth	Ga.s.	92	1912	Jan 10 1925	Stranded	Alacran Reef, Mexico.
1579	Ruth	St.w.	63	1903	Dec 22 1939	Stranded	Near Lock 16, Warrior River, Ala.
1580	Ruth Kay	Ol.s.	67	1945	Aug 5 1961	Burned	Due south of Galveston, Texas.
1581	Rutlidge	Ol.s.	71	1942	Aug 23 1957	Stranded	On Padre Island, 11 miles north of Brazos Santiago Pass, Texas.
1582	S-16	Sub	-	-	Mar 2 1945	"Sunk"	24-25-13 N. 82-02-24 W. Sunk for experimental purposes.
1583	S 631	Brg.	797	1955	Jul 26 1966	Foundered	At Mile 383.3 Ahp, in Mississippi River.
1584	S.B. Duncan	St.p.	432	1898	Jan 21 1912	Burned	Vicksburg, Miss.
1585	S.C. & N.O. 1504	Brg.	823	1953	Mar 7 1960	Foundered	At Mile 768.3 Ahp, Mississippi River. Steel vessel.
1586	S.C. & N.O. 1509	Brg.	823	1953	Sep 9 1965	Hurricane	In New Orleans Harbor, La.
1587	S.D,U.B. No.1	Ol.s.	187	1944	Nov 29 1954	Foundered	At Pass Cavallo, Matagorda Bay, Texas. 28-20-24 N. 98-23-00 W. Steel vessel.
1588	S.E. Swayze	St.p.	74	1907	Feb 26 1910	Burned	Jones Landing, La.
1589	S.F.J. Trabue	St.p.	577	1854	Apr 10 1856	Burned	Algiers, La.
1590	S.F. Vinton	St.p.	284	1850	Aug 27 1851	Burned	Grand View, La.
1591	S.J. Lee	St.p.	176	1866	Dec 6 1873	Stranded	Brownsville, Texas. Steel vessel. Another vessel with this same name was lost off Brazos, Texas in 1873 and said to be carrying a "treasure" worth $100,000.
1592	S.O. Co. No.87	Sch.	2,052	1911	Dec 15 1912	Foundered	Gulf of Mexico. All lives (10) lost.
1593	S.S. Louisiana	St.s.	2,840	1880		1905	Lost	Mississippi River. Iron vessel. Length 320'. Beam 39'.
1594	S.S. Paisano	St.s.	-	-		1873	Foundered	Sailed from Brazos Santiago bound for Galveston, Texas. Carried $200,000 in silver bullion.
1595	S.S. Prentiss	St.p.	272	1853	Feb 20 1858	Burned	Algiers, La.
1596	S.S.S. Viking	Ol.s.	79	1943	Sep 11 1961	Hurricane	At Seabrook, Texas.
1597	Sabine	St.p.	106	1843	May 1847	Snagged	Rio Grande, Texas.
1598	Sabine	St.s.	453	1901	Jun 28 1921	Burned	Tampico, Mexico.
1599	Saceharine	St.p.	98	1911	Sep 29 1915	Collided	With German st.s. ANDROMEDA. New Orleans, La.
1600	Saddie Downman	St.p.	86	1899	Jun 15 1913	Burned	Hanria, La.
1601	Sadie Lee	St.p.	179	1901	Nov 15 1912	Foundered	Dennis Landing, Mississippi River.
1602	Sadie S.	Ol.s.	63	1953	Nov 7 1966	Foundered	30 miles ESE of Freeport, Texas.
1603	St. Charles	St.p.	311	1850	Jun 4 1857	Snagged	Below Shreveport, La. 1 life lost.
1604	St. George	Ol.s.	65	1953	Jun 8 1963	Burned	Off coast of Campeche, Mexico.
1605	Saint Helena	St.p.	124	1846	Nov 10 1849	Foundered	Algiers, La.
1606	St. Hilda	St.s.	462	1902	Jul 21 1930	Foundered	Tampico, Mexico. Steel vessel. 2 lives lost (13).
1607	St. James	St.p.	347	1850	Jul 1 1852	Exploded	Lake Pontchartrain, La. 35 lives lost.
1608	St. James	St.p.	344	1898	Mar 20 1916	Burned	New Orleans, La.
1609	St. James	Ol.s.	63	1953	Sep 30 1953	Foundered	About 19-52-00 N. 90-40-00 W.
1610	Saint John	St.p.	85	1828	Feb 18 1832	Snagged	Black Bayou, La.
1611	St. John	Ol.s.	63	1952	Jan 22 1955	Collided	With LIBERTY. 20-15-00 N. 91-03-00 W.
1612	St. Joseph	Ga.s.	85	1917	Dec 9 1923	Burned	Pointe a la Hache, La.
1613	Saint Lawrence	St.p.	111	1835	May 7 1840	Stranded	Natchez, Miss.
1614	Saint Louis	Drg.	406	1912	Aug 17 1942	Burned	La Porte, Texas.
1615	St. Mark	Ol.s.	63	1953	Dec 21 1958	Collided	With AMARANTE. 25-37-00 N. 84-02-00 W.
1616	Saint Martin	St.p.	143	1832	Oct 31 1833	Burned	Donaldsonville, La. 31 lives lost.
1617	Saint Nicholas	St.p.	342	1856	Feb 5 1866	Snagged	Jackson, Ala.
1618	Saint Nicholas	St.p.	669	1865	Dec 23 1868	Stranded	Grand Ecore, Red River, La.
1619	St. Tammany	Ol.s.	104	1924	Sep 29 1928	Burned	Madisonville, La.
1620	Saline	St.p.	53	1845	Jun 5 1848	Foundered	Carrollton, La.
1621	Sallie List	St.w.	212	1860	Feb 19 1868	Snagged	Portland, Ala.
1622	Sallie Spann	St.p.	190	1852	Oct 1 1856	Burned	Mobile, Ala.
1623	Salmon	St.s.	63	1867		1873	Snagged	Mobile Bay, Ala.

NO.	NAME OF VESSEL	RIG	TONS	BUILT	DATE	CAUSE	PLACE AND COMMENT
1624	Sam A. Conner	St.p.	63	1901	Sep 21 1909	Foundered	Centennial Lake, Miss.
1625	Sam Dale	St.p.	276	1852	Feb 25 1854	Burned	Mobile, Ala.
1626	Sam Houston	-	-	-	Aug 16 1915	Burned	Galveston, Texas. 56 lives lost.
1627	Sam Houston	0l.s.	54	1948	Nov 9 1954	Stranded	On beach at Pass Cavalla, Texas.
1628	Sam Houston	0l.s.	71	1947	Nov 5 1957	Foundered	Gulf of Mexico, 140 miles SSE of Port Isabel, Texas. Steel vessel.
1629	Sammy H.	0l.s.	52	1956	Jul 2 1958	Collided	With 0l.s. PAPA DELTA, Gulf of Mexico, 37 miles southeast of Aransas Pass, Texas.
1630	Sammy J.	0l.s.	78	1957	Nov 22 1966	Foundered	Near Block 111, Gulf of Mexico, off Louisiana coast.
1631	Samuel M. Williams	St.p.	226	1846	Apr 12 1849	Stranded	Galveston, Texas.
1632	Samuel Q. Brown	St.s.	6,624	1921	Apr 8 1943	War Loss	20-15-00 N. 84-38-00 W. Steel vessel. Sunk by enemy action.
1633	San Diego	Ga.s.	81	1887	Apr 20 1928	Foundered	Dolores Bay, Mexico.
1634	San Gabriel	St.s.	561	1903	Sep 17 1918	Foundered	Off Cape Lucas, Mexico. Steel vessel. All lives (20) lost.
1635	San Jacinto	-	-	-	Aug 16 1915	Wrecked	Galveston, Texas. 50 lives lost.
1636	San Jacinto	0l.s.	69	1950	Jan 24 1960	Burned	At Aransas Pass, Texas.
1637	San Jorge (Span.)	Galleon	-	-		Foundered	Gulf of Mexico. Suggested that treasure was carried on this vessel.
1638	San Jose	St.s.	2,135	1882	Aug 9 1921	Stranded	San Roque Island, Mexico. Iron vessel.
1639	San Pedro	-	-	-	1717	Unknown	West of Gorda Key. Carried treasure, maybe.
1640	San Saba	St.s.	703	1943	Oct 15 1948	Burned	29-39-50 N. 94-01-00 W. 5 miles off Sabine Bar.
1641	Sandcrane	0l.s.	144	1941	Aug 3 1964	Foundered	19-06-00 N. 94-18-00 W. Steel vessel.
1642	Sandy Hook	0l.s.	188	1946	Aug 5 1956	Burned	In Mississippi Sound, 5 miles east of Calcasieu River jetties, 1 mile offshore of Broussard's Beach, Cameron, La.
1643	Santa Lucia	0l.s.	100	1952	Oct 13 1954	Burned	At southwest end of Lobos Island, Vera Cruz, Mexico.
1644	Santa Margarita (Span)	Galleon	-	-	1595	Foundered	Biscayne Bay, Miami, Fla. or Merritt Island or Palm Beach, Fla. Carried large quantity of precious metals.
1645	Santa Rita	St.s.	5,273	1902	Oct 20 1921	Foundered	Sailed from New Orleans, La., and has not since been reported. Steel vessel. All lives (35) lost.
1646	Santa Rosa (Span.)	Galleon	-	-	1815	Unknown	Off Matagorda, Texas. Valued at $250,000.
1647	Santa Rosa	-	-	-	1886	Unknown	Matagorda Bay, Texas. Also valued at $250,000.
1648	Santa Rosa (Span.)	Galleon	-	-	Unknown	Unknown	Due south of Key West, Fla. Unlikely this "wreck" exists.
1649	Santiago	0l.s.	59	1957	May 11 1967	Foundered	In Gulf of Mexico, 96 miles southeast of Port Isabel, Texas.
1650	Santiago De Cuba	St.s.	989	-	Aug 12 1942	War Loss	24-20-00 N. 81-50-00 W. Cuban registry.
1651	Santo Amaro	0l.s.	252	1930	Oct 19 1939	Burned	Magdalena Bay, Mexico.
1652	Santore	St.s.	7,117	-	Jun 19 1942	Unknown	24-05-00 N. 81-40-00 W. Freighter. Probable loss due to war.
1653	Sarah	St.p.	138	1850	Feb 21 1856	Exploded	Trinity River, Texas. 2 lives lost.
1654	Sarah Kimbrough	St.w.	65	1852	Jul 1 1852	Stranded	Muscle Shoals, Ala.
1655	Saratoga	St.p.	105	1828	Dec 4 1832	Burned	New Orleans, La.
1656	Saratoga	St.p.	339	1864	Aug 9 1866	Burned	New Orleans, La.
1657	Savanna	St.p.	337	1848	Nov 24 1849	Snagged	Waterloo, La. 1 life lost.
1658	Saxon	St.p.	479	1850	Feb 4 1854	Burned	New Orleans, La.
1659	Science	St.w.	116	1860	Jun 1866	Burned	Gretna, La.
1660	Scioto	St.w.	54	1863	1867	Snagged	Gretna, La.
1661	Scotland	St.p.	567	1855	Mar 22 1863	Burned	Fort Pemberton, Miss.
1662	Sea Boy	0l.s.	256	1933	Dec 25 1959	Foundered	In a westerly direction, 10 miles off Point San Pablo, Mexico.
1663	Sea Contractor	0l.s.	197	1942	Feb 6 1965	Foundered	In Gulf of Mexico. 28-53-00 N. 92-20-00 W.
1664	Sea Hornet	0l.s.	142	1943	Dec 22 1959	Burned	In Hog Bayou, about 1 mile west of Wax Lake Spillway, St. Mary Parish, La.
1665	Sea Horse	0l.s.	67	1942	Feb 14 1951	Stranded	On beach, 85 miles south of bar at Port Isabel, Texas.
1666	Sea Lady	0l.s.	133	1937	Nov 11 1953	Burned	In Ballenas Bay, Mexico.
1667	Sea Pack	0l.s.	378	1944	Nov 24 1952	Burned	About 18-55-00 N. 85-18-00 W. Steel vessel.
1668	Sea Star	0l.s.	65	1953	Jan 14 1964	Foundered	In Gulf of Mexico, about 90 miles southwest of Tortugas Light.

NO.	NAME OF VESSEL	RIG	TONS	BUILT	DATE		CAUSE	PLACE AND COMMENT
1669	Sea Turf	Ol.s.	63	1953	Mar 12	1965	Burned	Approximately 55 miles northeast of Point Palmas, Mexico.
1670	Seamaster	Ol.s.	134	1943	Sep 29	1967	Storm	At Port Mansfield, Texas.
1671	Selma	St.p.	227	1845	May 29	1850	Collided	With D.B. MOSBY. Cahawba, Ala.
1672	Selma	St.p.	320	1856	Jun 24	1868	Foundered	Off mouth of Brazos River, Texas. 6 lives lost.
1673	Selma	St.p.	600	1867	Jan 25	1875	Lost	New Orleans, La.
1674	Seneca	St.s.	193	1843	Nov 23	1870	Burned	Mobile, Ala. Used as ferryboat.
1675	Senorita	Ol.s.	73	1928	Mar 6	1952	Foundered	10 miles east of Los Fariles, Mexico.
1676	Sentinel	St.s.	297	1863	May 11	1896	Foundered	New Orleans, La.
1677	Seven Sons	Ol.s.	53	1951	May 11	1955	Stranded	Near Trinity Shoals, south of New Orleans, La.
1678	Sewance	St.w.	90	1904	Nov 18	1932	Burned	Patterson, La.
1679	Shamrock	St.p.	218	1832	Feb 8	1832	Collided	With BALTIC. New Orleans, La.
1680	Shamrock	St.p.	139	1848	Jun 29	1851	Burned	Lake Bistineau, La.
1681	Shamrock	Ol.s.	83	1951	Jan 23	1956	Stranded	On coast of Mexico, about 135 miles south of Port Isabel, Texas.
1682	Shangri-La	Ol.s.	179	1944	May 27	1946	Foundered	15 miles southwest of Cape Corrientes, Mexico.
1683	Shark	St.w.	228	1862	Jan 13	1871	Stranded	Liberty Island, Mississippi River.
1684	She-Bo	Ol.s.	66	1953	Mar 25	1960	Burned	In Campeche, Mexico. 20-19-00 N. 91-45-00 W.
1685	Sheherazade (Pan.)	St.s.	7,015	-	Jun 11	1942	War Loss	28-42-15 N. 91-23-00 W. Tanker. Steel vessel. Sunk by enemy action.
1686	Shell Driller	Ol.s.	61	1954	Jan 3	1958	Foundered	In Gulf of Mexico. 29-01-00 N. 91-28-00 W. Steel vessel.
1687	Shepherdess	-	-	-	Jan 1	1844	"Sank"	Mississippi River. 70 lives lost.
1688	Sherewog	Sc.b.	1,353	1918	Aug 4	1926	Burned	New Orleans, La.
1689	Sherrod	-	-	-	May 9	1837	Burned	Mississippi River. 200 lives lost.
1690	Sherry Ann	Ol.s.	56	1947	Mar 14	1961	Stranded	On Washington Beach, Mexico, 12 miles south of Port Isabel, Texas.
1691	Shoal Harbor	Ol.s.	194	1945	Sep 29	1955	Burned	In Gulf of Mexico, 10 miles offshore. 29-30-00 N. 92-38-00 W.
1692	Shreveport	St.p.	159	1852	Apr 20	1854	Snagged	Black Bayou, La. 1 life lost.
1693	Shrimp Carrier	Ol.s.	64	1954	Mar 20	1963	Collided	With Ol.s. MISS THELMA. 5 miles north of Champton, Mexico, in the Bay of Campeche.
1694	Siblsa	Bark	-	-	Jan 16	1891	Unknown	Progresso, Mexico.
1695	Siboney	Ol.s.	64	1954	May 25	1960	Foundered	About 25 miles offshore, between Campeche and Obregon, Mexico.
1696	Silver Cloud	St.w.	236	1862	Oct 2	1866	Snagged	Buffalo Bayou, Texas.
1697	Silver Dollar	Ol.s.	57	1951	Nov 20	1957	Foundered	At West Triangle in Gulf of Campeche, Mexico. 20-19-00 N. 92-17-00 W.
1698	Silver Heels	St.p.	267	1867	Oct 2	1860	Foundered	Carrollton, La.
1699	Silver Lake No.3	St.w.	212	1862	Feb 27	1866	Burned	Red River, La. Vessel changed to St.p. Sept. 28, 1865.
1700	Silver Liner	Ol.s.	225	1942	Aug 1	1951	Burned	7 miles off east jetty at Sabine, Texas.
1701	Silver Moon	St.p.	171	1857	Mar 7	1858	Burned	Bayou Goula, La.
1702	Silver Star	Ol.s.	87	1914	Oct 31	1956	Foundered	In Bayou Bienvenue, St. Bernard Parish, La.
1703	Sings Pride	St.w.	55	1950	Feb 4	1966	Foundered	Approximately 7 miles ESE of Tuxpan Reef, Mexico.
1704	Sir William Wallace	St.w.	255	1855	Mar 27	1866	Burned	Mobile, Ala.
1705	Skipjack	Ol.s.	64	1954	May 30	1958	Burned	About 90 miles west by north of Campeche, Mexico.
1706	Sonora	St.w.	229	1865	Nov 18	1866	Snagged	Atchafalaya River, La.
1707	South America	-	-	-	Dec 17	1850	Burned	Mississippi River. 30 lives lost.
1708	South Bay	St.s.	456	1901	Oct 29	1917	Foundered	Off Tampico, Mexico.
1709	South Carolina	Packet	580	1845	Jan 15	1859	Wrecked	On Mobile Bar. Sailing packet with auxiliary steam power.
1710	South Eastern	Ol.s.	71	1955	Aug 17	1964	Collided	With ol.s. NAVIGATOR. At Mile 530 Ahp, Mississippi River, at Greenville, Miss.
1711	South Sea	Ol.s.	67	1945	Sep 26	1954	Burned	About 10 miles ESE of Brazos Santiago Pass, Texas.
1712	Southern Belle	St.p.	525	1851	Oct 16	1857	Burned	Mobile, Ala.
1713	Southern Belle	Ol.s.	75	1952	Nov 12	1965	Stranded	On Alacran Reef, 90° northeast and 23 miles east of Campeche, Mexico.
1714	Southern Breeze	Ol.s.	93	1912	Mar 7	1944	Foundered	At Galveston, Texas.
1715	Southern Dawn	Ol.s.	53	1951	Apr 7	1964	Burned	27-00-00 N. 82-32-00 W.
1716	Southern Fisherman	Ol.s.	64	1957	Apr 26	1959	Burned	About 25 miles southwest of Morris Point, Campeche, Mexico.

NO.	NAME OF VESSEL	RIG	TONS	BUILT	DATE			CAUSE	PLACE AND COMMENT
1717	Southerner	St.p.	298	1836	May	21	1851	Snagged	New Orleans, La.
1718	Southerner	St.p.	393	1853	Jul	21	1862	Collided	College Point, La.
1719	Southerner	Ol.s.	52	1946	Mar	13	1959	Stranded	On Mexican coast, in vicinity of Ciudal del Carmen, Mexico.
1720	Southland	St.p.	673	1869	Aug	22	1925	Burned	Lake Pontchartrain, La. Iron vessel.
1721	Speedwell	St.s.	971	1912	Sep	29	1920	Foundered	25-00 N. 87-00 W. 9 lives lost (25).
1722	Sportfisher V	Ol.s.	63	1946	Jan	6	1948	Stranded	On San Geronimo Island, Mexico.
1723	Spot Pack	Ol.s.	147	1941	Apr	28	1954	Burned	24-56-04 N. 82-46-05 W.
1724	Springfield	Sch.	633	1901	Apr	8	1918	Foundered	Gulf of Mexico.
1725	Standard	St.w.	273	1915	Oct	26	1932	Foundered	Stack Island Light, Mississippi River. Steel vessel. 5 lives lost (18).
1726	Star	St.p.	147	1853	Aug	10	1856	Stranded	Last Island, La.
1727	Star	St.w.	94	1864	Jul		1865	Burned	Red Bayou, La.
1728	Star	Ol.s.	52	1920	Sep	2	1947	Stranded	About 11 miles north of Magdalena Bay, Mexico.
1729	Star of the Sea	Sch.	967	1887	Oct	26	1911	Stranded	Florida Reefs, Fla.
1730	Star of the West	St.p.	1,172	1852	Mar	17	1863	Scuttled	Fort Pemberton, Miss.
1731	Star Spangled Banner	St.p.	275	1845	Jun	29	1847	Snagged	Baton Rouge, La. 20 lives lost.
1732	Star State	St.p.	264	1851	Jun	4	1853	Foundered	Galveston, Texas.
1733	Stark D. Whiteman	Ol.s.	61	1872	Aug	5	1955	Burned	At Clarks Landing in Marrero, La. Iron vessel.
1734	Starke	Sch.	209	1876	Feb	5	1906	Stranded	Chandeleur Island, La.
1735	Starlight	St.p.	280	1858	Apr	23	1868	Burned	Algiers, La.
1736	Starlight	St.w.	214	1862	Apr	25	1868	Burned	Gretna, La.
1737	Stella	St.p.	82	1904	Dec	4	1906	Burned	Greenwood, Miss.
1738	Steven L.	Ol.s.	151	1936	Jul	7	1952	Stranded	About 18 miles north of Cape San Lazaros, Mexico.
1739	Storm	St.p.	247	1848	Feb	27	1857	Snagged	Campti, La.
1740	Stranger	Sch.	640	1893	Apr	22	1923	Burned	South-southwest of Mobile Bar Buoy, Ala.
1741	Stutz	Ga.w.	51	1926	Oct	31	1927	Burned	Baton Rouge, La.
1742	Sugarland	St.p.	100	1908	Sep	29	1915	Foundered	Morgan City, La.
1743	Sully	Brg.	–	–	Apr		1891	Unknown	Alvarado, Mexico.
1744	Sultan	St.p.	125	1845	Oct	25	1847	Snagged	Atchafalaya River, La.
1745	Sultana	–	–	–	Nov	21	1846	Collided	With MARIA, Mississippi River. 30 lives lost.
1746	Sultana	–	–	–	Apr	27	1865	Exploded	Mississippi River. 1,450 lives lost.
1747	Summit	St.w.	180	1855	Dec	5	1855	Burned	New Orleans, La.
1748	Sun	St.p.	136	1831	Aug	6	1840	Stranded	Mobile, Ala.
1749	Sun	St.p.	157	1852	Feb	21	1853	Snagged	Black Bayou, La.
1750	Sun	St.s.	9,002.	–	May	16	1942	War Loss	28-41-00 N. 90-19-00 W. Tanker. SALVAGED.
1751	Sun Beauty	Ol.s.	154	1937	Jul	11	1947	Foundered	20 miles off Cape Colnett, Mexico.
1752	Sun Dawn	Ol.s.	392	1945	Aug	31	1957	Foundered	Compass reading 253° True, 8 miles from Point Banda, Mexico.
1753	Sun Dial	Ol.s.	536	1945	Mar	26	1956	Foundered	About 2.5 miles from shore, off Banderas Bay, Mexico. Steel vessel.
1754	Sun Flower	St.p.	271	1865	Oct	3	1867	Stranded	Galveston, Texas.
1755	Sun Flower	St.s.	282	1863	Jan	29	1870	Collided	With JUNISTA. Southwest Pass, La.
1756	Sun Jewel	Ol.s.	72	1942	Mar	26	1952	Burned	18 miles from San Jose del Cabo, Mexico.
1757	Sun Maid	Ol.s.	101	1930	May	7	1948	Burned	In Guaymas Harbor, Mexico.
1758	Sun Pacific	Ol.s.	394	1945	Oct	23	1957	Storm	21-14-00 N. 107-56-00 W.
1759	Sun Valley	Ol.s.	88	1926	Dec	16	1949	Burned	Magdalena Bay, Mexico.
1760	Sunny South	St.p.	196	1847	Oct	1	1855	Snagged	Mobile, Ala.
1761	Sunny South	St.p.	270	1860	Jan	11	1867	Burned	Portland, Ala. 1 life lost.
1762	Sunny South	St.p.	372	1897	Apr	20	1916	Foundered	Mobile, Ala.
1763	Sunbeam	St.w.	167	1857	Feb	4	1858	Snagged	Bayou Pierre, La.
1764	Sunbeam	Ol.s.	69	1926	Jun	25	1948	Burned	28-59-40 N. 90-27-57 W.

NO.	NAME OF VESSEL	RIG	TONS	BUILT	DATE		CAUSE	PLACE AND COMMENT
1765	Sunflower	Ol.s.	64	1958	Nov 1	1959	Foundered	At Arcas Reef, Campeche, Mexico.
1766	Sunrise Ranger	Ol.s.	54	1929	May 13	1954	Burned	About 15 miles true, southwest of San Martin Island, Mexico.
1767	Sunset	Ol.s.	301	1947	Jan 21	1956	Foundered	About 38 miles south-southwest of Acapulco, Mexico. Steel vessel.
1768	Superior	Ga.s.	167	1902	Jun 20	1920	Stranded	Off Tampico, Mexico.
1769	Superior	St.w.	129	1917	Jun 12	1934	Foundered	Lower Grand River, La.
1770	Surcease	Ga.s.	79	1917	Oct 18	1943	Burned	Gulf of Mexico, south of the Rio Grande River.
1771	Susan & Gretta	Ol.s.	63	1944	Aug 12	1956	Burned	About 35 miles southeast of the Galveston, Texas, jetties.
1772	Susie B. Dantzler	Sch.	229	1901	Jan 14	1921	Stranded	Near Fronters, Mexico.
1773	Susie H. Davidson	St.s.	546	1883	Feb 9	1917	Foundered	Gulf of Mexico.
1774	Suwied	St.s.	3,249	1919	Jun 7	1942	War Loss	20-00-00 N. 84-48-00 W. Steel vessel. Sunk by enemy action.
1775	Swallow	St.p.	159	1844	Jul 15	1846	Stranded	New Orleans, La.
1776	Swallow	St.p.	337	1851	Jan 26	1853	Collided	With E. HOWARD. Bonnet Carre, La. 1 life lost.
1777	Swallow	St.w.	198	1854	Oct	1862	Burned	Glover, Miss.
1778	Swallow	Ol.s.	133	1943	May 19	1953	Foundered	185 miles northeast of Yucatan, Gulf of Mexico.
1779	Swamp Fox	St.p.	280	1851	Feb 4	1857	Snagged	McDade, La.
1780	Swan	St.p.	112	1836	Apr 4	1838	Foundered	Lake Chicot, La.
1781	Swan	St.p.	83	1840	Dec 5	1843	Stranded	Calcasieu, La.
1782	Sydonia	St.p.	235	1851	May 29	1857	Burned	Columbia, La. 2 lives lost.
1783	Sylvia H	Ol.s.	50	1947	Nov 17	1959	Foundered	In Gulf of Mexico, about 8 miles offshore, 30 miles southeast of Aransas Pass, Texas.
1784	Sylvia Shaw	Ol.s.	63	1953	Apr 11	1955	Foundered	85 miles southwest of Campeche, Gulf of Mexico.
1785	T.C.I.S.G. No.1	Brg.	428	1927	Dec 14	1927	Foundered	Mobile Bar, Ala.
1786	T.L. McGill	-	-	-	Jan 14	1871	Burned	Mississippi River. 58 lives lost.
1787	T.T. Co. No.11	Brg.	395	1904	Jan 13	1912	Abandoned	Gulf of Mexico.
1788	Tabasco	Ol.s.	1,184	1919	May 18	1933	Stranded	Alacran Reef, Gulf of Mexico. Steel vessel.
1789	Talleyrand	St.p.	593	1848	Dec 20	1850	Stranded	Bayou Goula, La.
1790	Tangipaho	St.w.	65	1837	Mar 2	1838	Burned	New Orleans, La. 3 lives lost.
1791	Tarquin	St.p.	165	1837	Nov 4	1841	Snagged	Princeton, Miss.
1792	Taurus	St.s.	228	1885	Feb 16	1912	Stranded	South Pass, Mississippi River, La. Steel vessel.
1793	Teche	St.p.	295	1820	Apr 14	1825	Exploded	Natchez, Miss. 20 lives lost.
1794	Tecumseh	St.p.	418	1852	Dec 1	1863	Burned	West Baton Rouge, La.
1795	Telegram	St.w.	205	1858	May 6	1861	Burned	Algiers, La.
1796	Telegraph	St.p.	188	1829	Dec 27	1833	Collided	With NEW ORLEANS. Palmyra Island, Miss.
1797	Temple	Drg.	168	1935	Sep 24	1956	Burned	In Drury Bay, near Dauphin Island, Ala.
1798	Tennessee	St.p.	416	1819	Feb 8	1823	Snagged	Natchez, Miss.
1799	Terrebonne	St.p.	91	1908	Aug 25	1926	Foundered	Donaldsonville, La.
1800	Terry Walker	Ol.s.	147	1953	Mar 31	1964	Burned	About 3 miles off Sabine Pass, Texas, in Sabine Pass Approach.
1801	Tessler	Ol.s.	68	1905	Jun 26	1949	Burned	About 86.2 miles on Upper Mississippi River. Steel vessel.
1802	Tetlin	St.p.	65	1908	Sep 4	1923	Stranded	Nabesna River, Ala.
1803	Texan	St.p.	96	1848	Mar 27	1849	Burned	Above Plaquemine, La.
1804	Texas	St.p.	184	1856	Sep	1860	Foundered	Galveston, Texas.
1805	Texas	St.p.	170	1859	Mar 8	1867	Snagged	Barbin Landing, La. 2 lives lost.
1806	Texas Queen	Ol.s.	75	1947	Jun 14	1952	Stranded	Off Campeche, Mexico.
1807	Texas Star	Ol.s.	74	1954	Jul 11	1956	Burned	In Gulf of Mexico, 10 miles east-southeast of Freeport, Texas.
1808	The Richards	Ol.s.	66	1953	Mar 6	1956	Burned	19-23-00 N. 91-26-00 W.
1809	Thelma	Sch.	525	1893	May 5	1925	Burned	29-38-00 N. 85-57-00 W.
1810	Thistle	St.w.	210	1863	Jul 31	1864	Snagged	Big Hurricane Island, Mississippi River.
1811	Thomas	Brg.	167	1899		1903	Foundered	Off Velasco, Texas.

NO.	NAME OF VESSEL	RIG	TONS	BUILT	DATE		CAUSE	PLACE AND COMMENT
1812	Thomas A. Edison	Ol.s.	75	1954	Apr 17	1954	Stranded	On Alcan Reef, Gulf of Mexico.
1813	Thos. B. Florence	Ga.w.	95	1875	Sep 30	1932	Burned	Natchez, Miss. Iron vessel.
1814	Thomas H. Benton	St.p.	84	1889	Apr 29	1917	Burned	Vidalia, La.
1815	Thomas J. Carroll	Sch.	71	1905	Aug 16	1915	Foundered	Galveston, Texas.
1816	Thomas Jefferson	St.p.	279	1846	Nov 8	1849	Stranded	Waterloo, La.
1817	Thomas L. Wand	St.s.	691	1906	Nov 10	1919	Abandoned	27-20-00 N. 88-58-00 W.
1818	Thomas McDaniel	St.p.	538	1853	Feb 26	1855	Exploded	English Turn, La. 7 lives lost.
1819	Thomas Pickles	St.w.	237	1892	Sep 9	1965	Hurricane	In Mississippi River, about 100 Mile Ahp, New Orleans, La.
1820	Thomas R. Buckham	St.p.	238	1901	Apr 6	1920	Burned	White Hall Point, La.
1821	Thos. R. Buckham	St.w.	166	1917	Feb 3	1928	Burned	Simmsport, La.
1822	Thomas Sparks	St.s.	373	1854	Jan 12	1866	Stranded	Mobile Bay, Ala. Steel vessel.
1823	Thomas W. Knight	Sch.	66	1881	Feb 14	1914	Foundered	Off Anclope, Gulf of Mexico.
1824	Three Brothers	Ol.s.	121	1951	Apr 3	1958	Foundered	About 120 miles south of Port Isabel, Texas. Steel vessel.
1825	Three Friends	Ol.s.	52	1945	Aug 11	1954	Burned	In Gulf of Mexico, 18 miles northeast of Port Isabel, Texas.
1826	Three Marys	Sch.	1,151	1891	Sep 29	1920	Foundered	27-14-00 N. 87-35-00 W.
1827	Three Sisters	Ol.s.	50	1956	Jan 27	1963	Foundered	Off mouth of Lonesome Bayou, La.
1828	Thunderbird	Ol.s.	122	1943	Jan 10	1962	Foundered	In Gulf of Mexico, about 15 miles south of Tuxpan, Mexico.
1829	Tiger	St.p.	364	1837	Nov 13	1844	Exploded	Southwest Pass, La. 3 lives lost.
1830	Tiger	St.p.	333	1858	Apr 2	1860	Snagged	Alexandria, La.
1831	Tigress	St.p.	321	1858	Apr 22	1863	Gunfire	Vicksburg, Miss.
1832	Time and Tide	St.w.	130	1853	May 28	1864	Burned	New Orleans, La.
1833	Tippah	St.p.	107	1851	Jan 13	1852	Burned	Point Pleasant, La. 1 life lost.
1834	Titan	St.s.	178	1897	Jul 27	1943	Foundered	Galveston, Texas. Steel vessel.
1835	Tombeckbe	St.p.	64	1821	Jan 20	1824	Snagged	Erie, Ala.
1836	Tomochichi	St.p.	236	1835	Apr 22	1843	Snagged	Poydras, La.
1837	Torando	Clipper	1,802	1852		1875	Burned	At New Orleans, La.
1838	Touchet	St.s.	10,172	1943	Dec 3	1943	War Loss	25-50-00 N. 86-30-00 W. Tanker. Steel vessel. 9 lives lost (80). Sunk by enemy action.
1839	Trade Wind	St.s.	426	1862	Sep 24	1869	Foundered	Belize, La. 1 life lost.
1840	Trans-Gulf No.10	Brg.	2,690	1958	Jan 10	1959	Foundered	In Block 21, South Timbalier Area, off Louisiana coast. Steel vessel.
1841	Transit	St.p.	104	1838	Oct 16	1842	Snagged	Coushatta, La.
1842	Transport	St.w.	91	1848	May 6	1849	Stranded	Donaldsonville, La.
1843	Traveler	Ol.s.	65	1946	May 21	1961	Burned	About 50 miles southeast of Port Arthur Lighthouse, Texas.
1844	Tremont	-	-	-	Oct 29	1837	Collided	With MONMOUTH. Mississippi River. 400 lives lost.
1845	Tribune	St.p.	251	1849	Nov 2	1849	Burned	Bayou Goula, La.
1846	Trinity	St.w.	238	1851	Nov 26	1851	Stranded	Last Island, La.
1847	Tulsa	Sch.	607	1909	Mar 10	1943	Foundered	30-09-00 N. 88-05-00 W. Steel vessel.
1848	Tuscaloosa	St.p.	320	1844	Jan 29	1847	Exploded	Mobile, Ala. 12 lives lost.
1849	Twilight	Ol.s.	77	1953	Dec 2	1965	Collided	With tug MISS GERALDINE and its tow. At Mile 26.5 Ahp, Mississippi River.
1850	Typhoon	Ol.s.	63	1953	Jun 28	1959	Burned	About 70 miles southwest of Campeche, Mexico.
1851	UM 105B	Brg.	1,005	1965	Sep 9	1965	Hurricane	In vicinity of Mile 124.5 Ahp in Mississippi River.
1852	Umpire	St.w.	87	1847		1852	Snagged	Aransas Pass, Texas.
1853	Una	St.p.	121	1863	Aug 12	1867	Stranded	Atchafalaya River, La.
1854	Uncle Ike	St.w.	68	1859	Dec 2	1860	Burned	Baton Rouge, La.
1855	Uncle Oliver	St.w.	156	1906	Dec 12	1929	Burned	Vicksburg, Miss.
1856	Unicorn	St.p.	185	1853	Dec 11	1855	Burned	Natchez, Miss.
1857	United States	St.p.	645	1819	Sep 3	1824	Stranded	New Orleans, La.
1858		Sch	2,384	1919	Nov 25	1920	Stranded	Off Port Aransas, Texas.

NO.	NAME OF VESSEL	RIG	TONS	BUILT	DATE		CAUSE	PLACE AND COMMENT
1859	Valley Belle	Ol.s.	67	1953	Mar 15	1959	Stranded	On Mexican coast at Point Juarez, 40 miles north of Tampico, Mexico.
1860	Valley King	Ol.s.	59	1953	Nov 8	1961	Stranded	On Mexican coast, about 60 miles south of Vera Cruz.
1861	Valley Prince	Ol.s.	57	1953	Apr 6	1956	Burned	In Gulf of Mexico, 20 miles southwest of Galveston, Texas.
1862	Valley Queen	Ol.s.	60	1953	Apr 4	1962	Burned	In Gulf of Mexico, about 30 miles north of Vera Cruz, Mexico.
1863	Valley Rio	St.s.	59	1952	Aug 19	1963	Burned	Between Aransas Pass and Pass Cavillos Light, Texas. 29-53-57 N. 85-27-50 W. Steel vessel. Freighter. Depth 30'.
1864	Vamar	St.s.	598	-		1942	Unknown	Ensenada, Mexico.
1865	Van Camp No.11	Brg.	190	1915	Feb 12	1926	Stranded	Off Campeche, Mexico.
1866	Vanguard	Ol.s.	60	1958	Mar 21	1967	Unknown	Off Tampico Bar, Mexico.
1867	Vaska	Sch.	285	1915	May 19	1917	Foundered	About 40 miles northeast of Palmas Point, Mexico.
1868	Vaya Con Dios	Ol.s.	75	1954	Jan 1	1955	Foundered	18-28-00 N. 93-07-00 W.
1869	Vega	Ol.s.	85	1956	Jan 18	1956	Foundered	On coast of Mexico, at Quintana Roo, 15 miles north of Port Xcalak, Mexico.
1870	Vega	Ol.s.	60	1958	Feb 18	1966	Stranded	Tabasco, Mexico.
1871	Velasco	Drg.	191	1923	Jan 19	1936	Foundered	21-20-00 N. 86-45-00 W. Freighter.
1872	Velma Lykes	St.s.	1,638	-	Jun 5	1942	Unknown	Pilcher Point, La.
1873	Venango	St.w.	120	1858	Dec 31	1864	Burned	With jetties, Tampico, Mexico.
1874	Vera Cruz	Sch.	1,934	1884	Apr 7	1918	Collided	Port Arthur, Texas.
1875	Versa	Ga.y.	79	1917	Apr 17	1933	Burned	Vicksburg, Miss.
1876	Vicksburg	St.p.	635	1857	Mar 29	1863	Burned	Vicksburg, Miss.
1877	Vicksburg	St.w.	73	1912	Jan 2	1932	Stranded	At foot of Walnut Street, New Orleans, La.
1878	Victor	Ol.s.	121	1917		1945	Foundered	Bayou d'Arbonne, La.
1879	Victoria	St.p.	487	1859	Jan	1866	Stranded	Algiers, La.
1880	Victoria	St.p.	405	1858	Feb 3	1869	Burned	Buras, La.
1881	Victoria	Ol.s.	117	1923	Nov 1	1927	Burned	About 15 miles northwest of Campeche, Mexico.
1882	Victoria	Ol.s.	63	1952	May 2	1964	Foundered	29-27-14 N. 80-52-50 W. Depth 80'.
1883	Victory	-	337	-	Pre-WWII		Unknown	40 miles southwest of Abriojos Point, Mexico.
1884	Victory	Ol.s.	143	1943	Aug 30	1956	Foundered	At Choctaw Point, mouth of Mobile River, Ala.
1885	Vigilant	Ol.s.	70	1935	Jul 14	1953	Burned	With steamer MOBILA. Gulf of Mexico. 29-00 N. 87-00 W.
1886	Vila Y. Hermano	Sch.	327	1891	Sep 5	1905	Collided	Off Long Key, Fla.
1887	Vincennes	St.p.	95	1833	Feb 10	1838	Snagged	Mobile, Ala.
1888	Vineyard	Brig	-	-		1830	Unknown	With AMERICA. Donaldsonville, La.
1889	Viola	St.p.	299	1846	Oct 27	1849	Collided	Lake Pontchartrain, La. 6 lives lost.
1890	Virginia	St.p.	642	1853	Aug 7	1858	Exploded	Claiborne, Ala.
1891	Virginia	St.w.	141	1860	Sep 11	1869	Snagged	28-53-06 N. 89-26-42 W. Tanker. Steel vessel. 27 lives lost (41). Sunk by enemy action. Wreck is completely silted over.
1892	Virginia	St.s.	10,731	1941	May 12	1942	War Loss	
1893	Virginia No.2	St.p.	228	1864	Mar 1	1868	Burned	Tombigbee River, Ala.
1894	Vitality	Ol.s.	93	1927	Mar 23	1931	Foundered	Guadelupe Island, Mexico.
1895	Volant	St.p.	136	1852	Nov 4	1853	Burned	Cardiff, Miss. 1 life lost.
1896	Volunteer	Ol.s.	65	1945	Nov 15	1951	Stranded	28 miles south of Port Isabel, Texas, on Mexican coast.
1897	Vona Mabry	Ol.s.	63	1950	Feb 5	1956	Collided	With Panamanian vessel LAMYRA. 29-12-00 N. 92-52-00 W.
1898	W-501	Scow	368	1913	Dec 18	1953	Foundered	In Lake Pontchartrain, La. Steel vessel.
1899	W.A. Bisso	St.s.	265	1907	Nov 10	1918	Collided	With Mexican st.s. COAHUILA. Point Celeste, La. 9 lives lost.
1900	W.A. Violett	St.p.	162	1848	Jan 24	1853	Burned	Torras, La.
1901	W.E. Hamilton	St.w.	129	1867		1883	"Sunk"	Red River, La. Used as ferryboat.
1902	W.F. Jewett	Sch.	474	1887	Aug 10	1928	Stranded	Magdalena Bay, Mexico.
1903	W.H. Marston	Sch.	1,100	1901	Dec 10	1927	Foundered	26-40-00 N. 88-09-00 W.
1904	W.M. Porter	St.p.	76	1906	Sep 24	1913	Burned	Teach Harbor, La.
1905	W.M. Wood	St.s.	58	1880	Sep 29	1906	Foundered	Poverty Point, La. Iron vessel.

NO.	NAME OF VESSEL	RIG	TONS	BUILT	DATE	CAUSE	PLACE AND COMMENT
1906	W.R. Carter	St.p.	563	1864	Feb 9 1886	Exploded	Island near Vicksburg, Miss. 125 lives lost.
1907	W.R. Douglas	St.p.	167	1856	Feb 28 1859	Foundered	Holcomb, Miss.
1908	W.T. Scovell	St.p.	244	1895	Dec 19 1906	Exploded	Vicksburg, Miss. 12 lives lost.
1909	Wade Allen	St.p.	129	1850	Jul 30 1855	Burned	Mobile, Ala. 1 life lost.
1910	Wakulla	Ol.s.	70	1929	May 15 1966	Burned	At Mile Post 89.0 of Intercoastal Waterway, east of Harvey, La.
1911	Walk in the Water	St.p.	290	1826	Dec 8 1835	Burned	Natchez, Miss.
1912	Walker	St.p.	112	1839	Dec 2 1843	Exploded	Lake Pontchartrain, La. 7 lives lost.
1913	Wanderer	St.p.	186	1831	Nov 11 1836	Snagged	Mobile, Ala.
1914	Warren Belle	St.p.	242	1865	Feb 6 1870	Snagged	Bayou Teche, La.
1915	Warrior	St.p.	96	1826	Jan 22 1829	Collided	With ERIE. Jackson, Ala.
1916	Warrior	St.p.	100	1832	1837	Snagged	Mississippi River.
1917	Washington	St.p.	100	1901	Sep 20 1909	Foundered	Donaldsonville, La. 1 life lost.
1918	Watchman	St.p.	129	1831	Jul 16 1836	Snagged	Bayou Plaquemine, La.
1919	Waul	Brg.	534	1892	Dec 24 1912	Foundered	Near St. Andrews Bar, Gulf of Mexico.
1920	Wave	St.p.	78	1844	Mar 7 1849	Stranded	St. James, La.
1921	Waw Hoss	Ol.s.	70	1924	Oct 3 1955	Foundered	In Mississippi River about Mile 384, from head of the Passes, which is about 24.5 miles north of Natchez, Miss. Steel vessel.
1922	Welcome	St.p.	449	1863	Aug 1871	Burned	New Orleans, La.
1923	Welfare	Ol.s.	53	1927	Sep 23 1930	Foundered	Point Canoas, Mexico.
1924	Welt 2	Brg.	841	1959	Jul 11 1962	Collided	With left bank of Mississippi River near Mile 584. Steel vessel.
1925	West Beaufort	Ol.s.	119	1938	Aug 10 1953	Burned	About 5.5 miles east by south of Calcasieu Pass, La.
1926	West Pointer	Ol.s.	65	1953	Jul 23 1957	Foundered	At Freeport, Texas.
1927	Western World	St.p.	338	1848	Dec 14 1852	Collided	With H.R.W. HILL. Princeton, Miss. 12 lives lost.
1928	Wetumpka	St.w.	313	1852	Feb 12 1854	Collided	With MAGNOLIA. Alabama River, Ala.
1929	White Water	Ol.s.	75	1875	Jan 30 1950	Burned	In Mississippi River at New Orleans, La. Iron vessel.
1930	Wild Duck	Ol.s.	58	1948	Dec 2 1948	Burned	About 6 miles SE of Biloxi, Miss., lighthouse.
1931	Will Davis	St.p.	150	1895	Sep 20 1909	Foundered	New Orleans, La.
1932	William Anthony	Ol.s.	67	1963	Feb 6 1967	Stranded	On reef at Cayo Arcus, Mexico.
1933	Wm. C. McTarnahan	St.s.	7,306	-	May 16 1942	War Loss	28-52-00 N. 90-20-00 W. Tanker. Steel vessel. 18 lives lost (45). SALVAGED.
1934	William Bradstreet	St.p.	247	1845	Mar 1852	Snagged	Aberdeen, Miss.
1935	William C. Young	St.p.	199	1854	Aug 15 1860	Foundered	Ship Island, Miss. 7 lives lost.
1936	William Campbell	St.p.	322	1856	May 27 1860	Burned	New Orleans, La.
1937	William Clarke Quinn	Ol.s.	108	1937	Sep 1961	Hurricane	Gilchrist, Texas.
1938	William E. Burnham	Sch.	772	1909	Nov 5 1927	Foundered	21-09-00 N. 84-40-00 W.
1939	Wm. Edenborn	St.p.	239	1906	May 5 1911	Foundered	Naples, Fla.
1940	William H. Webb	St.p.	655	1856	Apr 24 1865	Burned	23 miles below New Orleans, La.
1941	William Hays	Ol.s.	69	1912	Jul 16 1957	Foundered	Off Galveston Bar, Texas.
1942	William Hulburt	St.p.	107	1836	Jul 26 1839	Burned	Mobile, Ala. 2 lives lost.
1943	William J. Lewis	St.p.	503	1866	Apr 2 1873	Snagged	Liberty Island, Mississippi River.
1944	William Jones, Jr.	St.p.	391	1853	Mar 26 1855	Burned	Alabama River.
1945	William L. Douglas	Sch.	3,708	-	Dec 18 1917	Collided	At Sabine, Texas. Length 316'. 6-masted vessel. Sunk as "Delaware Sun".
1946	William M. Morrison	St.p.	662	1856	Aug 1861	Burned	New Orleans, La.
1947	William N. Sherman	St.p.	195	1855	Feb 20 1858	Burned	Algiers, La.
1948	William Penn	St.p.	160	1825	Dec 17 1827	Snagged	Bonnet Carre, La.
1949	William Penn	St.p.	113	1847	May 12 1854	Snagged	Red River, La.
1950	William R. King	St.p.	233	1846	Feb 5 1847	Collided	With WINONA. Tombigbee River, Ala. 2 lives lost.
1951	William R. Wilson	Sch.	1,385	1908	Jan 13 1912	Stranded	Pickles Reef, Fla.
1952	William Robinson, Jr	St.p	277	1839	Mar 20 1843	Collided	With CLARION. Fairfield, Ala.

NO.	NAME OF VESSEL	RIG	TONS	BUILT	DATE		CAUSE	PLACE AND COMMENT
1953	William S. Nelson	St.w.	324	1856	Nov	1859	Burned	Carrollton, La.
1954	William T. Barry	St.p.	148	1832	Mar 19	1836	Stranded	Lake Pontchartrain, La.
1955	William Tell	St.p.	80	1826	Mar 16	1830	Exploded	Torras, La.
1956	Wm. V. McDonald	Ol.s.	59	1924	Jan 15	1961	Foundered	On Alacran Reef (Campeche Banks), Gulf of Mexico.
1957	Willie	Brg.	230	1892	Feb 1	1914	Burned	Buffalo Bayou, Texas.
1958	Willie Gamage	St.w.	187	1864	Oct 11	1876	Burned	Plaquemine, La. 8 lives lost.
1959	Wilmington	St.p.	206	1837	Nov 8	1839	Exploded	Beulah Lake, Miss. 8 lives lost.
1960	Wilson B. Keene	St.s.	7,176	1944	Apr 17	1947	Burned	Texas City, Texas. Steel vessel.
1961	Wine Island	Ol.s.	61	1939	Aug 3	1954	Burned	In Intracoastal Waterway, Mile 81, west of Harvey, La.
1962	Winfield S. Shuster	Sch.	1,481	1904	Oct 27	1911	Stranded	Isaac Shoal, Fla.
1963	Winnifred	St.w.	129	1917	Sep 14	1936	Burned	Scottsbluff Landing, La.
1964	Winona	St.p.	135	1845	May 7	1847	Snagged	Warrior River, Ala.
1965	Winthrop	St.p.	352	1896	Jul 9	1947	Foundered	27 miles north of Port Isabel, Texas. Steel vessel.
1966	Wolf III	Ol.s.	253	1943	Sep 23	1953	Burned	4.5 miles south of Harvey Locks in Russell Wolf & Co. slip No.2, New Orleans.
1967	Wolf IV	Ol.s.	259	1943	Sep 23	1953	Burned	4.5 miles south of Harvey Locks in Russell Wolf & Co. slip No.2, New Orleans.
1968	Wolf V	Ol.s.	259	1943	Sep 23	1953	Burned	4.5 miles south of Harvey Locks in Russell Wolf & Co. slip No.2, New Orleans.
1969	Wyandotte	St.p.	314	1847	Nov 21	1848	Snagged	Vicksburg, Miss. 30 lives lost.
1970	Wychem 112	Brg.	765	1960	Mar 23	1961	Foundered	In Mississippi River at Mile mark 352.5, about 7 miles below Natchez, Miss.
1971	Yacht	St.p.	249	1844	Sep 23	1853	Stranded	Brazos Bar, Texas.
1972	Yakima	Sch.	108	1902	Mar 10	1924	Stranded	Alacrane Reef, Mexico.
1973	Yalobusha	St.p.	80	1837	Jan 18	1848	Burned	Donaldsonville, La. 35 lives lost.
1974	Yankee Pirate	Ol.s.	64	1953	Aug 11	1958	Burned	About 20 miles off Aransas Pass, Texas.
1975	Yankee Rebel	Ol.s.	63	1953	May 13	1955	Foundered	In Campeche Bay, Mexico, about 40 miles west of Campeche Flats.
1976	Yazoo	St.p.	304	1842	Apr 3	1848	Snagged	Carrollton, La. 1 life lost.
1977	Yazoo	St.p.	51	1914	Jun 25	1915	Burned	Bayou Sara, La.
1978	Yazoo Belle	St.p.	138	1855	Jun 23	1860	Snagged	Above raft, Red River, La.
1979	Yazoo City	St.p.	229	1843	Sep 3	1848	Snagged	Commerce, Miss.
1980	Yellowstone	St.p.	144	1831		1837	Stranded	Brazos River, Texas.
1981	Yetta	Ol.s.	69	1950	Feb 23	1965	Foundered	At Mile 91 Ahp, Mississippi River, 1.5 miles below Public Health Service Station.
1982	Young America	St.p.	138	1858	May 4	1867	Stranded	Saluria Island, Texas.
1983	Yuma	Brg.	123	1916	Nov 12	1920	Foundered	Tampico Bar, Mexico. Steel vessel.
1984	Yuma	St.s.	-	-	Mar 17	1926	Unknown	28-56-35 N. 89-26-37 W.
1985	Zalophus	-	300	-	Pre-WWII		Unknown	27-21-00 N. 82-38-00 W.
1986	Zerah, Jr.	St.p.	86	1901	Jul 16	1914	Foundered	Trotters Landing, Miss.
1987	35th Parallel	St.p.	419	1859	Mar 13	1863	Burned	Tallahatchie River, Miss.
1988	304	Brg.	386	1928	Mar 16	1947	Foundered	Cape Rock Light, Mile 54.1, Upper section of Mississippi River. Steel vessel.
1989	342	Brg.	463	1926	Mar 16	1947	Foundered	Cape Rock Light, Mile 54.1, Upper section of Mississippi River. Steel vessel.

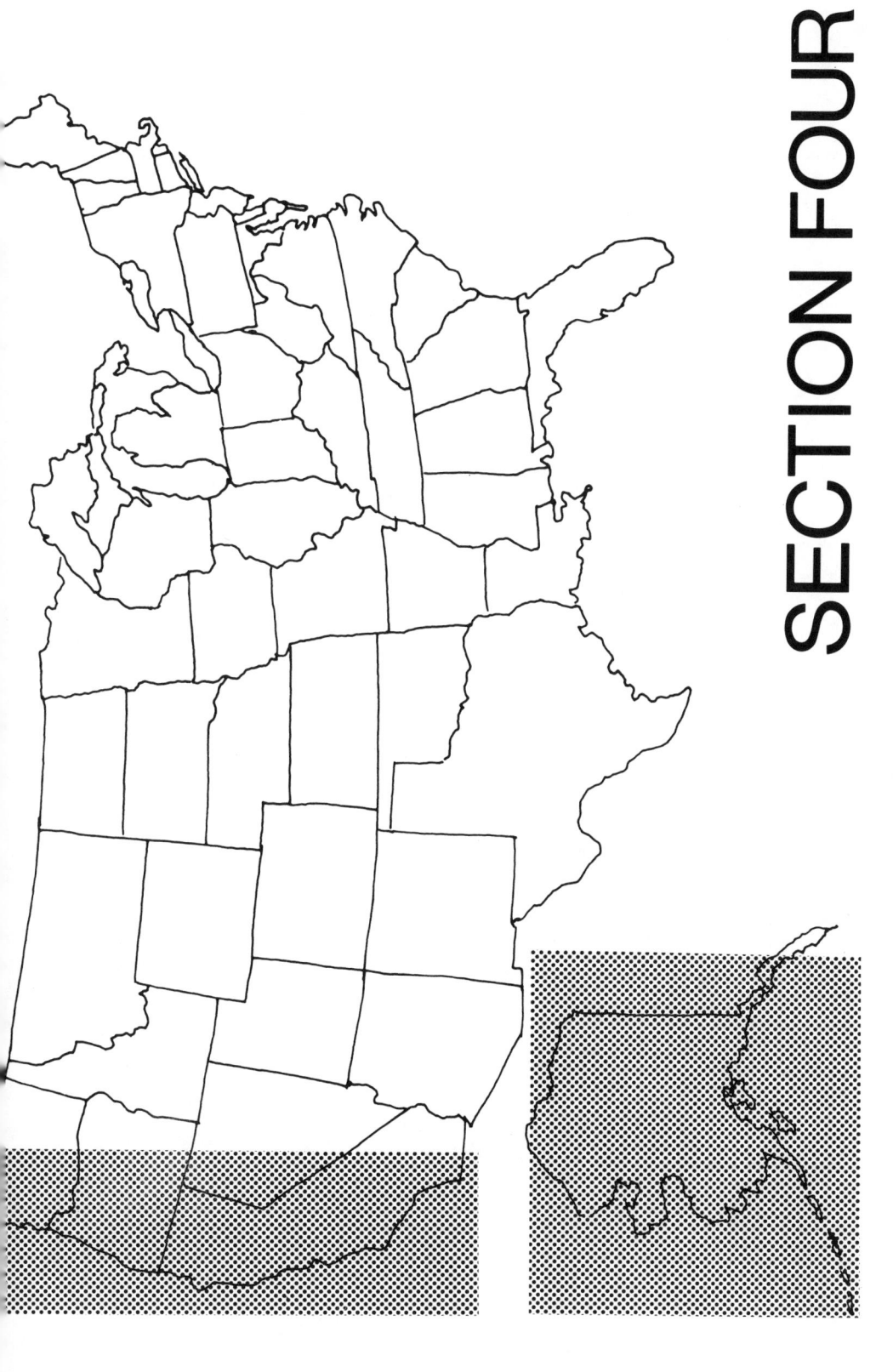

NO.	NAME OF VESSEL	RIG	TONS	BUILT	DATE		CAUSE	PLACE AND COMMENT
1	A.F.L. 1654	Brg.	1,007	1943	May 2	1954	Stranded	On Montague Island, Alaska. Wood vessel.
2	A.P.A. S-5	Scow	96	1947	Jun 16	1958	Foundered	In Bristol Bay, Alaska. Steel vessel.
3	A.P.A S-10	Scow	95	1948	Sep 11	1956	Stranded	Spanish Island, Sumner Strait, S.E. Alaska. 55-59-02 N. 134-05-06 W. Steel.
4	A.J. Fuller	Sch.	1,848	1881	Oct 30	1918	Collided	With Japanese st.s. MEXICO MARU. Seattle, Wash. (in Puget Sound).
5	ATB No.41	Scow	389	1944	Sep 2	1960	Stranded	At Ocean Cape Beach, Alaska. Steel vessel.
6	A.T.T. No.1	Brg.	3,577	1944	Nov 3	1946	Stranded	On northeast shore of Amukta Island, Alaska. Steel vessel.
7	Abbaroka	St.s.	5,695	-	Dec 24	1941	Unknown	Off San Diego, Calif. 33-40-00 N. 118-25-00 W.
8	Aberdeen	St.s.	499	1899	Jan 27	1916	Foundered	Golden Gate, Calif. All lives (7) lost.
9	Aberdeen	Scow	286	1912	Mar 16	1927	Foundered	Royal Bay, British Columbia.
10	Abraham Lincoln	Ga.s.	71	1925	Dec 20	1931	Burned	San Francisco, Calif.
11	Acalin	Ol.s.	87	1928	Aug 30	1934	Stranded	Golden Gate, Calif.
12	Ace I	Brg.	96	1944	Apr 28	1948	Foundered	At Dana Point, Calif. Steel vessel.
13	Achille Paladini	Ol.s.	98	1937	Sep 2	1956	Stranded	Off Point Laguna, Calif.
14	Acme	St.s.	416	1901	Oct 31	1924	Stranded	Coquille Light, Ore.
15	Adele Hobson	Ol.s.	73	1904	Jun 5	1934	Burned	Port Costa, Calif. 2 lives lost (3).
16	Admiral	Sch.	683	1899	Jan 13	1912	Stranded	Columbia River, Ore.
17	Admiral Benson	St.s.	3,049	1918	Feb 15	1930	Stranded	North jetty, Columbia River, Ore.
18	Admiral Evans	St.p.	2,393	1901	Mar 9	1918	Stranded	Hawk Inlet, Alaska.
19	Admiral Knight	St.s.	630	1916	Jul 27	1919	Burned	Straits of Georgia, British Columbia.
20	Admiral Nicholson	St.s.	678	1908	May 16	1924	Stranded	Umpqua River, Ore. Steel vessel.
21	Admiral Sampson	St.s.	262	1898	Aug 26	1914	Collided	With British S.S. PRINCESS VICTORIA. Off Point No Point, Puget Sound, Wash. 12 lives lost.
22	Advent	Sch.	431	1901	Feb 16	1913	Stranded	Coos Bay, Ore.
23	Aeine	Ga.s.	115	1914	Sep 25	1913	Burned	San Francisco Bay, Calif.
24	Afognak	Ol.s.	95	1889	Sep 15	1949	Foundered	On Palm Point, Controller Bay, Alaska.
25	Agnes	Ga.s.	53	1886	Dec 14	1931	Foundered	Stockton, Calif.
26	Ahrnklim	Ga.s.	64	1910	Sep 14	1922	Stranded	Acqua River, Alaska.
27	Alameda	St.s.	3,158	1883	Nov 28	1931	Burned	Seattle, Wash. Iron vessel.
28	Alaska	St.s.	60	1899	May 2	1906	Burned	Winter Quarters, Alaska. Steel vessel.
29	Alaska	St.s.	3,709	1899	Aug 6	1921	Stranded	Off Blunts Reef, Calif. Iron vessel. 42 lives lost.
30	Alaska	Ol.s.	67	1913	Feb 19	1928	Stranded	Kodiak Island, Alaska.
31	Alaska Cedar	Ol.s.	2,444	1944	Dec 2	1962	Stranded	On the north jetty, Coos Bay, Ore. Steel vessel.
32	Alaska Feefer	El.o.	962	1944	Aug 29	1961	Burned	About 470 yards off Walan Point, Puget Sound, Wash.
33	Alaska Roustabout	Ol.s.	119	1944	Sep 28	1962	Foundered	In Gulf of Alaska. Steel vessel.
34	Albatross	St.p.	661	1851	Apr 18	1853	Stranded	Cabegas Reef, off Vera Cruz, Calif.
35	Albert	Bark	682	1890	Apr 2	1919	Stranded	12 miles north of Point Reyes, Calif. 1 life lost.
36	Albion	St.s.	215	1892	Mar 21	1913	Stranded	Stewarts Point, Calif.
37	Albion	Ga.s.	86	1898	Sep 20	1924	Burned	Apple Tree Point, Wash.
38	Alcatraz	St.s.	255	1887	May 2	1917	Stranded	Mile Rock, Greenwood, Calif.
39	Alcazar	St.s.	263	1887	Jun 10	1907	Stranded	Needle Rock, Calif.
40	Alcoa Carrier	St.s.	5,588	-	May 25	1942	War Loss	Off Salina Cruz, Mexico. 18-45-00 N. 99-50-00 W.
41	Alden Anderson	St.s.	6,367	1908	Oct 29	1924	Burned	Avon, Calif. Steel vessel. 7 lives lost (41).
42	Alert	St.p.	65	1890	Sep 26	1919	Foundered	Near Rio Vista, Calif.
43	Aleutian	St.s.	5,708	1898	May 26	1929	Stranded	Amook Island, Alaska. 1 life lost (154).
44	Aleutian	Ol.s.	57	1926	Jul 16	1957	Storm	On Chiniak Rock, Kodiak, Alaska.
45	Alice B	-	-	-	Pre-WWII		Unknown	48-23-00 N. 124-37-00 W.
46	Alice Cooke	Sch.	782	1891	Nov 17	1931	Burned	Prince William Sound, Alaska.
47	Alice D. Snow	Clipper	1,425	1870	Sep	1881	Wrecked	Off California coast. Cargo of railroad iron.

NO.	NAME OF VESSEL	RIG	TONS	BUILT	DATE	CAUSE	PLACE AND COMMENT
48	Alice Gertrude	St.s.	413	1898	Jan 11 1907	Stranded	Ship Point Reef, Ore.
49	Alice H.	Ol.s.	61	1889	Sep 23 1950	Foundered	Near Port Orford, Ore.
50	Alice T.	Ol.s.	131	1943	Aug 5 1952	Stranded	On northwest corner of Perl Island, Chugach Passage, 30 miles from Seldovia, Alaska.
51	Aliceil	Ga.s.	709	1916	Dec 13 1916	Stranded	Point Loma, Calif.
52	Al-Ki	St.s.	1,259	1884	May 20 1917	Foundered	Fitzhugh Sound, British Columbia.
53	Allen A	Sch.	342	1888	Apr 3 1919	Stranded	Baranoff, Alaska.
54	Allenaire	Ga.s.	56	1915	Nov 30 1920	Burned	San Francisco, Calif. (Bay).
55	Alliance No.2	-	-	-	Oct 18 1915	Unknown	39-04-00 N. 123-44-00 W.
56	Alloway	St.s.	6,113	1918	Feb 12 1929	Stranded	Ugamak Island, Alaska.
57	Alma	Ol.y.	124	1909	Aug 16 1933	Stranded	Western tip of Pointe Vincente, Calif.
58	Alma	Ol.s.	118	1914	Mar 1 1964	Burned	About 20 miles southeast of Long Island, Chiniak Bay, Alaska.
59	Aloha	Sch.	814	1891	Nov 30 1913	Foundered	Destruction Island, Wash.
60	Alpha	Sch.	300	1903	Feb 3 1907	Stranded	9 miles north of Umpqua River, Ore.
61	Alpine	Ga.s.	95	1892	Oct 29 1924	Burned	Avon, Calif.
62	Alt Heidelberg	Ga.s.	102	1917	Jun 5 1935	Burned	Vank Island, Alaska.
63	Alta	Bkn.	1,381	1900	Feb 20 1923	Foundered	Sailed from San Pedro, Calif., for Bellingham, Wash., and has not since reported.
64	Alvarado	St.s.	1,994	1914	Mar 17 1945	Stranded	Steel vessel. All lives (15) lost. Steel vessel. 43-31-20 N. 124-15-00 W.
65							Vessel broke in two. Stern section 100 yards offshore and forward part on beach at low water.
66	Alviso	St.p.	197	1896	Dec 15 1920	Burned	Riverbank, Calif.
67	America	St.p.	922	1853	Jun 24 1855	Burned	Crescent City, Calif.
68	America	Sch.	2,054	1874	Aug 30 1914	Stranded	San Juan Island, Wash.
69	America	Ol.s.	116	1942	Oct 20 1946	Collided	Granville Channel, British Columbia.
70	America	Ol.s.	279	1910	Nov 14 1949	Burned	10 miles northwest of Point San Pablo, Baja California, Mexico.
71	America	Ol.s.	55	1938	Jul 11 1957	Foundered	About 1 mile north of Point Vincenti, Calif.
72	American Beauty	Ol.s.	442	1930	Jan 13 1965	Foundered	23-28-00 N. 111-18-00 W.
73	American Boy	Ol.s.	130	1930	Nov 26 1956	Burned	About 1 mile west of Malibu Dock. 34-01-00 N. 118-42-00 W.
74	American Boy	Ol.s.	325	1946	Mar 6 1966	Foundered	In Pacific Ocean. 07-40-00 N. 88-05-00 W.
75	American Rose	Ol.s.	120	1944	Dec 8 1952	Burned	Between San Clemente Island and Cortez Banks, 20 miles True 220° from northwest end of San Clemente Island, Calif.
76	Americana	Sch.	900	1892	Feb 28 1913	Foundered	Astoria, Ore. All lives (13) lost. Steel vessel.
77	Andrew D.	Ol.s.	116	1937	Nov 13 1953	Burned	About 5 miles south of Point Dume, Calif. 33-45-00 N. 118-50-00 W.
78	Andrew Foss	Ol.s.	125	1905	Aug 4 1951	Collided	With MICHAEL. In Greenville Channel, British Columbia.
79	Andrew Jackson	Ol.s.	71	1943	May 2 1954	Foundered	About 5 miles off coast, southwest of Gold Beach, Ore.
80	Ann B	Ol.s.	55	1942	Aug 19 1965	Burned	In Hecati Straits, Cape Scott, British Columbia.
81	Anna Barron	St.s.	82	1902	Jul 22 1930	Stranded	Ansley Point, Alaska.
82	Anna Helen	Ol.y.	80	1920	Nov 25 1930	Burned	North Seymour Narrows, Alaska.
83	Annadell	Ol.s.	163	1945	Mar 27 1964	Tidal Wave	At Seward, Alaska.
84	Annie Comings	St.p.	452	1887	Dec 30 1907	Collided	With French bark EUROPE. Willamette River, Ore.
85	Annie E Smale	Sch.	845	1903	Jul 9 1910	Stranded	Point Reves, Calif.
86	Ansonia	Ol.s.	50	1926	Jul 23 1955	Stranded	Struck rock and sank in Uyak Bay, Alaska.
87	Antelope	Sch.	123	1887	Sep 30 1907	Stranded	Nehalem River, Ore.
88	Aquilo	Ol.s.	199	1901	Sep 1966	Burned	About 4 miles offshore, 5 miles south of Fort Bragg, Calif.
89	Arcata	St.s.	2,722	-	Jul 14 1942	War Loss	North Pacific. 53-35-00 N. 157-40-00 W. Freighter. Steel vessel.
90	Arctic	St.s.	373	1901	Jul 5 1922	Stranded	Saunders Reef, Calif. Freighter. 38-47-00 N. 123-36-00 W.
91	Arctic Chief	Scow	775	1950	Dec 7 1950	Stranded	East of Marmot Island, Gulf of Alaska. Steel vessel.

NO.	NAME OF VESSEL	RIG	TONS	BUILT	DATE		CAUSE	PLACE AND COMMENT
92	Argo	St.s.	210	1898	Nov 26	1909	Stranded	Tillamook Bar, Ore. 3 lives lost.
93	Argo	St.s.	65	1906	Apr 1	1914	Collided	With tug MILWAUKEE. At Point Hudson, Wash.
94	Argus	Ga.s.	566	1902	Jun 13	1906	Burned	Near Destruction Island, Wash.
95	Argus	Brg.	505	1902	Jan 8	1916	Foundered	Gulf of Georgia, British Columbia.
96	Arispe	St.s.	280	1853	May 26	1854	Stranded	Punta Arenas, Calif.
97	Arlene S	Ol.s.	180	1945	Mar 28	1958	Foundered	In Gulf of California. 24-26-00 N. 109-32-00 W.
98	Armenia	Clipper	1,643	1877	Aug	1889	Unknown	At Port Costa, Calif. Wheat cargo.
99	Arr 738	Brg.	2,297	1944	Nov 8	1948	Stranded	Vicinity of Taylor Island, Gulf of Alaska. Steel vessel.
100	Artic	Ga.s.	669	1898	Aug 10	1924	Foundered	Point Barrow, Alaska.
101	Associated Oil Company No. 8	Brg.	487	1926	Jan 9	1952	Foundered	Off Point Richmond, Calif. Steel vessel.
102	Astorian	St.s.	255	1911	Dec 19	1923	Collided	With ga.s. LILLICO NO.20. Near Smiths Cove, Elliot Bay, Wash.
103	Astronaut	Ol.s.	77	1961	Feb 6	1967	Stranded	On Akutan Island, Aleutian Islands, Alaska.
104	Athlon	St.s.	157	1900	Aug 1	1921	Stranded	Port Ludlow, Wash.
105	Atomic	Ol.s.	86	1945	Sep 23	1946	Foundered	Off Cape Hook, Vancouver Island, British Columbia.
106	Aurora	Sch.	1,211	1901	Jan 18	1935	Stranded	Monterey, Calif.
107	Aurora	Ol.s.	122	1940	Nov 7	1952	Burned	Off Santa Cruz Island, near coast of Southern California.
108	Autocrat	Ship	1,130	1859	Apr	1868	Wrecked	In San Francisco Bay, Calif.
109	Avalon	St.s.	881	1912	Apr 29	1925	Stranded	Hillapa Harbor, Wash.
110	Avalon	St.s.	1,985	1890	Sep 16	1964	Foundered	At Palos Verdes Point, Calif.
111	B.D. Co. No.2	Scow	54	1938	Oct 12	1940	Foundered	70 miles south by southwest of Cape Etolin, Alaska.
112	B.D. Co. No.7	Scow	67	1945	Fall	1947	Foundered	On shores of Cape Suckling, Gulf of Alaska. Wood vessel.
113	B.M. Co. No.2	Scow	321	1928	Jun 1	1937	Stranded	Hinchinbrook Island, Alaska.
114	B.T. Co. 4	Ga.s.	59	1943	Jul 18	1944	Foundered	Gulf of Alaska.
115	B. & W. No.1	Ol.s.	188	1944	Sep 29	1956	Stranded	About 7 miles southeast of Mekoryuk Island, Bering Sea, Alaska. Steel vessel.
116	Babinda	Ga.s.	3,098	1919	Mar 3	1923	Burned	Off Santa Cruz, Calif.
117	Bacchus	Brg.	311	1916	Apr 8	1926	Stranded	Venice, Calif. All life (1) lost.
118	Bahada	St.s.	132	1902	Apr 22	1923	Collided	With American st.s. RICHMOND. Harbor of Los Angeles, Calif. Steel vessel. 1 life.
119	Bahada	St.s.	132	1902	Nov 21	1926	Foundered	Huckleberry Island, Wash. Steel vessel. All life (9) lost.
120	Balboa	Sch.	777	1901	Dec 1	1913	Stranded	Entrance to Grays Harbor, Wash.
121	Balboa	Ol.s.	128	1937	Jan 18	1949	Burned	Off California coast near Los Angeles.
122	Barbara K	Ol.s.	262	1947	Oct 30	1965	Foundered	30-50-00 N. 117-00-00 W.
123	Barcelona	Ol.s.	103	1941	Mar 21	1967	Foundered	Off coast of Baja California, Mexico, off Punta Abroejos.
124	Barge No.3	Brg.	383	1898	Sep 19	1907	Stranded	St. Michael, Alaska. Steel vessel.
125	Barge No.10	Brg.	573	1941	Mar 5	1964	Foundered	Off coast of Vancouver, British Columbia. Steel vessel.
126	Barge No.14	Brg.	1,473	1950	Jan 15	1956	Stranded	Off Port Orford, Ore.
127	Bay Island	St.s.	84	1900	Nov 30	1928	Foundered	Mukilteo, Wash.
128	Bear	St.s.	4,507	1910	Jun 14	1916	Stranded	Bear River, Calif. 5 lives lost.
129	Bella	Sch.	180	1896	Nov 25	1905	Stranded	Ocean Beach, Ore.
130	Belle	St.p.	66	1853	Jan 5	1856	Exploded	Sacramento, Calif. 30 lives lost.
131	Belle Isle	Ol.s.	169	1930	Jun 12	1934	Foundered	San Diego, Calif. All lives (12) lost.
132	Bellingham	Ol.s.	254	1891	Aug 13	1950	Burned	At Seattle, Wash.
133	Bender Brothers	Sch.	84	1889	Aug 21	1907	Stranded	Good News Bay, Alaska.
134	Benjie Boy	Ol.s.	64	1950	Apr 13	1955	Burned	2 miles south of west end of Catalina Island, Calif.
135	Bennington	–	–	–	Jul 21	1905	Exploded	San Diego, Calif. 65 lives lost.
136	Bering Sea	Ga.s.	59	1917	Feb 14	1933	Stranded	Prince of Wales Island, Alaska.
137	Berkeley	St.s.	571	1906	Nov 14	1907	Burned	7 miles east of Point Conception, Calif.
138	Berlin	Bark	1,634	1882	Apr 17	1922	Stranded	Ugaguk Flats, Alaska.

NO.	NAME OF VESSEL	RIG	TONS	BUILT	DATE		CAUSE	PLACE AND COMMENT
139	Bertha	St.s.	926	1899	Jul 18	1915	Stranded	Kodiak Island, Alaska.
140	Berwick	Ga.s.	100	1887	Mar 13	1908	Stranded	Siuslaw River Bar, Ore.
141	Bessie K	Ga.s.	98	1893	Feb 21	1907	Capsized	Off Coquille River, Ore. All lives (9) lost.
142	Betty	Ol.s.	55	1922	Dec 6	1964	Collided	With ol.s. EAGLE. About 21-3/4 miles southwest of Willapa Harbor, Wash.
143	Bianca	Sch.	2,139	1919	Dec 15	1924	Stranded	Strait of Juan de Fuca, Wash.
144	Bill	Brg.	624	1907	Aug 6	1917	Foundered	St. Michael, Alaska.
145	Billcona	Ol.s.	71	1943	Jun 23	1952	Stranded	At Santa Cruz Island, Calif., near Morse Point.
146	Blackford	St.s.	2,950	1918	Sep 17	1918	Foundered	Off Lower California.
147	Blakeley	Brg.	152	1872	Dec 23	1909	Stranded	Natividad Island, Mexico.
148	Bloomfield	Ol.s.	98	1920	Aug 15	1940	Burned	Empire Point, Empire Island, San Joaquin River, Calif.
149	Blue Fin	Ol.s.	94	1930	Sep 3	1944	Stranded	Near Santa Rosa Island, Calif.
150	Blue Fox	Ol.s.	56	1930	Dec 13	1937	Stranded	Southeast point of Beaver Bay. 55-28-00 N. 160-50-00 W.
151	Blue Sky	Ol.s.	99	1930	Nov 17	1952	Burned	2.5 miles off the east end of Santa Catalina Island, Calif.
152	Blunt	Brg.	96	1905		1921	Foundered	Point Partridge, Wash.
153	Bob-Don	Brg.	343	1929	Dec 15	1954	Foundered	At Sequim Bay, Wash.
154	Bohemia	Ship	1,633	1875	Aug 18	1931	Burned	San Diego, Calif.
155	Bolcom No.5	Scow	104	1909	Jun 28	1926	Stranded	Cedar Creek, Wash.
156	Bolcom No.8	Scow	63	1911		1924	Stranded	Bluff Point, Alaska.
157	Boobyalla	Ol.s.	3,099	1919	Mar 11	1929	Burned	Discovery Island, British Columbia.
158	Brant	Ol.s.	149	1926	May 8	1960	Burned	34-26-07 N. 120-01-05 W.
159	Bremerton	St.s.	191	1906	Nov 9	1926	Burned	Houghton, Wash.
160	Bridgit	Ga.s.	594	1913	May 1	1914	Burned	At Suisun Bay, Calif.
161	Brodie	Ol.s.	194	1931	Apr 11	1965	Burned	About 1/8 mile north of Frog Rock, Catalina Island, Calif.
162	Brooklyn	St.s.	333	1901	Nov 8	1930	Stranded	Humboldt Bar, Calif. 17 lives lost (18).
163	Brother Jonathan	St.p.	1,359	1851	Jul 30	1865	Stranded	Off Seal Rocks, St. Georges Reef, 8 miles from Crescent City, Calif. Wood vessel. 171 lives lost. Carried Army payroll and other monies, probably valued at more than $500,000. Vessel owned by California Steam Navigation Company.
164	Brothers	Scow	54	1890	Oct 10	1941	Foundered	Off Pebbly Beach, Catalina Island, Calif.
165	Brush	St.s.	5,115	1920	Apr 26	1923	Stranded	Cape Arago, Ore. Steel vessel. Freighter. 43-19-00 N. 124-30-00 W.
166	Bunker Hill	El.s.	10,590	1942	Mar 6	1964	Burned	In the Rosario Straits on a voyage from Tacoma to Anacortes, Wash. Steel vessel.
167	Burton	St.s.	97	1905	Feb 22	1924	Burned	Gig Harbor, Wash.
168	Buster	Brg.	230	1920	Oct 17	1940	Foundered	10 miles above Astoria, Ore.
169	Butcher	-	-	-		Pre-WWII	Unknown	44-37-00 N. 124-06-00 W.
170	Bydarky	Ga.s.	53	1910	Sep 4	1916	Burned	Bluff Point Coal Mine, Cook Inlet, Alaska.
171	C.A. Smith	St.s.	1,878	1917	Dec 16	1923	Foundered	Coos Bay, Ore. 9 lives lost (23). Freighter. 43-22-00 N. 124-21-00 W.
172	C.C. Co. 26	Brg.	111	1941	Apr 18	1961	Stranded	At Seal Beach, Calif.
173	C.C. Lindauer	-	-	-		Pre-WWII	Unknown	43-40-00 N. 124-14-00 W.
174	C.L. Anderson	Ol.s.	95	1939	Mar 25	1964	Storm	Near Kaline Rock, Kodiak Island, Alaska.
175	C-Trader	Ol.s.	2,392	1944	Dec 7	1963	Stranded	At entrance to the Columbia River, Portland, Ore. Steel vessel.
176	C.W.W. 26	Scow	60	1943	Dec 5	1943	Stranded	San Nicholas Island, Calif. Steel vessel.
177	Calcium	St.s.	51	1904	Aug 6	1913	Burned	Camano, Wash.
178	Caledonia	Ol.s.	164	1942	Sep 6	1948	Foundered	Near Icy Point, Southeast Alaska.
179	Californian	Ol.s.	74	1930	Jan 10	1932	Foundered	Half Moon Bay, Calif.
180	Camden	St.s.	6,653	1921	Oct 10	1942	War Loss	43-46-38 N. 124-31-15 W. Freighter. Steel vessel. Sunk by enemy action. 1 life lost (48). Also reported as tanker.
181	Camilla A	Scow	322	1908	Jun 15	1909	Foundered	Chignik Bay, Alaska.
182	Caoba	St.s.	683	1905	Feb 5	1925	Stranded	Columbia River Light, Ore.
183	Cape Spencer	Ol.s.	190	1940	Feb 10	1964	Stranded	On the south shore at Akun Bay, Alaska.

NO.	NAME OF VESSEL	RIG	TONS	BUILT	DATE	CAUSE	PLACE AND COMMENT
184	Capitol	Ol.s.	148	1921	Jun 15 1937	Burned	In Dana Passage, near Brisco Point, Puget Sound, Wash.
185	Captain Ludvig	Ol.s.	54	1945	Jun 25 1953	Burned	Off coast of Newport, Ore.
186	Caroga	Brg.	643	1944	Mar 29 1953	Stranded	On Portugese Bay, Calif., 6.5 miles north of Bodega Head. Steel vessel.
187	Caroline	St.p.	182	1868	Nov 18 1917	Burned	Sausalito, Calif.
188	Caroline	Ol.s.	61	1928	Aug 18 1944	Stranded	Walcott Reef, Kodiak Island, Alaska.
189	Carondelet	Sch.	1,368	1872	Dec 1 1911	Foundered	Prince Rupert, British Columbia.
190	Carrier Dove	Ga.s.	92	1884	Feb 23 1912	Stranded	Discovery Passage, British Columbia.
191	Carrier Dove	Ga.s.	90	1864	Apr 22 1927	Burned	Empire, Calif.
192	Carrier Pigeon	Ship	844	1852	1852	Unknown	South of San Francisco, Calif. Lost on maiden voyage.
193	Casco	St.s.	533	1906	Jun 27 1913	Stranded	Near Piedras Blancas Light, Calif.
194	Casco	Ga.s.	50	1913	Sep 27 1955	Burned	At Seattle, Washington.
195	Cassandra Adams	Ship	1,083	1876	Aug 1888	Wrecked	Off Cape Flattery, Wash.
196	Catherine M	Ga.s.	64	1902	Aug 21 1924	Foundered	Umatilla Light, Wash.
197	Celia	St.s.	173	1884	Aug 28 1906	Stranded	Point Pinos Light, Calif.
198	Celilo	Ol.s.	177	1944	Dec 27 1959	Burned	At Crescent City, Calif.
199	Centennial	Brg.	1,286	Jul 29 1930		Burned	Long Beach, Calif.
200	Central II	St.s.	59	1924	Aug 10 1931	Burned	Lummi Indian Reservation, Wash.
201	Chaco	Ga.s.	104	1916	Oct 16 1924	Burned	Colvas Pass, Wash.
202	Challamba	Ol.s.	2,400	1918	Jun 18 1927	Stranded	White Cliff Island, British Columbia.
203	Champlain	Ship	1,473	1874	Jun 17 1875	Wrecked	On Farallon Islands, off San Francisco, Calif. Total loss.
204	Charger	Sch.	1,376	1874	Oct 10 1909	Foundered	Karta Bay, Alaska.
205	Charles B. Kenney	Brg.	1,074	1878	1926	Foundered	Pillsburg, Calif.
206	Charles Brown	Brg.	72	1904	Apr 20 1932	Stranded	Laguna Beach, Calif.
207	Charles E. Falk	Sch.	298	1889	Mar 31 1909	Stranded	Cohalis Rocks, Wash.
208	Charles E. Moody	Ship	2,003	1882	Jun 28 1920	Burned	Naknek, Alaska, Bristol Bay.
209	Charles F. Crocker	Bkn.	860	1890	1929	Foundered	Santa Catalina Island, Calif.
210	Chas. L. Hutchinson	Brg.	80	1895	May 18 1910	Foundered	Kaltag, Alaska.
211	Chelan	St.p.	244	1902	Jul 8 1915	Burned	Columbia River, Wash.
212	Chetco	Ga.s.	103	1887	Feb 1918	Burned	Off Summerland, Calif.
213	Chicago	Ol.s.	75	1926	Dec 15 1943	Foundered	4 miles south of Catalina Island, Calif.
214	Chickasaw	St.s.	6,131	1942	Feb 7 1962	Stranded	Between Cluster Point and South Point, southwesterly portion of Santa Rosa Island, off California coast. Steel vessel.
215	Chico	St.s.	362	1890	Jul 18 1906	Stranded	Shelter Cove, Calif.
216	Chief	Ol.s.	157	1944	May 17 1961	Burned	In Johnstone Straits, near Alert Bay, British Columbia.
217	Chignik No.1	Scow	70	1908	Apr 28 1908	Foundered	Cape Cleatre, Alaska.
218	Chinook	Brg.	785	1904	Apr 12 1907	Stranded	Coos Bay Bar, Ore.
219	Chinook	Brg.	167	1907	Dec 12 1926	Foundered	Seattle, Wash.
220	Chirikof	Ol.s.	86	1945	Feb 28 1968	Foundered	Off Kodiak Island, Alaska.
221	Chris C.	Ol.s.	60	1927	Feb 4 1937	Foundered	Point Hueneme, Calif.
222	City of Clinton	St.s.	57	1922	Mar 23 1929	Burned	Mukilteo, Wash.
223	City of Honolulu	St.s.	10,688	1896	Oct 12 1922	Burned	400 miles off San Pedro, Calif. Steel vessel.
224	City of Mukilteo	St.s.	150	1927	Apr 18 1932	Burned	Columbia Beach, Wash.
225	City of Nome	Ol.s.	2,169	1919	Jun 3 1927	Burned	Aberdeen, Wash.
226	City of Rio De Janeiro	Steamer	–	–	Feb 22 1901	Unknown	Off Point Fort, near Mile Rock, San Francisco Bay, Calif. 130 lives lost. This vessel has been reported worth from $250,000 to $2 million. 37-49-00 N. 122-30-00 W.
227	City of Roede	–	–	–	Pre-WWII	Unknown	In North Castro Point, San Francisco Bay, Calif.
228	City of San Rafael	St.p.	484	1924	Jan 21 1943	Stranded	San Pedro Point, Santa Cruz Island, Calif.
229	City of Sausalito	Ol.s.	136	1936	Dec 11 1941	Burned	

NO.	NAME OF VESSEL	RIG	TONS	BUILT	DATE	CAUSE	PLACE AND COMMENT
230	Claremont	St.s.	747	1907	May 22 1915	Stranded	Coos Bay Bar, Ore.
231	Clarinda	Ol.s.	76	1913	Jan 12 1947	Burned	San Point, Alaska.
232	Cleone	St.s.	228	1901	Apr 9 1931	Stranded	Eureka, Calif.
233	Clevedon	St.s.	7,314	-	Jan 11 1942	Unknown	59-35-00 N. 139-48-00 W. Off Yakutat, Alaska. Passenger vessel. Steel vessel.
234	Clinton	St.p.	71	1854	Oct 27 1877	Collided	With PETALUMA. San Francisco, Calif.
235	Coast Trader	St.s.	3,286	1920	Jun 7 1942	War Loss	Tatoosh Island, Wash. 48-15-00 N. 125-40-00 W. Freighter. Steel vessel. Sunk by enemy action. 25% of lives lost.
236	Coldbrook	St.s.	5,104	1919	Jun 16 1942	War Loss	50-25-00 N. 145-30-00 W. Middleton Island, about 75 miles south of Cordova, Alaska. Freighter. Steel vessel. Sunk by enemy action.
237	Coloma	Bark	852	1869	Dec 7 1906	Abandoned	Off Cape Beale, British Columbia.
238	Col. Baker	Sch.	76	1864	Nov 6 1913	Stranded	Drakes Inlet, Calif.
239	Colonel Cross	St.p.	160	1846	Jan 29 1850	Snagged	San Francisco, Calif.
240	Columbia	St.s.	2,721	1880	Jul 21 1907	Collided	With st.s. SAN PEDRO. Point Arena, Calif. Iron vessel. 80 lives lost.
241	Columbia	Ship	1,471	1871	Apr 30 1909	Stranded	Unimak Bay, Alaska.
242	Columbia	St.p.	69	1907	Oct 1911	Burned	Near Northport, Wash.
243	Columbia	St.p.	341	1905	Jul 8 1915	Burned	Columbia River, Washington.
244	Columbia	St.s.	1,923	1912	Feb 17 1924	Foundered	Coos Bay, Ore. Steel vessel. 43-22-00 N. 124-21-00 W.
245	Columbia	St.s.	5,643	1915	Sep 13 1931	Stranded	Point Tasco, Calif. Steel vessel. Off Santa Margarita Island, Baja California, Mexico. Vessel reported to be valued at $250,000. Divers have recovered some $150,000. Depth reported between 60 and 90 feet.
246	Columbia Contract No. 41	Brg.	483	1916	Jun 7 1941	Foundered	5 miles off Redondo Beach, Calif.
247	Colusa	St.w.	795	1911	Sep 15 1932	Burned	Broderick, Calif.
248	Comet	Sch.	429	1886	Aug 30 1911	Stranded	San Miguel Island, Calif. 1 life lost.
249	Commander	Ol.s.	79	1929	Jun 6 1932	Stranded	San Roque Isle, Baja California, Mexico.
250	Commodore Preble	St.p.	282	1844	May 6 1851	Stranded	Humboldt Bay, Calif.
251	Compeer	Sch.	347	1877	Jul 17 1912	Stranded	Bristol Bay, Alaska.
252	Condor (Br.)	-	-	-	Dec 2 1901	Vanished	Esquimalt, British Columbia. 104 lives lost.
253	Conqueror	Ol.s.	163	1947	Aug 26 1949	Stranded	At Asuncion Bay, Baja California, Mexico.
254	Constance	Ga.s.	78	1913	Aug 23 1919	Stranded	25 miles east of Cape Suckling, Gulf of Alaska.
255	Continental	St.s.	1,636	1862	Sep 29 1870	Foundered	Gulf of California. 8 lives lost.
256	Coos Bay	St.s.	544	1884	Dec 19 1914	Stranded	Ventura, Calif.
257	Coos Bay	St.s.	3,011	1918	Sep 10 1918	Foundered	22-07-00 N. 110-45-00 W. Gulf of California.
258	Coos Bay	St.s.	5,149	1909	Oct 21 1927	Stranded	San Francisco Bay, Calif. Steel vessel. 37-48-00 N. 122-31-00 W.
259	Coquilee	Ga.s.	118	1883	May 21 1923	Abandoned	Bridgeport, Calif.
260	Coral Sea	Ol.s.	148	1943	Jul 19 1960	Burned	In Frederick Sound, Alaska.
261	Cordova	Brg.	66	1944	1957	Stranded	In Ensenada, Baja California, Mexico.
262	Cordova	Ol.s.	55	1935	Jun 6 1966	Burned	In Copper River Flats, near Cordova, Alaska.
263	Cordova Salvor	Ol.s.	180	1942	Nov 4 1957	Stranded	At Cape Sarichef, Alaska. Steel vessel.
264	Corinthian	Ga.s.	94	1892	Jun 11 1906	Stranded	Humboldt Bar, Calif.
265	Cornelia Cook	St.s.	51	1900	Jul 29 1925	Burned	Port Angeles, Wash.
266	Cornell 9	Scow	231	1921	Jun 1945	Burned	At Harper, Wash.
267	Corona	St.s.	1,492	1888	Mar 1 1907	Stranded	Humboldt Bar, Calif. Steel vessel. 1 life lost.
268	Corona	Ga.s.	79	1918	Apr 23 1924	Burned	Bodega Heads, Calif.
269	Coronado	Bkn.	1,058	1874	Nov 20 1913	Foundered	Near Sechett, British Columbia.
270	Coronado	St.s.	578	1900	Apr 27 1917	Foundered	Off Point Arena, Calif. Equipped with wireless radio.
271	Coryphene	Bark	811	1878	Aug 5 1905	Stranded	Off Prince of Wales Island, Alaska.
272	Cottage City	St.s.	1,885	1890	Jan 26 1911	Stranded	Willow Point, Vancouver, British Columbia.

NO.	NAME OF VESSEL	RIG	TONS	BUILT	DATE	CAUSE	PLACE AND COMMENT
273	Cottoneva	St.s.	1,113	1917	Feb 10 1937	Stranded	Port Orford, Calif.
274	Covina	Ga.s.	87	1902	Jul 30 1926	Burned	Collinsville, Calif.
275	Craig Foss	Ol.s.	179	1942	Nov 7 1965	Foundered	At Cook Inlet, Alaska.
276	Craig No.1	Scow	285	1923	Dec 25 1925	Foundered	Avalon, Calif. Iron vessel.
277	Crescent City	St.s.	701	1906	Jul 7 1927	Stranded	Santa Cruz Light, Calif.
278	Crowley No.64	Brg.	267	1913	Nov 1 1949	Foundered	In Santa Monica Bay, Santa Monica, Calif.
279	Crown No.2	Scow	1,295	1946	Feb 27 1954	Stranded	Near Tree Point, Alaska. Steel vessel.
280	Crown City	Ol.s.	5,433	1920	Sep 1 1942	Stranded	Sledge Island Light, Alaska. Steel vessel.
281	Crusader	Ol.s.	101	1937	May 1 1943	Foundered	Chumigan Island, Alaska.
282	Cuautemoc	Ga.s.	79	1916	Sep 3 1924	Stranded	Arena Cove, Calif.
283	Cuba	St.s.	3,168	1897	Sep 8 1923	Stranded	San Miguel Island, Calif. Steel vessel. Valued at $250,000 in gold and silver cargo. Depth averaging 75'.
284	Curacao	St.s.	1,503	1895	Jun 21 1913	Stranded	Prince of Wales Island, Alaska. Steel vessel.
285	Cynthia Olson	St.s.	2,140	1919	Dec 7 1941	War Loss	750 miles northeast of Seattle, Wash. Steel vessel. Sunk by enemy action.
286	Czarina	St.s.	1,045	1883	Jan 12 1910	Stranded	Coos Bay, Ore. Iron vessel. All lives (24) lost.
287	Czarina	Sch.	230	1891	Feb 15 1911	Stranded	Nagal Island, Alaska.
288	D.L. Co. III	Scow	80	1900	May 30 1915	Exploded	Seattle Harbor, Wash. Cargo of dynamite. All life (1) lost.
289	D.L. Co. VII	Scow	72	1904	Aug 1916	Stranded	Bering River, Alaska.
290	D.L. Co. XIV	Scow	281	1925	Jul 14 1939	Collided	With S.S. TEMPLE BAR. La Push, Wash.
291	D.L. Co. XLIX	Scow	297	1926	Feb 23 1948	Stranded	Makchanik Island, Chignik Bay, Alaska. Wood vessel.
292	D.L. Co. XXXIII	Scow	562	1918	Jan 23 1943	Foundered	Off Four Mountains Island, near Inaudak Bay, Ummak Island, Alaska.
293	D & M II	Brg.	84	1915	Sep 4 1962	Foundered	Off Ocean Cape, Alaska.
294	D.M. Renton	Ol.s.	68	1923	Jun 14 1965	Foundered	Approximately 10 miles southwest of Point San Luis Light, Calif.
295	Daisy Matthews	St.s.	933	1916	May 4 1940	Foundered	10.5 miles off New Trinidad Head, Calif.
296	Daisy Putnam	St.s.	886	1913	Nov 22 1929	Stranded	Point Gordon, Calif.
297	Dan	Brg.	255	1944	Mar 30 1949	Stranded	At Queen Charlotte Sound, British Columbia.
298	Danaco No.5	Brg.	88	1932	Jun 17 1956	Foundered	About 12 miles below Sleetmute, Alaska, on the Kuskokwim River.
299	Dante Alighieri II	Ga.s.	97	1937	Nov 30 1938	Foundered	Southwest of Santa Barbara Island, Calif.
300	Dart	St.s.	74	1911	Nov 9 1926	Burned	Houghton, Wash.
301	Dashing Wave	Brg.	1,054	1853	Mar 16 1920	Stranded	Vancouver Island, British Columbia.
302	Dauntless	Sch.	548	1898	Oct 13 1912	Collided	With st.s. ST. HELENS. 10 miles off Fort Bragg, Calif.
303	Dauntless	St.s.	127	1899	Jan 31 1923	Foundered	Meadows Point, Wash.
304	Dauntless	Ol.s.	91	1932	Apr 24 1948	Foundered	60 miles east-southeast of Gordo Point, near Cape San Lucas. 22-42-30 N. 108-33-30 W.
305	David C. Meyer	St.s.	2,510	1920	Mar 9 1926	Foundered	Point Firmin, Calif.
306	Deep Sea	Ol.s.	54	1919	Nov 26 1942	Stranded	Anchorage, Alaska.
307	Defiance	Ol.s.	297	1947	Jun 21 1956	Foundered	Near Roca Partida, Mexico, about 240 miles south of Cape San Lucas, Lower California. Steel vessel.
308	Del Monte No.3	Ol.s.	50	1939	Nov 30 1950	Stranded	At entrance to Noyo River, Calif.
309	Del Notre	St.w.	601	1865	Oct 21 1868	Stranded	Valdez, Alaska.
310	Del Notre	St.s.	450	1890	Jul 29 1917	Stranded	Point Arena, Calif.
311	Del Rio	Ol.s.	110	1935	Oct 28 1952	Burned	Off Anacapa Island, Calif.
312	Delhi	St.s.	986	1906	Jan 20 1915	Stranded	Strait Island, Alaska.
313	Denali	St.s.	3,432	1920	May 19 1920	Stranded	Zayas Island, British Columbia. Steel vessel.
314	Dentist	Brg.	274	1958	Nov 1963	Burned	At Nakawasina, 20 miles north of Sitka, Alaska.
315	Despatch No.5	Ga.s.	59	1913	Apr 5 1926	Stranded	Point Loma, Calif. 4 lives lost (5).
316	Destiny	Ol.s.	146	1937	Aug 1 1940	Stranded	Off coast of Lower California-Mexico.
317	Diamond	St.s.	650	1920	Apr 2 1926	Collided	With French st.s. INDIANA. Los Angeles, Calif.

NO.	NAME OF VESSEL	RIG	TONS	BUILT	DATE	CAUSE	PLACE AND COMMENT
318	Diamond Knot	Ol.s.	3,805	1944	Aug 13 1947	Collided	With st.s. PENN VICTORY. 3 miles from Race Rocks, Calif. Steel vessel.
319	Diamond O.	St.w.	442	1910	Apr 26 1934	Foundered	Portland, Ore.
320	Dirigo	Ol.s.	823	1898	Nov 16 1914	Foundered	40 miles east of Cape Lias, Alaska.
321	Discovery	Ol.s.	123	1936	Dec 20 1955	Burned	Off harbor, Los Angeles, Calif.
322	Dix	St.s.	130	1904	Nov 18 1906	Collided	With st.s. JEANIE. Al-ki Point, Wash. 45 lives lost.
323	Dode	St.s.	215	1898	Jul 20 1910	Stranded	Marrowstone Point, Wash.
324	Dolly C	Ol.s.	56	1922	Aug 11 1955	Collided	With barge. In Rosario Strait, southwest of Burrows Island, Wash.
325	Dolphin	Ga.s.	57	1918	Jul 11 1927	Burned	Stockton, Calif.
326	Donna Jo	Ol.s.	56	1936	Nov 7 1947	Stranded	At Abeojos, Ballerina Bay, Baja California, Mexico.
327	Dora	St.s.	320	1880	Dec 20 1920	Stranded	Noble Island, British Columbia.
328	Dora Bluhm	Sch.	330	1883	May 25 1910	Stranded	Santa Rosa Island, Calif.
329	Dorothy Joan	Ol.s.	50	1927	Sep 13 1945	Foundered	Yaquina Head, off coast of Oregon.
330	Dorothy Wintermore	St.s.	2,010	1918	Sep 17 1938	Foundered	Fish Rock, 10 miles south of Point Arena, Calif. Steel vessel. 38-42 N. 123-32 W.
331	Draecke (Dutch)	Frigate	-	-	Jun 12 1689	Foundered	Off southwestern tip of Tiburon Island, Sonora, Mexico. Valued at $250,000.
332	Dredge Kalama	Drg.	423	1937	Mar 14 1950	Burned	Carrolls, Wash.
333	Dredger No.1	St.p.	282	1898	Oct 1914	Burned	Near LaConner, Wash.
334	Drexel Victory	St.s.	7,607	1945	Jan 20 1947	Stranded	Columbia River Bar, 1/4 mile due north from No.6 Buoy, off coast of Oregon. Steel.
335	Dulcinea	Ol.s.	622	1944	Oct 9 1956	Stranded	On Buldir Island, Aleutian Islands, off coast of Alaska. Steel vessel.
336	Dupont	Ol.s.	71	1930	Jul 8 1961	Foundered	About 1 mile south of Cape Suckling, Alaska.
337	E-1	Brg.	203	1918	Sep 2 1941	Burned	Port Costa, Calif. 1 life lost (2).
338	E.A. Bryan	St.s.	7,212	1944	Jul 17 1944	Burned	Port Chicago, Calif. Steel vessel.
339	E. Edith Foss	Lighter	239	-	Dec 8 1944	Unknown	53-18-35 N. 128-53-40 W.
340	E. Jax	Brg.	219	1897	Jul 25 1907	Abandoned	Race Rock Light, British Columbia.
341	E.K. Wood	Sch.	519	1888	Nov 12 1912	Stranded	Barrier Island, British Columbia.
342	E.L. Dwyer	Ga.s.	54	1892	Oct 6 1913	Stranded	Port Clarence, Alaska.
343	E.L. Smith	Ol.s.	64	1917	Jan 1 1936	Foundered	1 mile north of Coquille River, Bandon, Ore.
344	E.S. Lucido	Ol.s.	160	1945	Jul 22 1959	Foundered	25-31-00 N. 113-38-00 W.
345	Eagle	Ol.s.	77	1917	Sep 29 1932	Burned	Brighton Beach, Calif.
346	Eagle	Ga.s.	77	1927	Jun 1937	Burned	Foot of 7th Street, Long Beach, Calif.
347	Eagle	Ol.s.	175	1904	Oct 2 1952	Burned	At Marysville, Wash.
348	Eclipse No.15	Brg.	302	1927	May 7 1962	Foundered	Everett, Wash.
349	Edith	St.s.	2,369	1882	Aug 30 1915	Burned	Off Cape St. Elias, Alaska. Iron vessel.
350	Edith	Brg.	245	1881	May 13 1926	Stranded	Big Port Walter Bay, Alaska.
351	Edith Foss	Ol.s.	172	1901	Dec 4 1944	Collided	With SS VICTORIA. Off Kingcome Point Light, northeast entrance to Fraser Beach, British Columbia.
352	Efin	Ol.s.	196	1914	May 11 1937	Burned	Ilwaco, Columbia River, Wash.
353	El Commodore	Ol.s.	117	1935	Oct 28 1946	Stranded	Surf, Calif.
354	El Dorado	Ga.s.	81	1913	Sep 8 1940	Burned	Bacon Island, near Stockton, Calif.
355	Eldorado	Sch.	881	1901	Jun 13 1913	Burned	At sea. 31-02-00 N. 121-37-00 W.
356	Eleanor W	Ga.s.	123	1917	Jun 25 1925	Burned	Point Lowell, Camano Island, Wash.
357	Electra	Ol.s.	72	1927	Jan 26 1944	Stranded	Columbia River, Ore.
358	Eliza Anderson	St.p.	279	1858	Dec 31 1898	Stranded	Unalaska, Alaska.
359	Elizabeth	Ship	1,773	1882	Feb 21 1891	Wrecked	Entering San Francisco Bay, Calif. 18 lives lost.
360	Elizabeth Olson	Ol.s.	275	1944	Nov 30 1960	Stranded	At entrance to harbor, Bandon, Ore.
361	Ella	St.p.	418	1905	Jul 17 1907	Foundered	Tolovana, on Tannana River, Alaska.
362	Ellamar	Ol.s.	148	1945	Jul 24 1953	Burned	Port Hardy, British Columbia.
363	Ellen	Ga.s.	80	1903	Oct 12 1927	Burned	San Francisco Bay, Calif. All life (1) lost.
364	Ellen Foster	Ship	996	1852	Dec 1867	Wrecked	Neah Bay, Wash.

NO.	NAME OF VESSEL	RIG	TONS	BUILT	DATE		CAUSE	PLACE AND COMMENT
365	Elna	St.s.	1,434	1920	Dec 27	1943	Stranded	Shektof Straits, Alaska. Steel vessel. Freighter. 58-30 N. 155-30 W.
366	Elsie	St.s.	159	1889	Dec 31	1910	Foundered	Valdez, Alaska.
367	Elsie	Ga.y.	64	1924	Oct 28	1924	Stranded	Partridge Island, Wash.
368	Elsie I	Brg.	79	1943	Apr 29	1951	Foundered	2410 magnetic from rnd of Huntington Beach Pier, Huntington Beach, Calif., and 3.5 miles offshore. Steel vessel.
369	Elsie II	Brg.	85	1944	Dec 3	1956	Stranded	At Long Beach, Calif. Steel vessel.
370	Elsie T	Ol.s.	149	1944	Dec 30	1958	Foundered	About 20 miles off coast of California, near Humboldt Bay, Eureka, Calif. Steel.
371	Emidio	St.s.	6,912	1921	Dec 20	1941	War Loss	40-34-00 N. 124-50-00 W. Tanker. Steel vessel. Sunk by enemy action. 5 lives lost (36).
372	Emily F. Bichard	Ga.s.	52	1867	Nov 17	1927	Burned	San Francisco Bay, Calif.
373	Emily Farnum	Clipper	1,119	1854	Nov	1875	Wrecked	Near Cape Flattery, Wash.
374	Emily Reed	Ship	1,564	1880	Feb 14	1908	Stranded	Nehalem Beach, Ore. 11 lives lost. Converted to bark. Coal cargo.
375	Emma	Sch.	80	1909		1916	Foundered	Manzanillo Bay, Mexico.
376	Emma Claudina	Sch.	195	1882	Nov 14	1906	Foundered	Off Cape Elizabeth, Grays Harbor, Wash.
377	Emma E. Thompson	St.s.	276	1875	May 28	1914	Burned	Ennis Island, Georgia Bay, British Columbia.
378	Emperor	Ol.s.	56	1927	Jul 15	1932	Foundered	Off Santa Barbara Island, Calif.
379	Empress	Ol.s.	71	1912	May 15	1962	Burned	Near Pleasant Island, Icy Straits, Alaska.
380	Empress	Ol.s.	169	1942	Jul 3	1966	Foundered	Off Point Joe, near Monterey, Calif.
381	Emrose	St.s.	67	1911	Jun 23	1929	Collided	With scow D.L. Co. XXXVI. Salmon Bay, Wash.
382	Ensign	Sch.	618	1904	Jan 21	1909	Foundered	Naples, Calif.
383	Enterprise (Br.)	Sch.	-	-	Mar 4	1892	Foundered	1/2 mile off Villami, south side of Galapagos Island, Calif. Carried a treasure valued at $250,000 in gold and silver.
384	Enterprise	St.p.	129	1903	Jul 12	1915	Foundered	Brewsters Ferry, Wash.
385	Eskimo	Ol.s.	61	1890	Jul 31	1956	Stranded	4 miles south of Cape Barnabas on Sitkalidak Island, near Kodiak Island, Alaska.
386	Esmeraldo	Ga.s.	92	1918	Jan 25	1943	Stranded	Bethel Island Bridge, Stockton, Calif.
387	Esperia III	Ol.s.	110	1944	Jan 25	1952	Foundered	Struck east Long Beach Harbor Breakwater, Calif.
388	Estebeth	Ol.s.	70	1918	Mar 31	1948	Burned	Off Port Converden, Alaska, 55 miles from Juneau, Alaska.
389	Esther Buhne	Brg.	428	1887	Feb 13	1927	Stranded	Newport Beach, Calif.
390	Eudora	Ol.s.	143	1944	Feb 26	1962	Stranded	At Cape Devine, Korovin Island, Alaska.
391	Eureka	St.s.	484	1900	Jan 8	1915	Stranded	Port Bonita, San Francisco Bay, Calif. 1 life lost.
392	Everett	St.s.	1,751	1920	Oct 29	1926	Burned	Eureka, Calif.
393	Excelsior	Sch.	348	1876	Aug 30	1906	Stranded	Nelsons Lagoon, Alaska.
394	Excelsior	St.s.	526	1893	Feb 7	1916	Collided	With st.s. HARVARD. San Francisco, Calif.
395	Express	Ol.s.	53	1927	Dec 14	1942	Foundered	Off Santa Cruz, Calif.
396	F-1	Ol.s.	-	-	Dec 17	1917	"Sunk"	San Diego, Calif. Submarine. 19 lives lost.
397	F.A. Douty	St.s.	227	1904	Aug 9	1944	Foundered	San Francisco Bay, Calif. Steel vessel.
398	F.F.F.	Ol.s.	93	1917	Feb 20	1921	Foundered	22-20-00 N. 111-04-00 W.
399	F.M. Smith	St.p.	295	1895	May 30	1909	Burned	Alameda Flats, Calif.
400	F.S.C. No.1	Brg.	62	1925	Feb 8	1958	Foundered	At Belmont Shore mooring, Long Beach, Calif. Wood vessel.
401	F.S. Redfield	Ga.s.	469	1887	Aug 27	1911	Stranded	Cape Prince of Wales, Alaska.
402	Fairhaven	St.p.	337	1889	Jun 9	1918	Burned	La Conner, Wash.
403	Fairweather	Ol.s.	73	1929	Oct 9	1965	Stranded	At the head of American Bay, Alaska.
404	Falcon	St.s.	74	1905	Aug 6	1906	Burned	Houghton, Wash.
405	Falcon	Ol.s.	106	1886	Mar 23	1945	Foundered	Standard Oil Pier, El Segundo, Calif.
406	Farallon	St.s.	749	1888	Jan 5	1910	Stranded	Cook Inlet, Alaska.
407	Farwest	Ga.s.	55	1925	Jun 7	1929	Burned	Orcas Island, Wash.
408	Fatima	Ol.s.	251	1946	Aug 12	1960	Storm	Of the coast of California.
409	Fay No.4	St.p.	309	1912	Jan 7	1920	Burned	Orwood, Calif.

NO.	NAME OF VESSEL	RIG	TONS	BUILT	DATE		CAUSE	PLACE AND COMMENT
410	Fearless	Ol.s.	68	1912	Aug 10	1949	Burned	In Columbia River, below Longview, Wash.
411	Fearless	Ol.s.	145	1942	Jan 31	1960	Foundered	Off Cape China, Kodiak Island, Alaska.
412	Fernstream (Br.)	Ol.s.	-	-	Dec 11	1952	Unknown	Off southwestern side of Alcatraz Island, San Francisco Bay, Calif.
413	Ferry Queen	Scow	62	1943	Oct 7	1953	Foundered	At Iliamna Bay, Cook Inlet, Alaska.
414	Fidalgo	St.p.	393	1904	Feb 12	1923	Foundered	Seattle, Wash.
415	Fidelity	Ga.s.	56	1885	Feb 18	1932	Burned	San Pablo Bay, Calif.
416	Fifield	St.s.	634	1908	Feb 21	1916	Stranded	South jetty of Coquille River, Ore.
417	Flavel	St.w.	967	1917	Dec 15	1923	Stranded	Point Carmel, Calif.
418	Flora	St.w.	185	1885	Sep 30	1932	Burned	Broderick, Calif.
419	Florence	St.p.	90	1898	Oct 10	1909	Foundered	St. Michaels Canal, Alaska.
420	Florian	St.s.	6,765	1915	Sep 1	1928	Collided	With st.s. ADMIRAL FISKE. Umatilla Lightship, Wash.
421	Flying Dragon	Ship	1,127	1853	Jan	1862	Wrecked	Entering San Francisco Harbor, Calif.
422	Forest No.37	Scow	225	1943	Apr	1948	Stranded	On rocks off Vancouver Island, south of Tashis, British Columbia.
423	Fort Bragg	St.s.	912	1910	Sep 7	1932	Stranded	Coos Bay jetties, Ore.
424	Fort Union	Brg.	2,654	1919	Sep 1	1930	Stranded	Port Conclusion, Alaska.
425	Foss 2	Scow	495	1926	Oct 24	1931	Foundered	Tillamook Head, Ore.
426	Foss 55	Brg.	233	1908	Oct 5	1965	Foundered	Off West Point Light, Seattle, Wash.
427	Foss 99	Brg.	463	1926	Nov 23	1945	Collided	With U.S. Navy vessel RAMPO. Off coast of Ballard, Wash.
428	Foss 99	Brg.	541	1943	Oct 2	1953	Stranded	On the south end of Calvert Island, Queen Charlotte Sound, British Columbia.
429	Foss 117	Scow	376	1914	Apr 13	1949	Foundered	At Tacoma Narrows Bridge, Tacoma, Wash.
430	Foss 125	Scow	81	1919	Nov 17	1958	Foundered	At mooring, Laguna Beach, Calif. Steel vessel.
431	Foss 130	Brg.	1,366	1918	May 2	1951	Foundered	36-33-00 N. 135-42-00 W.
432	Foss 138	Scow	382	1944	Aug 4	1951	Collided	With tug MACLOUFAY & barge P.T. & B. CO. 1597. In vicinity of Morning Reef Light, entrance to Klewnuggit Inlet, Greenville Channel, British Columbia. Steel vessel.
433	Foss 303	Brg.	89	1942		1950	Foundered	At Port Heiden, Alaska.
434	Francis H. Leggett	St.s.	1,606	1903	Sep 18	1914	Foundered	Off Columbia River, Ore. 65 lives lost (67).
435	Franconia	Ship	1,313	1874	Jun	1881	Wrecked	On Farallon Islands, off San Francisco, Calif.
436	Frank H. Buck	St.s.	6,076	1914	Mar 6	1937	Collided	With st.s. PRESIDENT COOLIDGE. In Golden Gate Channel, San Francisco, Calif. Steel vessel.
437	Frank Lawrence	Ga.s.	58	1886	Mar 24	1946	Foundered	10 miles off Point Sur, Calif.
438	Fred Ball No.4	Ga.s.	93	1916	Sep 27	1932	Burned	San Joaquin River, Calif.
439	Frederick C.	Brg.	369	1913	Apr 4	1914	Stranded	Sinslaw, Ore.
440	Frederick C.	Ol.s.	73	1919	Jun 8	1966	Stranded	East of Ocean Cape, Alaska. 59-32-00 N. 139-51-00 W.
441	Fresno	Sch.	1,244	1874	Apr 4	1923	Burned	Bellevue, Lake Washington, Wash.
442	Funchal	Ol.s.	185	1928	Mar 11	1938	Exploded	Off coast of Lower California.
443	G.C. Lindauer	St.s.	453	1901	May 16	1924	Stranded	Umpqua River, Ore.
444	G.C.T. Co. No.1	Brg.	143	1913	Jun 10	1922	Foundered	Off Tampico, Mexico.
445	G. Maroni	Ol.s.	100	1928	Sep 23	1931	Burned	Santa Barbara Channel, Calif.
446	Gabriel Winter	St.p.	73	1851	Apr 15	1854	Exploded	San Pablo Bay, Calif. 15 lives lost. Renamed "Secretary" in 1854.
447	Garfield No.6	Scow	112	1911	Oct 7	1937	Burned	La Push, Wash.
448	Garrison	Ol.s.	59	1945	Feb 3	1948	Foundered	5 miles south of Crescent City, Calif.
449	Gay Head	Bark	265	1877	Jun 27	1914	Stranded	Chignik Bay, Alaska.
450	Gem of the Ocean	Sch.	702	1852	Aug	1879	Wrecked	On Vancouver Island, British Columbia.
451	General Pershing	Ga.s.	2,450	1918	Jul 11	1921	Stranded	Endanion Shoal, Wash.
452	General Warren	Ol.s.	309	1844	Jan 31	1852	Stranded	Astoria, Ore. 42 lives lost.
453	Genevieve H. II	St.p.	112	1937	Jan 12	1956	Burned	15 miles southeast of east end of Catalina Island, Calif.
454	George C. Perkins	Bkn.	388	1880	Jul 1	1907	Stranded	Topolobampo Bar, Mazatlan, Mexico.
455	George L. Olson	St.s.	1,428	1917	Jun 23	1944	Stranded	Coos Bay, Ore.

NO.	NAME OF VESSEL	RIG	TONS	BUILT	DATE		CAUSE	PLACE AND COMMENT
456	George Loomis	St.s.	692	1895	Dec 19	1918	Foundered	Off Blunts Reef Light, Calif. Steel vessel. All lives (18) lost.
457	George Olson	Brg.	2,964	1919	Jan 30	1964	Foundered	On the Columbia River Bar, Ore. Steel vessel.
458	George U. Hind	Bkn.	1,389	1919	Sep	1936	Foundered	Off Carlsbad, Calif.
459	George W.	Ol.s.	117	1889	Aug 8	1967	Burned	At pier A, Everett, Washington.
460	George W. Elder	St.s.	1,709	1874	Jan 21	1905	Stranded	Reuben, Ore. Steel vessel.
461	George Walton	St.s.	7,229	1943	Nov 18	1951	Burned	Off coast of Vancouver Island, British Columbia. Steel vessel.
462	Georgia	St.s.	70	1914	Jun 1	1925	Exploded	Port Orchard, Wash. All lives (2) lost.
463	Georgia	Brg.	96	1902	Feb 22	1966	Foundered	Approximately 2 miles southwest of King Harbor, Redondo Beach, Calif.
464	Gerald C. Tobey	Sch.	1,459	1878	Jul 5	1914	Stranded	Seymour Narrows, British Columbia.
465	Gerome	St.p.	109	1902	Sep 2	1905	Foundered	Hoaniez Rapids, Wash.
466	Gig Harbor	St.s.	150	1925	Jun 10	1929	Burned	Gig Harbor, Wash.
467	Gipsy	St.s.	293	1868	Sep 27	1905	Stranded	China Point (Monterey), Calif.
468	Gipsy Girl	Ol.s.	56	1921	May 5	1945	Foundered	San Pedro, Calif.
469	Girlie Mahony	St.s.	382	1903	Dec 23	1919	Stranded	Albion Harbor, Calif.
470	Glen	Sch.	127	1883	Sep 30	1907	Stranded	Ikitak, Alaska. 1 life lost.
471	Glenn-Mayne	Brg.	431	1918	Jul 13	1939	Foundered	On beach at Carlsbad, Calif.
472	Gold	St.p.	324	1883	Nov 8	1920	Burned	Petaluma, Calif. 1 life lost (18).
473	Gold Hunter	St.p.	436	1849	Jun 6	1870	Stranded	Cape Mendocino, Calif. Renamed "Active" on June 12, 1862.
474	Gold Star	Brg.	168	1898	Jul 6	1906	Stranded	Tanana River, Alaska.
475	Golden City	Steamer	–	–	Feb 22	1870	Foundered	Off Cape Lazaro Point, Santa Margarita Island, Mexico. Reported to have carried large amounts of gold.
476	Golden City	Ol.s.	353	1920	Apr 24	1927	Collided	With st.s. NEWPORT. San Francisco Bay, Calif.
477	Golden Fleece	Clipper	968	1852	Apr 22	1854	Wrecked	San Francisco Bay, Calif.
478	Golden Forest	St.s.	5,658	1919	Sep 5	1929	Stranded	Shelikof Strait, Alaska.
479	Golden Gate	St.p.	2,057	1851	Jul 27	1862	Burned	North of Manzanillo, Mexico. 175 lives lost. Much has been written about this wreck, and it is not "positive" that any treasure in gold was carried.
480	Golden Gate	Ol.s.	120	1944	Jan 30	1952	Burned	About 1 mile southeast of Sand Stone Point, Santa Cruz Island, Calif.
481	Golden Shore	Sch.	699	1899	Apr 22	1928	Foundered	Pittsburg, Calif.
482	Golden West	Ga.s.	72	1923	Mar 29	1936	Burned	North jetty at Bandon, Ore.
483	Golden West No.2	Ga.s.	55	1918	Sep 22	1922	Burned	Eureka, Calif.
484	Goodnews	Ol.s.	63	1946	Nov 22	1948	Collided	With S.S. CATAWBA FORD. Off coast of Oregon.
485	Gotoma	Sch.	198	1872	Dec 25	1908	Abandoned	Willapa Harbor, Wash.
486	Governor	St.s.	5,474	1907	Apr 1	1921	Collided	With st.s. WEST HARTLAND. Near Point Wilson, Wash. Steel vessel. 9 lives lost.
487	Gov. Markham	Ol.s.	79	1892	Jan 9	1957	Foundered	About 10 miles west of La Jolla, Calif.
488	Gral S.C. Mariscal	Ga.s.	156	1916	Apr 13	1916	Burned	Acapulco, Mexico.
489	Granada	St.p.	1,058	1855	Oct 13	1860	Stranded	San Francisco, Calif.
490	Granger	Sch.	59	1875	Sep 17	1908	Foundered	San Mateo Beach, Calif.
491	Grant	St.s.	327	1871	Dec 27	1911	Stranded	Hecat Strait, British Columbia. Iron vessel.
492	Grapples	–	–	–	May 3	1883	Burned	Vancouver Islands, British Columbia. 70 lives lost.
493	Gratia	Brg.	1,582	1891	Apr 20	1932	Stranded	Redondo, Calif. Steel vessel.
494	Gravina Point	Ga.s.	59	1920	Aug 11	1947	Burned	At Cordova, Alaska.
495	Graywood	St.s.	915	1904	Oct 2	1915	Burned	Off Umatilla Lightship, Ore.
496	Great Admiral	Ship	1,575	1869	Dec 6	1906	Foundered	200 miles west of Cape Flattery, Wash. 2 lives lost.
497	Great Republic	St.p.	3,881	1867	Apr 18	1879	Stranded	Columbia River, Ore. 14 lives lost. 46-17-00 N. 124-08-00 W.
498	Greenland	Ol.s.	71	1929	Oct 26	1934	Stranded	East of Monterey, Calif.
499	Greyhound	Ol.s.	123	1942	Jul 9	1961	Burned	At foot of S.E. Division Street, Willamette River, Portland, Ore.
500	Guy Junior	Ol.s.	50	1927	Oct	1961	Foundered	Off Montague Island, Alaska.
501	Gypsy	Ol.s.	57	1921	Mar 27	1964	Tidal Wave	At Valdez, Alaska.

NO.	NAME OF VESSEL	RIG	TONS	BUILT	DATE	CAUSE	PLACE AND COMMENT
502	H.I.C. 5	Scow	51	1925	May 10 1946	Foundered	At Excursion Inlet, Alaska.
503	H.J. Cochrane	Steamer	—	—	Feb 14 1912	Collided	With iron steamer. Off southwest point of Angel Island, San Francisco Bay, Calif. Iron vessel. Also reported lost in 1911. Estimated value of cargo is $500,000 (gold). Also known as "H.J. Corcoran".
504	H.M. Adams	Ol.s.	58	1913	Oct 30 1945	Stranded	Off Cambria Pines, Calif.
505	H.M. Storey	St.s.	10,763	1921	Jul 10 1943	War Loss	En route, Noumea, New Caledonia to San Pedro, Calif. Steel vessel. Sunk by enemy action.
506	H & S No.5	Brg.	198	1911	Mar 29 1967	Foundered	In Whitewater Bay, southwest coast of Admiralty Island, Alaska.
507	H & S No.15	Scow	131	1913	May 17 1931	Foundered	Quillayute River, Wash.
508	H & S No.18	Scow	248	1917	Jul 9 1924	Foundered	Smith Island, Wash.
509	Hagemeister	Ga.s.	69	1943	Sep 19 1963	Foundered	About 12 miles southeast of Yaketaga, Alaska.
510	Halco	St.s.	970	1917	Nov 30 1925	Stranded	Grays Harbor, Wash.
511	Halcyon	Ga.s.	68	1887	Nov 12 1918	Foundered	Akutan Bay, Alaska.
512	Hanalei	St.s.	666	1901	Nov 23 1914	Stranded	Bolinas Point, California coast. 23 lives lost.
513	Harold Blekum	Sch.	192	1882	Mar 5 1917	Stranded	Eagle Harbor Rocks, Alaska.
514	Hartwood	St.s.	946	1916	Jun 27 1929	Stranded	Point Reyes, Calif.
515	Harvard	St.s.	3,818	1906	May 30 1931	Stranded	Point Arguello, Calif. Steel vessel.
516	Harvester	St.w.	638	1912	Oct 11 1938	Collided	With st.s. PRESIDENT MADISON. Seattle, Wash. Vessel was "crushed".
517	Hattie D.	Ga.s.	141	1943	Feb 5 1964	Foundered	Off Cape Mendocino, Calif.
518	Hayden Brown	Bark	864	1876	May 12 1912	Stranded	Montague Island, Alaska. 7 lives lost.
519	Hazel B. No.2	Ga.s.	135	1916	Jan 23 1932	Burned	Wrangell, Alaska.
520	Helen B.	Ol.s.	105	1938	Jun 9 1953	Burned	Halfway between Saook Bay and Rodman Bay in Perila Straits, Alaska.
521	Helen E.	Ol.s.	120	1943	Mar 9 1951	Stranded	On beach 4 miles north of Coos Bay Bar, Ore. Vessel destroyed by burning shortly after.
522	Helen Hale	St.p.	52	1912	Sep 20 1913	Burned	Kennewick, Wash.
523	Helori	Ol.s.	79	1911	Dec 21 1949	Burned	Off mouth of Umpqua River, Ore.
524	Henrietta	St.s.	53	1898	Nov 6 1927	Burned	Point Reyes, Calif.
525	Henrietta G. Martin	Sch.	52	1899	Mar 5 1911	Foundered	Alacran Reef, Mexico.
526	Henry Bergh	St.s.	7,176	1943	May 31 1944	Stranded	Farallon Island, Calif. Steel vessel. 37-45-00 N. 123-00-00 W.
527	Henry Foss	Ol.s.	136	1900	Feb 13 1959	Stranded	In the Strait of Georgia, off Saltspring Island, British Columbia.
528	Henry T. Scott	St.s.	1,596	1913	Jul 16 1922	Collided	With st.s. HENRY LUCKENBACH. East of Cape Flattery, Wash. Steel vessel. 4 lives lost.
529	Herald	St.p.	293	1878	Nov 4 1912	Burned	Oakland, Calif.
530	Hercules	St.w.	560	1899	Jan 5 1934	Foundered	Three Mile Rapid, Ore.
531	Hercules	Scow	80	1930	Jul 25 1952	Foundered	At Perl Island, off Chugack Island Group. Cook Inlet, Alaska.
532	Hercules	Ol.s.	275	1944	Oct 23 1966	Ice	At Clark South Point, Nushagak River, Alaska.
533	Hermine Blum	Ga.s.	52	1887	May 19 1938	Foundered	San Pablo Bay, Calif.
534	Hiawatha	Ol.s.	74	1909	Oct 1953	Foundered	In entrance of Port Etches, Alaska.
535	Holy Cross	Ol.s.	65	1947	Nov 14 1954	Burned	About 10 miles south of Deception Pass, Wash.
536	Hope	Ga.s.	66	1914	Sep 17 1917	Burned	Stockton, Calif.
537	Hopestill	Ol.s.	95	1916	Sep 21 1949	Stranded	On Purisima Point, off Camp Cook, Lopoc, Calif.
538	Horace	Scow	253	1904	Apr 14 1940	Foundered	Seattle, Wash.
539	Horizon	Ol.s.	69	1926	Aug 31 1932	Burned	Point Dume, Calif.
540	Howard Olson	St.s.	2,477	1917	May 14 1956	Collided	With MARINE LEOPARD. Off Point Sur, Calif. Steel vessel.
541	Humble SM1	Brg.	735	1943	Nov 25 1961	Storm	About 3 miles east-southeast of Government Point, Calif. Steel vessel.
542	Hunter	Ga.s.	63	1892	Aug 30 1917	Stranded	Foggy Cape, Alaska.
543	Hunter	St.s.	119	1883	May 12 1920	Foundered	Off Carroll Island, Cape Johnson, Wash.
544	Hunter	Ol.s.	118	1943	Sep 3 1962	Stranded	At Bodega Bay, Calif.

NO.	NAME OF VESSEL	RIG	TONS	BUILT	DATE		CAUSE	PLACE AND COMMENT
545	Husky	Drg.	277	1944	Jan 30	1954	Foundered	In Clarence Straits, Alaska. Steel vessel. During heavy storm.
546	Husky	Ol.s.	50	1940	Oct 13	1961	Stranded	On Amak Island, Alaska.
547	I.F. Co. No.1	Scow	138	1907	Nov 28	1911	Burned	Victoria, British Columbia.
548	Ida M.	Ol.s.	122	1943	Sep 23	1948	Stranded	About 10 miles north of Coos Bay Bar, Ore.
549	Ida May	Ga.s.	62	1908	Aug 29	1930	Stranded	Pacific Grove Beach, Calif.
550	Ida McKay	Sch.	187	1880	Feb 2	1912	Abandoned	40-59-00 N. 130-41-00 W.
551	Ida Schnauer	Sch.	215	1875	Jun 17	1908	Stranded	Tillamook Bar, Ore.
552	Idoneit	Ol.s.	59	1946	Jul 19	1955	Foundered	At Bahia Playa Maria, Mexico. 28-55-00 N. 114-28-00 W.
553	Ilwaco	Ga.s.	74	1891	Nov 5	1918	Stranded	Chatham Sound, Alaska.
554	Independent	St.s.	263	1911	Oct 6	1916	Stranded	Middleton Islands, Alaska.
555	Indiana	St.s.	3,335	1873	Apr 3	1909	Stranded	Cape Tosco, Santa Margarita Island, Mexico. Iron vessel.
556	Indiana	Ship	1,487	1876	Mar 12	1936	Stranded	Long Beach, Calif.
557	Indiana	St.s.	2,612	1920	May 18	1927	Stranded	Point Gorda, Calif. Steel vessel.
558	Infallible	Ol.s.	118	1936	Oct 26	1944	Foundered	2 miles north of Santa Cruz, Calif.
559	International No.1	Brg.	72	1916	Sep 13	1918	Stranded	Santa Cruz Island, Calif.
560	Iolanda	St.s.	53	1905	Oct 14	1923	Stranded	Pescadero Point, Calif.
561	Ione	St.w.	499	1911	Feb 4	1937	Foundered	3/4 mile above Copeys Rock, Ore.
562	Iowa	St.s.	5,724	1920	Jan 12	1936	Foundered	Peacock Spit, near Cape Disappointment, Wash. Steel vessel. All lives (34) lost. 46-16-30 N. 124-07-20 W.
563	Irene	St.p.	105	1903	Aug	1917	Foundered	Duwamish River, Wash.
564	Irene	Sch.	772	1900	Nov 1	1929	Burned	Long Beach, Calif.
565	Irene	Brg.	772	1900	Jan 28	1937	Foundered	Off Redondo, Calif.
566	Isabelita Hyne	Bark	350	1846	Jan 8	1856	Lost	Near San Francisco, Calif.
567	Iskum	Ol.s.	82	1912	Apr 15	1931	Stranded	Atka Island, Alaska.
568	Islander	Steamer	–	–	Aug 14	1901	Collided	With iceberg. In Steven's Passage, Alaska. Sailed from Juneau, Alaska and struck iceberg only after a minutes out of port. 70 lives lost. Reported to have carried between $1.5 and $3 million in gold. There have been reports that something has been salvaged and that attempts have followed. American registry.
569	Islander	Ga.s.	64	1928	Aug 30	1950	Burned	Off Skagit Island, near Deception Pass, Wash.
570	Isaac Reed	Brg.	1,491	1874	Jul 20	1924	Foundered	Bodega Bay, Calif.
571	Italic	Ol.s.	53	1928	Sep 8	1956	Burned	Near eastern spit of Kaliakh River, 12 miles west of Cape Yakutaga, Alaska.
572	Ituna	St.s.	201	1886	Mar 13	1920	Foundered	15 miles northwest of San Francisco Lightship, Calif. Iron vessel. 2 lives lost. 37-56-00 N. 122-55-00 W.
573	Ivy	Sch.	142	1882	Sep 1	1908	Stranded	Point Barrow, Alaska.
574	J.A. Chanslor	St.s.	4,938	1910	Dec 19	1919	Stranded	Cape Blanco, Ore. Steel vessel. 38 lives lost (41).
575	J.B. Stetson	St.s.	922	1905	Sep 3	1934	Stranded	Cypress Point, Calif.
576	J.C. Freese Co. No.7	Brg.	389	1930	Oct 23	1951	Foundered	In harbor at Richmond, Calif.
577	J.D. Loop No.1	Brg.	58	1911		1928	Foundered	Oceanside, Calif.
578	J.D. Peters	Sc.b.	1,085	1875	Apr 18	1930	Burned	Port Crescent, Wash.
579	J.H. Lunsmann	Sch.	1,090	1902	Jul 12	1913	Collided	With st.s. FRANCIS H. LEGGETT. San Francisco, Calif.
580	J.J. Loggie	St.s.	404	1908	Oct 19	1912	Stranded	Arguello Point, Calif.
581	J.M. Colman	Sch.	463	1888	Sep 3	1905	Stranded	San Miguel Island, Calif.
582	J. Marhoffer	St.s.	608	1907	May 18	1910	Burned	14 miles north of Yaquina, Ore.
583	J.R. McDonald	Brg.	609	1890	Aug 11	1940	Burned	Sequim, Wash.
584	Jabez Howes	Ship	1,648	1877	Apr 7	1911	Stranded	Chignik, Alaska.
585	Jacinto	St.w.	235	1889	Sep 30	1932	Burned	Broderick, Calif.
586	Jack Horner	Ga.s.	50	1911	Jul 13	1913	Burned	At Lynn Canal, Southeast Alaska.
587	Jacob Luckenbach	St.s.	7,869	1944	Jul 14	1953	Collided	With st.s. HAWAIIAN PILOT. About 7 miles southwest of the San Francisco Lightship,

NO.	NAME OF VESSEL	RIG	TONS	BUILT	DATE		CAUSE	PLACE AND COMMENT
587	Jacob Luckenback	Ol.s.	98	1949	Mar 27	1964	Tidal Wave	near San Francisco Bay, Calif. Freighter. Steel vessel. Cargo of steel. Depth ranges at 200'.
588	Jaguar	Sch.	1,520	1881	Oct 22	1914	Stranded	At Kodiak Island, Alaska.
589	James Drummond	Scow	96	1902	Mar 10	1960	Foundered	Dall Patch, Seaforth Channel, British Columbia.
590	Jas. F. McKenna	Sch.	586	1899	Aug 21	1910	Stranded	About 11 miles south of Long Beach, Calif.
591	James Rolph	Brg.	970	1892	Aug 30	1929	Collided	Point San Pedro, Calif.
592	Jane L. Stanford	St.s.	1,071	1883	Dec 19	1913	Stranded	With st.s. HUMBOLT. Santa Barbara, Calif. 34-23-00 N. 119-41-00 W.
593	Jeanie	Sch.	145	1869	Jan 10	1912	Stranded	At Calvert Sound, British Columbia.
594	Jennie Thelin	Sch.	261	1883	Sep 18	1911	Stranded	Punta Maria, Baja California, Mexico.
595	Jessie Minor	Ol.s.	72	1930	Oct 13	1963	Stranded	Nelsons Lagoon, Alaska.
596	Jinny C.	Brg.	896	1919		1948	Stranded	At Crescent Bay, Alaska.
597	Jitney	Ga.s.	250	1919	Feb 21	1928	Stranded	Whidby Island, Wash.
598	John						Burned	San Joaquin River, Calif.
599	John C. Kirkpatrick	St.s.	1,430*	-	Pre-WWII		Unknown	47-15-00 N. 124-50-00 W. Freighter.
600	John Currier	Ship	1,945	1882	Aug 9	1907	Stranded	Nelson Lagoon, Alaska.
601	John D. Spreckels	Sch.	266	1880	Mar 29	1913	Collided	With British st.s. STATESMAN. Point Reyes, Calif. 2 lives lost.
602	John Elliot Thayer	Ship	1,918	1854	Sep	1858	Burned	At Patos, Gulf of California.
603	John F. Miller	Sch.	179	1882	Jan 8	1908	Stranded	Bear Harbor, Alaska. 10 lives lost.
604	John H. Dwight	Brg.	221	1898	Aug	1920	Stranded	St. Michael Bay, Alaska.
605	John J. Mitchell	Brg.	90	-	Aug 5	1905	Stranded	Yokon Flats, Alaska.
606	John P. Gaines	St.s.	7,176		Nov 25	1943	Unknown	55-15-00 N. 159-00-00 W. Off Shumagin Island, Alaska. Freighter. Steel vessel.
607	John Reilly	St.p.	220	1898	Oct 13	1905	Stranded	Cape Blossom, Alaska.
608	John Straub	St.s.	7,176	1943	Apr 19	1944	Foundered	Off Sanak Island, Alaska. Steel vessel.
609	Johnnie Boy	Ol.s.	85	1937	Jan 28	1950	Burned	4 miles off Laguana Beach, Calif. 33-32-00 N. 117-52-30 W.
610	Joseph Pulitzer	Ga.s.	73	1894	Dec 18	1920	Foundered	Aniakchak, Alaska.
611	Joseph Russ	Sch.	247	1881	Apr 21	1912	Stranded	Cherikof Island, Alaska. 1 life lost.
612	Jubilee	Ol.s.	53	1885	Apr 24	1943	Stranded	26-47-00 N. 113-41-00 W.
613	Jugo Slavia	Ol.s.	80	1928	Nov 10	1940	Foundered	2 miles southeast of Point Montaro, Calif.
614	Junior	Ol.s.	60	1911	Oct 30	1955	Burned	At Deep Bay, near Cordova, Alaska.
615	K.F.C. No.1	Brg.	125	1946	May 9	1946	Foundered	Point Core, Alaska.
616	K.P. Co. Barge No.6	Brg.	57	1890	Jun 28	1933	Foundered	North Bear Harbor, Calif.
617	KSM No.1	Scow	63	1943	Dec 20	1958	Foundered	At Kindricks Bay, Alaska.
618	K & W No.1	Scow	68	1904	May 4	1929	Foundered	Pillar Point, Wash.
619	K & W No.4	Scow	55	1910	Dec 22	1913	Foundered	Queen Charlotte Sound, British Columbia.
620	Kamchatka	Ga.s.	552	1883	Apr 14	1921	Burned	51-57-00 N. 154-53-00 W.
621	Kanaga	Ol.s.	60	1925	Jul 27	1946	Stranded	6 miles south of Sitka, Alaska.
622	Kate Davenport	Brg.	1,248	1866	Jan 10	1916	Stranded	Cooks Inlet, Alaska.
623	Katherine Donovan	St.s.	993	1913	Jan 22	1941	Stranded	Vicinity of Seal Rocks, San Francisco, Calif.
624	Katie Flickinger	Bkn.	472	1876	Nov 20	1905	Stranded	Redondo Beach, Calif.
625	Kayak	St.s.	115	1901	Dec 19	1913	Stranded	At Cape Carew, Yukutat Bay, Alaska.
626	Kenai I	Ol.s.	163	1945	Aug 3	1948	Burned	At mouth of Kasiloff River, Cook Inlet, Alaska.
627	Kenmore	Ol.s.	70	1911	Aug 11	1957	Burned	As part of the Seattle, Wash., seafair exhibition.
628	Kennecott	Ga.s.	3,620	1921	Oct 8	1923	Stranded	Graham Island, British Columbia.
629	Ketovia	Ol.s.	53	1945	Sep 21	1962	Burned	Cook Inlet, Alaska.
630	King Cyrus	Sch.	717	1890	Jul 17	1922	Stranded	Chehalis Point, Grays Harbor, Wash.
631	Kingston	Ol.s.	204	1901	May 20	1933	Stranded	Whitestone Narrows, Alaska.
632	Kitsap	Ol.s.	526	1925	Nov 3	1921	Foundered	About 3/4 mile northwest of Tonki Cape Light, Alaska.
633	Kimesh	St.s	1,083	1909	Feb 5	1921	Stranded	Near Palmas Leading, Calif.

NO.	NAME OF VESSEL	RIG	TONS	BUILT	DATE		CAUSE	PLACE AND COMMENT
634	Klihyam	Ol.s.	111	1908	Sep 27	1958	Foundered	Off Siuslaw River, Ore.
635	Kopco Star	Ol.s.	60	1952	Oct 1	1963	Foundered	About 8 miles south of Port Hueneme, Calif.
636	Koto Hira Maru (Jap.)	St.s.	-	-	Jul 27	1917	Wrecked	Off Alaska. Unknown number of lives lost.
637	Kotzebue	Ol.s.	69	1946	Mar 10	1956	Ice	In Kotzebue Sound, Alaska. Steel vessel.
638	Koyukuk	St.p.	286	1902	May 20	1906	Stranded	Little Delta, Tanana River, Alaska.
639	Koyukuk	St.p.	260	1906	May 12	1911	Foundered	Tanana River, Alaska.
640	Kvichak	Ol.s.	1,063	1900	Jan 27	1941	Stranded	On reef of Sisters Island, Finlayson Channel, British Columbia. Steel vessel. 3 lives lost (63).
641	L.A. MacLeod	Ol.s.	56	1939	Mar 18	1951	Burned	Northport, Wash.
642	L.H. Coolidge	Ol.s.	282	1943	Oct 29	1951	Foundered	6.7 miles off coast of Yachats, Ore.
643	La Conner	St.s.	297	1898	Sep 24	1907	Burned	La Conner, Wash.
644	La Feliz	St.s.	102	1904	Oct 1	1924	Stranded	Santa Cruz Light, Calif.
645	Lady Alta	Ol.y.	102	1930	Sep 20	1931	Burned	Catalina Island, northwest side, Calif.
646	Lahaina	Brg.	1,067	1901	Oct 5	1933	Stranded	Point Vincent, Calif.
647	Laida	Ol.s.	58	1913	May 9	1942	War Loss	30 miles northeast of Port Moller, Alaska. Sunk by enemy action.
648	Lake Gebhart	St.s.	2,180	1919	May 3	1923	Stranded	North of Destruction Island, Wash. Steel vessel.
649	Larry Doheny	St.s.	7,038	1921	Oct 5	1942	War Loss	42-20-00 N. 125-02-00 W. Tanker. Steel vessel. Sunk by enemy action. 6 lives lost (44).
650	Larsen Bay No.3	Brg.	61	1943	Apr 19	1961	Stranded	At Swikshak Beach, near Kodiak, Alaska.
651	Lasata	Ga.y.	55	1905	Mar 21	1915	Burned	San Pedro, Calif.
652	Laura Madsen	Sch.	345	1882	Oct 14	1905	Ice	Off Point Barrow, Alaska.
653	Laurel	St.s.	5,759	1920	Jun 27	1929	Foundered	Portland, Ore.
654	Lawrence	Brg.	370	1913	Sep 22	1938	Foundered	15 miles southeast of Cape Fairweather, Alaska.
655	Lazy Days	Brg.	93	1943	May 9	1953	Foundered	1.5 miles west of Sunset Cliffs, San Diego, Calif. Steel vessel.
656	Leader	Ga.s.	50	1918	Jul 21	1955	Foundered	In Bering Sea, Alaska.
657	Leah	St.p.	477	1898	Sep 19	1906	Stranded	Quail Island, Yukon River, Alaska.
658	Leona	St.p.	145	1901	Feb 3	1912	Burned	La Center, Wash.
659	Lettitia	Sch.	245	1867	Feb 23	1915	Foundered	San Francisco Bay, Calif.
660	Lewis Cass	St.s.	7,176	-	Jan 26	1943	Unknown	29-11-00 N. 118-17-00 W. Guadalupe Island, Mexico.
661	Liberty	Ol.s.	66	1913	May 8	1958	Storm	At Cape Ecolic, Kodiak Island, Alaska.
662	Liberty Girl	Ol.s.	57	1919	Nov 2	1942	Stranded	San Pedro, Calif.
663	Lillebonne	Sch.	218	1883	Aug 29	1912	Foundered	San Francisco, Calif. 1 life lost.
664	Limit	Ol.s.	50	1927	Sep 28	1929	Foundered	In Chatham Strait, Alaska. All lives (8) lost.
665	Lincoln	Ol.s.	61	1912	Jan 1	1941	Foundered	1.25 miles west of Turn Rock Light, San Juan Island, Wash.
666	Lindbergh	Ol.s.	78	1928	Apr 7	1932	Burned	Lawson Reef, Wash.
667	Linde	Ol.s.	73	1928	Oct 5	1951	Stranded	1.5 miles west of breakwater at Port Hueneme, Calif.
668	Linnea	Ga.s.	51	1908	Sep 27	1927	Burned	Sacramento, Calif.
669	Lithgow	Brg.	370	1911	Aug 3	1924	Stranded	Yukon River, Alaska.
670	Little Glory	Ga.s.	50	1912	Aug 17	1937	Foundered	False Pass, St. Catherine's Cove, Alaska.
671	Lizzie S. Sorenson	Ga.s.	84	1898	May 10	1910	Foundered	Cape Addington, Alaska.
672	Lizzie Theresa	Ga.s.	64	1876	Jul 10	1920	Burned	Suisum Bay, Calif.
673	Llewellyn J. Morse	Ship	1,392	1877	Sep 11	1926	Burned	Santa Catalina Island, Calif.
674	Lois S	Ol.s.	55	1926	Apr 24	1934	Stranded	Lower California, Mexico. 4 lives lost (6).
675	Los Angeles	Drg.	199	1910	Aug 20	1942	Foundered	Point Arguello, Calif.
676	Los Angeles Tuna Canning Co. No.1	Brg.	52	1915	Feb 18	1921	Foundered	Ocean Park, Calif.
677	Lotta Talbot	St.p.	342	1898	May 22	1906	Stranded	Fairbanks, Alaska.
678	Louis	Sch.	831	1888	Jun 19	1907	Stranded	South Farallon Island, Calif.

NO.	NAME OF VESSEL	RIG	TONS	BUILT	DATE		CAUSE	PLACE AND COMMENT
679	Lourakis	Ol.s.	57	1931	Oct	2 1951	Stranded	At Anderson Cove, between Fort Bragg and Eureka, Calif.
680	Lucile	Ship	1,402	1874	Aug	19 1908	Stranded	Ugashik, Alaska.
681	Lucretia K	Ol.s.	54	1941	Sep	6 1958	Foundered	About 9 miles, bearing 251° True from Point Dume, Calif.
682	Luella	St.p.	115	1898	Sep	1910	Stranded	Tanana River, near Chena, Alaska.
683	Lumberjack	Brg.	6,009	1962	Oct	26 1963	Foundered	On the south jetty, at the entrance to Eureka Harbor, Eureka, Calif. Steel vessel.
684	Lumberjack	Brg.	4,924	1959	Oct	18 1966	Stranded	On Jorkins Point, Swindle Island, Milbank Sound, Inland Passage, Alaska.
685	Lurline	Brg.	358	1887	Jan	11 1915	Collided	With S.S. PANAMAN. Salina Cruz, Mexico.
686	Lyman Stewart	St.s.	5,919	1914	Oct	7 1922	Collided	With st.s. WALTER A. LUCKENBACH. Off Fort Point, San Francisco Bay, Calif.
687	M.F. Sterling	St.s.	2,360	1920	Nov	11 1931	Burned	Winslow, Calif.
688	M.L. Washburn	St.p.	284	1911	Oct	20 1920	Foundered	Little Salmon, Yukon River, Canada.
689	M.T. No.6	Brg.	1,315	1884	Dec	31 1949	Collided	With S.S. FAIRLAND. 1/2 mile east of Duwamish Head, Seattle, Wash. Iron vessel.
690	Maaroufa	Ol.s.	58	1947	May	2 1953	Burned	About 20 miles north of Ensenada, Mexico. 35-55-30 N. 116-48-30 W. Steel vessel.
691	Macray	Ol.s.	86	1922	Oct	16 1938	Stranded	South end of Kanak Island, Alaska.
692	Madelyn R.	Ol.s.	76	1941	Feb	27 1948	Foundered	About 5 miles southwest of Red Point, Baja California, Mexico.
693	Mahina Hou	Ol.s.	162	1944	Aug	24 1950	Stranded	On first cliff, west of Cape Suckling, Alaska. Steel vessel.
694	Major Tompkins	St.s.	151	1847	Mar	1855	Stranded	Esquimalt, British Columbia.
695	Majestic	St.s.	810	1908	Dec	5 1909	Stranded	Point Sur, Calif.
696	Majestic	Ol.s.	104	1934	Aug	12 1956	Stranded	12 miles out of Pualle Bay, Shelikoff Straits, Alaska.
697	Makawelia	Brg.	899	1902	Aug	15 1935	Stranded	Los Angeles, Calif.
698	Malahat	St.s.	991	1910	Sep	5 1956	Burned	At Zidell Machinery and Supply Co., Portland, Ore. Steel vessel.
699	Malina	Ol.s.	165	1943	Jun	14 1961	Stranded	Near Black Hills, Bristol Bay, Alaska.
700	Mandalay	St.s.	438	1900	Oct	27 1918	Stranded	Crescent City, Calif.
701	Manhattan	St.s.	291	1906	Nov	15 1917	Stranded	Lituya Bay, Alaska.
702	Mapele	St.s.	3,297	-	Jan	15 1943	Unknown	Off Shumagin Island, Alaska. 55-25-00 N. 160-12-00 W. Freighter.
703	Marconi	Sch.	693	1902	Mar	23 1909	Stranded	Coos Bay Bar, Ore.
704	Marconia	Ol.s.	115	1937	Mar	25 1962	Stranded	Vessel struck reef and sank in Unqa Strait, Alaska.
705	Margaret	Ga.s.	55	1920	Jul	6 1921	Burned	Katalla, Alaska.
706	Margaret C	Brg.	58	1880	May	3 1933	Burned	Catalina Harbor, Calif.
707	Marie	Ga.s.	161	1920	Jun	7 1925	Burned	Knights Landing, Calif.
708	Marion	Sch.	235	1882	Apr	11 1906	Foundered	Sannak Island, Alaska.
709	Mariposa	St.s.	3,158	1883	Nov	18 1917	Stranded	Sumner Strait, Alaska.
710	Markay	St.s.	10,342	1942	Jun	22 1947	Burned	Berth 168, Los Angeles Harbor, Calif. Steel vessel.
711	Martha A.	Ol.s.	128	1943	Apr	26 1949	Stranded	Near Mary Island, Alaska.
712	Martha Foss	Ol.s.	96	1886	May	21 1946	Collided	With st.s. IROQUOIS. In Straits of Juan de Fuca, British Columbia.
713	Martha W. Tuft	Sch.	173	1876	Oct	11 1907	Stranded	Kattala River, Alaska.
714	Mary V	Ol.s.	50	1947	Sep	24 1952	Foundered	Between Oceanside, Calif., and La Jolla, Calif. 8 miles offshore.
715	Mary Ann	Sch.	102	1852	Nov	13 1905	Stranded	Unga, Alaska.
716	Mary Ann No.2	Scow	111	1903	Jul	10 1943	Foundered	Prince Rupert Harbor, British Columbia.
717	Mary D.	Ol.s.	168	1940	Apr	28 1953	Foundered	About 22 miles north-northeast of Santa Catalina Island in the Gulf of California, Mexico.
718	Mary E. Moore	St.s.	1,783	1913	Feb	23 1927	Foundered	Coquille River Buoy, Ore.
719	Mary Hanlon	Ga.s.	458	1902	Jun	24 1924	Foundered	Off Mendocino City, Calif.
720	Mary L. Cushing	Bark	1,658	1883	Aug	21 1906	Stranded	Mazatlan, Mexico.
721	Mary S	Ol.s.	257	1949	Jan	1 1964	Collided	With submerged object. 30-19-00 N. 116-05-05 W.
722	Maryland	Ga.s.	51	1912	Jun	5 1913	Burned	San Rafael Creek, Calif.
723	Maui Girl	Ol.s.	63	1917	Nov	15 1960	Foundered	27-37-00 N. 114-59-00 W.
724	Mauna Ala	St.s.	6,256	1918	Dec	10 1941	Stranded	Clatsop Beach, Ore. Steel vessel. Freighter. 45-30-00 N. 122-45-00 W.
725	Maweema	Sch.	453	1895	Aug	19 1928	Stranded	St. Georges Island, Alaska.

NO.	NAME OF VESSEL	RIG	TONS	BUILT	DATE		CAUSE	PLACE AND COMMENT
726	Maxim	Sch.	117	1876	Jan	1901	Foundered	San Francisco, Calif. Sailed north for Eureka, Calif. Has not since reported. All lives (6) lost.
727	Melba	-	-	-	Pre-WWII		Unknown	44-36-00 N. 124-06-00 W.
728	Melvina	Ga.s.	63	1889	Oct 10	1920	Burned	San Francisco Bay, Calif.
729	Mendocino Woodsman	Brg.	3,400	1943	May 25	1963	Stranded	On south jetty, at entrance to Reedsport Harbor, Ore.
730	Merced	Ga.s.	994	1913	Oct 15	1913	Stranded	5 miles south of Punta Gorda, Calif.
731	Mercury	Ol.s.	73	1912	Jun 26	1958	Burned	Seldovia, Alaska.
732	Mermaid	Ol.s.	262	1949	Aug 3	1958	Foundered	22-15-00 N. 109-32-30 W.
733	Meteor	Ol.s.	83	1900	Aug 1	1963	Stranded	At Coal Harbor, Zacker Bay, Unga Island, Alaska.
734	Miami	St.s.	81	1898	Jun 10	1906	Stranded	Kvichak River, Alaska.
735	Michigan	Brg.	450	1898	May 12	1909	Foundered	Tanana River, Alaska.
736	Miduena	Ga.s.	71	1913	Sep 22	1924	Stranded	False River, Calif.
737	Mildred	Sch.	464	1897	Mar 16	1908	Stranded	Grays Harbor, Wash.
738	Milton Willis	St.s.	83	1859	Apr 27	1863	Exploded	San Pedro, Calif. 26 lives lost. Also known as "Ada Hancock".
739	Miner	St.p.	75	1850	Oct 8	1851	Burned	Sacramento River, Calif. 1 life lost.
740	Minnie A. Caine	Brg.	880	1900	Sep 24	1939	Stranded	6 miles west of Santa Monica, Calif.
741	Minnie E. Kelton	St.s.	632	1894	May 2	1908	Stranded	Yaquina, Ore. 11 lives lost.
742	Miss California	Ol.s.	193	1951	Nov 9	1952	Burned	64 miles northwest of Cape San Lazaro, Mexico.
743	Mississippi	-	-	-	Jun 12	1924	Exploded	Off San Pedro, Calif. 48 lives lost.
744	Mizpah	Ga.s.	64	1898	May 8	1910	Burned	Kvichak River, Alaska. 1 life lost. Vessel burned due to explosion.
745	Mobile Point	Ol.s.	1,117	1943	Dec 22	1944	Collided	With British ship SILVER STAR PARK. 44-43-00 N. 124-02-00 W. and also reported at 45-05-00 N. 124-24-00 W. Steel vessel. Reported as tug.
746	Mollie Stevens	Steamer	-	-	Jun 10	1878	Unknown	11 miles northwest of Lone Pine, in Owens Lake, Calif. Reportedly carrying gold valued at $100,000.
747	Monarch	St.p.	598	1901	Apr 13	1901	Foundered	San Paulo Bay, Calif.
748	Monarch	Ga.s.	91	1919	Jun 2	1929	Burned	Stockton, Calif.
749	Mondego	Ol.s.	306	1950	Jan 13	1967	Burned	San Diego, Calif. (Bay).
750	Montana	Ga.s.	65	1911	May 2	1914	Burned	Redoubt Bay, Sitka, Alaska.
751	Montara	Ol.s.	107	1937	Jul 23	1954	Foundered	140 miles southwest of San Diego, Calif. 31-00-00 N. 119-00-00 W.
752	Montebello	St.s.	8,272	1921	Dec 23	1941	"Sunk"	Off coast of California, near Moro Bay, Calif. Steel vessel. Attacked by submarine. 35-38-00 N. 121-17-00 W. Freighter. Also reported as tanker.
753	Montezuma	Ga.s.	73	1884	Aug 22	1925	Burned	Benicia Flats, Calif.
754	Morzhovoi	Ol.s.	81	1917	Jun 10	1955	Burned	At Funter Bay, Chatham Straits, Alaska.
755	Motormates	Ga.s.	273	1925	Mar 4	1944	Collided	With st.s. CARL G. BARTH. In San Joaquin River, Calif.
756	Mount McKinley	St.s.	4,861	1918	Mar 11	1942	Stranded	Off Scotch Cape Beach, Alaska. Steel vessel.
757	Mt. Baker	-	-	-	Feb 26	1944	Burned	54-49-30 N. 130-37-03 W. Fire occured at Prince Rupert, but was beached at above position.
758	Mt. Vernon	Scow	115	1911		1942	Foundered	In Skagit River, Wash.
759	Mountaineer	St.s.	57	1883	Oct 9	1925	Stranded	Hood Canal, Wash.
760	Multnomah	St.p.	312	1885	Oct 27	1911	Collided	With st.s. IROQUOIS. Seattle, Wash.
761	Multnomah	Frgt.	969	-	Pre-WWII		Unknown	46-53-00 N. 124-20-00 W. See No.760.
762	-Munleon	St.s.	2,606	1919	Nov 7	1931	Foundered	Point Reyes, Calif. Steel vessel. 38-00-00 N. 123-03-00 W.
763	Muriel	Brg.	536	1895	Jul 3	1925	Stranded	Balboa, Calif.
764	Myrtle	Ol.s.	52	1908	Apr 10	1968	Collided	With British OCEAN TRANSPORT. Off Kellet Bluff Light, Harpo Strait, Wash.
765	Myrtle Endresen	Ga.s.	86	1913	Sep 16	1915	Burned	Queen Charlotte Island, British Columbia, Canada.
766	McKinley	St.s.	66	1902	Oct 17	1911	Burned	Willochet Bay, Wash.
767	N. & K., No.2	Brg.	73	1918	Oct 18	1934	Burned	Drifted ashore at Huntington Beach, Calif.
768	Navajo	Ol.s.	55	1944	Jul 9	1963	Lost	Abandoned at sea. Off coast of San Pedro, Calif.

NO.	NAME OF VESSEL	RIG	TONS	BUILT	DATE	CAUSE	PLACE AND COMMENT
769	Nedra	Brg.	53	1918	Mar 23 1936	Foundered	6 miles from San Clemente Island, Calif.
770	Neenah	Scow	550	1905	May 23 1938	Foundered	6 miles south of Lituya Bay, Alaska.
771	Nefco 7	Brg.	80	1914	Mar 27 1964	Tidal Wave	At Point Shepard, Alaska.
772	Nefco 17	Scow	128	1951	Jul 10 1957	Burned	At Ketchikan, Alaska.
773	Nemaha	Ga.y.	81	1911	Jul 12 1925	Stranded	Shelter Cove, Calif.
774	Neponset No.2	St.p.	224	1884	Jan 4 1921	Foundered	Sacramento River, Calif.
775	Neptune	Brg.	365	1897	Oct 30 1918	Foundered	Gambier Island, Alaska.
776	Neptune	Ol.s.	415	1919	Nov 16 1948	Foundered	30 miles offshore from Willapa Harbor, Wash. Steel vessel.
777	Neptune	Ol.s.	54	1924	Aug 3 1951	Foundered	At Noblack Point, in Clarence Straits, Alaska.
778	Nerenta K	Ol.s.	60	1927	Sep 25 1941	Foundered	7 miles southwest of Davenport, Calif.
779	Nevada	St.s.	5,645	1920	Oct 3 1932	Stranded	Aleutian Islands, Alaska. Steel vessel. 34 lives lost (37).
780	New Crivello	Ol.s.	116	1936	Sep 18 1936	Foundered	Off Pescadero Point, Calif.
781	New Home II	Ol.s.	65	1948	Dec 6 1956	Foundered	5 miles south-southeast of Oceanside, Calif.
782	New Rex	Ol.s.	113	1936	Apr 29 1952	Foundered	About 3.5 miles off Laguna Beach, Calif.
783	New Saturnia	Ol.s.	116	1936	Nov 14 1955	Foundered	2.5 miles west of Dana Point, Calif.
784	New World	Ol.s.	55	1926	Mar 23 1945	Foundered	On south end of South Coronado Island. 32-23-30 N. 117-14-30 W.
785	Newberg	-	-	-	Oct 8 1913	Unknown	38-21-00 N. 123-05-00 W.
786	Newburg	St.s.	450	1898	Oct 8 1918	Stranded	7 miles north of Bodega, Calif. See No. 785.
787	Newsboy	St.s.	208	1888	Mar 31 1906	Stranded	Humboldt Bay Bar, Calif.
788	Niha	-	-	-	Pre-WWII	Unknown	48-00-00 N. 125-00-00 W.
789	Nika	St.s.	2,496	1919	Feb 14 1923	Burned	Off Vancouver Island, British Columbia. See No. 788.
790	Nonpareil	Ga.s.	52	1900	Mar 12 1915	Foundered	Unga, Alaska.
791	Noonday	Ship	1,189	1855	Jan 1 1863	Wrecked	Near San Francisco, Calif.
792	Nora	Ol.s.	62	1912	Oct 8 1948	Foundered	Off Middleton Island, Gulf of Alaska.
793	Norco	Ol.s.	615	1911	Mar 8 1944	Burned	Tongass Harbor, Annette Island, Alaska.
794	Nordic Pride	Ol.s.	105	1941	Oct 1 1941	Foundered	20 miles off Point Arenas, Calif.
795	Norlina	St.s.	4,523	1909	Aug 4 1926	Stranded	Point Reyes, Calif. Steel vessel.
796	Normandie	Ol.s.	123	1936	Mar 10 1937	Collided	With st.s. ALAMAR, Off Eureka, Calif.
797	North American	Ol.s.	155	1944	Jul 12 1959	Collided	With barge A.F. 1597 in tow of tug CHARLES. Off Bush Point, in Admiralty Inlet, Puget Sound.
798	North Bend	Brg.	976	1921	Oct 23 1940	Foundered	At entrance to Coos Bay, Ore.
799	North Cape	Brg.	85	1942	Nov 1 1966	Tidal Wave	In Cook Inlet, near Anchorage, Alaska.
800	North Fork	St.s.	322	1888	Sep 21 1919	Stranded	10 miles west of Shelter Cove, Calif.
801	North Head	Ol.s.	50	1942	Sep 25 1954	Burned	Off Catalina Island in southern California waters.
802	North King	Ol.s.	256	1943	Aug 10 1955	Stranded	On Unimak Island, Alaska, between Sennett Point and Scotch Cap.
803	North Sea	St.p.	3,133	1918	Feb 13 1947	Stranded	Porter Reef, Seaforth Channel, British Columbia, near Bella Bella. Steel vessel.
804	North Star	St.p.	198	1907	Jul 8 1915	Burned	Columbia River, Wash.
805	North Wind	St.s.	2,448	-	Dec 14 1944	Unknown	Simeonof Island, Alaska. 54-52-00 N. 159-10-00 W.
806	Northerner	St.p.	1,012	1847	Jan 6 1860	Stranded	Cape Mendocino, Calif. 36 lives lost.
807	Northland	St.s.	697	1908	Mar 3 1916	Stranded	North Reef, British Columbia. Steel vessel.
808	Northland	St.s.	1,387	1904	Jul 21 1927	Collided	With British st.s. PACIFIC TRADER. San Francisco Bay, Calif.
809	Northolm (Can.)	-	-	-	Jan 16 1943	Unknown	50-48-15 N. 128-27-27 W. Wreck reported to lie 1.5 miles northwest of Cape Scott. Depth at 20 fathoms.
810	Novelty	Sch.	592	1886	Oct 23 1907	Stranded	14 miles north of Cape Arago, Ore.
811	Noyo	St.s.	316	1887	Feb 26 1918	Foundered	Off Point Arena, Calif.
812	Noyo	St.s.	1,418	1913	Jun 10 1935	Stranded	Point Arena, Calif. Steel vessel.
813	Nuchek	Ol.s.	167	1943	Jun 8 1949	Burned	In Lake Washington Ship Canal, Seattle, Wash.
814	Nuestra Senora Ayuda	-	-	-	1641	Foundered	West of Santa Catalina Island, Calif. Reported to be worth $250,000. Spanish vessel.

NO.	NAME OF VESSEL	RIG	TONS	BUILT	DATE		CAUSE	PLACE AND COMMENT
815	No. 00	Brg.	98	1909	Jul 17	1931	Foundered	Cape Greig, Alaska.
816	Number Two	Scow	74	1929	Mar 13	1942	War Loss	Vicinity of Dutch Harbor, Alaska. Steel vessel. Sunk by enemy action.
817	Number Four	Scow	74	1927	Mar 13	1942	War Loss	Vicinity of Dutch Harbor, Alaska. Sunk by enemy action.
818	Nunivak	St.p.	681	1898	May 7	1909	Stranded	Nenena, Tanana River, Alaska.
819	O.M. Arnold	Ol.s.	74	1927	Aug 18	1939	Foundered	1/2 mile off Timbered Islets, southeast Alaska. 3 lives lost (8).
820	Oakland	Ga.s.	146	1905	Oct 23	1912	Stranded	Dry Bay, Alaska.
821	Ocean Pride	Ol.s.	393	1944	Nov 11	1955	Foundered	30 miles west of Cape Lookout, Ore.
822	Oduna	St.s.	7,252	1945	Nov 26	1965	Stranded	At Cape Pankof, Alaska.
823	Ohio	St.s.	3,488	1873	Aug 26	1909	Stranded	Finlayson Channel, British Columbia. Iron vessel. 4 lives lost.
824	Ohioan	St.s.	5,153	1914	Oct 8	1936	Stranded	San Francisco, Calif. Steel vessel.
825	Okanogan	St.p.	432	1907	Jul 8	1915	Burned	Columbia River, Wash.
826	Old Timer	Ol.s.	81	1928	Jan 17	1966	Stranded	At Avalon, Santa Catalina Island, Calif.
827	Olive	Scow	50	1905	May 15	1922	Stranded	Iditarod River, Alaska.
828	Olive	Ol.s.	59	1921	Jul 5	1932	Burned	Off Kodiak, Alaska.
829	Oliver J. Olson	Sch.	667	1900	Oct 3	1911	Stranded	Cape False, lower California.
830	Oliver Olson	St.s.	2,235	1918	Nov 3	1953	Stranded	Off the south jetty of the Coquille River, Bandon, Ore. Steel vessel.
831	Olivia H.	Ol.s.	51	1925	Dec 17	1941	Foundered	Dayville, Alaska.
832	Olympia	St.s.	2,837	1883	Dec 10	1910	Stranded	Bligh Island, Alaska. Iron vessel.
833	Olympic	Ol.s.	63	1927	Feb 16	1962	Burned	Off west side of Camano Island, Wash.
834	Olympic	Brg.	1,766	1877	Sep 4	1940	Collided	Off San Pedro, Calif. Steel vessel. 7 lives lost (18).
835	Omaney	Ol.s.	64	1912	Oct 6	1951	Collided	With ol.s. MASONIC. 78 miles southwest 1/4 west of Cape Blanco, Ore.
836	Omilak Chief	Ga.p.	65	1906	May 15	1917	Ice	Fish River, Alaska.
837	Onward	Ol.s.	51	1919	Feb 22	1950	Burned	5 miles southwest of Catalina Harbor, Calif. 33-22-00 N. 117-45-30 W.
838	Oregon	St.s.	2,335	1878	Sep 13	1906	Stranded	Cape Hinchinbrook, Alaska.
839	Oregon	Ol.s.	52	1927	Dec 26	1934	Stranded	Monterey, Calif.
840	Oregon Cove	Brg.	862	1943	May 9	1950	Foundered	475 miles southwest of San Francisco, Calif.
841	Oregon Trader	Brg.	861	1943	Dec 14	1949	Foundered	About 500 miles off Long Beach, Calif.
842	Orient	Ga.s.	57	1911	Sep 1	1930	Collided	With unknown vessel. Sisters Island Light, British Columbia. 10 lives lost (13).
843	Oriental	Ol.s.	66	1929	Jan 31	1930	Stranded	Point Dume, Calif.
844	Orion	Ol.s.	56	1927	Dec 25	1942	Stranded	Monterey Bay, Calif.
845	Orpheus	Clipper	1,272	1856	Nov 1	1875	Collided	With S.S. PACIFIC. Near Puget Sound.
846	Oshkosh	Ga.s.	145	1909	Feb 13	1911	Stranded	Mouth of Columbia River, Ore. 6 lives lost.
847	Ozmo	Ga.s.	765	1904	May 17	1922	Stranded	Oxford Reef, Ore.
848	P.A.F. No.27	Scow	70	1944	Apr 21	1944	Foundered	120 miles off Cape Spencer, Alaska.
849	P.C. No.1	Scow	94	1942	Sep 12	1950	Foundered	Off Cape Edwards, Herbert Graves Island, Alaska.
850	P.C.C. Co. No.II	Scow	79	1911	Oct 30	1920	Foundered	Madison Park, Wash.
851	P.J. Abler	Ga.s.	116	1900	Sep 29	1915	Burned	Douglas Island, Alaska.
852	P.L. Co. No.3	Scow	113	1912	Jul	1928	Foundered	Aberdeen, Wash.
853	PS No.76	Brg.	337	1943	Aug 27	1966	Storm	At east landing, St. Paul Island, Alaska.
854	P.S.B. & D. Co. No.5	Scow	150	1906	Nov 20	1943	Foundered	10 miles, 265° True from Yakutat entrance buoy, Alaska.
855	P.S.B. & D. Co. No.6	Scow	247	1924	Sep	1942	Stranded	Unimak Bight, Alaska.
856	P.S.B. & D. Co. No.8	Scow	185	1927	Nov 20	1943	Foundered	10 miles, 265° True from Yakutat entrance buoy, Alaska.
857	P.S.B. & D. Co. No.8	Scow	247	1924	Oct 16	1938	Stranded	Kanak Island, Controller Bay, Alaska.
858	P.S. & W.H. Ry. No.3	Brg.	167	1916	Jun 1	1964	Foundered	In the Kuskokwim River, near Bethel, Alaska.
859	P.T. & B. Co. 1651	Brg.	1,008	1944	Feb 26	1947	Stranded	Louis Reef, Tongass, 3.5 miles north of Ketchikan, Alaska.
860	P.T. & B. Co. 1652	Brg.	1,008	1943	Oct 17	1948	Foundered	About 20 miles north of Seguam Island, Aleutian Chain, Alaska.
861	P.T. & B. Co. 1655	Brg.	1,008	1944	Feb 11	1947	Foundered	31-00-35 N. 116-00-52 W.
862	Pacific	St.w.	875	-	Nov 4	1875	Collided	With ORPHEUS. Off Cape Flattery, Wash. 236 lives lost. Valued at $250,000.

NO.	NAME OF VESSEL	RIG	TONS	BUILT	DATE	CAUSE	PLACE AND COMMENT
863	Pacific	Ol.s.	89	1928	Oct 27 1951	Foundered	33-21-00 N. 119-19-00 W.
864	Pacific No.1	Brg.	3,238	1956	Dec 28 1960	Stranded	At Icy Bay, Alaska. Steel vessel.
865	Pacific No.5	Scow	97	1899	Jun 1931	Stranded	Mouth of Quilayute River, Wash.
866	Pacific No.13	Brg.	141	1924	Nov 4 1966	Foundered	At Anacortes, Wash.
867	Pal	Ol.s.	71	1926	Nov 27 1937	Foundered	6 miles north of Point Hueneme Lighthouse, Calif.
868	Palestine	Clipper	1,397	1877	Jan 27 1891	Wrecked	Off bar, San Francisco, Calif. Cargo of 2,500 tons of coal.
869	Palmyra	Clipper	–	1876	After 1908	Burned	Catalina Island, Calif. Converted to barge.
870	Palomar	Ol.s.	195	1945	Aug 23 1957	Foundered	Off Morro-Hermoso, Mexico. 27-18-00 N. 115-04-00 W.
871	Pan Pacific	Ol.s.	226	1948	Mar 6 1950	Foundered	33-46-45 N. 119-10-20 W.
872	Panama	Ol.s.	51	1911	Mar 26 1930	Stranded	Marmot Island, Alaska.
873	Panther	Ship	1,278	1854	Jan 1874	Wrecked	Vancouver Island, B.C. While under tow.
874	Paproco No.2	Brg.	91	1916	Dec 14 1917	Stranded	Long Beach, Calif.
875	Paproco No.3	Brg.	99	1917	Dec 14 1921	Stranded	Brighton Beach, Calif.
876	Paragon	Ol.y.	176	1929	Sep 24 1939	Stranded	Entrance to Newport Harbor, Calif. Steel vessel.
877	Paraminta	Bark	1,582	1879	May 14 1914	Stranded	Akin Island, Alaska.
878	Parker Barge No.1	Brg.	85	–	1934	Stranded	Astoria, Ore.
879	Parker Dredge No.2	Brg.	76	1908	Feb 26 1935	Foundered	Yaquina Bay Harbor, Ore. All lives (2) lost.
880	Pathfinder	Ga.s.	86	1900	Jan 15 1914	Stranded	Point Diablo, Calif.
881	Patterson	Ol.w.	604	1882	Dec 11 1938	Stranded	8 miles west of Cape Fairweather, Alaska.
882	Paul L.	Ol.s.	62	1926	Oct 26 1965	Storm	Near mouth of Italio River, Alaska.
883	Pavlof	St.s.	1,300	1889	Feb 17 1916	Stranded	Little Tugidak Island, Alaska.
884	Pawtucket	Ol.s.	141	1898	Dec 4 1965	Burned	Near Otter Island, Nuka Bay, Alaska.
885	Pearl	St.p.	78	1854	Jan 27 1855	Exploded	Yolo, Calif. 80 lives lost.
886	Pelican	Ol.s.	126	1942	Nov 15 1962	Foundered	In Half Moon Bay, Calif.
887	Pennsylvania	St.s.	7,608	1944	Jan 9 1952	Foundered	Off Vancouver Island, British Columbia. Steel vessel. Freighter.
888	Peralta	El.s.	2,075	1927	May 6 1933	Burned	Oakland, Calif. Iron vessel. Oil burner equipped.
889	Perdita	St.s.	286	1903	Oct 10 1911	Burned	Ludlow Rocks, Wash.
890	Pescawha	Ga.s.	93	1906	Feb 27 1933	Stranded	Cape Disappointment, Wash. 1 life lost (11).
891	Petaluma	St.p.	264	1884	Mar 22 1914	Burned	Petaluma, Calif.
892	Peter	Scow	458	1902	May 9 1919	Foundered	Chena, Alaska.
893	Peter Silvester	St.s.	7,176	1942	Feb 6 1945	War Loss	34-19-00 N. 99-37-00 W. Freighter. Steel vessel. Sunk by enemy action.
894	Philip F. Kelley	Ol.s.	126	1901	Aug 8 1954	Burned	By Seattle Seafair Pirates, at Seattle, Wash.
895	Philippine	Sch.	523	1899	Jan 1 1934	Stranded	Terminal Island, Calif.
896	Phoenix X	Ol.s.	70	1920	Oct 21 1957	Burned	Off Sukwan Island, southeast Alaska.
897	Phyllis	St.s.	1,266	1917	Mar 9 1936	Stranded	1 mile south of Humbug Mountain, Ore.
898	Phyllis	Ol.s.	82	1939	Dec 15 1952	Burned	At Gaviota, Calif.
899	Pierson Petroleum	Scow	85	1937	Oct 27 1950	Foundered	Off Naknek, Alaska.
900	Pioneer	St.p.	1,833	1851	Aug 15 1852	Stranded	San Simeon Bay, Calif.
901	Pioneer No.5	Scow	274	1909	Oct 26 1925	Foundered	Point Evans, Tacoma, Wash.
902	Point Arena	St.s.	245	1887	Aug 9 1913	Stranded	Pigeon Point, Calif.
903	Point Loma	Brg.	333	1888	Jul 18 1950	Foundered	In harbor at Crescent City, Calif.
904	Polar Bear	Ol.s.	162	1926	Jul 16 1935	Stranded	West end of Dry Spruce Island, Kupreanof Straits, southwest Alaska.
905	Polaris	Sch.	790	1902	Jan 16 1914	Stranded	Duksberry Reef, Calif.
906	Polynesia	Clipper	1,084	1852	Mar 1 1862	Burned	At San Francisco, Calif.
907	Pomo	St.s.	368	1903	Dec 31 1913	Foundered	Port Reyes, Calif.
908	Pomona	St.s.	1,264	1888	Mar 17 1908	Stranded	Fort Ross, Calif. Steel vessel.
909	Port Costa	Ga.s.	79	1899	Nov 13 1929	Burned	San Francisco, Calif.
910	Port Orford	St.s.	1,293	1917	Dec 26 1942	Foundered	Off Yacha Island, Alaska. 57-00 N. 1234-38 W. Freighter.

NO.	NAME OF VESSEL	RIG	TONS	BUILT	DATE	CAUSE	PLACE AND COMMENT
911	Port Saunders	St.s.	112	1905	May 6 1927	Collided	With USS MADRONO, San Francisco Bay, Calif.
912	Port Saunders	St.s.	112	1904	Sep 2 1941	Burned	Port Costa, Calif. Steel vessel.
913	Portland	Bkn.	493	1873	Jun 19 1906	Stranded	San Pedro Harbor, Calif.
914	Portland	St.s.	1,420	1885	Nov 12 1910	Stranded	Katalla Bay, Alaska.
915	Premier	Sch.	307	1876	May 13 1919	Stranded	Unimak Island, Alaska.
916	President	Ga.s.	50	1902	Jan 12 1923	Foundered	Bristol Bay, Alaska.
917	Prince of Wales	Ol.s.	99	1914	Jan 5 1944	Burned	Pt. Couverden, Alaska.
918	Princess Sophia (Can.)	-	-	-	Oct 25 1918	"Sank"	Off coast of Alaska. 398 lives lost.
919	Progress	Ol.s.	53	1927	Dec 25 1942	Stranded	Monterey, Calif.
920	Prospector	Ol.s.	78	1911	Aug 10 1930	Burned	Oceanside, Calif.
921	Prosper	Sch.	241	1892	Aug 2 1924	Burned	Off California coast.
922	Prosperity	Ol.s.	70	1926	Sep 18 1943	Foundered	San Francisco, Calif.
923	Puget	Brg.	175	1908	Mar 23 1951	Stranded	At Ward's Cove, Alaska.
924	Puritan	Ga.s.	78	1911	Mar 4 1918	Stranded	Montague Island, Alaska.
925	Putco-2	Brg.	90	1959	Sep 8 1959	Stranded	Near Dutch Harbor, Alaska. Steel vessel.
926	Quadra	Ol.s.	50	1912	Mar 27 1964	Tidal Wave	At Kodiak, Alaska.
927	Quinault	St.s.	582	1906	Oct 9 1917	Stranded	Point Gorda, Calif.
928	Quinault Victory	St.s.	7,608	1944	Jul 17 1944	Burned	Port Chicago, Calif. Steel vessel.
929	R.C.Co. No.2	Scow	402	1931	Apr 13 1939	Stranded	3 miles south of Point Huenemi, Calif.
930	R.C.Co. No.6	Scow	490	1934	Jan 23 1943	Stranded	Long Beach, Calif.
931	R.C.Co. No.10	Scow	402	1934	Jan 1 1944	Stranded	Vancouver, British Columbia.
932	R.D. Inman	St.s.	768	1907	Mar 20 1909	Stranded	Duxbury Reef, Calif.
933	Radio	Ol.s.	76	1923	Sep 27 1942	Stranded	Shuyak Straits, Alaska.
934	Radio	Sch.	137	1924		1950	Foundered	In harbor of San Diego, Calif.
935	Rainbow III	Ol.s.	139	1913	Jul 13 1947	Stranded	Marmouth Bay, Kodiak Island, Alaska.
936	Ramona	St.s.	1,061	1902	Sep 10 1911	Stranded	Christian Sound, Alaska.
937	Rampant	Ol.s.	425	1948	Aug 12 1968	Burned	At Vancouver, Wash.
938	Ranger	St.w.	199	1866		1869	Burned	Portland, Ore.
939	Ranger	Ol.s.	67	1936	Jan 25 1952	Stranded	Near Ceralbo Island, in western portion of Gulf of California.
940	Ravalli	St.s.	1,306	1906	Jun 14 1918	Burned	Lowe Inlet, Alaska.
941	Ray	Scow	142	1917	Sep 5 1924	Stranded	Marmot Island, Alaska.
942	Reaper	Bark	1,468	1876	Jul 21 1906	Burned	Port Ludlow, Wash.
943	Red Sails	Ol.s.	65	1944	Mar 10 1950	Foundered	8 miles southeast of west end of Cedros Island, Mexico. 28-03 N. 115-11 W.
944	Redwood	St.s.	679	1908	Sep 18 1939	Burned	Outside Humboldt Bay Breakwater, Eureka, Calif.
945	Regulator	St.p.	508	1891	Jan 24 1906	Burned	St. Johns Ways, Ore.
946	Reina	Ol.s.	94	1947	Nov 13 1965	Foundered	At Segum Island, Alaska.
947	Reliance	St.s.	98	1900	Nov 9 1926	Burned	Houghton, Wash.
948	Reliance	Ol.s.	234	1898	Dec 17 1945	Foundered	Pier 23, San Francisco Bay, Calif.
949	Reliant	Ol.s.	115	1935	Dec 21 1965	Foundered	12 miles southwest of west end of San Clemente Island, Calif.
950	Rescue	St.s.	139	1865	Oct 3 1874	Stranded	San Francisco, Calif. 1 life lost.
951	Resolute	Ga.s.	82	1887	Jan 21 1935	Stranded	Stephens Passage, southeast Alaska.
952	Resolute	Ol.s.	90	1948	May 30 1952	Burned	About 5 miles southwest from Gaviota Pier, Calif.
953	Retriever	Brg.	99	1922	Apr 29 1951	Foundered	About 1 mile south of Monstad Pier, Redondo Beach, Calif.
954	Richard III	Brg.	985	1859	Jan 23 1907	Stranded	Virago Sound, Alaska.
955	Richfield	St.s.	2,366	1913	May 8 1930	Stranded	Point Richmond, Calif.
956	Rio De Janeiro	Steamer	-	-	Feb 22 1901	Wrecked	San Francisco Bay, Calif. 128 lives lost. Reported to be worth substantial money.
957	Riverside	St.s.	1,838	1908	Jun 19 1913	Stranded	Near Cape Mendocino, Calif. Steel vessel.
958	Roamer	Ol.s.	57	1914	Sep 4 1951	Stranded	At Scraggy Point, Salisbury Sound, Alaska.

NO.	NAME OF VESSEL	RIG	TONS	BUILT	DATE	CAUSE	PLACE AND COMMENT
959	Roanoke	St.s.	2,354	1882	May 9 1916	Foundered	Port San Luis, Calif. Iron vessel. 45 lives lost.
960	Robarts	Ol.s.	58	1887	Jun 15 1948	Foundered	In Slough, near Portland, Ore.
961	Robert B.	Ol.s.	136	1923	Jun 15 1945	Burned	McDonald Island, San Joaquin River, Stockton, Calif.
962	Robert Lewers	Sch.	732	1889	Apr 11 1923	Stranded	East of Pachena Point, Vancouver Island, British Columbia.
963	Roberta	Ol.s.	56	1944	Dec 12 1961	Burned	About 22 miles off Vancouver Island, British Columbia.
964	Rochelle	St.s.	831	1894	Oct 21 1914	Stranded	Clatsap Strait, Columbia River, Ore.
965	Rock Island	St.p.	533	1898	May 16 1906	Ice	Chenoa, Alaska.
966	Rocona	Ol.s.	51	1934	Nov 27 1963	Burned	About 12 miles south of Point Fermin and 8 miles north of Long Point, Catalina Island, Calif.
967	Roderick Dhu	Sch.	1,534	1874	Apr 26 1909	Stranded	Point Pinos, Calif. Iron vessel.
968	Rodgers No.1	Scow	64	1900	Dec 23 1932	Foundered	Bellingham, Wash.
969	Rogue River	St.p.	80	1901	Nov 16 1902	Stranded	Rogue River, Ore.
970	Romanof	Brg.	114	1962	Nov 1965	Storm	Near St. Michael, Alaska.
971	Ronnie M.	Ol.s.	196	1944	Unknown	Unknown	Off Cape St. Elias, Alaska. Enroute from Sitka to Kodiak, Alaska.
972	Rosalie	St.s.	318	1893	Jun 22 1918	Burned	East Waterway, Seattle, Wash.
973	Rosanna	Ol.s.	105	1939	Feb 27 1953	Foundered	Near New Year's Point, off San Mateo coast, Calif.
974	Rose No.4	Scow	85	1912	Jun 8 1929	Foundered	Puget Sound, Wash.
975	Rose Marie	Ol.s.	50	1937	Sep 5 1942	Stranded	Off coast of lower California.
976	Rose Marie	Ol.s.	71	1938	Dec 10 1944	Foundered	Off coast of lower California, Mexico, 20 miles due north of Cape Lazarus.
977	Rosecrans	St.s.	2,976	1883	Jan 3 1913	Stranded	Columbia River Bar, Ore. Iron vessel. All lives (36) lost.
978	Rough and Ready	Ga.s.	64	1864	Apr 4 1923	Burned	Napa Creek, Calif.
979	Rubaiyat	Ga.s.	88	1923	Sep 30 1923	Foundered	Tacoma Harbor, Wash. 4 lives lost (12).
980	Ruby	Sch.	50	1888	Mar 21 1916	Foundered	San Francisco, Calif. All lives (5) lost.
981	Rudakof	Ol.s.	171	1943	Sep 4 1962	Storm	At mouth of Kaliak River, Alaska.
982	Ruth	St.s.	53	1897	1921	Burned	Ladysmith, British Columbia.
983	Ruth Ann	Ol.s.	135	1942	Oct 22 1959	Foundered	At Wornosky Island, Alaska.
984	Ruth C.	Ol.s.	61	1931	Feb 10 1939	Stranded	Chatham Point, British Columbia.
985	Ruth L	Ol.s.	55	1917	Nov 1 1961	Foundered	Near Cape Douglas, Alaska.
986	S. No.2	Scow	54	1918	Mar 1 1918	Foundered	Chignik, Alaska.
987	S. and C. No.9	Brg.	161	1925	Sep 24 1940	Foundered	Point San Vincente, Calif.
988	S.N. Castle	Sch.	514	1886	May 15 1926	Burned	Catalina Island, Calif.
989	SR 22	Brg.	659	1914	Oct 12 1962	Foundered	Near Chirikof Island, Gulf of Alaska, Alaska. Steel vessel.
990	S.S.F. Co. No.5	Scow	126	1928	Sep 24 1952	Foundered	Off Narrow Point, Clarence Straits, Alaska.
991	S.S. Lewis	St.s.	1,104	1851	Apr 9 1853	Stranded	Bolinas Bay, Calif.
992	Sachtleben	Ol.s.	57	1936	May 11 1940	Stranded	On rocks off Point Loma, Calif.
993	Sackett's Harbor	El.s.	10,488	1923	Feb 1926	Foundered	Off Anchorage, Alaska. Steel vessel.
994	Sacramento	Steamer	-	-	1872	Unknown	9 miles off Point San Antonio, Baja California, Mexico. Valued at over $1 million in gold and silver cargo. Many attempts made at salvage, but no evidence of being successful.
995	Sacramento	St.p.	373	1861	Nov 11 1874	Burned	San Francisco, Calif. Used as ferryboat.
996	Sacramento	Sch.	130	1868	Oct 15 1905	Stranded	Coos Bay Bar, Ore.
997	Sacramento	St.w.	760	1914	Sep 16 1932	Burned	Broderick, Calif. Oil burner equipped.
998	Sacramento	Brg.	87	1877	Dec 2 1968	Foundered	About 2 miles southwest of King Harbor Light in Santa Monica Bay, Calif.
999	Sagamore	St.p.	66	1850	Oct 29 1850	Exploded	San Francisco, Calif. 20 lives lost.
1000	Saginaw II	Scow	92	1920	1945	Foundered	Between Slocum Arm and Kaz Bay, Alaska.
1001	St. Anne of the Sunset	Ol.s.	100	1944	Oct 17 1955	Foundered	30 miles east of east end of Anacapa Island, Calif. 33-46-03 N. 118-40-09 W.
1002	St. Anthony	Ol.s.	63	1930	Dec 3 1967	Storm	At Puale Bay, Alaska.

NO.	NAME OF VESSEL	RIG	TONS	BUILT	DATE	CAUSE	PLACE AND COMMENT
1003	St. Croix	St.s.	1,993	1895	Nov 20 1909	Burned	Point Dume, Calif.
1004	St. David	Sch.	1,576	1877	Oct 31 1917	Stranded	Khantagg Island, Alaska.
1005	St. Frances	Ship	1,898	1882	May 14 1917	Stranded	Unimak Island, Alaska.
1006	St. George	Ol.s.	214	1941	May 2 1954	Foundered	12 miles west of La Jolla, Calif.
1007	St. James	Ol.s.	149	1940	Dec 11 1949	Burned	4 miles southwest of Point Firmin, Calif.
1008	St. Joseph	Ol.s.	125	1930	Apr 6 1948	Stranded	23-15-00 N. 109-25-00 W.
1009	St. Michael No.6	Brg.	240	1898	May 14 1910	Ice	Tanana River, Alaska.
1010	St. Michael No.9	Brg.	366	1898	Jul 21 1920	Foundered	St. Michael, Alaska.
1011	St. Paul	St.s.	2,440	1898	Oct 5 1905	Stranded	Point Gorda, Calif. Steel vessel.
1012	Salvator	Sch.	467	1890		1935	Stranded	Seldovia Bay, Alaska.
1013	Salvor	Ol.s.	56	1912		1948	Burned	In area of Petersburg, Alaska.
1014	Samoa	St.s.	377	1898	Jan 28 1913	Stranded	Near Point Reyes Light, Calif. 37-59-00 N. 122-58-00 W.
1015	San Augustine (Span.)	Galleon	-	-		1599	Foundered	On reefs off Point Reyes, Calif. Cargo consisted of gold, silver, ivory, & pearls valued at over $500,000.
1016	San Buenaventura	Sch.	180	1876	Jan 14 1910	Stranded	Rogue River Bar, Ore.
1017	San Carlos (Span.)	Patache	-	-		1797	Wrecked	Off Yerba Buena, California.
1018	San Domenico	Ol.s.	109	1935	Dec 26 1935	Stranded	Between Point Reyes, Calif., and Bolinas. 1 life lost (12).
1019	San Francisco	-	-	-	Dec 24 1853	Foundered	Off coast of California. 300 lives lost. See No.1019.
1020	San Francisco	Clipper	1,307	1853	Feb 8 1854	Foundered	Off San Francisco, Calif. Lost on maiden voyage. See No.1019.
1021	San Francisco	Ol.s.	128	1943	Oct 31 1949	Burned	About 2 miles west of west end of Anacapa Island, southern California. 34-01-00 N. 119-19-05 W.
1022	San Giuseppe	Ol.s.	109	1935	Dec 19 1950	Burned	About 4.5 miles south of Anacapa Island, Calif. 33-56-00 N. 119-22-00 W.
1023	San Joaquin	Ol.s.	519	1892	Nov 2 1951	Collided	With ol.s. SOLANO. At mouth of the Sacramento River in San Francisco Bay, Calif.
1024	San Joaquin No.2	St.w.	242	1875	Sep 30 1932	Burned	Broderick, Calif.
1025	San Joaquin No.3	St.p.	220	1877	Jul 25 1910	Burned	Sacramento, Calif.
1026	San Joaquin No.4	St.w.	365	1885	Sep 30 1932	Burned	Broderick, Calif.
1027	San Jose (Span.)	Caravel	-	-		1769	Foundered	Lost en route from La Paz to San Diego, Calif.
1028	San Jose	St.s.	1,115	1903	Mar 23 1919	Burned	Oakland, Calif.
1029	San Jose	St.w.	192	1898	Sep 30 1932	Burned	Broderick, Calif.
1030	San Juan	St.s.	2,152	1882	Aug 29 1929	Collided	With st.s. S.C.T. DODD. Pigeon Point, Calif. 71 lives lost (115).
1031	San Pedro (Span.)	Galleon	-	-	Jun 20 1598	Foundered	On reef off Arrow Point, Santa Catalina Island, Calif. Valued at $1 million.
1032	San Pedro	-	-	-	Jun 20 1907	Collided	With COLUMBIA. Off California coast. 100 lives lost. Also known as "San Petro".
1033	San Rafael City	Ga.s.	74	1910	Jun 3 1910	Burned	San Francisco Bay, Calif.
1034	San Salvador	Ol.s.	280	1931	Jan 9 1944	Foundered	16-53-00 N. 117-18-00 W.
1035	San Sebastian (Span.)	Galleon	-	-	Jan 7 1754	Foundered	On west side of Catalina Island, Calif.
1036	Santa Anna	Ol.s.	108	1944	Nov 26 1956	Foundered	About 3 miles south of Point Pfeiffer, near Monterey, Calif.
1037	Santa Cecilia (Span.)	Frigate	-	-	Sep 1852	Foundered	2.5 miles north-northwest of Ship's Rock, Calif. Valued at $100,000.
1038	Santa Clara	St.s.	1,588	1900	Nov 2 1915	Stranded	Coos Bay, Ore. 21 lives lost.
1039	Santa Lucia	Ol.s.	109	1937	Sep 28 1954	Burned	At Avila, Calif.
1040	Santa Maria	Ol.s.	84	1928	Mar 10 1955	Collided	With LST 306. In Puget Sound, off Point Wells, Wash.
1041	Santa Marta	-	-	-		1852	Stranded	On Santa Catalina Island, Calif. Valued at over $100,000.
1042	Santa Paula	Sch.	650	1900	Jul 8 1933	Burned	Hunters Point, Calif.
1043	Santa Rita	St.s.	1,600	1913	Feb 15 1923	Stranded	Northwest of Carmanah Light, Vancouver Island, British Columbia. Steel vessel.
1044	Santa Rita	Ol.s.	117	1939	Mar 12 1962	Burned	About 16 miles west of Punta Colnett, Baja California, Mexico.
1045	Santa Rosa (Span.)	Galleon	-	-	Oct 1717	Foundered	Off Bishop Rock, south of Cortes Bank, Calif. Valued at $500,000.
1046	Santa Rosa	St.s.	2,416	1884	Jul 7 1911	Stranded	Point Arguello, Calif. Iron vessel. 4 lives lost.
1047	Santa Rosa	Ol.s.	50	1950	Nov 23 1956	Foundered	About 12 miles southwest by west of Catalina Island, Calif. Steel vessel.
1048	Santiam	St.s.	946	1916	Oct 14 1936	Burned	Aberdeen, Wash.

NO.	NAME OF VESSEL	RIG	TONS	BUILT	DATE	CAUSE	PLACE AND COMMENT
1049	Santo Domingo (Span.)	Galleon	-	-	1540	Wrecked	5 miles off mouth of Escondido Creek, Calif. Valued at $1 million.
1050	Sanwan	Ol.y.	219	1917	Feb 11 1941	Foundered	Santa Barbara Harbor, Calif.
1051	Saratoga	St.s.	2,820	1878	Mar 20 1908	Stranded	Prince William Sound, Alaska. Iron vessel.
1052	Sausalito	Sch.	367	1903	Dec 27 1915	Stranded	Waaddah Island, Wash.
1053	Scandia	Ol.s.	116	1914	Feb 23 1927	Foundered	Kodiak, Alaska.
1054	Scotia	St.s.	181	1888	Aug 27 1914	Stranded	Purisima, Calif.
1055	Sea Eagle	St.s.	205	1889	Nov 20 1921	Foundered	Yaquina, Ore. Steel vessel. All lives (10) lost.
1056	Sea Foam	St.s.	339	1905	Feb 23 1931	Stranded	Point Arena, Calif.
1057	Sea Hawk	Ol.s.	83	1941	May 18 1945	Collided	Off Point Loma, Calif.
1058	Sea Horse	Ol.s.	142	1943	Dec 18 1955	Foundered	About 10 miles off East Chugach Island, Gulf of Alaska. Steel vessel.
1059	Sea King	Ol.s.	132	1946	Nov 28 1956	Foundered	In Santa Monica Bay, Calif.
1060	Sea Lion	Ol.s.	89	1935	Feb 1 1954	Burned	About 3 miles southeast of Point Conception, Calif.
1061	Sea Monarch	St.s.	471	1921	Dec 9 1925	Collided	With French st.s. ZENON. Admiralty Inlet, Wash.
1062	Sea Nymph	Clipper	1,215	1853	May 4 1861	Wrecked	Point Reyes, Calif.
1063	Sea Pirate	Ol.s.	87	1936	Feb 28 1946	Foundered	Off Point Gorda, Blunt Reef Light, Calif.
1064	Sea Products Co. No.1	Brg.	57	1912	Apr 16 1917	Foundered	Off Point Dume, Calif.
1065	Sea Products Co. No.2	Brg.	75	1915	Feb 17 1917	Stranded	Venice, Calif.
1066	Sea Products Co. No.3	Brg.	83	1915	1931	Foundered	San Diego, Calif.
1067	Sea Products Co. No.4	Brg.	111	1916	Feb 17 1917	Stranded	Playa de Rey, Calif.
1068	Sea Rose	Ol.s.	82	1949	Jun 2 1996	Stranded	3.5 miles east of Sister Island, Wash.
1069	Sea Rose	Ol.s.	128	1946	Jun 8 1963	Stranded	On reef at Seal Cape, Shumigan Island, Alaska.
1070	Sea Venture	Ol.s.	150	1906	Mar 15 1962	Foundered	About 20 miles north of Seguam Island, Alaska.
1071	Sea Wolf	Ol.s.	61	1928	Oct 27 1932	Foundered	Off Davenport, Calif.
1072	Seattle	Brg.	1,357	1909	1969	Burned	At Ugashik, Alaska.
1073	Secretary	-	-	-	Apr 15 1854	"Blown up"	San Pablo, Calif. 50 lives lost.
1074	Sehome	St.s.	809	1889	Dec 14 1918	Collided	With st.s. GENERAL FRISBIE. San Pablo Bay, Calif.
1075	Seldovia	Scow	144	1925	Oct 17 1928	Foundered	Barren Island, Alaska.
1076	Selkirk	St.p.	223	1899	May 15 1906	Stranded	Rock Island Rapids, Wash.
1077	Sequoia	St.s.	411	1898	Jan 14 1907	Stranded	Humboldt Bay, Calif.
1078	Servia	Bark	1,866	1883	Nov 6 1907	Stranded	Karluk, Alaska. 3 lives lost.
1079	Service	Ga.s.	92	1924	Apr 13 1934	Burned	Sausalito, Calif.
1080	Service	Ol.s.	110	1927	Jul 1967	Foundered	At Alameda, Calif.
1081	Sesnon No.5	Scow	58	1900	Jul 22 1920	Stranded	Lost River, Alaska.
1082	Seven Sisters	Sch.	129	1888	Sep 1 1905	Stranded	Kotzebue Sound, Alaska. Also reported at Cape Espenberg, Alaska.
1083	Shark	Ga.s.	122	1911	Oct 5 1924	Foundered	Crescent City, Calif.
1084	Shasta	St.s.	722	1903	Oct 5 1906	Stranded	Point Conception, Calif. 1 life lost.
1085	Shasta	St.s.	878	1908	Nov 14 1937	Stranded	At Bethlehem Yard, Alameda, Calif.
1086	Shasta	Ol.s.	160	1929	Jul 1 1965	Stranded	Near Crescente Island, Baja California, Mexico, at south end of Ofmadalena Bay.
1087	Sheila	Ol.s.	121	1943	Mar 8 1963	Stranded	Off Gleneden Beach, Ore.
1088	Shelikof	Ol.s.	92	1944	Dec 15 1966	Foundered	At Cape Lazaref, Unimak Island, Alaska.
1089	Shellco	Ga.s.	124	1917	Dec 1 1924	Burned	San Francisco Bay, Calif.
1090	Shna-Yak	St.s.	839	1907	Jul 21 1916	Stranded	Point Sur, Calif.
1091	Shoshoni	Ol.s.	55	1944	Mar 18 1960	Burned	In Mission Bay, Calif.
1092	Sibyl Marston	St.s.	1,086	1907	Jan 12 1909	Stranded	Surf, Calif. 2 lives lost.
1093	Sierra	St.s.	1,286	1917	Mar 3 1926	Burned	San Pedro, Calif.
1094	Sierra Neveda	St.p.	1,246	1852	Oct 17 1869	Stranded	San Simeon Bay, Calif.
1095	Signal	St.s.	475	1887	Jun 28 1911	Stranded	San Francisco, Calif.
1096	Silma	Sc.b.	2,237	1890	Jan 7 1930	Foundered	Oakland Harbor, Calif.

NO.	NAME OF VESSEL	RIG	TONS	BUILT	DATE		CAUSE	PLACE AND COMMENT
1097	Silver Sands	Ol.s.	52	1955	May 15	1967	Stranded	On Dauphin Island, Alaska.
1098	Sinaloa	Ga.y.	64	1917	Apr 10	1931	Burned	San Francisco, Calif.
1099	Sintram	Ship	506	1877	May 7	1915	Stranded	Egejak, Alaska.
1100	Skagit	Bkn.	502	1883	Oct 25	1906	Stranded	Vancouver Island, British Columbia. 2 lives lost.
1101	Skagit Chief	St.w.	502	1935	Oct 29	1956	Foundered	About 12 miles west of Grays Harbor, Wash.
1102	Skagway	St.s.	1,838	1908	Dec 15	1929	Burned	Tatoosh Island, Alaska.
1103	Skarstone	Ol.s.	261	1943	Oct 15	1948	Stranded	At Yakataga Beach, 40 miles west of Yakutat, Alaska.
1104	Smith	Ol.s.	94	1917	Aug 16	1951	Foundered	10 miles east of Middletown Island, Gulf of Alaska.
1105	Sockeye	Ol.s.	77	1928	Dec 11	1956	Burned	Off Westport, Wash.
1106	Solano	Sch.	728	1901	Feb 4	1907	Stranded	4 miles south of Willapa Bay, Wash.
1107	Sondra Lee	Ol.s.	296	1943	Mar 9	1947	Burned	Wrangell Narrows, Alaska.
1108	Sonoma	Sch.	1,063	1868	Jul 1	1911	Foundered	Point Reyes, Calif.
1109	Sonoma	Ol.s.	196	1914	May 21	1949	Foundered	In Pacific Ocean, off Ventura, Calif.
1110	Sophie McLane	St.p.	242	1858	Nov	1864	Exploded	Suisun, Calif. 5 lives lost.
1111	Soquel	Sch.	767	1902	Feb 22	1909	Stranded	Sea Bird Island, British Columbia.
1112	Sotoyome	Ga.s.	534	1905	Dec 7	1907	Burned	14 miles southwest of Cape Mendocino, Calif.
1113	South Coast	St.s.	301	1887	Sep 16	1930	Foundered	Off Oregon coast. All lives (19) lost.
1114	South Pacific	Ol.s.	240	1947	Sep 15	1953	Burned	11 miles west by north of San Pablo Point, lower California, Mexico.
1115	Southern Explorer	Ol.s.	130	1945	Oct 23	1968	Stranded	On the southeast side of the entrance to the breakwater, Los Angeles, Calif.
1116	Southland	Ol.s.	62	1930	Sep 25	1944	Foundered	Pescadero Point, Calif.
1117	Southland	Ol.s.	119	1937	Sep 24	1960	Foundered	About 15 miles from Anacapa Island, Calif.
1118	Spartan	Ol.s.	192	1941	May 3	1951	Foundered	110 miles from Cabo Falso Light, Lower California.
1119	Spencer	Ol.s.	61	1913	Dec 31	1947	Foundered	At Kanatak, Alaska.
1120	Sportfisher II	Ol.s.	88	1936	Apr 9	1945	Stranded	12 miles southwest of Point Banda, Baja California, Mexico.
1121	Standard	Ship	1,534	1878	May 14	1917	Stranded	Cape Constantine, Alaska.
1122	Standard II	Ol.s.	70	1927	Jul 2	1951	Foundered	35 miles southwest of Beggs Rock. 32-00-50 N. 120-00-15 W.
1123	Standard No.1	Brg.	226	1914	Mar 27	1964	Tidal Wave	At Copper River Flats, near Cordova, Alaska.
1124	Stanford	Ol.s.	59	1928	Dec 8	1943	Foundered	4 miles southwest of Davenport, Calif.
1125	Stanford	Ol.s.	122	1944	May 12	1958	Burned	About 12 miles off Shell Beach, Calif.
1126	Stanley	Sch.	355	1900	Mar 28	1910	Stranded	Pauloff Harbor, Sanak Island, Alaska. 5 lives lost.
1127	Stanwood	Ol.s.	78	1928	Aug 7	1954	Stranded	Beached at Petersburg, Alaska.
1128	Star of Bengal	Bark	1,877	1873	Sep 20	1908	Stranded	Coronation Island, Alaska. 112 lives lost.
1129	Star of Falkland	Ship	2,330	1892	May 23	1928	Stranded	Unimak Pass, Alaska. Steel vessel.
1130	Star of the Sea	Ol.s.	68	1937	Oct 22	1940	Foundered	2 miles west of Pedro Point, Calif.
1131	Star of the Sea	Ol.s.	55	1926	Nov 3	1953	Foundered	16 miles south of Turtle Bay, Baja California, Mexico.
1132	Star of the Sea	Ol.s.	242	1930	Oct 4	1961	Foundered	About 4 miles, 035° True from Point Arena Light, off the coast of California.
1133	State of California	St.s.	2,266	1879	Aug 17	1913	Foundered	Gambler Bay, Alaska. Iron vessel. 31 lives lost.
1134	State of Washington	St.p.	605	1889	Jun 23	1920	Foundered	Off Tongue Point, Oregon. 1 life lost.
1135	Steve Quinn No.1	Ga.s.	62	1918	Nov 10	1918	Burned	San Joaquin River, Calif.
1136	Stimson No.5	Brg.	145	1900		1942	Foundered	Smith's Slough, Quillayute River, Wash.
1137	Stockton City	Ga.s.	115	1898	Dec 28	1922	Stranded	Russia Gulch, Medocino County, Calif.
1138	Stocktonia No.2	Ga.s.	134	1916	Jan 28	1925	Burned	Brandt Bridge, San Joaquin River, Calif.
1139	Stranger	Ol.s.	90	1918	Jul 17	1948	Foundered	About 4 miles south by west of San Onofre, Calif.
1140	Stranger II	Ol.s.	121	1943	Sep 26	1966	Burned	Off Port Angeles, Wash.
1141	Success	Ol.s.	57	1928	Oct 29	1965	Burned	At Jap Bay, Kodiak Island, Alaska.
1142	Sujameco	St.s.	3,285	1920	Mar 1	1929	Stranded	Coos Bay, Ore. Steel vessel.
1143	Sun Beam	Ol.s.	59	1926	Jun 7	1946	Stranded	15 miles north of Cabo Falso, Baja California, Mexico.
1144	Sun Beam	Ol.s.	194	1948	Feb 25	1966	Storm	In Gulf of Alaska, about 130 miles from Kodiak City, Alaska.

NO.	NAME OF VESSEL	RIG	TONS	BUILT	DATE	CAUSE	PLACE AND COMMENT
1145	Sun Goddess	Ol.s.	76	1935	Dec 13 1943	Foundered	Coast of Lower California.
1146	Sun Venus	Ol.s.	237	1941	Nov 21 1961	Stranded	Off coast of Mexico. 25-40-00 N. 112-06-00 W.
1147	Sunbeam	Ol.s.	58	1927	Jul 17 1963	Stranded	Near Point Gardner, Alaska.
1148	Sun-D'E	Ol.s.	54	1927	Sep 4 1934	Collided	Granville Channel, British Columbia.
1149	Sundown	Ol.s.	270	1943	Aug 1 1952	Stranded	On Akun Island, Alaska.
1150	Sunlight	Ol.s.	57	1929	Dec 7 1937	Collided	With THREE STAR. 7 miles southeast of Southeast Lightship, San Francisco, Calif.
1151	Sunshine	Sch.	-	-	Unknown	Foundered	Offshore from North Beach Peninsula, Ore.
1152	Superior	Ga.s.	86	1912	Nov 9 1940	Burned	Dodd Narrows, Vancouver Island, British Columbia.
1153	Susan	Ol.s.	52	1920	Jan 21 1952	Stranded	500 yards west of jetty on Peacock Spit, on the north shore of Columbia River, mouth, Alaska.
1154	Susan Olson	St.s.	953	1911	Nov 15 1942	Foundered	41-52-00 N. 124-25-00 W.
1155	Susie M. Plummer	Sch.	920	1890	Dec 23 1909	Abandoned	Cape Flattery, Wash. All lives (10) lost.
1156	Swallow	Ga.y.	91	1918	Nov 30 1926	Burned	Los Angeles, Calif.
1157	Swastika	Ol.s.	148	1926	Nov 26 1933	Burned	Suisun Bay, Calif.
1158	Swifteagle	St.s.	8,206	1921	Feb 22 1934	Foundered	Off Cerros Island, Mexico.
1159	Sylvia de Grasse	Packet	641	1833	Sep 1849	Unknown	Mouth of Columbia River, Wash. Lumber cargo.
1160	T.G. Condare	Ol.s.	60	1914	Apr 11 1936	Stranded	Dark Gulch, near Albion, Calif.
1161	T.H. Trahey	Brg.	494	1910	Aug 26 1936	Stranded	In Yukon River, Alaska.
1162	T.M. Co. No.4	Scow	65	1903	Jun 5 1925	Burned	West Seattle, Wash.
1163	T.W. Lake	Ga.s.	104	1895	Dec 5 1923	Foundered	Rosario Straits, Wash. All lives (14) lost.
1164	Tagalak	Ol.s.	71	1928	Sep 10 1931	Burned	Sukkwan Straits, Alaska.
1165	Tahoe	Ol.s.	52	1938	Nov 11 1940	Foundered	1/2 mile off Humpback Light, toward Long Island, southwest Alaska.
1166	Taku	Ol.s.	60	1898	Oct 6 1942	Stranded	North end of Kayak Island, Alaska.
1167	Tanana	St.w.	495	1904	Oct 2 1921	Foundered	Minto, Alaska.
1168	Tanana Chief	St.p.	72	1898	May 10 1906	Stranded	Kautishua River, Alaska.
1169	Taurus	Sch.	551	1902	Jul 31 1924	Burned	Catalina Island, Calif.
1170	Teddy	Ga.s.	89	1937	Jan 24 1943	Foundered	Kodiak Island, Alaska.
1171	Teddy H	St.w.	153	1910	May 9 1930	Foundered	Tanana River, Alaska.
1172	Telegraph	St.p.	386	1903	Apr 25 1912	Collided	With st.s. ALAMEDA. Seattle, Washington.
1173	Tennessee	St.p.	1,275	1849	Mar 6 1853	Stranded	San Francisco, Calif.
1174	Texmar	St.s.	7,146	1945	Dec 30 1960	Stranded	Off coast of California. 140 lives lost.
1175	The Independence	-	-	-	Feb 16 1853	Burned	At Range No.4, in Grays Harbor, near Hoquiam, Wash. Steel vessel. Freighter.
1176	Theo. E.	Ol.s.	72	1929	Sep 2 1960	Foundered	At Yakutat, Alaska.
1177	Thistle	St.s.	102	1887	Apr 18 1917	Foundered	Pender Island, British Columbia.
1178	Thomas L. Wand	St.s.	691	1906	Sep 16 1922	Stranded	South of Point Sur, Calif.
1179	Thos. P. Emigh	Brg.	1,040	1902	Apr 20 1932	Foundered	Redondo, Calif.
1180	Thor	Ga.s.	59	1951	Apr 29 1963	Foundered	In the Behm Canal, Alaska. Steel vessel.
1181	Timberman	Ol.s.	53	1914	Oct 18 1952	Stranded	At Point Caamano, Alaska.
1182	Tiverton	St.s.	557	1906	Mar 13 1933	Stranded	Humboldt Bay, Calif.
1183	Tolo	St.s.	92	1906	Oct 5 1917	Collided	With tug MAGIC. Bremerton, Wash. 4 lives lost (63).
1184	Tom	Scow	134	1907	1931	Burned	Seattle, Wash.
1185	Tommy M	Ol.s.	76	1947	Aug 1 1958	Burned	In Greenville Channel, British Columbia.
1186	Tondeleyo	Ol.s.	432	1898	Oct 23 1941	Foundered	Three Islands, near Myers Chuck and Ship Island Lights, Wash.
1187	Transit	Sch.	547	1891	Aug 25 1913	Foundered	5 miles southwest of Point Barrow, Alaska. Crushed by ice.
1188	Transit	St.s.	57	1916	Jul 13 1925	Burned	Salmon Beach, Wash.
1189	Transport	St.s.	164	1899	Aug 27 1911	Foundered	Washington Sound, Wash. 1 life lost.
1190	Trilby	St.p.	80	1896	Nov 30 1911	Burned	Oakland, Calif.
1191	Trinidad	-	-	-	1540	Unknown	Off Point La Jolla, Calif. Reported to be worth 65 million

NO.	NAME OF VESSEL	RIG	TONS	BUILT	DATE	CAUSE	PLACE AND COMMENT
1192	Trinidad	St.s.	974	1917	May 7 1937	Stranded	Between buoys No.6 and No.7 on Willapa Harbor Bar, on North Spit, Wash.
1193	Tropic Bird	Bkn.	347	1882	Jan 10 1907	Stranded	Chamela Bay, Mexico.
1194	Tweed	-	-	-	Feb 2 1846	Lost	Yucatan, Alaska. 60 lives lost.
1195	Tyconda	St.p.	186	1901	Oct 11 1915	Burned	Anchorage, Alaska.
1196	U-S-1	Scow	91	1946	Jun 9 1948	Foundered	At Naknek anchorage, Bristol Bay, Alaska.
1197	U.S. Grant	St.s.	54	1866		Stranded	Cape Disappointment, Wash.
1198	USS Bennington	St.s.	-	-	1905	Unknown	Point Loma, entrance to San Diego Harbor, Calif.
1199	USS Bohemia	St.s.	-	-	1931	Unknown	Point Loma, entrance to San Diego Harbor, Calif.
1200	USS Despatch	-	-	-	1926	Unknown	Point Loma, entrance to San Diego Harbor, Calif.
1201	USS F1	Ol.s.	-	-	Unknown	Unknown	South of Point Loma, Calif. Submarine.
1202	USS Idaho	St.s.	-	-	1943	Unknown	Point Loma, entrance to San Diego Harbor, Calif.
1203	USS Kita	-	-	-	1937	Unknown	2 miles offshore on northwest side of Catalina Island, Calif.
1204	USS Pacific	-	-	-	1922	Unknown	Off Point Loma, Calif.
1205	USS Sea Hawk	-	-	-	1945	Unknown	Off Point Loma, Calif.
1206	USS Triton	St.s.	-	-	1943	Unknown	Point Loma, entrance to San Diego Harbor, Calif.
1207	U.S. Destroyers	-	-	-	Sep 3 1923	Collided	With rock. Off Santa Barbara, Calif. 22 lives lost. According to United States Coast Guard information, there were seven (7) destroyers that were lost. The above vessels (numbers 1198 thru 1206) should be researched for authenticity.
1208	Urania	St.s.	93	1907	Feb 12 1914	Burned	Houghton, Wash.
1209	Utility	Ol.s.	92	1915	Oct 3 1928	Burned	San Francisco, Calif.
1210	Uzbekistan (Rus.)	St.s.	-	-	Apr 1 1943	Unknown	48-42-55 N. 125-03-00 W. 2 miles southeast off Pachena Point, about 1/4 mile offshore, in about 30' of water.
1211	V O	Ol.s.	297	1943	Jan 9 1967	Foundered	Off Marmot Island, Alaska.
1212	Valdez	Brg.	5,051	1965	Dec 13 1967	Stranded	Near Yukatat, Alaska.
1213	Valencia	-	-	-	Jan 22 1906	Unknown	Vancouver Island, British Columbia. 129 lives lost.
1214	Valencia	Ol.s.	60	1927	Jun 29 1933	Burned	San Clemente Island, Calif.
1215	Valencia	Ol.s.	82	1927	Sep 11 1956	Stranded	On Spanish Island, southeast Alaska.
1216	Valiant	Ol.y.	444	1926	Dec 26 1930	Burned	Catalina Island, Calif. Steel vessel.
1217	Valletta	St.w.	419	1901	Sep 30 1932	Burned	Broderick, Calif.
1218	Valley Brew	Ga.s.	54	1917	Dec 8 1937	Burned	Burns Cutoff, San Joaquin River, Calif.
1219	Varsity	Ol.s.	90	1937	Feb 5 1940	Stranded	4 miles east of Pachena Point, Vancouver Island, British Columbia. 4 lives lost (7).
1220	Vasco De Gama	Ol.s.	90	1926	Dec 21 1935	Burned	80 miles west of Cape San Lucus, Calif.
1221	Vashon	St.p.	342	1891	Nov 28 1911	Burned	Victoria, British Columbia.
1222	Venture	Ol.s.	54	1927	May 8 1948	Foundered	10 miles northwest of Tugidak Island, Trinity Group, Alaska.
1223	Vermay	Ol.s.	50	1944	Aug 1950	Foundered	Near Cape Muzon, Alaska.
1224	Vincent	St.s.	6,210	1919	Dec 12 1941	War Loss	22-41-00 N. 112-19-00 W. Freighter. Steel vessel. Sunk by enemy action.
1225	Vindicator	Ol.s.	253	1942	Jul 8 1955	Stranded	Struck submerged reef at Cape St. Elias, Alaska.
1226	Vine	Sch.	228	1890	Sep 21 1907	Stranded	Deering, Alaska.
1227	Vingil G. Bogue	St.s.	170	1929	Jan 21 1939	Collided	With st.s. POINT LOBOS. In Oakland Bay, Calif.
1228	Virginia	Ol.s.	68	1929	Dec 14 1932	Burned	Half Moon Bay, Calif.
1229	Virginia IV	Ol.s.	92	1904	Apr 24 1935	Stranded	Yakobi Island, Alaska.
1230	Virginia E.	Ol.s.	70	1926	Nov 23 1964	Burned	At King Cove, Alaska.
1231	Vitanic	Ol.s.	131	1944	Oct 16 1967	Burned	At Charnofski, Alaska.
1232	Volant	Sch.	172	1883	Jan 21 1905	Stranded	Bristol Bay, Alaska.
1233	Volunteer	Sch.	585	1887	Jun 5 1906	Stranded	Near Bodega Head, Calif. 3 lives lost.
1234	W.A. Fletcher	Ga.s.	113	1918	Oct 7 1927	Burned	Mokelumne River, Calif.
1235	W.B. & T. Co. 50	Brg.	341	1913	Aug 4 1917	Stranded	Near Cape Flattery, Wash.
1236	W.H. Dimond	Sch.	390	1881	Feb 2 1914	Stranded	Bird Island, Alaska.

NO.	NAME OF VESSEL	RIG	TONS	BUILT	CAUSE	DATE	PLACE AND COMMENT
1237	W.H. Harrison	St.s.	91	1890	Stranded	Sep 22 1905	Alsea Bay, Ore.
1238	W.H. Kruger	St.s.	469	1899	Foundered	Jan 11 1906	Off Point Arena, Calif.
1239	W.H. McFadden	Ol.s.	92	1943	Foundered	May 19 1947	Straits of Juan de Fuca, Wash.
1240	W.H. Pringle	St.p.	575	1901	Stranded	Oct 9 1906	Entiat, Wash.
1241	W.L. & B. Co. No.1	Scow	68	1916	Stranded	Sep 1925	Gertrude, Wash.
1242	W.R. Todd	St.p.	172	1906	Collided	Jun 28 1912	With bridge. Pasco, Wash.
1243	W.T. Co. No.3	Brg.	264	1922	Foundered	Jul 25 1935	Between Long Beach, Calif., and San Miguel Island, Calif.
1244	W.T. Co. No.8	Brg.	173	1923	Foundered	Dec 24 1924	Catalina Island, Calif.
1245	W.T. Co. No.9	Brg.	173	1923	Foundered	Dec 10 1926	Catalina Island, Calif.
1246	W.T. Co. No.12	Brg.	330	1925	Foundered	Dec 10 1926	Catalina Island, Calif.
1247	W.T. Co. No.18	Brg.	330	1927	Foundered	Sep 17 1960	In the vicinity of Catalina Harbor, Santa Catalina Island, Calif.
1248	W.T. Co. No.18	Brg.	330	1927	Stranded	May 15 1961	On Brighton Beach, Los Angeles Harbor, Los Angeles, Calif.
1249	W.T. & B. Co. 3	Scow	194	1910	Foundered	May 25 1917	Puyallup River, Wash.
1250	W.T. & B. Co. 7	Brg.	488	1910	Burned	Jun 22 1937	Olga Straits, Alaska.
1251	W.T. & B. Co. 33	Scow	733	1902	Stranded	Mar 5 1927	Wards Cove, Alaska.
1252	W.T. & B. Co. 45	Scow	304	1911	Stranded	Nov 29 1919	Vancouver Island, British Columbia.
1253	W.T. & B. Co. 51	Brg.	390	1913	Stranded	Apr 18 1920	Swindle Island, British Columbia.
1254	W.T. & B. Co. 55	Scow	458	1915	Stranded	Apr 25 1926	Cape Hinchinbrook, Alaska.
1255	W.T. & B. Co. 60	Ol.s.	738	1914	Burned	Mar 24 1931	Gaviota, Calif.
1256	W.T. & B. Co. 66	Brg.	339	1924	Burned	May 30 1937	Puget Sound, Wash.
1257	Wahkeena	St.s.	1,030	1916	Stranded	Jan 24 1929	Grays Harbor, Wash.
1258	Wakena	Ga.s.	405	1911	Burned	May 27 1925	Gulf of Georgia, British Columbia.
1259	Waldero	Ol.s.	135	1936	Burned	May 14 1949	Off coast of Mexico at Cordo Point, Gulf of California.
1260	Wallacut	Sch.	708	1898	Stranded	Nov 2 1918	Coos Bay, Ore.
1261	Walworth	Ol.s.	148	1945	Burned	Aug 5 1968	Off Summer Strait, Alaska.
1262	Washington	St.w.	148	1866	Burned	1880	San Francisco, Calif.
1263	Washington	Sloop	708	1898	Stranded	Oct 10 1915	Kayak Island, Alaska.
1264	Washington	St.s.	539	1906	Stranded	Feb 15 1932	Eureka, Calif.
1265	Washington Mail	St.s.	7,943	1945	Lost	Mar 3 1956	Broke in two during storm and sank in Gulf of Alaska. Freighter. Steel vessel.
1266	Washtenaw	St.s.	2,896	1887	Abandoned	Sep 22 1928	Los Angeles Harbor, Calif.
1267	Washtucna	Sch.	710	1896	Stranded	Jul 4 1922	On Umpqua River Bar, South Spit, Ore.
1268	Watson A. West	Sch.	818	1901	Stranded	Feb 23 1923	San Miguel Island, Santa Barbara Channel, Calif.
1269	Webfoot	Clipper	1,091	1856	Wrecked	1886	On Cape Flattery, Wash.
1270	Welding	St.s.	211	1909	Burned	Jul 23 1913	At White Point, Graham Island, British Columbia.
1271	Weitchpec	St.p.	150	1904	Burned	Dec 15 1920	Riverbank, Calif.
1272	Western Clipper	Ol.s.	125	1939	Stranded	Feb 17 1964	On the beach at Atka, Alaska.
1273	Western Explorer	Ol.s.	166	1941	Foundered	May 14 1956	Off Socorro Island, Mexico, 3/4 mile northwest of Binner's Cove. 18-43-06 N. 110-58-03 W.
1274	Western Point	Ol.s.	113	1933	Burned	Nov 14 1953	8 miles south of Dana Point, Calif. 33-22-00 N. 117-45-00 W.
1275	Western Pride	Ol.s.	118	1930	Stranded	Jan 22 1967	At entrance to San Quintin Bay, Baja California, Mexico.
1276	Western Sun	Ol.s.	79	1937	Stranded	Dec 12 1954	56-27-00 N. 133-00-00 W. Near mouth of Kah Sheets Bay, sound end of Duncan Canal, Alaska.
1277	Westport	St.s.	116	1912	Stranded	Sep 14 1936	3 miles south of Lava Point on Akutan Island, Alaska.
1278	Whale	Brg.	97	1925	Stranded	Dec 20 1925	Port San Luis, Calif.
1279	Whittier	St.s.	1,295	1903	Stranded	May 1 1922	Saunders Reef, Calif. Steel vessel.
1280	Wildwood	St.s.	80	1902	Stranded	Sep 19 1910	Seattle, Wash.
1281	Wilhelmina	Ga.s.	112	1918	Burned	Dec 16 1935	In Fourteen Mile Slough, San Joaquin River, Calif.
1282	Willapa	St.s.	1,185	1917	Foundered	Dec 3 1941	8 miles south of Port Orford, Ore.

NO.	NAME OF VESSEL	RIG	TONS	BUILT	DATE	CAUSE	PLACE AND COMMENT
1283	Willard B.	Ol.s.	64	1913	Aug 29 1948	Stranded	In Lisianski Straits, 2 miles north of Pelican City, Alaska.
1284	Wm. Bowden	Brg.	778	1892	Feb 12 1926	Stranded	Redondo Beach, Calif.
1285	Wm. F. Witzemann	Sch.	473	1887	Feb 5 1907	Stranded	4 miles north of Bolinas, Calif.
1286	William G. Irwin	Sch.	348	1881	May 15 1926	Burned	Catalina Island, Calif.
1287	William H. Smith	Sch.	1,957	1883	Apr 14 1933	Stranded	Monterey, Calif.
1288	Wm. Nottingham	Sch.	1,204	1902	Oct 9 1911	Abandoned	Off Cape Disappointment, Wash.
1289	Willie A. Higgins	St.s.	863	1913	Dec 7 1922	Burned	Blaine, Wash.
1290	Willie R. Hume	Sch.	665	1890	Feb 22 1911	Stranded	Point Santa Maria, Mexico. 1 life lost.
1291	Wilmar	Ol.s.	56	1911	Mar 9 1950	Foundered	About 20 miles west of La Jolla, Calif.
1292	Wilmington	St.s.	990	1913	Oct 22 1931	Foundered	Blunts Reef, Calif. 40-54-00 N. 124-10-00 W.
1293	Windsor	Ol.y.	65	1926	Oct 3 1936	Foundered	Near Winchelsea Island, off Nanoose Harbor, British Columbia.
1294	Windward	Clipper	818	1854	Dec 1875	Wrecked	In Puget Sound, Wash.
1295	Windward	Ol.y.	63	1907	Jul 25 1931	Burned	Avalon, Calif. Steel vessel.
1296	Winifield Scott	St.s.	1,291	1851	Dec 2 1853	Stranded	Anacapa Island, off California coast.
1297	Winnebago	St.s.	1,065	1903	Jul 31 1909	Stranded	Point Arena, Calif. Steel vessel.
1298	Wizard	St.s.	139	1869	May 29 1907	Foundered	Punta Gorda, Calif.
1299	Wizard	Ol.s.	60	1924	Jul 22 1952	Stranded	Near Kodiak, Alaska.
1300	YBI	Brg.	701	1929	Oct 1 1950	Foundered	46-31-00 N. 129-02-00 W. Steel vessel.
1301	Yankee Blade	St.p.	1,767	1853	Oct 1 1854	Stranded	Point Arguello, Calif. 15 lives lost.
1302	Yankee Blade	St.p.	2,200	1853	Oct 1 1854	Unknown	Off Honda's Bridge Rock, Point Arguello, Calif. Wood vessel, Length 275'. Valued at $250,000 in gold and silver cargo.
1303	Yankee Mariner	Ol.s.	363	1945	Oct 19 1949	Burned	About 10 miles northwest of Point Arguello, Calif.
1304	Yellowstone	St.s.	767	1907	Mar 1 1933	Foundered	Eureka, Calif.
1305	Yosemite	St.p.	1,319	1862	Jul 9 1909	Stranded	Port Orchard Narrows, Wash.
1306	Yosemite	St.s.	827	1906	Feb 7 1926	Stranded	Point Reyes Light, Calif.
1307	Young America	St.p.	179	1856	Jan 13 1865	Snagged	Marysville, Calif.
1308	Yours Truly	Ga.s.	51	1930	Mar 25 1934	Burned	Balboa, Calif.
1309	Yukon	St.s.	1,238	1871	Jun 11 1913	Stranded	Sannak Island, Alaska. Iron vessel.
1310	Yukon	St.s.	5,746	1899	Feb 4 1956	Stranded	At Cape Fairfield, Alaska. Freighter. Steel vessel.
1311	Zapora	Ol.s.	485	1905	Feb 14 1937	Stranded	Rocky Point, Chatham Straits, Chaik Bay, Alaska.
1312	Zephyr	Ol.s.	104	1938	Oct 28 1960	Burned	About 5 miles southwest of west end of Catalina Island, Calif.
1313	Zilla May	Ga.s.	70	1896	Mar 31 1921	Stranded	Off Point Strait Island, Alaska.
1314	Zinfandel	St.p.	329	1889	Sep 5 1922	Foundered	Minner Slough, off Sacramento River, Calif.
1315	510 Port of Pasco	Brg.	526	1946	Dec 12 1953	Stranded	On North Jetty, Coos Bay, Ore. Steel vessel.
1316	519	Brg.	210	1944	Dec 1 1966	Foundered	At Takatz Island in Chatham Straits, Alaska.
1317	539	Brg.	5,864	1958	Oct 11 1963	Stranded	Off Hunter's Point, Queen Charlotte Islands, British Columbia. Steel vessel.
1318	4413	Scow	389	1944	Dec 5 1951	Stranded	At San Nicholas Island, off coast of California.

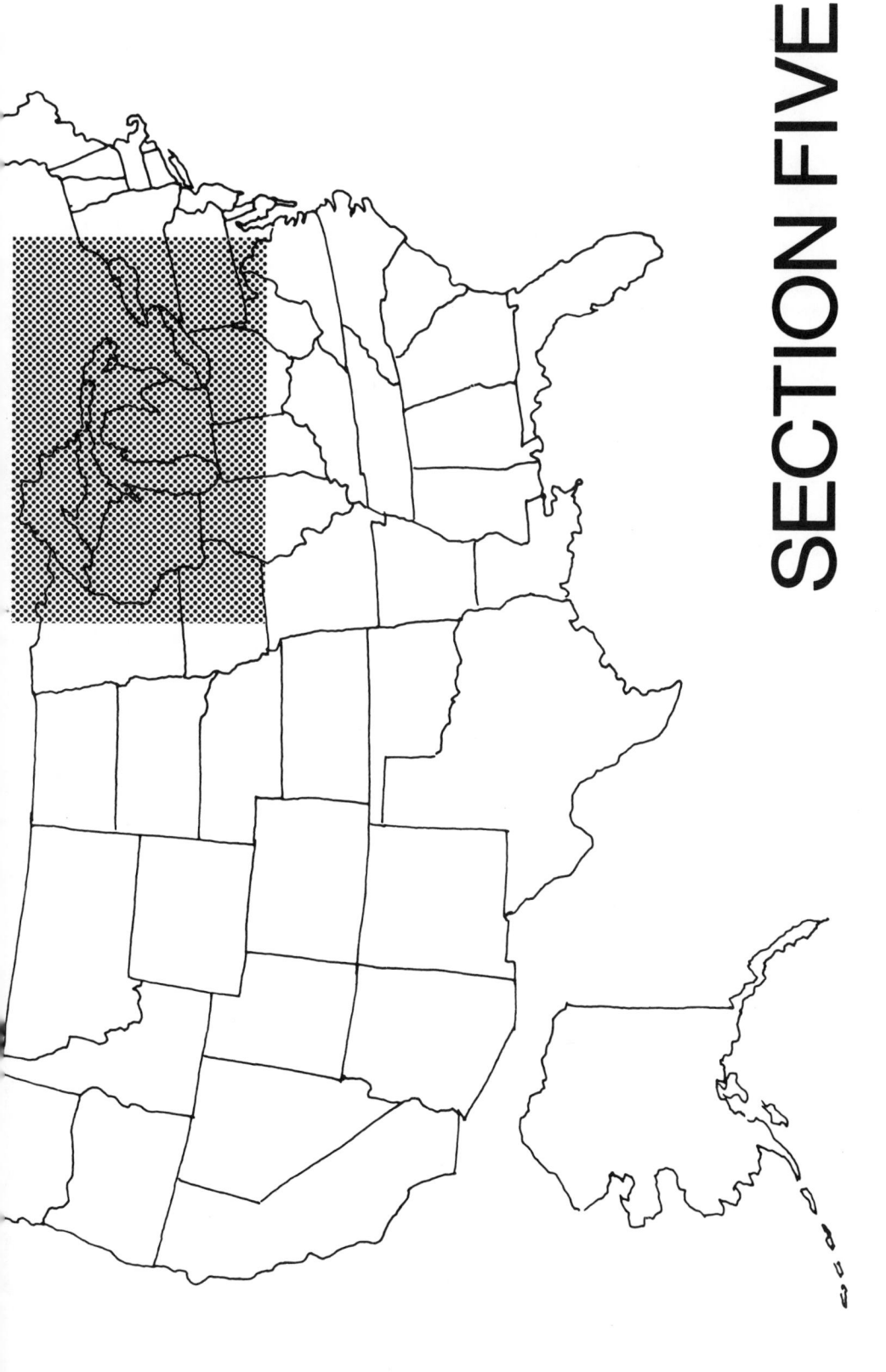

NO.	NAME OF VESSEL	RIG	TONS	BUILT	DATE		CAUSE	PLACE AND COMMENT
1	ABL 344	Brg.	400	1945	Nov 2	1959	Stranded	At Mile 250.1, Illinois River, above Kickapoo Creek Upper Light, Ill. Steel.
2	A. Bradley	Sch.	-	-	Dec 4	1866	Wrecked	Off Long Point, Lake Erie.
3	A. Buckingham	Sch.	-	-	Dec 4	1854	Unknown	Off Long Point, Lake Erie.
4	A.C. Ingersoll, Jr.	St.w.	128	1901	Aug 23	1940	Burned	4 miles above Lock 34, on Ohio River.
5	A.C. Maxwell	Sch.	469	1870	Nov 5	1908	Collided	With st.s. R.W. ENGLAND. Sault Ste. Marie River, Mich.
6	A.D. MacTier	St.s.	1,899	1913	Oct 20	1922	Foundered	Cape D'Espoir, Quebec. Steel vessel.
7	A.D. Patchen	St.p.	874	1846	Jun 11	1848	Stranded	Racine, Wisc.
8	A. Gebhart	Sch.	354	1869	Jun 4	1909	Burned	Drummond Island, Mich.
9	A.I. Baker	St.w.	140	1923	Dec 2	1943	Foundered	In Ohio River, off Marine Ways, Mound City, Ill.
10	A.J. McBrier	St.s.	111	1884	May 10	1907	Burned	Maxon Mill, Georgian Bay, Ontario, Canada.
11	A.L. Hopkins	St.s.	639	1880	Oct 2	1911	Foundered	Ontonagon, Mich.
12	A. Neff	St.p.	-	-	Oct 20	1886	Unknown	Edward Island, Ontario.
13	A. Rossetter	St.s.	200	1846	Oct 11	1855	Stranded	Calumet, Ill.
14	A.S. Field	St.s.	115	1853	Jul 6	1860	Exploded	Detroit, Mich. 4 lives lost.
15	Abbie	Sch.	87	1886	Nov 8	1905	Foundered	Portage Lake Harbor of Refuge, Mich.
16	Abeona	St.p.	206	1864	Mar 7	1872	Burned	Cincinnati, Ohio.
17	Abigail	St.p.	225	1898	Feb 15	1915	Burned	Ohio River, 30 miles below New Albany, Ind.
18	Abram Smith	Sch.	372	1892	Oct 8	1906	Stranded	Duck Island, Lake Huron.
19	Abyssinia	Sch.	2,037	1896	Oct 19	1917	Stranded	Tecumseh Reef, Ontario, Canada.
20	Acme	St.s.	762	1855	Nov 4	1867	Foundered	20 miles off Dunkirk, N.Y.
21	Acme	Sch.	58	1893	Apr 15	1902	Collided	With st.s. WILKESBARRE. Off Buffalo Breakwater, N.Y.
22	Ada Medora	Sch.	290	1867	Oct 6	1906	Stranded	Buffalo, N.Y.
23	Adair	Sch.	-	-		1891	Stranded	Oak Point, Mich.
24	Adam Schumann	Brg.	337	1910	Nov 4	1926	Foundered	Erie, Pa.
25	Adella Shores	St.s.	734	1894	May 1	1909	Foundered	Grand Island, Mich. All lives (14) lost.
26	Admiral	St.s.	130	1922	Dec 2	1942	Foundered	Lake Erie, between Shoal and Cleveland entrance.
27	Admiral Dewey	St.p.	99	1898	Feb 10	1918	Ice	Apple Grove, Ohio.
28	Advance	St.w.	96	1857	Jan 21	1862	Exploded	Matamoras, Ohio. 3 lives lost.
29	Agnes L. Potter	Sch.	279	1870	Aug 28	1906	Stranded	Cleveland, Ohio.
30	Agnes W	St.s.	1,593	1887	Jul 3	1918	Stranded	Drummond Island, Mich.
31	Ajax	St.p.	95	1864	Aug 9	1872	Burned	Saginaw Bay, Mich.
32	Alabama	St.p.	799	1849	Aug 28	1854	Foundered	Buffalo, N.Y.
33	Alaska	St.w.	670	1867	Dec 18	1873	Unknown	Cincinnati, Ohio.
34	Alaska	St.s.	-	-		1908	Burned	In Big and Little Tub Harbor, Tobermory, Lake Huron.
35	Albany	St.p.	669	1846	Nov 25	1853	Stranded	Presque Isle, Mich.
36	Albion	St.p.	-	-	Oct 3	1887	Stranded	Pointe Aux Barques, Mich., Lake Huron.
37	Alex Nimick	St.s.	1,968	1890	Sep 21	1907	Foundered	Vermilion, Mich. 6 lives lost.
38	Alexander	Steamer	-	-	Aug 13	1915	Foundered	Off Youngstown, N.Y.
39	Alexander Maitland	Brg.	3,351	1902	Dec 9	1924	Burned	Port Huron, Mich. Iron vessel.
40	Alfred P. Wright	St.s.	2,207	1888	Nov 16	1915	Burned	Portage Entry, Mich.
41	Algeria	Sch.	2,038	1806	May 9	1906	Stranded	Cleveland, Ohio. 2 lives lost.
42	Alice Hackett	Sch.	-	-		1828	Stranded	Lake Huron.
43	Allegheny	St.s.	468	1849	Oct 24	1855	Collided	With pier. Milwaukee, Wisc.
44	Allegheny	Sch.	689	1873	Jun 6	1913	Stranded	Crisp Point, Lake Superior, Wisc.
45	Allegheny Belle No.4	St.w.	143	1858	May 21	1874	Stranded	Portland, Ore.
46	Almighty	St.s.	-	-		1864	Stranded	On Long Point, Lake Erie. Demolished.
47	Alpena	-	-	-	Oct 16	1880	Foundered	Lake Michigan. All lives (60) lost.
48	Alpha Derrick No.1	Brg.	172	1932	Dec 5	1949	Burned	In Mississippi River, 800 North Front St., East St. Louis, Ill. Steel vessel.

NO.	NAME OF VESSEL	RIG	TONS	BUILT	DATE	CAUSE	PLACE AND COMMENT
49	Alphonse de Lamartine	St.p.	536	1848	Mar 23 1849	Burned	Bath, Ill.
50	Alta	Sch.	935	1884	Oct 20 1905	Stranded	Grand Island, Lake Superior.
51	Altadoc	Steamer	-	-	Dec 9 1927	Unknown	Isabelle Point Reef, Keweenaw Point, Mich.
52	Altamaha	Sc.b.	944	1913	Jul 13 1929	Burned	Muskegon, Mich.
53	Alton	St.w.	143	1904	Jan 1 1928	Foundered	Evansville, Ind.
54	Alva B	St.s.	83	1890	Nov 1 1917	Stranded	22 miles west of Cleveland, Ohio.
55	Alvarado	St.p.	134	1846	Dec 10 1850	Ice	Columbia, Ill.
56	Alvin A. Turner	St.s.	300	1873	Oct 18 1905	Stranded	St. Marys River, Mich.
57	Alzora (Can.)	Scow			Oct 1895	Stranded	1.5 miles west of light on Long Point, Lake Erie.
58	Amazon	St.p.	138	1847	Mar 24 1857	Snagged	Wood River, Ill.
59	Amboy	Sch.	893	1874	Nov 28 1905	Stranded	Thomasville, Minn.
60	America	Sch.	-	-	1827	Unknown	Off Long Point, Lake Erie.
61	America	St.p.	1,083	1847	Jan 12 1854	Stranded	Dunkirk, N.Y.
62	America	St.w.	142	1846	1852	Snagged	Niota, Ill.
63	America	St.w.	197	1863	Dec 23 1871	Ice	Madison, Ind.
64	America	St.s.	937	1898	Jun 7 1928	Stranded	Isle Royale, Mich.
65	America	St.p.	836	1900	Sep 9 1930	Burned	Port Fulton, Ind.
66	American	St.p.	55	1834	Jul 20 1836	Snagged	Illinois River.
67	American Sailor	Brg.	429	1918	Nov 2 1937	Foundered	Off Westfield, N.Y.
68	American Scout	Brg.	422	1918	Nov 2 1937	Foundered	Off Westfield, N.Y.
69	Amily (Can.)	St.s.	-	-	Oct 1864	Wrecked	On Long Point, Lake Erie.
70	Anabel II	Ol.s.	62	1928	Jan 12 1956	Burned	At Roon Steamship Co. dock, Sturgeon Bay, Wisc.
71	Andaste	St.s.	1,430	1892	Sep 9 1929	Foundered	Grand Haven, South Chicago, Ill. All lives (25) lost.
72	Andrew Jackson	St.p.	229	1845	Aug 7 1850	Burned	East St. Louis, Ill.
73	Andy	St.s.	53	1896	Dec 28 1917	Ice	Lockport, Ill.
74	Anglo Saxon	St.p.	214	1846	Feb 16 1848	Snagged	Chester, Ill.
75	Ann	Sch.	-	-	Nov 6 1827	Foundered	Off Long Point, Lake Erie.
76	Ann Arbor No.1	St.s.	1,127	1892	Mar 8 1910	Burned	Manitowoc, Wisc.
77	Anna C. Minch	St.s.			Nov 15 1940	Collided	With TOM B. DAVOCK, 1.5 miles south of Pentwater Pier. Freighter.
78	Anna O'Connor	Brg.	447	1923	Nov 15 1925	Foundered	Buffalo, N.Y. All life (1) lost.
79	Anne Livingston	St.p.	156	1849	Oct 27 1852	Snagged	Atlas Island, below Cincinnati.
80	Annie L	St.p.	90	1881	Jun 26 1907	Burned	Mount Vernon, Ind.
81	Annie Laura	St.s.	244	1871	Aug 10 1922	Burned	St. Clair Flats, Lake St. Clair, Mich.
82	Annie M. Peterson	Sch.	631	1874	Nov 19 1914	Foundered	Lake Superior. All lives (7) lost.
83	Annie Moiles	St.s.	72	1867	Feb 20 1929	Burned	Ecorse, Mich.
84	Annie Tague	C.bt.	108	1883	Oct 5 1909	Foundered	Lake St. Peter Canal, Quebec, Canada.
85	Anthony McCue	Brg.	485	1914	Nov 8 1925	Foundered	Dunkirk, N.Y.
86	Anthony Wayne	St.p.	390	1837	Apr 28 1850	Exploded	Vermilion, Ohio.
87	Anthony Wayne	St.p.	400	1849	Apr 28 1850	Exploded	Vermilion, Ohio. 22 lives lost.
88	Appomattox	St.s.	2,643	1896	Nov 2 1905	Stranded	North Point, Milwaukee, Wisc.
89	Aprentis	Ga.s.	50	1925	Sep 5 1954	Foundered	Near Mile 218, Upper Mississippi River, at Grafton, Ill.
90	Arabia	Sch.	-	-	Oct 4 1884	Foundered	North of Echo Island, Ontario, Canada.
91	Aragon	St.s.	1,450	1896	Nov 17 1921	Stranded	Salem Point, Lake Ontario. Steel vessel.
92	Araxes	St.s.	593	1856	1894	Stranded	Bay City, Mich.
93	Arcadia	St.s.	230	1888	Apr 13 1907	Foundered	Big Sable, Mich. All lives (12) lost.
94	Archer	St.p.	147	1844	Nov 27 1851	Collided	With DIE VERNON. Grafton, Ill. 34 lives lost.
95	Arcola	St.w.	170	1856	Apr 2 1857	Ice	Reeds Landing, Minn.
96	Arctic	St.p.	861	1851	May 29 1860	Stranded	Huron Islands, Mich.

NO.	NAME OF VESSEL	RIG	TONS	BUILT	DATE	CAUSE	PLACE AND COMMENT
97	Arcturus	Sch.	-	-	Apr 1868	Collided	At Long Point, Lake Erie.
98	Argand	St.w.	96	1896	Dec 6 1927	Burned	Lowell, Ohio.
99	Argo	St.p.	-	-	Nov 25 1905	Stranded	Entrance to Holland Harbor, Mich.
100	Argo	Brg.	421	1911	Oct 20 1937	Foundered	Off Pelee Island, Lake Erie. Steel vessel.
101	Argonaut	St.s.	1,118	1873	Oct 12 1906	Burned	Marysville, Mich., St. Clair River.
102	Argosy	St.w.	219	1863	Mar 7 1872	Burned	Cincinnati, Ohio.
103	Argus	St.s.	4,707	1913	Nov 9 1913	Foundered	Lake Huron. Steel vessel. All lives (24) lost.
104	Argyle	St.p.	319	1853	Jan 17 1867	Ice	Cincinnati, Ohio.
105	Ariel	St.p.	165	1854	Mar 31 1868	Burned	Belle Isle, Mich.
106	Arkansas	Sch.	-	-	Nov 15 1852	Wrecked	At Long Point Cut, Lake Erie. Railroad iron cargo.
107	Arlington	St.s.	-	-	May 1 1940	Foundered	South of Stannard Rock, Mich. All lives lost.
108	Armenia	Sch.	2,040	1896	May 9 1906	Foundered	Pelee Island Light, Lake Erie.
109	Arrow	St.p.	195	1839	1846	Snagged	Ohio River.
110	Arundell	St.s.	339	1878	Oct 18 1911	Burned	Douglas, Mich. Iron vessel.
111	Ashland	Brig	-	-	1854	Foundered	On Long Point, Lake Erie.
112	Asia	Sch.	-	-	Dec 3 1878	Wrecked	Off north end of Long Point, Lake Erie.
113	Asia	St.s.	-	-	Sep 14 1882	Foundered	Georgian Bay, Lake Huron. 125 lives lost.
114	Athens	Sch.	2,073	1897	Oct 7 1917	Foundered	Southampton, Ontario, Canada. 5 lives lost.
115	Atlanta	St.s.	-	-	May 6 1891	Foundered	North of Big Two Hearted River entrance, Mich. Coal cargo.
116	Atlanta	St.p.	1,129	1891	Mar 18 1906	Foundered	Near Sheboygan, Wisc. 1 life lost.
117	Atlantic	St.p.	1,155	1849	Aug 20 1852	Collided	With OGDENSBURG. Above Long Point, Ontario, Canada. 150 lives lost.
118	Atlas	St.s.	375	1851	Oct 26 1851	Stranded	Grand River, Ontario, Canada.
119	Atlas	St.s.	232	1903	Jun 26 1907	Collided	With abutment. Clark Street Bridge, Chicago, Ill.
120	Audubon	St.w.	191	1853	Dec 7 1858	Burned	Galena, Ill.
121	Augustus	Sch.	64	1885	Nov 24 1918	Burned	Red River, Wisc.
122	Augusta of Oswego	Sch.	-	-	Apr 18 1890	Unknown	7 miles northwest of Cleveland, Ohio.
123	Aurania	St.s.	3,218	1895	Apr 29 1909	Foundered	Whitefish Bay, Mich. Steel vessel.
124	Australia	Sch.	-	-	Sep 30 1888	Stranded	Near Holland, Mich.
125	Avalanche	St.p.	198	1847	Mar 16 1853	Burned	Peoria, Ill.
126	Ayecliff Hall (Br.)	St.s.	834	1889	Jun 11 1936	Foundered	At Long Point, Ontario, Lake Erie. Freighter.
127	Aztec	Scow	122	1898	Nov 8 1923	Burned	Bell River, Ontario.
128	B. No.17	St.s.	-	-	1914	Foundered	South Chicago, Ill.
129	B.B. Jones	St.s.	171	1864	May 25 1871	Exploded	Port Huron, Mich. 8 lives lost.
130	B.F. Bruce	St.s.	168	1852	Aug 1862	Burned	Port Stanley, Ontario, Canada.
131	B. Freeman	Sch.	-	-	Aug 13 1888	Unknown	Off Oswego, N.Y.
132	B.W. Lewis	St.p.	472	1858	Jun 24 1860	Exploded	Cairo, Ill. 40 lives lost.
133	B.W. Parker	Sch.	1,476	1890	Nov 13 1905	Foundered	Cleveland, Ohio.
134	B. West	Ga.s.	122	1905	Dec 16 1957	Foundered	About 1.5 miles, 69° from Grand Traverse Light Station, Mich. 45-13-00 N. 85-38-40 W. Steel vessel.
135	Badger State	St.s.	860	1862	Dec 6 1909	Burned	Marine City, Mich.
136	Badger State	St.s.	802	1862	Dec 6 1909	Burned	Marine City, Mich., St. Clair River.
137	Baltic	St.p.	206	1840	Sep 30 1841	Snagged	Cairo, Ill.
138	Baltic	Brg.	-	-	1872	Foundered	Off Long Point, Ontario, Canada.
139	Baltimore	St.p.	111	1836	Dec 1836	Snagged	Portsmouth, Ohio.
140	Baltimore	St.p.	513	1847	Sep 17 1855	Stranded	Sheboygan, Wisc.
141	Bannock City	St.w.	150	1866	Feb 12 1877	Ice	Ohio River.
142	Beardstown	St.p.	77	1847	Jun 8 1854	Exploded	Bath, Ill. 1 life lost.
143	Beaubien No.6	Scow	709	1907	Apr 15 1932	Foundered	Sandusky, Ohio.

NO.	NAME OF VESSEL	RIG	TONS	BUILT	DATE			CAUSE	PLACE AND COMMENT
144	Beaver	St.p.	143	1827	May		1834	Collided	With PLOUGHBOY, Steubenville, Ohio.
145	Beaver	St.p.	314	1886	Apr	7	1909	Burned	Cairo, Ill. 1 life lost.
146	Beaver	St.s.	121	1892	Apr	21	1915	Burned	Charlevoix, Mich.
147	Bedford	St.p.	82	1839	Apr	27	1840	Snagged	Wood River, Ill. 7 lives lost.
148	Bee	St.w.	254	1864	Dec	22	1877	Snagged	65 miles above Cairo, Ill.
149	Belle	St.p.	201	1837	Nov		1839	Burned	Liberty, Ill.
150	Belle (Can.)	Sch.	-	-	Nov		1864	Foundered	At Long Point, Ontario, Lake Erie.
151	Belle	St.s.	129	1860	Nov	20	1869	Burned	Port Washington, Wisc. 2 lives lost.
152	Belle	Sch.	105	1856	Dec	11	1908	Stranded	Point au Sable, Mich.
153	Belle Cash	Brg.	-	-	Sep		1877	Foundered	Off Long Point, Lake Erie.
154	Belle of Milton	St.p.	220	1865	Dec	24	1872	Ice	Madison, Ind.
155	Belle Mitchell	Sch.	-	-	Oct	14	1886	Foundered	22 miles west-southwest of Long Point, Ontario.
156	Belle of the West	St.p.	-	-	Apr	22	1850	Burned	Ohio River. 35 lives lost.
157	Ben Coursin	St.w.	161	1851	Aug	24	1857	Collided	With KEY CITY, La Crosse, Wisc. 7 lives lost.
158	Ben Franklin	St.p.	194	1836	Mar	13	1841	Foundered	Cincinnati, Ohio.
159	Ben Franklin	St.w.	212	1892	Dec	2	1935	Burned	Foot of Pike Street, Cincinnati, Ohio.
160	Ben W. Lewis	St.p.	-	-	Jun	24	1860	"Blown up"	Cairo, Ill. 50 lives lost.
161	Benjamin Franklin	St.p.	231	1842	Oct	9	1850	Stranded	Thunder Bay, Mich.
162	Benjamin Ives Gilman	St.p.	85	1836	Jun	17	1837	Exploded	Metropolis, Ill.
163	Benj. Noble	St.s.	1,481	1909	Apr	28	1914	Foundered	Near Knife Island, Lake Superior. Steel vessel. All lives (16) lost.
164	Bennington	Brg.	250	1891	Sep	5	1908	Foundered	Whitefish Point, Mich. All lives (2) lost.
165	Benton	St.s.	304	1867	Aug	1	1909	Burned	Riverrouge, Mich.
166	Berlin City	St.p.	74	1856	Jul	8	1861	Stranded	Oshkosh, Wisc.
167	Berwyn	Sch.	269	1866	Nov	22	1908	Foundered	Plum Island, Wisc.
168	Bessemer	St.p.	-	-	Oct	6	1889	Foundered	North of Keweenaw Waterway, Mich.
169	Bessemer and Marquette Ferry No.2	-	-	-	Dec	10	1909	Stranded	South of Point Stanley, Ontario, Lake Erie. Cargo of railroad cars.
170	Bessie Barwick	St.p.	-	-	Oct	28	1887	Stranded	West of Big Two Hearted River, Mich.
171	Betty Hedger	Brg.	460	1925	Nov	2	1937	Foundered	Off Westfield, N.Y., Lake Erie.
172	Betty L	St.s.	63	1863	Nov	6	1929	Burned	Wallaceburg, Ontario, Canada.
173	Billow	Sch.	-	-	Oct	17	1851	Wrecked	Off Long Point Cut, Ontario, Canada. Lumber cargo.
174	Black Hawk	St.p.	83	1852	Jun	13	1857	Snagged	Mount Vernon, Ind.
175	Blazing Star	Sch.	-	-	Nov		1887	Unknown	Port Detour Point, Wisc. Lumber cargo.
176	Blue Belle	Sch.	-	-	Sep	11	1887	Foundered	North of St. Joseph, Mich.
177	Blue Ridge	St.p.	138	1844	Jan	9	1848	Exploded	Gallipolis, Ohio. 11 lives lost.
178	Blue Wing	Ol.w.	51	1929	Jul	24	1953	Burned	On Mississippi River bank, at foot of "A" Street, Keokuk, Iowa.
179	Bob Ballard	St.p.	150	1890	Dec	8	1909	Collided	Below St. Clair, Mich. 2 lives lost.
180	Boscobel	St.s.	957	1867	Sep	3	1869	Burned	Below Cairo, Ill.
181	Boston	St.p.	163	1849	Jan	1	1850	Ice	Below Cairo, Ill.
182	Boston	St.p.	395	1856	Jul	25	1863	Burned	Portsmouth, Ohio.
183	Bostona	St.p.	468	1849	Nov	25	1852	Stranded	Evansville, Ind., Ford Ferry.
184	Bostona No.2	St.p.	304	1860	Oct	17	1865	Snagged	Craigs Bar, below Cincinnati, Ohio.
185	Bride	St.p.	295	1848	Apr	18	1853	Snagged	Vincennes, Ind.
186	Bridgebuilder X	Ol.s.	53	1911	Dec	15	1959	Foundered	In Lake Michigan. Steel vessel.
187	Bridget	Sch.	-	-			1862	Foundered	Off Long Point, Ontario, Canada.
188	Brightie	Sch.	600	1868	Aug	23	1928	Foundered	Whitehall, Mich. 1 life lost (7).
189	Britain (Can.)	Sch.	-	-			1855	Foundered	Off Long Point, Ontario.
190	British Lion (Can.)	Sch.	-	-	Oct	15	1877	Stranded	Near Old Cut Light, Long Point, Ontario, Lake Erie. Coal cargo.

NO.	NAME OF VESSEL	RIG	TONS	BUILT	DATE		CAUSE	PLACE AND COMMENT
191	British Lion	St.p.	-	-	Oct 27	1891	Unknown	1/2 mile north of Erie, Pa., Lake Erie.
192	Briton	St.s.	2,434	1891	Nov 13	1929	Stranded	Point Abino, Ontario, Canada.
193	Brooklyn	St.s.	466	1866	Oct 22	1874	Exploded	Detroit River, Mich. 20 lives lost.
194	Brown Brothers (Can.)	St.s.	-	-	Oct 28	1959	Wrecked	Northeast tip of Long Point, Ontario.
195	Bruce Mines	St.p.	-	-		1854	Unknown	Lake Huron.
196	Bruno	St.p.	-	-	Nov 13	1890	Collided	South of Cockburn Island, Ontario.
197	Brunswick	St.s.	512	1853	Aug 9	1856	Foundered	South Manitou, Mich. 1 life lost.
198	Brunswick	St.p.	-	-	Oct 4	1912	Unknown	12 miles north of Dunkirk, N.Y. Lumber cargo.
199	Bucephalus	St.s.	493	1852	Nov 12	1854	Foundered	Saginaw Bay, Mich. 10 lives lost.
200	Buckeye State	St.p.	1,274	1851	Jun 9	1855	Stranded	Point Abino, Ontario, Canada.
201	Buffalo	Sch.	-	-		1852	Wrecked	On Long Point, Ontario, Lake Erie.
202	Buffalo	St.s.	60	1887	Apr 29	1907	Foundered	Portage River, Mich.
203	Buffalo	Scow	193	1892	Apr 17	1918	Unknown	Niagara River, Black Rock, N.Y.
204	Bulgaria	St.s.	1,888	1887	Jun 4	1906	Stranded	Fisherman Shoals, Lake Michigan.
205	Burd Levi	St.w.	205	1864	May 19	1865	Exploded	West Franklin, Ind. 5 lives lost.
206	Burlington	St.p.	359	1863	Sep 7	1867	Snagged	Wabasha, Minn.
207	Burlington	St.s.	2,029	1897	Dec 6	1936	Stranded	200 feet off north breakwall, Holland, Mich. Steel vessel.
208	Burmadina King	St.p.	50	1896	Jul 24	1909	Burned	Evansville, Ind.
209	Burnside	Bark	-	-		1872	Unknown	Off Long Point, Ontario, Lake Erie.
210	C.B.C. 603	Brg.	469	1938	Feb 17	1950	Foundered	In Mississippi River, in vicinity of Mile Ahp 20, Chicago, Ill. Steel vessel.
211	C. Bealer	St.w.	262	1854	Mar 7	1858	Snagged	Carroll Island, Cairo, Ill.
212	C.C. Hand	St.s.	2,122	1890	Oct 6	1913	Burned	Big Summer Island, Lake Michigan.
213	C.F. Curtis	St.s.	691	1882	Nov 19	1914	Foundered	Lake Superior, Michigan. All lives (14) lost.
214	C.G. King	Sch.	457	1870	Jul 23	1913	Burned	Cleveland, Ohio.
215	C.J. Kershaw	St.p.	-	-	Sep 30	1895	Collided	With submerged object. At mouth of Chocolay River, Mich.
216	C.J. Sheffield	St.p.	-	-	Jun 15	1890	Collided	At mouth of Keweenaw Waterway, Mich.
217	C.W. Chamberlain	Sch.	-	-	Oct 11	1874	Unknown	South of Long Point, Lake Erie.
218	C.W. Elphicks	St.s.	2,406	1889	Oct 3	1913	Stranded	Long Point, Lake Erie.
219	California	St.p.	-	-	Oct 3	1887	Unknown	Straits of Mackinac, 1/2 mile offshore, Mich.
220	Calumet	Steamer	-	-	Nov 4	1886	Unknown	2.5 miles northwest of Evanston, Ill.
221	Camden	St.p.	103	1866	Nov 16	1869	Stranded	Evansville, Ind.
222	Cape Girardeau	St.p.	691	1892	Oct 21	1916	Collided	With obstruction. Fort Gage, Ill.
223	Cape Horn	Sch.	-	-	May	1873	Collided	Off Long Point, Ontario, Canada.
224	Cape May	St.p.	124	1850	Aug 2	1854	Snagged	Mt. Vernon, Ind. 18 lives lost.
225	Captain John	St.w.	84	1896	Jan 21	1937	Foundered†	Portsmouth, Ohio.
226	Caravan	St.p.	221	1825	Dec	1826	Snagged	Grand Chain, Ill.
227	Carl D. Bradley	El.s.	10,028	1927	Nov 18	1958	Storm	In Lake Michigan, approximately 12 miles southwest of Gull Island, and 25 miles southeast of the Port of Manistique. Steel vessel. 45-39-25 N. 86-04-28 W.
228	Carlingford	Sch.	-	-	Oct 4	1912	Collided	12 miles north of Dunkirk, N.Y.
229	Caroline	St.w.	77	1847	Mar 16	1849	Collided	With CONSIGNEE. Wellsville, Ohio. 3 lives lost.
230	Caroline	St.p.	271	1844	Mar 16	1849	Collided	With CONSIGNEE. Wellsville, Ohio. 7 lives lost.
231	Caroline	St.w.	122	1858	Jan 11	1861	Ice	Terre Haute, Ind.
232	Carol Marsh	Sch.	-	-	Nov 2	1890	Unknown	Off Oswego, N.Y.
233	Carrie A. Ryerson	St.s.	72	1883	Apr 23	1921	Burned	Willow Springs, Ill.
234	Carrie Brown	St.p.	92	1903	Nov 17	1913	Burned	Gallipolis, Ohio.
235	Cascaden	Sch.	-	-		1871	Unknown	Lake Huron.
236	Caspian	St.p.	921	1851	Jul 1	1852	Stranded	Cleveland, Ohio.
237	Castalia	Sch.	-	-	May	1871	Unknown	Off Cove Island, Ontario, Lake Huron.

NO.	NAME OF VESSEL	RIG	TONS	BUILT	DATE	CAUSE	PLACE AND COMMENT
238	Castle Garden	St.w.	161	1853	Jul 25 1862	Stranded	Mound City, Ill.
239	Cataract	Sch.	-	-	May 1857	Collided	Off Long Point, Lake Erie.
240	Cataract	St.s.	393	1852	Jun 16 1861	Burned	Erie, Pa. 4 lives lost.
241	Catchpole	Sch.	-	-	1858	Foundered	On Long Point, Ontario, Lake Erie.
242	Cavalier	St.p.	98	1832	Aug 10 1838	Snagged	Evansville, Ind. 2 lives lost.
243	Cayuga	St.s.	74	-	Apr 7 1925	Burned	Rochester, N.Y.
244	Cecelia Hill	St.s.	93	1896	Apr 7 1906	Burned	Fish Creek, Wisc.
245	Cedarville	St.s.	8,575	1927	May 7 1965	Collided	With Norwegian TOPDALSFJORD. In Mackinaw Straits, approximately 1.5 miles from Mackinaw City, Minn. 120°, 16,950 feet from south tower of Mackinaw Bridge. Steel vessel. 29' over wreck.
246	Central Barge Co. 10	Brg.	598	1939	Dec 4 1965	Foundered	At Mile 958.5, off Coffman Landing Light, 6.5 miles south of Cairo, Ill.
247	Central Barge Co. 16	Brg.	598	1939	Dec 4 1965	Foundered	At Mile 958.5, off Coffman Landing Light, 6.5 miles south of Cairo, Ill.
248	Challenge	St.s.	665	1853	Jun 22 1853	Exploded	Cheboygan, Mich. 5 lives lost.
249	Champion	St.w.	292	1864	Mar 7 1872	Burned	Cincinnati, Ohio.
250	Champlain	St.p.	128	1816	Sep 9 1817	Burned	Whitehall, N.Y.
251	Chancellor	St.p.	372	1850	Dec 7 1854	Snagged	Cairo, Ill.
252	Chapman	Sch.	-	-	1845	Foundered	Off Long Point, Ontario. Lumber cargo.
253	Charger	Sch.	-	-	Aug 7 1890	Foundered	Near light, mouth of Detroit River, Mich.
254	Charles A. Street	St.s.	512	1888	Jul 20 1908	Burned	Port Sanilac, Mich.
255	Charles B. Hill	St.s.	1,731	1878	Nov 22 1906	Stranded	Near Fairport, Ohio.
256	Charles H. Bradley	St.s.	801	1890	Oct 9 1931	Burned	Portage Lake, Mich.
257	Charles Horn	Steamer	930	1889	May 15 1926	Burned	Point Peter, Lake Ontario.
258	Charles M. Warner	Steamer	-	-	Nov 24 1905	Unknown	At Nine Mile Point, Cheyboygan, Mich.
259	Charles M. White	Steamer	-	-	1963	Aground	St. Marys River, Little Rapids Cut, at about 150 feet, 338° from Little Rapids Cut Lighted Buoy 104.
260	Charles Mears	St.s.	272	1856	Aug 7 1864	Burned	Muskegon, Mich.
261	Charles Merrian	St.p.	515	1883	Mar 27 1914	Burned	Cairo, Ill.
262	Charles P. Minch	Sch.	-	-	Oct 27 1898	Unknown	At Tecumesh Cove on Cove Island, Ontario.
263	Charles S. Price	St.s.	6,322	1910	Nov 9 1913	Foundered	Lower Lake Huron. Steel vessel. All lives (28) lost.
264	Charles Spademan	Sch.	306	1873	Dec 10 1909	Foundered	Put-in-Bay, Ohio.
265	Chas. Stewart Parnell	St.s.	1,739	1888	Nov 29 1905	Burned	Squaw Island, Lake Michigan.
266	Charleston	St.p.	344	1852	Dec 21 1855	Burned	Golconda, Ill. 1 life lost.
267	Charmer	St.w.	249	1863	Jun 23 1874	Burned	Evansville, Ind.
268	Charter	St.p.	197	1849	Aug 21 1852	Stranded	Mentor, Ohio. Rig changed to screw on March 22, 1852.
269	Chauncy Hurlbut	St.s.	1,009	1874	Sep 6 1908	Stranded	Whitefish Point, Mich.
270	Checotah	Sch.	658	1870	Oct 30 1906	Foundered	Off Harbor Beach, Mich.
271	Chesapeake	St.p.	412	1838	Jun 9 1847	Collided	With sch. GENERAL PORTER. Conneaut, Ohio. 7 lives lost.
272	Chesapeake	St.w.	216	1901	Oct 11 1931	Burned	Manchester, Ohio.
273	Chester A. Congdon	St.s.	6,530	1907	Nov 6 1918	Stranded	Isle Royal, Lake Superior. Steel vessel.
274	Chicago	St.p.	126	1842	Mar 14 1844	Collided	Grafton, Ill.
275	Chicago	Steamer	-	-	Aug 1 1849	Burned	In Buffalo Harbor, N.Y.
276	Chicago	Brig	-	-	1851	Unknown	Off Long Point, Ontario, Lake Erie.
277	Chicago	St.s.	3,195	1901	Oct 23 1929	Stranded	Michipicoten Island, Lake Superior.
278	Chickamauga	Sch.	2,472	1898	Sep 12 1919	Foundered	Harbor Beach, Mich.
279	Chickasaw	St.p.	309	1851	Apr 26 1852	Collided	With W.B. CLIFTON. French Island, Evansville, Ind. 20 lives lost.
280	Chilo	St.p.	94	1905	Nov 17 1921	Foundered	Lock 35, Ohio River.
281	Choctaw	St.s.	1,573	1892	Jul 12 1915	Collided	With British st.s. WAHCONDAH. Off Presque Island, Mich. Steel vessel.
282	Chris Greene	St.p.	99	1915	Nov 4 1922	Burned	Cincinnati, Ohio.

NO.	NAME OF VESSEL	RIG	TONS	BUILT	DATE	CAUSE	PLACE AND COMMENT
283	City of Bangor	St.s.	3,994	1896	Nov 30 1926	Stranded	Keweenaw Point, Mich.
284	City of Buffalo	St.s.	-	-	Nov 1864	Wrecked	Off Long Point, Lake Erie.
285	City of Buffalo	St.s.	2,026	1857	Jul 30 1866	Burned	Buffalo, N.Y.
286	City of Buffalo	St.p.	2,940	1896	Mar 20 1938	Burned	Cleveland, Ohio. Steel vessel.
287	City of Cairo	St.w.	199	1856	Apr 12 1858	Snagged	Grand Chain, Ill.
288	City of Charleston	St.p.	282	1898	May 8 1921	Burned	Gallipolis, Ohio.
289	City of Cincinnati	St.p.	816	1899	Jan 30 1918	Ice	Cincinnati, Ohio.
290	City of Concord	St.s.	385	1868	Sep 27 1906	Foundered	Off Pelee Island, Lake Erie. 2 lives lost.
291	City of Detroit	St.s.	-	-	Sep 21 1873	Unknown	2.5 miles north of Barcelona, N.Y. Cargo consisted of copper valued at about $100,000, and presumably $100,000 in gold.
292	City of Dresden (Can.)	St.s.	-	-	Nov 18 1922	Unknown	West of Old Cut Light, Long Point, Lake Erie.
293	City of Glasgow	St.s.	2,400	1891	Dec 3 1907	Burned	Green Bay, Wisc.
294	City of Grand Rapids	St.s.	-	-	Oct 1907	Burned	On bar at Little Tub Harbor, Lake Huron.
295	City of Green Bay	Sch.	-	-	Oct 4 1887	Unknown	Off South Haven, Mich.
296	City of Green Bay	St.s.	208	1880	Aug 19 1909	Burned	Whislters Point, Saginaw Bay, Mich.
297	City of Helena	St.w.	148	1931	Sep 6 1937	Burned	Cairo, Ill.
298	City of Hudson	St.p.	61	1899	Aug 29 1906	Burned	Brownsville, Minn.
299	City of Huntington	St.w.	58	1900	Jul 30 1926	Foundered	Manchester, Ohio.
300	City of Kalamazoo	St.s.	729	1893	Nov 11 1911	Burned	Manistee, Mich.
301	City of London	St.s.	2,005	1891	Sep 30 1913	Foundered	Lake Erie.
302	City of Louisville	St.p.	1,681	1894	Jan 30 1918	Ice	Cincinnati, Ohio.
303	City of Moline	St.s.	52	1905	Aug 7 1913	Foundered	Grafton, Ill.
304	City of Oswego	St.s.	357	1852	Jul 12 1852	Collided	With AMERICA. Willowick, Ohio. 15 lives lost.
305	City of Owen Sound	St.p.	-	-	Oct 24 1887	Unknown	Off Bear's Rump Island, Georgian Bay, 3 miles northeast of Tobermary, Ontario.
306	City of Parkersburg	St.p.	218	1899	Mar 8 1918	Collided	With obstruction. Ironton, Ohio.
307	City of Peoria	St.p.	113	1892	Sep 7 1914	Burned	Cairo, Ill.
308	City of Port Huron	St.s.	411	1867	Sep 9 1876	Unknown	Dunkirk, N.Y.
309	City of Rome	St.s.	1,908	1881	May 1914	Burned	Off Ripley, about 30 miles west of Dunkirk, N.Y.
310	City of St. Joseph	Brg.	833	1890	Sep 22 1942	Foundered	2 miles east of Eagle Harbor, Mich.
311	City of Sandusky	St.p.	-	-	Mar 24 1876	Burned	Point Stanley Harbor, Ontario.
312	City of Savannah	St.p.	293	1902	Dec 5 1911	Foundered	Mississippi River, 20 miles north of Cairo, Ill.
313	City of Superior	St.s.	578	1857	Nov 11 1857	Stranded	Copper Harbor, Mich.
314	City of Toledo	St.p.	315	1865	Aug 23 1874	Burned	Manistee, Mich.
315	City of Toledo	Sch.	245	1865	Jul 21 1906	Collided	With bridge. Detroit, Mich.
316	City of Wheeling	St.p.	439	1853	May 31 1856	Stranded	Pomeroy, Ohio.
317	Clara	St.p.	185	1848	Sep 8 1853	Burned	Cincinnati, Ohio.
318	Clara Hine	St.w.	79	1856	Jun 7 1866	Foundered	Lake City, Minn.
319	Clarence E. LaBeau	St.s.	275	1893	Jul 11 1922	Burned	Maumee River, Toledo, Ohio.
320	Clarion	St.w.	72	1851	1857	Unknown	St. Paul, Minn.
321	Clarion	St.s.	1,711	1881	Dec 8 1909	Burned	Lake Erie. Iron vessel. 15 lives lost.
322	Clarion	-	-	-	Jun 6 1918	Unknown	Off Point Moullie, Mich.
323	Clay Tile	Scow	206	-	Jul 11 1943	Foundered	In Saginaw River, Saginaw, Mich.
324	Cleveco	Brg.	2,441	1913	Dec 23 1942	Foundered	Lake Erie, between Southeast Shoal and Cleveland entrance. Steel vessel. 16-7/8 miles, 10-27-00 from the Cleveland East Entrance Light. Lies upside down. Depth 71'.
325	Clifton	St.p.	418	1864	May 12 1869	Burned	Cincinnati, Ohio.
326	Clifton	St.s.	1,713	1892	Sep 21 1924	Foundered	Lake Huron, Michigan. Steel vessel. All lives (27) lost.
327	Colgate Hoyt	St.s.	-	-	Nov 25 1894	Wrecked	At Long Point, Ontario.

NO.	NAME OF VESSEL	RIG	TONS	BUILT	DATE	CAUSE	PLACE AND COMMENT
328	Col. Brockett	Sch.	-	-	Apr 24 1890	Unknown	Harbor Beach, Mich.
329	Col. Cook	Steamer	-	-	Jul 15 1888	Unknown	Off Amherst Island, Ontario.
330	Colonna	St.w.	102	1859	Dec 1 1863	Burned	Newburg, Ind.
331	Columbia	St.p.	197	1893	Mar 25 1908	Collided	With log. Ohio River.
332	Columbia	St.p.	260	1892	Jan 20 1913	Burned	Jeffersonville, Ind.
333	Columbia	St.p.	222	1897	Jul 5 1918	Foundered	Wesley City, Ill. 89 lives lost (479).
334	Columbian	Brg.	356	1864	Sep 4 1913	Foundered	Dunkirk, N.Y.
335	Columbus	St.p.	312	1827	Oct 11 1828	Snagged	Cairo, Ill.
336	Columbus	St.p.	450	1819	Nov 11 1828	Snagged	Cairo, Ill.
337	Columbus	St.p.	391	1835	Mar 1848	Collided	With pier. Dunkirk, N.Y.
338	Comet	St.w.	116	1846	Sep 18 1850	Snagged	Grafton, Ill.
339	Commerce	St.p.	165	1836	Apr 13 1840	Burned	Cincinnati, Ohio.
340	Commerce	St.p.	-	-	May 1850	Collided	Cincinnati, Ohio.
341	Commerce	Sch.	327	1857	Nov 16 1909	Foundered	Off mouth of Grand River, Ontario, Canada.
342	Commercial	St.p.	266	1860	Jan 1 1872	Foundered	Sheboygan, Wisc.
343	Commodore	St.p.	225	1837	Jun 28 1842	Burned	Evansville, Ind.
344	Commodore	Sch.	550	1880	Jun 17 1918	Foundered	Cincinnati, Ohio.
345	Commodore Perry	St.p.	-	-	Jul 21 1835	Exploded	Off Southeast Shoal Light Vessel, Ontario, Canada.
346	Commonwealth	St.p.	690	1864	Aug 1889	Burned	Off Buffalo, N.Y.
347	Comrade	Sch.	-	-	Sep 13 1890	Foundered	Cincinnati, Ohio.
348	Concord	St.p.	58	1835	Jun 15 1837	Snagged	Off Blake Point, Minn. Lumber cargo.
349	Condor	St.p.	177	1899	Mar 4 1917	Snagged	Montezuma, Ind.
350	Conductor	Sch.	-	-	Nov 24 1854	Burned	Joppa, Ill.
351	Conemaugh	St.s.	1,609	1880	Nov 21 1906	Wrecked	1/2 mile off Long Point, Ontario.
352	Conqueror	St.w.	204	1916	Mar 21 1927	Stranded	Point Pelee, Lake Erie.
353	Constitution	Sch.	-	-	Sep 28 1848	Foundered	Sciotoville, Ohio.
354	Continental	St.p.	80	1865	Mar 19 1866	Unknown	Off Long Point, Ontario, Lake Erie.
355	Convoy	St.p.	170	1888	Jul 7 1915	Burned	Chicago, Ill.
356	Cora S	St.w.	201	1864	Oct 25 1869	Foundered	Cincinnati, Ohio. Iron vessel. 6 lives lost.
357	Coralia	-	-	-	Nov 25 1905	Snagged	Shawneetown, Ill.
358	Cormorant	St.s.	977	1873	Oct 30 1907	Unknown	On Point Isabelle, east side of Keweenaw Point, Mich.
359	Cornell	St.s.	65	1888	Dec 21 1922	Burned	Basswood Island, Wisc.
360	Cortland	Steamer	-	-	Jun 20 1868	Foundered	On Lake Erie. All lives (8) lost.
361	Cottonwood	Steamer	-	-	Dec 2 1926	Unknown	North of Lorain, Ohio.
362	Courier	St.w.	258	1857	Aug 22 1864	Burned	Off Coppermine Point, Ontario.
363	Courtland	Bark	-	-	Jun 20 1868	Collided	Mound City, Ill. With MORNING STAR. Between Black River and Vermilion Point, west of Lorain, Ohio. 31 lives lost. Cargo of iron ore. See No.360.
364	Cream City	St.s.	570	1884	Jul 1 1918	Stranded	North shore, Lake Huron.
365	Crescent City	-	-	-	Nov 26 1905	Unknown	2 miles east of Lester Park, Duluth, Minn.
366	Crusader	St.p.	89	1904	Mar 16 1917	Foundered	Cincinnati, Ohio.
367	Culligan	St.s.	1,748	1883	Sep 27 1912	Foundered	Grand Island, Lake Superior.
368	Cumberland No.2	St.w.	141	1849	1851	Stranded	Rising Sun, Ind.
369	Custodian	St.s.	359	1919	Jun 23 1925	Burned	West Sisters Island, Ohio.
370	Cutter	St.w.	92	1863	Oct 1869	Snagged	Stillwater, Minn.
371	Cyclone	St.p.	138	1891	Dec 2 1907	Burned	Wabasha, Minn.
372	Cyprus	St.s.	4,900	1907	Oct 11 1907	Foundered	18 miles north of Deer Park, Wisc. 22 lives lost. Steel vessel. Length 420'.
373	D.A. January	St.p.	440	1857	Dec 18 1867	Snagged	Chester, Ill. Renamed "Ned Tracy" in 1866.
374	D.C. Shaw	St.s.	64	1911	Jun 8 1926	Burned	Toledo, Ohio.

NO.	NAME OF VESSEL	RIG	TONS	BUILT	DATE		CAUSE	PLACE AND COMMENT
375	D.E. Callender	St.s.	3,522	1895	Nov 14	1933	Stranded	Lake Erie, Ontario. Steel vessel.
376	D.L. Filer	Sch.	357	1871	Oct 20	1916	Foundered	3 miles due east of Bar Point Light, Detroit River, Mich. 6 lives lost.
377	D. Leuty	St.s.	646	1882	Oct 31	1911	Stranded	Marquette, Mich.
378	D.C. Whitney	St.s.	-	-	Nov 25	1905	Stranded	Washington Island, Wisc. Freighter.
379	D.L. Couch (Can.)	Sch.	-	-	Jul 11	1872	Unknown	15 miles off Long Point, Ontario. Coal cargo.
380	D.M. Clemson	St.s.	5,531	1903	Dec 1	1906	Foundered	Near Whitefish Point, Mich. Steel vessel. All lives (24) lost. This was last position vessel was sighted after sailing from Lorain, Ohio on Nov. 28, 1908, bound for Duluth, Minn.
381	D.R. Hanna	St.s.	7,023	1906	May 16	1919	Collided	With st.s. QUINCY A. SHAW. Off Thunder Bay, Mich. Steel vessel.
382	D.R. Martin	Sch.	-	-		1904	Unknown	Southwest of Devil Island, Ontario.
383	Dacotah	St.s.	698	1857	Nov 23	1860	Stranded	Buffalo, N.Y. 24 lives lost. Cargo of copper.
384	Dan Kunz	St.s.	99	1888	Jun 5	1909	Stranded	Cleveland, Ohio.
385	Dan Marble	Sch.	-	-	Jul 21	1875	Foundered	8 miles east of Long Point, Lake Erie. Coal cargo.
386	Dan Pollard	St.w.	77	1857	Aug 3	1864	Snagged	Cairo, Ill.
387	Daniel Ball	St.s.	141	1862	Jan 14	1876	Burned	Saginaw, Mich.
388	Danube	St.p.	156	1847	Sep 6	1852	Foundered	Port Byron, Ill.
389	Darling	St.p.	401	1863	May 9	1869	Burned	Cincinnati, Ohio.
390	David Dows	Sch.	-	-	Nov 9	1889	Unknown	In North Chicago Harbor, Ill.
391	David F. Thomas	St.w.	60	1902	Apr 21	1929	Burned	Proctorville, Ohio.
392	David Foster	Brg.	447	1918	Nov 9	1936	Foundered	18 miles from Presque Island Light in Lake Erie. All life (1) lost.
393	David Stewart	Sch.	-	-	Oct 29	1891	Unknown	West of Fairport, Ohio.
394	David W. Mills	St.s.	925	1874	Aug 11	1919	Stranded	Ford Shoal, Lake Ontario. 1 life lost.
395	David Wagstaff	Sch.	293	1865	Nov 25	1890	Foundered	Off Sheboygan, Wisc.
396	David Watts	St.w.	68	1865		1870	Unknown	Cairo, Ill.
397	Daylight	St.p.	1,083	1864	Oct 7	1870	Burned	Ferrysburg, Mich.
398	Dean Richmond	St.s.	-	-	Oct 29	1871	Burned	Sault Ste. Marie, Mich. 1 life lost.
399	Dean Richmond	St.s.			Aug 14	1893	Foundered	North of Erie, Pa. This vessel has been written about several times and to provide the best opportunity for recovery, added research is a necessity. Last reported seen Van Buren Point, N.Y. and Erie, Pa. Lost during heavy winds. There were no survivors. Cargo has been reported being worth over $500,000 and consisted of copper, gold, with reports that there has been some salvage carried on.
400	Defiance	St.w.	135	1845		1848	Unknown	Liberty, Ill.
401	Defiance	Sch.	111	1905	Nov 16	1909	Stranded	Bark River, Mich.
402	Delaware	St.p.	177	1834	Jul 3	1836	Stranded	St. Joseph, Mich.
403	Delaware	St.s.	368	1846	Nov 3	1855	Stranded	Sheboygan, Wisc. 11 lives lost.
404	Delaware	St.w.	168	1862	Aug 6	1868	Burned	Cincinnati, Ohio.
405	Delaware	Sch.	-	-	Nov 25	1887	Unknown	North of Port Weller, Ontario.
406	Delegate	St.w.	208	1854	Jan 21	1859	Collided	With NATHANIEL HOLMES. West Franklin, Ind. 1 life lost.
407	Delta	Sch.	269	1890	Aug 25	1919	Stranded	Holland, Mich.
408	Detroit	St.p.	352	1846	May 25	1854	Collided	With bark NUCLEUS. Saginaw Bay, Mich.
409	Detroit	St.s.	398	1860	Oct 26	1867	Stranded	Thunder Bay, Mich.
410	Detroit	St.s.	398	1862	Oct 26	1867	Stranded	Off Thunder Bay, Mich.
411	Detroit	St.p.	1,039	1859	Sep 29	1872	Stranded	Harrisville, Mich. Rig changed to schooner and finally to a screw vessel in 1871.
412	Detroit	Sch.	-	-	Nov 4	1886	Foundered	Off Little Summer Island, Wisc.
413	Dickinson	Sch.	-	-	Nov	1886	Unknown	Frankfort, Mich.
414	Dixie	Brg.	152	1941	Dec 4	1964	Foundered	065°, 19,000 feet from Ashtabula Harbor East Breakwater Light, Lake Erie.
415	Doctor Franklin	St.p.	148	1847	May 7	1854	Collided	With GALENA. McCartney, Wisc.

NO.	NAME OF VESSEL	RIG	TONS	BUILT	DATE	CAUSE	PLACE AND COMMENT
416	Dolomite	Brg.	172	1881	Aug 5 1910	Foundered	Grafton, Ill.
417	Dorcas Pendell	Sch.	407	1884	Jan 5 1914	Burned	Harbor Beach, Lake Michigan.
418	Doris	St.y.	192	1903	May 3 1934	Burned	Chicago, Ill. Steel vessel.
419	Dormer No.2	Brg.	82	1918	Jul 7 1940	Foundered	Northern end of Crow Island, in Saginaw River, Mich.
420	Dorothy	St.p.	148	1916	Dec 1 1921	Burned	Golcondo, Ill.
421	Douglas Moir	C.bt.	103	1887	Oct 28 1913	Collided	With stone pier. At Three Rivers, Quebec, Canada.
422	Dover	St.p.	532	1890	Jul 23 1932	Burned	Ecorse, Mich.
423	Dudley	Drg.	95	1926	Nov 3 1934	Foundered	Au Sable Pierhead Light, Mich.
424	Duluth	Drg.	142	1872	Oct 12 1918	Burned	Duluth, Minn.
425	Dundee	Sc.b.	-	-	Sep 11 1900	Unknown	4 miles north of Girard, Pa.
426	E.A. Rae	Sch.	-	-	Oct 18 1889	Unknown	Off Braddock Point, N.Y.
427	E.H. Lemay	C.bt.	96	1901	Nov 3 1917	Collided	With pier. Quebec, Canada.
428	E.J. Laway, Jr.	St.s.	70	1914	Apr 19 1919	Foundered	North Channel, Lake Huron.
429	E.K. Collins	St.p.	942	1854	Oct 8 1854	Burned	Amherstburg, Ontario. 23 lives lost.
430	E.M. Foster	Sch.	-	-	Oct 18 1888	Stranded	Southeast of Pointe Aux Barques, Mich.
431	E.P. Dorr	Sch.	-	-	Nov 15 1881	Foundered	Northeast tip of Long Point, Ontario. Lumber cargo.
432	E.T. Carrington	St.s.	52	1876	Aug 23 1907	Foundered	15 miles northeast of Duluth, Minn.
433	E.W. Ogleday	St.s.	3,666	1896	Dec 8 1927	Stranded	Marquette, Mich. Steel vessel.
434	Eastland	St.s.	-	-	Jul 24 1915	Capsized	Chicago River. 812 lives lost.
435	Eclipse	St.s.	136	1852	Oct 20 1871	Burned	Lakeport, Mich.
436	Ed Jessey	Sch.	-	-	Sep 12 1848	Foundered	10 miles west of Long Point, Ontario.
437	Edmond Fitzgerald	Sch.	-	-	Nov 24 1883	Foundered	2 miles west of Old Cut Light, Long Point, Ontario.
438	Edmonia	St.w.	90	1856	Aug 20 1860	Snagged	Leavenworth, Ind.
439	Edna	Brg.	53	1866	Jul 15 1916	Burned	Algonac, Mich.
440	Edward E. Skeele	Sch.	199	1881	Sep 25 1921	Stranded	Barrie Island, Lake Huron.
441	Edward Kelley	Sch.	776	1874	Nov 25 1911	Stranded	Port Colborne, Ontario.
442	Edward Manning	St.w.	112	1856	Aug 10 1858	Burned	Alton, Ill.
443	Edw. U. Demmer	St.s.	4,651	1899	Mar 25 1923	Collided	With st.s. SATURN. Lake Huron. Steel vessel.
444	Edwin Hickman	St.p.	328	1842	Oct 13 1844	Burned	Cairo, Ill.
445	Effie Afton	St.p.	430	1855	May 6 1856	Burned	Rock Island, Ill.
446	Elgin	Brg.	330	1874	Oct 28 1906	Abandoned	Grand Marais, Minn.
447	Eliza R. Turner	Sch.	-	-	Oct 15 1877	Foundered	Off Long Point, Ontario.
448	Elizabeth (Can.)	Sch.	-	-	Dec 5 1854	Stranded	Off Long Point, Ontario.
449	Ellen Gray	St.w.	118	1859	Nov 5 1860	Collided	With ARKANSAS. Cairo, Ill.
450	Ellen Spry	Sch.	-	-	Nov 5 1886	Foundered	On South Manitou Island, Mich.
451	Ellen Stuart	Sch.	-	-	1851	Foundered	Off Long Point, Ontario.
452	Elmira	St.s.	700	1883	Jun 13 1930	Burned	Boyne City, Mich.
453	Elva	Sch.	69	1862	Jul 24 1911	Stranded	Sturgeon Bay, Wisc.
454	Emigrant	St.p.	65	1829	Dec 1834	Ice	Cincinnati, Ohio.
455	Emily	St.p.	68	1891	Jan 5 1910	Ice	Portsmouth, Ohio.
456	Emily and Eliza	Sch.	63	1874	Sep 9 1910	Stranded	Aral, Mich.
457	Emma	St.p.	101	1867	Dec 9 1872	Burned	Shawneetown, Ill.
458	Emma Floyd	St.w.	231	1863	Nov 28 1870	Snagged	Newburg, Ind.
459	Emma Graham	St.w.	162	1855	1872	Ice	Antiquity, Ohio.
460	Emma Harmon	St.w.	124	1854	Feb 7 1857	Ice	Peoria, Ill.
461	Emma L. Nielsen	Sch.	90	1883	Jun 26 1911	Collided	With st.s. WYANDOTTE. Pointe Aux Barques, Mich.
462	Empire	St.p.	90	1848	Nov 15 1853	Stranded	Monroe, Mich.
463	Empire	St.s.	70	1864	Jan 6 1869	Collided	Wolf Island, below Cairo, Ill.

NO.	NAME OF VESSEL	RIG	TONS	BUILT	DATE		CAUSE	PLACE AND COMMENT
464	Empire	St.p.	-	-	Oct 26	1870	Foundered	Off Long Point, Ontario.
465	Empress	St.w.	136	1849	Jun 20	1853	Snagged	Below Cincinnati, Ohio.
466	Enterprise	St.p.	111	1831	Mar 19	1833	Snagged	Grafton, Ill.
467	Envoy	St.w.	178	1852	Jul 21	1858	Collided	With MILWAUKEE. Coon Slough, Wisc.
468	Equality	St.w.	90	1860	May 11	1861	Snagged	Golconda, Ill.
469	Equator	St.w.	61	1853	Apr	1858	Unknown	Lake St. Croix, Wisc.
470	Equator	St.s.	620	1857	Nov 17	1869	Stranded	North Manitou Island, Mich.
471	Erie	St.p.	-	-	Aug 9	1841	Burned	Off Silver Creek, Lake Erie. 200 lives lost.
472	Erie	St.p.	149	1836	Mar 9	1844	Burned	Detroit, Mich.
473	Erie	Drg.	186	1900	Jun 2	1935	Burned	Off Duluth, Minn.
474	Essex	St.p.	158	1828	Oct 13	1829	Stranded	Grand Chain, Ill.
475	Eugene	Sch.	-	-	Oct 22	1890	Unknown	Off Port Austin Reef, Mich.
476	Euphrates	St.w.	136	1848	Oct 30	1850	Stranded	New Albany, Ind.
477	Euphrates	St.s.	587	1856	May	1862	Stranded	Sandusky, Ohio.
478	Evergreen City	St.s.	624	1856	Nov 18	1871	Stranded	Long Point, Ontario., 7.5 miles west of light.
479	Exile	Sch.	387	1867	Nov 26	1916	Foundered	7 miles south of Sturgeon Point, Lake Huron.
480	Explorer	Sch.	-	-		1867	Unknown	Lake Huron.
481	Export	St.p.	86	1841	Jun 15	1841	Collided	Rising Sun, Ind.
482	Ezra Porter	St.p.	451	1866	Aug 6	1868	Burned	Cincinnati, Ohio.
483	F.A. Meyer	St.s.	1,264	1888	Dec 18	1909	Foundered	22 miles east of Southeast Shoals, Lake Erie.
484	F.H. Prince	St.s.	2,047	1890	Aug 8	1911	Burned	Kelleys Island, Ohio. Length 240'.
485	F.J. King	Sch.	-	-	Sep 15	1886	Foundered	5 miles north of Cana Island Light, Wisc.
486	Fair Play	St.p.	135	1839	Nov 16	1842	Snagged	New Richmond, Ohio. 3 lives lost.
487	Fairport	St.p.	259	1838	Oct 12	1844	Burned	Newport, Mich.
488	Falcon	St.s.	663	1853	Oct 18	1856	Burned	Chicago, Ill.
489	Falcon	St.s.	865	1881	Nov 7	1909	Stranded	South Fox Island, Mich.
490	Fannie Fisk	St.p.	79	1856	Jul 16	1865	Burned	Cairo, Ill.
491	Fanny Fern	St.w.	190	1853	Jan 20	1858	Exploded	Lawrenceburg, Ind. 20 lives lost.
492	Fanny Harris	St.w.	159	1855	Dec 27	1862	Ice	Hastings, Minn.
493	Farmer	St.p.	180	1839	Nov 20	1842	Collided	With unknown object. Rosewood, Ind. 3 lives lost.
494	Farmer	St.p.	198	1848	Sep 19	1853	Snagged	Cairo, Ill. 3 lives lost.
495	Faustin	St.s.	256	1882	Sep 4	1912	Foundered	Detroit River.
496	Favourite	Sch.	-	-		1852	Wrecked	Mouth of Raisin River, into Lake Erie. Located off Monroe, Wisc.
497	Favorite	St.s.	409	1864	Jan 9	1907	Burned	St. Ignace, Mich.
498	Felix Grundy	St.p.	166	1845	Apr 20	1847	Snagged	Grand Chain, Ill.
499	Fenton	Sch.	-	-	Sep 29	1872	Unknown	Off Long Point, Ontario.
500	Ferdinand Schesinger	St.s.	2,607	1891	May 26	1919	Foundered	15 miles southeast of Passage Island, Lake Superior.
501	Fintry	St.s.	590	1853	Nov 8	1855	Exploded	Port Stanley, Ontario. 8 lives lost. Also known as "Finley".
502	Fleetwood	St.p.	212	1850	Feb 21	1852	Snagged	25 miles below Terre Haute, Ind.
503	Floating Palace	Brg.	215	1901	Apr 30	1917	Foundered	Newburg, Ind.
504	Floating Theatre	Brg.	192	1903	Jan 5	1918	Ice	Mount Vernon, Ind.
505	Flora	St.p.	561	1875	Dec 2	1912	Burned	Chicago, Ill. 2 lives lost.
506	Flora M. Hill	St.s.	623	1874	Mar 11	1912	Ice	Chicago, Ill. Steel vessel.
507	Florence Lister	Bark	-	-	Oct 1	1809	Foundered	1 mile west of Manistee, Mich.
508	Florida	Sch.	-	-	Sep	1868	Unknown	Long Point, Ontario.
509	Florida	St.p.	68	1914	Jul 8	1929	Foundered	Cairo, Ill.
510	Floyd H. Blaske	St.w.	98	1931	Oct 26	1940	Burned	Alton, Ill.
511	Forest City	St.s.	515	1851	Sep 18	1855	Collided	With sch. ASIA. Sturgeon Bay, Mich.

NO.	NAME OF VESSEL	RIG	TONS	BUILT	DATE	CAUSE	PLACE AND COMMENT
512	Forest City	St.p.	-	-	Apr 5 1856	Burned	Off Port Stanley, Ontario, Lake Erie.
513	Forest City	St.s.	-	-	Jun 5 1904	Unknown	North of Bears Rump Island, Ontario.
514	Forest Queen	St.s.	467	1852	Nov 13 1869	Ice	Clay Banks, Wisc.
515	Forester	St.w.	187	1854	Oct 22 1854	Burned	New Richmond, Ohio. 3 lives lost.
516	Fortune	St.s.	-	-	1884	Stranded	Off Long Point, Ontario.
517	Fox	St.p.	102	1851	Oct 1863	Burned	Newport, Mich.
518	Frances	Ga.y.	114	1910	Sep 1 1922	Burned	Monroe Piers, Mich. Steel vessel.
519	Frances Palms	Sch.	-	-	Nov 3 1874	Burned	Off Long Point, Ontario.
520	Francis Hinton	St.s.	397	1889	Nov 16 1909	Foundered	Manitowic, Wisc.
521	Francis P. Richie	Ga.s.	86	1888	Aug 29 1931	Stranded	Southampton, Ontario.
522	Francis Widlar	St.s.	4,682	1904	Nov 12 1920	Foundered	Pan Cake Shoals, Lake Superior. Steel vessel.
523	Frank E. Vigor	St.s.	4,067	1896	Apr 27 1944	Stranded	With st.s. PHILLIP MINCH. Lake Erie. Steel vessel.
524	Frank H. Goodyear	St.s.	4,815	1902	May 23 1910	Collided	With st.s. JAMES B, WOOD. Lake Huron. Freighter. Steel vessel. 17 lives lost.
525	Frank L. Vance	St.s.	1,952	1887	Oct 4 1910	Collided	25 miles southwest of Ludington, Mich.
526	Frank O'Connor	St.s.	2,340	1892	Oct 2 1919	Burned	Off Cana Island, Wisc.
527	Frank Perew	Sch.	-	-	Oct 25 1891	Burned	Mouth of Whitefish Bay, Mich. Coal cargo.
528	Frank Steel	St.p.	136	1857	Jun 2 1864	Foundered	La Crosse, Wisc. 2 lives lost.
529	Franklin	Sch.	-	-	1820	Exploded	Northeast of Fairport, Ohio.
530	Fred Hall	St.w.	88	1912	Dec 23 1932	Unknown	Madison, Ind.
531	Fred Pabst	St.s.	2,430	1890	Oct 11 1907	Burned	With st.s. LAKE SHORE. St. Clair River, Mich.
532	Fred Swain	St.p.	124	1900	Aug 20 1909	Collided	Peoria, Ill.
533	Free State	St.s.	768	1856	Sep 30 1871	Burned	Gray's Reef, Lake Michigan.
534	Freedom	Brg.	447	1917	Nov 4 1926	Burned	Erie, Pa.
535	Freighter	St.w.	93	1855	Jan 28 1860	Foundered	Big Stone Lake, Minn.
536	Frontenac	St.s.	626	1868	Jul 17 1908	Stranded	Lorain, Ohio.
537	Fulton	Sch.	256	1854	Jul 7 1908	Burned	Toledo, Ohio.
538	G.H. Breymann	St.s.	60	1903	Jun 8 1926	Foundered	Toledo, Ohio.
539	G.H. Wilson	St.w.	99	1857	Nov 27 1879	Burned	La Crosse, Wisc.
540	G.L. 35	Scow	339	1907	Mar 5 1927	Ice	With U.S.C. and G.S. st.s. LYDONIA. Lemong, Ill.
541	G.L. 37	Scow	242	1908	Oct 9 1913	Collided	At Soo Ste. Marie, Mich.
542	G.P. Griffin	St.s.	-	-	Jun 18 1896	Foundered	North of Willoughby, Ohio. Large quantity of copper valued at $250,000.
543	G.P. Griffith	St.p.	587	1848	Jun 17 1850	Unknown	North of Willoughby, Ohio. 286 lives lost.
544	G.W. McBride	St.w.	235	1932	Feb 22 1942	Burned	Mentor, Ohio.
545	Galatea	Sch.	610	1882	Oct 20 1905	Stranded	Grand Marais, Mich.
546	Galena	St.p.	297	1854	Jul 1 1858	Burned	Red Wing, Minn. 7 lives lost.
547	Galena	St.p.	690	1857	Sep 25 1872	Burned	Northport, Mich.
548	Garden City	St.p.	657	1853	May 16 1854	Stranded	Detour, Mich.
549	Gazelle	St.p.	422	1858	Sep 8 1860	Stranded	Eagle Harbor, Mich.
550	General	St.s.	132	1900	Nov 30 1910	Collided	With Canadian st.s. ATHABASCA. St. Marys River, Mich. 3 lives lost.
551	General	St.s.	143	1900	Apr 7 1930	Burned	Detour, Mich.
552	General Buell	St.p.	515	1862	Dec 24 1872	Ice	Madison, Ind.
553	General Burnside	St.p.	114	1863	Jun 10 1887	Burned	Sturgeon Bay, Wisc.
554	General Jesup	St.p.	374	1847	Dec 10 1849	Snagged	Chester, Ill.
555	General Porter	St.p.	342	1834	Sep 27 1847	Stranded	Buffalo, N.Y. Rig changed to screw in 1843.
556	General Scott	St.p.	200	1839	Oct 11 1848	Collided	Lake St. Clair, Mich.
557	General Taylor	St.s.	462	1848	Oct 1862	Stranded	Sleeping Bear, Mich.
558	General Vance	St.p.	75	1838	Jun 25 1844	Exploded	Windsor, Ontario, Canada. 9 lives lost.
559	Genevieve Ryan	Brg.	418	1917	Oct 17 1936	Foundered	Between Erie, Pa., and Ashtabula, Ohio. All life (1) lost.

NO.	NAME OF VESSEL	RIG	TONS	BUILT	DATE	CAUSE	PLACE AND COMMENT
560	Geo. B. Owen	Sch.	744	1893	Oct 1 1926	Foundered	Detroit River, Mich.
561	George C. Finney	Sch.	-	-	Oct 22 1891	Foundered	Off Long Point, Ontario, Lake Erie.
562	Geo. F. Bass	C.bt.	125	1910	Nov 7 1922	Collided	With STANDARD OIL barge. West of Rochester, N.Y.
563	Geo. G. Houghton	Sch.	332	1873	Sep 10 1907	Foundered	North-northwest of Bar Point Light, Mich.
564	Geo. Gardner	St.p.	72	1903	Apr 7 1909	Burned	Cairo, Ill.
565	George H. Van Vleck	St.s.	1,020	1875	Aug 3 1914	Burned	Duluth Harbor, Minn.
566	George Herbert	Scow	362	-	Nov 28 1905	Stranded	Two Islands, Minn. 3 lives lost.
567	Geo. J. Whelan	St.s.	1,293	1910	Jul 29 1930	Foundered	Erie, Pa. Steel vessel. 15 lives lost (21).
568	George King	St.s.	532	1874	Sep 20 1926	Burned	Buffalo, N.Y.
569	George M. Case	Sch.	-	-	Oct 14 1886	Foundered	Off Long Point, Ontario.
570	George M. Cox	St.s.	1,762	1901	May 27 1933	Stranded	Rock of Ages Light, Lake Superior. Steel vessel.
571	George M. Frost	St.p.	-	-	Sep 3 1879	Burned	In Erie Harbor, Pa.
572	George M. Humphrey	St.s.	8,004	1927	Jun 15 1943	Collided	With st.s. D.M. CLEMSON. In Straits of Mackinaw, Mich. Steel vessel.
573	George Nester	Sch.	790	1887	Apr 30 1909	Stranded	Huron Island, Mich. All lives (7) lost.
574	George Presley	St.s.	2,164	1889	Jul 26 1905	Burned	Washington Island, Green Bay, Wisc.
575	George Rogers IV	St.s.	4,010	1905	Mar 5 1923	Burned	Off Buffalo, N.Y. Steel vessel.
576	George S. Dodge	St.s.	61	1864	Sep 28 1870	Exploded	Oswego, N.Y.
577	George S. Smith	Sch.	577	1915	Nov 15 1919	Stranded	Pointe des Monts, Quebec, Canada.
578	George Sherman	St.p.	-	-	Oct 22 1887	Stranded	North of Presque Isle Harbor, Mich.
579	George Spencer	St.s.	1,360	1884	Nov 28 1905	Stranded	Thomasville, Minn.
580	George Stone	St.s.	1,841	1893	Oct 13 1909	Stranded	Grubb Reef, near Point Pelee, Ontario. 6 lives lost.
581	George W. Roby	Sch.	1,933	1899	Sep 19 1905	Burned	Lime Kiln Crossing, Detroit River, Mich.
582	George Washington	St.p.	605	1833	Oct 9 1833	Stranded	Long Point, Ontario. 50 lives lost.
583	Georgetown	St.p.	395	1850	Oct 17 1853	Snagged	Grand Tower, Ill.
584	Gerald Klein	St.w.	52	1910	Sep 20 1934	Burned	Manchester, Ohio.
585	German Fe	St.s.	-	-	Nov 24 1905	Stranded	Glencoe, Ill.
586	Germantown	St.p.	193	1846	Aug 25 1849	Burned	Shawneetown, Ill.
587	Gertrude Weightman	Brg.	254	1919	Nov 7 1941	Foundered	Buffalo, N.Y.
588	Gilbert W. Benedict	Brg.	447	1918	Oct 22 1930	Burned	Buffalo, N.Y.
589	Gipsy	St.w.	132	1855	Feb 7 1857	Ice	Cincinnati, Ohio.
590	Glad Tidings	Sch.	-	-	Oct 26 1870	Wrecked	On Long Point, Ontario.
591	Gladiator	St.p.	425	1857	Aug 14 1864	Stranded	Willard, Ill.
592	Glendy Burke	St.p.	425	1851	May 24 1855	Snagged	Bird Island, Cairo, Ill.
593	Glenora	Sch.	-	-	Nov 19 1887	Unknown	In Quinte Bay, off east end of Edwards Point, Ontario.
594	Globe	St.p.	1,223	1848	Nov 8 1860	Exploded	Chicago, Ill. 15 lives lost.
595	Globe	St.s.	313	1846	Aug 12 1865	Burned	Saginaw Bay, Mich.
596	Golden Eagle	St.w.	193	1904	May 18 1947	Stranded	At Mile 78, upper Mississippi River, near Grand Tower, Ill.
597	Golden Gate	St.p.	770	1852	Nov 29 1856	Burned	Erie, Pa. 1 life lost.
598	Golden West	Sch.	-	-	Oct 21 1884	Stranded	Southern portion of Snake Island, Ontario.
599	Goliath	St.s.	279	1846	Nov 3 1851	Stranded	Thunder Bay, Mich.
600	Goshawk	Sch.	501	1866	Jun 16 1920	Foundered	Off Tawas Point, Mich.
601	Goudreau	St.s.	2,298	1889	Nov 23 1917	Stranded	Lyal Island, Ontario, Canada.
602	Governor Breathitt	St.p.	125	1844	Jul 24 1849	Snagged	New Richmond, Ohio.
603	Governor Cushman	St.s.	384	1857	May 1 1868	Exploded	Buffalo, N.Y. 11 lives lost.
604	Governor Marcy	St.p.	161	1834	Jun 4 1847	Stranded	Dunkirk, N.Y.
605	Gov. Smith	St.s.	2,044	1889	Aug 19 1906	Collided	With st.s. URANUS. Off Point aux Barques, Mich.
606	Grace Holland	Sch.	629	1880	Jul 19 1918	Foundered	Wheeler Reef, Lake Huron.
607	Grace Whitney	Sch.	289	1866	Jul 30 1910	Collided	With st.s. OGDENSBURG. Bar Point, Mich. 2 lives lost.

NO.	NAME OF VESSEL	RIG	TONS	BUILT	DATE		CAUSE	PLACE AND COMMENT
608	Grand Tower	St.p.	569	1853	Nov 25	1854	Stranded	Cairo, Ill.
609	Granite State	St.s.	351	1852	Sep 3	1881	Stranded	Clay Banks, Wisc.
610	Gravel Gertie	Ol.w.	143	1926	Dec 2	1954	Foundered	At Mile 160.8, Illionois River. Steel vessel.
611	Grecian	St.s.	2,348	1891	Jun 15	1906	Foundered	Lake Huron. Freighter. Steel vessel.
612	Greenland	St.p.	294	1903	Jan 31	1918	Ice	Cincinnati, Ohio, Ohio River.
613	Greenville	St.w.	105	1857	Jun 6	1861	Snagged	Wabash River, Ind.
614	Greenwood	St.p.	264	1898	Nov 17	1925	Collided	With st.w. CHRIS. GREENE. Cincinnati, Ohio.
615	Grey Eagle	St.p.	382	1857	May 9	1861	Collided	With Bridge. Rock Island, Ill.
616	Grey Fox	St.w.	70	1857	Sep	1863	Snagged	Cairo, Ill.
617	Griffin	Sloop	75	–	Aug 7	1679	Foundered	Mississag Strait, Ontario. Belived to be first sailing vessel to traverse the Great Lakes. Of great value historically.
618	Griffith	St.p.	–	–	Jun 17	1850	Burned	Lake Erie. 300 lives lost.
619	Guyandotte	St.p.	90	1831	Apr 30	1833	Snagged	New Richmond, Ohio.
620	H.B. Hawgood	Steamer	–	–	Nov 12	1913	Stranded	On Corsica Shoal, north of Point Edward, Ontario.
621	H.B. Hulings	St.p.	53	1891	Apr 16	1923	Burned	Pipe Creek, Ohio.
622	H.C. Patter	Sch.	–	–	Nov 21	1887	Unknown	North of Pointe Aux Barques, Mich.
623	H.D. Moore	Sch.	143	1874	Sep 10	1907	Stranded	South Manitou Island, Mich.
624	H.D. Tupper	C.bt.	116	1881	Oct	1910	Collided	With unknown vessel. Chambly, Quebec.
625	H.E. Runnels	St.s.	889	1893	Nov 14	1919	Stranded	Grand Marias, Mich.
626	H. Houghton	St.s.	210	1889	Nov 20	1926	Burned	Hopps Point, Mich.
627	H.P. Smith	St.s.	55	1864	May 14	1872	Burned	Saginaw, Mich.
628	H.M. Score	Sch.	–	–	Nov	1891	Foundered	On Washington Island, Wisc.
629	H.S. Pickands	St.s.	625	1884	Dec 21	1912	Burned	Fairport, Ohio.
630	H.T. No.458	Brg.	399	1941	Dec 20	1951	Collided	While moored to bank of Chicago Sanitary Canal, Illinois Waterway, Mile 295.5.
631	H.T. Yeatman	St.w.	165	1852	Apr 10	1857	Stranded	Hastings, Minn.
632	Harmonia	St.w.	511	1856	Nov 10	1860	Snagged	Warsaw, Ill.
633	Harold	Sch.	718	1891	Nov 18	1915	Burned	Spragge, Ontario.
634	Harriet B	Brg.	2,340	1895	May 3	1922	Collided	With st.s. QUINCY A. SHAW. Two Harbors, Minn.
635	Harriette B.K.	Ol.s.	69	1918	May 30	1931	Burned	St. James Island, Mich.
636	Harvey Bissell	Sch.	496	1866	Nov 28	1905	Foundered	Thunder Bay, Mich.
637	Hattie Brown	Ga.p.	70	1884	Jan 30	1918	Ice	Cincinnati, Ohio.
638	Hattie Estelle	Sch.	–	–	Nov 16	1897	Foundered	Entrance to Manistee Harbor, Mich.
639	Hattie Wells	Sch.	376	1867	Oct 12	1906	Burned	Marysville, Mich., St. Clair River.
640	Hattie Wells	Sch.	376	1867	Nov 6	1912	Foundered	Lake Michigan.
641	Havana	St.w.	236	1863	Aug 16	1869	Burned	North Bend, Ohio.
642	Havana	Sch.	–	–	Oct 11	1887	Foundered	South of Beaver Island, Mich.
643	Hazel R. Knight	Brg.	236	1919	Nov 17	1927	Collided	With st.p. F.W. SARGENT. Buffalo, N.Y.
644	Helen C	St.s.	622	1874	Oct 14	1922	Foundered	Thunder Bay, Lake Huron.
645	Helen Mar	St.p.	88	1832	Jun 1	1836	Exploded	Peoria, Ill. 2 lives lost.
646	Helen Strong	St.p.	217	1845	Dec 4	1845	Stranded	Monroe, Mich.
647	Helen Taylor	St.s.	52	1894	Jan 1	1930	Foundered	Michigan City, Ind.
648	Helena	St.s.	2,083	1888	Sep 17	1918	Stranded	Sunken Chicken Reef, Lake Erie.
649	Henry A. Kent	St.s.	442	1850	May 19	1854	Burned	Off Port Colborne, Ontario.
650	Henry B. Martin	C.bt.	123	1911	Oct 8	1930	Stranded	Champlain, Quebec.
651	Henry B. Smith	St.s.	6,631	1906	Nov 9	1913	Foundered	Lake Superior. Freighter. Steel vessel. All lives (26) lost. Exact position is not known. Vessel lost during storm.
652	Henry Clay	St.s.	221	1849	Oct 23	1851	Foundered	Long Point, Ontario. 28 lives lost.
653	Henry Cort	St.s.	2,394	1892	May 20	1935	Stranded	Muskegon, Mich. Freighter. Steel vessel.

NO.	NAME OF VESSEL	RIG	TONS	BUILT	DATE	CAUSE	PLACE AND COMMENT
654	Henry M. Shreve	St.p.	567	1867	Nov 23 1872	Burned	Chester, Ill.
655	Henry M. Stanley	St.p.	293	1890	Sep 5 1907	Collided	With U.S. Engineer dredge OSWEGO. Gallipolis, Ohio, Ohio River.
656	Henry Steinbrenner	St.s.	4,719	1901	Dec 5 1909	Collided	With st.s. HARRY A. BERWIND. Mud Lake, St. Marys River, Mich. Freighter. Steel.
657	Henry Steinbrenner	St.s.	4,345	1901	May 11 1953	Foundered	In Lake Superior, 15 miles due south of Isle Royal Light. Freighter. Steel vessel.
658	Hercules	Sch.	-	-	Jul 7 1886	Foundered	North Manitou Island, Mich.
659	Hercules	Drg.	559	1904	Dec 23 1932	Foundered	Off Tawas Light, Mich.
660	Herman H. Hettler	St.s.	789	1890	Nov 23 1926	Stranded	Grand Island, Lake Superior.
661	Hero	St.p.	126	1820	Feb 20 1822	Stranded	Golconda, Ill. Also known as "Bezaleel Wells".
662	Hero	Sch.	-	-	Sep 17 1848	Foundered	On Long Point, Ontario.
663	Hibernia	St.w.	179	1856	Jan 1 1858	Burned	Martins Ferry, Ohio.
664	Hibou	St.s.	-	-	Nov 21 1936	Stranded	Mouth of Pottawatomi River, Ontario.
665	Hickory Stick	Drg.	260	1944	Nov 29 1958	Storm	On Lake Erie, approximately due north of Avon Point, Ohio.
666	Higginson Mfg. Co. 4	St.s.	148	1905	Jun 4 1941	Burned	Buffalo, N.Y.
667	Highland Chief	St.w.	342	1864	Aug 18 1864	Collided	With MAJOR ANDERSON. Vevay, Ind. 5 lives lost.
668	Highlander	St.w.	126	1847	Apr 1850	Snagged	Clinton, Ind.
669	Hippocampus	St.s.	152	1867	Sep 7 1868	Stranded	St. Joseph, Mich. 26 lives lost.
670	Hiram Powers	St.p.	225	1848	May 7 1853	Burned	Wabash River, Ind.
671	Hoboken	Sch.	299	1868	Aug 28 1920	Foundered	Brockville, Ontario, Canada.
672	Honduras	St.p.	296	1852	Jan 25 1855	Snagged	Hat Island, Chester, Ill.
673	Horace H. Bader	Sc.b.	-	-	Jun 11 1903	Foundered	1 mile north of Marblehead Lighthouse, Ohio.
674	Hornet	St.p.	-	-	Jun 2 1832	Capsized	Ohio River. 20 lives lost.
675	Howard	St.s.	195	1864	Jun 13 1921	Stranded	Victoria Isle, Lake Ontario.
676	Howard M. Hanna, Jr.	St.s.	5,905	1908	Nov 9 1913	Stranded	Port Austin Reef, Lake Huron. Freighter. Steel vessel.
677	Hudson	St.p.	741	1886	Feb 5 1905	Burned	Cincinnati, Ohio.
678	Humko	Ol.s.	128	1946	Jul 22 1956	Burned	In Lake Michigan, 6 miles off Two Rivers Point.
679	Hunter Willis	Brg.	83	1878	Oct 22 1931	Burned	Erie, Pa.
680	Huron	St.s.	-	-	1965	Unknown	Lake Erie, Detroit River entrance, 002°, 9,600' from East Outer Channel Light. Used as derrick barge by U.S. Army Corps of Engineers. Length 100'.
681	Huron City	St.s.	368	1867	Sep 21 1917	Foundered	Sandwich, Ontario, Canada.
682	Hydro	St.s.	-	-	Sep 12 1939	Unknown	Cleveland Harbor, Cleveland, Ohio.
683	Hydrus	St.s.	4,714	1903	Nov 9 1913	Foundered	Lake Huron. Freighter. Steel vessel. All lives (24) lost. Reported to be in area of Lexington, Mich.
684	I.N. Foster	Sch.	-	-	Aug 7 1887	Foundered	On Washington Island, Wisc.
685	I.W. Nichols	St.s.	2,624	1894	Nov 27 1913	Stranded	Lake Huron. Steel vessel.
686	Iatan	St.p.	172	1840	1844	Stranded	Cairo, Ill.
687	Ida	Sch.	169	1867	Sep 29 1908	Capsized	Frankfort, Mich.
688	Ida Keith	Sch.	489	1873	Jan 16 1922	Burned	Sandusky Bay, Ohio.
689	Idaho	St.s.	1,110	1901	Nov 5 1897	Foundered	7 miles southeast of Old Cut Light, Long Point, Ontario.
690	Illinois	St.w.	168	1901	Sep 14 1930	Burned	Alton, Ill.
691	Importer	St.p.	199	1842	Jun 11 1845	Burned	Cincinnati, Ohio.
692	Independence	Sch.	-	-	Oct 1818	Foundered	Mouth of Black River, near Lorain, Ohio. All lives lost.
693	Independence	St.s.	261	1843	Nov 21 1853	Exploded	St. Marys River, Mich. 4 lives lost. This was first steamer to enter service on Lake Superior.
694	Indiana	St.p.	534	1842	1848	Burned	Conneaut, Ohio.
695	Industry	Brg.	203	1905	Oct 6 1953	Foundered	In Lansing Shoals, Lake Michigan, Mich. Steel vessel.
696	Interlaken	Brg.	567	1893	Oct 1 1934	Stranded	White Lake Harbor, Mich.
697	International	St.p.	1,121	1857	Sep 20 1874	Burned	Detroit River.
698	International	St.s.	130	1889	Nov 2 1913	Burned	White City, Lake Superior, Mich.

NO.	NAME OF VESSEL	RIG	TONS	BUILT	DATE	CAUSE	PLACE AND COMMENT
699	Ione	St.p.	56	1853	Jun 6 1854	Snagged	Minnesota River, Minn.
700	Iosco	St.s.	2,051	1891	Sep 2 1905	Foundered	Off Huron Island, Lake Superior. All lives (19) lost.
701	Iowa	St.p.	454	1848	Mar 17 1856	Ice	Marietta, Ohio.
702	Iowa	St.s.	1,157	1896	Feb 4 1915	Foundered	3 miles east by northeast of Chicago, Ill.
703	Ira H. Owen	St.s.	1,753	1887	Nov 28 1905	Foundered	Off Apostles Island, Lake Superior. Steel vessel. 12 lives lost.
704	Irene	St.w.	124	1850	Feb 9 1857	Snagged	Portsmouth, Ohio.
705	Iris	Sch.	62	1897	Mar 1913	Stranded	Jackson Harbor, Wisc.
706	Irma L. Wheeler	St.s.	51	1877	Apr 1 1905	Burned	Pine Lake, Mich.
707	Iron Age	St.s.	1,114	1880	Jun 4 1909	Burned	Bar Point, Ontario.
708	Iron City	Sch.	648	1874	May 3 1913	Collided	With st.s. THOS. F. COLE, St. Claire River, Mich.
709	Ironsides	St.s.	937	1864	Sep 15 1873	Foundered	3 miles off Grand Haven, Mich.
710	Ironton	St.p.	70	1909	Jan 28 1918	Ice	Ironton, Ohio.
711	Isaac M. Mason	St.p.	114	1893	Mar 4 1913	Burned	Cooks Ferry, Ohio River.
712	Isaac M. Scott	St.s.	6,372	1909	Nov 9 1913	Foundered	Lake Huron. Steel vessel. All lives (28) lost. Has been reported in an area west of Point Elgin, Ontario.
713	Isaac Staples	St.p.	147	1878	Dec 2 1907	Burned	Wabasha, Minn., Mississippi River.
714	Isabella (Can.)	Sch.	-	-	Aug 1867	Unknown	Off Long Point, Ontario.
715	Isabella J. Boyce	St.s.	368	1889	Jun 16 1917	Burned	Off Middle Bass Island, Lake Erie.
716	Island Belle	St.s.	121	1879	Nov 20 1930	Burned	Buffalo, N.Y.
717	Island Maid	St.w.	363	1909	Dec 20 1932	Burned	Madison, Ind.
718	Island Queen	St.p.	1,446	1896	Nov 4 1922	Burned	Cincinnati, Ohio.
719	Isolde	Brg.	2,140	1891	May 1 1933	Stranded	Erie, Pa.
720	Itasca	St.p.	349	1857	Dec 27 1868	Burned	La Crosse, Wisc.
721	Ivanhoe	St.p.	298	1848	Nov 9 1849	Burned	Cincinnati, Ohio.
722	Iver Lawson	Sch.	149	1869	Oct 19 1905	Stranded	Horse Shoe Bay, Wisc.
723	J.A. Garfield	Sch.	-	-	Oct 1887	Foundered	Pelee Island, Ontario.
724	J.B. Carson	St.w.	185	1855	Feb 14 1859	Stranded	Alton, Ill.
725	J. Barber	St.s.	263	1856	Jul 19 1871	Burned	Michigan City, Ind. 2 lives lost.
726	J.B. Comstock	Sch.	325	1891	Oct 8 1906	Stranded	Duck Island, Lake Huron.
727	J.C. Daun	Sch.	-	-	Nov 1847	Unknown	Off Conneaut, Ohio.
728	J.C. Hill	Sch.	-	-	Nov 19 1869	Foundered	Off Long Point, Ontario.
729	J.D. Marshall	St.s.	531	1891	Jun 11 1911	Foundered	20 miles east of Gary, Ind. 4 lives lost.
730	J.D. Sawyer	Sch.	-	-	Oct 20 1891	Foundered	4 miles northeast of Lorain, Ohio.
731	J. Duvall	Sch.	131	1874	Dec 5 1905	Collided	With steamer JAMES B. COLGATE. Farsons Island, Ontario.
732	J.F. Johnson	St.s.	94	1866	Nov 25 1891	Stranded	South Haven, Mich.
733	J.H. Stevens	Ga.s.	77	1925	Jun 10 1927	Burned	Presque Isle, Mich.
734	J.J. Carroll	Ol.s.	548	1881	Nov 7 1929	Burned	Pelee Island, Ontario.
735	J.L. Crane	Sch.	71	1875	Nov 5 1925	Foundered	Crisp Point, Whitefish Bay, Mich. All lives (7) lost.
736	J.M. Jenks	St.p.	518	1867	Nov 12 1913	Stranded	North of Midland, Ontario, Georgian Bay, Lake Huron.
737	J.M. Spaulding	Sch.	113	1900	Nov 28 1905	Stranded	Fort Gratiot, Mich.
738	J.N. McCullough	St.p.	1,806	1913	Nov 17 1868	Collided	With TIGER. Madison, Ind. 3 lives lost.
739	J.O. Cole	St.p.	68	1911	Feb 8 1918	Ice	Elizabethtown, Ill.
740	J. Oswald Boyd	St.s.	82	1898	Nov 11 1936	Stranded	Simmons Reef, Straits of Mackinaw, Mich.
741	J.R. Ware	St.p.	312	1851	Jan 29 1918	Ice	Manchester Island, Ohio.
742	J.S. Crouse	St.s.	-	-	Nov 15 1919	Burned	Glen Haven, Mich.
743	J.W. Brooks	St.s.	227	1890	Nov 4 1856	Foundered	Duck Light, Ontario. 50 lives lost.
744	J.W. McGrath (Can.)	Sch.			Oct 28 1878	Foundered	East of light on Long Point, Ontario.
745	J.W. Van Sant	St.p.			Dec 2 1907	Burned	Wabasha, Minn., Mississippi River.

NO.	NAME OF VESSEL	RIG	TONS	BUILT	DATE		CAUSE	PLACE AND COMMENT
746	J. Wade	Sch.	-	-		1883	Foundered	Off Long Point, Ontario.
747	Jacob Bertschy	St.s.	467	1867	Sep 3	1879	Stranded	Point Aux Barques, Mich.
748	Jacob D. Early	St.p.	348	1853	Apr 29	1858	Burned	Alton, Ill.
749	Jacob Traber	St.w.	238	1856	May 8	1859	Burned	Cincinnati, Ohio.
750	James B. Colgate	St.s.	1,713	1892	Oct 20	1916	Foundered	About 25 miles east of Southeast Shoal, Lake Erie. Freighter. Steel vessel. 24 lives lost (25). Coal cargo.
751	James Carruthers	St.s.	-	-	Nov 10	1913	Unknown	Off Goderich, Ontario, Lake Huron.
752	James Dempsey	St.s.	847	1883	Dec 10	1922	Burned	Manistee, Mich.
753	James E. Eagle	St.s.	194	1860	Aug 8	1869	Burned	Saginaw Bay, Mich.
754	James F. Cahill	Brg.	396	1914	Sep 12	1928	Burned	Buffalo, N.Y.
755	James Fisk, Jr.	St.s.	914	1870	Nov 14	1906	Burned	St. Clair River, Mich.
756	James G. Worts (Can.)	Sch.	-	-	Nov 5	1895	Stranded	Western part of Devil Island, Ontario.
757	James Gayley	St.s.	4,777	1902	Aug 12	1912	Collided	With st.s. RENSSELAER. Lake Superior. Steel vessel.
758	James H. Hall	Ga.s.	100	1885	Nov 7	1916	Stranded	Thunder Bay River, Mich.
759	Jas. H. Pellett	Brg.	346	1905	Jul 2	1943	Foundered	Cleveland, Ohio. Steel vessel.
760	James H. Reed	St.s.	5,265	1903	Apr 27	1944	Collided	In Lake Erie, north of Ashtabula, Ohio. Steel vessel.
761	James Millinger	St.p.	285	1849	Jun 14	1853	Burned	Cincinnati, Ohio.
762	James Mowatt	Sch.	523	1884	Oct 10	1919	Foundered	Alpena, Mich.
763	James P. Farnum	St.p.	-	-	Jul	1889	Foundered	South of South Haven, Mich.
764	James Park	St.w.	258	1853	May 12	1856	Burned	Thebes, Ill.
765	James Paul	St.p.	70	1854	Dec 9	1855	Stranded	Palestine, Ill.
766	James Pitcher	St.p.	116	1843	Sep 10	1846	Snagged	Blue River, Ind. 1 life lost.
767	James R. Gilmore	St.w.	205	1863	Sep 18	1866	Snagged	Mound City, Ill.
768	James Robb	St.p.	593	1852	Feb 17	1855	Snagged	Grand Tower, Ill.
769	James Scott (Can.)	Sch.	-	-	Nov	1882	Foundered	Off Long Point, Ontario.
770	James Watt	St.w.	78	1852	Feb 7	1857	Ice	Cincinnati, Ohio.
771	James Wood	St.s.	286	1846	Sep 12	1852	Stranded	Ashtabula, Ohio.
772	Jane	St.s.	69	1923	May 30	1927	Foundered	Arcadia, Mich. Steel vessel.
773	Jay Gould	St.s.	840	1869	Jun 17	1918	Foundered	Off Southeast Shoal Light Vessel, Ontario, Canada.
774	Jennie	Ga.s.	70	1891	May 17	1921	Burned	Lake St. Clair, Mich.
775	Jennie Hopkins	St.w.	212	1863	Feb 27	1867	Burned	Evansville, Ind.
776	Jennie P. King	Sch.	-	-		1866	Unknown	Off Long Point, Ontario.
777	Jerry Petrie	Brg.	462	1916	Nov 15	1925	Stranded	Buffalo, N.Y. All lives (2) lost.
778	Jersey City	St.s.	633	1855	Nov 23	1860	Stranded	Long Point, Ontario. 17 lives lost.
779	Jessie Anderson	Sch.	-	-	Nov 28	1871	Foundered	10 miles southeast of Cut Light, Long Point, Ontario, Lake Erie.
780	Jessie Scarth	Sch.	-	-	Oct	1887	Stranded	East of North Manitou Island, Mich.
781	Jewell	St.p.	81	1906	Jan 5	1918	Ice	Mount Vernon, Ind.
782	Jimmijo VI	Ol.s.	62	1943	Jul 11	1953	Burned	In the lower Detroit River at the junction of the Amherstburg and Livingston Channels.
783	Joan of Arc	St.s.	2,375	1918	Nov 15	1920	Stranded	Rogue River Reef, Mich.
784	John A. McGean	St.s.	5,100	1908	Nov 9	1913	Foundered	Lake Huron, off Port Sanilac, Mich. Freighter. Steel vessel. All lives (23) lost.
785	John A. Styninger	St.s.	117	1913	Nov 12	1915	Burned	Grace Harbor, Mich.
786	John B. Cowle	St.s.	4,731	1902	Jul 12	1909	Collided	With st.s. ISAAC W. SCOTT. Whitefish Point, Mich. 14 lives lost.
787	John B. Lyon	-	-	-	Sep 11	1900	Unknown	Off Girard, Pa.
788	John Barrett	St.w.	102	1917	Oct 13	1935	Burned	Illinois River, Lacon, Ill.
789	John Breymann	St.s.	58	1885	Jun 8	1926	Burned	Toledo, Ohio.
790	John F. Eddy	Brg.	1,678	1886	Nov 13	1920	Foundered	Sister Island, Lake Erie.
791	John Gault	St.w.	108	1857	Mar 15	1862	Foundered	Cairo, Ill.

NO.	NAME OF VESSEL	RIG	TONS	BUILT	DATE	CAUSE	PLACE AND COMMENT
792	John H. Pauly	St.brg.	197	1880	Aug 10 1906	Burned	Marine City, Mich.
793	John Harvey	C.bt.	104	1896	1916	Foundered	St. Lawrence River.
794	John Herron	St.w.	56	1853	Jan 23 1859	Ice	Rock Island, Ill.
795	John J. Barlum	Sch.	1,184	1890	Sep 18 1922	Foundered	Off Marblehead, Lake Erie.
796	John L. Lowry	St.p.	88	1909	Jun 15 1911	Burned	Hamletsburg, Ill.
797	John Laddell	St.w.	160	1860	Dec 15 1860	Collided	With unknown object. Marietta, Ohio.
798	John M. Hutchinson	Sch.	980	1873	Aug 17 1905	Foundered	Off 14-Mile Point, Lake Superior.
799	John M. McKerchey	St.s.	506	1906	Oct 16 1950	Foundered	In Lake Erie, 6,680 feet, 298 degrees from Lorain, Ohio, West Breakwater Light. Steel vessel. Used as dredge. 6' of water over wreck. Lying north to south. Removed in 1954.
800	John M. Nicol	St.s.	2,126	1889	Dec 13 1906	Stranded	Big Summer Island, Mich.
801	John Mitchell	St.s.	4,468	1907	Jul 9 1911	Collided	With st.s. W.H. MACK. Vermilion Point, Mich. Freighter. Steel vessel. 3 lives lost.
802	John Moran	St.p.	284	1885	Apr 8 1907	Burned	Cairo, Ill.
803	John Owen	St.s.	2,127	1889	Nov 12 1919	Foundered	Lake Superior, near Caribou Island, Mich. All lives (22) lost.
804	John P. Tweed	St.p.	315	1851	Aug 14 1857	Snagged	Roth, Ill. 2 lives lost.
805	John Paul	Ol.s.	267	1927	Oct 31 1960	Foundered	At Mile 378.4, Upper Mississippi River, left side of Channel, near Nauvoo, Hancock County, Ill. Steel vessel.
806	John Plankinton	St.s.	1,821	1889	May 9 1917	Collided	With st.s. DETROIT. Detroit River, Mich.
807	John Pridgeon, Jr.	St.s.	1,173	1875	Sep 18 1909	Foundered	12 miles west of Cleveland, Ohio.
808	John R. Durkee	C.bt.	115	1879	Jun 15 1907	Foundered	Batiscan, Quebec, Canada.
809	John R. Parsons	Brg.	204	1891	Nov 29 1913	Foundered	In Lake Ontario, near Oswego, N.Y.
810	John Shuette	Sch.	269	1875	Jul 2 1909	Collided	With st.s. ALFRED MITCHELL. Ecorse, Mich., Detroit River.
811	John Stewart	St.s.	53	1867	Mar 12 1874	Burned	Port Huron, Mich.
812	John V. Jones	Sch.	200	1875	Oct 20 1905	Stranded	35 miles northeast of Milwaukee, Wisc. 2 lives lost.
813	John W. Lane	St.w.	65	1925	Jan 22 1947	Burned	In Ohio River, opposite Gallipolis, Ohio.
814	John Walters	Sch.	-	-	1883	Stranded	Southwest end of Russell Island, Ontario, Lake Huron.
815	Joliet	St.s.	1,935	1890	Sep 22 1911	Collided	With st.s. HENRY PHIPPS. St. Clair River, Mich.
816	Jordan Boys	Brg.	405	1907	May 4 1945	Foundered	Buffalo, N.Y.
817	Joseph A. Allore	C.bt.	103	1889	Jul 26 1913	Burned	At Bastican, Quebec, Canada.
818	Joseph C. Suit	St.s.	318	1884	May 30 1912	Collided	With st.s. CITY OF DETROIT III. Detroit River.
819	Joseph Fleming	St.w.	170	1864	Jun 11 1885	Burned	Lake DePere, Ill.
820	Joseph L. Hurd	Brg.	459	1869	Nov 8 1913	Stranded	Near Sturgeon Bay, Wisc.
821	Joseph S. Fay	St.s.	1,220	1871	Oct 19 1905	Stranded	Forty-mile Point Light, Lake Huron.
822	Josephine	St.p.	90	1834	Dec 27 1834	Snagged	Grand Tower, Ill.
823	Josephine Dresden	Ga.s.	84	1852	Nov 27 1907	Stranded	North Manitou Island, Mich.
824	Josh Cook	St.p.	384	1876	Jan 29 1918	Ice	Joppa, Ill.
825	Julia	St.w.	158	1863	May 10 1867	Snagged	Mankato, Minn.
826	Julia Dean	St.p.	145	1850	Sep 29 1856	Stranded	West Franklin, Ind.
827	Julia Dean	St.w.	117	1850	Apr 26 1857	Collided	With RAINBOW, Mt. Vernon, Ind. 5 lives lost.
828	Juliette	Brg.	414	1917	Aug 21 1923	Stranded	Lake Erie.
829	Julius D. Morton	St.p.	472	1848	Apr 8 1863	Burned	St. Clair River, Mich.
830	Junior	St.s.	339	1906	May 9 1915	Collided	With breakwater. Cleveland, Ohio. 6 lives lost.
831	Junius	Sch.	-	-	1866	Unknown	Off Long Point, Ontario.
832	Jupiter	Scow	444	1912	Dec 27 1933	Stranded	Wyandotte, Mich.
833	Jura	Sch.	227	1862	Oct 4 1911	Stranded	Near Cross Village, Lake Michigan.
834	K. of C.	Scow	56	1925	Aug 10 1937	Foundered	8 miles northeast of Ocoda, Mich.
835	Kaliyuga	St.s.	1,941	1887	Oct 19 1905	Foundered	Lake Huron. All lives (17) lost.
836	Kalkaska	St.s.	679	1881	Oct 10 1932	Burned	Marine City, Mich.

NO.	NAME OF VESSEL	RIG	TONS	BUILT	DATE		CAUSE	PLACE AND COMMENT
837	Kaloolah	St.p.	396	1858	Aug 27	1862	Stranded	Lake Huron.
838	Kansas	St.s.	835	1870	Oct 27	1924	Burned	Manistee, Mich.
839	Kate E. Howard	Sch.	96	1867	May 1	1911	Foundered	Port Washington, Wisc.
840	Kate Fleming	St.p.	76	1850	Oct 5	1850	Exploded	Walker Bar, Ohio River. 11 lives lost.
841	Kate Kinney	St.w.	508	1864	Oct 29	1872	Burned	New Albany, Ind.
842	Kate Lyons	Sch.	201	1866	Oct 19	1905	Stranded	Holland, Mich.
843	Kate May	St.w.	207	1859	Mar 31	1860	Burned	Cannelton, Ind.
844	Kate Putnam	St.w.	269	1864	Dec 31	1872	Ice	Cincinnati, Ohio.
845	Kate Robinson	St.w.	283	1863	Mar 7	1872	Burned	Cincinnati, Ohio.
846	Katherine M	Brg.	191	-	May 26	1906	Burned	Hastings, Minn.
847	Katie	St.w.	180	1864	Nov 22	1864	Collided	With DES MOINES. Diamond Island, Ohio River. 1 life lost.
848	Kanawha	St.p.	429	1896	Jan 5	1916	Stranded	Dam 19, Ohio River. Steel vessel. 16 lives lost.
849	Kellogg	Scow	489	1899	Sep 8	1910	Foundered	12 miles northwest of Point au Sable, Mich.
850	Kenosha	St.s.	645	1856	Oct 26	1864	Burned	Sarnia, Ontario.
851	Kent	St.p.	-	-		1845	Collided	Off Point Pelee, near entrance of Detroit River, Lake Erie.
852	Kentucky	St.p.	98	1849	Jul 4	1855	Burned	Rock Island, Ill.
853	Kentucky No.2	St.p.	148	1851		1858	Stranded	Prescott, Wisc.
854	Kenwood	St.w.	232	1863	Aug 14	1869	Exploded	Shawneetown, Ill. 18 lives lost.
855	Keokuk	St.w.	111	1907	Aug 16	1926	Burned	Davenport, Iowa.
856	Key West No.2	St.w.	205	1860	Oct 26	1863	Snagged	Chester, Ill.
857	Keystone	St.p.	1,923	1886	Jul 23	1932	Burned	Ecorse, Mich. Steel vessel.
858	Keystone State	St.p.	337	1850	May 31	1855	Burned	Florence, Ill.
859	Keystone State	St.p.	1,354	1849	Oct 30	1861	Stranded	Saginaw Bay, Mich. 33 lives lost.
860	Keystone State	Ol.s.	-	-		1952	Unknown	Lake Erie, Buffalo River, at the Great Lakes Dock & Dredge Co., at foot of Katherine Street. Tug.
861	Kingfisher	Sch.	517	1867	Oct 5	1905	Stranded	Cleveland, Ohio.
862	Kiowa	St.s.	2,309	1920	Nov 30	1929	Stranded	Point Au Sable, Mich. 5 lives lost (23).
863	Kittanning	St.s.	52	1922	Apr 13	1936	Burned	500 feet north of Cedar Street Bridge, Peoria River, Ill.
864	Knickerbocker	St.p.	169	1838	Dec 11	1839	Snagged	Cairo, Ill.
865	L.C. Butts	Sch.	-	-	Nov 12	1891	Unknown	Off Fish Island, near Rock Island Pass, Wisc. Coal cargo.
866	L.C. Smith	St.s.	-	-	Nov 25	1905	Stranded	Nine Mile Point, Mich., Lake Huron.
867	L.C. Waldo	St.s.	4,466	1896	Nov 8	1913	Stranded	Manitou Islands, Lake Superior, Wisc.
868	L. Jenison	St.p.	129	1867		1877	Burned	Grand Haven, Mich.
869	La Belle	St.w.	129	1853	Dec	1854	Snagged	Ohio River.
870	La Fourche	St.p.	186	1830	Sep 29	1833	Stranded	Cairo, Ill.
871	La Frienier	Sch.	-	1876	Nov 7	1886	Foundered	Hog Island Shoal, Mich.
872	La Rabida	St.s.	52	-	Nov 25	1906	Stranded	Naubinway, Mich.
873	Lac La Belle	St.s.	872	1864	Oct 13	1872	Foundered	Racine, Wisc. 9 lives lost.
874	Laclede	St.w.	179	1855	Nov 19	1862	Stranded	Chester, Ill.
875	Lady Elgin	St.p.	1,037	1851	Sep 8	1860	Collided	With sch. AUGUSTA. Off Waukegan, Ill. 282 lives lost.
876	Lady Franklin	St.p.	206	1850	Oct 23	1856	Snagged	Warren Ledge, about 200 miles below St. Paul, Minn. 5 lives lost.
877	Lady Gay	St.p.	1,406	1865	Jan 19	1870	Stranded	Grand Tower, Ill.
878	Lady Jane	St.s.	75	1864	Apr 19	1865	Collided	With pier. Rock Island, Ill. 1 life lost.
879	Lady of the Lake	St.s.	326	1846	Mar 26	1859	Exploded	Fairport, Ohio. 2 lives lost.
880	Lady Walton	St.w.	150	1858	Aug 2	1864	Collided	With NORMAN. Warsaw, Ind.
881	Lady Washington	Steamer	-	-	Sep 14	1890	Unknown	Off Seul Choix Point, Mich.
882	Lafayette	St.p.	84	1833	Aug 30	1833	Burned	Cairo, Ill.
883	Lafayette	St.s.	5,113	1900	Nov 28	1905	Foundered	Encampment Island, Lake Superior. Freighter. Steel vessel.

NO.	NAME OF VESSEL	RIG	TONS	BUILT	DATE		CAUSE	PLACE AND COMMENT
884	Lafayette	St.p.	77	1900	Jan 15	1908	Foundered	Mount Carmel, Ill.
885	Lake Grogan	St.s.	2,592	1919	Nov 19	1926	Stranded	Port Colbourne, Ontario. Steel vessel.
886	Lakeland	St.s.	2,425	1887	Dec 3	1924	Foundered	Lake Michigan. Steel vessel. Has been reported in vicinity of Sturgeon Bay, Wisc.
887	Laketon	St.p.	-	-	Nov	1888	Stranded	Grand Marais, Mich.
888	Langell Boys	St.s.	467	1890	Jun 13	1931	Burned	Fish Point, Mich.
889	Langham	St.s.	1,810	1888	Oct 23	1910	Burned	Keweenaw Point, Mich.
890	L'Anse Wreck	-	-	-		1964	Unknown	As reported by US Coast Guard: Lake Superior, Keweenaw Bay, 1,720 feet, 341.5° from tank in L'Anse, Mich. Depth 12'. Use chart 943.
891	Lansing	St.p.	83	1864	May 13	1867	Exploded	Hampton, Ill. 6 lives lost.
892	Laurel	St.p.	78	1846	Jan	1851	Stranded	Alton, Ill.
893	Le Claire No.2	St.p.	155	1864	Dec 29	1872	Ice	Evansville, Ind.
894	Lehigh	St.w.	210	1857	Jun 23	1861	Burned	Cincinnati, Ohio.
895	Leonidas	St.w.	364	1863	Jun 26	1871	Snagged	New Albany, Ind.
896	Levi Grant	Brg.	204	1872	Jul 11	1913	Stranded	Green Bay, Wisc.
897	Lewis Shickluna (Can.)	St.s.	-	-	Apr 28	1897	Collided	5 miles east of Long Point, Ontario.
898	Lexington	Sch.	-	-	Jun 11	1846	Unknown	Off Point Moullie, near mouth of Detroit River. Cargo valued at $100,000.
899	Lexington	St.p.	363	1838	Jun 15	1850	Stranded	Port Washington, Wisc.
900	Lexington	St.p.	312	1850	Jun 30	1855	Exploded	Rome, Ind. 30 lives lost.
901	Liberty	St.p.	96	1827	Oct 24	1831	Snagged	Wood River, Ill.
902	Liberty	St.s.	149	1889	Jul 9	1919	Burned	Grand Marias Harbor, Minn.
903	Linden	St.s.	894	1895	Nov 28	1923	Burned	Tawas Bay, Mich.
904	Little Belle	St.s.	-	-		1868	Foundered	West of light, at Long Point, Ontario.
905	Little Ben	St.p.	182	1841	Dec 7	1844	Stranded	Liberty, Ill.
906	Little Ben Franklin	St.p.	85	1842	Nov 29	1845	Snagged	Liberty, Ill.
907	Lizzie A. Law	Sch.	747	1875	Oct 19	1908	Stranded	Huron Island, Mich.
908	Lizzie Harvey	Brg.	426	1914	Nov 2	1937	Foundered	Off Westfield, N.Y., Lake Erie.
909	Lizzie Madden	St.s.	690	1887	Nov 22	1907	Burned	Saginaw Bay, Mich.
910	Lomie A. Burton	Sch.	203	1873	Nov 17	1911	Stranded	South Manitou Island, Mich.
911	Lorain	Ga.y.	50	1910	Sep 13	1929	Burned	Harbor Springs, Mich.
912	Loretta	Brg.	452	1917	Sep 27	1933	Collided	With steamer LEHIGH. Mouth of Detroit River.
913	Loretta B. Haber	Brg.	423	1916	Aug 21	1923	Stranded	Lake Erie.
914	Louis Igert, Jr.	Ol.w.	164	1939	Apr 2	1944	Stranded	Near Mile 438.6 in Mississippi River, below Cairo, Ill.
915	Louisa	St.w.	81	1851	Jun 18	1857	Snagged	Portsmouth, Ohio.
916	Louisiana	St.p.	306	1830	Jul 5	1837	Snagged	Cairo, Ill.
917	Louisiana	St.s.	1,929	1887	Nov 8	1913	Burned	Green Bay Harbor, Wisc.
918	Louisville	St.s.	366	1853	Sep 29	1857	Burned	Chicago, Ill. 1 life lost.
919	Lucerne	Sch.	-	-	Nov 18	1886	Foundered	North of Chequamegon Point, Wisc.
920	Lucia A Simpson	Sch.	227	1875	Dec 3	1935	Burned	Sturgeon Bay, Wisc.
921	Lucie May	St.w.	171	1855	May 6	1859	Collided	With CEDAR RAPIDS. Above Quincy, Ill. 3 lives lost.
922	Lucile	St.s.	71	1883	Aug 8	1906	Foundered	Lake Erie.
923	Lucky	Scow	109	1931	Sep 22	1951	Stranded	At Cordwood Point, 9 miles east of Cheboygan, Mich.
924	Lucy McConnell	St.p.	70	1852	Mar 6	1855	Snagged	Mount Carmel, Ill. Used as ferryboat.
925	Lucy Walker	St.p.			Oct 23	1844	Exploded	New Albany, Ind. 60 lives lost.
926	Lycoming	St.s.	1,448	1880	Oct 22	1910	Burned	Rondeau Harbor, Ontario.
927	Lydia Collins	St.w.	147	1849	Dec 10	1851	Snagged	Belpre, Ohio.
928	M.B. Spaulding	St.s.	419	1848	Jun 20	1860	Burned	Toronto, Canada, Lake Ontario.
929	M.C. Neff	St.s.	276	1888	Sep 20	1909	Burned	New Diluth, Minn.
930	M. Coo	Sch.	-	-		1851	Foundered	Off Long Point, Ontario.

NO.	NAME OF VESSEL	RIG	TONS	BUILT	DATE		CAUSE	PLACE AND COMMENT
931	M.F. Merrick	Sch.	-	-	May 7	1889	Collided	2 miles off Black River, Mich., Thunder Bay, Lake Huron.
932	M.I. Mills	St.s.	152	1867	Dec 30	1880	Foundered	Detroit, Mich.
933	M.I. Wilcox	Sch.	377	1868	May 8	1906	Stranded	Colchester Point, Ontario.
934	M.J. Bartelme	St.s.	3,400	1895	Oct 4	1928	Stranded	Cana Island Light, Wisc.
935	M.T. Greene	St.s.	523	1887	Mar 19	1928	Burned	Bridgeburg, Ontario.
936	M. Walton Trader	Brg.	87	1896	Apr 1	1916	Burned	Bellaire, Ohio.
937	Mable Wilson	Sch.	1,224	1886	May 28	1906	Foundered	Cleveland, Ohio. 1 life lost.
938	Madeira	Sch.	-	-	Oct 15	1877	Unknown	Off Long Point, Ontario.
939	Madeira	Sch.	5,039	1900	Nov 28	1905	Stranded	Split Rock, Lake Superior. Steel vessel. 1 life lost.
940	Madison	St.p.	168	1852	Jan 3	1859	Collided	With IOWA. Aurora, Ind.
941	Madison	St.p.	99	1855	Jan 3	1859	Collided	With IOWA. Aurora, Ind.
942	Madison	St.p.	292	1892	Jan 13	1910	Foundered	Venice, Ill.
943	Maggie McRae	Sch.	-	-	Jun 4	1888	Foundered	Thunder Cape, Ontario.
944	Magnetic	Sch.	1,946	1882	Aug 25	1917	Foundered	Long Point, Ontario.
945	Magnolia	St.p.	375	1858	Mar 18	1868	Exploded	California, Ohio. 35 lives lost.
946	Maid of Orleans	St.p.	276	1839	May 28	1841	Snagged	Hat Island, Chester, Ill.
947	Maine	Sch.	-	-	Oct	1887	Unknown	North of Milwaukee, Wisc.
948	Maine	St.s.	332	1862	Jul 16	1911	Burned	Marine City, Mich.
949	Maine	St.s.	392	1862	Jul 16	1911	Burned	Marine City, Mich.
950	Majestic	St.s.	1,985	1889	Sep 19	1907	Burned	12 miles west of Long Point, Ontario.
951	Majestic	St.w.	403	1906	May 7	1922	Burned	Havana, Ill. Steel vessel.
952	Major	St.s.	1,864	1889	Nov 13	1913	Foundered	30 miles northwest of White Fish Point, Lake Ontario, Niagara Falls, N.Y.
953	Major Anderson	St.p.	435	1861	Mar 7	1872	Burned	Cincinnati, Ohio.
954	Manhattan	St.s.	319	1847	Sep 1	1859	Foundered	Grand Marais, Minn.
955	Manistee	St.s.	561	1867	Nov 14	1883	Unknown	Lake Superior. 30 lives lost.
956	Manistee	St.s.	843	1882	Jun 28	1914	Burned	Ferryburg, Mich.
957	Manitou	Sch.	333	1873	Nov 3	1905	Foundered	Off Scotch Bonnet Light, Lake Ontario.
958	Mankato	St.w.	127	1864	May 8	1871	Snagged	Minnesota River, Minn.
959	Manola	St.s.	2,725	1890	Dec 3	1918	Foundered	5 miles south of False Duck, Ontario, Canada. Steel vessel. All lives (11) lost. This vessel was cut in two for passage through the Welland Canal, and bow section foundered.
960	Maplehurst	St.s.	-	-	Dec 1	1922	Unknown	West end entrance to Portage Entry Breakwater, Keweenaw Bay Peninsula, Mich.
961	Marengo	Sch.	648	1873	Oct 10	1912	Stranded	Port Colborn, Ontario.
962	Margaret Dall	Sch.	149	1867	Nov 16	1906	Stranded	South Manitou Island, Lake Michigan.
963	Margaret Olwell	St.p.	-	-	Jun 29	1899	Unknown	Off Lorain, Ohio.
964	Marie Barrett	St.p.	147	1908	Sep 27	1913	Burned	Cairo, Ill.
965	Mariner	St.p.	104	1860	Nov 20	1869	Burned	Chatham, Ontario.
966	Marinette	Sch.	-	-	Nov 18	1886	Stranded	Frankfort, Mich.
967	Marj III	Ga.y.	85	1908	Feb 20	1933	Burned	Chicago, Ill.
968	Marold II	Ga.y.	165	1911	Sep 21	1921	Burned	Marysville, Mich.
969	Marold II	Ol.s.	283	1911	Jan 1	1937	Burned	18 miles northeast of Beaver Island, Mich. Steel vessel. Explosion caused sinking.
970	Marquette and Bessemer No.2	St.s.	2,514	1905	Dec	1909	Foundered	Lake Erie. Steel vessel. All lives (31) lost.
971	Marquis Roen	St.s.	97	1921	Dec 7	1932	Burned	Bay City, Mich.
972	Mars	St.p.	132	1902	Aug 5	1912	Foundered	Winona, Minn.
973	Marshall F. Butters	St.s.	376	1882	Oct 20	1916	Foundered	Lake Erie. Many positions reported: Southeast Light, Quebec; Gull Island Shoal, Ohio; and Long Point, Ontario.
974	Martha Jewett	St.p.	408	1852	Jan 3	1859	Burned	Cairo, Ill.

NO.	NAME OF VESSEL	RIG	TONS	BUILT	DATE		CAUSE	PLACE AND COMMENT
975	Martha Putnam	St.w.	225	1857	Dec 29	1859	Burned	Cairo, Ill.
976	Mary A. McGregor	St.s.	816	1889	Aug 28	1920	Stranded	Magurtic Reef, Lake Huron.
977	Mary Ann	Ga.s.	85	1917	Oct	1933	Burned	Foot of Crane Avenue, Detroit, Mich.
978	Mary Catherine	Ga.y.	80	1907	Sep 19	1907	Burned	Chicago, Ill.
979	Mary E. McLachlan	Sch.	1,762	1893	Oct 20	1913	Stranded	Back Bay, Ontario, Lake Huron.
980	Mary Erwin	St.w.	308	1866	May 12	1869	Burned	Cincinnati, Ohio.
981	Mary N. Bourke	Sch.	920	1889	Sep 26	1914	Burned	Pine River, St. Ignace, Mich.
982	Mary Pell	St.p.	159	1845	Apr 12	1851	Collided	With PENNSYLVANIA. Lawrenceburg, Ind.
983	Mary Pringle	St.s.	166	1867	Aug 7	1893	Burned	Port Huron, Mich.
984	Mary Stewart	St.s.	442	1855	Nov 11	1866	Stranded	Pentwater, Mich.
985	Mary Ward	St.p.	-	-	Nov 22	1872	Unknown	North of Collingwood, Ontario, Lake Huron, on Nottawasaga Shoal.
986	Mary Woolson	Sch.	708	1888	Jul 18	1920	Collided	With st.s. CHARLES N. BRADLEY. Off Sturgeon Point, Lake Huron.
987	Marysville	St.s.	567	1894	Jun 25	1928	Foundered	Belle River, Mich.
988	Massasoit	Sch.	842	1874	Nov 24	1904	Stranded	Waterworks Crib, Niagara River, N.Y.
989	Mataafa	St.s.	6,900	-	Nov 27	1905	Unknown	Duluth Harbor, Minn. Iron ore cargo.
990	Maud	St.s.	98	1899	Nov 25	1917	Burned	St. Clair, Mich.
991	Mautehee	Sch.	647	1873	Oct 20	1905	Stranded	Pietou, Ontario.
992	May Flower	St.s.	57	1864	Nov 8	1865	Stranded	Detroit River, Mich.
993	May Queen	St.w.	92	1845	Feb 5	1847	Burned	Marietta, Ohio.
994	May Queen	St.p.	688	1853	Aug	1865	Stranded	Sheboygan, Wisc.
995	May Richards	Sch.	530	1880	Oct 7	1906	Stranded	North Bass Island, Lake Erie.
996	Mayflower	St.s.	-	-	Nov 4	1883	Foundered	Off Long Point, Ontario.
997	Mayflower	Sch.	-	-	Jun	1891	Foundered	South of Madeline Island, Wisc.
998	Mears	Sch.	-	-	Nov 27	1889	Unknown	East of Tawas Light, Mich.
999	Mecosta	St.s.	1,776	1888	Oct 29	1922	Foundered	Near Cleveland, Ohio.
1000	Mediterranean	Sch.	-	-	Oct 2	1891	Foundered	2 miles south of Sheboygan, Wisc.
1001	Medora	St.w.	101	1856	Jun 14	1861	Burned	Jeffersonville, Ind.
1002	Medora	Sch.	-	-	Oct	1870	Unknown	Near Long Point, Ontario, Lake Erie.
1003	Melnotte	St.w.	288	1856	May 12	1869	Burned	Cincinnati, Ohio.
1004	Melvin S. Bacon	Sch.	614	1874	Nov 6	1915	Collided	With st.s. JOSEPH SELLWOOD. Detroit River.
1005	Memphis	St.p.	196	1848	Jun 14	1853	Burned	Cincinnati, Ohio.
1006	Menekannee	Sch.	-	-	Nov 18	1886	Stranded	Point Betsie, north side of Frankfort, Mich.
1007	Merida	St.s.	3,329	1893	Oct 20	1916	Foundered	Between Southeast Shoal and Long Point, Lake Erie. Steel vessel. All lives (23) lost.
1008	Merrimac No.2	Sch.	-	-	Nov 3	1866	Foundered	Off Long Point, Ontario.
1009	Miami	Sch.	-	-	Nov 3	1874	Stranded	Off Long Point, Ontario.
1010	Miami	St.s.	228	1888	Aug 6	1924	Burned	Thunder Bay Island, Lake Huron.
1011	Michigan	St.p.	82	1854	Jul 11	1860	Burned	Grand Rapids, Mich.
1012	Michigan	St.s.	354	1852	Dec 3	1888	Burned	Kelley Island, Ohio.
1013	Michigan Central	Scow	1,478	1884	Oct 27	1926	Foundered	Lake Huron, Mich. Iron vessel.
1014	Midnight	Sch.	-	-	Nov 27	1889	Unknown	South of Tawas Light, Mich.
1015	Mike Corry	Sch.	380	1874	Jul 17	1916	Stranded	Georgian Bay, Lake Huron.
1016	Mike Dohearty	Scow	726	1899	May 23	1918	Foundered	Cedar River, Mich.
1017	Mildred	St.p.	92	1900	Jan 29	1918	Ice	Dam 31, Ohio River.
1018	Milton	St.w.	158	1850	Mar 23	1853	Burned	Ohio River.
1019	Milwaukee	St.p.	153	1845	Jan 1	1849	Ice	Naples, Ill.
1020	Milwaukee	St.p.	1,039	1859	Oct 9	1868	Stranded	Grand Haven, Mich.
1021	Milwaukee	St.brg.	-	-	Jul 8	1886	Collided	9 miles east of Grand Haven, Mich. See No.1020.

NO.	NAME OF VESSEL	RIG	TONS	BUILT	DATE		CAUSE	PLACE AND COMMENT
1022	Milwaukee	St.s.	2,933	1903	Oct 22	1929	Foundered	Milwaukee, Grand Haven, Wisc. Ferryboat. All lives (46) lost.
1023	Milwaukee Belle	Sch.	-	-	Nov 18	1886	Foundered	Off Brevort Point, Mich.
1024	Mingoe	Sch.	712	1893	May 21	1928	Foundered	Huron Island, Lake Superior.
1025	Minnehaha	Sch.	59	1872	Jul 3	1909	Stranded	Whiting, Ind.
1026	Minnesota	St.p.	749	1851	Sep 27	1861	Stranded	Green Bay, Wisc.
1027	Minnesota Belle	St.p.	225	1854	Mar 28	1862	Snagged	Liverpool, Ill.
1028	Minnie Will	St.p.	51	1866	Jun 30	1878	Unknown	St. Paul, Minn.
1029	Mioky	Ol.s.	52	1922	Feb 4	1863	Ice	At Mile 459, Ohio River, Sweetwine, Ohio.
1030	Missouri	St.p.	612	1840		1843	Stranded	Pointe aux Barques, Mich.
1031	Missouri	St.p.	856	1864	Jan 30	1866	Exploded	Newburg, Ind. 65 lives lost.
1032	Missouri	St.s.	588	1857		1881	Unknown	Detroit, Mich.
1033	Miztec	Sch.	777	1890	May 14	1921	Foundered	Lake Superior. All lives (7) lost.
1034	Mocking Bird (Can.)	Sch.	-	-		1876	Wrecked	Off Long Point, Ontario.
1035	Mohawk	St.w.	298	1866		1874	Unknown	Chicago, Ill.
1036	Mohawk	Brg.	334	-	May 12	1936	Burned	Indiana Harbor, Ind.
1037	Monguagon	Sch.	301	1874	Nov 18	1911	Foundered	Detroit River, Mich.
1038	Monkshaven	St.s.	-	-	Nov 27	1905	Unknown	Angus Rock, north end of Isle Royale, off Thunder Cove, Mich.
1039	Monohansett	St.s.	572	1872	Nov 23	1907	Burned	Thunder Bay Island, Mich.
1040	Monona	St.p.	173	1843	Oct 24	1847	Snagged	Chester, Ill.
1041	Monongahela	St.p.	335	1855	May 15	1859	Burned	East St. Louis, Ill.
1042	Monrovia	-	-	-		1959	Unknown	13.5 miles, 106 degrees from Thunder Bay Island. Buoyed. 34' of water over wreck. Wreck was to be removed.
1043	Montana	Sch.	-	1872	Nov 2	1890	Unknown	Near Middle Island Light, Mich.
1044	Montana	St.s.	1,212	1872	Sep 6	1914	Burned	Off Sulphur Island, Lake Huron, Mich.
1045	Montana	Ga.p.	50	1913		1921	Foundered	Cairo, Ill.
1046	Montcalm	Sch.	-	-	Nov 14	1891	Unknown	Off Long Point, Ontario.
1047	Monteagle	St.s.	1,273	1884	Sep 22	1909	Burned	Mud Lake, St. Marys River, Mich.
1048	Monticello	St.s.	364	1848	Sep 26	1851	Stranded	Ontonagon, Mich.
1049	Montpelier	Sch.	290	1866	Aug 11	1907	Foundered	Belle Isle, Detroit River, Mich.
1050	Montreal	St.p.	416	1856	Sep 3	1877	Burned	Maquam Bay, Vermont.
1051	Morania	Brg.	-	-		1951	Stranded	Lake Erie, Buffalo Harbor, 1,150', 90° from Buffalo North Breakwater South End Light. Gasolene cargo. REMOVED.
1052	Morning Star	St.p.	53	1860	May 23	1866	Burned	Mound City, Ill.
1053	Morning Star	St.p.	1,075	1862	Jun 20	1868	Collided	With bark COURTLAND. Oak Point, Ontario. 50 lives lost.
1054	Morning Star	St.p.	495	1901	Nov 4	1922	Burned	Cincinnati, Ohio.
1055	Moselle	St.p.	-	-	Apr 25	1838	Exploded	Ohio River. 200 lives lost.
1056	Mount Vernon	St.s.	577	1854	Oct 9	1860	Stranded	Point Pelee, Ontario. 2 lives lost.
1057	Munster	Scow	316	1909	Dec 6	1936	Foundered	Off Harbor Beach, Mich. Steel vessel.
1058	Muscatine	St.p.	322	1863		1880	Stranded	North La Crosse, Wisc.
1059	Muskegon	St.s.	941	1872	Oct 6	1910	Burned	Michigan City, Ind.
1060	Muskegon	St.p.	1,148	1881	Oct 28	1919	Collided	With pier. Muskegon, Mich. Iron vessel. 29 lives lost.
1061	Myosotis	Sch.	-	-	Nov 17	1886	Unknown	2 miles west of St. Joseph Harbor, Mich.
1062	Myron	St.s.	676	1888	Nov 22	1919	Foundered	Off Crisp Point, Mich. 16 lives lost (17).
1063	N.1	Scow	90	1884	Oct 12	1918	Burned	Duluth, Minn.
1064	N.2	Scow	84	1883	Oct 12	1918	Burned	Duluth, Minn.
1065	N.3	Scow	176	1892	Oct 12	1918	Burned	Duluth, Minn.
1066	N.4	Scow	192	1894	Oct 12	1918	Burned	Duluth, Minn.
1067	NBC 800	Brg.	1,112	1947	Mar 4	1963	Burned	At Hartford, Ill. Steel vessel.

NO.	NAME OF VESSEL	RIG	TONS	BUILT	DATE		CAUSE	PLACE AND COMMENT
1068	N.C. West	Sch.	-	-	Nov	1874	Foundered	Off Long Point, Ontario.
1069	N.J. Nessen	St.s.	440	1880	Oct 22 1929		Stranded	Pigeon Bay, Ontario.
1070	N. Mills	St.s.	391	1870	Sep 6 1906		Collided	With st.s. MILWAUKEE. McGregor Point, St. Clair River, Mich. 2 lives lost.
1071	N.P. Goddell	Sch.	-	-	Nov 27 1891		Foundered	On Yankee Reef, Lake Huron.
1072	Nadine	Brg.	-	-	May	1947	Unknown	Lies in channel about 1,000 feet downstream from Brush Point Front Range Light, St. Marys River, Point Aux Pins Range.
1073	Nagaho	St.s.	954	1888	Oct 27 1922		Foundered	South of Port Sollins, Ontario.
1074	Nannie Byers	St.w.	199	1863	Oct 2 1868		Collided	Into bridge. Quincy, Ill.
1075	Napoleon	St.p.	167	1831	Mar 2 1834		Snagged	Cairo, Ill.
1076	Naomi	St.s.	1,181	1881	May 21 1907		Burned	28 miles west of Grand Haven, Mich. Iron vessel. 5 lives lost.
1077	Narragansett	St.p.	184	1841	Jan 4 1845		Snagged	Willard, Ill.
1078	Nat Williams	St.w.	90	1866	Dec 24 1872		Ice	Madison, Ind.
1079	Negaunee	Sch.	640	1867	Sep 30 1906		Stranded	Lake Erie.
1080	Nellie Mason	Sch.	-	-	Nov 6 1887		Unknown	South Point, Mich., Thunder Bay, Lake Huron.
1081	Nellie Mason	Sch.	554	1882	Nov 13 1905		Stranded	Cleveland, Ohio.
1082	Nellie Sherwood	-	-	-	Sep 13 1880		Foundered	North of Russell Island, Ontario, Lake Huron. All lives were lost.
1083	Neptune	St.p.	180	1828	Oct 30 1830		Snagged	Cairo, Ill.
1084	Neptune	St.s.	636	1856	Nov 24 1874		Burned	East Saginaw, Mich.
1085	Neshoto	St.s.	2,225	1889	Sep 28 1908		Stranded	Crisp Point, Mich.
1086	Nettie Hartupee	St.w.	81	1863	Mar 4 1865		Burned	Pomeroy, Ohio.
1087	Nevada	St.p.	-	-	Nov 8 1890		Foundered	Off St. Joseph, Mich.
1088	Neville	St.w.	197	1865	Feb 25 1870		Exploded	North Bend, Ohio. 6 lives lost.
1089	New Brunswick	St.s.	-	-	Aug 6 1912		Unknown	10 miles north of Lorain, Ohio.
1090	New Dominion (Can.)	Sch.	-	-	Oct 26 1884		Stranded	Off Long Point, Ontario, Lake Erie.
1091	New Era	St.w.	157	1862	Jun 3 1868		Burned	Ship Island, Evansville, Ind.
1092	New Haven	Sch.	-	-	Nov	1852	Unknown	Long Point, Ontario. Railroad iron cargo.
1093	New Haven	St.p.	86	1841	Jan 24 1847		Foundered	Wood River, Ill.
1094	New Mexico	Ol.s.	-	-		1950	Unknown	Main entrance to Cleveland Harbor, Ohio. Tug. Removed.
1095	New Orleans	St.p.	610	1844	Jun 11 1849		Stranded	Thunder Bay, Mich.
1096	New Orleans	St.p.	299	1848	Jan 28 1855		Stranded	Cairo, Ill.
1097	New Orleans	St.s.	1,457	1885	Jun 30 1906		Collided	With st.s. WILLIAM R. LINN. Thunder Bay, Mich.
1098	New Ulm Belle	St.w.	50	1862	Aug	1862	Snagged	Minnesota River, Minn.
1099	New York	St.s.	665	1856	Oct 12 1876		Foundered	Sand Beach, Mich. 1 life lost.
1100	New York	St.s.	1,345	1879	Oct 1 1910		Foundered	Thunder Bay, Mich.
1101	Newaygo	St.s.	-	-		1903	Foundered	Off Northwest Bank, Cove Island, Ontario. Coal cargo.
1102	Newberg	Sch.	55	-	Dec 6 1891		Foundered	Off Long Point, Ontario.
1103	Newell Hubbard	Sch.	-	1867	Sep 25 1912		Foundered	Bar Point, Mich.
1104	Newsboy	Sch.	-	-	Nov 20 1891		Foundered	On Rock Island, Wisc.
1105	Niagara	-	-	-	Sep 24 1856		Burned	Lake Michigan. 60 lives lost.
1106	Niagara	Sch.	-	-	Sep 7 1887		Foundered	Off Manitou Island, Mich.
1107	Niagara	St.s.	-	-	Dec 6 1899		Foundered	East by about 12 miles of Long Point, Ontario.
1108	Niko	St.s.	814	1889	Nov 2 1924		Foundered	Garden Island, Mich.
1109	Nile	St.s.	650	1852	May 21 1864		Exploded	Detroit, Mich. 13 lives lost.
1110	Nirvana	Sch.	611	1890	Oct 20 1905		Foundered	Grand Marias, Mich.
1111	Nonpareil	St.p.	179	1840	Nov 23 1842		Snagged	Cairo, Ill.
1112	Noquebay	Sch.	684	1872	Oct 8 1905		Burned	Presque Isle Point, Mich.
1113	Norlond	St.s.	522	1890	Nov 13 1922		Foundered	East of South Point, Lake Michigan.
1114	Norman	St.w.	238	1863	Nov 21 1870		Burned	Evansville, Ind. 1 life lost.

NO.	NAME OF VESSEL	RIG	TONS	BUILT	DATE		CAUSE	PLACE AND COMMENT
1115	Norman	St.s.	431	1863	Oct 30	1883	Stranded	Manistee, Mich.
1116	North America	St.p.	361	1834	Jan 14	1847	Burned	Conneaut, Ohio.
1117	North America	St.p.	270	1852	Sep 8	1853	Burned	Cincinnati, Ohio.
1118	North America	St.s.	397	1857	Jul 1	1858	Foundered	Lake Saint Clair, Mich.
1119	North Shore	Ga.s.	63	1930	Sep 26	1930	Foundered	Racine, Wisc. Steel vessel. All lives (6) lost.
1120	North Star	Sch.	-	-	Oct 28	1855	Foundered	Off Long Point, Ontario.
1121	North Star	St.p.	1,106	1854	Feb 1	1862	Burned	Cleveland, Ohio.
1122	North Star	St.s.	2,476	1889	Nov 25	1908	Collided	With st.s. NORTHERN QUEEN. Port Sanilac, Ontario.
1123	North West	Ga.y.	66	1882	Oct 9	1943	Foundered	Harbor Beach, Mich.
1124	North Wind	St.s.	2,599	1888	Jul 17	1926	Foundered	Georgian Bay, Ontario.
1125	Northern Indiana	St.p.	1,475	1852	Jul 17	1856	Burned	Point Pelee, Ontario. 18 lives lost.
1126	Northern Light	St.p.	414	1857	Apr 11	1866	Ice	La Crosse, Wisc.
1127	Northern Queen	Steamer	-	-	Nov 13	1913	Stranded	Kettle Point, Ontario, Lake Huron.
1128	Northerner	St.p.	514	1851	Apr 21	1856	Collided	With FOREST QUEEN. Off Gratiot Light, Mich. 1 life lost.
1129	Northerner	St.p.	399	1853	Nov 8	1857	Stranded	Grand Chain, Ill.
1130	Northerner	Sch.	-	-		1860	Stranded	Off Long Point, Ontario.
1131	Northwest	St.s.	-	-	Jun 3	1911	Burned	In Buffalo Harbor, N.Y.
1132	Novadoc	St.s.	-	-	Nov 11	1940	Foundered	Juniper Beach, Pentwater, Mich.
1133	No.1	Brg.	1,544	1895	Nov 8	1918	Foundered	Thunder Bay, Mich.
1134	No.1	Drg.	179	1912	Jul 23	1932	Burned	Harsen's Island, Mich.
1135	No.2	Brg.	1,548	1895	Sep 29	1906	Foundered	Chicago, Ill. 3 lives lost.
1136	No.2	Drg.	403	1899	Dec 13	1907	Foundered	Sandusky, Ohio. 1 life lost.
1137	No.7	Scow	65	1895	Dec 14	1906	Collided	With st.s. MILWAUKEE. Lime Kiln Crossing, Detroit River.
1138	No.8	Scow	115	1913	Oct 11	1933	Stranded	Point Au Sable, Lake Superior.
1139	No.40	Scow	185	1891	Oct 12	1918	Burned	Duluth, Minn.
1140	No.80	Scow	365	1920	Oct 26	1941	Foundered	4.5 miles northeast of Thunder Bay Island, Lake Huron.
1141	No.300	Brg.	167	1922	Mar	1963	Storm	In Harbor, at Fairport, Ohio.
1142	Nyack	St.s.	1,188	1878	Dec 30	1915	Burned	Muskegon, Mich.
1143	O.E. Parks	Brg.	392	1891	May 3	1929	Foundered	Thunder Bay Island, Lake Huron.
1144	OR 929	Brg.	439	1955	Mar 5	1964	Foundered	At Mile 491.2, Ohio River. Steel vessel.
1145	OR 987	Brg.	413	1956	Jan 31	1968	Collided	With La Belle Bridge Pier. At Mile 68.8, Ohio River.
1146	Oakland	St.w.	141	1853	Dec 29	1859	Burned	Cairo, Ill.
1147	Oakwood	St.s.	2,051	1891	Jun 9	1925	Stranded	Millers Point, Ontario.
1148	Obion	St.p.	61	1851	Jan 1	1856	Collided	With NIAGARA. Liverpool, Ill.
1149	Ocean Wave	St.p.	-	-	Apr 30	1853	Burned	Off Kingston, Ontario, Lake Ontario.
1150	Ocean Wave	St.p.	235	1854	Jun 11	1868	Burned	Lake Pepin, Wisc.
1151	Ocean Wave	Sch.	96	1890	Nov 11	1890	Unknown	3 miles west of Oswego, N.Y.
1152	Oden	Scow	604	1864	Jul 8	1907	Foundered	Superior, Wisc., Lake Superior.
1153	Ogarita	Sch.	352	1852	Oct 25	1905	Burned	Thunder Bay Island, Mich.
1154	Ogdensburg	St.s.	-	-	Sep 30	1864	Collided	With sch. SNOW BIRD. Fairport, Ohio.
1155	Ogemaw	Steamer	594	1881	Dec 4	1891	Foundered	On Drisco Shoal, Green Bay, Wisc.
1156	Ogemaw	St.s.	157	1830	Dec 3	1922	Burned	Off Herson Island, abreast Algonac, Mich.
1157	Ohio	St.p.	441	1848		1842	Burned	Toledo, Ohio.
1158	Ohio	St.s.	235	1863	Nov	1859	Exploded	Buffalo, N.Y.
1159	Ohio Valley	St.w.	69	1909	Jan 3	1868	Exploded	Gallipolis, Ohio. 9 lives lost.
1160	Old Reliable	St.p.	220	1863	May 23	1914	Foundered	Golconda, Ill. 1 life lost.
1161	Olive	St.w.	1,271	1890	Jun 28	1865	Snagged	Golconda, Ill. 7 lives lost.
1162	Olive Jeanette	Sch.			Sep 2	1905	Foundered	Off Huron Island, Lake Superior, Mich. 7 lives lost. Iron ore cargo.

NO.	NAME OF VESSEL	RIG	TONS	BUILT	DATE		CAUSE	PLACE AND COMMENT
1163	Oliver No.1	Scow	75	1909	Oct 27	1920	Foundered	St. Marys River, Mich.
1164	Omar D. Conger	St.s.	196	1882	Mar 26	1922	Burned	Port Huron, Mich. All lives (4) lost.
1165	Omar Pasha	St.s.	343	1854	Oct 8	1869	Burned	Muskegon, Mich.
1166	Oneida	St.p.	140	1841	Mar 24	1842	Burned	Letart Falls, Ohio.
1167	Oneida	St.s.	345	1846	Nov 7	1852	Foundered	Fairport, Ohio. 17 lives lost.
1168	Onoko	St.s.	2,164	1882	Sep 14	1915	Stranded	Off Duluth, Minn. Iron vessel.
1169	Ontonagon	St.s.	560	1882	Sep 25	1883	Burned	St. Clair River, Mich.
1170	Oregon	St.p.	781	1845	Jan 19	1850	Burned	Chicago, Ill.
1171	Oregon	St.s.	312	1845	Apr 20	1855	Exploded	Detroit, Mich. 12 lives lost.
1172	Oregon	St.s.	779	1882	Aug 23	1908	Stranded	Thessalon, Ontario.
1173	Oriental	Sch.	–	–	Oct 23	1890	Foundered	In Quinte Bay, west of Edwards Point, Ontario.
1174	Orinoco	St.s.	2,226	1898	May 18	1924	Foundered	Lake Superior, Wisc. Also reported as being west of Point Albert, Ontario, Lake Huron. 6 live lost (22).
1175	Orion	St.p.	494	1866	Oct 16	1870	Stranded	Grand Haven, Mich.
1176	Orion	Sch.	–	–	Aug 31	1872	Foundered	Off Long Point, Ontario.
1177	Orphan Boy	Ga.s.	73	1876	Dec 17	1885	Unknown	3.5 miles south of Manistee, Mich.
1178	Oscar Newhouse	Ga.s.	73	1876	Jul 8	1927	Burned	Rocky Point, Mich.
1179	Oscar T. Flint	St.s.	823	1889	Nov 25	1909	Burned	Alpena, Mich.
1180	Oscoda	St.s.	529	1878	Nov 8	1914	Foundered	Espafette, Mich.
1181	Osprey	St.s.	56	1890	Apr 13	1915	Burned	Stony Point, Lake Superior.
1182	Oswegatchie	St.s.	436	1867	Dec 26	1891	Unknown	Detroit, Mich.
1183	Oswego	St.p.	187	1847	Feb 4	1852	Burned	Chester, Ill.
1184	Othello	St.w.	85	1837	Mar 23	1839	Collided	With PERU. Rome, Ind. 2 lives lost.
1185	Ottawa	Sch.	163	1874	Apr 13	1911	Stranded	Clay Banks, Mich. All lives (5) lost.
1186	Otto Marmet	St.w.	278	1898	Aug 19	1935	Burned	North Bend, Ohio.
1187	Our Son	Sch.	720	1875	Sep 27	1930	Foundered	Point Sable, Mich.
1188	Owen (Can.)	Sch.	–	–		1820	Foundered	Off Long Point, Ontario.
1189	Ozaukee	St.s.	102	1857	May 27	1884	Foundered	Bad River, Mich.
1190	P. C. Sherman	Sch.	–	–	Nov 15	1871	Collided	Long Point, Ontario.
1191	P. H. Birckhead	St.s.	495	1870	Sep 30	1905	Burned	Alpena, Mich., Lake Huron.
1192	P. J. Rolph	St.s.	964	1889	Sep 8	1924	Foundered	South Manitou Island, Mich.
1193	P.M. Ferry No.18	St.s.	–	–	Sep 8	1910	Unknown	Off Little Sable Point, Mich. Used for ferrying railroad cars.
1194	Pacific	St.p.	572	1850	Nov 23	1854	Snagged	Cairo, Ill.
1195	Pacific	Sch.	–	–	Nov 18	1887	Foundered	Mouth of Big Two Hearted River, Mich.
1196	Palm Beach	Drg.	203	1924	Feb 10	1943	Burned	Cleveland, Ohio.
1197	Palmyra	St.p.	101	1836	Nov 3	1838	Stranded	Rock Island, Ill. 1 life lost.
1198	Panama	St.s.	2,044	1888	Nov 21	1906	Stranded	Ontonagon Light, Mich.
1199	Paragon	St.p.	495	1863	Feb 28	1868	Snagged	Devils Island, Cairo, Ill.
1200	Pasadena	Sch.	2,076	1889	Oct 8	1906	Stranded	Portage Canal Breakwater, Mich. 2 lives lost.
1201	Pascal P. Pratt	St.s.	1,927	1888	Nov 18	1909	Burned	Long Point, Ontario.
1202	Passaic	St.p.	–	–	Nov 1	1891	Foundered	Off Dunkirk, N.Y.
1203	Pat Roger	St.s.	–	–	Jul 26	1874	Burned	Ohio River. 50 lives lost.
1204	Paugasset	St.s.	325	1847	Aug 23	1856	Burned	Dunkirk, N.Y.
1205	Paul Jones	St.p.	232	1843	Mar 10	1848	Stranded	Grand Chain, Ill.
1206	Peerless	St.p.	227	1864	Dec 15	1865	Burned	Mound City, Ill.
1207	Penelope	St.p.	54	1892	Dec 19	1909	Burned	Lorain, Ohio.
1208	Penguin	St.p.	60	1877	Aug 28	1908	Burned	Evansville, Ind.
1209	Peninsula	St.s.	354	1849	Nov 15	1854	Stranded	Eagle Harbor, Mich.

NO.	NAME OF VESSEL	RIG	TONS	BUILT	DATE	CAUSE	PLACE AND COMMENT
1210	Penobscot	St.s.	285	1880	Aug 19 1925	Burned	Marine City, Mich.
1211	Pentland	St.s.	827	1894	Nov 22 1921	Stranded	Weavers Point, Ontario.
1212	Peoria	St.p.	76	1832	1834	Snagged	Peoria, Ill.
1213	Pere Marquette 3	St.s.	924	1887	Mar 7 1920	Ice	Off Ludington, Mich.
1214	Pere Marquette 4	St.s.	941	1888	May 15 1924	Collided	With st.s. PERE MARQUETTE 17. Lake Superior, Wisc.
1215	Pere Marquette 8	St.s.	691	1888	Oct 26 1927	Burned	Manistee Lake, Mich.
1216	Pere Marquette 18	St.s.	2,090	1902	Sep 9 1910	Foundered	Sheboygan, Wisc. Steel vessel. 27 lives lost.
1217	Perryville	St.w.	77	1904	Jul 11 1925	Burned	Alton, Ill.
1218	Persian	St.s.	-	-	Aug 26 1875	Burned	8 miles south-southeast of Long Point, Ontario.
1219	Peshtigo	St.s.	817	1869	Oct 23 1908	Stranded	Mackinaw Island, Mich.
1220	Petoskey	St.s.	770	1888	Dec 3 1935	Burned	Sturgeon Bay, Wisc.
1221	Petrel	St.s.	237	1848	Oct 3 1850	Stranded	Ashtabula, Ohio.
1222	Petrel No.2	St.w.	137	1863	Mar 28 1873	Ice	Cincinnati, Ohio.
1223	Pewabic	St.s.	738	1863	Aug 9 1865	Collided	With METOUR. Thunder Bay, Mich. 40 lives lost. Between Thunder Bay Island and Crooked Island, Mich. Cargo of copper and general freight.
1224	Peytona	St.p.	109	1854	Mar 26 1859	Ice	Lake Peygan, Wisc.
1225	Peytona	St.w.	202	1867	Jun 30 1877	Unknown	Evansville, Ind.
1226	Phantom	St.w.	179	1864	Sep 15 1869	Exploded	New Liberty, Ind. 5 lives lost.
1227	Phil Sheridan	St.s.	710	1867	Dec 31 1875	Unknown	Detroit, Mich.
1228	Philetus Sawyer	St.s.	449	1884	Jul 11 1922	Burned	Toledo, Ohio.
1229	Philip	St.s.	54	1893	Mar 20 1933	Burned	Detour, Mich.
1230	Philip D. Armour	St.s.	1,900	1889	Nov 13 1915	Foundered	Lake Erie.
1231	Philip M.	Sch.	-	-	May 17 1889	Unknown	Off Port Weller, Ontario.
1232	Philip Walter	St.s.	-	-	Jun 27 1887	Unknown	3 miles north of Lorain, Ohio. 8 lives lost.
1233	Philo Scoville	-	-	-	Oct 6 1889	Unknown	Reported off Russell Island, Ontario. With active salvaging taking place.
1234	Phoenix	St.p.	336	1815	Jul 22 1819	Burned	Colchester, Ver.
1235	Phoenix	St.p.	302	1845	Nov 21 1847	Burned	Sheboygan, Wisc. 160 lives lost. Also reported as being of Dutch registry.
1236	Pilgrim	St.s.	299	1888	Apr 29 1907	Stranded	Fort Gratiot, Mich.
1237	Pilot	St.s.	77	1853	Nov 1865	Burned	Algonac, Mich.
1238	Pine Bluff	St.p.	153	1859	Nov 21 1870	Burned	Evansville, Ind.
1239	Pine Grove	St.w.	247	1864	Aug 6 1868	Burned	Cincinnati, Ohio.
1240	Pine Lake	St.s.	388	1895	Oct 21 1912	Collided	With st.s. FLEETWOOD. Lake St. Clair, Mich.
1241	Pioneer	St.p.	124	1825	Jul 9 1834	Stranded	St. Joseph, Mich.
1242	Platte	St.p.	158	1838	Sep 7 1841	Snagged	Thebes, Ill.
1243	Plymouth	St.p.	150	1844	Oct 27 1845	Collided	With LADY MADISON, Shawneetown, Ill. 25 lives lost.
1244	Plymouth	Sch.	-	-	Oct 24 1888	Stranded	West of Big Two Hearted River, Mich.
1245	Plymouth	Sch.	776	1854	Nov 8 1913	Foundered	Near Gull Island, Lake Michigan. All lives (7) lost.
1246	Pocahontas	St.s.	426	1846	May 27 1862	Stranded	Long Point, Ontario.
1247	Point Abino	St.s.	204	1872	Nov 14 1905	Stranded	St. Clair Flats Canal, Mich., Lake St. Clair.
1248	Polly M. Mayers	-	-	-	Nov 24 1890	Foundered	East of Scotch Bonnet Light, Lake Ontario.
1249	Polynesia	Steamer	-	-	Oct 23 1887	Foundered	Off Sheboygan, Wisc. Reported to have cargo valued at $50,000.
1250	Pontiac	St.p.	68	1856	May 1864	Exploded	Grand Haven, Mich. 3 lives lost.
1251	Pontiac	St.s.	229	1876	Jun 10 1934	Burned	Detroit, Mich.
1252	Portage	Sch.	-	-	Jul 27 1877	Stranded	Near Old Cut Light, Long Point, Ontario.
1253	Porter	-	-	-	Jun 5 1847	Collided	With CHESAPEAKE. Lake Erie. 15 lives lost.
1254	Portsmouth	St.s.	525	1853	Dec 5 1867	Stranded	Middle Island, Lake Huron.
1255	Post Boy	St.s.	94	1888	Aug 8 1905	Burned	Holland, Mich.
1256	Potomac	St.w.	974	1865	Aug 6 1868	Burned	Cincinnati, Ohio.

NO.	NAME OF VESSEL	RIG	TONS	BUILT	DATE		CAUSE	PLACE AND COMMENT
1257	Potosi	St.p.	115	1842	Sep 27	1844	Exploded	Quincy, Ill.
1258	Powhatan	St.p.	221	1829	Jun 26	1836	Collided	With NICHOLAS BIDDLE. Rising Sun, Ind.
1259	Prairie Bird	St.p.	213	1845	May 21	1851	Snagged	Keithsburg, Ill.
1260	Prairie State	St.p.	314	1849	Apr 25	1852	Exploded	Pekin, Ill. 20 lives lost.
1261	Prairie State	St.w.	287	1850	Jul 4	1855	Burned	Rock Island, Ill.
1262	Pretoria	Sch.	2,790	1900	Sep 2	1905	Foundered	Outer Island, Wisc. 5 lives lost.
1263	Pride of the West	St.p.	321	1846	Feb 13	1853	Ice	Cincinnati, Ohio. 6 lives lost.
1264	Prince	St.p.	146	1896	Nov 6	1918	Burned	Quincy, Ill.
1265	Prince Albert (Can.)	Sch.	-	-		1851	Stranded	Off Long Point Cut, Ontario.
1266	Princess Palms	Sch.	-	-	Nov 12	1889	Foundered	On Simmons Reef, Mich.
1267	Prins Willem V	-	-	-		1954	Unknown	Lake Michigan. 18,250 feet, 092 degrees from Milwaukee Breakwater Light, about 4 miles east of Milwaukee Harbor entrance. 31' over wreck. Lies northwest to southeast. Depth 69'.
1268	Prioress	St.p.	393	1859	Apr 16	1863	Burned	Cincinnati, Ohio. 1 life lost.
1269	Progress	St.s.	1,596	1880	Nov 24	1905	Stranded	Green Bay, Wisc.
1270	Progress	Drg.	235	1910	Jun 19	1942	Burned	Grand Haven, Mich.
1271	Protection	St.s.	161	1888	May 6	1924	Foundered	Cedar Point, Ohio. 3 lives lost (5).
1272	Pulaski	Sch.	-	-	Oct 3	1887	Foundered	North Manitou Island, Mich.
1273	Queen of the Lakes	St.s.	563	1853	Jun 12	1869	Burned	Marquette, Mich.
1274	Queen of the West	St.p.	291	1839		1843	Burned	Shawneetown, Ill.
1275	Quick Step	Sch.	-	-	Nov	1869	Unknown	Off Long Point, Ontario.
1276	R.G. Coburn	St.s.	-	-	Oct 17	1871	Unknown	In area of Six Fathom Reef, Mich., Lake Huron. Cargo valued at $100,000 in gold and copper. A vessel located off Harbor Beach, Mich. has not been positively identified as the vessel in question.
1277	R.H. Becker	Sch.	140	1867	May 1	1908	Capsized	Sheboygan Harbor, Wisc.
1278	R.J. Hackett	St.s.	1,129	1869	Nov 12	1905	Burned	Whaleback Shoal, Green Bay, Wisc.
1279	R.M. Bishop	St.p.	298	1866	Jul 15	1867	Snagged	Peru, Ill. 1 life lost.
1280	R.N. Rice	Sch.	-	-	Oct 3	1888	Stranded	North of Manitou Island, Mich.
1281	R.P. Mason	Brg.	155	1867	Jun 20	1917	Burned	Lake Michigan.
1282	Racine	St.s.	715	1856	Aug 10	1864	Burned	Rondeau, Ontario. 13 lives lost.
1283	Raleigh	St.s.	1,205	1871	Nov 30	1911	Foundered	Port Colborne, Ontario. 3 lives lost.
1284	Raphael	Brg.	643	1954	Jul 12	1966	Foundered	In Lake Erie, approximately 23 miles northwest of Fairport Harbor, Ohio.
1285	Rappahannock	St.s.	2,380	1895	Jul 25	1911	Foundered	Jackfish Bay, Lake Superior.
1286	Ray S. Farr	Sch.	-	-	Nov 30	1886	Foundered	On South Manitou Island, Mich.
1287	Reaper	St.w.	96	1906	Apr 26	1925	Foundered	Barrett Landing, Cairo, Ill.
1288	Rba Reeves	St.p.	63	1897	Feb 15	1918	Ice	Selitan, Ohio.
1289	Rebecca Foster (Can.)	Sch.	-	-	Winter	1863	Foundered	Off Long Point, Ontario.
1290	Redstone	Steamer	-	-	Apr 2	1852	Exploded	Ohio River. 40 lives lost.
1291	Reed Case	Sch.	-	-	Oct 20	1888	Stranded	Ship Canal, Portage Canal, Mich. 1 life lost.
1292	Regina	Sch.	-	-	Sep	1881	Foundered	Cove Island, Ontario.
1293	Regina	Steamer	-	-	Nov 12	1913	Unknown	Outer Hammond Bay, Mich., Lake Huron.
1294	Reindeer	St.p.	98	1831	Aug 19	1833	Burned	New Albany, Ind.
1295	Reindeer	St.p.	407	1851	Nov 12	1857	Snagged	Wood River, Ill.
1296	Reliable	St.s.	97	1880	Aug 16	1913	Foundered	Milwaukee Harbor, Wisc.
1297	Reliance	St.p.	156	1855	Dec	1862	Snagged	Steubenville, Ohio.
1298	Relief	St.s.	362	1855	Jun 18	1884	Burned	Sandusky, Ohio.
1299	Reomar II	Ga.y.	79	1912	Jun 27	1924	Burned	Cleveland, Ohio.
1300	Republic	St.s.	460	1848	Oct 3	1857	Burned	Sandusky, Ohio.

NO.	NAME OF VESSEL	RIG	TONS	BUILT	DATE		CAUSE	PLACE AND COMMENT
1301	Rescue	St.w.	168	1853	Sep 22	1857	Stranded	Derby, Ohio.
1302	Resolute	St.w.	62	1856	Nov 10	1867	Unknown	Alton, Ill.
1303	Resolute	Sch.	280	-	Nov 15	1871	Stranded	Opposite light, Long Point, Ontario.
1304	Resolute	Ol.w.	56	1936	Nov 30	1960	Foundered	In Ohio River at Mile 306.9. Steel vessel.
1305	Resumption	Sch.	293	1879	Nov 7	1914	Stranded	Plum Island, Lake Michigan.
1306	Return	Sch.	-	-		1863	Foundered	Off Long Point, Ontario.
1307	Revenue	St.p.	145	1844	May 21	1847	Burned	Peoria, Ill.
1308	Revenue	St.w.	236	1863	Aug 31	1866	Snagged	Buena Vista, Ohio.
1309	Revolution	St.p.	210	1848	May 16	1849	Burned	Peru, Ill.
1310	Rhine	St.p.	118	1838	Nov 20	1841	Snagged	Elizabethtown, Ill.
1311	Rialto	Scow	-	-	Lost	1800's	Foundered	Off Long Point, Ontario.
1312	Richard Burns	Sch.	565	1890	Nov 4	1921	Foundered	Lake St. Clair, Mich.
1313	Richard Henry Lee	St.w.	157	1850	Apr 23	1855	Collided	With OCEAN WAVE. Near Grafton, Ill.
1314	Richard Morwood	St.s.	-	-	Nov 19	1887	Stranded	Au Sable Point, Mich.
1315	Richard W	St.p.	52	1896	Feb 4	1917	Foundered	Evansville, Ind.
1316	Richmond	St.p.	347	1845	Nov 13	1845	Snagged	Grand Chain, Ill.
1317	Rienzi	St.p.	173	1836	Jan 24	1841	Snagged	Thebes, Ill.
1318	Rio Grande	St.p.	162	1846	Sep	1848	Snagged	Golconda, Ill.
1319	Risanco	St.w.	89	1911	Nov 7	1929	Foundered	Cincinnati, Ohio.
1320	Rising Star	Sch.	-	-	Oct 15	1877	Stranded	Near Old Cut Light, Long Point, Ontario.
1321	Rising Sun	St.s.	447	1884	Oct 29	1917	Stranded	Pyramid Point, Mich.
1322	Riverside	Sch.	-	-	Oct 14	1887	Foundered	South of Detroit Island, Mich., Porte des Morts.
1323	Rob Roy	Sch.	97	1868	Apr 27	1908	Stranded	Arthur Bay, Wisc.
1324	Robark	Ol.y.	74	1929	Apr 29	1937	Burned	Wyandotte, Mich.
1325	Robert C. Pringle	St.s.	141	1903	Jun 19	1922	Foundered	Off Sheboygan, Wisc.
1326	Robert C. Wente	St.s.	335	1888	Jul 11	1927	Burned	St. Clair River, Mich.
1327	Robert Holland	St.s.	423	1872	May 11	1915	Burned	Sturgeon Bay, Wisc.
1328	Robert L. Fryer	St.s.	1,810	1888	Apr 22	1914	Burned	St. Clair River, Mich.
1329	Rochester	St.p.	472	1838	Feb 2	1853	Stranded	Buffalo, N.Y. 7 lives lost.
1330	Rochester	St.w.	197	1855	Dec 8	1859	Snagged	Madison, Ind.
1331	Rolla	St.p.	130	1837	Nov 4	1837	Stranded	Rock Island, Ill. 1 life lost.
1332	Rosa Belle	Sch.	115	1863	Oct 30	1921	Foundered	Lake Michigan. All lives (11) lost.
1333	Roscoe	St.p.	255	1846	Mar 23	1849	Snagged	Rising Sun, Ind.
1334	Rosinco	Ga.y.	91	1916	Sep 19	1929	Collided	With unknown obstruction. Kenosha, Wisc.
1335	Rouse Simmons	Sch.	205	1868	Nov 23	1912	Foundered	Near Two River Point, Wisc. All lives (11) lost.
1336	Royal Arch	St.p.	212	1852	Jun 2	1856	Collided	With EMPIRE CITY. Above Savanna, Ill.
1337	Russia	St.s.	1,501	1872	Apr 30	1909	Foundered	Point Detour, Mich. Iron vessel.
1338	Ryan	St.s.	-	-	Jun 12	1890	Foundered	Thunder Bay Island, Mich., Lake Huron.
1339	S.A. Wood	Sch.	294	1868	Jun	1907	Foundered	Chicago River, Ill.
1340	S.C. Baldwin	Brg.	412	1871	Aug 27	1908	Foundered	Twin River Point, Wisc. 1 life lost.
1341	S.K. Martin	St.s.	302	1883	Oct 12	1912	Foundered	Near Erie, Pa.
1342	S.R. Kirby	St.s.	2,338	1890	May 8	1916	Foundered	Off Eagle Harbor, Mich. Iron vessel. 20 lives lost.
1343	S.S. Rumage	St.s.	101	1863	Nov 6	1929	Burned	Wallaceburg, Ontario.
1344	S.S. Wisconsin	St.s.	1,921	1881	Oct 29	1929	Unknown	Off Kenosha, Wisc., Lake Michigan. Length 210'. Beam 40'. 16 lives lost.
1345	S.V.R. Watson	Bark	-	-	Jul 4	1874	Collided	0360 True (bearing) 1,966 yds. from Dunkirk Light, in Lake Erie, between Buffalo and Dunkirk, N.Y. Steel vessel. Tug. Removed in 1951.
1346	Sachem	Ol.s.	85	1907	Dec 18	1950	Foundered	This vessel reported located in 1934. Demolished. With unknown steamer. Off Point Pelee, Ontario.

NO.	NAME OF VESSEL	RIG	TONS	BUILT	DATE		CAUSE	PLACE AND COMMENT
1347	Sachem	St.s.	739	1889	Oct 25	1928	Burned	Roberts Landing, Mich.
1348	Sailor Boy	St.s.	162	1891	May 12	1924	Burned	Hancock, Mich.
1349	St. Andrew	Sch.	-	-	May	1882	Foundered	East of New Cut Light, Long Point, Ontario.
1350	St. Catherine	Brg.	466	1914	Nov 4	1926	Foundered	Lake Erie, N.Y. All life (1) lost.
1351	St. Charles	St.p.	764	1864	Mar 7	1872	Burned	Cincinnati, Ohio.
1352	St. Clair	St.s.	236	1867	Jul 9	1876	Burned	14-Mile Point, Mich. 27 lives lost.
1353	St. Clair	Sch.	-	-	Oct 1	1888	Foundered	Off Sand Beach, near Harbor Beach, Mich.
1354	Ste. Genevieve	St.p.	611	1903	Mar 1	1918	Burned	Kellogg Incline, Ill.
1355	Saint Joseph	St.p.	460	1846	Nov 10	1856	Stranded	Fairport, Ohio.
1356	St. Lawrence	St.p.	1,844	1853	Sep 18	1855	Stranded	Fort Niagara, Ontario.
1357	St. Lawrence	St.w.	259	1855	Mar 22	1858	Stranded	Pomeroy, Ohio.
1358	St. Lawrence	Sch.	-	-		1900	Unknown	Off Lorain Light, Lorain, Ohio.
1359	St. Louis	St.p.	618	1844	Nov 8	1852	Stranded	Sandusky, Ohio.
1360	St. Magnus	St.s.	-	-	Jun 7	1895	Unknown	Cleveland Harbor, Cleveland, Ohio.
1361	Saladin	St.p.	346	1846	Jan 1	1851	Snagged	Thebes, Ill.
1362	Saltillo	Sch.	-	-		1853	Wrecked	In St. Clair River, Lake Erie.
1363	Salvor	Brg.	1,731	1896	Sep 26	1930	Foundered	Muskegon Pier, Mich. Steel vessel. 5 lives lost (14).
1364	Sam Flint	Sch.	499	1868	Oct 23	1916	Stranded	Cockburn Island, Ontario.
1365	Samoa	St.s.	1,096	1880	Sep 20	1909	Burned	Torch Lake, Mich.
1366	Samson	St.s.	250	1843	Nov 12	1852	Stranded	Buffalo, N.Y.
1367	Sampson	St.p.	61	1849	May 31	1855	Exploded	Calumet, Wisc. 2 lives lost.
1368	Sampson	Brg.	235	1901	Jan 19	1914	Stranded	Saginaw Bay, north of Pigeon River, Mich.
1369	Samuel H. Foster	Sch.	672	1873	Oct 9	1906	Stranded	Portage Canal, Mich.
1370	Samuel J. Christian	St.s.	55	1868	Oct 16	1907	Burned	Detroit River, Mich.
1371	Samuel Mather	Steamer	-	-	Oct 19	1889	Collided	Southern portion of Whitefish Bay, Mich.
1372	Samuel P. Hibbard	St.w.	178	1856	Jul 26	1860	Collided	With CHANCELLOR. New Albany, Ind. 1 life lost.
1373	Sanderson	St.p.	389	1894	May 29	1933	Foundered	Brookport, Ill.
1374	Sandusky	Sch.	-	-	Oct 26	1848	Foundered	Off Long Point, Ontario. Coal cargo.
1375	Sandusky	St.s.	370	1848	Oct 30	1856	Stranded	Conneaut, Ohio.
1376	Santiago	Sch.	2,600	1899	Sep 16	1918	Foundered	14 miles off Pointe aux Barques, Mich.
1377	Sappho	St.s.	223	1883	Mar 23	1929	Burned	Ecorse, Mich.
1378	Sarah E. Sheldon	St.s.	693	1872	Oct 20	1905	Stranded	Off Lorain, Ohio. 2 lives lost.
1379	Sarah J. Easton	Sch.	-	-	Nov	1852	Foundered	Off Long Point, Ontario.
1380	Saratoga	St.p.	130	1840	Nov 28	1842	Snagged	Mound City, Ill.
1381	Saronic	St.s.	-	-	Aug 21	1926	Burned	Cockburn Island, Ontario, Lake Huron.
1382	Satellite	St.s.	233	1864	Jul 21	1879	Foundered	Whitefish Point, Mich.
1383	Satellite	St.p.	60	1890	Feb 4	1917	Foundered	Mississippi River.
1384	Saxon	Bark	-	1871	Nov 12	1871	Foundered	South of light, Long Point, Ontario.
1385	Saxona	St.s.	4,716	1903	May 14	1917	Collided	With st.s. PENTECOST MITCHELL. St. Marys River, Mich.
1386	Schylkill	Sch.	-	-	Oct	1889	Unknown	Mouth of Keweenaw Waterway, Mich.
1387	Scioto	St.s.	389	1848	Sep 2	1864	Collided	With ARCTIC. Dunkirk, N.Y. 9 lives lost.
1388	Sciota	-	-	-	Jul 4	1882	Collided	Ohio River. 57 lives lost.
1389	Scioto Valley	St.p.	194	1840	Feb 24	1844	Burned	Cincinnati, Ohio.
1390	Scotland	St.p.	-	1848	Nov	1848	Unknown	Near Port Stanley, Ontario.
1391	Sea Bird	St.p.	638	1859	Apr 9	1868	Burned	Off Waukegan, Ill. 72 lives lost.
1392	Sea Gull	St.p.	149	1846	Apr	1854	Snagged	Marietta, Ohio.
1393	Sea Gull	St.s.	441	1863	Apr 30	1893	Burned	Mackinaw, Mich.
1394	Sea Wing	Steamer	-	-	Jul 13	1890	Storm	Lake Papin, Minn. 97 lives lost.

NO.	NAME OF VESSEL	RIG	TONS	BUILT	DATE	CAUSE	PLACE AND COMMENT
1395	Seabreeze	St.s.	87	1907	Dec 3 1946	Unknown	Sugar Island, Detroit River, Mich. Steel vessel.
1396	Seaman	Sch.	181	1848	Nov 15 1908	Stranded	Pilot Island, Wisc.
1397	Sebastpool	St.p.	863	1855	Sep 18 1855	Stranded	Milwaukee, Wisc. 4 lives lost.
1398	Selah Chamberlain	Steamer	-	-	Oct 14 1886	Foundered	Off Sheboygan, Wisc., Lake Michigan.
1399	Selden E. Marvin	Sch.	618	1881	Nov 7 1914	Foundered	Lake Superior. All lives (7) lost.
1400	Senator	St.p.	181	1831	Jan 14 1835	Stranded	Sandy Island, Ohio River.
1401	Senator	St.s.	3,632	1896	Nov 6 1929	Collided	With st.s. MARQUETTE. Milwaukee, Wisc. 8 lives lost (27).
1402	Senator Blood	Sch.	230	-	Nov 21 1894	Unknown	Near Lorain, Ohio.
1403	Service	Scow	169	1921	Jan 22 1958	Foundered	In the Buffalo River, 200 feet above the entrance of the old Ohio Basin. Steel.
1404	Seventy-Six	St.p.	257	1854	Feb 6 1859	Stranded	Alton, Ind.
1405	Sevona	St.s.	3,166	1890	Sep 2 1905	Stranded	Sand Island, Wisc. Steel vessel. 7 lives lost.
1406	Shamrock	St.s.	403	1875	Jun 26 1905	Stranded	Near Thunder Bay, Lake Huron.
1407	Shawmut	Brg.	250	1889	Nov 1 1909	Collided	With st.s. AMERICA. Buffalo Harbor, N.Y.
1408	Shawnee	Sch.	571	1873	May 16 1911	Stranded	Cleveland, Ohio.
1409	Shelby	St.p.	225	1850	Oct 1 1852	Foundered	Below Cairo, Ill.
1410	Shepherdess	St.p.	133	1842	Jan 3 1844	Snagged	East St. Louis, Ill. 70 lives lost.
1411	Sherman V. Petrie	Brg.	421	1914	Nov 15 1925	Stranded	Buffalo, N.Y. All life (1) lost.
1412	Siberia (Can.)	Sch.	-	-	Oct 30 1883	Stranded	Long Point, Ontario.
1413	Siberia	St.s.	-	-	Oct 20 1895	Unknown	Off Bar Bluff, Long Point, Ontario.
1414	Siberia	St.s.	1,892	1882	Oct 20 1905	Foundered	Long Point, Ontario. See No.1413.
1415	Silver Cloud	Sch.	-	-	Jul 8 1891	Unknown	Port Washington, Wisc.
1416	Silver Spray	St.s.	95	1894	Jul 15 1914	Stranded	Lake Michigan.
1417	Silver Star	St.w.	150	1856	May 12 1860	Burned	Evansville, Ind. 5 lives lost.
1418	Simon Langell	Steamer	-	-	Oct 10 1898	Unknown	Mouse Island, Ohio.
1419	Sinaloa	St.s.	-	-	Nov 11 1940	Stranded	Off Sac Bay, Garden Peninsula, Mich.
1420	Sioux	Ol.s.	-	-	Oct 24 1930	Foundered	Off Long Point, Ontario. Reported as tug.
1421	Smith	Sch.	-	-	Jun 13 1889	Foundered	Grand Island, Mich.
1422	Smith Moore	Steamer	-	-	Oct 1888	Stranded	North Manitou Island, Mich.
1423	Solon H. Johnson	St.s.	74	1889	Nov 24 1912	Foundered	Lake Superior.
1424	South Shore	St.p.	550	1847	Oct 18 1853	Stranded	Ashtabula, Ohio.
1425	Southerner	Sch.	-	-	Oct 25 1891	Foundered	Off Pie Island, Minn., Lake Superior.
1426	Sovereign	St.s.	3,942	1902	Nov 5 1940	Stranded	1 mile west of Grand Portal, Lake Superior, Mich. Steel vessel.
1427	Sparta	Ga.y.	59	1915	Mar 28 1919	Burned	Cleveland, Ohio.
1428	Speejacks	St.s.	2,356	1886	Oct 28 1907	Stranded	Gull Rock, Manitou Island, Mich. Steel vessel.
1429	Spokane	St.w.	232	1864	Feb 17 1871	Exploded	Evansville, Ind.
1430	Spray	Drg.	107	1926	Sep 14 1962	Foundered	In Ohio River, at Mile Point 232.5.
1431	Standard	St.p.	138	1837	1845	Burned	Buffalo Harbor, Buffalo, N.Y.
1432	Star	St.p.	122	1842	Jan 17 1844	Collided	Cairo, Ill. 3 lives lost.
1433	Star of the West	Steamer	-	-	Nov 1888	Stranded	Grand Island, Mich.
1434	Starucca	St.p.	1,221	1880	May 20 1924	Burned	Cleveland, Ohio. Iron vessel. 1 life lost (2).
1435	State of Ohio	Brg.	623	1880	Dec 17 1929	Stranded	Lorain, Ohio.
1436	State of Ohio	Ol.s.	1,695	1923	Sep 3 1942	Foundered	Lake Superior, 18 miles, 68 degrees, Manitou Island. Steel vessel.
1437	Steelvendor	St.s.	81	1853	Aug 1865	Burned	Bear Creek, Mich.
1438	Stockman	St.p.	879	1866	Oct 27 1869	Burned	45 miles above Cairo, Ill. 209 lives lost.
1439	Stonewall	St.s.	89	1863	Oct 27 1885	Burned	Detroit, Mich.
1440	Stranger	St.w.	128	1850	Jun 1 1853	Foundered	Cincinnati, Ohio.
1441	Summit	St.w.	153	1846	Oct 2 1847	Collided	With MOTIVE. Portsmouth, Ohio. 8 lives lost.
1442	Sunbeam	St.p.	398	1861	Mar 28 1863	Foundered	Near Eagle Harbor, Mich. 34 lives lost.

NO.	NAME OF VESSEL	RIG	TONS	BUILT	DATE		CAUSE	PLACE AND COMMENT
1443	Sunbeam	Ga.y.	79	1917	May 19	1923	Foundered	Near Niagara Falls, below Chippewa, Canada.
1444	Sunflower	St.p.	90	1841		1843	Snagged	Ironton, Ohio.
1445	Sunnyside	St.p.	330	1860	Nov 13	1863	Burned	Pomeroy, Ohio.
1446	Sunrise	St.s.	74	1921	Oct 16	1929	Stranded	Lake Bluff, Ill.
1447	Superior	Steamer	567	1845	Oct 29	1856	Stranded	Grand Island, Mich. 34 lives lost.
1448	Superior	St.s.	327	1916	Jun 11	1929	Burned	Detour, Mich.
1449	Superior City	St.s.	4,795	-	Aug 20	1920	Collided	With st.s. WILLIS L. KING. Off Whitefish Point, Lake Superior. Steel vessel. 29 lives lost (32). Freighter. Depth approximately 40'.
1450	Surveyor	Ol.s.	-	-		1965	Unknown	Lake Erie, 066 degrees, 6,660 yards from Ashtabula Harbor East Breakwater Light. Depth 43'. 36' of water over wreck.
1451	Susan W. Hughes	Ol.w.	65	1926	Dec 6	1932	Burned	Off Ottawa, Ill.
1452	Suwanee	St.p.	384	1846	Nov 19	1848	Stranded	Grand Chain, Ill.
1453	Swallow	St.p.	359	1862	Dec 21	1869	Collided	With CHAMPION NO.6. Cincinnati, Ohio.
1454	Swan	St.p.	102	1846	Nov	1848	Snagged	Marietta, Ohio.
1455	Swan	St.s.	94	1888	Nov 5	1914	Burned	At pier, Saginaw River, Mich.
1456	Swatara	St.p.	144	1846	Mar 11	1848	Collided	With YAZOO. America, Ill.
1457	Sweepstakes	Sch.	209	-	Jun	1896	Foundered	Big Tub Harbor, Tobermory, Ontario, Lake Huron.
1458	Sweetheart	Brg.	538	1867	Jul 6	1913	Foundered	St. Clair River, Mich.
1459	Swift	St.s.	886	1893	Dec 3	1935	Burned	Sturgeon Bay, Wisc.
1460	Swiftsure No.4	St.p.	141	1846	Oct 21	1851	Snagged	Utica, Ind.
1461	Sydney C. McLouth	St.s.	2,220	1880	Jun 27	1912	Stranded	8 miles northeast of Pensaukee, Wisc.
1462	Sylph	Sch.	-	-		1825	Stranded	On North Bass Island, Ohio, Lake Erie.
1463	Sylvan Stream	St.p.	330	1863	Jun 25	1903	Burned	Kingston, Ontario.
1464	Syracuse	St.s.	85	1897	Aug 26	1908	Stranded	Maumee Harbor, Ohio.
1465	T.G. Lester	Sch.	257	1868	Mar 30	1908	Foundered	Detroit, Mich.
1466	T.H. Davis	St.p.	240	1898	Dec 23	1915	Collided	With unknown obstruction. Joppa, Ill.
1467	T.H. Orton	Brg.	249	-	Jul 14	1891	Foundered	East of Marblehead Light, near Sandusky, Ohio, Lake Erie.
1468	T.L.D. No.1	Scow	195	1913	Nov 4	1928	Burned	Detour, Mich.
1469	T.S. Christie	St.s.	517	1885	Nov 8	1933	Stranded	Manistee, Mich.
1470	Tacoma	St.s.	1,879	1881	Aug 23	1914	Burned	Ludington, Mich.
1471	Tacoma	St.p.	276	1897	Nov 4	1922	Burned	Cincinnati, Ohio.
1472	Tacoma	St.s.	76	1894	Nov 4	1929	Foundered	Chicago, Ill.
1473	Talisman	Steamer	-	-	Nov 19	1847	Collided	With TEMPEST. Ohio River. 100 lives lost.
1474	Tampa	St.s.	1,972	1890	Jul 18	1911	Collided	With st.s. JOHN W. GALES. Walkerville, Ontario.
1475	Tashmoo	St.p.	1,344	1900	Jun 18	1936	Foundered	Near Amberstburg, Ontario, in Sugar Island Channel, Canada. Sinking caused by collision with unknown obstruction. All lives (1,529) were saved.
1476	Tasmania	Sch.	979	1871	Oct 20	1905	Foundered	South of Pelee Passage Light, Lake Erie. All lives (8) lost.
1477	Tawas	St.s.	122	1864	May 14	1874	Exploded	Sand Beach, Mich. 6 lives lost.
1478	Tchula	St.p.	203	1840	Aug 24	1841	Snagged	Cairo, Ill.
1479	Tecumseh	St.p.	285	1845	Nov 14	1850	Stranded	Buffalo, N.Y.
1480	Telegraph	St.p.	181	1849	Aug 2	1858	Collided	With sch. MARQUETTE. 40 miles north of Cleveland, Ohio.
1481	Telegraph No.2	St.p.	375	1848	Jul 12	1855	Burned	New Albany, Ind.
1482	Tell City	St.p.	574	1911	Apr 6	1917	Collided	With dam 19, Ohio River. 1 life lost.
1483	Tempest	Steamer	-	-	Nov 19	1847	Collided	With TALISMAN. Ohio River. 100 lives lost.
1484	Tempest	St.w.	144	1857	Oct 12	1860	Snagged	Mt. Vernon, Ind.
1485	Tempest	St.w.	63	1856	Mar 28	1864	Ice	Cincinnati, Ohio.
1486	Tempest	St.s.	412	1872	Aug 27	1918	Foundered	Erie, Pa. 1 life lost.
1487	Tennessee	St.w.	57	1849	Dec 2	1849	Foundered	Cincinnati, Ohio.

NO.	NAME OF VESSEL	RIG	TONS	BUILT	DATE		CAUSE	PLACE AND COMMENT
1488	Texas	Sch.	-	-		1845	Foundered	Off Long Point, Ontario.
1489	Thames No.1	Scow	548	1930	Mar 3	1959	Foundered	About 100 feet northward and 600 feet offshore of the Canadian Rock Salt dock, at Ojibway, Ontario, Canada. Steel vessel.
1490	The Craftsman	Brg.	165	1920	Jun 3	1958	Foundered	Lake Superior. 35 lives lost.
1491	The Superior City	St.s.	-	-	Aug 20	1920	Collided	at Ojibway, Ontario, Canada. Steel vessel.
1492	Theseus	St.s.	58	1886	Oct 29	1924	Exploded	Cairo, Ill.
1493	Thomas Cranage	St.s.	2,219	1893	Sep 25	1911	Stranded	Watcher Island, Georgian Bay, Ontario.
1494	Thomas Friant	St.s.	81	1884	Dec 22	1908	Burned	Sault Ste. Marie, Mich.
1495	Thomas Friant	St.p.	70	1884	Jan 6	1923	Foundered	Lake Superior.
1496	Thomas H. Larkin	Sch.	1,096	1855	Jul 28	1856	Burned	Chester, Ill.
1497	Thomas Hume	Sch.			May 22	1891	Foundered	Off Holland, Mich.
1498	Thomas J. Feeney	Brg.	500	1917	Sep 28	1937	Stranded	Near Peace Bridge, Buffalo, N.Y.
1499	Thomas Quayle	Sch.	722	1872	Sep 18	1910	Burned	Cleveland, Ohio.
1500	Thomas Scott	St.w.	149	1856	Jul 13	1863	Snagged	Warsaw, Ind.
1501	Thomas Shriver	St.p.	153	1850	Feb 7	1857	Ice	Cincinnati, Ohio.
1502	Three Brothers	St.s.	583	1888	Sep 27	1911	Stranded	South Manitou Island, Mich.
1503	Three Sisters	Ga.s.	52	1901	Nov 23	1912	Stranded	Red River Bluffs, Wisc. All lives (3) lost.
1504	Tiger	Scow	102	1915	Jul 28	1929	Burned	Lakeside, Mich. Steel vessel.
1505	Tigress	St.p.	215	1829	May 19	1830	Burned	Troy, Ohio.
1506	Tioga	St.s.	2,320	1885	Nov 26	1919	Stranded	Keweenaw Point, Mich.
1507	Tipple Boat No.1	Brg.	509	1925	Jan 1	1946	Burned	Shadyside, Ohio.
1508	Tiskilwa	St.p.	88	1834	Mar 15	1837	Collided	With WISCONSIN. Illinois River. 7 lives lost.
1509	Tobacco Plant	St.p.	207	1843	Mar 7	1853	Stranded	Chester, Ill.
1510	Toledo	St.s.	585	1854	Oct 24	1856	Foundered	Port Washington, Wisc. 40 lives lost.
1511	Toltec	St.s.	767	1889	Sep 4	1919	Burned	Windmill Point, Quebec, Canada.
1512	Tom B. Davock	St.s.	-	-	Nov 11	1940	Collided	With MINCH. About 2.5 miles south of Pentwater, Mich.
1513	Tom C. Powell	St.p.	99	1915	Jan 31	1924	Foundered	Off Wilson Light, Ill. 5 lives lost (45).
1514	Tom Metcalf	St.p.	131	1844	Feb 23	1847	Stranded	Aurora, Ind. 2 lives lost.
1515	Tonawanda	St.s.	822	1856	Oct 18	1870	Foundered	Buffalo, N.Y.
1516	Topeka	St.s.	1,476	1889	Aug 15	1916	Collided	With st.s. CHRISTOPHER. Detroit River, off Sandwich, Ontario, Canada.
1517	Tornado	St.s.	102	1863	Aug 6	1870	Exploded	Oswego, N.Y. 3 lives lost.
1518	Tourist	St.p.	66	1897	Aug 18	1911	Burned	Riverdale, Ill., Calumet River.
1519	Trade Wind	Sch.	-	-	Dec 4	1854	Collided	Off Long Point, Ontario.
1520	Trader	Scow	291	1903	Jul 8	1908	Foundered	Strawberry Island, Niagara River, N.Y.
1521	Transfer	St.s.	-	-	May	1896	Unknown	Off Lorain, Ohio.
1522	Transport	Brg.	1,397	1880	Sep 22	1942	Foundered	Eagle Harbor, Mich. Iron vessel.
1523	Traveler	St.p.	603	1852	Aug 17	1865	Burned	Eagle Harbor, Mich.
1524	Trenton	St.s.	517	1905	May 1	1923	Foundered	St. Clair River, Mich. Steel vessel.
1525	Troy	St.s.	340	1849	Oct 26	1859	Foundered	Point Dubuque, Lake Huron. 23 lives lost.
1526	Trude R. Wiehe	St.s.	786	1885	Jul 11	1910	Stranded	Portage Bay, Mich.
1527	Turret Chief	St.p.	-	-	Nov 11	1913	Stranded	West of Copper Harbor, Keweenaw Peninsula, Mich.
1528	Two Brothers	Sch.	71	1884	Jan 12	1908	Foundered	Lock No.4, Ohio River, Pa.
1529	Two Fannies	Sch.			Aug 10	1890	Foundered	Mouth of the Detroit River, Mich.
1530	U.S. 104	Brg.	306	1919	Jul 15	1921	Foundered	Buffalo, N.Y. Concrete vessel.
1531	U.S. 240	Brg.	294	1919	Sep 13	1923	Foundered	Off Port Colburns, Ontario.
1532	U.S. Mail	St.p.	139	1841	Sep 25	1841	Snagged	Chester, Ill.
1533	Uganda	St.s.	2,298	1892	Apr 19	1913	Foundered	Lake Michigan.
1534	Unadilla	Sch.	396	1862	Nov 15	1915	Burned	Cleveland, Ohio.

NO.	NAME OF VESSEL	RIG	TONS	BUILT	DATE		CAUSE	PLACE AND COMMENT
1535	Uncle Sam	St.p.	78	1914	Oct 16	1914	Burned	Near Florence, Ind., Ohio River.
1536	Uncle Tom	Sch.	-	-	Sep 17	1848	Stranded	Off Long Point, Ontario.
1537	Union	St.p.	139	1857	Apr 2	1861	Snagged	Clinton, Ind.
1538	Union	St.p.	116	1855	Dec 30	1865	Burned	Detroit, Mich.
1539	Union	St.s.	84	1863	Nov 14	1870	Burned	Saginaw, Mich.
1540	Unique	St.s.	91	1900	Nov 7	1913	Burned	Shelburne Harbor, Vermont.
1541	United States	St.p.	366	1835	Mar 7	1849	Burned	Buffalo, N.Y.
1542	United States	St.s.	2,058	1909	Dec 8	1927	Burned	Sarnia Harbor, Ontario. Steel vessel. Also reported lost March 5, 1928.
1543	United Workman	C.bt.	101	1891	Nov 14	1912	Burned	Near Rochester, N.Y.
1544	Ursula	Brg.	177	1902	May 15	1923	Foundered	Buffalo Creek, Buffalo, N.Y.
1545	V.H. Ketchum	Brg.	1,699	-	Sep 15	1905	Burned	Parisien Island, Lake Superior. 2 lives lost.
1546	Val P. Collins	St.p.	119	1901	May 31	1918	Ice	Selitan, Ohio.
1547	Van Valkenburgh	Sch.	-	-	May 11	1887	Unknown	Off North Point, Thunder Bay, Mich.
1548	Vega	Sch.	200	1856	Oct 20	1905	Stranded	Ludington, Mich.
1549	Vega	St.s.	2,143	1893	Nov 28	1905	Foundered	South Fox Island, Lake Michigan. Steel vessel.
1550	Venture	St.p.	61	1851	Apr 12	1858	Foundered	Gallipolis, Ohio. 6 lives lost.
1551	Venus	Sch.	-	-	Oct	1887	Unknown	Off Black River, Thunder Bay, Mich.
1552	Verano	Ga.s.	102	1925	Aug 28	1946	Foundered	8 miles north of South Haven, Mich.
1553	Vermillion	St.p.	385	1839	Nov 7	1842	Burned	Huron, Ohio. 5 lives lost.
1554	Vermont	St.p.	167	1809	Oct 15	1815	Foundered	Isle aux Noir, Quebec, Canada.
1555	Vernon	Steamer	-	-	Oct 29	1887	Foundered	Lake Michigan. 41 lives lost.
1556	Victor	Sch.	-	-	May 30	1888	Unknown	West of Forty Mile Point, Mich., Lake Huron.
1557	Vienna	St.w.	169	1853	Feb 7	1857	Ice	Illinois River.
1558	Vigilant	St.w.	90	1842	Oct 6	1843	Snagged	Warsaw, Ind.
1559	Virginia	St.p.	109	1819	Sep 19	1823	Snagged	Chester, Ill.
1560	Virginia	Brig	-	-	Fall	1855	Foundered	Off Long Point, Ontario.
1561	Virginia	Ga.y.	50	1902	Oct 5	1914	Burned	Mouth of Clinton River, Lake St. Clair, Mich.
1562	Virginia C	C.bt.	102	1888	Jul	1911	Collided	With unknown vessel. Chambly, Quebec, Canada.
1563	Virginia Home	St.w.	70	1858	May 21	1860	Foundered	Cincinnati, Ohio.
1564	Visitor	St.p.	141	1848	May 30	1851	Collided	With HIRAM POWERS. Terre Haute, Ind.
1565	Volant	St.p.	76	1831	Aug 19	1833	Burned	New Albany, Ind.
1566	Vulcan	Steamer	-	-	Jun 7	1882	Unknown	North of Lorain Harbor, Ohio.
1567	Vulcan	St.s.	1,759	1889	Oct 30	1918	Stranded	Pointe Abbaye, Lake Superior. Steel vessel.
1568	W.B. Castle	St.s.	218	1862	Jul 24	1906	Collided	With ROBERT HOLLAND. Belle Isle, Mich. Also reported as 124 Gross Tons.
1569	W.C. Kimball	Sch.	-	-	May 12	1891	Foundered	Point Betsie, near Frankfort, Mich.
1570	W.C. Mitchell	St.w.	121	1907	Feb 18	1945	Burned	Kentucky side of Ohio River, 7 miles east of Manchester, Ohio.
1571	W.C. Richardson	St.s.	3,818	1902	Dec 8	1909	Foundered	Buffalo, N.Y. Steel vessel. 5 lives lost.
1572	W.C. Trotter	C.bt.	103	1893	Oct 12	1920	Stranded	St. Anne, Quebec, Canada.
1573	W.C. Wiley	C.bt.	98	1889	Oct 5	1918	Foundered	St. John's de Shion, Quebec, Canada.
1574	W.G. Keith	Sch.	-	-	Oct 31	1870	Stranded	Off Long Point, Ontario.
1575	W.H. Denny	St.w.	276	1855	Sep 16	1858	Burned	Quincy, Ill.
1576	W.H. Gilbert	St.s.	2,820	1902	May 22	1914	Collided	With st.s. CALDERA. 15 miles below Hamden Bay Island, Lake Huron. Steel vessel.
1577	W.H. Sawyer	St.s.	746	1890	Sep 20	1928	Foundered	Harbor Beach, Mich.
1578	W.H. Warwick	St.p.	92	1900	Nov 27	1923	Foundered	Cincinnati, Ohio.
1579	W.L. Wetmore	St.s.	-	-	Nov 29	1901	Foundered	On Russell Reef, in Devil Island Channel, Ontario, Lake Huron. Demolished.
1580	W.P. Thew	St.s.	206	1884	Jun 22	1909	Collided	With st.s. WILLIAM LIVINGSTONE. Thunder Bay Island, Mich.
1581	W.W. Stewart	Sch.	294	1866	Oct 12	1909	Burned	Buffalo, N.Y.
1582	Wabash	St.s.	721	1863	Jun 5	1870	Collided	With EMPIRE STATE. Lexington, Mich. 1 life lost.

NO.	NAME OF VESSEL	RIG	TONS	BUILT	DATE		CAUSE	PLACE AND COMMENT
1583	Wabash Valley	St.s.	593	1856	Nov 22	1860	Stranded	Muskegon, Mich.
1584	Walcolken	Sch.	-	-		1887	Foundered	Off Long Point, Ontario.
1585	Walk in the Water	St.p.	338	1818	Nov 1	1821	Stranded	Buffalo, N.Y. First steamer on the Great Lakes above Niagara, N.Y.
1586	Walter Needham	St.p.	142	1901	Oct 17	1910	Foundered	Brookport, Ill.
1587	Walter R. Pringle	St.s.	199	1890	May 6	1920	Burned	Stag Island, St. Clair River, Mich.
1588	War Eagle	St.p.	296	1854	May 15	1870	Burned	La Crosse, Wisc. 2 lives lost.
1589	Warrington	St.s.	375	1868	Aug 21	1911	Stranded	Charlevoix, Mich.
1590	Washington	-	-	-	Jun 16	1838	Burned	Lake Erie. 50 lives lost.
1591	Water Witch	St.s.	369	1862	Oct	1863	Foundered	Saginaw Bay, Mich. 20 lives lost.
1592	Waterloo	St.p.	98	1840		1849	Stranded	Georgian Bay, Ontario, Canada.
1593	Waunita	St.w.	318	1864	Feb 14	1872	Ice	Cincinnati, Ohio.
1594	Wave	St.p.	78	1835	Jun 21	1837	Burned	Peru, Ill. 1 life lost.
1595	Wave	St.p.	207	1850	Nov 7	1851	Stranded	Grand River, Ontario.
1596	Wave	St.s.	153	1864	Aug 29	1874	Burned	Saginaw Bay, Mich.
1597	Wayne	Sch.	708	1882	Oct 9	1906	Stranded	14 miles southwest of Portage Canal, Mich.
1598	West Newton	St.p.	163	1849	Oct 13	1853	Snagged	Alma, Wisc.
1599	West Side	Sch.	324	1870	Unknown		Stranded	Near Parry Sound, Georgian Bay, Ontario.
1600	Western	St.p.	116	1845	Jan	1849	Snagged	Wabash River, Ind.
1601	Western Reserve	St.s.	-	-	Aug 30	1892	Foundered	South of Caribou Island, Mich.
1602	Western Star	Steamer	-	-	Nov 25	1905	Stranded	East of Fourteen Mile Point, near Ontonagon, Mich.
1603	Western Star	St.s.	4,764	1903	Sep 24	1915	Stranded	Georgian Bay, Lake Huron. Steel vessel.
1604	Westmoreland	St.s.	665	1853	Dec 2	1854	Foundered	Sleeping Bear, Mich. 17 lives lost.
1605	Westmoreland	St.p.	432	1860	May 12	1869	Burned	Cincinnati, Ohio.
1606	Wexford	Steamer	-	-	Nov 13	1913	Unknown	Northwest of Kettle Point, Ontario, Lake Huron.
1607	Wheel of Fortune	St.p.	165	1845		1847	Burned	Enterprise, Ind.
1608	White Bluff	St.w.	142	1856	Mar 27	1857	Collided	With GEORGE ALBREE. Cairo, Ill. Also known as "White Bluffs".
1609	White Rose	St.p.	194	1847	Jul 24	1848	Burned	Cairo, Ill.
1610	White Swan	Ol.s.	99	1922	Nov 30	1956	Stranded	On reef called De Aux Galete in Lake Michigan.
1611	Wild Rover	Sch.	-	-	Nov 2	1874	Unknown	West of light on Long Point, Ontario.
1612	William A. Reiss	St.s.	4,498	1901	Nov 13	1934	Stranded	Sheboygan, Wisc. Steel vessel.
1613	Wm. A. Young	Sch.	434	1883	Nov 7	1911	Foundered	Between Middle and Thunder Bay Islands, Lake Huron.
1614	William Aldrich	Sch.	177	1856	Jun 7	1916	Stranded	Davenport, Mich.
1615	William B. Davock	St.s.	4,220	1907	Nov 11	1940	Foundered	Lake Michigan, between Ludington and Pentwater, Mich. Steel vessel.
1616	William C. Moreland	St.s.	7,514	1910	Oct 18	1910	Stranded	Eagle River Reef, Mich. Steel vessel.
1617	William Case	Sch.	266	1855	Jul 26	1906	Foundered	50 miles northeast by north of Colchester Light, Lake Erie.
1618	Wm. Crosthwaite	Sch.	371	1866	Sep 6	1906	Collided	With st.s. HOMER WARREN. Lake Erie.
1619	Wm. Dickinson	St.s.	78	1893	Sep	1923	Burned	Marine City, Mich.
1620	William E. Corey	St.s.	-	-	Nov 26	1905	Unknown	On Gull Island Reef, Mich., Lake Superior.
1621	William Glasgow	St.p.	249	1837	Apr 23	1839	Burned	Mound City, Ill.
1622	William Grandy	Sch.	464	1867	Aug 28	1906	Stranded	Cleveland, Ohio.
1623	Wm. H. McAllister	Ol.s.	140	1942	Nov 17	1963	Collided	With submerged object. In Lake Champlain, N.Y. Steel vessel.
1624	William H. Simons	Brg.	471	1919	Sep 16	1933	Burned	4 miles southwest of Thunder Bay Island, Lake Huron, Mich.
1625	Wm. H. Vanderbilt	Sch.	-	-	Sep 24	1883	Unknown	Near Old Cut, Long Point, Ontario.
1626	Wm. H. Wolf	St.s.	2,265	1887	Oct 20	1921	Burned	St. Clair River, Mich. 2 lives lost.
1627	Wm. L. Parkhurst	St.s.	50	1906	Oct 11	1932	Burned	Pearl Beach, Mich.
1628	William M. Hatch	Ol.s.	107	1919	Oct 3	1935	Foundered	12 miles south by southwest of Point Aux Pins, Lake Erie.
1629	William P. Rend	Brg.	2,323	1888	Sep 22	1917	Foundered	Alpena, Mich.
1630	William Paris	St.p.	172	1839	Sep 1	1841	Snagged	Grand Chain, Ill.

NO.	NAME OF VESSEL	RIG	TONS	BUILT	DATE	CAUSE	PLACE AND COMMENT
1631	William Peacock	St.p.	-	-	Sep 16 1830	Unknown	Off Buffalo, N.Y.
1632	William Penn	St.p.	214	1826	May 28 1836	Stranded	Erie, Pa.
1633	Winchester	St.p.	190	1837	Aug 18 1837	Snagged	Grand Chain, Ill.
1634	Winchester	St.p.	560	1866	Feb 23 1866	Burned	East Liverpool, Ohio. 5 lives lost.
1635	Windsor	St.p.	223	1856	Apr 26 1866	Unknown	Detroit, Mich. 28 lives lost. Used as ferryboat.
1636	Winnipeg	St.s.	1,108	1878	Oct 21 1922	Foundered	Lachine Canal, Quebec, Canada.
1637	Winslow	St.s.	265	1862	Nov 1864	Stranded	Cleveland, Ohio. 6 lives lost.
1638	Winslow	St.s.	919	1863	Oct 1891	Burned	Duluth, Minn.
1639	Wisconsin	St.p.	87	1834	Mar 15 1837	Collided	With TISKILWA. Illinois River.
1640	Wisconsin	St.p.	490	1838	Aug 24 1853	Collided	With BRUNSWICK, Toledo, Ohio.
1641	Wisconsin	St.p.	139	1849	Oct 31 1857	Snagged	Grafton, Ill.
1642	Wisconsin	St.s.	352	1852	May 21 1867	Burned	Grenadine Island, Lake Ontario. 23 lives lost.
1643	Wisconsin	St.s.	1,921	1881	Nov 11 1929	Foundered	Kenosha, Wisc. 9 lives lost (68).
1644	Wonder	St.s.	99	1899	Sep 6 1908	Stranded	Ashtabula, Ohio.
1645	Wyoming	St.p.	198	1846	Dec 16 1853	Burned	Pekin, Ill.
1646	Yonkers	Brg.	1,209	1879	Oct 4 1917	Stranded	Ashtabula, Ohio.
1647	York State	St.p.	247	1852	Sep 1 1859	Snagged	Madison, Ill.
1648	Young America	St.w.	127	1853	Jun 13 1855	Snagged	Bath, Ill.
1649	Young America	St.s.	-	-	Sep 2 1873	Unknown	At Oak Orchard, Lake Ontario.
1650	Young America		-	-	Aug 20 1880	Unknown	Off Kelleys Island, Ohio.
1651	Young Farmer	Sch.	-	-	Nov 5 1827	Unknown	Off Long Point, Ontario.
1652	Young Phoenix	Sch.	-	-	Sep 14 1818	Foundered	2 miles off Long Point, Ontario.
1653	Yuba	St.p.	348	1852	Dec 27 1856	Stranded	Wood River, Ill.
1654	Yukon	Sch.	1,602	1893	Oct 20 1905	Foundered	3 miles north of Ashtabula piers, Ohio.
1655	Zach Chandler	Steamer	-	-	Oct 30 1892	Foundered	4 miles east of Deer Park, Mich.
1656	Zachary Taylor	St.p.	174	1848	Dec 21 1853	Foundered	Lawrenceburg, Ind. 3 lives lost.
1657	Zephyr	St.p.	92	1840	May 15 1843	Snagged	Portsmouth, Ohio.
1658	Zillah	St.s.	748	1890	Aug 29 1926	Foundered	Whitefish Point, Minn.
1659	43	Brg.	546	1911	May 24 1961	Foundered	In Buffalo Harbor, N.Y. Steel vessel.
1660	102	Brg.	407	1950	Jan 1959	Foundered	In Ohio River at Montgomery Lock, Industry, Pa. Steel vessel.
1661	361	Brg.	386	1935	Nov 30 1950	Foundered	At Lemont Light, Mile 302.9, above Grafton, Ill. in the Illinois Waterway. Steel.

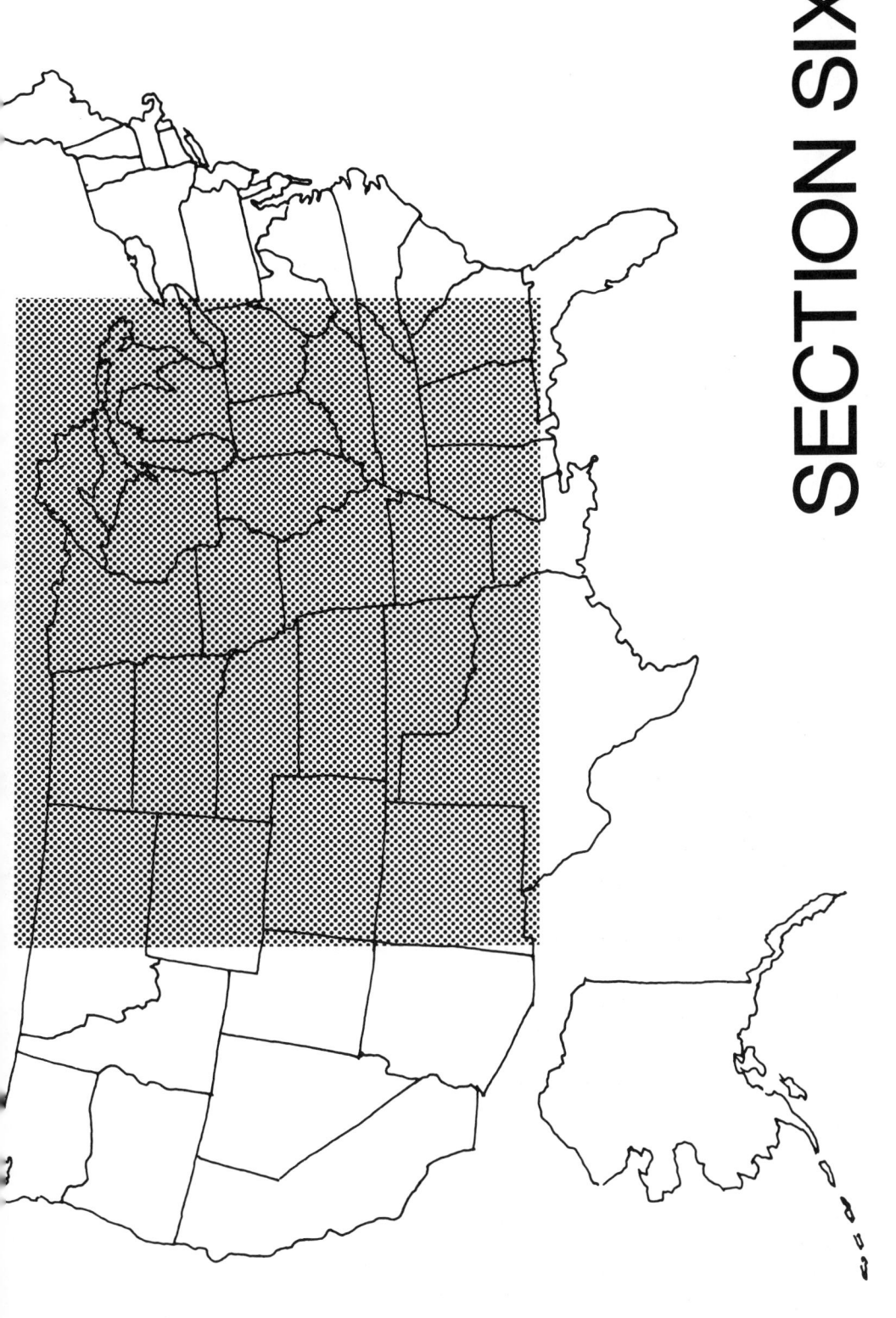

NO.	NAME OF VESSEL	RIG	TONS	BUILT	DATE		CAUSE	PLACE AND COMMENT
1	ABL 122	Brg.	486	1936	Oct 2	1953	Stranded	Near Stewart Bar, Mile 870.6 Ahp, Mississippi River, off Caruthersville, Mo.
2	ABL 212	Brg.	550	1935	May 16	1967	Collided	With the Markland Dam. At Mile 532, on the Ohio River.
3	A.B. Shaw	St.p.	67	1847	May 20	1850	Burned	Memphis, Tenn.
4	A.C. Goddin	St.p.	351	1855	Apr 27	1857	Snagged	Hamburg, Mo.
5	A.C. Jaynes	St.w.	148	1925	May 9	1960	Burned	At mouth of Helena Harbor, Helena, Ark. Steel vessel.
6	ACO 47	Brg.	597	1955	Nov 27	1966	Foundered	Approximately Mile 372.4, lower Mississippi River.
7	A.G. Mason	St.w.	170	1855	Oct 30	1857	Snagged	Davenport, Iowa.
8	AGS 103	Brg.	620	1950	Aug 3	1960	Foundered	In Mississippi River at a point just above Clarksville, Mo. Steel vessel.
9	A.H. Sevier	St.w.	193	1860	Dec 31	1860	Snagged	Pine Bluff, Ark.
10	A.J. Sweeney	St.w.	244	1862	Mar 9	1864	Burned	Clarksville, Tenn.
11	A.L. Davis	St.w.	102	1852	Mar 23	1857	Snagged	Shelbyville, Tenn.
12	A.L. Shotwell	St.p.	582	1852	Mar 24	1857	Snagged	Memphis, Tenn.
13	A.M. Phillips	St.p.	174	1836	Sep 11	1841	Snagged	Doolen Slough, Mo.
14	A.N. Johns	St.p.	199	1847	Dec 29	1847	Exploded	Trinity, Ky. 60 lives lost.
15	A.W. Armstrong	St.w.	81	1925	Jun 25	1930	Foundered	Genevieve, Mo.
16	A.W. Van Leer	St.p.	160	1847	Oct 23	1850	Snagged	Henderson, Ky.
17	Acadia	St.w.	118	1845	May 17	1849	Burned	St. Louis, Mo.
18	Accentor	Ol.s.	142	1941	Jun 12	1966	Foundered	At Star Landing, about Mile 91 Ahp, Mississippi River.
19	Ad Hine	St.w.	94	1860	Apr 25	1866	Snagged	Sioux City, Iowa.
20	Admiral	St.p.	242	1843	Dec 28	1847	Collided	Clarksville, Ark.
21	Admiral	St.p.	244	1852	Apr 5	1862	Burned	Columbus, Ky.
22	Aid	St.p.	60	1860	Jan 28	1861	Snagged	St. Francis River, Ark.
23	Airline	Ga.w.	53	1929	Jan 31	1945	Foundered	In the 14th pool, left bank of the Ohio River.
24	Alabama	St.p.	297	1850	Aug 12	1855	Burned	Louisville, Ky.
25	Alabama	St.w.	250	1912		1932	Foundered	Memphis, Tenn.
26	Albany	St.p.	98	1912	Oct 30	1918	Burned	Nonconnah Creek, Tenn.
27	Albertine	St.p.	160	1855	Feb 24	1856	Unknown	Covington, Ky.
28	Alert	St.w.	92	1845		1847	Snagged	Arkansas River, Ark.
29	Alert	St.w.	66	1874	Aug 9	1928	Foundered	Musick Ferry, Mo.
30	Alert No.2	St.w.	94	1848	Nov 24	1849	Collided	With JAMES MILLINGER. Smithland, Ky.
31	Alexander Hamilton	St.p.	212	1847	May 17	1849	Burned	St. Louis, Mo.
32	Algoma	St.p.	209	1846	May 28	1849	Burned	St. Louis, Mo.
33	Alhambra	St.w.	187	1854		1863	Burned	Commerce, Mo.
34	Alhambra	St.p.	290	1845	Jan	1851	Burned	Commerce, Mo.
35	Alice	St.p.	232	1848	May 17	1849	Burned	St. Louis, Mo.
36	Alice	St.p.	130	1904	Dec 26	1921	Burned	Arkansas City, Ark.
37	Alice Dean	St.p.	411	1863	Jul 7	1863	Burned	Brandenburg, Ky.
38	Alice L. Barr	St.s.	50	1884		1924	Foundered	Delaware, Ky.
39	Alida	St.w.	94	1853	Jun 9	1857	Collided	With FASHION. Smithland, Ky.
40	Alliance	St.w.	136	1852	Apr 17	1863	Stranded	Devil Island, Cape Girardeau, Mo.
41	Allie	St.p.	53	1903	Jan 23	1914	Burned	Morgantown, Green River, Tenn.
42	Alone	St.w.	211	1863	Jun 13	1867	Foundered	St. Louis, Mo. 3 lives lost.
43	Alpha A. Knight	Ol.w.	57	1928	Apr	1947	Foundered	At Reidland Road Landing, Paducah, Ky.
44	Alton	St.p.	800	1906	Jan 29	1918	Foundered	Paducah, Ky.
45	Altona	St.p.	402	1852	Feb 26	1856	Foundered	St. Louis, Mo.
46	Amanda	St.p.	390	1865	Nov 3	1867	Burned	Omaha, Neb.
47	Amarath	St.w.	160	1863	Nov 17	1867	Snagged	Doniphan, Kan.
48	Amazon	St.p.	231	1838	Feb 21	1843	Snagged	Bird Point, Mo.

NO.	NAME OF VESSEL	RIG	TONS	BUILT	DATE	CAUSE	PLACE AND COMMENT
49	Amazonia	St.p.	257	1849	Feb 16 1854	Stranded	St. Louis, Mo. 2 lives lost.
50	Ambassador	St.p.	473	1843	Apr 25 1847	Burned	Luxemburg, Mo.
51	Amelia	St.p.	151	1846	Dec 11 1849	Snagged	Fayette, Mo.
52	Amelia	St.p.	92	1847	Dec 11 1849	Snagged	Glasgow, Mo.
53	Amelia Poe	St.w.	321	1865	May 23 1968	Snagged	Oswego, Montana.
54	America	St.p.	263	1827	Nov 12 1827	Snagged	Plum Point, Tenn.
55	America	St.p.	740	1849	Jan 20 1857	Snagged	St. Francis River, Ark.
56	America	St.p.	1,256	1866	Dec 4 1868	Collided	With UNITED STATES (which lost 70 lives). Warsaw, Ky. 4 lives lost.
57	America	St.w.	277	1854	Jan 28 1870	Snagged	Arkansas River, Ark.
58	American Eagle	St.p.	295	1842	May 17 1849	Burned	St. Louis, Mo.
59	American Eagle	St.p.	216	1847	May 17 1849	Burned	St. Louis, Mo.
60	Andrew Fulton	St.p.	360	1848	Feb 21 1849	Stranded	Crystal City, Mo. 3 lives lost.
61	Andy Fulton	St.w.	146	1858	Jul 29 1861	Burned	Carrollton, Ky.
62	Anna	St.p.	110	1860	Oct 30 1864	Burned	Johnsonville, Tenn.
63	Anna S. Cooper	Ol.s.	85	1882	Mar 24 1955	Foundered	At Mile 1002, Johnsville, Tenn.
64	Annabell King	St.p.	86	1903	Dec 31 1911	Collided	With pier, Knoxville, Tenn.
65	Annie Jacobs	St.w.	148	1863	May 10 1868	Burned	Memphis, Tenn.
66	Antelope	St.p.	400	1866	Apr 12 1869	Burned	20 miles above Yankton, S.D. 2 lives lost.
67	Anthony Wayne	St.p.	164	1846	Apr 11 1851	Snagged	Independence, Mo.
68	Appleton Belle	St.w.	103	1856	Feb 6 1862	Burned	Fort Henry, Tenn.
69	Arabia	St.p.	222	1853	Sep 1 1856	Snagged	Parkville, Mo.
70	Arabian	St.w.	305	1866	May 8 1868	Snagged	Missouri River.
71	Arago	St.p.	268	1860	Feb 6 1865	Burned	Commerce, Mo.
72	Arcola	St.w.	203	1863	Nov 4 1864	Burned	Johnsonville, Tenn.
73	Argo	St.p.	84	1832	Dec 17 1841	Stranded	Frankfort, Ky.
74	Argos	St.w.	84	1864	Jul 27 1871	Foundered	Batesville, Ark.
75	Arkansas	St.p.	229	1841	Mar 29 1844	Snagged	Lewisburg, Ark.
76	Arkansas	St.w.	223	1860	Sep 10 1863	Burned	Little Rock, Ark.
77	Arkansas Mail	St.p.	107	1843	Dec 29 1848	Burned	Louisville, Ky.
78	Arkansas Traveler	St.w.	170	1856	Mar 21 1860	Snagged	Pine Bluff, Ark. 1 life lost.
79	Armenia	St.w.	297	1863	Mar 29 1869	Burned	St. Louis, Mo.
80	Artizan	St.p.	144	1839	Oct 10 1841	Snagged	Van Buren, Ark.
81	Asia	St.p.	199	1849	Feb 2 1854	Foundered	St. Louis, Mo.
82	Assiniboin	St.p.	149	1833	Jun 1 1835	Burned	Heart River, N.D.
83	Astoria	St.p.	148	1836	1840	Snagged	Blue River, Mo.
84	Atlanta	St.w.	311	1855	Dec 20 1860	Snagged	Platin Rock, below St. Louis, Mo.
85	Atalanta	St.p.	141	1853	Mar 2 1863	Collided	With bridge. Clarksville, Tenn.
86	Atlas	St.p.	135	1844	Mar 8 1847	Snagged	Clarksville, Mo.
87	Auburn	St.p.	120	1841	Apr 22 1842	Burned	Maysville, Ky. 1 life lost.
88	Augustus McDowell	St.w.	451	1860	Oct 27 1862	Burned	St. Louis, Mo.
89	Aurora	St.p.	331	1857	Nov 4 1864	Burned	Johnsonville, Tenn.
90	Australia	St.p.	289	1853	Apr 1 1859	Burned	St. Louis, Mo.
91	Banner State	St.p.	254	1850	Apr 11 1855	Snagged	Brickhouse Bend, Mo.
92	Bart Tully	St.p.	63	1891	Sep 3 1922	Foundered	Craighead Point Light, near Osceola, Ark. Steel vessel. 1 life lost (16).
93	Baton Rouge	St.w.	65	1860	Jun 1862	Burned	Tennessee River.
94	Bayard	St.p.	200	1864	Dec 13 1876	Ice	St. Louis, Mo.
95	Bayou Boeuf	St.w.	104	1847	Mar 25 1848	Foundered	Clear Lake, Ark.
96	Beaver	St.w.	100	1847	Apr 28 1854	Collided	With L.M. KENNETT. Ste. Genevieve, Mo.

NO.	NAME OF VESSEL	RIG	TONS	BUILT	DATE			CAUSE	PLACE AND COMMENT
97	Beaver	St.p.	148	1865	Apr	18	1885	Snagged	St. Louis, Mo.
98	Bedford	St.w.	180	1852	Jun	1	1854	Burned	Harpeth Shoals, Tenn.
99	Belfast	St.p.	435	1829	Apr	8	1836	Burned	Louisville, Ky.
100	Belle of Calhoun	St.w.	283	1895	Mar	22	1930	Burned	Alton Slough, Mo.
101	Belle of Clarksville	St.p.	250	1843	Dec	14	1844	Collided	Memphis, Tenn. 31 lives lost.
102	Belle Creole	St.w.	206	1856	Feb	1	1864	Snagged	Plum Point, Tenn. 1 life lost.
103	Belle Golding	St.w.	189	1854	Jun	14	1855	Snagged	Missouri River.
104	Belle Isle	St.p.	219	1846	May	17	1849	Burned	St. Louis, Mo.
105	Belle Peoria	St.p.	263	1858	Apr	19	1866	Snagged	Fort Randall, S.D.
106	Belle of Pike	St.p.	614	1866	Dec		1872	Ice	Memphis, Tenn.
107	Belle Quigley	St.p.	132	1852	Feb	5	1856	Burned	Carrollton, Ky.
108	Belle Vernon	St.w.	90	1910	Jan	25	1926	Foundered	New Madrid, Mo.
109	Belle of the West	St.p.	249	1841	Apr	23	1850	Exploded	Warsaw, Ky. 34 lives lost.
110	Ben Franklin No.8	St.p.	473	1848	May	1	1854	Collided	With GALENA, North Buena Vista, Iowa.
111	Ben Johnson	St.p.	525	1866	May	29	1869	Burned	St. Louis, Mo.
112	Ben South	St.p.	176	1860	Dec	9	1864	Burned	Cumberland City, Tenn.
113	Ben West	St.p.	241	1849	Aug	10	1855	Collided	With bridge. Washington, Mo.
114	Benton	St.w.	246	1864	May	19	1869	Snagged	Sioux City, Iowa.
115	Bertha	St.w.	218	1863	Jun	24	1872	Snagged	St. Joseph, Mo.
116	Bertrand	St.w.	251	1864	Apr	1	1865	Snagged	Omaha, Neb.
117	Bessie Smith	St.p.	127	1897	Mar	20	1911	Burned	Parkersburg, W.Va.
118	Bettie Owen	St.p.	344	1891	Feb	5	1910	Burned	Paducah, Ky.
119	Betty Lord	St.w.	300	1921	Sep	28	1924	Burned	Owens Island, Ky. Used as ferryboat.
120	Birdie Brent	St.p.	152	1866	Nov	24	1887	Unknown	Boonville, Mo. Used as ferryboat.
121	Bismarck	St.p.	1,450	1867	Nov	2	1877	Burned	St. Louis, Mo.
122	Bismarck	Ga.p.	93	1896	Jun	30	1913	Burned	At Ree, N.D., Missouri River.
123	Black Hawk	St.p.	125	1909	Jan	29	1918	Ice	Livingston Point, Tenn.
124	Blanche Lewis	St.w.	155	1855	Nov		1860	Foundered	Nashville, Tenn.
125	Blue Wing No.2	St.p.	170	1850	Dec	28	1862	Burned	Napoleon, Ark.
126	Bluff City	St.p.	396	1853	Jul	27	1853	Burned	St. Louis, Mo.
127	Bob Dudley	St.p.	196	1897	Dec	20	1916	Foundered	Wharf, Nashville, Tenn.
128	Bob White	St.w.	70	1908	Sep	1	1930	Ice	St. Louis, Mo.
129	Boonslick	St.p.	-	1835	Oct	24	1834	Collided	With MISSISSIPPI BELLE. St. Louis, Mo. 30 lives lost.
130	Boonville	St.p.	114	1835	Nov	19	1837	Snagged	Kansas City, Mo.
131	Boreas No.3	St.p.	264	1847	May	17	1849	Burned	St. Louis, Mo.
132	Boston	St.p.	148	1839	Nov	28	1842	Snagged	Cape Girardeau, Mo.
133	Bostona	St.p.	355	1854	Jun	2	1866	Burned	St. Louis, Mo.
134	Bostona No.3	St.p.	375	1863	Aug	8	1866	Burned	Maysville, Ky.
135	Bowling Green	St.p.	148	1839	Dec	12	1842	Stranded	Osage River, Mo.
136	Bowling Green	St.p.	123	1904	Mar	31	1926	Foundered	Off South Carrollton, Ky.
137	Boyd C. Taylor	St.w.	242	1891	Feb		1926	Foundered	Wheeling, W.Va.
138	Bracelet	St.p.	169	1857	Sep	10	1863	Burned	Little Rock, Ark.
139	Brandywine	St.p.	483	1829	Apr	9	1832	Burned	Randolph, Tenn. Also reported at Memphis, Tenn. 155 lives lost.
140	Bridge City	St.w.	199	1854	Nov	29	1860	Burned	Napoleon, Ark.
141	Bridgeport	St.w.	184	1864	Jun	1	1868	Snagged	Sioux City, Iowa.
142	Brilliant	St.p.	398	1850	Dec	3	1855	Burned	Memphis, Tenn.
143	Brilliant	St.p.	440	1863	Oct	16	1865	Burned	New Madrid, Mo.
144	Brilliant	St.w.	226	1862	Dec	6	1867	Burned	Prarie Landing, Ark. 1 life lost.

NO.	NAME OF VESSEL	RIG	TONS	BUILT	DATE	CAUSE	PLACE AND COMMENT
145	Brunette	St.p.	228	1852	Oct 15 1859	Burned	Bloody Island, St. Louis, Mo.
146	Buckeye	St.p.	74	1896	Jul 27 1921	Burned	Point Pleasant, W.Va.
147	Buckeye Belle	St.p.	155	1852	Nov 26 1857	Exploded	Columbus, Ky.
148	Buffalo	St.p.	249	1809	Mar 2 1820	Exploded	Owensboro, Ky. 17 lives lost.
149	C 91	Brg.	742	1959	Dec 2 1964	Foundered	At Mile 851, lower Mississippi River.
150	C.C. Bowyer	St.p.	72	1909	Dec 3 1919	Collided	With obstruction. Rampeys Landing, Ky.
151	C.E. Taylor	St.p.	79	1899	Jul 23 1907	Foundered	Black River, Ark.
152	C.S. Pearcy	St.p.	148	1910	Sep 13 1917	Burned	Little Kanawha River, W.Va.
153	C.T. 425	Brg.	440	1936	Oct 4 1949	Foundered	At foot of Market Street, St. Louis, Mo. Steel vessel.
154	C.T. 429	Brg.	416	1936	Feb 28 1950	Foundered	Sunk while under load at Mile 836.7, Slim Island Towhead, Ohio River, Mo.
155	C.T. 431	Brg.	416	1936	Feb 22 1949	Foundered	At Dycusburg, Ky. Steel vessel.
156	C.W. Sombart	St.p.	411	1857	Jun 27 1859	Burned	St. Louis, Mo.
157	Caddo	St.p.	194	1839	Apr 13 1842	Snagged	Fort Towson, Okla.
158	Caledonia	St.p.	371	1824	Apr 21 1833	Snagged	New Madrid, Mo.
159	Caledonia	St.w.	124	1848	Aug 9 1851	Foundered	Paducah, Ky.
160	Calvin B. Beach	St.w.	138	1877	Feb 19 1939	Burned	Ravenswood, W.Va.
161	Calypso	St.p.	254	1863	Dec 16 1865	Ice	St. Louis, Mo.
162	Cambria	St.p.	203	1845	Feb 3 1851	Snagged	Ste. Genevieve, Mo.
163	Cambridge	St.w.	242	1856	Feb 23 1862	Snagged	Grand Glaise, Ark. 42 lives lost.
164	Camden	St.p.	103	1835	Oct 20 1839	Snagged	Newport, Mo.
165	Camden	St.w.	122	1855	Apr 1857	Snagged	Fulton, Ark.
166	Camelia	St.w.	204	1863	Apr 20 1874	Snagged	Raleigh, Ky.
167	Cando	St.p.	74	1899	Jun 10 1907	Foundered	Huntington, W.Va.
168	Cantonia	St.p.	75	1891	Nov 30 1910	Burned	Canton, Mo.
169	Capitol	St.p.	133	1844	Dec 27 1844	Burned	Seventy-Six, Mo. 3 lives lost.
170	Captain John Brickell	St.w.	188	1863	Nov 11 1863	Snagged	West Columbia, W.Va.
171	Car of Commerce	St.p.	160	1827	May 8 1832	Snagged	Portage des Sioux, Mo.
172	Car of Commerce	St.p.	294	1848	Jan 1849	Stranded	Louisville, Ky.
173	Caroline	St.p.	407	1841	Aug 6 1841	Snagged	Plum Point, Tenn. 37 lives lost.
174	Caroline	St.w.	103	1853	Mar 5 1854	Burned	White River, Ark. 45 lives lost.
175	Carrie	St.w.	189	1863	Apr 14 1868	Snagged	Indian Mission, Missouri River.
176	Carrier	St.p.	345	1855	Aug 12 1861	Snagged	St. Charles, Mo.
177	Catahoula	St.p.	227	1858	Oct 4 1863	Burned	St. Louis, Mo.
178	Cataract	St.p.	283	1851	Nov 18 1857	Exploded	Lisbon, Mo. 12 lives lost.
179	Catawba	St.w.	60	1862	Feb 7 1866	Snagged	Jacksonport, Ark.
180	Catherine	Ga.p.	85	1914	Jan 30 1918	Ice	Mouth of Kentucky River, Ky.
181	Cedar Rapids	St.w.	131	1858	Feb 12 1861	Snagged	Douglas Landing, Ark.
182	Celeste	St.w.	79	1863	Apr 1865	Snagged	Duvalls Bluff, Ark.
183	Central Barge Co. 26	Brg.	598	1940	Oct 9 1966	Collided	With row of timber used as underwater barrier. In vicinity of De Witt, Ark.
184	Central Barge Co. 30	Brg.	598	1942	Aug 31 1965	Foundered	At Mile 10, in vicinity of De Witt, Ark.
185	Centralia	St.w.	239	1864	May 27 1868	Snagged	Auburn Landing, Ark.
186	Ceylon	St.p.	257	1836	Nov 14 1837	Burned	Salt River, Ky.
187	Challenge	St.w.	229	1854	Feb 25 1860	Burned	Above St. Louis, Mo.
188	Champion	St.p.	319	1843	Jun 7 1847	Snagged	Cape Girardeau, Mo.
189	Champion	St.p.	676	1858	Aug 21 1863	Burned	Memphis, Tenn. 1 life lost.
190	Champlain	St.p.	86	1832	Dec 11 1834	Snagged	Ste. Genevieve, Mo.
191	Chancellor	St.p.	392	1856	Oct 4 1863	Burned	St. Louis, Mo.
192	Charilton	St.p.	112	1834	Jul 27 1837	Exploded	St. Louis, Mo. 3 lives lost.

NO.	NAME OF VESSEL	RIG	TONS	BUILT	DATE		CAUSE	PLACE AND COMMENT
193	Charles C. Smith	Brg.	473	1942	Apr 16	1947	Burned	On Miller's Bar, 20 miles above Greenville, Miss. Steel vessel.
194	Charles Carroll	St.p.	349	1846	Jan 13	1850	Snagged	Eddyville, Ky.
195	Charleston	St.p.	94	1887	Feb 10	1906	Stranded	Wolf Island Shute, Mo.
196	Charley Curlin	St.p.	92	1895	Oct 28	1906	Burned	Caruthersville, Mo.
197	Charlie Kremer	St.p.	77	1908	Dec 23	1920	Foundered	Ashland Landing, Miss.
198	Charlie Potwin	St.w.	52	1860	Nov 28	1864	Foundered	Point Pleasant, W.Va.
199	Charter	St.w.	114	1856	Jan 15	1863	Burned	Dozier, Tenn.
200	Cherokee	St.p.	137	1839	Aug 9	1851	Burned	Paducah, Ky.
201	Cherokee	St.w.	261	1864	Jul 13	1864	Stranded	St. Louis, Mo.
202	Cherokee	St.s.	59	1863		1869	Burned	White River, Ark.
203	Chester	St.p.	214	1832	Mar 8	1841	Snagged	Cape Girardeau, Mo.
204	Chester	St.p.	218	1839	Mar 8	1841	Snagged	Cape Girardeau, Mo.
205	Chester Ashley	St.w.	192	1860	Sep 10	1863	Burned	Little Rock, Ark.
206	Chevalier	St.p.	67	1901	May 22	1907	Burned	Huntington, W.Va. (Ohio River).
207	Chicago	St.p.	52	1895	Jan 5	1909	Snagged	Rob Roy, Ark.
208	Chief Black Hawk	Ol.s.	62	1938	Aug 24	1948	Burned	In Ohio River at Mile 420.
209	Choctaw	St.p.	99	1899	Dec 21	1916	Burned	Palo Alta Ledge, Mississippi River.
210	Cincinnati	St.p.	157	1818	Nov 5	1823	Snagged	Ste. Genevieve, Mo.
211	Circassian	St.p.	178	1845	Feb 27	1848	Burned	Maysville, Ky. 4 lives lost.
212	Citizen	St.p.	170	1849	Dec	1850	Snagged	Arkansas River, Ark.
213	City of Fulton	Ga.p.	67	1907	Oct 8	1907	Burned	Fulton, Ark.
214	City of Huntsville	St.p.	238	1852	May 12	1858	Snagged	Palmyra Island, Tenn. 8 lives lost.
215	City of Louisiana	St.p.	564	1857	Sep 14	1860	Snagged	Hat Island, below St. Louis, Mo.
216	City of Memphis	St.p.	865	1857	May 31	1866	Exploded	Buck Island, Memphis, Tenn. 5 lives lost.
217	City of Mondak	Ga.p.	64	1909	Apr 5	1917	Ice	Sanish, N.D.
218	City of McGregor	St.p.	98	1867	Jan 5	1911	Burned	Greenfield Landing, Mo.
219	City of Providence	St.p.	1,303	1880	Jan 20	1910	Foundered	St. Louis, Mo.
220	City of Salitto	St.p.	372	1905	May 11	1910	Stranded	Glen Park, Mo. 12 lives lost (66).
221	City of Savannah	St.p.	293	1902	Dec 11	1911	Foundered	Mississippi River, about 20 miles north of Cairo, Ill.
220	City of Warsaw	St.p.	93	1895	Dec 11	1909	Stranded	Rays Landing, Mo.
221	Clara	St.p.	248	1850	Feb 26	1856	Ice	St. Louis, Mo.
222	Clara	St.p.	342	1864	May 23	1870	Snagged	Missouri River.
223	Clara Dolson	St.w.	938	1860	Feb 4	1868	Burned	St. Louis, Mo.
224	Clara Poe	St.w.	208	1859	Apr 15	1865	Burned	Eddyville, Ky.
225	Clarksville	St.p.	484	1845	May 27	1848	Burned	Napoleon, Ark. 21 lives lost.
226	Clermont	St.p.	121	1845	Dec 9	1851	Unknown	White River, Ark. 20 lives lost.
227	Clermont	St.p.	79	1863	Mar 8	1867	Snagged	Helena, Ark. 1 life lost.
228	Clipper	St.w.	216	1859	Jul 23	1866	Snagged	Quick Run, Ky.
229	Clyde	St.w.	99	1903	Jan 29	1930	Burned	Point Pleasant, W.Va.
230	Colbert	St.w.	164	1850	Jun 26	1855	Burned	Bayne, Tenn.
231	Colonel Crossman	St.p.	415	1857	Feb 4	1858	Exploded	New Madrid, Mo. 14 lives lost.
232	Colonel Gus Linn	St.w.	83	1859	Apr	1860	Snagged	Sioux City, Iowa.
233	Colonel King	St.w.	67	1849		1852	Exploded	Tennessee River.
234	Colorado	St.p.	172	1845	Jun 18	1850	Stranded	Memphis, Tenn.
235	Colossus	St.w.	183	1863	Dec 17	1866	Snagged	Pine Bluff, Ark.
236	Columbia	St.w.	253	1863	Feb 24	1872	Ice	St. Louis, Mo.
237	Columbia	St.p.	197	1893	Mar 25	1908	Collided	With lock wall. Ohio River.
238	Comet	St.p.	100	1857	Feb 19	1859	Foundered	18 miles below Memphis, Tenn.

NO.	NAME OF VESSEL	RIG	TONS	BUILT	DATE		CAUSE	PLACE AND COMMENT
239	Commander	St.w.	138	1906	Apr 3	1929	Foundered	Boonville, Mo.
240	Commodore Perry	St.w.	193	1857	Aug 2	1862	Exploded	Louisville, Ky. 1 life lost.
241	Companion	St.p.	89	1831		1835	Snagged	Barnhart, Mo.
242	Compromise	St.p.	132	1833	Apr 16	1837	Snagged	Little Rock, Ark.
243	Confidence	St.p.	139	1845	Sep 18	1849	Unknown	St. Louis, Mo.
244	Consignee	St.p.	196	1848	Jan 10	1852	Stranded	Cape Girardeau, Mo.
245	Constitution	St.p.	536	1848	May 20	1850	Burned	Memphis, Tenn.
246	Control	St.p.	103	1904	Mar 15	1921	Stranded	Near Owensboro, Ky.
247	Convoy	St.w.	170	1888	Jul 7	1915	Foundered	Cincinnati, Ohio. Iron vessel. 6 lives lost (23).
248	Conway	St.p.	103	1859	Dec 15	1860	Snagged	Badgett Landing, Ark.
249	Coosa	St.p.	173	1826	May 14	1831	Collided	With HUNTRESS, Caruthersville, Mo. 13 lives lost.
250	Cora	St.p.	144	1846	Apr 28	1850	Snagged	Council Bluffs, Iowa. 15 lives lost.
251	Cora	St.w.	215	1864	Aug 15	1869	Snagged	Mouth of Missouri River.
252	Cora L. Roberts	St.p.	157	1910	Oct 15	1914	Foundered	Big Rock, Arkansas River, Ark.
253	Cornelia	St.p.	255	1851	Mar	1855	Stranded	Keokuk, Iowa.
254	Corsair	St.p.	193	1841	Nov	1844	Snagged	Ste. Genevieve, Mo.
255	Corwin H. Spencer	St.p.	1,609	1887	Oct 12	1905	Burned	Ivory Station, Mo.
256	Cote Joyeuse	St.p.	142	1842	Aug 20	1847	Collided	Big Cypress Bend, Ark. 2 lives lost.
257	Cotton Plant	St.p.	295	1846	May 22	1852	Burned	Napoleon, Ark.
258	Courtland	St.p.	230	1848	May 6	1851	Burned	Shippingport, Ky.
259	Crescent	St.p.	356	1888	Nov 17	1920	Burned	Spottsville, Ky.
260	Cricket No.4	St.w.	171	1863	Sep 7	1869	Burned	Licking River, Ky.
261	Cuba	St.p.	157	1853	Sep 29	1856	Snagged	West Franklin, Tenn.
262	Cumberland Valley	St.p.	176	1842	Sep 22	1849	Snagged	Kansas City, Mo.
263	Cutter	St.p.	148	1843	Oct	1847	Snagged	Ste. Genevieve, Mo. 7 lives lost.
264	D.H. Morton	St.p.	173	1856	Mar 11	1859	Burned	Dardanelle, Ark.
265	D.M. Armstrong	St.w.	103	1921	Apr 26	1932	Burned	Memphis, Tenn.
266	D.M. Sechler	St.w.	111	1864	Dec 4	1868	Burned	Carrollton, Ky.
267	Dacotah	St.p.	90	1857	Apr 15	1862	Foundered	St. Joseph, Mo. 4 lives lost.
268	Dan Able	St.p.	647	1866	Jul 21	1870	Burned	Columbus, Ky.
269	Dan Converse	St.p.	163	1852	Nov 15	1858	Snagged	Amazonia, Mo.
270	Daniel G. Taylor	St.p.	543	1855	Feb 5	1864	Burned	Louisville, Ky. 1 life lost.
271	Dardanelle	St.p.	170	1856	Feb 6	1859	Burned	Pine Bluff, Ark.
272	Dart	St.p.	113	1835	May 6	1836	Snagged	St. Louis, Mo.
273	David Gibson	St.p.	414	1854	Mar 28	1859	Collided	With NATHANIEL HOLMES. Petersburg, Ky.
274	Decatur	St.w.	66	1924	Dec 5	1929	Burned	Miami, Mo.
275	Decotah	St.w.	230	1858	Mar 25	1864	Burned	Paduch, Ky.
276	Defender	St.w.	295	1855	Apr 13	1860	Snagged	Laconia, Ark. 5 lives lost.
277	Defender	St.p.	514	1881	Jan 3	1905	Exploded	Huntington, W.Va. 9 lives lost (45).
278	Delphine	St.p.	137	1832	Jun 21	1833	Burned	Louisville, Ky.
279	Delta	St.p.	97	1881	Apr 16	1907	Burned	Lock No.4, Great Kanawha River, W.Va.
280	Denmark	St.p.	283	1856	Oct 8	1862	Snagged	Atlas Island, below Keokuk, Iowa.
281	Denver	St.p.	410	1863	May 16	1867	Burned	St. Joseph, Mo.
282	De Soto	St.p.	569	1898	Jan 21	1918	Burned	Memphis, Tenn.
283	De Soto	St.w.	141	1915	Sep 16	1926	Foundered	Tamms Landing, Tenn.
284	Des Moines City	St.w.	122	1859	Jan	1865	Snagged	Arkansas River, Ark.
285	Desoto	St.w.	82	1918	Jul 15	1928	Burned	Memphis, Tenn.
286	Dew Drop	St.w.	148	1857	Jun 12	1860	Burned	Osage River, Mo.

NO.	NAME OF VESSEL	RIG	TONS	BUILT	DATE		CAUSE	PLACE AND COMMENT
287	DeWitt Clinton	St.p.	265	1847	Jan 25	1852	Snagged	Memphis, Tenn. 36 lives lost.
288	Diana	St.p.	103	1833		1836	Snagged	Missouri River.
289	Dick C. Page	St.p.	98	1897	Jan 31	1918	Foundered	Tenemo Landing, Tenn.
290	Dick Clyde	St.p.	76	1881	Mar 22	1918	Collided	With obstruction. St. Louis, Mo.
291	Dick Williams	St.w.	99	1927	Dec 22	1932	Burned	Potsville, Ky.
292	Diligence	St.p.	124	1845	Feb 28	1849	Snagged	Fort Coffee, Ark.
293	Diligent	St.p.	140	1859	Jan 10	1865	Snagged	Helena, Ark.
294	Diurnal	St.p.	199	1850	Sep 12	1863	Burned	St. Charles, Ark.
295	Doan No.2	St.w.	250	1863	Nov 4	1864	Burned	Johnsonville, Tenn.
296	Doctor Buffington	St.p.	262	1857	Dec	1862	Foundered	White River, Ark.
297	Doctor Franklin No.2	St.p.	189	1848	Jul 7	1853	Burned	St. Louis, Mo.
298	Dolphin	St.w.	120	1848	Jan 6	1850	Stranded	Hawesville, Ky. 3 lives lost.
299	Donald T. Wright	Ol.s.	55	1949	Jan 6	1959	Burned	In the Ohio River at Benwood, W.Va.
300	Donna Lee	Ol.s.	201	1941	Jan 24	1956	Burned	At Mile 100, on Cumberland River. Steel vessel.
301	Dorothy Barrett	St.p.	391	1896	Feb 7	1918	Ice	Randolph, Tenn.
302	Douglas Hall	St.p.	122	1900	Sep 12	1914	Burned	Leon, W.Va.
303	Dover	St.w.	80	1847	Aug 9	1851	Foundered	Paducah, Ky.
304	Dresden	St.p.	548	1852	Feb 15	1855	Snagged	New Madrid, Mo.
305	Duke	St.w.	123	1862	Nov 4	1864	Burned	Johnsonville, Tenn.
306	Duke of Orleans	St.p.	307	1842	Apr 29	1848	Burned	Ste. Genevieve, Mo.
307	Duncan S. Carter	St.p.	428	1858	Aug 27	1859	Snagged	Augusta, Mo.
308	Dunkirk	St.p.	377	1851	Jan 7	1852	Snagged	Ste. Genevieve, Mo.
309	E.A. Ogden	St.p.	399	1855	Feb 22	1860	Snagged	Jefferson City, Mo.
310	E.H. Fairchild	St.p.	496	1857	Feb 13	1867	Ice	Carondelet, Mo.
311	E.M. Ryland	St.p.	267	1857	Oct 8	1861	Burned	St. Louis, Mo.
312	E.P. McNeil	St.p.	203	1850	Aug 30	1851	Burned	Memphis, Tenn.
313	Eau Claire	St.w.	130	1857	Mar 25	1857	Collided	With SOUTH AMERICA. Barnhart, Mo.
314	Eclipse	St.p.	223	1862	Jan 27	1865	Exploded	Johnsonville, Tenn. 27 lives lost.
315	Eclipse	St.p.	57	1903	Nov 3	1910	Burned	Drakes Station, Mo.
316	Eclipse	St.w.	182	1901	Sep 12	1925	Stranded	Osceola, Ark. 2 lives lost (39).
317	Edinburgh	St.p.	382	1854	May 15	1859	Burned	St. Louis, Mo.
318	Edward Bates	St.p.	299	1848	May 17	1849	Burned	St. Louis, Mo.
319	Ed. Myer	St.p.	66	1909	Jan 23	1918	Foundered	Helena, Ark.
320	Effie Dean	St.w.	238	1863	Apr 7	1866	Burned	St. Louis, Mo.
321	El Paso	St.p.	260	1850	Apr 10	1855	Snagged	Boonville, Mo.
322	Eleanora Carrel	St.p.	1,165	1865	Jan 5	1866	Burned	Louisville, Ky.
323	Eleonore	St.p.	97	1902	Jun 5	1916	Foundered	Eastman Landing, Tenn. 12 lives lost (24).
324	Eliza	St.p.	206	1841	Oct 13	1842	Snagged	Bird Island, Mo. 30 lives lost.
325	Eliza	St.p.	349	1852	Jan 25	1855	Snagged	Plum Point, Tenn.
326	Eliza Stewart	St.p.	169	1847	May 17	1849	Burned	St. Louis, Mo.
327	Elk	St.w.	61	1851	Aug 9	1851	Stranded	Paducah, Ky.
328	Elk	St.p.	100	1894	Oct 13	1905	Stranded	Mississippi River, between Vicksburg and Davis Bend.
329	Ella	St.w.	173	1854	Dec 13	1865	Snagged	Little Rock, Ark.
330	Ella	St.p.	72	1858	Aug 3	1868	Foundered	Leavenworth, Kan. Used as ferryboat.
331	Ella Faber	St.w.	198	1862	Oct 9	1867	Burned	Portland, Ky.
332	Ellwood	St.p.	171	1860	Apr 16	1865	Burned	Hatchie River, Tenn.
333	Elvira	St.p.	222	1851	Oct 11	1863	Snagged	Below St. Louis, Mo.
334	Emerson	St.p.	192	1880	Oct 3	1908	Collided	With barge. Osceola, Ark. 1 life lost (9).

NO.	NAME OF VESSEL	RIG	TONS	BUILT	DATE		CAUSE	PLACE AND COMMENT
335	Emigrant	St.p.	343	1856	Nov 19	1860	Burned	Dozier Landing, Mo.
336	Emilie	St.p.	220	1841	Apr 3	1843	Snagged	Washington, Mo.
337	Emily	St.p.	160	1849	Aug 6	1852	Snagged	White River, Ark.
338	Empire City	St.w.	268	1854	Jan 12	1866	Ice	St. Louis, Mo.
339	Enos Taylor	St.p.	64	1893	Mar 15	1912	Burned	De Koven, Ky.
340	Enterprise	St.p.	180	1848	May	1850	Burned	Licking River, Ky.
341	Era No.6	St.w.	83	1860	Dec 27	1862	Burned	Van Buren, Ark.
342	Ernestine	Ol.w.	110	1941	Sep 3	1961	Foundered	In the Kanawha River, at Point Pleasant, W.Va.
343	Esso Barge No. 244; 245;246;247;248; 252;254;255;256; & 259							
344	Estella	Brgs.	620	1944	Oct 2	1954	Burned	All barges lost at Standard Oil Plant on Mississippi River, Memphis, Tenn.
345	Eudora	St.p.	414	1862	Oct 27	1862	Burned	St. Louis, Mo.
346	Eugene	St.p.	420	1847	May 17	1849	Burned	St. Louis, Mo.
347	Europa	St.p.	298	1860	Nov 1	1862	Burned	Plum Point, Tenn. 15 lives lost.
348	Evansville	St.w.	348	1849		1858	Stranded	Augusta, Ark.
349	Evening Star	St.p.	155	1854	Jan 28	1864	Snagged	Memphis, Tenn.
350	Excel	St.w.	343	1864	Aug 24	1869	Burned	St. Louis, Mo.
351	Excelsior	St.p.	79	1851	Mar 25	1856	Snagged	Osage River, Mo.
352	Exchange	St.w.	155	1864	Dec 30	1872	Ice	Memphis, Tenn.
353	Exchange	St.w.	127	1852	Jan 13	1858	Snagged	White River, Ark.
354	Expansion	St.p.	211	1862	Apr 25	1869	Snagged	Decatur, Neb.
355	Express	St.p.	78	1900	Mar 13	1910	Ice	Bismarck, N.D.
356	FBL 623	Brg.	192	1850	Jun 15	1855	Snagged	Spar Island, Missouri River.
			811	1954	Dec 10	1959	Stranded	At Mile 44.8, above Cairo, upper Mississippi River, about 525 feet off Missouri shore. Steel vessel.
357	F.Y. Batchelor	St.p.	313	1878	Feb 16	1907	Ice	Running Water, S.D.
358	Fairmount	St.p.	184	1846	May 12	1850	Snagged	Brandenburg, Ky.
359	Fairy Queen	St.w.	106	1866	Jul 31	1870	Stranded	Black River, Ark.
360	Falcon	St.p.	79	1832		1832	Collided	With SENATOR. Henderson, Ky.
361	Falls City	St.w.	170	1867	Feb 3	1872	Collided	With J.W. GARRETT. Sand Island, Ky.
362	Fame	St.p.	140	1832	Oct 27	1836	Snagged	Louisiana, Mo.
363	Fannie Scott	St.w.	253	1866	Apr 9	1869	Burned	St. Louis, Mo.
364	Fanny Barker	St.p.	174	1863	Mar 24	1873	Stranded	St. Louis, Mo.
365	Fanny Bullitt	St.p.	438	1854	Mar 15	1864	Snagged	Napoleon, Ark.
366	Fanny Farrar	St.w.	134	1852	Jan 24	1855	Snagged	Canton, Ky.
367	Fanny Ogden	St.p.	417	1862	Apr 7	1866	Burned	St. Louis, Mo.
368	Fashion	St.p.	474	1847	May 8	1852	Stranded	Louisville, Ky.
369	Fashion	St.p.	415	1851	Jun 16	1859	Stranded	Sand Island, Louisville, Ky.
370	Federal Arch	St.p.	195	1850	Feb 26	1856	Ice	St. Louis, Mo.
371	Fire Canoe	St.p.	166	1854	Nov 13	1858	Snagged	Wyandotte, Kan.
372	Flag	St.w.	235	1853	Feb 24	1856	Ice	Covington, Ky.
373	Florence	St.p.	399	1857	Mar 29	1864	Snagged	Atchison, Kan.
374	Florence	St.p.	170	1889	Jan 13	1910	Stranded	St. Louis, Mo.
375	Florence Miller No.2	St.p.	189	1863	Dec 23	1867	Burned	Clarendon, Ark.
376	Florence Taber	St.w.	241	1866	Dec 31	1868	Snagged	Arkansas River, Ark.
377	Floyd	St.p.	56	1914	Mar 3	1920	Foundered	6 miles below Boonville, Mo.
378	Flying Cloud	St.p.	537	1854	Dec 9	1860	Burned	Memphis, Tenn.

NO.	NAME OF VESSEL	RIG	TONS	BUILT	DATE			CAUSE	PLACE AND COMMENT
379	Flying Dutchman	St.p.	169	1840			1840	Stranded	Dubuque, Iowa.
380	Forest Queen	St.p.	282	1851	Oct	4	1863	Burned	St. Louis, Mo.
381	Forest Queen	St.p.	419	1858	Oct	4	1863	Burned	St. Louis, Mo.
382	Forest Rose	St.w.	205	1852	Mar	25	1857	Exploded	Napoleon, Ark. 6 lives lost.
383	Forest Rose	St.w.	203	1862	Feb	4	1868	Ice	St. Louis, Mo.
384	Fort Pitt	St.p.	158	1840	Sep	28	1842	Snagged	Cape Girardeau, Mo.
385	Fort Smith	St.w.	244	1866	Oct	27	1871	Snagged	White River, Ark.
386	Fountain City	St.p.	65	1905	May	5	1913	Collided	With obstruction. Robertsport, Ky.
387	Francis Fisher	St.p.	154	1861	Jan	12	1873	Foundered	St. Louis, Mo.
388	Frank Bates	St.p.	538	1866	Apr	7	1866	Burned	St. Louis, Mo.
389	Frank W. Phillips	St.w.	130	1929	Aug	24	1930	Foundered	St. Louis, Mo.
390	Franklin	St.p.	131	1816	Jan	24	1819	Snagged	Ste. Genevieve, Mo.
391	Frederic Notrebe	St.w.	190	1860	Dec	27	1862	Burned	Van Buren, Ark.
392	French	St.p.	92	1903	Nov	14	1914	Burned	Tennessee River, Tenn.
393	Friendship	St.p.	195	1866	May	10	1873	Snagged	Hannibal, Mo.
394	Frolic	St.w.	126	1844	May	17	1849	Burned	St. Louis, Mo.
395	Frontier City	St.w.	144	1860	Jan	4	1861	Snagged	Napoleon, Ark.
396	G.A. Thomson	St.p.	366	1865	Apr	9	1869	Snagged	Pine Bluff, Ark. 4 lives lost.
397	G.B. Allen	St.p.	593	1866	Mar	29	1869	Burned	St. Louis, Mo.
398	G.M.	St.p.	51	1906	Nov		1919	Collided	With obstruction. Near Onawa, Iowa.
399	G.W. Graham	St.p.	508	1861	Jul	11	1867	Burned	St. Louis, Mo.
400	G.W. Sparhawk	St.p.	282	1851	Feb	26	1856	Ice	St. Louis, Mo.
401	Galenian	St.p.	133	1834			1839	Burned	St. Louis, Mo.
402	Gallatin	St.w.	131	1864	Apr	21	1868	Snagged	50 miles above Omaha, Neb.
403	Garden City	St.p.	409	1853	Jan	14	1855	Burned	35 miles below Napoleon, Ark.
404	Gayoso	St.p.	236	1850	Nov	30	1850	Burned	Memphis, Tenn.
405	Gazelle	St.p.	129	1832	Mar	4	1838	Ice	St. Louis, Mo.
406	Gem	St.p.	145	1863	Nov	9	1869	Unknown	St. Louis, Mo.
407	General Bem	St.p.	116	1849	Jan	9	1854	Snagged	Walnut Bend, Arkansas River. 10 lives lost.
408	General Brooke	St.p.	143	1842	May	7	1849	Burned	St. Louis, Mo.
409	General Grant	St.w.	172	1863	Mar	18	1866	Ice	Plattsmouth, Neb.
410	General Greene	St.p.	305	1820	Feb	11	1824	Snagged	Harpeth Shoals, Tenn.
411	General Halleck	St.w.	66	1862	Feb	5	1866	Burned	Memphis, Tenn.
412	General Harrison	St.p.	184	1841	Nov		1842	Exploded	Chattahoochee River. 3 lives lost.
413	General Jackson	St.p.	142	1818	May	30	1821	Snagged	Clarksville, Tenn.
414	General Lane	St.p.	240	1848	Dec	30	1851	Snagged	Mouth of St. Francis River, Ark.
415	General Pike	St.p.	366	1851	Sep	23	1853	Snagged	Cape Girardeau, Mo.
416	General Pratte	St.p.	342	1840	Nov	25	1842	Burned	Memphis, Tenn.
417	General Robertson	St.p.	237	1819	Apr	17	1823	Snagged	New Madrid, Mo.
418	General Scott	St.p.	293	1847	May	13	1853	Burned	New Madrid, Mo.
419	General Shields	St.w.	75	1849	Jun		1851	Snagged	Arkansas River.
420	Geneva	St.w.	121	1848	Sep	30	1856	Snagged	Nebraska City, Neb.
421	Geneva	St.p.	127	1864	Dec	16	1865	Ice	St. Louis, Mo.
422	Genoa	St.p.	226	1854	Sep	13	1856	Snagged	Nebraska City, Neb.
423	George Collier	St.p.	538	1851	Dec	3	1855	Burned	Memphis, Tenn.
424	George R. Gettys	Ol.s.	57	1936	Jun	5	1952	Foundered	In Tennessee River at Mile Post 608.7.
425	George R. Gettys II	Ol.s.	56	1951	Mar	13	1959	Burned	At Mile Post 641, Tennessee River. Steel vessel.
426	George W. Kendall	St.p.	280	1849	Feb	27	1853	Stranded	Louisville, Ky.

NO.	NAME OF VESSEL	RIG	TONS	BUILT	DATE		CAUSE	PLACE AND COMMENT
427	Georgia Lee	St.p.	595	1898	Jan 21	1918	Ice	Memphis, Tenn.
428	Georgetown	St.w.	183	1852	May 11	1855	Snagged	Bellefontaine, Mo.
429	Geraldine	St.p.	74	1908	Aug 20	1910	Burned	Little Kanawha River, W.Va.
430	Gipsy	St.s.	79	1835	Apr 19	1841	Stranded	Keokuk, Iowa.
431	Gladys	St.p.	60	1896	Dec 4	1905	Collided	With wharf. Frankfort, Ky.
432	Glaucus	St.p.	191	1839	Aug 12	1842	Snagged	Hannibal, Mo.
433	Glaucus	St.w.	154	1849	Mar 30	1852	Burned	Montrose, Iowa.
434	Glencoe	St.p.	428	1846	Apr 3	1852	Exploded	St. Louis, Mo. 60 lives lost.
435	Glendale	St.w.	481	1866	Dec 29	1870	Unknown	Ste. Genevieve, Mo.
436	Glenmore	St.p.	208	1897	Mar 5	1909	Stranded	Harlem, Mo.
437	Globe	St.p.	150	1830		1834	Snagged	Missouri River.
438	Golden Gate	St.p.	317	1852	Sep 6	1857	Burned	Sulphur Springs, Mo.
439	Golden Girl	St.p.	77	1911	Apr 12	1917	Burned	Owensboro, Ky.
440	Gondolier	St.p.	198	1847	Nov 1	1848	Collided	With JOSEPH LAWRENCE. St. Louis, Mo.
441	Goody Friends	St.w.	196	1857	Nov 4	1864	Burned	Johnsonville, Tenn.
442	Grace Virginia	St.p.	75	1900	Nov 5	1905	Burned	Ohio River.
443	Gracey Childers	St.p.	215	1895	Sep 3	1909	Burned	Paducah, Ky.
444	Grampus	St.p.	96	1850	Mar 23	1852	Snagged	Hatchie River, Tenn.
445	Grampus	St.p.	100	1857	Jan 11	1863	Burned	Wolf River, Memphis, Tenn.
446	Grand Turk	St.p.	688	1848	Jul 2	1856	Burned	St. Louis, Mo.
447	Grapeshot	St.w.	153	1855	Jun 10	1859	Snagged	Van Buren, Ark.
448	Grey Eagle	St.p.	65	1857	Apr 9	1869	Foundered	Winfield, Mo. Used as ferryboat. 3 lives lost.
449	Grey Eagle	St.p.	555	1892	Jan 29	1918	Ice	Livingston Point, Ky.
450	Greyhound	St.p.	132	1910	Dec 22	1917	Ice	Ashland, Ky.
451	Grosse Tete	St.p.	399	1858	Jun	1862	Snagged	St. Charles, Ark.
452	Guidon	St.w.	240	1864	Mar 23	1870	Snagged	90 miles up Arkansas River.
453	Gulnare	St.p.	276	1840	Sep 8	1844	Collided	With WESTWOOD. Helena, Ark. 3 lives lost.
454	H. Clay Wilson	St.w.	315	1865	Nov 24	1872	Snagged	Mouth of White River, Ark.
455	H.D. Bacon	St.p.	370	1860	Oct 27	1862	Burned	St. Louis, Mo.
456	H.H. Cole	St.s.	76	1915	Oct 23	1931	Burned	Memphis, Tenn.
457	H.K. Bedford	St.p.	139	1885	Feb 27	1911	Ice	Waverly, W.Va., Ohio River.
458	H.N. Sherburne	Ga.w.	111	1916	Jul 3	1928	Burned	Carrsville, Ky.
459	Halcyon	St.p.	121	1832	Nov 14	1834	Snagged	St. Charles, Mo.
460	Hannibal City	St.p.	563	1858	Sep 4	1862	Snagged	Louisiana, Mo.
461	Harrison Bridges	St.p.	176	1856	Jun 25	1859	Snagged	Cromwell, Ky.
462	Harry Lee	St.s.	200	1900	May 16	1914	Burned	Memphis, Tenn.
463	Hattie May	St.p.	230	1864	Jan 12	1866	Ice	St. Louis, Mo.
464	Hattie R	Ol.w.	75	1934	Sep 7	1954	Foundered	At Paducah, Ky.
465	Helen Blair	St.p.	213	1897	Apr 28	1920	Burned	Memphis, Tenn.
466	Helena	St.p.	199	1866	Oct 16	1868	Snagged	Sioux City, Iowa.
467	Hendrick Hudson	St.p.	246	1846	Feb 27	1848	Burned	Maysville, Ky.
468	Henry A. Jones	St.w.	193	1856	Feb 27	1858	Burned	Augusta, Ky.
469	Henry Adkins	St.w.	528	1867	Mar 29	1869	Collided	St. Louis, Mo.
470	Henry C. Yeiser, Jr.	St.w.	158	1901	Aug 15	1940	Burned	With pier. At Charleston, W.Va.
471	Henry Choteau	St.p.	623	1853	Sep 26	1863	Burned	Columbus, Ky.
472	Henry Clay	St.p.	310	1841		1843	Snagged	Randolph, Tenn.
473	Henry Fitzhugh	St.w.	217	1857	Sep 5	1864	Snagged	Licking River, Ky.
474	Henry Logan	St.w.	75	1860	May 28	1868	Stranded	Parkersburg, W.Va.

NO.	NAME OF VESSEL	RIG	TONS	BUILT	DATE	CAUSE	PLACE AND COMMENT
475	Henry S. Dickerson	St.s.	57	1863	Oct 6 1864	Exploded	St. Louis, Mo. 5 lives lost.
476	Hercules	St.w.	151	1854	Feb 18 1863	Burned	Memphis, Tenn.
477	Heroine	St.p.	96	1832	Jun 4 1837	Stranded	Keokuk, Iowa.
478	Hesperian	St.p.	360	1857	Aug 19 1860	Burned	Atchison, Kan.
479	Hiawatha	St.p.	767	1856	Sep 13 1863	Burned	St. Louis, Mo.
480	Hiawatha	St.p.	256	1882	Nov 30 1911	Burned	Louisville, Ky.
481	Hibernia	St.p.	162	1844	Mar 10 1848	Burned	St. Louis, Mo.
482	Hickman	St.p.	227	1855	Mar 2 1860	Burned	Below Little Rock, Ark. 2 lives lost.
483	Highland Mary	St.p.	158	1848	Jul 27 1853	Burned	St. Louis, Mo.
484	Highland Mary	St.p.	158	1848	Feb 26 1856	Ice	St. Louis, Mo.
485	Highlander	St.p.	346	1842	Jun 1 1849	Burned	St. Louis, Mo.
486	Highlander	St.w.	241	1864	Dec 16 1865	Ice	Johnsonville, Tenn.
487	Hindoo	St.p.	199	1849	Jan 28 1855	Ice	Ste. Genevieve, Mo.
488	Hodge	St.s.	113	1945	Nov	Foundered	On Flathead Lake, Polson, Montana.
489	Home	St.w.	70	1855	Jul 27 1868	Snagged	Clarksville, Mo.
490	Homer	St.p.	410	1832	Mar 18 1841	Snagged	Cape Girardeau, Mo.
491	Homer C. Wright	St.w.	72	1920	Aug 18 1927	Abandoned	St. Louis, Mo.
492	Houma	St.p.	159	1837	Sep 28 1842	Snagged	Fulton, Ark.
493	Hugh L. White	St.p.	175	1839	May 20 1850	Burned	St. Louis, Mo.
494	Huntsville	St.p.	344	1845	Aug 21 1854	Snagged	Ste. Genevieve, Mo.
495	Huntsville	St.p.	898	1853	Mar 24 1855	Burned	Hamburg, Tenn.
496	I.N. Flesher	St.p.	99	1908	Jan 12 1913	Burned	Uniontown, Ky.
497	I Go	St.w.	101	1862	Jun 12 1864	Burned	Arkansas River, Ark.
498	I Go	St.w.	104	1860	Jun 12 1864	Burned	Arkansas Post, Ark.
499	Ida Handy	St.p.	684	1864	Jun 2 1866	Burned	Carondelet, Mo.
500	Illinois	St.p.	85	1839	Apr 30 1842	Stranded	Montrose, Iowa.
501	Imperial	St.p.	907	1858	Sep 13 1863	Burned	St. Louis, Mo.
502	Importer	St.w.	428	1866	Jan 15 1872	Snagged	150 miles above Little Rock, Ark.
503	India Givens	St.p.	228	1900	Jan 27 1907	Burned	Hickman, Ky.
504	Ingomar	St.p.	254	1864	Dec 30 1868	Snagged	Below Wheeling, W.Va. Converted barge.
505	Inland	St.w.	257	1927	Dec 22 1937	Stranded	Near right bank of river at Warwood, W.Va.
506	Interchange	St.w.	251	1854	Oct 1860	Snagged	Newport, Ark.
507	Ion	St.p.	99	1837	Feb 27 1842	Snagged	Deer Creek, Ky.
508	Irene	St.p.	158	1858	Sep 24 1859	Snagged	Little Rock, Ark.
509	Irene	St.p.	117	1867	1877	Snagged	Omaha, Neb. Used as ferryboat.
510	Iris	St.p.	95	1839	Nov 27 1842	Snagged	Eddyville, Ky.
511	Iron City	St.w.	118	1844	Dec 31 1848	Ice	St. Louis, Mo. 5 lives lost.
512	Iron City	St.p.	118	1903	Sep 8 1911	Stranded	Laurie Bar, Ohio River.
513	Ironton	St.p.	187	1850	Dec 24 1854	Snagged	Washington, Mo.
514	Irvin S. Cobb	Ol.w.	155	1923	Feb 17 1951	Burned	At Mile 16, Tennessee River, Ky. Steel vessel.
515	Isaac M. Mason	St.p.	114	1893	Mar 4 1913	Burned	Cooks Ferry, Ohio River.
516	Isaac Shelby	St.p.	100	1856	Jun 21 1860	Snagged	Swan Lake, Ark.
517	Isabella	St.p.	361	1857	Apr 15 1868	Snagged	Dozier Landing, Mo.
518	Island City	St.w.	139	1863	Jul 25 1864	Stranded	Buford, N.D.
519	Izetta	St.p.	301	1859	Jan 20 1867	Burned	St. Louis, Mo.
520	J.B. Finley	St.p.	679	1899	Aug 1 1918	Burned	Paducah, Ky.
521	J.B. Richardson	St.p.	191	1889	Nov 18 1913	Burned	Paducah, Ky., Mississippi River.
522	J.G. Morrow	St.p.	163	1861	Sep 1 1861	Snagged	St. Joseph, Mo. Used as ferryboat.

NO.	NAME OF VESSEL	RIG	TONS	BUILT	DATE	CAUSE	PLACE AND COMMENT
523	J.H. Donals, Jr.	St.w.	235	1920	Dec 23 1925	Stranded	South Ripley, Ky.
524	J.H. Lacy	St.p.	269	1863	Oct 10 1867	Snagged	Nodaway, Mo.
525	J.H. Miller	St.w.	68	1863	Aug 1864	Burned	Pine Bluff, Ark.
526	J.M. Bowell	St.p.	94	1882	Mar 8 1909	Burned	Henderson, W.Va.
527	J.M. Clendenin	St.p.	276	1851	Nov 1 1853	Snagged	Bates Ledge, Mo.
528	J.M. Linder	St.p.	73	1899	Jun 16 1911	Burned	Memphis, Tenn.
529	J.N. Harbin	St.p.	152	1895	Aug 25 1911	Stranded	Lake Landing, Mississippi River.
530	J.P. Webb	St.w.	171	1865	Sep 17 1868	Collided	With bridge. Louisville, Ky.
531	J.R. Wells	St.p.	92	1898	Jan 29 1920	Ice	St. Louis, Mo.
532	J.S.	St.p.	292	1901	Jun 25 1910	Burned	Bad Axe Island, Mississippi River. 2 lives lost (1,219).
533	J.T. Hatfield	St.w.	153	1904	Oct 4 1929	Stranded	Dann, W.Va.
534	J.W. Cheesman	St.w.	251	1856	Nov 3 1864	Burned	White Oak Island, Tenn.
535	Jacob Musselman	St.w.	144	1860	Jan 8 1863	Burned	Memphis, Tenn.
536	James Dick	St.p.	272	1845	May 7 1850	Burned	Nashville, Tenn.
537	James E. Woodruff	St.p.	612	1855	Feb 25 1858	Ice	Hat Island, below St. Louis, Mo.
538	James Hewitt	St.p.	356	1843	Aug 18 1851	Foundered	Carondelet, Mo.
539	James Johnson	St.p.	526	1856	Feb 23 1862	Burned	Nashville, Tenn.
540	James Laughlin	St.p.	187	1853	Sep 13 1856	Foundered	Memphis, Tenn.
541	James Lyon	St.w.	187	1853	Dec 26 1858	Foundered	St. Louis, Mo.
542	James M. Niles	St.p.	266	1848	Feb 20 1854	Stranded	Louisville, Ky.
543	James Monroe	St.p.	140	1817	1820	Snagged	Smithtown, Ky.
544	James Montgomery	St.p.	536	1856	Dec 11 1861	Snagged	Devil Island, Cape Girardeau, Mo.
545	James Nelson	Ol.w.	76	1935	Mar 4 1939	Burned	Near Maysville, Ky.
546	James Ross	St.p.	269	1818	Feb 18 1823	Ice	St. Louis, Mo.
547	James Woods	St.p.	585	1860	Feb 23 1862	Burned	Nashville, Tenn.
548	Jamestown	St.p.	338	1845	Jan 9 1853	Stranded	Columbus, Ky.
549	Jayhawker	St.w.	147	1925	Jan 25 1939	Foundered	240 miles from the mouth of Tennessee River.
550	Jeanie Deans	St.p.	485	1852	May 12 1866	Burned	Carondelet, Mo.
551	Jefferson	St.p.	66	1832	Feb 23 1835	Snagged	Nashville, Tenn.
552	Jefferson	St.p.	232	1851	Feb 26 1852	Snagged	Pine Bluff, Ark.
553	Jennie Lewis	St.w.	509	1864	Mar 29 1869	Burned	St. Louis, Mo.
554	Jesse K. Bell	St.p.	325	1856	Sep 13 1863	Burned	White River, Ark.
555	Jesse Lazer	St.w.	72	1854	Jan 1858	Snagged	Green River, Ky.
556	Jewel	St.p.	201	1893	Feb 2 1910	Burned	St. Louis, Mo.
557	Jewess	St.p.	248	1847	Jan 1 1852	Ice	St. Louis, Mo.
558	John A. Fisher	St.w.	122	1859	Oct 27 1864	Snagged	Carroll Island, below St. Louis, Mo.
559	John B. Gordon	St.p.	57	1848	Jun 8 1851	Snagged	Arkansas River.
560	John Bell	St.w.	209	1855	Sep 28 1863	Snagged	St. Charles, Mo.
561	John Golong	St.w.	144	1844	Mar 8 1846	Stranded	Camden, Mo.
562	John Hancock	St.p.	100	1835	Nov 28 1836	Snagged	Bellefontaine, Mo.
563	John Hancock	St.p.	293	1845	Mar 25 1851	Snagged	Cape Girardeau, Mo.
564	John J. Hardin	St.p.	206	1845	Mar 10 1848	Burned	St. Louis, Mo.
565	John J. Roe	St.p.	691	1856	Sep 12 1864	Snagged	Above New Madrid, Mo.
566	John M. Stockwell	St.p.	352	1853	Jul 2 1856	Burned	St. Louis, Mo.
567	John McFaden	St.w.	221	1852	Apr 3 1854	Collided	With S.F.J. TRABUE. Wolf Creek, Ky. 4 lives lost.
568	John Ross	St.w.	94	1906	Aug 8 1925	Foundered	Spottsville, Ky.
569	John S. Hall	St.w.	110	1864	Jun 22 1866	Stranded	Little Rock, Ark.
570	John S. Hopkins	St.p.	593	1880	Jan 11 1917	Burned	Green River, Tenn.

NO.	NAME OF VESSEL	RIG	TONS	BUILT	DATE		CAUSE	PLACE AND COMMENT
571	John Strader	St.p.	205	1852	Nov 18	1857	Burned	Above Gaines Ledge, Ark.
572	John Swasey	St.w.	236	1864	Aug 31	1864	Snagged	Above Cape Girardeau, Mo.
573	John Tompkins	St.w.	199	1855	Dec 13	1860	Burned	Louisville, Ky.
574	John Trendly	St.w.	255	1860	Jan 12	1866	Ice	St. Louis, Mo.
575	Joseph H. Oglesby	St.p.	389	1856	Aug 28	1858	Snagged	Above Glasgow, Mo.
576	Josephine	St.p.	124	1844	May 16	1850	Snagged	Clarksville, Tenn.
577	Josie	Brg.	197	1882	Feb 27	1905	Foundered	St. Louis, Mo.
578	Judge Torrence	St.p.	419	1857	Feb 19	1868	Snagged	Ozark Island, Napoleon, Ark.
579	Julia	St.p.	234	1846	Sep 14	1850	Snagged	Bellefontaine, Mo.
580	Julia	St.p.	77	1848	Dec 17	1860	Snagged	Arkansas River.
581	Julia Roane	St.w.	181	1859	Sep 10	1863	Burned	Little Rock, Ark.
582	Juliet	St.w.	157	1862	Dec 31	1865	Stranded	White River Cutoff, Ark.
583	Julius Fleischmann	St.w.	564	1897	Mar 21	1945	Stranded	Near Catlettsburg, Ky.
584	Julius H. Smith	St.w.	224	1859	Feb 6	1862	Burned	Fort Henry, Tenn.
585	Jumbo	Brg.	107	1915	Apr 1	1917	Burned	Owensboro, Ky.
586	Junius	St.p.	129	1833	Dec 7	1836	Burned	St. Louis, Mo.
587	Kansas	St.p.	276	1847	Apr 25	1853	Stranded	Brownville, Neb.
588	Kare Kearney	St.p.	-	-	Feb 14	1854	Exploded	St. Louis, Mo. 15 lives lost.
589	Karlina	St.w.	118	1922	Apr 10	1933	Burned	White River, Ark.
590	Kate Adams	St.p.	595	1898	Jan 8	1927	Burned	Memphis, Tenn. Steel vessel.
591	Kate B. Porter	St.w.	241	1864	Jun 21	1867	Stranded	300 miles below Fort Benton, Montana.
592	Kate Bruner	St.w.	118	1861	Sep 15	1866	Snagged	St. Charles, Ark.
593	Kate Howard	St.p.	504	1857	Aug 11	1859	Snagged	Osage City, Mo.
594	Kate Kearney	St.p.	304	1847	Feb 16	1854	Exploded	St. Louis, Mo. 6 lives lost. See No.588.
595	Kate Swinney	St.p.	280	1852	Jul 31	1855	Snagged	300 miles above Council Bluffs, Iowa.
596	Kenois	St.p.	53	1901	Apr 27	1914	Foundered	Cumberland River.
597	Kenton	St.w.	215	1860	Jun 10	1870	Snagged	Helena, Ark.
598	Kentucky Home	St.w.	207	1855	Jul 30	1855	Collided	With TELEGRAPH NO.3. Carrollton, Ky. 3 lives lost.
599	Keokuk	St.p.	89	1838	Aug 29	1841	Burned	Ste. Genevieve, Mo. 12 lives lost.
600	Keokuk	St.p.	434	1855	Apr 22	1858	Burned	St. Louis, Mo.
601	Key West	St.w.	169	1857	Dec 27	1862	Burned	Van Buren, Ark.
602	Keystone	St.p.	69	1839	Jun 24	1841	Burned	Arkansas City, Ark.
603	Keystone	Ol.w.	93	1937	Sep 26	1960	Collided	With barge. In Ohio River near Parkersburg, W.Va.
604	Kit Carson	St.p.	280	1848	May 17	1849	Burned	St. Louis, Mo.
605	L.T.C. No.22	Brg.	452	1937	Dec 17	1938	Burned	Paducah, Ky.
606	La Salle	St.w.	196	1860	Aug	1864	Snagged	Cape Girardeau, Mo.
607	Laclede	St.p.	239	1845	Mar 10	1848	Burned	St. Louis, Mo.
608	Lady Franklin	St.p.	204	1830	Dec 2	1835	Collided	With CLEOPATRA. Owensboro, Ky. 18 lives lost.
609	Lady Grace	St.w.	387	1865	Jan 3	1870	Burned	Omaha, Neb.
610	Lady Jackson	St.w.	207	1860	Oct 14	1863	Snagged	White River, Ark.
611	Lake City	St.w.	171	1857	Dec 8	1862	Burned	Carson Landing, Ark.
612	Lamartine	St.p.	174	1848	Feb 26	1856	Ice	St. Louis, Mo.
613	Lancaster No.4	St.p.	218	1861	Nov 18	1864	Snagged	Below Portland, Mo.
614	Leander	St.p.	137	1840	Jan	1844	Snagged	Ste. Genevieve, Mo.
615	Lebanon No.2	St.w.	264	1862	Jun 24	1863	Snagged	Big Hurricane Island, Ky.
616	Legal Tender	St.p.	539	1867	Jun 30	1876	Snagged	Memphis, Tenn.
617	Leni Leoti	St.w.	174	1863	May 10	1869	Snagged	Arkansas River, Ark.
618	Leodora	St.p.	158	1864	May 26	1866	Burned	20 miles below Yankton, S.D.

NO.	NAME OF VESSEL	RIG	TONS	BUILT	DATE	CAUSE	PLACE AND COMMENT
619	Leon	St.w.	87	1859	Mar 1864	Snagged	Barnum, Ark.
620	Leonora	St.w.	259	1861	May 29 1866	Burned	Junction City, Kan.
621	Leonora No.2	St.w.	182	1864	Dec 28 1869	Collided	With MARY HOUSTON, Louisville, Ky.
622	Leslie Combs	St.w.	99	1860	Apr 8 1872	Stranded	Kentucky River, Ky.
623	Leviathan	St.p.	987	1864	Feb 26 1866	Burned	St. Louis, Mo.
624	Lewiston	St.p.	548	1904	Jul 12 1922	Burned	Lewiston, Idaho.
625	Liberator	St.p.	240	1826	Jun 8 1826	Exploded	St. Louis, Mo.
626	Liberty No.3	St.w.	54	1860	Dec 17 1876	Snagged	Memphis, Tenn.
627	Lillie Martin	St.w.	210	1863	Feb 4 1867	Burned	St. Louis, Mo.
628	Lilly	St.w.	256	1864	Oct 24 1868	Snagged	Rushbottom Bend, Missouri River.
629	Linn Boyd	St.w.	227	1859	Feb 6 1862	Burned	Fort Henry, Tenn.
630	Linnie Drown	St.w.	229	1864	Sep 7 1866	Snagged	Helena, Ark. 4 lives lost.
631	Linton	St.w.	285	1867	Oct 25 1869	Snagged	Cut off, Arkansas River, Ark.
632	Little Missouri	St.p.	198	1846	Apr 1848	Snagged	Glasgow, Mo.
633	Little Rock	St.w.	183	1858	Sep 10 1863	Burned	Little Rock, Ark.
634	Little Rock	St.p.	125	1865	Dec 1 1872	Snagged	Pine Bluff, Ark. Used as ferryboat.
635	Lizzie Gardener	St.p.	82	1871	Oct 16 1909	Burned	Davenport, Iowa.
636	Lizzie Gill	St.p.	489	1865	Jan 10 1870	Foundered	Mouth of White River, Ark.
637	Lizzie Simmons	St.p.	454	1859	Sep 10 1863	Burned	Little Rock, Ark.
638	Lorena	St.p.	287	1895	Feb 2 1916	Burned	Point Pleasant, W.Va.
639	Lotus	St.w.	170	1864	Aug 8 1868	Snagged	St. Louis, Mo.
640	Louisville	St.p.	327	1831	Oct 10 1832	Snagged	Cape Girardeau, Mo.
641	Louisville	St.p.	378	1839	Jun 13 1842	Stranded	St. Louis, Mo.
642	Louisville	St.w.	288	1863	May 1864	Snagged	Omaha, Neb.
643	Low Water	St.w.	177	1856	Nov 27 1857	Snagged	Hills Landing, Mo.
644	Lucie Marmet	St.p.	185	1903	Oct 5 1914	Burned	Charleston, W.Va.
645	Lucie Bertram	St.p.	268	1847	Jan 18 1853	Burned	St. Louis, Mo.
646	Lucy Holcombe	St.p.	440	1858	Nov 11 1859	Burned	Helena, Ark.
647	Lucy Long	St.w.	82	1843	Nov 19 1845	Stranded	Louisville, Ky.
648	Luella	St.w.	122	1850	Sep 17 1855	Collided	With JESSE LAZEAR, White River, Ark.
649	Luna	St.p.	561	1864	Feb 26 1886	Burned	St. Louis, Mo.
650	Lunette	St.p.	166	1852	Oct 13 1853	Burned	St. Louis, Mo.
651	Lynx	St.p.	124	1844	1849	Snagged	Clarksville, Mo.
652	M.S. Mepham	St.p.	683	1864	Mar 2 1868	Burned	St. Louis, Mo.
653	MST 31	Brg.	883	1959	Mar 30 1963	Collided	With bridge. At Helena, Ark. Steel vessel.
654	M.T. Bryan	St.p.	97	1903	Oct 5 1922	Burned	Cumberland River, near Paducah, Ky.
655	Mackie	St.p.	77	1906	Apr 26 1915	Burned	Nashville, Tenn.
656	Madison Belle	St.p.	169	1847	Mar 19 1851	Snagged	Salt River, Ky.
657	Madonna	St.p.	94	1852	Feb 24 1856	Ice	Covington, Ky.
658	Magenta	St.p.	424	1863	May 22 1863	Snagged	DeWitt, Mo.
659	Magenta	St.p.	843	1864	Jan 1 1871	Burned	St. Louis, Mo.
660	Magic	St.p.	122	1845	Oct 26 1846	Snagged	Plum Point, Tenn.
661	Magnolia	St.w.	120	1853	Apr 24 1856	Stranded	Shippingport, Ky.
662	Magnolia	St.p.	1,255	1865	Jun 14 1866	Burned	St. Louis, Mo.
663	Mail	St.p.	211	1844	May 9 1848	Burned	St. Louis, Mo.
664	Majestic	St.p.	648	1863	May 6 1863	Burned	Hickman, Ky. 1 life lost.
665	Majestic	St.p.	600	1899	Jun 20 1914	Foundered	Chain of Rocks, Mo. 3 lives lost (30).
666	Malta	St.p.	114	1839	Sep 30 1841	Snagged	Teetsaw Bend, Missouri River.

NO.	NAME OF VESSEL	RIG	TONS	BUILT	DATE		CAUSE	PLACE AND COMMENT
667	Mameluke	St.p.	570	1848	May 17	1849	Burned	St. Louis, Mo.
668	Mandan	St.p.	204	1847	May 17	1849	Burned	St. Louis, Mo.
669	Mansfield	St.w.	166	1854	Aug 16	1858	Snagged	White Cloud, Neb.
670	Margaret	St.p.	100	1896	Mar 10	1914	Foundered	Arkansas City, Ark.
671	Margaret Hall	St.p.	140	1922	Jun 24	1941	Stranded	Owens Island, opposite Pudacah, Ky.
672	Maria	St.w.	254	1864	Dec 11	1864	Exploded	Carondelet, Mo.
673	Mariner	St.w.	193	1856	Jul 4	1864	Burned	Above Helena, Ark.
674	Marjorie	St.p.	54	1908	Jul 8	1917	Burned	Lexington, Mo.
675	Market Boy	St.w.	70	1862	May 25	1866	Foundered	Helena, Ark.
676	Marquette	Ol.w.	64	1925	Feb	1947	Foundered	At Cement Manufacturing Company dock, Cape Girardeau, Mo. Steel vessel.
677	Mars	St.p.	329	1856	Jul 8	1865	Snagged	Cogswell Landing, Mo.
678	Martha	St.p.	180	1847	May 17	1849	Burned	St. Louis, Mo.
679	Mary	St.p.	130	1845	Jul 29	1849	Burned	St. Louis, Mo.
680	Mary	St.p.	276	1847	Jul 28	1849	Burned	St. Louis, Mo.
681	Mary Agnes	St.p.	374	1853	Mar 1	1854	Burned	Memphis, Tenn.
682	Mary Alice	St.w.	559	1867	Apr 5	1875	Unknown	St. Louis, Mo.
683	Mary B.	St.p.	90	1890	Aug 5	1915	Burned	Wolf River, Tenn.
684	Mary B.	Ol.s.	465	1940	Apr 20	1961	Foundered	At Mile 152, on Missouri River.
685	Mary Blane	St.p.	181	1847	Sep 10	1851	Burned	St. Louis, Mo.
686	Mary Cole	St.p.	93	1851	Apr 22	1855	Snagged	Plattsmouth, Neb.
687	Maryland	St.w.	118	1856	Oct 24	1857	Burned	Louisville, Ky.
688	Mason	St.p.	57	1863	Jun	1887	Stranded	St. Francis River, Ark.
689	Mat II	Brg.	602	1951	Mar 30	1963	Collided	With bridge. At Helena, Ark. Steel vessel.
690	Mattie Cabler	St.w.	128	1864	Dec 26	1872	Ice	Memphis, Tenn.
691	May Flower	St.p.	890	1855	Dec 3	1855	Burned	Memphis, Tenn. 3 lives lost.
692	May Queen	St.w.	68	1850	Aug 13	1852	Snagged	45 miles below Little Rock, Ark.
693	Mayflower	St.s.	100	1841	Dec 3	1855	Burned	Memphis, Tenn.
694	Mazeppa	St.w.	185	1864	Oct 29	1864	Burned	Fort Helman, Tenn.
695	Melrose	St.w.	177	1856	Jan 24	1861	Snagged	Below Uniontown, Ky. 1 life lost.
696	Mendota	St.p.	157	1844	Jan 29	1848	Snagged	Ste. Genevieve, Mo.
697	Mengel Box Company	St.p.	164	1909	Feb 28	1918	Foundered	Off Plum Point, Tenn.
698	Mentor	St.p.	270	1841	Sep 11	1842	Snagged	Commerce, Mo.
699	Mercury	St.w.	184	1863	Mar 13	1867	Stranded	Cut Off, Ark. 2 lives lost.
700	Mervyn	Ga.y.	96	1911	Jul 11	1924	Stranded	St. Joseph, Mo.
701	Meteor	St.p.	165	1844	Aug 24	1848	Collided	With PARIS. Stephensport, Ky. 4 lives lost.
702	Metropolis	St.w.	254	1856	Dec 26	1858	Stranded	Louisville, Ky.
703	Metropolis	St.w.	254	1855	Dec 26	1858	Stranded	Sugar Creek, Ky.
704	Metropolis	St.w.	97	1911	Feb 1	1925	Burned	Caruthersville, Mo.
705	Miami	St.w.	175	1863	Jan 28	1866	Exploded	Napoleon, Ark. 40 lives lost.
706	Michigan	St.p.	482	1853	Dec 9	1859	Exploded	New Madrid, Mo. 2 lives lost.
707	Mildred	St.p.	92	1900	Jan 29	1918	Ice	Dam 31, Ohio River.
708	Mill Boy	Brg.	86	1857	Jan 31	1864	Snagged	Jacksonport, Ark. Converted steamer.
709	Miner	St.p.	258	1864	Jun 8	1869	Snagged	Skunk River, Iowa.
710	Minnetonka	St.w.	158	1857	Feb 23	1862	Burned	Nashville, Tenn.
711	Minnesota	St.p.	482	1866	Feb	1866	Unknown	St. Louis, Mo.
712	Minnesota	St.s.	1,332	1921	Jun 21	1951	Foundered	Mile 336.3, Missouri River, near mouth of Fishing River, Mo. Steel vessel.
713	Minnie	St.w.	445	1865	Nov 18	1873	Snagged	Leavenworth, Kan.
714	Miriam	St.p.	65	1906	Apr 29	1908	Capsized	Hardins Point, Ark. 11 lives lost (65).

NO.	NAME OF VESSEL	RIG	TONS	BUILT	DATE		CAUSE	PLACE AND COMMENT
715	Mishawaka	Ol.s.	88	1939	Nov 11	1955	Burned	Near Harrods Creek, Ky. Steel vessel.
716	Mississippi	St.p.	378	1819	May 26	1825	Snagged	Ste. Genevieve, Mo.
717	Mississippi Belle	-	-	-	Oct 24	1834	Collided	With BOONSLICK. St. Louis, Mo. 30 lives lost.
718	Missouri	St.p.	110	1828	May 1	1831	Snagged	Bonnots Mill, Mo.
719	Missouri	St.p.	886	1845	Jul 8	1851	Burned	St. Louis, Mo.
720	Missouri Mail	St.p.	209	1843	May 9	1848	Burned	St. Louis, Mo.
721	Moderator	St.w.	231	1856	Jan 28	1864	Ice	St. Louis, Mo.
722	Mogul	St.p.	292	1847	Sep 30	1848	Stranded	Cloverport, Ky.
723	Mokita	Ol.s.	196	1935	Jul 25	1961	Burned	On right bank of Ohio River, near Dam 53, at Mile 963, below Pittsburg, Ky. Steel vessel.
724	Mollie Dozier	St.p.	384	1865	Oct 3	1866	Snagged	Plattsmouth, Neb.
725	Molly Grath	St.w.	75	1851	Nov 29	1851	Collided	With PONTIAC NO.2. Below Owensboro, Ky. 20 lives lost.
726	Monongahela	St.p.	74	1863	Feb 11	1870	Foundered	Leavenworth, Kan.
727	Montauk	St.p.	175	1847	May 17	1849	Burned	St. Louis, Mo.
728	Montauk	St.w.	237	1853	Oct 13	1853	Burned	St. Louis, Mo.
729	Montezuma	St.p.	175	1828	Feb 28	1829	Snagged	Helena, Ark.
730	Montgomery	St.p.	162	1828	Jun 10	1829	Snagged	Smithland, Ky.
731	Morgan	St.p.	60	1908	Sep 29	1911	Burned	Haddux Ferry, Ky.
732	Morning Star	St.p.	465	1856	Jun 21	1859	Burned	St. Louis, Mo.
733	Mountaineer	St.w.	211	1864	Nov 4	1864	Burned	Johnsonville, Tenn.
734	Muscatine	St.w.	274	1915	Jul 29	1945	Burned	Barge plant, West Kentucky Coal Co., Paducah, Ky. Steel vessel.
735	Mustang	St.p.	128	1848	Oct 9	1850	Snagged	Brunswick, Mo.
736	Mustang	St.p.	138	1848	Aug 18	1851	Stranded	Paducah, Ky.
737	McGhee	St.w.	145	1924	Aug 18	1927	Burned	Barren River, Ky. 1 life lost (10).
738	Nancy F	Ga.s.	64	1925	Dec 3	1929	Burned	Westover, Ark. 1 life lost.
739	Nathaniel Holmes	St.w.	215	1856	Mar 29	1859	Collided	With DAVID GIBSON. Petersburg, Ky. 15 lives lost.
740	National	St.p.	189	1844	Mar 30	1847	Burned	Carrollton, Ky. 1 life lost.
741	Native	St.p.	104	1835	May 23	1837	Stranded	Harpeth Shoals, Tenn.
742	Native	St.p.	50	1834	Nov 21	1838	Exploded	Dover, Tenn. 2 lives lost.
743	Naugatuck	St.w.	295	1864	Dec 31	1866	Snagged	St. Marys, Mo.
744	Nebraska	St.p.	683	1854	Jan 12	1860	Ice	St. Louis, Mo.
745	Nellie Miller	St.w.	146	1854	Feb 4	1858	Snagged	Nashville, Tenn.
746	Nellie Moore	St.w.	226	1863	Nov 25	1863	Stranded	Cumberland Island, Ky.
747	Neosho	St.p.	88	1834	Feb 11	1837	Snagged	Arkansas River. 1 life lost.
748	Neptune	St.p.	227	1841	Dec 12	1845	Snagged	Plum Point, Tenn.
749	Neptune	St.w.	211	1857	Mar 19	1862	Collided	With bridge. Clarksville, Tenn.
750	Nettie	St.p.	94	1897	Oct 30	1905	Foundered	Little Rock, Ark.
751	Neva	St.p.	71	1898	Jul 26	1908	Burned	Wheeling, W.Va.
752	Nevada	St.w.	299	1863	Apr 7	1866	Burned	St. Louis, Mo.
753	New England	St.w.	306	1847	Jan 18	1853	Burned	St. Louis, Mo.
754	New Hampshire	St.w.	125	1845	May 6	1847	Exploded	Pine Bluff, Ark. 12 lives lost.
755	New Jersey	St.p.	152	1830	Nov 1	1830	Snagged	Ste. Genevieve, Mo.
756	New Lucy	St.p.	416	1852	Nov 22	1857	Burned	DeWitt, Mo.
757	New Orleans	St.p.	306	1840	Sep 12	1842	Snagged	Commerce, Mo.
758	New York	St.p.	298	1827	Jan	1832	Snagged	Plum Point, Tenn.
759	Niagara	St.p.	213	1847	Jan	1856	Stranded	Randolph, Tenn.
760	Niagara	St.p.	797	1864	Oct 20	1865	Collided	With POST BOY. Above Helena, Ark. 75 lives lost.
761	Nile	St.p.	454	1866	Apr 8	1874	Stranded	St. Louis, Mo.

NO.	NAME OF VESSEL	RIG	TONS	BUILT	DATE		CAUSE	PLACE AND COMMENT
762	Nina F.	Ol.s.	80	1945	Aug 7	1961	Foundered	At Mile 404, Missouri River, Ft. Leavenworth, Kan. Steel vessel.
763	Nora	St.w.	214	1864	May 28	1867	Snagged	DeSoto, Neb.
764	North America	St.p.	273	1844	Oct 8	1849	Burned	St. Louis, Mo.
765	North Missouri	St.p.	348	1865	May 25	1872	Unknown	Ingleside, Ark.
766	Northerner	St.p.	332	1859	Jul 13	1864	Burned	St. Louis, Mo.
767	No.300	Brg.	438	1926		1943	Flood	At Point Pleasant, W.Va. Steel vessel.
768	No.501	Brg.	635	1911		1947	Unknown	Ohio River, near West Columbia, W.Va.
769	O.K.	St.p.	59	1899	Jun 21	1908	Burned	Fort Benton, Montana.
770	O & K 637	Brg.	417	1938	Aug 15	1940	Foundered	In Kanawha River, W.Va.
771	OR 215	Brg.	664	1962	May 16	1967	Collided	With Markland Dam. At Mile 532, Ohio River.
772	OR 438 and 44	Brg.	694	1963	May 16	1967	Collided	With Markland Dam. At Mile 532, Ohio River.
773	OR 248;270;280 and 40	Brg.	640	1962	May 16	1967	Collided	With Markland Dam. At Mile 532, Ohio River.
774	Ocean Spray	St.p.	371	1857	Apr 22	1858	Burned	St. Louis, Mo. 23 lives lost.
775	Ocean Wave	St.p.	205	1845	Aug 12	1851	Burned	Louisville, Ky.
776	O'Connell	St.p.	107	1833	Jul 31	1836	Snagged	Trinity, Ky.
777	Odd Fellow	St.p.	70	1862	Jan 1	1865	Snagged	Columbus, Ky.
778	Ohio	St.p.	122	1841	Oct 3	1846	Ice	Arrow Rock, Mo.
779	Ohio	St.w.	90	1852	Jun 1	1854	Snagged	Quick River, Ky.
780	Ohio	St.p.	361	1898	Feb 9	1910	Burned	Parkersburg, W.Va.
781	Ohio Valley	St.p.	201	1841	Nov 28	1842	Snagged	Ste. Genevieve, Mo.
782	Olive Branch	St.p.	312	1819	Apr 28	1827	Burned	Louisville, Ky.
783	Ollie Neville	St.p.	70	1887	Jan 3	1905	Foundered	Ripley, Ohio.
784	Ollie Sullivan	St.w.	91	1862	Oct 5	1870	"Sunk"	Paducah, Ky.
785	Omaha	St.p.	307	1856	Dec 16	1865	Ice	St. Louis, Mo.
786	Omaha City	St.p.	147	1857	Jan 12	1866	Ice	St. Louis, Mo.
787	Only Chance	St.p.	219	1865	Nov 23	1869	Foundered	Douglas Landing, Ark.
788	Ontario	St.w.	265	1864	Sep 25	1866	Snagged	15 miles below Nebraska City, Neb.
789	Onward	St.p.	85	1912	Apr 7	1919	Burned	6 miles above Highbridge, Ky.
790	Oregon	St.p.	225	1827	Jan 31	1832	Snagged	Trinity, Ky.
791	Oregon	St.p.	382	1841	Jun 13	1841	Snagged	Ste. Genevieve, Mo.
792	Orient	St.w.	222	1862	Feb 17	1864	Snagged	Commerce, Mo. 14 lives lost.
793	Orion	St.p.	158	1914	Jan 31	1918	Ice	Randolph, Tenn.
794	Osage Valley	St.p.	166	1841	Oct 5	1842	Stranded	St. Louis, Mo.
795	Oswego	St.p.	117	1835	Feb 16	1839	Snagged	Carrollton, Ky.
796	PB 1412	Brg.	735	1952	Jan 28	1966	Foundered	At Mile 82.5, Upper Mississippi River, on the side at Wittenberg, Mo.
797	Pacific	St.p.	603	1857	Nov 18	1860	Burned	Uniontown, Ky. 8 lives lost.
798	Palace	Ga.p.	83	1907	Jan 20	1912	Foundered	Weston, Ky.
799	Papa Lere	Ol.s.	81	1936	Jul 21	1956	Tornado	At Randolph Bluff Light, 39 miles north of Memphis, Tenn., on Mississippi River.
800	Park City	St.p.	197	1883	Dec 6	1909	Foundered	Sunnyside Landing, Ky.
801	Parthenia	St.w.	154	1854	Dec 7	1855	Burned	St. Louis, Mo.
802	Pathfinder	St.p.	62	1882	Nov 13	1916	Foundered	St. Joseph, Mo.
803	Patriot	St.p.	268	1825	May 6	1829	Exploded	Trinity, Ky.
804	Patrol	St.p.	144	1883	Sep 8	1918	Stranded	Harmons Creek Shoals, Ky.
805	Paul Anderson	St.p.	310	1850	Jul 2	1856	Burned	St. Louis, Mo.
806	Pavonia	St.p.	132	1892	Jan 29	1918	Ice	Little Chain, Ky.
807	Pearl	Drg.	307	-	Aug 4	1948	Burned	On left bank of Mississippi River, near Charleston, Mo.
808	Pennsylvania	St.p.	486	1854	Jun 13	1858	Exploded	Ship Island, Helena, Ark. 20 lives lost.
809	Pensacola	St.p.	128	1839	Nov 14	1841	Snagged	Smithland, Ky.

NO.	NAME OF VESSEL	RIG	TONS	BUILT	DATE			CAUSE	PLACE AND COMMENT
810	Peoria	St.p.	490	1914	Jan 29	1918		Ice	Paducah, Ky.
811	Persia	St.p.	255	1852	Mar 23	1860		Burned	Memphis, Tenn.
812	Peter Balen	St.w.	545	1866	Jul 22	1869		Burned	Camp Crook, Missouri River.
813	Peytona	St.p.	747	1864	Feb 26	1866		Burned	St. Louis, Mo.
814	Philip Pennywith	St.p.	246	1849	May 13	1851		Snagged	Van Buren, Ark.
815	Philip Ritchie	Ol.w.	95	1905	Dec 3	1948		Burned	At Alpha Landing, on Tennessee River. Steel vessel.
816	Phoenix	St.p.	189	1846	Jul 28	1849		Burned	St. Louis, Mo.
817	Pike	St.p.	245	1852	May 10	1854		Snagged	Big Eddy, Ste. Genevieve, Mo. 10 lives lost.
818	Pike	St.p.	94	1867		1872		Unknown	St. Louis, Mo.
819	Pilgrim	St.w.	139	1864	Dec 6	1867		Snagged	30 miles below Helena, Ark.
820	Pilot	St.p.	129	1825	Jan 17	1829		Stranded	Ste. Genevieve, Mo.
821	Pilot	St.w.	72	1845		1848		Snagged	Arkansas River, Ark.
822	Pizarro	St.p.	107	1839	Dec 13	1839		Burned	St. Louis, Mo.
823	Plough Boy	St.p.	248	1848	Oct 6	1848		Snagged	Providence, Mo.
824	Pocahontas	St.p.	163	1857	Aug 9	1866		Snagged	Fort Randall, S.D.
825	Pontiac No.2	St.p.	269	1850	Nov 29	1851		Collided	With MOLLY GRATH. Below Owensboro, Ky. 20 lives lost.
826	Portland	St.p.	57	1847	May 6	1851		Burned	Portland, Ky. 1 life lost.
827	Portsmouth	St.w.	168	1857	Feb 26	1860		Snagged	Weston, Mo.
828	Post Boy	St.p.	348	1859	Sep 13	1863		Burned	St. Louis, Mo.
829	Potomac	St.p.	54	1828		1832		Ice	Newport, Ky.
830	Prairie City	St.w.	198	1852	Dec 7	1855		Burned	St. Louis, Mo.
831	Prairie Rose	St.w.	247	1854	Jan 12	1866		Ice	St. Louis, Mo.
832	Preemption	St.p.	181	1840	Sep 21	1842		Snagged	Plum Point, Tenn.
833	President	St.p.	288	1824	Feb 7	1829		Stranded	2 miles south of Clarksville, Mo.
834	President	Ol.s.	70	1931	May 2	1937		Burned	White Oak Shoals, Red River, Ark.
835	Preston	St.p.	144	1852	May 4	1853		Snagged	Hickman, Ky. 74 lives lost.
836	Prince	St.p.	223	1859	Feb 27	1862		Snagged	With GREAT WESTERN. Raleigh, Ky.
837	Princess	St.w.	138	1856	Mar 14	1858		Collided	Napoleon, Ark.
838	Princess	St.w.	185	1863	Jun 1	1868		Stranded	Carrollton, Ky. 1 life lost (2).
839	Princess	St.s.	687	1900	Jan 30	1918		Ice	Louisville, Ky.
840	Princess	St.w.	335	1888	Jan 15	1928		Burned	Arkansas River, Ark.
841	Progress	St.w.	217	1854	Dec	1865		Snagged	Arkansas River, Ark.
842	Progress	St.p.	59	1862	Jan 2	1866		Burned	Memphis, Tenn.
843	Progress	St.w.	90	1882	Jul 20	1926		Foundered	Nashville, Tenn.
844	Quaker City	St.w.	213	1853	Feb 17	1859		Burned	Little Rock, Ark.
845	Quapaw	St.w.	245	1857	Feb 11	1861		Snagged	Licking River, Ky.
846	R.H. Winslow	St.p.	335	1851	Jun 1	1859		Foundered	At Mile 592.1, right side bank of Missouri River, near Peru, Neb.
847	R.J.B.	Ga.w.	112	1929	Feb 6	1951		Stranded	St. Louis, Mo.
848	R.J. Lockwood	St.p.	417	1864	Feb 26	1872		Ice	With LAST CHANCE. Chattanooga, Tenn.
849	R.P. Converse	St.w.	69	1865	Mar 21	1872		Collided	Louisville, Ky.
850	Rambler	St.w.	91	1832	Jun 21	1833		Burned	Tennessee River.
851	Rapidan	St.w.	236	1866	Mar 14	1870		Snagged	Paducah, Ky.
852	Rapids	St.p.	148	1905	Dec 12	1917		Ice	Tennessee River.
853	Reaper	St.p.	126	1831	Jan 28	1832		Snagged	With bridge. Parkersburg, W.Va. 5 lives lost.
854	Rebecca	St.p.	341	1864	Dec 7	1869		Collided	St. Louis, Mo.
855	Red Wing	St.p.	142	1846	May 17	1849		Burned	Smith Cut Off, Ark.
856	Red Wing	St.w.	150	1856	May 25	1860		Snagged	Carrollton, Ky. 14 lives lost.
857	Redstone	St.p.	181	1851	Apr 2	1852		Exploded	

NO.	NAME OF VESSEL	RIG	TONS	BUILT	DATE		CAUSE	PLACE AND COMMENT
858	Rees Lee	St.p.	463	1899	Jan 22	1906	Collided	With obstruction. Burns Landing, Tenn.
859	Reliance	St.w.	95	1918	Jul 21	1924	Burned	Calhoun, Ky.
860	Relief	St.p.	68	1848	Nov 8	1853	Snagged	Louisiana, Mo.
861	Republic	St.w.	107	1850	Jun 23	1854	Snagged	Near Dover, Tenn.
862	Republic	St.p.	147	1842	Jun 12	1846	Snagged	Lewisburg, Ark.
863	Resolute	St.w.	203	1857	Apr 10	1859	Snagged	Van Buren, Ark.
864	Return	St.w.	219	1852	Jul 27	1859	Foundered	Duvall Bluff, Ark.
865	Return	St.p.	50	1848	Jul 27	1859	Snagged	Duvall Bluff, Ark.
866	Return	St.w.	76	1840	Nov 19	1842	Snagged	Pine Bluff, Ark.
867	Rialto	St.p.	82	1846	Jan 17	1850	Burned	Pee Dee, Ky.
868	Richland	St.p.	1,645	1867	Dec 31	1874	"Wrecked"	St. Louis, Mo.
869	Richmond	St.p.	212	1846	Feb	1848	Snagged	Arkansas River, Ark.
870	Ringgold	St.w.	141	1926	Dec 22	1932	Burned	Potsville, Ky.
871	Rival	St.w.	266	1864	Dec 17	1865	Stranded	Commerce, Mo.
872	Roanoke	St.p.	–	–	Jun 9	1836	Exploded	Mississippi River. 17 lives lost.
873	Rob Roy	St.p.	268	1849	Oct 13	1853	Burned	St. Louis, Mo.
874	Robert Campbell	St.w.	178	1864	Nov 3	1864	Snagged	De Witt, Mo.
875	Robert Emmet	St.p.	199	1845	Dec 12	1851	Snagged	Bainbridge, Mo.
876	Robert Fulton	St.p.	158	1860	Oct 7	1863	Burned	Union Point, Red River, Ark.
877	Robert Fulton	St.p.	173	1860	Aug 19	1863	Exploded	Savannah River. All lives lost.
878	Robert Habersham	St.w.	68	1860	Feb 5	1864	Burned	Louisville, Ky. 3 lives lost.
879	Robert Lee	St.w.	238	1864	May 8	1870	Snagged	Cumberland Island, Ky.
880	Robert Moore	St.p.	178	1850	Apr 14	1852	Collided	With REPUBLIC. Dover, Ky.
881	Robert Rogers	St.w.	92	1927	Apr 26	1946	Burned	Benzal, Ark. Steel vessel.
882	Robert Sanford	St.p.	249	1864	Dec	1865	Snagged	15 miles below Little Rock, Ark.
883	Rodolph	St.p.	67	1843	Nov 17	1845	Snagged	Pine Bluff, Ark.
884	Rolla	St.p.	140	1850	Dec 31	1851	Snagged	Campagnolle, Ark.
885	Romeo	St.w.	158	1854	Dec 16	1865	Ice	St. Louis, Mo.
886	Rosalie	St.w.	123	1860	Dec	1862	Burned	Van Buren, Ark.
887	Rose Douglas	St.w.	126	1856		1858	Collided	With MONONGAHELA. Napoleon, Ark.
888	Rough and Ready	St.p.	230	1847	Mar 12	1850	Snagged	St. Charles, Mo.
889	Rowena	St.p.	435	1858	Apr 18	1863	Snagged	Devil Island, above Cape Girardeau, Mo.
890	Rubicon	St.p.	164	1838	Oct 9	1841	Snagged	Ste. Genevieve, Mo.
891	Ruth	St.p.	702	1862	Aug 4	1863	Burned	Columbus, Ky. 30 lives lost.
892	Ruth	St.p.	173	1910	Jan 31	1918	Ice	McMechen, W.Va.
893	SC No.1524	Brg.	932	1955	Jul 2	1965	Foundered	At Mile 189.5, Missouri River.
894	S.C. Pomeroy	St.w.	205	1863	Mar 27	1877	Unknown	Harlem, Mo. Used as ferryboat.
895	Sadie Lee	St.p.	179	1901	Nov 15	1912	Foundered	Dennis Landing, Mississippi River.
896	Saint Ange	St.p.	254	1849	Feb 2	1854	Ice	St. Louis, Mo.
897	Saint Charles	St.p.	127	1835	Jun 21	1836	Burned	Lexington, Mo.
898	Saint Charles	St.p.	290	1843	Dec 7	1844	Exploded	St. Louis, Mo. 1 life lost.
899	Saint Clair	St.p.	320	1852	Jul 2	1856	Burned	St. Louis, Mo.
900	Saint Cloud	St.w.	291	1859	Jan 24	1867	Snagged	Plum Point, Tenn.
901	St. Francis No.2	St.p.	162	1853	Sep 16	1860	Foundered	Memphis, Tenn.
902	Saint Francis No.3	St.p.	219	1858	Sep 10	1863	Burned	Little Rock, Ark.
903	Saint Joseph	St.p.	217	1846	Jan 12	1850	Exploded	Napoleon, Ark. 8 lives lost.
904	St. Louis	St.p.	199	1918	Dec 28	1820	Burned	New Madrid, Mo.
905	St. Louis	St.p.	210	1847	Feb 20	1851	Exploded	St. Louis, Mo. 20 lives lost. Used as ferryboat.

NO.	NAME OF VESSEL	RIG	TONS	BUILT	DATE	CAUSE	PLACE AND COMMENT
906	St. Louis	St.p.	937	1850	Dec 9 1860	Foundered	Memphis, Tenn.
907	Saint Louis	St.p.	374	1912	Sep 2 1918	Foundered	Sulphur Springs, Mo. 1 life lost (91).
908	St. Mary	St.p.	295	1855	Sep 7 1859	Snagged	Above St. Joseph, Mo.
909	St. Nicholas	St.p.	666	1853	Apr 24 1859	Exploded	St. Francis Island, Helena, Ark. 60 lives lost.
910	St. Patrick	St.p.	414	1862	Apr 18 1868	Burned	Memphis, Tenn.
911	Saint Paul	St.p.	265	1852	Aug 12 1857	Snagged	St. Aubert, Mo.
912	St. Paul	St.p.	83	1864	Apr 16 1865	Burned	Hatchie River, Tenn.
913	St. Peters	St.p.	163	1847	May 17 1849	Burned	St. Louis, Mo.
914	Salem	St.w.	147	1851	Feb 24 1856	Ice	Covington, Ky.
915	Sallie Anderson	St.p.	62	1846	Sep 24 1849	Burned	Little Rock, Ark.
916	Sallie West	St.w.	286	1853	May 5 1859	Snagged	Kickapoo, Kan.
917	Saluda	St.p.	233	1846	Apr 9 1852	Exploded	Lexington, Mo. 35 lives lost.
918	Sam Brown	St.p.	491	1903	Feb 2 1916	Burned	Huntington, W.Va. 11 lives lost (32).
919	Sam Cloon	St.p.	301	1851	Feb 26 1856	Ice	St. Louis, Mo.
920	Sam Kirkman	St.w.	271	1857	Feb 6 1862	Burned	Fort Henry, Tenn.
921	Sam Walker	St.p.	126	1846	Jun 5 1849	Burned	Memphis, Tenn.
922	Samson	St.p.	198	1832	Jun 28 1836	Burned	New Madrid, Mo.
923	Samuel Gaty	St.p.	295	1853	Jun 29 1868	Burned	Arrow Rock, Mo.
924	San Francisco	St.p.	263	1849	Jul 28 1849	Burned	St. Louis, Mo.
925	Sangamon	St.p.	85	1853	Feb 12 1856	Snagged	St. Charles, Ark.
926	Sarah	St.p.	442	1849	May 17 1849	Burned	St. Louis, Mo.
927	Saranac No.2	St.p.	295	1850	Jul 2 1856	Burned	St. Louis, Mo.
928	Saxonia	St.s.	60	1863	Apr 8 1863	Burned	Clarksville, Tenn.
929	Scioto No.2	St.p.	265	1851	Jun 1 1860	Burned	Shippingport, Ky.
930	Sea Bird	St.p.	261	1844	Jan 5 1848	Burned	Cape Girardeau, Mo.
931	Sea Lion	St.p.	92	1880	Oct 27 1919	Burned	Boone's Ferry, Ky.
932	Senate	St.p.	106	1845	Sep 1847	Snagged	Brandenburg, Ky.
933	Sentinel	St.p.	151	1832	Jun 21 1833	Burned	Louisville, Ky.
934	Shenandoah	St.p.	179	1848	Feb 26 1856	Ice	St. Louis, Mo.
935	Shipper	St.w.	78	1849	Oct 26 1853	Stranded	Harpeth Shoals, Tenn.
936	Silver Cloud No.2	St.w.	287	1863	Jan 11 1869	Burned	Point Pleasant, W.Va. 1 life lost.
937	Silver Heels	St.w.	50	1858	Oct 14 1868	Snagged	Vanceburg, Ky.
938	Silver Lake	St.w.	70	1858	Sep 3 1862	Burned	Osage River, Mo.
939	Silver Spray	St.w.	352	1864	Apr 10 1870	Exploded	Pacific Place, Tenn. 9 lives lost.
940	Siren	St.p.	110	1838	Feb 8 1845	Exploded	Chattachooche River. 10 lives lost.
941	Skylark	St.p.	371	1858	Aug 9 1862	Burned	Duck River, Tenn.
942	Sligo No.2	St.p.	170	1849	Jan 22 1853	Burned	Smithland, Ky.
943	Sonoma	St.p.	139	1897	Jun 27 1913	Foundered	Collided with snag in Kentucky River. 4 lives lost (41).
944	Sonora	St.p.	363	1851	Feb 1856	Snagged	Portland, Mo.
945	Sophia M. Gardner	St.s.	91	1912	Apr 2 1917	Collided	With snag. Missouri City, Mo.
946	South Bend	St.w.	150	1859	Dec 13 1860	Collided	With GOODY FRIENDS. Fulton, Tenn. 2 lives lost.
947	Southerner	St.p.	347	1856	Jul 12 1856	Burned	St. Louis, Mo.
948	Southland	St.w.	256	1922	Dec 22 1932	Burned	Potsville, Ky.
949	Spokane	St.p.	561	1899	Jul 12 1922	Burned	Lewiston, Idaho.
950	Spread Eagle	St.p.	389	1857	Mar 20 1864	Snagged	Washington, Mo.
951	Spread Eagle	St.p.	223	1911	Jan 29 1918	Ice	Paducah, Ky.
952	Stacker Lee	St.p.	710	1902	Oct 21 1916	Foundered	Mississippi River, Ark.
953	Star	St.w.	210	1863	Jan 19 1870	Snagged	Benwood, W.Va. 1 life lost.

NO.	NAME OF VESSEL	RIG	TONS	BUILT	DATE		CAUSE	PLACE AND COMMENT
954	Star of the West	St.p.	435	1855	Apr 22	1858	Burned	St. Louis, Mo.
955	Stephen Bayard	St.p.	155	1851	Mar 6	1865	Burned	Memphis, Tenn.
956	Steve Click, Jr.	St.s.	161	1903	Jul 3	1947	Foundered	At Helena, Ark. Iron vessel.
957	Submarine No.4	St.p.	226	1850	Feb 26	1856	Ice	St. Louis, Mo.
958	Success	St.w.	280	1867	Dec 13	1868	Unknown	Arkansas River, Ark.
959	Sully	St.p.	280	1867	Oct 22	1869	Stranded	St. Joseph, Mo.
960	Sultan	St.p.	349	1854	Unknown		Burned	Ste. Genevieve, Mo. 23 lives lost.
961	Sultana	St.p.	924	1848	Jun 12	1851	Burned	St. Louis, Mo. 1 life lost.
962	Sultana	St.p.	565	1852	Mar 25	1857	Burned	Hickman, Ky.
963	Sultana	St.p.	660	1863	Apr 27	1865	Exploded	Above Memphis, Tenn. 1,547 lives lost.
964	Sunset	St.w.	103	1865	Jul 18	1869	Snagged	Sioux City, Iowa.
965	Sunshine	St.p.	354	1860	Jul 13	1864	Burned	St. Louis, Mo.
966	Superior	St.p.	74	1822	Dec 20	1832	Exploded	Brandenburg, Ky. 3 lives lost.
967	Susan	St.p.	198	1896	Sep 17	1907	Collided	With snag. Fort Calhoun, Neb.
968	Susie A	Ol.w.	92	1936	Oct 9	1942	Burned	Pan-Am. docks, Nashville, Tenn.
969	Susquehanna	St.p.	141	1845	Feb 2	1852	Snagged	Harpeth Shoals, Tenn.
970	Swallow	St.w.	83	1847	Nov 30	1850	Burned	Memphis, Tenn.
971	T.D. Horner	St.w.	123	1859	Jan 1	1868	Collided	With bridge. Louisville, Ky.
972	T.L. Crawford	St.w.	155	1858	Nov 12	1860	Snagged	Boonville, Mo.
973	T.L. McGill	St.p.	598	1857	Jan 16	1871	Burned	Memphis, Tenn. 40 lives lost.
974	Taglioni	St.p.	253	1847	May 17	1849	Burned	St. Louis, Mo.
975	Tahlequah	St.p.	92	1860	Sep 10	1863	Burned	Little Rock, Ark.
976	Talisman	St.p.	116	1828	Apr 22	1832	Burned	St. Louis, Mo.
977	Talisman	St.p.	173	1846	Nov 19	1847	Collided	With MOTIVE. Cape Girardeau, Mo. 51 lives lost.
978	Talma	St.p.	306	1843		1848	Snagged	New Madrid, Mo.
979	Tamerline	St.p.	122	1846	Nov 16	1849	Snagged	St. Louis, Mo.
980	Tampico	Ol.s.	591	1947	Jul 2	1965	Foundered	Near Mile 12, Missouri River.
981	Tarascon	St.p.	358	1896	Dec 26	1917	Foundered	Off Cottonwood Point, Mo.
982	Teche	St.w.	106	1911	Aug 30	1937	Burned	Louisville, Ky. Steel vessel.
983	Telegraph	St.p.	313	1848	Feb 14	1852	Foundered	St. Charles, Mo.
984	Telegraph No.3	St.p.	747	1853	Nov 25	1863	Exploded	Osceola, Ark. 3 lives lost.
985	Tennessee	St.p.	334	1897	Sep 11	1908	Collided	With snag. Kansas City, Mo.
986	Tennessee Belle	St.p.	248	1855	Apr 27	1860	Burned	Above Paducah, Ky.
987	Tennessee Belle	St.w.	436	1923	Nov 2	1942	Burned	300 miles below Natchez Island Light.
988	Tennessee Valley	St.p.	496	1842	Aug 7	1843	Snagged	Ste. Genevieve, Mo.
989	The Elk	Ga.p.	77	1912	Oct 14	1918	Stranded	Decatur, Neb.
990	Thomas E. Tutt	St.p.	351	1855	Dec 9	1864	Burned	Cumberland City, Tenn.
991	Thomas J. Patten	St.w.	118	1860	Jan 25	1864	Burned	Walker's Bend, below Memphis, Tenn.
992	Thomas Jefferson	St.p.	224	1819	Oct 4	1824	Snagged	Helena, Ark.
993	Thomas Parker	St.p.	57	1894	Dec 16	1908	Burned	Owensburg, Ky.
994	Thomas Yeatman	St.p.	113	1830	Oct 24	1833	Exploded	Memphis, Tenn. 7 lives lost.
995	Time	St.p.	263	1860	Feb 9	1862	Burned	Duck Creek, Tenn.
996	Time and Tide	St.p.	161	1847	Apr 21	1853	Stranded	St. Louis, Mo.
997	Timour	St.p.	232	1849	Aug 26	1854	Exploded	Jefferson City, Mo. 17 lives lost. Also reported as "Timour No.2".
998	Toledo No.2	St.w.	80	1851	Jan 31	1855	Ice	St. Louis, Mo.
999	Tom Brierly	St.p.	163	1856	Feb 13	1868	Unknown	Missouri River. Used as ferryboat.
1000	Tom Corwin	St.p.	194	1846	Oct 9	1846	Stranded	Plum Point, Tenn.
1001	Tom Farrow	St.w.	119	1863	Jan 9	1879	Ice	Coalburg, W.Va.

NO.	NAME OF VESSEL	RIG	TONS	BUILT	DATE			CAUSE	PLACE AND COMMENT
1002	Tom Rees No.2	St.p.	327	1869	Feb	5	1910	Foundered	New Cumberland, W.Va.
1003	Tom Williams	St.w.	97	1895	Dec	22	1932	Burned	Potsville, Ky.
1004	Transit	St.p.	81	1880	Jan	26	1920	Ice	Jeffersonville, Ky.
1005	Trenton	St.p.	207	1847	Feb	27	1848	Burned	Marysville, Ky.
1006	Tributary	St.p.	148	1845	Dec	29	1848	Burned	Louisville, Ky.
1007	Trio	St.w.	150	1857	Jan	14	1863	Burned	Nashville, Tenn.
1008	Trpoic	St.p.	242	1853	Oct	15	1857	Burned	Waverly, Mo. 8 lives lost.
1009	Trustee	St.p.	146	1849	Feb	18	1852	Snagged	Van Buren, Ark.
1010	Tuscumbia	St.p.	291	1846	Oct	10	1852	Snagged	Memphis, Tenn.
1011	Twilight	St.p.	230	1865	Sep	10	1865	Snagged	Napoleon, Mo.
1012	Twin City	St.w.	209	1852	Dec	7	1855	Burned	St. Louis, Mo.
1013	Tycoon	St.p.	332	1860	Oct	9	1865	Burned	Tiptonville, Tenn.
1014	Umpire	St.w.	124	1854	Jun	12	1860	Burned	Osage River, Mo.
1015	Umpire No.2	St.w.	101	1850	Aug	1	1854	Snagged	Above Little Rock, Ark.
1016	Uncle Sam	St.p.	360	1898	May	18	1910	Collided	With dredge. Kansas City, Mo.
1017	Uncle Steve	Ol.w.	64	1926	Dec	9	1939	Burned	Westover, Ark. All life (1) lost.
1018	Undine	St.p.	158	1859	Nov	3	1864	Burned	Johnsonville, Tenn.
1019	Union	St.p.	240	1845	Jan	11	1850	Stranded	Cape Girardeau, Mo.
1020	Universe	St.p.	399	1857	Oct	30	1864	Snagged	Plum Point, Tenn. 17 lives lost.
1021	Urilda	St.w.	169	1863	Apr	24	1869	Snagged	Sioux City, Iowa.
1022	U.S. Mail	St.p.	196	1852	Jun		1857	Snagged	Atchison, Kan.
1023	Vagabond	Ol.s.	69	1940	Nov	6	1945	Burned	At Davenport, Iowa. Steel vessel.
1024	Valley Gem	St.p.	156	1897	Feb		1919	Ice	Morgantown, W.Va.
1025	Valley Queen	St.w.	156	1913	May	17	1934	Foundered	Omaha, Neb.
1026	Van Buren	St.w.	229	1866	Oct	30	1869	Snagged	Above Pine Bluff, Ark.
1027	Venus	St.w.	235	1863	Nov	4	1864	Burned	Fort Hidman, Tenn. 17 lives lost.
1028	Vermont	St.p.	158	1835	Sep	11	1841	Snagged	Doolen Slough, Mo.
1029	Vermont	St.p.	161	1848	Feb	5	1856	Burned	Carrollton, Ky.
1030	Verne Swain	St.w.	120	1904	Aug	26	1929	Stranded	Dismal Point, Ark.
1031	Victor	St.p.	100	1894	Feb	23	1907	Foundered	Pendleton, Ark.
1032	Victor	Ga.w.	92	1926	Jul	5	1930	Burned	Leavenworth, Kan.
1033	Victor No.2	Ga.p.	67	1907	Oct	27	1868	Snagged	20 miles above Memphis, Tenn.
1034	Victoria	St.p.	60	1907	Apr	2	1912	Foundered	Buford, N.D.
1035	Vienna	St.p.	155	1839	Oct	30	1841	Snagged	Owensboro, Ky.
1036	Violett	St.w.	89	1856	Dec	27	1862	Burned	Van Buren, Ark.
1037	Virginia	St.p.	890	1865	Oct	7	1871	Snagged	Osceola, Ark.
1038	Virginia Barton	St.p.	219	1864	Oct	27	1870	Snagged	Bow River Bend, Mo.
1039	Vixen	St.w.	232	1856	Dec	25	1859	Burned	Louisville, Ky.
1040	W.A. Caldwell	St.w.	297	1866	Dec	10	1870	Unknown	Arkansas River, Ark.
1041	W.A. Moffitt	St.p.	553	1865	Nov	17	1865	Burned	St. Louis, Mo.
1042	W.B. Clifton	St.p.	341	1851	Apr	1	1854	Collided	With OHIO. Columbus, Ky. 4 lives lost.
1043	W.B. Terry	St.w.	175	1856	Sep	3	1862	Burned	Dick River, Tenn.
1044	W.I. ,aclay	St.w.	245	1856	Nov	19	1861	Snagged	Below St. Louis, Mo.
1045	W.W.	St.p.	212	1882	May	9	1923	Foundered	Off Brush Creek Island, Carrs, Ky. 1 life lost (10).
1046	Wacouta	St.w.	239	1922	Mar	27	1950	Foundered	At Helena, Ark. Steel vessel.
1047	War Eagle	St.p.	446	1858	Aug	24	1869	Burned	St. Louis, Mo.
1048	Warrenn	St.p.	98	1900	Oct	9	1907	Stranded	Burnside, Ky.

NO.	NAME OF VESSEL	RIG	TONS	BUILT	DATE			CAUSE	PLACE AND COMMENT
1049	Warrior	St.p.	204	1844	Feb 20	1852		Exploded	Meramec River, Mo. 2 lives lost.
1050	Warsaw	St.p.	65	1842	Mar 25	1846		Snagged	St. Charles, Mo.
1051	Warsaw	St.w.	457	1858	Jan 12	1886		Ice	St. Louis, Mo.
1052	Washburn	St.p.	57	1901	Jan 12	1918		Ice	Crocketts Bluff, Ark.
1053	Washington	St.w.	160	1850	Jan 31	1852		Ice	Rock Island, below Louisville, Ky.
1054	Washington	St.p.	74	1847	Feb	1867		Ice	Covington, Ky.
1055	Water Queen	Brg.	165	1900	Jan 23	1936		Foundered	Point Pleasant, W.Va., at Great Kanawha.
1056	Watossa	St.w.	127	1857	Sep 26	1858		Snagged	Nodaway, Mo.
1057	Waverly	St.w.	452	1866	Nov 24	1867		Snagged	Glasgow, Mo.
1058	Webster	St.w.	78	1860	Dec 28	1872		Ice	Helena, Ark.
1059	Wenona	St.p.	63	1893	Jan 29	1918		Ice	Ashland, Ky.
1060	West Wind	St.p.	350	1860	Oct 17	1864		Burned	Glasgow, Mo.
1061	Western	St.p.	154	1838	Jun 1	1843		Burned	St. Charles, Mo.
1062	Westerner	St.p.	461	1853	Jan 3	1855		Stranded	Commerce, Mo.
1063	Weston	St.p.	209	1843	Mar 21	1844		Collided	With ALIQUIPPA. Ste. Genevieve, Mo. 3 lives lost.
1064	Weston	St.p.	89	1882	Sep 7	1909		Foundered	Bismarck, N.D.
1065	Whisper	St.p.	55	1907		1924		Stranded	Tennessee River.
1066	White Cloud	St.p.	259	1843	May 17	1849		Burned	St. Louis, Mo.
1067	White Cloud No.2	St.p.	545	1864	Feb 13	1867		Snagged	St. Louis, Mo.
1068	White River	St.w.	71	1852	Jan 21	1854		Snagged	Barren River, Ky.
1069	William Armstrong	St.w.	89	1846	Nov	1849		Snagged	Little Rock, Ark.
1070	William Baird	St.w.	286	1855	Apr 19	1858		Snagged	Waverly, Mo.
1071	William Butler	St.w.	205	1864	Oct 14	1868		Burned	Wheeling, W.Va.
1072	William Garvin	St.p.	299	1853	Nov	1859		Burned	St. Louis, Mo.
1073	William H. Russell	St.p.	405	1856	Oct 27	1862		Burned	St. Louis, Mo.
1074	William Henry	St.w.	95	1857	Jun 2	1861		Snagged	Fort Smith, Ark.
1075	William L. Ewing	St.p.	355	1856	Nov 25	1864		Stranded	Hardscrabble, St. Louis, Mo.
1076	William Parsons	St.p.	116	1831	Apr 12	1835		Snagged	Little Rock, Ark.
1077	Wilmington	St.p.	-	-	Nov 18	1839		Exploded	Arkansas River. 10 lives lost.
1078	Winifrede	St.w.	125	1854	Mar 28	1860		Snagged	Sobel, Tenn.
1079	Wonderland	Brg.	259	1906	Jul 8	1917		Foundered	Belleville, W.Va.
1080	Wyaconda	St.p.	239	1865	Jul 14	1865		Burned	Ste. Genevieve, Mo.
1081	Yankee	St.w.	205	1857	Nov 28	1867		Snagged	Plum Point, Tenn.
1082	Yellowstone	St.p.	378	1864	Jul 11	1867		Burned	St. Louis, Mo.
1083	Youghiogheny	St.w.	65	1850	Dec 25	1853		Snagged	White River, Ark.
1084	356	Brg.	227	1930	Aug 2	1945		Foundered	In Mississippi River, at Mile Post No.656, Helena, Ark. Steel vessel.
1085	441	Brg.	399	1940	Apr 15	1953		Foundered	Mile 29.3, on Tennessee River. Steel vessel.

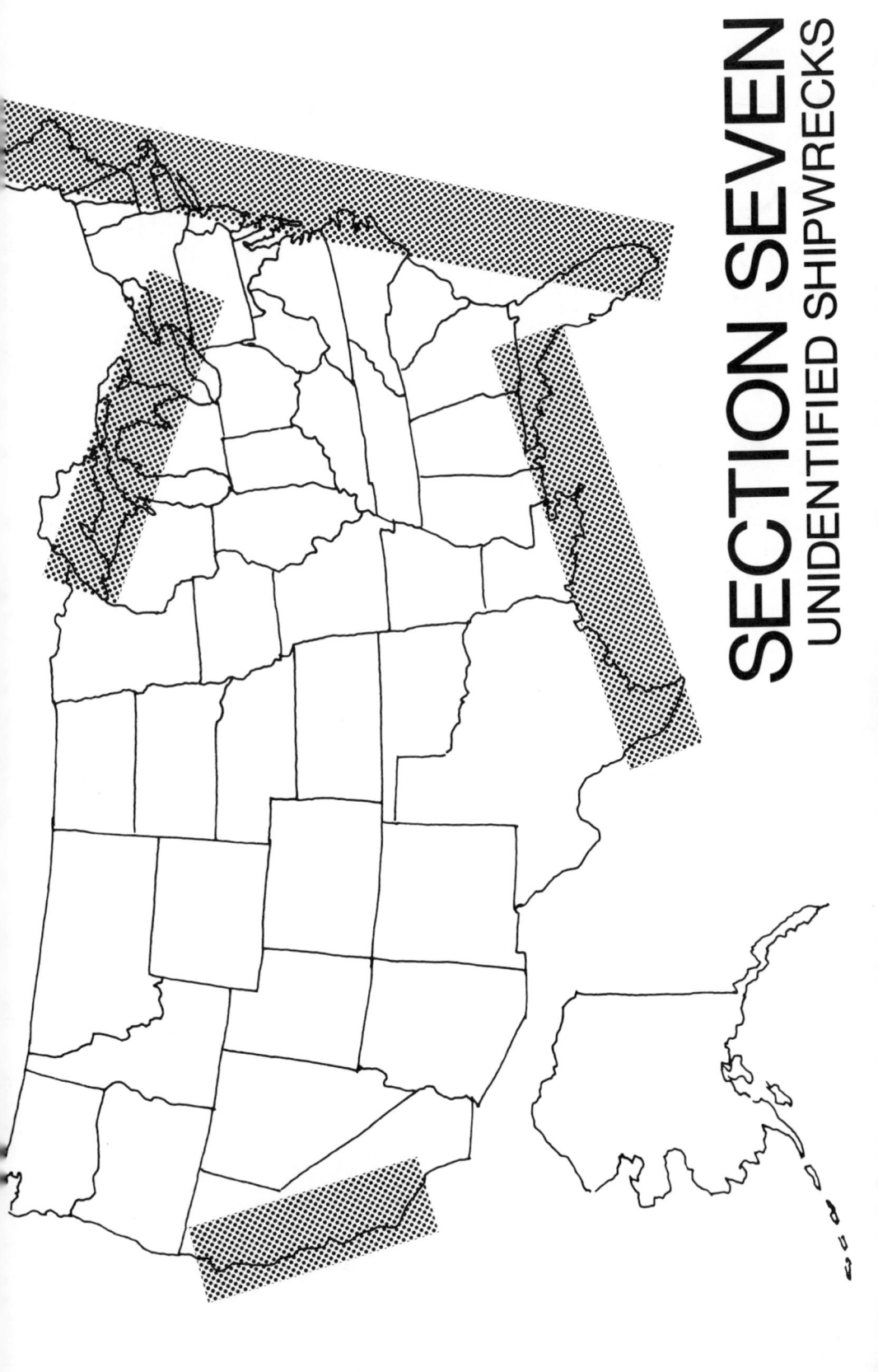

NO.	PLACE AND COMMENT
	SECTION ONE
1	36-53-54 N. 76-23-19 W.
2	36-54-30 N. 76-23-20 W.
3	36-58-00 N. 76-22-05 W.
4	36-59-00 N. 76-05-00 W.
5	37-27-10 N. 74-12-49 W.
6	37-02-20 N. 75-56-25 W.
7	37-03-20 N. 75-53-25 W.
8	37-15-15 N. 75-43-00 W.
9	37-56-35 N. 75-57-30 W.
10	37-01-20 N. 76-10-25 W.
11	37-13-25 N. 76-09-40 W.
12	37-15-25 N. 76-20-25 W.
13	37-15-45 N. 76-11-20 W.
14	37-17-45 N. 76-11-40 W.
15	37-22-55 N. 76-09-55 W.
16	37-23-00 N. 76-10-05 W.
17	37-40-00 N. 76-13-25 W.
18	37-57-40 N. 76-35-00 W.
19	38-05-29 N. 74-49-00 W.
20	38-09-00 N. 74-56-16 W. Bow section of ship.
21	38-22-00 N. 74-32-40 W.
22	38-26-30 N. 74-46-30 W. Old wreck. Approximately 7,000 net tons. Wreck lies bottom up.
23	38-26-30 N. 74-59-18 W. Fisherman.
24	38-27-22 N. 74-56-24 W. Sunk pre-WWII.
25	38-27-26 N. 74-56-04 W. Sunk pre-WWII.
26	38-28-00 N. 74-58-45 W.
27	38-31-30 N. 74-31-54 W. Stands 37' high in 124' of water.
28	38-32-00 N. 74-33-25 W.
29	38-33-20 N. 74-59-45 W.
30	38-36-00 N. 74-56-18 W. Barge. Stands 18' high in 58' of water.

NO.	PLACE AND COMMENT
31	38-36-18 N. 74-39-36 W. Sunk pre-WWII. Stands 15' high in 92' of water.
32	38-36-20 N. 74-57-00 W.
33	38-38-35 N. 74-55-35 W.
34	38-39-36 N. 74-26-36 W. Stands 9' high in 110' of water.
35	38-40-06 N. 74-27-48 W. Pre-WWII. Stands 14' high in 108' of water.
36	38-51-54 N. 74-23-06 W. Stands 29' high in 97' of water.
37	38-54-20 N. 75-08-25 W.
38	38-56-30 N. 75-10-20 W.
39	39-39-30 N. 72-34-30 W. Reported October 1943.
40	39-43-54 N. 73-56-42 W. Stands 3' high in 83' of water.
41	39-45-30 N. 73-58-28 W. Barge. Depth 69'.
42	39-56-00 N. 73-55-40 W. Depth 58'.
43	39-57-00 N. 73-55-00 W. Pre-WWII. Depth 60'.
44	39-02-25 N. 74-40-01 W.
45	39-03-28 N. 74-39-09 W. Depth 10'.
46	39-04-30 N. 74-38-06 W. Stands 9' high in 54' of water.
47	39-06-24 N. 74-06-24 W. Dispersed wreckage. Stands 5' high in 71' of water. Thought to be barges.
48	39-08-36 N. 74-33-18 W. Small wreck. Stands 11' high in 61' of water.
49	39-11-48 N. 74-31-00 W. Yacht. Depth 55'. Length 73'.
50	39-12-48 N. 74-15-42 W. Stands 6' high in 85' of water.
51	39-14-45 N. 74-23-00 W. Sunk pre-WWII. Depth 38'.
52	39-17-30 N. 74-26-30 W. Fisherman. Depth 43'.
53	39-19-54 N. 74-14-36 W. Dispersed wreckage. Stands 4' high in 58' of water.
54	39-20-18 N. 74-19-12 W. Sunk pre-WWII. Car float. Depth 35'.
55	39-21-07 N. 74-17-06 W.
56	39-21-12 N. 74-12-54 W. Sunk pre-WWII. Large freighter. Depth 38'.
57	39-21-12 N. 74-17-09 W. Barge. Cargo of pig iron. Depth 42'.
58	39-21-15 N. 74-11-25 W. Depth 43'.
59	39-25-54 N. 74-12-12 W. Stands 5' high in 60' of water.
60	39-26-20 N. 74-08-18 W. Sunk pre-WWII. Depth 32'.

NO.	PLACE AND COMMENT
61	39-51-00 N. 74-01-45 W.
62	40-06-00 N. 69-55-00 W. Sunk pre-WWII. Stands 48' high in 387' of water.
63	40-26-20 N. 69-29-30 W.
64	40-26-50 N. 69-45-30 W.
65	40-06-42 N. 69-31-36 W. Off Nantucket Shoals.
66	40-48-50 N. 69-59-00 W.
67	40-34-09 N. 70-10-37 W. Arthur Kill, Richmond Creek, Staten Island, New York. Lies east to west across channel.
68	40-55-00 N. 70-54-30 W. Fisherman. Burned. Depth 180'. Length 82'.
69	40-59-00 N. 70-36-00 W. Fisherman. Depth 156'. Length 96'.
70	40-04-30 N. 73-58-20 W. Wooden barge. Depth 50'.
71	40-08-00 N. 73-53-35 W.
72	40-09-00 N. 73-21-00 W. 28 miles, 130 degrees from Ambrose Lightship.
73	40-12-42 N. 73-45-42 W. Depth 50'.
74	40-12-45 N. 73-44-25 W.
75	40-25-12 N. 73-15-18 W.
76	40-16-12 N. 73-56-30 W. Depth 42'.
77	40-16-54 N. 73-56-24 W. Depth 45'.
78	40-17-00 N. 73-57-00 W. Depth 42'.
79	40-21-18 N. 73-56-06 W. Depth 35'.
80	40-21-24 N. 73-49-18 W. Sunk pre-WWII.
81	40-25-12 N. 73-45-18 W. Depth 70'.
82	40-27-22 N. 73-59-13 W.
83	40-27-24 N. 73-53-06 W. Derrick barge.
84	40-28-00 N. 73-09-00 W. Barge. Reported sunk 2 miles, 105 degrees from Fire Island Lighted Whistle Buoy 2FI.
85	40-30-08 N. 73-51-40 W. Depth 7'.
86	40-32-00 N. 73-51-00 W. Pre-WWII. Depth 24'.
87	40-35-45 N. 73-11-30 W. Derrick barge. Depth 66'. About 2.5 miles, 150 degrees from Fire Island Lighthouse.
88	40-49-30 N. 73-47-10 W. Eastchester Bay, N.Y. Depth 52'.
89	40-00-00 N. 74-05-36 W. Barge. Depth 42'.

NO.	PLACE AND COMMENT
90	40-41-10 N. 74-07-12 W. Branch Channel, Newark Bay, N.J. Wooden scow. Depth 19'. Lies NW to SW. Cargo of scrap steel. May have been removed.
91	41-10-18 N. 67-22-42 W. Georges Bank.
92	41-00-00 N. 69-27-00 W. Depth 55'.
93	41-20-12 N. 69-44-54 W. Rose and Crown Shoal, Mass. Depth 15'.
94	41-23-56 N. 69-55-32 W.
95	41-26-20 N. 69-29-30 W.
96	41-40-15 N. 69-55-00 W.
97	41-42-30 N. 69-51-08 W. Sunk pre-WWII.
98	41-17-23 N. 70-05-27 W. Barge. 3,400 yards, 32 degrees from Brant Point Light, Nantucket Sound, Mass.
99	41-19-06 N. 70-50-12 W. Fisherman. Depth 45'.
100	41-19-52 N. 70-55-09 W. Aircraft.
101	41-23-55 N. 70-08-45 W.
102	41-23-24 N. 70-02-42 W. Barge. Depth 26'.
103	41-24-30 N. 70-57-18 W.
104	41-26-54 N. 70-17-30 W. Barge. Stone cargo.
105	41-28-42 N. 70-32-48 W. On side. Vineyard Sound, Mass.
106	41-29-05 N. 70-55-05 W.
107	41-29-11 N. 70-37-30 W. Fisherman.
108	41-30-00 N. 70-54-00 W. 185' length.
109	41-30-06 N. 70-50-55 W. Barge. Wood vessel. Length 90'.
110	41-30-27 N. 70-48-40 W. Fisherman.
111	41-30-36 N. 70-54-28 W.
112	41-30-55 N. 70-22-20 W. Patrol craft 1203.
113	41-31-43 N. 70-33-40 W. Fisherman.
114	41-32-36 N. 70-36-30 W. Visible.
115	41-33-34 N. 70-51-39 W. Depth 9'.
116	41-34-33 N. 70-14-41 W. Barge.
117	41-37-38 N. 70-54-47 W.
118	41-39-59 N. 70-42-18 W. Barge.
119	41-46-30 N. 70-27-45 W. Barge.

NO.	PLACE AND COMMENT
120	41-46-24 N. 70-23-36 W. Airforce plane.
121	41-48-40 N. 70-27-52 W. Fisherman. Depth 55'.
122	41-57-37 N. 70-39-46 W. Tug. 14' of water over wreck. Lies north to south direction. Plymouth Harbor, Mass.
123	41-59-12 N. 70-38-54 W.
124	41-02-30 N. 71-29-45 W. Barge. Depth 140'. Cargo of sulphuric acid. Length 240'. Block Island vicinity, R.I.
125	41-05-07 N. 71-26-33 W. Fisherman. Ol.s. Lost in 1962.
126	41-06-20 N. 71-45-19 W.
127	41-05-48 N. 71-33-18 W. Fisherman.
128	41-08-58 N. 71-32-54 W. Southeast Point, Block Island, R.I.
129	41-09-17 N. 71-32-45 W. Freighter. Steel vessel. Wreck demolished.
130	41-12-07 N. 71-36-03 W. Schooner.
131	41-12-20 N. 71-31-30 W. Barge.
132	41-12-37 N. 71-18-30 W.
133	41-13-10 N. 71-33-50 W.
134	41-15-50 N. 71-49-45 W. Tug. Depth 100'. Fishers Island, Block Island Sound, 5,570 yds., 150 degrees from Watch Hill Light.
135	41-16-22 N. 71-49-12 W. Derrick barge. Depth 33'. About 1,200 yards, 330 degrees from northern tip of No Mans Land.
136	41-17-43 N. 71-51-58 W.
137	41-19-01 N. 71-37-09 W. Dump barge. Depth 60'. Length 85'.
138	41-19-45 N. 71-33-06 W.
139	41-20-10 N. 71-55-00 W. Fisherman. Lost September 1948.
140	41-21-33 N. 71-30-30 W. Scow.
141	41-23-42 N. 71-05-28 W.
142	41-24-30 N. 71-22-30 W. Depth 94'. 1 mile south of Brenton Reef Lightship.
143	41-25-37 N. 71-14-37 W. Trawler.
144	41-25-45 N. 71-23-08 W.
145	41-26-00 N. 71-21-00 W. Narragansett Bay, R.I. Depth 30'.
146	41-26-30 N. 71-26-15 W.
147	41-26-42 N. 71-14-30 W.
148	41-27-30 N. 71-06-10 W.
149	41-31-53 N. 71-19-18 W. Barge. Granite cargo.
150	41-36-47 N. 71-20-25 W. Barge. Depth 22'.
151	41-36-47 N. 71-20-27 W.
152	41-37-58 N. 71-12-29 W. Depth 20'.
153	41-37-58 N. 71-12-52 W.
154	41-38-00 N. 71-12-30 W. Derrick barge.
155	41-42-37 N. 71-09-59 W. Barge. 1,110 yards, 52.5 degrees True from Borden Flats Lighthouse.
156	41-47-54 N. 71-23-12 W. Scow.
157	41-14-39 N. 72-50-23 W. Scow.
158	42-00-00 N. 70-30-00 W. Barge.
159	42-00-23 N. 70-35-21 W.
160	42-08-06 N. 70-40-54 W. Aircraft.
161	42-18-26 N. 70-53-08 W. 975 yards, 201 degrees 30 minutes from the tower, Point Allerton, Mass.
162	42-18-55 N. 70-53-16 W. Sunk pre-WWII. Depth 22'.
163	42-19-27 N. 70-56-22 W. Barge. Steel vessel.
164	42-19-28 N. 70-56-20 W. Barge. Steel vessel. Off pier on Gallops Is., Boston Harbor.
165	42-20-10 N. 70-54-13 W. Barge.
166	42-20-12 N. 70-57-35 W. Small craft.
167	42-20-15 N. 70-54-18 W. Barge.
168	42-21-06 N. 70-42-15 W. Scow. Concrete vessel. Sunk pre-WWII.
169	42-21-35 N. 70-39-35 W. Lighter. Sunk pre-WWII.
170	42-21-50 N. 70-42-17 W. Mud scow. Sunk pre-WWII.
171	42-22-00 N. 70-49-24 W.
172	42-22-22 N. 70-51-39 W.
173	42-22-39 N. 70-59-40 W. Tug. East side of harbor.
174	42-23-00 N. 70-54-00 W.
175	42-23-16 N. 70-51-49 W. Salvage completed. 60-ton mass of steel remains.
176	42-27-30 N. 70-54-25 W. Yawl. Depth 34'.

NO.	PLACE AND COMMENT	NO.	PLACE AND COMMENT
177	42-27-31 N. 70-54-24 W.	202	Buzzards Bay, Mass. 5.25 miles, 110 degrees from Dumpling Rock Lighthouse. 37' of water over wreck.
178	42-33-18 N. 70-36-36 W. Fisherman.	203	Between Sow & Pigs and Vineyard Lightship, Mass. Lost February 18, 1895.
179	42-36-52 N. 70-39-15 W. Seine boat.	204	5.5 miles southeast of Bishops & Clerks Ledge, Mass. Lost 1800's.
180	42-39-13 N. 70-41-00 W. Fisherman.	205	In Edgartown Harbor, Mass. Lost 1800's.
181	42-40-25 N. 70-34-18 W.	206	Nantucket Island, Mass. Lost April 30, 1885. Brig.
182	42-40-39 N. 70-35-02 W.	207	In Nantucket Harbor, Mass. Lost 1800's.
183	42-17-49 N. 71-02-37 W.	208	Block Island Sound, R.I. 1-1/2 miles northeast of Block Island North Reef Lighted Bell Buoy 1B1. Barge. Wood vessel.
184	42-17-56 N. 71-00-12 W. Wooden vessel. Length 75'.	209	Narragansett Bay, R.I. 4,800 yds., 168 degrees True from Conimicut Lighthouse. Reported in 1943. Depth 16'.
185	42-18-00 N. 71-02-30 W. Barge.	210	Approximately 1 mile south of Brenton Reef Lightship, R.I. Barge. Depth 94'.
186	42-21-17 N. 71-02-54 W. Barge.	211	Point Judith, R.I. British brig. Lost April 7, 1862.
187	42-21-18 N. 71-02-43 W. May have been removed.	212	Beaver Tail, R.I. Brig. 250 Gt. Lost winter of 1865.
188	43-04-36 N. 70-45-30 W.	213	Catumb Reef, Watch Hill, R.I. Schooner. Lost 1800's.
189	43-32-27 N. 70-19-36 W. Broken up.	214	Mussel Bar, Watch Hill, R.I. Schooner. Lost January 3, 1882.
190	43-32-48 N. 70-12-30 W. Lighter. Depth 45'. Seal Cove, Cape Elizabeth, Maine.	215	Watch Hill, R.I. Sloop. Lost March 23, 1888.
191	43-38-08 N. 70-12-33 W. Barge. Depth 44'. Length 100'. Portland Harbor, Me.	216	Brentons Reef, R.I. Schooner. 75 Gt. Lost June 1870.
192	43-38-53 N. 69-59-18 W. At least 160' of water over wreck.	217	Brentons Reef, R.I. Schooner. 100 Gt. Lost winter of 1865.
193	43-48-54 N. 69-24-56 W. Barge. 104' of water over wreck. Length 115'.	218	Block Island Light, R.I. Schooner. 200 Gt. Lost spring of 1870.
194	Gloucester Harbor, Mass. 1,335 yds. 212 degrees True from Tenpound Island Lighthouse. Depth 33'.	219	Harbor Neck Point, Block Island, R.I. Schooner. Lost December 16, 1879.
195	Nantucket Sound, Mass. 666 yds. northwest of Cross Rip Lighted Horn Buoy 21. Barge. Stone cargo. Length 100'.	220	Napatree Point, R.I. Sloop. Lost March 24, 1880.
196	6,600 yards, 251 degrees from Cuttyhunk Lighthouse, Mass. Depth 68'.	221	Point Judith, R.I. Brig. Lost April 16, 1862.
197	Cape Cod Bay, Mass. Approximately 1 mile. 332 degrees True from Cape Cod Canal Breakwater Light. Barge.	222	The Thimbles, L.I.S., Conn. 880 yds., 190 degrees from house, Johnson Point. Wreck lies north to south with 10' of water over it.
198	Neponset River, Boston Harbor, Mass. Located 400' downstream from Granite Avenue Bridge.	223	L.I.S., Conn. 2,350 yds., 40 degrees True from Kelsey Point Breakwater Light. Depth 16'. Wreck lies northwest to southeast.
199	Cleveland Ledge Channel, Buzzards Bay, Mass. 2,050 yds., 203 degrees True from Cleveland Ledge Channel Range Front Light. Depth 29'. Identified as tug.	224	About 2.2 miles, 146 degrees from Branford Reef Light. Depth 50'.
200	Vineyard Haven, Mass. Barge. Coal cargo. Sunk after collision with Norwegian st.s. GEZINA on November 14, 1934.	225	Conn. & N.Y., Long Island Sound. South side, in vicinity of Mattituck Inlet.
201	Plymouth Harbor, Mass. 1,375 yds., 198 degrees True from Duxbury Pier Lighthouse. Dragger. Depth 18'.	226	Bergen Basin, Jamaica Bay, N.Y. 110 yds., 088 degrees from tank, Hamilton Beach. Scow. Depth 17'. Wreck lies northeast to southwest. Length 110'.
		227	L.I.S., N.Y. Between Hart Island Light and Stepping Stones Light. Area has 900 tons of scrap steel. Depth 68'.

NO.	PLACE AND COMMENT
228	Approaches to New York, 18.1 miles, 174 degrees from Montauk Point Light. Aircraft owned by Republic Aircraft Corporation. Depth 178'.
229	Jamaica Bay, N.Y. 150 yds., 099 degrees from tank at Hamilton Beach. Depth 23'.
230	Lower Hudson River, N.Y. 2,245 yds., 013 degrees from Lower Hudson River Light 23. Barge.
231	East River, L.I.S., New York. 675 yds., 071 degrees from Throgs Neck Light. Tug. Wreck lies north to south. Depth 50'.
232	New York Harbor. 990 yds., 188 degrees from tank at Hoffman Island. Wreck lies north to south. Depth 12'. Other obstructions in area.
233	Great South Bay, N.Y. About 720 yds., 113 degrees from Brown Point West Breakwater Light.
234	Gerritsen Inlet, Jamaica Bay, N.Y. Above Plum Beach Bridge. Several barges in area.
235	Oyster Bay, Mill Neck Creek, N.Y. About 75' west of draw opening of the Mill Neck Highway Bridge. Unknown obstruction. May have been removed.
236	Jamaica Bay, N.Y. Off Nova Scotia Bar, about 2,200 yds., 046 degrees from Cupola, Rockaway Point. Unknown object.
237	New York Harbor. At northwest corner of Shooters Island. Barge. Depth 34'.
238	Great Peconic Bay, N.Y. 300 yds., 77 degrees True from Shinnecock Canal. Barge. Depth 9'.
239	New York Harbor, Upper Bay, N.Y. 865 yds., 40 degrees True from Robbins Reef Light. Barge. Wreck lies north to south. Depth 18'.
240	New York Approaches. 52 miles, 116 degrees True from Sandy Hook Light. Tug. Stands 32' high in 70' of water.
241	Fire Island Inlet, N.Y. 1200 yds., 258 degrees True from Fire Island Breakwater Light.
243	New York Harbor, Upper Bay, N.Y. 925 yds., 29 degrees True from Robbins Reef Light. Barge. Coal cargo.
244	Hudson River, New York & New Jersey. 1,955 yds., 22 degrees True from mast of Englewood Yacht Club. Barge. Depth 15'. Wreck lies north to south. May have been removed.
245	East River, N.Y. 490 yds., 92 degrees True from Hunts Point Light. Depth 19'. Wreck lies east to west.
246	Long Island Sound, Eastchester Bay, N.Y. In special anchorage west of City Island, about 800 yds., 213 degrees True from spire.
247	New York Harbor, N.Y. 4,520 yds., 68-1/2 degrees True from Sandy Hook Light. Dump scow. Depth 20'. Wreck lies southeast to northwest.
248	Hudson River, N.Y. 390 yds., 144 degrees True from Van Wies Point Light #93. Tug. Wreck lies southwest to northeast.
249	Hudson River, N.Y. 2,485 yds., 21 degrees True from Crossover Light #97. Grain barge. Depth 16'.
250	Buttermilk Channel, Upper Bay, N.Y. 950 yds., 30 degrees True from Buttermilk Rear Range Light. Barge.
251	East River, N.Y. 475 yds., 348 degrees True from Blackwells Island Reef Light. Barge. Depth 55'. Wreck lies east to west.
252	Hudson River, N.Y. 800 yds., 337 degrees True from spire, Poughkeepsie. 30' of water over wreck.
253	Hudson River, N.Y. 165 yds., 56 degrees True from tunnel ventilator, Erie Railroad Pier 9, Hudson River. Barge. Depth 30'. Wreck lies north to south.
254	Great South Bay, Fire Island, N.Y. 1,650 yds., 339-1/2 degrees True from tank, Point O Woods. Depth 15'. Wreck lies north to south.
255	Raritan River, N.J. Vicinity of Raritan Light #41. Small vessel.
256	Beach Haven Inlet, N.J. 7,800 yds., 111 degrees from Lookout Tower, Holgate. Depth 62'. Barge.
257	Upper Bay, Hudson River, N.J. 410 yds., 231 degrees from tower, Central Railroad Yard, Jersey City. Crane barge. Depth 30'. May have been removed.
258	Passaic River, N.J. 660 yds., 120 degrees from dome, Newark. Derrick barge. Wreck lies north to south. Depth 20'.
259	Beach Haven Inlet, New Jersey seacoast. 7,800 yds., 111 degrees from lookout towers, Holgate. Drydock. Broken up.
260	Manasquan Inlet, N.J. About 6,100 yds., 120 degrees from Manasquan Inlet South Breakwater Light. Barge. Depth 60'. Mast 10' below water.
261	Newark Bay, N.J. 680 yds., 208 degrees True from southerly of twin chimneys, Kearney Point, Passaic River. Barge. Depth 27'. Wreck lies north to south direction.
262	Barnegat Inlet, N.J. 1,600 yds., 87 degrees True from Barnegat Inlet North Breakwater Light. Small craft.
263	Barnegat, N.J. Southerly Wreck Lighted Gong Buoy, 9,000 yds., 116.25 degrees True from abandoned lighthouse. Depth 50'.
264	Manasquan Inlet, N.J. 975 yds., 292-1/2 degrees True from Manasquan Inlet South Breakwater Light. Barge.

NO.	PLACE AND COMMENT
265	Off New Jersey coast. 9.2 miles, 107 degrees True from standpipe, Highpoint, N.J.
266	Maurice River Cove, N.J. & Del. 9,150 yds., 094 degrees from Egg Island Point.
267	Delaware River. 300 yds. north of Reedy Island Light on Reedy Island Dike. Fisherman.
268	Delaware Bay, N.J. & Del. 11,200 yds., 42.5 degrees True from Brandywine Shoal Light. Barge. Depth 18'.
269	Delaware River. 1,710 yds., 95 degrees True from Reedy Island Jetty Light. Tug. Depth 25'. Mast and stack visible. May have been removed.
270	Delaware Bay. 3.5 miles, 314.5 degrees True from Brandywine Shoal Light. Barge. Depth 42'.
271	Delaware. About 6 miles, 087 degrees from Indian River Inlet. Tug.
272	Delaware. About 4 miles southeast of standpipe, Avalon (Indian River). Depth 48'. Barge.
273	Ocean City, Md. 3.5 miles, 135 degrees from lookout tower. Depth 50'.

SECTION TWO

NO.	PLACE AND COMMENT
1	24-03-30 N. 79-09-00 W. Schooner.
2	24-42-00 N. 80-52-00 W. Depth 96'.
3	24-34-40 N. 81-24-35 W. Wreck demolished.
4	24-45-00 N. 82-01-30 W. Sunk 1942.
5	25-13-00 N. 79-07-45 W.
6	26-10-00 N. 81-51-00 W. Barge. Depth 21'. May have been removed.
7	27-03-08 N. 80-04-00 W.
8	27-04-10 N. 80-03-41 W. Depth 60'.
9	27-58-00 N. 83-07-00 W. Sunk 1943.
10	28-23-30 N. 80-02-30 W. Wreck cleared.
11	30-45-00 N. 80-11-30 W.
12	30-33-00 N. 81-09-15 W. Depth 60'.
13	30-06-00 N. 81-00-00 W. Depth 66'. May have been removed.
14	30-26-48 N. 81-19-06 W. Sunk pre-WWII. Depth 65'.
15	32-36-00 N. 79-40-06 W. 13 miles, 137 degrees off Sullivan's Island light, Charleston, S.C.

NO.	PLACE AND COMMENT
16	32-36-00 N. 79-40-06 W.
17	33-38-30 N. 76-30-30 W.
18	33-29-00 N. 77-40-00 W.
19	33-58-30 N. 77-41-12 W.
20	33-55-30 N. 77-14-00 W.
21	33-59-00 N. 77-03-00 W.
22	33-18-00 N. 77-51-00 W.
23	33-54-00 N. 77-49-00 W.
24	33-12-36 N. 77-48-30 W.
25	33-58-30 N. 77-39-30 W. Wreck estimated to be 375' in length.
26	33-57-45 N. 77-36-00 W. Wreck estimated to be 185' in length.
27	33-57-18 N. 77-39-02 W. Wreck estimated to be 220' in length.
28	33-51-00 N. 77-28-50 W. Wreck estimated to be 385' in length.
29	33-59-00 N. 77-00-00 W. Depth 25'.
30	33-35-58 N. 77-27-59 W. Wreck estimated to be 381' in length. Depth 60'.
31	33-35-30 N. 77-28-30 W. Wreck lying on side. Depth 84'.
32	33-55-30 N. 77-14-00 W. Lost May 2, 1942. Depth 60'.
33	33-51-20 N. 77-26-30 W. Wreck estimated to be 180' in length.
34	33-45-00 N. 78-05-05 W.
35	34-54-30 N. 73-55-45 W.
36	34-19-36 N. 76-42-00 W. Wreckage estimated to be 10 to 12 feet above bottom.
37	34-13-42 N. 76-34-06 W.
38	34-19-01 N. 76-27-00 W.
39	34-10-00 N. 76-36-30 W. Wood vessel. Depth 100'.
40	34-37-10 N. 76-32-37 W.
41	35-01-36 N. 75-17-48 W. 3.9 miles, 161 degrees from buoy 12A, off Diamond Shoals. Depth 260'.
42	35-04-42 N. 75-23-42 W. Large vessel lying on its side. Depth 95'.
43	35-05-30 N. 75-35-00 W. Schooner. Lost pre-WWII. Reported to lie 10 miles southwestward of Cape Hatteras Lighthouse.
44	35-08-42 N. 75-35-30 W.

NO.	PLACE AND COMMENT
	SECTION THREE
1	17-49-24 N. 76-57-42 W.
2	21-16-30 N. 86-38-30 W.
3	22-55-00 N. 78-27-00 W.
4	23-34-00 N. 79-44-00 W.
5	24-27-57 N. 81-59-12 W. Sunk pre-WWII.
6	24-56-30 N. 81-57-35 W. Small wreck.
7	24-27-30 N. 82-09-54 W. Sunk pre-WWII.
8	24-27-30 N. 82-15-12 W. Sunk pre-WWII.
9	24-45-00 N. 82-01-30 W. Sunk 1942.
10	25-13-00 N. 79-07-45 W.
11	27-03-09 N. 80-04-00 W.
12	27-05-12 N. 82-41-00 W. Depth 35'.
13	27-58-00 N. 83-07-00 W. Dredge. Sunk 1943.
14	28-13-00 N. 83-43-00 W. Sunk pre-WWII.
15	28-50-00 N. 91-05-00 W. About 5 miles south of Ship Shoal Light. Depth reported at 25'.
16	28-50-00 N. 92-10-00 W. Depth 56'.
17	28-00-00 N. 96-46-12 W. Derrick barge. Sunk pre-WWII.
18	29-38-00 N. 85-49-00 W. Sunk pre-WWII.
19	29-28-26 N. 93-16-52 W. 2 miles northeast of Sabine Bank East End Lighted Whistle Buoy.
20	29-35-42 N. 93-18-36 W. Trawler. Depth 36'.
21	29-15-12 N. 94-45-45 W. Wreck lies on its side in 33' of water. May have been removed.
22	30-05-45 N. 85-56-00 W. Sunk pre-WWII. Depth 45'.
23	30-00-00 N. 87-21-00 W. Barge. Demolished.
24	30-11-48 N. 87-56-30 W. Sunk pre-WWII. Barge used for decking seaplanes is located at; 265 degrees, 5.8 miles from Sand Island Lighthouse, 292 degrees, 4.8 miles from Mobile Point Beacon Light.
25	30-12-00 N. 87-13-30 W. Wreck may have been removed.
26	30-12-09 N. 87-13-32 W.

NO.	PLACE AND COMMENT
45	35-08-48 N. 75-26-48 W. Depth 44'.
46	35-10-12 N. 75-19-50 W. Iron vessel. 5 miles, 357 degrees from Diamond Shoal Lightship. This vessel was reported capsized by visual observation on July 17, 1918.
47	35-13-30 N. 75-11-42 W. Small wreck. Lost August 4, 1944. Stands 15' high in 85' of water.
48	35-24-00 N. 75-07-12 W.
49	35-24-12 N. 75-07-00 W. Lost pre-WWII.
50	35-32-35 N. 75-16-35 W.
51	35-53-12 N. 75-17-00 W.
52	35-54-00 N. 75-24-30 W.
53	36-43-48 N. 74-45-00 W. Depth 252'.
54	36-58-00 N. 75-54-30 W.
55	36-49-36 N. 75-52-06 W.
56	36-57-33 N. 75-57-21 W.
57	36-49-36 N. 75-23-00 W.
58	36-57-33 N. 76-01-17 W. Reported lost July 24, 1944. Depth 40'.
59	37-02-20 N. 75-56-12 W. Sunk pre-WWII.
60	37-02-30 N. 75-29-30 W.
61	37-03-00 N. 75-55-00 W.
62	37-10-30 N. 74-33-30 W. The presence of two wrecks approximately 3 miles apart on a line bearing (195 degrees - 15 degrees) are located in 360' depths.
63	Blackfish Bank, Va. About 1,400 yds., 350 degrees from buoy 8A.
64	Cape Henry, Va. 6,700 yds., 300 degrees from lighthouse.
65	Willoughby Spit, Hampton Roads, Va. Submarine used as artificial jetty.
66	Bodie Island, N.C. Area has many unidentified wrecks.
67	Cape Lookout, N.C. 10 miles, 080 degrees from light.
68	Cape Lookout, N.C. 18 miles, 170 degrees from light.

NO.	PLACE AND COMMENT
	SECTION FOUR
1	32-26-15 N. 117-08-30 W. Wreck was surveyed as "bombing" target.
2	33-51-00 N. 118-30-00 W. Sunk pre-WWII.
3	33-59-53 N. 118-31-12 W. Wreck lies 2,270 yds., 246.5 degrees from Santa Monica Breakwater East End Light.
4	37-47-13 N. 122-39-37 W.
	SECTION FIVE
1	Fairport Harbor, Ohio. In Grand River at B & O Railroad Bridge (Mile 2.18). Barge. Wooden vessel. May have been removed.
2	Vermilion Harbor. 1 mile northwest of entrance. Small vessel.
3	Approximately 2 miles northeast of Cleveland East Entrance Light and 2,000' offshore. Dredge.
4	Toledo, Ohio. Northeast corner of Lake Front Ore Dock. Steel vessel.
5	Off Lorain Harbor. 3,500', 349 degrees from Lorain East Breakwater Light. Scow. Depth 26'.
6	Buffalo River. 7,225', 128.5 degrees from Buffalo River South Entrance Light. Barge. May have been removed.
7	Off Avon. About 100', 142 degrees from Avon Intake Breakwater Light. Barge. Depth 12'. Visible.
8	2 miles east of Port Clinton, Ohio.
9	2 miles south of Colchester, Ont.
10	South of Stony Point, Mich., near mouth of the Detroit River.
11	South of Bar Point, Mich., near mouth of Detroit River.
12	Racine, Wisc. Sunk east side of the Root River, directly below 4th Street Bridge. Fishing tug. Depth 12'. May have been removed.
13	Cathead Point, Mich. About 1 mile southwest of Cathead Point. Barge.
14	Milwaukee Harbor, Wisc. 300' off Milwaukee Harbor entrance. Sloop. Depth 31'.
15	Off Sturgeon Point, Mich., about 7 miles east. Sloop.
16	24,000 yards, 105.5 degrees from Thunder Bay Island Light. 26' of water over wreck.

SELECTED LIST OF SOURCES

Books

Anderson, Romola and R.C., *The Sailing Ship,* New York, R.M. McBride, 1926.

Bowen, Dana Thomas, *Memories of the Lakes,* Daytona Beach, Fla., D.T. Bowen, 1946.

Bowen, Dana Thomas, *Shipwrecks of the Lakes,* Cleveland, Ohio, Freshwater Press, 1952.

Bradlee, Frances B.C., *Blockade Running During the Civil War,* Salem, Mass., The Essex Institute, 1925.

Burgess, Robert F., *Sinkings, Salvages, and Shipwrecks,* New York, American Heritage Press, 1970.

Coffman, Ferris L., *Atlas of Treasure Maps,* New York, Thomas Nelson & Sons, 1957.

Fairburn, William Armstrong, *Merchant Sail* (Vol. 1-6), Center Lovell, Maine, Fairburn Marine Educational Foundation, 1945-1955.

Gardner, Arthur H., *Wrecks Around Nantucket,* Nantucket, Mass., Gardner, 1877.

Hoehling, Adolph A., *Great Ship Disasters,* New York, Cowles Book Co., 1971.

Horner, Dave, *Shipwrecks, Skin Divers and Sunken Gold,* New York, Dodd, Mead & Company, 1965.

Howe, J., *Awful Calamities of December 15, 21, and 27, 1839,* Boston, 1840.

Howland, S.A., *Steamboat Disasters and Railroad Accidents in the United States,* Worcester, Dorr, Howland & Co., 1840.

Jones, Virgil Carrington, *The Civil War at Sea,* New York, Holt-Rinehart-Winston, 1960.

Lloyd's Register of Shipping, *Merchant Ships Totally Lost,* London, Lloyd's, 1890.

Lonsdale, Adrian L., and Kaplan, H.R., *A Guide to Sunken Ships in American Waters,* Arlington, Virginia, Compass Publications, Inc., 1964.

Lubbock, Basil, *The Last of the Windjammers,* Boston, Mass., Charles E. Lauriat Company, 1927.

Lytle, William M., *Merchant Steam Vessels of the United States, 1807-1868,* Mystic, Conn., Steamship Historical Society of America, 1952.

Neider, Charles, *Great Shipwrecks and Castaways,* New York, Harper and Brothers, 1952.

Nesmith, Robert I., *Dig for Pirate Treasure,* New York, The Devin-Adair Company, 1958.

Paine, Ralph D., *The Book of Buried Treasure,* New York, Sturgis and Walton Company, 1911.

Peterson, Mendel, *History Under the Sea,* Washington, D.C., Smithsonian Pub. 4538, 1965.

Parker, W.J. Lewis, *The Great Coal Schooners of New England, 1870-1909,* (Vol. 2 No. 6), Mystic, Conn., Marine Historical Association, 1948.

Potter, John S., *Treasure Divers Guide,* New York, Doubleday and Company, 1960.

Small, Isaac M., *Shipwrecks on Cape Cod,* Chatham, Mass., Chatham Press, 1967.

Stick, David, *Graveyard of the Atlantic,* Chapel Hill, The University of North Carolina Press, 1952.

Public Documents

U.S. Coast Guard, *Bibliography,* Washington, D.C., Public Information Division, July 1945.

U.S. Coast Guard, *Notice to Mariners,* Washington, D.C., Department of Transportation.

U.S. Coast Guard, *Principal Marine Disasters 1831-1932,* Washington, D.C., Public Information Division.

U.S. Coast Guard, *U.S. Merchant Ship Losses December 7, 1942 through August 14, 1945,* Washington, D.C., Public Information Division.

U.S. Coast Guard Annual Reports, Washington, D.C., Government Printing Office, 1915-1932.

U.S. Engineer Office, *Index of Marine Disasters from Fishers Island, Conn. to Cape Cod, Mass.,* Newport, R.I., Army Corps of Engineers, 1904.

U.S. Hydrographic Office, *Wreck Information List,* Washington, D.C., Government Printing Office, March 10, 1945.

U.S. Hydrographic Office, *Corrections and Additions,* Washington, D.C., Government Printing Office, 1946.

U.S. Life Saving Service Annual Reports, Washington, D.C., Government Printing Office, 1872-1914.

U.S. Bureau of Navigation, *Merchant Vessels of the United States 1906-1968,* Washington, D.C., Department of Commerce.

U.S. Naval Oceanographic Office, *Nautical Chart Symbols and Abbreviations,* Washington, D.C., Government Printing Office, 1963.

U.S. Revenue Cutter Service Annual Reports, Washington, D.C., Government Printing Office, 1912-1913.

U.S. Steamboat Inspection Service Annual Reports, Washington, D.C., Government Printing Office, 1871-1934.

Charts

U.S. Coast Guard and Geodetic Survey, *Wreck Charts,* Washington, D.C., Government Printing Office, 1945-1947.

> 1007-A: Gulf of Mexico. Sept. 1947.
> 1106-A: Bay of Fundy to Cape Cod. Sept. 1947.
> 1107-A: Georges Bank and Nantucket Shoals. Sept. 1947.
> 1108-A: Approaches to New York-Nantucket Shoals to Five Fathom Bank. Jan. 1945.
> 1109-A: Cape May to Cape Hatteras. Sept. 1947.
> 1110-A: Cape Hatteras to Charleston Light. March 1945.
> 1111-A: Charleston Light to Cape Canaveral. Sept. 1947.
> 1112-A: Cape Canaveral to Key West. Sept. 1947.
> 1207-A: Massachusetts Bay. Sept. 1947.

U.S. Hydrographic Office, Bureau of Navigation, *Wreck Chart of the North Atlantic Coast of America,* Washington, D.C., Feb. 20, 1893.

U.S. Weather Bureau, *Wreck and Casualty Chart of the Great Lakes,* Washington, D.C., Department of Agriculture, 1895.

U.S. Weather Bureau, *Wreck Chart of the Great Lakes,* Washington, D.C., Department of Agriculture, 1886 to 1891.

NOTES

NOTES

NOTES

NOTES